THE SPORT **AMERICANA**

PRICE GUIDE
TO THE

Non-Sports Cards

By
CHRISTOPHER BENJAMIN

NUMBER FOUR

EDGEWATER BOOK COMPANY • CLEVELAND

SPORT AMERICANA® is a registered trademark of

EDGEWATER BOOK COMPANY
P.O. BOX 40238
CLEVELAND, OHIO 44140

Manufactured in the United States of America
Second Printing
ISBN 0-937424-57-9

TABLE OF CONTENTS

Acknowledgements 6
Introduction 7
Modern Cards 8
What's In A Name 8
How To Collect 9
Prices And Dealers 9
Set Price Versus Single Price 10
Wrapper Prices 10
Display Boxes 10
Price Presentations In This Book 11
Measurements 11
Advertising In The Price Guide 11
Errata 11
How To Use The Price Guide 12
Addams Family (1991) 13
Addams Family (1964) 14
African Wild Animals 14
Air-Lines Cards 15
Airplanes 15
Alf - 1st Series 16
Alf - 2nd Series 17
Alf Album Stickers 18
Alien 20
Alien Nation 21
All My Children 21
All-Pro Skateboard 22
Alvin Tattoos 23
American History Trading Cards 23
American Zoo Animals 23
An American Tail - Fievel Goes West (Impel) 24
An American Tail - Fievel Goes West (Pizza Hut) 25
An American Tail - Fievel Goes West (Diamond) 25
Andy Gibb Posters 26
Andy Griffith - 1st Series 27
Andy Griffith - 2nd Series 28
Andy Griffith - 3rd Series 29
Angry Stickers 30
Animals Heroes Card Collection 30
Animal Posters 31
Animals 32
Animals and Flags of the World 32
Animals of the World 33
Annie Album Stickers 34
Archie Tattoos 35
Aristocats 36
Astro Boy Tattoos 36
Astronauts 37
Astronauts 38
A-Team 38
Autos of 1977 39
Awesome All-Stars 40
Baby 42
Back-Slapper Stickers 43
Back To The Future II 43
Barbie Album Stickers (1983) 44
Barbie Album Stickers (1987) 45
Barbie Album Stickers (1989) 46
Barbie Trading Cards - Series 1 46
Barbie Trading Cards - Series 2 47
Barbie Trading Cards (Panini / Action) 47
Baseball's Greatest Grossouts 48
Baseball Stickers 49
Baseball Super Freaks - 1st Series 49
Baseball Super Freaks - 2nd Series 50
Baseball Weird-Ohs 50
Basketball Stickers 51
Batman 52
Batman - A Series 52
Batman - B Series 53
Batman Deluxe Reissue Edition 53
Batman - Riddler Back 54
Batman - Color Photos 54
Batman Movie - 1st Series 54
Batman Movie - 1st Series Collectors' Edition 56
Batman Movie - 2nd Series 56
Batman Movie - 2nd Series Collectors' Edition 57
Battle 58
Battlestar Galactica (Topps) 59
Battlestar Galactica (Wonder Bread) 60
Batty Book Covers 61
Batty Buttons 62
Bay City Rollers 62
Beatles - B&W 63
Beatles - Color 64
Beatles Diary 65
Beatles Movie - "A Hard Day's Night" 65
Beatles Plaks 67
Beatles Candy Boxes 68
Beautiful People 68
Beauty and the Beast 69
Beetlejuice 70
Beetlejuice Album Stickers 71
Believe It Or Not (Fleer) 71
Believe It Or Not (Milk Duds) 72
Belly Buttons 73
Beverly Hillbillies 74
Beverly Hills 90210 75
Bicentennial Daze 76
Big Bad Buttons 76
Bill & Ted's Excellent Adventure & Bogus Journey 76
Bionic Woman 77
Birds and Flowers 78
Black Hole 78
Blackstone's Magic Tricks 79
Blockheads 80
BMX Bikes 81
Bobby Sherman "Getting Together" 81
Bobby Sherman Plaks 82
Body Shop 83
Boris - Series 1 83
Brady Bunch 84
Brave Star Album Stickers 85
Buck Rogers 86
Bugs Bunny Roadrunner Tattoos 87
Bugs Bunny Tattoos 88
Bugs Bunny Tattoo Transfers 89
Bullwinkle Tattoo Transfers 89
Bumper Stickers 89
Busch Gardens Cards 90
Bush League 90
Button Factory 91
Cabbage Patch Kids Trading Cards 92
Captain Nice 92
Care Bears 93
Casey & Kildare 93
CB Convoy Code 94
CB Jeebies / Iron Ons 94
CB Stickers 95
CB Talk 95
Charlie's Angels 97
Chester Cheetah Cards 99
Chip 'n Dale Rescue Rangers 99
Chips 100
Choppers & Hot Bikes 101
Cinderella Album Stickers 101
Civil War News 102
Civil War Picture Cards 103
Civil War Scenes 103
Classic Aircraft Collector Cards 104
Close Encounters (Topps) 105
Close Encounters (Wonder Bread) 105
Comic Images 106
Combat 108
Comic Ball - Series 1 109
Comic Ball - Series 2 110
Comic Book Foldees 111
Comic Book Foldees 112
Comic Book Heroes Stickers 113
Comic Book Tattoos 114
Comic Cover Stickers 114
Coup D'Etat 115
Cover Ups 115
Cowboy & Cowgirl Trading Cards 116
Cracked Magazine 116
Crazy Cards 117
Crazy College Pennant Stickers 118
Crazy Comic Stick-Ons 118
Crazy Hang Ups 119
Crazy Labels Stickers 119
Crazy Magazine Covers 120
Crazy Stick-Ons 121
Crazy TV 122
Cyndi Lauper 123
Daktari 124
Dallas 124
Dallas Cowboy Cheerleaders 125
Daniel Boone 125
Dark Crystal 126
Dark Shadows - Pink 126
Dark Shadows - Green 127
Dark Shadows Giant Pinups 128
Darkwing Duck Album Stickers 128
D.C. Cosmic Cards 129
DESERT STORM SECTION
Desert Storm: The Mother of All Trading Card Themes 130
Damn Saddam The Wacky Iraqi 131
Defenders of Freedom 132
Desert Storm (ProSet) 133
Desert Storm 1st Series (Topps) 134
Desert Storm 2nd Series - "Victory" (Topps) 138
Desert Storm 3rd Series - "Homecoming" (Topps) 139
Desert Storm Card & Map Set 140
Desert Storm Trading Cards 140
Desert Storm Weapons Set 142
Gulf War Fact Cards 143
Heroes of the Persian Gulf 143
Landforce 145
Operation Desert Shield 145
Operation Yellow Ribbon 146
Seaforce 147
Skyforce 147
The Desert Storm Card Collection 148
Triumphs & Horrors of the Gulf War 149
Victory 149
Development of Naval Flight 150
Dick Tracy 151
Dick Tracy Deluxe Collector's Edition 151
Dick Tracy Collector Cards 152
Dick Tracy Crimestopper Game Cards 153
Dick Tracy Giant Stickers & Poster Set 154
Dinomac Collector Cards 154
Dino-Mite Facts 155
Dinosaur Action Card Collection 155
Dinosaur Album Stickers 156
Dinosaur Bones 156
Dinosaur Cutouts 157
Dinosaurs (Wacky Wax) 157
Dinosaurs (Sunkist) 158
Dinosaurs (Willy Wonka) 158
Dinosaurs (Golden Press) 159
Dinosaurs (MPM) 159
Dinosaurs (ProSet) 160
Dinosaurs Album Stickers 160
Dinosaurs Attack! 161
Dinosaur Series 162
Disgusting Disguises 163
Disney Collector Cards 164
Disneyland 166
Doctor Dolittle Tattoos 167
Donkey Kong 167
Dopey Books 168
Drag Nationals 169
Dragon's Lair 169
Dragstrips / Stick Shift 170
Dream Machines 171
Duck Tales 173
Duck Tales Album Stickers 173
Dukes of Hazzard (1980) 174
Dukes of Hazzard Stickers 175
Dukes of Hazzard (1983) 175
Dumb Dabs / Dumb Dots 176
Dumb Dabs 176
Dune 177
Dungeons & Dragons 178
Duran Duran 179
Dynamite Sports Cards / Dynamite Trading Cards 179
Early Jazz Greats 181
Elephant Jokes 181
Elephant Laughs 182
Elvis Presley 183
Empire Strikes Back (Hershey) 183
Empire Strikes Back (Topps) 184
Empire Strikes Back Giant Photo Cards 187
Endangered Animals 188
Endangered Species 189
Enviromints 190
Environmental Action Cards 190
E.T. 191
E.T. Album Stickers 191
E.T. Magic Motion Stickers 192
E.T. Rainbow Reflection Stickers 193
E.T. Stand-Ups 193
E.T. Stickers - Hershey 194
Evel Knievel 195
Everybody Wins Trading Cards 196
Exciting Science Facts 196
Fabulous Odd Rods 454
Fabulous Rock Records 197
Family Fun Games 199
Famous American Indian Chiefs 200
Famous Americans 201
Famous Monsters Series 202
Fancy Pants 202
Fantastic Firsts In Sports 203
Fantastic Fun With Science 203
Fantastic Odd Rods 1 455
Fantastic Odd Rods 2 456
Far-Out Iron-Ons 204
Fern Gully 205
Fiends and Machines 207
50 Fun Stamps 207
Fighter Planes 208
Fink Buttons 208
Flag Midgee Cards 209
Flags of All Nations 210
Flags of America 210
Flags of the World 211
Flag Stickers & International Communities 212
Flashdance Stickers 213
Flash Gordon (Topps) 213
Flash Gordon (Jasinski) 214
Flintstones Cards 214
Flipper 215
Flipper's Magic Fish 215
Flip-Ups 215
Flower Power 216
Flying Nun 216
Flying Things 217
Fold-A-Roos 218
Foldees 219
Fool 'Ems 220
Football Stickers 220
Football Super Freaks 221
Frankenstein Stickers 221
Freddie & The Dreamers 222
Friendly Dictators 223
Fright Flicks 223
Fun Buttons 225
Fun Cards 226
Fun Gum Monsters 226
Fun 'n Donuts 227
Funny Cars 227
Funny Doors 227
Funny Fotos 229
Funny Li'l Joke Books 229
Funny Rings 230
Funny Travel Posters 230
Fun Projects 231
Future of Rock 231
Galaxy Wars 232
The Garbage Pail Kids Story 233
Garbage Pail Kids, Series 1 234
Garbage Pail Kids, Series 2 236
Garbage Pail Kids, Series 3 237
Garbage Pail Kids, Series 4 238
Garbage Pail Kids, Series 5 240
Garbage Pail Kids, Series 6 241
Garbage Pail Kids, Series 7 242
Garbage Pail Kids, Series 8 243
Garbage Pail Kids, Series 9 244
Garbage Pail Kids, Series 10 245
Garbage Pail Kids, Series 11 245
Garbage Pail Kids, Series 12 246
Garbage Pail Kids, Series 13 247
Garbage Pail Kids, Series 14 248
Garbage Pail Kids, Series 15 249
Card and Print Run Variations in Garbage Pail Kids 250
Garbage Pail Kids Buttons 253
Garbage Pail Kids Chewy Candy 253

TABLE OF CONTENTS

Garbage Pail Kids Giant
  Stickers 253
Garbage Pail Kids Giant
  Stickers 254
Garbage Pail Kids Posters 255
Garbage Pail Kids 3-D Wall
  Plaks 256
Garfield Album Stickers 257
Garfield NFL Mini Posters 257
Garrison's Gorillas 258
Get Smart 259
Ghostbusters Album Stickers .260
Ghostbusters II 260
Giant Plaks 261
Giant Size Funny Valentines .263
G.I. Joe Album Stickers 263
G.I. Joe (Hasbro) 265
G.I. Joe (Impel) 265
Gilligan's Island 267
Glitter Glove 268
Glow Worms 269
Go-Go Buttons 269
Gomer Pyle 270
Gong Show 271
Good Guys & Bad Guys 271
Good Times 272
Goofy Gags 273
Goofy Goggles 274
Goonies 275
Grande Illusions 276
Grease 277
Great Americans 278
Great Moments in American
  History 279
Green Berets 280
Green Hornet 280
Green Hornet Playing Cards .281
Green Hornet Stickers 282
Gremlins 283
Gremlins 2 284
Gremlins 2 Collectors Edition .285
Gremlins Album Stickers 286
Gremlins Movie Stickers 286
Gremlins Stickers 287
Groovy Stick-Ons 288
Gross Bears 288
Grossville High 289
Growing Pains 289
Gruesome Greeting Cards 291
Guiness World Records 291
Gum Berries Lids 292
Gumby and Pokey Tattoos ...293
Gummi Bears Stickers 293
Hang-Ups 294
Hanna-Barbera Magic Trick
  Cards 295
Hanna-Barbera 3-D Stickers ...295
Happy Birthday Bugs.........296
Happy Days 297
Happy Days A Series 298
Happy Horoscopes 298
Happy Stickers 299
Harlem Globe Trotters 300
Harry and the Hendersons ...301
Hee Haw 302
Here's Bo 303
Heroes of the Blues 304
Hippie Tattoos 304
Hogan's Heroes 305
Hollywood Slap Stickers 306
Hook 307
Horrible Horoscopes 308
Horror Heads 309
Horror Monster Series 309
Hot Hunks 311
Hot Rods 311
Hot Seat Stickers 312
Hot Wheels Tattoos 312
Howard the Duck 313
Hysterical History 314
Idiot Cards 315
I Love Lucy 315
I Love Snoopy Album Stickers .317
Incredible Hulk 318
Indiana Jones & The Temple
  of Doom 319
Insult Post Cards 320
Iran Contra Scandal 321
Jake's Jokes 322
James Bond 323
James Bond - Thunderball ...324
Jaws 2 325
Jaws 3-D 326

Jem Album Stickers 326
Jet Set Stickers 327
Jiggly Buttons 328
Johnny Clem 329
Johnson vs. Goldwater 330
Julia 331
Justice League of America ...332
John F. Kennedy (Rosan) ...333
John F. Kennedy (Topps) ...334
Robert F. Kennedy 335
Kids Around the World 336
Killer Cards 337
King Kong (Test) 338
King Kong (Donruss) 339
King Kong (Movie) 339
Kiss 340
Kitchen Sink Cards 341
Knight Rider 342
Know The Presidents 342
Know Your U.S. Presidents . .342
Know Your 50 States 343
Kookie Plaks 343
Kooky Awards 344
Krazy Kards 345
Krazy Little Comics 345
Krazy Pennants 346
Krazy People Posters 346
K2 Factory Workers 347
Kung Fu (Test) 347
Kung Fu 348
Kustom Cars 1 348
Kustom Cars 2 349
Labyrinth 351
Laffs 351
Land of the Giants 353
Laugh-In 353
Laugh-In Rings 354
Laugh N' Tell 356
Laurel & Hardy 356
League of Nations -
  1st Series 356
League of Nations -
  2nd Series 357
Leave It To Beaver 357
Little Mermaid 358
Little Mermaid Album
  Stickers 359
Little Shop of Horrors 360
Lone Ranger Tattoos 360
Looney Labels 361
Looney Labels & Stamps ...362
Looney Tunes Magic Fun
  Books 363
Looney Tunes Stickers
  & Scenes 363
Looney Tunes Trading Cards . .364
Looney Tunes Trivia Games ..364
Looney Series Cards 365
Lost in Space 366
Love Initials 366
Love Notes 366
Mad Ad Foldees 367
Mad Cards 368
Mad Medals 369
Mad Mod Buttons 369
Mad Stickers 370
Magic Card Tricks 371
Magic Funny Fortunes 371
Magic Tatoos 371
Magnum p.i. 372
Magoo Tattoos 373
Make Your Own Name
  Stickers 374
Man from U.N.C.L.E. 375
Man on the Moon 376
The Joy of Collecting Mars
  Attacks 377
Mars Attacks 379
Mars Attacks Mini Comic
  Books 381
Mars Attacks - The
  Unpublished Version 381
Marvel Comics 382
Marvel Comics 382
Marvel Comics Super Heroes
  Tattoos 383
Marvel Flyers 384
Marvel Super Heroes 385
Marvel Superheroes First
  Issue Covers 386
Marvel Super Heroes Stickers .387
Marvel Universe I 388
Marvel Universe II 390

A Sport Americana Special
  Feature 391
Mash 392
Mask Album Stickers 392
Masters of the Universe 393
Masters of the Universe 394
Masters of the Universe
  Album Stickers 395
Masters of the Universe
  Movie Album Stickers 396
Masters of the Universe
  Trading Cards 396
Matchbook Car & Driver
  Collector Cards 396
Max Headroom 397
Maya 398
McHale's Navy 398
Men of Apollo XI 399
Men of the Old West 399
Menudo 400
Michael Jackson 1st Series ...401
Michael Jackson 2nd Series ..402
Michael Jackson Super
  Stickers 403
Mickey Memorability 404
Mickey Mouse and His
  Friends 405
Mickey Mouse and His Pals . .405
Mickey Story 405
Mickey's Magic Moments
  Mobile 406
Micro Machines 407
Midnight Madness 410
Mighty Hercules Tattoos 411
Mighty Heroes Tattoos 411
Mighty Mouse & His Pals
  Tattoos 411
Mighty Mouse - The New
  Adventures 412
Military Emblems 412
Milton the Monster and
  Fearless Fly 413
Miniature Comic Book
  Collection 413
Mini Stickers & Nutty
  Tickets 414
Mini-Toons 414
Minnie 'n Me 415
Mod Generation Stickers ...416
Mod Initials 417
Mod Squad 417
Monkees 417
Monkees Series A, B, & C. ...418
Monkees Badges 419
Monkees Flip Movies 419
Monkey Shines 420
Monogram Models Cards ...421
Monster Cards 421
Monster Flip Movies 422
Monster Greeting Cards 423
Monster Initial Stickers 424
Monster in My Pocket......424
Monster Laffs (Midgee) 425
Monster Laffs 426
Monster Legends 427
Monster Marks 427
Monster Tattoo 427
Monster Tattoos 428
Monstickers 428
Moon Mars 429
Moonraker 430
Mork & Mindy 431
Movie Posters 432
Mr. Freeze Fun Quiz 433
Mrs. Grossman's Sticker Art
  Trading Cards 433
Ms. Pac Man 433
Munsters 434
Muscle Cards 436
Musclecars 437
My Kookie Klassmates 438
My Little Pony 439
Nabisco's Wildlife Card
  Collection 440
Nasty Notes 440
Nasty Valentine Notes 441
National Fungus Football
  League 441
National Geographic World ..442
National Periodical / Warner
  Bros. Cards 443
New Kids On The Block -
  Series 1 443

New Kids On The Block -
  Series 2 444
New Kids On The Block
  Album Stickers 446
New Kids On The Block
  Bubble Gum Cassettes 446
New York World's Fair 447
Nice Or Nasty Valentines ...447
Nickelodeon 449
Nightmare On Elm Street ...450
Night Of The Living Dead ...450
Nintendo 451
Nintendo Album Stickers ...452
Nutty Awards 452
Nutty Initial Stickers 453
Odd Rods 453
Odder Rods / Fabulous Odd
  Rods 454
Oddest Odd Rods / Fantastic
  Odd Rods 1 455
Fantastic Odd Rods 2 456
Odd Rod All Stars 456
Official Drag Champs 458
101 Dalmations 459
Orders and Decorations of
  the World 459
Osmonds 460
Outer Limits 460
Pac-Man 461
Partridge Family 462
Partridge Family Posters 463
Peanuts 464
Peanuts Characters 465
Peanuts Comic Cards Game . .465
Peanuts Klakkers 465
Peanuts Presidential Stickers . .466
Pee Wee's Playhouse 467
Perlorian Cats Stickers 470
Pez Stickers 470
Phoney Records 471
Phoney Records Stickers 471
Pioneers of Country Music . .472
Pirates Bold 472
Pirate Tattoo 473
Pixies 473
Planet of the Apes (1969) ...474
Planet of the Apes (1975) ...475
Playboy 475
Poker Hands 476
Pom Pom Riddles 476
Pop Guns 477
Popples 478
Pop-Ups 478
Prehistoric Scenes 479
Premiere Magazine Collectors'
  Cards 480
Presidential Series 480
Presidents 481
Presidents and Famous
  Americans 481
President Stickers 482
Pro Cheerleaders 482
Push-Pull 484
Put-On Stickers 485
Quentin 486
Race Toons 487
Race USA 488
Racing Track Cards / Soda
  Fountain Cards 489
Rad Dudes 489
Raiders of the Lost Ark 490
Rambo 491
Rambo Album Stickers 492
Rat Fink Greeting Cards 492
Rat Patrol 494
Real Cloth Patches 494
Real Road Signs Stickers 495
Real Wood Plaks / Valentine
  Plaks 496
Red Barn Space Cards......496
Remember Pearl Harbor 497
Return of the Jedi I 497
Return of the Jedi II 499
Return of the Jedi Album
  Stickers 500
Return to Oz 501
Riddle Run 501
Riddle Time 502
Ringer Dingers 502
Rip Into Rock 502
Robin Hood Prince of Thieves .503
Robocop 2 504
Robocop 2 Collectors' Edition .506

TABLE OF CONTENTS

Robot Wars ... 506
RockCards ... 507
Rock Bottom Awards ... 509
Rocketeer (Topps) ... 509
Rocketeer (Pizza Hut) ... 511
Rocketship X-M ... 512
Rock Stars (Donruss) ... 512
Rock Stars (Wonder Bread) ... 513
Rock Express ... 514
Rocky Horror Picture Show ... 515
Rocky II ... 515
Rocky IV ... 516
Rodda Cards ... 517
Roger Rabbit ... 517
Roger Rabbit Album Stickers ... 519
Rookies ... 519
Room 222 ... 520
Rotten Eggs ... 520
Saturday Night Fever ... 521
Saturday Night Live ... 522
Saturday Serials - Series 1 ... 523
Saturday Serials - Series 2 ... 523
Savings & Loan Scandal Trading Cards ... 524
School-Daze Stickers ... 524
School Stickers ... 525
Screamin Gleamin Glitter Iron-Ons ... 525
Sea World Character Cards ... 526
Secret Origin Stories ... 527
Secret Wars ... 527
Sgt. Pepper's Lonely Hearts Club Band ... 527
Shadoworld ... 528
She-Ra Album Stickers ... 529
Shock Theater ... 529
Silly Cycles ... 531
Silly Stickers ... 531
Silver Hawks Album Stickers ... 532
Six Million Dollar Man (Donruss) ... 532
Six Million Dollar Man (Topps) ... 533
Skateboard Stickers ... 534
Slimer & The Real Ghostbusters ... 534
Slob Stickers ... 535
Smellies ... 536
Smurf Album Stickers ... 536
Smurf Supercards ... 537
Smurf Tattoos ... 537
Sneekies ... 538
Snoots ... 538
Snotty Signs ... 539
Snotty Signs Stickers ... 540
Snow White Album Stickers ... 541
Songbirds of the United States ... 542
Soupy Sales ... 542
Space Candy ... 543
Space Defenders ... 543
Space: 1999 ... 544
Space Pak ... 544
Space Shots - Series 1 ... 545
Space Shots - Series 2 ... 546
Spec Sheet ... 547
Speed Wheels ... 547
Spooking Size Candy Cigarettes ... 548
Spook Stories ... 549
Sport Goofy Trading Cards ... 552
Sports Cars ... 552
Stacks of Stickers ... 553
StarCom Stickers ... 553
Star Trek (1967) ... 554
Star Trek (1976) ... 555
Star Trek (1979) ... 556
Star Trek (Colonial) ... 557
Star Trek II - Wrath of Kahn ... 558
Star Trek III - Search for Spock ... 559
Star Trek IV - The Voyage Home ... 560
Star Trek 1991 - Series 1 ... 561
Star Trek 1991 - Series 2 ... 563
Star Trek - The Next Generation Album Stickers ... 564
Star Wars (Topps) ... 565
Star Wars (Wonder Bread) ... 568
Star Wars Movie Photo Pin-Ups ... 568
State License Plates ... 570
Stick-Its ... 570
Stick-It-To-'Em Insult Stickers ... 571
Sticky Feet ... 572
Stop Stamps ... 572
Stupid Buttons ... 572
Stupid Scratch-Offs ... 573
Stupid Smiles Stickers ... 573
Stupid Soaps ... 574
Stupid Stamps ... 575
Super Cycles ... 576
Super Defenders ... 576
Super Girl ... 577
Super Heroes ... 577
Super Hero Stickers ... 578
Super Powers Stickers ... 579
Superman ... 579
Superman ... 580
Superman In The Jungle ... 581
Superman Tattoos ... 583
Superman - The Movie (Topps) ... 583
Superman - The Movie (Drake) ... 585
Superman II ... 585
Superman III Stickers ... 586
Superman III ... 588
Super Pac-Man ... 589
Super Sneekies ... 589
Super Stars MusiCards ... 590
Superstar Tattoo Transfers ... 592
Tac-It-To-Me Spooky Tattoos ... 592
Tac-It-To-Me Tattoos ... 592
Tacky Tattoos / Ticky Tacky Tattoos ... 593
Tale Spin Album Stickers ... 594
Tarzan ... 595
Teddy Bear Collector Cards ... 596
Teenage Mutant Ninja Turtles - Series 1 ... 596
Teenage Mutant Ninja Turtles - Series 1 Collectors' Edition ... 597
Teenage Mutant Ninja Turtles - Series 2 ... 598
Teenage Mutant Ninja Turtles - The Movie Series 1 ... 598
Teenage Mutant Ninja Turtles - The Movie Collectors' Edition ... 599
Teenage Mutant Ninja Turtles - The Movie Series 2 ... 600
Teenage Mutant Ninja Turtles Album Stickers ... 601
Teenage Mutant Ninja Turtles - The Movie Album Stickers ... 601
Teenage Mutant Ninja Turtles II Album Stickers ... 602
Teenage Mutant Ninja Turtles Action Figures ... 603
Teenage Mutant Ninja Turtles Collector Cards ... 604
Teenage Mutant Ninja Turtles Stickers ... 605
Teenage Mutant Ninja Turtles Stickers ... 605
Teenage Mutant Ninja Turtles Movie Stickers ... 606
Teenage Mutant Ninja Turtles Vending Machine Stickers ... 606
Terminator 2 (Topps) ... 606
Terminator 2 (Impel) ... 607
Terrorist Attack ... 608
Terror Monsters ... 609
Terror Tales ... 610
The Air Power Series ... 610
The Amazing Ocean ... 611
The California Raisins ... 612
The California Raisins Album Stickers ... 612
The Civil War ... 613
The Dean Gunnarson Collection ... 613
The New Archies ... 614
The Real Ghostbusters ... 614
The Simpsons ... 615
The Simpsons Album Stickers ... 616
The Simpsons & Bart Bubble Gum ... 617
The True West ... 618
Three's company ... 618
Three Stooges ... 619
Thundercats ... 619
Tiny Toon Adventures ... 620
Tiny Toon Adventures Album Stickers ... 621
Tom and Jerry Tattoos ... 621
Top Pilot Cards ... 621
Topps Pak O' Fun ... 622
Toppscience ... 624
Topps Scratch-Offs ... 625
Topps Winners ... 626
Total Recall ... 626
Toxic Crusaders ... 627
Toxic High ... 628
Toxic Waste Zombies ... 628
Trading Card Treats ... 629
Transformers ... 630
Trivia Battle ... 630
Trivia Quiz ... 631
Tron ... 632
Truckin' ... 632
True Fact Series ... 633
TSR Trading Cards ... 633
TV Cartoon Tattoos ... 637
TV Smelly Awards ... 638
24 Tattoos ... 638
Special Feature: "A Non-Sports Mystery" ... 639
21 Jump Street ... 639
Twin Peaks ... 640
200 Years of Freedom ... 642
Ugly Buttons ... 642
Ugly Stickers (1965) ... 643
Ugly Stickers (1973-74) ... 644
Ugly Stickers (1976) ... 645
Underdog ... 646
Universal Monsters ... 646
Untouchables ... 647
Uranus Strikes ... 647
U.S. Congress Cards ... 648
U.S. Customs Canine Enforcement ... 648
U.S. Of Alf ... 649
U.S. Presidents ... 650
V ... 651
Valentine Foldees ... 651
Valentine Post Cards ... 653
Valentine Stickers ... 654
Vette Sette ... 655
Video City ... 656
Vietnam Fact Cards - Volume I ... 656
Vietnam Fact Cards - Volume II ... 657
Voltron Album Stickers ... 658
Voltron Tattoos ... 658
Vote ... 659
Voyage To The Bottom Of The Sea ... 659
Wacko-Saurs ... 660
Wacky Baseball Players ... 661
Wacky Basketball Players ... 661
Wacky Football Players ... 661
Wacky Labels ... 662
WACKY PACKAGES SECTION
Introduction ... 662
Wacky Ads ... 663
Wacky Packages Album Stickers ... 664
Wacky Package Posters ... 665
1967 Die-Cuts ... 666
1973 Stickers - 1st Series ... 666
1973 Stickers - 2nd Series ... 667
1973 Stickers - 3rd Series ... 667
1973 Stickers - 4th Series ... 668
1974 Stickers - 5th Series ... 668
1974 Stickers - 6th Series ... 669
1974 Stickers - 7th Series ... 669
1974 Stickers - 8th Series ... 670
1974 Stickers - 9th Series ... 670
1974 Stickers - 10th Series ... 671
1974 Stickers - 11th Series ... 671
1975 Stickers - 12th Series ... 672
1975 Stickers - 13th Series ... 672
1975 Stickers - 14th Series ... 673
1975 Stickers - 15th Series ... 673
1977 Stickers - 16th Series ... 674
Alphabetical Directory of "Original" Stickers, Series 1-16 ... 674
1979-80 Stickers ... 678
1985 Stickers ... 679
1991 Stickers ... 680
Wacky Package Tattoos ... 681
Wacky Stickers ... 682
Wacky TV Show Cards ... 682
Walt Disney Characters Tattoos ... 683
Walt Disney's Character Collecting Cards ... 683
Waltons ... 684
Wanted Posters ... 684
Wanted Stickers ... 686
War Bulletin ... 686
Washington Dudes ... 687
Water World Heroes ... 687
Way-Out Wheels ... 688
Weird Ball Trading Cards ... 688
Weird-Ohs ... 689
Weird Wheels Stickers ... 689
Welcome Back Kotter ... 690
Wendy's Old West Trading Cards ... 691
What's My Job? ... 691
Wheels, Wings and Things ... 692
Where's Waldo? ... 692
Who Am I? ... 692
Wierd World of Baseball ... 694
Wild Animals ... 694
"Wildlife" Baby Animals ... 694
Wild Wheel Collector Cards ... 695
Wild Wonders Animal Cards ... 695
Willow Album Stickers ... 696
Willow Movie Stickers ... 696
Willow Trading Cards ... 696
Window Pains ... 697
Wings of Fire ... 697
Wings of Gold ... 698
Wisecrackers ... 698
Wise Guy Buttons ... 699
Wise Ties ... 699
Wizard of Oz ... 699
WNEW Superstars ... 700
Woody Woodpecker Tattoos ... 701
World of Stamps ... 701
World War II ... 701
World War II Propaganda ... 702
X-Men ... 704
Yo! MTV Raps ... 705
You'll Die Laughing - 1973 ... 706
You'll Die Laughing - 1980 ... 707
Your Latest Picture ... 708
Yuckies ... 709
Zero Heroes ... 710
Zilly-Zereal Boxes & Stickers ... 711
Zoo Card Series ... 712
Zoo Life Zoo Cards ... 712
Zoo-Per Card Series ... 714
Zoo's Who ... 714
Manufacturers Index ... 715
Condition Guide ... 718
Glossary ... 719

ACKNOWLEDGEMENTS

Each successive edition of **The Sport Americana Price Guide to the Non-Sports Cards** has been acclaimed by hobbyists as "the finest card catalog ever published." The current edition, containing 720 pages and over 4900 separate illustrations, surpasses any work we have done in the past and will instantly become an invaluable guide for established collectors and newcomers alike.

Christopher Benjamin, the author of this Price Guide, is responsible for collecting and developing the material presented herein, but a project of this scope would be impossible to attempt without the contributions of other individuals. We continue to be inspired by the past efforts of legendary collectors like Jefferson Burdick, Buck Barker, John Wagner, et al. We also salute those contemporary hobbyists who have directly aided us in putting together this volume. Their names read like a "Who's Who" of the non-sports hobby: Roxanne Toser, Robert and Jeffrey Marks, John Neuner, Bill Nielsen, Marty Ballistreri, Brian Bigelow, Larry Fortuck, Bill Mullins, and Gordon Burns.

Many other collectors have assisted the author by sending checklists, photocopies, price information, background material, and cards for us to study and record. With gratitude we salute the following people who have helped with past and present volumes:

Bill Ackers	Robert Dubois	Duncan Holmes	Jack Pollard
Jerry Adamic	Shirley Eross	George Hunter	Stephen Powers
Lyn Adamic	Ronald Evans	Orve Johansson	Robert Price
Mark Angert	John Farnetti	Buck Kane	Tom Reid
Jimmy Austin	Robert Foster	Dotty Kaufman	Frank Reighter
George Bammer	Mike Gallela	Jeff Kilian	Steve Roden
Diana Beckman	Leon Geisler	Charles Koble	Kieran Sala
Paul Brenner	Pete Gilleeny	Paul Koch	Tony Salamone
Marvin Brown	Alan Gillman	Ruth Kohn	Tony Seger
Ken Bush	Sheldon Goldberg	Jim Kroeger	Jody Slates
Jack Byrd	Steve Goldman	Mike Kucharski	Conrad Somerville
Tony Cento	Jeff Goldstein	Chuck Ladoucer	Mike Strauss
David Chamberlain	"Mo" Goldstein	Lew Lipset	Paul Tenpenny
Wanda Chan	Mike Gordon	Kenneth Lunn	H.G. Treacher
Lou Chericoni	Howie Gordon	James Macumber	Sal Visalli
Tom Church	Clayton Grimm, Jr.	Paul Marchant	George Wallace
Bob Conway	John Grossman	Chris McCann	Bernard Wermers
Jim Cuthbert	Travis Haagen	Todd McWilliams	Ernie White
Melva Davern	Bill Hall	John Newbraugh	Stephen Woods
Les Davis	Linda Hardman	Bob Nolan	Maryann Wolf
Val DeCarlo		Dennis Owyang	Robert Youhouse
Bill Dodge		Enzo Palombit	

We must also single out the following people: Mary Hall, who sends us cartons of new material every year; Sherryl Schmick, who proofreads our copy and is a champion card finder; and Paul Schmick, who photographed many of the cards and wrappers appearing in these volumes.

The author, and collectors everywhere, express their appreciation to the companies past and present who have produced cards: the inventiveness and quality of your trading cards has exerted a profound influence upon our lives. We also salute the collector, for without him the cards themselves are meaningless.

With fondness, we recall my talented, hard-working co-author, Denny Eckes, who passed away suddenly in the prime of his life. Denny made many friends throughout the hobby and is sorely missed.

Finally, I dedicate this book to "Boo" for her seventeen years of friendship and devotion. You helped me every step of the way and I will never forget you.

INTRODUCTION

Welcome to the fifth edition of *The Sport Americana Price Guide to the Non-Sports Cards*. The information in this book has been carefully researched by Christopher Benjamin and is presented in the illustrated format which has made the Sport Americana line the best selling trading card price guides of all time. The result is an attractive and interesting volume which is as useful and comprehensible to the novice collector as it is to the veteran. The cards of every set in this book are illustrated front and back (except where the cards are blankbacked), with wrappers, display boxes, and checklists included in the presentations whenever possible.

With the exception of one set, all the cards listed in this book were issued in the United States. This is not ethnocentrism but a simple desire to identify and catalog American cards for the American collector.

The contents of this volume encompass all types of trading cards issued between 1961 and the early part of 1992, EXCEPT those issued with cereal. Cards distributed with magazines, bakery products, ice cream, foodstuffs, etc., have been added to the "traditional" ones appearing with gum and confections. The decision to include all types of cards was easy since we have now moved into a period when nearly all the major and minor card producers are distributing cards without gum or any other product or service.

Questions about the cards, wrappers, and boxes appearing in this book, or about any trading cards not described or pictured, or comments, suggestions, etc., should be directed to Christopher Benjamin, P.O. Box 4020, Saint Augustine, FL 32085-4020. Please include a self-addressed, stamped envelope with your letter (photocopies of cards are always preferable to written descriptions).

Most of the illustrations for the sets presented herein were shot at 50% of original size, with some small-size cards at 66%. Many of the pictures appearing on the 304 pages which have been added to this book since the 1988 volume have been reduced or enlarged as necessary to fill space rather than adhere to a specific formula. Precise measurements for each set of cards are listed in the headings or card summaries.

The author thanks you for purchasing this volume. I have worked diligently to provide collectors with accurate information and reasonable prices. Please remember these very important points:

This book is a guide. It is not the "for sale" list of anyone. The prices are not thoughts or desires of the author, publisher, distributors or advertisers. They are what the marketplace, through the law of supply and demand, has determined. Throughout the year prices on "any" card might increase or decrease. You and you alone are the final judge as to whether you should or should not buy or sell a particular card at a particular price.

MODERN CARDS

In the last two years, the traditional world of non-sport card collecting has undergone major changes. For one thing, bubble gum - the very substance which used to define our hobby - has disappeared from trading card packages. More importantly, a number of major and minor card manufacturers have entered the market and are pumping out card sets at an incredible pace. Before 1991, there were, perhaps, twenty new non-sports sets issued per year. Now we have that many released to the public during the course of a single month.

In the last volume of this price guide, issued in 1988, I described the demise of the artwork trading card in favor of photographic imagery. The infusion of new card producers has changed that trend and collectors have been treated in the last year and a half to a variety of interesting and attractive artwork sets. Since artwork, and the creative requirements supporting it, are far more expensive than photography, it may be that this renaissance will be short-lived. The battle for licensing rights has also heated up and has caused some manufacturers to overextend themselves financially, while others have opted for less interesting, but less expensive themes. All this benefits the collector, who now has a far wider range of products to choose from than ever before.

Sets with adult-only themes are another feature of the modern hobby. These are inconsistent with the perspective and goals of this book and they will not be reviewed or advertised herein.

The other major trend in post-1960 card production is the flowering of so-called "exaggerated humor." I suppose that in the not too distant future there will be an entire generation of Earthlings who believe that satire, on the trading card level, was invented by the Garbage Pail Kids. Not so. In fact, GPK is tame compared to some of the themes and insults appearing in the 19th century card sets. In those pre-lawsuit days, illustrators actively employed caricature and dialogue to discredit individuals, social classes, and racial and ethnic groups. This vindictive social philosophy, which often vented itself in comic strips and popular characters like the Yellow Kid and Buster Brown, persisted into the 1930s: bubble gum card sets like Comic Gum (R33), Novelty Cut Out & Trick Cards (R102), and Comic Jokes and Pictures (R159-2) all contained artwork and dialogue that would now be considered unacceptable. Today's satire is rooted in the irreverence pioneered by *Mad Magazine*, and many of the exaggerated humor sets issued since 1960 were inspired to some degree by that magazine.

The appeal of non-sports card collecting can be summed up in one word: variety. There are thousands of sets to choose from and each set poses its own particular challenge. Most remarkably, the majority of cards remain within the limitations of a modest budget. The entire world - and perhaps, the entire universe, if one counts the science fiction sets - lies within the grasp of the non-sports card collector.

WHAT'S IN A NAME?

Recently there has been considerable discussion among collectors as to the attractiveness of the term "non-sports." Several alternative names have been suggested for this category of cards. However, the author confesses to having no difficulty with the original term, not only because of the irrefutable Shakespearean logic, but also with respect to the very etymology of the word. The prefix "non" merely means "not" and carries no derogatory meaning by itself. (Words such as non-flammable, non-toxic, and non-smoker certainly carry no antagonizing meaning). When connected by a hyphen to the word "sports" it becomes a generic term which is more accurate than any alternative yet coined. Most "non-sports" collectors feel no real or imagined inferiority to their counterparts in the sports card hobby because of this name. Pragmatically speaking, the word "non-sports," no matter what its origin, is the term that has been and is being used, understood, and accepted.

HOW TO COLLECT

There are no set rules on how to collect non-sports cards. Card collecting is a hobby, a leisure pastime. What you collect, how much you collect, and how much time and money you spend collecting are entirely up to you. The amount of time you wish to spend, the funds you have available for collecting, and your own personal likes and dislikes determine how you collect. What will be presented here is information and ideas that might help you in your enjoyment of the hobby.

Several avenues are open to you for obtaining cards. You can purchase current issues in the traditional way at the local candy, grocery, or drug store with the bubble gum or other products included. If you live near a food or candy wholesaler, it is well worth the effort to purchase cards directly from this source. Many companies which offer cards in their products also offer complete sets in premium offers listed on the packaging. You can purchase complete sets from mail order dealers or collectors who advertise in publications like *The Wrapper, The Card Collector's Bulletin,* and *Non-Sport Update.* Advertising in local newspapers is another way of obtaining cards and meeting other collectors. Local flea markets and antique shops often have cards on hand. Finally, the card conventions staged in various cities around the country provide an excellent opportunity for the collector to purchase cards in a price-competitive atmosphere.

VALUE

The value of a trading card is determined by many factors. Among these factors are the age of the card, the subject(s) depicted on the card, the amount of the card printed, the attractiveness and popularity of the set in which the card appears, and most importantly, the physical condition of the card.

None of these factors has an absolute influence on value except for physical condition. For example, cards from some sets issued in the 1880's are extremely durable and were printed in great quantities. They might be worth far less than cards from a 1970's set which were distributed on a limited basis or withdrawn from the market. Some cards - like those picturing Hitler in the Horrors of War series (R-69) — have a higher value due to subject matter. However, condition is an absolute determinant of value. Given two of the same card, the one in the best condition ALWAYS has the higher value.

PRICES AND DEALERS

The prices in *The Sport Americana Price Guide to the Non-Sports Cards* are the retail "going rates" for the cards and sets listed in this book as of May 1992. However, pricing — like grading — is subject to a number of variables, including personal opinion, regionalism, and where and from whom the cards are purchased. We've all heard stories of fabulous buys at flea markets, antique shops, etc., but in reality, most collectors obtain their cards from card dealers. Dealers are profit seekers who perform the very important service of providing collectors with cards. They have expenses — travel, advertising, postage, convention fees, sorting and handling, etc. The prices that some dealers charge may vary from those listed in this book. In some cases, this may be due to cost factors, but they may also reflect different opinions about specific sets or cards in general. Other factors, such as the discovery of large quantities of a certain set, may drastically reduce some prices overnight. The best approach to buying cards is to know exactly what you want and what you want to pay for it, give or take a little. This guide and the hobby periodicals advertised in it should enable you to keep up with all the "trends" and to make intelligent decisions.

SET PRICE VERSUS SINGLE PRICE

The prices charged for some modern issues may seem paradoxical at first, but they are based on proven experience with card production and distribution rather than personal theories. The pricing system in this book is based on the "single card" axiom: specifically, that the labor costs involved in maintaining card inventories, and pulling certain cards from them on request, are equal to or exceed the value of the card (or cards) requested. This explains why cards and stickers of even the most recent sets are listed at 10 - 35 cents each in mint condition, when their actual value straight from the gum pack is far less. It also accounts for the fact that the sum of the individual card and sticker prices in most recent issues is higher than the set price listed. It is far more economical for card dealers to sell sets than singles; it may be less fun, but it is also far more economical for collectors to buy sets from dealers than to try to assemble them card-by-card. It is also much easier to deal with prices expressed in certain increments; pegging prices to absolute values would result in dealers and collectors requiring calculators to make simple sales and purchases. As the card hobby continues to grow, there is a corresponding impetus to separate cards and wrappers into general price groups. The prices in this book reflect that trend.

The other side of the coin applies to high demand and/or scarce card sets. Here the individual card values are well established and the "extra" value attached to a complete set is widely recognized and accepted. Collectors can expect to find premium charges of 10-25% over the sum of individual card values for high demand sets in the grades of "excellent" or "mint." Another point to remember: the No. 1 card of any set is worth AT LEAST double the "regular" card price.

WRAPPER PRICES

The interest in wrapper collecting expanded at a phenomenal pace in the 1980s and we have made a special effort to illustrate and to price the wrappers for all the sets listed in this book. A word of caution: quantities of wrappers from the period 1961 to date are constantly being discovered. What was "scarce" yesterday may be all too common today, and the wrapper collector must be on his toes to keep up with the latest "finds" in this highly active part of the hobby. Prices for these items fluctuate widely, and prospective buyers are advised to proceed with caution when contemplating a major purchase.

DISPLAY BOXES

Collecting display boxes from bubblegum sets is not a new idea — some collectors have been doing it for years. There has been a dramatic increase in this field in recent times, however, and it is nothing more than a logical step in progression: first cards, then wrappers, now boxes. Perhaps the biggest boost to box collecting came from wrapper collectors. They were the first people in the hobby to point out the disproportionate relationship between wrappers and boxes. Most wrappers, no matter how scarce they are today, came packed in quantity in a single box. Even on a one-to-one basis, a wrapper has more chance of survival than a box. A crushed or crumpled wrapper can be redeemed because wax paper can be smoothed (and even ironed); a box that is smashed or "modified for display" (i.e., lid torn off) may not be salvageable even if it escapes the trash bin. The remarkable thing is that many boxes have survived these perils and have found their way into the hands of collectors. We have made a determined attempt to illustrate the boxes from various sets and price them according to market trends and we owe a debt of thanks to Bob Marks, "The Box King," and Roxanne Toser for their efforts on this project.

PRICE PRESENTATIONS IN THIS BOOK

Cards in *The Sport Americana Price Guide to the Non-Sports Cards* are priced in the manner they are normally found in a buy-sell environment. Set prices are provided for each set for which the sum total of items has been established. The typical, individual card and/or sticker in each set listed is always priced. A wrapper and box price is also presented whenever such items are illustrated in the display. If more than one wrapper or box exists for a set or series, each is individually priced. Collateral items such as 3-D glasses, decoders, etc., are also priced, but selling (or order) sheets are not. The latter exist for many sets but the level of public interest in them does not warrant pricing at this time. Most complete sets in this volume include the stickers if issued with the set. Exceptions to this are clearly noted.

The two columns of prices correspond to "mint" and "excellent." For a description of condition grades, consult the condition guide on page 718. There are no prices for hybrid conditions such as "very good to excellent" or "excellent to mint." Collectors must judge for themselves if the cards fall into such grades and should consult the price levels in this guide for possible adjustments to accommodate them. Since all the sets in this volume were printed after 1961, collectors should be able to find cards from them in the top grades. Lesser condition cards should be avoided unless they are extremely scarce, and even then price must match condition. The "mint" price column is for cards of that grade only, and cards not meeting the strict requirements of that category must be priced accordingly.

Only one price is given for wrappers: "excellent." Rather than debate why or why not wrappers could be graded "mint," we must point out that wrappers for some sets — Mars Attacks, for example — have been found completely flat and unfolded. Most wrappers, however, do have some imperfections which are to be expected from the nature of their use as packaging. Some defects are allowable in the excellent grade but collectors are advised that the discussion in the "Value" summary applies to wrappers as well as cards.

Boxes are also priced in the "excellent" column only. As more and more collectors are attracted to this fascinating part of the hobby, we expect that a more definitive set of criteria for judging grades and values will ensue. The "excellent" stated in our display refers to intact items with minor defects or damage. Boxes with lids or other parts detached cannot be placed in this category. However, boxes which have been folded flat — either by removing side staples or compacting along pre-scored joints — are acceptable for this grade.

MEASUREMENTS

Every card in this book has been measured personally by the author down to a scale of 1/32". Exact measurements are an important tool in identifying card sets, as many previous books contain grossly inaccurate dimensions. Although the reader should have no difficulty identifying card sets using our index and illustrated text, the measurements given with every set constitute a confirmation of the other data presented. The authors recognize the fact that the dimensions for cards from the same set may vary as much as one-eighth inch in either direction, especially in older series.

ADVERTISING IN THE PRICE GUIDE

The advertisements appearing in this Price Guide were accepted in good faith; however, neither the author, the publisher, the distributors nor the other advertisers in this book accept any responsibility for any particular advertiser not complying with the terms of his or her ad. Should you come into contact with any of the advertisers in this Guide as a result of their advertisement herein, please mention that you found out about them from this source.

ERRATA

In a book of this scope, it is inevitable that errors in typing, sequence, and spelling have occurred. If you find a mistake, if you can provide a missing checklist title, or if you wish to comment about any part of the book, please write to Chris Benjamin, P.O. Box 4020, Saint Augustine, FL 32085-4020.

HOW TO USE THE PRICE GUIDE

FRONT VIEW OF TYPICAL CARD IN SET

BACKVIEW OF TYPICAL CARD IN SET

WRAPPER FROM SET

NUMBER & TITLE OF CARD (THE CHECKLIST)

NUMBER OF CARDS IN SET

TITLE OF SET (AND ACC. DESIGNATION WHERE APPLICABLE)

NUMBER OF SUPPLEMENTAL ITEMS (FOIL CARDS & STICKERS) IN SET

HOWARD THE DUCK (77 & 22)

The trouble with buying license rights for a product based on a film is that you sink or swim together. Topps had high hopes for "Howard the Duck" (issued in 1986), but neither the movie or the card set attracted much of a following. There are 75 story-cards in the series; these have

photos from the movie on front and text on back. The first and last cards are a title card and a checklist. The 22 stickers have diecut center designs with yellow borders. They are numbered but not captioned. Eleven stickers have "film clip" side frames; the remaining eleven are photos set on green, blue, or purple backgrounds. Note: set price includes stickers.

2 1/2" X 3 1/2"

ITEM	MINT	EX
Set	8.00	4.00
Card	.10	.05
Sticker	.25	.15
Wrapper	—	.25
Box	—	2.00

1 Howard the Duck
2 Introducing Howard!
3 Beverly Switzler
4 Phil Blumburtt
5 Dr. Jenning
6 Howard on Duck World
7 Duck-O-Vision: Crazy Webby
8 Duck-O-Vision: Teen Bandstand
9 Duck-O-Vision: Medical Program
10 Duck-O-Vision: Public Affairs
11 Duck-O-Vision: Count Duckula
12 Landing on an Airport!
13 Motorcycle Man
14 Cherry Bomb's Best Lady!
15 Bev in a Jam!
16 No More Mr. Nice Duck!
17 Little Duck Lost
18 Weird...But Cute!
19 Special Delivery!
20 A Feathered Phenomenon!
21 At The Dynasthetics Lab
22 'Ascent of Duck'
23 Waddling Off in a Huff
24 Bug Off, Blumburtt!
25 Humans...Phooey!
26 So Long, Ducky!
27 How a Duck Can Make a Buck
28 Howard in Hot Water
31 Hi-wie & Bev...Together Again!
32 A Scientist Possessed!
33 Jenning's Mad Lab
34 A Fowl Shakedown!
35 Beverly's Packin'!
36 Master of Quack Fu
37 The Thing within Jenning
38 Diner Dilemma
39 Bottoms Up!
40 Eggs? You're Kidding!
41 Duck Vs. Truckers
42 Stop That Duck!
43 Doctor of Doom!
44 Ketchup Catastrophe!
45 Howard the Swinger!
46 Destroying a Duck
47 He's Not on the Menu!
48 Dr. Destructo!
49 Earth Vs. The Flying Cleavers
50 Howard Gets a Lift!
51 The Dark Overlord
52 Everything's Ducky!
53 "Help Us, Howard!"
54 Hell On the Highway
55 Hit Me with Your Best Shots
56 The Imminity Syndrome
57 Facing the End
58 Howard Is the Rescue!
59 How About Plan "B"?
60 The Switch Sacrifice
61 The Girl of Problems...
62 Diabolical Jenner!
63 "He's Uncontrollable!"
64 Zapped!!
65 Howard's Last Chance
66 Howard... Hero!
67 Overloads Overlord
68 Duck, You Sucker!
69 Spectronics Disaster
70 One Last Chance!
71 Ka-Blooo!!
72 Quack to Howard!
73 Lord Love a Duck!
74 Cleveland Triumphant!
75 I Want My MTV!
76 A Comic Classic!
77 Checklist

191

CHECKLIST OF SET CONTINUED FROM PREVIOUS PAGE

DIMENSIONS OF CARD

SUPPLEMENTAL INFORMATION ON THE SET

CONDITION CATEGORIES MINT, EXCELLENT

PRICES FOR EACH ITEM LISTED

CHECKLIST OF STICKERS IN SET

STICKER FROM SET

BOX FROM SET

Brady Bunch

1 The Brady Bunch
2 The Brady Girls
3 The Brady Boys
4 Eve Plumb as Jan
5 Mike Lookoland as Peter
6 Christopher McKnight as Peter
7 Gerard and Mike
8 The Family Pet
9 Sweet Treat
10 Peter, Greg and Bobby
11 Stuck in Stockade!
12 Reporting for Duty
13 Here Comes My Fast
14 Big Prize for Little Bobby
15 Break It Up! It's Bedtime!
16 What's Cooking, Alice
17 Big Noise
18 Inferior Decorators
20 Guess Who?
21 Make up for Marcia!
22 Big Brother's Advice
23 Long Distance Phone
24 The Murphy Bed
25 Christmas Celebration
26 Musical Consecration
27 Ain't Love Wonderful
28 Someone's Here to Learn
29 Homework Huddle
30 A Couple of Hungry Kids
31 Backyard Playground
32 Lollipop Lovers
33 I'm Ready for Action
34 Running a Fever
35 King of the Day
36 Uh-oh... Here Comes Indians!
37 Tired of Prayers
38 Who Stole My Toothbrush?
39 I'm in Trouble
40 Kristy Conference
41 Something Smells Good
42 Trying to Get a Glimpse
43 Someone in the Tub
44 Big Brother's Advice
46 Say Something
47 Man-to-Man Talk
48 Flopped Your Wig?
49 Sandlot Stars
50 A Boy's Room in His Car
51 "Alice, You Grew a Bean!"
52 Where's My Greasy Kid Stuff?
53 Houswkeeper
54 Someday Let's Eat Alone
55 Photo of the Brady Kids
56 You Did It Again
57 Sloppy but Fun
58 Come and Get it
59 Big Sister
60 Talking It Over
61 A Small Disagreement
62 A New Rock Star
63 What's the Noise
64 Can I Keep the Bird?
65 Meet Marcia Brady
66 Meet Bobby Brady
67 Meet Jan Brady
68 Meet Cindy Brady
69 Meet Peter Brady
70 Trimming the Tree
71 Meet Greg Brady
72 Marcia's Pajama Party
73 Having a Ball
74 Christmas
75 A Guitar Lesson
76 Alice's Coffeebreak!
77 No Man Talk
78 Back Home
79 Greg's Plate
80 Practice Makes Perfect
81 What Was
82 Bedtime Snack
83 A Guitar Lesson
84 Checking Homework
85 Greg Listens In
86 A Tired Young Man
87 Feeling Better Yet?
88 Say Cheese!

BUCK ROGERS (88 & 22)

2 1/2" X 3 1/2"

Topps produced the Buck Rogers set in 1979. The cards — of which there are 88 — have color pictures taken from the TV series. Each photo-graph is surrounded by a jag-ged white frame line which has small portraits of the series characters inserted at the cor-ners. The borders are red and the caption is printed in yel-low. The card number appears both front and back. The re-verses are green and gray and contain a sequential gray line. The set of 22 stickers has color pictures with red frame lines and blue borders. They are numbered but un-captioned (captions are iden-tical card pictures as used in the checklist below). Note: set price includes stickers.

ITEM	MINT	EX
Set	10.00	5.00
Card	.15	.07
Sticker	.50	.35
Wrapper		.35
Box		3.50

1 Buck Rogers
2 Suspended in Time
3 Capt. Buck Rogers
4 The Lost Space Shuttle
5 Frozen Alive
6 Draconian Fortress
7 The Interrogators
8 A Delirious Spaceman!
9 The Man Called Kane
10 Destination: Earth
11 Toward the Inner City
12 The Land Beg
13 Wilma's Chilly Reception
14 "Remove This Barbarian!"
15 The Brilliant Dr. Huer
16 "(Gulp) the 20th Century?"
17 Dr. Theopolis
18 Culture Shock for Buck
19 Twiki's Tonic
20 The World of Tomorrow
21 A New Beginning
22 Remains of Yesteryear
23 The Mutant Peril
24 Fate of Buck's Family
25 Surrounded!
26 Bizarre Rescue
27 The Monsters Repelled
28 Run for Cover!
29 Wilma to the Rescue!
30 "Thanks Alot, Colonel"
31 Bitten by the Love Bug
32 City of the Future
33 Buck...A Traitor?
34 Observing the Trail
35 The Computer Council
36 Buck's Plan
37 The Enemies Meet
38 Visions of Ardela
39 "I Believe You Know Capt. Rogers"
40 The Ace of Space
41 "Look Out World—Lucky Buck is Back!"
42 The Combat Computer
43 Heavy Losses for Wilma!
44 "Get Off the Air, Buck!"
45 Outrunning the Enemy
46 "Sorry About That, Guys!"
47 Zapping the Space Forces
48 "Hey Wilma—How'm I Doing?"
49 Party for a Princess
50 The Party Girl Herself!
51 Dressed in Style
52 They...You Guys Know Any Rock?"
53 "C'mon, Princess...Let's Boogie!"
54 The Princess Gets Down!
55 "He Makes Me Soooo Mad!"
56 Buck Makes a Late Date
57 Twiki Catches Disco Fever!
58 The Princess' Play
59 "We Shall Take Them by Surprise"
60 Disguised as a Space Pirate!
61 Sabotage!
62 Landing Bay in Flames
63 Days of Destruction
64 Wilma Gets the Message!
65 Here Come the Earth Forces!
66 The Starfighter
67 Zeroing in!
68 The Draconian Armada
69 Wilma in Command!
70 Zap! Blam! Pow Power!
71 Death Throes of the Fortress
72 Battle with Tigerman
73 Dogfight in Space!
74 Hunter and the Hunted
75 Battle Skills of Col. Deering
76 Target on Computer
77 Caught in Laser Light!
78 Ardela's Defeat
79 The Battle Rages
80 Futuristic Warfare
81 Explosion in Space
82 Last-Minute Rescue!
83 Off to New Adventures!
84 Gil Gerard as Buck
85 Erin Gray as Wilma
86 Felix Silla as Twiki
87 Pamela Hensley as Princess
88 Henry Silva as Kane

1 Buck Rogers
2 Toward the Inner City
3 A New Beginning
4 Erin Gray as Wilma
5 The World of Tomorrow
6 Dr. Theopolis
7 "Get Off the Air, Buck!"
8 Battle with Tigerman
9 The Lost Space Shuttle
10 The Starfighter
11 The Brilliant Dr. Huer
12 Twiki Catches Disco Fever!
13 Dressed in Style
14 The Party Girl Herself!
15 Gil Gerard as Buck
16 Death Throes of the Fortress
17 Sabotage!
18 "We Shall Take Them by Surprise"
20 Suspended in Time
21 Felix Silla as Twiki
22 Disguised as a Space Pirate!

60

My how times have changed! When the original Addams Family television series debuted on ABC in 1964, the producers tapped Carolyn Jones, John Astin, and Jackie Coogan to play the leads. Solid performers all, but mostly known for their comedic performances over the years. Their counterparts in the spectacular 1991 motion picture - Raul Julia, Anjelica Huston, and Christopher Lloyd - are known primarily for their dramatic talents, but they have proved beyond a doubt that comedy is also within their metier.

Topps issued the series of 99 cards and 11 stickers and the company's response to the fierce competition which mushroomed among card manufacturers in 1991 is evident in certain production details. Most conspicuously, the card obverses are super glossy, a finish which Topps used exclusively for special production sets in the past. This surface luster brings out the details of the images and makes the cards themselves far more attractive than the old flat-finish types. The backs on the stickers are also super glossy, thereby enhancing the clarity of the puzzle picture which can be assembled from the individual parts. Another "first" is the use of a horizontal cellophane envelope as a wrapper (code = 0-485-15-01-1). This is another step away from the folded edge wrapper style, which Topps used for Batman, Robin Hood, and Beverly Hills 90210. Wrapper collectors who bemoaned the switch from folded wax wrappers to folded cello, watch out! This cello uni-pack may become the wrapper of the future. Needless to say, there was no bubble gum packaged with Addams Family cards.

According to copy on the nicely-designed box and the wrappers, the cards are "creepy, kooky, spooky, ooky." This monstrous baby-talk is typical of the captions which appear on the fronts of the cards, where Topps has resorted to the time-honored company tradition of banal one-liners to complement the pictures. Luckily, the backs are more intelligently written. The purple borders surrounding the color photographs on the card fronts are sure to remind collectors of other classic horror sets, and the spider web corner accents, done in gold filigree, are a nice touch. The stickers are an elegant gray, with oval photo frames in the center and puzzle piece backs. They are all numbered, but strangely, sticker number one is missing the caption. Note: Since Topps has already dumped overstocks (boxes) on the market, the values for this set are lower than originally contemplated, even in spite of the bad collation.

1 Addams Family Header Card
2 Gomez
3 Morticia
4 Uncle Fester
5 Lurch
6 Granny
7 Pugsley
8 Wednesday
9 Thing
10 Seasonal Spirit
11 Woe to the World
12 The House That Addams Built
13 A Meeting of Minds
14 The Sensual Snipper
15 Off to School
16 Tully Pays a Call
17 Care for a Bite?
18 En Garde!
19 Touché!
20 Lord and Monster
21 Abigail's Offspring
22 A Geek Named Gordon
23 Electrical Storm Playtime
24 What a Lovely Night ...
25 The Maddest Scheme
26 Gate Extends a Welcome
27 Seance for Screwballs
28 Who's That Knockin' ...?!
29 Egad! It's Fester Addams!
30 Semi-Safe at Home
31 Festering Memories
32 Early to Dead ...
33 Handy Around the Kitchen
34 A Feast for Fester
35 The Little One Suspects
36 "Greed" Triggers It ...
37 Vault Trek
38 The (Weird) Way We Were
39 Boys Will Be Ghouls
40 Pugsley on the Hotseat
41 Shocking Experiment
42 Bidding Wars

43 The Imposter ... Snagged
44 Loco Motorman
45 On Trouble's Track
46 Granny's Strange Brew
47 Look Before You, Lurch
48 Deadtime Stories
49 Hobbies ... A Bad Sign!
50 Tanks Alot!
51 A Walk in the Cemetery
52 Proud Heritage
53 What About "Plan B"?
54 Comforting House Call
55 The Joys of Gangrene
56 Hacking and Slicing
57 An Uncle's Advice
58 Aim for a Major Artery!
59 Tonight's the Night!
60 Brotherly Love
61 Fore!
62 Excellent, My Man!
63 The Ghouls in School
64 Horrors of Hamlet
65 A Kiss Before Spying
66 All Wrapped Up
67 Gordon's Turmoil
68 Night of the Big Bash
69 Granny's Goodies
70 The Addams Assemble
71 Waltzing Weirdos
72 The Oddest Couple
73 Beside Herself Again!
74 Meet Dexter and Donald
75 Romanced By Cousin It
76 Another Close Shave
77 After Wednesday!
78 Siamese, If You Please
79 Danding the Mamushka
80 Uncle Fester's Triumph
81 Little Girl Found
82 Barred From Their Mansion!
83 Thing's Things
84 Motel From Hell
85 Funked-Out Gomez
86 A Soapy Snack
87 Doing Their Part
88 A Simple Exchange
89 Shot from the Coal Chute
90 Wheel of Misfortune
91 Thing Spills the Beans
92 Tully's Last Stand
93 Gomez to the Rescue!
94 One False Move ...
95 Storm Warning!
96 Their Happiest Halloween
97 Margaret's New Boyfriend
98 Uncle Fester Lights Up!
99 A Happy, Haunted Home

STICKERS
1 [No caption]
2 Gomez
3 Morticia
4 Uncle Fester
5 Wednesday
6 Pugsley
7 Granny
8 Lurch
9 Thing
10 Uncle Fester
11 Cousin It

ITEM	MINT	EX
Set	12.50	9.00
Card	.10	.07
Sticker	.25	.20
Wrapper	---	.10
Box	---	2.00

ADDAMS FAMILY (66)

One of the Donruss Company's earliest trading card issues was The Addams Family set of 66 cards marketed in 1964. It contains black and white photos taken from the TV series and from the pro-

2 1/2" X 3 1/2"

motional department of Filmways Productions. The name "The Addams Family" is written in "scary" red ink on the picture area, and the card number appears at the right. The card has a large white area at the bottom containing the caption and the line "Watch The Addams Family on your local ABC station." Below that is a statement in red print advising that all 66 cards have puzzle backs. The wrapper is black with red print.

ITEM	MINT	EX
Set	350.00	250.00
Card	4.00	3.00
Wrapper	––	40.00
Box	––	150.00

1 "Gomez"
2 Somebody Drank My Embalming Fluid!
3 Feeding the Tropical Fish!
4 Will the Real Granny Please Stand Up!
5 You Rang?
6 I Always Look Better by Candlelight.
7 I'm Your New Neighbor!
8 Ever Seen a Train in Orbit?
9 Of Course I play the Piano!
10 This Will Stop His Headache!
11 My Brother-in-Law!
12 Only 3 More and the Cemetery Is Filled
13 Next Time—Use Your Zip Code!
14 Want Some Lizard Soup?
15 Your Slab Will Be Ready in a Moment.

16 I Really Dig You Mortica!
17 Got Any Ghostly Numbers?
18 Which One?
19 "Fester"
20 Don't Move, You'll Spoil My Shot!
21 Here He Comes...Now Do Your Stuff!
22 Yes, We Have a Room for Rent!
23 I Can't Stand a Lumpy Mattress!
24 I Always Use Live Bait!
25 My Own Graveyard!
26 He'll Get the Point Now!
27 Your Kids Ate My Spiders.
28 A Few More and We'll Have Our Own Boot-Hill.
29 Yes, the Real Estate Is Getting Cheaper.
30 Of Course I Ride a Broom!

31 It's So Nice and Gloomy in Here!
32 What Do You Mean—Get a Receipt!
33 What'll I Wear for Halloween?
34 A Friend of Lurch.
35 I Always Play in Poison Ivy!
36 "Thing"
37 Just Think, Our First Dead Letter.
38 Let's Tell Scary Stories
39 The African Strangler
40 It Only Hurts When I Cough!
41 Two Heads Are Always Better Than One.
42 It's Only the Monthly Bill from the Blood Bank.
43 Bury the Next One Over There!
44 "Mortica"
45 Yea, Yea, Yea!

46 I Need a Real Hair-Raising Story.
47 He Saw Lurch!
48 Look, No Dandruff!
49 Weaving a Wig for Fester.
50 You're a Real Cut-Up Fester!
51 My Favorite! Devil's Food Cake.
52 Whaddya Mean, I Need a Man's Deodorant?
53 Son, Now Don't Scalp Fester!
54 Get Their Vote (Dead or Alive).
55 Gotta Be Sharp for Company.
56 I Won't Be Home for Dinner!
57 Lurch Lowers the Body so Beautifully!
58 Let's Eat Before He Wakes Up!
59 Come on in the Playroom and See Our Guillotine.
60 What Do You Mean, Follow You?
61 You've Never Heard of Guillotine
62 Hang Around and I'll Call the Butler!
63 Go Past the Second Grave and Turn Right.
64 House for Sale...
65 The Family Hearse.
66 Quit Shaking the Coffin!

AFRICAN WILD ANIMALS (25)

1 Rhinoceros
2 Wart-hog
3 Aardvark
4 Cheetah
5 Kudu
6 Mandrill
7 Eland
8 Zebra
9 Spotted Hyena
10 Jackal
11 Leopard
12 African Elephant
13 Sable Antelope

14 Chimpanzee
15 Impala
16 Hippopotamus
17 Cape Buffalo
18 White-bearded Gnu
19 Giraffe
20 Gorilla
21 Klipspringer
22 Barbary Sheep
23 Sacred Baboon
24 Crested Porcupine
25 African Lion

1 1/8" X 2 3/4"

In 1964, this set of 25 cards was marketed by Nabisco in packages of Sugar Daddy caramel candy. The artwork and text were created by H. Wayne

Trimm and a 20-page album was offered via the mail to store the collection. The card fronts contain color artwork with a tiny dated copyright line in the bottom white border. On the backs are printed the series number, set title, card number and title (including Latin binomial) and text––all in green print on white stock.

ITEM	MINT	EX
Set	18.00	13.50
Card	.60	.45
Album	15.00	12.00

AIR-LINES CARDS (24)

The title for this set, "Air-Lines Cards," comes from advertising printed on Testor Model Airplane kit boxes and does not appear on the cards. There are 24 planes pictured in the set and a three-card panel was packed inside every model kit associated with the promotion; two cards were airplanes and the third was an unnumbered checklist card. The set is rife with errors: the card illustrated, for example, is incorrectly identified as a Miles Master Advanced Trainer, but is listed and described correctly on the back as a Fairey Barracuda. The "note" which appears on the back of this card - "Name on face of card is incorrect" - indicates that the manufacturer did not bother to correct the mistakes which occurred, and not enough of the cards have been seen to establish that there is a "corrected" version for each error.

The fronts of the cards are finely-detailed, color paintings of the various planes in flight. The caption and card number (which apparently refers to the model kit) are printed in one white border. The backs are tan cardboard with black-print sections detailing the "history" and "specifications" of each aircraft.

Note: only cards found intact in three-card panels can be considered mint.

ITEM	MINT	EX
Sets		
Cards	— —	55.00
Panels (8)	80.00	60.00
Cards		
Single	— —	2.00
Panel	8.00	6.00

3900	Miles Magister I Primary Trainer	7901	Blackburn Skua Dive Bomber
3901	Dewoitine D520C Fighter	7902	Fairey Barracuda
3902	Fokker D21 Fighter	7903	Westland Wallace
3903	Macchi M.C. 202 Folgore Fighter	7904	Hotspur II Training Glider
		7905	Westland Wessex Anti-Sub Air Rescue
4900	Supermarine S6B Racer		
4901	DH 88 Comet Racer	7906	Airspeed Oxford Trainer
4902	Morane Saulnier 406 Fighter	7907	Bristol Beaufort Torpedo Bomber
4903	Hawker Sea Fury Naval Fighter	9800	Martin Baltimore Bomber
4904	Miles Master Advanced Trainer	9801	Junkers JU 88 Bomber
		9802	Bristol 138
4905	Percival Proctor IV Trainer	12900	North American Mitchell Bomber
7900	Spirit of St. Louis	12901	Vickers Vimy
		12902	Martin Marauder II Bomber

AIRPLANES (20)

The first reaction of collectors, when told that these airplane cards were distributed by Esskay Hot Dogs (Baltimore), is that they can't be hot dog cards because they're not stained, or crumpled, or heavily waxed. The reason that Esskay airplanes are found in nice condition, however, is simple: they were premiums available only by sending in to the company via a mail offer. The cards were sent out in five small envelopes (marked "Set 1," "Set 2," etc.) with each envelope containing four cards. Details of the offer were printed on the hot dog packages and the regional distribution of Esskay products to the northeastern United States explains why many collectors have not seen the series before now.

The card fronts contain color artwork drawings of various World War I aircraft in flight and each airplane is identified in large, stylized print within the picture area. A black frame line encloses each picture and separates it from the surrounding white borders. A brief description of the plane is centered on the eggshell white backs, along with an Esskay seal. The cards are not numbered, and only by obtaining the original envelopes with cards can the collector determine which planes belong to each of the five original sets. The cards were issued in 1979 and no reference number has been assigned as of this date.

AEG Dr1
AEG G111
Albatross D111
Albatross Dr1
Armstrong Whitworth FK8
Bristol F2B
Caproni Ca42
Fokker Dr1
Fokker DV11
Hansa Brandenburg FB
"Jenny"
Macchi M7
Nieuport 11 Bebe
Siemens Schuckert DIV
Sopworth 1½
Sopworth 2B2
Sopworth Triplane
Spad Type XIII
Vickers FB5
Vickers Vimy

ITEM	MINT	EX
Set	27.50	22.50
Card	1.25	1.00

Fokker Dr1
Flown by Manfred von Richthofen, Germany's famous "Red Baron", who said it "climbed like a monkey, and maneuvered like the devil". Engine: 110 hp Le Rhone. Armament: twin Spandau machine guns. Maximum speed: 102½ mph. Climb: 3,300 feet in 1 minute 36 seconds. Ceiling: 20,000 feet. Endurance: 1½ hours.

ESSKAY

ALF — 1ST SERIES (47 & 22 & 18)   2 1/2" X 3 1/2"

Topps latched onto one of the hottest television personalities of 1987 when it produced this

series about Gordon Shumway, a.k.a. Alf. The set consists of 69 cards and 18 stickers. Cards 1-46 introduce us to the Alien Life Form and tell about "His Life & Times" (card No. 47 is a checklist). A shorter series of

22 cards, numbered 1B-22B, profiles the stars of Melmac's National Pastime, "Bouillabaseball." The 18 stickers have blue starry backgrounds and diecut centers picturing characters from the TV show. All the cards and stickers in the set are numbered and captioned. Note: set prices include stickers.

ITEM	MINT	EX
Set	15.00	10.00
Cards		
1-47	.10	.05
1B-22B	.35	.25
Sticker	.35	.25
Wrapper	--	.35
Box	--	5.00

Bouillabaseball Cards

1B Gordon "No Problem" Shumway
2B Sally "Queenie" Shankwipple
3B Arnold "P.U." Garlic
4B G. Hamilton Chickpea III
5B Bob Lundquist
6B Ester "The Tomato" Dink
7B Hap Frizzbain
8B Howard "Slap" Happer
9B Brad "Hippity" Hopper
10B Reginald "Hoots" Fang
11B Mickey Mackerel
12B Thor "The Tank" Tankersly
13B Lyle "The Finger" Huck
14B Tyrone "The Shoe" Horner
15B Simus "Goobers" Wadsworth
16B Stanley "Mousebreath" Yikes
17B Ben "Choo-Choo" Tramer
18B Erno "What's It To Ya" Sludge
19B Ron Oyster
20B Wilber "Scooter" Pyz
21B Egbert "Tiny" Cartwheeler
22B Skippy "The Terror" Meltzer

1   How About A Hug For The Old Alfer?
2   I'm Only 229. I Haven't Hit My Prime!
3   You're Out Of This World!
4   Let's Have A Snack. You Got A Cat?
5   Gimme Four!
6   Be There Or Be Square
7   Have A Seat...Let's Have A Chili Cat!
8   Willie's Okay...For Someone Without Fur.
9   I'm A People Alien!
10 A Whisker For Your Thoughts.
11 You Remind Me Of Someone I Knew Back On Melmac—
12 Happy Light Year!
13 Hey, No Problem!
14 Don't Be Repulsed...It's A Turkey!
15 Season's Greetings From Alf
16 Alf A Girl's Best Friend
17 What Can I Say? The Kid Adores Me!
18 Alf

1   Introduction Card
2   Whaddya Mean This Isn't A Piano?
3   I Can See It's A Cat...But Where's The Soy Sauce?
4   I Think I'll Order The Cat Of The Day.
5   I Use It For Scanning Hi-Frequency Interplanetary Modulations...And Watching Dr. Ruth.
6   Hey, How Come My Bowtie Doesn't Spin?
7   I Think I'll Take A Little Catting Practice.
8   What Do You Mean, "Willie Is The Fairest Of Them All"?
9   Hey, I'm Supposed To Be The One With The Silly Hair.
10 Hi, Honey, I'm Home.
11 You're Right! TV Is A Lot Better When It's Plugged In!!
12 Smile When You Call Me Repulsive!
13 Now Smile And Say "Cheese Cat!"
14 Don't Look Now, But There's An Alien Behind The Couch.
15 Don't Come In Yet. The Kitchen Needs A Second Coat Of Spaghetti Sauce.
16 Cheer Up. We'll Stop Falling Off The Couch Eventually.
17 Wash The Laundry? I Thought You Said Toss The Laundry!
18 Would You Buy A Used Car From This Family?
19 Are We Having Fun Yet?
20 Alf, You Can't Dry Dishes By Putting Them In The Toaster.
21 My Earth Family Doesn't Understand Me, Doctor.
22 Tastes A Lot Like Calicoquille-St. Jacques.
23 I Told You, I Didn't Eat Lucky. Do You See A Tail Down There?
24 TV Dinner? Isn't The Picture Tube A Little Tough To Get Down?
25 Siamese On Rye, Stella. Tuck In The Tail.

26 Hi There. Do You Come Here Often?
27 Who Needs A Pot Of Gold At The End Of The Rainbow. I've Got A Refrigerator!
28 I'm Taking This To Remember You By! You Mean Our Portrait? No... Your Camera!
29 Operator, I'd Like To Place A Collect Call To The Man In The Moon.
30 I Wonder If I Can Deduct Flea Powder As A Business Expense?
31 Get My Lawyer! Nobody Calls Me A Litterbug!
32 C'Mon, Let's Build Something Fun... Like A Blonde.
33 This Isn't Your Shirt, Willie. I Borrowed It From A Neighbor's Clothesline.
34 What A Shame. Nothing Left To Eat...Except That Pillow.
35 Who Ordered The Grilled Broccoli And Tuna-Flavored Soda?
36 I'm A Melmac Doodle Dandy!
37 Alf, Do You Ever Stop Eating? Can't Talk Now, Willie...My Mouth's Full.
38 So The Cat's Missing. Why Is Everybody Looking At Me?
39 Siamese & Mayo. Oh! I Thought You Said Cinco De Mayo.
40 Whaddya Mean You're Trying To Get Cable? There's Tons of It Lyin' Around!
41 I Wanted A New Car For My Birthday...But This Is Ridiculous!
42 I Don't Mind If You Go Steady. Just Not With Each Other!
43 Want Some Anchovies? No, But I'll Eat The Can!
44 Hey, Did You Stop Using Hair Spray And Switch To Jell-O?
45 O.K. Who's The Wise Buy Who Made Off With My Persian On Rye?
46 I Can't See The Future, But I Am Getting A Rerun Of "Diff'rent Strokes".
47 Checklist

Alas, the chronicle of the Alien Life Form, more commonly known to millions of Earthlings as "ALF," has been relegated to the status of syndicated rerun. However, collectors have two series of ALF cards, produced by Topps in 1987 and 1988 when the show was at its peak, to keep the memory of Gordon Shumway alive.

This second series, like the first, is divided into three categories: regular cards, "Bouillabaseball" cards, and stickers. The regular cards (numbered 48-91) have red borders and contain color photos from the TV show, with black-letter captions printed in yellow panels beneath the pictures (1st series colors were reversed: yellow borders & red panels with white letters). There are 47 regular cards in 1st series ALF; the 2nd series has but 44.

There are 22 "Bouillabaseball" cards in the 2nd series, the same number as in the 1st, and these follow the same format and are numbered 23B to 44B. The team and player names are very funny and show more wit and imagination than do the regular cards of the set. The eleven stickers (numbered 19-29) are all photographs of ALF in portrait or in costume; the color centers are surrounded by black, starry borders. Since all the captions read "ALF," there is no point in printing a separate checklist for 2nd series stickers. Note: set price includes stickers.

ITEM	MINT	EX
Set	15.00	10.00
Cards		
48-91	.10	.05
23B-44B	.35	.25
Sticker	.35	.25
Wrapper	––	.35
Box	––	4.00

CARDS:
48 2nd Series Header Card
49 It's Tough Being A Living Legend!

50 You Know, Mummies Were the First Ones to Sing "Wrap" Music!
51 Watsa Matter? Cat Got Your Tongue! Har Har!
52 You Know What They Say: "Hair Today, Gone Tomorrow!"
53 I Think They Left the Cat in the Dryer!
54 As the Karate Experts Say: "Ouuuuuuch!!!"
55 I Knew I Had Fans ... But Not *These* Kinds of Fans!
56 It's Important to Eat Your Food ... Otherwise I will!
57 He's Not Sick. He Just Needs to Chase the Cat for Awhile!
58 Brother, Can You Spare a Cat?
59 I Ate the Phone? Well, That Explains the Ringing Sensation in My Head!
60 I Was Too Small to Play Quarterback. So They Made Me a One-Eight Back! Har Har!
61 No More Coffee for Me! I Had Too Much Yesterday ... and I Thought We Were Having an Earthquake!
62 Wait! Dinner Isn't Over! I Think I Smell a Cat!
63 If We're Gonna Play Hide-and-Seek, You Have to Cover Your Eyes!
64 Karate is All Mind Over Matter. Sure, If You Don't Mind the Pain, It Won't Matter!
65 Let's Play Cards! Everything's Wild for Guys from Melmac!
66 We'll Throw Alf a Surprise Party! Better Yet, Let's Just Throw Alf!
67 I Never Met a Cat I Didn't Like ... for Dinner!
68 Did You Get Shorter, or Is Your Son Growing Very, Very Fast?
69 Did You Know I Wear a Size 44 Suit. Extra Squat?
70 Say, Don't I Know You from Another Planet?
71 What Bowling Ball? I'm Not Letting My Cat Out of the Bag!
72 Trust Me! I'll Be More than Happy to Babysit for Your Cat!
73 I've Got a Pair of Aces and This Replica of My Birth Certificate!
74 I Only Dress Like This So I Can Carry a Briefcase. It's Perfect for Big Lunches!
75 Are You Sure I Can't Order a Fudge Ripple Sundae Here?
76 If You Can't Eat It, Forget It!
77 Who Would Eat All the Canned Food Without Opening the Can? Gee, Ya Got Me?!

78 Hey, I Told You to be Careful with those Velcro Eyebrows!
79 What Can I Tell You? The Girl Who Sold Me this Shirt was Very Cute!
80 The Winner! You Actually Finished Your Meal Before Alf Could Finish It for You!
81 Is This a Bowtie or am I being Choked by a Snake in Formal Wear?
82 Vote for Me! I'm for a Cat in Every Pot and Two Aliens in Every Garage!
83 Who Says You're Not Supposed to Eat the Bag After You Dunk It?
84 Is There Such a Thing as Being "Too Cool"?
85 There's No Worse Feeling than When a Meal is Over!
86 Watch Out, Spuds! The *Real* Party Animal has Arrived!
87 If I Get Any Better Looking, We May Have to Sell Tickets!
88 What Happened? No More Ring Around the Collar?
89 I Was So Hungry, I Ate the First Chapter of this Book!
90 When You're Like Me, Finding Hair in Your Food is an Occupational Hazard!
91 A Hair Dryer? I Thought It was a Bagpipe that Went Berserk!

BOUILLABASEBALL CARDS:
23B Dirk "That Swell Guy" Twink
24B Biff "Lucky" Delrish
25B Abner "The Big Hucker" Knarp
26B Artie "The Sponge" Fern
27B Nina "Dropsies" Zynk
28B Fafner "That Goofy Guy" Pelt
29B Wilky "The Salad Bar" Wartlap
30B Sid "The Mad Bunny" Tenny
31B Heather "Leather" Labat
32B Benny "The Ball" Baldelli
33B Homer "The Gooch" Twang
34B Timmy "The Fist" Shrapknuckle
35B Chuck "The Chucker" Stang
36B Earl "Rat Lips" Flick
37B Sondra "The Wank" Proudfoot
38B Marty "Dandy" Torpedos
39B Seymore "The Stick" Faz
40B Spilvey "The Rock" Glik
41B Chester "Spunky" Thread
42B Bart "The Swollen Egg" Lobb
43B Barbie "The Lobster Bib" Coals
44B Sean "The Munchkin" Splat

ALF ALBUM STICKERS (180)   1 3/4" X 2 9/16"

Diamond Toy began distribution of this Alf album sticker set immediately after its "U.S. of Alf" series hit the market in January 1988. Each album sticker measures 1 3/4" X 2 9/16" and depicts the Alien Life Form in photographs or artwork. There are 180 stickers in the set and all are numbered on the back. Diamond also printed a 24-page album in which to affix the stickers. Two SLIDE-O-SCOPE Movie Viewers are provided with every album; these allow the viewer to see Alf in animation when looking at special-format drawings printed on album pages and stickers.

Note: set price includes album.

ITEM	MINT	EX
Set	30.00	22.50
Sticker	.15	.10
Wrapper	--	.35
Album	3.00	2.00
Box	--	4.00

ALIEN (84 & 22)

2 1/2" X 3 1/2"

Alien, issued in 1979, is composed of 84 cards and 22 stickers showing scenes from the Twentieth Century Fox movie of the same name. The cards have red borders on the front, with the caption underneath the picture in a yellow area and the number in a blue circle. The backs are two varieties: one is a series of 44 story cards (story in "egg" on blue background) and the other is a series of 36 puzzle backs and four puzzle promotion cards (backs show completed puzzle). The sticker pictures have yellow frame lines and green borders and are numbered but not captioned. Since they correspond to pictures found in the card series, they have been assigned captions in the checklist below. Note: set prices include stickers.

ITEM	MINT	EX
Set	18.00	14.00
Card	.15	.10
Sticker	.35	.25
Wrapper	--	.50
Box	--	7.00

1 The Nostromo
2 Halls of Silence
3 The Ship...Deserted
4 Activated Star Helmet
5 Electronic Conversation
6 Emerging from Hypersleep
7 Nostromo Interiors
8 Captain Dallas
9 Warrant Officer Ripley
10 Executive Officer Kane
11 Science Officer Ash
12 Navigator Lambert
13 Engineer Parker
14 Technician Brett
15 Introducing 'Jones'
16 Crew of the Nostromo
17 A Message from 'Mother'
18 "Where's Earth?"
19 Signals from Deep Space
20 Ready to Land
21 Asteroid Colony Design
22 The Refinery
23 The Planet in Sight
24 Searing Electrical Fire!
25 The Steamy Peril
26 A Pensive Kane
27 Furturistic Spacesuit
28 Space Tug, Disengaged
29 The Landing
30 The Asteroid Explorers
31 Walking to Derelict
32 Bizarre Alien Landscape
33 Grotesque Rock Formations
34 Ash's Deception
35 Explorers...Or Invaders?
36 Nightmare Planet
37 Dawn on the Devil World
38 Dallas, Kane and Lambert
39 The Derelict Spaceship
40 Entrance to Derelict
41 At Death's Door
42 Mind-boggling Sight!
43 Fantastic Space Jockey
44 Face of the Space Jockey
45 Inspecting the 'Jockey'
46 Sculpting the 'Jockey' Prop
47 Creating a Space Jockey
48 The Chamber Entrance
49 Enter...the Hell Chamber!
50 Egg Hatchery
51 Kane's Discovery
52 "Don't Touch It, Kane!"
53 Unearthly Assault!
54 Dressing a Movie Set

SCIENCE FICTION SHOCKER OF THE YEAR!

55 Nostromo Tug Lifting Off
56 Returning to the Refinery
57 The Face Grabber
58 Remains of a Monster
59 The Last Supper
60 The Thing Within Kane!
61 The Chest Burster
62 Alien Search Weapons
63 The Search Begins
64 "Oh God...No! NO!"
65 Hunting the Beast
66 Dallas' Fate
67 Ash...An Enemy?
68 Struggle with Ash
69 Ash Runs Amok!

70 The Murderous Android
71 The Secret Revealed
72 "Where Can It Be?"
73 Corridors of Nostromo
74 Organic Starcraft Design
75 The Monster at Bay
76 Unstoppable Horror!
77 Escape Shuttle Narcissus
78 It Lives to Destroy!
79 Walking Nightmare!
80 Spacesuit Storage Area
81 Ripley Strikes Back!
82 The Final Stand
83 Blown into Oblivion!
84 The Survivor

1 Engineer Parker
2 Executive Officer Kane
3 Captain Dallas
4 Navigator Lambert
5 Alien Search Weapons
6 Escape Shuttle Narcissus
7 Face of the Space Jockey
8 Bizarre Alien Landscape
9 Crew of the Nostromo
10 The Refinery
11 Ash's Deception
12 Technician Brett
13 Science Officer Ash
14 Warrant Officer Ripley
15 Fantastic Space Jockey
16 "Where Can It Be?"
17 The Nostromo
18 Asteroid Colony Design
19 Dawn on the Devil World
20 "Where's Earth?"
21 Dallas, Kane and Lambert
22 It Lives to Destroy!

ALIEN NATION (60)

Alien Nation, a Fox Television Network series with a devoted following of fans, is the subject of this 60-card set produced in 1990 by Mark Macaluso of the Fantasy Trading Card Co. (FTCC). The header card (#1) and cards 2-12 depict various Alien Nation characters on the front and have character/actor identifications on the back. Cards 13-60 show more actors and scenes from the program but have puzzle backs. None of the cards carries an obverse caption and card numbers are printed only on the fronts.

The series was issued in poly "bag" packs in counter display boxes. This means that all wrappers distributed to the public will have sides cut off or the back slit open to get to the cards inside. A minimum amount of damage to the wrapper will give it "excellent" status under these circumstances, but wrappers with excessive damage must be downgraded and priced accordingly.

ITEM	MINT	EX
Set	10.00	7.50
Card	.15	.10
Wrapper	—	.50
Box	—	2.00

Lovely Cathy Frankel played by Terri Treas

ALL MY CHILDREN (72)

"All My Children," the legendary ABC soap opera with millions of fans (including many NFL players, who selected it as their favorite daytime soap) has been crafted into a 72 card set by Star Pics. The series incorporates all the excellent production values of Star Pics' "CardArt" projects: sharp images, super glossy finish, stylish layout, and clear, readable text. Soap buffs will enjoy the diverse components of the set: Characters, Famous Scenes, Family Trees, Local Sites, Famous Couples, and Love Triangles, to name a few. Of special interest is the subset of seven cards devoted to Erica Kane, the character that eleven million women love to hate (probably all of them vote against her in the Emmys!). Star Pics distributed this 1991 set in two ways: in ten-card foil packs and as a complete set in a small collector's box. Cards bearing the authentic signatures of AMC actors were randomly inserted into packs and a two-card promotional strip was given to dealers and the media. Collectors will be interested to know that there are six unnumbered cards in the set: 3, 8, 18, 38 & 50 (you can tell where they belong in the sequence by the subject matter).

ITEM	MINT	EX
Sets		
From packs	15.00	11.00
In box	20.00	15.00
Card	.20	.15
Wrapper	—	.15
Display box	—	2.00
Autographed cards		
Susan Lucci	25.00	20.00
All others	15.00	10.00

All My Children

1 In The Beginning	36 Jeremy and Natalie	53 Adam and Erica
2 All About Pine Valley	37 Trevor and Natalie	54 McKay's
3 Martin Family Tree*	38 Wallingford Family Tree*	55 Jackson Montgomery
4 Joe Martin	39 Phoebe Wallingford	56 Jackson and Erica
5 Ruth Martin	40 Langley and Phoebe	57 A Fire at the Montgomery's
6 Joe and Ruth	41 Trivia	58 Caught in the Middle
7 Trivia	42 Myrtle Fargate	59 Jeremy and Erica
8 Chandler Family Tree*	43 The Boutique	60 Erica at the Circus
9 Adam Chandler	44 Ceara Connor	61 Trivia
10 Stuart Chandler	45 Jackson and Ceara	62 Erica
11 Chandler Mansion	46 Don't Drink and Drive	63 Electrifying / Pure
12 Adam and Brooke	47 Brooke English	64 Playful / Hot
13 Adam and Dixie	48 Tom and Brooke	65 Inspired / Seductive
14 Hayley Vaughn	49 Tom Cudahy	66 Fragile / Aggressive
15 Brian Bodine	50 Kane Family Tree*	67 Sultry / Flirtatious
16 Brian and Hayley	51 Erica Kane	68 Confident / Bewitching
17 The Masked Ball	52 Tom and Erica	69 Behind the Scenes
18 Cortlandt Family Tree*		70 Behind the Scenes
19 Cortlandt Manor		71 Actor Awards
20 Palmer Cortlandt		72 Checklist
21 Trivia		
22 Dixie Martin		
23 Craig Lawson		
24 Love Triangle		
25 Opal Cortlandt		
26 Trivia		
27 The Glamorama		
28 Palmer and Opal		
29 Trivia		
30 Palmer and Natalie		
31 Natalie Chandler		
32 Janet Green		
33 Trevor Dillon		
34 Derek Frye		
35 Jeremy Hunter		

ALL-PRO SKATEBOARD (44)

2 1/2" X 3 1/2"

There are actually 44 sticker-cards in the All-Pro Skateboard set issued by Donruss in 1978. Of these, 42 are numbered; the remaining two have identical fronts (the International Skateboard Association logo) but different backs. The number and caption for each card is located within the score line of the sticker design on front. On the reverse side, the set is composed of 38 profiles of skateboarders, three "Basic Rules" cards (6-7-37), and three ISA membership forms (27-30-41). Note: this set was issued after "Skateboard" but leftover stickers from that set were also placed in packages of this series.

	EX	ITEM	MINT
Set		10.00	8.00
Sticker-card		.25	.20
Wrapper		---	1.00
Box		---	5.00

BASIC RULES FOR SAFE SKATEBOARDING

TAKE GOOD CARE OF YOUR EQUIPMENT

1. Check your bearings and wheels.
2. Look the board over, check for cracks or splits.
3. Use a non-skid material on the deck of your board.

DRESS COMFORTABLY IN PROTECTIVE EQUIPMENT

1. Always skateboard in athletic shoes.
2. Wear a helmet, gloves, and knee and elbow pads.
3. *Protect your weak spots.* If it is your hips, wear hip padding. If it is your wrists, wear wrist guards. Protect any area of likely impact.

INTERNATIONAL SKATEBOARD ASSOCIATION

APPLICATION FOR MEMBERSHIP

I would like to become an Official Member of the ISA. Enclosed is $10.00; please send me an ISA Decal, Poster, T-shirt, Membership Card and my one year subscription to "National Skateboard Review".

NAME

PHONE   SHIRT SIZE

ADDRESS   AGE

CITY   STATE   ZIP

INTERNATIONAL SKATEBOARD ASSOCIATION
711 W. 17th, Suite E7
Costa Mesa, California 92627

All-Pro Skateboard

1 Three Wheels Over
2 Samoan Squat Nose Wheelie
3 Tail Tapper
4 Speed Slalom
5 Wired!
6 Forearm Handstand
7 Helicopter
8 Boogie Down!
9 Pipeline Fever
10 Do Not Touch This Skate Board
11 Off The Rocks
12 Wind Sailor
13 Gutter Jumping
14 Confucius Say Wiseman Use Helmet
15 UFO
16 High Jump
17 Catamaran
18 Frontside 360
19 Street Serpent
20 Kiss The Rim
21 Stoked!
22 Thirst For Skateboarding
23 Kick Tail
24 Street Freak
25 Backside 360
26 Locomotion
27 Bunny Hop
28 Concrete Surfer
29 Powerslide
30 360 Arial
31 Wild Child
32 One Foot Nose Wheelie
33 Bail Out
34 Salvage
35 Double Handstand
36 On The Ceiling
37 Make Skateboarding an Olympic Sport 1984
38 Smokin
39 Barbarian
40 Free Spirit
41 Pure Speed
42 High Flyer

ALVIN TATTOOS (?)

SIZE UNKNOWN

Very little is known about the set of tattoos based on Ross Bagdasarian's character "Alvin the Chipmunk." It was produced by Fleer, and unlike most of the other "tattoo" sets on the market, the "transfer picture" was printed on a separate piece of paper rather than on the inside of the wrapper.

ITEM	MINT	EX
Tattoo	--	5.00
Wrapper	--	35.00
Unopened pack	--	45.00

AMERICAN HISTORY TRADING CARDS (24) 2 1/2" X 3 1/2"

"American History Trading Cards" were issued as special inserts in Scholastic Magazine during 1976. The magazine was distributed to junior high and high schools across the country and not many of the cards have "survived" to filter into the non-sport hobby. The fronts contain captioned, artwork scenes and subjects using duller color schemes than many mainstream card issues, but the details of each picture are well-drawn and interesting. The backs have black-print text on brown stock and some edges will be rouletted since the cards were issued in strips or sheets. None of the cards are numbered. Note: only cards intact in original sheets or strips can be graded "mint"; since we have not seen any of these and are unable to determine the original form, we can not list prices for this grade.

ITEM	MINT	EX
Set	--	20.00
Card	--	.75

Benjamin Franklin
Chief Sitting Bull
Crossing the Delaware
Declaration of Independence
Elizabeth Cady Stanton
First at the North Pole
George Washington
John Paul Jones
Lindbergh Flies the Atlantic
Marquis de Lafayette
Men Land on the Moon
Patrick Henry
Paul Revere
Paul Revere's Ride
Racing Cars Old and New
Rockets Old and New
The Battle of Lexington
The Bombing of Pearl Harbor
The Boston Tea Party
The San Francisco Earthquake
The Statue of Liberty
The United States Enters World War I
The Wright Brothers' Airplane
Thomas Jefferson

AMERICAN ZOO ANIMALS (25) 1 1/8" X 2 3/4"

This was the premiere set of Nabisco's annual nature series which was initiated in 1963. The obverse of each card contains striking color artwork; a dated copyright line is located below. The backs contain the series number and title, the card number and title (including the Latin binomial), and text. The series was prepared by H. Wayne Trimm and distributed in packages of Sugar Daddy caramel pops. An album to house the collection is available through the mail.

ITEM	MINT	EX
Set	18.00	13.50
Card	.60	.45
Album	15.00	12.00

1 Bobcat
2 Gray Fox
3 Timber Wolf
4 Moose
5 Sea Lion
6 Mountain Lion
7 Black-tailed Deer
8 Black Bear
9 Bighorn Sheep
10 Mink
11 Ringtail Cat
12 Shorttail Weasel or Ermine
13 Alligator
14 Antelope or Pronghorn
15 Grizzly Bear
16 Wolverine
17 Sea Otter
18 Armadillo
19 Florida Key Deer
20 Blacktail Prairie Dog
21 American Elk or Wapiti
22 Mountain Goat
23 Lynx
24 Coyote
25 Bison

AN AMERICAN TAIL —
FIEVEL GOES WEST (150)

2 1/2" X 3 1/2"

Fievel and his family, the Mousekewitzes, have fled the oppression and Cossacks of Imperial Russia and made a daring trip to America. They find a home on Hester Street, in New York City, but are constantly terrorized by a gang of cats. Seeking a better life, they accept free railway tickets to the western town of Green River, only to find they are being "imported" to feed a bunch of western cats, led by Cat R. Waul. Fievel, who has romantic notions of western life from books he has read, must now foil these feline desperados with the help of his family, a friendly cat from back east, and a cowardly dog. Fievel and his

friends win the showdown and turn their efforts into making Green River a happy home for all peaceable critters.

Such is the story told by Impel's 1991 series of 150 cards entitled "An American Tail - Fievel Goes West." Children were the "target" market for this heartwarming story and they are sure to be pleased with the color artwork and text of the cards. The set is divided into several subgroups: cards 1-14 introduce the characters; cards 15-25 show various characters together; cards 26-102 carry the main story; cards 103-134 are "Fievel's Diary;" cards 135-143 show how the animated film was made;

cards 144-147 give safety tips and advice; card #148 depicts the movie poster; and cards 149 and 150 are checklists. The glossy front and back surfaces bring out the details which make this set so attractive. The cards were distributed in 12-count poly bag wrappers and five bonus holograms were randomly inserted into packs. The latter are not part of the regular set and prices for them had not yet been established by the time this book was printed.

ITEM	MINT	EX
Set	15.00	10.00
Card	.10	.07
Wrapper	—	.15
Box	—	2.00

We Need You!

1 Fievel
2 Tanya
3 Papa
4 Mama
5 Yasha
6 Cat R. Waul
7 T.R. Chula
8 Wylie Burp
9 Tiger
10 Miss Kitty
11 "One Eye"
12 "Earless"
13 "Frenchy"
14 Geronimouse
15 Fievel & Tiger
16 Fievel & Tanya
17 Fievel & Wylie Burp
18 Mama & Papa
19 The Architect & Cat R. Waul
20 Cat R. Waul & Chula
21 Miss Kitty & Tiger
22 Tanya & Miss Kitty
23 Mousekewitz Family
24 The Waul Gang
25 The Wylie Bunch
26 New York, 1885
27 Hester Street
28 Tanya Sings for Supper
29 Reading About Wylie
30 Fievel's Fantasy
31 "Filly the Kid"
32 Miss Kitty & Tiger
33 Miss Kitty's Farewell
34 Mousekewitzes at Dinner
35 Alarm!
36 Cat Attack!
37 Mice on the Run
38 Escape Devices
39 Tiger's Aborted Rescue
40 Fievel Faces "One-Eye"
41 Fievel is Cornered
42 Papa to the Rescue
43 Rolling Tuna Tin
44 Escaping From "One-Eye"
45 Shooting the Rapids
46 Hustler the Mouse
47 The Crowd Goes Crazy

48 Fievel's Note
49 Grand Central Station
50 Fievel Says Goodbye
51 Tiger Dodging Dogs
52 The Dog Pound
53 Tiger Leaps on the Train
54 Tiger in the River
55 Tiger on Stage
56 Fievel Explores the Train
57 Fievel Entangled
58 Playing Poker
59 "Mouseburgers"
60 "What Do We Have Here?"
61 Mouse Overboard
62 Green River
63 Cats are Nice in the West
64 The Raging Sun
65 Tiger and Fievel's Mirage
66 Indian Village
67 The Indian Chief
68 Hawk Dive-Bombs Fievel
69 Fievel & Scorpions
70 The Hawk Gets Fievel
71 The Indian God
72 Fievel's Rescue?
73 Fievel Un-eaten
74 Talkin' Tumbleweed
75 Home at Last
76 Saloon Raising
77 Blueprints

78 The Giant Mousetrap
79 Catching the Spy
80 A Talent Discovered
81 Tanya Transformed
82 Tanya's Debut
83 Fievel & the Dawg
84 We Need You!
85 Desperado Gulch
86 Practice Makes Perfect

LOOK OUT PARDNERS, THERE'S A NEW MOUSE IN TOWN

AN AMERICAN TAIL
FIEVEL GOES WEST

AN AMERICAN TAIL
FIEVEL GOES WEST

The Characters Come to Life!

AN AMERICAN TAIL
FIEVEL GOES WEST

Play It Safe!

87 Bark School
88 Lazy Eye
89 Dog Practice
90 Heroes Are Born
91 Ruff & Ready
92 Town Square
93 Mousetrap in Disguise
94 Just in Time!
95 The Paw Fight
96 Showdown
97 Tanya's Warning
98 Tiger the Hero
99 Cat-a-pult
100 Prairie Dog Hill
101 Fievel Gets His Badge
102 Sunset
103 Happy in Russia
104 Hanukkah Gifts
105 Papa's Stories
106 Cossack Attack
107 Leaving Russia
108 The Boat Trip
109 The Storm at Sea
110 Overboard
111 Floating in a Bottle
112 Immigration
113 Henri the Pigeon
114 Showing Fievel America
115 Warren T. Rat & Digit
116 Putting Fievel to Work
117 Tony Toponi
118 Looking for Papa
119 Lost in America
120 Reunion with Tony
121 The Mayor

122 Thinking of Tanya
123 The Town Meeting
124 Fievel's Idea
125 The Museum
126 Papa?
127 Trapped
128 A Sensitive Cat
129 The Chase
130 Giant Mouse of Minsk
131 Soaking Cats
132 Family Reunion
133 Flying with Henri
134 Statue of Liberty
135 The Story & The Screenplay
136 Story Sketches & Early Visuals
137 Character Development
138 The Characters Come to Life!
139 Backgrounds & Scene Painting
140 Animation Drawing
141 Coloring Ink & Paint
142 Painting & Finishing Cels
143 Final Assembly & Filming
144 Play It Safe!
145 Making Friends
146 Fun Adventures
147 Family of Friends
148 Movie Poster
149 Checklist 1
150 Checklist 2

24

AN AMERICAN TAIL — FIEVEL GOES WEST (3)

2 1/2" X 3 1/2"

Impel, the manufacturer of the regular trading card series starring Fievel, joined Pizza Hut in a kid's meal promotion in late 1991 and early 1992. Purchasers of a "Kid's Pizza Pack" received a theme box containing a two-page newsletter and a single trading card (the meal also came with a plastic character cup). Three different cards have been reported to date; the one pictured here is borderless (the regular cards have borders) and it does not appear in the regular Impel series. The back contains a small introductory text, advertising copy for the Impel set, and Impel and Pizza Hut logos. None of the Pizza Hut cards are numbered and because of the limited duration of the promotion and the manner of distribution (many are bent), excellent grade cards are valued at $1.00 each. The theme box and plastic cup are also worth $1.00 each, while the newsletter sells for 50 cents.

AN AMERICAN TAIL — FIEVEL GOES WEST ALBUM STICKERS (150)

1 3/4" X 2 1/2"

Diamond Toy obtained a license from MCA Merchandising to issue "An American Tail - Fievel Goes West" in album sticker format. Released to the public in late 1991, the series consists of 150 small stickers plus an album with corresponding spaces to house them. Each sticker front has a color artwork picture which is surrounded by two, three, or four yellow borders, depending on whether or not it stands alone or is grouped with other stickers in the album. The backs are numbered and carry collecting advice in both English and French (the set was also issued in Canada). All of the text is printed in the album under the appropriate space or spaces. The package containing six stickers sold for 40 cents in the U.S. and 49 cents in Canada. Help in assembling a complete set was available via the "Diamond Sticker Trading Club" advertised on the back cover of the album. Note: set price includes album.

ITEM	MINT	EX
Set	15.00	10.00
Sticker	.10	.07
Wrapper	--	.15
Album	1.00	.75

Knowledgeable collectors are well aware of the difficulty involved in completing the Andy Gibb poster set. Produced in 1978 by Donruss, each of the 42 large paper posters bears a full-color photo of the youngest of the singing Gibb brothers. None of the posters is captioned but each is numbered. The wrapper is blue with a red title and a red and yellow design. Note: since the posters were folded several times to fit into the standard size wrapper, we have not listed a "mint" price for this item.

ITEM	MINT	EX
Set	--	60.00
Poster	--	1.00
Wrapper	--	1.00
Box	--	5.00

A nostalgia set produced by Pacific Trading Cards in 1990, the first series of "Andy Griffith" contains 110 cards. Of these, 50 have color pictues; the rest are black & white (color cards are marked with an asterisk in the checklist below). The photos are a mix of show scenes, publicity stills, and "set takes."

All cards are captioned on the front and have a logo reading "The Andy Griffith Show" in the lower left corner of the frameline. The backs have a red ink sketch of the show's four principal characters, text, and the card number (in a Mayberry police badge). The series was distributed both in individual (gumless) packs and as a boxed set.

ITEM	MINT	EX
Set	15.00	10.00
Cards		
Color	.15	.10
B&W	.10	.05
Wrapper	—	.35
Set box	—	.50
Display box	—	2.00

1 Catch of the Day*
2 Bee Leaving Mayberry*
3 Sheriff Without a Gun*
4 Barney Fife*
5 "Two Chairs, No Waiting"*
6 Eagle-Eye Annie*
7 "Nip It in the Bud!"*
8 Tailored Taylor*
9 Aunt Bee Taylor*
10 Andy and Warren on Call*
11 Shazam!*
12 Mayberry Sweethearts*
13 Great Casting*
14 Keeper of the Flame*
15 The Tomahawks*
16 Howard Sprague*
17 Outstanding Outdoorsman*
18 The Return of Barney Fife*
19 Mayberry Double Take*
20 Heart for Heart's Sake*
21 Kid Stuff*
22 All in a Day's Work*
23 Civil Servants*
24 Two Men and a Lady*
25 Down by the Duck Pond*
26 Nature Study*
27 The Fishin' Hole*
28 Colorful Couples*
29 Opie Taylor*
30 Happy Camper*
31 Goober Says Hey!
32 Class Reunion
33 "Hello Sarah? Get Me a Bluebird Diner."
34 Gomer Pyle
35 "Well, Come On Now, Don't Give Him My Mr. Cookie Bar."
36 What's Shakin' in Mayberry
37 Sign of the Times
38 Barney's Bloodhound
39 Otis Campbell
40 All Smiles
41 Helen Crump
42 Party Animal
43 "Lover Sheriff!"
44 Thelma Lou
45 TV Time at the Taylors
46 Mayberry Due Process
47 Out Shopping
48 Opie Welcomes Aunt Bee Home
49 Opie Reacts to Andy's Blackened Eggs
50 Andy Taylor on Mayberry
51 "You Beat Everything, You Know That!"
52 The Taylor Family
53 Salt and Pepper Deputy
54 "No Children, No Pets and No Cooking"
55 Howard Land ..d Sam
56 Mayberry Hold-Up
57 Read My Lips
58 Leon
59 Quick-Draw Experts
60 Aunt Bee at the Controls
61 Andy Taylor*
62 Just Deserts*
63 Back to Nature*
64 Floyd Lawson*
65 Breakfast with the Taylors*
66 Front Porch Portrait*
67 Goober Pyle*
68 Go Fish*
69 A Standing "O" for Andy*
70 Like Father, Like Son*
71 The Omen of the Owl*
72 Mayberry Stare Case
73 Warren Ferguson
74 Red-Headed Ranger*
75 Love Birds*
76 Let's Go Fly a Kite*
77 "You Belong in the Funny Papers, You Know That!"*
78 Ready for the Esquire Club*
79 The Darlings
80 Floyd's Barbershop*
81 The Taylor Men*
82 Service with a Smile
83 A Kid'll Eat Ivy*
84 Mayberry Sunshine*
85 "Millions for Defense, But Not One Cent for Tribute."
86 Justice of the Peace
87 "If I Ever Have to Use this Baby, I Want to Teach It to Come to Papa in a Hurry."
88 The Few. The Proud. The Gomer.
89 Tune in to Mayberry
90 Mayberry Ghostbusters
91 The New Housekeeper
92 Having a Blast!
93 Mrs. MacGruder's Cousin
94 Briscoe Darling
95 Andrew Paul Lawson and Floyd
96 Batman
97 "Pipe Down, Otis!"
98 Dummy Detective
99 "Next!"
100 "They're All Keyed Up!"
101 Alert at All Times
102 Chalk Talk
103 Fireside Chat
104 "How Do You Do, Mrs. Wiley?"
105 Ernest T. Bass
106 Maximum Security
107 A Basket Case for Opie
108 Empty Nest
109 The Wedding
110 Have Beard, Will Think

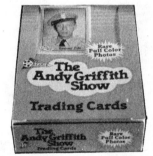

Tailored Taylor

ANDY GRIFFITH — 2ND SERIES (110)   2 1/2" X 3 1/2"

Buoyed by the success of Andy Griffith I, Pacific Trading Cards followed up with AG-II in 1991. Once again, the series contains 110 cards (numbered 111-220) but collectors may be disappointed to find that there are no color cards in the set. The fronts have the same glossy surface, format, and coloration of the first series and the backs are also identical in design to cards 1-110.

The set was issued in packs via retail outlets as well as in specially-boxed complete editions. The small box for the latter has a cellophane wrap with a "Series #2" label attached.

ITEM	MINT	EX
Set	10.00	6.00
Card	.10	.05
Wrapper	––	.25
Set Box	––	.50
Display box	––	1.50

111 Standing Tall
112 Say Watt?
113 Evening News
114 Mayberry Waltz
115 Deputy Dosage
116 Chance of a Ghost?
117 Picnicking Pals
118 "Hey! Stop It, You! Can't You See I'm Holding Up the Rosy Red?"
119 Cabin Fever
120 Calls of Concern
121 "Not Now Leon. I'm on a Case."
122 Posse
123 "Suck in that Gut!"
124 Mr. McBeevee
125 On Patrol
126 "East to West! East to West!"
127 No Loitering
128 "Five."
129 "Hit One for the Ol' Goober."
130 "Ten-hut!"
131 "Relax. Set. One, Two, Throw!"
132 Steamy Situation
133 Fife and Harmonica Blues
134 Ernest T. Studies Ernestly
135 Law on the Crawl
136 Gomer Gets the Blues
137 "Giddy-up Old Paint!"
138 Warren and Andy on Call
139 "Barney!"
140 Mayberry Getaway
141 Extra! Extra!
142 Opie Taylor Sr. and Dr. Pendyke
143 "You Get a Line and I'll Get a Pole, Babe!"
144 Family Time
145 Keeper of the Door
146 A Sinking Feeling
147 Firewater
148 Breathtaking Situation
149 Mr. Goss Cleans His Plate
150 Debonair Deputy

151 Forget Something, Barn?
152 The New Mayberry Minstrels
153 Pep Talk
154 "Say It Again."
155 Lone Trombone
156 Hello Dolly!
157 Snack Time
158 Otis with Andy's Fixer-upper
159 "Everybody on the Truck."
160 Red Barn
161 Classified
162 Blooey!
163 Miracle Salve
164 A Set
165 Window Shopping
166 Fast-gun Fife
167 On Guard!
168 Fun Girls
169 Fields of Investigation
170 Recaptured ... Again
171 Seasoned Greetings
172 Mayberry Friends and Grins
173 Rafe Hollister
174 Oh My, Darlings!
175 Waiting for the Gold Shipment
176 Life at "The Rock"
177 "No Hunt Beware Open and Closed No Credit"
178 Chili Time
179 "Here It Comes, Here It Comes."
180 Double Deputies
181 Mountain Wedding
182 Deputy Otis
183 Duelling Guitars
184 Sidecar Express
185 To Bee or Not to Bee
186 Stumped
187 "Oh, Andy, I Know a Lot about Baseball. Who Do You Think I Am — a Ninny?"
188 We the People
189 Courthouse Cousins

190 Barney and the Cave Rescue
191 Double-barrelled Deputy
192 Wall Partners
193 Classic Clerk
194 Bee Pouring It On
195 Stick 'Em Up!
196 Bee Lines
197 Bee's Birthday
198 A Door, Able Kid
199 The Darling Baby
200 Andy and the Woman Speeder
201 Down by the Duck Pond
202 All Set
203 Two Boys and a Baby
204 At the Ballpark

205 Barney Fife, Realtor
206 Not Pleased
207 Bee Sting
208 Understanding English
209 Play More
210 Largemouth Bass Fishing
211 Staggering Success
212 "This Car's Just Been Sitting on a Velvet Pillow."
213 Lemon Fresh and Mrs. Lesh
214 Sunday Drive Way
215 Pillar of the Community
216 Mortar Fire
217 Southern Draw
218 Tannenbaum Barn
219 Sketch of the Imagination
220 Let's Face It

ANDY GRIFFITH — 3RD SERIES (110)   2 1/2" X 3 1/2"

The third series of Andy Griffith, distributed by Pacific Trading Cards in 1991, has 110 cards and runs in number sequence from 221 to 330. There are 17 color cards among the 110 titles and the most interesting of these are five character drawings which appear late in the set (#'s 321-325). In terms of appearance, the cards do not differ front or back from series I and II. The color cards of this set are marked by an asterisk in the checklist below. Andy Griffith III was

issued both in gumless packs and as boxed sets (the small box is the same as AG-II except that the cellophane wrap has a "Series #3" sticker on it.)

ITEM	MINT	EX
Set	10.00	6.00
Cards		
Color art	.35	.25
Color photo	.15	.10
B&W	.07	.03
Wrapper	--	.10
Set Box	--	.50
Display box	--	1.50

221 The Deadly Game
222 Eye Spy
223 Class Act
224 The Legend Returns
225 No Funning Around
226 Weight Just a Second
227 "You're Right. This is No Place for Us! Let's Get Out of Here!"
228 Outstanding Salesmen
229 Gron and Bearings
230 Fez to Face
231 Spot Reporting
232 Birthday Boy
233 Lunch at Home
234 No Go
235 No Rock Enrolled
236 Mayberry Diplomacy
237 Casual Court
238 Get a Bottle of Pop
239 "Welcome to Checkpoint Chickle!"
240 Check Mates
241 Sidecar Sidelines
242 "Don't Look Back."
243 Fisherman Floyd
244 Mr. 300
245 Friendly Feeding
246 "There's Dud!"
247 Guardian Andy*
248 Draw Play
249 Bench Grinch
250 Still Life in Mayberry
251 Reliable Barney Fife
252 "I'd Appreciate for You to Dance with Me."
253 "Come, Fish, Come"
254 Jim Lindsey
255 "Jubal, Jubal, Jubal. Ju-ball"
256 Having a Ball*
257 Gomer Solo — Just Hymn
258 Grin and Bear It
259 Howard Makes His Point
260 Two Cheers
261 Bearded Wonder
262 Sky's the Limit
263 Sign of a Goober
264 Silver (Carp) Lining
265 The Last Straw
266 Goober's Brain Trust
267 Shock Absorber
268 Faces in the Crowd
269 "A One and a Two and a ..."
270 Drive Bye
271 Lucky Day
272 "Mayberry: Gateway to Danger"

273 "Quiet! We Know How to Deal with Unruly Prisoners!"
274 Where Credit's Due
275 A Little Tied Up
276 Overdrawn
277 Mayor Pike
278 "Now There's Bullet Maintenance."
279 Ellie Walker
280 Citizens Arrested!
281 Rafe Hollister Sings
282 Emmett Clark
283 Mechanical Difficulty
284 Smoked Out
285 Backfiring Sparks
286 The Dipsy-doodle
287 Courthouse Conversation
288 Candid Shot
289 Mayor Roy Stoner

290 Homecoming Hug
291 Fountain of Youth
292 Blue to the Rescue
293 The Barber Civil
294 Double Trouble
295 Three Chairs for Mayberry
296 Music in Mayberry
297 Andy's Open Door Policy
298 Peaceful Officer
299 Deputy Opie?
300 Fine Pine Rose
301 Danny Meets Andy
302 Very Local Call
303 Andy Knows Danny
304 Brass and Copper
305 Country Fathers
306 Dukes of Hazard?
307 Fit to be Tied
308 Facing a Bout
309 Malcolm Merriweather

310 Family Visit
311 Yo-Yo Man
312 Rushin' for Russians
313 Goober SAYS How*
314 Christmas Present*
315 Shoes and Rice Time*
316 Out on a Limb*
317 The Goob*
318 Howard Knows Bowling*
319 Goober Pose*
320 Mayberry Friends*
321 Otis the Artist*
322 Back to Local Call*
323 Floyd the Barber*
324 Gun-Crazy Barney*
325 Mayberry Pride*
326 Pair of Aces
327 Opie, Crackle and Pop*
328 Without Ceremony
329 Irresistible Andy
330 Made in the Shade*

ANGRY STICKERS (88)   1 3/4'' X 2 1/2''

Former Topps spokesman Norman Liss first told us that "Angry Stickers" were issued in 1967 (on a test basis) and this has been confirmed by the "482-85-01-7" code on the wrapper owned by John Neuner. Collector Mark Angert recently obtained a small number of stickers in pairs, thereby proving that the single stickers that exist are actually tandems that were cut apart (single stickers have no "mint" listing for this reason). Angry Stickers are so difficult to obtain that even the box pictured here comes from a photocopy from Topps' archive and no collector is known to have one (the price listed is merely an estimate). Only the factor of limited demand keeps Angry Stickers within a reasonable price range; a complete set commands a special premium.

ITEM	MINT	EX
Sets		
Singles	--	350.00
Pairs	525.00	400.00
Stickers		
Singles	---	3.00
Pairs	10.00	7.00
Wrapper	--	300.00
Box	--	300.00

1 Save Belly Button Lint
2 Bribe A City Official
3 Kick A Dog Today
4 Support Meanness
5 Homework Causes Pimples
6 Santa Claus Is Alive
7 Smokey The Bear Is A Firebug
8 Smack Your Sister
9 Demonstrate For Hate
10 Give To Mental Health Or I'll Kill You
11 Teachers Are Dropouts
12 Cleanliness Is Disgusting
13 Buy Brand X
14 Build Slums
15 Cheat On Exams
16 Flake Off
17 Blow Your Horn Near A Hospital
18 Betray A Friend Today
19 Cut Class Today
20 Down With Everything
21 Snow White Has Bad Breath
22 Take A Fink To Lunch
23 Drop Out Of Everything
24 Be Kind To The Hoods
25 Help Support Low Averages
26 I Support Mental Cruelty!
27 School Causes Sleeping-Sickness
28 I Love Hate
29 Punch A Small Kid Today
30 Warning: Reading Can Be Habit Forming
31 Help Stamp Out School
32 Be A Bully
33 Ban Friendship
34 Think Unpleasant
35 Pray For A Teacher's Strike
36 Smash Violence
37 Bomb The Bans
38 Stamp Out Soap!
39 Brush Twice A Month
40 Studying Kills
41 Slurp Your Soup
42 Lose Your Temper
43 Avoid Responsibility
44 Guard Against Clean Habits
45 Strike Somebody
46 Support Tantrums
47 Act Fresh
48 Avoid Work
49 See Evil/Hear Evil/Speak Evil
50 Down With Grownups
51 Be A Big Mouth
52 Make Friends With A Fink Today
53 Don't Clean Up Your Room
54 Encourage Laziness
55 Fun, Si, Homework, No!!
56 Say "No" To Everything
57 Only Finks Get Good Marks
58 Irritate A Parent Today
59 My Teacher Hates Me
60 Down With Haircuts
61 Pout!!
62 My Teacher Is A Public Nuisance
63 Are Adults Necessary?
64 Knowledge Is Junk
65 Don't Talk, Yell!
66 Cleanliness Is A Disease
67 Same To You, Bub
68 Dirt Don't Hurt
69 Down With Vitamins
70 Practice Lying
71 Support Unpleasantness
72 Soap And Water Ruins The Skin
73 Freckles Are Catching
74 Math Can Make You Sick
75 B.O. Is Fun
76 Up With Allowances
77 Books Rot Minds
78 Think One Evil Thought A Day
79 Santa Claus Hits Reindeer
80 Park Statues Are For The Birds
81 Encourage Back-Talk
82 Spread A Vicious Rumor Today
83 Hooray For Spoiled Brats
84 Would You Let Your Sister Marry A Teacher?
85 Speak With A Forked Tongue
86 Equal Rights For Kids
87 Snitch On A Friend
88 Drive Parents Crazy

ANIMAL HEROES CARD COLLECTION (50)   1 1/16'' X 2 3/4''

A set of 50 cards designated as Series No. 8 in Nabisco's nature-based card program. It was marketed in 1970 in packages of Sugar Daddy and Sugar Mama caramel pops. The obverses contain artwork by Charles L. Ripper, with his last name appearing on each scene. A dated copyright line is beneath the picture. The reverses are printed in brown ink and carry the set title, card title (including the Latin binomial) and number, and text (also prepared by Ripper. The card set could be mounted on a 24'' X 36'' wall chart available via the mail.

ITEM	MINT	EX
Set	35.00	25.00
Card	.60	.45
Wall chart	12.00	9.00

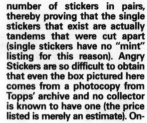

ANIMAL POSTERS (12)   12" X 20"

Adorable Kittens! Cuddly Cubs! Playful Pandas! Perky Puppies! All of the above were depicted in Topps' set of twelve "Cute & Cuddly Animal Posters" which targeted the pre-teen market in 1981. The large bag wrapper (paper) contained one poster (but no gum). The posters are numbered but are not captioned; our checklist consists of simple descriptions of the color photos appearing on each. Note: since the posters were folded to fit the packaging, no mint price is given.

ITEM	MINT	EX
Set	--	10.00
Poster	--	.75
Wrapper	--	.60
Box	--	5.00

1 Orange Kitten Clutching Pole
2 Bunny Rabbit
3 Kitten and Duckling
4 Fawn
5 Lioness and Cub
6 Two White Kittens
7 Two Dachshound Puppies
8 Unhappy Puppie Having Bath
9 Two Tabby Kittens
10 Mountain Lion Cub
11 Baby Lamb
12 Panda

ANIMALS (45)   2 1/2" X 2 7/8"

Collectors who are familiar with the "Presidents" and "Baseball Hall of Fame" sets issued by Golden Press already know that those sets, plus the "Animals" set listed here, were originally issued in "book" form. The "book" actually was a set of covers with sheets of cards inside and the edges of the individual cards were scored by machine for easy removal. The Golden Press series of "books" sold for 59¢ to 79¢ in 5 & 10's and other variety stores during the 1961 season. The condition of single cards in the Animals series varies greatly and probably is related directly to the age of the person removing them from the sheets. The card fronts depict various animals from around the world in gorgeous color, with each animal named in a white panel beneath the picture area. The backs contain the card number and a description of the subject. These cards, like those of the "Presidents" series, are easily

CAMEL

10 CAMEL
Height: 7 feet to top of humps

The temperamental camel is well adapted to the hard life of the desert. It can eat thorny desert plants and drink dirty, muddy water. It stores food in its hump and water in its stomach and can go without water for over a week. Walking on the soft sand is made easier for the camel by its wide, cushioned feet. The Arabian camel has one hump; the Bactrian camel of Central Asia has two.

identified by their proportions, which is fortunate since the company name is not printed on the cards. Note: the price for "mint" grade refers only to cards intact in the original book.

ITEM	MINT	EX
Set	30.00	18.00
Card	---	.35

1 Tiger	24 Giraffe	
2 African Elephant	25 Polar Bear	
3 Flamingo	26 Kangaroo	
4 Red Fox	27 Raccoon	
5 Walrus	28 Gorilla	
6 Anteater	29 Boa Constrictor	
7 Mountain Goat	30 Opossum	
8 Zebra	31 Reindeer	
9 Penguin	32 Ostrich	
10 Camel	33 Crocodile	
11 Porcupine	34 Grizzly Bear	
12 Wolf	35 Bull Frog	
13 Spider Monkey	36 Puma	
14 Leopard	37 White-tailed Deer	
15 Blue Whale	38 Ermine	
16 Skunk	39 American Buffalo	
17 Llama	40 Gray Squirrel	
18 American Eagle	41 Hippopotamus	
19 Rhinoceros	42 Koala	
20 Wapiti	43 Lion	
21 Beaver	44 Musk Rat	
22 Seal	45 Giant Panda	
23 Galapagos Tortoise		

ANIMALS AND FLAGS OF THE WORLD (100)   1 1/8" X 2 3/4"

The 1965 entry in Nabisco's yearly nature series was this 50-card set depicting animals alongside the flag of their country of origin. The color artwork and text were created by H. Wayne Trimm, and the color of the print on back is light blue. The reverse contains the set title, card number and title (including the Latin binomial and country of origin) and descriptive text. A 32-page album to store the cards was available through the mail.

ITEM	MINT	EX
Set	35.00	25.00
Card	.60	.45
Album	15.00	12.00

19 Chamois (Switzerland)
20 Otter (Norway)
21 Flying Fox (Cambodia)
22 Polecat (France)
23 Polar Bear and Walrus (Russia)
24 European Bison (Western Russia)
25 Brown Bear (Siberia)
26 Meercat (South Africa)
27 Mongoose (India)
28 Indian Rhinoceros with Tiger (India)
29 Camel (Mongolia)
30 Indian Elephant (Ceylon)
31 Maned Wolf (Argentina)
32 European Wild Boar (Germany)
33 Red Deer (Scotland)
34 Chital or Axis Deer (Thailand)
35 Vicuna (Peru)
36 Gaur (Viet Nam)
37 Hartebeest (Sudan)
38 Bongo (Ethiopia)
39 Chinchilla (Bolivia)
40 Peccary (Guatemala)
41 Snow Leopard (Nepal)
42 Siberian Ibex (Nepal)
43 Manatee (Venezuela)
44 Dolphin (Greece)
45 Pangolin (Thailand)
46 Giant Anteater (Brazil)
47 Hedgehog (England)
48 Fisher (United States)
49 Tiger (Burma)
50 Ocelot (Mexico)

1 Dall Sheep (United States)
2 White-tailed Sheep (United States)
3 Caribou (Canada)
4 Raccoon (Canada)
5 Musk Ox (Greenland)
6 European Badger (Denmark)
7 Yak (Tibet)
8 Giant Panda (China)
9 Killer Whale (International)
10 Blue Whale (International)
11 Kangaroo (Australia)
12 Duck-billed Platypus (Australia)
13 Tasmanian Devil (Australia)
14 Koala (Australia)
15 Tapir (Indonesia)
16 Capybara (Panama)
17 Black Howler Monkey (Colombia)
18 Sloth (Brazil)

ANIMALS OF THE WORLD
ALBUM STICKERS (192)

2 1/8" X 2 3/4"

This Panini set of album stickers was distributed in foreign markets before it finally reached the United States and Canada. There are two distinct elements to the series. The first of these is a run of stickers, numbered 1-180, which have corresponding spaces in the sticker album. In addition , there are 12 un-numbered "multiple plastic stickers" containing a pair of animals which are designed to be stuck on (and lifted off) the six "natural habitats" pictured on the centerfold page of the album. The album also contains an offer to sell specific stickers for 10 cents each (limit 30 stickers per letter), a handy way to fill in those missing numbers. Note: set price includes album.

ITEM	MINT	EX
Set	32.00	20.00
Stickers		
Numbered	.15	.10
Not numbered	.35	.20
Wrapper	—	.35
Album	2.00	1.50

Produced in 1982, the Annie series of 120 album stickers utilizes color photos from the Columbia Pictures movie directed by John Huston. Each corner-peel sticker is numbered and is assigned a space in the 24-page album (which retailed for 25 cents). The stickers have four red borders surrounding the picture except where two or more stickers are required to make a larger scene. The album contains sketches and dialogue and has a space on the inside back cover to paste the owner's photo. This entire set was manufactured for Topps in Italy by the Panini Company. Note: set price includes album.

ITEM	MINT	EX
Set	17.50	12.50
Sticker	.15	.10
Wrapper	—	.35
Album	2.00	1.50
Box	—	4.00

In 1969, Topps produced a set of 16 fold-out sheets containing color skin transfers based on the characters Archie, Veronica, Betty and Jughead. The individual paper sheets were folded accordian-style into a standard-size, wax gum package selling for five cents. Unfolded, they measure 3 7/16" x 14 3/8". Each is numbered and has a thematic title. The sheet illustrated contains six "large" designs measuring 1 11/16" x 2 3/8" and eight smaller designs measuring 1 3/16" x 1 11/16". If this pattern holds true for all sheets, there would be 224 different tattoos in the set.

ITEM	MINT	EX
Set	27.50	20.00
Sheet	1.50	1.00
Wrapper	––	15.00

LOOK FOR
"THE NEW ARCHIES"
ON PAGE 614
OF THIS BOOK

ARISTOCATS (225)

2 1/16" X 2 9/16"

In March, 1987, the American division of Panini began distribution of this 225-sticker set based on the Disney animated movie. The stickers have the standard Panini multi-language back, on which here the sticker number appears in a box. The 32-page album contains monochrome illustrations among the numbered spaces and text. On the inside back cover of the album, the company offers to supply collectors with the stickers they need for 10 cents apiece. Note: set price includes album.

ITEM	MINT	EX
Set	25.00	20.00
Sticker	.15	.10
Wrapper	--	.35
Album	2.00	1.50

ASTRO BOY TATTOOS (?)

1 9/16" X 3 1/2"

The value of this set of wet-skin-and-apply tattoos is gauged solely on the demand for the exterior wrapper designs, which come with the three pictures illustrated. All the wrappers are yellow with red, blue, green, orange, black and pink details and print. A set of visually-enhanced directions for applying the tattoos appears on every wrapper. The inside of each wrapper contains a color design which is not numbered or systematically captioned. Note: All "unwrapped" wrappers will have a small tear or slit at the glue point.

ITEM	MINT	EX
Wrappers		
3 dif. each	--	10.00

ASTRONAUTS (55)

2 1/2'' X 3 1/2''

The Astronauts set of 55 cards was issued by Topps in 1963. The pictures are color NASA photographs of America's space explorers, their training exercises, and their equipment. The caption and text appear in a yellow block on the front of the card, with a starry blue circle containing the card number attached to one side. The backs are 3-D sketches in orange and green, which must be viewed with cellophane and cardboard eyeglasses. Cards with the line "Popsicle Space Cards" on the back were issued at a later date with ice cream by the Joe Lowe Corporation and are worth double the values listed below.

THE FLOATING TOOLS
Look Thru Viewer and See This Picture in 3-D

SPACE HERO

LOOK THRU THIS SIDE. LONGER YOU LOOK, MORE YOU SEE!
3-D VIEWER
LEFT EYE — RED   RIGHT EYE — BLUE

ITEM	MINT	EX
Set	265.00	200.00
Card	4.00	3.00
3-D viewer	10.00	7.00
Checklist card	20.00	10.00
Wrapper	––	100.00
Box	––	175.00

Popsicle Space Card Wrapper
  Value in "EX" = $175.00

Popsicle Space Cards
  Value in "EX" = $4.00 each

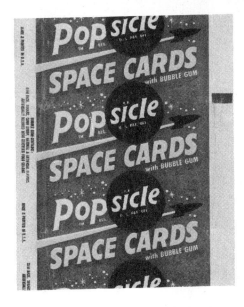

ASTRONAUTS (7) 2 1/2" X 3 9/16"

This set of seven color photographs of America's pioneering astronauts was produced by the Williamson Candy Company. The cards were printed on stiff cardboard trays of O'Henry multi-bar packages and were designed with brown dotted lines to act as cutting guides. They are blank-backed and unnumbered and only the astronaut's last name is used as a caption. The set price reflects the difficulty involved in acquiring all seven cards in contrast to finding singles.

ITEM	MINT	EX
Set	--	37.50
Card	--	4.00

SCHIRRA — SLAYTON — SHEPARD — GRISSOM

CARPENTER — GLENN — COOPER

A-TEAM (66 & 12) 2 1/2" X 3 1/2"

The A-Team set of 66 cards and 12 stickers was issued by Topps in 1983. The obverses of the cards have blue borders with thin red, yellow, and black frame lines enclosing the picture. The caption is printed in black ink within a yellow panel to the right of the set title, which is printed on every card. The reverses are a combination of red, yellow and blue with black print on a dull finish stock. The card number is located at upper right. The stickers are diecut, with the color picture surrounded by a red border. Both the sticker caption and number are printed on the portion of this border resting inside the score line. Note: set price includes stickers.

ITEM	MINT	EX
Set	8.00	5.00
Card	.10	.05
Sticker	.35	.25
Wrappers (2) each	--	.50
Box	--	5.00

1 Introducing The A-Team
2 He's Bad
3 A Wild Ride!
4 Crash!!!
5 "Up Against The Wall!"
6 "What?"
7 "You Turkey!"
8 "No Way!"
9 "Put It In Gear!"
10 "Are You Nuts?"
11 "No Sweat!"
12 Strong Man!
13 A New Assignment!
14 "What's So Funny?"
15 In Disguise!
16 "A Likely Story!"
17 Too Bad For Howling Mad!
18 "What The Heck!"
19 Ready For Action
20 Pretty As A Picture!
21 Beautiful, But Deadly!
22 "Say Cheese!"
23 A Busy Lady!
24 "Wouldn't You Like To Know?"
25 "Tha Faceman's Here!"
26 "Sure You Don't Want A Bite?"
27 "Time To Go!"
28 "Move It Or Lose It!"
29 A Lucky Break!
30 The A-Team's In For It!!
31 "Eeeeeyahh!"
32 B.A.'s Biggest Van!
33 A Smash Hit!
34 No Escape!
35 "Out Of The Way!"
36 "Comin' Through!"
37 Over The Top!
38 One That Got Away!
39 The Deadly Getaway!
40 Ready For The Mission!
41 "I Won't Fly!"
42 Take Off!
43 Ready To Land!
44 A Heavy Load!
45 "What's This?"
46 "You'll Get Yours!"
47 "Don't Gimme No Bull!"
48 On With The Mission!
49 Heavy Traffic!
50 Crashing The Gates!
51 It's A Knockout!
52 Out Of Control!
53 Roll Out!
54 Mad Man!
55 "Oop! Wrong Turn!"
56 Fast Break!
57 A Close Call!
58 On Target!
59 The Darkest Moment!
60 It's A Blast!
61 Fiery Getaway!
62 Explosive Escape!
63 Two Cool Customers!
64 B.A.'s Little Joke!
65 Mission Accomplished!
66 Checklist

A-Team Stickers

1 B.A. (Bad Attitude) Baracus
2 Templeton (The Faceman) Peck
3 Amy Amanda Allen
4 Colonel "Hannibal" Smith
5 "Howling Mad" Murdock
6 Don't Miss With B.A.!
7 Fearless Five
8 B.A.—The Baddest
9 The A-Team
10 The A-Team
11 The A-Team
12 Trio For Trouble!

AUTOS OF 1977 (99 & 20)

2 1/2" X 3 1/2"

This nicely designed set is an automobile enthusiast's dream come true. There are 98 cards containing color photographs of the year's best domestic and imported cars, with the model named above the photo and the manufacturer below it. The silver foil stickers, 20 in number, have brightly colored logos of ten domestic and ten import models or makers. The last numbered card in the set is a checklist. Note: set price includes stickers. Stickers are often found with a patterned strip or band across the surface—these cannot be rated higher than "excellent."

ITEM	MINT	EX
Set	45.00	35.00
Card	.35	.25
Sticker	.50	.35
Wrapper	--	1.50
Box	--	7.00

Autos of 1977

1 AMC Pacer X	26 Chrysler Cordoba	51 Oldsmobile Starfire GT	76 Peugeot 504 SL Sedan
2 Matador 4-Door Sedan	27 Chrysler Newport	52 Omega Brougham Sedan	77 504 Station Wagon
3 AMC Matador Coupe	28 New Yorker Brougham	53 Oldsmobile Toronado	78 Porsche Turbo Carrera
4 Hornet D/L 2-Door Sedan	29 Royal Monaco Brougham	54 Cutlass Colonade Hardtop	79 Porsche 911S
5 AMC Gremlin	30 Ford LTD Landau	55 Delta 88 Royale	80 Porsche Audi Fox
6 Buick Skylark	31 Dodge Aspen R/T	56 98 Regency Sedan	81 Porsche Audi 100
7 Buick Skyhawk	32 Dodge Charger SE	57 Volare Premier Wagon	82 Renault 5
8 Buick Electra	33 D100 Club Cab Adventurer	58 Volare Road Runner	83 Saab 99 EMS
9 Buick Riviera	34 Ford LTD II	59 Plymouth Fury Sport	84 Triumph TR7
10 Cadillac Eldorado	35 Econoline Cruising Van	60 Plymouth Fury Salon	85 Triumph Spitfire
11 Cadillac Seville	36 Ford Ranchero GT	61 Gran Fury Brougham	86 Corolla Sport Coupe
12 Cadillac Coupe deVille	37 Ford Thunderbird	62 Pontiac Sunbird	87 Toyota Celica ST
13 Cadillac Brougham	38 Ford Mustang II Cobra II	63 Pontiac Grand Prix	88 Toyota Celica GT
14 Nova Coupe	39 Ford Granada	64 Pontiac Bonneville	89 Corona Four-Door Sedan
15 Monte Carlo Landau	40 Ford Maverick	65 Alfa Romeo Alfetta	90 Volvo 264 GL
16 Malibou Classic Landau	41 Pinto 3-Door Runabout	66 Alfa Romeo Spider Veloce	91 Volvo 265 5-Door
17 Camaro LT Coupe	42 Ford Mustang II Ghia	67 Alfa Romeo Alfetta GT	92 Volvo 244 DL
18 Chevette Hatchback Coupe	43 Continental Mark V	68 Jaguar XJ-S	93 VW Campmobile
19 Corvette Coupe	44 Continental	69 Mazda Mizer	94 VW Beetle
20 Caprice Classic 4-Dr. Sedan	45 Mercury Marquis	70 Cosmo Sports Coupe	95 VW Rabbit
21 Monza Towne Coupe	46 Mercury Cougar XR-7	71 RX-4 Four Door Sedan	96 VW Scirocco
22 Monza 2+2 Hatchback	47 Mercury Monarch Ghia	72 Mercedes-Benz 450SE	97 VW Dasher
23 Impala Coupe	48 Mercury Comet	73 Mercedes Benz 450 SL	98 VW Beetle Convertible
24 Vega Estate Wagon	49 Mercury Bobcat	74 Mercedes Benz 280S	99 Checklist Card
25 Caprice Classic Wagon	50 Mercury Capri II	75 MG MGB	

Foil Stickers

Alfa Romeo
Buick
Cadillac
Chevrolet
Chevrolet Corvette
'Cuda
Demon
Dodge
Gremlin
HM
Jaguar Coventry
Mercedes Benz
MG
Oldsmobile
Peugeot
Plymouth
Saab
Triumph
VW
Volvo

AWESOME! ALL-STARS (127)

2 1/2" X 3 1/2"

The latest non-sports set from Donruss, Awesome! All-Stars is a welcome break from the company's string of photo sets. The format is a revival of the "Baseball Super Freaks" series issued more than a decade ago; indeed, some of the players from the older sets are still "in the league." Although there are 99 numbered cards in the set, 28 cards were printed with both text and puzzle piece backs, making a total of 127 different. Cards with text backs are numbered on back; puzzle back cards are numbered on front. The cards marked *2 in our checklist have both backs; a single * indicates that the card has been reported only with a puzzle back.

ITEM	MINT	EX
Set	18.00	13.00
Sticker	.15	.10
Wrappers (3) ea.	—	.35
Box	—	5.00
Poster	—	5.00

1　Phil The Fanatic
2　Net Head Nelson
3　Ned The Nose
4　Sèan The Second Sacker
5　Todd The Tooth
6　Norman The Nose
7　Steve The Second Sacker
8　Ozzie The Outfielder
9　Freddie Fats
10　Nat The Nose
11　Charlie The Chomper
12　Hot Breath Henry
13　Norris The Nibbler
14　Ollie The Outfielder*2
15　Benny The Boxer*2
16　Handy Harold*2
17　Strike Out King*2
18　Oliver The Ump*2
19　Baldy Bob*2
20　Greg The Gluck*2
21　Bob The Bomber
22　Sarah The Second Sacker
23　Ernie Eyeballs
24　Gene The Giant
25　Billy Big Mouth*2
26　Alert Adam*2
27　Weird William*2
28　Ted The Intimidator*2
29　Glenn The Glob*2
30　Richard The Runner*2
31　Jack Boxley*2
32　Matt The Mole
33　Peter The Pounder
34　Scott Scooper
35　Voo Doo Vernon
36　Paul The Ball*2
37　Randy The Reader*2
38　What's His Name*2
39　Hatchet Harry*2
40　Michael The Midget*2
41　Larry Line Drive*2
42　Speed E. Ed*2
43　Warren Wine Brain
44　Bobby Backswing
45　Sammy Springer
46　Chris The Center Fielder
47　Evil Eye Eric*2
48　William The Wombat*2
49　Spider Sam*2
50　Bo The Bookmaker*2
51　Benny The First Baseman*2
52　John The Jet*2
53　Long Arm Larry*2
54　Steve The Switcher
55　Neal The Negotiator
56　Unethical Alan
57　Second Baseman (Two-Bagger)
58　Stuart The Stealer
59　Big Mouth Bruce
60　David The Dominator
61　Blooper Looper
62　Shane The Shortstop
63　Gavin The Goof-Off
64　Sperry The Spitball
65　Perry The Persuader
66　Benny Bolts
67　Elbert The Eyes
68　Barney The Bat Eater
69　Fingers Frankie
70　Freddie Farout
71　Checklist
72　Death Wish Dan*

73　Bob The Slob
74　Robust Robert*
75　Pat The Pitcher*
76　Forgetful Fred*
77　Slimey Sam*
78　Prickley Paul*
79　Lightening Larry*
80　Ball-Brain Bruce*
81　Ugly Ursala*

82　Shawn The Sissy*
83　Carl The Contra*
84　Winged Wayne*
85　Jerry Jabber-Jaws*
86　Corey The Bat Corker*
87　Brian The Bat Boy*
88　Stubby Stan*
89　Robert The Robber*
90　Fireball Frankie*

91　Mighty Small Michael*
92　Junk Food Jimmy*
93　Shell-Shocked Shawn*
94　Gary Garlic Breath*
95　Ball Licker Lee*
96　Tommy Tummy*
97　Machine Gun George*
98　Harry The Hypnotist*
99　Glove-Head Glenn*

41

BABY (66 & 11)

Although the "Great New Adventure Movie" of 1984 was a bust at the box office, it has been preserved for us in cardboard by Topps. There are 65 red-bordered photo cards, each bearing the series title in yellow print and the card caption in black. The backs (blue print on green) contain the card number, series title, and a short text. None of the eleven black-bordered stickers bears a caption but nine of them have pictures identical to those appearing on cards (Nos. 10 & 11 do not). Card No. 66 is a checklist. Note: set price includes stickers.

ITEM	MINT	EX
Set	8.00	6.00
Card	.10	.05
Sticker	.35	.25
Wrapper	--	.35
Box	--	5.00

1 Title Card
2 Land of Mystery
3 Rivals!
4 Death of a Scientist
5 Susan's Discovery
6 George Isn't Thrilled!
7 Kiviat's Plan
8 "Susan, Come Back Here!!"
9 Poisoned by...What?
10 Treacherous Trek!
11 Besieged by Natives!
12 "Don't...It's Their Soul!"
13 Guests of the Kaleri
14 Stomping Ground!
15 A Living Legend
16 Where Time Stands Still
17 Awesome Sight!
18 A Family of Brontos
19 Introducing...Baby!
20 Chow Time!
21 Curious Critter!
22 Who Turned Out the Lights?
23 Swimming Companions
24 Making Friends!
25 Three of a Kind
26 Rage of the Creature!
27 Papa Bronto Attacks!
28 Kiviat, the Evil Scientist!
29 Mama Bronto...Captured!
30 Baby Needs a Friend!
31 Stubborn as a Dino!
32 Malombo Snack!
33 The Perilous River
34 Journey to Freedom!

35 Unexpected Guest!
36 ...And Baby Makes Three!
37 Another Fine Mess!
38 Three's a Crowd
39 A Familiar Face?
40 Friends from Different Eras
41 Sorry...Wrong Mama!
42 Captured!
43 Baby Is Sighted!
44 The Great Escape
45 Operation: Save Baby!
46 Pursued by Kiviat
47 The Cave of Bats
48 Tending Baby's Wounds
49 Nursing the Bronto
50 Wake Up, Sleepyheads!
51 Quiet, Kiddo!
52 Freeing Mama!
53 Mama on the Rampage!
54 Under Attack!
55 A Dream in Flames!
56 George Flies into Danger!
57 "Give It Up, Kiviat!"

58 Crashing the Gates!
59 Hot Pursuit!
60 Mama Gets Even!
61 Fate of the Evil One
62 Is Baby Okay?
63 Mama and Baby...Together Again!
64 Mother Love, Monster-Style!
65 A Final Farewell
66 Checklist

BACK-SLAPPER STICKERS (60) 2 1/2" X 3 1/2"

Collectors often become confused about this set since Fleer issued it in both the United States and Canada. The 60 sticker captions in the American set are checklisted below. While both the American and Canadian stickers have a brown paper backing, the U.S. variety has a vertical peel break, as opposed to the horizontal peel break on the Canadian type. In addition, the Canadian sticker is noticeably smaller, measuring 2 1/2" X 3 3/8". The Canadian captions and numbers often do not match up with the American set.

A series of unnumbered cards was included in both the American and Canadian Back-Slapper packs. These cards have a bold face introduction line—"This Will Introduce"—under which is a blank space for a name and an insulting title (for example, "Chicken Plucker"). The American card is printed in black ink on shell-white stock; it's Canadian counterpart uses red ink on off-white cardboard (with a gray back). Both types are blank-backed; it is believed, but not confirmed, that

there are ten cards in the set. Note: a follow-up set called "School Daze Back-Slapper Stickers" is listed in the "S" section of this book. The prices below are for the American set only. The set price does not include the cards.

ITEM	MINT	EX
Set	85.00	65.00
Sticker	1.25	.90
Card	1.00	.75
Wrappers (2)		
Without "New"	--	8.00
With "New"	--	25.00
Box	--	30.00

This Will Introduce

World's Greatest Lover

1 I Am So Fit To Eat With Pigs
2 Kiss Me...You Fool!
3 Please Pick My Pockets
4 My Father Can Beat Up Your Mother
5 I Just Escaped From the Nut House
6 I'm The World's Tallest Midget
7 Help Stamp Out Schools!
8 Quiet Please!
9 I'm Teachers Pet!!
10 I Took Ugly Pills This Morning
11 I'm Not Doing the Frug
12 If This Looks Funny You Need Glasses
13 My Brother Can Beat Up Your Sister!!
14 Danger Falling Dandruff!
15 Somebody Turn Me Around
16 I'm No Dope
17 Help Stamp Out Teachers
18 I've Got Nothing But Muscle
19 Somebody Give Me a Sock
20 I'm Yours!
21 This Side Up
22 Call Me Stinky
23 I'm The Best Speller in My Skool!!
24 My Sister Can Beat Up Your Brother
25 I'm Lost! Take Me to the Nearest Policeman
26 Please Scratch My Back!
27 Look at This Green Picture
28 I'm a Worm
29 Tilt! I'm Out of Order
30 I am Not a Boy!!
31 My Back Looks Funny
32 Help Stamp Out Parents
33 I'm a Nut!
34 I Was Just in a Beauty Contest
35 I'm an Official Spitball Target
36 Danger! Bad Breath!
37 You're Looking at The World's Biggest Coward.
38 I'm Ugly But Bright 2 x 3 = 7
39 Me Speak With Forked Tongue
40 My Mother Can Beat Up Your Father
41 I Just Flunked Out of Kindergarten
42 I'll Be a Movie Star
43 My Brain is Like the Alphabet M.T.
44 How Ugly Can You Get?
45 Help Stamp Out Children
46 I'm Playing Hookey Tomorrow!
47 Unless You're a Cop Stop Following Me!
48 I've Got B.O.
49 I'm No Good But You're No Gooder
50 They Charged Me $4.00 For a Haircut...
51 Want to Fight My Friend?
52 Please Drop in the Nearest Mailbox
53 Please Yell at Me
54 I am Not a Girl!
55 I Collect Old Cigar Butts.
56 Find Me in the Yellow Pages
57 Please Tap Me on this Shoulder
58 Wanna Know Where I'm Going Crazy!
59 Sing Class of 1978
60 You Wanna Fight?

BACK TO THE FUTURE II (88/11) 2 1/2" X 3 1/2"

Back To The Future II, the least succesful film of the movie trilogy starring Michael J. Fox as Marty McFly, was selected by Topps for a card set in 1989. The 66 cards contain captioned scenes from the movie and have interesting red-to-yellow phased borders. The card backs are blue and red on gray stock and have the card number in the top left corner above the movie logo. The stickers have color photos on white backgrounds: ten have partial-picture backs, while the back of sticker no. 11 shows "what your yellow border pic-

Back to the Future II

9 MOVIE CARDS • 1 STICKER
1 STICK BUBBLE GUM

ture will look like." The wrapper is mostly blue, with red, yellow, white, and black accents.

ITEM	MINT	EX
Set	15.00	11.00
Card	.10	.07
Sticker	.35	.25
Wrapper	—	.35
Box	—	2.50

1 The Return of Marty McFly
2 Onward, to the Future!
3 The DeLorean Takes Off!
4 Tomorrow's Mission *Today!*
5 Hill Valley, 2015
6 The New, Improved Town Square
7 A Peek into the Future
8 Wonders of Tomorrow
9 Future Shocks
10 Incredible, Isn't It?
11 A Must for Nostalgia Freaks
12 Check This Place Out!
13 "Hello, Anybody Home?"
14 Griff Makes the Scene
15 Griff's Criminal Plan
16 Makeshift Escape!
17 The Pit Bull Brigade
18 Hoverboarding Marty!
19 Here Comes Trouble ...!
20 "Whew! That Was Close!"
21 "Yeeeeoooowwwww!!!"
22 Griff is Fully Foiled
23 A Timely Idea
24 Purchasing the Past
25 Returning to Town Square

26 The Times They Are A'Changing
27 Mission (Somehow) Accomplished
28 The Capture of Jennifer
29 Biff's Outlandish Scheme
30 "Follow that DeLorean!"
31 Jennifer is ... Home?!
32 Marlene Comes to Call
33 Future Family
34 A Possible Paradox?!
35 Stealing Some Time!
36 I Want My F-TV!
37 Marty McFly Junior
38 Spotted by Jennifer
39 Marty McFly, Age 47
40 A Peekaboo from Guess Who?
41 Doc Has His Hands Full!
42 Back from the Past
43 "What Could be Wrong?"
44 Mr. Strickland Takes Aim!
45 "This is *Nuts*...!"
46 Everything's Different --!
47 The Whole Town has Changed!

48 Tannen's Henchmen
49 A Family Squabble
50 Mom ... and Dad?!
51 "Where's George McFly?"
52 Dear, Departed Dad
53 Biff Hits the Jackpot!
54 Doc Brown's New Plan
55 Mad, Murderous Biff
56 Not *This* Time, Tannen!
57 The Rescue
58 Back in '55
59 Marty in Disguise!
60 Biff is Scorned!
61 Biff's Mysterious Benefactor
62 Another Way to Travel!
63 A Familiar Scene
64 Retrieving the Almanac
65 Their First Kiss
66 Go, Marty, Go!
67 Man in the Shadow
68 "Somethin' Weird's Going On...!"
69 Seeing Double!
70 When Time Trippers Collide!
71 Saved by Doc (Again)
72 Burning the Almanac
73 Good News!
74 More Good News!
75 Western Union Delivers!
76 Trapped in the Past!

77 Marty's Original Escape
78 "No ... Not Again!!"
79 Next Stop ... 1985!
80 The Once and Future Car
81 No title [Spider Car]
82 No Title [Scat Hovercraft]
83 No title [Taxi Cab]
84 No title [Ford prototype]
85 No title [Chevrolet prototype]
86 Cafe '80s (Interior Set)
87 Michael J. Fox is Marty McFly
88 Until *Next* Time ...!

None of the 11 stickers have titles so there will be no checklist.

BARBIE ALBUM STICKERS (216)   2" X 3"

This set of 216 album stickers, produced by Panini for Topps, is one of the most imaginative and well-designed sets of the modern card era. There are 150 "story" stickers; the remaining 66 stickers are: die-cut logos, slogans or uncaptioned art (6); fashion overlays (18); two-on-ones (4); and die-cut dolls (38). The story cards are distributed among 18 different themes in the 36-page album, and although the "fashion" perspective is always emphasized, there is a serious effort made to show the characters in responsible and constructive roles. Note: set price includes the album. A filled album is valued at 50% of the excellent price.

ITEM	MINT	EX
Set	25.00	15.00
Sticker	.15	.07
Wrapper	—	.35
Album	2.50	1.50

BARBIE ALBUM STICKERS (240)

2 1/16" X 2 9/16"

American Panini decided to cash in on the current popularity of female rock groups with this 240-sticker series released in May, 1987. The 32-page album tells of Barbie's rise to rock'n' roll stardom with her group, "The Rock-ers," managed by—who else?—Ken. The best feature of this implausible set is a three-dimensional "Pop-Up Hot Rockin' Stage" designed as an album insert. There are 15 lettered plastic stickers designed to fit spaces on and around the stage. Note: set price includes album & stage.

ITEM	MINT	EX
Set	25.00	15.00
Sticker	.10	.07
Wrapper	--	.35
Album	2.00	1.50

BARBIE ALBUM STICKERS (204)   2 1/8" X 3"

The second exclusively Panini "Barbie" series to be issued in the U.S. (the original Barbie was made by Panini, but issued through Topps), this 1989 set contains a total of 204 stickers. Of these, 180 are multi-color artwork pictures designed to be placed onto corresponding spaces in the album. Another 24 stickers are center-diecut, "peel and place" figures which Panini suggests can be randomly positioned onto eight postcards of foreign countries which are stapled in sheet form in the center of the album. The rest of the album is composed of two-page sections with specific themes: "Looking Back," "Formal Affairs," etc. Note: set price includes album.

ITEM	MINT	EX
Set	22.00	16.50
Sticker	.10	.07
Wrapper	--	.20
Album	1.50	1.00

BARBIE TRADING CARDS — SERIES 1 (300)   3 1/2" X 5 1/2"

This 1990 set of "Barbie Trading Cards," produced by Mattel, is a perfect example of the dilemma created by non-traditional card manufacturers. For Barbie collectors, the 300-card series is an excellent presentation of "Barbie dolls and fashions through the years," and the cost of 10 cents per card and $35 per set might seem very reasonable. For the general trading card collector, however, the subject is too specific, the cost too high, and the cards themselves seem repetitive and dull. Complete sets were not offered by the manufacturer and assembling sets via "randomly packed" has proved difficult. Luckily, Mattel also produced a large poster showing all 300 card fronts and this reasonably-priced item (less than $4) is a much better buy. As of this printing, Barbie Trading Cards were still being sold in 10-card poly bag packages at some retail stores.

ITEM	MINT	EX
Set	50.00	35.00
Card	.15	.10
Wrapper	--	.15

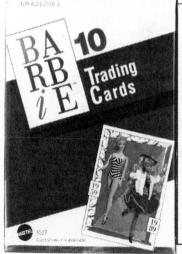

BARBIE TRADING CARDS — SERIES 2 (300) 3 1/2" X 5"

Mattel wasted no time in producing another 300-card Barbie set for release in 1991. The series follows the same basic format and size as the first set, with the notable exception that all second series cards have the card number prominently displayed in a pink panel on the reverse of every card (the card numbers on series 1 cards were hidden below the copyright line at the bottom). The product was issued in 10-card (gumless) plastic packages, with 24 packages in each box. The second series wrapper has more pink and less white than its series 1 counterpart and shows a different card, plus a "puzzle-piece" design which advertises a bonus puzzle card included in the package. Each puzzle card contains eight numbered puzzle pieces which are part of a 64-piece puzzle, and the card itself is also numbered (1-8). A combination of spotty collation and steady demand from doll collectors makes it likely that both series of Mattel Barbie cards will increase in price in the near future. Note: Series 2 set price does not include the eight puzzle cards. The information for this presentation was furnished by Melva Davern.

ITEM	MINT	EX
Sets		
Cards	50.00	35.00
Puzzle cards	2.50	1.75
Card	.15	.10
Puzzle card	.25	.20
Wrapper	--	.15

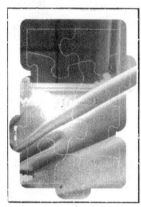

BARBIE TRADING CARDS (196)

2 1/2" X 3 1/2"

Panini entered the "Barbie" market in 1992 with a splendid 196-card set produced in standard 2-1/2" X 3-1/2" size. Cards 1-194 contain color pictures of different Barbie dolls issued from 1959 to 1991 and the production year is printed on both sides of each card. The backs are mostly white with pink accents and there are three categories of text: "Fashion Facts," "Barbie Facts," and "Fun Facts." The individual card number is printed in the upper right corner. Card #'s 195-196 are checklists which list the "Fashion Facts" subtitle for each card. The cards bear the company name "Action," which is the card producing arm of Panini, Canada Ltd. The series was made available in eight-card (gumless) packs and as a complete, boxed set as well. Panini's Barbie series was produced in limited quantities and Dart Flipcards, the Canadian distributor, reports that the issue had completely sold out as of the time we went to press.

ITEM	MINT	EX
Set	20.00	--
Card	.10	--
Wrapper	--	.10
Display box	--	2.00

BASEBALL'S GREATEST GROSSOUTS (88)　　2 1/2" X 3 1/2"

BEANBALL BIFF

The ink had hardly dried on Donruss-Leaf's "Awesome! All-Stars" series before the company started printing a sequel, entitled "Baseball's Greatest Grossouts." There are 88 zany characters pictured on the corner-peel stickers and each has a number printed in a tiny circle on the front. The backs of the cards on which the stickers sit present a confusing situation. Most have descriptions of the character pictured on front but a number of cards have both descriptive and puzzle piece backs (see card illustrations). Those with puzzle piece backs are marked * in the checklist; numbers confirmed to have both types of backs are marked *2. Baseball's Greatest Grossouts has not attracted much attention from collectors and for this reason the set price is lower than the sum of individual card values. Three wrappers were issued for the set. Note: set price is for 88 different sticker fronts, regardless of back variations.

ITEM	MINT	EX
Set	5.00	2.75
Card	.05	.03
Wrappers (3) each	--	.25

BEANBALL BIFF

1 Jumpin' Jack Trash	15 Rex the Runner	29 Cardinal Carl
2 Dogface Donald	16 Kiel D. Ump*	30 Hard Luck Harry
3 Tiger Tad	17 Moosehead Melvin*	31 Combat Conrad
4 Wolfman Jerk	18 Benny the Blob	32 Horseface Henry
5 Leon the Chameleon	19 Colin the Coward	33 Billy the Brain
6 Bat Boy Bobby*	20 Winnie the Windbag	34 Gordie the Ghoul
7 Laidback Larry	21 Dynamite Daryl	35 Four Eyes Freddie
8 Whirlwind Walter	22 Long Arm Lenny*	36 Stinkin' Seth
9 Mark the Maniac	23 Karate Ken	37 Sad Sack Sal
10 Abominable Adam*	24 Ryan the Rhino*	38 Russ T. Armor
11 Leapin' Louie	25 Joker Joe	39 Frank N. Stine
12 Whacko Willie	26 Mitts Michael	40 Elvis Pelvis
13 Garlic Breath Gary*	27 Cory the Cub	41 Dynamite Daryl
14 Stickyfingers Steve	28 Ollie the Oaf	42 Snakey Pete*

43 Snoozin' Sean	49 Charlie the Chewer	69 Ernie the Elephant
44 Gross Out Glenn	50 Lips Leroy	70 Orville the Oozer
45 Phil the Fly	51 Grouchy Gregg*	71 Vernon the Vamp
46 Handy Andy	52 Brad the Bunter	72 Evan the Terrible
47 Pirate Perry	53 Rightey Whitey	73 Nervous Nickie *2
48 Tricky Dicky*	54 Skinny Vinny*	74 Speedy Spike
	55 San Quentin Chicken	75 Twisted Brother
	56 Underground Eric	76 Ratface Robert
	57 Rich Kid Richie	77 Beanball Biff *2
	58 Tobacco Tony	78 Loony Lyle
	59 Fans Farley	79 Chipmunk Chuck
	60 Hogface Homer	80 Slowball Scott
	61 Peekaboo Paul	81 Allen the Alien
	62 Towering Tommy	82 Artie the Announcer
	63 Tongue-Twister Tony	83 Ralph D. Rocker*
	64 Brain Rot Bruce	84 Tiptoer Tim
	65 Chainsaw Jason	85 Airhead Arnie
	66 Samurai Sam	86 Johnny Reb*
	67 Pigskin Patrick	87 Radar Roy
	68 Backwards Barry*	88 Dull David

BASEBALL STICKERS (?)

2 1/2" X 3 1/2"

This is the first of several sets with sports themes which are included in this volume because they are ignored by "serious" sports card collectors and catalogers. There are two types of thin stickers with brown paper backing in this set: one has a complete humorous caption; the other has a sentence with a blank space for placing a name sticker. The name stickers (each measuring 11/32" X 1 1/4") are mounted on the bottom half of a blankback card. There are six name stickers and one 2 1/2" sq. "All Star" sticker on each of these cards. All of the paper-backed and "All Star" stickers are numbered (No. 59 seen) but the length of the set has not been established.

ITEM	MINT	EX
Sticker	1.50	1.00
Sticker-card	1.50	1.00
Wrapper	--	7.00

BASEBALL SUPER FREAKS 1ST SERIES (42)

2 1/2" X 3 1/2"

There are 42 freaks in this first series baseball parody produced by Donruss. They are called both "picture cards" and "bubble gum stickers" on the wrapper: they are actually sticker-card combinations with a corner peel sticker on the front and a printed cardboard back. While the sticker on front may or may not be captioned, the card title is always printed on the back under the card number. The back also contains a small yellow-tone copy of the front design, plus text. A line advises "Collect All 42 Stickers." Each unpriced pack contained five cards and a piece of gum.

ITEM	MINT	EX
Set	27.50	20.00
Sticker-card	.55	.40
Wrapper	--	3.00
Box	--	20.00

1 Monte the Mole	15 Benny Bolts	29 Hatcher Hooper
2 Jack Boxley	16 Unethical Unger	30 Net Head Nelson
3 John the Jet	17 George the Gluck	31 Blooper Looper
4 Freddie Fats	18 Crusher Lewis	32 Long Arms Larson
5 Paul the Ball	19 Fingers Frankie	33 Voo Doo Vernon
6 Tom the Tooth	20 Charlie the Chomper	34 Wierd McBeard
7 Hot Breath Harrigan	21 George the Giant	35 Norman the Nose
8 Rock Grossiano	22 Fatsy Felix	36 Bobby Backswing
9 Conrad the Cow	23 The Per-suader	37 Steven the Stomper
10 Wendell Wine Brain	24 Tommy the Fireball	38 Melvin the Midget
11 Spider Smith	25 Baldy Ben	39 Handy Harold
12 Big Mouth Johnson	26 Elbert the Eyes	40 Ernie Eye-balls
13 Zap Zoroff	27 Barney the Bat Eater	41 Nelson the Nose
14 Connie the Coach	28 Power-ful Powell	42 Warren the Wombat

BASEBALL SUPER FREAKS 2ND SERIES (44)

2 1/2" X 3 1/2"

This follow-up to the original series contains 44 sticker-cards portraying a whole new gallery of baseball freaks. The wrapper has a red center section with "All New! 2nd Series" over part of the design. The cards backs have black print on white stock in contrast to the black-on-yellow of the 1st series. The card number, caption, text and "Collect All 44 Stickers" line all appear on the reverse.

ITEM	MINT	EX
Set	27.50	20.00
Sticker-card	.55	.40
Wrapper	--	3.50
Box	--	20.00

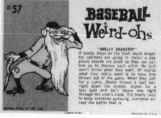

1 Norris the Nibbler	25 Stude the Second Sacker	35 Sammy Springer
2 Arnie the Agile	26 Marvin the Mouth	36 Pork E. Pine
3 Shecky the Short Stop	27 Freddie Far-out	37 Sis E. the Second Sacker
4 Sted the Stealer	28 Larry Line Drive	38 Second Baseman
5 Ozzie the Outfielder	29 Harry the Horrible	39 George the Glob
6 Paul the Pitcher	30 Sam the Slammer	40 Gavin the Goof-off
7 Ned the Negotiator	31 Speed E. Freak	41 Bernard the First Baseman
8 Slurp the Second Baseman	32 Sylvester the Center Fielder	42 Alert Albert
9 Sam the Switch Hitter	33 Strike Out King	43 Foul Ball Fred
10 Oink the Ump	34 The Nose	44 Herman the Hideous
11 Benny the Base Runner		
12 Ollie the Out-fielder		
13 The Bomber		
14 Whats His Name		
15 Barney Big-mouth		
16 Hank the Hitter		
17 Richard the Runner		
18 Bo the Book-maker		
19 Sperry the Spit-ball		
20 Nevin Nothing		
21 Ronnie the Reader		
22 Bob the Slob		
23 Harry the Hypnotist		
24 Super Scooper		

BASEBALL WEIRD-OHS (66)

2 1/2" X 3 1/2"

Fleer adopted the "Weird-Oh" designs developed by the Hawk Model Company (a toy-maker) to poke fun at baseball in this 66-card set. The fronts have color artwork with the caption located below it in a large white border. The backs contain the set title, the card title (which is different from the caption on front) and text. The card number is situated in the upper left corner of a monocolor block containing a humorous character sketch.

ITEM	MINT	EX
Set	150.00	115.00
Card	2.00	1.50
Wrapper	--	40.00

Baseball Weird-Ohs

THE GREATEST FUN UNDER THE SUN
IS TO WATCH THIS MORON TRY TO RUN!

Special Note: Stickers with fronts identical to some of the cards in this set have been reported. They may have been inserts in Weird-Oh packs, but it is more likely that they were distributed inside Hawk model boxes.

BASKETBALL STICKERS (?)

TWO SIZES

As the wrapper of this Fleer product states, these funny basketball stickers were designed to be attached to "Backs, Books 'n Bikes." That advice may explain why only limited quantities have survived. Type 1 stickers measure 2½" x 2¾", have a caption and a (blank) name box on front, and the backs are brown paper with a machine-scored center break. Type 2 stickers are attached to a card: each has a single caption-and-name-box sticker above and two columns of names below (six names in all). The card is white and is devoid of printing; once the stickers are removed, it is a blank piece of cardboard. Unlike Fleer's "Baseball Stickers," none of the stickers in this set are numbered. The length of the set is not known and our partial checklists below are divided into sticker captions and sticker names.

ITEM	MINT	EX
Sticker	1.50	1.00
Sticker-card	1.50	1.00
Wrapper	---	7.00

TYPE 1

TYPE 2

Stickers — partial checklist with type in ( ).

Best Center (1)
Big Slob (2)
Blind Referee (2)
Clumsiest Player (1)
High Scorer (2)
Hook Shot (1)
Jump Shot (2)
Slowest Player (1)
Sneak Player (1)
Team Mates (1)

NAMES — partial checklist

Art	Paul
Carl	Pete
Charlie	Phil
Don	Ricky
Doug	Ronnie
Fred	Roy
Gary	Scotty
Joe	Stan
John	Steve
Johnny	Terry
Larry	Tim
	Tony

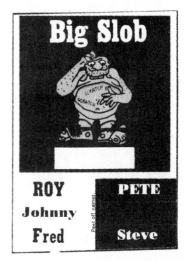

BATMAN (55)

2 1/2" X 3 1/2"

Topps produced this 55-card Batman series in 1966. The cards are color drawings of the Caped Crusader and his side-kick in action against various enemies of law and order. The caption appears in a black bat design on the front of the card. The backs are light orange in color and have a design of Batman (running) on the right side. The card number appears above the text in another black bat design.

ITEM	MINT	EX
Set	160.00	125.00
Card	2.50	2.00
Wrapper	--	30.00
Box	--	90.00

1 The Batman
2 Robin—Boy Wonder
3 The Bat Signal
4 Midnight Conference
5 Rooftop Vigil
6 Chloroform Victim
7 Grim Realization
8 Into the Batmobile
9 Face of the Joker
10 Crime Czar
11 Poison Pellet
12 Batman Strikes!
13 The Joker in Jail
14 Nightly Patrol
15 Batman in Action
16 The Penguin's Trap
17 Spikes of Death
18 Robin in Action
19 Fiery Encounter
20 Robin to the Rescue
21 Narrow Escape
22 Double Cross

23 Umbrella Duel
24 Penguin Captured
25 The Cat Woman
26 Queen of Crime
27 Sinister Smile
28 "Let's Go!"
29 Robin Is Kidnapped
30 Fighting Back
31 Threat of the Catwoman
32 Bat-A-Rang Bulls-eye
33 The Enemies Clash
34 Deadly Claws
35 Cat Women Defeated
36 The Riddler
37 A Trap for Batman
38 Robin Rescued
39 "To the Batcave"
40 Following the Clue
41 Time for Rescue
42 Robin in Peril
43 The Bat-Gasmask
44 Flying Fists

45 Trap for the Riddler
46 The Bat-A-Rang
47 Deadly Robot
48 Monstrous Illusion
49 Decoy
50 Beastly Encounter
51 Flaming Welcome

52 Winged Giant
53 Race Against Death
54 Whirlpool
55 Hidden Loot

BATMAN—A SERIES (44)

2 1/2" X 3 1/2"

"A" series Batman cards are numbered 1A to 44A and have the card caption in a red bat design on the obverse. In addition, the color drawing on the front is surrounded by a purple frame line. The backs are approximately sixty percent puzzle piece and forty percent text area. The card number is found in a black circle located underneath the text. The A series Batman set was marketed by Topps in 1966.

ITEM	MINT	EX
Set	125.00	100.00
Card	2.50	2.00
Wrapper	--	30.00
Boxes		
Small sticker	--	115.00
Large sticker	--	130.00

1A The Ghostly Foe
2A Grappling a Gator
3A The Menacing Mummy
4A Target of the Trapper
5A Pendulum Peril
6A Facing the Ace
7A The Batline Lifeline
8A Tentacled Terror
9A Knighting a Thief
10A Cycling Crusader
11A Landing a Big One

12A Boiling Bath
13A Out on a Limb
14A Danger in the Depths
15A Gotham Gallants
16A Portable Bat Signals
17A Link to Lincoln
18A Death Spins a Web
19A Leap for Life
20A Surfing Sleuths
21A Batman Wins a Prize
22A Death Skis the Slopes
23A Battling Nature's Fury
24A Tight Squeeze
25A In the Batlab
26A The Joker's Last Laugh
27A Striking Out the Cobra
28A Victorious Duo
29A Danger from the 25th Century
30A Undone by an Umbrella
31A Flying Foes
32A Captain Kidd's Caper
33A Dynamite in Robin's Nest
34A The Batman Baby Sitter
35A Crime Above the Harbor
36A Cliff Hangers
37A Watery Warfare
38A In the Path of Death
39A Stopping the Sub
40A Inferno of Flame
41A Duel of Death
42A Counterfeit Caped Crusader
43A Menace in Fairyland
44A Batman on Broadway

BATMAN–B SERIES (44)

2 1/2" X 3 1/2"

The Batman "B" series is not as confusing as it might appear at first. There are 44 cards numbered 1B to 44B, and each card was issued with two separate backs: one has a large blue bat design containing a text, with the card number (also in blue print) at the upperleft; the other is a puzzle back wth about forty percent of the area given to caption, text, and card number (in a black circle). The obverse pictures of both types are identical to one another, having a blue frame line and the card caption in a blue bat design.

ITEM	MINT	EX
Sets		
Bat back	150.00	125.00
Puzzle back	150.00	125.00
Cards (all)	3.00	2.50
Wrapper	--	30.00
Box	--	125.00

1B	The Joker's Icy Jest			
2B	The Penguin Prevails			
3B	Hydro-foil Hotspot			
4B	Branded Boy Wonder			
5B	Caged by the Catwomen			
6B	Canape for a Cobra			
7B	The Grim Gladiator			
8B	Snaring the Sheik			
9B	Bashed on a Billboard	23B	The Joker's Juggernaut	
10B	Amphibious Attackers	24B	Fangs of the Phantom	
11B	To Robin's Rescue	25B	Dragged from Death's Door	
12B	Renegade Roulette	26B	Jack Frost's Jinx	
13B	Batman's Coffin	27B	Pasting the Painter	
14B	Neanderthal Nemesis	28B	Concrete Conquest	
15B	Joker Wishes Robin Well	29B	A Wretched Riddle	
16B	Penned by the Penguin	30B	Jostled by the Joker	
17B	Prehistoric Peril	31B	Batman Bucks Badman	
18B	The Penguin's Prey	32B	Frozen by Frost	
19B	Cornered on a Cliff	33B	Gassed by a Geranium	37B	Riddler on the Roof	41B	Aquatic Attack!
20B	Distorted Dynamic Duo	34B	A Fatal Joust	38B	Beware the Bat-A-Rang	42B	Inhospitable Hatter!
21B	Toll of Torture	35B	Holy Rodents	39B	Caught in a Cavern	43B	The Perilous Penny
22B	Routing the Riddler	36B	A Pressing Position	40B	Batman Bails Out!	44B	Riddler Robs a Rainbow

BATMAN DELUXE REISSUE EDITION (143)

2 1/2" X 3 1/2"

Regardless of the continuing debate about the role and value of reprints and reissues in the hobby, many people will find this "Batman Deluxe Reissue Edition" to be a convenient and inexpensive addition to their collections. Produced by Topps in 1989, it is composed of 143 cards and is a modern version of the first three Batman sets issued by the company in 1966 (the "B" series cards are puzzle backs only).

The fronts have super glossy surfaces and the backs are marked "1966 Deluxe Reissue Edition" and "reissue 1989." Originally issued as a boxed set for $19.95, the value has since risen to its present level of $30 per set (price includes box). Note: there is no logic in offering these cards for sale as singles unless the seller is trying to pass them off as original 1966 cards.

BATMAN — RIDDLER BACK (38)　　　2 1/2" X 3 1/2"

The 38 cards in the "Riddler Back" series of Batman were another 1966 Topps issue. The front design is a color photograph with white borders; it has red photo mounts drawn at the corners and black card borders. There is no printing on the obverse. The backs are black, with the card number in a white bat design. There is a written riddle feature at the top, and an illustrated riddle at the bottom. The latter could only be deciphered by using a decoder provided in the gum packs.

ITEM	MINT	EX
Set	160.00	135.00
Card	3.50	3.00
Decoder	8.00	6.00
Wrapper	--	35.00
Box	--	175.00

1 Batman's Butler
2 The Boy Wonder
3 Robin's Time Out
4 Rarin' to Go
5 A Lesson for Robin
6 Bookworm Batman
7 A Batly Gesture
8 The Caped Crusader
9 Batmobile Breakdown
10 Beaming Batman
11 Studious Crimefighter
12 The Clown Prince of Crime
13 A Dual Decision
14 Convention Caper
15 To the Bat-Foil
16 Hide-and-Go-Riddle
17 Cautious Caped Crusader
18 A Fearsome Foursome
19 A Purr-fect Plot
20 Attacked
21 United Underworld
22 Awesome Foursome
23 Boy Wonder's Bat-cart
24 A Desperate Leap
25 The Princess of Plunder's Prey
26 A Nefarious Note
27 De-clawed
28 Close Call
29 A Riddle for Robin
30 Dashing Dick Grayson
31 Bat on a Buoy
32 Whacking Robin's Wings
33 The Pudgy Penguin
34 Docking the Bat-Foil
35 A Dastardly Duo
36 A Catly Caper
37 Showdown on the Sea
38 Rescued by Robin

BATMAN—COLOR PHOTOS (55)　　　2 1/2" X 3 1/2"

There are 55 cards in this series of white-bordered color

Batman photos issued by Topps in 1966. The pictures are numbered on the front (in red ink in a white circle) and the backs are either puzzle pieces or "Bat Laffs."

A credit line on the reverse mentions Greenway Productions and 20th Century Fox Television.

ITEM	MINT	EX
Set	190.00	160.00
Card	3.00	2.50
Wrapper	--	35.00
Box	--	150.00

∫ BATMAN MOVIE — 1ST SERIES (132/22)　　　2 1/2" X 3 1/2"

Topps hoped to cash in on the blockbuster movie hit of 1989 by printing a 154-item set of "Batman" that same year. The 132 cards in the set have color photographs surrounded by white borders; a Batman logo and the card title appear beneath each picture. The backs are mustard yellow with black print and color-reversal headings. The 22 stickers contain color photos of movie scenes, Bat equipment and logos, plus some artwork pictures. All of the stickers are

numbered, but only three are captioned, so there is no checklist listed for them here. Sticker backs are divided into two groups of ten partial pictures which can be assembled to form yellow and red-bordered pictures. The remaining two sticker backs show the completed pictures. There are two different wrappers and each design was manufactured in both wax and cellophane (99¢) versions. The wax display boxes have been seen with and without a 45¢ tab at upper right.

The cellophane pack display box is smaller than the wax version and is more difficult to find.

ITEM	MINT	EX
Set	18.00	13.50
Card	.10	.05
Sticker	.35	.25
Wrappers		
Wax (2), ea.	--	.35
Cellophane (2), ea.	--	.75
Boxes		
Wax	--	2.00
Cellophane	--	4.00

Batman Movie - 1st Series

1 Introduction
2 Darknight Detective
3 Bruce Wayne
4 The Clown Prince of Crime
5 Jack Napier
6 Vicki Vale
7 Alexander Knox
8 Commissioner Gordon
9 Alfred the Butler
10 D.A. Harvey Dent
11 Crime Boss Carl Grissom
12 Alicia Hunt
13 Gotham City After Dark
14 Mugged!!
15 Rooftop Rendezvous
16 Night of the Bat
17 Nailed by the Dark Avenger
18 "Who...What are You?!!"
19 Gotham City's Dark Knight
20 The New D.A.
21 Knox on the Job!
22 The Set-Up
23 Bruce in Wayne Manor
24 Meeting Their Host
25 View from the Batcave
26 The Axis Chemical Factory
27 Mysterious Manhunter
28 Batman's Weapon
29 Toxic Food!
30 In the Batman's Clutches
31 Commissioner Gordon - Hostage
32 Holding Batman at Bay!
33 Hero and the Horror
34 Jack Loses His Grip!
35 Plunge into Toxic Oblivion!
36 Rising Above It All
37 Spotted by Commissioner Gordon!
38 Front Page Story!
39 Ghastly Revelation
40 Back from the Dead
41 No Deals, Grissom!
42 "Call Me...Joker!"
43 Grissom's Gruesome Demise
44 "Wait'll They Get a Load of Me"
45 "Hi Honey!"
46 The New Crime Boss
47 Gotham City's Gang Lords
48 Joy-Buzzed to Death!
49 Evil of the Joker
50 Fried Alive!
51 "I'm in Charge Now!"

52 A Final Farewell
53 Lord of Wayne Manor
54 Outside City Hall
55 The Mine of Mayhem
56 Funny Meeting You Here!
57 City Hall Massacre!
58 Outrageous Assault!
59 Who's the Wildest One of All?
60 The Joker's Lair
61 Vicki's Most Devoted Fan
62 "Keep Up the Bad Work!"
63 Smylex Attack!
64 The Joker Conquers TV!
65 "Love That Joker!"
66 "Let's Go Shopping!"
67 At The Flugelheim
68 The Are of Crime
69 A Date with Vicki
70 You Light Up My Life
71 Alicia's New Look
72 "No! No! I'm Melting!!"
73 Crash!!!
74 The Rescue
75 Swing to Safety!
76 A Daring Escape!
77 The Batmobile
78 Fantastic Chase!
79 The Batmobile Tears Away!
80 Cocooned!
81 "Is It Halloween?"
82 "How Much Do You Weigh?"
83 Death-Defying Duo!
84 Hang On, Vicki!
85 Batman Overpowered!
86 The Challenge
87 Urban Warriors
88 Slashing Assault!
89 Photographed by Vicki
90 Friend...Or Mad Vigilante?
91 Within the Batcave
92 Vicki in a Jam!
93 The Joker is Wild!
94 Haunting Memory
95 Fate of the Wayne Family
96 Gearing Up For Danger!
97 Knight Patrol!
98 Sabotage!
99 The Axis Fireball!
100 Escape from Flaming Death
101 The Master of Disaster
102 Becentennial Nightmare!
103 Twisted Terrorists!
104 Flight of the Batwing
105 Batwing Cockpit
106 The Joker's Secret Weapon
107 Taking Aim at the Batwing!

108 Super-Sleek Craft!
109 Crash Dive!
110 Vicki to the Rescue!
111 The Joker Takes a Hostage
112 Batman Lives!
113 Grim Vendetta
114 In Danger's Domain
115 Watch Out Behind You...!
116 Assault on the Caped Fury
117 Desperate Struggle!
118 Grip of Death!
119 Perilous Plunge!
120 Batman in Action!
121 No Match for Batman!
122 Bruised But Not Beaten!
123 The Joker's Final Stand
124 Dance of Death
125 Vicki Imperiled!
126 The Titans Clash!
127 Batman vs. Madman
128 The Dark Knight Triumphs
129 The Joker - Over the Edge!
130 He Who Laughs Last...
131 The Bat-Signal
132 The Guardian of Gotham City

HERE IS WHAT YOUR COMPLETED YELLOW BORDER PICTURE WILL LOOK LIKE:

COLLECT ALL 10 CARDS OF PICTURE A

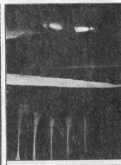

55

BATMAN MOVIE — 1ST SERIES
COLLECTORS' EDITION (143/22)

2 1/2" X 3 1/2"

This "Collectors' Edition" of 1989 1st Series "Batman Movie Cards" is essentially an upgraded version of the regular set. The 132 cards are exactly the same as those in the regular issue EXCEPT that they have a high gloss finish on front and a bright yellow background on back. The 22 stickers have slightly more obverse gloss and a more pronounced matte finish on the back than do their regular-issue counterparts. Apart from the changes in surfaces and ink color, the major difference between the regular set and the Collectors' Edition is that the latter has an eleven card "Bonus" set included in the box. These cards, lettered A through K, are attractive miniature copies of production artwork used to set up specific scenes in the film. All in all, the Collectors' Edition is far more attractive than the regular issue card set and is probably a better buy in the long run. Note: sold as a boxed set only.

ITEM	MINT	EX
Set	30.00	25.00

BATMAN IN BATWING COCKPIT

BONUS CARDS:

A Batman in Batwing Cockpit
B The Batwing Swoops Down
C Canyons of Gotham City
D Zeroing In on the Joker
E Setting the Missile Sights
F Hitting the Switch
G Firing Away!
H The Joker Avoids the Onslaught
I The Dark Knight Reacts
J The Batwing Bounces
K Cathedral Directly Ahead!

BATMAN MOVIE — 2ND SERIES (132/22)

2 1/2" X 3 1/2"

Topps immediately followed up its premiere series of "Batman Movie Cards" with a second set of 132 cards and 22 stickers. The former are numbered 133-264 and have yellow borders surrounding the color photos taken from the movie and the movie set. Second series card backs are basically a soft greenish-blue, which is even harder on the eyes than the dull yellow color background of Series 1. The stickers for this issue are numbered 22-44 and have color photos and artwork centered on white backgrounds (Since only three are captioned, there is not a checklist below). Sticker backs are partial pictures which can be assembled into two ten-piece views of Batman (orange borders) and the Joker (blue borders). The wrappers have an "All New 2ND Series" line on front and come in both wax and cellophane versions. As with the first series, the second series cello pack display box is harder to find than the wax variety.

ITEM	MINT	EX
Set	18.00	13.50
Card	.10	.05
Sticker	.35	.25
Wrappers		
Wax (2), ea.	--	.35
Cellophane (2), ea.	--	.75
Boxes		
Wax	--	2.00
Cellophane	--	4.00

CONTINUED ON CARD #223: EVERYONE NEEDS A HOBBY!

Batman Movie - 2nd Series

133 Batman - The 2nd Series
134 The Man and his Quarry
135 Hand of Vengeance
136 Parked in the Batcave
137 Fistfuls of Funny Money
138 Onward, To His Fate ...
139 Doppelganger
140 Time to Die, Grissom!
141 "Armadillo" Effect
142 The Last of Eckhardt
143 Leer of the Clown Prince
144 "I've Got to Work Tonight"
145 Leap from the Belltower
146 March of the Misfits
147 Meltingly Beautiful
148 You Know Who I Mean ...!
149 Power of the Batmobile
150 Flugelheim Aftermath
151 Alley Bat
152 Aiming to Kill!
153 News of the Battle
154 The Wayne Manor Party
155 Of Mimes and Memories
156 Danger in the Streets
157 The Oddest Couple
158 Knight and the Damsel
159 Hanging on for Life!
160 Murder ... Just for Laughs
161 Twisted Pitchman
162 'Copter Escape
163 Instructions for Alfred
164 Gotham City Landscape
165 Flugelheim Museum
    Interior
166 Elevated Subway Exterior
167 Flugelheim Museum
    Exterior
168 Grissom's Office
169 Their Final Bow?
170 The Batmobile — Head On
171 Dancing Devil
172 See Rotelli Roast
173 The Defeat of Batman
174 Sneaking Up Behind Jack ...
175 Festival of Madness
176 Battered but Unbowed!
177 Mission Accomplished
178 Retreat into Darkness
179 "You Want to Get *Nuts* ...!"

180 The Master's Mimes
181 Knox Chats with Alfred
182 Savage Sneak Attack!
183 Madness Wears a Smile
184 The Batmobile Escapes
185 Jack and Alicia
186 Trick or Treat!
187 The Fiend Flies High!
188 His Card ...
189 Silent but Deadly
190 The Phantom Avenger
191 A New Mad Plan!
192 Friends and Lovers
193 Fiery Finale
194 Another Man Down
195 The Batwing Soars!
196 The Joker [By Tim Burton]
197 Batman Costume Design
198 The Joker Costume Design
199 Batman Design Concept
200 Metal Walkway
201 Tugging the Line
202 The Hanging Hood
203 Over the Gantry
204 The Joker Knocked
    Backwards
205 Danger Directly Ahead!
206 Clearing the Trigger
207 Preparing for an Assult
208 Cathedral Dead Ahead!
209 Goons in Hot Pursuit!
210 Mysterious Millionaire
211 Alleys of Gotham City

212 The Villain Supreme!
213 Who is Jack Napier?
214 The Joke's on Alicia
215 Weapon Against Evil
216 His Foul and Fiendish Grin
217 Armor Inspiration
218 Grotesque Reflections
219 A Gift for Vicki
220 The Night is His Again!
221 Kids Playing 'Batman'
222 Brains + Beauty = Vicki
223 Everyone Needs a Hobby!
224 Throttling a Punk
225 An Artist Most Bizarre
226 Batman's Public Service
227 A Goon and His Tune
228 City of Light and Danger
229 Heroic Escape!
230 How the Joker Lives
231 Batman in the Belfry
232 Classic First Issue!
233 Directing Grissom's Murder
234 The Clown and the
    Clapboard
235 The Director's Vision
236 Maniacal Murderer
237 Knox Takes a Shot at
    Heroism
238 What Tim Burton Wants ...

239 Getting the Worst from
    Grissom
240 Directing Helicopter Escape
241 Special Advice for Batman
242 Directing Michael Keaton
243 Flight of the Dark Avenger
244 Interviewed by Knox
245 Tim Burton, Filmmaker
246 Alicia — Exquisite!
247 Presenting the Batmobile!
248 Relaxing with Key Players
249 Filming the Dance Macabre
250 Shooting the Rescue Scene
251 Dining at Wayne Manor
252 Secret Life of Bruce Wayne
253 City Street Miniature
254 At the Nerve Center
255 Computerized SFX
256 Fantastic Miniature Set
257 Trail of the Mystery Man
258 Directing Jack Nicholson
259 Dance of the Deranged
260 From Burton to Batman
261 Batman's Revenge
262 Gruesome Grimace
263 Buildings of Gotham City
264 The Killer Clown's in Town!

Stickers 23-44 have no titles

BATMAN MOVIE — 2ND SERIES
COLLECTORS' EDITION (143/22)

2 1/2" X 3 1/2"

BONUS CARDS:

L Grappling Hook, Spring
   Action Reel
M Batarang [Folded and
   Unfolded]
N Darkly Humorous Pistols
O Batman's Time Bomb
P Smoke Capsules
Q Handset & Tracer
R Batmobile Communicator
S Cocooned Batmobile [Front
   and Rear]
T Acid-Squirting Flower
U Batman's Gauntlet
V Utility Belt, Body Armor

As described on the back panel of the box, this 2nd Series "deluxe movie card set" contains "11 exclusive weapons and gadgets cards which will not appear elsewhere." These are the so-called "bonus cards" (lettered L through V) which, along with the super-glossy surfaces and improved-visibility backs of the 132 cards and 22 stickers, allow Topps and card dealers to charge a premium for the set. According to Topps, it was produced in limited quantities and is the ideal compliment [sic!] to the 1st Series Collectors' Edition. The excellent production values of this set make it much more attractive and interesting than the regular issue, and in the long run, it probably is a better buy. Note: sold as a boxed set only.

ITEM	MINT	EX
Set	30.00	25.00

The 66-card Battle set was issued by Topps in 1965. Except for numbers 54-66 — which are types of servicemen, generals, statesmen, and 2 checklist cards — the typical color drawing of this series depicts a violent war scene in realistic detail. The caption appears in a yellow panel on the front and the cards have white borders. The backs are brown and gray, and there is a sketch of a running soldier next to the text. One 2″ X 3 5/16″ "U.S. Military Cloth Emblem" was inserted into each gum pack as a bonus; there are 24 emblems altogether. Note: the card checklist (#66) and the emblem checklist (#65) must be unmarked to be graded "mint" or "excellent."

JUNGLE DUEL

JUNGLE DUEL

Pvt. Lon Brown, sole survivor of a scouting mission, had been awake for over 24 hours...

ITEM	MINT	EX
Card set	450.00	350.00
Card	5.00	4.00
Card checklist	35.00	25.00
Emblem set	300.00	225.00
Emblem	10.00	7.50
Emblem checklist	25.00	20.00
Wrapper	---	100.00
Box	---	400.00

LEADERS OF WORLD WAR II
PRES. FRANKLIN ROOSEVELT

FIGHTING MEN OF WORLD WAR II
U.S. PARATROOPER

BATTLE CHECKLIST

1. "Fight to the Death"
2. Attack on Pearl Harbor
3. Execution at Dawn
4. Grenade of Death
5. Collision in the Sky
6. Watery Doom
7. Ambushing the General
8. Death of a Frogman
9. Hiding from the Nazis
10. Medic Under Fire
11. Death Rides the Wing
12. Death on the Bridge
13. Death in the Street
14. "Stop Those Planes"
15. Dog Warrior
16. The Ocean's Victims

BATTLE
the story of WORLD WAR II
EXTRA
MILITARY EMBLEM IN EACH PACK
BUBBLE GUM 5¢

U.S. MILITARY CLOTH EMBLEM
CHECKLIST

DECORATE YOUR BOOKS, BIKE AND ROOM.
WET THE BACK OF THE EMBLEM AND APPLY.

1. ☐ 7th Army
2. ☐ Army Air Forces
3. ☐ Hq. European Theater
4. ☐ 2d Division
5. ☐ 17th Airborne Division
6. ☐ 59th Division
7. ☐ 63d Division
8. ☐ 10th Mountain Division

1 "Fight to the Death"
2 Attack on Pearl Harbor
3 Execution at Dawn
4 Grenade of Death
5 Collision in the Sky
6 Watery Doom
7 Ambushing the General
8 Death of a Frogman
9 Hiding from the Nazis
10 Medic under Fire
11 Death Rides the Wing
12 Death on the Bridge
13 Death in the Street
14 "Stop Those Planes"
15 Dog Warrior
16 The Ocean's Victims
17 Attack on Nazi Convoy
18 Jungle Duel
19 Hand to Hand Combat
20 Snipers in the Snow
21 Saved in Time
22 Stockade Attack
23 Suicide Dive
24 Trapped!
25 Stopped by Grenades
26 Blasting the Nazis
27 Train of Death
28 Caught While Escaping
29 Smashing Thru the Guards
30 Cossack Charge
31 Battlefront Transfusion
32 Confession by Force
33 Nazi Terror
34 Saving His Buddies
35 Terror from the Sky
36 Helpless Paratrooper
37 Jungle Execution
38 School Bombing
39 Death Blow
40 The Flaming Sea

41 Hospital Raiders
42 Fiery Death
43 Disaster in the Street
44 The Torture Chamber
45 Train Yard Bombing
46 Assassin in the Sky
47 Battle on the Beach
48 Exploding Grenade
49 Death Struggle
50 Bomb Victims
51 Tangled on a Tree
52 Flames of Death
53 Beautiful Spy
54 United States Sailor
55 U.S. Commando
56 U.S. Marine
57 U.S. Paratrooper
58 Japanese Soldier
59 Nazi Soldier
60 Charles DeGaulle
61 Winston Churchill
62 Gen. Douglas MacArthur
63 Pres. Franklin Roosevelt
64 Gen. Dwight Eisenhower
65 Cloth Emblem Checklist
66 Battle Checklist

1 7th Army
2 Army Air Forces
3 Hq. European Theater
4 2d Division
5 17th Airborne Division
6 59th Division
7 63d Division
8 10th Mountain Division
9 11th Airborne Division
10 77th Division
11 187th Airborne Reg. Team
12 4th Air Force
13 Alaska Air Command
14 Aviation Cadet
15 Air Material Command
16 99th Infantry Battalion
17 442d Regimental Combat Team
18 One Hundred First Division
19 Armored Force
20 U.S. Wing Marking
21 73d Air Base
22 31st Bombardment
23 3d Observation
24 VF-2

BATTLESTAR GALACTICA (132 &22)   2 1/2" X 3 1/2"

It has been the practice of Topps in the last few years to issue card sets with a variety of features on the backs of the cards. In Battlestar Galactica, a series of 132 cards and 22 stickers produced in 1978, the reverses contain not only puzzle pieces but also presentations entitled "Story Summary," "TV Facts," and "Character Profile." The fronts are color pictures from the Universal movie and have the set title emblazoned in yellow letters across the bottom. The caption appears in blue print in the white panel at the bottom, and the card number is located in the bottom-right corner. The main design of the stickers is surrounded by a purple color form and is set upon a "starry universe" background. Each sticker is numbered and captioned in the yellow area underneath the picture. Note: set prices include stickers.

ITEM	MINT	EX
Set	30.00	22.50
Card	.15	.10
Sticker	.35	.25
Wrapper	--	.35
Box	--	5.00

1 Lorne Greene Is Commander Adama
2 Dirk Benedict Is Lt. Starbuck
3 Richard Hatch Is Captain Apollo
4 Lew Ayres Is the Colony President
5 A Day of Peace...or Betrayal?
6 Preparing to Blast a Battlestar!
7 For the Love of Gold Cubits!
8 Sneak Attack!
9 President Adar Endangered!
10 Blasting the Planet Caprica!
11 A World in Flames!
12 "They're Bombing the City!"
13 Adar's Final Moments!
14 The President's Council—Destroyed!
15 Panic in Caprica Mall
16 Doomsday on Caprica
17 Blasted by the Cylon Warships!
18 Caught in the Middle of a Star Battle
19 Annihilation of the Human Colonies
20 The Cylon Centurions
21 The Imperious Leader
22 Fate of the Traitor Baltar
23 Serina Survives the Onslaught!
24 Leveling a Planet
25 The Escape Plan
26 Adama's Dream
27 The Colonial Battlestars
28 Charting the Exodus
29 Laurette Spang Is Cassiopea
30 Fleet of Colonial Vipers

31 Adama and Col. Tigh
32 Galactica Under Fire!
33 The Commander and His Daughter, Athena
34 Muffit 2, the Cybernetic Daggit!
35 Boxey's New Daggit!
36 Boosting Boxeys Morale!
37 Destination: Earth
38 Deep Inside the Planet Carrillon
39 Speeding Toward Carillion
40 Starbuck's Landram
41 The Big Bash on Carillon
42 Pig-faced Tourist!
43 Chamber of the Imperious Leader
44 At the Gambling Casino
45 Carillon—A Nice Place to Visit!
46 Intergalactic-Gambler
47 Bizarre Wonderland
48 Boxey Attacked by Alien Creatures!
49 Behold...the Ovion Insectoids!
50 Ovion Guards Escort Boxey!
51 Boxey and Muffit Are Reunited!
52 Captured by Ovion Warriors
53 One of Lotay's Musicians
54 Lothay, Queen of the Ovions
55 Conferring with Seetol

56 The Colonists and the Insectoids
57 Escape from Fiery Death!
58 Bridge of the Galactica
59 An Ovion Warrior
60 Profile of an Ovion
61 An Elaborate Party for the Colonists
62 The Space Supremes
63 Trio of Tucanas
64 Where the Elite Meet!
65 Jane Seymour Is Serina
66 Serina Arrives at the Carillon Bash
67 Maren Jensen is Athena
68 Flamboyant Lovers: Starbuck and Cassiopea
69 The War of the Wiles
70 Hitting Outrageously High Notes!
71 The Lord of Galactica
72 Galacticans Discuss Their Dilemma
73 Lotay and Her Centurion Allies
74 Nourishment for Newborn Ovions!
75 Brood of the Insectoids!
76 Starbuck and Boxey...to the Rescue!

77 Lt. Starbuck Posed for Action!
78 Metallic Monster
79 Attack of the Cylons!
80 Shoot-out in the Ovion Catacombs!
81 "My Blaster Is Quick..."
82 Inside the Chosen Chamber
83 Creatures of Destruction
84 A Narrow Escape!
85 Covered by Lt. Boomer!
86 The Human Exterminators
87 Army of Evil
88 Destroying the Human Refuse?
89 Unstoppable Invaders!
90 Night of the Metal Monsters
91 Clipped by a Laser Blast!
92 Seetol's Fate
93 The Colonists' Counterattack!
94 Don't Mess with Starbuck!
95 Centurions on the March
96 The Cylon War Machine
97 The Destructors
98 Emissaries of Hate
99 Attacking our Heros!
100 "Destroy the Human Vermin!"

Battlestar Galactica

101 A Planet In Peril!	119 Monitoring the Battle	1 Commander Adama
102 Fantastic Weapons of the Cylons	120 Athena in Action!	2 Lt. Starbuck
	121 Troubled Colonial Elder (Wilfred Hyde-White)	3 Captain Apollo
103 Holding the Enemy at Bay!		4 Lt. Boomer
104 Man of Destiny	122 A Day of Deliverance!	5 Athena
105 Everything's A-OK!	123 Landrams to the Rescue!	6 An Ovion Warrior
106 Flight of Oblivion!	124 The Battle Is Ours!	7 The Imperious Leader
107 Preparing the Colonial Ships	125 Picking Up the Last Stranded Colonists	8 Casino Patron
108 The Moment of Truth!		9 President Adar
109 Colonial Star Pilots	126 The Odyssey of Battlestar Galactica	10 Serina
110 Facing Incredible Odds		11 Android Sister
111 The Cylon Supreme Star Force	127 Stars Dirk Benedict and Richard Hatch	12 Cylons on the March!
		13 Survivor of Carillon
112 Blasted by the Enemy!	128 Dirk Benedict Portrait Shot	14 Alien Warrior
113 The Destroying Ray!	129 A Boy and His...Err...Daggit?	15 Cassiopea
114 The Fate of Human Kind before Them!	130 Self-reliant Athena (Maren Jensen)	16 Cylon Centurion
		17 Starbuck (Dirk Benedict)
115 Cylon Warships Closing In!	131 Lovely Jane Seymour Takes a Breather	18 Galactican Warrior
116 A Direct Hit!		19 Boxey
117 Athena on Galactica	132 Photographing a Colonial Viper	20 Space Warrior
118 The Battlestar Quakes!		21 Galactican Elder
		22 Spirit of Salvation

GALACTICAN WARRIOR

BATTLESTAR GALACTICA (36)   2 1/2" X 3 1/2"

Although this 36-card "Battlestar Galactica" set is generally associated with Wonder Bread, there is no mention of that brand on the cards. The fronts contain color photographs taken from the 1978 Universal Studios movie and the borders are red. The series title is printed at center below the picture but there are no individual card captions. The backs are simply designed: there is a line or two of text, the card number, and some copyright and trademark credits. No retail advertising appears anywhere on the cards. A generous supply of sets, plus very moderate demand, has kept the price of this set at reasonable levels.

ITEM	MINT	EX
Set	10.00	8.00
Card	.25	.20

1 A gambler and daredevil, Starbuck is one of BATTLESTAR GALACTICA'S best fighter pilots and destroyed many an evil Cylon Raider with his marksmanship.

2 Boxey smiles approvingly at Muffit, the daggit created by Scientist Winkler, as he trains the droid to do all the tricks a real daggit can do.

3 Snowrams are a necessity for traveling in the sub-freezing temperatures on ARCTA. On foot, no one could survive on the asteriod's surface.

4 Space Cadet Cree was captured alive by the Cylons, but refused to reveal BATTLESTAR GALACTICA'S location despite cruel torture.

5 Cylon warships look like bats in the night, but they proved to be no match for a colonial warship in the hands of a capable fighter like Starbuck.

6 Known as Boom Boom to his friends because of his shooting abilities, Boomer is Starbuck's closest friend in the Red Squadron.

7 Athena was an Ensign on the BATTLESTAR GALACTICA because of her ability, not her father, Commander Adama.

8 During a red alert, the control room took on an eerie cast as the crew raced to their stations.

9 Scientist Winkler can fix the most complex wiring systems on the BATTLESTAR GALACTICA — he can also make a daggit out of fur, wiring, metal and love.

10 B.R. SER 5-9 leads his fellow Clones in their revolt to gain freedom from the tyranny of Vulpa, the Cylon dictator.

11 Starbuck thought the Android Sisters would make a fortune on the Star Circuit, but could he feed all those mouths?

12 Croft had been in prison, but he heroically led the assault against the Laser Spear when Apollo faltered on Mt. Hekla.

13 Of the five BATTLESTARS, only the GALACTICA survived to safeguard the human race.

14 Ravashol was the one human tolerated by the Cylons, but only because his genius mind created the Laser Spear; but to the Clones, he was Father-Creator.

15 Nadil was interested in Starbuck's offer, but kept her eyes open for spies in the nightclub.

16 Since the croupier at Carillon's gambling casino had eyes big enough to see everything, why did every gambler win?

17 Surviving humans came in all sorts of guises from the BATTLESTAR GALACTICA, resolved to avenge their friends' deaths.

18 Commander Adama and Colonel Tigh have served together for many years. Not only are they a most capable team, they are close friends.

19 No one knows what was behind the metallic mask of the Cylon warriors; the red scanner beam served as eyes to the clumsy, but strong aliens.

20 The Jondrew loved the gambling on Carillon, even though it did not show on his face.

21 Capricans hopelessly try to evade the blasts from the evil Cylon's sneak attack.

22 Starbuck shows Boomer his perfect pyramid, but the alert was called before he could collect his winnings from the Gemons.

BattlestaR GALACTICA

Nadil was interested in Starbuck's offer, but kept her eyes open for spies in the nightclub.

#15 of Thirty-six

23 The Imperious Leader was the only Cylon with a third brain — unfortunately he devoted it to the extermination of all humanoid forms of life.

24 Lotay, Queen of the Ovions, ruled a world in which male Ovions were not tolerated.

25 Although badly beaten by the Cylon's devious treachery, the surviving Capricans resolve to fight rather than surrender.

26 Seetol uses her many hands to play soothing music on the Ovion harp.

27 Humans were not the only visitors to Carillon; life forms came from everywhere to enjoy Carillon's parties and replenish their supply of Tylium.

28 Unfortunately, not everyone was brave. Sire Uri, who partied while others starved, wanted to lay down all weapons and trust the Cylons.

29 Serina and her son Boxey came to depend on Apollo, who promised to help the boy become a full-fledged Colonial warrior.

30 The Cylons trained hard in their deadly arts; "Attack" and "Kill" were their favorite words.

31 From his control room, the Imperious Leader orders squadrons of Cylon Raiders on Borallus to attack BATTLESTAR GALACTICA and the surviving humans.

32 Pledging themselves to serve their people, Commander Adama and the Council seek out the original source — Earth.

33 Apollo and Starbuck, an unbeatable team, are planning the attack against Vulpa's forces on Mt. Hekla.

34 A Colonial viper ship was the sleekest, fastest and most potent ship in the BATTLESTAR GALACTICA'S arsenal.

35 Muffit tried hard, but learning all those tricks was not an easy thing to do, even for a droid.

36 Zac and Apollo were the first to see the Cylons treachery, but Zac never made it back to warn the others.

How do you drive a teacher crazy? Wrap up all your schoolbooks in Topps' series of Batty Book Covers, that's how! This innovative set of 24 paper bookcovers has features like phoney headlines, frac- tured history lessons, kooky klassified ads, and other wacky themes. A checklist of all 24 titles appears on the wrapper and on each cover, and every cover is numbered. Note: no mint price is given since the covers were folded to fit into the gum pack.

ITEM	MINT	EX
Set	--	215.00
Bookcover	--	7.50
Wrapper	--	35.00
Box	--	75.00

Batty Book Covers

1 Crazy History
2 Believe It Or Nuts No. 1
3 Kooky Klassified Ads
4 Dracula For President
5 Wacky Packages
6 I Want You
7 Nutty Newspaper
8 Flour Power
9 Funny Famous Paintings No. 1
10 Crazy Literature
11 Believe It Or Nuts No. 2
12 Tippy Through Tulips
13 15-7/8 Magazine
14 How To Succeed In School
15 Classroom Creeps No. 1
16 Reader's Disgust
17 Brain Surgery Made Simple
18 Calendar
19 Funny Mail-Order Catalog
20 Classroom Creeps No. 2
21 Hip Parader Magazine
22 Funny Famous Paintings No. 2
23 National Geografink
24 Classroom Creeps No. 3

BATTY BUTTONS (24)   2" DIA.

A series of 24 tin buttons issued by Topps, without gum, in blue paper envelopes. The button and wrapper both bear a "Made in Japan" line. A numbered checklist of the button captions is located on the back of the wrapper but the buttons themselves are un-numbered. They are 2" in diameter and have a horizontal

"spike" pin held by a retainer. There is no manufacturer identification on the buttons and the date of issue is thought to be 1973.

ITEM	MINT	EX
Set	55.00	40.00
Button	2.00	1.50
Wrapper	--	6.00
Box	--	40.00

Ain't I Cute
Bite On!
Fly Me!
Get Lost
Get Off My Back
Greatest Kid On Earth
I'm A Brain
I'm Available
I'm A Winner
I'm Wonderful
I've Got My Eye On You
I Want You
Keep On Truckin'
Kiss Me
Peace
Pray For A Teacher's Strike
Remember Mummy's Day
Stake Gives Me Heartburn
Stop Pollution! Shut Your Mouth

You Make Me Drool
You Win Me
U.S. Kissing Team
U.S. Navel Academy
Warning · Full Moon Tonight

BAY CITY ROLLERS (66)   2 1/2" X 3 1/2"

This set of 66 cards was tested in the U.S. by Topps in 1975 (test wrapper is white with sticker and T-96-5 code). Reports indicate that the regular wrapper packs, which carry a 0-413-21-01-05 code, were marketed here only in Fun Packs, with the bulk of the cards produced going to England. The fact that no box has been seen supports this theory. The cards have color pictures of various band members on the front. The card number appears on back, where the layout is apportioned on a 55/45 basis between puzzle piece and text.

ITEM	MINT	EX
Set	37.50	25.00
Card	.50	.35
Wrappers		
Test	--	30.00
Regular	--	6.00
Box	--	75.00

1 Rock Sensation	11 Alan's Dream	21 Big Rock Star!	44 Takin' Off
2 Singing Star	12 Groovy Group!	22 Alan Cracks Up!	45 Hot Dog!
3 Rollin' On	13 Eric the Great!	23 Singin' Pals!	46 Eric Relaxes
4 The Fab Five!	14 Call to Eric!	24 Eric Faulkner	47 Phone Freaks
5 Cool Group!	15 Secret Wish	25 Alan Longmuir	48 Midday Break!
6 The Rollers	16 Brushin' Up	26 Les McKeown	49 Happy Times!
7 Success Sighted!	17 The Big Apple!	27 Derek Longmuir	50 Rollers Hit N.Y.!
8 Copter Trip	18 A Sign of Thanks!	28 "Woody" Wood	51 Thinking of You
9 Woody's Blues	19 Taking It Easy!	29 Cool Concert!	52 Sneaker City!
10 Fab Musicians	20 Break for Lunch!	30 Fab Songsters	53 Teen Idols!
		31 Concert Event!	54 Visit to the U.S!.
		32 Balad...To You	55 One More Time!
		33 Havin' A Ball!	56 Boss Guitar!
		34 Roller Star!	57 Camera Catcher!
		35 In New York!	58 Real Cool Cat!
		36 Take a Bow!	59 Rockin' Rollers!
		37 Shoe Shopping!	60 Up and Away!
		38 Down the Hatch!	61 Beat Those Drums!
		39 Time to Relax!	62 That's Show Biz!
		40 Singin' Brothers	63 Pop Idol!
		41 Manhattan Fun!	64 Best-Dressed Feet!
		42 Take a Break!	65 Hello, World!
		43 Concert Classic!	66 'Till Next Time!

BEATLES — B&W (60-55-50)   2 1/2" X 3 1/2"

In 1964 Topps issued the 165-card Beatles set of black and white photos in three separate series. The fronts

are photographs with facsimile autographs printed in blue ink. The backs are empty except for a small box at the bottom which identifies the series and the card number. Series 1 (1-60) has a blue line box which says "...series of 60 photos." Series 2 (61-115) has either an orange or green box with "2nd Series" inset at the top. Series 3 (116-165) has a green box and is marked "3rd Series."

ITEM	MINT	EX
Sets		
Series 1	175.00	150.00
Series 2	165.00	140.00
Series 3	145.00	125.00
Cards		
All Series	2.50	2.00
Wrapper	--	30.00
Boxes		
No sticker	--	100.00
"New Series"	--	100.00

BEATLES—COLOR (64)

2 1/2" X 3 1/2"

Since there are no captions on this 64-card Beatles set, we have arranged the checklist according to card descriptions.

Each picture is a color photograph surrounded by white borders; there is no printing on the fronts of the cards. The backs contain the card number and a question-and-answer feature (except for 1-4, which introduce the Beatles individually and provide their vital statistics). The backs are orange and white in color and have a sketch of the "Fabulous Four" on the left side.

ITEM	MINT	EX
Set	190.00	160.00
Card	2.50	2.00
Wrapper	—	30.00
Box	—	100.00

1 Meet John Lennon
2 Meet Paul McCartney
3 Meet George Harrison
4 Meet Ringo Starr
5 Front—John, Paul, George, Ringo/Back—Question—Paul Speaking
6 Front—John, Paul, George, Ringo/Back—Question—John Speaking
7 Front—George and Paul/Back—Question—Ringo Speaking
8 Front—Paul/Back—Question—George Speaking
9 Front—Ringo and John/Back—Question—Paul Speaking
10 Front—John/Back—Question—John Speaking
11 Front—George—Back—Question—Ringo Speaking
12 Front—John, Paul and Ringo/Back—Question—John Speaking
13 Front—John and Paul/Back—Question—Paul Speaking

14 Front—John/Back—Question—George Speaking
15 Front—John, Paul, George and Ringo/Back—Question—Ringo Speaking
16 Front—Ringo, Paul and John/Back—Question—John Speaking
17 Front—Ringo, George, John and Paul/Back—Question—George Speaking
18 Front—Ringo, George, John and Paul/Back—Question—George Speaking
19 Front—John/Back—Question—Ringo Speaking
20 Front—Ringo/Back Question—John Speaking
21 Front—George, John, Ringo and Paul/Back—Question—Paul Speaking
22 Front—Paul, George, John and Ringo/Back Question—George Speaking
23 Front—John, Paul and Ringo/Back—Question—Ringo Speaking
24 Front—John, Ringo and Paul/Back—Question—John Speaking
25 Front—John, Paul, Ringo and John/Back—Question—Ringo Speaking
26 Front—George/Back—Question—Paul Speaking
27 Front—Paul, Ringo and John/Back—Question—Paul Speaking
28 Front—Ringo/Back—Question—George Speaking
29 Front—Paul, John, Young Boy, and Ringo/Back—Question—Ringo Speaking
30 Front—Paul, George, John and Ringo/Back—Question—Paul Speaking

31 Front—Ringo, George, John and Paul/Back—Question—George Speaking
32 John, Dog and Ringo/Back—Question—John Speaking
33 Front—Ringo, George, John and Paul/Back—Question—John Speaking
34 Front—Paul, John and Ringo/Back—Question—Ringo Speaking
35 Front—Paul, Ringo, George and John/Back—Question—Ringo Speaking
36 Front—Paul, John, George and Ringo/Back—Question—Paul Speaking
37 Front—Paul, George and John/Back—Question—Ringo Speaking
38 Front—Paul/Back—Question—John Speaking
39 Front—John and George/Back—Question—John Speaking
40 Front—John, Ringo and Paul/Back—Question—Paul Speaking
41 Front—Paul/Back—Question—Paul Speaking
42 Front Ringo, John and Paul/Back—Question—George Speaking
43 Front—Paul, Ringo, John and George/Back—Question—Ringo Speaking
44 Front—Paul, George and John/Back—Question—John Speaking
45 Front—Ringo/Back—Question—Paul Speaking
46 Front—Paul, George, John and Ringo/Back—Question—Ringo Speaking
47 Front—Ringo and John/Back—Question—John Speaking

48 Front—Ringo, John and Paul/Back—Question—George Speaking
49 Front—Paul/Back—Question—Ringo Speaking
50 Front—Paul, George and Ringo/Back—Question—John Speaking
51 Front—Paul and Ringo/Back—Question—Ringo Speaking
52 Front—Ringo, Paul and John/Back—Question—Paul Speaking
53 Front—Ringo, Paul, John and George/Back—Question—Paul Speaking
54 Paul and Ringo/Back—Question—John Speaking
55 Front—Paul, Ringo, George and John/Back—Question—John Speaking
56 Front—Ringo/Eack—Question—Paul Speaking
57 Front—Paul, Ringo and John/Back—Question—John Speaking
58 Front—Ringo and Paul/Back—Question—George Speaking
59 Front—John, Paul and Ringo/Back—Question—Ringo Speaking
60 Front—John, Ringo and Paul/Back—Question—Paul Speaking
61 Front—Paul, George, John and Ringo/Back—Question—Paul Speaking
62 Front—John, Paul, Ringo and George/Back—Question—Paul Speaking
63 Front—George and John/Back—Question—Paul Speaking
64 Front—Ringo, Paul and John/Back—Question—John Speaking

BEATLES DIARY (60)

2 1/2" X 3 1/2"

There are 60 cards in the Beatles Diary set issued by Topps in 1964. Each obverse has a color photograph surrounded by white borders and is devoid of print. The backs are blue and white and are styled like a diary page. Upon this page design is a short story relating the adventures of the English rockers on tour. The cards are numbered 1A to 60A. The checklist below is a listing of the individual facsimile autographs appearing on the fronts of the cards. No wrapper has been confirmed for this set.

ITEM	MINT	EX
Set	175.00	145.00
Card	2.50	2.00

1	George Harrison	16	John Lennon	31	Paul McCartney	46	George Harrison
2	John Lennon	17	John Lennon	32	Ringo Starr	47	John Lennon
3	Paul McCartney	18	Paul McCartney	33	John Lennon	48	George Harrison
4	Paul McCartney	19	Ringo Starr	34	John Lennon	49	Ringo Starr
5	John Lennon	20	John Lennon	35	Paul McCartney	50	John Lennon
6	Ringo Starr	21	Paul McCartney	36	George Harrison	51	Ringo Starr
7	John Lennon	22	Paul McCartney	37	Paul McCartney	52	George Harrison
8	Ringo Starr	23	George Harrison	38	Ringo Starr	53	George Harrison
9	George Harrison	24	Ringo Starr	39	Paul McCartney	54	Paul McCartney
10	George Harrison	25	Paul McCartney	40	John Lennon	55	John Lennon
11	Paul McCartney	26	Ringo Starr	41	George Harrison	56	George Harrison
12	Ringo Starr	27	Paul McCartney	42	John Lennon	57	John Lennon
13	Ringo Starr	28	Ringo Starr	43	Ringo Starr	58	Paul McCartney
14	George Harrison	29	Ringo Starr	44	John Lennon	59	Ringo Starr
15	George Harrison	30	George Harrison	45	Paul McCartney	60	Paul McCartney

BEATLES MOVIE (55) "A HARD DAY'S NIGHT"

2 1/2" X 3 1/2"

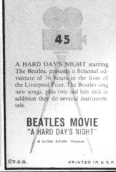

The pictures in the "A Hard Day's Night" set are sepiatone photographs taken from the United Artists movie. They have white borders but no printing. The backs are white with a camera design running through the body of the text. The card number is printed on the camera at the top, and there is an advertisement for the movie near the bottom. The set was issued by Topps in 1964. The checklist below lists the first sentence of the text on the back of each card. The cellophane combination-pack header card illustrated below has a value of $10.

ITEM	MINT	EX
Set	165.00	135.00
Card	2.50	2.00
Wrapper	--	30.00
Box	--	125.00

Be In The Know!

★ **Complete Line of Non Sport**
Call or write (please include a SASE) to check on availability of items.

★ **Full-time Mail Order** (not a store)

★ **Buying Collections**

MasterCard and Visa for orders of $25.00 or more.
By Phone, Mail or Fax (717) 238-3220

ROXANNE TOSER
Dept. 92, 4019 Green Street
Harrisburg, PA 17110
(717) 238-1936
Mon.-Fri. 10-9, Sat. 10-5 E.S.T.
No Sunday Calls

3/10¢ PACKS

BEATLES MOVIE "A HARD DAY'S NIGHT"

A UNITED ARTISTS RELEASE

29¢

1 There were always spectators on the set of A HARD DAY'S NIGHT.

2 All the boys proved to skeptics that they had fine acting ability, besides being fine singers.

3 The Beatles left the studio sets to film this scene outdoors.

4 Here's a close-up of George Harrison.

5 John Lennon and George Harrison chat on the set after doing one of the musical numbers from A HARD DAY'S NIGHT.

6 Paul McCartney and Ringo Starr pose in front of the cameras during a brief break in the filming of A HARD DAY'S NIGHT.

7 Don't get excited!

8 In this candid snapshot, George Harrison of the fabulous Beatles speaks to one of the technicians on a sound stage.

9 Paul gets set to dance with the young actress that plays a girl friend in A HARD DAY'S NIGHT.

10 Ringo Starr is having a one-way conversation with himself as he speaks into a phone that doesn't work.

11 Paul is snapped in a reflective mood on the set of A HARD DAY'S NIGHT.

12 Ringo gets some last minute instruction from a movie technician.

13

14 Look out, because here comes another Beatle!

15 Here's one of the wildest scenes from A HARD DAY'S NIGHT.

16 It's early in the morning and most people are still fast asleep...But not The Beatles!

17 Ringo Starr speaks to a young admirer in a scene from A HARD DAY'S NIGHT.

18 George, John, Paul and Ringo get some last minute instructions from the movie's director.

19 Paul's Grandfather is the villain in A HARD DAY'S NIGHT.

20 Who is the man in the beard?

21 Beatles...Beatles...everywhere!

22 One of the funniest sequences in A HARD DAY'S NIGHT involves Paul and his grandfather on a railroad station.

23 Here comes the big fight scene.

24 Paul gets a call from his song publisher on the set of A HARD DAY'S NIGHT.

25 Ringo takes a coffee break on the set of A HARD DAY'S NIGHT.

26 The final chore for the boys was to make a trailer.

27 Paul, Ringo and George are getting ready to shoot their favorite scene in A HARD DAY'S NIGHT.

28 Ringo looks a little unhappy, according to the script, because Grandfather has been up to his old tricks again.

29 Ringo Starr is in trouble with the police...but in the movie only.

30 The Beatles get their famous hair combed just before the day's shooting begins on A HARD DAY'S NIGHT.

31 Meet The Beatles

32 In A HARD DAY'S NIGHT, Ringo Starr disappears, and the three Beatles are frantic.

33 John Lennon gets ideas for new songs almost everywhere.

34 Beatle George Harrison poses for a publicity shot.

35 Beatle George Harrison takes a welcome break between scenes in A HARD DAY'S NIGHT.

36 Paul McCartney is on a train in this scene from A HARD DAY'S NIGHT.

37 Paul McCartney, in his movie debut, is dressed as a London banker in this scene from A HARD DAY'S NIGHT.

38 In The Beatles' first movie, Ringo Starr makes his film debut.

39 The Beatles are onstage in The Scala Theatre in Soho performing CAN'T BUY YOU LOVE.

40 John, Paul, George and Ringo are getting set to run through the title song from their movie A HARD DAY'S NIGHT.

41 In this scene from A HARD DAY'S NIGHT, it is just before The Beatles are scheduled to appear on a live television show.

42 Movie grandfather John McCartney is going to work on Ringo to try to split up the group.

43 John Lennon has met Paul's grandfather for the first time in their train compartment.

44 Paul McCartney has his eye on his grandfather in this scene from A HARD DAY'S NIGHT.

45 A HARD DAY'S NIGHT starring The Beatles, presents a fictional adventure of 36 hours in the lives of the Liverpool Four.

46 Ringo Starr has quit The Beatles!

47 Which one is the real Beatle?

48 Popular Beatle John Lennon poses for publicity shots for The Beatles' first motion picture, A HARD DAY'S NIGHT.

49 The Beatles are actors now and they mug it up for the cameras during a shooting break.

50 Here come all four Beatles on the dead run.

51 Beatle George Harrison relaxes in his dressing room waiting for the word to begin the next scene of A HARD DAY'S NIGHT.

52 Paul McCartney holds a clapboard on the set of A HARD DAY'S NIGHT.

53 In this scene from A HARD DAY'S NIGHT, Paul, John, George and Ringo open fan mail and relax in their hotel suite.

54 The Beatles are on stage during a live television show performing several of their numbers.

55 The Beatles are about to board a train and this is where their troubles start in A HARD DAY'S NIGHT.

BEATLES PLAKS (55)

2 1/2" X 4 11/16"

INSTRUCTIONS FOR HOOKING UP PLAKS

1 Tear along perforated lines, leaving hooks intact.

2 Slide hooks into slots in next plak.

3 Make 'em as long as you want—2 ft, 5 ft, 10 ft!!!

"Hook 'Em Up!" suggests a line on the wrapper of this 55-card set glorifying the Fab Four. Each card contains a picture or slogan about the Beatles set against a woodgrain background (the wavy edges are simulated). The cards could be hooked together in a chain by punching out three pre-scored cardboard pieces and inserting the "hooks" thus exposed into the slots on another card (the directions for doing this are on the reverse of each plak). The cards are numbered on the back and cards without pictures (sayings only) are marked in the checklist by an asterisk. Note: mint and excel cards must be complete (no parts missing). A "find" of Beatles Plaks has resulted in lower prices for this set than were printed in the 1988 Price Guide.

ITEM	MINT	EX
Set	950.00	700.00
Cards		
Picture	15.00	11.00
No picture	12.50	9.00
Wrapper	--	100.00
Box	--	200.00

Beatles Plaks

1 I Dig The Beatles
2 Paul, John, George, Ringo
3 Seal of Approval Beatles Are OK
4 The Beatles for Congress
5 Ringo! Ringo! Ringo!
6 Beatles 4 Ever
7 Love That Ringo
8 The Greatest Ever
9 I Love You
10 George Harrison
11 The Chairmen of the Board
12 The Beatles are the Gear
13 Paul Is All
14 John! John! John!
15 Keep the Beatles Here
16 Go-Go-Go with Ringo
17 Beatles!!! Beatles!!! Beatles!!!
18 Hail The Beatles
19 I Pledge Allegiance to The Beatles
20 John Lennen [sic]
21 The Worlds Fairest
22 Thank You England
23 John Sends Me
24 I Have Beatlemania

25 Beatles*
26 George is Gorgeous
27 John is Fab
28 I Love The Beatles

29 Beatles You're Beautiful
30 The Boys from Liverpool are Real Cool
31 Hats Off to The Beatles
32 The 8th Wonder of the World-The Beatles

33 I Go Ape for the Beatles
34 Paul is the Living End
35 Smile-The Beatles are Singing*
36 Next to Me, I Love the Beatles
37 Paul McCartney
38 I Flip for George
39 I'm Hooked on The Beatles
40 Stamp Out Everyone Who Wants to Stamp Out the Beatles*
41 I Flip My Beatles Wig
42 Paul! Paul!! Paul!!!
43 A Gas
44 Ringo is the Cutest
45 George! George!! George!!!
46 The Beatles are Real Boss
47 Ringo Starr
48 Fab! Fab! Fab!
49 Never Leave Me
50 Silence I'm Listening to The Beatles*
51 The U.S.A. Wants You to Stay
52 The Beatles are Happening
53 Ringo for Kingo
54 Yeah Yeah Yeah
55 Think How Wonderful The Beatles Are*

BEATLES CANDY BOXES (4)

To exploit the beatle craze sweeping the country, World Candies (of New York) issued four small "Yeah Yeah Candy" boxes bearing caricatures of the Mod Rockers. The first name of each band member is printed beneath his picture; "The Beatles" is printed below the names of George, John and Paul, but is printed above Ringo's name on his drum. Note: the box picturing John Lennon (not illustrated) is very often found priced higher than the others.

ITEM	MINT	EX
Set	250.00	175.00
Box	50.00	35.00

BEAUTIFUL PEOPLE (50/14)

2 1/2" X 3 3/8"

Of course they're not beautiful! They're grotesque and distorted and they say insulting, ill-mannered things. They encourage gum-chewing in class and give the juvenile mind another weapon to mistreat friends, enemies and innocent bystanders. There are 50 of these corner-peel "ugly stickers" in the set, 28 with yellow backgrounds and 22 with white backgrounds. None of the stickers is numbered and both color varieties have identical instructions printed on their tan paper backs. A subset of 14 cards offering a range of suspect "free" services is also unnumbered. Note: set price stated is for 50 stickers and 14 cards.

ITEM	MINT	EX
Set	35.00	25.00
Card	.50	.35
Sticker	.50	.35
Wrapper	--	2.00

YELLOW STICKERS
My Name Is [blank] Body Beautiful (Fly Me!)
My Name is [blank] (Call Me Fatso)
My Name is [blank] (Call Me Slurpy!)
My Name is [blank] (I'm a Yo-Yo)
My Name is [blank] (I Stink!)
My Name is [blank] (Kick Me!)
My Name is [blank] (Kiss Me)
My Name is [blank] (Let's Do It!)
My Name is [blank] (Let's Streak Baby!)
My Name is [blank] (Me Worry?)
My Name is [blank] Pimplehead (Lick Here)
[blank] Big Lover? (I'm Yours!)
[blank] Did It! (Sniff...Who Did It?)
[blank] Dumbbell (Me Worry?)
[blank] 46-56-96 (Call Me Fatso!)
[blank] Got Caught!
[blank] Has Bad Breath (Come Close!)
[blank] I Eat Anything
[blank] is a Big Mouth! (You Jive Turkey)
[blank] is a Dirty Person (Kiss Me Now!)
[blank] is a Dumbbell
[blank] is a Hunchback
[blank] is a Loser
[blank] is a Pinhead (Math Teacher)
[blank] is Lumpy (Hi Stupid!)
[blank] is Slimy!
[blank] My Favorite Teacher (Fly Me!)
[blank] Needs a Bath! (Smell Here)
[blank] Needs a Kleanex

DUMBBELL

Beautiful People

WHITE STICKERS

My Name is [blank] (Call Me Big Nose!)
My Name is [blank] Godzilla Breath!
Wants You!
[blank] Eats Soap
[blank] Eats Trash (Eat Here!)
[blank] Has a Hole in his Head!
[blank] Has Athletes Foot (Kiss My Foot)
[blank] Has Big Ears
[blank] Has Buck Teeth (Kiss Me!)
[blank] Has Pop-Eyes!
[blank] Loves Boys
[blank] is a Bone Head
[blank] is All Wet
[blank] is a Pimplehead

[blank] is a Sweathog (Kick Me!)
[blank] is a Swinger (Let's Do It!)
[blank] is Ugly! (Kiss Me Baby!)
[blank] Needs a Bath! (I Stink)
[blank] Wears a Girdle
[blank] Worlds Fastest Lover!

"FREE" CARDS

Free Dance Lessons
Free Haircut by Roto-Matic
Free Helen Rinkleskin Cosmetics
Free Manicure by Wanda the Wacker
Free Massage
Free Mud Pack
Free Pass Bob D. Builders
Free Pass Dr. Shocks Group Encounter
Free Pass to Charlie's Charm Center
Free Sample Course
Free Sample Dr. Ungawah's Head Shrink
  Special
Free Shoe Shine
Free Tailoring Service
Free Treatment!

BEAUTY AND THE BEAST (95)   2 1/2" X 3 1/2"

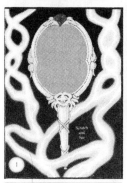

Lumiere
Color-In Card

The Walt Disney Studio has earned many accolades over the years for its gorgeous and innovative animated films, but it may have topped all previous efforts with "Beauty and the Beast." Pro Set's series of 95 cards based on this movie captures all the brilliant color and charm of the movie. There are 75 story cards in the set, each with a gorgeous artwork illustration made even more striking by the absence of surrounding borders. The text on back is short and is positioned to the left of a "magic mirror" which has a small color artwork insert. The card number is printed in a fireworks-burst design at the upper right. Speaking of magic mirrors, there is a 10-card subset of these with scratch-off surfaces which reveal various characters from the film. Another ten cards are double-sided "color-in" items to use with crayons or paint. Pro Set released the set in early 1992 in foil "fin" packs containing eight story cards and one each of the mirror and color-in cards.

ITEM	MINT	EX
Set	12.00	--
Cards (all)	.10	--
Wrapper	--	.10
Box	--	2.00

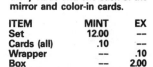

BEAUTY AND THE BEAST STORY CARDS

1 Love's Magic Tale
2 The Selfish Prince
3 A Terrible Spell
4 An Enchanted Rose
5 A Peculiar Mademoiselle
6 Books and Big Dreams
7 A Braggart's Boast
8 Positively Primeval!
9 A Fine Invention
10 A Fond Farewell!
11 Lost in the Woods
12 Hunted by Wolves!
13 A Narrow Escape!
14 An Odd Welcoming Committee
15 An Angry Host!
16 Wedding Bells for Belle?
17 Gaston Pops the Question
18 A Spurned Suitor
19 Belle's Dreams
20 Belle's Adventure Begins
21 Papa, Where Are You?
22 There's a Girl in the Castle!
23 Belle Finds Her Father
24 A Brave Bargain
25 Heartbroken Prisoner
26 Gaston's Boasts
27 A Cry for Help!
28 No Help in Sight
29 An Evil Plan
30 No Date for Dinner

Beauty and the Beast

31 Etiquette Lessons for the Beast
32 A Rough Beginning
33 A Hopeless Moment
34 A Midnight Snack
35 Entertainment a la Carte
36 The Show Goes On
37 Happy to Serve Again
38 The Grand Finale
39 A Strange Discovery
40 An Angry Meeting
41 Danger in the Forest
42 A Surprise Rescuer
43 A Moment of Trust
44 A Vicious Plot
45 A Precious Gift

46 A Tender Lesson in Manners
47 Something Different
48 New Feelings
49 Quiet, Happy Hours
50 A Big Night Ahead
51 A "Belle Mademoiselle"
52 A Handsome Beast
53 An Enchanted Dance
54 Song as Old as Rhyme
55 Bad News in the Mirror
56 A Family Reunion
57 A Little Stowaway
58 The Villains Strike!
59 The Beast is Revealed
60 Gaston Incites the Mob

61 Gaston's Prisoners
62 The Mob Attacks
63 Cogsworth in Command
64 Hot Water for the Invaders
65 Top-Drawer Maneuvers
66 A Victory Cheer
67 Gaston's Treachery
68 Chip Starts Chopping
69 A Beloved Face
70 End of a Villain
71 Words of Love
72 The Spell is Broken
73 Human Again!
74 Another Dance
75 And of Course ...

MAGIC MIRROR CARDS
1 Beast
2 Belle
3 Lumiere
4 Cogsworth
5 Mrs. Potts
6 Chip
7 Feather Duster
8 Phillipe
9 Maurice
10 Gaston

COLOR-IN CARDS
1 Beast / Belle & Beast
2 Mrs. Potts / Chip
3 Lumiere / Feather Duster
4 Belle / Cogsworth
5 Belle / Beast
6 Belle / Lumiere
7 Footstool / Mrs. Potts & Chip
8 Cogsworth / Lumiere & Feather Duster
9 Beast / Belle & Beast
10 Belle / Armoire

BEETLEJUICE (100/20)   2 1/2″ X 3 1/2″

This colorful "Limited Collector's Edition" of 100 cards and 20 stickers was produced by Dart Flipcards in 1990. The numbered, high gloss cards contain artwork pictures taken from the Beetlejuice television cartoon show (Geffen Film Co.). There are 20 unnumbered and uncaptioned stickers that accompany the cards and these were designed to glow in the dark. The set was issued in a special presentation box which also contained two bonus stickers and a sequentially-numbered "Certificate of Authenticity." The latter states that only 3000 sets of the Beetlejuice Collector's Set were produced, and you can really on that since Dart is one of the few card producers that actually destroys EVERYTHING (including the film) used to create their sets.

ITEM	MINT	EX
Boxed set	20.00	---

1 Header card
2 Lydia
3 Delia
4 Charles
5 Prudence ("Prune")
6 Bertha ("Burp") Goes Camping
7 Jacques Lalean
8 Ginger, Toe Tapping Fool
9 The Monster Across the Street
10 Claire Brewster, "Valley Girl"
11 Home Sweet Home
12 Panic at the Shocking Mall
13 I Get a Kick Out of Life!
14 Snack Time!
15 Now That's One Sharp Kid!
16 Gross-Out Meter Record!
17 Babysitting!
18 Starring Barf Bendman!
19 Lydia's Haunted House
20 Where'd They Go?
21 ...I'm an Old Cow Hand...
22 Bully's Back in Town!
23 "Where's the Sheriff?!"
24 Chickenjuice on Boot Hill

25 I'm Really into Art!
26 MMMMM..., Lunch!
27 Double Deluxe Lung Tosser
28 "You Look Bad, Beetlejuice"
29 Double Trouble
30 Neitherworld Beauties!
31 Slimy Beauty
32 "Shrimp Shells & Chicken Bones Please"
33 Who Invited You?!
34 The Best Part!
35 Beetlejuice Strikes Again
36 Buzzface
37 Dancing Fools
38 Where've I Smelt That?!
39 Door to The Neitherworld
40 I Love a Buffet!
41 Spooky Sunset
42 Dead Letter Box
43 Nice Smile!
44 Bettyjuice's Ballad
45 Crab Grass Attack
46 Back Pack Surprise
47 Hedgehogs!
48 Nice Muscles!
49 Creepy Camping
50 Timber Wolves

51 Terrifying Sandworm
52 Bertha to the Rescue
53 The Rot Tub
54 Scummin' Through!
55 Goin' to Pieces!
56 Coffin Break
57 Scared My Pants Off!
58 The Thing in the Tub
59 Howdy Clare!
60 Skeleton of the Year
61 Morning Breath
62 An Upset Stomach
63 Breakfast of Champion Ghouls
64 Howdy!
65 Need a Hand?!
66 Neighborhood Surprise
67 Toe Truck
68 Bug Attack
69 Neitherworld Neighbors
70 It's Showtime!
71 Spare a Quarter?
72 Snakes Alive!
73 What's Cookin'?
74 Waiting Room Weirdos
75 Wake Up, Stinky
76 Pea Brain

77 Thanks for the Warning!
78 No Problem!
79 I Screamed My Head Off!
80 I'm a Monkey's Uncle!
81 All Snaked Up!
82 Twist My Arm, Lydia!
83 Armpit Musician
84 Neitherworld Rock Stars
85 Egomaniac
86 Party Animal Arrives
87 Party Bats!
88 Punk-in-Pie
89 How 'bout that Punch?!
90 Tall, Dark & Hairy
91 Make My Day!
92 Shake!
93 Watch those Extra Toppings!
94 Loosen Up!
95 Cousin B.J.
96 B.J.'s Candy Bar
97 Foot Doctor
98 Garbageman
99 Proud Parents
100 Skull checklist

BEETLEJUICE ALBUM STICKERS (48)

1 15/16" X 3 1/8"

In recent times, Panini has been testing a new format for some of its sticker sets, one in which a complete set of stickers is stapled directly into the center of the album. "Beetlejuice," issued in 1990, employs this system and the end result is that it resembles a child's activity book rather than a traditional Panini set. The 48 numbered, "peel and lift" stickers found in sheet form in the middle of the album make 33 different pictures when left in original condition or placed on the appropriate album pages. Other features printed in the album include Halloween Safety Tips, a board game, a mask, and a contest. Considering how difficult it can be to put together a Panini set by purchasing individual packages of stickers, this complete, albeit smaller, set format may be the wave of the future. Note: this album may still be found at discount in some retail stores.

ITEM	MINT	EX
Album set	7.00	5.00

BELIEVE IT OR NOT (84)

2 1/2" X 3 1/2"

HERE LIES MY 4 HUSBANDS
ALL IN A ROW
AND HERE LET THEM KEEP
WITHOUT MAKING A BOTHER
WHILE I LOOK ABOUT ME
TO FIND ME ANOTHER

TOMBSTONE in Wheldrake Cemetery England

Fleer issued this 84-card Believe It Or Not series in 1970. The benchmark Ripley's panel is situated at the top of each card and the picture area contains several illustrated facts from the Ripley's storehouse of amazing facts. The artwork might be more visually striking were it not for the wide yellow borders that dominate the color scheme of these cards. The Fleer name does not appear on the card and the set is not numbered. The backs contain a simple ink sketch of another Ripley's feature. Note: some cards may have been double printed since single cards are much easier to find than complete sets.

ITEM	MINT	EX
Set	60.00	50.00
Card	.50	.35
Wrapper	--	8.00
Box	--	35.00

A Savage Stallion
A Strain of Donkeys
A Witch Doctor
Aztec Warriors
Big Mouth
Bono
C.G. Wilson
Chief Monguba
Doctors
Doctors of Death
El Cid
Emperor Aurelian
First Lady Kidnapped by a Orangutan!
4 Elephants
General Atha Mossana
Girls
Half a Shoe
Harry Morse
Howard Hill
John Johnstone
John McCollam
John Sayre
King Alexander
Knights
"La Grand'Mere"
Marotte Beaupre
Most Amazing Archer in all History
Rab Hamilton

A Bullfight that Decided a War!
Agesilas
Ali Sali
Allen Bradley
Angelo Corsaro

Siward the Strong
Star Point
Sultan Ahmad
The Amazing Frogman of El Obeid
The Amazing High Divers of Cape Dukato
The Ancient Persians
The Big One That Didn't Get Away
The Blind Warrior
The Dellis
The Dog Soldiers
The Drunkard's Fountain
The Duel Fought for a Kingdom!
The Elephant that Defeated an Army
The Executioner of Charlotte Corday
The Fabulous Fakir of Sipi
The Human Carpet!
The Human Haystacks Dancers
The Human Tigers
The Human Snowball
The Knight Who was Killed by His Own
  Trap!

The Largest Elephant in the World
The Man in the Goldfish Bowl!
The Man Who Always Bathed in Full
  Uniform!
The Man Who Burned His Tongue with a
  Red-Hot Iron 95,000 Times
The Man Who Could Not Be Hanged
The Man Who Dueled with a Fan!
The Man Who Killed a Bear with his Bare
  Hand!
The Man Who Outwrestled a Tiger!
The Man Who Really "Said a Mouthful!"
The Man Who Sentenced Himself to Life
  Imprisonment!
The Man Who Was Saved by a Railroad
  Wreck!
The Most Deadly Duels in History - Vikings
The Most Powerful Woman in History!
The Most Sensitive Bald Man in History -
  Emperor Theophile
The Nightmare That was a Fatal Prophecy!

The People Who Laugh Themselves to
  Death!
The Roman Firebrand!
The Skeleton that Ruled the Roman
  Empire!
The Ski Rescue Staged 762 Years Ago!
The Strangest Coming-Out Parties in the
  World
The Strangest Dance in the World
The Structure That was Designed by a
  Nightmare
The Suitor Who Had to Fight 17 Rivals!
The Viking Who Had Legs Like Steel
  Springs
Thomas Parnell
Thomas Schweicker
3 Bodies
2-Headed Turtle
Vijeya
Young Couples
Zobeida

BELIEVE IT OR NOT (23-23-18)

1 2-Headed Turtle/Vanilla Beans/
  Crocodile
1 Signey Wigfall/The Spotted Bower
  Bird/Girls
2 The Ocotillo/The Human Haystacks/
  The Pineapple
2 The Ancient Persians/Zinc Ore
  Crystals/The Sloth
3 Monument to a Woman's Right to
  Change Her Mind/Half a Shave/The
  Walrus
3 Zobeida/Bucky/The Light of the Sun
4 The Suitor/Tom Turkey/The Saracen's
  Tent
4 Elephant Feet/The Man Who Always
  Bathed in Full Uniform/Apple
5 Earwig/Siward the Strong/Sis
5 An Oyster/The Anchor Inn/El Cid
6 Marotte Beaupre/Trees/Aeoliscus
  Punctulatus
6 The Witch Doctor/The Guernsey Lilly/
  Raspberries & Blueberries
7 Emperor Aurelian/The Cockroach/
  The Cave Cathedral
7 Mr. Corn/The Human Carpet/
  Tombstone
8 The Living Arch/Mzilikaze's Bird/John
  Johnstone
8 Thomas Parnell/Pearl/A Regiment of
  Submarine Soldiers
9 Start Point/A Rake/The Grizzly Bear
9 The Most Sensitive Artist in all History/
  The Camel/John Sayre

10 2 Siamese Cats/9 Temples/The Man
  Who Could Not be Hanged
10 Harry Morse/The Penitents
11 Rev. Ritchie D. Ocheltree Sr./The
  Human Snowball/The Nighthawk
11 Oars/The Strangest Coming-Out Parties
  in the World
12 The Cattail/Tiberio Fiurelli/John
  McCollam
12 Thomas Schweicker/A Piece of Blue
  Glass
13 Angelo Cosaro/Women/Northwest
  Telephone
13 Big Mouth/The Church Cave/Six
  O'Clock Shooter
14 4 Elephants/The Chair that Collected
  Taxes
14 Doctors/Pushkar/The Landing of
  Columbus
15 The Human Tigers/The Lucin Railroad
  Cutoff/Southern Ontario
15 The Roman Firebrand/World's Biggest
  Hot Dog
16 The Tower/The Balancing Boulder/
  3 Bodies
16 The Knight Who was Killed by His Own
  Trap/The Wall
17 The Man Who was Saved by a Railroad
  Wreck/The Blind Benthosaurus/Rev. J.
  F. Benson
17 The Big One/Peter Paddock
18 Aztec Warriors/Early Compass/Stone
  Pyramid

TWO SIZES

There were two sizes of Ripley's cards printed on Milk Duds boxes during the summer of 1974. The smaller, or 5-cent box size, measures 1 7/8" X 2 3/4" and was issued in two groups of 23 titles each, 46 cards in all. The larger, 10-cent box size, is 2 3/16" X 3 1/4" and was issued in a single series of 18 designs. The card numbers for both sizes of cards were printed on box flaps. Once the cards were cut off, they would, in fact, be unnumbered. Since there is no way to determine which of the 23-card small-size boxes was issued first, we have listed both titles together under one number. Both 5-cent and 10-cent boxes had an order form for a 190-page Ripley's book printed on the inside of each box. All 64 designs found in the Milk Duds series are duplicated in the Fleer set listed above. Note: collector Jeff Kilian provided the information and checklist for this summary.

ITEM	MINT	EX
Card	--	1.00
Full Box		
5 cent	6.00	5.00
10 cent	7.50	6.00

18 First Lady Kidnaped by an Orangutan
19 Young Couples/The Marsupial Mole/
  The Great Anteater
19 Cow/The Nun and the Monk/The
  Drunkard's Fountain
20 "La Grend'Mere"/Jack Clapp/
  Hailstones
20 The Frog Fish/Bono/Cruelest Husband
  in All History
21 Blue Laws/Tomato Head/The Dellis
21 The Stucture That was Designed by a
  Nightmare/Giacomo Meyerbeer/The
  Sword-Billed Hummingbird
22 Agesilas/Tiger Bird/The Castle of
  Pragstein
22 Allspice/The Man Who Burned his
  Tongue with a Red Hot Iron 95,000
  Times/Blood
23 The Largest Elephant in the World/
  The First Cook Book/Wolf Fish
23 Elm Tree/The Crown of Thorns/The
  Executioner

1 The Most Bizarre Act of Proof in all History!/General Atha Mossana
2 The Fabulous Fakir of Sipi/The Tartolten
3 Tomato Doughnut/A Strain of Donkeys
4 A Bullfight That Decided a War/Apple
5 Tibetian Monks/Ali Sali
6 Knights/The Petrified Waterfall
7 The Man Who Killed a Bear with his Bare Hands/Spot
8 The Skeleton That Ruled the Roman Empire
9 The Nightmare That was a Fatal Prophecy/The Spirobis Worm
10 The Elephant That Defeated an Army/Ancient Letter Box
11 Howard Hill/The Upside-Down Catfish
12 The Blind Warrior/The Bamboo and Straw Huts
13 The Prophecy That Killed a King/The Largest Loaf of Bread in the World
14 The Death's Head Moth/Vijeya
15 Chief Monguba/James Crow
16 Rab Hamilton/The Broken-Hearted Oak
17 The Dog Soldiers/H.M.S. Bounty
18 Vinegar Falls/A Savage Stallion

BELLY BUTTONS (20 & 14)

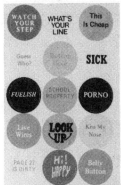

Antiques - Treasures
Antraks Railroad
Bacteria Baking Company
Bill Telephone
Endless Advertising Inc.
Generally Defective
Greedy Grocer
Last National Bank
Midnight Auto
Miss Fortune's
Monster Movies
Shortservice
Sid's Barber Shop
Ye Olde Ice Cream Shoppe

Army Surplus
Big Tummy
Button Up
Do Not Touch
Enter There
Fly Me
Forget It
Hi Dude (blue)
Hi Dude (purple)
Kick To Start
Lo-Calorie
Real Sick
Rotten
Sale 99
Sisters Are Ugly
Watch Your Step
What's Your Line
You Smell (blue)
You Smell (green)
You're Too Fat

TWO SIZES

There are two distinct parts to the Belly Buttons set distributed by Fleer. First, there are twenty 2 1/2" X 4" paper sheets, each containing 15 diecut "buttons," According to the illustration on the wrapper, and to the set title, these have a specific anatomical function (although a kid would certainly find other applications). Second, there are fourteen 2 1/2" X 4" cards printed in "business" or "calling card" style. Neither the sticker sheets or cards are numbered. The sticker checklist below is alphabetized according to the top, upper left "button" on every sheet. Note: set price includes sticker sheets and cards.

ITEM	MINT	EX
Set	50.00	35.00
Sticker sheet	1.50	1.00
Card	1.00	.75
Wrapper	--	4.00
Box	--	12.50

BEVERLY HILLBILLIES (66)

GRANNY, I'M GROWING MY OWN LEOPARD COAT.

Lookee there! There's Jed 'n Granny 'n Jethro 'n Elly May an' they's all standin' down by the cement pond...and

2 1/2" X 3 1/2"

it's all in this Topps set of 66 cards issued in 1963. The color photographs are taken from the TV series and are captioned at the bottom. The set title appears in a black oval in the field of every picture. The backs are brown and gray and contain a feature named "Hillbilly Gags." The card number is located in a barrel design near the bottom of the reverse side.

ITEM	MINT	EX
Set	415.00	330.00
Card	5.00	4.00
Wrappers		
1 cent	--	50.00
5 cent	--	125.00
Box	--	175.00

1 People in California Sure Dress Funny.
2 Officer, Granny Meant No Harm Climbing Up the Telephone Pole.
3 Don't Fret. We'll Get You a New Slingshot for Christmas.
4 There Ain't a Possum in All of Beverly Hills!
5 Granny.
6 You Stop Beating Up Jethro, Hear?
7 "It's Great for Cracking Walnuts?"
8 Strangest Looking Prison Bars I Ever Saw.
9 Now, No More Rassling, You Two.
10 Granny, I'm Growing My Own Leopard Coat.
11 That Telephone Pole Makes Good Fire Wood.
12 But Granny, You're Too Old to Slide Down the Bannister.
13 Home Sweet Home
14 Let's Shoot Something for Breakfast
15 Ow, I Hit the Wrong Nail!!
16 Elly May and Jethro.
17 We Give Up—Where Is the Water Pump?
18 I Gave Him a Bath and He Just Wrinkled All Up.

19 Got Any Spare Parts for a 1921 Touring Car?
20 The Folks at This Drive-In Ain't Watching the Movie.
21 Why Can't I Take My Pet for a Walk?
22 I Don't Care if It Is Your Job, Just Touch Our Garbage & I'll Shoot.
23 These Californy Bathtubs Are a Bit Snug.
24 I'd Be a Good Executive—If I Knew What "Executive" Meant.
25 Elly May, Stop Putting the Wash in the Television Machine.
26 This Car's Been in Our Family for 40 Years!
27 Why'd They Put a Harp in This Wood Box?
28 We Get 10 Gallons Per Mile.
29 We Use This for Washing & the Outside Pool for Rinsing.
30 That Picture Is by Rembrant—Mebbe He Can Paint One of You.
31 I Got Fine Antiques—My Furniture and Granny.

32 So That's a Bikini Bathing Suit!!
33 You Can Get Pretty Thirsty, Sunning Yourself.
34 If I Knew You Two Were Dressing Up, I'd Have Put on My New Dungarees.
35 They're Fun, but Not Much for Hunting Bears.
36 Ain't They Ever Seen a Convertible Before?
37 Aw Granny, That's Not a Giant Bug—That's a Hely-copter.
38 Elly May, It's Easier to Iron My Coat after I Take It Off.
39 It Musta Been a Pretty Sick Chicken for Such a Bandage.
40 Who Says My Coat Ain't in Style—It Has Been for the Past 25 Years.
41 Jethro
42 Magazines Are Great for Swatting Flies.
43 Jethro, You're Going to Get in Trouble Bathing in the Park Fountain.

44 Everybody Got Cadillacs, but We Got Something Special.
45 This New House Is Bigger'n Our Old Farm
46 Jethro and Jed.
47 Get Fresh with Me, Will Ya!
48 Race You Up One of Them Palm Trees.
49 Maybe We Could Get Jobs as Models
50 We Can Always Throw Darts at It.
51 This'll Go Great in My Possum Stew.
52 Today I Bagged 2 Squirrels and a Mink Coat.
53 Spread-Out, You Two You're Scrunching Me!
54 The Letter Would Make More Sense if You Could Read.
55 We're Going to a Fancy Nightclub.
56 Elly May, Jed, Granny and Jethro.
57 Jed, You Look Fine in Sports Clothes.
58 I Don't Know What a Parking Attendant Is, but You Just Stay Away from Our Car.
59 That "One Way" Sign Is Wrong—It's Pointing the Other Way.
60 When My Date's Car Stopped, I Fixed the Motor.
61 Jed Clampett.
62 We've Been Posing for 2 Hours—You Sure Paint Slow.
63 When That Ice Melts We're in for a Flood!
64 Elly May.
65 You Mean Some People Play Games with These Pot Holders?
66 There's Someone in This Thing—I Can Hear Him Talking.

THE BEAUTY OF BEVERLY

Shannen Doherty, who has been on several TV shows and movies, plays Brenda Walsh, twin sister to Brandon and a girl trying to fit in at West Beverly Hills High.

HERE IS WHAT YOUR COMPLETED BLUE BORDER PICTURE WILL LOOK LIKE.

COLLECT ALL 10 CARDS OF PICTURE A.

Hey, here's an idea. Let's take Rebel Without a Cause, Fast Times at Ridgemont High, The Flamingo Kid, and Beach Blanket Bingo, mix em all up together in- to a soap opera for teenagers and name it after a zipcode!! Lucky for us there's a television network that caters to such im- probable shows, so we'll fit right in between Aresenio, Bay Watch, Alien Nation, Bill & Ted, Paul Rodriguez, In Living Color, 21 Jump Street, et al. No wonder the Japanese, who have an affinity for bizarre theatre, are buying up Los Angeles for their own private theme park!

Topps apparently thought this was a hot property and purchas- ed a license to produce a 90210 card set in 1991. The series con- sists of 88 cards and 11 stickers which were sold in cello fold-flap packs (8 cards & 1 sticker per pack). The entire series of cards are publicity shots (not from episodes); they have black and orange borders and a turquoise "wave" with a 90210 logo. Seven of the stickers show photo cut- outs superimposed on blue logo backgrounds, while three of the remaining four simply repeat pictures used on the cards. The reverse sides are puzzle parts (10) plus a puzzle preview picture.

Collectors, take note of the foul-up involving card #'s 46, and 47. Cards 35-66 were supposed to be a sub-series with ver- tical/pink "Quick Quiz" backs (cards 1-34 & 67-88 have horizontal/blue/text backs). Both #46 and #47 are sub- headed "Trivia Question #12," meaning that card #'s 47-65 are numerically out of sequence question-wise. Since no correc- tion has been reported (or is like- ly), these have no special value. In addition, card #66 has no trivia question but still has a pink, ver- tical back because it has a trivia answer. Note: set price includes stickers.

ITEM	MINT	EX
Set	12.50	9.00
Card	.10	.07
Sticker	.35	.25
Wrapper	--	.25
Box	--	2.00

STICKERS		
1 Brandon	6	Kelly
2 Dylan	7	No caption
3 Brenda	8	No caption
4 Brandon	9	Dylan
5 Andrea	10	No caption
	11	No caption

QUICK QUIZ

TRIVIA QUESTION #12:
Which two male cast members are the best cooks?
Find the answer on Card #47.

Answer to Trivia Question #11:
Bagels! When Luke lived in New York City for three years, he fell in love with them. "Now I have to drive three miles out here—in Los Angeles—just to get bagels!" he says.

46

QUICK QUIZ

TRIVIA QUESTION #12:
What was Tori's first role?
Find the answer on Card #48.

Answer to Trivia Question #11:
Luke and Jason! Luke loves hav- ing people over for special din- ners, and Jason is a whiz at whip- ping up Chinese and Mexican meals.

47

1	Rock 'N' Roll High School	34	Gill Guy
2	He's a Rebel	35	Quick Quiz #1
3	New Kid in Town	36	Quick Quiz #2
4	The Beauty of Beverly	37	Quick Quiz #3
5	That Smarts!	38	Quick Quiz #4
6	Beach Boy	39	Quick Quiz #5
7	Silver's Gold	40	Quick Quiz #6
8	California Girl	41	Quick Quiz #7
9	Head of the Clique	42	Quick Quiz #8
10	Terrific Trio	43	Quick Quiz #9
11	Cute Couple	44	Quick Quiz #10
12	Expect the Unexpected	45	Quick Quiz #11
13	Girl Group	46	Quick Quiz #12
14	Time Off	47	Quick Quiz #12
15	The Dynamic Duo	48	Quick Quiz #13
16	Music Lover	49	Quick Quiz #14
17	Main Dudes	50	Quick Quiz #15
18	The Pet Set	51	Quick Quiz #16
19	Wave Watching	52	Quick Quiz #17
20	Hog Wild	53	Quick Quiz #18
21	Now You're Styling!	54	Quick Quiz #19
22	Tube Talk	55	Quick Quiz #20
23	Happy Together	56	Quick Quiz #21
24	Character Actress	57	Quick Quiz #22
25	Getting Better All The Time	58	Quick Quiz #23
26	Growing Up	59	Quick Quiz #24
27	Offscreen Athletes	60	Quick Quiz #25
28	Siblings	61	Quick Quiz #26
29	Hard at Work	62	Quick Quiz #27
30	Great Guys	63	Quick Quiz #28
31	Water Babies	64	Quick Quiz #29
32	Get on Board	65	Quick Quiz #30
33	Schooldaze	66	Social Climber
		67	Earth First
		68	Family Affair
		69	Happy Actress
		70	Work and Play
		71	Like Alike
		72	I Am What I Am
		73	Horsing Around
		74	Poor Rich Boy
		75	Fun in the Sun
		76	Face It
		77	Nothing is Perfect
		78	Words of Wisdom
		79	Book Nook
		80	Hobby Horse
		81	In The Beginning
		82	The Real BH
		83	Animal Farm
		84	Thrill Seeker
		85	Movie Man
		86	Puck Stuck
		87	Green Team
		88	Staying on Top

BICENTENNIAL DAZE (24)

2 1/2" X 3 1/2"

Collectors have advanced several theories about the manner in which "Bicentennial Daze" was distributed, but it seems most likely that the cards were issued with bread. The series carries a "1976 Gamecraft" copyright credit and was produced by Arnold Harris Associates of Cherry Hill, N.J. The fronts of the cards contain artwork portraits of 24 patriots, soldiers, and statesmen of the American Revolution. The title,

"Bicentennial Daze," is an attempt to attract interest by being witty; the front of every card poses a question about the subject pictured, to which a humorous answer is given on back. The card reverses contain biographical summaries and the card number. No packaging of any sort has been reported for this set.

ITEM	MINT	EX
Set	17.50	12.50
Card	.60	.45

Count Casimir Pulaski was born in Poland. What part?

All of him.

CASIMIR PULASKI (1748-79)

Revolutionary war hero. Born Poland. Pulaski, a Polish nobleman, fought desperately to preserve his country's freedom from Russian domination. When the cause was lost, he fled Poland to save his life. Learning of the fight for freedom in the United States, he sailed to America with a letter of introduction to George Washington written by Benjamin Franklin.

Having been a brilliant cavalryman in his own country, he was commissioned brigadier general and assigned a cavalry unit. He proved to be such an outstanding leader that Washington requested him to form his own independent force composed of European trained cavalry and infantrymen. Two years later he was mortally wounded while leading a cavalry charge in the attack on Savannah on October 11, 1779.

Because of the love and esteem held for this beloved patriot who gave his life for the American cause at the age of 31, Congress has honored his memory by proclaiming October 11th as "Pulaski Day."

NO.2 IN A BICENTENNIAL SERIES OF 24 CARDS

© 1976 GAMECRAFT. Produced in U.S.A.

1 George Washington	13 George Rogers Clark
2 Casimir Pulaski	14 John Paul Jones
3 Thomas Jefferson	15 Nathanael Greene
4 John Adams	16 Marquis de Lafayette
5 James Madison	17 Deborah Sampson Ganett
6 Alexander Hamilton	18 Betsy Ross
7 Ethan Allen	19 Robert Morris
8 Benjamin Franklin	20 Paul Revere
9 Thomas Paine	21 John Hancock
10 Samuel Adams	22 Benedict Arnold
11 Nathan Hale	23 Baron Friedrich Von Steuben
12 Patrick Henry	24 Crispus Attucks

BIG BAD BUTTONS (24)

2 1/4" Diameter

"Big Bad Buttons" is one of those mysterious sets which no one knew about until very recently. We can tell from the "T-75-16" code printed on the paper packet that the series was issued by Topps in 1975. That it was not reported until 1991 suggests that the packs that have been discovered are part of a very small quantity which was test marketed seventeen years ago. Luckily, the titles of all 24 buttons are printed on the

reverse side of the button packet and we have arranged them alphabetically below. The values listed are tentative since the number of packets and buttons discovered has yet to be determined and the marketplace has not had sufficient time or information to react.

ITEM	MINT	EX
Set	215.00	170.00
Button	7.50	5.00
Packet (empty)	20.00	15.00

Beat It!	Hi, Good Lookin'	Visit The Zoo
Bug Off	I Wish You Would Disappear	Where's Your Leash?
Button Your Lip	Jive Turkey	You Dirty Rat!
Change Your Deodorant	Kiss My Button!	You Dummy
Drop Dead	Official Streaking Champ	You're Cracked
Go Fly A Kite	Quit Hanging Around	You're Spaced Out
Go Haunt A House	Shut Up	You Turn Me Off
Go Jump In A Lake	Stop Air Pollution	You've Gone Bananas

BILL & TED'S EXCELLENT ADVENTURE & BOGUS JOURNEY (100)

2 1/2" X 3 1/2"

Pro Set figured it would kill two birds with one stone by combining an older film and its sequel into a single card set. The original film, "Bill & Ted's Excellent Adventure," chronicled the exploits of two California high school dudes who arrange to travel through time to absorb the history they were incapable of learning in the classroom. Cards 1-46 of the Pro Set series deal with these close encounters of the 12th grade. In the sequel, covered by cards 47-100, we are catapulted into the future (2691 A.D.), where evil dudes attempt

to alter the course of history by having Bill & Ted killed by their own evil clones! The righteous duo, now quite dead, must defeat the Grim Reaper in quintessential California style - by beating him at Battleship, Electric Football, and Twister - in order to return to the land of the living. They do this and get back just in time to win the Battle of the Bands, marry their Princesses, and bask in the glory of their accomplishments until another sequel beckons. Both these movies had a certain charm about them which has

not translated well into the trading card format. Collectors will note that card #96, which has the cartoon-character versions of Bill and Ted on the front, is nothing more than than an advertisement for the Fox Television Network. Since none of the cards are properly captioned, we are unable to provide a checklist for this set.

ITEM	MINT	EX
Set	15.00	10.00
Card	.15	.10
Wrapper	--	.10
Box	--	2.00

BIONIC WOMAN (44)

2 1/2" X 3 1/2"

Alas, the ratings for the TV show were not nearly as bionic as the main character, but Donruss has preserved the memory of the Bionic Woman in this 44-card set marketed in 1976. Each card contains a color photograph from the TV series and is numbered and captioned in a white panel situated in the lower corner, right. The backs are puzzle pieces.

ITEM	MINT	EX
Set	12.00	9.00
Card	.25	.20
Wrapper	––	1.00
Box	––	10.00

1 Jaime as a beauty queen.
2 Jaime rips open a bomb container.
3 With the Bionic leg, Jaime can leap over buildings.
4 Jaime easily handles rough terrain.
5 Jaime is played by Lindsey Wagner
6 Jaime has tremendous strength.
7 The Bionic woman hurls a bomb at enemy.
8 The Bionic arm bends bars to escape enemy.
9 The Bionic woman is beautiful and powerful.
10 Jaime rips loose a high voltage cable.

11 Oscar gives Jaime new information.
12 Jaime and Oscar discuss plans.
13 Jaime escapes through underground passage.
14 The Bionic arm can split logs.
15 Jaime ponders her next move.
16 Jaime leaps up to a high platform.
17 Jaime is a teacher when she isn't fighting crime.
18 Jaime leaps from a high cliff.
19 The Bionic arm slips through stone wall to escape enemy.
20 The Bionic arm protects Jaime and Friend from falling rock.
21 Jaime leaps from house to chase outlaws.
22 With the Bionic arm, Jaime easily pushes auto.

23 Jaime gives important news to Oscar.
24 Jaime leaps over two story house.
25 Jaime attacks airborne enemy.
26 With Bionic strength, Jaime can run like the wind.
27 Jaime at the controls of a locomotive.
28 Jaime drives a nail with her hand.
29 Jaime controls runaway elephant.
30 The Bionic ear hears sound from long distance.
31 Enemy approaches Jaime through jungle.
32 The Bionic arm crashes through door.

33 A real threat to the Bionic woman.
34 Jaime subdues king of the jungle.
35 Jaime hears enemy on the mountain above her.
36 Jaime leaps to the roof.
37 Jaime rips door off flaming auto.
38 The Bionic arm bends metal pipe with ease.
39 Jaime peers through fence at enemy hideout.
40 Jaime lies unconscious.
41 Oscar and Jaime pleased with success.
42 Jaime crashes through brick wall.
43 Jaime rips lock off enemy's hideout.
44 Jaime leaps from second story house.

BIRDS AND FLOWERS (50)

Virginia Hobby Supply and Bon Air Collectibles are the team which brought us this handsome series of state birds and flowers in 1991. The attractive card fronts are enlargements of "actual postage stamps produced by the U.S. Postal Service" in 1982. The backs relate interesting facts about each state and the card number is situated in the upper right corner. The card-deck size box which houses the collection is marked "Limited Edition," but we are not given any specifics. A second stamp-related set, entitled "American Wildlife," was in development as we went to press.

1	Alabama	26	Montana
2	Alaska	27	Nebraska
3	Arizona	28	Nevada
4	Arkansas	29	New Hampshire
5	California	30	New Jersey
6	Colorado	31	New Mexico
7	Connecticut	32	New York
8	Delaware	33	North Carolina
9	Florida	34	North Dakota
10	Georgia	35	Ohio
11	Hawaii	36	Oklahoma
12	Idaho	37	Oregon
13	Illinois	38	Pennsylvania
14	Indiana	39	Rhode Island
15	Iowa	40	South Carolina
16	Kansas	41	South Dakota
17	Kentucky	42	Tennessee
18	Louisiana	43	Texas
19	Maine	44	Utah
20	Maryland	45	Vermont
21	Massachusetts	46	Virginia
22	Michigan	47	Washington
23	Minnesota	48	West Virginia
24	Mississippi	49	Wisconsin
25	Missouri	50	Wyoming

ITEM	MINT	EX
Boxed set	9.00	--

BLACK HOLE (88 & 22)

Walt Disney Productions created the 1979 movie upon which this series is based. There are 88 cards and 22 stickers in the set, which was produced by Topps. The cards have color photos taken from the movie and are surrounded by a starry blue border. The card number is placed in a small red spaceman design in the upper right-hand corner and the caption appears in yellow print beneath the picture. The card backs are divided into 19 "Story Summary" backs, 64 puzzle backs (making three different puzzles), and four puzzle preview backs. The sticker backs have two groups of ten puzzle pieces (which make the same yellow-bordered puzzle twice) and two puzzle preview cards.

Note: Set price includes stickers.

ITEM	MINT	EX
Set	16.00	12.00
Card	.15	.10
Sticker	.35	.25
Wrapper	--	.35
Box	--	5.00

Black Hole

1 Title Card/Checklist
2 Capt. Dan Holland
3 Dr. Alex Durant
4 Kate and V.I.N.Cent
5 Harry Booth
6 Recreational Break!
7 Plotting a Star Course
8 Holographic Image
9 Lt. Charles Pizer
10 Force of Black Hole
11 Repairing Damaged...
12 Cygnus — a Ghost Ship?
13 Approaching Starcraft
14 Landing Platform
15 Deserted Passageway
16 In the Cygnus Air Car
17 Journey Across Cygnus
18 Humanoid Creatures
19 Crew of Robotoids
20 Cygnus Command Center
21 Awesome Spectacle
22 Behold...Maximillian!
23 Instant Adversaries
24 Enigmatic Host
25 Pizer Apprehended
26 An Offer of Aid
27 A Truce...for Now!
28 B.O.B.

29 Courageous B.O.B.
30 Holland's Discovery
31 Burial in Space
32 Limping Humanoid
33 Dr. Hans Reinhardt
34 A Very Special Dinner
35 Capt. S.T.A.R.
36 Sharpshooting Robot
37 Defeated by V.I.N.Cent
38 Galactic Hospital
39 An Urgent Report
40 "Prepare to Enter
41 "He's a Genius
42 Secret Revealed
43 Durant Under Attack!
44 Fatal blast
45 Death of a Scientist
46 Reinhardt's Scheme
47 Condemned...
48 Fear Chamber
49 Escorted by Robot...
50 Kate's Cruel Fate!
51 Holland to th Rescue!
52 Capt.'s Fight for Life!
53 Sneak Attack...
54 Victorious Holland
55 Kate...Unharmed!
56 Escape from Hospital

57 Destination: Black Hole
58 Warriors of Space
59 Ready for Action!
60 Powerful Laser Blast!
61 Robot War
62 A Hidden V.I.N.Cent
63 Hydroponic Gardens
64 The Search Begins.
65 Frozen Wasteland
66 "Help Us, B.O.B.!"
67 Deadly Plunge
68 Blasting the Enemy
69 Army of Evil
70 Dangerous Trek
71 Kate's Escape
72 "Gimmie All..."
73 Heroes at Bay
74 Power of the Enemy
75 Booth's Deception
76 Cowardly Act
77 Destruction of Palomino
78 His World Torn Asunder!
79 Reinhardt's Folly
80 Death of a Mad Genius
81 Last Hope for Escape!
82 Metallic Monster
83 The Confrontation
84 Fate of the Cygnus
85 Battle of Nonhumans
86 Vanquished!
87 Escape to Infinity
88 The Mind's Eye

TOPPS 20¢ MOVIE PHOTO CARDS BUBBLE GUM

1 Metallic Monster
2 "Gimmie All You've Got, V.I.N.C.E.N.T.
3 The Enigmatic Host
4 Death of a Mad Genius
5 Courageous B.O.B.
6 The Warriors of Space
7 Destruction of the Palomino
8 Humanoid Creatures
9 "Prepare to Enter the Black Hole"
10 Fate of the Cygnus
11 The Mind's Eye
12 The Heroes at Bay
13 Pizer Apprehended!
14 "He's a Genius, Not a Madman!
15 Captain Dan Holland
16 Robot with Tripoid Legs
17 Sharpshooting Robot
18 Blasting the Enemy
19 Dr. Alex Durant
20 Harry Booth
21 Ready for Action!
22 The Cygnus...A Ghost Ship?

BLACKSTONE'S MAGIC TRICKS (24) 2 7/16" X 3 1/2"

Ten years after issuing "Amazing Tricks" in 1953, the Philadephia Chewing Gum Company brought out a similar set of 24 folders explaining various feats of legerdemain. The series was marketed in 5-cent packages of "Magic Trick Bubble Gum" and the tricks

and illusions were ostensibly prepared by Harry Blackstone, "Dean of Magicians." Packed in each folder was an insert: the actual card or other item needed to perform the trick being explained. The folders have red covers and are numbered on both front and back.

Note: prices are for folders with inserts. Folders without inserts are worth $1.00 each (Mt.).

ITEM	MINT	EX
Set	90.00	60.00
Folder	3.00	2.00
Wrapper	--	5.00
Box	--	50.00

1 Broken Toothpick Restored	7 Hindoo Magic Hook	13 Vanishing Coin	19 Crazy Money!
2 Handkercheif Restored	8 Jumping Card	14 Wine to Water Mystery	20 Magic Animal Whell
3 5 Cards Change Into 2	9 Spirit Writing	15 Great Mind Reading Mystery	21 S-t-r-e-t-c-h It!
4 Traveling Cards	10 Chinese Laundry Ticket	16 Cigarettes From Thin Air	22 Water Defies Gravity
5 Card Changes To Matchbox	11 Chinese Magic Paddle	17 Magic Square Puzzle	23 Vanishing Card
6 Candle Vanishes	12 Great Ball of Wool Trick	18 Diminishing Card	24 The Telephone Message

BLOCKHEADS (12) 7 1/4" X 8 5/8"

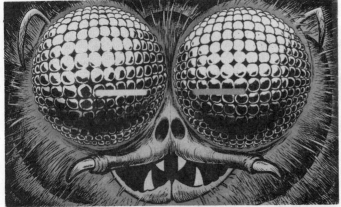

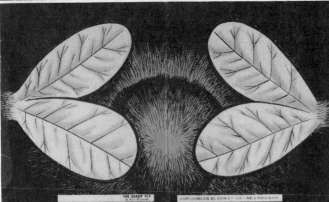

Most children, and even some adults, could fit into these over-the-head cardboard masks produced by Topps in 1967. Each is numbered and captioned and there are twelve designs in the set. They were sold for 15 cents apiece—without gum or wrappers—from a large eight-count display box. Pulled from the box flat, a mask was "popped" open into a cube by simple lateral pressure. "Blockheads" were one of many novelty items distributed by Topps without gum and they are considered by some collectors to be "toys," not "cards."

ITEM	MINT	EX
Set	200.00	160.00
Mask	15.00	12.00
Boxes		
10¢	--	250.00
15¢	--	150.00

1 Green Monster	7 The Hippie
2 The Pirate	8 Three-Eyed Monster
3 Mad Scientist	9 The Giant Fly
4 Witch Doctor	10 The Bleech
5 The Martian	11 The Ape
6 Moon Creature	12 The Skull

BMX BIKES (59)

Bicycle Motorcross Racing, BMX for short, is the subject of this 59-card set marketed by Donruss. The card fronts contain pictures of bikes or racers, with their brand or team affiliation printed below.

The backs contain endorsements, specifications, and biographical information, plus brand advertising. The card number is located on the back only. Card No. 59 is entitled "checklist'" but simply gives a breakdown of the bike brands appearing in the set. The checklist below is based on the card backs.

2 1/2'' X 3 1/2''

ITEM	MINT	EX
Set	6.50	3.00
Card	.10	.05
Wrapper	--	.35
Box	--	3.00

1 600B & 700P
2 500A
3 R. L. Osborn
4 D. D. Leone
5 Pro-Styler
6 1984 Factory Team
7 Carrera II
8 Torker 280
9 "Torker Magnum 200"
10 Hutch Pro Star
11 Michael Joseph Buff
12 Joseph Durwood Itson
13 Tim Judge
14 Brian Deam
15 Christy Anderson
16 Monte Gray
17 Team Murray 330
18 Team Murray X20R
19 Team Murray X20FS
20 Team Murray
21 Jeff Ruminer
22 Keith Gaynor
23 Jeff Botema
24 Scott Clark
25 Mike Horton
26 Anthony Sewell
27 Rusty Cable
28 Predator
29 Predator Team
30 Predator Sting Frameset
31 Schwinn BMX Action
32 Schwinn BMX Action
33 Schwinn BMX Action
34 Predator P2000
35 Kuwahara Laser Lite
36 Cline Miller, Brent Patterson, Turnell Henry
37 Clint Miller
38 Gary Ellis
39 Gary Ellis
40 Deric Garcia
41 Deric Garcia
42 Doug Davis
43 Brent Romero
44 Brent Romero
45 Doug Davis
46 Turbo
47 Diamond Back Formula One
48 John Piant
49 Andrew Soule
50 Mike King
51 Stu Thomsen
52 Rodney Cooper
53 Raleigh Airborne Division
54 Sam Arellano
55 George Antill
56 Don Johle
57 Ron House
58 Sam Arellano
59 Checklist

BOBBY SHERMAN "GETTING TOGETHER" (55)   2 1/2" X 3 1/2"

A set of 55 standard-size cards "tested" by Topps in 1971. The card fronts have color pictures with "exuberant"

captions (all have exclamation marks), while the borders are magenta with a flashy multi-colored design at the top. The backs contain a variety of features: puzzle pieces (A-B-C), Fan Club information, and "Ask Bobby Sherman." Each card is numbered and carries a dated copyright line on the back. The test wrapper has blue & yellow sticker affixed to white waxpaper.

Test Issue: Values Are Speculative

Card, each . . . . 20.00 +
Set. . . . . .1100.00 +
Wrapper 200.00

1 Meet Bobby!	20 Laughing with Wes!	39 Mr. Songwriter!
2 Bobby and Wes!	21 Bobby Sherman!	40 Towers of Talent!
3 Together with Wes!	22 Teen Favorite!	41 Bobby's Latest Hit!
4 Groovin' Together!	23 Weary Travelers!	42 Enjoying the Guitar!
5 Caught in the Act!	24 Wes Stearn!	43 Pinup of Bobby!
6 Our Favorite Star	25 Talking It Over!	44 Pure Bobby!
7 Singing Sensation!	26 The Swingin' Singer	45 Susan Neher!
8 Singin' and Strummin'!	27 Clowin' Around!	46 Sweet Sue!
9 On Stage!	28 Hittin' the Road!	47 Meet Susan!
10 Top Recording Star!	29 Practicing with Wes!	48 Jack Burns!
11 Adventurous Bobby!	30 Harmonizing!	49 Pat Carroll!
12 Rappin' Together	31 Hollywood Celebrities!	50 Peace Brother
13 Singing for a Fan!	32 A Couple of Stars!	51 Loving Nature!
14 Gettin' Together!	33 Bobby and his Buddy!	52 Bobby's Best Friend!
15 Thinking It Over!	34 Looking Ahead!	53 Bobby's Buddy!
16 "This Suits Me Fine!"	35 Enjoying Life!	54 Meet Wes!
17 Recording a Hit!	36 Rock Songwriters!	55 Smilin' Bobby!
18 Autograph Time!	37 Taking It East!	
19 Happy Together!	38 Composing a Hit!	

BOBBY SHERMAN PLAKS (?) (35)   3 1/8" X 5 1/4"

It is not clear what Topps was trying to accomplish with the plak-size Bobby Sherman set. We have illustrated two cards: both have the same black &

white picture and facsimile autograph printed on heavy, rounded-corner cardboard. The type with the clear photo has a postcard back, is numbered, and states the length of the set as 35. The dull, grainy photo has a blue-print "Ask Bobby Sherman" back and a 1970 copyright date. Notice that the same picture has a different number in each variety. Note: the plak price given is for either type and no set price will be listed until more facts are known.

Test Issue: Values
Are Speculative

Plak, each . . . . 20.00 +
Set . . . . 700.00 +
Wrapper 225.00
Box 250.00

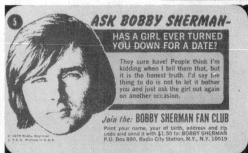

BODY SHOP (?)

Did your Mom go out and buy one of those polo shirts with a little animal on the pocket that only geeks wear? Well, you can make that shirt look really neat by heating up Mom's iron and pressing on some of these "Groovy Iron-Ons" sold by Fleer for five cents. They come three to a sheet in each pack, plus you get a stick of gum and a card

2 1/8" X 2 9/16"

that tells you how to put them on. What a bargain! (Parents, are you listening?) Each iron-on is 1 13/16" square and is rendered in psychedelic colors. The length of the set is unknown.

ITEM	MINT	EX
Sheet	1.00	.75
Instruction card	.50	.35
Wrapper	--	3.00
Box	--	10.00

BORIS — SERIES 1 (90)

History will record that two of the finest artist-illustrators of this century both emigrated to the United States from Peru, and that both of their names began with a "V": Varga and Vallejo. In the latter's case - according to the back of one of these cards - "When Boris came to the United States, he knew no English, had no friends, and [had] only $80 ... in his pocket." How times have changed! Vallejo is now recognized as one of the foremost fantasy illustrators of all time, is probably a millionaire, and speaks about "effective composition and propitious use of color and light." The man who once supported himself by drawing diagrams for how-to-assemble instruction sheets has come a long, long way.

The 1991 card set, simply called "Boris" by collectors, is a "first" in the realm of trading cards. True, other series have contained science fiction and comic book material, but this is the first set to depict artwork from the genre aptly described as "barbarian science fiction." The varied subject matter among the 89 numbered cards comes from different Vallejo

2 1/2" X 3 1/2"

projects: book covers, folios, illustrated adventures, etc. It derives its inspiration from astrology, modern gothic tales, and classic and modern mythology. The artwork fronts are borderless and are not captioned. The card title, number, a short quote or description, and a black and white drawing appear on the back. The 90th card is an unnumbered checklist (with multi-color accents on a black background on front and an uncolored back). Note: Boris 2 was about to be released by Comic Images as this book was going to press. The second series consists of 90 cards and the company has informed us that it contains artwork considered more "daring" than that of Series 1. Under the circumstances, responsible collectors should review both these sets to decide for themselves whether or not they are appropriate for viewing by family members or friends.

ITEM	MINT	EX
Series 1		
Set	13.50	--
Card	.15	--
Wrapper	--	.10
Box	--	2.00

Boris

1 The Torch
2 The Magnificent
3 Night
4 Gryphon's Eerie
5 Death Stalker
6 Taurus, The Bull
7 Egyptian Warrior
8 Runners
9 Capricorn, The Goat
10 I Am A Barbarian
11 Elephant
12 Weight Lifting
13 Swordsman
14 Sagittarius, The Archer
15 Nubian Warrior
16 Ape's Land
17 Through The Reality Warp
18 Tarnsman
19 The High Couch Of Silistra
20 Domes
21 Dungeon
22 Wrestling
23 The Lavalite World
24 White Eagle
25 Tower
26 Witch And Her Familiar
27 Genie
28 Beast And The Butterfly
29 Haesel The Slave
30 Mercenary
31 Unicorn
32 Cave Battle
33 Dragon's Knight
34 Tattoo
35 Jade Manikin

36 Alpnu
37 Colossus
38 Curl
39 Space Guardian
40 Wilderness
41 Queen Of The Amazons
42 Lord Of The Wolves
43 Dumbell
44 Magic Crystal
45 Discus Thrower
46 Torso
47 Bursting Out
48 Mother & Daughter
49 Against The Odds
50 Gemini, The Twins
51 Secrets Of Synchronocity
52 Berserker
53 Stone Idol

54 Scarlet Menace
55 Behind The Walls Of Terra
56 Phantom Of The Sea
57 White Magic
58 Golden Wings
59 Red Amazon
60 Yesterday And Tomorrow
61 She Vampire
62 Two-Headed Beast
63 Heavy Metal
64 Hatchett
65 The Bride
66 Enchantment
67 Mayan Serpent
68 Exterminator
69 The Last Stand
70 Knight On Wheels
71 The Siege Of Faltara
72 The Siege of Faltara
73 Football Hero
74 Apache Wells
75 The General Zapped An Angel
76 Nomads
77 Elijah
78 Crystal Griffin
79 The Victorious
80 Hammer Throw
81 Celestial Cab
82 Backstage
83 Nyankopong And Elohda
84 Leda And The Swan
85 Atlas
86 Es And The Creation
87 The Amazons
88 Deianeira And Nessus
89 Daphne And Apollo
Unnumbered checklist

BORIS TRADING CARDS
By Comic Images

The most beautiful fantasy artwork of Boris Vallejo is collected into this dreamlike 90 trading card collection.

10 Cards/Pack

© 1991 Boris Vallejo

BRADY BUNCH (88)

2 1/2" X 3 1/2"

After several years of debate, it has finally been established that there is no second series of Topps' Brady Bunch. There was, however, a "test" series of 55 cards issued in 1970 (either in cellophane or in Fun Packs). The "regular" series of 88 cards was sold in 1971 according to Topps' spokesman Norman Liss. The confusion about both sets arises from the Paramount Pictures copyright dates appearing on each type of card. Our enlargement shows an identical card (No. 12) from the test (top) and regular set (bottom). The Paramount copyright date on the test issue is 1970; on the regular card, it is 1969. The 1969 date refers to the original license granted for 88 designs. When Topps "tested" only 55 designs, a new license/copyright was required: 1970. When the 88-card set was finally made, the original 1969 copyright was still valid and was printed on the cards released in 1971. Note: the prices below are for the 1971 regular issue. Text cards (no wrapper seen) are worth at least $10.00 each.

ITEM	MINT	EX
Set	425.00	315.00
Card	4.00	3.00
Wrapper	--	40.00
Box	--	150.00

Greg Listens In!

85 PUZZLE No. 3 ©1969 Paramount Pictures Corporation
COLLECT ALL 88 CARDS — ©T.C.G. PRTD. IN U.S.A.

the BRADY BUNCH

WITH 1 STICK BUBBLE GUM

12 ©1970 Paramount Pictures Corporation
COLLECT ALL 55 CARDS — ©T.C.G. PRTD. IN U.S.A.

12 PUZZLE No. 1 ©1969 Paramount Pictures Corporation
COLLECT ALL 88 CARDS — ©T.C.G. PRTD. IN U.S.A.

the BRADY BUNCH BUBBLE GUM

Brady Bunch

1 The Brady Bunch
2 The Brady Girls
3 The Brady Boys
4 Ann B. Davis as Alice
5 Eve Plumb as Jan
6 Mike Lookinland as Bobby
7 Christopher McKnight as Peter
8 Carol and Mike
9 The Family Pet
10 Sweet Treat
11 Peter, Greg and Bobby
12 Stuck in Stockade!
13 Reporting for Duty
14 Here Comes My Fast Ball!
15 Big Prize for Little Bobby
16 Break It Up! It's Bedtime
17 What's Cooking, Alice?
18 Big Noise
19 Inferior Decorators
20 Guess Who?
21 Make-up for Marcia!
22 Big Brother's Advice

23 Long Distance Phone Call
24 The Music Man
25 Christmas Celebration
26 Musical Depreciation
27 Ain't Love Wonderful?
28 Sometimes I Hate Ice Cream
29 Homework Huddle
30 A Couple of Hungry Kids
31 Backyard Playground!
32 Lollipop Lovers
33 I'm Ready for Action
34 Running a Fever
35 King for a Day
36 Uh-oh, Here Comes the Indians!
37 Tired Ballplayers
38 Who Used My Toothbrush?
39 I'm the Umpire
40 Kitchen Conference
41 Something Smells Good
42 Trying to Get a Date
43 Sorry for the Turkey
44 Daydreaming

45 Say Something
46 Man-to-Man Talk
47 Sandlot Stars
48 Flipped Your Wig?
49 Soothing Greg
50 A Boy's Room is His Castle
51 "Alice, You Grew a Beard"
52 Where's My Greasy Kid Stuff?
53 Housekeeper
54 Someday Let's Eat Alone
55 Photo of the Brady Kids
56 You Did It Again
57 Sloppy but Fun
58 Come and Get It
59 Big Sister
60 Talking It Over
61 A Small Disagreement
62 A New Rock Star
63 What's the Noise
64 Can I Keep the Bird?
65 Meet Marcia Brady
66 Meet Bobby Brady

67 Meet Jan Brady
68 Meet Cindy Brady
69 Meet Peter Brady
70 Trimming the Tree
71 Meet Greg Brady
72 Marcia's Pajama Party
73 Having a Ball
74 Christmas
75 A Guitar Lesson
76 Alice's Coffeebreak!
77 Man-to-Man Talk
78 Trouble at Home
79 Greg's Big Date
80 Practice Makes Perfect
81 What Was That?
82 Bedtime Snack
83 A Guitar Lesson!
84 Checking Homework
85 Greg Listens In
86 A Tired Young Man
87 Feeling Better Yet?
88 Say Cheese!

BRAVE STAR ALBUM STICKERS (204)   2 1/8" x 2 3/4"

"It was the roughest of planets. They needed a thousand lawmen. They got one. He was enough." Is this the lead-in for a story in some tawdry 1950's men's magazine or advertising for an Italian western? No, it's an introduction to a children's cartoon character, "Brave Star," the hero of this 1987 Panini sticker set. The series contains 204 color artwork stickers divided into three varieties: regular, foil, and diecut. Each is numbered and fits onto a specific space in the 32-page album. The wrapper is purple and has a multi-color inset picture of Brave Star dressed in a ten-gallon hat and a flak vest. Ain't science fiction westerns grand?! Note: set price includes album.

ITEM	MINT	EX
Set	22.00	14.00
Sticker	.10	.07
Wrapper	--	.25
Album	2.00	1.50

Topps produced the Buck Rogers set in 1979. The cards — of which there are 88 — have color pictures taken from the TV series. Each photograph is surrounded by a jag-ged white frame line which has small portraits of the series characters inserted at the corners. The borders are red and the caption is printed in yellow. The card number appears both front and back. The reverses are green and gray and contain a sequential story line. The set of 22 stickers has color pictures with red frame lines and blue borders. They are numbered but un-captioned (captions from iden-tical card pictures are used in the checklist below). Note: set price includes stickers.

THE PRINCESS GETS DOWN!

ITEM	MINT	EX
Set	16.00	12.00
Card	.15	.10
Sticker	.35	.25
Wrapper	––	.50
Box	––	6.00

1 Buck Rogers
2 Suspended in Time
3 Capt. Buck Rogers
4 The Lost Space Shuttle
5 Frozen Alive
6 Draconian Fortress
7 The Interrogators
8 A Delirious Spaceman!
9 The Man Called Kane
10 Destination: Earth
11 Toward the Inner City
12 The Land Bay
13 Wilma's Chilly Reception
14 "Remove This Barbarian!"
15 The Brilliant Dr. Huer
16 "(Gulp) the 25th Century?"
17 Dr. Theopolis
18 Culture Shock for Buck
19 Twiki's Tonic

20 The World of Tomorrow
21 A New Beginning
22 Remains of Yesteryear
23 The Mutant Peril
24 Fate of Buck's Family
25 Surrounded!
26 Bizarre Rescuer
27 The Monsters Repelled
28 Run for Cover!
29 Wilma to the Rescue!
30 "Thanks Alot, Colonel"
31 Bitten by the Love Bug
32 City of the Future
33 Buck...A Traitor?
34 Observing the Trail
35 The Computer Council
36 Buck's Plan
37 The Enemies Meet
38 Visions of Ardala
39 "I Believe You Know Capt. Rogers"
40 The Ace of Space
41 "Look Out World—Lucky Buck Is Back!"
42 The Combat Computer
43 Heavy Losses for Wilma!
44 "Get Off the Air, Buck!"
45 Outrunning the Enemy
46 "Sorry About That, Guys!"
47 Zapping the Space Pirates
48 "Hey Wilma—How'm I Doing?"
49 Party for a Princess
50 The Party Girl Herself!
51 Dressed in Style
52 "Hey...You Guys Know Any Rock?"
53 "C'mon, Princess...Let's Boogie"
54 The Princess Gets Down!
55 "He Makes Me Soooo Mad!"
56 Buck Makes a Late Date
57 Twiki Catches Disco Fever!
58 The Princess' Ploy

59 "We Shall Take Them by Surprise"
60 Disguised as a Space Pirate!
61 Sabotage!
62 Landing Bay in Flames
63 Days of Destruction
64 Wilma Gets the Message!
65 Here Come the Earth Forces!
66 The Starfighter
67 Zeroing in!
68 The Draconian Armada
69 Wilma in Command!
70 Zap! Blam! Pa-Towww!
71 Death Throes of the Fortress
72 Battle with Tigerman
73 Dogfight in Space!
74 Hunter and the Hunted
75 Battle Skills of Col. Deering
76 Target on Computer
77 Caught in Laser Light!
78 Ardala's Defeat
79 The Battle Rages
80 Futuristic Warships
81 Explosion in Space
82 Last-Minute Rescue!
83 Off to New Adventures!
84 Gil Gerard as Buck
85 Erin Gray as Wilma
86 Felix Silla as Twiki
87 Pamela Hensley as Princess
88 Henry Silva as Kane

HERE IS WHAT YOUR COMPLETED BLUE BORDER PUZZLE WILL LOOK LIKE:

COLLECT ALL 10 CARDS OF PUZZLE B.

1 Buck Rogers
2 Toward the Inner City
3 A New Beginning
4 Erin Gray as Wilma
5 The World of Tomorrow
6 Dr. Theopolis
7 "Get Off the Air, Buck!"
8 Battle with Tigerman
9 The Lost Space Shuttle
10 The Starfighter
11 The Brilliant Dr. Huer
12 Twiki Catches Disco Fever!
13 Dressed in Style
14 The Party Girl Herself!
15 Gil Gerard as Buck
16 Death Throes of the Fortress
17 Sabotage!
18 "We Shall Take Them by Surprise"
19 Henry Silva as Kane
20 Suspended in Time
21 Felix Silla as Twiki
22 Disguised as a Space Pirate!

BUGS BUNNY ROADRUNNER TATTOOS (96)

1 1/4" X 2 7/16"

There are 96 different tattoos, printed two inside each wrapper, in this Topps set distributed in 1980 (the 1975 & 1979 dates on either side of the wrapper refer to Warner Bros. licensing, not date of issue). The exterior wrappers show either Bugs Bunny, done in lavender or yellow, or the Roadrunner, done in red. Sixteen of each color wrapper, 48 in all, make up a complete set. The tattoos are not numbered or captioned. The wrapper was designed with a tear strip for opening but unused wrappers are avilable in quantity and the prices below refer to them.

ITEM	MINT	EX
Set	30.00	--
Wrapper	.50	--

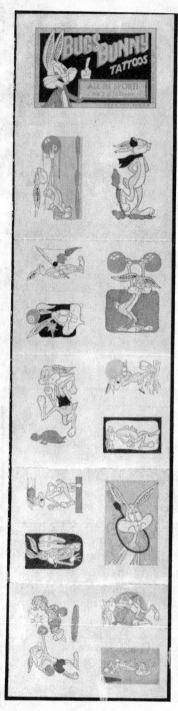

There are fourteen different tattoos—six large and eight small—on each sheet of Topps' Bugs Bunny Tattoos. The 3 7/16'' X 14 3/8'' sheets came folded in a standard size wax wrapper. Perforations around each tattoo allowed for easy removal. The wrapper carries a 1970 production code number and a 1971 Warner Bros. copyright. The length of the set is stated as 16 sheets but No. 16 does not appear to have been issued.

ITEM	MINT	EX
Set	40.00	32.50
Sheet	2.50	2.00
Wrapper	--	7.00
Box	--	30.00

1 Way Out West!
2 All In Sport!
3 In Hollywood!
4 Rock & Roll Racket!
5 Happy Holidays!
6 In The Haunted House!
7 Bugs And His Pals!
8 Moon Bound!
9 School Daze!
10 On The Pirate Ship!
11 Back In History!
12 Snowbound!
13 At The Circus!
14 Around The World!
15 Beach Fever
16 Not Issued

BUGS BUNNY TATTOO TRANSFERS (?) 1 1/2" 3 5/16"

The wrapper pictured is light blue with the words "Bugs Bunny" printed in white. The Fleer "crown" logo, colored red, is located in a white area at the base beneath a set of written 3-step instructions for applying the "transfers." Printed directly on the inside surface of the wrapper, the multi-colored tattoos are not numbered or captioned and the length of the set is not known. Note: prices are for exterior wrappers, not tattoos.

ITEM	MINT	EX
Wrapper	--	10.00

BULLWINKLE TATTOO TRANSFERS 1 9/16" X 3 3/8"

The color of this wrapper is yellow; Bullwinkle himself is brown and his name is orange. A copyright line, "1965 P.A.T. Wood," is printed under the words "Bubble Gum." The 3-step directions for applying tattoos appear above the red Fleer logo. The length of set is not known (tattoos are neither numbered or captioned). Note: the value of this item refers to the exterior wrapper, not the tattoos.

ITEM	MINT	EX
Wrapper	--	10.00

BUMPER STICKERS (96 & ?) TWO SIZES

Who says the gum companies aren't constantly devising ways to get your kids in trouble? Take this item for example: kids don't have cars, so where are they going to stick these 2 1/2" X 8" bumper stickers? On Dad's car, on police cars, on lockers, on the refrigerator, etc. Fleer produced this set of 96 stickers and simultaneously started your kids on the path to fiscal irresponsibility by inserting with them a series of "Krazy Kredit Cards". The latter measure 2 1/2" X 3 1/2", are blank-backed, and are printed in green and black on white cardboard. the bumper stickers originally came attached in pairs with a dotted cutting line in between. Note: set price does not include cards and is for paired stickers. Single stickers are priced but cannot be considered mint.

ITEM	MINT	EX
Sets		
In pairs	85.00	70.00
Singles	--	60.00
Stickers		
In pairs	1.50	1.25
Singles	--	.50
Card	.50	.35
Wrapper	--	7.50

BUMPER STICKERS — PARTIAL CHECKLIST

Get-Away Car
Go Man!
"Honest John" Lied
Lady Driver
Malibu Beach
No Man!
Radio Controlled
Scratch Here
Secret Agent 703½
Welcome Wagon

KRAZY KREDIT KARDS — PARTIAL CHECKLIST

Biggest Eaters Club
Charge-A-Drink
Grease Card
Hippie Card
Idiot Signature Card
krazy DRIVER unLICENSEd
Locker Inspection Card
Perfectly Useless Card

BUSH GARDENS CARDS (19K)   2 1/2″ X 3 1/2″

Judging from the brands of bread associated with these cards — "Colonial" and "Rainbo" — we can only assume that this Busch Gardens series was aimed at attracting tourists from out of state. The fronts have color photos of various animals found in the Tampa wildlife/theme park and these are named in the lower left corner. The brand of bread is identified only in a small red, blue, and yellow ribbon design under the lower right corner of the picture. The backs are printed with blue ink on white stock and give information about the animals pictured on front. The checklist below is considered incomplete since 19 cards is an unlikely set total.

ITEM	MINT	EX
Card	.50	.35

Addax
American Flamingo
Asian Elephant
Beisa Oryx
Black-capped Capuchin
Black Rhinoceros
Black Spider Monkey
Douroucoulli
Gerenuk   Scarlet Ibis
Greater Kudu   Stanley Crane
Grevy's Zebra   Toco Toucan
Impala   White Tiger
Ostrich
Reticulated Giraffe
Rose-breasted Cockatoo

BUSH LEAGUE (36)   2 3/4″ X 3 3/4″

"Bush League" is a non-mainstream set produced in 1989 by Eclipse Enterprises, a California company whose products exhibit a very strong political bias, most of it directed against the Republican Party. The set is composed of 36 art-work cards depicting various Republican politicians, influence-peddlers, covert operators, etc., and Jesse Jackson (their token Democrat!). The backs relate stories "gleaned from the New York Times, the Washington Post," and a variety of other less reliable publications. The set, which is sold in its own small box, follows a baseball theme and the final card has a sobering message for us all.

ITEM	MINT	EX
Boxed set	10.00	--

1 George Bush	19 James Baker
2 J. Danforth Quayle	20 C. Boyden Gray
3 Prescott Bush	21 The Bush Brothers
4 The Gas Pump Gang	22 Robert Mosbacher
5 Richard Nixon	23 Tower Out — Cheny In
6 Gerald Ford	24 William Webster
7 Langley Longhorns	25 William Sessions
8 Manuel Noriega	26 Henry Kissinger
9 Murderer's Row	27 Brent Scowcroft
10 Paula Parkinson	28 Edward Derwinski
11 October Surprise	29 William Bennett
12 Oliver North	30 Nicolas Brady
13 Lee Atwater	31 Dick Thornburgh
14 Jackson Benched	32 Dole — Sullivan — Lujan
15 Stu Spencer	33 Donald Gregg
16 Free Agents Released	34 Jack Kemp
17 Michael Dukakis	35 Farm Club Brawl
18 John Sununu	36 Peewee Takes the Mound

HONEST ...
SPORT AMERICANA GUIDES ARE TOPS!

"Shock Your Friends!" reads the propaganda on the paper envelope housing Fleer's "Button Factory." Inside were five metal tab-back pin blanks, and one sheet of directions. A button was made by transferring the press-ons of your choice from the sheet to the pin blank. Note: the sheet containing the press-ons is made of parchment paper and the items on it are easily ruined.

ITEM	MINT	EX
Sheets		
Press-ons	1.50	1.00
Directions	.50	.35
Pin Blank	.35	.25
Envelope	——	10.00
Box	——	15.00

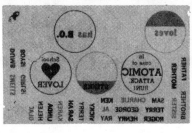

CABBAGE PATCH KIDS TRADING CARDS (?) 2 1/2" X 3 1/2"

In 1985 and 1986, Coleco (the toy manufacturer) and Original Appalachian Artworks (the creators of "Cabbage Patch Dolls") distributed trading cards inside the packages containing Astronaut, Baseball, and "Cuddly Crinkles" dolls. It is not known how many were produced of each series at this time; however, it is assumed that all major league baseball teams were represented in the baseball series and Aldrin, Armstrong, Glenn, and Shepard have been confirmed for the Astronaut set. As you can see by the illustrations, the baseball and "Cuddly Crinkles" are pictures of dolls, while the Astronaut series uses actual NASA photos of America's space pioneers. Since the only way to obtain cards was to purchase expensive dolls, it is likely that quantities of these cards are limited. It is also true that they are not in high demand. The cards of all three types are standard size and are printed on thin cardboard stock.

ITEM	MINT	EX
Cards		
Astronaut	2.00	1.50
Baseball	1.00	.75
Cuddly Crinkles	.75	.50

CAPTAIN NICE (?)   2 1/2" X 3 1/2"

Seldom seen are the cards from the Topps test set "Captain Nice." Based on the T.V. show starring William Daniels, the card fronts have captioned black & white pictures framed by blue and red lines. The card number is located on the reverse in the title area above a beautifully-colored 4-panel "Adventure" story. The date of issue is estimated to be 1967. The test wrapper is a yellow sticker with red, white & blue accents centered on white wax paper.

ITEM	MINT	EX
Card	30.00	25.00
Wrapper	--	350.00

IF I REALLY HURRY I CAN MAKE IT HOME ON TIME TO SEE A SUPER HERO SHOW ON T.V.

CARE BEARS (216)

2 1/8" X 3"

American Panini released this 216-sticker series to the general public in January, 1986. Although the subject matter may not appeal to adult collectors, the beautifully illustrated and thoughtfully written "Care Bear" philosophy is ideal for younger children. The 36-page album contains numbered spaces for each standard peel-back sticker, plus four glossy pages to hold a run of stickers (93-128) with diecut designs on front. When Care Bears was "tested" in November, 1985, some bear stickers had a fuzzy texture, but this feature was never incorporated into the regular set. Note: set price includes album.

ITEM	MINT	EX
Set	27.50	20.00
Sticker	.15	.10
Wrapper	---	.35
Album	2.00	1.50

CASEY & KILDARE (110)

2 1/2" X 3 1/2"

In 1962, Topps produced this Casey & Kildare set of 110 black and white photos taken from the popular TV show. Numbers one to 55 have Ben Casey as the subject matter, and numbers 56 to 110 feature Dr. Kildare. Each card in the set carries the facsimile autograph of the star. The backs are blank except for a small blue-line box which contains the card number and a copyright line (Bing Crosby Productions). Note: cards are found printed on either dull or glossy stock. Both the cellophane and wax wrapper bear the identical design.

ITEM	MINT	EX
Set	315.00	250.00
Card	2.50	2.00
Wrappers		
Cellophane	---	20.00
Wax	---	40.00
Box	---	65.00

CB CONVOY CODE (44)

The 44 titles in our checklist refer to the diecut stickers found on the fronts of these cards. The titles are printed inside the score line of each sticker but the sticker number is printed only on the card back (at the bottom). The cardboard backs contain a feature called "CB Dictionary," which has 23 parts and its own numbering system. Since there are 44 cards in the set, 21 of the dictionary cards are repeated. The series was produced by Donruss and has two wrappers, one portraying a trucker and the other depicting a "Smokey Bear" cop.

1 Tijuana Taxi
2 Breaker Breaker
3 Part Your Hair
4 Bear in the Air
5 Ten-Four Good Buddy
6 Sick Horse
7 Breaker 8
8 Smokey on Four Legs
9 Two Wheeler
10 Mercy Sakes
11 Eyeball to Eyeball
12 Steamer
13 Ratchet Jaws
14 Channel Hog
15 Six Wheeler
16 Bear in the Bushes
17 Blow the Doors Off
18 Ears On!
19 Peanut Butter Ears
20 Smokey Takin' Pictures
21 Handle
22 Shake the Leaves
23 Drop the Hammer
24 Battery Acid
25 Local Yokel
26 Country Cadillac
27 Super Dude
28 Moon Dog
29 Love Bug
30 Night Hawk
31 Feeding the Bears

32 Show Your Cards
33 Chatter Rabbit
34 Fat Rollerskate
35 Bear Cave
36 Happy Hobo
37 CB Addict
38 Asphalt Pilot

39 Mad Dog
40 Bear
41 Walked On
42 Crazy Horse
43 Green Stamps
44 88's

ITEM	MINT	EX
Set	25.00	17.50
Card/Sticker	.50	.35
Wrappers (2) ea.	—	1.00
Box	—	7.00

CB JEEBIES IRON ONS (25)

This clever series of 25 designs carries a built-in bonus: after the sticker on front is pulled off and put on Mom's refrigerator, the front door, or on the cat ... THEN you still have the same picture on the back which you can iron onto your favorite shirt! Each sticker is numbered and captioned and the brand of bread which distributed the series is printed in the lower left corner. The iron-on decal has dotted "cut here" lines to indicate that the area containing the heading, "Have parents apply" disclaimer, and copyright date and manufacturer should be cut away before application. The sample in our illustration was issued in 1977 by Sunbeam Bread. Note: values are for complete, undetached sticker/iron-ons.

ITEM	MINT	EX
Set	30.00	22.50
Sticker/Iron-on	1.00	.75

CB STICKERS (15)

"Davey Crockett was a famous pioneer from Tennessee who could have used a CB radio while he was a scout for Andrew Jackson." Yes, and Joan of Arc could have used a fire extinguisher, but the absurdity of the events suggested on the back of these "CB Stickers" was surely lost on the children at whom they were aimed. The color drawings and text of the 15 numbered stickers mix humor and history in an appealing manner following a CB radio theme. The set was prepared for Tip Top Bread in 1976 by Bakery Incentives of Philadelphia. The area of distribution has yet to be established and some stickers may have stains due to the oil in the bread.

ITEM	MINT	EX
Set	17.50	13.00
Sticker	1.00	.75

CB TALK (60 & 7)

The dialogue in this 60-card Fleer set spoofs citizen's band radio as it is practiced by the trucking community. Each card front has color artwork showing a trucker broadcasting a message to his "buddies." A black & white photo insert of a trooper makes wisecrack remarks and warns of future trouble. The reverses have a feature called "C.B. Talk Dictionary" and the card number. There are two wrapper designs and one of a sub-series of eight 1 1/2" X 3 1/2" side-peel "Official Truck Stickers" came in each pack. Note: set price includes stickers.

ITEM	MINT	EX
Set	25.00	17.50
Card	.35	.25
Truck Sticker	.50	.35
Wrappers (2) ea.	—	1.00
Box	—	7.00

1 And I'm Here to Make Sure the Only Speeding in Indianapolis is Done on the Race Track!
2 An' When You See It Flashing You Know Smokey Bear Will Chew on You!
3 That Convoy's Got Me Shut Out but I'll Get Them Yet!
4 They Think They're Safe but They Ain't Seen my Eye-in-the-Sky Yet.
5 Better Slow Down 'Cause Us Bears Eat Up Big Dogs if They Get Too Sassy!
6 But I'll Reel Him In - Hook, Line and Sinker Even If He Does Have Two Antennas!
7 Yo' Right Big Mouth Rubber Duck! I'm Listenin' to Every Word You Say!
8 I'll Get Rubber Duck This Time in this Unmarked Police Car.
9 That's What Happens When Everybody Tries to Go to the Same Place at the Same Time!
10 When I'm Flashing My Lights I'm Advertising and It's Gonna Cost You Some Green Stamps, Boy!
11 You Can Bet Ol' Junkyard Joe is Watching His Rear View Mirror for Me
12 He Means He'll Be Lookin' for Him on the Return Trip...and So Will I!
13 That Means He's Goin' to L.A. in his International Harvester...and I'm Waitin' for Him!
14 This Is What You Get When I Take It Out of the Brown Paper Bag!
15 That Silver Bullet's Comin' In Loud and Clear and I'm Listenin' to Every Word!
16 He's Signing Off for a Rest Room Stop
17 You're In a Heap o' Trouble When I Finish My Lunch!

CB Talk

18 Ha! Ha! I Told You I'd Give You a Ticket Rubber Duck!

19 After He Fuels and Showers He'll be Clean for the Judge!

20 I'd Jump Over the Grand Canyon to Get You Rubber Duck!

21 Ol' Rubber Duck Better Watch Out or That Gal Will Get Him in a Heap o' Trouble

22 I'll Get You Yet, Big Mouth Rubber Duck!

23 I'm the Sheriff of Chattanooga and Y'all Better Behave While I'm Around!

24 If You Speed Too Much You'll End Up on the Hooks!

25 But I'm Waitin' on the Other Side of the Tunnel!

26 He's Takin' His Truck in for Some Fuel Now, But I'll Have an Eyeball on Him When He Comes Out!

27 I Didn't Catch Yo' Today But I'll be Waitin' for You Tomorrow!

28 I May be Fat But I'm Mean!

29 "One-Nine" Means Channel 19. "Blue Fox" is His Handle. 10-77 Means Negative Contact.

30 ...And I'm Waitin' with a Pocket Full of Green Stamps!

31 I Confuse 'Em When I Patrol Both Sides of the Highway!

32 He's Got a Big Motor Under His Hood, But I'll Get Him Before Atlanta!

33 He Really Thinks He's Sumpthin' in that Rig. Even Takes It to the Drive-In Movies!

34 You Better Drive Safely Boy!

35 Cause I'm Gonna Catch Him Long Before He Gets to Boston!

36 I'm Gonna Park That Car Carrier for Him Before He Reaches Chicago!

37 Sorry Boy! They're Not Your Type!

38 He Means Big Mouths an' No Ears!

39 An' I Guarantee It'll Cost You Some Money to Get Out of Jail!

40 I Missed Them Again! Rubber Duck, I'll Get You Yet!

41 The Boy Has Some Monkey Business in the Big City!

42 That's What It Will Cost You if I Catch You in the Passin' Lane!

43 I'm Gonna Give Him Enough Tickets to Paper the Walls of his Truck!

44 He Better Keep That GMC Refrigerator-On-Wheels at 55 or I'll Get Him!

45 This Boy's Gonna Collect Some Green Stamps Too!

46 He Ain't Answerin' His Good Buddies But He'll Answer Me!

47 Ol' Smokey's Got an Eyeball on You When you're Speedin' Boy!

48 I Just Love Doin' This When the Boys Do Somethin' Foolish!

49 Ol' Smokey Can Still Teach Him a Few Lessons!

50 And You Better Keep It at 55 Boy!

51 That Means I Ain't Been Where He's Just Been!

52 An' I Got Your Picture for the Judge, Baby!

53 He Thinks He'll Make It to Nashville, But I'll Catch Him First!

54 Just Because You're Runnin' Empty, Don't think You Can Speed, Boy!

55 Ha! Ha! I'm Waitin' at Milwaukee City Limits!

56 And If You Don't Slow Down, You'll be Feedin' the Bears!

57 It'll Take More than Strong Coffee to Get from Little Rock to Las Vegas... Probably a Bunch of Speeding Too!

58 And I'm Gonna Beat the Pants off You Boy!

59 Ha! Ha! I Eat Speeders for Breakfast!

60 That Means That Speedin' Car has No "CB" and That's Good for Me!

Airborne
Allied Van Lines
A-P-A
Global Van Lines
North American Van Lines
P-I-E
Smith's Transfer Corporation
Trailways

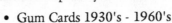

CHARLIE'S ANGELS (253 & 44)   2 1/2" X 3 1/2"

The Charlie's Angels series might well be one of the most popular card sets ever issued in terms of mass appeal. Overall, there are 253 cards and 44 stickers in the complete set, which was distributed in four series by Topps during 1977-78. Regardless of series, the card number is always located on the obverse. The stickers from each series are numbered and captioned on the front and are blank on the back. The first two series (1-121) are in higher demand than the last two (122-253). Note: all series prices include stickers.

ITEM	MINT	EX
Sets		
Series I (1-55)	25.00	18.00
Series II (56-121)	22.00	16.50
Series III (122-187)	18.00	13.00
Series IV (188-253)	18.00	13.00
Cards		
1-55	.35	.25
56-121	.25	.20
122-253	.20	.15
Stickers		
1-11	.50	.35
12-44	.35	.25
Wrappers (4)		
Series I	--	1.50
Series II	--	1.00
Series III	--	.50
Series IV	--	.50
Boxes		
Series I	--	10.00
Series II	--	5.00
Series III	--	5.00
Series IV	--	5.00

COURAGEOUS CRIMEFIGHTER!

AN ANGELIC POSE!

SUPER DETECTIVE!

A SATISFIED SLEUTH!

COMING SOON!
UPDATE TO THE 1930-1960 NON-SPORT PRICE GUIDE

Charlie's Angels

1 A Job Well Done!
2 Charlie's Beautiful Angels
3 Policewoman Jill!
4 Time for a Ticket
5 She Aims for Danger!
6 Spotting a Crime!
7 The Fastest Thing on Wheels!
8 Time Out to Relax!
9 Fast-Gun Sabrina!
10 Confident Angel!
11 Ready to Nab a Creep
12 Jill Gets a Brainstorm
13 Freeze!
14 Angels Do Their Homework
15 Jill—Caught by Surprise!
16 Reviewing the Plan...
17 Jill in a Jam!
18 Jill Solves Another Mystery
19 Kelly Swings into Action!
20 Kelly, Bikini-clad Beauty!
21 Posing as a Fashion Model
22 Escape by Skateboard!
23 Two Lovely Angels!
24 Jill and Some Ransom Money
25 Sabrina Makes a Point
26 One Pretty Angel
27 An Angel Says Her Prayers!
28 Another Success for the Angels!
29 Farrah Fawcett-Majors
30 Jaclyn Smith
31 Kate Jackson
32 Two Terrific Angels!
33 The Best Boss an Angel Ever Had!
34 A Peek-a-boo from Kelly!
35 Sabrina Bakes—An Angel Cake!
36 Ready for a New Assignment!
37 An Angel in Trouble!
38 Awaiting the Bad Guys!
39 Focusing on Danger!
40 Bosley Spiffing Up!
41 Tearing Up the Road!
42 Chalk Up Another One for the Angels!
43 Don't Mess with Kelly
44 Kelly Smells a Rat!
45 A Funny Caper!
46 A Cop in Hot Pants!
47 A Heavenly Girl!
48 Angels Take a Ride!
50 Cycle Freak Kelly!
50 One for the Angels!
51 Jill, the Tennis Star!
52 The Angels Get an Assignment
53 Gorgeous Jill!
54 Sabrian Cracks Another Case!
55 An Angelic Pose!

56 Having a Wonderful Crime!
57 Sorry Dummy—You Can't Join the Angels!
58 "The Killer Is Loose!"
59 Angels at Dinner
60 Wonderful Kelly
61 Discussing a New Case
62 The Angels Celebrate!
63 A Rough Day for Bosley!
64 Jill Gets an Idea
65 An Exhausted Angel
66 "Who Can the Killer Be?"
67 Kelly Steams Up!
68 Danger Is Their Business!
69 Trio for Danger!
70 On the Trail of a Mad Killer!
71 Bosley and Jill
72 Super Detective

73 Two Cool Angels!
74 The Angels on a Cruise!
75 A Dangerous Case!
76 The Mystery Deepens!
77 Awaiting Charlie's Call
78 Ready for Danger!
79 Beautiful Kelly!
80 Angelic Actress!
81 Jaclyn Smith as Kelly
82 Dreamy Angel!
83 Pretty Detective!
84 Kelly Clobbers a Crook!
85 Pistol Packing Angel
86 Hold It Right There, Creep!
87 Kelly Poses as a Cop
88 Kelly's Hunch
89 Kelly Smells a Rat!
90 Now Here's the Rain!
91 Ready for a New Assignment!
92 Freeze!!!
93 Sabrina Smiles at Danger
94 Kate Jackson as Sabrina
95 Surprised Angel!
96 Sabrina Gets a Clue!
97 On to a New Adventure!
98 Beautiful Sleuth!
99 The Hidden Room!
100 Another Job Well Done!
101 A Worried Angel!
102 Farrah Fawcett-Majors as Jill
103 An Angel at Play!
104 Sabrina Cracks the Case!
105 An Angel in Trouble!
106 Sabrina Under Cover!
107 Sabrina Takes a Break
108 Defusing a Bomb!
109 Jil Nabs a Crook!
110 Caught in the Act!
111 Lovely Angel!
112 A Bullet for Jill
113 A Confusing Assignment!
114 A Rose Is a Rose!
115 The Dynamite Trap!
116 Jill, the Swingin' Angel!
117 A Fun Assignment for Jill!
118 "What's the New Job, Bosley?"
119 Cracking Another Case!
120 About to Get Her Wings Clipped!
121 Chased by a Killer
122 Charlie's Beautiful Angels!
123 The Angels Relax
124 Going Over a Case
125 Clowning Around in the Office
126 Bosley and Sabrina
127 A Pair of Super-Sleuths!
128 "Look Out! It's the Killer!"
129 A Get-Well Visit from Bosley!
130 "Keep Your Eyes Peeled, Sabrina!
131 Sabrina's Plan
132 Angels in Paradise
133 Kelly and Kris
134 Breaking in the New Angel!
135 Beautiful Crimefighters!
136 Vacationing Angels!
137 On the Trail of a Killer
138 An Angel Does Her Thing!
139 Freeze!
140 A Heavenly Cop!
141 A Daring Damsel!
142 Sabrina on a Movie Set!
143 "Hey Bos—Get Me Through to Charlie"
144 Closing in on the Crooks
145 Sabrina Duncan
146 Sabrina—Smart as a Whip!
147 Lovely Sabrina Duncan!
148 Angel Has Plans...
149 Beautiful Cop
150 Time Out for Sabrina!

151 Devising a Plan!
152 One Clever Angel!
153 Heads Up, Sabrina!
154 Kelly in a Daze!
155 A Narrow Escape!
156 Lovely Crimefighter!
157 Awaiting New Instruction!
158 Kelly in a Jam!
159 Ride to Danger
160 Desperate Hours for Kelly!
161 Kelly in Trouble!
162 Calling for Help!
163 Kelly Has Her Doubts!
164 Escape from Fiery Death!
165 Super-Sleuth Kelly!
166 A Satisfied Sleuth!
167 Kelly Gets a Lead!
168 Cute Angel
169 Lovely Kelly!
170 One Beautiful Angel!
171 Knife Throwing Peril!
172 A lovely Reflection!
173 Watch Out, Kris!
174 A Day at the Circus
175 Kris Does Some Snooping
176 Vivacious New Angel!
177 Jill's Young Sister Kris!
178 Hunting for Clues!
179 Beautiful Kris!
180 Kris in the Tropics
181 Charlie's Newest Angel!
182 Spotting a Crime!
183 The Lovely New Angel!
184 Kris Cracks the Case!
185 Lovely Kris!
186 Beautiful New Sleuth!
187 Courageous Crimefighter!

188 Sabrina Aims for Trouble
189 Sabrina Takes a Break
190 Waiting for Charlie's Call
191 "Don't Shoot...I'm a Private Eye!"
192 Bottoms Up, Sabrina!
193 Super Sleuth!
194 Another Case Solved!
195 Sabrina...Stalked by a Killer!
196 Pert Angel!
197 "Wait 'Il Charlie Hears About This!"
198 Sabrina Takes a Vacation
199 All's Well That Ends Well!
200 Winsome Crimefighter!
201 A Funny Moment for Sabrina!
202 Kris on Ice!
203 Spectator Kris!
204 Kris Smells a Rat!
205 Pursued by a Murderer!
206 Cute Kris!
207 A New Outfit for Kris!
208 "Aww, C'mon Charlie!"
209 Watch Out, Angel!
210 Kris—Charlie's Newest Angel!
211 A Brand New Angel!
212 "Who Says I'm Inexperienced?"
213 Kris Listens to the Plan...
214 Fun Loving Angel!
215 Plucky Angel Kris!
216 "Crimefighting Is Rough Work!"
217 Adorable Angel!
218 Spotting the Crime!
219 Pole-vault to Danger!
220 Gorgeous Girl!
221 Be Careful, Kelly!
222 Kelly Overhears a Murder Plot!
223 Lovely Sleuth!
224 Kelly—Out to Win!
225 Kelly and Friend!
226 Mixing Business with Pleasure!
227 A Concerned Kelly!
228 Having Fun on the Job
229 Kelly—in Top Form!
230 Joking with Charlie!
231 An Athletic Angel!
232 Problems for Kelly...
233 Kelly—What a Gal!
234 "Now Put the Gun Down... Slowly!"
235 A Phone Call to Charlie!
236 The Angels Discuss Their New Caper!
237 The Terrific Trio!
238 Angels Get a New Wardrobe!
239 Sabrina and Bosley
240 Anxious for Danger!
241 Crimefighting Camera-Bugs
242 A Dangerous Assignment!
243 Going Undercover
244 Angels, Hawaiian Style!
245 "Consider the Odds, Angels..."
246 "Charlie Should Call Soon...!"
247 Tackling Their Newest Case!
248 Breaking in Kris!
249 Charlie's Youngest Angel!
250 Devising a Plan!
251 Taking It Easy!
252 Bosley's Beautiful Crimefighters!
253 Charlie's Angels—We'll Be Back!

1 Jill
2 Kelly
3 Sabrina
4 Heavenly Kelly!
5 Jaclyn Smith
6 Beautiful Angel!
7 Heavenly Smile!
8 Angels Get It Together!
9 Pretty Detective!
10 Kate Jackson
11 Farrah Fawcett-Majors
12 Charlie's Angels
13 Two Heavenly Angels!
14 Dynamite Sabrina
15 Kate Jackson as Sabrina
16 Sabrina
17 Farrah Fawcett-Majors Is Jill
18 Beautiful Jill
19 Angelic Jill
20 Jaclyn Smith as Kelly
21 Lovely Girl!
22 Cool Angel

23 Beautiful Sabrina Duncan
24 Kate Jackson as Sabrina
25 Kelly—A Real Dreamboat!
26 Lovely Detective Kris!
27 Charlie's New Angel
28 Kris, Jill's Little Sister!
29 Kelly Means Business!
30 Jaclyn Smith as Kelly
31 Gun-toting Angel!
32 The Lovely New Angel!
33 Charlie's Angel Sabrina
34 Lovely Sleuth Kelly
35 Jaclyn Smith as Kelly
36 Sabrina in a Jam
37 Kate Jackson as Sabrina
38 Radiant Angel!
39 Charlie's Angels
40 Cute Kris!
41 Kris, the Rookie Angel
42 Kelly on the Job
43 Kelly and Kris
44 Cheryl Ladd as Kris

CHESTER CHEETAH CARDS (?)

2 1/2" X 2 3/4"

There is no mistaking a "Chester Cheetah" card: the wide borders surrounding the picture area are bright orange with 24 black paw prints on them. The center of each card is a color drawing of

Chester engaging in skate-boarding, surfing, etc. The backs have a black-line frame in the middle which holds a poem; an example: "I'm Chester Cheetah, The hang ten kitty, Got Cheetos on board, I'm rollin' into surf ci-ty." The cards are standard size and are not numbered. Since they were distributed in bags of "Cheetos," collectors may find supplies rather limited. Date of issue: 1987.

ITEM	MINT	EX
Card	1.00	.75

CHIP 'N DALE RESCUE RANGERS (242)

2 1/8" X 2 9/16"

Panini and Walt Disney combined to produce the "Chip 'n Dale Rescue Rangers" set of album stickers in 1990. Inside the 32-page album, there are eight different stories with a total of 228 spaces for color artwork album stickers. In addition, there is a four-page center sec-tion entitled the "Treasure Hunt Game," which has spaces for 14 diecut foil stickers (lettered A-N). The inside back cover contains "The Sticker Exchange," an offer to send in 20 duplicates for 20 stickers that you need ($1 handling fee plus stamp for each exchange). Note: set price includes album.

ITEM	MINT	EX
Set	22.50	16.50
Stickers		
Artwork	.10	.07
Foil	.15	.10
Wrapper	--	.25
Album	1.50	1.00

CHIPS (60 & 6)   2 1/2" X 3 1/2"

The Chips set, produced by Donruss, consists of 60 numbered, corner-peel stickers and six unnumbered diecut stickers. The numbered stickers are photos from the TV series; there are no captions but the word "Chips" is printed in red in the field of every picture. The diecut stickers have "head" views of Jon and Ponch. The reverses on both types of stickers are puzzle pieces.

ITEM	MINT	EX
Set	15.00	12.00
Stickers (all)	.25	.20
Wrapper	--	.35
Box	--	5.00

CHOPPERS & HOT BIKES (66)

2 1/2" X 3 1/2"

Two magazines, "Street Chopper" and "Hot Bikes," provided Donruss with the photos and information to produce this set. The obverse pictures show motorbikes on the road or in "showroom" poses and each photo is surrounded by fancy frame lines. Card numbers are always stationed in the upper left corner of the reverse. The backs may contain simple text or a feature entitled "Bike Digest." The line "Collect All 66 Cards" is printed on every card.

ITEM	MINT	EX
Set	40.00	27.50
Card	.50	.35
Wrapper	--	5.00
Box	--	10.00

1 Refinement of a Classic
2 Kawasaki 100
3 Yamaha AT2
4 Baja 100
5 Honda Mini Trail
6 Chopper Scrambler
7 BMW 750
8 47-74
9 Suzuki 250
10 Harley Davidson
11 Honda 100
12 Low Flyer
13 Drag Racer
14 Moto Guzzi 750
15 Beyer's Beauty
16 California Flash
17 Dragster
18 Four Square
19 BMW
20 Amani
21 BMW 750
22 Stretched and Strong
23 The Shovelhead
24 Honda 350
25 Yamaha JT2
26 Record Holder
27 Barn Job
28 Kawasaki 100
29 Big Twin
30 XL-ent Shovelhead
31 Pantastic 74
32 Boris Murray's Twin Triumph
33 "Wow"
34 Super Sport
35 Moto Guzzi 750
36 Honda XL-250
37 47-74
38 Cycletron
39 Honda Half-Breed
40 On My Own 74
41 Barn Job
42 BMW
43 Shortster
44 Suzuki 750
45 Honda 750
46 Exercise in Originality
47 Embryo Sportster
48 Home Brew
49 Woman's Pride
50 Kawasaki 350
51 Production Road Racer
52 AEE Trike
53 Kawasaki 500
54 Full House Sportster
55 Suzuki 250
56 Blue Wild Fire
57 Suzuki 500
58 Yamaha LS2
59 Action Four's Double Threat
60 Easy Rider
61 Gladiator Scorpion
62 Dragster
63 Yamaha JT2-MX
64 Panhead Engine
65 Honda 500
66 The Mindbender

CINDERELLA ALBUM STICKERS (225)

2 1/16" X 2 9/16"

The "Cinderella" album sticker series was marketed in the United States by Panini in 1988. The set consists of 225 brightly-colored, artwork stickers designed to fit into numbered spaces in a 32-page album. All the drawings were taken from the full-length Disney film which the studio released in 1950 (and again in 1988). Panini's marketing technique at this point in time allowed for mixing foreign language packages in with the U.S. version, so collectors found German, Dutch, Italian, French, and Spanish titles on sticker packs sold in American stores. The stickers themselves have Panini's "universal" back, which has the set title translated into six languages and everything else printed in English. Note: set price includes album.

ITEM	MINT	EX
Set	24.00	18.00
Sticker	.10	.07
Wrappers (6), ea.	--	.35
Album	2.00	1.50

Cinderella Album Stickers

CIVIL WAR NEWS (88)

2 1/2" X 3 1/2"

The Civil War centennial celebration was still going strong in 1962 when Topps issued the Civil War News set of 88 cards. Each card has a color printing of a battle or historical event, which is captioned in a white box set inside the picture area. The backs are gray with a red-brown border; the card number is located in this border at the bottom corner on the right side. The text is arranged in newspaper fashion. A piece of facsimile Confederate currency was folded into every pack (17 different). Note: set price does not include currency.

ITEM	MINT	EX
Set	525.00	420.00
Card	5.00	4.00
Currency		
Each	6.00	5.00
Set of 17	135.00	110.00
Wrappers		
1 cent	--	250.00
5 cent	--	200.00
Boxes		
5 cent	--	400.00
1 cent	Not Seen	

GENERAL LEE
SOUTHERN HEADQUARTERS—APR. 1, 1863

1 The Angry Man	17 The Flaming Raft	33 Fight for Survival	49 The Explosion	63 Ambushed	76 Blazing Cannon
2 President Jeff Davis	18 Death to the Enemy	34 Wall of Corpses	50 Stolen Secrets	64 Jaws of Death	77 Trapped
3 The War Starts	19 Pushed to his Doom	35 Gasping for Air	51 Horse Thieves	65 Flaming Death	78 Sudden Attack
4 Confederate Power	20 Death Fall	36 Midnight Raid	52 Friendly Enemies	66 Victim of the War	79 Council of War
5 Exploding Fury	21 Painful Death	37 Death Barges In	53 Train of Doom	67 Deadly Duel	80 City in Flames
6 Pulled to Safety	22 Wave of Death	38 General Grant	54 A Horseman Falls	68 The Will to Win	81 Deadly Defense
7 Death at Sea	23 Crushed by Wheels	39 General Lee	55 The Silent Drum	69 Death in the Water	82 Destroying the Rails
8 Destructive Blow	24 After the Battle	40 Bullets of Death	56 Burst of Fire	70 The Sniper	83 The Looters
9 Savages Attack	25 Hanging the Spy	41 Protecting Family	57 Hand Combat	71 No Escape	84 Deadly Arrows
10 Destruction at Sea	26 Messenger of Death	42 The Battle Continues	58 Angel of Mercy	72 The Cannon's Victim	85 Attacked from Behind
11 Attack	27 Bloody Massacre	43 Costly Mistake	59 Submarine Attack	73 Through the Swamp	86 Dynamite Victim
12 Bloody Combat	28 The Cannon Roars	44 Shot to Death	60 Suicide Charge	74 Fighting for Victory	87 The War Ends
13 Dying Effort	29 Bridge of Doom	45 Riverboat Explodes	61 The Flaming Forest	75 The Family Flees	88 Checklist
14 Fight to the Finish	30 Charging the Bullets	46 Vicious Attack	62 The General Dies		
15 Nature's Fury	31 Terror of the Sea	47 Death Battle			
16 Direct Hit	32 Death Struggle	48 Smashing the Enemy			

CIVIL WAR PICTURE CARDS (55)   2 1/2″ X 3 7/16″

PICKETT'S CHARGE

This anonymous set of 55 cards contains black and white photographs provided by the Bettman Archives. The pictures are tinted pink, and the captions are found directly below in a red panel decorated with a hat design. The backs are mostly gray in color with a dark red frame surrounding the text. The card number is found on the reverse in the upper left corner.

1 Abraham Lincoln	20 The Ironclad Cairo	38 The Dictator
2 Jefferson Davis	21 Battle of Gaines Mill	39 Federal Depot
3 Ulysses S. Grant	22 McClellan at Malvern Hill	40 Grant at Wilderness
4 Robert E. Lee	23 Battle of Cedar Mountain	41 Battle of Cold Harbor
5 Philip Sheridan	24 Dejected Yankees	42 The Alabama Sinks
6 Thomas Jackson	25 Fiercest Battle of the War	43 Victory at Mobile Bay
7 David Farragut	26 Battle of Antietam	44 Atlanta Destroyed
8 Lincoln's Generals	27 Stonewall at Antietam	45 Rip Up Atlanta's Rails
9 Fire on Star of the West	28 Rest After Battle	46 Remains of Atlanta
10 Fire on Fort Sumter	29 Lincoln Visits McClellan	47 Sherman's March
11 Defending Fort Sumter	30 Lincoln Visits Gettysburg	48 Marching through Georgia
12 Confederate Capitol	31 Battle of Fredericksburg	49 Lincoln Visits Grant
13 Drummer Boy	32 Burnside's Bridge	50 Charleston in Ruins
14 Fire Zouaves	33 Gettysburg Charge	51 Defeat Becomes Victory
15 Newspaperman	34 Pickett's Charge	52 Richmond in Ruins
16 The Cumberland Sinks	35 Vicksburg Falls	53 Lee Surrenders
17 Monitor and Merrimac	36 Battle of Chickamauga	54 Formal Surrender
18 Monitor and It's Crew	37 Battlefield Newspaper Stand	55 Lincoln's Assassins
19 Battle of Fair Oaks		

ITEM	MINT	EX
Set	260.00	200.00
Card	4.00	3.00

CIVIL WAR SCENES (36)   2 1/2″ X 3 1/2″

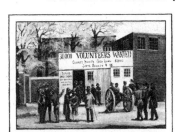

Few collectors will have seen this interesting 36-card set of "Civil War Scenes" since it was only distributed in boxes of "Delish-us" potato chips in the Wisconsin area. Produced by Jim Nicewander, the fronts of the cards feature vignettes of the American civil conflict in an engaging homespun style of artwork. The backs are nicely designed with miniature Union and Confederate flags and several paragraphs of accurate text. The set was created in 1986 and card #36, featuring excellent framed portraits of Grant and Lee, has a checklist on back.

ITEM	MINT	EX
Set	25.00	20.00
Card	.65	.50

1 Fort Sumter
2 Call to Arms
3 Philippi, Virginia
4 1st Bull Run
5 Berdan's Sharpshooters
6 General Zollicoffer
7 Fort Donelson
8 Pea Ridge
9 Mississippi Action
10 Andrew's Raid
11 Seven Days' Campaign
12 Rebel Raiders
13 2nd Bull Run
14 The Aeronautic Corps
15 Antietam
16 General McCellan
17 Fredericksburg
18 The Monitor
19 Grierson's Raid
20 Vicksburg
21 Port Hudson
22 Gettysburg
23 After the Battle
24 General Thomas
25 The Bristoe Campaign
26 Missionary Ridge
27 Winter War
28 Field Telegraphs
29 The Wilderness
30 Petersburg Siege
31 Mobile Bay
32 Sherman's March
33 Five Forks
34 Richmond
35 The Rebellion Ends
36 Generals Grant and Lee

CLASSIC AIRCRAFT COLLECTOR CARDS (TWO SETS)

2 1/2" X 3 1/2"

This is the title which appears on both sets of aircraft cards produced by Universe Games, Inc. (Selah, WA) as of this date (more sets are promised). The first series, issued in 1988 and marketed as a complete set in j-hook "window" packs, carries the title "Classic Warbirds and Military Jets" on the package. It contains 48 cards with blue borders and red frame lines surrounding color artwork scenes of planes in flight. The majority of planes pictured are propeller-driven, although various jets from the World War II period up until 1974 are also included. The backs, done in red accents and blue print on white stock, give specifications and history for each type of plane. A vertical panel under the card number carries aircraft facts and quizzes. The header card for this set bears the snappy, if misguided, phrase: "The 'Baseball Card' of Aviation History."

The second series of "Classic Aircraft Collector Cards" carries a 1989 copyright date and was also sold in set form in j-hook packages. The elegant gray borders of this issue set off artist Bob Hill's drawings to better advantage than the blue perimeter used in series one. The pictures have also been "uncluttered" by moving the captions outside of the picture area. The backs carry specifications and history of each aircraft, written in black print on the same gray background. The card number appears in a black and white aircraft star in the lower left corner. Due to the preponderance of jets in this series, the title on the packaging was flip-flopped and the header card more appropriately reads " 'The Trading Card' of Aviation History." Note: since both series are found pre-packaged as sets, only values for "mint" grade are listed.

ITEM	MINT	EX
Sets		
Series 1	6.00	--
Series 2	6.00	--

CLASSIC AIRCRAFT COLLECTOR CARDS, Series 1

1 Republic P-47 (Thunderbolt)
2 Hawker (Sea Fury)
3 Republic P-47D (Thunderbolt)
4 Mitsubishi A6M3 (Zero)
5 Grumman F-9F (Panther)
6 Boeing B-17 (Flying Fortress)
7 McDonnell Douglas F-4B (Phantom)
8 Boeing B-29 (Superfortress)
9 Curtiss P-40E (Kittyhawk)
10 Douglas A-20
11 General Dynamics F-16 (Falcon)
12 Boeing P-12E
13 Consolidated Vultee PB4Y
14 Martin B-26 (Marauder)
15 North American P-51B (Mustang)
16 North American P-51D (Mustang)
17 Focke Wulf Fw 190A-6
18 Focke Wulf Fw 190-8
19 North American B-25 (Mitchell)
20 Yakoviev Yak-9
21 Mitsubishi A6M5 (Zero-sen)
22 North American F-100 (Super Sabre)
23 North American NA-16 (T-6 Texan)
24 Boeing B-52 (Stratofortress)
25 Nakajima Ki-84 (Hayate)
26 Lockheed P-38J (Lightning)
27 Grumman F4F-3 (Wildcat)
28 Grumman F8F (Bearcat)
29 Messerschmitt Me 262
30 General Dynamics (Convair) F-106 (Delta Dart)
31 Vought F4U-1 (Corsair)
32 Messerschmitt Bf 109F-4
33 Kawasaki Ki-61 (Hien)
34 Boeing B-50 (Superfortress)
35 Mitsubishi J2M (Raiden)
36 Messerschmitt Bf-109E
37 Messerschmitt Me-410
38 Bell P-63 (Kingcobra) P-39 (Aircobra)
39 Grumman F-14 (Tomcat)
40 Douglas SBD-5 (Dauntless)
41 Grumman F6F (Hellcat)
42 Supermarine (Spitfire MK II)
43 Curtiss P-40B (Tomahawk)
44 Boeing P-26
45 Junkers Ju87B
46 Lockheed P-38G (Lightning)
47 Curtiss SB2C (Helldiver)
48 McDonnell Douglas A-4 (Skyhawk)

CLASSIC AIRCRAFT COLLECTOR CARDS Series 2

1 McDonnell Douglas F-15 (Eagle)
2 Tupolev TU-22 (Backfire-B)
3 Cessna A-37 (Dragonfly)
4 Lockheed S-3 (Viking)
5 Rockwell T-2 (Buckeye)
6 Grumman EA-6 (Prowler)
7 LVT (Vought) A-7 (Corsair II)
8 Rockwell International B-1B
9 Panaviamrca (Tornado)
10 Dassault Mirage III
11 Sukhoi SU-27 (Flanker)
12 General Dynamics F-111
13 Lockheed SR-71 (Blackbird)
14 Sepecat (Jaguar)
15 Northrop F-5
16 Mikoyan MiG-23 (Flogger)
17 McDonnell Douglas / Northrup F-18
18 Hawker Siddeley AV-8 (Harrier)
19 Grumman F11F (Tiger)
20 Lockheed F-117A (Stealth Fighter)
21 Sukhoi Su-15 (Flagon)
22 Hawker Siddeley (Hawk)
23 Fairchild Republic A-10A
24 U.S.A.F. Thunderbirds
25 Lockheed C-130 (Hercules)
26 British Aero / McDonnell Douglas T-45
27 Boeing B-47 (Stratojet)
28 Mikoyan MiG-21
29 Republic F-105 (Thunderchief)
30 Lockheed F-104 (Starfighter)
31 Douglas Skyray F-6
32 Convair F-84 F (Thunderstreak)
33 Convair F-102A
34 Hawker Siddeley (Buccaneer)
35 de Havilland (Vampire)
36 Mikoyan MiG-19
37 Bell P-59 (Airacomet)
38 Lockheed F-80 (Shooting Star)
39 North American F-86A (Sabre)
40 SAAB 29
41 Douglas DC-3 (C47)
42 Northrup P-61 (Black Widow)
43 Mikoyan MiG-15
44 Republic (Seversky) P-35
45 Mitsubishi G4M
46 Heinkel HE 162 (Salamander)
47 de Havilland Mosquito
48 Republic F-84 (Thunderjet)

CLOSE ENCOUNTERS (66 & 11)　　2 1/2" X 3 1/2"

There are 66 cards and 11 stickers in the Close Encounters set produced by Topps in 1978. The color photos used for this series were taken from the movie of the same name. Each picture has a red frame line and black borders and is captioned in yellow print underneath. The card number is located on the front in a small Close Encounters design. There are 44 puzzle and 22 "Movie Facts" backs. Except for sticker no. 1, which has a red frame line and starry border, the sticker set is characterized by yellow frame lines and black borders. The stickers are not captioned so the titles appearing in the checklist were taken from identical pictures in the card set. Note: Set prices include stickers.

ITEM	MINT	EX
Set	12.00	9.00
Card	.15	.10
Sticker	.35	.25
Wrapper	—	.35
Box	—	5.00

1 Vanished Planes reappear in the desert!
2 Monitoring a UFO
3 UFOs disrupt telephone service
4 Neary's truck is engulfed in eerie lights!
5 Strange disturbances caused by the UFOs
6 Ear-splitting sounds from the saucer!
7 A confused Ronnie tries to comfort her children
8 Fear of the unknown grips Ronnie!
9 Jillian Guiler searches for her little boy
10 Returning home
11 Jillian at Devil's Tower
12 Highway encounter
13 "It's like Halloween...for grown-ups!"
14 Image of the Devil's Tower
15 Display of cosmic beauty
16 Jillian senses the approach of a UFO!
17 A frightened Jillian calls for help!
18 The aliens arrive
19 Unearthly light bathes Jillian's home!
20 The aliens seek a subject
21 Scout Ships arrive at Devil's Tower

22 Alien visitors at the door...
23 Aliens in the eyes of innocence
24 Jillian's child is kidnapped by the aliens.
25 Exciting new star Melinda Dillon
26 Teri Garr stars as Ronnie Neary
27 Jillian and the Devil's Tower
28 National Guard alert!
29 Closing off the area for the aliens' arrival
30 Speeding toward the Devil's Tower
31 Midnight trek
32 A contaminated area...or is it?
33 A masked Jillian pushes onward!
34 Melinda Dillon stars as Jillian Guiler
35 Climbing to the top of Devil's Tower!
36 Jillian hides from military 'copters!
37 Earth scientists await the aliens
38 "Keep watching the skies..."
39 A great event in the history of man begins.
40 The giant spacecraft dwarfs the Devil's Tower!
41 The mother ship appears!
42 Awesome spectacle of the mother ship!

43 Man stares in wonder at the giant spaceship!
44 The implanted image
45 The spacecraft prepares to land
46 Scientists gather around the mother ship
47 Fantastic underside of the giant starship!
48 Jillian and her son observe the incredible event!
49 Scientists of the world stare in wonder!
50 Releasing abducted humans from the past
51 The aliens appear!
52 Earthmen watch the strange, childlike aliens!
53 Aliens walk among the humans!
54 The bizarre but benevolent space visitors
55 The alien visitors!
56 Her son returned, Jillian watches the aliens in awe!
57 The alien leader materializes
58 Goodwill toward the people of Earth!
59 Friendship lies in the outer reaches of space!
60 Steven Spielberg, Director of "CLOSE ENCOUNTERS"
61 The landing—a moment of triumph and beauty
62 Small spaceships hail the aliens' arrival
63 The road to tomorrow
64 The mother ship releases smaller vehicles
65 Artist's conception of the mother ship
66 "We are Not Alone!!!"

1 Greetings from the Limitless Universe
2 Jillian and the Devil's Tower
3 The road to tomorrow
4 Small spaceships hail the aliens' arrival
5 "We are not alone!!!"
6 The landing—a moment of triumph and beauty
7 The mother ship releases smaller vehicles
8 Artist's conception of the mother ship
9 Alien visitors at the door
10 The spacecraft prepares to land
11 Jillian and her son observe the incredible event

CLOSE ENCOUNTERS (24)　　2 1/2" X 3 1/2"

"Free ... Close Encounters of the Third Kind ... 24 Trading Cards ... One each in specially marked loaves of Wonder Bread." That's how the advertising on the shelf-hanger sign reads for this 24-card set issued in 1977. Yet collectors have never had to worry about assembling the set card by card, because sets of CE3K have flooded the market for years. The obverses of the cards have blue borders with a color picture; the set title is printed on the left-hand margin. The reverse sides have the number spelled out, a short caption, and a solicitation to join the "CE3K Skywatchers" club. The Club Portfolio and the bread loaf wrapper with CE3K advertising are far more difficult to find than the cards.

ITEM	MINT	EX
Set	5.00	4.00
Card	.25	.20

1 Barry Guiler
2 Jillian Guiler
3 Ronnie Neary
4 Claude Lacombe
5 The Leader
6 The Visitors
7 Neary's first encounter
8 Barry's first encounter
9 At the toll booth
10 The light
11 A close encounter for Barry
12 The sound is heard in India
13 Barry's model
14 Neary's model
15 Devil's Tower
16 Hiding from the helicopter
17 The base camp
18 Visitors examine the base camp
19 A small space ship
20 The red space ship
21 The mother ship at Devil's Tower
22 The mother ship at the base camp
23 The light board
24 A friendly greeting

Comic Images
By Russell Roberts

What do underwear and trading cards have in common? Nothing ... unless you're part of a company called Comic Images.

Before Comic Images began making a name for themselves in the non-sports hobby through sets such as "History of X-Men," "The Flaming Carrot," and "Boris," the Saddle Brook, New Jersey-based company was called Transcolor. They produced the colorful images used on "Underoos," the popular Fruit of the Loom kid's underwear line.

But while it may seem like a long leap between underwear and trading cards, in fact the "Underoos" experience familiarized the company with the various licensors — Marvel Comics, D.C. Comics, Paramount Pictures, etc. — whose characters and images were used for the garments. This familiarity led Marvel Comics in 1984 to invite them to take a license to manufacture Marvel-related products (stickers, buttons, pens, etc.) that would primarily be sold in comic book stores. From here it was a natural segue into producing trading card sets featuring Marvel characters. However, the company remained true to their comic book roots by placing their card sets only in stores that derived a significant part of their income from the sale of new comic books.

Today, although Comic Images is one of the most active non-sport card companies, you won't find stacks of their cards in convenience and discount stores. Although they've had success with selling both sport and non-sport sets in markets other than comic book stores, they've decided to go back to putting their products only into stores with a high concentration of comic book sales. This reflects their philosophy of trying to create a specific product geared toward the comic book market that is also collectible.

"We don't want to produce twenty-five or fifty thousand cases of an item," says Hank Rose, co-founder of the company. "We want to produce five thousand or seventy-five hundred cases maximum of an item. Let it be very collectible, a premium product, well-thought out; (we want to) build up the collectibility of the product."

Rose sums up the Comic Images strategy as: "Specializing in product that is related to our comic industry, and also desired by the hobby." The company sells more product to comic book stores, other than comics themselves, than anybody else in the world. They use this expertise to help them determine what type of card sets might appeal to comic book fans.

Over the past several years, comic book stores have evolved into comic book/trading card stores. This leads Rose to believe that the comic book fan and the trading card fan are now one and the same. Thus he feels that anything Comic Images aims at comic fans will most likely interest non-sport collectors as well.

Although his company is relatively new to the non-sports field, Rose sounds like many a veteran hobbyist when he talks about the pleasure he gets in producing a set that relies on artwork, like the classic sets of old.

"I'm a connoisseur of talent," he says. "I find it remarkable that someone can sit down at an absolutely blank board, and all of a sudden, from nothing, is created something that people will look at for years and years to come. It gives me a great kick to see that kind of talent translated to something that I have a part in."

While comic-oriented sets make up the bulk of Comic Images' card output, the success of the Boris cards has opened up a new area for the company to explore. Hard on the heels of Boris were card sets by two other well-known artists: Frazetta and Olivia.

Rose feels that, while growth in any hobby is cyclical, non-sport cards will never return to the limited visibility of the past. This is because at least some of the new fans that the hobby has picked up will remain during a slowdown, even as others drop out. However, he also knows that hobby downturns are inevitable, and that non-sports cards are no different than any other aspect of collecting.

But if and when the non-sports boom does level out, Rose and Comic Images will have no regrets. The explosion in the hobby, and the company's success with their cards, have helped Comic Images become a force to be reckoned with in non-sports cards. In the future, Rose hopes to always give Comic Image cards that little extra something that will make them stand-out from the crowd.

"If we can find something to appeal to people who want something a bit new, we're going to do that," he says.

COMIC IMAGES — SET LISTINGS

Comic Images has been producing sticker and card sets since 1986, but the terms of the company's licensing agreements have limited the target market in most cases to comic book stores. This explains why most Comic Images sets are unknown to the majority of non-sports collectors. The following is a chronological list of the company's issues; we will attempt to provide complete presentations of these sets in future editions if collectors demonstrate enough interest. The only Comic Images set with a full description in this book is Boris I, located on pages 83-84.

THE OFFICIAL MARVEL UNIVERSE STICKERS
[July 1986] set of 75 stickers and album

HISTORY OF THE X-MEN
[February 1987] 75 stickers and album

MARVEL UNIVERSE TRADING CARDS
[May 1987] 90 cards, Series No. 1

THE G.I. FILES
[May 1987] 55 cards, all from G.I. Comic Books

MARVEL'S MAGIC MOMENTS
[July 1987] 75 stickers and album

COLOSSAL CONFLICTS
[September 1987] 90 cards, Series No. 2 of the Marvel theme

MUTANT HALL OF FAME
[December 1987] 75 stickers and album

∗∗

WOLVERINE
[February 1988] 50 cards; Series No. 3 of Marvel theme

THE HONEYMOONERS
[March 1988] 50 card set

THE PUNISHER
[April 1988] 50 cards

THE WORLD OF SPIDER-MAN
[April 1988] 50 stickers and poster

THE FLAMING CARROT
[May 1988] 40 card set

CONAN TRADING CARDS
[June 1988] 50 cards of comic book covers

WOLVERINE
...re-offer of the February 1988 set

A NIGHTMARE ON ELM STREET
[September 1988] 264 stickers and album

HEROIC ORIGINS
[October 1988] 90 cards

TODD McFARLANE TRADING CARD SET NO. 1
[April 1989] 45 cards

MIKE CZEK TRADING CARD SET
[May 1989] 45 cards

THE JOHN BYRNE TRADING CARD SET
[August 1989] 45 cards

ARTHUR ADAMS TRADING CARD SET
[October 1989] 45 cards

EXCALIBUR
[November 1989] 45 card set

X-MEN COVERS
[January 1990] 90 cards

WOLVERINE UNTAMED
[February 1990] 75 stickers and album

SPIDER TEAM UP TRADING CARDS
[March 1990] 45 cards

CAPTAIN AMERICA TRADING CARDS
[May 1990] 45 cards

THE PUNISHER PAPERS
[June 1990] 75 stickers and 24-page album

JIM LEE TRADING CARDS NO. 1
[July 1990] 45 cards

TODD McFARLANE TRADING CARD SET NO. 2
[August 1990] 45 cards; Spiderman

GHOSTRIDER TRADING CARDS
[September 1990] 45 cards

X-MEN COVERS SERIES 2
[November 1990]

∗∗

WEBS
[January 1991] 75 stickers and album

WOLVERINE — FROM THEN TO NOW
[February 1991] Series 1; 45 cards

JIM LEE TRADING CARD SERIES 2
[March 1991] 45 cards

BORIS
[April 1991] actually did not appear until June; originally scheduled to be a 45-card set; 5-card packs; 48 pack boxes; one generic sticker; first of the 90-card sets

HULK
[May 1991] 90 cards; Dale Keown was the artist

X-FORCE
[June 1991] by Rob Liefeld; 90 cards

MARVEL FIRST ISSUE COVERS SERIES 2
[July 1991] (FTCC Series was Series No.1); 100 covers

X-MEN TRADING CARDS
[August 1991] 45 cards

SPECIAL EDITIONS OF X-FORCE AND BORIS
[September 1991] the 90 original cards plus autographed cards by Boris or Rob Liefeld (1000 of each)

HEAVY METAL COVERS
[October 1991] 90 cards

FRAZETTA
[November 1991] 90 cards

BORIS 2
[December 1991] 90 cards

COMBAT (132)

The 132-card Combat series—based on the TV show—was marketed by Donruss in 1964. The front of each card has a black and white photo surrounded by white borders. The card number and caption are located on the back above a short narrative. Cards 1-66 are marked "Series I," and cards 67-132 are marked "Series II." The wrapper appears in two varieties: an identical picture captioned "Lt. Hanley" and "Sgt. Saunders" or captioned "Rick Jason" and "Vic Morrow." Note: The recent death of Morrow has caused some speculative pricing on Combat cards and the Morrow wrapper.

ITEM	MINT	EX
Set	380.00	300.00
Card	2.50	2.00
Wrappers		
Series I	--	15.00
Series II	--	10.00
Boxes		
Series I	--	85.00
Series II	--	75.00

1 Rick Jason as the Fighting Lt.
2 Vic Morrow as the Tough Sgt.
3 The "Real" Rick Jason
4 The "Real" Vic Morrow
5 Training Camp
6 Troop Ship
7 Recon Landing
8 Hitting the Beach!
9 Combat!
10 Smoking Them Out!
11 Hand Fighting
12 Tanks Advance!
13 Devastation
14 Take Them!
15 Advancing
16 Hornet's Nest!
17 Killer Tank!
18 Death of a Killer!
19 Morrow Calls for Orders
20 "Let's Go!"
21 Through Enemy Fire!
22 Cut Off!
23 Wounded!
24 Morrow Finds a Way
25 Clearing the Way!
26 Scouting a Command Post!
27 Moving In!
28 Stop That Man!
29 Mortar Fire!

30 Destruction!
31 Fighting—House to House!
32 Retreat!
33 Watch—Out—Germans!
34 Taking a Prisoner!
35 An Anxious Prisoner!
36 "Come Out;" Morrow Commands
37 Storm Trooper
38 It's All Clear!
39 This One's Okay!
40 Run for Cover!
41 Surprise!
42 Where's Morrow?
43 Out of Action!
44 Captured!
45 S.S. Commander Jodl
46 Lt. Jason Studies a Map
47 How to Escape!
48 Planning an Escape!
49 Digging Out!
50 Die American!
51 After Them!
52 Getting New Rifles!
53 A French Farmer
54 Watch Out!
55 Fire from the Sky!
56 Run!
57 Death of a Friend

58 Let's Blast Out!
59 Get 'Em!
60 A Real Soldier
61 Watching Eyes
62 Friends
63 Back Home
64 Together Again!
65 Good Soldiers!
66 Victory
67 Plan of Attack
68 Assembling the Patrol
69 Take the Point!
70 Move Out!
71 Spread Out! Watch Out!
72 Death Walk
73 Caution!
74 Take Cover!
75 All Clear!
76 Deadly Surprise!
77 Close Up!
78 Blasted Country
79 Compass Check
80 Barrage!
81 Soldier's Luck!
82 Check with Command Post
83 New Danger!
84 Rear Guard
85 Take a Break!
86 Sniper!
87 First Aid
88 Target in Sight
89 Radio Check
90 Quiet-Sentries!
91 Enemy Contact
92 On Your Toes!
93 German Guns!
94 Yankees Coming!
95 Ready Now!

96 Enemy Eyes
97 Fire Fight!
98 Pinned Down!
99 Fall Back!
100 Missing in Action
101 Bad News!
102 Out Flanked!
103 One Way Out!
104 Stalking the Enemy
105 Cover Them!
106 Surprise!
107 German Bombs
108 Fighting Time!
109 Open Fire!
110 Calling for Help
111 Halftrack, Coming Up!
112 The Big Guns Speak!
113 Zeroing In
114 Bombardment!
115 Crash!
116 Fighter Support
117 Extra Firepower
118 The Chips Are Down!
119 Heavy Tanks Move Up
120 Too Much!
121 Heavy Fire
122 Low on Ammo
123 Prisoner
124 Getting Tough
125 Dangerous Journey
126 Danger Under the Stars
127 Flares!
128 Radio Out!
129 Charge!
130 Grenades!
131 Mopping Up!
132 Victory!

The "Comic Ball" series issued by Upper Deck in 1990 was an obvious attempt to wed sport and non-sports elements into a single set which would appeal to all types of collectors. Although the market will eventually reveal the success or failure of this attempt, preliminary indications are that collectors have broken down into traditional camps regarding this set. Serious sports card collectors have rarely embraced humorous treatments of professional sports and the static price response to Comic Ball artwork cards has probably disappointed card dealers accustomed to dramatic short-term increases in sports-related material. Non-sports collectors, on the other hand, seem to be genuinely delighted by the marvelous color artwork and the idea of the two-sided card.

The set consists of 297 actual cards; each is numbered front and back, so the number total is 594. The cards with obverse numbers 1-9 and reverse numbers 10-18 introduce the Looney Tunes characters with artwork (front) and biography (back). The rest of the set is compartmentalized into 17 baseball episodes, each with its own title and header card. Three cards — #'s 198, 396, & 594 — are story checklists on the reverse side. Since the characters in all these stories are dressed in major league uniforms, the Major League Baseball Players Association (MLBPA) logo appears on every card.

Three albums, each with the same basic design but in different colors, were available to house the cards ("Make Your Own Comic Books"). Each album has plastic pages to accommodate 99 actual cards (198 different numbers).

In addition to the regular cards in the series, a set of nine hologram cards was inserted randomly into packs. Since these are a marketing device intended to promote sales, they are not considered to be part of the set. Six of the holograms are basically "center-cuts" of artwork from cards 1-6, with minor detail changes; the other three seem to have been developed from unused scenes. Since holograms do not photograph well, we are unable to provide an illustration in this presentation.

ITEM	MINT	EX
Card set	25.00	18.50
Card	.10	.05
Hologram	2.00	--
Hologram set	20.00	--
Wrapper	--	.15
Box	--	1.50

Comic Ball

1 & 16. . . Bugs Bunny	199-234. . "Father Knows Worst"
2 & 17. . . Daffy Duck	235-259. . "Evening Ralph, Evening Sam"
3 & 18. . . Road Runner	260-278. . "Hold the Mustard"
4 & 13. . . Wile E. Coyote	279-305. . "Trick Baseballs"
5 & 14. . . Sylvester	306-333. . "Calamity Jane"
6 & 15. . . Porky Pig	334-357. . "Rabbit Season"
7 & 10. . . Tweety	358-395. . "Mighty Angelo"
8 & 11. . . Yosemite Sam	396 . . . . . Series One Story Checklist
9 & 12. . . Tasmanian Devil	
	397-424. . "Hopalong Casualty"
19-99. . . . "Porky Pig and Charlie Dog"	425-464. . "Which Pitch is Witch"
100-153. . "Magnetic Field"	465-494. . "The Diamond and the Gruff"
154-166. . "Swidel Swide"	495-545. . "Squeeze Play"
167-197. . "Acme Battle"	546-565. . "Baseball According to Daffy Duck"
198 . . . . . Series One Story Checklist	566-593. . "Curve Ball"
	594 . . . . . Series One Story Checklist

COMIC BALL — SERIES 2 (198)

2 1/2" X 3 1/2"

Upper Deck made some major adjustments from the Series 1 format before releasing Comic Ball 2 in 1991. The first important change is that Series 2 cards are one-sided like most other trading card issues (each Series 1 card had two "fronts" with two different numbers). In addition, the company decided to mix the cartoon artwork with two of baseball's most popular personalities, Nolan Ryan and Reggie Jackson, rather than continue dressing Looney Tunes characters in major league baseball uniforms. Finally, the nine holograms randomly inserted into packs as a bonus feature Ryan and Jackson with cartoon characters. Collectors seem to have responded to these changes positiively, although it is still too soon to say how the series will fare in the marketplace over the long term.

The 198-card set is compartmentalized into twelve separate stories, which take up 196 cards, plus two "checklists" which do nothing more than list the story titles on one side and describe the set on the other. Each story has a header card bearing the very same obverse illustration; the only detail differences are the story title at top and the background color (orange for stories in the 1-99 group, purple for the stories in the 100-198 part). The backs of all the story cards are either puzzle pieces or single photos with a trivia question printed at top (the answer is given in a small-letter, upside-down line at bottom).

Comic Ball 2 could be purchased in individual 12-count foil packs or as a complete set of 198 cards. Upper Deck arranged for nine holograms to be randomly inserted into their foil packages and these are priced separately in the value section below. Two albums were manufactured, complete with plastic pages, to house the set and they are available from hobby dealers at varying prices. As a note of interest to collectors, it appears that Upper Deck is planning to issue at least three more series of Comic Ball cards. It is assumed, but not confirmed at this time, that these future sets will feature other ballplayers besides Ryan and Jackson.

ITEM	MINT	EX
Card set	15.00	--
Card	.10	--
Hologram set	25.00	--
Hologram	2.50	--
Wrapper	--	.10
Box	--	2.00

1-18 . . . . "Favorite Interplanetary Pastime"	100-117 . . . . "Burger Ball"	
19-36 . . . . . . "Road Games"	118-135 . . . . "Chicken Wing Ding"	
37-54 . . . . . . "Couch Potato Baseball"	136-153 . . . . "Patch of Greens"	
55-72 . . . . . . "Monster Flyball"	154-171 . . . . "Baseball Appreciation"	
73-90 . . . . . . "Batting Twoubles"	172-189 . . . . "Get Your Souvenirs"	
91-98 . . . . . . "Seventh Inning Stretch"	190-197 . . . . "Seventh Inning Stretch"	
99 . . . . Set 1 Checklist Card	198 . . . . Set 2 Checklist Card	

COMIC BOOK FOLDEES (44)   2 1/2" X 4 11/16"

This set of 44 color metamorphic cards was produced by Topps in 1966. The artwork depicts a wide range of subjects—some taken from other Topps sets—including Babe Ruth, Green Arrow, Dracula, Fidel Castro, Tarzan, and Gandhi! Each card is numbered on the back of the solid center piece and the various appendages can be arranged to produce nine different "pictures."

ITEM	MINT	EX
Set	220.00	165.00
Foldee	4.00	3.00
Wrapper	--	20.00
Box	--	80.00

1 Western Explorer/Evil Devil/Speedy Flash
2 Graceful Dancer/Grubby Beatnik/Jimmy Olsen
3 Fat Lady/Pistol-Packin' Marshall/Super Hero
4 Viking Warrior/Flea-Bitten Dog/Youthful Kid Flash
5 Beautiful Starlet/—Crying Baby/Heroic Green Arrow
6 Bear Named Sam.../Slugger Hits 8.../Riddler Elected...
7 Evil Witch Doctor/British Queen/Speedy Old Flash
8 Scary Frankenstein/Beautiful Bathing Beauty/Powerful Green Lantern

9 Mahatma Gandhi/Fido the Pooch/Atom the Tiny Super Hero
10 Cross-Eyed Clod/Beautiful Betsy Ross/Handsome Green Lantern
11 Clucking Chicken/Dancing Elephant/Super Krypto
12 Wanda the Witch/Babe Ruth the Slugger/Wonder Woman the Amazon
13 Roman Emperor/Sloppy Hobo/High-Flying Supergirl
14 Western Marshall/Snappy Hot Rodder/Mischievous Imp
15 Indian Chieftan/Loud Singer/Martian Man Hunter
16 Ulysses S. Grant/Pork Chops the Pig/Saturn Girl the Legionnaire
17 Honest President/Fanged Dracula/Crime-Fighting Batman
18 Sinbad the Sailor/Lawrence of Arabia/Penguin the Evil Villain

19 Oriental Criminal/Leo, the Lion/Gold, the Metalman
20 Blackbeard the Pirate/Hoppy the Kangaroo/Alfred the Butler
21 Bucking Bronco/Pretty Skater/Evil Joker
22 Dutch Governor/Western Cowboy/High-Flying Hawkgirl
23 Silent Comedian/Russian Politician/Adventurous Super Girl
24 Bath Tub/Jack-in-the-Box/Bat Mobile
25 Decaying Mummy/Fighting Soldier/Crusading Editor
26 Jet Plane/Spotted Pup/Super Man
27 Mysterious Secret Agent/Barnyard Pig/Sharp-shooting Green Arrow
28 Russian Dancer/Shouting Paul Revere/Ugly Bizarro
29 Charity Raffle.../Scientist Finds.../the Evil Penguin...

30 Queen of the Egyptians/Mangy Rats/Leader of the Blackhawks
31 Benjamin Franklin/Metal Robot/Robin Boy Wonder
32 Prehistoric Cave Man/Aging Scrubwoman/Winged Hawkman
33 Rock'N'Roll Singer/Dopey Dunce/Beautiful Wonder Woman
34 Hawaiian Dancer/Bizarre Martian/Scheming Riddler
35 Happy Singer/Pretty Actress/Leering Luthor
36 Kiddie Bicyclist/Smiling Pianist/Stretching Hero
37 Balancing Bicyclist/Swimming Dolphin/Metamorpho the Element Man
38 Graceful Giraffe/Chief Sitting Bull/Elastic Plastic Man
39 Cuban Dictator/18th Century President/Comic Book Reporter
40 Beautiful Starlet.../Ugly Monster.../The Aqua Man...
41 Ape Man in the Jungle/Astronaut in Space/Flash in Action
42 19th Century Champion/Bad-Tempered Hermit/Mysterious Spectre
43 DeGaulle the General/Tipsy Drunk/Catwoman, the Princess of Plunder
44 Baseball Hero Autographing Ball/Boy Eating Ice Cream Cone/Superman Holding Deadly Kryptonite

COMIC BOOK FOLDEES (43)

3 1/4" X 6"

This set is easily distinguished from the preceding one on the basis of physical size: when open, each card measures 3 1/4" X 6", in contrast to the 3 1/2" X 4 5/8" dimensions of the smaller version. In addition, the small-size variety is a series of 44 and has the words "Printed in U.S.A." after the T.C.G. initials on the center panel. The large-size set contains 43 cards and has no "Printed in U.S.A." line after Topps' initials. All other details of the sets—artwork, card numbers, & text—appear to be identical (except for the "missing" 44th card).

ITEM	MINT	EX
Set	240.00	185.00
Foldee	4.50	3.50

1 Western Explorer/Evil Devil/Speedy Flash
2 Graceful Dancer/Grubby Beatnik/Jimmy Olsen
3 Fat Lady/Pistol-Packin' Marshall/Super Hero
4 Viking Warrior/Flea-Bitten Dog/Youthful Kid Flash
5 Beautiful Starlet/—Crying Baby/Heroic Green Arrow
6 Bear Named Sam.../Slugger Hits 8.../Riddler Elected...
7 Evil Witch Doctor/British Queen/Speedy Old Flash
8 Scary Frankenstein/Beautiful Bathing Beauty/Powerful Green Lantern
9 Mahatma Gandhi/Fido the Pooch/Atom the Tiny Super Hero
10 Cross-Eyed Clod/Beautiful Betsy Ross/Handsome Green Lantern
11 Clucking Chicken/Dancing Elephant/Super Krypto
12 Wanda the Witch/Babe Ruth the Slugger/Wonder Woman the Amazon
13 Roman Emperor/Sloppy Hobo/High-Flying Supergirl
14 Western Marshall/Snappy Hot Rodder/Mischievous Imp
15 Indian Chieftan/Loud Singer/Martian Man Hunter
16 Ulysses S. Grant/Pork Chops the Pig/Saturn Girl the Legionnaire
17 Honest President/Fanged Dracula/Crime-Fighting Batman
18 Sinbad the Sailor/Lawrence of Arabia/Penguin the Evil Villain
19 Oriental Criminal/Leo, the Lion/Gold, the Metalman
20 Blackbeard the Pirate/Hoppy the Kangaroo/Alfred the Butler
21 Bucking Bronco/Pretty Skater/Evil Joker
22 Dutch Governor/Western Cowboy/High-Flying Hawkgirl
23 Silent Comedian/Russian Politician/Adventurous Super Girl
24 Bath Tub/Jack-in-the-Box/Bat Mobile
25 Decaying Mummy/Fighting Soldier/Crusading Editor
26 Jet Plane/Spotted Pup/Super Man
27 Mysterious Secret Agent/Barnyard Pig/Sharp-shooting Green Arrow
28 Russian Dancer/Shouting Paul Revere/Ugly Bizarro
29 Charity Raffle.../Scientist Finds.../the Evil Penguin...
30 Queen of the Egyptians/Mangy Rats/Leader of the Blackhawks
31 Benjamin Franklin/Metal Robot/Robin Boy Wonder
32 Prehistoric Cave Man/Aging Scrubwoman/Winged Hawkman
33 Rock'N'Roll Singer/Dopey Dunce/Beautiful Wonder Woman
34 Hawaiian Dancer/Bizarre Martian/Scheming Riddler
35 Happy Singer/Pretty Actress/Leering Luthor
36 Kiddie Bicyclist/Smiling Pianist/Stretching Hero
37 Balancing Bicyclist/Swimming Dolphin/Metamorpho the Element Man
38 Graceful Giraffe/Chief Sitting Bull/Elastic Plastic Man
39 Cuban Dictator/18th Century President/Comic Book Reporter
40 Beautiful Starlet.../Ugly Monster.../The Aqua Man...
41 Ape Man in the Jungle/Astronaut in Space/Flash in Action
42 19th Century Champion/Bad-Tempered Hermit/Mysterious Spectre
43 DeGaulle the General/Tipsy Drunk/Catwoman, the Princess of Plunder

COMIC BOOK HEROES STICKERS (40 & 9)

It appears that this Topps set of 40 diecut stickers and nine combination checklist/puzzle piece cards was both "tested" and regularly issued in 1975. As a result we have two varieties of stickers and cards with minor detail differences. One sticker version has a thin white cardboard backing and two stars preceding the Topps copyright line; checklists for this type are also printed on white stock, have bright hues, and are easily read.

The second variety of stickers has a tan paper backing, only one star preceding the Topps copyright, and a dull-colored, hard-to-read checklist printed on gray stock. The debate about which variety came first has little more than theoretical meaning in light of the fact that both types seem to be equally plentiful. Note: set price includes all stickers and cards.

ITEM	MINT	EX
Set	30.00	22.50
Sticker	.50	.40
Card	.40	.30
Wrappers		
Test	--	40.00
Regular	--	1.50
Box	--	25.00

Black Widow (I'm Natasha Fly Me to Miami!)
Captain America - 1 (I'm a Yankee Doodle Dandy!)
Captain America -2 (Look, Ma, No Cavities!)
Captain Marvel (Fly the Friendly Skies of United!)
Conan (Trick or Treat?!
Daredevil (Badness Makes Me See Red!)
Dracula - 1 (Sure Doesn't Taste Like Tomato Juice!)
Dracula - 2 (Flying Drives Me Bats!)
Dr. Doom (I'm Dressed to Kill!)
Dr. Octopus (I'm Just a Well-Armed Crook!)
Dr. Strange (Darn Those House Calls!)
Frankenstein's Monster (Maybe It's My Breath!)
Ghost Rider (Peter Fonda Look Out!)
Hawkeye (Annie Oakley I Ain't!)
Hulk - 1 (Who Stole My Right Guard?)
Hulk - 2 (Green Power!)
Human Torch - 1 (Tan...Don't Burn!)
Human Torch - 2 (When You're Hot, You're Hot!)
Iron Fist (Kung Fooey!)
Iron Man (Fight Rust!)
Ka-Zar (Be Kind To Animals...Or Else!)
Kull (These Pants Don't Fit!)
Luke Cage (I Was a 98 Lb. Wealking!)
Man-Thing (I Dropped the Soap in the Shower!)

Medusa (Darn That Cheap Hairspray!)
Moribus, Living Vampire (Which Way to the Blood Bank?)
Mr. Fantastic (I'm the Long Arm of the Law!)
Shang-Li, Kung Fu (All Aspirin is Not Alike!)
Spider-Man-1 (Who'd You Expect? Little Miss Muffet?)
Spider-Man-2 (You Drive Me Up a Wall!)
Sub-Mariner (Don't Pollute My Waters!)
The Falcon (You Bet Your Bird!)
The Living Mummy (Which Hand Has the M&M's?)
The Son of Satan (The Devil Made Me Do It!)
The Thing-1 (It's Clobberin' Time!)
The Thing-2 (I'm Going to Pieces)
Thor-1 (Support Your Local Thunder-God!)
Thor-2 (Who Said Blondes Have More Fun?)

COMIC BOOK TATTOOS (?)

1 9/16" X 3 1/2"

When this tattoo set portraying D.C. Comic characters was issued by Topps in 1967, the tattoos on the insides of the wrappers were the major attraction. Times have changed: now the exterior wrappers are far more interesting and valuable to collectors than the transfers. The Superman and Batman designs are red with a yellow panel; Wonder Woman is blue with a yellow panel; and Aquaman is yellow with a blue panel. All the wrappers carry a one-cent price. The multi-colored tattoos on the interior sides are not numbered or captioned.

ITEM	MINT	EX
Wrappers (4)		
Each	——	10.00

COMIC COVER STICKERS (44)

2 1/2" X 3 1/2"

FOLD CORNER ON DOTTED LINE

Slowly peel sticker from FRONT of card.

The revival in the late 1960's of interest in comic books and their characters led to several bubble gum sets dealing with this subject. "Comic Cover Stickers," issued by Topps in 1970, is one of the best ever produced. There are 44 corner peel stickers in the set. Of these, 16 have single subject fronts with instruction backs. The remaining 29 are multiple formats, each showing four different comic book covers. The backs of these have no print. The 5-cent wrapper is red with a yellow title and a multi-color sticker design.

ITEM	MINT	EX
Set	190.00	135.00
Sticker	3.50	2.50
Wrapper	——	20.00
Box	——	55.00

SINGLE STICKERS
Batman
Detective Comics
Enemy Ace
Falling In Love
Flash
Girls' Love
Green Lantern
Superman
Teen Titans
The Unexpected
   Wonder Woman
Young Love (Lisa St. Claire)
Young Love (20 Miles to Heartbreak)
Young Romance (Have a Fling With...)
Young Romance (Two Different Worlds)

FOUR-ON-ONES
Batman, Aquaman, Falling in Love, Hellcats
Batman, Enemy Ace, Teen Titans, Girls' Love
Batman, G.I. Combat, Girls' Romances, The Witching Hour
Batman, Sgt. Rock, Girls' Romances, Debbi
Batman & Robin, Strange, Young Love, Action Comics
Batman & Robin, Young Love, Strange, Adventure
Binky, Batman, Falling in Love, Young Romance
Binky's Buddies, Girls' Romances, Batman, Superman
Enemy Ace, Wonder Woman, Binky, Batman
Girls' Love, Detective, Tomahawk, Teen Titans

Girls' Love, The House of Secrets, Batman, Jimmy Olsen
Girls' Romances, The House of Mystery, Challengers of the Unknown, Batman and Batgirl
Girls' Romances, The Phantom Stranger, Batman and Batgirl, Action Comics
Girls' Romances, Wonder Woman, Aquaman, The Phantom Stranger
Green Lantern, Batman and Robin, Beyond the Unknwn, Girls' Romances
Jimmy Olsen, Strange, Jason's Quest, Young Love
Lois Lane, Debbi, Witching Hour, Young Romance
Lois Lane, Scooter, Falling in Love, The Witching Hour
Sgt. Rock, Batman and Batgirl, Girls' Romances, Action Comics
Teen Titans, Scooter, Tomahawk, Adventure Comics
The House of Secrets, Beyond the Unknown, Girls' Love, Batman and Batgirl
The House of Secrets, Tomahawk, Superboy, Girls' Love
The Unexpected, Falling in Love, Batman, Binky
The Witching Hour, Binky's Buddies, World's Finest, Wonder Woman
The World's Finest, Scooter, Young Love, The Phantom Stranger
Young Love, Adventure, Tomahawk, Batman and Batgirl
Young Love, Superman, Binky, The House of Secrets
Young Romance, Lois Lane, Binky's Buddies, The Witching Hour
Young Romance, Superman, The Unexpected, Challengers of the Unknown

COUP D'ETAT (36)

Another 36-card set with a certain political perspective, "Coup D'Etat" was issued in 1990 by California-based Eclipse Enterprises. The title of the set refers to the notion that the assassination of President John F. Kennedy was, in fact, a toppling of a legitimate government by subversives at home and abroad. Writer Paul Brancato explores all the conspiracy theories and artist Bill Sienkiewicz accompanies the narrative with eerie drawings of people and places. The cards are slightly bigger than standard size and our checklist reflects the fact that front and back captions for each card are different. The series is sold as a boxed set only; for this reason, single values are not listed and there is no price given for the set in "excellent" grade. Note: set price includes box.

ITEM	MINT	EX
Set	10.00	—

1 F: "Wanted For Treason"	11 F: CIA — KGB	21 F: Military Intelligence	29 F: Future Target
B: The Assassination	B: James Jesus Angleton	B: General Charles Cabel	B: Robert Kennedy
2 F: Ambushed!	12 F: Control Agent	22 F: The Cuba Question	30 F: Goddess
B: The Secret Service	B: George De Mohrenschildt	B: Fidel Castro	B: Marilyn Monroe
3 F: Best Evidence	13 F: Control Agent II	23 F: Codename: Bishop	31 F: Among the Missing
B: The Autopsy	B: Guy Banister	B: David Atlee Phillips	B: James Hoffa
4 F: The Sniper's Nest	14 F: Misguided Plot	24 F: The Three Tramps	32 F: Mafia Kingfish
B: Crossfire	B: David Ferrie	B: E. Howard Hunt & Frank Sturgis	B: Carlos Marcello
5 F: Patrolman Murdered	15 F: Mysterious Traveler	25 F: Oil Money	33 F: The Arranger
B: J.D. Tippett	B: "Oswald" in Mexico	B: Haroldson Lafayette Hunt	B: I. Irving Davidson
6 F: Alias Alek Hidell	16 F: Doppelganger in Dallas	26 F: The Policeman's Pimp	34 F: The Untouchable
B: The Mail-Order Rifle	B: Too Many Oswalds	B: Jack Ruby	B: J. Edgar Hoover
7 F: The Other Assassination	17 F: The Other Widow	27 F: The French Connection	35 F: Ballots and Bullets
B: Ruby Kills Oswald	B: Marina Oswald	B: Jean Souetre	B: Lyndon Johnson
8 F: Whitewash	18 F: FBI Shadows	28 F: The Mob	36 F: Silenced!
B: The Warren Commission	B: James Hosty	B: CIA — Mafia Plots	B: Dead Witnesses
9 F: Suppressed Evidence	19 F: Texas Uber Alles		
B: The Zapruder Film	B: General Edwin Walker		
10 F: Just A Patsy?	20 F: The Permindex Plot		
B: Lee Harvey Oswald	B: Clay Shaw		

CONTROL AGENT I

COVER UPS (?)

A typical sheet of "rub-offs" found in a 5-cent pack of "Cover Ups" (Fleer) contained a variety of signs, names, expressions, numbers, etc. These could easily be applied to book covers, or any other surface, by rubbing a pencil point over the chosen designs. As a bonus, each pack also contained a 2-card panel of numbered and captioned "Book Marx."

TWO SIZES

ITEM	MINT	EX
Rub-offs	1.00	.75
Book Marx		
Panel	1.00	.75
Single	—	.35
Wrapper	—	3.00
Box	—	15.00

COWBOY & COWGIRL TRADING CARDS (6) 2 3/8" X 4 1/8"

This interesting set of six cards, printed in color on heavy paper stock, was the fourth in a series of trading cards printed for pre-teens in WOW magazine. The artwork has a Victorian look to it and each picture is captioned in the bottom panel. The background behind the text on back is parchment brown and each card has a different piece of western gear as an accent below the final paragraph. Only the word "WOW" in an arc design above the text gives a clue to the origin of the set. Other WOW magazine 6-card sets include Pirates, American Indians, Bears, and Endangered Animals. Since single cards had to be cut from the insert page with scissors, collectors may find uneven edges (such cards cannot be graded " excellent").

ITEM	MINT	EX
Uncut sheet	4.00	3.00
Set (cut)	3.00	2.00
Card	.50	.35

Bill Pickett
Buffalo Bill — Annie Oakley
Calamity Jane
Nat Love
Theodore Roosevelt
Will Rogers

CRACKED MAGAZINE (56 & 10)   TWO SIZES

Of the 56 numbered cards in this set produced by Fleer, 28 depict "Cracked Magazine" covers, four feature "Great Moments," and the remaining 14 are "Shut-Ups." The backs of all 56 cards are puzzle pieces of a "Giant 2 Ft. Poster." The ten stickers in the set are unnumbered, have tan paper backing, and measure 2 3/8" X 2 3/4". Note: set price includes stickers.

ITEM	MINT	EX
Set	20.00	16.50
Card	.25	.20
Sticker	.60	.50
Wrapper	--	.50
Box	--	6.00

116

The Topps gold mine of humorous issues continued with the 66-card set of Crazy Cards issued in 1961. The front of each card contains a full-color drawing with an apparently factual statement; the back, printed in blue on white stock, delivers a punch line. The cards are numbered, on the back, in a black circle.

ITEM	MINT	EX
Set	190.00	150.00
Card	2.50	2.00
Wrappers		
1-cent	--	250.00
5-cent	--	75.00

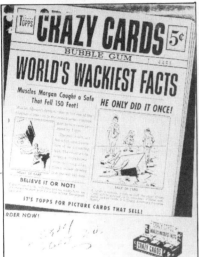

1 Basher Brown Had Over 2500 Fights!
2 An Eating Champ Ate 53 Pies at One Meal!
3 Ben Franklin Did Not Discover Electricity!
4 A Stuntman Jumped from a Jet Plane and Landed Unhurt!
5 Muscles Morgan Caught a Safe That Fell 150 Feet!
6 A Man Was Shot from a Cannon in N.Y. His Feet Touched the Ground in Maine!
7 A Ten Year Old Smoked 25 Cigars...They Didn't Stunt His Growth!
8 Astronaut Cole Reached a Speed of 25,000 MPH!
9 Though He Failed in Medical School a Famous Doctor Did 300 Operations!
10 A 75 Year Old Shoeshine Man Retired as a Millionaire!
11 99 Year Old Zeke Meek Still Has His Hair and Teeth!

12 In Detroit a Man Sleeps Upside Down Because of a Strange Illness!
13 A Denver Man Lay on a Bed of Nails for 45 Days!
14 Mr. Juggles Can Toss Up 25 Dumbbells at One Time!
15 Mr. Memory Amazed People in His First Appearance!
16 A New York Policeman Never Had an Injury in Over 40 Years on the Police Force!
17 A Dallas Salesman Had One Blue Eye and One Brown Eye!
18 In 1947 "Amazo" the Famous Magician Was Tied and Thrown in the River!
19 An Animal Trainer Won 300 Fights with Lions!
20 A Texas Man Has Seen a Three Headed Cow!
21 A Man-eating Shark Will Not Eat a Man!
22 An Alaska Man Never Wore a Coat and Never Had a Cold!
23 In Maine a Man Lived Inside a Whale!
24 A Swiss Climber Fell Off Mt. Everest and Only Broke One Finger!
25 Jockey Jones' Horse Could Go Safely Through a Flaming Hoop!
26 Mr. Fabulous Threw Knives at His Wife Blind-folded!
27 In N.Y. a Man Was Arrested for Throwing Shoes in the River!
28 A 6 Year Old Girl Blew a Bubble Gum Bubble 20 Feet Wide!
29 Mr. Hercules Had the World's Strongest Teeth!

30 Every Time You Breathe Someone Dies!
31 A N.Y. Artist Can Paint Pictures with His Feet!
32 A Man Once Stayed Up for 97 Hours without Sleeping!
33 A Girl in Dallas Read an Entire Book Upside Down!
34 In Rome a Man Stayed Under Water for 10 Minutes!
35 A Noted Astronomer Saw 53 Stars in the Daytime!
36 An Ohio Farmer Never Hits Any of His 12 Children!
37 A Berlin Man Put 15 People in His Volkswagon!
38 A Master Carpenter Drove a Nail Through a 12 Inch Board with One Blow!
39 A Paris Scientist Saw Flying Saucers for 3 Days!
40 "Quick Draw" Lee Was the Fastest Gun in the West!
41 Movie Star Rex Huff Never Uses a Stunt Man!
42 Dr. Zilch Was Famous as the First Painless Dentist!
43 In 61 Years Doctor Roy Peters Never Lost a Human Life!
44 A Fisherman Reeled in a Man with His Fishing Rod!
45 A Man Once Drove His Car Through the City Blindfolded!
46 In 1922 a Man Was Arrested for Bathing on a Saturday!
47 Casper Blip's Act was Sawing his Wife in Half!
48 A Lion Will Not Bite a Human!
49 In 1959 a Man Broke His Neck Getting Out of a Car!

50 A Troy Housewife Hurt Her Eye While Drinking Tea!
51 There's a Man Who Is Actually as Strong as An Ox!
52 William Tell Was the World's Greatest Archer!
53 Stare at This for 15 Minutes and You'll Discover Something Interesting!
54 A Man in Idaho, Age 105, Never Wore Glasses!
55 A Dutch Scientist Claimed He Could Eat Tarantulas!
56 Mr. Fearless Walks on Hot Coals Once a Year!
57 100 Year Old "Pop" Atlas Hasn't Visited a Dentist for 75 Years!
58 In 1938 a Man Hooked a 65 Ft. Whale with a Fishing Pole!
59 Bullfighting Diaz Didn't Have a Scratch on his Body!
60 A Man Lost 185 Pounds of Ugly Fat in One Day!
61 A Miami Man Swam 5 Miles Through Shark Filled Water!
62 Army Scout Reed Fought 8 Indians Single-handed!
63 A U.S. Sub Commander Sank 12 Jap Ships in 1 Day!
64 An Ace Skier Went Down a 150 Foot Hill in 33 Seconds!
65 A Boston Man Was Run Over by a Steam Roller and Went Home an Hour Later!
66 A Doctor Once Performed a Delicate Brain Operation for 13 Hours!

CRAZY COLLEGE PENNANT STICKERS (25) 2 1/2" X 2 7/8"

The title for this set is printed on a 2½" x 3½" checklist card, but does not appear on the stickers themselves. There are 25 stickers in the set, each with a humorous version of a well-known college spelled out on a pennant design. The latter is scored around the edges for easy removal from the backing; once the sticker is peeled away, the bread company, secondary caption, and sticker number remain behind and the only writing on the pennant itself is a "Walt Disney Productions" credit line. Note: the values listed below are for unpeeled stickers with the backing intact. Set price does not include the checklist card, which must be unmarked to fit into either "mint" or "excellent" grade.

ITEM	MINT	EX
Set	45.00	32.50
Sticker	1.50	1.00
Checklist card	10.00	7.50

1	Wonder Bread Yell	14	Aw Burn
2	Dart Mutt	15	M.I. Tea
3	Prince Ton	16	S.M. Mew
4	Stamp Ford	17	Purr Due
5	Minnie Soda	18	I Owl A
6	Rich Man	19	Mar Cat
7	Oregon Snake	20	E. See L.A.
8	De Paw	21	Noted Dame
9	Ala Bambi	22	Dook
10	Wash A Ton	23	Too Lane
11	Ho Hi Ho State	24	Vest Point
12	Georg A Tack	25	Mickey Can Skate
13	Mary Land-ing		

CRAZY COMIC STICK-ONS (96) 1 3/4" X 2 1/2"

This metamorphic set issued by the Philadelphia Chewing Gum Co. consists of 96 "half-cards." Fifty percent of these are "heads" (1-48) and fifty percent are bodies (49-96); a complete "Crazy Comic Stick-On" was constructed by attaching any "head" to any "body." You don't have to be a genius to figure out the potential here: with 2304 different combinations possible, the kids could be occupied for hours! There are two different wrappers for the set—one blue, one yellow. Note: prices are for "halves" with attachment strips intact.

ITEM	MINT	EX
Set	60.00	50.00
1/2 card	.50	.35
Wrappers		
Blue	--	6.00
Yellow	--	8.00
Box	--	25.00

CRAZY HANG UPS (24)   3 3/4" X 10 1/2"

"Crazy Hang Ups" were sold directly from a display box without wrappers or gum. Each 5-cent cardboard folder had to be opened by a pull-tab located on the back. Printed on the inside were two 3 3/4" X 10 1/2" full color cards with funny scenes and captions. Each card is numbered and has a pre-punched hole for hanging on "bikes, bulletin boards, door handles or...anything." There are 24 titles in the set, which was produced by Donruss. Note: mint price is valid for unopened folders only.

ITEM	MINT	EX
Sets		
Folders (12)	100.00	80.00
Cards (24)	--	70.00
Folder	8.00	6.00
Card	--	2.50
Box	--	20.00

1 School Closed 'Til Further Notice	13 Danger Jungle Rot!
2 This School Lunch Room is a Health Hazard	14 Sign Up Here for the Draft
	15 Quarantine Bad Breath!
3 Closed for Repairs - Use Other Mouth	16 Pull
4 Save Water - Shower with a Dog!	17 In Case of Atomic Attack Blow This Room Up!
5 Monster's Pad!	18 Push Cart for Sale
6 Do Not Enter My Life!	19 Ladies Room
7 Private Keep Out - This Room Belongs To:	20 Attention Car Thieves - This Car is Junk
8 O.T.L. (Out to Lunch)	21 Wet Paint
9 No Trespassing (State Prison)	22 Danger 45,000 Nuts!
10 Beware Vicious Dog	23 Warning A-Bomb Factory
11 No Parking	24 Danger Man Eating Pig (boy)
12 Danger Man Eating Pig (girl)	

CRAZY LABELS STICKERS (64)   2 1/2" X 3 1/2"

In most sets, if a sticker is removed from it's backing there is no longer any record of what it looked like. Fleer solved that dilemma in the Crazy Labels set by printing each design twice. Each piece of artwork spoofing various products was created as a removable glossy, diecut sticker on the front of one card, and as the dull-finish cardboard back of another card (the same design is never front & back on the same card). The stickers and the cards have different numbering systems; we have chosen the sticker system for our checklist. (The number in parentheses indicates the design's place in the cardboard set.)

ITEM	MINT	EX
Set	20.00	15.00
Sticker/card	.35	.25
Wrappers (3) ea.	--	.50
Box	--	7.00

Crazy Labels

1 Ex-Con Motor Oil (32)
2 Crampfire Mushmallows (28)
3 Liptune (23)
4 Sad Trash Bags (20)
5 This Drink Is a Joke (31)
6 Chef Boy-R-These Sad Spitghetti (27)
7 Bullseye Green Beans (25)
8 Swish Fizzlelean (19)
9 Cannibal's Jungle Soup (30)
10 Dessert X (26)
11 Elastic — Pickles That Stretch (22)
12 Grillette Flamey (18)
13 Perspiration H (17)
14 Binds Tomato Catch-Up (21)
15 Lowbrow (24)
16 Swet Ones (29)
17 Pierre's (13)
18 Embalmed Chopped Steak Lips (12)
19 Schlepps Bionic Water (8)
20 Smell Sham-Phew (4)
21 You Risk Everything (14)
22 Weak Thins (11)
23 Coaloil Herbicidel Essence (3)
24 BO-5
25 Nobull Fake Motor Oil (7)
26 Fan Anti-Perspirant (10)
27 Bananacin (6)
28 Done-In Yogurt (2)
29 Fatal Touch (16)
30 Soggies (9)
31 Gullotine Krac II (5)

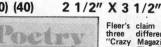

32 Swansong (1)
33 Windy's Burgers (61)
34 21st Century (62)
35 Sik Lighter (63)
36 If? Crumby Peanut Plaster (64)
37 Maimed Toothwaste (57)
38 Singeford Charcoal (58)
39 Ty-One-On Tablets (59)
40 Nausea Zit Cream (60)
41 Bugs (56)
42 Nice & Sleazy (55)

43 Saggies (54)
44 Sunburnt (53)
45 Hamburger Belcher (49)
46 Draines Burpers (50)
47 Litely Watered Beer (51)
48 Strip-Ex (52)
49 Dr. Scorch (45)
50 U-8 Juice (46)
51 Hi Temperature Fear (47)
52 Cannon (48)
53 U.S. Fail (44)

54 Kracked Barrel (43)
55 Instant Stanka (42)
56 Max-Smell House (41)
57 Dare Eat Those (37)
58 Sealed Best Heavy Slush (38)
59 American Distress (39)
60 Dandi-Flush (40)
61 Just Booze (33)
62 Colorots Bleech (34)
63 Fool Koffin Nails (35)
64 Miracle Whiffs (36)

CRAZY MAGAZINE COVERS (30) (30) (40) 2 1/2" X 3 1/2"

Fleer's claim that there are three different series of "Crazy Magazine Covers" is untrue. The first series consists of 30 stickers (with a blue band or bands across the tan paper back) and nine combination cards (blue-print checklist on one side, puzzle piece on the other). The assembled first series puzzle is "Bad."

The second series has 30 stickers with entirely new magazines (tan backs with orange-brown band or bands), plus nine checklist/puzzle cards forming the puzzle "Pearents'." In the so-called "3rd series," there are 30 stickers with tan paper backs and orange-brown bands that are identical to those of the 2nd series. However, there are ten entirely new stickers that have either 3rd series checklists or puzzle pieces printed on cardboard backs. The 3rd series puzzle is "New Math" and several different puzzle backs may exist for each of the ten "true" 3rd series stickers. Note: the number of bands on the backs of 2nd and 3rd series tan-back stickers varies and is irrelevant in determining "true" 2nd or 3rd series issuance. Set prices include complete puzzles (9 cards).

ITEM	MINT	EX
Sets		
1st series (30)	20.00	15.00
2nd series (30)	20.00	15.00
3rd series (40)	20.00	15.00
Stickers		
Paper back	.50	.35
Cardboard back	.50	.35
Checklists/		
puzzle pieces (all)	.25	.15
Wrappers		
Regular	--	2.00
"All New"	--	2.00
Box	--	7.00

Crazy Magazine Covers

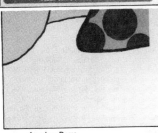

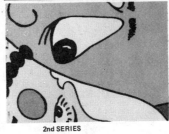

2nd SERIES

American Dome	Agony
Bad	Blandie
Bedbook	Bloating
Betty Cooker Crock Book	BlunderWoman
Bitter Homes and Garbage	Bugs Baloney
Business Freak	Confusing Reports
Chicken Souperman	Cosmopelican
Expire	Custom Hoppers
Family Cycle	Fail
Fatman and Bratboy	Hot Bod
Field & Cream	Jarhead's Jokes
Good Housepeeping	Ladies Room Jourbal
Jerk and Jill	Lice
Mechanix Illiterate	Mademosoil
Newsleak	Man, Myth & Maniac
Penhouse	McStall's
Reader's Disgust	Mi$fortune
Rears	Modern Bribe
Road & Crack	Mouse Beautiful
Rolling Stoned	My Brother Bullfinkle
Saturday Evening Pole	Pearents'
Seventons	Peephole
Shorts Illustrated	Playtoy
Slime	Screem Stories
Smacked	Smelly Pages
Snort	The Banana Spits
The New Forker	Underhog
True Romantic Confusion	Waist Watchers
T.V. Died	Webfoots Dictionary
U.S. Booze and World Report	Woman's Say

3rd SERIES

Art
Basic Science
Civics
Geography
Health & Higene
New Math
Poetry
Social Studies
Spelling Bouk
Weakly Reader

CRAZY STICK-ONS (48)

1 1/8" X 3 3/8"

Each Crazy Stick-On" is a paper strip containing one large sticker flanked by two smaller ones. The large sticker may be oval or rectangular; the smaller stickers are always rectangular. Each strip is numbered and carries a 1979 copyright line. These "peel-off" stickers were inserts in packages of Bazooka Sugar Free Bubble Gum. There are 48 in the set.

ITEM	MINT	EX
Set	60.00	45.00
Stick-On	1.00	.75
Wrapper	--	1.00
Box	--	10.00

CRAZY TV (?)　　　　　　　　　2 1/2" X 3 1/2"

The fact that Crazy TV was marketed in both Canada and the U.S. does not fully explain the variety of cards associated with the set. There are three varieties of cards with "TV screen" fronts. Type 1 has a woodgrain TV cabinet and a printed back containing the card number, set total (55), and a feature entitled "TV Knock-Knocks." Type 2 has a woodgrain TV front, but is not numbered and has a blank back. Type 3 has a salmon-colored front and also is unnumbered and blank-backed. Although the Type 1 cards state that there are 55 cards in the set, only 22 skip-numbered titles have been reported for this variety. Most of these titles are also confirmed to exist in both blank-backed series (no new titles discovered in these sets).

The 22 "TV Knock-Knocks" jokes printed on the backs of Type 1 cards also appear by themselves with the title shortened to "Knock-Knocks." These cards have salmon-colored fronts and blank backs. A third series of cards, called "Ton 'O' Laffs," was also printed with salmon fronts and blank backs. It is believed that there are also 22 cards in thi series, but only 19 titles have been reported to date. ["Ton 'O' Laffs" cards with red fronts and blank backs were issued in Canada, possibly with a completely different set.]

A woodgrain-front card was visible in a recently examined unopened test pack, but the back of the card could not be seen. Some collectors believe that Type 2 TV screen cards were issued in Canada, and that all salmon-colored cards were distributed in U.S. Fun Packs. These theories remain to be proven, and the best we can do for now is evaluate the cards on the basis of demand and scarcity.

TV Cards

1 Commercial – Zilch Cigarettes are Cough! Definitely (Sput!) Milder!!
2 News Flash – ...And Here's a Bulletin Just Handed Me! A TV Announcer Has Just Been...Stabbed...
4 News Flash – Here's a Bulletin...Russia Has Just Invaded the United States... But First a Word from Our Sponsor!
8 What's Up Doctari? – I'm Sorry, He's on Another Lion...
9 Gunstroke – Matt, I Think You've Been Marshall, Too Long!!
12 Eye Spy – Let's Try Not to Attract Attention!
16 Bazanza – Did You Feel an Arrow?
17 Cowpoke in Afrida - Okay...Draw!!
20 Man From A.U.N.T. – That's a Pretty Silly Disguise, Solo!
22 Lazzie – O.K., Mom! We'll Come Eat Supper as Soon as Lazzie Finds a Cure for Mumps!
28 Eye Spy – I Know She's a Deadly Foreign Agent, But What a Way to Go!
30 Beverly Sillybillies – What D'Ya Mean the Dinner's Ruined – I'm Burning the Garbage
35 Dragged Net – Hm...The Victim Was Stabbed, Shot, Beaten and Strangled! Looks Like Foul Play, Eh, Joe?
36 Gut Smart – All Right, 98, When I Count Three, We Attack!
37 Gently, Ben! Ben! Ben! Have You Seen Mark? We Can't Find Him Anywhere? Burp!
41 Commercial – You Can Fire Me for This, Boss, But You Have Bad Breath! O.K.! You're Fired!
43 Fun For Your Life – It's the Doctor Who Told Me I Only Had a Year to Live!
45 Steelside – I Never Should Have Taken This Bonnie and Clyde Case!
47 May I? – If I Hear One More Elephant Joke, Terry, You Go the Rest of the Way on Foot!
50 Daniel Boob – Look...Who's Side Are You On, Anyway?
53 Gut Smart – Deposit 15 cents for the Next Three Minutes, Please...
55 Weather Report – ...And Here's a Cold Front Moving in from the East

ITEM	MINT	EX
TV Screen cards		
Type 1	10.00	8.00
Type 2	6.50	5.00
Type 3	6.50	5.00
Knock-Knocks	2.50	2.00
Laffs	2.50	2.00
Wrapper	--	75.00
Box	--	250.00

Knock Knocks

Anita!	Jed!
Barry	Jess!
Bertha!	Max!
Cassius!	Milly!
Clarence!	Oliver!
Diane!	Phyllis!
Ellie Max!	Rita!
Gary!	Scott!
Hoss!	Stan!
Hugo!	Wendy!
Ida!	Yvonne!

122

CYNDI LAUPER (33/33)   2 1/2" X 3 1/2"

The Cyndi Lauper set distributed by Topps in 1985 is composed of 33 cards and 33 stickers. The former have color photos of the entertainer set on a "spotty" pink background. The card number and a short text are printed on back. The stickers have a die-cut center design containing a color picture and are numbered on front outside the score line. Sticker backs are puzzle pieces needed to assemble a 15-piece puzzle (two different fronts have identical backs) and there are three "puzzle preview cards." Note: set price includes all 66 items.

ITEM	MINT	EX
Set	10.00	7.50
Card	.10	.07
Sticker	.25	.15
Wrappers (2) ea.	--	.35
Box	--	4.00

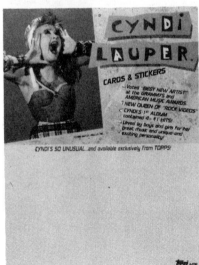

DAKTARI (66)

DON'T BE A BULLY

2 1/2" X 3 1/2"

The "Daktari" television series provided the black and white photos used in this 66-card set. The copyright line on the reverse reads "1966" but these cards were issued in 1967 by the Philadelphia Chewing Gum Company. The card caption is located on the obverse, but everything else — the card number, text, and a "Pet Command" feature — appear on the back. The reverses are also puzzle pieces.

ITEM	MINT	EX
Set	95.00	75.00
Card	1.25	1.00
Wrapper	--	40.00
Box	--	90.00

43 Sick Call
44 Recovery Complete
45 Another Life Saved
46 Hello and Goodbye
47 Medical Marksman
48 Command Performance
49 High Riding Taxi
50 Leopard Collar Deluxe
51 Front Porch Pals
52 Chimp Nears Death
53 Dying Lion
54 Little Lively Leopards
55 Hello Hyena
56 No Way to Say Thank You
57 Walk into Danger
58 Grumpy Goat
59 Fully Recovered
60 How Do You Feel Today?
61 Lion Napper
62 Angry King
63 Ticklish?
64 Good to See You, Friend
65 Can I Help?
66 Meet My Doctor

1 Jungle Scientist	15 Monkey Business	29 Just Call Me Smiley
2 Jungle Miss	16 And Away We Go!	30 Spare That Spare
3 Able Assistant	17 Elephant Power	31 Tranquilized Zebra
4 Smile Please	18 Did you Say It's Dinnertime	32 Hospital Bound
5 Serious Medical Problems	19 Big Patient, Big Pain	33 No More Peanuts
6 Calling Wameru—Urgent!	20 Nurse's Little Helper	34 Rooster Roost
7 Don't Keep the Doctor Waiting	21 Hold Your Hat	35 Playful Pachyderm
8 It Won't Hurt	22 Parting Shot	36 The Pause That Refreshes
9 Dinnertime, Gang!	23 Jungle Search	37 Murder Suspect Subdued
10 Taking the Cat for a Walk	24 Under Attack	38 Hold on Tight
11 Alert to Danger	25 Natural Enemies Dine	39 Race for Survival
12 Sad-Eyed Departure	26 Sympathy for a Sick Tiger	40 Fancy Hood Ornament
13 Don't Be Afraid	27 Hold That Tiger!	41 You're Doing Fine
14 Clever and Cunning	28 Fighting Like Cats and Dogs	42 Don't Be a Bully

DALLAS (56)

DALLAS

2 1/2" X 3 1/2"

The super "Soap" of nighttime television was made into a card set by Donruss in 1981. The cards are printed on thin stock and the pictures, which are color photos from the TV show, are surrounded by red or blue borders. The cards are numbered 1-56 but are not captioned. The backs are puzzle pieces.

ITEM	MINT	EX
Set	8.00	5.00
Card	.15	.10
Wrapper	--	.35
Box	--	5.00

DALLAS COWBOYS CHEERLEADERS (30)

4 7/8" X 6 7/8"

Topps clearly envisioned more success for the Dallas Cowboy Cheerleader set than it actually achieved. The cards are marked "1981 Series"—as if this might become a yearly project—but the product was largely ignored by the public. The large blue paper wrapper has a checklist of 30 titles printed in a yellow panel on the back. The card fronts are giant glossy photos of the cheering squad; the backs contain, the series title, card caption, text, and card number.

ITEM	MINT	EX
Set	20.00	15.00
Card	.65	.50
Wrapper	--	1.00
Box	--	6.00

1 A Pensive Moment for Angela	16 Today Dallas...Tomorrow the World!
2 Always in Demand!	17 From Nervousness to Joy
3 Admired by Thousands!	18 Those Fabulous Fans
4 First-Rate All the Way!	19 For the Love of Sports
5 When the Going Gets Tough...	20 Poms Away!
6 The Right Stuff!	21 Up, Up and Away!
7 A Tirade of Talents!	22 Dancing Demands
8 No Rest for the Best!	23 This Year's Rookie, Next Year's Vet!
9 Cowboys' Two Minute Drill!	24 Three Cheers for America!
10 Beginnings	25 Behind Every Dark Cloud...
11 Next Stop...Television!	26 The Joy of Victory
12 Cheerleader Fever!	27 The Winning Look!
13 Cheer Up, Judy!	28 Time for a Quick Change!
14 Trim is "In"	29 For Openers...
15 The Mark of a Pro	30 Until Next Season...!

DANIEL BOONE (55?)

2 1/2" X 3 1/2"

COMING OUT OF HIDING

One of the scarcest of all the Topps issues, Daniel Boone was tested and withdrawn from the marketplace in 1965. The card fronts have black and white photos with black print captions below. The brown print backs contain the card number, caption, and a short text. The card photos were taken from the TV series, which debuted on NBC on Sept. 9, 1964. No wrapper or box has been reported and the set total is thought to be 55 cards.

ITEM	MINT	EX
Card	50.00	40.00

DARK CRYSTAL (78)   2 1/2" X 3 1/2"

The 78-card set of color photos from the motion picture "The Dark Crystal" was produced by Donruss in 1982. It is the first gum card set in many years to employ round (rather than square) edges and this should make the cards very durable. Each card has wide purple borders surrounding the picture on front and the text on back. The cards are numbered on the front at the bottom-right corner.

ITEM	MINT	EX
Set	10.00	6.00
Card	.15	.10
Wrapper	--	.35
Box	--	4.00

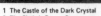

1 The Castle of the Dark Crystal	20 Aughra, Keeper of Secrets	39 The Making of a Pod Slave—I
2 The Skeksis Power Ceremony	21 Aughra's Observatory	40 The Making of a Pod Slave—II
3 The Mystic Ritual-Guardian	22 Aughra's Explanation	41 The Making of a Pod Slave—III
4 The Valley of the Standing Stones	23 Selecting the Shard	42 Essence, the Life-Force
5 The Mystic Scribe	24 Garthim Attack	43 The Skeksis Slave-Master
6 Jen the Gelfling	25 Jen's Escape	44 The Black River
7 The Dying Mystic Master	26 The Swamp	45 Crystal Bat
8 The Quest Begins	27 Fissgig	46 Jen, Kira, and Fizzgig
9 The Master's Funeral	28 Another Gelfling	47 Pod Village
10 The Skeksis Emperor's Death	29 Kira the Gelfling	48 Kira at Home
11 A Grab for Power	30 Jen's Dreamfast	49 Jen at Pod Village
12 The Dying Skeksis Emperor	31 Kira's Dreamfast	50 Jen and Ydra
13 The Emperor's Funeral	32 The Banqueting Hall	51 Garthim
14 The Skeksis Ritual-Master	33 An Unexpected Prisoner	52 Garthim Raid
15 The Battle of the Stone	34 Aughra in the Castle	53 Escaping the Garthim
16 The Skeksis Chamberlain	35 The Garthim-Master	54 In the Forest
17 The Skeksis Garthim-Master	36 Aughra in the Chamber of Life	55 The Gelfling Ruins
18 The Disgraced Chamberlain	37 Aughra's Eye	56 The Wall of Prophecy
19 Jen is Captured	38 Pod Slave	57 The Outcast Chamberlain
		58 The Trek of the Mystics

59 Kira Atop a Landstrider
60 Jen Rides a Landstrider
61 Landstrider Assault
62 Landstrider Defeat
63 No Exit
64 Flight to Safety
65 The Teeth of Skreesh
66 The Secret Tunnel
67 Kira's Capture
68 Kira in the Chamber of Life
69 The Mystics at the Castle
70 Jen in the Crystal Chamber
71 The Leap
72 The Lost Shard
73 Kira's Act of Heroism
74 Kira's Sacrifice
75 "The two made one, by Gelfling hand"
76 The Great Conjunction
77 The Mystics and the Dark Crystal
78 Harmony Restored

DARK SHADOWS—PINK (66)   2 1/2" X 3 1/2"

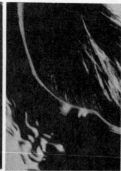

The borders on the cards in this Dark Shadows set are vibrant pink. There are 66 cards in the series, which was marketed by Philly Gum in 1968. The card number is located on the front of the card in the bottom left-hand corner. There are no captions and the backs, when all placed together, form a poster.

ITEM	MINT	EX
Set	400.00	325.00
Card	5.00	4.00
Wrapper	--	30.00
Box	--	175.00

The wrapper of the green-bordered Dark Shadows set has "2nd Series" marked in a diagonal line, but since the cards are marked 1-66 it would be more apt to call them a "new" series. The cards are captioned in a panel which is of the same deep pink color as the border of the "pink" series illustrated above. The card number is in the lower left corner, and the backs are poster pieces. Philly Gum distributed this set in 1969.

ITEM	MINT	EX
Set	400.00	325.00
Card	5.00	4.00
Wrapper	--	25.00
Box	--	175.00

1 Barnabas: "I must go back to the past to save the boy's life."
2 Barnabas: "We are dealing with a pagan thing."
3 Barnabas: "I have lived long, I doubt nothing."
4 Barnabas: "I have no answer to this terrible thing."
5 Barnabas: "Why is the ghost possessing Jamison?"
6 Barnabas: "I have no choice, I must find Quentin's secret."
7 Barnabas: "Go to Quentin's grave, see for yourself."
8 Judith: "When will Quentin rise again?"
9 Barnabas: "Quentin may yet live again."
10 Judith: "I can't look at him like this."
11 Barnabas: "Are you still a zombie, Quentin?"
12 Barnabas: "I've failed. He's not alive!"
13 Barnabas: "Come with me, Quentin, there is still hope."
14 Judith: "Quentin holds the key to my life."
15 Judith: "We poured cement over Quentin's coffin."
16 Judith: "Quentin's dead, yet walks the earth again."
17 Trask: "Good evening, I'm Gregory Trask."
18 Trask: "It's urgent the children leave Collinwood."
19 Trask: "We must protect the children from evil."
20 Judith: "No one can harm the children."
21 Judith: "But I saw them bury him myself."
22 Trask: "The Devil's work is beyond belief."
23 Trask: "Perhaps I can end this horrible situation."
24 Jamison: "I feel Quentin's body here."
25 Jamison: "I knew you'd come, Quentin."
26 Jamison: "Barnabas, is Quentin with you?"
27 Trask: "I sense an alien spirit here."
28 Trask: "A dead body that once was a man."

29 Trask: "The boy has nothing to fear from me."
30 Jamison: "Why am I in this cemetery."
31 Barnabas: "Take his hand in yours, Jamison."
32 Jamison: "I'm not Jamison, my name is Quentin."
33 Jamison: "His hand is so cold."
34 Jamison: "I want him to live again."
35 Jamison: "Spirit, depart from this body."
36 Barnabas: "I'm thinking of Barnabas Collins and when he lived."
37 Trask: "I must know the true facts to help him."
38 Barnabas: "It will take a miracle to save him now."
39 Jamison: "What is he going to do?"
40 Trask: "This boy is possessed by a giant evil force."
41 Quentin: "I'll die when the moon is full."
42 Quentin: "My spirit is in Jamison's body."
43 Quentin: "What strange power guides my life?"
44 Quentin: "Perhaps Barnabas knows the answer."
45 Quentin: "Am I a zombie? A walking dead man?"
46 Quentin: "There's my grave, my home."
47 Quentin: "Jamison, come to me, help me."
48 Quentin: "It's too late, my life is slipping away."
49 Quentin: "Judith, have you thought of murder?"
50 Quentin: "The gypsy was just speaking of you."
51 Dirk: "You have still another secret, Judith?"
52 Judith: "She must never leave this room...alive!"
53 Judith: "That music will drive me mad!"
54 Magda: "Quentin, you have no future."
55 Quentin: "You see the mark of death?"
56 Quentin: "Who will kill me? When? How?"
57 Magda: "Quentin, there is another world."
58 Quentin: "This will help you see the future better."
59 Jenny: "These aren't my dolls, they're my babies."
60 Jenny: "Quentin...Quentin..... is Quentin here?"
61 Jenny: "The keys! My keys to freedom!"
62 Jenny: "Where is he...where is Quentin?"
63 Werewolf: "I must hurry, dawn means death."
64 Carolyn: "Oh, please won't someone save me?"
65 Werewolf: "It must be this house...the curse of Collinwood!"
66 Werewolf: "What is happening to me?"

DARK SHADOWS GIANT PINUPS (16)   9 1/2" X 18 9/16"

Philly Gum was determined to capitalize on the Barnabas craze, so this poster set — 16 in number — was issued in 1969 in conjunction with their Dark Shadows card sets. Each poster has a black and white photo in an ornate green and purple frame design. A fac-simile autograph, printed in green ink, is found at the bottom. The number of the poster is printed in a small line at the bottom left.

ITEM	MINT	EX
Set	--	80.00
Pinup	--	4.00
Wrapper	--	12.00
Box	--	50.00

1 Reverend Trask
2 Quentin Collins
3 Charles Tate
4 Charity Trask
5 Judith Collins
6 Quentin Collins
7 The Men of Collinwood
8 Jamison Collins
9 Count Petoji
10 Barnabas
11 Edward Collins
12 Evon Hanley
13 Quentin Collins
14 Barnabas
15 Angelique
16 Magda

DARKWING DUCK ALBUM STICKERS (216)   2 9/16" X 2 1/8"

OK gang, here's the setup. Darkwing Duck and his sidekick, Launchpad McQuack, work for SHUSH!, an organization headed by J. Gander Hooter which fights against international espionage around the world. All of this spying seems to be the handiwork of the Fiendish Organization of World Larceny, or F.O.W.L. Panini's 1991 series of album stickers follows the exploits of Darkwing and Launch-pad as they battle F.O.W.L. in seven different adventures. All of the 216 stickers have complete or partial artwork and fit into spaces with corresponding numbers in the 32-page album. The color scheme of the 39¢ packet is two shades of purple with orange and red accents. As we went to press, Darkwing Duck packets (39¢) and albums (89¢) were still available in grocery and variety stores; complete sets offered by dealers are likely to cost in the $15-$18 range (album included).

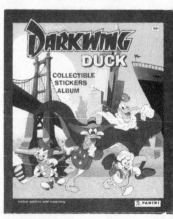

Darkwing Duck

D.C. COSMIC CARDS (180)

2 1/2" X 3 1/2"

The snappy advertising copy from Impel portrays DC Cosmic Cards as "good news and bad news all rolled into one." What the company means by this is that their new 180-card series contains "DC's all-time good guys and bad guys, from A to Z and old to new." In fact, there are more than 130 of "the most popular comic book characters of all time" in the set and the stylish artwork pictures are surrounded by elegant gray borders. The backs contain an "Identikit" profile of each character, a short story about one of his or her adventures, and a Q & A feature. Each card is clearly marked

"1992 Series 1" and is numbered in two different locations at upper right. According to Impel's press release, "ten out-of-this-world DC Hologram Hall of Fame Cards will be included in a limited number of randomly selected 12-card packs." These holograms are bonus cards and are not part of the regular set.

ITEM	MINT	EX
Card set	15.00	---
Card	.10	---
Hologram	3.00	---
Hologram set	35.00	---
Wrappers (each)	---	.10
Box	---	2.00

HERO HERITAGE
1 Golden Age Blue Beetle
2 Silver Age Blue Beetle
3 Modern Age Blue Beetle
4 Golden Age Flash
5 Silver Age Flash
6 Modern Age Flash
7 Golden Age Green Lantern
8 Silver Age Green Lantern
9 Modern Age Green Lantern
10 Golden Age Hawkman
11 Silver Age Hawkman
12 Modern Age Hawkman
13 Golden Age Shazam!
14 Silver Age Shazam!
15 Modern Age Shazam!
16 Golden Age Superman
17 Silver Age Superman
18 Modern Age Superman
19 Golden Age Wonder Woman
20 Silver Age Wonder Woman
21 Modern Age Wonder Woman

VILLAIN HERITAGE
22 Golden Age Cheetah
23 Silver Age Cheetah
24 Modern Age Cheetah
25 Golden Age Luthor
26 Silver Age Luthor
27 Modern Age Luthor
28 Golden Age Mr. Mxyzptlk
29 Silver Age Mr. Mxyzptlk
30 Modern Age Mr. Mxyzptlk

EARTH'S MIGHTIEST HEROES
31 Animal Man
32 Aqualad
33 Aquaman
34 Black Condor
35 Black Lightning
36 Blackhawk
37 Blue Devil
38 Booster Gold
39 Bronze Tiger
40 Changeling
41 The Creeper
42 Crimson Fox
43 Cyborg
44 Deathstroke The Terminator
45 Dove
46 Dr. Light
47 Elongated Man
48 Fire
49 Firehawk
50 Firestorm
51 Gangbuster
52 Geo-Force
53 The Guardian

54 Guy Gardner
55 Hawk
56 Hawkwoman
57 Hourman
58 Ice
59 Jade
60 John Stewart
61 Katana
62 Metamorpho
63 Mr. Bones
64 Nightshade
65 Nightwing
66 Northwind
67 Nuklon
68 Pantha
69 Peacemaker
70 Phantom Lady
71 Power Girl
72 Ragman
73 Raven
74 Rocket Red
75 Speedy
76 Troia
77 Vixen
78 Wildcat

EARTH'S MIGHTIEST VILLAINS
79 Amazo
80 Big Sir
81 Black Manta
82 Blockbuster
83 Bolt
84 Brainiac
85 Captain Boomerang
86 Chemo
87 Chronos
88 Copperhead
89 Count Vertigo
90 Deadline
91 Deadshot
92 Dr. Light
93 Dr. Polaris
94 Eclipso
95 Goldface
96 Gorilla Grodd
97 Houngan
98 Jericho
99 Kestrel
100 Monarch
101 Ocean Master
102 Parasite
103 Phobia
104 Plasmus
105 Psycho-Pirate
106 Shadow Thief
107 Silver Swan

108 Sonar
109 Toyman
110 Vandal Savage
111 Warp

HEROES FROM BEYOND
112 Adam Strange
113 Arisia
114 Big Barda
115 Black Racer
116 Fastbak
117 G'nort
118 Kilowog
119 Lightray
120 Lobo
121 Martian Manhunter
122 Metron
123 Mr. Miracle
124 Orion
125 Starfire

VILLAINS FROM BEYOND
126 Ares
127 Blackfire
128 Darkseid
129 Desaad
130 Despero
131 Glorious Godfrey
132 Granny Goodness
133 Kalibak
134 Kanjar Ro
135 Manga Khan
136 Maxima
137 Mr. Nebula
138 Sinestro
139 Starro
140 Steppenwolf
141 Yuga Khan

GREAT BATTLES
142 Crisis on Earths One and Two (A)
143 Crisis on Earths One and Two (B)
144 Crisis on Earths One and Two (C)
145 Crisis on Infinite Earths (A)
146 Crisis on Infinite Earths (B)
147 Crisis on Infinite Earths (C)
148 Legends (A)
149 Legends (B)
150 Legends (C)
151 Millenium (A)
152 Millenium (B)
153 Millenium (C)
154 Invasion! (A)
155 Invasion! (B)
156 Invasion! (C)
157 Cosmic Odyssey (A)
158 Cosmic Odyssey (B)
159 Cosmic Odyssey (C)
160 The Great Darkness Saga (A)
161 The Great Darkness Saga (B)
162 The Great Darkness Saga (C)
163 Armageddon 2001 (A)
164 Armageddon 2001 (B)
165 Armageddon 2001 (C)
166 War of the Gods (A)
167 War of the Gods (B)
168 War of the Gods (C)

CLASSIC COVERS
169 Action Comics #1
170 All-American Comics #16
171 All Star Comics #3
172 The Brave and The Bold #34
173 New Gods #1
174 Sensation Comics #1
175 Showcase #22
176 Showcase #34
177 Superman #1
178 Wonder Woman #1

CHECKLIST
179 Checklist #1
180 Checklist #2

DESERT STORM:

THE MOTHER OF ALL TRADING CARD THEMES   by Bill Mullins

At the end of 1991, when the media reviews the major events of the year, the War in the Persian Gulf will far and away be the leading story. The same could be said when reviewing the non-sport hobby. Nothing has attracted attention like Desert Storm cards since Garbage Pail Kids. No other event has been the subject of so many cards and sets since the Second World War. Within a six month period, over 1000 different Desert Shield and Desert Storm cards and stickers were issued by a dozen card manufacturers.

Topps, long the dominant force in trading cards, challengers like Pacific and Pro Set, and newcomers like Lime Rock and Spectra Star all manufactured Desert Storm sets. Card formats ranged from the "homegrown" artwork of sets like "Damn Saddam" and other Crown Sports releases to the slick photographic sets of Pro Set and DSI. Photographs came from a variety of sources: the Defense Department pool, military contractors, the wire services, free-lance photographers, etc., and a number of them were duplicated in various sets. Subject matter was both serious and comic. People, places, events, weapons, flags, and scenes, from the Allies and the enemy, were documented through the cards. Oddball items like variations, errors, multiple printings, insert and promotional cards showed up. While the focus of all sets was on the war, Desert Storm demonstrated how diverse the non-sport hobby can be.

The war happened to occur at a time when the trading card industry had about run out of ideas. In addition to the traditional "big four" of baseball, football, basketball, and hockey, the last few years have seen sports sets for golf, tennis, bowling, deer hunting, bass fishing, boxing, all types of motor sports, and horse racing. Even without the war cards, 1991 has seen more non-sport sets issued than in any time in recent memory. Card companies old and new were looking for new projects when world events sent the largest military power in the world across the globe to wage war — a war featuring heroic leadership and dastardly enemies, and space age weapons against ditches filled with burning oil. Given the circumstances, it is amazing that so few Desert Storm cards were issued!

Several of the major sets captured the attention of baseball cards dealers like no other non-sport set in recent memory: significant quantities of cards, particularly Topps 1st Series Desert Storm, were purchased for reasons ranging from curiosity to investment / speculation. Some dealers even displayed a growing awareness of the non-sport hobby. After the initial surge of interest died down and serious collectors completed their sets, a great deal of unsold material was left, ensuring that most of the Desert Storm issues would be available in the marketplace for some time to come.

The various Desert Storm sets attracted a great deal of attention from both local and national media. Stories and news segments appeared on network and cable news shows, in USA Today, and Money magazine, and were matched by hometown coverage in small newspapers, on radio, and on UHF television. Nearly all of the sports and non-sports card magazines carried articles and press releases as the different sets were issued. Several publications also printed letters from irate collectors who vowed to boycott Topps and every other company who sought to profit by issuing Gulf War cards. The editorial responses by sports card magazines to such letters were hardly adequate, demonstrating a disturbing lack of knowledge about the history of non-sport cards.

Since the introduction of trading cards in the late 1800's, sets of "war cards" have been released in commemoration of, and often contemporaneous with, the armed conflicts of mankind. Several sets have pictured the soldiers and weapons of wars throughout history (for example, Allen & Ginter's tobacco card set "Arms of All Nations"). Cards have also been issued for specific wars including the Civil War, The Spanish-American War, World War I, the Spanish Civil War, World War II, the Korean War, the Cold War, and the Viet Nam conflict. [It is interesting to note that it took more than a decade for a Viet Nam set to be issued, and that a Canadian company performed the deed.] None of these sets glorify war and its horrors, but many do reflect the attitudes of society at the time of issue, when national pride demanded that enemies be described in brutal and racist terms. Almost all of the war cards of the twentieth century were issued concurrently with the hostilities they portrayed and all are prized by collectors, not only for their artwork and text, but also because they, like sports cards, form a collectible means of documenting their respective subjects. In years to come, hobbyists will hold the best of the Desert Storm sets in the same high regard.

The collector who aims to complete a full run of all the Desert Storm cards has a tall mountain to climb. Not all of the cards referring to the war are found in the sets we have listed below. Some card producers acknowledged the war in their sports sets: Score's 1991 baseball card #737 has a U.S. flag and a patriotic message, for example, and Topps printed ten million 1991 baseball cards with "Operation Desert Shield" logos on front for shipment to the Persian Gulf. Pro Set's Winston Cup series of stock cars (1991) showed five cars from the 1991 Daytona 500 race which honored the five branches of the armed forces. One Pro Set 1991 football card showed servicemen watching the Super Bowl on TV and another one portrayed Whitney Houston's amazing rendition of the National Anthem. In addition to these sports issues, there were Desert Storm sets manufactured in England, France, Australia / New Zealand, and Portugal, and there may be other foreign series that have not yet come to our attention.

All of the Desert Storm sets which fit the traditional "non-sports" classification are checklisted and priced below. No single card prices are given where cards were sold only as sets. Although prices were demand-driven and speculative early on, especially in respect to Topps 1st series cards, the market for the most part has established reasonable values based on supply. With the exception of the promotional, variation, and special insert cards, none of the items listed should be too difficult to find, since all appear to have been printed in quantities sufficient to satisfy both the collector market and the general public.

Bill Mullins is a member of the Sport Americana Non-Sport Advisory Board. Comments and information about Desert Storm cards are welcome and should be addressed to Bill at P.O. Box 16164, Huntsville, AL 35802.

DAMN SADDAM — THE WACKY IRAQI (36)   2 1/2" X 3 1/2"

SCUM ON A SCUD

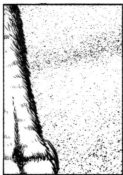

This set of 36 black and white artwork cards, issued by Potshot Productions, was sold in complete sets only. The series features insulting cartoons about Saddam Hussein, some of which are risque. The backs of the cards are picture puzzle pieces which form a drawing of a camel relieving himself on the dictator of Iraq. The cards are not numbered and many are not formally captioned, so no checklist is provided. No wrapper or packaging have been seen.

ITEM	MINT	EX
Set	10.00	7.00

In chronological terms, "Defenders of Freedom," a 144-card series issued by Historical Images, is the latest entry to the pantheon of Desert Storm sets. Given the advantage of time and perspective, you might expect this set to contain something new and exciting, or at least, interesting. However, only about 30% of the cards actually picture events in the theater of operations; the rest are the usual Pentagon press pool photos of equipment and

training exercises. Moreover, the "in country" images include five blown-up Iraqi T-72 tanks, five different shots of burning oil wells, and the obligatory camel. Defenders of Freedom was distributed in 36-pack boxes and each gumless pack contained eight cards. Some reports of spotty collation have been received but the box I opened contained one full set plus part of another (as the manufacturer specified it would). This set is an

example of another problem posed for collectors by the now-numerous small companies producing trading cards: the company's profit is made up front on case sales and the company, not the marketplace, sets the retail price. Compared to other Desert Storm sets, "Defenders of Freedom" may not seem such a good deal at the asking price of $25 per set, but collectors who feel compelled to add it to their Persian Gulf anthology will no doubt ante up.

1 B-1 Bomber
2 CH-47 Chopper
3 F-15 Eagle Soars
4 Phantom Refuels
5 B-52's On Flightline
6 B-52 On Line
7 B-52H Takes Off
8 EF-111A Raven
9 M-9 Beretta Pistols
10 F-16 Falcon Tail
11 E-3 AWACS at Sundown
12 F-16 Hangars
13 Destroyed T-72
14 Loading M-2 Bradley
15 Kuwait Airport
16 Oil Fields Afire
17 Hussein's Legacy
18 Oil Fields Burn

19 Dead in the Sand
20 U.S. 7th Corps Rolls
21 Hueys
22 Gen. Schwarzkopf & Prince Khalid
23 Cease Fire Talks
24 Gen. Schwarzkopf Makes a Point
25 Ordinance Disposal
26 Barracks Destroyed
27 Out of Control
28 Borgan Magwa
29 Loading USNS Cuato
30 Patriot Missile Launcher
31 1st Cav. Colorguard
32 UH-1 Iroquois
33 Victim of U.S. 7th Corps.
34 Multiple Launch Rocket System
35 Destroyed Iraqi APC
36 Desert Victim
37 Awarding Medals
38 Gen. Powell
39 Charleston Welcome
40 Daily Duties
41 Kuwaiti "V" Sign
42 Iraqi Gun Emplacement
43 Kuwaiti Troops
44 Damaged Hangar
45 Hangar Doors Kayoed
46 AVC Shelters Damaged
47 Air Base Damaged
48 Iraqi Choppers Damaged
49 Damaged SU-17
50 Damaged Iraqi Plane
51 Damage At Tallil
52 Iraqi Tank Smashed
53 Security Police
54 Protective Mask
55 Fire Team
56 M16A2
57 Carrier Power
58 C-5A Galaxy
59 USS Eisenhower
60 The Eagle Lifts Off
61 C-130 On Runway
62 Old Reliable F-4
63 Avenger
64 Sea Knights Take Off
65 M-1A1 Abrams MBT
66 Apache Tank Killer
67 Patriot Missile
68 Decontamination
69 Harrier Jet Landing
70 USS Missouri
71 General Powell Inspects
72 M-2 Bradley
73 Night Vision
74 M-60 Main Battle Tank
75 M-109 155 mm SP Howitzer
76 M-60 Tank
77 B-52 Refuels
78 F-14 Tomcat Roars
79 M-9 Ace
80 USS Iowa-16" Guns

81 Tomahawk Missile
82 USS Texas
83 Hercules Takes Off
84 M998 (HMMWV)
85 M-198 Howitzer
86 Gen. Schwarzkopf
87 Chaparral Missile
88 Hawk Missile
89 F-16 Fighting Falcons
90 AH-64A Apache
91 M-1 Tank
92 Multiple Launch Rocket System
93 Pack of Warthogs
94 C-130 Hercules
95 Stealth Mission
96 Stealth Refuels
97 M-113 APC
98 AV-88 Harrier II
99 B-1 Bomber
100 USS Conolly
101 USS Jarrett
102 USS Iowa
103 AH-1S Huey Cobra
104 M-1A1 Abrams
105 B-2 Stealth Top View
106 F-4 Phantom Lurks
107 OH-58C Scout
108 Ready for Action
109 A-10 Warthog
110 AWACS in Saudi
111 AWACS Protection
112 B-1 Swing Wing
113 Full Back Pack
114 F-111's
115 Flight of A-10 Warthogs
116 Pair of F-16 Falcons
117 Soldier and Mortar
118 F-16 Loaded for Bear
119 F-4 on Approach
120 M-60 Tank in Saudi
121 Chemical / Biological Protection
122 Tomahawk Cruise Missile
123 Ship of the Desert
124 82nd Abn. Div. Physical Training
125 Troops Fill Sandbags
126 F-18 Hornet Buzzes
127 A-7D Corsair II
128 Falcons on the Roll
129 Bronco Soars
130 OV-10A Bronco
131 A-6 Intruder Takes Off
132 Lance Missile
133 C-130 Ninja Turtle
134 Falcon on the Prowl
135 F-14 Tomcat
136 A-6 Intruders
137 F-18 Hornet Landing
138 T-30 Talon
139 USS Virginia
140 Twin F-16 Falcons
141 Tomcat on the Prowl
142 USS Hewitt
143 82nd Abn. Division Trains Checklist

The distinction of having the largest single-series Desert Storm set goes to Pro Set, whose 250 cards feature leaders, military skills, countries involved in the conflict, and other topics related to the war. The cards are full color on front and back, with desert camouflage backgrounds and accents. They were issued in poly bags, with ten cards per bag and 36 bags per box. The bags were heat sealed and could not be opened without damage, so the price listed below for "wrapper" pertains to a neatly trimmed bag. Nine unnumbered prototype cards were distributed to dealers to promote the set (see list below). These prototype cards have the same pictures as their counterparts in the regular set, but are unnumbered and some have different titles and text. A checklist sheet (8-1/2" x 11") with photo credits and a bibliography for the information presented on the cards was available free via the mail.

Pro Set also produced two special edition boxed sets of Desert Storm. The first was sold only at service commissaries and contains six additional cards not included in the regular set. The second variety of boxed set featured boxes with serial numbers and the autograph of Pro Set president Lud Denny, plus a three dimensional, lucite version of the dove card, complete with stand. Quantities of both types of boxed sets were limited and prices for each are speculative at this time.

ITEM	MINT	EX
Set	20.00	14.00
Card	.10	.07
Commissary set	Speculative	
Signed set	Speculative	
Prototype cards	Speculative	
Wrapper	--	.10
Display box	--	2.00
Paper checklist	1.00	.75

GEOGRAPHY
1 Afghanistan
2 Argentina
3 Australia
4 Austria
5 Baghdad
6 Bahrain
7 Bangladesh
8 Basra
9 Belgium
10 Bulgaria
11 Canada
12 China
13 Czechoslovakia
14 Denmark
15 Diego Garcia
16 Egypt
17 Finland
18 France
19 Germany
20 Greece
21 Honduras
22 Hungary
23 Iceland
24 Iran
25 Iraq
26 Israel
27 Italy
28 Japan
29 Jerusalem
30 Jordan
31 Kuwait
32 The City of Kuwait
33 Lebanon
34 Libya
35 Luxembourg
36 Malaysia
37 Morocco
38 Netherlands
39 New Zealand
40 Niger
41 Norway
42 Oman
43 Pakistan
44 Persian Gulf
45 Philippines
46 Poland
47 Portugal
48 Qatar
49 Riyadh
50 Saudi Arabia
51 Senegal
52 Sierra Leone
53 South Korea
54 Soviet Union
55 Spain
56 Sweden
57 Syria
58 Taiwan
59 Tel Aviv
60 Turkey
61 U.A.E.
62 United Kingdom
63 United States
64 Washington, D.C.
65 Yemen

PROTOTYPES
Header / Set Title
F-117A Stealth Fighter
The Rt Hon John Major
Radio Alphabet
United States Air Force
General Colin L. Powell
United Kingdom
Canada
United Nations

LEADER
66 Brian Mulroney
67 Ali Akbar Hashemi
   Rafsanjani
68 Tariq Aziz
69 Saddam Hussein
70 Yitzhak Shamir
71 His Majesty King Hussein I
72 Sheik Jaber al-Ahmed
   al-Sabah
73 King Fahd Bin 'Abdulaziz
74 Mikhail Gorbachev
75 Hafez al-Assad
76 John Major
77 Javier Perez de Cuellar
78 James Baker
79 George Herbert Walker Bush
80 Richard B. Cheney
81 Marlin Fitzwater
82 General Alfred M. Gray
83 Lieutenant General
   Charles A. Horner
84 Margaret Hilda Thatcher
85 Admiral Frank B. Kelso II
86 General Merrill A. McPeak
87 Brigadier General
   Richard I. Neal
88 General Colin L. Powell
89 General H. Norman
   Schwarzkopf

GOVERNMENT
90 Canadian Executive Branch
91 Canadian National Anthem
92 Canadian System
93 Iraqi System
94 Kuwait System

95 Saudi Arabia System
96 United Nations History
97 United Nations Organization
98 United Nations Resolutions
99 United Nations Sanctions
100 United Nations Security
    Council
101 United Kingdom System
102 Central Intelligence
    Agency
103 Congress
104 U.S. Constitution
105 Department of Defense
106 Pentagon
107 Judicial System
108 National Anthem
109 National Security Act
110 The Pledge of Allegiance
111 President and Cabinet
112 Department of State

PERSONNEL
113 Fire Fighters
114 Military Police
115 Radar Operators
116 The Chaplains' Corps
117 The Infantryman
118 United States Air Force
119 United States Army
120 United States Coast Guard
121 United States Marine
    Corps
122 United States Navy
123 United States Air
    Force Academy
124 U.S. Marine Warrior

125 United States Military
    Academy at West Point
126 U.S. Naval Academy
127 U.S. Navy Seals

INTELLIGENCE FILE
128 Amphibious Assault
129 Arabic Language
130 Arab League
131 Chemical/Biological
    Warfare
132 Christianity
133 Chronology of Events
134 Conserving Energy
135 Dog Tags
136 Donating Blood
137 Islam
138 Journalism
139 Judaism
140 Mideast Greeting Customs
141 Middle East History
    Colonial
142 Middle East History
    Present
143 Middle East History
    Ancient
144 Oil
145 Palestinians
146 Reconnaissance
147 Red Cross
148 Reserves
149 Rank
150 United Service
    Organization
151 Yellow Ribbons

MILITARY SKILL
152 Camouflage
153 Collect/Report Information
154 Courtesy
155 Discipline
156 Education
157 First Aid
158 Fitness
159 Greenwich Mean Time
160 Hand Signals
161 Health & Hygiene
162 Heroes Don't Do Drugs
163 Inspection
164 Latitude and Longitude
165 Map Reading
166 Women in Combat
167 Military Time
168 Moon Phases
169 Navigation
170 Noise, Light & Litter
   Discipline
171 Phonetic Alphabet
172 Range
173 Recognition Cards
174 Survival
175 Teamwork

MILITARY ASSET
176 USS Blue Ridge (LCC-19)
177 Kilauea Class Ammunition
   Ship (AE)
178 USS England (CG-22)
179 USS Inchon (LPH-12)
180 USS John F. Kennedy
   (CV-67)
181 USS Midway (CV-41)
182 USS Wisconsin (BB-64)
183 USS Theodore
   Roosevelt (CVN-71)
184 USS Saratoga (CV-60)

185 USS Ranger (CV-61)
186 USS Richmond K.
   Turner (CG-20)
187 USS Missouri (BB-63)
188 Aggressive Class
   Mine Sweeper (MS0)
189 Farragut Class
   Destroyer (DDG)
190 USNS Hospital Ship (TAH)
191 Knox Class Frigate (FF)
192 Newport Class Tank
   Landing Ship (LST)
193 USS America (CV-66)
194 Ticonderoga Class
   Cruiser (CG)
195 Spruance Class
   Destroyer (DD)
196 Oliver Hazard Perry
   Class Frigate (FFG)
197 LCAC
198 M60 Machine Gun
199 M2/M3 Bradley
   Fighting Vehicle
200 T-62 Main Battle Tank
201 Challenger Main Battle
   Tank
202 T-72 Main Battle Tank
203 AMX-30 Tank
204 Multiple Launch
   Rocket System (MLRS)
205 M109 DSWS Howitzer
206 M113 Armored
   Personnel Carrier
207 M998 Hummer
208 M1 Main Battle Tank
209 M1A1 Abrams Tank
210 M551 Sheridan
211 M60 Main Battle Tank
212 F1M-92A Stinger
213 Hawk Guided Missile
   System

214 M1M-104 Patriot
215 Tomahawk Cruise
   Missile
216 SS-1C Scud B/C
217 AIM-9 Sidewinder
218 AGM-65 Maverick
219 M220A1 TOW
220 FB-111 Aardvark
221 F-14 Tomcat
222 F-15 Eagle
223 F-16 Fighting Falcon
224 F-4G Wild Weasel
225 F/A-18 Hornet
226 KC-10A Extender
227 MIG-21 Fishbed
228 MIG-23 Flogger
229 Mirage 2000
230 UH-1 Iriquois
231 UH-60A Black Hawk

232 Tornado
233 F-117A Stealth
   Fighter
234 C-5 Galaxy
235 A-7 Corsair
236 A-10 Thunderbolt II
237 A-6 Intruder
238 AH-1 Cobra
239 AH-64 Apache
240 AV-8B Harrier II
241 B-52 Stratofortress
242 C-130 Hercules
243 C-141B Starlifter
244 CH-46 Sea Knight
245 CH-47D Chinook
246 E-2C Hawkeye
247 E-3 Sentry AWACS
248 EA-6B Prowler
249 Bombs
250 Peace

DESERT STORM — 1ST SERIES (88/22)   2 1/2" X 3 1/2"

Of all the Gulf War sets, the three series issued by Topps have received the most attention, both in the media and from dealers and collectors. The first series, entitled "Desert Storm," began distribution only a few days after the commencement of hostilities, and the rapidity with which it was produced is evident in the various errors that appeared in the first printing. The novelty of the cards and the great commercial advantage Topps gained by being the first major producer to market a Gulf War set, have muted the criticism which the company justifiably deserves for creating so many errors and variations on the cards. In all, Topps distributed five distinct print runs of first series Desert Storm.

The first two printings had brown letters in the "Desert Storm" logos which appear on the wrapper, the cards, and (only) on sticker #17; these are designated "1PB" [1st printing/brown] and "2PB" [2nd printing/brown] in the descriptions below. After only a few weeks, a third printing appeared in which the brown letters of the Desert Storm logos were changed to yellow. This run,

designated "3PY" [3rd printing/yellow], is identical to brown letter run 2PB except for the new color of the letters. In a fourth print run, designation "4PY" [4th printing/yellow], Topps finally got around to correcting some of the errors which appeared in 1PB, 2PB, and 3PY. The fifth run, labelled "5PY" [5th printing/yellow], was a boxed "Deluxe Collectors' Edition" printed on glossy stock. This final edition contained corrections for two more error cards which had not been rectified in previous print runs: straightening out Cheney's biography on card #3 and properly identifying the aircraft on card #19 as a Harrier, not a Tornado.

The same set of 22 stickers accompanied the cards of all five printings. These depict the insignia of divisions active in the conflict, the Congressional Medal of Honor, the Desert Storm logo, service and command logos, and two American flags. The only known variation among the stickers is #17, which was issued with brown letters in 1PB and 2PB and with yellow letters in all subsequent printings. The brown letter #17

Desert Storm — 1st Series

sticker is the KEY to completing any brown letter set; brown letter sets with yellow letter #17 stickers cannot be considered as legitimate 1PB or 2PB sets. All the stickers of the Deluxe Collectors' Edition have a slightly different surface finish than the stickers issued in wax packs, but collectors are not likely to encounter these as singles.

The first four print runs of Desert Storm were all issued in wax packages. Sets 1PB and 2PB were distributed in wax packs with brown letter logos and the wrapper code 0-459-21-01-1. Sets 3PY and 4PY came in yellow letter packs with the wrapper code 0-459-21-02-1. The display boxes also came in brown and yellow letter varieties.

In light of the errors confirmed to exist so far in Topps' first series Desert Storm, it is likely that collectors will continue examining the photographs and print of each and every card in hopes of discovering more anomalies. Collector Richard Laino, for example, has reported finding a #7, yellow-letter McPeak card with a Gabriel biography on back. Moreover, at some point in time, Topps aired a television ad offering a Deluxe Collectors' Edition of Desert Storm in a red, white & blue box and a Desert Storm Binder containing plastic pages to house the set, along with four 11" X 14" prints ("Sea," "Land," "Air," and a map). This has yet to turn up at any convention as of this writing.

BROWN CAMOUFLAGE LETTERS   YELLOW LETTERS

1 The Commander in Chief
2 General Colin Powell
3 Secretary of Defense Dick Cheney
4 General H. Norman Schwarzkopf
5 General Richard G. Graves
6 Admiral Frank Kelso
7 Chief of Staff Charles Gabriel
8 Stallion Helicopter
9 CH-53 Helicopter
10 SH-60B Helicopter
11 AH-64 Apache
12 CH-47 Chinook
13 UH-1 Huey Navy Bell
14 CH-53 Super Stallion
15 Helicopter Formation
16 Cobra 'Copter
17 Canadian Air Force CF-18
18 French Mirage Fighter
19 Britain's Tornado
20 State of the Art Stealth Fighter Bomber
21 F-117A Stealth
22 F-14 Flies in Formation
23 Phoenix Missiles on F-14
24 Pilots-Eye View
25 B-52 Stratofortress
26 Ready for Takeoff
27 Flying High — The F-18
28 Taking off in an F-18
29 An F-18 Waits to Fly

30 Wild Blue Yonder
31 Wings Over Egypt
32 The Amazing AV-8B Harrier
33 The Sentry — An E3A
34 A-10s in Formation
35 EA-6B Prowler
36 F-111 Bombers
37 F-15 Fighter Plane
38 M-2 Bradley Tank
39 Manning the M-110
40 Tanks Take a Strong Hold
41 Sunset on the Desert
42 Lining up the Tanks
43 M-1 Abrams
44 Hummer Land Vehicle
45 TOW Anti-Tank Gun
46 The Power of the Tomahawk
47 Tomahawk Missile in Flight
48 The Patriot Missile
49 The Sidewinder Missile
50 Scud Missile (A)
51 Scud Missile (B)
52 HAWK Missile
53 Phoenix Missile
54 Army Supply Ship
55 Carrier Plane at Night
56 USS Midway
57 USS America
58 Destroyers
59 USS Iowa
60 USS Wisconsin
61 USS Ouellet Frigate
62 Moving In
63 Night Vision Goggles
64 F-18 Cockpit
65 At the Controls
66 Patriot Control Center
67 Aegis Control Center
68 Airborne Unit
69 Preparing to Jump
70 Paratrooper in Flight
71 Anti-Aircraft Chemical Gear

72 Satellite Dish
73 Machine Gunner
74 Marine Firefighters
75 Ready in the Cockpit
76 Wearing the Gas Mask
77 Patriot Missile Command Center
78 Machine Guns Ready
79 Mid-Air Refueling
80 In Flight with A-7s
81 The View from Above
82 Mission Accomplished
83 Dawn in the Desert
84 Heat Storm in the Gulf
85 A Quiet Moment
86 Sunset on the F-14
87 The Pentagon
88 Checklist

STICKERS
1 American Flag
2 37th Field Artillery
3 75th Infantry
4 8th Field Artillery
5 320th Field Artillery
6 73rd Armor
7 504th Infantry
8 34th Armor
9 506th Infantry
10 48th Infantry
11 41st Field Artillery
12 503rd Infantry
13 17th Cavalry
14 62nd Air Defense Artillery
15 6th Field Artillery
16 2nd Infantry
17 Desert Storm Logo
18 U.S. Air Force Emblem
19 Congressional Medal of Honor
20 U.S. Navy
21 U.S. Central Command
22 American Flag

VALUES FOR SETS, CARDS, WRAPPERS, AND ANOMALIES IN TOPPS' 1ST SERIES DESERT STORM

KEY:
1PB...1st print run, brown letters in logo.
2PB...2nd print run, brown letters in logo.
3PY...3rd print run, yellow letters in logo.
4PY...4th print run, yellow letters in logo.

SET PRICES:

Set 1 PB...Brown letters in card logos; Card #73 lists 16 countries on back; Sticker #17 has brown letters in logo; 88 cards & 22 stickers: $42 mint ($30 excellent).

Set 2PB...Brown letters in card logos; Card #73 lists 14 countries on back; Sticker #17 has brown letters in logo; 88 cards & 22 stickers: $32 mint ($24 excellent).

Set 3PY...Same as 2PB, EXCEPT letters in card logos are yellow; Sticker #17 has yellow letters in logo; 88 cards & 22 stickers: $15 mint ($10 excellent).

Set 4PY...Same as 3PY, EXCEPT cards 7-33-55-58-88 are revised and card #73 has no spaces where deleted countries were removed from list; Sticker #17 has yellow letters in logo; 88 cards & 22 stickers: $20 mint ($15 excellent).

CARD VALUES:

(1) All cards with brown letter logos EXCEPT the celebrities, demand cards, & anomalies listed below: 15¢ mint (10¢ excellent).

(2) All cards with yellow letter logos EXCEPT the celebrities, demand cards, & anomalies listed below: 10¢ mint (7¢ excellent).

STICKER VALUES:

(1) All stickers EXCEPT #17 with brown letters in logo: 25¢ mint (20¢ excellent);

(2) Sticker #17 with brown letters in logo: $7.00 mint ($5.00 excellent).

WRAPPER VALUES:

(1) "Desert Storm" in brown letters (1PB & 2PB), wrapper code = 0-459-21-01-1): 35¢.

(2) "Desert Storm" in yellow letters (3PY & 4PY), wrapper code = 0-459-21-02-1): 15¢.

"CELEBRITY" & "DEMAND" CARDS:

(1) Brown letters in logo:
#1 Bush $2.00 mint ($1.00 excellent);
#2 Powell $1.00 mint (50¢ excellent);
#4 Schwarzkopf $4.00 mint ($3.00 excellent);
#48 Patriot   50¢ mint (35¢ excellent);
#50 Scud   50¢ mint (35¢ excellent);
#51 Scud   50¢ mint (35¢ excellent).

(2) Yellow letters in logo:
#1 Bush $1.00 mint (75¢ excellent);
#2 Powell   50¢ mint (35¢ excellent);
#4 Schwarzkopf $2.00 mint ($1.50 excellent);
#48 Patriot   25¢ mint (20¢ excellent);
#50 Scud   25¢ mint (20¢ excellent);
#51 Scud   25¢ mint (20¢ excellent).

ANOMALIES:

#3 Incorrectly states that Secretary of Defense Dick Cheney was a congressman from Nebraska (should have read Wyoming). This card was finally corrected in the Deluxe Collectors' Edition, but not on the regular issue cards. The incorrect card, therefore, has no special value.

#7 (1) Pictures Charles Gabriel, brown letters in logo (1PB & 2PB), value: 50¢ mint (35¢ excellent).
(2) Pictures Charles Gabriel, yellow letters in logo (3PY), value: 25¢ mint (20¢ excellent);
(3) Pictures Merrill McPeak, yellow letters in logo (4PY), value: $1.50 mint ($1.00 excellent).

#8 Reads "HH53B only" — the word "only" should not be there. Not corrected, no special value.

#19 The jet pictured on all regular issue cards is a Harrier Jump Jet, not a Tornado. This was not corrected EXCEPT in the Deluxe Collectors' Edition. No special value.

Desert Storm — 1st Series

Card #19 also has a vertical blue line which appears in part or whole on some cards, and not at all on others, between the words "and" and "dump" in the text. This is a printing process anomaly and it has no special value.

#20 In the second-to-last line of text, the word "within" is misspelled "withing." Not corrected, no special value.

#33 (1) The backs of brown letter logo cards (1PB & 2PB) read "An EA-3B Sentry" — no special value;
   (2) The backs of 3rd printing yellow letter logo cards (3PY) read "An EA-3B Sentry" — no special value;
   (3) The backs of 4th printing yellow letter logo cards (4PY) read "An E3A Sentry" — value: $1.00 mint (75¢ excellent).

#55 All cards have the same text on the back, but the captions differ:
   (1) Brown letter logo cards (1PB & 2PB) ... front caption reads "Carrier Plane at Night" ... back caption is "Aircraft Carrier" — no special value;
   (2) Yellow letter logo cards of the 3rd printing (3PY) have the same captions as (1) — no special value;
   (3) Yellow letter logo cards of the 4th printing (4PY) have the same caption, "Carrier Ship at Night," front and back; value: $1.00 mint (75¢ excellent).

#58 (1) Brown letter logo cards (1PB & 2PB) have "Destroyers" caption on front and "Destroyer Ships" caption on back — no special value.
   (2) Yellow letter logo cards of the 3rd printing (3PY) have the same front & back captions as (1) — no special value;
   (3) Yellow letter logo cards of the 4th printing (4PY) have the caption "Frigates" front and back and the text describes frigates — value: $1.00 mint (75¢ excellent).

#60 On cards of all print runs, the fourth sentence of the text ends with the word "mem." No special value.

#63 (1) On brown letter logo cards (1PB & 2PB), the last word in the text is "vision." No special value.
   (2) On yellow letter logo cards of the 3rd printing (3PY), the last word in the text is "vision." No special value.
   (3) On yellow letter logo cards of the 4th printing (4PY), the last word in the text is "missions." Value: $1.00 mint (75¢ excellent).

#73 (1) Brown letter logo cards of the 1st printing (1PB) have 16 countries listed on the back. Value: $10.00 mint ($8.00 excellent).
   (2) Brown letter logo cards of the 2nd printing (2PB) have 14 countrires listed & spaces where two countries, France and Bulgaria, were deleted. Value: $3.00 mint ($2.25 excellent).
   (3) Yellow letter logo cards of the 3rd printing (3PY) have 14 countries & spaces where France and Bulgaria were deleted. Value: $1.00 mint (75¢ excellent).
   (4) Yellow letter logo cards of the 4th printing (4PY) have 14 countries listed and there are NO spaces where France and Bulgaria used to be. Value: $2.00 mint ($1.50 excellent).

#88 (1) Checklists of 1PB, 2PB and 3PY all list the following:
   #7..."Chief of Staff General Charles Gabriel"
   #55..."Carrier Plane at Night"
   #58..."Destroyers"
   (2) Checklists of 4PY list the following changes:
   #7..."Chief of Staff General Merrill McPeak"
   #55..."Carrier Ship at Night"
   #58..."Frigates"
   NOTE: All checklists say that #21 is "F-177A" although the card actually is captioned "F117A."

137

DESERT STORM — "VICTORY" (88/11)   2 1/2" X 3 1/2"

The Gulf War, and much of the mania over Gulf War cards, was over by the time Topps released the second series of Desert Storm. The cards, numbered 89-176, have darker desert camouflage borders on the front than first series cards and the back format is an exuberant mix of red, white, & blue colors and designs. Variations have been reported for card #'s 140, 142, 148, 157, & 160. Of these, only the so-called "smiling Schwarzkopf" has attracted any attention, and it is selling in the $2-$3 range. The eleven stickers show flags of coalition members on front and have "puzzle C" picture piece backs. The wrapper is basically yellow, with a blue panel at bottom and red lettering at top (wrapper code = 0-459-21-03-1). Note: set price includes stickers.

ITEM	MINT	EX
Set	15.00	11.00
Card	.10	.07
Sticker	.35	.25
Wrapper	—	.15
Box	—	2.00

89 Stinger Missile
90 Carpet Bombing*
91 Rolling Out
92 M-551 Sheridan
93 M-2 Bradley Fighting Vehicle
94 Laying An M-21 Mine
95 Machine Gun
96 M-1s Move Out
97 The Mighty M-1A1
98 TOW Missile
99 HMMWV - The Hummer*
100 LAV - Light Armored Vehicle
101 Iraq's Scud Missile
102 Battleship Cannons
103 LCAC
104 A-6 Intruder
105 Dragon Missile Launcher
106 M-60's Reactive Armor
107 M-109 Howitzer
108 F-16 Fighter/Bomber
109 F-15 Eagle
110 F-14 Fighter
111 F-4 Phantom
112 A-7 Avenger
113 Wild Weasel

114 The Agile F-14
115 F-16 Fighting Falcon
116 F/A-18 Hornet
117 F-15 Dual-Role Eagle
118 A-10 Warthog*
119 Stealth F-117A*
120 USS Eisenhower
121 USS Longbeach
122 USS Wisconsin
123 USS Goldsborough
124 Marine APCs
125 CH-47 Chinook
126 USS Sides
127 Desert Hawk*
128 Apache Attack 'Copter
129 The Cobra*
130 UH-60A
131 Chaparral Missile Launch System
132 F/A-18 Fighter
133 F-111 Aardvark*
134 Tried & True B-52
135 B-52 In Formation*
136 AV-8B Harrier
137 Prowler - The EA-6B*
138 KC-10 — The Flying Gas Can
139 E-3 AWACS

140 What Is A Tank?
141 Unit Sizes - A
142 Unit Sizes - B
143 Military Terms - A
144 Military Terms - B
145 Desert Storm Slang
146 Allied Forces
147 Working Together
148 Becoming a Fighter Pilot
149 Top Gun
150 LVTP
151 The Marines Land
152 Harpoon Launch
153 Medical Support
154 Desert Drink
155 In The Cockpit
156 Mail Call
157 Gen. Schwarzkopf
158 Gen. Powell & Sec. Cheney
159 Lt. Gen. Horner
160 Lt. Gen. Kelly
161 Gen. Yeosock
162 Paratroopers Land
163 Multi-Launch Rocket System
164 AH-64 Apache Helicopter

165 Bomb's-Eye View
166 Patriot - The Scud Interceptor
167 Tomahawk Cruise Missile
168 Hawk Missile
169 In The Trenches
170 Stopping The Oil's Flow
171 Anti-Chemical Gear
172 E-2C Hawkeye
173 Satellite Communications
174 Huey Cobra
175 Tent City
176 Checklist

DESERT STORM STICKERS
23 U.S.A.
24 U.K.
25 Canada
26 Egypt
27 France
28 Kuwait
29 Morocco
30 Saudi Arabia
31 Syria
32 U.S.S.R.
33 United Nations

DESERT STORM — "HOMECOMING" (88/11) 2 1/2" X 3 1/2"

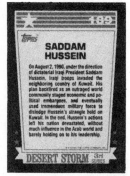

By the time the "Homecoming Series" arrived from Topps, people were beginning to realize that Desert Storm cards were not a license to print money. The fact that this set was carried by far fewer dealers than were series 1 & 2 does not mean that it is numerically scarce. In fact, certain areas of the country are reporting boxes of "Homecoming" sitting on store shelves in abundance. The lack of attention to detail which plagued the first series from Topps returned with a vengeance in series 3. Card #'s 200, 202, 204, 209, 212, 222, 226, & 260 all have errors in spelling or misidentify photos, but only #'s 202 and 204 seem to have been corrected and these are selling for 50 cents apiece. The stickers, numbered 34-44, depict various service medals (very few of which have anything to do with the Persian Gulf) and several other patriotic items. Sticker backs are picture pieces of "puzzle D." Note: set price includes stickers.

ITEM	MINT	EX
Set	12.00	9.00
Card	.10	.07
Sticker	.35	.25
Wrapper	––	.15
Box	––	2.00

HERE IS WHAT YOUR COMPLETED GREEN BORDER PUZZLE WILL LOOK LIKE:

COLLECT ALL 10 CARDS OF PUZZLE D.

177 President George Bush
178 General Norman Schwarzkopf
179 Dick Cheney
180 General Colin Powell
181 Emir Jaber Al Sabah
182 John Major
183 Francois Mitterand
184 Hosni Mubarak
185 Mikhail Gorbachev
186 King Fahd
187 Hafez Assad
188 Javier Perez De Cuellar
189 Saddam Hussein
190 Kuwaiti Troops
191 Qatari Troops
192 British Troops
193 French Forces
194 Egyptian Forces
195 Saudi Soldiers
196 Syrian Soldiers
197 AH-1 Cobra
198 AH-64 Apache
199 CH-47D Chinook
200 A-6 Intruder
201 AV-8B Harrier
202 A-10 Thunderbolt
203 B-52 Stratofortress
204 F-4G Wild Weasel
205 F-14 Tomcat

206 F-15 Eagle
207 F-16 Fighting Falcon
208 F/A-18 Hornet
209 M-198 Howitzer
210 Paratroopers Jump
211 F-117A Stealth
212 TOW Missile
213 Light Armored Vehicle
214 LVTP
215 M-1A1 Abrams
216 M-2 Bradley
217 Multi-Launch Rocket System
218 M-60 Tank
219 Night Vision Goggles
220 Working Dogs
221 Reporting Center
222 M-110 Howitzer
223 Scuds Explode
224 Vulcan System
225 Dragon Missile
226 E-3 Sentry
227 C-58 Galaxy
228 Tomahawk Cruise Missile
229 KC-10 Extender
230 Hummer
231 Bomb's-Eye View*
232 FB-111 Aardvark
233 M48A1 Chaparral Missile System
234 M-551 Sheridan
235 The Burning Fields
236 Ecological Warfare
237 M-113 Armored Personnel Carrier
238 Working Together
239 The Ground War*

240 Schwarzkopf's Plan*
241 Iraqis Surrender - A
242 Iraqis Surrender - B
243 Iraqis Surrender - C
244 Target Markings
245 Mood at Home
246 Rally of Support
247 Liberation Day - A
248 Liberation Day - B
249 Liberation Day - C
250 Anticipation Grows
251 82nd Airborne Returns
252 USS Mississippi Comes Home*
253 The Wisconsin Returns
254 Pride in the Troops
255 Meeting the Crowd
256 Safe at Home
257 Tomcats Fly In
258 Home Again
259 Worth Fighting For
260 Marines Return
261 Heroes' Welcome
262 Reunited!
263 Daddy's Home!
264 Checklist

DESERT STORM Stickers checklist
34 Southwest Asia Service Medal
35 National Defense Service Medal
36 Purple Heart
37 Prisoner-of-War Medal
38 The United States Army Silver Star Medal
39 Joint Service Achievement Award
40 Medal of Honor
41 Top Gun
42 These Colors Don't Run!
43 Let Freedom Ring
44 Welcome Home

DESERT STORM CARD & MAP SET (110)

2 1/2" X 3 1/2"

All the elements of this set — 110 cards and a large map/poster (20" X 31") — came packaged in a nicely-designed cardboard box (approx. 3-3/4" X 10-1/2"). The cards have color photo fronts with blue framelines and sand-colored borders; most of the pictures appear to have come from the standard Pentagon pool of training exercises and publicity stills. The American flag and a "Desert Storm" logo unique to this set are located in the top right and lower left corners, respectively. The card numbers, located only on the backs, are each followed by a "V" (for "victory?"). According to a credit line which appears on the cards, the set was produced by America's Major Players, Inc. Note: sold only as a boxed set, so no single or "excellent" prices are given.

ITEM	MINT	EX
SET	20.00	--

1 General Schwarzkopf
2 General Powell
3 Secretary Cheney
4 President Bush
5 Chemical Protective Gear
6 M224 60mm Mortar
7 Patriot SAM
8 M2 / M3 Bradley
9 AH-64 Apache
10 M1 Abrams
11 F-14A Tomcat
12 EA-6B Prowler
13 A-6E Intruder
14 F-15C Eagle
15 TOW Missile Carrier
16 F / A-18 Hornet
17 F-16C Fighting Falcon
18 A-7E Corsair II
19 F-15E Strike Eagle
20 AIM-9 Sidewinder
21 F-117A Stealth
22 F-111E / F Aardvark

23 EF-111A Raven
24 F-14A + Tomcat
25 B-52G Stratofortress
26 CH-53E Super Stallion
27 CH-46D Sea Knight
28 CH-47D Chinook
29 UH-1H Iroquois "Huey"
30 AH-1S "Huey" Cobra
31 C-5 Galaxy
32 LAV-25 "APC"
33 M551A Sheridan
34 M1A1 Abrams
35 OV-1D Mohawk
36 CH-46F Sea Knight
37 E-3 AWACS (Sentry)
38 OH-58 Kiowa
39 SH-60B Seahawk
40 AV-8B Harrier II
41 Rockeye Mk20 Cluster Bomb
42 M113 "APC"
43 AAV-7 "Amtrack"
44 M110 A-2 Howitzer
45 M109 SP Howitzer
46 HAWK SAM
47 M48A1 Chaparral
48 M163 Vulcan
49 MLRS

50 M901 Improved TOW Vehicle
51 SH-3 Sea King
52 OV-10A Bronco
53 HH-53B Sea Stallion
54 S-3A Viking
55 RF-4C Phantom
56 F-4G Wild Weasel
57 M198 Howitzer
58 Stinger
59 M102 105mm Howitzer
60 M47 Dragon
61 AH-1W Sea Cobra
62 UH-60B Blackhawk
63 RC-135 "Recon"
64 M60A1 / A3 Battle Tank
65 AIM-54 Phoenix
66 HH-3 Jolly Green Giant
67 AIM-7 Sparrow
68 AC-130 Spectre
69 A-10 Thunderbolt II "Warthog"
70 U.S.S. John F. Kennedy (CV-67)
71 Mirage 2000C
72 Jaguar GR.1
73 Tornado GR.1
74 Victor Tanker
75 BB-64 U.S.S. Wisconsin
76 M269 "SAW"
77 P-3 Orion
78 Cargo / Troop Carrier

79 LPH 12 U.S.S. Inchon
80 FFG-47 U.S.S. Nicholas
81 SA 341 Gazelle
82 Mirage IIIR
83 Mirage 5
84 F-4E Phantom II
85 Hunter
86 A-4KU Skyhawk
87 C-130E Hercules
88 F-5F Tiger II
89 F-5E Tiger II
90 Hawk 50
91 SU-25 Frogfoot
92 SU-22M-4 Fitter K
93 Mirage F.1
94 MiG-29 Fulcrum A
95 MiG-29 Fulcrum C
96 MiG-25 Foxbat
97 MiG-23 Flogger B
98 MiG-21 Fishbed K
99 Tornado IDS
100 Tornado F.3
101 Mi-8 "Hip-C"
102 Mi-24 Hind E
103 T-62 Battle Tank
104 BMP-1 Early
105 T-55 Battle Tank
106 T-54 Battle Tank
107 BTR-60 "APC"
108 SA-8 Gecko
109 ZU-23 A / A Gun
110 SS-1 Scud B

DESERT STORM TRADING CARDS (60) (60)

2 1/2" X 3 1/2"

The conflict in the Persian Gulf promoted several companies with no previous card manufacturing experience to try their hand. Perhaps the strangest was Spectra Star, a kite maker based in Pacoima, California. Spectra Star advertised a series of 300 cards on its packaging, but when the dust had settled only two 60-card runs had emerged. The first printing cards came in five categories — Aircraft, Armor, Ships, Troops, and

Desert Storm Trading Cards

Weapons — with each category sold in J-hook bubble packs of 12 cards with its own package header. The cards within were connected in strips and single cards from these packs will have "nubs" on their edges. The cards were also sold in 60-card rack packs by Treat Hobby World, and these have machine cut edges with no nubs. In addition, uncut sheets of six cards were included as a bonus in kites made by Spectra Star, which retailed for about $3.00 in variety and toy stores.

Spectra Star issued a second series of 60 cards several months after their first hit the market. These are numbered 61-120 and have red framelines on the back, but are mostly more pictures of ordinance, soldiers, aircraft, equipment, etc. In addition, there are photographs of some of the U.S. statesmen and soldiers involved in war: Bush, Powell, Schwarzkopf, Cheney, and Horner. Second series cards, although packed in J-hook bubble packs like first series cards, have machine cut edges devoid of nubs. In the final analysis, the ten header cards — and especially the five belonging to the second series — may prove to be more collectable than the cards themselves. Note: the word "Troops" is printed in the right corner of the picture area of every card, and some collectors prefer to call these sets by that name.

ITEM	MINT	EX
Series 1 set	8.00	6.00
Series 2 set	12.00	9.00
Series 1 card	.10	.07
Series 2 card	.15	.10
Series 1 header	.35	.25
Series 2 header	.50	.35

1 Stealth Fighter
2 A-10 Warthog
3 Strike Eagle
4 Apache
5 Intruder
6 AV-8B
7 Wild Weasel
8 B-52
9 Tomcat
10 Falcon
11 E-3A AWACS
12 Tornado
13 U.S.S. Long Beach
14 U.S.S. Brewton
15 U.S.S. Kittyhawk
16 U.S.S. Halsey
17 U.S.S. Charles F. Adams
18 U.S.S. Luce
19 U.S.S. Oliver Perry
20 U.S.S. Blue Ridge
21 U.S.S. Hermitage
22 U.S.S. Wisconsin
23 U.S.S. Arkansas
24 U.S.S. New Jersey
25 LAV
26 M551
27 M1A1
28 M113
29 LVTP-7
30 M110-A2
31 MLRS
32 T-72
33 T-62
34 ZSU-23-4
35 BMP-1
36 M2
37 Tomahawk Firing
38 Patriot
39 Patriot Firing
40 BGM-71 (TOW-2)
41 Tomahawk
42 Cluster Bombs
43 MK83
44 M249
45 AT-4
46 MK-19-3
47 Hellfire
48 Maverick
49 Gen. Schwarzkopf
50 Gen. Powell
51 President Bush
52 Saddam Hussein
53 Lt. Gen. Horner
54 Flight Crew
55 Stormin Norman / King Fahd
56 Troops Deploy
57 Live Fire
58 Combat Patrol
59 Howitzer Crew
60 Deck Crew
61 Checklist Series I & II
62 CH-47
63 Black Hawk
64 Hornet
65 Galaxy
66 A-4M
67 Herky Bird
68 MiG 29
69 Gen. Kelley
70 Gen. McCaffrey
71 AWACS
72 High Tech
73 Hovercraft
74 U.S.S. Spruance
75 U.S.S. Pensacola
76 U.S.S. Vincennes
77 U.S.S. America
78 U.S.S. Saratoga
79 U.S.S. Inchon
80 Failed Diplomacy
81 High Command
82 Norman Before the Storm
83 Corsair II
84 Jaguar
85 Humvee
86 AMX-30
87 T-55
88 MCV-80
89 Challenger
90 M-60 A3
91 M-109
92 Desert Stealth
93 Thanksgiving
94 America Cheers
95 Powell Before the Storm
96 82nd Returns
97 Scud
98 G-5
99 Milan
100 HAWK
101 HARM
102 GAU-8 / A
103 Avenger Turnaround
104 Combat Graffiti
105 Schwartzkopf [sic] Strategy
106 Desert Surrender
107 Behind Enemy Lines
108 Bronco
109 Raven
110 Super Cobra
111 Iraqi Vandalism
112 Scud Terror
113 No Escape
114 Line in the Sand
115 Deploy Forward
116 War Zone
117 Coalition Commanders
118 Baghdad AAA
119 Gas Mask
120 Eight Stars

DESERT STORM WEAPONS SET (50)   2 1/2" X 3 1/2"

M2/M3 Bradley Fighting Vehicle

Desert Storm

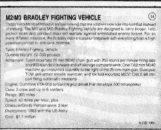

M2/M3 BRADLEY FIGHTING VEHICLE (14)

Desert Storm

F-117A Stealth Fighter

The "Desert Storm Weapons" series is probably the most visually attractive of all the Gulf War sets. The outstanding color of the photographs, which benefit greatly from being borderless, is the selling point for this set. Of the 50 cards, one shows a Saudi jet, two depict British hardware, nine picture Iraqi weapons and machines, and 38 cards display elements of the American military arsenal. Four unnumbered promotional cards, corresponding to card #'s 20, 23, 35, & 50, were issued and have a slightly different Desert Storm heading on the front. The back of regular issue card #50 contains a checklist, while its promotional counterpart has a descriptive text on the reverse. The complete set of "50 plastic laminated cards" was sold in J-hook blister packs and singles or lesser grade cards will not likely be encountered by collectors.

ITEM	MINT	EX
Set	7.00	---

1 Patriot Anti-Missile Missile
2 A-6E Intruder
3 M-16A2 Battle Rifle
4 F-117A Stealth Fighter
5 John F. Kennedy Carrier
6 SCUD Missile
7 F-14 Tomcat
8 AIM-9 Sidewinder Missile
9 MiG-29 "Fulcrum"
10 A-10 Thunderbolt II
11 AC-130 Spectre Gunship
12 E-3 AWACS
13 MD-530 Defender
14 M2 / M3 Bradley Fighting
   Vehicle
15 M9 Personal Sidearm
16 Iowa-Class Battleship
17 F / B-111 Aardvark
18 M-1A1 Abrams Tank
19 Tornado GR.MK 1
20 M60 Tank
21 Los Angeles-Class SSN
   Submarine
22 F-16 Fighting Falcon
23 F-15 Eagle
24 Amphibious Assault Vehicle
25 Iwo Jima Helicopter Carrier
26 M998 HMMWU "Hummer"
27 MiG-25 "Foxbat"
28 AH-1 Cobra Helicopter
29 Challenger
30 AIM-7 Sparrow Missile
31 F-1 Mirage
32 AV-8B Harrier II
33 M-113 Armored Personnel
   Carrier
34 AK-47 Battle Rifle
35 Aegis Cruiser
36 B-52 Stratofortress
37 Tomahawk Cruise Missile
38 LAV-25 Light Assault Vehicle
39 C-5 Galaxy
40 TOW Missile
41 M60 Machine Gun
42 T-55 Tank
43 AH-64 Apache
44 T-72 Tank
45 British Hawk
46 F / A-18 Hornet
47 T-62 Tank
48 F-4G Phantom "Wild
   Weasel"
49 AM-39 Exocet Missile
50 M60-A1 Tank and CH-53
   Helicopter [and Checklist on
   back]

Desert Storm WEAPONS & Specifications

US Allies and Iraqi Systems

50 plastic laminated cards

M60 Machine Gun

Desert Storm

50 card set   DSI, Inc.

GULF WAR FACT CARDS (100)　　　　2 1/2" X 3 1/2"

The war in the Persian Gulf prompted the creation of more than a dozen trading card sets aimed at collectors. These range in scope and quality from B&W caricatures of Saddam Hussein to color photographs of soldiers and military hardware. Most, if not all, of the sets using photos relied heavily on pictures from the Pentagon media pool, which were available to everyone. Only one company, Dart Flipcards,

dared to be different and produced a set using actual wire service action shots taken in the theater of operations.

Obtaining real wartime imagery is more expensive and time-consuming than using pool photos or training exercise pictures, but the results, as seen in Dart's "Gulf War Fact Cards," are spectacular. Here we see General Schwarzkopf talking to the troops, Saudis intently

reading a "war edition" newspaper, dejected Iraqi commanders hearing the terms of surrender, and Coalition troops in Khafji ducking hostile fire. No other Gulf War set comes close to matching this realism: these are real pictures of real events!

The flip side of the 100-card series is equally impressive. Dart reports the facts accurately in a compact, easy-to-read format which refrains from any glorification of the war. The set was printed in Canada and was sold only in complete, factory-sealed boxed editions, so collectors are not likely to encounter single or lesser grade cards.

ITEM	MINT	EX
Boxed set	18.00	—

1 Introduction
2 Colonial Era
3 The Middle East Divided
4 Iraq Invades Kuwait
5 Road to Independence
6 Saddam's Rise to Power
7 U.N. Speaks Out
8 Call to Action
9 USS Independence
10 Defense Secretary Dick Cheney
11 Saddam Hanged in Effigy
12 Egyptians Bolster Coalition
13 USS Dwight D. Eisenhower
14 General H. Norman Schwarzkopf
15 U.S. Military Build-up
16 M2 Bradley
17 A-10 Thunderbolt "Warthog"
18 Control of the Seas
19 Battleship USS Missouri
20 F-14 Tomcat
21 French Helicopters Land
22 USS Ticonderoga
23 Iraqi Popular Army
24 Midair Refueling
25 Chemical Warfare Threat
26 Praying on the Frontlines
27 Troubled Kuwaiti Emir
28 Refugees Flee Invaders
29 Letters from Home
30 TOW Antitank Missile
31 AWACS — Eyes in the Sky
32 British Army "Desert Rats"
33 Apache Attack Helicopter
34 Syrian T-62 Tanks Arrive
35 M-47 Dragon Anti-Tank Missile
36 President Bush Visits Troops
37 Stock Market Frenzy
38 Last-Ditch Peace Talks
39 Desert Storm Begins
40 Baghdad Attacked
41 Scud Missile Alert!
42 "No Blood for Oil"
43 Saddam Hussein
44 Smart Bomb on Target
45 F-15 Eagle
46 Supporting the Troops
47 B-52 Stratofortress
48 War Fears Hit Super Bowl

49 A-7E Corsair Attack Plane
50 General Colin Powell
51 Saddam Hussein's Bunker
52 Scud Missile Hits Tel Aviv
53 Patriot Anti-Missile Battery
54 Patriot in Pursuit
55 Shamir Surveys Damage
56 F-4G Wild Weasel
57 Marine Reinforcements Arrive
58 Hit the Dirt
59 Marines Fire 155mm Howitzer
60 Cobra Attacks Iraqi Positions
61 Fire-Fight at Khafji
62 Ecological Disaster
63 F-16 Fighting Falcon
64 Victims of the Oil Slick
65 Clearing the Minefields

66 Battleship USS Wisconsin
67 Battleship Bombs Ressurected
68 Scud
69 Baghdad Devastated
70 Supply Lines
71 Zoo Tragedy
72 Arming the F-117 Stealth
73 Tornado Fighter
74 Final Check
75 Kuwaiti Valentine Card
76 Gorbachev's Peace Efforts
77 Pilot's Nightmare
78 Israel Prepares for the Worst
79 Tomahawk Cruise Launcher
80 F/A-18 Hornet Fighter-Bomber
81 M1-A1 Battle Tank
82 Marines Guard POWs

83 British PM John Major
84 Harriers Prepare for Action
85 Ground War Begins
86 Allied Strategy - Map 1
87 Allied Strategy - Map 2
88 Multi-National Effort
89 Taking Aim
90 Evacuating the Wounded
91 Scorched-Earth Campaign
92 "The Mother of All Surrenders"
93 Carnage of War
94 Skeleton of Retreat
95 Kuwait Liberated
96 Cease-Fire Talks
97 America's Pride Reborn
98 Marines Retake U.S. Embassy
99 Schwarzkopf's Finest Hour
100 Checklist

HEROES OF THE PERSIAN GULF (110)　　　　2 1/2" X 3 1/2"

Lime Rock, a commercial printing company in Providence, Rhode Island, came up with the most dramatic set name of any of the Gulf War sets. Don't expect to see pictures of valiant fighting men, however, because military hardware is what this set is all about. The color photograph fronts shown navy ships, aircraft, assault craft, tanks, helicopters, and a varie-

Heroes of the Persian Gulf

1 F-117A Stealth Fighter
2 F-117A Stealth Fighter
3 Tomahawk Cruise Missile
4 Tomahawk Cruise Missile
5 F-14 Tomcat
6 F-14 Tomcat
7 E-3 Sentry (AWACS)
8 E-3 Sentry (AWACS)
9 B-52 Stratofortress
10 B-52 Stratofortress
11 C-141B Starlifter
12 C-141B Starlifter
13 A-10 Thunderbolt II
14 A-10 Thunderbolt II
15 OV-10 Bronco
16 OV-10 Bronco
17 EA-6B Prowler
18 EA-6B Prowler
19 A-7E Corsair II
20 A-7E Corsair II
21 A-6 Intruder
22 A-6 Intruder
23 F/A-18 Hornet
24 F/A-18 Hornet
25 F-15 Eagle
26 F-15 Eagle
27 F-4 Phantom II
28 F-4 Phantom II
29 C-5 Galaxy
30 C-5 Galaxy
31 KC-135 Stratotanker
32 KC-135 Stratotanker
33 F-16 Fighting Falcon
34 F-16 Fighting Falcon
35 C-130 Hercules
36 C-130 Hercules
37 F-111
38 F-111
39 AV-8B Harrier II
40 M60A1 Main Battle Tank
41 Stinger
42 M993 HMMWV "Hummer"
43 M1A1 Abrams Tank
44 M1A1 Abrams Tank
45 M2 Bradley IFV
46 M2 Bradley IFV
47 M102
48 M198 155mm Howitzer (T)
49 M110 8-Inch Cannon
50 M110 8-Inch Cannon
51 M109 Self Propelled Howitzer
52 Hawk Missile System
53 Harpoon Cruise Missile
54 AIM/RIM-74 Sparrow Missile
55 AIM-(9M) Sidewinder Missile
56 Landing Craft Air Cushion
57 Landing Craft Air Cushion
58 UH-1N Huey
59 UH-1N Huey
60 CH-46E Sea Knight
61 CH-47 Chinook
62 CH-47 Chinook
63 CH-53D Sea Stallion

64 CH-53E Super Stallion
65 SH-3H Sea King
66 AH-64A Apache
67 AH-64A Apache
68 UH-60 Black Hawk
69 UH-60 Black Hawk
70 USNS Comfort (AH-20)
71 USS Midway
72 USS America
73 USS Ranger
74 USS Theodore Roosevelt
75 USS Saratoga
76 USS John F. Kennedy
77 USS David Ray (DD-971)
78 USS Normandy (CG-60)
79 USS Antietam (CG-54)
80 USS Richmond K. Turner (CG-20)
81 USS Bunker Hill (CG-52)
82 USS England (CG-22)
83 USS Sterret (CG-31)
84 USS Biddle (CG-34)
85 USS Nitro (AE-23)
86 USS Seattle (AOE-3)
87 USS Missouri
88 USS Wisconsin

89 USS Shreveport (LPD-12)
90 USS Austin (LPD-4)
91 USS Vancouver (LPD-2)
92 USS Nashville (LPD-13)
93 USS Pensacola (LSD-38)
94 USS Saint Louis (LKA-116)
95 USS Mobile (LKA-115)
96 USS Okinawa (LPH-3)
97 USS Inchon (LPH-12)
98 USS New Orleans (LPH-11)
99 USS Guam (LPH-9)
100 USS Blue Ridge (LCC-19)
101 USS San Bernardino (LST-1189)
102 USS Vreeland (FF-1068)
103 USS Elmer Montgomery (FF-1082)
104 USS Brewton (FF-1086)
105 USS Curtis (FFG-38)
106 USS White Plains (AFS-4)
107 The Pentagon (Checklist I)
108 Helicopter (Checklist II)
109 Refueling at Night (Checklist III)
110 Lightning over Eisenhower (Checklist IV)

PROTOTYPE CARD

REGULAR CARD

...ty of other weapons and vehicles, and each picture is surrounded by a red, white & blue frameline. The card number is printed only on the back, where the text is printed over an American flag design. The cards were sold only in consecutively numbered boxed sets and the company reports that 100,000 were printed. Two unnumbered variations of cards #9 and #25 were given away as promotional cards before the regular set was released to the public.

ITEM	MINT	EX
Boxed Set	20.00	--

LANDFORCE (10)

General Colin Luther Powell

BONUS CARD

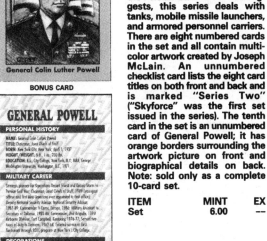

1 Multiple Launch Rocket System
2 M2 Bradley Fighting Vehicle
3 M60 Main Battle Tank
4 M1A1 Abrams Main Battle Tank
5 M113 Armored Personnel Carrier
6 M109 Self-Propelled Howitzer
7 V-600 Commando
8 Chieftain MK-5 Main Battle Tank
* Landforce Checklist (no #)
* General Powell (no #)

"Landforce" is one of three Crown Sports Card Company sets devoted to picturing components of the U.S. military arsenal which was employed in the Persian Gulf. As the title suggests, this series deals with tanks, mobile missile launchers, and armored personnel carriers. There are eight numbered cards in the set and all contain multi-color artwork created by Joseph McLain. An unnumbered checklist card lists the eight card titles on both front and back and is marked "Series Two" ("Skyforce" was the first set issued in the series). The tenth card in the set is an unnumbered card of General Powell; it has orange borders surrounding the artwork picture on front and biographical details on back. Note: sold only as a complete 10-card set.

ITEM	MINT	EX
Set	6.00	--

OPERATION DESERT SHIELD (110)

Ready For Action

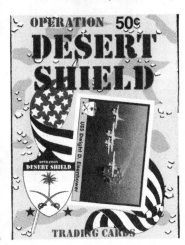

This is the only Gulf War set to be named "Desert Shield," reflecting Pacific Trading Card's early commitment to producing a Persian Gulf series. Except for a few photographs that were obviously taken in the theater of operations, most of the color pictures appear to have come from Pentagon publicity stocks.

Pacific, however, has composed these to better advantage than many of its competitors, and collectors will be pleased with the crisp look and feel of the cards and the excellent layouts on the backs (22 cards even have small color photos on the reverse). The series was distributed in wax packs and as factory sets (in three different boxes, two used by Pacific and one used by Treat Hobby Products). To promote sales, the company inserted the following types of Schwarzkopf cards randomly into wax packages: 30,000 white-bordered, 10,000 gold-bordered, four silver-bordered, and three cards with hologram borders. The "camouflage" collectors' set also contained white-bordered Schwarzkopf cards. Since prices for these bonus cards tend to be very active, collectors are advised to check the hobby publications for news about their values.

ITEM	MINT	EX
Set	16.00	12.00
Boxed set	18.00	--
Card	.10	.07
Wrapper	--	.15

Operation Desert Shield

1. President George Bush
2. Vice President Dan Quayle
3. General Colin Powell
4. USO Show [Thomas Hearns]
5. Marines Dig In
6. The Backbone
7. U.S. Airborne Infantrymen
8. Ready for Action
9. "Big Mo"
10. "Protection"
11. "Mail Call"
12. Front Line Defense
13. House-to-House Assault
14. Evacuation Exercise
15. Sidewinder Missile
16. "Time Out"
17. Medical Exercise
18. Returning from Patrol
19. "Forming Up"
20. "Night Fighter"
21. Marine Assault
22. Mock Casualty Exercise
23. F-15 Eagle
24. "Modern Day Desert Rat"
25. Marine Corps M1A1 Abrams Tank
26. Multiple Launch Rocket System
27. M60A3 Tank
28. "Marine Armor"
29. M119 105mm Howitzer
30. Marine Landing Craft
31. "The Scud's Deadliest Enemy"
32. Bomb Preparation
33. U.S. Navy Air Cushioned Landing Craft
34. Marine Light Armored Vehicle
35. Thanksgiving in the Desert [Bush]
36. HMMWV with TOW Missile Launcher
37. Maintenance on the Move
38. 155mm Howitzer
39. Armor Comes Ashore
40. HAWK Missile
41. "Home Away from Home"
42. M-60 Machine Gun
43. Chemical Decontamination Exercise
44. Phoenix AIM Missile
45. "Knock Out Punch"
46. "Top Brass" [Powell and Schwarzkopf]
47. "FIRE!"
48. "Sidewinder"
49. M551 Sheridan Tank
50. "The Dragon Strikes"
51. USS Dwight D. Eisenhower
52. USS Nimitz
53. USNS Mercy
54. USS Missouri
55. USS LaSalle
56. Aircraft Carrier USS Saratoga
57. USS Forrestal
58. "Secretary and Foreign Minister"
59. Amphibious Assault Ship USS Iwo Jima
60. Close Air Defense Drill
61. U.S. Navy Seals
62. "Coming Ashore"
63. Battleship USS Iowa
64. USS Boston
65. USS Wisconsin
66. Harpoon Cruise Missile
67. "First Ashore"
68. "The Prowler"
69. F-16 Fighting Falcons
70. C-5A Galaxy
71. "Loaded for Action"
72. C-141B Starlifter
73. F-117A Stealth
74. "Free Kuwait"
75. S-3 Viking
76. "Eyes and Ears"
77. "Ready for Attack"
78. "Pinpoint Bombing"
79. UH-46 Sea Knight
80. "Feeding the Wild Weasels"
81. "Fangs of the Cobra"
82. "RECON Patrol"
83. F-14 Tomcat
84. "A MIG's Worst Nightmare"
85. F-117A Stealth
86. F-15 Eagle
87. F-111 Aardvark
88. EF-111A Raven
89. A-10 Warthog
90. F-4 Phantom II
91. C-130 Hercules
92. A-10 Thunderbolt II Refuels
93. B-52 Stratofortress
94. A-6 Intruders in Formation
95. F-14A Tomcat
96. A-7E Corsair II
97. F-16 Fighting Falcon
98. F/A-18 Hornet
99. SH-60 Seahawk
100. CH-47 Chinook
101. F-4 Phantom
102. B-52G with Cruise Missiles
103. Tomahawk Cruise Missile
104. Tomahawk Cruise Missile Attack
105. Harpoon Cruise Missile
106. USS Wisconsin
107. F-4Gs Over Bahrain
108. F/A-18 Fires Sidewinder
109. Saudi Air Force Pilots
110. AV-8B Harrier

OPERATION YELLOW RIBBON (60)

2 1/2" X 3 1/2"

"Operation Yellow Ribbon," produced by AAA Sports, was sold in complete, boxed sets of 60 cards. Some of the proceeds from sales were donated to OYR, a support agency for servicemen and their families. The color photographs are a blend of Pentagon stocks and some Persian Gulf views but the only unique cards picture servicemen whose parents are officials in the OYR organization. The manufacturer made an obvious attempt to cash in on the promotional/bonus card craze by creating 15 different special cards which are not part of the regular set. These are: (1) a ten card set numbered P1-P10; (2) a Schwarzkopf card, numbered P11, with silver foil borders; (3) unnumbered, foil-bordered cards of Bush (gold), Cheney (silver), Powell (silver), and Schwarzkopf (silver). The foil cards were packed in cases as dealer incentives and all of the "special issue" cards are too market-active to be listed here.

ITEM	MINT	EX
Boxed set	7.00	--

Brian S. Economy
GMG2 Navy Diver

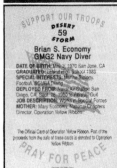

M-1 ABRAMS Tank

M-1 ABRAMS Tank

Operation Yellow Ribbon

1 Commander in Chief
2 Stealth Fighter F-117A
3 Gas Mask
4 HAWK Missiles
5 M-1 Abrams Tank
6 Troops at "Ready"
7 U.S. Aircraft Carrier
8 Harrier AV-8B
9 Tomcats F-14
10 Patriot Missile (Scud Buster)
11 Ready to Go
12 U.S. Guided Missile Frigate
13 U.S. Marines in Saudi Desert
14 Maximum Control
15 Maximum Protection
16 Air Superiority
17 Air to Air Refueling
18 Sea Superiority
19 Allied Ground Forces
20 Black Hawk UH-60A Helicopter
21 Allied Troops in Action
22 U.S.S. Wisconsin
23 Free Kuwaiti Air Force
24 Mid-Air Refueling

25 "The Hummer"
26 US Troops in Saudi Arabia
27 Intra-Arab Forces
28 The Battle of Khafji
29 Nimrod Laser Guided Missile
30 A-7's on Patrol
31 F-18 Hornet
32 F-15 Eagle
33 Super Stallion
34 Awaiting the Next Mission
35 The "BIG GUNS"
36 On the Alert
37 On the Offense
38 Comrades in Arms
39 The Invisible Fighter
40 B-52 Bomber
41 AH-64 Apache
42 Air to Air Action
43 The Stinger Missile
44 F-14 Tomcat A-6E Intruder
45 Iraqi P.O.W.s
46 UH-60 Black Hawk
47 Carrier Landing
48 A-10 Warthog
49 Pilot's View
50 Standing Guard

51 Desert Watch
52 President George H. Bush
53 Richard Cheney Secretary of Defense
54 Colin Powell Chrm. Joint Chiefs of Staff
55 General H. Norman Schwartzkopf
   Desert Storm Field Commander
56 First Lieutenant Patrick K. Milligan USMC
57 James Paul Seith Lance Corporal USMC
58 HM3 Derek L. Sauer
59 Brian S. Economy GMG2 Navy Diver
60 SP4 Thomas E. Alcorn 1st CAV DIV Army
P1 Commander In Chief
P2 Stealth Fighter F-117A
P3 Gas Mask
P4 HAWK Missiles [sic]
P5 M-1 Abrams Tank
P6 Troops at "Ready" in the desert
P7 U.S. Aircraft Carrier
P8 Harrier AV-8B
P9 Tomcats F-14
P10 Patriot Missile (SCUD Buster)
P11 Gen. Norman Schwarzkopf
Gold Foil President George H. Bush
Silver Foil Richard Cheney
Silver Foil Gen. Colin Powell
Silver Foil Gen. H. Norman Schwarzkopf

SEAFORCE (10)   2 1/2" X 3 1/2"

Series Three of the Crown Sports Card Company anthology of Desert Storm weaponry is entitled "Seaforce." There are ten cards in the set: eight numbered, artwork pictures of naval vessels, an unnumbered checklist card, plus an orange-bordered card of the "Commander In Chief." Joseph McClain created the artwork for the cards, which were sold only in complete sets.

ITEM	MINT	EX
Set	6.00	---

President George Herbert Bush

BONUS CARD

1 LCAC Landing Craft Air Cushion
2 Carrier USS America (CV-66)
3 MSO Mine Sweeper
4 Amphibious Assault Vehicle
5 Cruiser USS Longbeach
6 Frigate USS Reid (FFG-30)
7 Carrier USS Inchon (LPH-12)
8 Battleship USS Wisconsin (BB-64)
* Seaforce Checklist (no #)
* Commander In Chief (no #)

SKYFORCE (9)   2 1/2" X 3 1/2"

In chronological terms, "Skyforce" was the first of three Crown Sports Card Company sets depicting U.S. military hardware and the unnumbered checklist for this nine-card set is clearly marked "First Series." The production run was limited to 15,000 sets and the color artwork was drawn by Joseph McLain. Collectors will find that each card has a serial number written in pencil on the back. A special promotional card of General Schwarzkopf was distributed to dealers; according to the company, 1250 were printed. The "Skyforce" set is complete at eight numbered cards and one unnumbered checklist and was issued in a blue paper wrapper (both "Landforce" and "Seaforce" are ten card sets).

ITEM	MINT	EX
Set	6.00	---

1 A-10 Thunderbolt II "Warthog"
2 F-117A Stealth Fighter
3 F-14 Tomcat
4 F/A-18 Hornet
5 F-15 Eagle
6 A-6 Intruder
7 A-7 Corsair
8 A-4 Skyhawk
No # Checklist

THE DESERT STORM CARD
COLLECTION (20)

2 1/2" X 3 1/2"

The distinction of being the first Desert Storm card series belongs to the initial nine-card group of "The Desert Storm Card Collection," a creation of Crown Sports Card Co. The black and white drawings were produced by Joseph McLain and each is surrounded by wide "camouflage" borders. A second series of ten cards, in the same style, was distributed at a later date, but is now being packaged with the first printing to form a 20-card set (the 20th card is an unnumbered checklist). Note: although this set is listed as a 20-card set below, collectors may encounter it divided into a 1st series (9 cards) and 2nd series (11 cards) for $3.00 each.

ITEM	MINT	EX
Set	6.00	--

SERIES I SET
1 "In Your Face"
2 Quarterback Sack
3 Foiled Again
4 "Make My Day"
5 Over the Top
6 "Dance, Pilgrim"
7 Rambush
8 Cutting Remarks
9 First Round TKO

SERIES II SET
Header/Checklist card
10 "Scudbusters"
11 "USA - Leading the Way"
12 "An Easy Strike"
13 "Record Time"
14 "Batter Up"
15 "A Major Achievement"
16 "Stormin' Norman"
17 "Behind the 8 Ball"
18 "World Championship Team"
19 "Been Keepin' Bad Company Boys"

TRIUMPHS & HORRORS OF THE GULF WAR (50)

2 1/2" X 3 1/2"

You may not like the results, but you have to credit TNTL Studios for producing a card set which lives up to its name. Some of the more graphic wire photos which eluded the American public during the Gulf War have showed up on these cards. Collectors have voiced different opinions about the motive for creating the set: was it controversy designed to sell cards or to promote peace? Certainly, the donation of a portion of the profits to the Feinstein World Hunger Center is a positive indicator, but collectors are warned that the contents of this set may be unsettling to children. The 50 cards in the set have glossy obverse surfaces with color photos surrounded by blue borders. The matte finish backs contain a short text, the card number, and a Brown University/Feinstein Center logo. Note: sold as boxed sets only.

ITEM	MINT	EX
Set	25.00	--

1 Man of the Hour
2 An Allied Tank under Fire
3 Greek Riot Police Clash with Protestors
4 Demonstrators for Saddam
5 Scud Damage in Saudi Arabia
6 Israelis Brace for Scud Attacks
7 Kuwaitis Demonstrate Against Hussein
8 Bombs Burst in Baghdad
9 U.S. Barracks after a Scud Hit
10 Refugee Camp Violence
11 Israeli Woman Hit by Scud Attack
12 A Time to Pray
13 Scud Attacks Wreak Havoc
14 Bombed out Building in Baghdad
15 Dead Iraqi Civilians
16 Faith in God Survives
17 Scuds Hit Israel Again
18 Hungry Refugees Hoping for Food
19 Israeli Women - Homeless But Alive
20 Exploding Iraqi Bunker
21 Captured in the Desert
22 U.S. Marine with Iraqi Prisoner
23 The Victor Leading the Vanquished

24 Iraqi Prisoners Guarded by Kuwaitis
25 Returning in Triumph
26 Burned Bus & Iraqi Bodies
27 The Face of Hell
28 Wartime Horrors Spare No Creature
29 Liberation Celebration
30 Cheering the U.S. Troops
31 Stoning Saddam
32 An Iraqi Torture Victim
33 A Gift for Her Savior
34 Cheering Kuwaiti Children on Destroyed Tank
35 The Ugly Face of Pollution
36 Head of Our Victorious Forces
37 At Last - Kuwait Freed
38 The Winner and the Losers
39 Charred Limbs Hang from Wrecked Truck
40 After the War - Devastation Continues
41 The Vice President Speaks Out
42 Hungry, Cold and Desperate
43 Kurdish Refugees Clamoring for Food
44 The Hideous Scars of War
45 Starving Kurds Storm Bread Trailer
46 New Life Surrounded by Death
47 The Innocent Suffer and Die
48 The Face of Death
49 Refugees Devour Bread Crumbs
50 Turned Back at the Turkish Border

VICTORY (1)

2 1/2" X 3 1/2"

"Victory" — a "one card set" commemorating the U.S. military triumph in the Persian Gulf War — was specifically designed to target collectors of "special issue" cards. The card contains a color artwork portrait panorama of Bush, Powell, and Schwarzkopf which is embellished with gold foil borders. The back carries a sentence of dedication to these "United States Commanders" and mentions the three weaponry sets also produced by Crown Sports Card Co. of Virginia ("Skyforce," "Landforce," and "Seaforce"). This single card arrived in the marketplace with a manufacturer-induced value of $6.00 and only time will tell how collectors respond to it at that price.

According to the advertising printed on each card, this set is a "Limited Edition of 24 Historic Collectors' Cards Commemorating the Development of Naval Flight." The cards are printed on thick paper and have glossy surfaces on both sides. The fronts contain uncaptioned multi-color pictures of aircraft carriers and carrier aircraft. The card number, card caption, and a short text are printed on the reverse. Revell distributed the series by inserting a two-card panel in specific model kits (each card will have at least two rouletted edges). Collectors who sent in a complete set of 24 cards to the company received a free science book ("The Wonderful World") and we cannot confirm that sets were returned. Since cards could be obtained only by purchasing model kits, supplies of them in the current marketplace are limited. Note: the prices listed below are for single cards; add 20% value for panels.

ITEM	MINT	EX
Set	90.00	67.50
Card	3.00	2.25

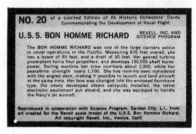

1 U.S.S. Essex
2
3
4 North American A3J-1 Vigilante
5 U.S.S. Franklin D. Roosevelt
6 U.S.S. Forrestal
7 Martin Seamaster P6M-1
8
9 Douglas A3D Skywarrior
10 Martin PBM-5 Mariner
11 Douglas A4D Skyhawk with Bullpup Missiles
12 Lockheed WV-2 Radome
13 Chance Vought F8U-2N Crusader
14 Grumman F9F-8 Cougar
15 Grumman F11F-1 Tiger
16 Chance Vought F7U-3 Cutlass
17
18
19 U.S.S. Saratoga
20 U.S.S. Bon Homme Richard
21
22 U.S.S. Coral Sea
23 U.S.S. Ranger
24

How This Program Makes Science EASY and FASCINATING!

As a member of the Science Program, you are going to be taken on an interesting "field trip" every month in the world of science—with a top science writer, artist and photographer to act as your guides. Sometimes you will go up in an X-15 with a jet pilot to see how the earth looks from miles up in the air. Sometimes you will go with a chemist into his laboratory to see how he makes a special glass-like material to use in rocket noses. On other "trips" your guides will be electronic engineers, doctors, oceanographers, cartographers, test pilots, atomic scientists. These thrilling adventures will come to you in monthly ALBUMS and beautiful FULL COLOR PHOTO-PRINTS illustrating the subject. You will also receive an informative SCIENCE BULLETIN each month to keep up-to-date on recent developments. All of this is yours for the low cost of $1.00 a month. And you take no risk. You may stop the program at any time simply by dropping us a note.

ACT NOW ON THIS AMAZING 10¢ OFFER. Fill out the card below and mail it today. We will send you the entire 6-part FLIGHT package shown on this page and described on the other side—all for 10¢. (Don't send the dime now—we'll bill you later.) You will also receive the current science set to examine, and you'll be enrolled in the Science Program on a no-risk basis. If you decide not to continue, return the introductory package in 10 days and your subscription will be cancelled. Start on this exciting adventure now—mail the card today to join the Science Program.

All This for 10¢ with membership

SEE OTHER SIDE... THEN MAIL POSTAGE-FREE CARD BELOW

SCIENCE PROGRAM
Garden City, L. I., N. Y.
ACCEPT THIS 10¢ OFFER NOW!

Rush me the introductory 6-part FLIGHT package described on other side, for which I will later send you only 10¢ to help cover shipping. Also enroll me as a member of the Science Program and send me the current science kit with a bill for only $1 plus shipping. After examining this package I may cancel membership simply by writing you within 10 days. In this case I will return everything and owe nothing. As a member I will receive a new science kit every month for only $1 each plus shipping. I do not have to take any minimum number of future kits, and may resign any time I wish.

SIGNATURE
NAME
ADDRESS
CITY
REV-4

BREATHLESS MAHONEY

WANTED

INFLUENCE

BLACKMAIL

Dick Tracy, "The Movie Event of Summer 1990," did not achieve the blockbuster success that some box office buffs predicted. Detective Tracy, described as "a timeless hero" on card #2 of the set, failed to have the built-in name recognition of Batman among modern movie-goers, especially children. Stylish camera work and some excellent acting, plus a dose of Madonna, will keep this film alive as a campy favorite for years to come.

Topps' success with the Dick Tracy series of 88 cards and eleven stickers also appears to have been limited. Card fronts have color photos from the film surrounded by a deco style frame; a Dick Tracy logo sits in one corner and each picture is captioned. The heading on the back reads "Dick Tracy Calling," below which there is a short text. The stickers are made up like wanted posters and name various hoodlums and their crimes. The reverses of the cards on which the stickers sit are puzzle picture pieces. Note: set price includes stickers.

ITEM	MINT	EX
Set	15.00	11.00
Card	.10	.07
Sticker	.35	.25
Wrappers (2), ea.	—	.35
Box	—	2.00

Topps

8 GLOSSY MOVIE CARDS • 1 STICKER

1 "The Movie Event of Summer 1990"
2 Dick Tracy
3 Al "Big Boy" Caprice
4 Breathless Mahoney
5 Tess Trueheart
6 The Kid
7 Lips Manlis

8 Flattop
9 Jake "Itchy" Rossi
10 Influence
11 Pruneface
12 Littleface
13 The Bwow
14 The Rodent
15 Shoulders
16 The Stooge
17 Steve the Tramp
18 The Blank
19 The Games Felons Play
20 Crashing the Poker Party
21 Machine Gun Maniac
22 The Party's Over
23 Calling Dick Tracy!
24 Cop on the Scene
25 Gangland Revenge
26 The Kid and His Captor
27 Dinner at Mike's Diner
28 "Arresting" Lips Manlis
29 Big Boy in Command
30 Lips in a Fix
31 The Cement Bath
32 A Not-So-Friendly Visit
33 The Interrogation
34 Partners in Crime
35 New Boss of the Ritz
36 Tracy Tracks His Man
37 A Confident Crook
38 Woman of Mystery
39 At City Hall
40 The Cop and the Kid
41 Family Outing
42 Dropping Tess Off
43 Flattop's Revenge
44 "Tracy, Watch Out!"
45 Unexpected Caller
46 Friend ... or Gorgeous Foe?
47 The Gang's All Here
48 Roll Call of Evil
49 Lawman on the Ledge

50 Spying on the Bad Guys
51 Blast from Below
52 Terror in the Streets
53 Mysterious Observer
54 "Behave Yourself, Kid!"
55 A Ride into Danger
56 Surrounded by His Foes
57 Captive Crimefighter
58 The Bribe
59 A Hot Time for Tracy!
60 The Kid to the Rescue!
61 Narrow Escape
62 Confronting Breathless
63 Sultry and Seductive
64 Tracy Takes Aim Against Crime
65 "You're Under Arrest!"
66 "We Gotta Deal with Tracy!"
67 Hard-Driving Detective
68 Bug Bailey
69 Observed from Above
70 Bug's Blunder
71 Another Cement Shower?
72 On the Waterfront
73 Tracy ... Tarnished!
74 Honest Cop in the Slammer
75 His Faith Restored
76 Back in Action
77 The Party's Over ...!

78 Tess at Gunpoint
79 A City Beseiged
80 Fighting Fire with Fire
81 Flattop's Final Stand
82 Death of a Mobster
83 Abducted by Big Boy!
84 Behind Closed Doors
85 Trussed Tess!
86 Tracy's Gamble
87 A Damsel in Distress
88 One Last Kiss

STICKERS
1 The Brow ... International Espionage
2 Jake "Itchy" Rossi ... Assault & Battery
3 Steve the Tramp ... Vagrancy & Assault
4 The Blank ... Faceless Felon
5 Al "Big Boy" Caprice ... Notorious Gangster
6 Pruneface ... Sabotage
7 Littleface ... Manslaughter
8 Influence ... Blackmail
9 The Stooge ... Considered Armed & Dangerous
10 Flattop ... Murder
11 The Rodent ... Larceny

DICK TRACY DELUXE COLLECTOR'S EDITION (110/11)

2 1/2" X 3 1/2"

What better way to describe the set but in Topps' own words: "This full-color collection captures all the excitement and action [of Dick Tracy] on 88 movie cards, 11 stickers and is lavishly produced with ultra-glossy coating on white card stock. As

an added bonus, there are 22 behind-the-scenes cards not available elsewhere. Issued in limited quantities, the Complete Collectors' Edition is a state-of-the-art movie card collectible and a must for all DICK TRACY fans."

All of the cards of the regular Dick Tracy series are repeated here, but the color on front and the readability of the back text is far better due to the glossy surface coating. The "bonus" cards have red borders and show eight painted backdrops

and 14 scenes. They are lettered A-V, rather than numbered, and have the words "Dick Tracy Bonus Card" printed on the back. Topps issued the Deluxe Collector's Edition as a boxed set with a suggested retail price of $19.95 and the market has not yet demanded a higher value. Compared to the regular set, the Deluxe Edition is a very good buy for collectors who must choose between the two.

ITEM	MINT	EX
Boxed set	20.00	--

A Matte Painting: City by Night	M "Framing" Big Boy
B Matte Painting: Greenhouse	N Lighting the Rooftop Set
C Matte Painting: Street (Green)	O Building an Interior Set
D Matte Painting: Smokestacks	P Against a Blue Screen
E Matte Painting: Street (Red)	Q Gangland in Focus
F Matte Painting: Trees	R Casting Ominous Shadows
G Matte Painting: Rooftop	S Filming the "Ledge"
H Matte Painting: The Bridge	Sequence
I Filming the Blank	T Shooting Flattop's Demise
J Touching Up the Brow	U Directing Breathless
K Shooting Tracy's Leap	V Zeroing In on the Kid
L Setting Up the Cement Bath	

DICK TRACY COLLECTOR CARDS (?)　　2 7/8" X 3 15/16"

"Dick Tracy Collector Cards," a series of color photographs from the Disney movie, were printed on the back covers of the following Dick Tracy activity books by Golden: "Giant Sticker Fun," "Giant Paint With Water," and "Giant Color/Activity." The books were sold for $2.00 or less in supermarkets and variety stores. The cards are not numbered and must be removed from the back covers by cutting.

ting. Collectors may be disappointed by the lack of details — there are no card numbers or captions and the backs are blank — but the pictures themselves are clear and attractive. The set total is not known at this time. Note: cards must be carefully trimmed to be graded excellent.

ITEM	MINT	EX
Card	--	.50
Complete book	3.00	2.00

DICK TRACY CRIMESTOPPER
GAME CARDS (12)

2 1/2" X 5 7/8"

Thanks to the efforts (and cast iron stomachs) of Wanda Chan and "Greenie" Smith, we are able to catalog all of the "Crimestopper Game" cards distributed by McDonald's during the spring and summer of 1990. Each card originally had two sections: a "Part 1" scene, measuring 2-1/2" X 4-1/2", and a "Part 2" tab, 2-1/2" tall by 1-7/16" wide. Each scene had five scratch-off boxes which required proper sequencing to win a prize. The tab portion had a

single "Rub Off To Reveal Mug Shot" box. Since the Dick Tracy promotion ran for more than eight weeks, and supplies varied among restaurants, it was not easy to assemble a complete set of cards then, and it is proving even more difficult to do so now. Note: prices are given for cards with and without tabs. Cards cannot be graded mint if any of the silver coating on the boxes has been removed or tabs have been removed. Detached "Part 2" tabs are valueless.

ITEM	MINT	EX
SETS:		
With tabs & coating	30.00	22.00
With tabs & missing		
some or all coatings	--	15.00
No tabs & coating	--	7.00
No tabs & no coating	--	3.00
CARDS:		
With tabs & coating	2.00	1.50
With tabs & missing		
some or all coatings	--	1.00
No tabs & coating	--	.50
No tabs & no coating	--	.25

DICK TRACY GIANT STICKERS & POSTER SET (27)

2 1/2" X 3 1/4"

The format of this Dick Tracy set from Panini is a radical departure from most of the company's previous sets. Instead of having several hundred small stickers and an album to put them in, the Tracy series consists of 27 large (2-1/2" X 3-1/4") stickers and a two-sided poster on which they can be mounted. Collectors will most likely prefer to keep their stickers "unpeeled" on the original sheets which, with the poster, is stapled between the covers of the folder. When it was marketed in 1990, Panini's Dick Tracy ensemble retailed for $3.99 or less, depending on the type of store. Collectors may still encounter it in some stores specializing in overstocks, at a considerable discount, but purchasing it from hobby dealers is likely to cost double or triple the cover price.

DINOMAC COLLECTOR CARDS (3)

2 1/8" X 2 3/4"

"Dinomac Collector Cards" are one of three different 3-card sets printed by Kraft on the backs of Macaroni & Cheese Dinner boxes in 1991. The cards are smaller than standard size and have blank backs. The fronts contain multi-color artwork paintings of dinosaurs with cartoon-like expressions and facsimile autographs. Despite this bit of anthropomorphism, the text underneath the picture actually explains some facts about the subjects. Collectors are advised to look for intact boxes containing these cards since there are other dinosaur-related features printed on them.

ITEM	MINT	EX
Set of complete boxes	2.00	1.50
Set of cards	1.00	.75
Complete box	.65	.50
Card	.35	.25

CHECKLIST
Brontosaurus
Stegosaurus
Tyrannosaurus Rex

DINO-MITE FACTS (?) 3 1/2" X 6 1/2"

The "T-76-11" code on the side of this interesting Topps wrapper indicates that it was marketed in 1976. The color illustration and text are located on the reverse of a glossy paper pouch entitled "Leapin' Lizards Prehistoric Candy." If the number of surviving wrappers is any indication, the product does not appear to have been long-lived.

ITEM	MINT	EX
Wrapper	--	25.00

DINOSAUR ACTION CARD COLLECTION (60) 3" X 4"

The set title for this series of 60 cards is printed on the wrapper and in advertising copy, but not on the cards themselves. The set was one of many dinosaur-related products issued through the "Dinosaur Club," a promotion of Illuminations (Cambridge, MA). The cards were distributed in twelve different glossy-paper envelopes which were sold from J-hooks in toy and variety stores. The card fronts were borderless and show a variety of dinosaurs in excellent color and detail. The backs contain the name and pronunciation for each dinosaur, a description, and a subject-specific "Dino-Quiz." Each card has a hyphenated number on back which indicates the series it belongs to and its place within the series. There are twelve different series, each containing five cards: Meat Eaters (3 dif.), Plant Eaters (3 dif.), Horned Dinos, Giant Dinos, Dwarf Dinos, Duckbills, Crested Duckbills, and Armored Dinos. The cards are larger than standard size and have rounded corners and glossy surfaces.

ITEM	MINT	EX
Set	20.00	15.00
Card	.30	.20
Envelopes (12), ea.	--	.50

DINOSAUR ALBUM STICKERS (240)   1 15/16" X 2 9/16"

Anyone interested in natural history would be thrilled by this set of 240 dinosaur album stickers issued by Panini in 1986. The stickers themselves have the "international" back design written in six languages, but the actual "text" explaining each sticker, or group of stickers, is printed by the corresponding numbered space in the 32-page album. Each 25-cent gumless package contained six stickers and these packs can still be found in stores at this time. Note: set price includes album.

ITEM	MINT	EX
Set	25.00	18.50
Sticker	.10	.05
Wrapper	--	.25
Album	1.50	1.00
Box	--	2.00

DINOSAUR BONES (7) (7)   TWO SIZES

World Candies, the manufacturer, issued two separate sizes of candy boxes under this title. The large size illustrated at top is 1-7/8" wide, 2-1/2" tall, and 3/8" deep. The smaller and thinner variety, illustrated below, is the same size as the Beatles Candy Boxes listed earlier in this volume. The larger type has "connect-a-dot" pictures on the reverse and the name of the dinosaur is printed on one flap. The smaller boxes have the name of the subject printed right on the picture panel. Both series of boxes appear to have been issued in 1989-1990 and they are currently selling for $1.00 each.

CHECKLIST OF
LARGE BOXES:

Ankylosaurus
Brontosaurus
Elasmosaurus
Pterosaurus
Stegosaurus
Triceratops
Tyrannosaurus

SMALL SIZE CHECKLIST
Ankylosaurus
Brontosaurus
Elasmosaurus
Pterosaurus
Stegosaurus
Triceratops
Tyrannosaurus

DINOSAUR CUTOUTS (5)

VARIOUS SIZES

Country Oven Cookies has adorned its cookie boxes with this impressive set of five "Dinosaur Cutouts" since the latter part of 1990. The cutouts range in height from five to seven inches, depending upon the specific animal, and each subject is drawn in full color against an appropriate background. The dotted lines indicating the cutting line extend to the side panels of the box; these side panels are the supports which allow the dinosaur to stand independently once it is free of the box. As of this writing, Country Oven boxes with Dinosaur Cutouts were still available in grocery stores and collectors are advised to save complete boxes, if possible.

ITEM	MINT	EX
Set of complete boxes	6.00	4.50
Set of cutouts	--	3.00
Cutout	--	.50

CHECKLIST
Brontosaurus
Dimorphodon
Protoceratops
Stegosaurus
Tyrannosaurus

DINOSAURS (36)

2" X 3 1/4"

The dimensions given in the heading refer to the entire Wacky Wax card; the dinosaur sticker itself is approximately 2" square. There are 36 black-ink drawings in the set and each design appears on both green and blue backgrounds. The green stickers, however, have a blank white back; the blue stickers have a green patterned back with the words "Wacky Wax" printed in angled rows. The sticker number is located on the bottom part of the card: the sticker itself is unnumbered. Note: prices listed are for either color variety. Stickers were sold in a clear cello pack devoid of design or writing.

ITEM	MINT	EX
Set	14.00	10.00
Sticker	.35	.25

1	Elasmosaurus	10	Monoclonius	19	Protoceratops
2	Stegosuarus	11	Tylosuarus	20	Geosaurus
3	Corythosaurus	12	Pteranodon	21	Plesiosaurus
4	Camptosaurus	13	Plateosaurus	22	Brontosaurus
5	Teratosaurus	14	Allosaurus	23	Gorgosaurus
6	Archaeopteryx	15	Antosaurus	24	Struthiomimus
7	Hesperosuchus	16	Styracosaurus	25	Glyptodon
8	Coelophysis	17	Triceratops	26	Doedicuris
9	Ornitholestes	18	Ankylosaurus	27	Proganochelys

28	Dimorphodon
29	Rhamphorhynchus
30	Elasmosaurus
31	Ceratosaurus
32	Tyrannosaurus
33	Diplodocus
34	Dimetrodon
35	Scolosaurus
36	Palaeoscincus

DINOSAURS (10) (10)

Issued by Sunkist 'Fun Fruits' between 1987 and 1989, these attractive cards provided a collecting challenge. One card was inserted in each six-pack box of fruit candy: the 'A' series appeared first, followed by 'B', and, finally, a reissue of modified 'A' cards. The second issue of 'A' cards featured the addition of green borders to the originally

borderless design. Several print-size variations have been identified on the backs of these cards, but have generated little interest among collectors.

ITEM	MINT	EX
Sets (all)	6.00	4.00
Cards (all)	.50	.35

A1	Ankylosaurus	B1	Allosaurus
A2	Apatosaurus	B2	Camarasaurus
A3	Brachiosaurus	B3	Dilophosaurus
A4	Coelophysis	B4	Diplodocus
A5	Deinonychus	B5	Iguanodon
A6	Parasaurolophus	B6	Maiasaura
A7	Pterodactyl	B7	Pachycephalosaurus
A8	Stegosaurus	B8	Protoceratops
A9	Triceratops	B9	Senonychosaurus
A10	Tyrannosaurus	B10	Struthiomimus

GREEN BORDER

NO BORDER

DINOSAURS (12)

Here is an example of some of the hidden treasures to be found in the candy section of any store. On the surface, boxes of "DinaSour Eggs," a Willy Wonka product, look like your average candy aisle selection. The front panel has a cute, blue-spotted dinosaur baby hatching from an egg and there is a "DinaSour Quiz" feature printed on the other side of the box. The answer to the "Fun Clues" in the

"Who Am I?" quiz, however, is a "Collector's Card" printed on a hidden panel inside the box. There are twelve cards in the set, each a nicely detailed B&W drawing accompanied by three lines explaining the dinosaur's name, its pronunciation, and its origin. The cards are not numbered and they are smaller than standard size, with an unusual notch in one corner. Willy Wonka distributed the series beginning in 1987.

ITEM	MINT	EX
Set of complete boxes	15.00	12.00
Set of cards	7.00	4.50
Complete box	1.00	.75
Card	.50	.35

CHECKLIST
Allosaurus
Ankylosaurus
Brachiosaurus
Brontosaurus
Camarassaurus
Diplodocus
Iguanodon
Pteranodon
Stegosaurus
Trachodon
Triceratops
Tyrannosaurus Rex

DINOSAURS (45)

2 1/2" X 2 13/16"

In addition to its Baseball Hall of Fame, Presidents, and Animals sets, Golden Press also issued a 45-card set of Dinosaurs in "book" form. The book actually was a front and back cover with sheets of cards inside. Juvenile owners rarely left these sheets intact — these were designed as trading cards, after all — so collectors most often encounter Golden Press dinosaurs as singles or sets of single cards with rouletted edges. A variety of dinosaurs are portrayed in multi-colored artwork on front; backs carry the card number and text. The "Golden Press" name is not printed on the card; they can be identified by the checklist printed below and by their size (smaller than standard). Note: the price for "mint" grade refers only to cards in the original book.

ITEM	MINT	EX
Set	30.00	18.00
Card	--	.35

1 Fossils	16 Icnthyosaur	31 Moropus
2 Trilobite and Lampshell	17 Ornithopod	32 Merychippus
3 Sea Lily	18 Stegosaurus	33 Baluchithere
4 Sea Scorpion	19 Brontosaurus	34 Amphicyon
5 Coiled Ammonite	20 Allosaurus	35 Shovel-Tusker
6 Lobe-fin Fish	21 Protoceratops	36 Giant Ground Sloth
7 Armored Fish	22 Giant Mossasaurus	37 Saber-Toothed Tiger
8 Diplovertebron	23 Pteranodon	38 Glyptodont
9 Seymouria	24 Tyrannosaurus	39 Woolly Rhinoceros
10 Cockroach	25 Triceratops	40 Woolly Mammoth
11 Plesiosaur	26 Astrapothere	41 Royal Bison
12 Dimetrodon	27 Eohippus	42 Long-necked Camel
13 Saltoposuchus	28 Early Mammal	43 Three-horned Grazer
14 Archaeopteryx	29 Diatryama	44 American Mastodon
15 Rhamphorhynchus	30 Brontothere	45 Musk-ox

DINOSAURS (28)

2 1/2" X 3 1/4"

One of the nicest dinosaur series produced in recent years is also one of the hardest to collect. In 1982, The Milwaukee Public Museum — aided by one of its employees, collector Paul Tenpenny — decided to hand out dinosaur cards to visitors in order to promote an exhibit called "The Third Planet" which was scheduled to open in October, 1983. Since that time, MPM has distributed 28 different cards; the only way to obtain them is to visit the museum itself.

The first four cards issued were unnumbered and bear a 1982 date on the reverse. In 1984, a total of eight cards were distributed, and these are numbered 5-12. Four more cards, numbers 13-16, were released in 1986. In 1988, cards 17-22 were created. All of the cards cited so far have the year of issue printed on them and this is important because somehow numbers 17-21 were used again when the museum issued a five card set of dinosaurs in 1990. This means that there are two different cards for each of the following numbers: 17, 18, 19, 20, & 21. In addition, MPM also issued an unnumbered "gimmick" card showing Milwaukee Brewers manager Tom Trebelhorn riding a torosaurus. It's easy to see why collectors find this set confusing.

A total of 28 cards have been issued to date. The fronts all have excellent artwork depictions of dinosaurs and the pictures are surrounded by white borders. The backs contain the names of the subjects and some descriptive text about them. All of the cards except the redundant number group have the year of issue printed at bottom on the back. Due to the method of distribution, very few samples have reached the trading card market. Demand for MPM dinosaur cards is limited, however, and the few cards which become available sell for $1.00 each.

—	Anatosauruus copei
—	Ankylosaurus magniventris
—	Triceratops prorsus
—	Tyrannosaurus rex
5	Archaeopteryx
6	Dromaeosaurus
7	Stegosaurus
8	The Last of the Dinosaurs
9	Mammut Americanum
10	Othnielia
11	Camptosaurus
12	Diplodocus
13	Pterichthyodes
14	Casteroides
15	Plesiosaurus
16	Megaloceros
17	Torosaurus
17	Mammuthus primigenius
18	Pteranodon
18	Smilodon
19	Stygimoloch
19	Platybelodon
20	Albertosaurus
20	Eobasileous
21	Struthiomimymus
21	Coelodonta
22	Diatryma
—	Major Leaguers Tom Trebelhorn & the Torosaurus

DINOSAURS (65)

2 1/2" X 3 1/2"

"It's The Next Big Thing." That was the message of the relentless television advertising which preceded "Dinosaurs" to network television. Other projects that have used this style of "ooh, you're gonna love it" commercials - Ishtar and Willow - fell flat on their faces. Luckily, Dinosaurs has more going for it than either of those turkeys.

Pro Set introduced its 65-card Dinosaurs set early in 1992. The majority of the series is composed of "television cards" which are numbered from 1 to 50 (on the back). The fronts of these contain color photos set on four colors of marbled backgrounds. The backs have a gray-tan marbled surface with a short, easy-to-read text printed on top. The five numbered trivia cards have the same background color or on both the "questions" and "answers" sides. Each of the ten puzzle cards is a complete six-piece jigsaw which can be punched out and assembled. The entire set was obviously designed as a "prehysterical and fabrosaurously fun" set for children. The cards were distributed in (gumless) foil "fin packs" containing eight television cards, plus one each of the trivia and puzzle cards. Note: set price includes all three types of cards.

ITEM	MINT	EX
Set	10.00	--
Television card	.10	--
Trivia card	.10	--
Puzzle card	.50	--
Wrapper	--	.10
Box	--	2.00

DINOSAURS ALBUM STICKERS (150)

1 3/4" X 2 1/2"

Diamond Publishing obtained the rights to produce a sticker set based on the "Dinosaurs" television show and this was released to the public in early 1992. All of the 150 paper album stickers in the set have color photographs on front: these may be complete or partial, depending on how they are arranged in the sticker album. The latter is 24 pages in length and it has numbered spaces which correspond to the numbers on the backs of the stickers. Product was distributed in blue "packet" envelopes containing six stickers each (40¢) and the packet design is repeated on the 50-count box. The album (79¢) has large color photos on the front and back covers and there is a line of text for each sticker printed under the appropriate space. Diamond's "Dinosaurs" was still available in retail stores as we were going to press; complete sets (including album) should be available from card dealers in the $15 range.

"A hundred million years into the future they came, swept through time by an accident of science! Can the human race survive? Or will these towering monarchs from the dawn of creation once again inherit the earth ... this time for ALL time? The ultimate nightmare is now a reality." That's the snappy introduction Topps created for their "Dinosaurs Attack!" series.

Maybe it should read like this: "Three years ago they came, a modern version of "Mars Attacks" hoping to capitalize on the dinosaur fad! Can collectors survive? Or will these deja vu-like cards from Topps' dungeon of creation again inherit our wallets ... until NEXT time?" Topps was right about the ultimate nightmare becoming reality ... they did succeed in producing a series which rivals "Here's Bo" and "Menudo" in terms of collector indifference.

Well, read my lips, pilgrims. I knew "Mars Attacks," and "Dinosaurs Attack!" is no "Mars Attacks," but it is an astonishingly underestimated set. We are talking great artwork and hilarious text here ... displaying more imagination and creativity than any other set issued in the decade of the eighties. The problem is that Topps overestimated the potential demand and printed zillions of cards, and while they are still in abundance, the set will never rise in price. This makes "Dinosaurs Attack!" one of the best buys in the current marketplace (but not a good set to speculate in for the future). This set is a throwback to the "golden days" of collecting and is a bargain to boot! Note: set prices include stickers.

ITEM	MINT	EX
Set	10.00	7.00
Card	.10	.07
Sticker	.35	.25
Wrappers (3), ea.	––	.25
Box	––	2.00

1 Forward (Header card)
2 Experiment in Space!
3 Time Scanner Disaster!
4 The Past Comes Alive
5 Homeroom Horror
6 Police Precinct Assaulted!
7 D.C. Holocaust
8 Crushing a Canine
9 Nuptial Nightmare
10 Italy Under Seige!
11 Trapped in the Basement!
12 Panic in the Stadium
13 Rock Concert Carnage
14 Lunch Break!
15 The Colonel ... Shredded!
16 Heartland Horror
17 Blue Water, Savage Death
18 Tourist Trap
19 Madness in the Streets
20 Bashing the BMT
21 Fast Food Frenzy
22 The Behemoth Fries
23 The Perfect Wave
24 London in Flames

The TRUTH about PARASAUROLOPHUS
(pa-ra-sor-OL-uh-fus)

LENGTH: 11 meters
SIZE OF HEAD CREST: as much as 92 cm.
ERA: Cretaceous
75 million years ago
MEANING OF NAME: 'Parallel Crested Reptile'

Curious-looking Parasaurolophus belonged to the species Hadrosaur (Trachodon is also a member of this group). A gentle, plant-eating creature, he lived only in North America. The impressive crest on his head is made up of two hollow tubes, one on top of the other and joined at the far end. The front end of these tubes link up with the nostrils. Similar to a trombone, this crest might have been used to produce a highly distinctive 'hooting' sound.

© 1988 THE TOPPS COMPANY, INC.

Dinosaurs Attack!

25 Day of the Duckbill
26 Coasting to Calamity
27 Soviets VS. Dimetrodons
28 Saurian Secrets
29 Monster in the Museum
30 A Kid Strikes Back!
31 Our Forces - Flattened!
32 Cat Lady's Revenge
33 Manhattan Island Swamped!
34 Animal Wars

35 A Lady in Distress
36 Comics Con Catastrophe!
37 Picnic of Peril
38 "We Can't Hold Them Back!!"
39 Trilobite Terror
40 Wrestling Riot
41 Entombed!!
42 Lights! Camera! Carnage!
43 Business Lunch
44 Meltdown!!

45 Anchorman's Peril
46 Grip of Horror
47 Supreme Evil
48 "You Can't Let Them Win!!"
49 Ripped Out of Time!
50 Gruesome Fate
51 Time Twister
52 The Ultimate Sacrifice
53 Prometheus Explodes!
54 Rebuilding Our World
55 Dinosaurs Attack! Synopsis

STICKERS
1 Allosaurus
2 Ankylosaurus
3 Dimetrodon
4 Brontosaurus
5 Parasaurolophus

6 Plesiosaurus
7 Pteranodon
8 Stegosaurus
9 Trachodon
10 Triceratops
11 Tyrannosaurus

DINOSAUR SERIES (80) 2 1/2" X 3 1/2"

Although the wrapper says "Dinosaur Trading Cards," the cards themselves are marked "Dinosaur Series." There are 80 cards in the set and the obverses have a strange greenish-blue coloration. The card number appears on the front in a white dinosaur design, and on the back at the beginning of the text. An album for mounting the set could be obtained free of charge by sending in eight cards bearing the letters of the word "dinosaur" (one letter per card in box on reverse). The set was issued by Nu-Cards Sales in 1961.

ITEM	MINT	EX
Set	375.00	300.00
Card	4.00	3.00
Wrapper	--	20.00
Box	--	125.00

52 SABRE TOOTH TIGERS

80 WHAT IS IT?

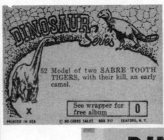

52 Model of two SABRE TOOTH TIGERS, with their kill, an early camel.

See wrapper for free album   O

FREE ALBUM TO MOUNT ALL YOUR DINOSAUR CARDS
to get your FREE album

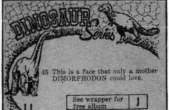

DINOSAUR TRADING CARDS

1 Phobosuchus crocodilla Chamosaurus saurischia ceratopsia
2 Prehistoric Man
3 Wooly Mammoth
4 Dryptosauri
5 Brontosaurus
6 Dimetrodon
7 Tyrannosaurus
8 Phororhacos
9 Hoplophoneus
10 Lycaenops
11 Smilodon
12 Allosaurus
13 Pteradodon - Tylosaurus
14 Peteranodons Elasmosaurus - Tylosaurus
15 Pterodactylus
16 Gorgosuarus - Scolosaurus
17 Giant Elk

18 Nothrotherium Smilodon
19 Mesosaurus
20 Neanderthan Man - Cave Bears
21 Indricotherium
22 Duck-Billed Trachodon Tyrannosaurus
23 Mahcairodus
24 Arsinoitherium
25 Monster Fishes
26 Brontotherium
27 Iguandon
28 Rhamphorhynchus
29 Styracosaurus
30 Triceratops
31 Smilodon Prehistoric Elephant
32 Deinotherium
33 Corythosaurus
34 Brachiosaurus

35 Ceratosaurus - Stegosauri
36 Plesiosaurid
37 Ornitholestes - Archaeopteryx
38 Dire Wolf - Arsinoitherium
39 Sabre-Toothed Tigers
40 Emperor Mammoth
41 Mammoths
42 Sabre-Toothed Cat
43 Wooly Mammoth
44 Dinosaur
45 Dimorphodon
46 Monoclonius
47 Protoceratops
48 Smaller Dinosaurs
49 Pachycephalosaurus
50 Corypihodon

51 Stegosaurus
52 Sabre Tooth Tigers
53 Mochops
54 Diplodocus
55 Hesperonis Regalis
56 Giant Tylosaurus
57 Early Reptiles
58 Mischelokolk
59 Sabre-Tooth Tiger Giant Sloth
60 Tyrannosaurus
61 Ground Sloth Sabre-Tooth Tiger
62 Stegosaurus - Ceratosaurus
63 Giant Bison
64 Hyaenodons - Arsinotherium
65 Agathaumas Monoclonium
66 Protoceratops
67 Trachodon
68 Triceratops
69 Diatryma
70 Plesiosaurus
71 Mystriosuchus
72 Struthiomimus
73 Baluchitherium
74 Giant Sloth Short Faced Bear
75 Dinornis
76 Prehistoric Men
77 Giant Beavers
78 Phytosaur
79 Entelodon
80 What is it?

45 DIMORPHODON

45 This is a face that only a mother DIMORPHODON could love.

See wrapper for free album   J

DISGUSTING DISGUISES (24 & 27)

TWO SIZES

Although Topps issued this product on two separate occasions—1967 & 1970—the cards and stickers from both issues are identical. In fact, the only evidence available to prove this double marketing is on the wrappers. The 1967 wrapper has a 5-cent price, a 1967 product code, and a "Topps Brooklyn" credit; the 1970 wrapper is unpriced, has a 1970 product code, and was made by "Topps Duryea." The set consists of 24 cards and 27 stickers—all numbered—depicting a variety of disguises and disfigurements. Note: set price includes all cards & stickers.

ITEM	MINT	EX
Set	185.00	140.00
Card	2.00	1.50
Sticker	4.00	3.00
Wrapper		
1967	--	25.00
1970	--	10.00
Box	--	40.00

FISH FACE

SEE OTHER SIDE

SAFETY PIN AND RAZOR BLADE
NO. 6 IN A SERIES OF 27 STICKERS

Masks
1 Bolt Thru Head
2 Sloppy Moustache
3 Tiger Mask
4 Wind Up Ear Key
5 Bloody Bandage
6 Nose Moustache
7 Diamond Earrings
8 Ape
9 Arrow Thru Head
10 Tearing Mask
11 Pirate Mask
12 Horn Eyes
13 Blue Monster Mask
14 Dagger In Ear
15 Skull Earrings
16 Crossed Eyes
17 Octopus Mask
18 Sun God
19 Cannibal
20 Oriental Mask
21 Three Eye Mask
22 Skull Mask
23 Tongue Moustache
24 Fish Face

Stickers
1 Monster Fingernails
2 Creepy Crawlers
3 Accidents
4 Scalp
5 Dragonfly & Caterpillar
6 Safety Pins and Razor Blade
7 Anchors and Mermaid
8 Flies and Bees
9 Hearts
10 Arrow Target & Nail
11 Butterflies
12 Scar-Face
13 Beetles and Flying Ant
14 Devil's Disguise
15 Traffic Signs No. 1
16 Beards and Moustache
17 Spiders and Ants
18 Loser's Kit
19 Eyes
20 Flowers
21 Good Luck
22 Scar-Face
23 Big Eyes
24 Traffic Signs No. 2
25 Dragonfly & Caterpillar
26 Loser's Kit
27 Moths and Butterfly

Snooze Power...

Brave Little Tailor

The honor of being the most colorful and attractive set of 1991 belongs to Impel's "Disney Collector Cards." The series consists of 210 cards divided into three categories: "Favorite Stories" (1-99, double-sided), "Family Portraits" (100-171), and "World Tour" (172-207). Card #'s 208, 209, & 210 are checklists for each of these themes. All the cards have glossy surfaces front and back and contain original Disney artwork, plus information about the various characters and the movies and cartoons in which they appeared. Disney Collector Cards are currently being sold in grocery and variety stores in 15-count foil packages. A special Disney Collector Album, complete with 24 standard plastic card pages to house the cards, was available through the mail via an offer on the wrapper. Two different double-sided holograms were inserted randomly into packs as a bonus to collectors. These are not numbered and are not part of the regular set. No specific price is listed for the holograms since they are subject to intense demand and rapidly-changing values.

ITEM	MINT	EX
Set	15.00	11.00
Card	.10	.07
Hologram	Speculative	
Wrapper	––	.10
Box	––	2.00

FAVORITE STORIES

BRAVE LITTLE TAILOR
1 On the heels of disaster
G "A giant-killer — me!?"

2 Time for a giant break...
H A hero's sendoff...

3 A tasty morsel!
I "How to catch a giant?"

4 Nose to nose with trouble...
D "Oh boy, seven in one blow!"

5 The mighty sword...
E Gloom in the throne room...

6 A stitch in time...
F "Conquer the giant — marry my daughter!"

7 Snooze Power...
A BRAVE LITTLE TAILOR

8 Happily ever after!
B A sign of trouble...

9 Brave Little Tailor
C Bothered by flies...

BONE TROUBLE
10 "Ouch!"
G A place to hide...

11 Is it a mirage?
H A tall story...

12 After awhile, crocodile!
I "Smile..."

13 Out for revenge...
D A bone to pick...

14 What a team!
E Caught in the act...

15 A bright idea...
F Run for your life!

16 Scared stiff!
A BONE TROUBLE

17 A just reward...
B Breakfast for the birds...

18 Bone Trouble
C A guarded treasure...

CLOCK CLEANERS
19 On the edge...
G A bundle of joy?

20 Goofy takes the plunge!
H Father Time!

21 On the rebound...
I Time out of mind...

22 A joint effort!
D Spring cleaning...

23 Touchdown!
E In the works!

24 Spring has sprung...
F A fine-feathered friend...

25 Out of gear...
A CLOCK CLEANERS

26 Mumbo jumbo...
B Making a clean sweep...

27 Clock Cleaners
C Getting in gear...

THRU THE MIRROR
28 A grand finale!!
G "Aw, nuts!"

29 "Forward, march!"
H Feeling small...

30 What a card!
I Hats off to Mickey!

31 "Dancin' cheek to cheek..."
D The true reflection...

32 A two-faced opponent!
E Through the looking glass...

33 The pen is mightier than the sword!
F A tasty treat?

34 Going home...
A THRU THE MIRROR

35 Awake at last!
B A book of wonder...

36 Thru the Mirror
C A dream unfolds...

ORPHANS' BENEFIT
37 Giving Donald a hand...
G Caveman ballet...

38 A knockout!
H Swan dive or belly flop?!

39 A singing sensation...
I A poet's reprise...

40 Tickling the ol' ivories!
D "Little Boy Blue..."

41 Encore! Encore!
E "Come blow your horn..."

42 Mischief is in the air!
F Donald blows his stack!

43 A sitting duck...
A ORPHANS' BENEFIT

44 "Aw, phooey!"
B Fun and games...

45 Orphan's Benefit
C "Introducing Donald Duck..."

PLUTO'S JUDGEMENT DAY
46 Seeing Double...
G A real cat-astrophe!

47 The verdict!
H "Swear in the prisoner!"

48 Poor Pluto!
I Public Enemy Number One!

49 A devilish ploy...
D A perplexed pooch...

50 In the hot seat...
E Scared out of his skin...

51 A rude awakening...
F A taunting tomcat...

52 "Kiss and make up!"
A PLUTO'S JUDGEMENT DAY

53 Friends at last...
B The chase is on...

54 Pluto's Judgement Day
C In the doghouse...

SYMPHONY HOUR
55 Sour notes...
G The big night...

56 A blow out...
H Money is in the air...

57 Musical mayhem!
I A disaster waiting to happen...

58 Bird's - eye view...
D Donald on drums...

59 All fiddled out...
E On first bass with Clara Cluck

60 Sweating it out...
F Music to his ears!

61 Drumming up trouble!
A SYMPHONY HOUR

62 Bravo! Bravo!
B Playing a mean horn...

63 Symphony Hour
C Stringing along with Clarabelle...

LONESOME GHOSTS
64 Surf's Up!
G "Is anybody home?"

65 "Put up your dukes!"
H "One for all...All for one!"

66 A goulish reflection...
I A spooky shadow...

67 Running for cover...
D A ghostly persuasion...

68 A sticky solution...
E "We're on the case!"

69 Who's scaring who?
F "A-ghosting we shall go!"

70 Ghosts on the run!
A LONESOME GHOSTS

71 A job well done!
B Open for business...

72 Lonesome Ghosts
C Napping ghostnabbers...

THE MAD DOCTOR
73 Pluto's Dilemma!
G Caught in the middle...

74 The great experiment!
H A skeletal staircase

75 A bone-chilling chase...
I A mad doctor!!

76 A sticky situation...
D "Oh, no, Pluto's missing!"

77 A real cut-up!
E "Let me in!"

78 What's that buzz?
F A skeleton's welcome...

79 "Where's Pluto?"
A THE MAD DOCTOR

80 Joyful reunion!
B One dark, stormy night...

81 The Mad Doctor
C A dog is nabbed...

DONALD'S CRIME
82 "You forgot to kiss us good-night!"
G Fork it over!

83 Feeling like a skunk...
H In the money!!

84 Dream date with Daisy!
I A guilt-ridden uncle...

Disney Collector Cards

85 "You're a public enemy, pal!"
  D Money in the bank...
86 A life of crime!!
  E A devilish scheme...
87 A real jailbird!!
  F Working on his cut...
88 Cleaning up his debt!
  A DONALD'S CRIME
89 The Payback!
  B "A date with Daisy!
90 Donald's Crime
  C Flat broke!

THE ART OF SKIING
91 Hangin' in there...
  G And we're off...

92 Up and at 'em...
  H Divided he stands...
93 Over the hill...
  I A real twister!
94 At the peak of his form.
  D A striking pose!
95 Up a tree...
  E Something up his sleeve...
96 Down a tree...
  F Head over heels!
97 A crash landing!
  A THE ART OF SKIING
98 Home at last!
  B Sleeping like a log...
99 The Art of Skiing
  C The ultimate back scratcher...

FAMILY PORTRAITS
100 Mickey Mouse
101 Minnie Mouse
102 Goofy
103 Pluto
104 Donald Duck
105 Daisy Duck
106 Mickey Mouse
107 Donald Duck
108 Goofy
109 Brave Little Tailor (1938)
110 Magician Mickey (1937)
111 The Sorcerer's Apprentice (1940)
112 The Nifty Nineties (1941)
113 Brave Little Tailor (1938)
114 Hawaiian Holiday (1937)
115 Society Dog Show (1939)
116 Mickey's Kangaroo (1935)
117 Pluto's Quin-Puplets (1937)
118 Sea Scouts (1939)
119 Fire Chief (1941)
120 Modern Inventions (1937)
121 Don Donald (1937)
122 Donald's Diary (1954)
123 Mr. Duck Steps Out (1940)
124 Hawaiian Holiday (1937)
125 Clock Cleaners (1937)
126 The Olympic Champ (1942)
127 "I only have eyes for you"
128 Lonesome Ghosts (1937)
129 Goofy and Wilbur (1939)
130 Brave Little Tailor (1938)
131 Old MacDonald Duck (1941)
132 Hawaiian Holiday (1937)
133 "The Princess of Polka Dots"
134 Pluto, Junior (1942)
135 Boat Builders (1938)
136 Cartoon: Mickey's Fire Brigade (1935)
137 Cartoon: The Olympic Champ (1942)
138 Cartoon: Truant Officer Donald (1941)
139 Cartoon: Mr. Duck Steps Out (1940)
140 Cartoon: Pluto's Quin-Puplets (1937)
141 Cartoon: Self Control (1938)
142 Cartoon: The Nifty Nineties (1941)
143 Cartoon: Society Dog (1939)
144 Cartoon: Donald's Better Self (1938)
145 Cartoon: Hawaiian Holiday (1937)
146 Cartoon: The Art of Skiing (1941)
147 Cartoon: The Sleepwalker (1942)
148 Cartoon: Mickey's Amateurs (1937)
149 Cartoon: Don Donald (1937)
150 Cartoon: Donald's Golf Game (1938)
151 Cartoon: Beach Picnic (1939)
152 Cartoon: How to Swim (1942)
153 Cartoon: Donald's Ostrich (1937)
154 Sunday Comic strip (1935)
155 Sunday Comic Strip (1939)
156 Daily Comic Strip (1940)
157 Sunday Comic Strip (1939)
158 Sunday Comic Strip (1941)
159 Sunday Comic Strip (1936)
160 Sunday Comic Strip (1940)
161 Sunday Comic Strip (1939)
162 Sunday Comic Strip (1940)
163 Sunday Comic Strip (1937)
164 Sunday Comic Strip (1939)
165 Sunday Comic Strip (1934)
166 Sunday Comic Strip (1939)
167 Sunday Comic Strip (1936)
168 Sunday Comic Strip (1936)
169 Sunday Comic Strip (1939)
170 Sunday Comic Strip (1940)
171 Sunday Comic Strip (1940)

The "Goofy Express"

WORLD TOUR
172 Mickey's World Tour - 1001 Hellos!
173 Seeing Red
174 Wrestling, Japanese Style
175 Safari Surprise
176 A Camel Built for Two
177 The "Goofy Express"
178 Donald's Calypso Beat!
179 Ooh La La, Can They Can-Can!
180 Donald Goes for the Gold
181 Donald the Gondolier
182 Mickey's Crash Course in Greek
183 A Moscow Chorus Line
184 Mickey Scores Again!
185 Pluto's Tail of India
186 Ancient Egyptian Comic Strips
187 Have Bagpipes, Will Travel
188 G'Day, Mate!
189 Daisy Diva
190 Paris Originals
191 Luau Ladies
192 Samurai Duck
193 Hanging Around the Alps with Goofy
194 The Sombrero Stomp
195 Mickey in Russia
196 Mickey's Passport
197 Goofy's Alpine Antics
198 Flight 110
199 Pasta a la Pluto
200 Goofy Guards the Guard
201 Gold Medal Goofy
202 Miki Tiki
203 Mickey's Dutch Dilemma
204 Time on His Hands
205 Flamenco Fun!
206 Chiquita Minnie
207 Mickey's Oom-Pah Band
208 Favorite Stories Checklist
209 Family Portraits Checklist
210 World Tour Checklist

There are two varieties of Disneyland cards, both of which were distributed by Donruss in 1965. The more common type has the card number and caption printed on front and a puzzle piece back. The obverse of the scarcer variety is devoid of print; instead, the card caption and number are printed on the back in a white center area surrounded by dark blue borders. This second type of card was once considered to be a Topps issue, but that rumor has been dispelled.

ITEM	MINT	EX
Sets		
Puzzle back	100.00	80.00
Blue back	200.00	160.00
Cards		
Puzzle Back	1.25	1.00
Blue back	2.50	2.00
Wrapper (1)	--	50.00

1 Santa Fe and Disneyland Railroad Trains Take You Through the Grand Canyon Diorama

2 Goofy and His Disney Character Pals Are Reflected in the Sun Glasses of a Young Disneyland Guest.

3 Sleeping Beauty's Castle in Disneyland Marks Entrance to Fantasyland.

4 Departing from the Swiss Chalet in Fantasyland Guests on Disneyland Skyway Travel High Above the Magic Kingdom of Disneyland.

5 Indians Greet the Santa Fe and Disneyland Railroad Train as the 1890 Locomotive Pauses for Water at the Frontierland Depot.

6 Three of Disneyland's Most Popular Attractions—the Matterhorn Mountain, Disneyland Alweg Monorail and the Submarine Voyage

7 Alice and the White Rabbit Begin a Ride through the Alice in Wonderland Attraction at Disneyland.

8 Western Mine Train Takes Disneyland Visitors through Nature's Wonderland.

9 Disneyland Guests Board Doubledeck Bus for Trip Down Main Street to Town Square.

10 Spaceman Greets Tommorrowland Visitors at Disneyland.

11 Storybookland Miniatures Are Viewed from the Colored Casey Jr. Circus Train at Disneyland.

12 Alice in Wonderland and Her Friends, White Rabbit and Mad Hatter, Greet Guests at Disneyland.

13 Disneyland Submarine Passes through Waterfall as Guests Explore "Liquid Space."

14 "Old Faithful" Geyser Erupts as the Western Mine Train Makes Its Way through Nature's Wonderland at Disneyland.

15 "Fantasy in the Sky" Fireworks Explore Nightly Over Sleeping Beauty's Castle During Summertime at Disneyland.

16 Disneyland Mountain Climbers, Fritz and Otto, Ascend the 90 Feet Height of Matterhorn Mountain.

17 Gaily Decorated Tree Brings Christmas to Disneyland Town Square During Yuletide Season.

18 Snow White and the Seven Dwarfs Welcome Guests to Fantasyland in Disneyland.

19 Corps of Toy Soldiers Marches Down Main Street During Disneyland's Christmas Season's Parades.

20 Disneyland African Veldt Is Viewed from Aboard Jungle Cruise Launches in Adventureland.

21 Walt Disney's Enchanted Tiki Room Marks the Entrance to Adventureland.

22 Actual Sets Used in the Making of Walt Disney's Motion Picture "20,000 Leagues Under the Sea" Are on Display for Tomorrowland Visitors.

23 Sleeping Beauty's Castle in Disneyland Marks Entrance to Fantasyland.

24 The Trapped Safari at Disneyland as Viewed by Disneyland Passengers Aboard Jungle Cruise in Adventureland.

25 Visitors Aboard Disneyland Mark Twain View Life-Like Indian Villiage.

26 Viewed from Dutch Canal Boats, Story Bookland Features Miniature Settings from Disney Animated Motion Pictures.

27 Mickey Mouse and His Dog Pluto Take a Ride on Disneyland Fire Engine.

28 White Rabbit and Mrs. Rabbit On an Egg Hunt During Disneyland Easter Season.

29 Western Mine Train Crosses Trestle over Bear River Going Through Nature's Wonderland.

30 Disneyland Astrojet Provides Thrilling Ride in Tomorrowland.

31 Indian Elephants Play in Sacred Wading Pool as Seen by Passengers Aboard Disneyland Jungle Cruise.

32 Deluxe Passenger Train of the 1890 Vintage Leaves Main Street Station on the Santa Fe and Disneyland Railroad.

33 Disneyland's Gonzales Trio Entertain Guests at Mexican Village in Frontierland.

34 A Disneyland Future Attraction Under Construction for Opening in 1967, The Haunted House.

35 Disneyland Skyway Passes through Matterhorn Mountain.

36 Disneyland's Swiss Family Robinson Treehouse Towers 80 Feet Above Adventureland.

37 The Wonders of Liquid Space Are Viewed Aboard the Nautilus, One of the Disneyland Submarine Fleet.

38 Brightly Canopied Launches Carry Passengers Past a Native Hut in the Jungle Cruise at Disneyland.

39 Disney Characters Meet in Front of Disneyland Main Gate with a Flower Portrait of Mickey Mouse.

40 Colorful Disneyland Band Marches Down Main Street.

41 Aboard Brightly Canopied Launches Disneyland Visitors Become explorers on Jungle Cruise.

42 King Arthur's Carousel in Disneyland Is America's Largest Carousel.

43 An Aerial View of the Rivers of America in Disneyland.

44 Guests Thrill to Climax of Disneyland Bobsled Ride as Sleds Race to a Splashing Halt in Glacier Lake.

45 Western Mine Train Departs for Tour of Nature's Wonderland at Disneyland.

46 Golden Horseshoe Revue is Staged Several Times Daily in This Ornate Frontier "Saloon" at Disneyland.

47 Startlingly Lifelike in Appearance and Movement, These Animals Inhabit the Rivers of America at Disneyland.

48 Old-Fashioned Stands and Popcorn Vendors Can Be Found Along Main Street and Town Square.

49 Viewed from Dutch Canal Boats, Storybookland Features Miniature Settings from Disney Animated Motion Pictures.

50 The White Rabbit and Mrs. Rabbit Surprise Alice in Wonderland with an Easter Basket.

51 Santa Fe and Disneyland Trains Depart from 1890 Main Street.

52 Storybookland Miniatures Are Viewed from the Gaily Colored Casey Jr. Circus Train at Disneyland.

53 Disneyland Mark Twain Carries Frontierland Visitors Along Rivers of America.

54 Disneyland Indian Village Features Ceremonial Dancing by the Rivers of America.

55 The Columbia Is a Full-Size Authentic Replica of the First American Ship to Sail Around the World.

56 Disneyland's Mighty Matterhorn Mountain Towers Above the Submarine Lagoon in Tomorrowland.

57 Comical Reindeer Greets Guests During the Disneyland Annual Character Parade.

Disneyland

58 Mickey Mouse Leads the Disneyland Band in Front of Sleeping Beauty's Castle.
59 Squid "Attacks" Shark in Disneyland's Submarine Lagoon as Viewed by Passengers Aboard Authentic Air-Conditioned Submarines.

60 Peter Pan Welcomes Disneyland Visitors to Fantasyland.
61 Disneyland Astrojet Enables Guests to "Pilot" Their Own Jet Through a Fast-Moving Journey.

62 Indian War Canoes Transport Disneyland Visitors Down the Rivers of America in Frontierland.
63 Disneyland Tour Guide Points Out Exhibits and Shops Along Town Square and Main Street.

64 Davy Crockett Fort Marks Entrance to Frontierland at Disneyland.
65 Disneyland Mad Hatter's Tea Party Features a Merry Whirl in Spinning Cups and Twirling Saucers.
66 Tomorrowland Autopia Allows Drivers Some "Freeway" Fun.

DOCTOR DOLITTLE TATTOOS (?)   1 9/16" X 3 1/2"

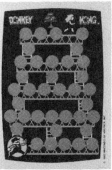

Like most of the older tattoo sets, this series is collected for the outside wrappers, not the transfers. The production code printed on the attachment flap indicates this item was marketed in 1967. The designs illustrated are the only

two reported to date: the "parrot-in-hand" design is yellow & the "hat-in-hand" design is red. The tattoos depict various Dolittle animals and characters. They are not numbered or captioned.

ITEM	MINT	EX
Wrappers (2) each	--	15.00

DONKEY KONG (4 & 32)   2 1/2" X 3 1/2"

The Donkey Kong set is composed of four game cards and 32 stickers. The former are miniature arcade screens: players advance by scratching off dots which conceal game moves. The 32 stickers are not numbered and contain Donkey Kong humor and slogans on front and puzzle pieces (30) and puzzle previews (2) on back.

ITEM	MINT	EX
Set	7.00	5.00
Card	.10	.05
Sticker	.25	.15
Wrapper	--	.35
Box	--	3.00

DOPEY BOOKS (42)

2 1/2" X 3 1/2"

The title on the front cover of each Dopey Book is a setup (straight line) for the joke (or punch line) within. There are 42 cardboard folders in the set and each is numbered on the left interior page. The wrapper is green with a yellow book and red title. Dopey Books hit the retail market in 1967 and sold for 5 cents a pack.

ITEM	MINT	EX
Set	150.00	125.00
Book	3.00	2.50
Wrapper	--	20.00
Box	--	65.00

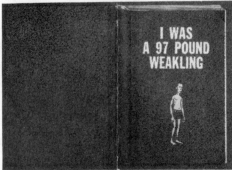

This large "Dopey Book Shop" card appeared i another Topps set, "Funn Doors."

1 How to Make People Look Up to You (...Become a Window Washer!)
2 How to make a Million Dollars (...Print Them!)
3 How to Stop Children from Biting Their Nails (Knock Their Teeth Out!)
4 How to Catch Flies (Swat Them!)
5 Smile Thru Life and Gain Fame (...As a Grinning Idiot!)
6 I Worked 40 Years for the U.S. Government (...In a Federal Jail!)
7 I Live with Wild Beasts (My Family!)
8 I Own 5,000 Head of Cattle (...No Bodies, Just Heads!)
9 It's Easy to Speak Chinese (If You Were Born in China!)
10 How to Take Care of Your Teeth (... Put 'Em in a Glass!)

11 The Ostrich, The Worlds Largest Living Bird (It's Also the World's Largest Dead Bird!)
12 Open in Case of Fire (Not Now, Stupid...in Case of Fire!)
13 How to Repair a Broken Water Pipe (Call a Plumber!)
14 Your Future in Electricity (...An Electric Chair!)
15 How to Survive a Blizzard (Stay Home!)
16 You Can Be as Smart as the Next Man (...If the Next Man Is an Idiot!)
17 I Never Worked a Day in My Life (I'm a Night Watchman!)
18 How to Control Your Temper (...Argue with Someone Bigger!)
19 They Said It Couldn't Be Done (They Were Right!)
20 How to collect Coins (...Beg)
21 What to Do in Case of Air-Raid (Hide!!)
22 I Went Thru College in Record Time (...3½ Minutes!)
23 How to Get Your Name in Headlines (...Rob a Bank!)

24 School Can Be Fun (If You Don't Have to Go!)
25 I Married a Handsome 6-Footer (...But Who Wants Someone with 6 Feet!)
26 I Haven't an Enemy in the World (...But My Friends Hate Me!)
27 How to Put a Lasting Finish on Your Car (...Try to Beat a Train to the Crossing!)
28 How to Avoid Making Mistakes (Don't Do Anything!)
29 I Won 100 Fights in a Row (Then I Fought a Man!)
30 I Traveled into Space (...When I Sat on a Tack!)
31 How to Get Rid of Dishpan Hands (Let Your Sister Do the Dishes!)
32 You Can Have a Job in the Movies (...As an Usher)
33 What Every Girl Should Know (A Rich Bachelor!)
34 Honesty Is the Best Policy (...If You're Too Nervous to Steal!)
35 How to Keep Your Bills Down (Use a Paper Weight!)
36 I Hunted for Buffalo (But I Got Lost and Wound Up in Albany!)
37 I Was a 97 Pound Weakling (Now I'm Down to 57 Pounds!)
38 You Don't Have to Work for a Living (...You Can Starve!)
39 You Can Fly Your Own Plane ('Till the Rubber Band Breaks!)
40 Instructions for Back-Seat Drivers (Shut Up!)
41 Make Money (By Using Your Head ...in a Carnival!)
42 Why I Went to College (Because I Didn't Get a Boyfriend in High School!)

DRAG NATIONALS (70)

2 1/2" X 3 1/2"

Drag Nationals, produced by Fleer in 1972, have color action photos of dragstrip racing on the front. The backs (blue print on white stock) contain a large AHRA logo, the set title, card caption, text, and card number. Although this is a sport card set, it has been listed in the Non-Sport Guides for years because the sport card guides have chosen to ignore it. Now that racing cards are "hot," collectors can expect to find it included in more and more sport listings. PRICE ADVISORY: the prices listed here pertain to the non-sports market; they will be lower than the values found among those who exclusively deal in or collect racing cards.

ITEM	MINT	EX
Set	160.00	120.00
Card	2.00	1.50
Wrappers (2) ea.	—	12.00

1 STICK GUM

1 STICK GUM

1 Don Garlits' "Swamp Rat" Fuel Dragster
2 Don Garlits' "Swamp Rat" Fuel Dragster
3 Don Garlits' "Swamp Rat" Fuel Dragster
4 "Cyr & Schofield" Fuel Dragster
5 Charlie Thurwanger's "Hombre" Chevy Funny Car
6 Bill Leavitt's "Quickie too" Mustang Funny Car
7 "CKC" Vega Funny Car
8 "Blue Max" Mustang Funny Car
9 Kansas John Wiebe Fuel Dragster
10 Steve Carbone Fuel Dragster
11 "Mr. Norm" Dodge Charger Funny Car

12 Jim Hayter Pro-Stock Vega
13 Sox & Martin Pro-Stock Dodge
14 Don Grotheer's "Cable Car" Pro-Stock Duster
15 "Rod Shop Dodge" Pro-Stock Demon
16 "The Boss" Pro-Stock Plymouth
17 Rundle's "Speed Goodies" Chevrolet
18 "Grumpy's Toy" Pro-Stock Vega
19 "Landy's Dodge" Pro-Stock Dodge
20 "Mo-Town Missle" Pro Stock Dodge
21 "Drag-On Vega" Vega Funny Car
22 "Revell Snowman" Dodge Charger Funny Car

23 "Mo-Town Shaker" Vega Funny Car
24 Mickey Thompson Vega Funny Car
25 "Paddy Wagon" Vega Wheelstander
26 "The Mongoose" Plymouth Funny Car
27 "The Snake" Plymouth Funny Car
28 Gary Cochran Fuel Dragster
29 "White Bear Dodge" Dodge Charger Funny Car
30 "Revell Snowman" Dodge Funny Car
31 Steve Carbone Fuel Dragster
32 "Courage of Australia" Rocket Dragster
33 Kansas John Wiebe Fuel Dragster
34 "Carpet Bagger" Fuel Dragster
35 "Smokin' Sun Devil" Chevy Funny Car
36 "Drag-On Vega" Vega Funny Car
37 Chris Karamesines Fuel Dragster
38 Gary Cochran Fuel Dragster
39 Don Cook Fuel Dragster
40 Creitz & Dill Fuel Dragster
41 Chris Karamesines Fuel Dragster
42 "The Boss" Pro-Stock Plymouth
43 "White Bear Dodge" Dodge Charger Funny Car
44 Braskett & Burgin Camaro Funny Car
45 "Lil' John's Chevy" Vega Funny Car

46 "Hot Wheels Snake" Plymouth Cuda Funny Car
47 "Hot Wheels Mongoose" Plymouth Duster Funny Car
48 Candies & Hughes Plymouth Funny Car
49 "Telstar" Dodge Funny Car
50 Walton, Cerny & Moody Fuel Dragster
51 "Stardust" Plymouth Funny Car
52 "Green Mamba" Jet Dragster
53 "Arizona Wildcat" Funny Car
54 Tom Grove Mustang Funny Car
55 Dunn & Reath Funny Car
56 "El Diablo" Fuel Dragster
57 "California Flash" Pro-Stock Plymouth
58 "Grumpy's Toy" Pro-Stock Vega
59 Walton, Cerny & Moody Fuel Dragster
60 "Ramchargers" Dodge Funny Car
61 "Researcher" Vega Funny Car
62 "Brand-X" Mustang Funny Car
63 "Special Edition" Fuel Dragster
64 "Trojan Horse" Dodge Funny Car
65 "Peter Paul Vega" Vega Funny Car
66 "Whipple & Mr. Ed" Plymouth Funny Car
67 "Smokey Joe's Charger" Dodge Funny Car
68 "Green Mamba" Jet Dragster
69 Mickey Thompson Funny Car
70 "Paddy Wagon" Vega Wheelstander

DRAGON'S LAIR (63 & 30)

TWO SIZES

Fleer produced the Dragon's Lair set in 1984. There are 63 numbered, front-peel stickers, each measuring 2 1/2" X 3 1/32" (the captions for these are listed below). In addition, there are 30 untitled rub-off games, which have instructions on the back for single or multi-person play and scoring. The striking artwork makes this an excellent set for collectors interested in fantasy themes. Note: set price includes stickers and game cards.

ITEM	MINT	EX
Set	24.00	15.00
Game card	.15	.10
Sticker	.30	.20
Wrapper	—	.35
Box	—	4.00

1 Come On Big Guy, Make My Day!	23 This'll Tickle Your Tentacles!
2 Help! Save Me!	24 Are You Guys Sure This Is A Hot Tub?
3 Dragor's Lair Is Great	25 Please Don't Squeeze The Dirk!
4 Psst...Your Deodorant Hath Failed!	26 Ouch! This Better Be Worth It!
5 Reach Out And Touch Somebody!	27 Dirk's Key To Happiness
6 You're So Brave	28 Dirk The Daring
7 I Vant To Bite Your Neck!	29 Princess Daphne
8 Here Comes That Night Rider!	30 Please Dont Feed The Dragon
9 Charge	31 Prepare To Die! Just Try It Lizard Lips!
10 Dirk In the Cornerpocket	32 ...And Away Goes Dirk Down The Drain!
11 Princess Daphne	
12 Squinch! I Can't Stand The Pressure	33 Take A Dragon To Lunch Dragons Need Love Too!
13 I've I Got It!	
14 I'm Watching You	34 The Dragon
15 This Way To...Dragon's Lair	35 Dirk Meets The Dragon
16 Yuck! Spider Breath	36 Say Ah!
17 Will You Guys Stop Picking On Me!	37 Ride 'em Dirk
18 Go For It!	38 Here Comes Trouble
19 Feet Don't Fail Me Now!	39 The Demons Castle
20 Peekaboo Dirk!	40 The Black Knight
21 You're My Key Man	41 The Magic Sword
22 Oh! Please Hurry!	

42 Maximus Joyus Stikus
43 Dirk Battling The Snakes
44 Beat It!
45 Let's Play Dragon's Lair
46 Dirty Old Mud Men
47 Pow
48 It's A Thriller
49 The Smithie
50 You Drive Me Batty
51 This Way Out
52 Keep Out This Is A Private P[
53 Be My Princess
54 So This Is Detention Hall!
55 The Whirlpools
56 Home Sweet Home!
57 Surprise!
58 Oh! Ah! Eee! Uh!
59 Take A Dunk With Dirk
60 You Think You Had A Bad [
61 The Grim Reaper
62 Dirk Is Bad!
63 Dragon's Lair Is The Real Or[

DRAGSTRIPS/STICK SHIFT (?)

TWO SIZES

The similarities between these two Fleer products are so pronounced that we have grouped them together here. The wrappers are the same size and color and both have identical instructions for peeling and applying the stickers. The sticker "sheets" measure 2" X 4 1/2" and each contains four front-peel stickers (with tan paper backs). The black & white cards from both sets are blank-backed and measure 2 1/2" X 4 1/2". Those from "Dragstrips" have no printing and have a gray back; those from "Stick Shift" have captions on front and white backs. Dragstrips was issued first, retailing for 5 cents a pack. After improving the card format, the set was reissued in 1971 as "Stick Shift" at 10 cents per pack.

ITEM	MINT	EX
Stickers (all)	3.00	2.00
Cards		
Print	3.00	2.00
No print	3.00	2.00
Wrappers		
Dragstrips (2)		
each	--	15.00
Stick Shift (2)		
each	--	25.00

PLYMOUTH GTX — Comes Standard With A 440 4-Barrel High Performance V-8, Automatic Transmission, Wide Tread Tires And Bucket Seats.

Fuel Dragster — Wheelstand!!!   Courtesy of RACING GRAPHIS Magazine.

Checklist of known stickers (Listed alphabetically starting with the top name on each sticker. Information provided by Robert Marks.)

A.J. Foyt's Pit Stop
Wynn's
Super Stock
Bear Racing Service

Bear Official "500" Service
Bendix
Dual Controls
Sealed Power Piston Rings

Bear Official "500" Service
Funny Car
Tuned For Trouble
Alemite CD-2

Bear Official "500" Service
Super Stock
Approved By The Board Of
  Health
McCord

Bear Official "500" Service
Wild One!
Twister
Filko

Borg Warner
Hit The Binders
Grey-Rock Brake Lining
The Rapid Transit System

Buckle Your Seat Belt
Wynn's
Go...Go with Alemite CD-2

Burn Rubber
Tuned For Trouble
Close Windows Above
  105 MPH
Plymouth Racing Team

Champion Spark Plugs
Chevy Eater
Wynn's [checkered flags]
Purolator Filters

Champion Spark Plugs
Mean Machine
GTO
Gumout

Chevy Eater
Hauler
Fram Filters
Love Is A High Performance
  Thing

Columbus Shock Absorbers
Hemi Powered
Catch Me If You Can
American Hammered Piston
  Rings

Dual Controls
Fuelie
Duotone by Walker
Dragster

Full Bore
Grey-Rock Brake Lining
Plymouth Makes It
Catch Me If You Can

Funny Car
Good Year
You're Wiped
Monroe

Gasser
Purolator Filters
Digger
Cuda

Grrl
High Rev
Auto Stick
Grizzly Brakes

Gumout
Fuel Burner
Super Bee
Walker Exhaust Systems

Gumout
Rest Room
Dragster
Bush Whacker

Gunk
Rrr-i-p!
Beep Beep
Porsche

Hauler
Four On The Floor
Good Year
Datsun

Hot Dog
Champion Spark Plugs
Hemi Powered
Hurst

Hot Rod
Reserved For Lovers
Gunk
Jeep

Kick To Start
Do It Now
Exide Go
Casite

Love-In-HQ
Wiped
Duster
Top Eliminator

Mean Machine
Gumout
Champion Spark Plugs
Triumph

Plymouth Makes It
4 On The Floor
Champion Spark Plugs
Amalie Pro Racing Oil

Purolator Filters
Super Stock
Full House
Cyclone

Ram Rod
No Riders
Handler
Cherry Bomb

Rest Room
Four On The Floor
Good Year
DuPont Golden 7

76 Union
Fuel Injection
Cougar Country
SW Instruments

76 Union
Buckle Your Seat Belt
Good Year
Grey-Rock [checkered flags]

STP
Close Windows Above
  105 MPH
Grrrr!
Pure

STP
Reserved For Lovers
Street Rod
Wagner Lockheed

STP
Wide Track
Good Year
McQuay-Norris Piston
  Rings

Twister
Fram Filters
Wide Track
MG

2 + 2
Funny Car
Just Ask Me
Plymouth Racing Team

Wynn's [checkered flags]
T-Bucket
Digger
Fram Filters

Wynn's
Wheeler
I Stop At All Drive-Ins!
Golden Ram

DREAM MACHINES (110)   2 1/2" X 3 1/2"

If you like automobiles, then "Dream Machines" by Lime Rock is the set for you! Each of the 110 cards carries a full color photograph of a classic car and all eras, from the turn of the cen-

tury to modern times, are represented. The "Dream Machines" logo and card caption are printed within the picture area on each card; the lavender borders add a distinctive air to

1957 Ford Thunderbird Convertible: 7

The Thunderbird symbolizes power, swiftness and prosperity in Indian legend and on February 15, 1954, the name was officially incorporated as the name of the new Ford sports car. The 1957 model was redesigned, the first time major changes were made to the car since the introduction. The rear section was enlarged so that, unlike the 1956 model, the spare tire was kept inside the trunk and tail fins were featured on the rear fenders. A unique feature of the 1957 model was the automatic radio volume control. As the speed of the car increased, so did the radio volume. The original factory price was $3408 and 21,380 were produced in 1957. A fully restored model is priced in the high $30,000s today.

© 1991 LIME ROCK COMPANY, INC. Prov. R.I. • Printed in U.S.A.

the set. The backs are printed in lavender and white and contain the caption, card number, and descriptive text. Lime Rock produced the series in a limited edition of 100,000 sets and each comes in a factory-sealed presentation box with a serial number on the seals. Note: as of October, 1991, Dream Machine cards were only available in factory sets.

ITEM	MINT	EX
Set	20.00	--
Display box	--	2.00

Dream Machines

HOT...FAST...CLASSIC...
CARS!

LIMITED 100,000 SET EDITION!

1971 Jaguar E-Type

1971 Jaguar E-Type

PROTOTYPE CARD AND COUNTERPART IN REGULAR ISSUE.

1 1931 Ford Sedan
2 Corvette 1953-1990
3 1971 Jaguar E-Type
4 1971 Ford Capri
5 Mercedes-Benz 300SL Gullwing
6 Ferrari Monza 1954
7 1957 Ford Thunderbird Convertible
8 1931 Bugatti Type 50T Coupe
9 1930 Cadillac V16 Roadster
10 Porsche 930 SE
11 1957 Chevrolet Bel-Air
12 1910 Chadwick Touring
13 1941 Cadillac Fleetwood Sixty Special
14 1934 Alpha Romeo 8C-2300
15 Jaguar D type 1954-1957
16 Lamborghini Countach
17 1970 GTO Judge
18 1948 Ferrari 166 Corsa 12 Cylinder
19 1953 Studebaker Starliner Coupe
20 1968 Ford Mustang
21 1968 Shelby GT-500
22 1963 Chevrolet Impala
23 1932 Stutz DV32
24 1956 Jaguar XK140
25 1954 Porsche 356 Speedster
26 1927 Daimler
27 1989 Porsche 911 Speedster
28 BMW 507 1956-1959
29 1970 Dodge Challenger
30 1967 Camaro SS
31 1969 Buick GS
32 Pontiac GTO
33 1970 Ford Boss 429
34 Plymouth "Wedge"
35 1956 Mercedes-Benz 300SC
36 1971 Mercedes-Benz 280SL
37 1956 Chrysler 300B
38 1970 Chevrolet Chevelle
39 1986 Lagonda
40 1960 Corvette
41 1974 Porsche 911 RS
42 1938 BMW 328
43 Ferrari 365 GTB Daytona Spyder
44 1955 Ferrari 250 GT
45 1990 Nissan 300 ZX
46 1933 MG K3 Magnette
47 1987 Ferrari Testarossa
48 1953 Corvette
49 1989 Corvette Challenge Race
50 Ferrari
51 1969 Ford GT40
52 1960 Ferrari Spyder
53 1936 Dusenberg
54 1957 Corvette Super Sport
55 Imperial Palace Collection Las Vegas Nevada
56 1938 Cadillac Sixteen
57 1931 Pierce-Arrow
58 1981 Delorean
59 1906 Pope-Waverley
60 1904 Eldredge Runabout
61 1908 Firestone Columbus
62 1903 Ford Model A

63 1941 Chrysler Newport Dual Cowl Phaeton
64 Ford Popcorn Wagon
65 1953 Mercury
66 1936 Maybach Type W6 DSG Cabriolet
67 1916 Ford Model T Town Car
68 1946 Ford Woody
69 1933 Horch Type 670 Sport Cabriolet
70 1909 Mercedes Town Car
71 1939 Mercedes 770K Town Car
72 1911 Stanley Touring Car
73 1928 Cadilllac Town Car
74 1910 Rolls-Royce
75 1931 Cadillac V16
76 1907 Packard 30
77 1929 Cadillac Dual Cowl Phaeton
78 1932 Buick Town Car
79 1904 Pierce Arrow
80 1907 Franklin Type D
81 1905 Columbia Electric
82 1951 Nash Ambassador Custom
83 1934 Ford Brewster
84 1910 Thomas Flyer
85 1957 Cadillac Convertible
86 1939 Alfa Romeo
87 1908 Halsman Rope Drive
88 1956 Chrysler Imperial Parade Phaeton
89 1938 Graham Model 97
90 1947 Delahaye Type 175S Aerodynamique
91 1938 Packard Model 1605 Super Eight
92 1948 Tucker Model 48
93 1935 Hispano-Suiza Type J112 Transformable
94 1937 Cord Model 812 Phaeton
95 1950 Muntz Jet Convertible Coupe
96 1934 Dusenberg Model SJ Dual Cowl Phaeton
97 1936 Mercedes-Benz Type 500K Special-Roadster
98 1938 Mercedes-Benz Type G4 Gelandewagen
99 1955 Mercedes-Benz 300SL Coupe
100 1920 Daimler Model 45 Convertible Saloon
101 1916 Crane-Simplex
102 1933 Indian
103 1940 Indian
104 1914 Harley-Davidson
105 1922 Harley-Davidson Sidecar
106 Classic Express
107 Pantera
108 Checklist #1 (Hot!)
109 Checklist #2 (Fast!)
110 Checklist #3 (Classic!)

DUCK TALES (16)

2 5/8" X 2 3/4"

Collectibles can be found in the strangest places, even on the applesauce shelves in your supermarket. That's where these multicolor artwork drawings of characters from Disney's "Duck Tales" appeared in 1986-87. Each design was printed on the plastic lid of an individual-serving tub of Lucky Leaf applesauce (regular or natural). The character is named beneath each picture, but there are no numbers, advertising, or any other clues to identify the manufacturer or determine the length of the set (16). You just had to be there, as they say, and collector Gloria Smith was there and collected the titles that appear on our checklist. It is suspected, but not confirmed, that all 16 characters may also have appeared as small insets on Lucky Leaf jar labels (see illustration). Note: since lids have to be removed from their tubs, no prices are listed for "mint."

ITEM	MINT	EX
Set	--	20.00
Lid	--	1.00

Baggy Beagle	Gyro Gearloose
Big Time Beagle	Huey
Burger Beagle	Launchpad McDuck
Dewey	Little Bulb
Doofus	Louie
Duckworth	Magicia De Spell
Flintheart Glomgold	Scrooge McDuck
Gladstone Gander	Webby

DUCK TALES ALBUM STICKERS (240)

1 15/16" X 2 9/16"

Panini issued this set of 240 album stickers based on Disney's "Duck Tales" in 1987. Each multi-color artwork sticker is numbered and has a corresponding space in the nicely-designed, 32-page album. As is customary with Panini stickers, the dialogue or description for each sticker is printed beneath the appropriate space in the album, not on the sticker itself. Seven distinct adventures comprise the series: "Back to the Klondike" (1-35), "Dinosaur Ducks" (36-73), "Hero for Hire" (74-111), "Bermuda Triangle Tangle" (112-141), "Send in the Clones" (142-179), "Hotel Strangeduck" (180-209), and "Duckman of Aquatraz" (210-240). There are six different wrappers for the set. Note: set price includes album.

ITEM	MINT	EX
Set	27.50	20.00
Sticker	.10	.07
Wrappers (6) ea.	--	.25
Album	2.00	1.50

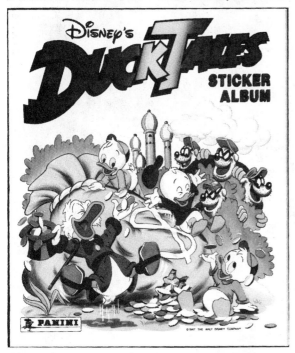

Duck Tales Album Stickers

DUKES OF HAZZARD (66)

2 1/2'' X 3 1/2''

The blue-bordered set of 66 cards was issued by Donruss in 1980. The color photographs are taken from the television series and are numbered inside the frame line. The set title is printed in blue in a yellow panel on the front of the card. The backs are poster pieces.

ITEM	MINT	EX
Set	15.00	11.00
Card	.25	.20
Wrapper	--	.35
Box	--	6.00

  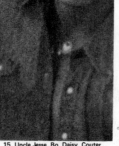 

* No. 1 show in it's time period
* No. 4 rated show on TV
* Features live action comedy
* Watched by over 30 million viewers weekly.

BASED ON THE POPULAR CBS TV SERIES

1. Car Crash at Carnival Race
2. Bo Duke Holding Cards
3. Daisy Duke
4. Bo and Luke Duke
5. Friend, Bo, Daisy on Motorcycle and Luke
6. Bo Playing Guitar
7. Daisy and Luke
8. Cleatus
9. Bo, Daisy and Luke
10. The General Lee at Carnival Race
11. The General Lee
12. Car Crash Explosion
13. Luke and Bo
14. Luke Riding Horse
15. Uncle Jesse, Bo, Daisy, Couter, Luke, Boss Hog, and Policeman
16. Bo, Sheriff Roscoe and Luke
17. The General Lee Flying through Air
18. Luke and Daisy
19. Luke Duke
20. Bo, Daisy and Luke—Country Style
21. Bo Duke
22. Luke, Uncle Jesse, Daisy and Bo
23. Daisy Standing with Cannon
24. A Wrecked General Lee
25. Daisy Sitting on Counter Top
26. Luke, Daisy and Bo
27. Daisy Duke
28. The General Lee
29. Sheriff Roscoe
30. Daisy and Bo and the General Lee
31. Flash—Sheriff Roscoe's Dog
32. Bo
33. Sheriff Roscoe, Boss Hog, Bo, Luke and Daisy
34. Daisy Leaning on General Lee
35. Sheriff Roscoe and Flash
36. Sheriff Roscoe and Boss Hog
37. Boss Hog Speaking
38. Luke, Cleatus and Bo
39. Boss Hog
40. Luke and Bo
41. Daisy with Horse
42. Sheriff Roscoe
43. Luke and Bo Outside Court House
44. Couter and Daisy
45. Daisy Duke
46. Daisy Standing in Doorway
47. Flash and Sheriff Roscoe
48. Daisy and Luke
49. Sheriff Roscoe Jumping with Joy
50. Daisy and Luke
51. Motorcycle Going through Loup-Topped Car
52. Luke and Bo
53. Carnival Car Race (Crash)
54. Boss Hog Pointing
55. Daisy and Luke
56. Carnival Car Race Crash
57. Bo Relaxing
58. Wrecked Car Lying Upside Down
59. Luke, Daisy and Bo Leaning on General Lee
60. Boss Hog
61. Daisy Wearing Heart Imprinted Blouse
62. General Lee Sitting on Hillside
63. Jesse Duke
64. Police Car Taking Flying Leap
65. Daisy Duke
66. Flash and Sheriff Roscoe Playing Checkers

DUKES OF HAZZARD STICKERS (66)   2 1/2" X 3 1/2"

Donruss followed up the success of its Dukes card series by issuing this set of 66 stickers in August 1981. There are 60 numbered stickers, with large color pictures from the TV show, and six unnumbered die-cut stickers of characters, cars, etc. The backs of all 66 stickers form a large poster when properly arranged. Collectors should note that there is no number 60 in this set; the stickers are numbered 1-59 and 61.

ITEM	MINT	EX
Set	10.00	7.50
Card	.20	.15
Wrapper	––	.35
Box	––	6.00

DUKES OF HAZZARD (44)   2 1/2" X 3 1/2"

Donruss released yet another Dukes of Hazzard set in 1983. It is composed of 44 cards containing color photographs encircled by log fence framelines. Several of the pictures are cropped from photos which appeared previously in the Dukes sticker set. Each card is numbered on front in the white border area but there are no captions. The reverses are puzzle backs which can be combined to form the picture appearing on card no. 8.

All the stickers issued with this set are leftovers from the sticker set produced in 1980. For this reason, they are not considered a part of this set and are not priced.

ITEM	MINT	EX
Set	17.50	13.00
Card	.35	.25
Wrapper	––	.35
Box	––	6.00

DUMB DABS/DUMB DOTS (?)   2 1/2" X 4 1/2"

A 1969 Fleer issue marketed in two similar wrappers with different titles. Each sticker sheet holds 20 "Dabs"/"Dots" and has plain brown paper backing. The "License" cards are blank-backed (10 different seen). Our sticker checklist denotes the title of the upper-left sticker on each sheet.

ITEM	MINT	EX
Sticker sheet	2.00	1.50
License	2.00	1.50
Wrappers (2) each	--	10.00

STICKERS

Alice	Idiot Works Here	Spitball Target
Contents: Worms	Lousy	Tease Me
Feed Trees	Mental Institution	Ted
For Sale Cheap	Pete	Turn Me Around
Hold Tight	Protect Bugs	Your Feet Stink

LICENSES

Bad Report Card License	License To Go Without Bath 1 Week
Broken Window License	License To Rob Piggy Bank
Gold Fishing License	Messy Room License
Hookey License	One Month Without A Haircut License
Late Show License	Skin Diving In The Bathtub

DUMB DABS (63?)   2 1/2" X 3 1/2"

We have not included a checklist for Fleer's modern version of Dumb Dabs because many of the sticker designs are pictures which would be difficult to describe. On the front of each card are nine oval stickers: 63 different fronts have been reported ("Over 300 Stickers In All!" says the wrapper). The backs contain a "Dumb Dab Funnies" feature which is printed in "shocking" purple: we have printed all 13 drawings below. Note: in sorting, it was determined that specific fronts always came with specific backs, except for two sticker/cards containing the stickers "Hug Me!" and "No!" in the upper left corner. These two sticker/cards could be found with either of two different back drawings. The set price given does not include these two minor variations.

ITEM	MINT	EX
Set	15.00	12.00
Sticker / card	.25	.20
Wrapper	--	.35
Box	--	3.00

BRING IN THAT FLOATING
FAT MAN . . . THE BARON

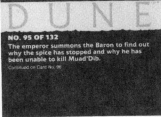

NO. 95 OF 132
The emperor summons the Baron to find out why the spice has stopped and why he has been unable to kill Muad'Dib.
Continued on Card No. 96

"He who controls the spice, controls the Universe," but he who buys cases of "Dune" cards will be stuck with them forever. Make no mistake about it, the Fleer set of 132 cards and 44 stickers is nicely designed, but that alone could not possibly overcome the stigma left by Hollywood's mistreatment of this science fiction classic. The stickers are slightly smaller than standard size (2 1/2" X 3 5/16") and were much more difficult to complete in sorting than the cards. For this reason, the set price does not include stickers.

ITEM	MINT	EX
Card set	12.50	9.50
Card	.10	.07
Sticker	.50	.35
Wrappers (3)		
each	---	.35
Box	---	4.00

DUNE CHECKLIST
CARD No. 129 of 132

1. 3RD STAGE NAVIGATOR
2. PRINCESS IRULAN
3. EMPEROR & R. M. MOHIAM
4. FACE HIM ALONE
5. GUILDSMEN ENTER
6. NAVIGATOR REVEALED
7. A WARNING
8. R. M. MOHIAM
9. PAUL ATREIDES
10. DUKE LETO
11. LADY JESSICA
12. GURNEY HALLECK
13. THUFIR HAWAT
14. DR. YUEH
15. DUNCAN IDAHO
16. FIGHTER ROBOT
17. SHIELD PRACTICE
18. FATHER & SON
19. PAUL & R. M. MOHIAM
20. THE TEST
21. KWISATZ HADERACH?
22. THE BARON'S TREATMENT
23. PITER DELIVERS
24. RABBAN & FEYD
25. THE BARON FLOATS
26. THE BARON'S GOO!
27. FAREWELL CALADAN
28. ARRIVAL ON ARRAKIS
29. UNPACKING
30. INSPECTING SERVANTS
31. PAUL EXPLORES
32. SHADOUT MAPES
33. HUNTER-SEEKER

TERMS & DEFINITIONS CARD

FEDAYKIN: Fremen death commandos, pledged to give their lives for Paul Muad'Dib.
FREMEN: the free tribes of Arrakis, dwellers in the desert.
FREMKIT: desert survival kit of Fremen.
GIEDI PRIME: the planet of Odtachs B (36) homeworld of House Harkonnen.
GLOW GLOBE: suspensor-buoyed illuminating device, self-powered.
GUILD: the Guild monopoly on space travel and transport and upon international banking made them a powerful force in the universe.
HARVESTER: a large spice mining machine.
HEIGHLINER: major cargo carrier of the Guild system.
HUNTER-SEEKER: a sliver of metal guided as a weapon by a near-by control console.
IMPERIAL CONDITIONING: from the Suk Medical Schools; the highest conditioning against taking human life.
KANLY: formal feud.

ITEM 521 36 CT.

FLEER
10 CARDS-1 STICKER-1 STICK GUM

FLEER
10 CARDS-1 STICKER-1 STICK GUM

FLEER
10 CARDS-1 STICKER-1 STICK GUM

1 3rd Stage Navigator
2 Princess Irulan
3 Emperor & R. M. Mohiam
4 Face Him Alone
5 Guildsmen Enter
6 Navigator Revealed
7 A Warning
8 R. M. Mohiam
9 Paul Atreides
10 Duke Leto
11 Lady Jessica
12 Gurney Halleck
13 Thufir Hawat
14 Dr. Yueh
15 Duncan Idaho
16 Fighter Robot
17 Shield Practice
18 Father & Son
19 Paul & R. M. Mohiam
20 The Text
21 Kwisatz Haderach?
22 The Baron's Treatment
23 Piter Delivers
24 Rabban & Feyd
25 The Baron Floats
26 The Baron's Goo!
27 Farewell Caladan

28 Arrival On Arrakis
29 Unpacking
30 Inspecting Servants
31 Paul Explores
32 Shadout Mapes
33 Hunter-Seeker
34 Searching
35 Harkonnen Spy
36 Thufir Reports
37 Arriving For Tour
38 Dr. Kynes & Gurney
39 Entering' Thopter
40 A Harvester
41 Wormsign!
42 Carryall
43 To The Rescue
44 Worm Attacks
45 Harvester Destroyed
46 Treachery Begins
47 Sardaukar Attack
48 The Battle Rages
49 Piter's Orders
50 Rabban Eliminates
51 Baron Harkonnen
52 Dr. Yueh's Reward
53 Rabban & Kr. Kynes
54 Mean Rabban
55 Leto's Chance
56 Dangerous Flight
57 Crash Landing
58 Worm Attack?
59 We've Gutted Them!
60 Show No Mercy

61 Run From Worm
62 Into the Rocks
63 Meeting Fremen
64 Stilgar
65 Jessica Holds 'Em
66 Paul Meets Chan!
67 Accepted By Tribe
68 Sietch Tabr
69 Fremen Water Monk
70 Paul Speaks
71 Weirding Way
72 Chuksa!
73 Pass Within?
74 R. M. Ramallo
75 Witness the Change
76 Hall of Rites
77 Thufir Is Mine
78 Fedaykin Red!
79 Paul Watches
80 Better in Battle
81 Who Is Muad'Dib
82 Fremen Trail
83 Mounting Worm
84 A Sandrider!
85 Rabban in Desert
86 Rabban & Boys
87 "...Find Muad'Dib!"
88 You Yound Pup!
89 Guild Ship
90 Last Chance
91 Alia
92 The Fighters
93 Paul & Company

94 Harkonnen Ship
95 Emperor's Orders
96 Floating Fatman
97 Poor Rabban
98 ...But Your Highness!
99 Muad'Dib's Messenger
100 Paul Atreides Lives?!
101 Into Battle
102 Release Sardaukar
103 Fremen Secret Weapon
104 ...To The Storm
105 Helpless
106 Worms Come Closer
107 And Closer
108 Crushed
109 Ate The Baron
110 Run for Lives
111 Alia Inspects
112 Paul Enters Hall
113 Face to Face
114 Kill Him Thufir!
115 Take My Life
116 Thufir's Sacrifice
117 Last Battle
118 Harkonnen Animal
119 Feyd Attacks
120 Fight Back
121 My Blade
122 Feyd Gets Stung!
123 How It Will Be
124 I Sit on Throne
125 Paul Comforts
126 Brother & Sister
127 Muad'Dib's Word
128 Rain On Arrakis
129 Checklist
130 Checklist
131 Terms & Definitions
132 Terms & Definitions

Dune

1 A Spicescout
2 Paul and Lady Jessica
3 Lady Jessica
4 Feyd Rabban
5 Jessica as Reverend Mother
6 Feyd Challenges Paul
7 Feyd and The Emperor's Blade
8 Paul With Weirding Module
9 Rabban And Troops
10 Beast Rabban
11 Rabban The Conqueror
12 Feyd...The Baron's Nephew
13 The Baron Harkonnen
14 Baron Vladimir Harkonnen
15 Piter The Assassin
16 Princess Irulan
17 Emperor Shaddam IV
18 Princess Irulan
19 Bene Gesserit Sisterhood
20 Dr. Kynes
21 Chani
22 Harrah And Sons

23 Alia, Paul's Sister
24 Gurney Halleck
25 Dr. Yueh
26 ...That Floating Fat Man!
27 Fremen Monk
28 Reverend Mother Gaius Helen Mohiam
29 Sardaukar
30 Paul Muad' Dib
31 ...The Sleeper Must Awaken
32 Paul Sets A Thumper
33 Third Stage Navigator
34 Feyd..Ready To Fight
35 Sandrider Express
36 Charging Worm
37 A Harkonnen Ship
38 Duke Leto and Friend
39 Thufir Hawat
40 Guildsman
41 Shadout Mapes
42 Piter Inspects The Troops
43 Paul Fires His Weapon
44 Fremen Fighters

DUNGEONS & DRAGONS (6)   2 3/16" X 2 7/8"

We have illustrated all six of the package backs in this 1983 Amurol set based on the popular fantasy game. The cards were designed to be cut away from the boxes but many collectors prefer them to be intact. There are only three different box fronts and the product was called "Dungeons & Dragons Fantasy Candy Figures."

ITEM	MINT	EX
Card	--	.50
Boxes (6) each	2.00	1.50

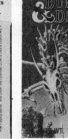

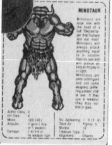

DURAN DURAN (33/33)

Like the Cyndi Lauper set, Duran Duran is made up of 33 cards and 33 stickers. The former have color photos of various group members in publicity and action poses. The borders are gray and the angled frame lines are either red or blue. The card backs contain a short text and the card number. The stickers are diecut and are numbered outside the score line beneath the picture. The reverses of the sticker/cards are puzzle pieces of a 15-piece puzzle, plus three puzzle preview cards. Note: set price includes all cards and stickers.

ITEM	MINT	EX
Set	10.00	7.50
Card	.10	.07
Sticker	.25	.15
Wrapper	---	.35
Box	---	4.00

DYNAMITE SPORTS CARDS (6)
DYNAMITE TRADING CARDS (6)

"Dynamite" is the name of a magazine that targets juvenile minds across America. It is filled with articles, features, games etc., and on two separate occasions six-card sheets of faux bubblegum cards were distributed as a bonus to readers. The first set to be issued - "Dynamite Sports Cards" - portrayed five klutzy athletes and one crooked hot dog vender. The second set to appear - "Dynamite Trading Cards" - poked fun at various professions: telephone operator, radio DJ, TV repairman, dog

Dynamite Sports Cards / Dynamite Trading Cards

catcher, politician, and fast food franchise operator. The people who posed for these pictures look like they probably work for the magazine, or at best, were pulled right off the street. The backs, printed in black ink on gray stock, are mildly humorous. Note: it is not uncommon to find intact sheets of six cards.

ITEM	MINT	EX
Sets		
"Sports"	3.50	2.50
"Trading"	3.50	2.50
Intact sheet		
each set	5.00	4.00
Cards, all	.50	.35

DYNAMITE SPORTS CARDS
Clete M. Goode
Fielding Flize
Grace Fullfall
Ollie Infree
Rex Karz
Robb M. Blynde

DYNAMITE TRADING CARDS
Biff Bergers
Isabel Ringing
Moe Tormouth
Phil O. Hoddair
Ray Beeze
Rip U. Hoff

ISABEL RINGING
TELEPHONE OPERATOR

MOE TORMOUTH
RADIO DJ

RIP U. HOFF
TV REPAIRMAN

RAY BEEZE
DOG CATCHER

BIFF BERGERS
FAST FOOD FRANCHISE OPERATOR

PHIL O. HODDAIR
POLITICIAN

EARLY JAZZ GREATS (36)

2 3/4" X 3 3/4"

"Early Jazz Greats," drawn by artist Robert Crumb for Yazoo Records in 1982, is a definite must for collectors of music cards and for jazz afficionados. There are 36 cards in the set and each features a prominent musician or singer in elegant, multi-color artwork portraiture. The title of the series is printed beneath each picture and the backs contain the card number, a short biographical sketch, and advertising for Yazoo Records. Although the initial run of sets was issued more than ten years ago, boxed sets of Early Jazz Greats are still available in quantity and commonly sell for $10 per set. According to our in-formation, the set is still being printed as demand requires, so the price should not increase from present levels. Collector advisory: individual cards from this set have been seen glued into albums and picture frames and offered as original 1930's cards at very high prices.

1 "Bix" Beiderbecke
2 Coleman Hawkins
3 "Jelly Roll" Morton
4 Louis Armstrong
5 Lil Hardin
6 Johnny Dodds
7
8 Junie C. Cobb
9 Joe "King" Oliver
10 Ikey Robinson
11 Roy Palmer
12 Jack Teagarden
13 Jabbo Smith
14 Joseph "Wingy" Mannone
15 "Pops" Foster
16 Steve Brown
17 Earl Hines
18 Jimmy Blythe
19 James P. Johnson
20 "Tiny" Parham
21 "Duke" Ellington
22 Sidney Bechet
23 Freddie Keppard
24 Thomas "Fats" Waller
25 "Muggsy" Spanier
26 Lammar Wright
27 Bennie Moten
28 Frank Trumbauer
29 Mary Lou Williams
30 Ernest "Punch" Miller
31 Eddie South
32 Alex Hill
33 Joe Venuti
34 Fletcher Henderson
35 Jimmy Noone
36 Benny Goodman

ELEPHANT JOKES (50)

2 3/8" X 3 1/2"

During the 1960's, the L.M. Becker Company of Wisconsin distributed a variety of cards in their paper-wrapper "surprise packages." The most famous of these is the series of 50 Elephant Jokes, which came three to a package. The cards are simple black and white drawings on solid color backgrounds (each title can be found on yellow, green, blue and red); the straight line is located on the front and the punch line on the back. The card number is located on the back, as is an offer to buy new elephant jokes for $1 each.

ITEM	MINT	EX
Set	150.00	120.00
Card	2.50	2.00
Wrapper	--	50.00
Box	--	75.00

1 How Do You Make an Elephant Float?
2 Why Do Elephants Have Flat Feet?
3 Why Do Elephants Walk Sideways Through the Grass?
4 Why Do Elephants Have Tusks?
5 Why Can't an Elephant Ride a Tricycle?
6 Why Do Elephants Have Wrinkles on Their Ankles?
7 What Did the Elephant Say to the Bluebird?
8 How Can You Tell if There's an Elephant in the Bathtub with You?
9 How Do Elephants Get into Trees?

Elephant Jokes

10 Why Do Elephants Wear Sneakers?
11 How Do You Make a Statue of an Elephant?
12 How Do You Get Six Elephants in a Volkswagon?
13 Why Don't Elephants Play Basketball?
14 How Do You Know if You Have an Elephant in the Refrigerator?
15 Why Are Elephants Gray?
16 What Did Tarzan Say When He Saw the Elephants Coming?
17 What Did Jane Say When She Saw the Elephants Coming?
18 How Do You Stop a Charging Elephant?
19 What Is the Difference Between an Elephant and an Orange?
20 How Is an Elephant Like a Volkswagon?

21 Why Doesn't an Elephant Drink Whiskey?
22 Why Doesn't an Elephant Have a Glove Compartment?
23 Why Did the Elephant Wear Pink Tennis Shoes?
24 Why Don't Elephants Fly?
25 How Do You Know If You Have an Elephant in Your Oven?
26 How Do You Raise a Baby Elephant?
27 Why Do Elephants Swim on Their Backs?
28 Why Do Elephants Have Wrinkles in Their Backs?
29 Why Do Elephants Wear Green Socks?
30 How Can You Tell When There Are Three Elephants in the Bathtub with You?
31 Why Did the Elephant Make Friends with the Owl and the Goat?

32 Why Are an Elephant's Toes Split?
33 How Do You Get Down from an Elephant?
34 Why Did the Elephant Change His Socks?
35 What Do Elephants Do with Old Volkswagons?
36 What Time Is It When an Elephant Sits on a Fence?
37 Why Do Ducks Have Webbed Feet? To Stamp Out Forest Fires. Why Do Elephants Have Flat Feet?
38 Why Didn't the Elephant Have Any Pajamas?
39 What Did the 500 Pound Canary Say to the Elephant?
40 What Did the Worm Say When He Got Under the Elephants Foot?
41 Who Started the Elephant Jokes?

42 Why Don't Elephants Wear Bow Ties?
43 Why Didn't the Elephant Go Water Skiing?
44 Why Does an Elephant Eat Peanuts?
45 Why Do Elephants Have Big Ears?
46 What's the Best Way to Catch an Elephant?
47 Why Do Elephants Have White Tusks?
48 How Do You Tell an Elephant from a Dozen Eggs?
49 Why Do Elephants Have a Trunk?
50 What Did the Elephant Say to the Cannibal?

ELEPHANT LAUGHS (?)

1 5/8" X 3 15/16"

The first reference to Nabisco's "Elephant Laughs" series appeared in Buck Barker's "Catalog Additions" printed in The Card Collectors Bulletin of June 1, 1971. The delay involved in compiling lists of new issues for that newsletter makes it likely that the set was issued in 1970. The "card" is actually the entire back of the candy box and the answer to the elephant joke is printed on the left end flap. If the format is consistent with other Nabisco candy card sets, there are 24 jokes in the series (but this is unconfirmed) and the cards probably appeared on both "Junior Mints" and "Pom-Poms" boxes. Intact boxes are occasionally found and these are far more valuable than single cards that have been cut away.

ITEM	MINT	EX
Card	—	1.00
Box	5.00	4.00

ELVIS PRESLEY (66)

2 1/2" X 3 1/2"

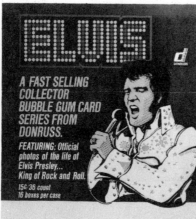

Donruss produced the 66-card Elvis Presley set in 1978. The fronts have an elegant frame surrounding color or blue-tone photographs of the popular entertainer. The backs are numbered and contain two types of features: "Elvis Facts" (cards 1-48) and "Elvis Records" (cards 49-66). In a moment of candor, card No. 48 states: "The death of Elvis Presley spawned a billion dollar industry of Elvis products. It included everything from real money with Elvis' likeness to t-shirts and of course bubble gum cards." Card No. 24 appears with two different pictures, one of which is identical to the photo on Card No. 59.

ITEM	MINT	EX
Set	15.00	12.00
Card	.25	.20
Wrapper	--	1.00
Box	--	7.00

EMPIRE STRIKES BACK (5)

3" X 4 3/4"

This striking set of five color photographs from the Star Wars sequel appeared on 6-pack candy bar trays marketed by Hershey and it's Reese's subsidiary. A dotted line is printed around the perimeter of the cards to facilitate cutting them from the tray. They are captioned but are not numbered. A copyright line appearing on each tray is dated 1980 (Lucasfilm). The "wrapper" is a piece of clear cellophane with the brand name and "card notice" printed on it.

ITEM	MINT	EX
Sets		
Cards	12.50	9.50
Trays	30.00	22.50
Card	2.00	1.50
Tray	5.00	4.00
Wrapper	--	5.00

Boba Fett
Chewbacca
C3PO and R2D2
Darth Vader
Luke on a Tauntaun

EMPIRE STRIKES BACK (352 & 88)

2 1/2" X 3 1/2"

The Stars Wars epic has spawned two "mega-sets" from Topps Chewing Gum, one of which is this 352-card, 88-sticker series of The Empire Strikes Back issued in 1980. Series 1 has gray-bordered cards with red-framed color pictures, and yellow-bordered stickers. Series 2 cards have gray borders and blue frame lines, with blue-bordered stickers. Series 3 cards are yellow-bordered with green frame lines, and the stickers are green. The wrappers, in order of issuance, are red, blue and yellow in color. Note: set and series prices include stickers.

ITEM	MINT	EX
Sets		
Series I	30.00	22.50
Series II	30.00	22.50
Series III	20.00	15.00
Cards (all)	.15	.10
Stickers (all)	.35	.25
Wrappers (3) ea.	—	.35
Boxes (3) ea.	—	7.00

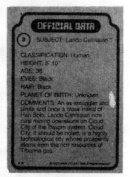

SPACE PAINTINGS by RALPH McQUARRIE

LUKE BATTLING DARTH

1 Ist Series — Introduction
2 Luke Skywalker
3 Princess Leia
4 Han Solo
5 Chewbacca
6 See—Threepio
7 Artoo—Deeto
8 Lando Calrissian
9 Yoda
10 Darth Vader
11 Boba Fett
12 The Imperial Probot
13 Planet of Ice
14 "Where's Luke?"
15 Droids on Patrol
16 The Hidden Rebel Base
17 New Rebel Strategy
18 General Rieekan
19 Leia's Plan
20 Prey of the Wampa
21 Examined: Luke's Tauntaun
22 "But Sir, I Mmh...Mffh..."
23 In Search of Luke
24 Frozen Death
25 Skywalker's Rescue
26 Luke's Fight for Life
27 Rejuvenation Chamber
28 Surgeon Droid
29 Artoo's Icy Vigil
30 Metal Monster
31 Zeroing in on Chewie!
32 Han Aims for Action!
33 Destroying the Probot
34 Death of Admiral Ozzel
35 The Freedom Fighters
36 Rebel Defenses
37 Armed Against the Enemy
38 Joined by Dack
39 The Sound of Terror
40 Suddenly...Starfire!
41 Rattled by the Enemy
42 Might of the Imperial Forces
43 The Snow Walkers
44 Luke... Trapped!
45 Escape from Icy Peril
46 "Retreat! Retreat!"
47 Headquarters in Shambles
48 Solo's Makeshift Escape
49 Invaded!
50 Vader and the Snowtroopers
51 Snowtroopers of the Empire
52 Millennium Falcon: Getaway Ship!
53 Emergency Blast Off!
54 Battle of the Star Destroyer
55 Fix-It Man Han Solo!
56 A Sudden Change of Plan

57 Misty World of Dagobah
58 The Creature Called Yoda
59 "Welcome, Young Luke!"
60 Journey Through the Swamp
61 Yoda's House
62 Artoo Peeking Through
63 The Secret of Yoda
64 The Princess Lends a Hand
65 Repairing Hyperdrive
66 Star Lovers
67 "Pardon Me Sir, But...Ohhh!"
68 Mysterious and Deadly Chamber
69 Attacked by Batlike Creatures!
70 "Use the Force, Luke!"
71 Raising Luke's X-Wing
72 A Need Beyond Reason
73 A Gathering of Evils
74 The Bounty Hunters
75 IG-88 and Boba Fett
76 Enter Lando Calrissian
77 Warm Welcome for an Old Buddy
78 Conniving Pals
79 "Greetings, Sweet Lady"
80 Calrissian's Main Man
81 Pretty as a Princess!
82 A Swarm of Ugnaughts
83 Threepio...Blasted to Bits!
84 A Pile of See-Threepio!
85 Escorted by Lando
86 Dinner Guests
87 Host of Horror
88 Deflecting Solo's Blasts
89 Alas, Poor Threepio!
90 The Ordeal
91 The Prize of Boba Fett
92 His Day of Triumph
93 The Carbon-Freezing Chamber
94 End of the Star Warriors?
95 Pawn of the Evil One
96 "No! This Can't Be Happening!"
97 The Fate of Han Solo
98 Boba's Special Delivery
99 Observed by Luke
100 Luke Arrives
101 Ready for Action!
102 The Search for Vader
103 "Where Are You, Skywalker?"
104 Dark Lord of the Sith
105 Weapon of Light
106 The Confrontation
107 Duel of the Lightsabers
108 Escape from Their Captors
109 Lando..Friend or Foe?

110 Leia Takes Control!
111 Blasting the Stormtroopers!
112 Artoo to the Rescue!
113 Spectacular Battle!
114 "Embrace the Dark Side!"
115 "Hate Me, Luke! Destroy Me!"
116 Luke's Last Stand
117 "Do You Have a Foot in My Size?"
118 Probot
119 Falcon on Hoth
120 Snow Walkers
121 The Pursued
122 Darth Vader
123 Swamps of Dagobah
124 Cloud City
125 Lando's Greeting
126 Threepio's Destruction
127 Luke Battling Darth
128 The Final Stand
129 Rescue
130 Ion Cannon
131 Checklist — 1-66
132 Checklist — 67-132

"WELCOME, YOUNG LUKE!"

133 2nd Series — Introduction
134 Millennium Falcon
135 The Executor
136 Imperial Star Destroyer
137 Twin-Pod Cloud Car
138 Slave I
139 Rebel Armored Snowspeeder
140 The Avenger
141 Tie Fighter
142 Rebel Transport
143 Tie Bomber
144 Preparing for Battle
145 Seeking the Missing Luke
146 The Searcher
147 Star Pilot Luke Skywalker
148 Luke's Patrol
149 Shelter on Icy Hoth
150 Imperial Spy
151 Tracking the Probot
152 Han Solo, Rescuer
153 Medical Treatment
154 Worried Droids on Hoth
155 Imperial Assault!
156 Narrow Escape!
157 Fighting Against the Empire
158 Roar of the Wookiee

159 Chewie's Task
160 Moments Before the Escape
161 Last Stages of the Battle
162 Gallant Warrior
163 "Raise Those Ships!"
164 The Awesome One
165 Vader and His Snowtroopers
166 Takeover of Rebel Base
167 The Man Called Han Solo
168 The Falcon in Repairs
169 Skills of the Star Pilot
170 "Sir...Wait for Me!"
171 Han's Desperate Plan
172 An Overworked Wookiee?
173 "Oh, Hello There, Chewbacca!"
174 Artoo's Bumpy Landing
175 Mysterious Planet
176 "Luke...in Trouble?"
177 Working Against Time
178 Han and the Princess
179 Soldiers of the Empire
180 The Wookiee at Work
181 Vader and a Bounty Hunter
182 World of Darkness
183 Taking no Chances!
184 Farewell to Yoda and Dagobah
185 Racing to the Falcon
186 The Ominous Vader
187 The Dark Pursuer
188 Young Senator from Alderaan
189 Don't Fool with Han Solo
190 Kindred Spirits
191 Lobot's Task
192 A Brave Princess
193 Corridors of Bespin
194 Lando's Aide, Lobot
195 "Get Back Quick...It's Vader!"
196 Held by the Stormtroopers
197 Han's Torment
198 Lando's Game
199 Deadly Device
200 In Vader's Clutches
201 A Tearful Farewell
202 Han Faces His Fate
203 Into the Carbon-Freezing Pit!
204 An Ugnaught
205 Tears of a Princess
206 Suspended in Carbon Freeze
207 Gruesome Fate!
208 Evil Threatens!
209 "This Deal is Getting Worse!"
210 The Captor, Boba Fett
211 Fear on Cloud City
212 A Warrior Driven
213 Courage of Skywalker
214 The Pursuer
215 Stalked by Vader!
216 A Droid Gone to Pieces
217 Threepio's Free Ride
218 Stormtrooper Takeover!
219 Princess Leia Under Guard!
220 Bounty Hunter Boba Fett
221 Lando Covers Their Escape!
222 Tumbling to an Unknown Fate
223 On the Verge of Defeat!
224 Gifted Performer
225 Actress Carrie Fisher
226 Han Solo (Harrison Ford)
227 Anthony Daniels as C-3PO
228 Our Favorite Protocol Droid

229 R2-D2 (Kenny Baker)
230 "Mynocks Outside? Oh My!"
231 Actor Billy Dee Williams
232 Galaxy's Most Loyal Droids
233 Dashing Han Solo
234 The Force and the Fury
235 Yoda's Squabble with R2-D2
236 Blasted by Leia!
237 The Art of Levitation
238 Snowswept Chewbacca
239 Dreamworld...or Trap?
240 Swampland Peril!
241 "Tried, Have You?"
242 Encounter on Dagobah
243 Captain Solo Senses a Trap
244 A Test for Luke
245 R2-D2 on the Misty Bog
246 Confronting the Dark Side
247 Luke Battles...Himself?
248 Blooming Romance
249 Chewie Retaliates
250 Stormtrooper Battle
251 Director Irvin Kershner
252 Spiffing up a Wookiee
253 Filming the Falcon
254 Kershner Directs Mark Hamill
255 Shooting the Exciting Climax
256 Filming Vader in His Chamber
257 Dagobah Comes to Life
258 Building the Falcon
259 Hoth Rebel Base Sequence
260 Filming an Explosion
261 Spectacular Swampland Set
262 Acting Can be a Dirty Job!
263 Checklist — 133-198
264 Checklist — 199-264

265 3rd Series — Introduction
266 Han Solo
267 Princess Leia
268 Luke Skywalker
269 C-3PO
270 R2-D2
271 Darth Vader
272 Boba Fett
273 Probot
274 Dengar
275 Bossk
276 IG-88
277 FX-7
278 Chewbacca
279 Lando Calrissian
280 Stormtrooper
281 Yoda
282 Imperial Ships Approaching!
283 The Courageous Trench Fighters!
284 Too-Onebee
285 Rebel Protocol Droids
286 Within the Hidden Base
287 Calrission of Bespin
288 Testing the Carbon-Freezing Process
289 Flight of the X-Wing
290 Dodging Deadly Laserblasts!
291 The Lovers Part
292 Canyons of Death!
293 Magnificent Rebel Starship
294 Old Friends...or Foes?
295 Power of the Empire
296 Threepio in a Jam!
297 Swamp Plane!
298 A Hasty Retreat!
299 Hostile World of Hoth
300 Descent into Danger!
301 Luke...Long Overdue!
302 Toward the Unknown

303 In Search of Han
304 Luke's Desparate Decision
305 Emerging from the Pit
306 Busy as a Wookiee!
307 Portrait of an Ugnaught
308 The Wizard of Dagobah
309 Emergency Repairs!
310 Han on the Icy Wasteland
311 The Walkers Close In!
312 Toward Tomorrow...
313 In the Path of Danger!
314 The X-Wing Cockpit
315 Hero of the Rebellion
316 Vader's Private Chamber
317 Aboard the Executor
318 The Ominous One
319 Lord Vader's Orders
320 "He's Still Alive!"
321 Lando's Warm Reception
322 The Landing
323 Their Last Kiss?
324 Bounty Hunter IG-88
325 The Icy Plains of Hoth
326 Luke Astride His Tauntaun
327 Rebel Snowspeeders Zero In!
328 Champions of Freedom
329 Inside the Falcon
330 The Training of a Jedi
331 Yoda's Instruction
332 The Warrior and the Jedi Master
333 Imperial Snow Walker Attack!
334 The Asteroid Chase
335 Approaching Planet Dagobah
336 Power Generators
337 Beauty of Bespin
338 Dreamlike City
339 Luke's Training
340 Snow Walker Terror
341 Tauntaun
342 Cloud City Reactor Shaft
343 Yoda's Home
344 Escape from Bespin
345 Deadly Stompers
346 Snow Walker Model
347 Of Helmets and Costumes
348 Filming the Star Destroyer
349 Millennium Falcon Miniature
350 Launching an X-Wing
351 Model Star Destroyer
352 Checklist — 265-352

• EMPIRE FORCES •

1 F O
2 R I
3 A E
4 B X
5 U I
6 W U
7 M N
8 C D
9 O U
10 H E
11 E O
12 Y U
13 A K
14 A V
15 E S
16 Q L
17 A I
18 I O
19 Z T
20 G J
21 E I
22 A P
23 Montage — Luke Skywalker, Darth Vader, Luke Skywalker, C-P30
24 C-P30
25 Luke with Yoda and Han Solo Tauntaun
26 Stormtrooper and Boba Fett
27 Trooper Luke Skywalker and Yoda
28 Montage — Too-Onebee, Bossk and Lobot
29 Montage — Princess Leia, Luke Skywalker, Han Solo, and Chewbacca
30 Boba Fett
31 Stormtrooper and IG-88
32 Montage — C-3PO, Lando Calrissian and R2D2
33 Darth Vader
34 F O
35 R I
36 A E
37 B X
38 U I
39 W U
40 M N
41 C D
42 O U
43 H E

44 E O
45 Y U
46 A K
47 A V
48 E S
49 Q L
50 A I
51 I O
52 Z T
53 G J
54 E I
55 A P
56 Empire Forces — Darth Vader
57 Empire Forces — Boba Fett
58 Empire Forces — Probot

59 Rebel Forces — Luke Skywalker
60 Rebel Forces — Princess Leia
61 Rebel Forces — Han Solo
62 Rebel Forces — Lando Calrissian
63 Rebel Forces — Chewbacca
64 Rebel Forces — R2D2
65 Rebel Forces — C-3PO
66 Rebel Forces — Yoda
67 F O
68 R I
69 A E
70 B X
71 U I
72 W U
73 M N

74 C D
75 O U
76 H E
77 E O
78 Y U
79 A K
80 A V
81 E S
82 Q L
83 A I
84 I O
85 Z T
86 G J
87 E I
88 A P

25¢

NEW SERIES!

25¢

MOVIE PHOTO CARDS BUBBLE GUM

SERIES 3

ONCE AGAIN...

TOPPS OFFERS THE MOST EXCITING FORCE IN THE UNIVERSE...

EMPIRE STRIKES BACK (30)
GIANT PHOTO CARDS

4 7/8" X 6 7/8"

After issuing a 440-item ESB series in standard card size, Topps followed up with this magnificent 30-card collection of 5" X 7" color glossies showing scenes from the movie. There are two versions of the cards and wrappers: "test" and "regular issue." The test wrapper is made of wax paper and folds like a normal-size gum pack; the regular wrapper is a paper en-velope with crimped end flaps. The obverses of both the test and regular cards are identical, but the backs are completely different. The regular card reverse is marked checklist No. 1 or No. 2 and shows black & white photos of either cards 1-15 or 16-30 (these numbers do not appear on the cards themselves). The test backs contain 16 small drawings surrounding a short text, and a card number.

ITEM	MINT	EX
Sets		
Regular	18.00	14.50
Test	80.00	65.00
Cards		
Regular	.50	.35
Test	2.50	2.00
Wrappers		
Regular	––	.50
Test	––	30.00
Box	––	4.00

ENDANGERED ANIMALS (10 & 8) 2 5/8" X 4 1/4"

The title of this set derives from the "Endangered" symbol in the corner of the picture on each card; it is not printed on cards of either of the two series issued to date. There are ten cards in series one, each bearing a small red circle design in the lower right corner of the reverse. In contrast, the eight cards belonging to series 2 have the numbers "002" printed in the same location. Other than this detail, the cards of both series share an identical format: color photos, yellow borders, and red letter captions on front and "question" backs with a habitat map and "What You Can Do" feature. Both series were distributed in boxes of "Small World Animal Grahams" (two box sizes exist) on a one-card-per-package basis. The values listed below are based on one-half the retail price of the smallest box of cookies (99¢).

ITEM	MINT	EX
Cards, all	.50	.35
Sets		
Series 1	6.00	4.50
Series 2	5.00	3.75
Boxes		
Large	––	.35
Small	––	.25

SERIES 1		SERIES 2	
Blue Whale	Parrot	Bald Eagle	Snow Leopard
Crocodile	Rhinoceros	Cheetah	3 Toed Sloth
Elephant	Sea Turtle	Manatee	Wallaby
Giant Panda	Spotted Owl	Orangutan	Woodland Caribou
Gorilla	Tiger		

ENDANGERED SPECIES TRADING CARDS (36)

2 1/2" X 3 1/2"

"The habits and habitats of our planet's threatened wildlife in a unique 36 card set." That is what you get when you buy this colorful series created by Calico Graphics in 1990. The card fronts contain 35 different artwork pictures (34 animals & one plant); the borders are black and the card number is printed to one side. The backs are nicely laid-out and deliver a wealth of information about each subject, including the Latin binomial. Card #36 is a checklist. It is unlikely that collectors will encounter single cards since the series is currently sold only in complete, boxed sets at a retail price of $7.00 each.

AYE-AYE *Daubentonia madagascariensis*
Class: **Mammal**   Order: **Primate**
Family: Daubentonia Weight: 6½ lbs
Head/Body Length: 16" Tail: 16"
Range: East coast rain forests of Madagascar and the island of Nosy Mangabe.

The Aye-aye is the sole representative of its family and one of the strangest primates. It has teeth which grow continuously like a rodent's and claws rather than nails. The Aye-aye is nocturnal and the object of much superstition. It feeds on fruit and insect larvae which it hears under the bark of trees with its large ears. An enormously long thin middle finger is used to dig out the larvae and to scoop the meat out of coconuts.
The Aye-aye was thought to be extinct but was rediscovered in 1957. In 1966 French biologists captured nine individuals to be released for better protection on the island of Nosy Mangabe. Evidence suggests Aye-ayes have survived.

© 1990 CaliCo Graphics   NO. 18

1 Arabian Oryx
2 Indus Dolphin
3 Yak
4 Black Rhino
5 Peregrine Falcon
6 Onager
7 Texas Blind Salamander
8 Malayan Tapir
9 Leadbeater's Possum
10 Engelmann Oak
11 River Otter
12 Lion
13 Red Wolf
14 Humpback Whale
15 Pigmy Rabbit
16 Maryland Darter
17 Vicuna
18 Aye-aye
19 Green Turtle
20 Kakapo
21 Cheetah
22 Latifi's Viper
23 Spotted Bat
24 Giant Panda
25 European Stag Beetle
26 Simien Jackal
27 Zetek's Frog
28 California Condor
29 African Elephant
30 Mexican Grizzly Bear
31 Long-beaked Echidna
32 West Indian Manatee
33 Morelet's Crocodile
34 Muriqui
35 Greater Prairie Chicken
36 Check List

ENVIROMINTS (48)

WESTERN HARE WALLABY

Placed on the Endangered
Species list December 2, 1970

Historic Range: Australia

For more information on how you can help
endangered and threatened species, write
for your FREE "Wildlife Action Guide".

Send your request to:

Enviromintal Candy Company
P.O. Box 95730   Set 1
Seattle, WA 98145   Card 34 of 48

1 Desert Bandicoot
2 Southern Sea Otter
3 African Elephant
4 Black Rhinoceros
5 Scarlet Chested Parrakeet
6 Guam Kingfisher
7 Northern Flying Squirrel

8 Wood Stork
9 American Crocodile
10 Mountain Zebra
11 Grizzly Bear
12 Lowland Gorilla
13 Woods Bison
14 Costa Rican Puma

15 Orangutan
16 Jaguarundi
17 Snow Leopard
18 Chimpanzee
19 Brown Pelican
20 Giant Panda
21 African Wild Dog
22 Spider Monkey
23 Tiger
24 Woodland Caribou
25 Bald Eagle
26 California Condor
27 Peregrin Falcon
28 Western Gray Kangaroo
29 Asian Elephant
30 Humpback Whale
31 Giant Sable Antelope
32 Key Deer
33 Slender-horned Gazelle
34 Western Hare Wallaby
35 Hairy-nosed Wombat
36 Eastern Cougar
37 Fan Skink
38 Central American Tapir
39 Utah Prairie Dog
40 Whooping Crane
41 Cheetah
42 Guadalupe Fur Seal
43 Arabian Tahr
44 Desert Tortoise
45 Gray Wolf
46 Ocelot
47 Black-footed Ferret
48 Jaguar

1 1/2" SQUARE

This interesting set of endangered animals was brought to our attention by Brian Bigelow, a member of the Sport Americana Non-Sport Advisory Board. One 1-1/2" square card was packed inside individually-wrapped chocolate mints produced by the Enviromintal Candy Company of Seattle, Washington. The fronts have borderless color pictures of each subject. On the back, the animal is identified along with a pertinent fact about it and its habitat. The cards seen so far are marked "Set 1" and each is numbered by using the "card 1 of 48, card 2 of 48" format. Although individual cards are priced inexpensively, it is difficult to assemble a set, and this accounts for the premium placed on a completed collection.

ITEM	MINT	EX
Set	7.00	--
Card	.10	--
Wrapper	--	.05

ENVIRONMENTAL ACTION CARDS (50)

GELADA BABOON

01 Jaguar
02 Galapagos Tortoise
03 Black Rhinoceros
04 Chesapeake Bay Area
05 Siberian Tiger
06 White-Naped Crane
07 Leopard Cat
08 Mugger Crocodile
09 Wattled Crane
10 Grevy's Zebra
11 Brown Pelican
12 Wildlife Conservation Int'l
13 Indian Elephant
14 South American Condor
15 Proboscis Monkey
16 Bald Ibis
17 White Handed Gibbon
18 Bronx Zoo
19 Hartmann's Mountain Zebra
20 Komodo Dragon
21 Tuatara
22 Banded Iguana
23 Pygmy Chimpanzee
24 Koala
25 Asiatic Lion
26 Bactrian Camel
27 Tropical Rain Forest
28 Gelada Baboon
29 Babirusa
30 Milwaukee County Zoo
31 African Elephant
32 Malayan Tapir
33 Giant Panda
34 Indian Gavial
35 Sumatran Orangutan
36 Cotton Topped Tamarin

37 Chinese Monal
38 Przewalski's Horse
39 Black Footed Cat
40 Cheetah
41 Radiated Tortoise
42 San Diego Zoo
43 Snow Leopard
44 Pheasant Pigeon
45 Kodiak Bear
46 White Cheeked Gibbon
47 Sumatran Tiger
48 Piping Plover
49 Rothschild's Starling
50 Symbols and Checklist

2 1/2" X 3 1/2"

It has been said that there can never be too much of a good thing, but the rash of "environmental" cards that have flooded the hobby lately is beginning to make me think otherwise. Endangered animal species are one of the nature-conscious topics attracting the attention of card manufacturers, and to date we've seen a number of sets issued in both artwork and photographic formats. Among the card sets issued so far, the "Environmental Action Cards" series created by Mundus Amicus rates the highest marks. That accolade is even more remarkable considering that this is the company's very first card issue. The blend of color photography, format, design details, and text is outstanding. True, the manufacturer's inexperience shows in some ways - the set title is not printed on the cards and there are some spelling and nomenclature errors to be found - but if you like animal cards, this is the set to buy. A portion of the revenues from these cards benefits the American Association of Zoological Parks and Aquariums (AAZPA) and fifty percent of the first series print run of four million cards is being sold through the "Toys R Us" chain of stores.

ITEM	MINT	EX
Set	7.50	--
Card	.15	--
Wrapper	--	.10
Box	--	2.00

E.T. (87 + 12)

AN ALARMED E.T.!

THE EXTRA-TERRESTRIAL

NEW! HIT MOVIE!

MOVIE PHOTO CARDS BUBBLE GUM

2 1/2" X 3 1/2"

Topps issued the E.T. set in 1982 hard on the heels of the fabulously successful movie. There are 87 numbered cards plus 12 stickers in the series. Each card contains a color photograph from the movie surrounded by a "starry" blue border. A bicycle logo appears on the front and the card number and text are located on the back. The stickers have scenes from the movie, E.T. close-ups, and two sheets of mini-stickers. Stickers nos. 10, 11 and 12 are in short supply compared to nos. 1-9. Note: Set price includes stickers.

ITEM	MINT	EX
Set	15.00	12.00
Card	.10	.07
Stickers		
1-9	.35	.25
10-12	1.00	.75
Wrapper	--	.35
Box	--	4.00

1 Title Card	26 Time for a Snack!
2 Alien Visitors!	27 Unearthly Thirst!
3 Stranded!	28 Elliott in School
4 Mysterious Glow!	29 E.T. Lives It Up!
5 Elliott's Search	30 E.T. Watching T.V.!
6 Fright in the Woods!	31 Frog Madness!
7 An Alarmed E.T.!	32 The Tipsy Alien!
8 The Vigil	33 Trouble for Elliott!
9 E.T. Approaches...	34 What's Wrong with Elliott?
10 Fear of the Unknown	35 Uplifting Moment!
11 A Trail of Candy	36 Dressed Up By Gertie!
12 The Friends Meet	37 Comic Strip Strategy!
13 A Boy's Best Friend?	38 They're Coming to Get Us!
14 The E.T. and Me	39 The Listeners
15 Among Elliott's Toys	40 A Present for "Mom"!
16 Reading a Comic Strip!	41 It's Halloween!
17 Where Do You Come From?	42 Elliott's Disguise!
18 E.T. and the Flower	43 Off on Their Mission
19 A Hungry E.T.!	44 Trick or Treat!
20 Gertie Says "Hi!"	45 Night Ride
21 A Quick Disguise!	46 In the Woods
22 Alone in the House	47 E.T. Phones Home!
23 Up to Mischief!	48 Testing the Communicator
24 A New Found Friend!	49 Message into Space!
25 What's in the Fridge?	50 "Did They Hear You?"
	51 Their Home Besieged!
	52 Spaceman at the Door!
	53 The Investigators
	54 Sterilizing the House
	55 The Air Hose
	56 "How Can We Save Him?"
	57 "You're Killing Us Both"

58 The Emergency Ends	
59 "Don't Die, E.T.!"	
60 The Escape Plan	
61 All Bundled Up!	
62 Van to Freedom!	
63 "They're Gaining!"	
64 To the Landing Site!	
65 Bicycle Chase!	
66 For the Love of E.T.!	
67 A Mother's Concern!	
68 E.T.'s Glowing Heart	
69 Sighting the Aliens!	
70 "The Spaceship Is Coming!"	
71 Cosmic Landing	
72 Michael's Farewell	
73 A Present for E.T.	
74 Gertie's Goodbye Kiss	
75 The Friends Depart	
76 A Final Farewell	
77 Entering the Ship	
78 E.T. and His Gift	
79 Spaceship Interior	
80 Interstellar Garden	
81 Return to Outer Space	
82 Elliott's Family	
83 E.T.'s Director	
84 Filming the Aliens	
85 An Amazing New Star!	
86 Friendly Face from Space!	
87 Checklist Card	

E.T. ALBUM STICKERS (120)

Of the 120 stickers in this Topps E.T. set, only 33 depict complete scenes from the movie. The remaining 87 stickers must be placed together to form larger pictures and there is an album for this purpose. Each sticker is numbered in tiny print on the front and in large print on the back. The stickers themselves were produced by Panini of Italy for Topps. The album contains an offer to supply specific numbers plus an ad for the "Official E.T. Fan Club."

2 1/8" X 3"

ITEM	MINT	EX
Set	24.00	18.00
Sticker	.20	.15
Wrapper	--	.35
Album	2.50	2.00
Box	--	4.00

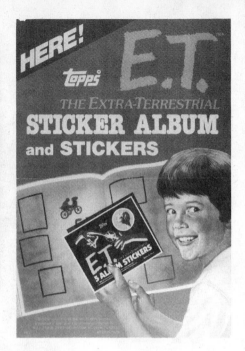

E.T. MAGIC MOTION STICKERS (8)   1 5/16" SQ.

They used to be called "vari-vues" or "wiggle pictures" but the Reese's promotional team came up with the name "Magic Motion Stickers." There are eight in the set: seven are artwork representing scenes or symbols from the movie; the other design shows a bag of Reese's Pieces and the words "E.T.'s Favorite Candy." They are true stickers—there is a thin peel-off backing—and they were mar- keted in 1983-84.

ITEM	MINT	EX
Set	15.00	10.00
Sticker	1.50	1.00
Wrapper	—	2.00

E.T. RAINBOW REFLECTION STICKERS (8) 2" SQ.

An offshoot of laser technology, holograms are finding their way into the card collecting market in a variety of products. This set of eight "Rainbow Reflection Stickers," issued in Reese's Pieces, was one of the first to arrive (1983). Like the "Magic Motion" set, seven of these holograms depict scenes or symbols from the movie; the eighth sticker is an ad for the candy. The stickers do have a peel-away back and can be applied to various surfaces.

Note: since the surfaces of holograms are easily scratched, no mint price is stated below.

ITEM	MINT	EX
Set	--	20.00
Sticker	--	2.00
Wrapper	--	2.00

E.T. STAND-UPS (6) 3 1/2" X 5 5/16"

Perhaps the most heartwarming and successful movie of all time, E.T. has given rise to an amazing group of collectibles and memorabilia. One of the best and, strangely, least known of the "card" collectibles is this series of six "E.T. Stand-Ups" issued by Papercraft Invisible Tape. As you can see in the illustrations, the various color artwork scenes are printed directly on the packages which held the plastic tape dispensers. They are not numbered and each has machine-scored lines to remove the main design from the rest of the cardboard. Note: the prices listed below are for undetached stand-ups; those that are detached from the rest of the cardboard are valued at 50% of the prices given below.

ITEM	MINT	EX
Card	3.00	2.00
Set	22.50	15.00

E.T. STICKERS—HERSHEY (12)   3 5/8" X 4 5/16"

The Hershey E.T. Sticker set of 12 large stickers was marketed in 1982 and could be obtained from the company via a premium offer contained on packages of E.T.'s favorite candy, "Reese's Pieces." Each "Collector Set" of four stickers—A, B and C—contains color photos from the movie surrounded by white borders. The stickers of each set are numbered 1-4 and there are no captions for the pictures. Each sticker has a small Reese's Pieces package at bottom-left, with a Universal Studio's credit line underneath.

ITEM	MINT	EX
Set	15.00	12.00
Sticker	1.00	.75
Panel	3.00	2.00

EVEL KNIEVEL (60 & 22)   2 1/2" X 3 1/2"

Topps released the Evel Knievel series in 1974 as a "test set" to gauge public reaction and to measure product durability and design. Each card has a color photo of the daredevil flanked by starry edges and blue borders. A caption printed in yellow appears underneath the picture. The blue and gray backs contain the card number and a biographical text. In a masterpiece of understatement, a line on the back advises "Caution; Motorcycle and Bike Stunting Can Be Dangerous. Don't Take Chances."

In addition to the cards, a series of 22 black-background "Auto Stickers" was inserted as a bonus in the gum packs. Each one of these numbered stickers has a tan paper back and contains 16 smaller (5/8" sq.) stickers depicting logos and names of various automobile companies and products. They are similar, but not identical, to stickers issued in 1970 with "Way Out Wheels." The stickers from "Wheels," however, have white backs and a different arrangement of mini-stickers for each number. The Evel Knievel wrapper is cellophane; no wax wrapper has been seen. Note: separate set prices are listed for cards and stickers.

ITEM	MINT	EX
Set		
Cards	140.00	100.00
Stickers	40.00	30.00
Card	2.00	1.50
Sticker	1.50	1.00
Wrapper	--	10.00
Box	--	40.00

Evel Knievel

1 Evel Knievel	13 Facing the Fans	25 Snake River Canyon	37 Checking the Ship	49 Boarding the Sky Cycle
2 The Evel Wheelie	14 Robert Craig Knievel	26 The X-2	38 Last Minute Tests	50 All Systems Go
3 Riding High	15 Fast and Furious	27 Driver's Seat	39 In the Cockpit	51 Blast-off
4 Movin' On	16 No. 1 Hero	28 Launching Site	40 Man of Action	52 Up, Up, and Away
5 Idol of Millions	17 Interviewing Evel	29 It's A-ok	41 High Horizons	53 Evel's Eye View
6 Way-out Wheelie	18 Profile in Courage	30 The Challenger	42 The Dream Machine	54 In Flight
7 Cycle Super-hero	19 Checking the Site	31 Awesome Task	43 Root of All Evel	55 Across the High Horizon
8 Easy Rider	20 Making Tracks	32 The Super Cycle	44 Many Happy Returns	56 Parachute to Safety
9 Along Came Evel	21 Public Appearance	33 Fantastic Voyage	45 Momentous Moment	57 Retrieving the Sky Cycle
10 Tall in the Cycle	22 Fearless Flyer	34 Man of Determination	46 Ascent to Danger	58 Evel Lives
11 Evel Speaks	23 The Living Legend	35 Star Spangled Hero	47 Until We Meet Again	59 Bruised but not Beaten
12 The Supervan	24 Confident Crusader	36 Aiming for Success	48 I Shot an Arrow	60 Man of the Hour

EVERYBODY WINS TRADING CARDS (36) 2 1/2″ X 3 1/2″

CONTEST CARD

HAN AND CHEWIE MEAN BUSINESS!

EVERYBODY WINS™ TRADING CARDS
There are 36 Different Trading Cards in the Everybody Wins™ Game, so you can save them or trade them with your friends.
Play Everybody Wins™ again the next time you visit BURGER KING®. Game ends July 30, 1981 or when game card supplies run out.

Battle of the Lightsabers!
Cantina Denizens!
Captured by the Jawas!
Chase through the Asteroids!
Darth Vader and Boba Fett
Droids Inside the Rebel Base
Flight of the Millennium Falcon
Han and Chewie Mean Business!
Han Solo in Action!
Imperial Stormtrooper
Jawas of Tatooine
Jedi Warrior Ben Kenobi
Luke Astride His Tauntaun
Luke Disguised as a Storm Trooper!
Luke Instructed by Yoda
Luke's Training
One of the Sandpeople
Princess Leia Organa
Pursued by the Empire!
R2-D2 and C-3PO
Raid on the Death Star!
Search for the Droids
Seduced by the Dark Side!
Space Adventurer Han Solo!
Snowswept Chewbaca
Star Pilots Prepare for Battle!
Storm Trooper Attack!
The Bounty Hunters
The Dark Lord of the Sith
The Dashing Han Solo
The Defenders of Freedom!
The Imperial Snow Walkers!
The Wonderful Droid, R2-D2
Weird Cantina Patrons!
Yoda on Dagobah
Yoda, The Jedi Master

Burger King confused everyone in 1980-81 by producing a "Star Wars" trading card set to promote the motion picture "The Empire Strikes Back." There are 36 cards in the set and they were issued in strips containing three cards each. The fronts of the cards are excellently designed, with full color pictures surrounded by white borders and captions printed in red. The backs, however, are a dismal gray stock with nothing but advertising copy from top to bottom. The heading "Star Wars" appears on the reverse at top-left and the cards are not numbered. The fact that Burger King used the title "Star Wars" on the cards but printed "The Empire Strikes Back" on its contest cards (see illustration) has created too much confusion, so we have decided to list these cards by the name of the promotion. Note: complete sets of intact strips are more commonly encountered than are single cards.

ITEM	MINT	EX
Set	10.00	7.50
Strip	.75	.60
Card	--	.20

EXCITING SCIENCE FACTS (?) 4 1/8″ X 6 7/8″

The wrapper illustrated doesn't look like much but the implica- tions of the data printed on it are frightening to diehard wrapper collectors. "What Makes a Volcano Erupt?" is listed as "Exciting Science Fact No. 139" ... folks, that's an awful lot of facts and wrappers to collect, and it gets worse, because No. 165 has now been reported to the Hobby Card Index. The series was first mentioned by "New Issues" Editor Buck Barker in a 1961 edition of The Card Collectors Bulletin. Despite the numbering system, very few of these wrappers have found their way in collectors' hands, which is not surprising given the nature of the product and the subject matter of the set. As far as value is concerned, a single wrapper in excellent condition will sell for $20-$25 as long as supply remains limited.

In terms of originality and attractiveness, this set of 16 "Fabulous Rock Records" is one of Topps' finest productions ever. Issued in 1968, each record is 6 3/4" in diameter and is pressed on thin cardboard stock. The reverse is magenta in color and contains a short biography of the group, directions for playing the record, and a list of eight of the 16 titles in the set. The checklist below has been alphabetized for convenience since the individual record numbers appear on the tiny circle of cardboard which is punched out of the spindle hole (the record number is also listed below the "Collect All 16 Titles" line). These records were originally packaged in blue sleeves and sold directly from the box for 15 cents apiece (no gum). Note: all prices are for records in sleeves.

ITEM	MINT	EX
Set	450.00	350.00
Record	25.00	20.00
Box	--	125.00

Baby I Need Your Loving - Four Tops (9)
Baby Love - Diana Ross & The Supremes (1)
Come See About Me - Diana Ross & The Supremes (15)
Dancing In The Streets - Martha & The Vandellas (7)
Fingertips - Part Two - Stevie Wonder (8)
How Sweet It Is (To Be Loved By You) - Marvin Gaye (6)
I Can't Help Myself - The Four Tops (5)
Love Is Like A Heat Wave - Martha Reeves & The Vandellas (14)
My Girl - The Temptations (4)
My World Is Empty Without You - Diana Ross & The Supremes (16)
Please Mr. Postman - The Marvelettes (12)
Shop Around - Smokey Robinson & The Miracles (11)
Stop In The Name Of Love - Diana Ross & The Supremes (2)
The Way You Do The Things You Do - The Temptations (13)
Uptight (Everything's Alright) - Stevie Wonder (10)
Where Did Our Love Go - Diana Ross & The Supremes (3)

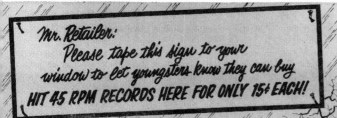

FAMILY FUN GAMES (11K)

1 1/2" X 2 1/2"

Baseball Fun
Boxing Fun
Darts
Eraso
Fishin' Fun
Football
Shooting Gallery
Ten Pins
Tic-Tac-Toe
Wheel O' Fortune
Word Game

Recently discovered by John Neuner, "Family Fun Games" is a series of small game cards with different themes issued by Eveready Batteries. Each card has a number of "Spot-O-Gold" rub-off dots which reveal the player's progress in the game being played. The cards original-ly came in attached pairs, so the left or right end of every card will have a rouletted edge. Rules for each game are printed on the reverse. The 1972 copyright date printed on every card may possibly indicate the year of issue but it is more likely that it refers to the "Spot-O-Gold" pa-tent. No packaging has been found and the number of cards in the series is not known. Note: cards with any gold dots rub-bed off cannot be graded mint.

ITEM	MINT	EX
Card	.75	.50
Panel	2.00	1.50

For 2 players: Players select "bowling lanes" (No. 1 or 2). 1st player erases (with regular pencil eraser) any 1 of his gold pins to discover his score, and enters total points in first frame (other side). 2nd player erases any one of his gold pins and writes score in his 1st frame. Players take turns until all bowling pins are erased. Player with highest total score wins.

Scoring: Top number under gold pin represents score for 1st ball "thrown," bottom number is for 2nd ball. A ◫ is a spare; a ⊠ is a strike. If last pin erased is a ◫ add 10 points, if it's a ⊠ add 20 points to final score.

© 1972 Spot-O-Gold Corporation, Phila., Pa. U.S. Patent No. 3281165

"Get the Cat 🐱 ...Not a copy cat"

FAMOUS AMERICAN INDIAN CHIEFS (3K)   2 5/8" X 3 1/2"

SPECIAL!

Learn about famous
American Indian Chiefs!
Full-color cards—
FREE with Hires cartons.
Collect a complete set—
limited time only.

Podner—here's a right refresher!
Sparkling Hires Root Beer, made
the real oldtime way. It's balanced
refreshment—blended as only
Hires has done it since 1876.
Have a Hires today! It's wonderful
with snacks or any time you need
refreshment. At your dealer's
or at fountains and dispensers
everywhere. Hires to you!

Hires *Refreshes RIGHT!*

Partial Checklist
Geronimo ... Chief of the Apache Tribe
Osceola ... Chief of the Seminole Tribe
Pontiac ... Chief of the Ottawa Tribe
Quanah Parker ... Chief of the Commanche Tribe
Sitting Bull ... Chief of the Dakota Sioux Tribe

Most collectors have never seen a card from this series of "Famous American Indian Chiefs" issued by Hires Root Beer. As you can see by the illustration, each card was actually part of a much larger panel which had a ring tab (to attach it to a bottle in the carton of root beer), a large heading, and a considerable amount of printed text. All of the titles, save one, that have been reported to the Hobby Card Index have come from cards that were cut away from the panel. Such cards are blank-backed and have no reference to set or issuer printed on them, nor are they numbered. Neither the advertising page, provided by Brian Bigelow, nor the panel reveal the length of the set. The values listed below reflect the scarcity of single cards in general and panels in particular. Note: single cards cannot be graded mint since they were cut away from the original panel.

ITEM	MINT	EX
Card	--	3.00
Panel	20.00	15.00

QUANAH PARKER
CHIEF OF THE COMANCHE TRIBE

"Comanche," a name that struck terror in the hearts of the settlers on the plains, a tribe that committed most of the Indian horrors of the southwest.

The Comanches were expert riders and horse-breeders, originally obtaining their mounts from Spanish settlers. They waged constant war, first against Spaniards, then with other tribes, carried on bloody relentless persecution of the white settlers. When a great epidemic wiped out many Comanches, they increased their tribe by kidnapping and adopting Mexican boys and girls.

Comanche, meaning "people," were led for many years by Chief Quanah Parker reared in war. He refused to accept a treaty that would confine him to a reservation and by a series of daring raids, extending over many years, terrorized frontier settlements. Ruthless in his determination to rid the land of the whites, he led an attack of 700 warriors against a small band of whites in the Battle of Adobe Walls. The Comanche's surprise attack on the whites failed because buffalo hunters there had six shooters and heavy rifles enabling them to pick off the Indians as they attacked. In 1875, after a series of defeats, he surrendered. He converted to the white man's ways immediately, and later achieved the reputation of being the richest Indian in the nation.

"Famous Americans all - explorers, pioneers, sports heroes - featuring color portraits combined with action scenes and authentic facts." That's how the advertising card (see illustration) describes this set, but the actual product is less impressive. The "color portraits" are really monochrome blue, the "action scenes" are interesting line-drawings that are limited by the tiny format, and the "authentic facts" are simple one or two line statements pertaining to the subject. This is one of Topps' first stamp sets and it is relatively scarce and difficult to complete, but most collectors regard it with indifference. The frame lines and panel beneath the picture are blue in color on all but six stamps: these have black frame lines and panels and are marked by an asterisk in our checklist. Note: the prices listed below are for "common" stamps in the set. Collectors will encounter premium prices for certain political personalities and celebrities, and especially for sports stars. Collectors interested in those stamps must decide for themselves whether the prices asked are reasonable. No set price is given since there are wide differences of opinion concerning the value of specific "high demand" stamps.

ITEM	MINT	EX
Stamp	2.50	2.00
Wrapper	—	100.00
Box	—	150.00

1 George Washington	21 Chester A. Arthur	41 Thomas A. Edison	61 Billy Mitchell
2 John Adams	22 Grover Cleveland	42 Dolly Madison	62 Andrew Carnegie*
3 Thomas Jefferson*	23 Benjamin Harrison	43 Alexander Graham Bell	63 John Paul Jones
4 James Madison	24 William McKinley	44 Clara Barton	64 James Fenimore Cooper
5 James Monroe	25 Theodore Roosevelt	45 Eli Whitney	65 Alexander Hamilton
6 John Quincy Adams	26 William Taft	46 Daniel Boone	66 Harriet Beecher Stowe
7 Andrew Jackson	27 Woodrow Wilson	47 Washington Irving	67 Adlai Stevenson
8 Martin Van Buren	28 Warren Harding	48 General Lee*	68 Richard Nixon
9 William Henry Harrison	29 Calvin Coolidge	49 Betsy Ross	69 Alan Shepard
10 John Tyler	30 Herbert Hoover	50 Babe Ruth	70 Jonas Salk
11 James Polk	31 Franklin D. Roosevelt	51 Robert Fulton	71 John Pershing*
12 Zachary Taylor	32 Harry S. Truman*	52 Frank Lloyd Wright	72 Buffalo Bill
13 Millard Fillmore	33 Dwight D. Eisenhower	53 John L. Sullivan	73 Kit Carson
14 Franklin Pierce	34 John F. Kennedy	54 Gen. George Custer	74 Annie Oakley
15 James Buchanan	35 Wright Brothers	55 Edgar Allan Poe	75 Jim Corbett
16 Abraham Lincoln	36 Benjamin Franklin	56 Davy Crockett	76 Peter Stuyvesant
17 Andrew Johnson	37 Albert Einstein	57 Richard Byrd	77 Dr. Walter Reed
18 Ulysses S. Grant	38 Charles Lindbergh	58 Lewis & Clark	78 Admiral Dewey
19 Rutherford B. Hayes	39 Mark Twain	59 Jim Thorpe	79 Nathan Hale
20 James Garfield	40 Henry Ford	60 Lou Gehrig	80 Douglas MacArthur

FAMOUS MONSTERS SERIES (64)   2 1/2" X 3 1/2"

The fact that it is easier to find a complete set of Famous Monsters than it is to build a set card by card is attributable to the fact that the full set was originally sold via the mail. The obverse format is a black & white monster picture with orange borders, caption, and card number. The backs state the series title, have a 1963 Rosan copyright, and carry offers for merchandise such as rubber monster masks. Although the Rosan Company made trading cards, it did not manufacture bubble gum or arrange to have gum packed with these cards.

ITEM	MINT	EX
Set	150.00	110.00
Card	2.00	1.50

1 Konga	21 Educated Skeleton
2 The Red Planet	22 The Melting Head
3 I Was a Teenage Frankenstein	23 The Head Shrinker
4 Amazing Colossal Man	24 The Giant Lizard
5 Invasion of Saucerman	25 Teenage Frankenstein
6 Konga	26 Cruel Terror
7 Night of the Blood Beast	27 How to Make Monster
8 The Undead	28 Creation of Frankenstein
9 Goliath and the Dragon	29 Goliath and the Dragon
10 The Blood of Dracula	30 The Blood of Dracula
11 War of the Colossal Beast	31 The Devil's Curse
12 The Blood of Dracula	32 The Devil's Curse
13 Konga	33 Invasion of Saucerman
14 Terror From Year 5,000	34 How to Make a Monster
15 Return of Saucerman	35 The Claw
16 Headless Ghost	36 The Werewolf and Frankenstein
17 Goliath and the Barbarians	37 Teenage Werewolf
18 Konga	38 Werewolf Meets Teenage Frankenstein
19 Goliath and the Dragon	39 Invasion of Saucerman
20 Circus of Horrors	40 Coffin of Terror

41 The She Creature
42 The Hook
43 Unknown Terror
44 Horrors of the Black Museum
45 Circus of Horrors
46 The Iron Mask
47 I Was a Teenage Frankenstein
48 The Iron Mask
49 The Snake Pit
50 Reptilicus
51 Circus of Horrors
52 The Sea Monster
53 Dracula's Daughter
54 The Ghost
55 The Colossal Beast
56 Konga
57 The Corrugated Brute
58 Invasion of Creatures
59 Star Creatures
60 The Yelloe Serpant

61 The Devil's Doll
62 The Beastly Horror
63 Haunted Fear
64 Horrors from the Black Museum

FANCY PANTS (31)   2 1/2" X 3 1/2"

"Fancy Pants," a product test marketed by Topps in 1975, was recently brought to light by John Neuner, "The Wrapper King." The series is composed of 31 "real cloth jean stickers" designed to be temporarily applied to "jeans, jackets, t-shirts, any place!" Each pack contained one cloth patch, a checklist card with application instructions on the back, and a stick of gum. The wrapper follows the standard test format: a multi-color product label centered on white wax paper, with an issuer/ingredients label used to seal the back. The wrapper code is T-85-5 and the checklist card bears a copyright date of 1976. No box has been seen. Until more of this product is found and enters the marketplace, we can only make suggestions about values based on past experience: patch ... 3.00; checklist/instruction card ... 2.00; wrapper ... 100.00.

Big Wheel	I Don't Give A Hoot	Official Bully
Beat It!	I Hope You Croak	Poison
Comb Your Face!	I Love Frankenstein	Seal Of Approval
Cruisin'	I'm A Heavy Dude!	Smile
Cycle King	I'm A Pussycat	Spaced Out!
Drop Dead	I'm Fresh	Super Star
Fly Me	I'm No Angel	Vampire Lib!
Foxy Lady!	I Want My Mummy!	What A Bummer
George Washington	Jive Turkey	You Stink!
For President	Kick Me!	You Turn Me On!
Hot Dog!	Let's Neck!	

FANTASTIC FIRSTS IN SPORTS (50)

1 5/8" X 3 5/16"

A set which has not been reviewed in a sports card reference book since 1979, "Fantastic Firsts In Sports" is an interesting candy box series which deserves more attention. The "cards" are actually the entire back panel of the candy box and each is numbered and titled (see the all caps words of the first sentence of text). Each subject has an illustration which covers about 40% of the card area; the color scheme is green, brown and white. The series was issued by Nabisco in 1969 and appears only on "Junior Mints" brand candy (none reported on "Pom Poms"). Note: cards cut away from the box cannot be graded mint. No set price is given since values for some of the events vary greatly depending upon the sport and individuals involved. The prices listed below refer to "common" cards.

ITEM	MINT	EX
Card	--	1.00
Box	5.00	4.00

1 Discus Throwing
2 Longest Successful Run
3 Grand Slam Home Runs
4 Most Points Scored
5 Bicycle Speed Record
6 Distance Flight Shooting
7 Fastest Automobile Race
8 Highest Three-Game Score
9 Longest World Championship Fight
10 Equestrian High Jump
11 Longest Hole In One
12 Longest Home Run
13 College Football Records
14 Greatest Distance
15 Fastest Player
16 Fastest Horses
17 Fastest Ice Boat
18 Greatest Female Figure Skater
19 Motorcycle Speed Record
20 World's Water Speed Record
21 Fastest Human Racer
22 Fastest Revolver Marksman
23 Downhill Speeds
24 Most Consecutive Free Throws Scored
25 Land Speed Record
26 Longest Surfboard Ride
27 Longest Swim
28 Highest Kites
29 Fastest Service
30 Barrel Jump
31 Fastest Eight Car Crew
32 Water Skiing Speed Record
33 Most Consecutive Speed Record
34 Quickest Knockout
35 Place Kicking
36 Sailplane Altitude Record
37 Most Consecutive Perfect Innings
38 Longest Ski Jump
39 Longest Singles Match
40 Drag Racing Records
41 Deepest Spelunkers
42 Largest Catch
43 Long Jump
44 Longest Jump
45 Passing Record Holder
46 Greatest Lift
47 Flight Endurance Record
48 Deepest Dive
49 Free Fall
50 World's Finest Athlete

FANTASTIC FUN WITH SCIENCE (25)

1 5/8" X 3 15/16"

The "Fantastic Fun With Science" series, printed on the backs of "Junior Mint" candy boxes, appears to have been issued in 1971. There are 25 subjects in the set but many of the titles are still unknown at this time (eight are printed in our checklist below). Unlike the "Fantastic Firsts In Sports" set previously reviewed, cards of this science-theme series are mostly white, with brown-print text and a small green and brown illustration. All cards are numbered and the series title is printed in bold red letters on each. The words "Series No. 1" are found on each card, but no subsequent sets have been reported to The Hobby Card Index. The series currently holds the catalog reference number R757-12. Note: cards cut away from the box cannot be graded mint.

ITEM	MINT	EX
Card	--	.50
Box	3.50	2.50
Sets		
Cards	--	15.00
Boxes	110.00	75.00

Partial Checklist

3 Magic Window Pane
9 Magic Wand
12 Pearl Divers
13 Invisible Glue
14 Anti Gravity Water
15 Magic Ice Cube
18 Tightrope Walker
19 Water-Powered Elevator

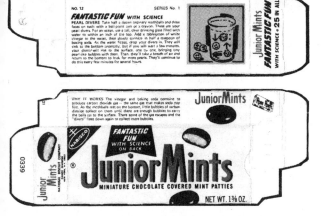

FAR—OUT IRON—ONS (24)   IRREGULAR

Mom's got her hands full with this set! First, the instructions say "Get your mom to help you apply your Far-Out Iron-Ons." Not only does she suffer through your temper tantrum (you want to put it on your brand new tee shirt) but after giving in, she has to drag out the ironing board and iron and do all the work. Then she gets to iron this tee shirt and it's constantly deteriorating iron-on INSIDE OUT for years to come because one can't touch the rubberized transfer with a hot iron and you won't trash that grungy shirt! Each iron-on is approximately 4" X 6" and came packaged in a 6 3/8" X 8 1/2" paper envelope (two different). Rather than list the titles, we have illustrated the visual checklists appearing on each package.

ITEM	MINT	EX
Unopened pack	5.00	4.00
Wrappers (2)		
each	––	2.50
Iron-On	1.00	.75

4-902-59-01-5   4-921-59-01-5

KEEP AMERICA CLEAN

ECCCH

BAZOOKA

KUNG FU

LOOKING AT YOU

I'M KOOL

DRACULA FOR PRES.

LET'S STREAK

WHO'S A CHICKEN

I'M HOT STUFF

CHOPPER KING

HI, DOLL

LET'S CUDDLE

PEACE ON MARS

DROP DEAD

DONATE BLOOD

HOT ROD

I'M REVOLTING

I'M DYNAMITE

JIVE TURKEY

KING OF THE ROAD

THE SPIRIT OF 76

FAR OUT

MONSTER MASH!

FERN GULLY (100)   2 1/2" X 3 1/2"

The message of this environmental saga is set forth on card #1 of the series: "FernGully is a fantasy, but there is nothing imaginary about the depletion of the forest's resources. Think globally and act locally. You can make a difference!" The story involves a 17-year-old city kid named Zak who takes on a job with a logging company for the summer. Accidentally shrunk to a fraction of his normal size, Zak becomes aware that the forest is teeming with miniature life

forms and that the logging company is destroying their habitat. After Zak realizes that he must change his outlook and work for preservation and reforestation, he regains his former size, but not before introducing rock and roll to Crysta and the rest of the forest creatures. Such is the plot of the full-length animated film which is currently playing in movie theaters throughout North America.

The 100-card series, produced by Dart Flipcards, is divided in-

to the following categories: 81 story cards, 8 character cards, 9 coloring cards, and a single card each for checklist and header / introduction. More importantly, Dart itself made a remarkable commitment by producing FernGully in a manner designed to save resources. The company not only used recycled paper, vegetable-based inks, and water-based varnish to create the set, but is also donating a percentage of the profits to selected environmental groups. The cards were issued in 8-card packs (gumless) and could also be purchased in limited-edition, numbered sets directly from the manufacturer.

ITEM	MINT	EX
Sets		
From packs	12.50	—
Limited Edition	15.00	—
Card	.10	—
Wrapper	—	.10
Box	—	2.00

1 Think Globally, Act Locally
2 Collision Course
3 Lungs Of The Earth
4 A New Day
5 The Forest Song
6 Life Is A Magic Thing
7 Magical Creatures
8 Crysta
9 Zak
10 Pips
11 Batty Koda
12 Magi Lune
13 The Beetle Boys
14 Stump
15 Twig
16 Knotty
17 Bark
18 Symphony Of Noise
19 Sky's The Limit
20 Above The Canopy
21 Warning On The Horizon
22 Look Out, Below!
23 Spread The News
24 Rock And Ock
25 Endless Sky
26 The Web Of Life
27 The Balance Of Nature
28 The Spirit Of Destruction
29 The Powers Of Nature
30 Music To Her Ears
31 Batty Koda Arrives
32 Dazed And Confused
33 Flying Free
34 Human Tales
35 Battered And Bruised
36 Batty Raps
37 Erratic Logic
38 Last Place In The World
39 X Marks The Spot
40 At The Controls
41 Ants Don't Wear Shoes
42 Bat Dreams
43 Who's The Monster?
44 Leaf It To Zak
45 Dinner Time!
46 I'm Gonna Eat Ya
47 Welcome To The Food Chain
48 He's Got Good Taste
49 Never Eat Your Friends
50 I.O.U.
51 New Friends
52 All Ears
53 Welcome To FernGully
54 Fools Rush In
55 Looks Can Be Deceiving!
56 There Goes The Neighborhood!

57 Machine Or Monster?
58 Partners In Grime
59 Crysta's Missing
60 Amazing Discovery
61 Givers Of Life
62 Stumped Again!
63 Hair-Raising Experience
64 The Sound Of Music
65 Catch The Beat
66 Rock On!
67 FernGully Wild Life
68 Tense Times
69 Making A Splash
70 Fairy Tag
71 Breath Of Death
72 Guilty!
73 Crysta's Pain
74 Guardians Of The Forest
75 The Seed Of Life
76 Magi's Power
77 Frozen By Fear
78 FernGully Beseiged
79 Clouds Of Poison
80 No Escape
81 Bat Rescue
82 Inside The Monster
83 Never Forget
84 Beetle Boys Bid Goodbye
85 The Seed Of Creation
86 Fairy Magic
87 The Forest Floor

88 Water Life
89 Giants Of The Forest
90 Crysta's Power
91 Coloring Card
92 Coloring Card
93 Coloring Card
94 Coloring Card
95 Coloring Card

96 Coloring Card
97 Coloring Card
98 Coloring Card
99 Coloring Card
100 Checklist

The SIXTH International
NON-SPORTS Convention

IF YOU COLLECT NON-SPORTS...
DON'T MISS THIS CONVENTION!

3 BIG DAYS

Thursday	Friday	Saturday
JULY	**JULY**	**AUG.**
30TH	**31**ST	**1**ST
SNEAK PREVIEW	10 AM to	10 AM to
8 PM to	10 PM	4 PM
10 PM		
$10 Admission		

$3 Admission
Show Closed 5-7 pm for Dinner Break

1992 SHOW

★ NON-SPORTS CARDS
★ WRAPPERS
★ UNOPENED PACKS

* OVER 60 NON-SPORTS CARD TABLES
* OVER 40 INTERNATIONAL DEALERS

WILL BE HELD AT

PARSIPPANY HILTON
One Hilton Court
Parsippany, N.J. 07054

I-80 to I-287 South to
Exit 35B-Route 10 West
Hotel is about 1/2 mile
on right * 201-267-7373

SHIRLEY EROSS
MEMORIAL AUCTION
Saturday, Aug. 1st
8:00 PM
QUALITY LOTS ACCEPTED
FOR CONSIGNMENT
Viewing Begins 7:30 PM

HOSPITALITY SUITE AVAILABLE
For Dealers & Overnight Hotel Guests
Thurs, Fri & Sat eves 10 PM until ???

MIKE GORDON
GORDON SPORTS COLLECTIBLES
680 Speedwell Ave., Morris Plains, NJ 07950

11 AM to 8 PM Weekdays
Saturdays 10 AM to 5 PM
(201) 540-0004

FIENDS AND MACHINES (66)   2 1/2" X 3 1/2"

"Fiends and Machines," marketed by Donruss in the early 1970's, is a perfect example of how suddenly a "find" of cards can cause a rapid drop in value. The series was listed in the 1988 guide at $60 per set and $35 per wrapper and people not familiar with the way the non-sport market works assumed that these prices would hold even when several unopened cases were found. That was a severe miscalculation: the set was never popular to begin and non-sport collectors are very resistant to items with low demand

profiles, regardless of the supply. In other words, you can't talk somebody into buying something they don't want. The new prices listed below reflect the current supply-demand status of Fiends and Machines.

The idea behind this set, as stated on the wrapper, was to "mix and match your favorite cars and monsters to create your own F&M cartoon." Stickers 1-33 are "tops" depicting various "Fiends;" stickers 34-66 are "bottoms" picturing different "Machines." More than 1000 wacky combinations can be made by putting various tops and bottoms together.

ITEM	MINT	EX
Set	27.50	20.00
Sticker	.35	.25
Wrapper	--	15.00

1	Turn On With	22	Dragin Machine
2	It's Only A	23	Made in Detroit To Win
3	Take Your Next Trip In A	24	Mad Over My
4	Shut 'Em Down With A	25	Fords Breakfast Of
5	Have A Better Idea, Burn A	26	Mopar To Ya
6	Chevys Never Die They Just Go Faster	27	Hungry For
7	Beware Of The Bug	28	Color Me Gone
8	Happiness Is A Low E.T.	29	Camaros Kill
9	It's Duces Wild	30	King Of The Road
10	Your Friendly Local Plymouth Eater	32	Take The Worry Out Of Being Close
11	The Great 1	33	Drive A
12	Blow Your Mind With A	34	Wind Out In A
13	Fords Lite Your Tires	35	T-Bird
14	Chevys Beware Of The	36	Duster
15	Hot Stuff By	37	Torino
16	AMX Destroys Any	38	Firebird
17	Fire Up A	39	Firebird Trans-Am
18	Dynamite Comes In Small Packages	40	s/s 454 Chevelle
19	I Love My	41	Pinto
20	Make Mine A	42	Hornet
21	Evil Mean and Nasty	43	Gremlin
		44	Vega
			Camaro

45	Charger
46	Manx Power
47	Monte Carlo
48	Montego
49	Nova s/s
50	Super Cuda
51	Cougar XR-7
52	AMX
53	Demon 340
54	
55	Mustang
56	Challenger
57	Vette
58	Grand Prix
59	Super Bee
60	Cyclone
61	Olds 442
62	Mustang Mach 1
63	Mustang Boss 429
64	Maverick Grabber
65	Comet-GT
66	Road Runner

50 FUN STAMPS (500)   VARIOUS SIZES

A package of Fleer's "50 Stamps" sold for 5 cents and contained one sheet of 50 gummed stamps and a blank piece of cardboard to stiffen the package. Each sheet measures 4 1/16" X 14 5/8" when unfolded and consists of six smaller panels: to fit into the gum pack, the sheet was folded five times. There are 10 different sheets, totaling 500 stamps, in the set. The stamps come in four different sizes and the position of each size stamp is the same on every sheet. Our checklist enumerates the title of the first large stamp on every sheet.

ITEM	MINT	EX
Set	25.00	18.00
Sheet	2.00	1.50
Wrapper	--	3.00
Box	--	7.50

50 Fun Stamps

(1) Do Not Disturb — I'm Sleeping
(2) Help Stamp Out School!
(3) I Dare You to Mess My Hair
(4) I Have Personality...But No Brains [Blue]
(5) I Have Personality..But No Brains [Pink]
(6) I'm a V.I.P.
(7) Our Principal Has an Open Mind
(8) Panic Button — Push Hard!
(9) Teacher's Pest
(10) This Movie Is Rotten

FIGHTER PLANES (12)

Bell X-1 (USA)	Hawker Hunter (English)
F-51 Mustang (USAF)	M-109 (German)
F-86 Saber Jet (USAF)	MIG 15 (Russian)
F-100F Super Sabre (USAF)	X-15 (USAF)
Flying Tiger (USA)	XF3D-1 Skynight (US Navy)
Gruman Avenger (USAF)	Zero (Japan)

IRREGULAR

Collectors in our hobby are more interested in the wrapper—actually a paper envelope of this Topps product than in the toy plane packaged within. The envelope carries a 10-cent price tag and a Topps Duryea credit. The set consists of twelve planes of the "gliding model" variety, each approximately 6" long; simple assembly was required. They were manufactured for Topps in Japan. Note: this was a non-gum issue.

ITEM	MINT	EX
Unopened pack	35.00	30.00
Wrapper	––	25.00

FINK BUTTONS (24)

2" DIAMETER

There was no gum to be found in a 5-cent pack of Leaf's "Fink Button." The only thing inside the glossy paper envelope was a tin button (2" in diameter) with humorous artwork and caption. The buttons are devoid of any other detail except for a "Made in Japan" line printed on the rim. The attachment mechanism is a standard half-moon spike with retainer bar. The wrapper bears a 1965 copyright date.

ITEM	MINT	EX
Unopened pack	15.00	12.00
Wrapper	––	10.00
Button	4.00	3.00
Box	––	100.00

Checklist Compiled by Bob Marks	Big Joker	Deodorant Tester	Mother's Helper	Private Eye	Teacher Tamer
	Blind Date	Gym Teacher	News Commentator	Short Sighted	The Silent Type
Baby Sitter	Chicken Plucker	Honor Student	Peace Corps	Surf Stomper	T.V. Fan
Bargain Hunter	Chow Hound	Jay Walker	Pill Tester	Sword Swallower	Wheeler Dealer
	Clock Watcher	Landscape Gardener			

FLAG MIDGEE CARDS (99)

1 9/16" X 2 1/2"

In 1963, Topps produced this series of Flag Midgee Cards in panels of three cards each, four panels to a 5 cent pack. The cards are color drawings of flags representing "Countries from the 4 Corners of the World." The backs are blue and gray in color, with the card number, vital statistics of the country, and text printed in black ink. A set of similar cards, with blank backs, was issued pre-cut into singles in cereal (several cards in a plain white wax wrapper).

ITEM	MINT	EX
Sets		
Cards	55.00	40.00
Panels	95.00	75.00
Card	.50	.35
Panel	2.50	2.00
Wrapper	--	25.00
Box	--	75.00

1	Afghanistan	12	Canada	23	Dominican Republic
2	Albania	13	Ceylon	24	Ecuador
3	Argentina	14	Chile	25	Egypt
4	Australia	15	China (Peoples' Republic of)	26	El Salvador
5	Austria	16	China (Nationalist)	27	Ethiopia
6	Belgium	17	Colombia	28	Finland
7	Bhutan	18	Costa Rica	29	France
8	Bolivia	19	Cuba	30	Ghana
9	Brazil	20	Cyprus	31	Great Britain
10	Bulgaria	21	Czechoslovakia	32	Greece
11	Burma	22	Denmark	33	Guatemala

34	Guinea	45	Israel
35	Haiti	46	Italy
36	Holland	47	Japan
37	Honduras	48	Jordan
38	Hungary	49	Laos
39	Iceland	50	Lebanon
40	India	51	Liberia
41	Indonesia	52	Libya
42	Iran	53	Liechtenstein
43	Iraq	54	Luxembourg
44	Ireland	55	Malagasy Republic

56	Malaysia	87	Thailand
57	Mexico	88	Tibet
58	Monaco	89	Togo
59	Mongolia	90	Tunisia
60	Morocco	91	Turkey
61	Nepal	92	U.S.S.R.
62	New Zealand	93	United States
63	Nicaragua	94	Uruguay
64	Niger	95	Venezuela
65	Nigeria	96	Yemen
66	Norway	97	Yugoslavia
67	Pakistan	98	West Germany
68	Panama	99	United Nations
69	Paraguay		
70	Peru		
71	Phillippines		
72	Poland		
73	Portugal		
74	Republic of Congo		
75	Republic of Vietnam		
76	Romania		
77	San Marino		
78	Saudi Arabia		
79	Somali Republic		
80	South Africa		
81	South Korea		
82	Spain		
83	Sudan		
84	Sweden		
85	Switzerland		
86	Syria		

FLAGS OF ALL NATIONS (?)

1 7/16" X 3 3/8"

There are two parts to this flag series issued by Leaf. First, there is a set of unnumbered peel-back flag stickers with adhesive backs. The color flag design is printed on clear acetate so the sticker takes on the background color of the surface onto which it is affixed. The other element of the set is a numbered series of blank-backed, "Fact Cards." These show the physical outline (or geographical shape) of the country and list information about population, language, money, and capital city. The wrapper is blue and bears a 5-cent price (one stick-on & one "Fact Card per pack).

ITEM	MINT	EX
Sticker	1.00	.75
Card	.65	.50
Wrapper	––	10.00
Box	––	35.00

FLAGS OF AMERICA (31)

2 1/2" X 3"

Viking Banner 1003 A.D.

To celebrate the United States Bicentennial, Schafer Bread produced a series of stickers entitled "Flags of America" in 1976. The multi-color designs on front were reproduced from models provided by the National Flag Foundation and the stickers were printed for Schafer by Fleer. The set contains battle flags, various renditions of the American flag, and flags from other countries who once held possessions in present U.S. territory. The backs have a descriptive text for each subject, printed in black ink on brown paper stock. None of the stickers are numbered and most that are encountered have minor stains from contact with the bread. An album was available via the mail from Schafer. Note: stickers with stains cannot be graded mint or excellent.

ITEM	MINT	EX
Sticker	1.00	.75
Set	37.50	27.50

Alamo Flag
Bedford Flag
Bennington Flag
British Union Jack
Bunker Hill Flag
Commodore Perry Flag
Confederate Battle Flag
Cross of St. George Flag
Cowpens Flag
First Stars and Stripes
Fleur-de-lis Flag
Fort Moultrie Flag
Gadsden Flag
General Fremont Flag
Grand Union Flag
Green Mountains Flag
Guilford Courthouse Flag
Iwo Jima Flag
Peary Flag
Philadelphia Light Horse Flag

Rattlesnake Flag
Rhode Island Flag
Royal Standard of Spain
Serapis Flag
Sons of Liberty Flag
Star Spangled Banner

Taunton Flag
The Flag of the United States of America
United East India Co. Flag
Viking Banner
Washington's Cruisers Flag

The Green Mountains 1775

FLAGS OF THE WORLD (77 & 5 & 17)   2 1/2" X 3 1/2"

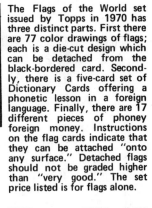

The Flags of the World set issued by Topps in 1970 has three distinct parts. First there are 77 color drawings of flags; each is a die-cut design which can be detached from the black-bordered card. Secondly, there is a five-card set of Dictionary Cards offering a phonetic lesson in a foreign language. Finally, there are 17 different pieces of phoney foreign money. Instructions on the flag cards indicate that they can be attached "onto any surface." Detached flags should not be graded higher than "very good." The set price listed is for flags alone.

1 How They Say It in Italian
2 How They Say It in Spanish
3 How They Say It in Japanese
4 How They Say It in Chinese
5 How They Say It in Hebrew

ITEM	MINT	EX
Sets		
Flags	90.00	67.50
Currency	20.00	15.00
Dictionary	10.00	7.50
Flag Card	1.00	.75
Currency	1.00	.75
Dictionary	1.50	1.00
Wrapper	—	15.00
Box	—	35.00

1 Honduras	21 Dominican Republic	41 Malaysia	61 Romania
2 Albania	22 Guinea	42 Kenya	62 Colombia
3 Algeria	23 El Salvador	43 Liberia	63 Spain
4 Argentina	24 Ethiopia	44 Libya	64 Sweden
5 Australia	25 Finland	45 Luxembourg	65 Thailand
6 Austria	26 France	46 Lebanon	66 Ecuador
7 Belgium	27 Greece	47 Mexico	67 Trinidad and Tobago
8 Bolivia	28 Guatemala	48 Chile	68 Turkey
9 Brazil	29 Haiti	49 Netherlands	69 Uganda
10 Burma	30 United Arab Rep.	50 New Zealand	70 U.S.S.R.
11 Canada	31 South Africa	51 Nicaragua	71 Morocco
12 Ceylon	32 Hungary	52 Nigeria	72 United Kingdom
13 Afghanistan	33 Iceland	53 Norway	73 United States
14 China	34 India	54 Pakistan	74 Uruguay
15 Tunisia	35 Iran	55 Panama	75 Venezuela
16 Congo	36 Ireland	56 Paraguay	76 Yugoslavia
17 Costa Rica	37 Israel	57 Peru	77 United Nations
18 Cuba	38 Italy	58 Philippines	
19 Czechoslovakia	39 Jamaica	59 Poland	
20 Denmark	40 Japan	60 Portugal	

WHEN YOU BUY CARDS ...
MAKE SURE THE CONDITION MATCHES THE PRICE.

FLAG STICKERS & INTERNATIONAL COMMUNITIES (28/12)

TWO SIZES

This interesting promotion for the 1992 Olympic Games was on the shelves of grocery stores as this book was going to press. The set is composed of two elements: a sheet of 10 flag stickers packed inside each carton and a back panel containing three views of foreign countries and the U.S. Each scene has a flag pole with a place to mount the appropriate sticker at top. These items are found in and on specially-marked boxes of Minute Maid 9-count juice boxes. The backs of each "International Community" have a map, details of past Olympic accomplishments, and Olympic symbols and facts. Another panel of the carton has a checklist of flags and communities printed on the reverse side. Since the product carrying these collectibles is still being offered, suggested values are as follows (total = 50% of retail price): community panel of three scenes ... $1.00 each; strip of ten flag stickers ... 50 cents.

FLAG STICKERS	INTERNATIONAL COMMUNITIES
Argentina	Australia
Austria	Brazil
Australia	Canada
Brazil	China
Canada	France
China	Germany
Czechoslovakia	Italy
Finland	Spain
France	Switzerland
Germany	United Kingdom
Indonesia	United States (2)
Jamaica	
Italy	
Japan	
Kenya	
Norway	
Pakistan	
Peru	
Romania	
South Korea	
Spain	
Sweden	
Switzerland	
The Netherlands	
United Kingdom	
U.S.A.	
U.S.S.R.	
Yugoslavia	

FLASHDANCE STICKERS (104)

2 11/16" X 3 7/8"

 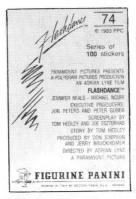

Despite being panned by film critics, Flashdance was a tremendous box-office hit and Panini, the Italian sticker manufacturer, decided to produce an album sticker series based on the movie. They did a magnificent job: each of the 100 oversized stickers has a beautiful technicolor photograph set upon a black background. The backs of the stickers contain only the sticker number and film credits and are written entirely in English. There are also four unnumbered stickers (3 glossy finish, 1 felt finish) with the word "Flashdance" printed across the front. This set was never issued in the U.S. but we have listed it here because it is an American set in terms of form and content.

ITEM	MINT	EX
Set	75.00	55.00
Sticker	.60	.45
Wrapper	—	5.00

FLASH GORDON (24)

2 1/2" X 3 1/2"

1 Arrival on Mongo
2 Break for Freedom
3 Fight for Life
4 Flash and Aura
5 Firing Squad
6 Slaves of the Hawkmen
7 Ming Demands Death
8 Tournament of Death
9 Flash and the Hawkmen
10 Barin, Flash and Aura
11 Time Bomb
12 Ming the Merciless
13 The Forests of Mars
14 News of Ming
15 Attacked by Robots
16 Saved
17 Air Battle
18 Plotting Ming's End
19 Final Plans
20 Beneath the Palace
21 Preparing to Charge
22 Preliminary Victory
23 Final Encounter
24 Heading Home

It is safe to say that this black and white Flash Gordon series produced by Topps in the mid-1960's is one of the most valuable and least-known sets of the modern era. According to Bob Marks, Test Issues Consultant of the Sport Americana Non-Sport Advisory Board, most of the cards released to the public were concentrated in the hands of just a few collectors and the movement of those cards over the years is traceable. Each card depicts a scene from the Buster Crabbe matinee serial, with the caption underneath the picture and a planet logo in one corner. The salmon-colored backs contain the card number and a short text and there is a credit line for King Features at the bottom. No wrapper or box have been seen. Price Advisory: cards of this series are subject to extreme demand and collectors will encounter asking prices of $100 or more per card.

FLASH GORDON (36)

A nostalgia set produced by Michael Jasinski and copyrighted in 1990. There are 36 cards in the series, each with a black and white photograph on the front. The card number, set title, and text are printed on the back. According to a statement on the back of a sample card included with the set, a Limited Edition of 6000 sets was produced, and the sample card for each set bears a stamped consecutive number. Note: sold in complete sets only.

ITEM	MINT	EX
Set	10.00	---

FLINTSTONES CARDS (4)

2 1/2" X 3 1/2"

Card collectors got their first glimpse of the "Flintstones" series by Mother's Cookies when representatives of the company gave away thousands of these cards as samples at the 1990 national sports card convention in Dallas. The giveaway created a slight problem, however, since only the first three of the four cards in the set were handed out; the fourth card, "Dino," could only be obtained by buying bags of Mother's Cookies, in which all four cards were randomly inserted. Since Mother's is marketed on a regional basis, many collectors and dealers have been unable to finish off the sets started for them by the manufacturer.

The cards have multi-colored cartoon-artwork fronts with uneven frame lines, white borders and no captions. The obverse finish is glossy and the corners are rounded. The backs are flat-finished and contain the caption, biographical data, and the card number. The clear cello sleeve in which the card was packed also contained an "Official Flintstones Trivia Sweepstakes" entry form. Note: the numerical scarcity of card #4, "Dino," relative to the other three cards in the set has not been confirmed, but it does seem to be harder to obtain at the present time.

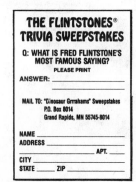

1 Fred and Wilma Flintstone
2 Barney and Betty Rubble
3 Pebbles and Bamm Bamm
4 Dino

ITEM	MINT	EX
Set	6.00	4.00
Cards		
#1-3	1.00	.75
#4	2.00	1.00

FLIPPER (30)

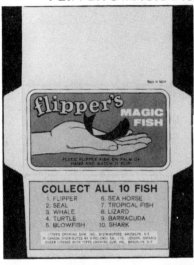

THE RICKS AND FRIEND

1 Bud Rows Home
2 Flipper the Trickster
3 World's Most Famous Dolphin
4 Flipper Surfaces
5 Flying High
6 Flipper's Journey
7 Bud and Sandy
8 Feeding Time
9 The Lookout
10 Strange Seacraft

11 Searching for Flipper
12 Po Ricks
13 Bud Spots Flipper
14 Bud's Sea Cruise
15 Family Talk
16 The Undersea Ranger
17 The Young Ricks
18 Ship to Shore Talk
19 Skyward Leap
20 Flipper and Sandy

21 Looking for Adventure
22 Flipper's Friends
23 Exploring Team
24 Flipper and Sandy
25 Loyal Pal
26 The Ricks and Friend
27 The Ricks Take a Breather
28 Father and Sons
29 Bud Ricks
30 Man-to-Man Talk

Flipper is another black and white "test" issue from Topps. There are 30 cards in the set, which is composed of photographs from the M-G-M television series. There is a black frame line around each picture and the cards have white borders. A Flipper logo appears on the front. The card backs are numbered and are puzzle pieces. The set was produced in 1966. No wrapper or box have been seen.

ITEM	MINT	EX
Set	1300.00	925.00
Card	35.00	25.00

FLIPPER'S MAGIC FISH (10)

COLLECT ALL 10 FISH

1. FLIPPER   6. SEA HORSE
2. SEAL   7. TROPICAL FISH
3. WHALE   8. LIZARD
4. TURTLE   9. BARRACUDA
5. BLOWFISH   10. SHARK

The title of this set refers to the "amazing" properties of the toys inserted into the papper wrapper illustrated here. They are shaped like different fish (see checklist for varieties) and are made of a material engineered with a set of surface dynamics which makes it "move." The ten "Flipper Fish" are assigned numbers on the wrapper checklist but are not themselves numbered. They were manufactured in Japan for Topps, who distributed them in gumless packages.

ITEM	MINT	EX
Fish	10.00	7.50
Wrapper	25.00	20.00

Barracuda
Blowfish
Flipper
Lizard
Sea Horse
Seal
Shark
Tropical Fish
Turtle
Whale

FLIP—UPS (?)

This is decidedly one of the most unusual containers ever used by Topps to market a product. It is a 2" X 2 1/4" cardboard box with artwork and a "set-up" (or straight line) printed on top. On the front side is a pull-tab to slide out a drawer containing candy (or gum). When the drawer is fully extended, a flap "flips" up exposing the "punch line" artwork and caption. The tension which holds the drawer in the box is provided by a rubber band and the box was manufactured for Topps in Japan.

ITEM	MINT	EX
Flip-up	50.00	35.00
Wrapper	--	150.00

FLOWER POWER (?)

2 1/2" X 3 1/2"

"Flower Power," by Donruss, is one of those sets that prompts the question, "Why did they bother?" The "cards" are pieces of blank-backed cardboard with one or more circular diecut stickers on front. They are not numbered or captioned and the length of the set is not known. The series title appears to make an association with "hippie" philosophy, but the "stick-ons" themselves look like hex sign bathtub appliques. However, this is an early Donruss set (1968) and there is some interest among collectors in acquiring these items.

ITEM	MINT	EX
Sticker/card	1.00	.75
Wrapper	—	25.00

FLYING NUN (66)

2 1/2" X 3 1/2"

The cast of the FLYING NUN

In 1968, Donruss collaborated with Screen Gems to produce this 66-card set based upon the television series "The Flying Nun." Each color photograph is surrounded by blue borders and the white frameline is decorated with fancy scrollwork. The caption, printed in black ink, is located in the field of the picture, and the card number is found in the lower right-hand corner. The backs of the cards are puzzle pieces.

ITEM	MINT	EX
Set	200.00	160.00
Card	2.50	2.00
Wrapper	—	8.00
Box	—	35.00

For a safe flight!

1 Sour Grapes
2 Wheee-e-e-e!
3 The School Teacher
4 Of Course, I Can Fly!
5 For a Safe Flight!
6 All I Said Was, "I Bet I Can Fly!..
7 Full Speed Ahead!
8 Tell the Captain His Wing Just Fell Off
9 No, I Don't Give Flying Lessons!
10 Up, Up and Away!
11 Santa's Little Helper!
12 Cowboys Don't Fly!
13 Sour Grapes
14 Are You Certain a BIRD FLEW in Your Ear?
15 The Case of the FLYING NUN
16 The Control Tower
17 More Bounce to the Ounce!
18 Alejandro Rey
19 Sally Fields
20 Flying Lessons Are Fun!
21 Short Runway!
22 Air Mail Presents!
23 I Can't Look Down!
24 I Need a Clearing to Take Off
25 Now I Can Taxi Before Takeoff!
26 Sister Jacqueline and Her Dog
27 Sister Jacqueline Played by Marge Redmond
28 I Don't Think I Can Fly Blind
29 License? What License?
30 Mother Superior, Played by Madeline Sherwood
31 A Thorn Among the Roses!
32 Of Course It Will Fly!
33 I Want to Fly Too!
34 Sister Sixto

35 Watch Out for That Branch!
36 Sure! Everyone Drives a Pink Car!
37 No, I Don't Get Air Sick!
38 Around the Island in 80 Minutes
39 But It Matches the Car
40 Not Just Everyone Can Fly
41 You Throw Me a Pass As I Fly Over the Goal
42 Good Day for Flying
43 I'd Rather Be an Airplane Mechanic
44 The Easy Way to Raise the Flag
45 Looks Like a Storm Up Ahead
46 I Think I Should Have Turned LEFT at the Last Cloud
47 Bad Landing
48 Sky Surfing
49 An Eagle Bit My Finger
50 Just Thought I Would Drop In
51 Testing My Wings
52 This Way Your Lesson Will Stay in Your Head
53 Now, What Did I Do?
54 Sally Fields
55 Sister Sixto, Played by Shelly Morrison
56 Guess I Landed Short!
57 It's a Bird, It's a Plane, It's...!
58 The Control Tower Goofed
59 You're Grounded!
60 One for the Road-er, the Sky That Is
61 Inspecting the Property!
62 You Call This the Bathtub Boo-Ga-Loo!
63 I Can't Take Passengers
64 I Like to Paint by Number!
65 Come Fly with Me!
66 I Won't Even Make a Splash!

FLYING THINGS (48?)

Over the ten-year period 1965-1975 Topps issued "Flying Things" on at least five different occasions. It is very difficult to determine the exact year of distribution for any of these sets, except for the cellophane-wrapped issue bearing a 1975 product code. Illustrated below are six wrappers (courtesy of Stephen Powers and John Neuner) which are lettered A-F for purposes of identification.

We have listed the titles of every "Flying Thing" reported to us (48 in all) alphabetically, and the letter or letters in parentheses indicate the wrapper or wrappers in which they came. The "Flying Hotdog" wrapper — labeled "D" — has no back checklist so no titles are confirmed for it. Wrapper "F" does not have the Topps logo and may have been a Topps "test" issue or another company's effort under license to Topps.

IRREGULAR

ITEM	MINT	EX
Wrappers		
A & D	--	25.00
B, C, & G	--	35.00
E	--	5.00
F	--	20.00
Flying Things		
A, E, & F	8.00	6.00
B & G	10.00	8.00
C	12.50	10.00
Boxes (2) each	--	40.00

A

B

C

D

E

F

G

Bacon 'n Eggs (B)
Banana (B)
Bathtub (B)
Bridge (C)
Can O' Beans (C)
Carpenter Kit (C)
Carpet (B)
Cigar (B)
Dachshund (B)
Drive-In-Movie (C)
Empire State Building (C)
Eyeball (A, F)

Firecracker (C)
Fist (C)
Fly-Swatter (B)
Football Field (C)
Goof-Off (C)
Guitar (C)
Hammer & Nail (C, F)
Hands Brinker (A, F)
Hero Sandwich (C)
Hippie (C)
Hotdog (A, E, F)
Kiss (B)

Lady Fish (A)
Letter (B)
Monstermobile (A, F)
Moon-Rocket (B)
Mop (A, F)
Nose (A, E, F)
Pencil (B)
Salami (C)
Schmohawk (A, E, F)
Scissors (C. F)
Shaving Kit (C)
Shoe & Sock (C)

Skeleton (A, E, F)
Soap Bar (C)
Soda Bottle (C)
Steak (A, E, F)
Strike (C)
Toothbrush & Toothpaste (C)
Twinkle Toes (A)
Uncle Sam (B)
Vampire (C)
Watermelon (C)
Witch (C)
Yicch (A, E, F)

FOLD—A—ROOS (24)

2 1/2" X 4 11/16"

Through exhaustive research, collectors Bob and Jeffrey Marks have determined that there are only 24 cards in the Topps test set "Fold-A-Roos." Apparently designed as a 36-card set, the artwork and titles for certain numbers were dropped. Keep this in mind when you use the skip-numbered checklist printed below. The dimensions listed in the heading are for a "closed" card; when the bottom flap is pulled down to reveal the punch line, the card measures 3 9/16" X 4 11/16". The test wrapper has a multi-colored sticker centered on white wax paper.

ITEM	MINT	EX
Set	750.00	575.00
Card	25.00	20.00
Wrapper	--	75.00

1 I'd walk the desert for you...you little devil!

2 Do you know what I think...you're a real blast!

3 You're my knight in shining armor... even if you are a strange bird!

4 You're a big baby...really big!

5 You're really a strange chick...ya old witch!

6 I really like you a lot...and I'm not horsing around!

7 You'd make some points with me... if it wasn't for the one on your head!

9 It's hard to believe that in this day and age...there's someone as stupid as you!

11 You're quite a sight at night...but during the daytime, yeccch!

13 You sleep like a bear...but why must you eat like a hog?

15 I cleaned up on Wall Street...I've been doing it for years!

17 Thanks for the unusual gift...wait'll you see yours!

20 We know someone who likes you... because he's bats!

22 Come into my garden...baby!

24 You're noble as a viking...but I wish you wouldn't bug me!

26 No matter how you slice it...you're just a ratfink!

28 You're as cute as a bunny...too bad you smell like an old hound!

30 You've got the endurance of a camel... and hairy knees too!

31 You're a real swinger...so go find a tree!

32 You're the caveman type...you're smelly and you've got scales!

33 You're invited to our party...you big ape!

34 I'll come clean with you...you're not my type!

35 You will meet a handsome stranger... who will turn you into a frog!

36 I got up to 100 M.P.H. in my sports car...the day I saw a fire breathing dragon!

This 44-card set containing metamorphic designs was assigned the reference number R708-8 by Buck Barker in his list of new issues printed in the July, 1962 issue of The Card Collectors Bulletin. Each color card has a solid center panel over which split end pieces may be folded, thereby creating different funny pictures, ads, and headlines (nine different on each card). The back of the center panel bears the card number and the set title, plus the statement "Collect The Entire Set!" We are no longer listing a set price because certain cards (especially #11, picturing Babe Ruth) are subject to speculative pricing. The price listed below for single cards is for "common" cards of the series (no quantitative scarcities have been reported).

ITEM	MINT	EX
Card	4.00	3.00
Wrapper	---	90.00

1 Nikita Khruschev
Mahatma Gandhi
General Charles de Gaulle
2 Monstrous Martian
Hairy Dancer
Curvy Miss America
3 High Stepping Horse
Bearded General
Charming Lady
4 Worried Bull-Thrower
Horrible Monster
Cuban Dictator
5 Awful Wild Man
Graceful Ballerina
Rock 'n' Roll Singer
6 Giraffe
Whale
Elephant
7 Turkey in Shopping Cart
Driving in Automobile
Man Bathing in Bathtub
8 Porcupine
Caterpillar
Rhinoceros
9 Wheel I'm a Trickster
Bald Headed Bone Crusher
Cute Doll
10 Skinny Kid
Grouchy Teacher
Sweet Bathing Beauty
11 Theodore Roosevelt
Benjamin Franklin
Babe Ruth
12 Pretty Wac
African Ubangi
German Soldier
13 Queen Elizabeth
Nikita Khrushchev
Fidel Castro
14 Fuzzy Old Crank
Bald Headed Slob
America's Favorite
Beauty Queen
15 Abraham Lincoln
George Washington
Franklin D. Roosevelt
16 America's Favorite Bandleader
Lady Vampire
Comic Hobo
17 Scary Savage
Roman Emperor
Egyptian Sphinx
18 Gentleman Hunter
Fierce Gorilla
Pretty Huntress
19 Richard Nixon
John Kennedy
Dwight Eisenhower
20 Weird Skeleton
Pretty Nurse
Friendly Doctor

21 Winston Churchill
Queen Elizabeth
Ferocious Bulldog
22 Adolf Hitler
Frankenstein the Monster
Blackbeard the Pirate
23 Daredevil Dives 150 Feet Into 6 Foot Deep Flaming
Tank of Water
Kids Enjoy Bathing in a
Shallow Rubber Wading
Pool
Boy Rushed to Hospital
After Swallowing a Small
Cast Iron Thimble
24 Millionaire to Live Near the
Newly Elected Mayor and
His Wife
Astronaut Lands Safely on
the Far Surface of the
Moon
Garbage to be Unloaded on
the City's New Downtown
Garbage Dump
25 A 70 Year Old Millionaire
Marries 22 Year Old
Hollywood Starlet
In Maine A 9 Year Old Boy
Graduates with Honors
from High School
A small Tan Cocker Spaniel
Gives Birth to Twenty
Healthy Puppies
26 Famous Baby Doctor Treats
3 Year Old Son of a Local
Congressman
Olympic Star Set to Wrestle
a 650 Pound Ferocious
Alligator
Zoo's Anteater Arrives to Eat
Bugs in the County's New
Park
27 titles unreported
28 Talent Contest Winner Gets
a Prize of a $10,000
Beautiful Mink Coat
Man Ruled Insane After Giving Wife a Bone Crushing
Punch in the Nose
United States President
Asks Congress for
Another New $50,000,000
Atomic Sub
29 A Tornado Blows Down Our
Town's 60 Year Old
School House
Mayor to Get Rid of Top of
Our Town's Local Police
Department
Women's Group Ask Action
Against Teenagers Skimpy Bathing Suit Bikini

30 Principal Asks Help with Our
Town's Juvenile
Delinquents
Man Injured Trying to Kiss
Wife Who Objects to His
Being Drunk
Zoo Keeper Eaten by
Ferocious Man-Eating
Bengal Tiger
31 Former President of the
U.S.A. Called in for White
House Conference
12 Year Old Ballet Dancer
Will Dance at Opera
House in New York City
French Horse Named Pierre
Takes Spill and Breaks
Leg in Kentucky Derby
32 Brush Your Teeth Twice a
Day with Shiny Tooth
Paste
Patch Up Holes in Your Roof
with Black Tar
Shine Your Shoes with Nifty
Shoe Polish
33 titles unreported
34 Use Jones' Ointment to Prevent Getting Painful
Blisters and Infections
Use Mel's Dog Powder and
Your Dog will Have Thick
Fur All Over the Body
35 Kill off Pesky Rodents with
Brown's Rat Poison
Police Need the Best! They
Always Use a "Quick-
Firing" Revolver
Surprise Guests Who Drop
In Unexpectedly With
Woodbury's Liquor
36 Smith's Cream Cheese is
Delicious in Sandwiches
Nilson's Iodine is Wonderful
When Applied to Cuts and
Bruises
Gordon's Flea and Tick Killer
Kills on Contact
37 Stick Pictures on Your Wall
with Ace Thumb Tacks
Fill Holes in Your Driveway
with Mason's Cement
Kids Love to Have a
Mouthful of Burpy Mashed Potatoes

38 Your Pens Write Smoother
Filled with Waterbury's
Black Ink
For a Quick Snack, Try a
Sandwich Made of
Creamy Peanut Butter
Komfy Beach Chairs are
Great When You Are Sitting in Sand
39 Muriel Eye Wash Works Like
Magic When Applied to
Tired Eyes
Whiz Floor Wax is Great
when rubbed on Kitchen
Floors
Lumberger Cheese is
delicious on Crackers
40 Give Your Smelly Pet a Bath
with Fay's Dog Soap
For Mother's Day Give Dear
Old Mom a Big Kiss and a
Pair of Nylon Stockings
Take Strongheart's Muscle
Course and You Can Beat
a Bully by Giving Him a
Punch in the Nose!
41 An Allen Girdle Gives You a
Figure Like a Curvy Movie
Star
The Apex Disposal Unit
Grinds Up Even a 200
Pound Bag of Garbage
With a Crane Model Kit You
Can Make Your Own
Navy Blimp
42 Shore's Hamburgers are
Made from Fresh Ground
Red Chopped Meat
James' Rash Powder Makes
Infants Feel Like Happy
Babies
Dunn's Animal Tonic Makes
Your Pets Look Like New
Cats and Dogs
43 titles unreported
44 For an unusual gift, give the
one you love Tropical Fish
Tasteless Cough Syrup
tastes like Nothing At All!
Dr. Brown's Anti-Germ Pills
kill cold germs

FOOL 'EMS (25)

1 5/8" X 3 5/16"

Our research indicates that "Fool 'ems," a 25 card series printed on the back of "Pom Poms" candy boxes, was issued by Nabisco in 1972. There are two varieties of boxes and cards known: both say "Series 1" on the card, but the type with the set title printed in red letters is slightly larger than the variety with the letters of the set title printed in brown. Since we have very few captions for this series recorded in The Hobby Card Index, we cannot say at this time if the two types contain similar or different card titles. Note: cards cut away from the box cannot be graded mint.

ITEM	MINT	EX
Card	--	1.00
Box	4.00	3.00

FOOTBALL STICKERS (?)

2 SIZES

Alphabetically speaking, this is the third sport to be spoofed by Fleer in a humorous sticker set. It has the same format as that company's baseball and basketball sets previously listed. First, there are a group of 2 1/2" X 3 1/2" cards containing six small name stickers and a larger (2 1/2" Sq.) sticker with a funny picture and a blank name panel. Secondly, there are two types of 2 1/2" X 2 3/4" stickers with tan paper backs. One variety has a blank name panel for placement of one of the small name stickers; the other has the title "All Star" within a star outline. None of the items mentioned are numbered and the set total is not known.

ITEM	MINT	EX
Name card	1.50	1.00
Sticker	1.50	1.00
Wrapper	--	10.00

LARGE SIZE WITH NAME PANELS		LARGE STICKERS WITHOUT NAME PANELS	Andy	Dick	Harry	Larry	Ricky
Bench Warmer	Sock It To Me	Defensive Guard	Art	Don	Henry	Lou	Roy
Butter Fingers	Substitute	No Fair Biting	Bart	Doug	Howie	Marty	Sam
Couldn't Catch a Cold	Team Mascot	Offensive Back	Bill	Ed	Jack	Mike	Stan
Crazy Legs	300 Lbs. Of Cement	This End Up	Bobby	Frank	Jeff	Nick	Steve
Dirty Player	Water Boy		Bruce	Fred	Jerry	Pat	Ted
4 Letterman	Worst Blocker	"ALL STAR" STICKERS	Butch	Gary	Jimmy	Paul	Terry
Here Come Da Judge	Worst Coach	Full Back	Charlie	Gene	Joe	Pete	Tom
Out Of Gas	Worst Halfback	Interceptor	Dan	George	John	Phil	Tony
Pure Chicken	Worst Place Kicker	Pass Receiver	Dave	Gus	Ken	Ralph	Walt
	Worst Referee	Quarterback					

FOOTBALL SUPER FREAKS (42) 2 7/16" X 3 1/2"

"Freak Football" is the game and Donruss brings us the brightest stars of the gruesome gridiron in this 42-sticker set. The stickers are multi-color artwork of the grotesque variety and they peel away from the cardboard backing at the corners. The "SF" logo seen on several cards and uniforms stands for "Super Freaks." The backs of the cards are found with either white or green stock (no difference in value) and have a small B&W picture of the front design, the card number (the stickers themselves are not numbered), and a short text. There are three wrappers recorded for the set; on these, the center designs are identical but the panels have different information or are blank.

ITEM	MINT	EX
Set	25.00	17.50
Card	.50	.35
Wrappers (3)		
each	--	4.00
Box	--	30.00

1	Ronnie the Receiver	22	Alvin Awful
2	Benny the Baby	23	Billy the Biter
3	Richard the Ram	24	Weird Wendell
4	Troy the Trojan	25	Vernon the Viking
5	Jimmy the Jet	26	Wilson the Wreck
6	Barney the Bear	27	Frightening Finklestein
7	Larry Lightfoot	28	Quinton the Quarterback
8	Hectic Harold	29	Dennis the Dinasour
9	Joe the Toe	30	Leonard the Lion
10	Terry the Tailback	31	Amos the Awesome
11	Pearson the Passer	32	Perry the Perforator
12	Freaky Freddy	33	Zonka
13	Text the Terrible	34	Tommy the Turfeater
14	Stinson the Steeler	35	Ike the Spike
15	Cedric the Center	36	Linda Lovely
16	Donald Dum-Dum	37	Arms Armbruster
17	Morgan the Mouth	38	Ernie the End
18	Irving the Indian	39	Richard the Record Holder
19	Ollie the Oiler	40	Bobby the Blimp
20	Durwood the Dolphin	41	Cecil the Center
21	Ned Nimble-fingers	42	Conrad the Kicker

FRANKENSTEIN STICKERS (44) 2 1/2" X 3 1/2"

Over the years, the use of comedy to counter-balance horror has been one of Topps' blueprints for success in producing non-sports cards. The Frankenstein Stickers set, issued in 1966, is a classic example of this formula. Each sticker is a color artwork rendition of an Universal Pictures monster, with a humorous caption below. The stickers are numbered and have tan paper backs (blank). The wrapper is green, with a gray tombstone, magenta-colored monster, and yellow title.

ITEM	MINT	EX
Set	150.00	125.00
Sticker	3.00	2.50
Wrapper	--	20.00
Box	--	100.00

Frankenstein Stickers

1 Be My Ghoul Friend
2 Take Me Back
3 I'll Keep an Eye out for You
4 Don't Make a Monkey out of Me
5 I Love Your Silky Skin
6 Let's Swing Together
7 You Send Me to the Moon
8 Without You, It's Curtains
9 We'd Make a Splash Together
10 I Vant You
11 You're just What the Doctor Ordered
12 Mad About You
13 I Admire your Brains
14 You're a Real Prince
15 I've Got my Eye on You
16 You've Changed Me
17 I'll Love You Forever
18 You're the Strong Silent Type
19 Don't Hyde From Me!
20 You Set my Heart Aflame
21 You Look Like Cleopatra
22 I'm Sinking Without You

23 I Love You in Vein
24 I've Flipped Over You
25 You Remind Me of My Mummy
26 You've Tied Me Down
27 Give Me a Bite, Love
28 I Love Your Toothy Smile
29 I'm All Wrapped Up In You
30 You Make My Heart Sing
31 Pucker Up
32 I Wanna Hold Your Claw
33 You Bring Out the Beast in Me
34 Hug Me
35 I'm No Wolf
36 You're My Type
37 Let's Be Friends
38 Let's Stroll in the Moonlight
39 Don't Keep Me in the Dark
40 Hello Old Pal
41 I Dig You
42 I'm Stuck on You
43 String Along with Me
44 Oh Well, Looks Aren't Everything

FREDDIE & THE DREAMERS (66)   2 1/2" X 3 1/2"

At the height of their popularity, the English rock group Freddie and the Dreamers was captured in cardboard by Donruss in 1965. Each card has a black and white photo printed on a simple white background. The caption and number appear directly below the picture in red print. The backs of the cards were black and white poster pieces which — when all 66 were collected and placed together — formed a "giant" autographed photograph of the band.

ITEM	MINT	EX
Set	75.00	55.00
Card	1.00	.75
Poster	5.00	4.00
Wrapper	--	5.00
Box	--	25.00

FRIENDLY DICTATORS (36)

FERDINAND MARCOS

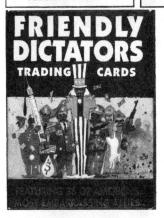

20 FERDINAND MARCOS
President of the Philippines

Ferdinand Marcos began his career with a bang: At age 21, convicted of gunning down Julio Nalundasan, his father's victorious opponent in the Philippines' first national elections, he went to prison. He was later released by a Supreme Court Justice who, like Marcos and his father, was a Nazi collaborator. Despite Marcos's record as murderer, false WW II hero, and Nazi agent, he was elected Philippine President in 1965.

Under Marcos, the Philippine national debt grew from $2 billion to $30 billion (and his wife Imelda's shoe collection grew along with it to over 1,000 pairs), but U.S. corporations in the Philippines prospered, perhaps explaining why the U.S. didn't protest Marcos's imposition of martial law in 1972.

The Carter Administration engineered an $86 million World Bank loan to Marcos, increased military aid to him by 300% and called him a "soft dictator." But a 1976 Amnesty International report identified 88 government torturers and stated that alleged subversives had their heads slammed into walls, their genitals and pubic hair touched, and were beaten with clubs, fists, bottles and rifle butts.

By 1977, the armed forces had quadrupled and over 60,000 Filipinos had been arrested for political reasons, yet in 1981, Vice President George Bush praised Marcos for his "adherence to democratic principal and to the democratic processes". Marcos was defeated and his rule overthrown in 1986 by the followers of Corazon Aquino, widow of an assassinated opposition leader. Ferdinand and Imelda fled to Hawaii, only to be indicted in 1988 for fraud and tax evasion.

FRIENDLY DICTATORS TRADING CARDS
Text © 1989 Dennis Bernstein & Laura Sydell. Art © 1989 Bill Sienkiewicz
Eclipse Enterprises, P.O. Box 1099, Forestville, California 95436

1 The Friendly Dictators
2 Maximiliano Hernandez Martinez
3 Fulgencio Batista
4 Rafael Leonidas Trujillo
5 General Humberto Branco
6 Colonel Hugo Banzer
7 Anastasio Somoza, Sr. and Jr.
8 General Jorge Rafael Videla
9 General Efrain Rios Mont
10 Roberto Suazo Cordova
11 Francois & Jean Claude Duvalier
12 Alfredo Stroessner
13 General Augusto Pinochet
14 General Manuel Noriega
15 Vinicio Cerezo
16 Alfredo Cristiani
17 Chiang Kai-Shek
18 Ngo Dinh Diem
19 Park Chung Hee
20 Ferdinand Marcos
21 Mohammed Zia Ul-Haq
22 Sir Hassanal Bolkiah
23 General Sitiveni Rabuka
24 General Suharto
25 Halie Selassie
26 Ian Smith
27 P.W. Botha
28 General Samuel Doe
29 Mobutu Sese Seko
30 Mohammad Reza Pahlevi
31 Hussan II
32 Adolf Hitler
33 General Francisco Franco
34 Antonio de Oliveira Salazar
35 George Papadopoulos
36 Turgut Ozal

Here we have another of the policitally-biased theme sets produced by Eclipse Enterprises of California. Writers Dennis Bernstein and Laura Sydell excel in relating the excesses of mostly Third World despots and artist Bill Sienkiewicz has produced another string of off-beat, thought-provoking artwork portraits of the crooks and goons who found themselves as heads of state. The set should actually be entitled "Friendly Right Wing Dictators," because there is very little representation of the ultra-leftists who have plagued civilization during the past eighty years (they don't seem to have the staying power of the right wingers). And, yes, there is a Hitler card included for those collectors who think that no set should be without one. Note: sold as a boxed set only.

ITEM	MINT	EX
Set	10.00	---

FRIGHT FLICKS (90/11)

Not all the cards in Fright Flicks are as innocent as the "Mr. Stay Puft" illustrated here. In fact, some of these images taken from 15 different horror movies are so graphic that they may be disturbing to some children and adults in spite of the "humorous" captions. For this reason, we have posted a CONTENT ADVISORY for "Fright Flicks" and suggest that the set be reviewed for content before purchase.

There are 90 cards and eleven stickers in the set. The card fronts have color photographs taken from 15 different horror movies; the captions are printed in red and the borders are white. The backs are green and yellow with a monster drawing above a fabricated story. According to the disclaimer printed on the wrappers, "The characters, companies and events depicted in these cards are fictional. Any resemblance to actual persons living or dead or to any companies or events is purely coincidental." The card number is printed on a "Now Playing" marquee design which identifies the movie from which the scene on front was taken. The stickers are red with color photo centers that have captions printed in various colors. The backs of stickers 1-5 and 7-11 are puzzle pieces, while the reverse of sticker #6 shows the completed puzzle picture. There are four different wax wrappers. Note: set price includes stickers.

I WANNA ROAST ME A BOY SCOUT!

DID IT EVER HAPPEN?

Private Hart pulled his ripcord, but his parachute failed to open. Then he saw a yellow beam of light coming toward him from below. Falling into the beam, his rapid descent was halted and he floated gently to earth.

NOW PLAYING
GHOSTBUSTERS

ITEM	MINT	EX
Set	15.00	12.00
Card	.15	.10
Sticker	.35	.25
Wrappers (4) each	---	.35
Box	---	3.00

Fright Flicks

CARDS

1 Header card
2 Man, That Soup is Hot!
3 Gotta Quit This Nailbiting Habit!
4 I Really Oughta Stop Gargling with Kerosene!
5 I Visit My Dentist Once a Year ... Unfortunately, He Died!
6 Doc, How Do I Get a Head in This Life?
7 Baby, You're the Greatest!
8 Talk About Obscene Phone Calls!
9 Okay, Who Took a Bite Out of My Bran Muffin?
10 Darn! Now I'll Have to Learn Shorthand!
11 Open Wide and Say Aaaah!
12 I Ordered a Pizza — Not a Pizza Face!
13 I Gotta Stop Hammering Nails with My Head!
14 Do I Get Extra Sauce with These Ribs?
15 Must Have Been Someone I Ate!
16 Hi! I'm the New Babysitter!
17 I've Got a Stake in Your Future!
18 Hey - Who Swiped My Undershirt?
19 Let Your Fingers Do the Walking!
20 Better Fix that Broken Window, Paul — A Fly Could Get In!
21 Now Don't Get Cross!
22 I Tell You, that Nuclear Plant is Safe!
23 Eek! A Mouse!
24 Well, I'll be a Monkey's Uncle ... Oh Yeah, I Am.
25 She's Not Exactly a "10" — but She's a Perfect 1/10th!
26 Sorry — Wrong Answer!

27 The Singles Scene is Murder!
28 Warning: I Brake for Small Animals — and Eat Them!
29 Now You Put on the Bunny Outfit!
30 That's a Heck of a Hangnail You Got There, Pal!
31 Mirror, Mirror, On the Wall — Who's the Grossest One of All!
32 Hello, I'm from Acme Pest Control!
33 Oh No — Now I'll Need to Buy New Gloves!
34 Mayhem? I'm Up for It!
35 One Tube of Acne Gel — King Size!
36 What Do You Mean? I Just *Had* a Manicure!
37 By the Way, How's the Meatloaf Here?
38 They Sure Have Ugly Girls in this Neighborhood!
39 Give Grandma a Great Big Sloppy Kiss!
40 No Job is Too Big for Your Local Exterminator!
41 Darn It, I Forgot the Marshmallows!
42 By the Way — Are You Insured?
43 Honey, Shut the Window — I Feel a Draft in Here!
44 Trick or Treat!
45 Dishwashing Liquid? I'm Soaking in It!
46 Braces? Really, You Think So?
47 Next Time I'll Use an *Electric* Razor!
48 The Unkindest Cut of All!
49 Okay Everybody, Arms Extended — and Stretch, 1-2-3!
50 Okay Everybody, Arms Extended — and Stretch, 1-2-3!
51 Is This the Line for Ballet Tickets?

52 When You Said You'd Have Me for Dinner, I Thought You Meant —
53 Am I Tired — *Dead* Tired!
54 Nancy! Come Sit Down Next to Daddy!
55 When I Said "Hand Me that Screwdriver" —
56 Billy ... Suzie? Okay, I Give Up. Who is It?
57 Mommy! You Forgot to Pay the Paper Boy!
58 I Should Have Passed on that Last Egg Cream!
59 The Label Said *Not* to Open Before Christmas!
60 I Wanna Roast Me a Boy Scout!
61 Whew, I'm Really Shot!
62 Charlene, Something Inside Me is Yearning to be Released!
63 Can You Spare a Dime for a Bite?
64 It Takes a Lot of Guts to Do This!
65 "Cheese!"
66 All Right — Bring Back the Lighter for a Refund!
67 Okay Dudes, Let's Take It from the Top!
68 But Why Can't I Join the Boy's Choir?
69 What Big Teeth You Have, Grandma!
70 But Leave the Side Burns!
71 Stay for Coffee?
72 I've Had It with those Miracle Diets!
73 I Said I'd Give Blood but This is Ridiculous!
74 I'll Call You Later, Something Just Came Up!
75 "And for my Next Shadow Picture..."
76 I've Gone All to Pieces Over You, Honey!

77 Mommy, I Want a Glass of Water — Make that Two!
78 Who Said You Could Touch My Toys?
79 Phooey — Nothing's Good on TV Tonight!
80 Have You Seen Your Dentist This Year?
81 Hey, You're Right — I Can See Myself!
82 Hey Pop, That Microwave Really Works!
83 Try the Shrimp Tempura — It's Delicious!
84 Gary Will Be Here at 8:00 and I Can't Do a Thing With My Hair!
85 Later, Kids!
86 Whadda You Mean, Success Has Gone to My Head?
87 There's Just Never Enough Pate to Go Around!
88 I've Got a Bone to Pick with You!
89 Man, My Dogs are Killing Me!
90 Thank You, Thank You, Thank You!

STICKERS

1 T.V. Can Be Hazardous to Your Health
2 Long Live the Queen (Alien)
3 Fright Night
4 Freddy for President
5 Do The Freddy
6 The Fly
7 Freddy vs. Dream Warriors
8 Predator
9 The Man of Your Dreams is Back!
10 Slimer
11 Pumpkinhead

FUN BUTTONS (144)

Once upon a time, "Fun Buttons" were everywhere: drug stores, groceries, card conventions, card publications ... everyone seemed to have them. Then a funny thing happened ... the company that produced them went out of business and collectors found that they hadn't paid enough attention to the buttons while supplies were plentiful. Now there is renewed interest and people are finding that assembling a complete set of 144 is quite a challenge.

Each tin button measures 1-1/8" in diameter and has a visual or written statement, logo, word or phrase printed in a multicolor format on front. The pin apparatus is a half-moon with a full-length spike and a protective "U" retainer. The buttons are not numbered and there is no credit line or manufacturer identification on the rim or in the well. The wrapper is made of paper and each pack contained six buttons (nothing else was included, although the producer was "Fun Foods"). The most interesting buttons in the series refer to Garbage Pail Kids and Michael Jackson.

ITEM	MINT	EX
Set	60.00	45.00
Button	.35	.25
Wrapper	—	.35

Board of Health Approved — Try Me
Boogie
(No) Boys
Break Dance
Brothers are Bullies
Brothers Stink
Buzz Off
Candy Taster
Certified Clown
Cheap Button
Chow Hound
Coach
Computer Whiz
Danger
Danger Keep Out!
Do (Eye) Know U?
Don't Ask
Don't Ask Me!
Do Not Enter — School
Don't Follow Me I'm Lost
Don't Step In It
Drop Dead You Jerk!
Eight Ball
Emergency Button
(Fire hydrant & dog)
Follow Me!
Garbage Patch Kid
Gas Attack
Genius
Genius Behind This Button!
Get Lost
Get Lost!
Get Lost You Creep
Girl Inspector
(No) Girls
Give Me a Break
Give Me a Break!
Give Me a Buck!!
Go Crazy
Go For It!
Good Stuff

Gross
Gun Control
Gym Locker Inspector
Have You Hugged a Teacher Today?
(No Homework)
Homework Off Limits
Hot Stuff
I Ate School Lunch Today
I Dare You!
I Dare You To Rip-Off This Button!
I Don't Want To!
I Got Junk Food Mania
I (Love) My Shirt
I (Love) My Brother
I (Love) My Sister
I (Love) L.A. Until I Was Mugged!!
I (Love) N.Y. Until I Was Mugged!
I Smell Gas
I'm a Trivia Treat
I'm Back by Popular Demand
I'm Famous
I'm Not Deaf I'm Ignoring You
I'm The Best!
If I Followed You Home Would You Keep Me?
It's Fun To Be Superior
Keep It Clean
Kidz Have Rights Too!
Kiss Me!
Kissing Permitted in This Area Only!
Legal in Most States!
Let's Go Out 2 Night
Lifetime Warranty
Macho
Make My Day!
Michael Who?
Mirror / Monkey

Misplaced Belly Button!
Nobody's Home
No One Asked You!
No Parking Beyond This Button!
No Way
Not My Job!
Nuke the Whales (Just Kidding Stupid!)
(Nuts) 2 U
Official Boy Watcher
Official Genius
Official Visitor From Another Planet
100% Pure Flubber
Out of Order
Perfect Ten
Pizza Power
Press Here If You Dare!
Press Here See What Happens
Private Property Keep Away Stupid
Punk Rocker
Question Mark
Radio Active
Rock-It
Rock (Rock) Rock
Rock Roll
Runaway Hotline 800-231-6949
Shut Up!
Shut Up Genius At Work!
Sisters Are Stuck-up
Sisters Stink
Sit on It!
Slow Is More Fun!
Smell My Gym Sox
Smoking (No)
Space 4 Rent
Spitballs Are Forbidden Under Penalty of Death
Spoiled Rotten
Stop
Take a Bath

Teach Me!
Teacher's Pest
This Button Holds Up My Pants!
This Button is Bugged
Thriller
Try Me!
Uh-Huh!
Veteran Food Fighter
Video Game Ace
Wake Me When You're Through!!
Warning ... Neighborhood Crime Watcher
Weird
What Are You Lookin' At?
What Crawls and Goes Ding-Dong? A Wounded Avon Lady!
What Do You Do with a Green Monster? You Wait Until He Ripens!
What Do You Say to a 2-Headed Monster? Hello-Hello, What's New? What's New?
What's a Monsters Normal Eye Sight? 20-20-20
What's That Odor?
Where Do Baby Monsters Come From? Frankenstorks!
Who Did It?
Why Won't a Skeleton Cross the Road? No Guts!
Wink If You Can Read This
Yeah!
You Creep
You Got Bad Breath!
You're a Turkey!
You're Such a Jerk
You're Wrong I'm Right
Your Feet Stink!

FUN CARDS (12)

2" X 3 3/4"

"Fun Cards," a series of twelve activity cards for young children, came attached (via gummed flaps at top and bottom) to individual-serving size Ocean Spray juice boxes. The promotion began at the end of 1985 and continued into the early months of 1986. The fronts of the cards are yellow, blue, and white and about 40% of the area is devoted to advertising for "an all-in-one windbreaker and tote bag." This is significant because eight Fun Cards plus $2.95 were required to redeem this mail offer and it does not state that the cards would be returned. The card number and caption are located only on the obverse side.

ITEM	MINT	EX
Set	--	3.50
Card	--	.25

1 What is Your Riddle-Solving IQ?
2 Figure Your Age with "Birthday Math!"
3 Can You Change the Word Burn into the Word Mark?
4 Get Ready for Some Challenging Brain Teasers!
5 Can You Crack the Secret Code?
6 Can You Find the Ocean Spray Fruit?
7 What Do School Kids Look Forward To?
8 Play the Ocean Spray Mini Maze Game?
9 How Good of a Detective are You?
10 Put Your Spelling Skill to the Test!
11 Solve the Tricky Triangle Game!
12 Can You Solve the Ocean Spray Puzzle?

FUN GUM MONSTERS (36)

2 1/2" X 3 1/4"

Glenn Confections (Buffalo, NY) marketed this series of funny monster stickers for the Halloween season in both 1989 and 1990. Each 2-3/8" X 2-1/2" sticker is mounted on thin cardboard backing; the ingrediants/UPC panel below is separated from the picture by a machine-scored line and it remains in place when the sticker is removed. The color-artwork characters have their name and sticker number printed at bottom-left and bottom-right, respectively. One sticker was packed in each clear cello package containing a "Wowee Fun Gum Whistle" or wax mustache, lips, etc. The retail price range of 79¢-99¢ plus the poor sort of titles in each box made completing a set difficult. Note: a sticker that has been removed from the backing cannot be graded mint or excellent.

ITEM	MINT	EX
Set	45.00	32.50
Sticker	1.00	.75

1 "Richard"	13 "Golfball Gremlin"	25 "Tank"
2 "Squeeker"	14 "Chris"	26 "Otto"
3 "Wally"	15 "Albert"	27 "Mr. Cactus"
4 "Frigid Freddy"	16 "Ken"	28 "Hairball"
5 "Barry"	17 "Toofer"	29 "Carmel Clam"
6 "Jed"	18 "Snap"	30 "Ripley"
7 "Snooker"	19 "Gerd"	31 "Piggerbull"
8 "Shelly"	20 "Mr. Lewis"	32 "Sam"
9 "Mr. Snout"	21 "Tony"	33 "Wyatt"
10 "Bubbles"	22 "Gary"	34 "Ormand"
11 "Ronald"	23 "Frazzle Cat"	35 "Seadoo"
12 "Bart"	24 "Pretz"	36 "Mrs. Boonha"

FUN n' DONUTS (5)

Here is another set from Fun Foods, the short-lived company whose financial standing was more limited than its imagination. Each "Fun N' Donuts" box has an amazing amount of detail. There is a joke question printed on one panel which requires the owner to pull up the entire front panel to reveal the hidden answer. One side flap has two printed jokes and the back has one more printed Q&A joke plus five illustrated gags. The color scheme is purple, white, and black and the candy inside the box was shaped like miniature donuts. The five front panel titles in the set are: "Hanging Out,"

1" X 1 1/2" X 2 3/4"

"Monster Snack," "Skool Bus," "Skool Lunch," and "Watching TV." Note: generally found intact, boxes with front panel flaps pulled up cannot be graded mint or excellent.

ITEM	MINT	EX
Set	6.00	4.50
Box	1.00	.75

FUNNY CARS (20)

This nifty set of twenty cards spoofing various automobiles does not have a series title printed on the cards and no packaging or advertising has been found, so we have simply called them "Funny Cars." The fronts contain color artwork parodies of well-known models, accompanied by bogus logos (look closely!). On back, a credit line reads "(copyright symbol) ITT C.B.C. 1976," indicating the issuer to be the Continental Baking Co. The artwork, plus the "Safety Fax," "Funny Fax," and

2 1/2" X 3 1/2"

"Car Fax" features on the reverse suggest that elementary/pre-teen children were the target audience. Cards were distributed on a one-per-loaf basis and many are found with light stains (these may be graded excellent, but not mint).

ITEM	MINT	EX
Set	50.00	25.00
Card	2.00	1.00

Blunderhead	Monsta
Boltswagen	Moosetang
Booick	Muck Trucks
Coldsmobile	Pincho
Dirt	Purrsche
Furrari	Shoverolet
Grumplin	Sobb
Hounda	Stinkin' Continental
Ickonoline	Toybota
Monkey Carlo	Voltvo

FUNNY DOORS (24)

"Open the Door for Laffs!" advises the wrapper of the Funny Doors set released to the public by Topps in 1970. The instructions for doing this —which are printed on the back of a standard-size check-list card—explain why Funny

2 1/2" X 4 11/16"

Door cards are seldom found in top condition. The two-step directions, in effect, tell the owner to bend the card in an arc and pry open the doors with his nails. We have illustrated all 24 cards in the set since the captions on the checklist card may differ from those actually printed on the cards. Note: cards with doors that have been opened cannot be graded mint. Door flaps are easily damaged after being opened: strict grading applies.

ITEM	MINT	EX
Set	180.00	120.00
Card	6.00	4.00
Wrapper	--	35.00
Box	--	200.00

Funny Doors

1 Antville

2 X-Ray Machines

3 Cemetery

4 Hospital

5 Nutty Plane

6 Billboard

7 Haunted House

8 Castle

9 Newsstand

10 Flying Saucer

11 Office Doors

12 Tree House

13 Circus Wagon

14 Paintings

15 Circus Tent

16 Big Ol' Shoe

17 Ship Portholes

18 Sewer Manholes

19 Record Rack

20 Book Store

21 Protest Poster

22 Automat

23 Crystal Balls

24 Barn

228

FUNNY FOTOS (7)

"Funny Fotos" cards could be found in boxes of Fun Fruits snacks at the time this book was going to press. They measure 3-1/2" X 4" and have color artwork drawings printed on thin cardboard stock. The face of each character is either blank or drawn, but in each case that area can be "popped out" and replaced by a photo of your choice (attached on the back of the card). Each card also has a small half-circle machine cut at the bottom to serve as a stand should you care to display your handiwork. There are four "Rock 'n Roll" cards and three "Wacky Players" cards in the series and none of these are numbered. Keeping with our formula of pricing current material at one-half the retail cost of the product, the suggested price per card for Funny Fotos is $1.00 per card.

FUNNY LI'L JOKE BOOKS (44)

What did the beaver say to the tree? Nice gnawing you! If that's your kind of humor you'll certainly appreciate this "joke book" series distributed by Topps in 1970. Each numbered book is actually an eight-sided folder which looks like a miniature comic book, but is not stapled in the center. Two or three theme jokes (Knock-Knocks, Rotten Riddles, etc.) appear on every page. A checklist of six other titles in the set appears on the back cover. This set was also issued abroad in true folder format (accordian-style pages) on coated paper.

ITEM	MINT	EX
Set	125.00	100.00
Folder	2.50	2.00
Wrapper	--	35.00
Box	--	200.00

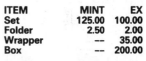

1 Knock-Knock Jokes No. 1
2 Rotten Riddles No. 1
3 Hippie Jokes No. 1
4 School Daze No. 1
5 Crazy Poems
6 Sick Jokes No. 1
7 The Cops and Robbers Jokebook
8 Puns!?!
9 Nutty Proverbs No. 1
10 Rotten Riddles No. 2
11 Mom and Pop Jokes
12 Moron Jokes No. 1
13 Tramp Tramp Tramp
14 Sick Jokes No. 2
15 Animal Antics No. 1
16 Waiter, There's a Fly in My Soup!
17 Loony Limericks No. 1
18 Hillbilly Jokes No. 1
19 Moron Jokes No. 2
20 Fatso Jokes
21 Animal Antics No. 2
22 Crazy Horoscope No. 1

23 Elephant Jokes No. 1
24 Silly Songs
25 Dopey Dictionary A-H
26 Dopey Dictionary I-P
27 Dopey Dictionary Q-Z
28 Looney Limericks No. 2
29 Sports Jokes No. 1
30 School Daze No. 2
31 Doctor Jokes
32 Hillybilly Jokes No. 2
33 Little Willies Jokes
34 Bazooka Joe's Joke Book
35 Rotten Riddles No. 3
36 Loony Limericks No. 3
37 Grape Jokes
38 Elephant Jokes No. 2
39 Knock-Knock Jokes No. 2
40 Nutty Proverbs No. 2
41 Hippy Jokes No. 2
42 Crazy Horoscope No. 2
43 Drunk Jokes
44 Sport Jokes No. 2

FUNNY RINGS (24)

"Funny Rings" are a perfect example of what happens when market values become distorted. In the 1988 edition of this guide, ring cards were listed at $3.00 each and there was scant interest in the set (possibly because collectors on both sides of the fence were put off by the fact that a non-sport set was issued as a bonus in a football series). How times have changed! Now we see ads in sports publications offering ring cards for $50 apiece (or more) and the checklist card at the same price or higher. Such an extreme jump in value is the result of speculation and would appear to be a short-term phenomenon. Therefore, we advise non-sport collectors to look carefully for "Funny Rings" in the $10 price range and to avoid jumping on the inflationary bandwagon.

The series, consisting of 24 punch-out finger rings, was distributed as bonus inserts in packs of 1966 Topps football cards. The ring designs are approximately 3" long and are 1" to 1-5/16" in height. A checklist card illustrates all 24 rings and assigns them captions which are not actually printed on the rings or on the rest of the card. The cards — not the rings — are numbered and the card reverses are blank.

1	Kiss Me	13	Scram!
2	Bloodshot Eye	14	Nuts to You
3	Big Mouth	15	Get Lost
4	Tooth-ache	16	You Fink
5	Fish Eats Fish	17	Hole in Sole
6	Mrs. Skull	18	One-Eyed Terror
7	Hot Dog	19	Mr. Ugly
8	Nail Thru Head	20	Mr. Fang
9	Say "Ah"	21	Mr. Fright
		22	Mr. Boo
11	The Snake	23	Mr. Glug
12	Yicch!	24	Mr. Blech

FUNNY TRAVEL POSTERS (24)

Issued by Topps in 1967, the Funny Travel Posters set employs the theme (and some of the same material) that appeared one year later in "Silly Stickers": travel can be hazardous to your health! Each large poster is captioned and numbered and was folded five times to fit into the 3" X 4 3/4" gum pack. Note: no mint price is given since these posters were pre-folded to fit into smaller packaging. It has been suggested from the quantity of wrappers and boxes seen that this set was "re-issued" at a later date. This has not been confirmed.

ITEM	MINT	EX
Set	--	60.00
Poster	--	2.00
Wrapper	--	10.00
Box	--	35.00

1 See Los Angeles If You Can
2 Visit Old England...Land of Tradition
3 America's Most Exciting City...Chicago
4 Visit the Everglades...You ll Never Go Anywhere Else
5 See the Canals of Venice...For Sheer Beauty
6 Take a Trip to San Francisco
7 Come to Florida and Learn to Swim (Fast)
8 Come to Hawaii...It Will Surf You Right!
9 Visit Africa...But Not at Dinner Time
10 When in Italy Visit the Leaning Tower of Pizza
11 Visit Paris...City of Hospitality?
12 Visit New York...Fun City
13 Visit Transylvania and You'll Never Leave
14 Visit Our School Cafeteria...It's a Nice Place to Visit But You Won't Want to Eat There
15 Visit Sunny Cuba...But Not During the Execution Season
16 See the Ruins of Rome...If You Can Find Them!
17 You'll Be Charmed with India
18 Visit Sing Sing and Feel Wanted
19 Visit Kansas...Land of Gentle Breezes
20 Visit My Dining Room...You'll Never Eat Anyplace Else!
21 See Niagara Falls by Boat
22 Visit Hollywood and See the Stars
23 Visit the Home of Advertising... Madison Avenue
24 Visit Mexico...Where the Action Is!

FUN PROJECTS (12)

"Fun Projects" were a "Make-It-Yourself Bonus Feature" printed on the back panels of Bazooka Gum boxes in 1972. As you can see in the illustration, each project card was surrounded by a dotted line to guide the owner in cutting the card away from the package. Each project was designed to be constructed by using materials found around the home, such as used cardboard, milk cartons, pins, string, etc. The card number appears twice: in the dot circle at top left and in the line located at bottom right. The card itself is mostly white, with blue print, but the color of the panel around it is yellow. Twelve project cards comprise the set; we do not list a set value, however, since all the titles are not known.

ITEM	MINT	EX
Card	--	2.00
Box	10.00	7.50

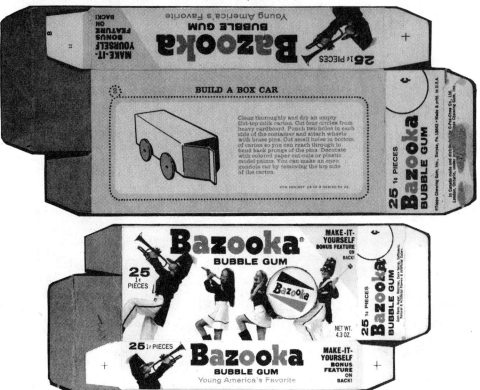

FUTURE OF ROCK (4/3K)

The "Future of Rock" series of cards distributed in 1990 and 1991 by Kellogg's Pop Tarts is a promotion to generate greater recognition for several "up-and-coming" recording artists and groups. The 1990 series consists of four titles (see checklist

One of the most exciting new groups from Atlantic Records today is Troop. Their second album, *Attitude*, has gone Gold thanks to four hit singles: "Spread My Wings," "I'm Not Souped," "All I Do Is Think Of You" and "That's My Attitude." Troop, based in Southern California, is known for their great vocal harmonies and spectacular dancing.

1990 Series

THE PARTY

Their combination of styles is as diverse as the members of the hot, new group — The Party. Each member takes their turn in the spotlight and the result is a pop, rock, rap, rhythm and blues, hip-hop performance that will bring you to your feet. Take a listen to The Party available now from Hollywood Records.

1991 Series

1990 CHECKLIST
En Vogue
Linear
Tommy Page
Troop

1991 CHECKLIST
Keedy
The Party
Tracie Spencer

TWO SIZES

below) and each card measures 2-3/16" X 3-3/8". The cards came two per box, on the back panel, and had dotted guide lines around the perimeter for cutting them away from the package. For 1991, three titles have been reported so far and the cards have slightly different measurements: 2-1/16" X 3-3/8". These are clearly marked "1991" and are more stylish than the series of the previous year. Collectors will find that the printed backs on cards of both years may not line up exactly with the fronts. Cards of both years are valued at approximately one-half the retail cost of the product ($1.00-$1.29), so collectors should be able to find them at about 50 cents each.

GALAXY WARS (40)

2 3/8″ X 3 3/16″

"Galaxy Wars" was distributed by Donruss and has the same format as that company's "Tacky Tattoos" series. Each tattoo sheet has one large and two small tattoos on it; the sheet back has "scissor" lines printed to enable accurate separation of the designs. A cardboard "How To Apply Tattoos" card was inserted in every pack. According to a line printed on the back of every sheet, there are 40 different sets of tattoos in the set.

None of the individual tattoos has a caption and there are three different wrappers for the set.

ITEM	MINT	EX
Set	35.00	25.00
Tattoo sheet	.75	.50
Card	.25	.15
Wrappers (3)		
each	––	1.00
Box	––	7.00

THE GPK STORY

Not too long ago, the children of America were embarked on a collision course with Terminal Cuteness. They started playing with toys designed to stimulate their minds or provide positive role models. They stopped throwing temper tantrums, said "Please" and "Thank You" whenever possible, and ate everything served them at meals. Kids even came in from the playground with clean clothes! This unorthodox behavior disoriented and confused parents. Some reacted by wandering about aimlessly and replying "Good for you, dear," whenever addressed. Others rebelled by throwing temper tantrums, being rude, and refusing to eat their vegetables.

Among adults as a whole, teachers were the hardest hit. Day after day, they faced classrooms full of smiling, attentive children eager to answer questions, recite lessons, and write on the blackboard. Schools were fast becoming Institutions of Learning! Newspaper headlines screamed about rising test scores, awards, and merit badges. Politicians raved about conspiracies and psychologists appeared on talk shows to answer questions about the "Apple Pie Syndrome." The nation was on the verge of collapse.

But then a miracle happened...from within Corporate America emerged a champion to battle the Forces of Niceness: Topps Gum. While other companies caved in and produced cute toys that summer, Topps designed an amazing card series depicting the worst aspects of juvenile existence. No detail, no matter how disgusting or gross, was overlooked by the Braintrust at Topps.

At first, the children collecting Garbage Pail Kids were an underground movement. Then, as the number of collectors increased, kids began to carry their cards openly, shocking their parents back to normal behavior and returning schools to the tumultuous atmosphere of the pre-cute era. Newspaper headlines screamed about falling test scores, gum-chewing, and detention. Politicians raved about conspiracies and psychologists debated the effects of GPK on youthful psyches. Many people hailed GPK as "The Fad That Saved America."

Topps made bundles of money by producing series after series of Garbage Pail cards. The licensing rights sold to other companies brought in additional revenues. A major television network announced plans for a Saturday-morning cartoon series and a film company produced a full-length GPK movie.

As Garbage Pail mania swept the country, rival card and toy companies tried to "catch the wave" by marketing their own gross and disgusting products. Soon stores bulged with shelf after shelf of items extolled for their slimy and repulsive attributes. "Gross" had not only kayo'd "cute" — but was stomping it into the ground. It was time, as the stock marketeers say, for a "correction" to occur.

Bowing to public reaction, some stores refused to sell GPK. The cartoon show flopped and the movie played mostly to empty seats. Cabbage Patch Dolls took Topps to court. More importantly, the novelty of GPK wore off where it counted most, with the pre-teen gum chewers of America. GPK has lost the power to shock; it became a familiar, even venerable, commodity. Although it still has a strong following in the card-collecting hobby, the quantities of unsold GPK cards and toys attest to a waning public interest. As time goes on, these "overstocks" will doubtless return as authentic collectibles and GPK will be remembered as the card set that saved America from Terminal Cuteness.

GARBAGE PAIL KIDS   2 1/2" X 3 1/2"

Goodbye penny loafers, Slinkies, hula hoops, and mini skirts — each was once The Fad. So long "Monsters of the Midway," Jim and Tammy, giant pandas and the rest of you media darlings. America has been transfixed by any number of short-term sensations since the days of P.T. Barnum, but none has fascinated us any more than The Most Amazing Bubble Gum Cards of all time: Garbage Pail Kids.

These are trading cards that polarized society and uncovered the Jekyll and Hyde in all of us. They are not only The Set We Hate To Love but also The Set We Love to Hate. And despite predictions of imminent collapse, the series is still going strong. At 918 cards (not counting variations), it is the largest single-theme card set of the bubble gum era (and the most profitable). Nothing has stemmed the tide, not parents or preachers, not lawyers or boycotters.

The set is so famous that millions of Americans refer to it simply as "GPK;" so popular that toys based on it have flooded stores for years; so newsworthy that some people considered it deserving of a cover from "Time." How long can GPK last? No one knows, but Topps will release the 12th series soon and reportedly has a couple more "in the can." GPK has invaded Europe, South America, and the Middle East and now appears in French, Dutch, German, Spanish, and Hebrew. The "Kids" have gained a permanency that few fads ever achieve, and even though the controversy which once swirled about them has ebbed, they will likely retain a certain status and collectibility among a whole generation of Americans.

PRICE ADVISORY: SERIES 1. The initial market response to GPK was so disappointing that considerable amounts of Series 1 cards were never shipped to wholesale outlets. This unsold material has recently entered the hobby; the majority of it is in the hands of baseball card dealers who are "dumping" off sets at "bargain" prices ($50-60). What a contrast to the "panic" price tags ($200) posted by greedy amateurs and "collectibles" dealers on the other end of the scale! Prospective Series 1 buyers are best served by purchasing these cards from an established non-sports dealer, at a figure midway between these extremes. Be sure to inquire whether or not the set price includes all variations (ask for a signed receipt to that effect). Series 1 overstocks have temporarily unbalanced the normal process of supply and demand, but the market will return to it when the overstocks eventually disappear.

PRICE ADVISORY: CARD VARIATIONS. The set prices listed in this book for GPK **Series 2-15** include all the card variations enumerated in the display for each Series, except where they are specifically marked "Not included in set price." No prices are listed for individual variation cards. To some dealers, sales of single variation cards damage potential set sales, resulting in large supplies of slow-moving cards, and encourage speculative pricing on certain cards as well. Some dealers are willing to sell variations singly, others are not. In any case, the buyer should seek out a reputable non-sport dealer for help on this matter. Note: all "sticker" values listed in our price sections are for the regular (non-variation) stickers of each series.

Series 1

SERIES 1

Sequence...1A-41A and 1B-41B
Variations ..5A, 5B, 8A, 8B, 29A, 29B — all these are included in the set price listed at right.
Set total ...88 stickers (82 regular, plus 6 variations).

ITEM	MINT	EX
Set	see Price	Advisory
Sticker	1.00	.75
Wrappers (2)		
25 cents	—	1.50
no price	—	2.00
Box	—	10.00

NOTE: Boxes with covers "crossed out" by marker lines *cannot* be graded excellent.

1A	Nasty Nick	22A	Junky Jeff	1B	Evil Eddie	22B	Stinky Stan
2A	Junkfood John	23A	Drippy Dan	2B	Ray Decay	23B	Leaky Lou
3A	Up Chuck	24A	Nervous Rex	3B	Heavin' Steven	24B	Nerdy Norm
4A	Fryin' Brian	25A	Creepy Carol	4B	Electric Bill	25B	Scary Carrie
5A	Dead Ted	26A	Slobby Robbie	5B	Jay Decay	26B	Fat Matt
6A	Art Apart	27A	Brainy Janie	6B	Busted Bob	27B	Jenny Genius
7A	Stormy Heather	28A	Oozy Suzy	7B	April Showers	28B	Meltin' Melissa
8A	Adam Bomb	29A	Bony Joanie	8B	Blasted Billy	29B	Thin Lynn
9A	Boozin' Bruce	30A	New Wave Dave	9B	Drunk Ken	30B	Graffiti Petey
10A	Tee-Vee Stevie	31A	Run Down Rhoda	10B	Geeky Gary	31B	Flat Pat
11A	Itchy Richie	32A	Frigid Bridget	11B	Bugged Bert	32B	Chilly Millie
12A	Furry Fran	33A	Mad Mike	12B	Hairy Mary	33B	Savage Stuart
13A	Ashcan Andy	34A	Kim Kong	13B	Spacey Stacy	34B	Anna Banana
14A	Potty Scotty	35A	Wrinkly Randy	14B	Jason Basin	35B	Rockin' Robert
15A	Ailin' Al	36A	Wrappin' Ruth	15B	Mauled Paul	36B	Tommy Tomb
16A	Weird Wendy	37A	Guillotina	16B	Haggy Maggie	37B	Cindy Lopper
17A	Wacky Jackie	38A	Slimy Sam	17B	Loony Lenny	38B	Lizard Liz
18A	Cranky Frankie	39A	Buggy Betty	18B	Bad Brad	39B	Green Jean
19A	Corroded Carl	40A	Unstitched Mitch	19B	Crater Chris	40B	Damaged Don
20A	Swell Mel	41A	Mean Gene	20B	Dressy Jesse	41B	Joltin' Joe
21A	Virus Iris			21B	Sicky Vicky		

SERIES 2: GPK.

Some collectors say there are three distinct sets in Series 2 GPK; other collectors reply that there is only one set which has a number of variations. Whatever camp you choose to join, the fact remains that Series 2 was issued in three different print runs. All three runs have the same "minor" variation for cards 42A and 42B — two different backs. In the first run, the puzzle back cards form a puzzle Messy Tessy and this is shown on the puzzle preview backs of cards 43A and 43B; the checklist cards, 46A&B and 47A&B, list card 49B as Schizo Fran. The second print run had Live Mike Puzzle backs and puzzle preview cards, but still showed Schizo Fran as 49B on the checklist cards. The third print run had Live Mike puzzle backs and puzzle preview cards but listed card 49B as Fran Fran. Some dealers sell these print runs as separate sets not only to accommodate the "purists," but to avoid having unsellable racks of Series 2 common stickers. Other dealers will sell the 42A/42B, 43A/43B, 46A/46B, 47A/47B, and 49B variation cards singly or as a group, plus whatever puzzle back cards you require, but prices vary greatly according to subjective evaluations. The collector must choose his own "medicine" when collecting the variations in GPK Series 2.

Series 2

SERIES 2

Sequence. . .42A-83A and 42B-83B
Variations. .Three different print runs: all three have Nos. 42A & 42B with two different backs.
   1st print run: 49B is Schizo Fran and puzzle is Messy Tessy.
   2nd print run: 49B is Schizo Fran and puzzle is Live Mike.
   3rd print run: 49B is Fran Fran and puzzle is Live Mike.
Set totals. . .There are 84 regular cards and 2 variations in each print run. If you have set 1 and set 3, you already have everything in set 2.

ITEM	MINT	EX
Sets		
1st printing	60.00	40.00
2nd printing	50.00	35.00
3rd printing	35.00	25.00
Sticker	.50	.35
Variations	see Price Advisory	
Wrappers (2)		
25 cents	——	.50
no price	——	1.00
Box	——	5.00

NOTE: Boxes with covers "crossed out" by marker lines *cannot* be graded excellent.

42A	Patty Putty	42B	Muggin' Megan
43A	Smelly Kelly	43B	Doug Plug
44A	Sy Clops	44B	One-Eyed Jack
45A	Leaky Lindsay	45B	Messy Tessie
46A	Rappin' Ron	46B	Ray Gun
47A	Disgustin' Justin	47B	Vile Kyle
48A	Tongue Tied Tim	48B	Marty Mouthful
49A	Double Heather	49B	Schizo Fran (1st & 2nd print run)
50A	Mad Donna	49B	Fran Fran (3rd print run)
51A	Russell Muscle	50B	Nutty Nicole
52A	Dirty Harry	51B	Brett Sweat
53A	Jolted Joel	52B	Rob Slob
54A	Fryin' Ryan	53B	Live Mike
55A	Hairy Gary	54B	Charred Chad
56A	Hairy Carrie	55B	Brutal Brad
57A	Tommy Gun	56B	Brutal Bridget
58A	Cracked Jack	57B	Dead Fred
59A	Clogged Duane	58B	Soft Boiled Sam
60A	Prickly Rick	59B	Bye Bye Bobby
61A	Jolly Roger	60B	Cactus Carol
62A	Greaser Greg	61B	Pegleg Peter
63A	Spacey Stacy	62B	Chris Hiss
64A	Hot Scott	63B	Janet Planet
65A	Shrunken Ed	64B	Luke Warm
66A	Matt Ratt	65B	Cheeky Charles
67A	Phony Lisa	66B	Rachel Rodent
68A	Oliver Twisted	67B	Mona Loser
69A	Jenny Jelly	68B	Dizzy Dave
70A	Brad Breath Seth	69B	Sara Slime
71A	Odd Todd	70B	Foul Phil
72A	Mad Max	71B	Bent Ben
73A	Gorgeous George		
74A	Mark Bark	73B	Dollar Bill
75A	Off-The-Wall Paul	74B	Kennel Kenny
76A	Bonnie Bunny	75B	Zach Plaque
77A	Ghastly Ashley	76B	Pourin' Lauren
78A	Wrinkled Rita	77B	Acne Amy
79A	Sewer Sue	78B	Ancient Annie
80A	Tattoo Lou	79B	Michelle Muck
81A	Split Kit	80B	Art Gallery
82A	Slain Wayne	81B	Mixed-Up Mitch
83A	Ugh Lee	82B	Ventilated Vinnie
		83B	Sumo Sid

49B ☐ SCHIZO FRAN   49B ☐ FRAN FRAN

Series 3

SERIES 3

Sequence. . .84A-124A and 84B-124B

Variations . .84A, 84B, 110A, 110B, 113A, 113B

Set total . . .88 stickers (82 regular, plus 6 variations).

ITEM	MINT	EX
Set	20.00	15.00
Sticker	.35	.25
Variations	see Price Advisory	
Wrappers (2)		
25 cents	---	.50
no price	---	1.00
Box	---	3.00

NOTE: Boxes with covers "crossed out" by marker lines *cannot* be graded excellent.

84A	Joe Blow	105A	Juicy Jessica	84B	Rod Wad	105B	Green Dean
85A	Stuck Chuck	106A	Fowl Raoul	85B	Pinned Lynn	106B	Mack Quack
86A	Horsey Henry	107B	Totem Paula	86B	Galloping Glen	107B	Tatum Pole
87A	Hot Head Harvey	108A	Smelly Sally	87B	Roy Bot	108B	Fishy Phyllis
88A	Dinah Saur	109A	Toady Terry	88B	Farrah Fossil	109B	Croakin' Colin
89A	Hurt Curt	110A	Snooty Sam	89B	Pat Splat	110B	U.S. Arnie
90A	Stoned Sean	111A	Target Margaret	90B	Thick Vic	111B	Bullseye Barry
91A	Blake Flake	112A	Frank N. Stein	91B	Hippie Skippy	112B	Undead Jed
92A	Marvin Gardens	113A	Alice Island	92B	Spittin' Spencer	113B	Liberty Libby
93A	Drew Blood	114A	Starin' Darren	93B	Bustin' Dustin	114B	Peepin' Tom
94A	Bruised Lee	115A	Warmin' Norman	94B	Karate Kate	115B	Well Done Sheldon
95A	Grim Jim	116A	Eerie Eric	95B	Beth Death	116B	Berserk Kirk
96A	Distorted Dot	117A	Rocky N. Roll	96B	Mirror Imogene	117B	Les Vegas
97A	Punchy Perry	118A	Half-Nelson	97B	Creamed Keith	118B	Glandular Angela
98A	Charlotte Web	119A	Ned Head	98B	Didi T.	119B	Still Jill
99A	Beaky Becky	120A	Babbling Brooke	99B	Picky Mickey	120B	Jelly Kelly
100A	Ali Gator	121A	Apple Cory	100B	Marshy Marshall	121B	Dwight Bite
101A	Mushy Marsha	122A	Broad Maud	101B	Basking Robin	122B	Large Marge
102A	Mugged Marcus	123A	Glooey Gabe	102B	Kayo'd Cody	123B	Sticky Rick
103A	Wriggley Rene	124A	Hugh Mungous	103B	Curly Carla	124B	King-Size Kevin
104A	Silent Sandy			104B	Barren Aaron		

Series 4

MOUTH PHIL   TOOTH LES

SERIES 4

Sequence... 125A-166A and 125B-166B

Variations.. Two print runs: four names in original print run were withdrawn and replaced in the 2nd printing (2nd print run checklists also changed).

Wrappers: commonly appear with either white or purple cloud above Adam Bomb's head.

Set totals... 84 stickers in each print run.

ITEM	MINT	EX
Sets		
1st printing	20.00	15.00
2nd printing	25.00	20.00
Sticker	.35	.25
Variations	see Price Advisory	
Wrappers (4)		
25 cents (both)	--	.50
no price (both)	--	1.00
Box	--	3.00

NOTE: Boxes with covers "crossed out" by marker lines *cannot* be graded excellent.

125B □ WOODY ALAN   **149A □ REESE PIECES**   **158B □ CRYSTAL GALE**   **164B □ SALVATORE DOLLY**

125A	Holly Wood	146A	Baked Jake
126A	Armpit Britt	147A	Amazin' Grace
127A	Travellin' Travis	148A	Turned-On Tara
128A	Sloshed Josh	149A	Reese Pieces (1st print run)
129A	Second Hand Rose	149A	Puzzle Paul (2nd print run)
130A	Nicky Hickey	150A	Hairy Harriet
131A	Stuffed Stephen	151A	Losing Faith
132A	Bony Tony	152A	Whisperin' Woody
133A	Furry Murray	153A	Jack O. Lantern
134A	Hip Kip	154A	Basket Casey
135A	Rock E. Horror	155A	Spikey Mikey
136A	Swollen Sue Ellen	156A	Warrin' Warren
137A	Max Axe	157A	Larry Lips
138A	Alien Ian	158A	Meltin' Elton
139A	Double Iris	159A	Catty Kathy
140A	Mouth Phil	160A	Decapitated Hedy
141A	Ashley Can	161A	Shorned Sean
142A	Bruce Moose	162A	Yicchy Mickey
143A	Melba Toast	163A	Trish Squish
144A	Horny Hal	164A	Teddy Bear
145A	Dale Snail	165A	Dana Druff
		166A	Gored Gordon

125B	Woody Alan (1st print run)	146B	Dry Guy
125B	Oak Kay (2nd print run)	147B	Muscular Molly
126B	Shaggy Aggie	148B	Tiffany Lamp
127B	Flat Tyler	149B	Incomplete Pete
128B	Low Cal	150B	Bushy Bernice
129B	Trashed Tracy	151B	Dyin' Dinah
130B	Hank E. Panky	152B	Van Triloquist
131B	Rutherford B. Hay	153B	Duncan Pumpkin
132B	Unzipped Zack	154B	Dribblin' Derek
133B	Foxy Francis	155B	Nailed Neil
134B	Walt Witless	156B	Brett Vet
135B	Marty Gras	157B	Distortin' Morton
136B	Bloated Blair	158B	Crystal Gale (1st print run)
137B	Deadly Dudley	158B	Ig Lou (2nd print run)
138B	Outerspace Chase	159B	Kitty Litter
139B	4-Eyed Ida	160B	Formalde Heidi
140B	Tooth Les	161B	Hy Gene
141B	Greta Garbage	162B	Barfin' Bart
142B	Hunted Hunter	163B	Ruby Cube
143B	Hy Rye	164B	Salvatore Dolly (1st print run)
144B	Rudy Toot	164B	Battered Brad (2nd print run)
145B	Crushed Shelly	165B	Flakey Fay
		166B	No Way Jose

239

Series 5

SERIES 5

Sequence...167A-206A and 167B-206B
Variations..168A, 168B, 169A, 169B, 175A,
175B, 178A, 178B
Set total...88 stickers (80 regular, plus 8
variations).

ITEM	MINT	EX
Set	20.00	15.00
Sticker	.35	.25
Variations	see Price Advisory	
Wrappers (2)		
25 cents	---	.50
no price	---	1.00
Box	---	3.00

NOTE: Boxes
with covers
"crossed out"
by marker
lines *cannot*
be graded
excellent.

167A	Mick Dagger	167B	Slayed Slade
168A	Handly Randy	168B	Jordan Nuts
169A	Dee Faced	169B	Terri Cloth
170A	Richie Retch	170B	Luke Puke
171A	Willie Wipe-Out	171B	Spencer Dispenser
172A	Nat Nerd	172B	Clark Can't
173A	Menaced Dennis	173B	Wormy Shermy
174A	Fred Thread	174B	Repaired Rex
175A	Windy Winston	175B	Johnny One-Note
176A	Condo Minnie	176B	Bill Ding
177A	Meltin' Milton	177B	Lazy Louie
178A	Earl Painting	178B	Blue-Boy George
179A	Moe Skeeto	179B	Sting Ray
180A	Haunted Hollis	180B	Batty Barney
181A	Cliff Hanger	181B	Neck Ty
182A	Sprayed Wade	182B	Tagged Tad
183A	Diaper Dan	183B	Pinned Penny
184A	Upside Down Donald	184B	Hugh Turn
185A	Fran Furter	185B	Hot Doug
186A	Iron-Jaw Aaron	186B	Jean Machine
187A	Ginger Snapped	187B	Edible Ernie
188A	Mel Meal	188B	Ross Roast
189A	Brenda Blender	189B	Juicy Lucy
190A	Gory Rory	190B	Gil Grill
191A	Ben Bolt	191B	Fried Franklin
192A	Delicate Tess	192B	Hamburger Pattie
193A	Shattered Shelby	193B	Cracked Craig
194A	Nasty Nancy	194B	Razzin' Roslyn
195A	Lucas Mucus	195B	Dotty Dribble
196A	Dangling Dolly	196B	Surreal Neal
197A	Doughy Joey	197B	Starchy Archie
198A	Gore May	198B	Connie Sewer
199A	Ruptured Rupert	199B	Gassy Gus
200A	Fluoride Floyd	200B	Dental Daniel
201A	Michael Mutant	201B	Zeke Freak
202A	Ultra Violet	202B	Tanya Hide
203A	Toothie Ruthie	203B	Dental Flossie
204A	Jules Drools	204B	Kit Spit
205A	Hot Rod	205B	Bud Buggy
206A	Deaf Geoff	206B	Audio Augie

SERIES 6

Sequence...207A-250A and 207B-250B
Variations..None reported for stickers to date. Wrappers: 25 cent type found with yellow (normal) or white (variation) background inside price star.

Set total ...88 stickers

NOTE: Boxes with covers "crossed out" by marker lines *cannot* be graded excellent.

ITEM	MINT	EX
Set	15.00	12.00
Sticker	.25	.20
Wrappers (3)		
25 cents type		
yellow star	--	.50
white star	--	1.00
no price	--	1.00
Box	--	2.50

207A Over Flo	229A Claire Stare	207B Moist Joyce	229B Bloodshot Scott
208A Joel Hole	230A Manuel Labor	208B Teed-Off Tom	230B Handy Andy
209A Whacked-Up Wally	231A Ashley Tray	209B Paddlin' Madeline	231B Bernie Burns
210A Intense Payne	232A Pam Ham	210B First Ada	232B Cole Cut
211A See More Seymour	233A Wes Mess	211B Coy Roy	233B Trash-Can Ken
212A Upliftin' Clifton	234A Harry Canary	212B Air-Head Jed	234B Burt Cage
213A Otto Whack	235A Ugly Hans	213B Elliot Mess	235B Jan Hand
214A Off-Color Clara	236A Trina Cleaner	214B Brushed-Off Brenda	236B Suckin' Sybil
215A Gnawing Nora	237A Totaled Todd	215B Nervous Nellie	237B Towin' Owen
216A Tiny Tim	238A Marc Spark	216B Small Saul	238B Cherry Bomb
217A Trashy Trudy	239A Jerry Atric	217B Rose Dispose	239B Abraham Wrinklin'
218A Tom Thumb	240A Radar Ray	218B Bridget Digit	240B Eve Droppin'
219A George Washingdone	241A Old Gloria	219B Pressed Preston	241B Jose Can You See
220A Joan Clone	242A Clean Maureen	220B Warty Ward	242B Dryin' Ryan
221A Cracked Crystal	243A Lee Tree	221B Shrill Jill	243B Sherwood Forest
222A Troy Toy	244A Welcome Matt	222B Loose Spring	244B Muddy Maude
223A Lolly Poppy	245A Shisk K. Bob	223B Lily Popped	245B Barbie Q.
224A Monte Zuma	246A John John	224B Pagan Megan	246B Flushing Floyd
225A Nasal Hazel	247A Rusty Heap	225B Snotty Lottie	247B Rustin' Justin
226A Pierced Pearl	248A Hector Collector	226B Cheap Jewel	248B G.P. Kay
227A Bea Sting	249A Many Lenny	227B Screaming Mimi	249B Lotta Carlotta
228A Casper Gasper	250A Newly-Dead Ed	228B Uncool Carl	250B Dyna Mike

SERIES 7

Sequence. . .251A-292A and 251B-292B
Variations . .253A, 253B, 265A, 265B — all included in set price listed at right.
In addition, 260B and 261B are found with either blue or purple letters in GPK title; 289B found with card number in top center (black print) or top right (white print): not included in set price at right.

Set total . . .88 stickers (84 regular, plus 4 back variations).

ITEM	MINT	EX
Set	15.00	12.00
Sticker	.25	.20
Variations	see Price Advisory	
Wrappers (2)		
25 cents	---	.50
no price	---	1.00
Box	---	2.50

NOTE: Boxes with covers "crossed out" by marker lines *cannot* be graded excellent.

251A	Barfin' Barbara	272A	Elastic Elwood
252A	Milky Wayne	273A	Haunted Forrest
253A	Russ Pus	274A	Reptilian Lillian
254A	Chris Mess	275A	Wheel Barry
255A	On The Mark	276A	Venessa Undresser
256A	Jack Pot	277A	Reuben Cube
257A	Cut–Up Carmen	278A	Have A Nice Dave
258A	Mickey Mouths	279A	Short Mort
259A	Grilled Gil	280A	Shut-Up Sherwin
260A	Adam Boom	281A	Soured Howard
261A	Gooey Huey	282A	Screwey Dewey
262A	Brainless Bryan	283A	Alien Alan
263A	Vincent Van Gone	284A	Manny Heads
264A	Pete Seat	285A	Wind Sheila
265A	Curly Shirley	286A	Haley Comet
266A	Roy L. Flush	287A	Christine Vaccine
267A	Tongue Tied Tina	288A	Grant Ant
268A	Phil Grim	289A	Stair Casey
269A	Sharpened Sheena	290A	Busted Armand
270A	Cannibal Stu	291A	Homer Runt
271A	Bratty Maddy	292A	Staple Gunther

251B	Valerie Vomit	272B	Fletcher Stretcher
252B	Dairy Cari	273B	Sappy Sarah
253B	Louise Squeeze	274B	Jay Prey
254B	Sandy Clod	275B	Rollin' Roland
255B	Bull's Ira	276B	Banana Anna
256B	Monte Carlo	277B	Blockhead Blake
257B	Dotted Lionel	278B	Miles Smiles
258B	Oral Laurel	279B	Noah Body
259B	Well Don	280B	Filled Up Philip
260B	Blasted Billy II	281B	Paul Bunion
261B	Bobbi Booger	282B	Bent Brent
262B	Jughead Ted	283B	Martian Marcia
263B	Modern Art	284B	Max Stacks
264B	Noel Bowl	285B	Hit N' Ronni
265B	Blown Joan	286B	June Moon
266B	Shuffled Sherman	287B	Medi Kate
267B	Braided Brandy	288B	Sticky Nikki
268B	William Penned	289B	Alexander The Grate
269B	Cranky Kristin	290B	Jim Nauseum
270B	Brewin' Bruno	291B	Screwball Lew
271B	Dirty Birdie	292B	Clipped Claude

SERIES 8

Sequence. . .293A-334A and 293B-334B
Variations . .298A, 298B, 318A, 318B
Set total . . .88 stickers (84 regular, plus 4 variations).

ITEM	MINT	EX
Set	15.00	12.00
Sticker	.25	.20
Variations	see Price Advisory	
Wrappers (2)		
25 cents	––	.50
no price	––	1.00
Box	––	2.50

NOTE: Boxes with covers "crossed out" by marker lines *cannot* be graded excellent.

293A	Explorin' Norman	314A	Shifting Sandy	293B	Drillin' Dylan	314B	Grainy Janey
294A	Weird Wendell	315A	Messy Bessie	294B	Luke At Me	315B	Unclean Helene
295A	Charlie Horse	316A	Flowin' Owen	295B	Amusement Parker	316B	Russell Spout
296A	Plucked Daisy	317A	James Flames	296B	Wiltin' Milton	317B	Burnin' Vernon
297A	Yul Tied	318A	Haley's Vomit	297B	Murray Christmas	318B	Inter Stella
298A	Bloody Mary	319A	Chopped Susie	298B	Donna Donor	319B	Shana Saw
299A	Buck Puck	320A	Pumping Aaron	299B	Lowell Goal	320B	Will Explode
300A	Corrina Corona	321A	Squashed Josh	300B	Smoky Joe	321B	Squoze Rose
301A	Bowling Elaine	322A	K.O.'D Karl	301B	Mike Strike	322B	Sparrin' Warren
302A	Mixed-Up Mick	323A	Piece O' Lisa	302B	Artificial Mitchell	323B	Wedding Bella
303A	Hung Up Hank	324A	Waffle Ira	303B	Coat Rack Zack	324B	Griddled Greta
304A	Rubbin' Robyn	325A	Marcel Parcel	304B	Soapy Opie	325B	Handle With Caren
305A	Grate Scott	326A	Leather Heather	305B	Reggie Veggie	326B	Chained Shane
306A	Midge Fridge	327A	Needled Nina	306B	Leftover Grover	327B	Knittin' Brittany
307A	Divin' Ivan	328A	Glowing Amber	307B	Walter Sport	328B	Bright Dwight
308A	Fritz Spritz	329A	Lem Phlegm	308B	Ella P. Record	329B	Gezundt Heidi
309A	Heartless Hal	330A	Lotta Lotta	309B	Bowen Arrow	330B	Dupli-Kit
310A	Stinkin' Stella	331A	Page Cage	310B	Smellin' Helen	331B	Tommy Ache
311A	Stu Spew	332A	Sling Scott	311B	Slimin' Simon	332B	Teddy Aim Fire
312A	Moe Bile	333A	Ortho Donny	312B	Dang Len	333B	Ruth Canal
313A	Graham Bell	334A	Ashley To Ashes	313B	Death Nell	334B	Dustin To Dust

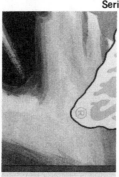

243

SERIES 9

Sequence. . .335A-378A and 335B-378B

Variations . .Not included in set price listed at right: No. 355B (Semi Colon) without number.

Wrappers: both 25 cents and "All New" (no price) types are found with either a U.S.A. or Canada line.

Set total . . .88 stickers

ITEM	MINT	EX
Set	15.00	12.00
Sticker	.25	.20
Variation	see Price Advisory	
Wrappers (4)		
25 cents		
U.S.A.	--	.50
Canada	--	.50
"All New"		
U.S.A.	--	1.00
Canada	--	2.00
Box	--	2.50

NOTE: Boxes with covers "crossed out" by marker lines *cannot* be graded excellent.

335A	Cute Tippi	357A	3-Dee
336A	Laser Ray	358A	Mac The Knife
337A	Early Bert	359A	Kerosene Kerry
338A	See-Sawyer	360A	Marcus Mucus
339A	Snot Rope Hope	361A	Diced Brice
340A	Half-Baked Betty	362A	Doug Food
341A	Juicy Bruce	363A	Slidin' Sloan
342A	Jim Equipment	364A	Sticky Ricky
343A	Con Vic	365A	Shrap Nell
344A	Perry Chute	366A	Low-Life Lola
345A	Cyril Bowl	367A	Dent Al
346A	Peeled Paul	368A	Nat Splat
347A	Dam Dan	369A	Scalped Ralph
348A	Plane Jane	370A	Cementin' Quentin
349A	Polluted Percy	371A	Grippin' Griffin
350A	Misty Suds	372A	Jack Frost
351A	Cheryl Peril	373A	Desi Island
352A	Herman Hormone	374A	Swiss Kris
353A	Bazooka Joanne	375A	Trap Dora
354A	Clark Shark	376A	Retchin' Gretchen
355A	Beasty Boyd	377A	Closet Clyde
356A	Momma Mia	378A	Empty Emmy

335B	Waxy Wendy	357B	Blurry Blair
336B	Sizzlin' Sid	358B	Wade Blade
337B	Rotten Robin	359B	Blazin' Blake
338B	Teeter Todd	360B	Gun Beryl
339B	Drippy Debbie	361B	Chopped Chet
340B	Rollin' Rolanda	362B	Nick Yick
341B	Fruity Ruby	363B	Flamin' Damon
342B	Buddy Builder	364B	Gooey Louie
343B	Al Catraz	365B	Hanna Grenade
344B	Rip Cord	366B	Sis Pool
345B	Soggy Doggie	367B	Fluoride Ida
346B	Skin Les	368B	Jugglin' Jud
347B	Mike Dike	369B	Bone-Head Fred
348B	Woody Shop	370B	Minus Hans
349B	Barnacle Bill	371B	Ren Wrench
350B	Amelia Airhead	372B	Window Payne
351B	Deflatin' Nathan	373B	Marooned Maureen
352B	Turned-On Ron	374B	Cheesy Chandra
353B	Bubbly Babs	375B	Rear View Myra
354B	Manny Eater	376B	Ill Jill
355B	Semi Colin	377B	Hooked Howie
356B	Electric Shari	378B	Ragged Aggie

Series 10

SERIES 10

Sequence. . .379A-417A and 379B-417B
Variations. . .379A and 379B have three different backs; 385A, 385B, 408A, and 408B have two different backs.
Set total . . .86 stickers (78 regular, plus 8 variations).

ITEM	MINT	EX
Set	15.00	12.00
Sticker	.25	.20
Variations	see Price Advisory	
Wrappers (2)		
25 cents	--	.50
no price	--	1.00
Box	--	2.50

NOTE: Boxes with covers "crossed out" by marker lines *cannot* be graded excellent.

379A	Locked Dorian	399A	Dirty Flora	379B	Sidney Kidney	399B	Gina Cleaner
380A	Vermin Herman	400A	Varicose Wayne	380B	Gullivered Travis	400B	Elaine Vein
381A	Ground Chuck	401A	Viv E. Section	381B	Lean Jean	401B	Disect Ed
382A	Good-Bye Hy	402A	Lunchpail Gail	382B	Farewell Mel	402B	Lunchbox Stu
383A	Itchy Mitch	403A	Hunter Punter	383B	Raked Jake	403B	Fractured Francis
384A	Flamin' Raymond	404A	Airy Mary	384B	Hot Toddy	404B	Hissy Missie
385A	Phil 'Er Up	405A	Over-Ripe Melanie	385B	Chuckin Charlie	405B	Walter Melon
386A	Snotty Dotty	406A	Shopping Carter	386B	Frozen Flo	406B	Super Marcus
387A	Fatty Maddie	407A	Cracked Sheldon	387B	Cora Corset	407B	Wally Walnut
388A	Facey Tracie	408A	Lickin' Leon	388B	Heads Upton	408B	Rat-Sucker Randall
389A	Dire Rita	409A	Tiltin' Milton	389B	Overflow Joe	409B	Amazing Mason
390A	Connecting Dots	410A	Scratching Pole Paul	390B	Twinny Vinnie	410B	Clawed Claude
391A	Glass Isaac	411A	Van Pire	391B	False Iris	411B	Bud Sucker
392A	Ann Chovie	412A	Mixed-Up Trixie	392B	Sardine Candice	412B	Doughy Chloe
393A	Jess Express	413A	Barnyard Barney	393B	Choo-Choo Trina	413B	Dick Hick
394A	Barb Wire	414A	Umbilical Courtney	394B	Play Penny	414B	Yo Yolanda
395A	Paved Dave	415A	Erased Erica	395B	Run-Over Grover	415B	Wiped Out Winnie
396A	Creamed Gene	416A	Shootin' Newton	396B	Clobbered Bob	416B	Sherman Tank
397A	Cleaned Up Clint	417A	Hangin' Harriet	397B	Sucked Up Stefan	417B	Swingin' Sophie
398A	Skiin' Ian			398B	Sheared Sherwood		

Series 11

SERIES 11

Sequence. . .418A-459A and 418B-459B
Variations. . .None reported to date
Set total . . .84 stickers

ITEM	MINT	EX
Set	15.00	12.00
Sticker	.25	.20
Wrappers (2)		
25 cents	--	.35
no price	--	.75
Box	--	2.50

NOTE: Boxes with covers "crossed out" by marker lines *cannot* be graded excellent.

418A Lucy Lock-It	439A Jack Splat	418B Shut Up Shirley	439B Abstract Art
419A Meg-A-Volt	440A Bert Squirt	419B Charged Marge	440B Fritzie Zits
420A Spanked Hank	441A Loose Leif	420B Spikey Sondra	441B Composition Booker
421A Groovy Greg	442A Rugged Roy	421B Combin' Harry	442B Bare Barry
422A Sheri Cola	443A Wet Whit	422B All-Night Dinah	443B Wee-Wee Willie
423A Hungry Ivan	444A Fairy Tale Dale	423B Sy Sty	444B Nose Drip Skip
424A Rainy Storm	445A Colette Coldcut	424B Lightning Linda	445B Ellie Deli
425A Denny Saur	446A Mean Marlene	425B Rip Tile	446B Punk Rocky
426A Quenching Quincy	447A Gushing Garfield	426B Squirtin' Burton	447B Drained Blaine
427A Ripped Fletch	448A Touch Toni	427B Taped Tate	448B Phoney Joni
428A Lotta Litter	449A Bert Food	428B Garbage Mouth Gilbert	449B Gutsy Gus
429A Laundry Matt	450A Ike Spike	429B Drip-Dry Dru	450B Mason Mace
430A Taste Bud	451A Destroyed Lloyd	430B Salivatin' Sal	451B Tinsel Tim
431A Pollutin' Newton	452A Impaled Gail	431B Empty Head Jed	452B Magic Wanda
432A Packed Mac	453A Dead End Kit	432B Sue Case	453B Slidin' Clyde
433A Porcelain Lynn	454A Lynched Lyndon	433B Arlene Latrine	454B Bruce Noose
434A Holly Daze	455A Charred Cole	434B Joyous Noel	455B Deviled Egbert
435A London Bridget	456A Split Cord	435B Toxic Wes	456B William Won't Tell
436A Scaldin' Alden	457A Sally Suction	436B Steamy Mimi	457B Teethin' Trina
437A Sliced Brad	458A Dental Hy Gene	437B Dead Lee	458B Rudy Canal
438A Hallie Ween	459A Vomi-Ted	438B Trick or Tricia	459B Juicy Jules

Series 12

SERIES 12

Sequence ... 460A-500A and 460B-500B.
Variations ... 469A, 469B, 472A, 472B, 481A, and 481B have two different backs.
Set total ... 88 stickers (82 regular, plus 6 variations).

ITEM	MINT	EX
Set	12.00	9.00
Sticker	.20	.15
Variations	see Price Advisory	
Wrappers (2)		
25 cents	---	.35
no price	---	.75
Box	---	2.00

NOTE: Boxes with covers "crossed out" by marker lines *cannot* be graded excellent.

460A Ball 'N Shane	481A Car-Stick Karla	460B Hard Rocky	481B Cruisin' Susan
461A Marathon	482A Lickin' Leo	461B Racy Lacey	482B Lappin' Lenny
462A Half Price	483A Seedy Sydney	462B Checked-Out Chet	483B Fertile Myrtle
463A Phooey to Hugh	484A Tim Can	463B Razzin' Ross	484B Rusty Bolts
464A Tongue Tied Teddy	485A 12 O'Clock Hy	464B Dressed to Killian	485B Midnight Dwight
465A Upsy Daisys	486A Chiseler Chad	465B Barfy Barbies	486B Julius Sneezer
466A Seasick Cecil	487A Dead Letter Debbie	466B Dinner at Eytan	487B Maimed Mamie
467A Tongue in Chico	488A Telly Scope	467B Nick Lick	488B Peek-A-Boo Beau
468A Mummified Clyde	489A Irate Ira	468B Twyla Paper	489B Angry Annie
469A Upset Tommy	490A Kinky Kristine	469B Tub 'O Lars	490B Knot the Norm
470A Quick Sandy	491A Sunken Trevor	470B Abraham Sinkin'	491B Anchored Hank
471A Freestyle Kyle	492A Cory on the Cob	471B Rad Rod	492B Hot Buttered Corinne
472A Walter Fall	493A Peanut Butter 'N Kelly	472B Ronny Nose	493B Out-To-Lunch Lance
473A Heavy Meryl	494A Mitch Match	473B One-Night Stan	494B Hot Dot
474A Sole Food Sol	495A Gloppy Glen	474B Gooey Stuey	495B Slop Top Todd
475A Road-Kill Will	496A Allison Waterland	475B Stop Sy	496B Jon Pond
476A Barf Band Ben	497A Lame Lem	476B Off Key Lee	497B Edward Hopper
477A Ingrid Inc.	498A Rolls Royce	477B Smokestack Zach	498B Piston Pete
478A Bizarre Lamar	499A Abandoned Amanda	478B Rearranged Raymond	499B Please Give Me a Homer
479A Gulpin' Gabe	500A Winkless Wally	479B Over Eatin' Ethan	500B Sight Les
480A Robby Rubbish		480B Garbage Pail Kitty	

Series 13

SERIES 13

Sequence ... 501A-540A and 501B-540B.
Variations ... 507A, 507B, 518A, 518B, 534A, 534B, 538A, and 538B have two different backs.
Set total ... 88 stickers (80 regular, plus 8 variations.)

ITEM	MINT	EX
Set	12.00	9.00
Sticker	.20	.15
Variations	see Price Advisory	
Wrappers (2)		
25 cents	––	.35
no price	––	.75
Box	––	2.00

NOTE: Boxes with covers "crossed out" by marker lines *cannot* be graded excellent.

501A	Missing Marcia	521A	Dee Odorant	501B	Hidden Heidi	521B	Stan Can
502A	Gory Laurie	522A	Bloody Murray	502B	Undead Ned	522B	Juan For the Road
503A	Louise Trapeze	523A	Meltdown Meryl	503B	3-Ring Cyril	523B	Steamed Piper
504A	Cooper Scooper	524A	Pop Connie	504B	Jess Desserts	524B	Poppy Corn
505A	Sucked Chuck	525A	Cocktail Dale	505B	Unsani-Terry	525B	Party-Pooper Patty
506A	Tire Jack	526A	Ripped Kip	506B	Crankin' Franklin	526B	Torn Shaun
507A	Target Prentice	527A	Toilet Bo	507B	Blow Hardy	527B	Butt-bit Brandon
508A	Barry Bomber	528A	Daniel Prune	508B	Hi-flyin' Brian	528B	Dried-Fruit Newt
509A	Misfortune Cookie	529A	Corkscrewed Drew	509B	Chow Maynard	529B	Champ-pain Dwayne
510A	Grim Kim	530A	Fun Gus	510B	Taffy Pull	530B	Warty Morty
511A	Puffy Buffy	531A	Stormy Skye	511B	Busty Dusty	531B	Claude Burst
512A	Seymour Barf	532A	Fertile Liza	512B	Kent Stand It	532B	Horace Manure
513A	Repeatin' Pete	533A	Jiggley Jennifer	513B	Round Robyns	533B	Spooned June
514A	Ampu-Ted	534A	Jayne Drain	514B	Hans Off	534B	Eda Mouthful
515A	Wretched Richard	535A	Howie Hanging	515B	Billy Ache	535B	Rush Hour Russ
516A	Bubblin' Lynn	536A	Scrambled Aggie	516B	Heavin' Heather	536B	Sonny Side Up
517A	Chester Drawers	537A	Miriam Migraine	517B	Natty Dresser	537B	Head Buster
518A	Barfin' Marvin	538A	Cat-cradle Cathy	518B	Over Etan	538B	Gooey Gwen
519A	Paddlin' Adeline	539A	John John	519B	Rikki Racket	539B	All Wet Walt
520A	Sprinkling Jose	540A	Ill Windsor	520B	Jay Spray	540B	Horatio Hornblower

Series 14

ALIEN ED

PHONE HOMER

SERIES 14

Sequence ... 541A-580A and 541B-580B.
Variations ... 541A, 541B, 548A, 548B, 562A, 562B, 573A, and 573B have two different backs.
Set total ... 88 stickers (80 regular, plus 8 variations).

ITEM	MINT	EX
Set	12.00	9.00
Sticker	.20	.15
Variations	see Price Advisory	
Wrappers (2)		
25 cents	--	.35
no price	--	.75
Box	--	2.00

NOTE: Boxes with covers "crossed out" by marker lines *cannot* be graded excellent.

541A Rocco Socko	561A Marsh Room	541B Destroyed Boyd	561B Todd Stool
542A Jugglin' Julian	562A Post No Bill	542B Up In The Aaron	562B Bulletin Boris
543A Undersea Lee	563A Potato Chip	543B Sailin' Waylon	563B Dick Tater
544A Zipped Kip	564A Millie Meter	544B Jack Tracks	564B Asa Rule
545A Artie Party	565A Easter Bonnie	545B Driftin' Clifton	565B Hard-boiled Meg
546A Modern Marlise	566A Swarmin' Armin	546B Abstract Abby	566B Infested Lester
547A Cuckoo Clark	567A Doomsday Dom	547B Bile Lyle	567B A-bomb Tom
548A Walt to Wall	568A Glut Tony	548B Nailed Noel	568B Phil Swill
549A Shannon Cannon	569A Cut Curt	549B Bomb Shelly	569B Electric Fanny
550A Violent Viola	570A Ava Shaver	550B Sawin' Susan	570B Holly Hormone
551A Rah Rah Roni	571A Rubber Robert	551B Sis Boom Bonnie	571B Inside Otto
552A Half Whit	572A Fake Jake	552B Lead-head Ned	572B Sham Sam
553A Cold Sore Lenore	573A Snotwich Sandra	553B Kissy Missy	573B Hedda Spreader
554A Rufus Refuse	574A Shattered Shell	554B Cleaned Up Parker	574B Fractured Frank
555A Alien Ed	575A Brain Drain Brian	555B Phone Homer	575B Pick a Winnie
556A Mothy Martha	576A Croaked Kaye	556B Nailed Natalie	576B Sporty Morty
557A Stu Brew	577A Sown Sonya	557B Empty Ken	577B Stitchin' Tyne
558A Hans Off	578A Dial-a-Twyla	558B Numb Nate	578B Phone Bella
559A Dwayne Stain	579A Judd Cud	559B Spilled Gil	579B Spearmint Mindy
560A Lappin' Larry	580A Burnt-out Brett	560B Guzzlin' Guy	580B Burne Toast

Series 15

SERIES 15

Sequence ...581A-620A and 581B-620B.
Variations ...581A, 581B, 582A, 582B, 583A, 583B, 584A and 584B have two different backs.
Set total ....88 stickers (80 regular, plus 8 variations).

ITEM	MINT	EX
Set	12.00	9.00
Sticker	.20	.15
Variations	see Price Advisory	
Wrappers (2)		
25 cents	---	.35
no price	---	.75
Box	---	2.00

NOTE: Boxes with covers "crossed out" by marker lines *cannot* be graded excellent.

581A Shel Game	601A Losin' Wade	581B 3-Card Monte	601B Hy Cholesterol
582A Take-out Dinah	602A Upside Donna	582B Chow Mame	602B Two-fer Juan
583A Lyle Tile	603A Mitch Mitt	583B Harry Glyph	603B Foul Bill
584A Slimy Hymie	604A Sandi Box	584B Crawlin' Rollin	604B Cat Litter
585A Picky Nick	605A Windy Mindy	585B Beulah Ghoul	605B Birthday Kate
586A Peter Cheater	606A Foul-towel Raoul	586B Dean List	606B Muddy Buddy
587A Cornelia Flake	607A Kit Video	587B Mala Nutrition	607B Ham Actor
588A Yo! Gert	608A Fairy Mary	588B Ice Cream Connie	608B Stinker Belle
589A Ecch Benedict	609A Dewy Dewey	589B Brain Les	609B Dank Frank
590A Little Leak Len	610A Beau Constricted	590B Snot-ball Saul	610B Coiled Carl
591A Frank Footer	611A Acid Wayne	591B Dog Bites Boyd	611B Polluted Paul
592A Extra Dexter	612A Shoe Lacey	592B Flabby Abby	612B Weird Walker
593A Footloose Fred	613A Bag Piper	593B Lucky Lew	613B Great Scott
594A Tied Di	614A Fillin' Dylan	594B Knotty Lottie	614B Cutting Juan
595A Mal Practice	615A Preston Change-o	595B Intensive Carrie	615B Sleight of Hans
596A Sani Klaus	616A Alec Gator	596B Sick Nick	616B Croco-Dale
597A Harry Armpits	617A Claude Flesh	597B Under Arnie	617B Slasher Asher
598A Vise Guy	618A Paper Dolly	598B Hugh Fix-it	618B Catie Cut-up
599A Bern-out	619A V.C. Arnie	599B Dim-bulb Bob	619B Cassette Casey
600A Vendo-Matt	620A Ada Bomb	600B Doug Slug	620B Blasted Betty

CARD AND PRINT RUN VARIATIONS IN GPK

SERIES 1

5A Dead Ted......two different backs:
(1) Checklist
(2) Stupid Student Award

5B Jay Decay.....same as 5A

8A Adam Bomb...two different backs:
(1) Checklist
(2) Cheaters License

8B Blasted Billy...same as 8A

29A Bony Joanie...two different backs:
(1) Checklist
(2) Reform School Diploma

29B Thin Lynn.....same as 29A

SERIES 2

42A Patty Putty....appears with same two back variations in all three print runs:
(1) Sneak Award
(2) Spaz Award

42B Muggin' Megan .same as 42A

43A Smelly Kelly...puzzle preview back varies according to print run:
1st print run=Messy Tessy
2nd print run=Live Mike
3rd print run=Live Mike

43B Doug Plug.....same as 43A
44A Sy Clops......same as 43A&B
44B One-Eyed Jack .same as 43A&B and 44A

46A Rappin' Ron...checklist back lists 49B differently according to print run:
1st print run=Schizo Fran
2nd print run=Schizo Fran
3rd print run=Fran Fran

46B Ray Gun......same as 46A
47A Vile Kyle......same as 46A&B
47B Disgustin' Justin.......same as 46A&B and 47A

49B Schizo Fran....appears in 1st and 2nd print runs only

49B Fran Fran.....appears in 3rd print run only

SERIES 3

84A Joe Blow......two different backs:
(1) Wanted for Brain Washing
(2) Wanted for Running A Clip Joint

84B Rod Wad.....same as 84A
110A Snooty Sam.....two different backs:
(1) Wanted for Blocking Traffic
(2) Wanted for Mental Cruelty

110B U.S. Arnie.....same as 110A
113A Alice Island....two different backs:
(1) Wanted for Creating A Public Nuisance
(2) Wanted For Running A Clip Joint

113B Liberty Libby ..same as 113A

SERIES 4

125A Holly Wood....1st print run checklist has the following:
    125B=Woody Allan
    149A=Reese Pieces
    158B=Crystal Gale
    164B=Salvatore Dolly
2nd print run checklist has the following changes:
    125B=Oak Kay
    149A=Puzzled Paul
    158B=Ig Lou
    164B=Battered Brad

125B Woody Alan ...appears in 1st print run only; checklist back has original names for 125B, 149A, 158B, and 164B

125B Oak Kay .....appears in 2nd print run only; checklist back has new names for 125B, 149A, 158B, and 164B.

138A Alien Ian.....same as 125A checklist

138B Outerspace Chase.......same as 125A and 138A

149A Reese Pieces .appears in 1st print run only

149A Puzzled Paul ...appears in 2nd print run only

158B Crystal Gale...appears in 1st print run only

158B Ig Lou.......appears in 2nd print run only

164B Salvatore Dolly.......appears in 1st print run only

164B Battered Brad ..appears in 2nd print run only

SERIES 5

168A Handy Randy ..two different puzzle pieces on back (red letters)

168B Jordan Nuts....same puzzle pieces as 168A but with blue letters

169A Dee Faced.....two different puzzle pieces on back

169B Terri Cloth ....two different puzzle pieces on back (not like 169A pieces)

175A Windy Winston .two different puzzle pieces on back

175B Johnny One-Note.....two different puzzle pieces on back (not like 175A pieces)

178A Earl Painting ...two different backs:
    (1) puzzle piece
    (2) Acne Amy

178B Blue-Boy George .two different backs:
    (1) puzzle piece (not like 178A piece)
    (2) Acne Amy

SERIES 6 — NO VARIATIONS REPORTED

SERIES 7

253A Russ Pus ......two different puzzle piece backs

253A Louise Squeeze .same two pieces as 253A

260B Blasted Billy II........found with either blue or purple set title on front of card

261B Bobbi Booger ..same as 260B

265A Curly Shirley...two different puzzle piece backs

265B Blown Joan....same two pieces as 265A

289B Alexander The Grate........1st print run:
    card number top center in black print
    2nd print run:
    card number at top right in white print

SERIES 8

298A Bloody Mary ...two different puzzle pieces on back

298B Donna Donor ..same two pieces as 298A

318A Haley's Vomit..two different puzzle pieces on back

318B Inter Stella ....same two pieces as 318A

SERIES 9

355B Semi Colon ....found with and without a card number

SERIES 10

379A Locked Dorian .three different backs:
    (1) puzzle L preview
    (2) Rob Slob & Double Iris
    (3) Zach Plaque & Still Jill

379B Sidney Kidney..three different backs:
    (1) puzzle K preview
    (2) Rob Slob & Double Iris
    (3) Zach Plaque & Still Jill

385A Phil 'Er Up ....title of back feature ("The Garbage Gang") found in both blue and red letters

385B Chuckin' Charlie.......same as 385A

408A Lickin' Leon ...title of back feature ("The Garbage Gang") found in both blue and red letters

408B Rat-Sucker Randall ......same as 408A

SERIES 11 —NO VARIATIONS REPORTED

SERIES 12

469A Upset Tommy .. two different backs:
    (1) checklist
    (2) "The Garbage Gang"
469B Tub o' Lars .... same as 469A
472A Walter Fall .... two different backs:
    (1) puzzle P preview
    (2) "The Garbage Gang"
472B Ronny Nose .. two different backs:
    (1) puzzle O preview
    (2) "The Garbage Gang"
481A Car-Stick Karla . two different backs:
    (1) puzzle P preview
    (2) "The Garbage Gang"
481B Cruisin' Susan .. two different backs:
    (1) puzzle O preview
    (2) "The Garbage Gang"

SERIES 13

507A Target Prentice . two different backs:
    (1) "Puzzle Puke"
    (2) puzzle Q preview
507B Blow Hardy ..... two different backs:
    (1) "Puzzle Puke"
    (2) puzzle R preview
518A Barfin' Marvin ... two different backs:
    (1) "Color in the letters"
    (2) "Solve this puzzle"
518B Over Etan ...... same as 518A
534A Jayne Drain .... two different backs:
    (1) checklist
    (2) "Puzzle Puke"
534B Eda Mouthful ... same as 534A
538A Cat-Cradle
  Cathy .... two different backs:
    (1) "Puzzle Puke"
    (2) puzzle Q preview
538B Gooey Gwen .... two different backs:
    (1) "Puzzle Puke"
    (2) puzzle "R" preview

SERIES 14

541A Rocco Socco .... two different backs:
    (1) puzzle T preview
    (2) "Would we lie to you?"
541B Destroyed Boyd . two different backs:
    (1) puzzle S preview
    (2) "Would we lie to you?"

548A Walt to Wall .... two different backs:
    (1) checklist
    (2) "Would we lie to you?"
548B Nailed Noel ..... same as 548A
562A Post No Bill .... two different backs:
    (1) "Would we lie to you?" (Fried Franklin)
    (2) "Would we lie to you?" (Baked Jake)
562B Bulletin Boris ... same as 562A
573A Snotwich
  Sandra .... two different backs:
    (1) puzzle T preview
    (2) "Would we lie to you?"
573B Hedda Spreader . two different backs:
    (1) puzzle S preview
    (2) "Would we lie to you?"

SERIES 15

581A Shel Game ..... two different backs:
    (1) checklist
    (2) "Horrible Horoscopes"
581B 3-Card Monte ... same as 581A
582A Take-out Dinah .. two different backs:
    (1) "Asinine Astrology"
    (2) puzzle piece
582B Chow Mame .... same formats as 582A but puzzle piece is different
583A Lyle Tile .... two different backs:
    (1) puzzle V preview
    (2) puzzle piece
583B Harry Glyph .... two different backs:
    (1) puzzle U preview
    (2) puzzle piece (different than 583A-(2)
584A Slimy Hymie .... two different backs:
    (1) puzzle V preview
    (2) puzzle piece
584B Crawlin' Rollin .. two different backs:
    (1) puzzle U preview
    (2) puzzle piece (different than 584A-(2)

GARBAGE PAIL KIDS BUTTONS (12)   1 7/8" X 2 5/8"

Topps took twelve illustrations from GPK stickers to produce this button set marketed in 1986. Each "button" is a plastic case with an attach-

Awesome!
Bad!
Bless You!
Drop Dead!
Fresh!
Gross!
Hot Stuff!
Mutant!
Ouch!
Radio Active!
Smile!
Squeeze Me!

ment pin on back. All the plastic cases are the same shape and the dimensions in our heading were obtained by measuring between the tallest and widest points. The buttons were sold in clear cellophane bags without gum. Each

bag also contained a 2" X 2 1/2" checklist card printed on gray, blank-backed stock. Although the buttons are assigned numbers on this card, they are not actually numbered and we have listed them alphabetically below.

ITEM	MINT	EX
Set	15.00	12.00
Button	1.25	1.00
Box	--	4.00

GARBAGE PAIL KIDS (16)   2 1/8" X 3 3/4"
CHEWY CANDY

The Confex Company of New Jersey obtained a license from Topps to use GPK artwork on candy wrappers and marketed "Garbage Pail Kids Chewy Candy" in 1987. The product was made in Argentina by Stani and imported to the U.S. for distribution. There are 16 different center designs in the set and some of these appear on more than one flavor of

candy. Note: no mint price is given since these wrappers were folded and twisted around the candy. The prices listed are for wrappers with the GPK design centered (many wrappers are miscut so that the design is off-center).

ITEM	MINT	EX
Set	--	6.00
Wrapper	--	.35

Adam Bomb
Brett Sweat
Brutal Brad
Brutal Bridget
Chris Hiss
Dressy Jesse
Fat Matt
Fran Fran

Jenny Genius
Muggin' Megan
One-Eyed Jack
Pegleg Peter
Ray Decay
Savage Stuart
Spacey Stacy
Thin Lynn

GARBAGE PAIL KIDS (15)   4 7/8" X 6 7/8"
GIANT STICKERS

Some collectors have labeled this set of 15 giant size stickers a "test" issue simply because the 39-sticker set which followed it was entitled "1st Series Kids." That is not an accurate description, however,

because this set has its own theme (no cards are repeated in the series of 39) and it is not in short supply, as a test set would be. Except for sticker No. 1, the artwork sticker fronts all have the style of advertising posters promoting the GPK series. Three stickers were packed in every clear cellophane wrapper.

ITEM	MINT	EX
Set	18.00	15.00
Sticker	1.50	1.00
Wrapper	--	.50
Box	--	2.00

Garbage Pail Kids Giant Stickers-15

1 Bazooka Jerk and his Garbage
2 Bony Joanie
3 Garbage Pail Kids Rule!
4 Garbage Pails Foul Bill
5 Have A Nice Day
6 Hooked on Garbage Pail Kids
7 Why Fight It? Collect Garbage Pail Kids
8 Take A Garbage Pail Kid to Lunch!
9 Visit Garbage Pail National Park
10 Garbage Pail Circus!
11 How To Be A Garbage Pail Kid
12 It Takes Guts To Be A Garbage Pail Kid
13 And The Winner Is...Miss Garbage Pail Kid
14 Busted!
15 Garbage Pail School Senior Class

GARBAGE PAIL KIDS (39) GIANT STICKERS
4 7/8" X 6 7/8"

The second group of giant stickers marketed by Topps was issued in wrappers and boxes bearing the title "1st Series Kids." The 39 designs are simply enlargements of regular GPK 1 Series A stickers. By studying an uncut sheet, we have determined that 15 giant stickers were double printed; these are marked by an asterisk in our checklist. The checklist on the back of the cellophane wrapper incorrectly lists No. 17 as "Mean Jean;" this is spelled correctly ("Mean Gene") on the actual sticker. In the first print run, sticker No. 8 appeared with a "Most Unpopular Student Award" on back; this was changed to "Most Unlikely to Succeed Award" in subsequent printings. Note: set price includes No. 8 with "Most Unpopular" back only.

ITEM	MINT	EX
Set	40.00	30.00
Stickers		
1-4, 15-18 & 29-35	.75	.60
No. 8	3.00	2.00
All others	1.50	1.00
Wrapper	—	.50
Box	—	2.00

1 Nasty Nick*
2 Junkfood John*
3 Up Chuck*
4 Fryin' Brian*
5 Dead Ted
6 Art Apart
7 Stormy Heather
8 Adam Bomb
9 Unstitched Mitch
10 Tee-Vee Stevie
11 Itchy Richie
12 Furry Fran
13 Ashcan Andy
14 Potty Scotty
15 Ailin' Al*
16 Weird Wendy*
17 Mean Jean*
18 Cranky Frankie*
19 Corroded Carl
20 Swell Mel
21 Virus Iris
22 Junky Jeff
23 Drippy Dan
24 Nervous Rex
25 Creepy Carol
26 Slobby Robbie
27 Brainy Janie
28 Oozy Suzie
29 Bony Joanie*
30 New Wave Dave*
31 Run Down Rhoda*
32 Frigid Bridgit*
33 Mad Mike*
34 Kim Kong*
35 Wrinkly Randy*
36 Wrappin' Ruth
37 Guillo Tina
38 Slimy Sam
39 Buggy Betty

GARBAGE PAIL KIDS POSTERS (18)

12" X 17"

This imaginative series of 12" X 17" glossy paper posters is an excellent mix between original designs and artwork taken from other GPK sets. The most interesting posters are the satires — spoofing food products, Gone With The Wind, cosmetics, etc. — evidence of the pervasive influence of Topps Wacky Packages (the set from which GPK evolved). Each glossy yellow paper envelope contained one folded poster, but no gum.

ITEM	MINT	EX
Set	--	25.00
Poster	--	1.50
Wrapper	--	1.00
Box	--	6.00

Double-crossing the Delaware

1. Drink All-Natural Garbage Pail Kola
2. Hang In There Baby!
3. Garbage Pail Kids Sugar Crusted Sewage
4. The Inside Dope
5. Visit Garbage Pail Land
6. Garbage Pail Kids Headquarters Keep Out!
7. Eat My Face!
8. Slime
9. Miss Dumpster
10. Double-crossing the Delaware
11. National Garbage Pail
12. I [Love] Garbage Pail Kids
13. "Beauty Is Only Skin Deep"
14. Look Like Garbage
15. Gone With The Garbage
16. How To Be A Garbage Pail Kid
17. Garbage Pail Kids Want You!
18. Busted!

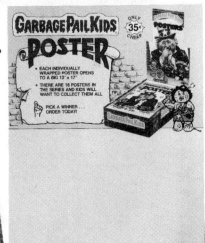

255

GARBAGE PAIL KIDS (12)
3-D WALL PLAKS

Topps was not content with publishing two-dimensional Garbage Pail Kids; they had to go and manufacture a set of "3-D Wall Plaks" for children to nail on bedroom walls (kids deface bedroom walls anyway, so why not use a GPK?). The plaks measure 6 1/4" X 9" and with their molded wood-like frames, resemble classic oil paintings in a grotesque sort of way. This series was not widely distributed, yet prices for it have stayed low because of lack of recognition. Each plak was issued in a plastic bag with a J-hook style header card at top (no gum).

ITEM	MINT	EX
Set	40.00	30.00
Plak	3.00	2.25
Wrapper w.		
Header	––	1.50
Box	––	6.00

GARFIELD ALBUM STICKERS (180)

ANIMATED STICKER

1 3/4" X 2 1/2"

Diamond Toy used an Italian sticker manufacturer to produce its "Garfield" series of album stickers marketed in 1989. There are 180 stickers in the set, each with a numbered spot for placement in the 24-page album. Of these, 156 are regular multi-color artwork types which follow an album-long story entitled "Garfield in Paradise." Another 24 stickers are special "animated" formats which fit into a "Family Album" feature in the center of the album. These "move" when viewed through the "slide-o-scope" viewer stapled inside the spine. The album also contains 21 "animated" sketches spread throughout the pages and a "jumping for joy" connect-the-dots picture on the last page. "Garfield in Paradise" was a television special and Diamond's license apparently was restricted to portraying it in this format (Panini also made a Garfield sticker set). Note: set price includes album.

ITEM	MINT	EX
Set	22.50	18.00
Sticker	.10	.07
Wrapper	––	.25
Album	2.00	1.50

GARFIELD NFL MINI POSTERS (28)

1990 Schedule	
Philadelphia	
1989 record: 11-5-0	Eagles/Opponent
Sept. 9	at N.Y. Giants
Sept. 16	Phoenix
Sept. 23	at L.A. Rams
Sept. 30	Indianapolis
Oct. 7	OPEN DATE
Oct. 15	Minnesota
Oct. 21	at Washington
Oct. 28	at Dallas
Nov. 4	New England
Nov. 12	Washington
Nov. 18	at Atlanta
Nov. 25	N.Y. Giants
Dec. 2	at Buffalo
Dec. 9	at Miami
Dec. 16	Green Bay
Dec. 23	Dallas
Dec. 29	at Phoenix

1990 Argus • 6888 RES. © 1978 United Features Syndicate, Inc.

NFC	AFC
Atlanta Falcons	Buffalo Bills
Chicago Bears	Cincinnati Bengals
Dallas Cowboys	Cleveland Browns
Detroit Lions	Denver Broncos
Green Bay Packers	Houston Oilers
Los Angeles Rams	Indianapolis Colts
Minnesota Vikings	Kansas City Chiefs
New Orleans Saints	Los Angeles Raiders
New York Giants	Miami Dolphins
Philadelphia Eagles	New England Patriots
Phoenix Cardinals	New York Jets
San Francisco 49ers	Pittsburgh Steelers
Tampa Bay Buccaneers	San Diego Chargers
Washington Redskins	Seattle Seahawks

2 1/2" X 3 1/2"

Garfield, the wide-body cat, has finally found an appropriate use for his impressive bulk: he has joined the National Football League! The premise of this set is quite simple ... take two basic illustrations — Garfield running back and Garfield pass receiver — and dress them up in the uniform of all the teams in the NFC and AFC, with matching team backgrounds. The "mini posters" are actually standard size cards and the best feature on either side is the schedule on back, which has slots to record the score of every game in the 1990 season. Complete cello-wrapped sets of both NFL conferences sold in grocery and variety stores for $2.00 per pack. This is the "official" value we have listed below, but collectors may be able to find sets drastically reduced in "discounted" bins. Note: cards with scores filled in cannot be graded excellent.

ITEM	MINT	EX
Set (both conferences)	4.00	3.00
Conference set	2.00	1.50
Card	.15	.10

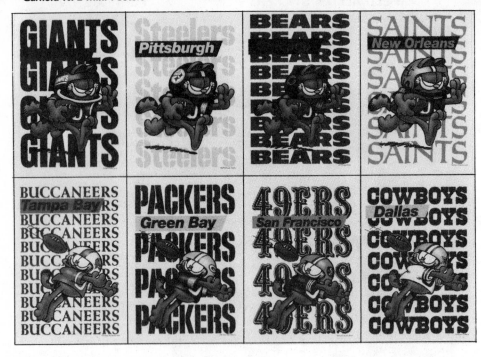

GARRISON'S GORILLAS (72)

2 1/2" X 3 7/16"

Leaf Brands, a company which has produced more card sets in black and white than in color, created the Garrison's Gorillas

series in 1967 from photographs taken from the television show. Each photo is surrounded by white borders and is captioned in a black panel underneath. The backs are horizontally aligned and contain a short narrative and the card number.

ITEM	MINT	EX
Set	105.00	85.00
Card	1.25	1.00
Wrapper	—	5.00
Box	—	35.00

1	Unplugged	25	Blast for Freedom
2	Escape Cover	26	Finders Keepers
3	Break for Freedom?	27	Alert for Ambush
4	Firing an Ammo Dump	28	Outsmarting the Nazis
5	Laying Low	29	Baby Sitters
6	Deadly Aim	30	Journey in Style
7	Playing It Cool	31	Finishing Off Nazis
8	Mining a Bridge	32	Rehearsal for a Mission
9	Inside a Nazi Prison	33	Casino Sets a Trap
10	Fast Draw Goniff	34	Wine Barrel Affair
11	Out of Ambush	35	Chief Bags a Nazi
12	Blast 'Em Casino	36	Goniff Goes Nazi
13	Fight or Prison	37	Chief Blasts the Enemy
14	Discovered	38	One Blast Ahead
15	Trapped	39	Chief Drops a Nazi
16	Pistol Point	40	Clearing the Way
17	Mission Briefing	41	In Fast, Out Fast
18	Rooftop Lookout	42	Garrison Tries a Bluff
19	Knock Out	43	No Laughing Matter
20	No Warm Welcome	44	Ready for the Getaway
21	Underwater Pursuit	45	Goniff on Guard
22	"Hold It, Chief!"	46	On the Alert
23	Actor Strikes a Pose	47	Garrison Covers Chief
24	Garbage Collectors	48	Borrowing a Tank

49	Hot Cargo	61	Desperate Wait
50	Search for a Code	62	Split Second Timing
51	Casino on the Alert	63	Taking a Big Risk
52	Goniff Captured	64	A Rise in Rank
53	Fight to Save Bridge	65	Dynamite Charge
54	Actor Covers Escape	66	Warden Falls Dead
55	Lookout Goniff	67	Germans Again!
56	Chief Takes a Break	68	Bank Job
57	Risky Bluff	69	Nazis Overhead
58	Rehearsal for Trouble	70	Stealing a Tank
59	High Jinks	71	Into a Nazi Trap
60	Time Running Out	72	Ready for Action

The Get Smart set of 66 photo cards and 16 artwork "Secret Agent Kits" was marketed by Topps in 1966. The photo cards contain black & white pictures taken from the TV series, and they came out of the 5-cent gum pack in two-card 'panels. When separated into singles, the cards may vary in width from one another as much as 3/16". The backs contain a "Get Smart Quiz": the answer is obtained by rubbing a coin over the blank space (see illustration below). The "Secret Agent Kits"—actually parts of disguises—were inserted, one to a pack, as a bonus. Special notes: Bob Marks reports that certain cards in this set were double-printed and these are marked by an asterisk in the checklist. Single-printed cards (SP) are valued higher than double-printed cards (DP). No set price is given for panels since this would depend upon the specific combinations of cards involved. Secret Agent Kits with punch holes missing cannot be considered mint; detached masks or parts are valued at 50% of the excellent price.

ITEM	MINT	EX
Sets		
Cards	250.00	190.00
Kits	160.00	120.00
Cards		
SP	3.50	2.50
DP	2.50	2.00
Kit	5.00	4.00
Panels		
2 SP's	8.00	6.00
SP/DP	6.50	5.00
2 DP's	5.00	4.00
Wrapper	—	30.00
Box	—	150.00

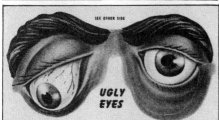

1 If It Goes Off, I'm in Trouble.*
2 Going Down!
3 Finger Isometrics
4 The Super Snooper*
5 Pardon My Foot!
6 Cone of Silence
7 The Arsenal
8 K-13 and Friend*
9 On His Way to Headquarters
10 Smart Punches In
11 Oops, Wrong Number!
12 Chief, One False Move and I'm Dead
13 Planning Her Next Move*
14 Something Fishy About This*
15 Gad, This Gun is a Toy, Too!
16 I'll Wait for Tomorrow's Flight. I Already Saw the Movie.
17 We See Eye to Eye on Everything.
18 X86 + X99 = Formula for Trouble
19 Control's Top Agents
20 Max Smart — Control's Problem
21 Don Adams and Barbara Feldon

22 Two Heads Are Better Than One?*
23 Agent X99*
24 Atta Boy K13, Go Get 'em.
25 Maxwell Smart
26 You Trying to Tell Me Something?
27 Max Smart's Secret Weapon*
28 I Must Be Gaining Weight
29 That Fat Gentleman Looks Familiar.
30 Come on K-13, Open Up.*
31 We Got Them or Vice Versa.
32 Adorable Agent
33 Max, You've Found the Lost Chord
34 Everyone Up on Her Toes.*
35 Ow, My Karate Needs More Work
36 Think They'll Recognize Us?*
37 Never Trust a Ticking Doll
38 This is No Way to Punish an Agent.*
39 Just in Time To Be too Late
40 It Sounds Like Coffee.
41 Oops, I Shot a Hole in the Roof!*
42 X99—Western Style
43 When You Call Me an Idiot, Smile*
44 Figuring Out His Next Mistake.*
45 Low Level Conference.
46 Is He Trying to Attract My Attention?
47 Mister, Are You a Secret Agent?*
48 It Only Hurts When I Laugh.
49 I'll Shoot When I Count 3... Maybe 4?
50 Maxwell in Control*

51 Where Do You Want Your Head Sent?*
52 Think You Got Me? I Think So Too!
53 There's 1 Way I'll Talk—That's It!
54 All This Protection is Killing Me.
55 Be Quiet, I'll Do the Panicking.
56 Careful with Your Shave Cream*
57 Wonder Why It's So Quiet in Here?*
58 This Beats Working
59 Smart Hits the Jackpot
60 Something's Suspicious—Five Aces
61 Calling for Help
62 Smart Gets His Man
63 Posing as a Big Gambler
64 Hold It Chief, I'm Coming*
65 Don't You Know I Have Hay Fever?*
66 Gee, I Wish This Gun Were Loaded.

GET SMART SECRET AGENT KITS
1 Arrow through the neck
2 Left ear
3 Right ear
4 Stake through the head
5 Screw through the neck
6 Thick mustache
7 Pop eyes
8 Ugly eyes
9 Cross eyes
10 Knife through the neck
11 Left horn
12 Right horn
13 Three eyes
14 Droopy mustache

15 Droopy eyes
16 Dandy mustache

GHOSTBUSTERS ALBUM STICKERS (264)

The animated cartoon series, not the movie, is the subject of this series issued on a test basis by American Panini in 1987. There are 240 numbered album stickers in the set and they have the usual multi-language Panini back. In addition, there is a sub-series of 24 diecut plastic stickers (lettered A-X on back) designed to be placed onto a special four-page feature entitled "Do It Yourself Terror." Note: set price includes album.

ITEM	MINT	EX
Set	25.00	18.00
Sticker	.10	.07
Wrapper	--	.35
Album	2.00	1.50

GHOSTBUSTERS II (88/11)

2 1/2" X 3 1/2"

Guess what? The sequel to the original Ghostbusters movie was pretty much a dud, but that didn't stop Topps from making a card set about it. The series is composed of 88 cards and eleven stickers and it was issued in 1989. The cards are a mixture of color photographs, artwork pictures of various ghostly creatures, and special "wide screen SFX shots." The backs are mostly covered by a large "Ghostbusters II" logo and title; a short text is printed underneath. The stickers, likewise, are a mixture of color photos and artwork and all have puzzle piece backs, except for #8, which shows the completed puzzle. The wrapper is blue, yellow, black and red and carries the wrapper code 0-416-21-01-9. Note: set price includes stickers.

ITEM	MINT	EX
Set	12.00	9.00
Card	.10	.07
Sticker	.30	.20
Box	--	2.00

Ghostbusters II

1 Ghostbusters II
2 Bill Murray is Venkman
3 Dan Aykroyd is Stantz
4 Sigourney Weaver is Dana
5 Harold Ramis is Spengler
6 Rick Moranis is Louis
7 Ernie Hudson is Winston
8 Runaway Carriage!
9 Kiddie Celebrities!
10 A New Job for Dana
11 Janosz' Secret
12 Egon on the Job!
13 In Ray's Bookstore
14 Supernatural Check-up!
15 Dr. Venkman's House Call
16 Portrait of a Monster
17 Possesed by Vigo!
18 Descent into Danger!
19 The Van Horne Station
20 Sinister Caller
21 Tully for the Defense!
22 Ghostbusters on Trial
23 Spectral Assault!
24 Scoleri's Ghost
25 A Courtroom in Chaos!
26 Struck by (Finger) Lightning!
27 The Judge-Found Guilty!
28 Ghostly Brothers on a Rampage!
29 No Order in *This* Court!
30 Who Ya Gonna Call, Judge?
31 Spengler Means Business!
32 Back in Action!
33 Boxed In!
34 TV Commercial (Part 1)
35 TV Commercial (Part 2)
36 TV Commercial (Part 3)
37 TV Commercial (Part 4)
38 TV Commercial (Part 5)
39 The Grand Re-opening!
40 Emergency Ghost-call!

HERE IS WHAT YOUR COMPLETED
BLUE BORDER PICTURE WILL LOOK LIKE:

COLLECT ALL 10 CARDS OF PICTURE A

41 The Ghost Jogger
42 Ghost Catcher Supreme!
43 A Job Well Done!
44 Merry Christmas, New York!
45 Spengler Under Glass
46 At the Museum
47 What *Is* This Stuff?
48 No Sign of Life!
49 All Squeaky Clean?
50 Janine's New Scheme
51 The Return of Slimer
52 The New Ghostbuster?
53 Sorry, Guys!
54 Dana Wows 'Em!
55 Love, Manhattan-style!
56 The Baby-Sitters
57 Hate, Manhattan-style!

58 Engulfed by Mood Slime!
59 To the New Year...
60 Restaurant Crashers!
61 Vigo's Master Plan
62 Oscar in a Jam!
63 The Evil of Vigo
64 Dana's Gamble
65 The Monstrous Mink!
66 Heads Up!
67 The Titanic Has Arrived!
68 Racing to the Rescue!
69 Psycho-reactive Slime Flood!
70 Facing the Unknown
71 Levitating Oscar
72 Tully's Big Chance
73 The Libby Express!

74 Venkman's Favorite Lady
75 The Party's Over!
76 The Confrontation
77 Eat This, Vigo!
78 Janosz - What a Drip!
79 Stantz Survives a Sliming!
80 Her Hero ... Again!
81 Bizarre Revelation
82 The Fabulous Four!
83 Filming Lady Liberty's "Walk"
84 Filming the Subway Interior
85 Artwork: Slimer
86 Artwork: Scoleri Ghost 1
87 Artwork: Scoleri Ghost 2
88 Until Next Time...!

GIANT PLAKS (50)

TWO SIZES

There are two varieties of Giant Plaks: one is printed on cardboard 1/16" thick, has a prepunched hole for hanging, and has wavy edges cut to shape; the other variety is printed on thin cardboard, has no "hang" hole, and has simu- lated (printed) wavy edges. The checklist for both types is identical and there are two wrappers for the set. The "test" wrapper is a paper en- velope with a large artwork sticker attached; it bears a 10- cent price and contained an unknown number of thin plaks. The "regular" wrapper is wax, bears a 5-cent price, and carried a 1968 product code. This wrapper plainly states "Contents: 1 Plak" and did indeed contain one of the thick, wavy-edged type, but no gum.

ITEM	MINT	EX
Sets		
Thick	500.00	375.00
Thin	375.00	250.00
Plaks		
Thick	8.00	6.00
Thin	6.00	4.00
Wrappers		
Test (10¢)	--	150.00
Regular 5¢	--	25.00
Regular 10¢	--	75.00

THICK TYPE

THIN TYPE

Giant Plaks

1. Do It Tomorrow - You Made Enough Mistakes Today!
2. **What's on Your Mind? — If You Will Forgive the Overstatment**
3. I'd Like To Help You Out - Which Way Did You Come In?
4. I Spend 8 Hours a Day Here - Do You Expect Me to Work Too?
5. Whether You're Rich or Poor It's Good to Have Money.
6. I'm Not Hard of Hearing - I'm Just Ignoring You.
7. If You Ever Need a Friend - Buy a Dog.
8. Come In - Everything Else Has Gone Wrong Today.
9. Be An Optimist - So Far Not Bad At All!
10. Silence
11. Your Visit Has Climaxed An Already Dull Day.
12. You Must've Been a Beautiful Baby. But What Happened?
13. We Aim for Accuracy.
14. Smile - Later Today You Won't Feel Like it.
15. Some People Can't Do Anything Right!
16. Mistakes Will Happen. Oops, Sorry!
17. Somebody Goofed
18. Nobody Tells Me What To Do!
19. I'd Rather Be Handsome Than Rich.
20. You're Head and Shoulders Above Everyone.
21. I Was Born This Way - What's Your Excuse?
22. Think - Maybe We Can Dodge This Work.
23. The Marines Build Men - But Even They Couldn't Help You!
24. Stop Talking When I'm Interrupting
25. This Is a Non Profit Organization - We Didn't Plan It That Way.
26. **Think — It May Be a New Experience**
27. I'd Give $1,000 Dollars To Be a Millionaire
28. Tell Me All You Know - I've Got a Minute to Spare.
29. In Case of Fire - Please Yell "Fire"
30. Don't Let School Work Get You Down - Flunk Now and Get It Over With.
31. Think You Got Troubles?
32. I'd Like To See You Get Ahead - You Need One!
33. Keep Your Temper - Nobody Else Wants It.
34. Work Fascinates Me - I Can Sit and Watch It For Hours.
35. Keep Calm!
36. I Never Forget a Face. But In Your Case I'll Make an Exception.
37. Quiet - Genius at Work
38. I May Look Busy - But I'm Only Confused!
39. Join Me for Dinner...at Your House.
40. If You're So Smart Why Ain't You Rich?
41. Concentrate
42. Why Be Difficult? With a Little Effort You Can Be a Real Stinker.
43. I'm a Genius - Do I Have to Prove It?
44. Who's Excited?
45. Money Isn't Everything - But It's Way Ahead of Whatever's In Second Place!
46. Time Wounds All Heels
47. If At First You Don't Succeed - To Heck With It!
48. Remember the Old Chinese Saying:
49. Don't Just Do Something — Stand There
50. Not Everyone Has Your Brains - Some People Are Smart.

GIANT SIZE FUNNY VALENTINES (55) 2 1/2" X 4 3/4"

With the Funny Valentine craze still going strong, the dilemma for Topps in 1961 was to create a card similar enough to play on the basic theme, but different enough to keep up the interest. The result was this 55-card set of Giant Funny Valentines (first reported by Barker in the 2nd Catalog Updates, 6-26-61). Each card has a color drawing and "straight line" on the front, and the punch line is printed on the orange-colored back. There is a space provided for each card to be personalized should it really be "delivered."

ITEM	MINT	EX
Set	75.00	60.00
Card	1.25	1.00
Wrapper	---	25.00
Box	---	125.00

1 All Year Round You Work Your Fingers to the Bone and What Do You Get?
2 Dear Valentine I Want You to Accept the Check on the Other Side
3 Have You Ever Thought of Getting Married to Me?
4 I've Never Met Anyone Like You.
5 A Good Man Is Hard to Find
6 I Picked Up a Real Nice Gift for You
7 Valentine to My Teacher—I Think You're Wonderful
8 With a Friend Like You...
9 A Valentine for My Teacher—You Made Me What I Am Today
10 You're Just What the Doctor Ordered
11 How Does It Feel to Know You're Wanted?
12 To a Dad Who Has Given Me Everything

13 I'd Like to Invite You to Dinner
14 Today Is Your Day Mom
15 You're Invited to a Masquerade Party
16 I Just Said the Word That Describes You
17 Invitation—If You Have No Date on Saturday Night...
18 I Couldn't Let This Valentine Day Go by without Buying Something
19 You Give Me a Feeling No One Else Does
20 I Thought of Something Funny the Other Day!
21 I'm Glad You're Out of Bed
22 They Say Two Heads Are Better than One.
23 To My Valentine—You Have So Many Wonderful Points.
24 It Isn't the Words that Count
25 Thank You for Your Unusual Valentine Gift.
26 Invitation—We're Having a Beach Party by the Lake.

27 You're as Lovely as a Rainbow
28 I Love Your Beautiful Long Blond Curls.
29 When I Think of You I Think of Music
30 You Are Invited to a Surprise Party
31 You Are My Sunshine
32 You'll Be Out of the Hospital in no Time
33 You're Invited to a Wild Valentine Party
34 To Mom My Favorite Valentine
35 You're the Worlds Greatest Dad!
36 I Hope You Like My Present
37 When I See You I Can Think of Only One Thing to Do
38 You've Got the Sweetest Lips
39 There's Something About You That Makes Me Swoon!
40 Someday You Will Make One Girl Very Happy
41 Don't Read the Other Side of This Card Until Valentine Day

42 A Present For You on Valentine Day, Dad!
43 You Have a Peach of a Complexion
44 I Like You Because
45 Happy Valentine Day, Mom
46 Success Certainly Hasn't Changed You
47 You May Not Be a Beauty
48 Tonight I'd Like to Pick You Up at Your House

49 You're Not the Type to Wear My School Ring
50 I Can't Forget the Day I Met You
51 I'm Going to Pick Out a Little Gift for You
52 You Have Beauty and Brains
53 I Get a Thrill When I Watch You Play Football
54 You Really Deserve a Better Kid than Me.
55 I'll Always Care for You!

G.I. JOE ALBUM STICKERS (225) 1 3/4" X 2 1/2"

Of the 225 stickers in the G.I. Joe set, produced by Diamond, 24 have special fronts which can only be "read" by using the special "Magic Decoder" which comes with the album. In fact, all of the sticker spaces in the 32-page album, plus all the supplemental illustrations, are "coded" in this manner. The set was released to the retail market in October 1987, in gumless green envelopes containing seven stickers each. Note: set price includes album.

ITEM	MINT	EX
Set	30.00	20.00
Sticker	.15	.10
Wrapper	---	.20
Album	2.00	1.50

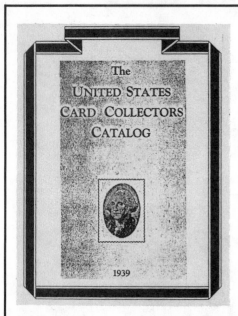

G.I. JOE (180?)

2 1/2" X 3 1/2"

We have very little information at this time about the "G.I. Joe" series of trading cards issued by toy-maker Hasbro in 1986. Sales of the cards were limited almost exclusively to toy stores and they did not reach the card collecting public in general. All the cards in our possession are marked "Series 1" and #180 is the highest seen so far. The fronts have color artwork scenes without captions or borders and the subject matter is described on back. Corners are rounded and the obverses are glossy; the cardboard stock is thin but is standard size. Until more information is obtained, we recommend a market value of 25 cents per card.

G.I. JOE (200)

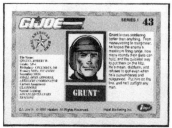

Impel released this 200-card set of "G.I. Joe" cards in 1991; it is marked "Series 1," so another set is being planned. The cards

2 1/2" X 3 1/2"

feature multi-color artwork fronts and are divided into a number of different themes: Patrols, Rank & File, Original G.I. Joe Team, Battle Gear, Special Missions, Recruits, Famous Battles, and Honor Roll. The surfaces, front and back, are so glossy that each standard-sized card seems to be made of thin plastic. The series was sold on a retail basis in poly bags (12 cards) and collectors could order (1) a free 8-1/2" X 11" checklist page (see illustration) or (2) a special "Premier Edition Collector's Album," with 23 plastic sheets, for $19.95 from offers printed on the back of the wrapper. Samples of the set were also packed in clear cello packs and distributed to collectors and dealers at various card conventions (the cards in these packs are all regular issue).

ITEM	MINT	EX
Set	25.00	18.00
Card	.10	.07
Wrapper	--	.10
Box	--	1.50
Checklist page	1.00	.75

1 Cesspool	37 Dr. Mindbender
2 Flint	38 Firefly
3 Toxo-Viper II	39 Zap
4 Sludge Viper	40 Breaker
5 Clean Sweep	41 Snake-Eyes
6 Septic Tank	42 Scarlet
7 Ozone	43 Grunt
8 Skystriker	44 Flash
9 Rolling Thunder	45 Rock & Roll
10 Tomhawk	46 Short-Fuze
11 M.B.T. Mobile Battle Tank	47 Stalker
12 Snowcat	48 Clutch
13 A.W.E. Striker	49 Steeler
14 Night Raven	50 Grand Slam
15 Rattler	51 Viper
16 H.I.S.S.	52 Cobra Officer
17 Cobra Hydrofoil, Moray	53 Hawk
18 G.I. Joe Headquarters	54 Jet Pack, J.U.M.P.
19 Bazooka	55 Rapid Fire Motorcycle, R.A.M.
20 Shockwave	56 Attack Cannon, Flak
21 Dusty	57 Attack Vehicle, V.A.M.P.
22 Duke	58 Heavy Artillery Lazer, H.A.L.
23 Tripwire	59 Mobile Missile System, MMS
24 Alpine	60 Motorized Battle Tank, Mobat
25 Shipwreck	61 Wet-Suit
26 Spirit	62 Gung-Ho
27 Deep Six	63 Payload
28 Storm Shadow	64 Deep Six
29 Captain Gridiron	65 Light Foot
30 Roadblock	66 Fast Draw
31 Gung-Ho	67 Salvo
32 Cobra Commander	68 Hard Ball
33 Televiper	69 Outback
34 Metal-Head	70 Air-Tight
35 Snow Serpent	71 Charbroil
36 Baroness	72 Ambush

73 Pathfinder	109 Mexican Holiday
74 Hit & Run	110 Condor
75 Desert Scorpion	111 Badger
76 Techno-Viper	112 Paralyzer
77 Toxo-Viper I	113 Attack Cruiser
78 Hydro-Viper	114 Ice Sabre
79 Range Viper	115 Brawler
80 Astro Viper	116 Battle Wagon
81 T.A.R.G.A.T.	117 Interrogator
82 Night Viper	118 Major Altitude
83 That Sinking Feeling	119 Sky Creeper
84 Words of Honor	120 Night Vulture
85 Burn-Out	121 Cloudburst
86 No Holds Barred	122 Skymate
87 Showdown	123 General Hawk
88 Evasion	124 Sci-Fi
89 The Old Switcheroo	125 Heavy Duty
90 Ambush	126 Crimson Guard Immortal
91 Plausible Denial	
92 Turnabout	127 Incinerator
93 Sheep's Clothing	128 Big Ben
94 Airshow	129 Red Star
95 Washout	130 Desert Scorpion
96 In From The Cold	131 Low-Light
97 And Into The Fire	132 Dusty
98 Tight Circle	133 Cobra Commander
99 All In A Night's Work	134 B.A.T.H.
100 Extraction	135 Snake-Eyes
101 Getting There	136 Tracker
102 Snowblind	137 Grunt
103 The Lower Depths	138 Mercer
104 Decisions	139 Law
105 Scoop	140 Tunnel Rat
106 Ladies' Day	141 Dial Tone
107 Forced Play	142 Dodger
108 Passing of the Guard	143 Viper
	144 Lamprey

G.I. Joe

145 Major Bludd
146 Falcon
147 Road Pig
148 Rock & Roll
149 Zap
150 Psyche-Out
151 Assault on Cobra Island I
152 Battle of Cobra Robot in Pit I
153 Operation: Wingfield
154 Battle on Fifth Avenue
155 Battle of Hindu Kush
156 Code Name: Sea Strike
157 First Battle of Springfield
158 Alaskan Pipeline Battle
159 First Battle of Sierra Gordo
160 Battle of Washington, D.C.
161 Operation: Scarface
162 First Battle of Pit I
163 Solo Assault on Destro's
    Citadel
164 Battle of Lucca, Italy
165 Dreadnok's Assault on
    McGuire Air Force Base
166 Battle at Snake-eye's
    Cabin
167 Firefight at Staten Island
    Mall
168 Air Battle: Skystriker vs.
    Rattler
169 Sea Battle: Whale vs.
    Hydrofoils
170 Firefight at the Carnival
171 Raid into Sierra Gordo
172 Battle of Joe Air-Sea Base
173 First Assault of New Cobra
    Island

174 Serpentor
175 Zartan
176 Dr. Mindbender
177 Raptor
178 Golobulus
179 Nemesis Enforcer
180 Royal Guard
181 Crystal Ball
182 General Flag
183 Breaker
184 Quick Kick
185 Heavy Metal
186 Thunder
187 Crank Case

188 Blocker
189 Avalanche
190 Blaster
191 Crazy Legs
192 Maverick
193 Knockdown
194 Doc
195 Sneak Peek
196 Croc Master
197 Voltar
198 Firefly
199 Checklist 1
200 Checklist 2

A REAL AMERICAN HERO®

1991 TRADING CARD CHECKLIST

SPIRIT

PATHFINDER™

PATROLS
ECO-WARRIORS™
1 Cesspool
2 Flint
3 Toxo-Viper II
4 Sludge Viper
5 Clean Sweep
6 Septic Tank
7 Ozone

RANK & FILE
8 Skystriker
9 Rolling Thunder
10 Tomahawk
11 Mobile Battle Tank,
   Mauler
12 Snowcat
13 A.W.E. Striker
14 Night Raven
15 Rattler
16 H.I.S.S.
17 Cobra Hydrofoil
   Moray
18 G.I. Joe Headquarters
19 Bazooka
20 Shockwave
21 Dusty
22 Duke
23 Tripwire
24 Alpine
25 Shipwreck
26 Spirit
27 Deep Six
28 Storm Shadow
29 Captain Gridiron
30 Roadblock
31 Gung-Ho
32 Cobra Commander
33 Televiper
34 Metal-head
35 Snow Serpent
36 Baroness
37 Dr. Mindbender
38 Firefly

ORIGINAL JOE TEAM
39 Zap
40 Breaker
41 Snake-Eyes
42 Scarlett
43 Grunt
44 Flash
45 Rock & Roll
46 Short-Fuze
47 Stalker
48 Clutch
49 Steeler
50 Grand Slam
51 Viper
52 Cobra Officer

53 Hawk
54 Jet Pack, J.U.M.P.
55 Rapid Fire Motorcycle,
   R.F.M.
56 Attack Cannon, Flak
57 Attack Vehicle,
   V.A.M.P.
58 Heavy Artillery Laser,
   H.A.L.
59 Mobile Missile System,
   M.M.S.
60 Motorized Battle Tank,
   MOBAT

BATTLE GEAR
61 Wet Suit
62 Gung-Ho
63 Payload
64 Deep Six
65 Light Foot
66 Fast Draw
67 Salvo
68 Hard Ball
69 Outback
70 Air-Tight
71 Charbroil
72 Ambush
73 Pathfinder
74 Hit & Run
75 Desert Scorpion
76 Techno-Viper
77 Toxo-Viper I
78 Hydro-Viper
79 Range Viper
80 Astro Viper
81 T.A.R.G.A.T
82 Night Viper

SPECIAL MISSIONS
83 That Sinking Feeling
84 Words of Honor
85 Burn-out
86 No Holds Barred
87 Showdown
88 Evasion
89 The Old Switcheroo
90 Ambush
91 Plausible Denial
92 Turnabout
93 Sheep's Clothing
94 Airshow
95 Washout
96 In From the Cold
97 And into the Fire
98 Tight Circle
99 All in a Night's Work
100 Extraction
101 Getting There
102 Snowbird
103 The Lower Depths

104 Decisions
105 Scoop
106 Ladies' Day
107 Forced Play
108 Passing of the Guard
109 Mexican Holiday
110 Condor

1991 RECRUITS
111 Badger
112 Paralyzer
113 Attack Cruiser
114 Ice Sabre
115 Brawler
116 Battle Wagon
117 Interrogator
118 Major Altitude
119 Sky Creeper
120 Night Vulture
121 Cloudburst
122 Skymate
123 General Hawk
124 Sci-Fi
125 Heavy Duty
126 Crimson Guard
    Immortal
127 Incinerator
128 Big Ben
129 Red Star
130 Desert Scorpion
131 Low-Light
132 Dusty
133 Cobra Commander
134 B.A.T. II
135 Snake-Eyes
136 Tracker
137 Grunt
138 Mercer

PATROLS
SONIC FIGHTERS™
139 Law
140 Tunnel Rat
141 Dial Tone
142 Dodger
143 Viper
144 Lamprey

PATROLS
SUPER SONIC FIGHTERS™
145 Major Bludd
146 Falcon
147 Road Pig
148 Rock & Roll
149 Zap
150 Psyche-Out

FAMOUS BATTLES
151 Assault on Cobra Island I
152 Battle of Cobra Robot
    in Pit I

153 Operation: Wingfield
154 Battle on Fifth Avenue
155 Battle of Hindu Kush
156 Code Name: Sea Strike
157 1st Battle of Springfield
158 Alaskan Pipeline Battle
159 1st Battle of Sierra
    Gordo
160 Battle of Wash., D.C.
161 Operation: Scarface
162 First Battle of Pit I
163 Solo Assault on
    Destro's Citadel
164 Battle of Lucca, Italy
165 Dreadnoks' Assault on
    McGuire Air Force Base
166 Battle of Joe at Snake-Eyes'
    Cabin
167 Firefight at Staten Island
    Mall
168 Air Battle: Skystriker vs.
    Rattler
169 Sea Battle: WHALE vs
    Hydrofoils
170 Firefight at the Carnival
171 Raid into Sierra Gordo
172 Battle of Joe Air-Sea
    Base
173 First Assault of New
    Cobra Island

HONOR ROLL
174 Serpentor
175 Zartan
176 Dr. Mindbender
177 Raptor
178 Golobulus
179 Nemesis Enforcer
180 Royal Guard
181 Crystal Ball
182 General Flagg
183 Breaker
184 Quick Kick
185 Heavy Metal
186 Thunder
187 Crank Case
188 Blocker
189 Avalanche
190 Blaster
191 Crazy Legs
192 Maverick
193 Knockdown
194 Doc
195 Sneak Peek
196 Croc Master
197 Voltar
198 Firefly
199 Checklist 1
200 Checklist 2

Distributed exclusively by Impel Marketing Inc.

FACTORY CHECKLIST

GILLIGAN'S ISLAND (55)

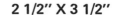

The antics of Bob Denver and the rest of the Gilligan's Island crew have been preserved for collectors and fans in this Topps set of 1965. The fronts contain black and white photos surrounded by white borders. The backs are done in "filmclip" style so that a complete set could be fanned to produce a short action sequence. The cards are numbered on the back only.

Complete sets are difficult to find in top grade and command a 35% premium, which is reflected in the set prices listed below.

ITEM	MINT	EX
Set	480.00	375.00
Card	6.50	5.00
Wrapper	--	30.00
Box	--	150.00

1 You'll Be Safe Skipper! Only if Stand behind You!
2 Gee Skipper, You Pop Up in the Strangest Places!
3 Somebody Call for a Handy Man?
4 Are You Sure this Will Go Up? Yeah! But I Don't Know if It'll Come Down!
5 Don't Hit Them Too Hard! They're Only Eggs!
6 Stop Crying, Skipper, I'll Always Be with You! That's Why I'm Crying!
7 Gee, I Thought You Were the Statue of Liberty!
8 You Said Drop Everything, so I Dropped the Logs on the Radio!
9 It's a Bird! It's a Plane! No, It's Gilligan!
10 You First!
11 If You Say One Word I'll Kill Myself! What's the Word?
12 What Could Go Wrong with Me at the Wheel?
13 It's the Footprint of a Horrible Monster! You Ought to Know, Skipper, You Just Made It!
14 Always Happy to Lend a Hand, Skipper!
15 Drink this and You'll Feel Like a Million Dollars! Yeah, All Green and Wrinkled!
16 My Gosh, It Does Look Like Gilligan!
17 There's Something Fishy about this Place!
18 Bob Denver
19 You're So Strong, So Brave, So Fearless! You're So Wrong!
20 Are You Sure We're Safe from Gilligan in Here?
21 Everything I Say to You Goes in One Head and out the Other!
22 Does Neatness Count?
23 Why Did I Sit on that Ant Hill?
24 Are You Sure Tarzan Started this Way?
25 Bang
26 I Think the Radio Is Fixed! Yeah? See if You Can Get Some Rock 'n Roll Music!
27 A Sentry Must Always Be Alert!
28 Ever Have a Fish in Your Mouth?
29 Gilligan, Investigate those Strange Noises. Those Are My Knees Knocking!
30 Where Are We Going on this Raft? Straight Down!
31 Gee, We Could Be Stuck Here for Years!
32 One False Move and I'll Shoot!
33 Where'd Everybody Go?
34 I Wonder What the Skipper Had in Mind with this?
35 I Don't Know What I'd Do without You, but I'd Love to Try!
36 I'm a Witch Doctor Making a House Call!
37 Gilligan to the Rescue! Don't Bother. Oh No! We've Got Enough Troubles Right Now.
38 Can You See Anthing? Yeah, the Back of Your Head!
39 What a Crazy Time to Gargle!
40 Only an Idiot Would Fly this Plane! Happy Landing, Skipper!
41 Why'd I Have to be Stuck on the Same Island with You? I Guess You're Just Lucky!
42 Anyone for a Showdown!
43 Aw Come One, Stick 'em Up!!
44 Uh-oh, the Skipper Stepped in My Animal Trap!
45 They'll Never Find Me in this Poison Ivy!
46 I'm Starting My Own Fan Club!
47 I Think I'm Losing My Mind! Don't Worry! You'll Never Miss It!
48 Who's the Wise Guy Who Said "Go Jump in the Lake"?
49 It's Time You Learned Something about Sailing! I Think It's Time I Learned Something about Swimming.
50 Let Me at Him! Let Me at Him! Don't Listen to Him! Don't Listen to Him!
51 I'm the Brains of this Outfit!
52 I'm Plane Crazy about Flying!
53 I Shouldn't Have Made a Hole in the Boat to Let the Water Out!
54 I Think I'm Seasick. When We're Stuck in the Sand?
55 The Castaways

REGULAR CARD   PROOF PHOTO

REGULAR CARD

PROOF PHOTO

Photos courtesy of "The Original Gilligan's Island Fan Club."

GLITTER GLOVE (14 & 28 & ?)

TWO SIZES

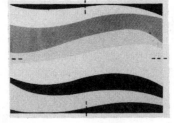

Fleer's "Glitter Glove" appears to be a take-off inspired by Michael Jackson's famous piece of apparel. The component parts of this set are two sizes of paper-backed, glitter-finish stickers (2 1/2" X 3 1/2" and 1 3/4" X 2 1/2") and standard size cardboard "Wild Cards." The big sticker sheets have large diecut glove designs of different colors plus an additional small diecut design. The smaller sticker sheets have either two or three diecut designs each. The peel-off stickers from either size sheet can be placed on the "Wild Cards," which are designed to be cut, on the lines provided, and assembled into a mobile or other "Wild Sculpture." There are 14 different large and 28 different small sticker sheets in the set. Since the Wild Cards are all identical and may be used in a variety of ways, no set price is listed.

ITEM	MINT	EX
Stickers		
Large	.25	.20
Small	.25	.20
Wild Card	.15	.10
Wrapper	--	.35
Box	--	4.00

GLOW WORMS (?)   2 1/16" X 3 9/16"

"Magic Glow Worms and Bed Bugs" is the full description of this Fleer set as it appears on  the wrapper. The insects and related signs ("Beware of the Bug," etc.) are rub-off tattoos with adhesive backs that can be applied directly to the skin without using water. One sheet of tattoos (2 1/16" X 3 9/16") and one instruction card (2 1/2" X 3 15/16") came in each 5-cent pack. The "glow in the dark" properties of the tattoos are activated by holding them close to light.

ITEM	MINT	EX
Sheet	1.00	.75
Instruction card	.35	.25
Wrapper	––	3.00
Box	––	10.00

GO–GO BUTTONS (24)   2 3/8" DIA.

This set, manufactured in Japan and distributed by Topps, consists of 24 cardboard buttons wth plastic overlays engineered to make the designs appear to move. The buttons are assigned numbers on the checklist printed on the back of the box but are themselves not numbered. The attachment mechanism is a safety pin and the word "Japan" is printed below it. Go-Go Buttons were sold in 10-cent boxes without gum.

ITEM	MINT	EX
Set	160.00	120.00
Button	6.00	4.50
Box	35.00	25.00
Display box	––	100.00

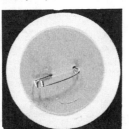

COLLECT THE ENTIRE SET OF GO GO BUTTONS

1 I'm A Lover	13 Drive You Crazy
2 Greatest Authority	14 Action
3 Come Into My Arms	15 Get On The Ball
4 I'm A Big Wheel	16 Confused?
5 Genius	17 Do Not Disturb
6 Get Moving!	18 I Dig You
7 Pull Yourself Together	19 Get Lost
8 Let's Twist	20 Ain't I Grand
9 Keep Calm	21 Cool It!
10 Don't Bug Me	22 Yicch!
11 Kiss Me Quick!	23 I'm A Swinger
12 I Love Me.	24 Nuts To You

GOMER PYLE (66)   2 1/2" X 3 1/2"

The television series "Gomer Pyle" provided the inspiration for this Fleer set issued in 1965. The photographs are black and white, and the cards have white borders. A line of dialogue is located underneath the picture. The backs have the "Sergeant-yelling-in-Gomer's ear" design imprinted in blue, and a blue-line box encloses a joke (printed in black ink). The 66 cards are numbered on the reverse. Gomer Pyle was predominantly distributed in cellophane vending packs and boxes rather than in regular gum packs, which accounts for the low value of the cards in comparison to the value of the wrapper.

ITEM	MINT	EX
Set	60.00	47.50
Card	.75	.60
Wrapper	--	50.00
Box	--	150.00

1 I Can See You'll Need My Special Attention, Pyle!
2 You Mean They Taught Him To Cut Hair This Way??
3 Every Marine's Creed: May That Lousy DI Choke On His Stinkin' Whistle!
4 Sergeant, I Hates To Say It, But You Just Don't Whistle Pretty!
5 Pyle, Am I In Good Voice Today?
6 I Must Be Slippin'...Two Days With Me and You Can Still Smile!
7 Pyle, Only You Could Get A Mop Stuck In A Bucket!
8 Ah Sure Love It Here in the Marines. Ah Kin Be Workin' and Layin' Down at the Same Time.
9 Sergeant Told Me I Was In G-2. That Ain't Intelligence. I'm In Garbage.
10 On This Entire Base We Got the Cleanest Area and Ah Got the Wettest Socks.
11 The Sergeant Is All For Safety. He said Dig A Hole 6' Wide, 6' Long and 6' Deep—To Bury A Match.
12 Cain't Remember What the Sergeant Said: 'Paint the Door-Post or Paint Every Door on the Post?'
13 That Funny Sergeant Put Me In G-2 Again!
14 The Big Wind From Winnetka!
15 It's Got So Ah Sweep When Ah Sleep and Sleep When Ah Sweep.
16 Pyle You've Got To Stop Eating Those Garlic and Onion Sandwiches!
17 What'd Ya Mean Ya Can't Count Past 50...I'll Count...48, 49, 50, 1, 2, 3, 4, 5.
18 While You're Down There Pyle, Check Those Cracks For Dirt.
19 I'm So Tired, Mah Hair Won't Even Stand Up.
20 Sorry Sergeant, But I Thought the General Would Like A Piece of My Licorice.
21 I'd Sure Hate to Meet the Spider That Spun This Web.
22 Guess the Sergeant Was Right When He Called Me Leadfoot.
23 Don't Look So Miserable, Pyle...Be Happy and Smiling Like Me.
24 That Simple Grin Won't Get You Out of This Goof Up, Pyle.
25 No, Not For Cleaning Your Toenails....Guess Again, Pyle!
26 Pyle, I'll Pick My Own Teeth, Thanks!
27 Ain't Anybody Can Look As Mean and Vicious As You Sergeant.
28 Pyle, What Could Possibly Make You Think of Me As Your Enemy?
29 Here, Just Take A Whiff of Mah Letter.
30 Ah Sure Hope She Didn't Get Carried Away...It'd Be Embarrassin'.
31 SHAZAM!
32 Looky Here Sergeant What I Got In the Mail.
33 Don't Grind Your Teeth Like That Sergeant...You'll Wear 'Em Right Down to the Nubbins.
34 Happy Days, Happy Days, A Four Leaf Clover.
35 Mah Aunt Ruby Found A Four Leaf Clover Once and Now She's 110 Years Old.
36 Cousin Icabod Never Found A Four-Leaf Clover and Cother Day he Fell Down the Well and ' Most Drown.
37 Ever Since I Come Here Sergeant, I Noticed You Ain't Been Very Happy.
38 Look, Sergeant, Guess Who Won?
39 Golly, Sergeant, You and Uncle Sam are Just Too Generous.
40 SHAZAM! Looky Here!!
41 Gosh Did Your Momma Get Herself Lost Little Feller?
42 Now. You Just Pretend You're A Regular Pussy-cat.
43 Ain't He Jest the Cutest Little Feller You Ever Saw?
44 It Ain't the Smell So Much, Sergeant, It's Just That It Makes Your Eyes Water.
45 I Don't Make the Rules... You Jest Cain't Enlist.
46 Hey There, Li'l Ol' King Snake. Don't It Feel Good To Get Up Off Your Belly For A While?
47 Snakes Are Just Like People. You Grin At 'Em and They'll Grin Right Back At'cha.
48 From Uncertainty Directly to Confusion.
49 If I Thought It Was Possible, Pyle, I'd Ask You To Help Me By Thinking.
50 The Smell of That Cigar Sure Takes Me Home. Sort'a Like Leaves Burnin' in the Fall.
51 Do You Always Turn Green on the First Puff Sergeant?
52 In the Field, Pyle, You Eat Berries, Roots, Fruit All Raw!
53 Hope Sergeant Carter Found Some of Those Fruits and Berries for Dessert.
54 All I Need Now Is Some Turnip Greens, Hush Puppies and Black Eyed Peas.
55 Pyle, I Might Make A Marine Out of You Yet!
56 I Said I'd Find Us Water If I Hadda Dig to China. And I Think I Just Hit A Rickshaw.
57 A Drip Looking For A Drop.
58 No, Pyle, I'm Not Doing Anything Important. I Just Like to Get All Hot, Dirty and Sore Digging Holes.
59 Water?? I Don't Believe It Pyle. The Only Water You Could Find Is the Water On Your Brain.
60 What'd You Say, Sergeant? I'm Surrounded By What Kinda Ivy?
61 'Do I Look Like A Big, Ugly Bear, Pyle?' 'Well, Sir...' 'Don't Answer That Pyle!'
62 Miss, This Little Two-Seater Was Made For You and Sergeant Carter. Let's Try and Forget Private Pyle.
63 I'll Kill Him, 1001; I'll Kill Him, 1002; I'll Kill Him, 1003...
64 Wipe the Stupid Look Off Your Face, Stupid!
65 Gomer Pyle and Friend.
66 Well, I Finally Made It Fellers... Gomer Pyle, USMC—SHAZAM!

Looky Here Sergeant What I Got In the Mail.

Don't Grind Your Teeth Like That Sergeant . You'll Wear 'Em Right Down to the Nubbins

GONG SHOW (66 & 10)

2 1/2" X 3 3/8"

An then there was the Gong Show. Any TV show which has so much impact that it adds expressions to the English language ("You're gonna get gonged," "Careful or I'll gong you," etc.) deserves a trading card set. Fleer responded to this dubious calling by producing this 66-card, 10-sticker series in 1979. The cards are white-bordered and have captions in a yellow strip below the color picture. The number is situated in a gong-mallet design on front. The backs are poster pieces of memorable Gong Show performances. The stickers have yellow borders and are not numbered. Note: set price includes stickers.

ITEM	MINT	EX
Set	15.00	12.00
Card	.15	.10
Sticker	.35	.25
Wrapper	—	.50
Box	—	6.00

1 "That's the Last Time I Eat Beans for Lunch"!!!
2 "I'll Have One Order of Fries, a Coke and a Tourist with Cheese to Go"!!!
3 "I Was Bald 'til I Saw the Folks at Harry's Hair Research..."
4 "Everybody Makes Fun of Me Because I Wear Glasses..."
5 "No Thank You, I Brought My Own"
6 Oh! I Swallowed My Bubble Gum!
7 "My Teeth Itch"
8 "That's the Last Time I Gong a Chicken."
9 "...Call Me That Again and I'll Peck Your Eyes Out!"
10 "Did Anybody Happen to Find One Contact Lens?"
11 "It's Not Nice to Fool Mother Nature"!!!
12 "I Don't Mind Walking This Way But I Keep Crushing My Hat".
13 "Excuse Me, But I Have to Blow My Eyes".
14 "Is It Hot in Here Or Am I the Only One Melting."
15 "That's Her...the Old Lady with the Knitting Needles in Her Hand".
16 "This Hat Is Just a Little too Tight."
17 "Love That Gong!"
18 "That's the Biggest Zit I Ever Popped"

19 "Mirror Mirror on the Wall... Oh, Forget It!"
20 "What a Fuzzy Lolly Pop"!
21 "Is This the Gong Show or the Gag Show"?
22 "Say...Who's Your Gardener?"
23 "Can't a Girl Have Any Privacy?"
24 "Why Do I Wear Two Pair of Glasses? So I Can See Past My Nose, Stupid"!
25 "Now Try and Get Me You Pigeons"
26 "Your What"?
27 "You Bite Me and I'll Have You Made into a Belt, Sweetie"!
28 "I've Never Seen Anyone Do That on TV Before"!
29 "Someday They'll Love Me for My Talent Not Just My Good Looks"!
30 "Jamie, Looking Up Your Nose Is Like Looking Into the Grand Canyon!"
31 "I Took Guitar Lessons from a Contortionist."
32 "Next I'll Attempt the 100 Meter Dive!"
33 "Does Anyone Have an Ouchless Bandaid?"
34 "That Does It...No More Exploding Twinkies on the Show"
35 "My Nose Was Always Running Until I Got This Chain."
36 "Take Me to Your Leader"

37 "The Only Problem with Large Ears, Is That I Have to Use a Mop for a Q-Tip."
38 "Oh I Love It"!
39 Jaye P. Morgan's Hair by Your Local Florist."
40 "What Do You Mean I've Been Gonged?"
41 "Sometimes We Get Some Real Trash on This Show"
42 "This Show Wasn't My Idea, I Wanted to Do "Operation Petticoat"
43 "Are You Sure Peter Pan Started This Way?"
44 "Call Me a Sissy Again, Jaye, and I'll Gong You!"
45 "At Last, My Very Own Barbey Doll"
46 "Would Someone Get This Caterpillar off My Nose!"
47 "I Guess If I Don't Make It as a Singer, I Can Always Sell My Feet for Key Chains"
48 "I Guess If I Don't Make It In Show Business I Can Always Become a Chandelier"!!!
49 "I Don't Care What Anybody Says, Before That Magician Did His Act I Had Five Fingers"!!!
50 "It's Tough Being Siamese Twins, But We've Managed to Lead Our Own Lives."
51 Jamie's Gonna' Gong Ya!
52 "Help! I'm Being Followed by a Flock of Pigeons"

53 "We'll Hide Out at the Gong Show. They'll Never Notice Us There!"
54 "Sometimes I Get So Mad I Could Punch Myself in the Face"
55 "I Don't Care If You Are the Green Giant, Get Off My Toe!"
56 "They Told Me There Would Be Days Like This"
57 "Hey You...Put That Down, You Never Gong the Host"
58 Sometimes the Acts on This Show Are Real Killers
59 You're Probably Wondering Why I Wear All These Funny Hats—So Do I?
60 "I Left My Horse Backstage... Actually He's on Next!"
61 "Would the Ballerina I'm Sharing a Dressing Room with Please Return My Clothes."
62 "Don't Feel Bad Harriet, We've Been Gonged in Better Places"
63 "Hey, Look at the Weirdo in the Funny Lookin' Hat"
64 "Mr. Barris—Have You Anything for a Headache?"
65 "Before I Went into Show Business, I Had a Job Proof Reading Eye Charts."
66 "It's The Best Way to Watch Most of the Acts on this Show."

GOOD GUYS & BAD GUYS (72)

2 1/2" X 3 1/2"

Leaf produced this 72-card Good Guys and Bad Guys set for distribution in 1966. Each card has the portrait — drawn in color — of a famous western character. The picture has white borders and the subject is named. The card number is located on the reverse, next to a data list and above a written biography. The cards are numbered from one to 73, with No. 40 not issued.

ITEM	MINT	EX
Set	100.00	87.50
Card	1.25	1.00
Wrapper	—	100.00
Box	—	175.00

1	Robert Ford	25	Crazy Horse
2	Tiburcio Vasquez	26	Red Cloud
3	Butch Cassidy	27	Pat Garrett
4	Sundance Kid	28	Samuel Colt
5	Frank Leslie	29	Jim Bowie
6	Richard Broadwell	30	Cochise
7	Texas Jack	31	Clay Allison
8	Santa Anna	32	Joel Collins
9	Rattlesnake Dick	33	Virgil Earp
10	Black Bart	34	Wild Bill Hickock
11	Joaquin Murieta	35	Johnny Ringo
12	Emmet Dalton	36	Elfago Baca
13	Pancho Villa	37	Jack Behan
14	Bill Anderson	38	Kit Carson
15	Ben Thompson	39	Luke Short
16	Reuben Boyce	40	NOT ISSUED
17	Elijah Briant	41	Sitting Bull
18	Bill Brocius	42	Jess Chisholm
19	Bill Carver	43	Bill Clanton
20	Thomas Ketchum	44	Allen Pinkerton
21	Yellowstone Kelley	45	General George Custer
22	The Younger Brothers	46	Geronimo
23	John Hardin	47	Chief Jeseph
24	William Longley	48	Davey Crockett

49	Frank James	62	Calamity Jane
50	Bat Masterson	63	Belle Starr
51	Quantrell	64	Judge Bean
52	William Brady	65	Cherokee Bill
53	Wyatt Earp	66	Rube Burrows
54	Robert Dalton	67	William Doolin
55	Henry Plummer	68	Apache Kid
56	Joe Slade	69	Ben Kilpatrick
57	Tom O'Folliard	70	Kid Curry
58	Sam Bass	71	Buffalo Bill Cody
59	John Chisum	72	Doc Hoiday
60	Colonel Mackenzie	73	Billy the Kid
61	Jesse James		

GOOD TIMES (55 & 21)

2 1/2" X 3 1/2"

The Good Times set of 55 cards and 21 stickers was issued by Topps in 1975. The color photos are taken from the television series and feature dialogue inserted in comic strip style. Of the 55 cards in the series, 11 have backs with a "Good Times Behind the Scenes" feature, and 44 backs are poster pieces with a small written section about the show. All the cards are numbered on the reverse. The unnumbered stickers are white-bordered and blank-backed. Note: set price includes stickers.

ITEM	MINT	EX
Set	25.00	18.00
Card	.15	.10
Sticker	1.00	.75
Wrapper	—	1.00
Box	—	7.00

1 Gee, Dad, You Look Cleaner than the Board of Health.

2 Michael, Don't You Know Any Little Words?

3 That Jacket's So Loud They Can Hear You Three Blocks Away!

4 What a Great Game—"Pin the Tail on the Jackass"!

5 Whatta Ya Call That New Cologne—Odor De Stench?

6 I Thought You Would Make Porridge Not Library Paste!

7 Son, You're Skinnier than a Stringbean with Malnutrition.

8 Now Remember, J.J. Looks Aren't Everything!

9 What's for Dinner? Ghetto Goulash?"

10 Well Strike Me Dumb—The King Has Come!

11 I Just Lost a Close Friend, My Appetite!

12 Cook Something That'll Do You Some Good, Sis—Like Brain Food!

13 Ever Get the Feeling We're Being Watched?

14 It's No Earthquake—That's My Stomach on the Growl!

15 Face It, J.J.—You're Just a Flag Pole with Teeth!

16 Do I Wear It, or Fly It?"

17 That's the Last Time I Say Anything Nice to Thelma!

18 Thelma, You Oughta Make It in Hollywood—in Horror Movies!

19 We're a Close Knit Family—Always in Stitches!

20 This Must Be for Thelma—"Learn to Improve Your Personality!"

21 J.J.'s Doing What He Does Best "Nothing"

22 Junior, Only You Could Make a Woman Dislike a Man in Uniform.

23 Don't Be too Eager—It's Only a Letter from My Principal!

24 My Report Card's Underwater Again—Below "C" Level!

25 Take It from Me, Michael, You'll Like Being a Sex Symbol.

26 This Family Sticks Together through Thick and Thin—Mostly Thin!

27 You'd Better Put Some Clothes on That Picture Before Your Mother Gets Home!

28 Militant Midget—You Will Not Boycott Breakfast!

29 I've Just Been Voted "Man of the Ghetto!"

30 Just Call Me the "Van Gogh Of the Ghet-to!"

31 Thanks for the Gifts—You Couldn't Have Given Them to a Nicer Guy!

32 I'd Borrow the Car Tonight, Pop—If You Had One!!

33 Things Are Pretty Bad—Even the Muggers Are Afraid to Go Out at Night!

34 Thelma, You're Outta Sight—and You Oughta Stay That Way!

35 You Think You've Got Problems? J.J.'s My Brother!

36 No, This Is Not the City Dump—Not Yet!

37 You're in Luck, Fella, Thelma's Not Home!

38 Hmmmpp...She Buys Her Face at the Cosmetics Counter!

39 Black is Beautiful, Thelma, But You're an Exception!

40 I Must Have the Wrong Notebook—This One Has Work in It!

41 Hey Clan—Papa Bear Is Home!

42 I Would've Painted Thelma, Dad, But I'm Not into Cartooning!

43 Don't Tell Junior, But I Think You're the Prettiest!

44 Says Here, Ned the Wino Fell Down Four Flights of Stairs and Didn't Spill a Drop!

45 Who Do You Think You Are? The Galloping Gourmet of the Ghetto!

46 Hey, J.J.—Is That Your Nose or Are You Eating a Banana?!

47 Ma, I Think the Chores Should Be Distributed in Order of Intelligence—the Brighter the Lighter!!

48 The Kids Voted Me Scarecrow for the Class Play!

49 Protest This Picture and I'll Paint You a Bright Shade of Red!

50 Say, Mama, Why Isn't "Jive Turkey" in the Dictionary!

51 There's Only One Boss in This Family, Son—My Belt!

52 Begone—You Jive Turkeys!

53 In My Crowd I'm Known as the Playboy of the Projects!

54 Cheer Up Folks, I'm Not Getting Older...I'm Getting Better!

55 J.J.'s So Skinny, He Can Use a Donut for a Life Preserver!

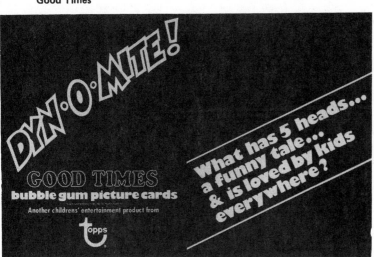

Good Times Stickers

"Are You Sure Don Juan Started This Way?"
BernNadette (Thelma) Stanis
"Call Me the Playboy of the Projects!"
Esther (Florida) Rolle
"Foxes of America - Eat Your Hearts Out!"
Good Times
"I'm Handsome & Bright...and Pure Dyn-O-Mite!"
"I'm King of this Castle & You're Gonna Be Crowned."
"I'm Michael - Also Known as the Millitant Midget!"
"I'm the Jaws of the Ghetto."
"In This Cruel World, Gook Looks Aren't Enough'"
"In This House the Belt is Boss."
Jimmie (J.J.) Walker
J.J. Is Dyn-O-Mite!
"Just Call Me Kid Dyn-O-Mite!"
"Thelma, You're a Jive Turkey!"
The Pint-sized Protester
We Love J.J.
Who's a Pipe Cleaner with Teeth?
"With a Face like Yours, J.J., Who Needs Enemies?"
"Yeechh! Ghetto Goulash!"

GOOFY GAGS (55)

1 3/4" X 2 7/8"

The "gag" cards of this series were placed as a bonus insert in packages of 1963 Fleer football cards, but are ignored by sports card collectors. The expressions are the usual mix of vaudeville jokes, insults, and witicisms and many of them have appeared in similar sets marketed by Topps, Price, and other trading card entrepreneurs. The print colors are black and red on cream or tan stock. The cards are not numbered and there are 55 in the set.

ITEM	MINT	EX
Set	30.00	22.50
Card	.50	.35

Goofy Gags

1. A Fisherman Is a Jerk at One End of a Line..Waiting for a Jerk at the Other End
2. As an Outsider, What Do You Think of the Human Race?
3. Avoid Tension
4. Be Neat!
5. Be Reasonable...Do It My Way!
6. Danger...Contains Radioactive Material
7. Don't be Unkind to Your Enemies... Remember, You Made Them.
8. Don't Just Sit There - Worry
9. Don't Think It Hasn't Been Pleasant To Meet You...Because It Hasn't
10. Get A Head...You Need One!
11. I'd Like to Help You Out...Which Way Did You Come In?
12. I'd Horsewhip You...If I Had a Horse!
13. I'd Send My Dog to an Analyst But He's Not Allowed on the Couch
14. I Don't Have Ulcers...I Give 'Em!
15. I Don't Make a Habit of Forgetting Faces..But In Your Case, I'll Make an Exception
16. If You Had Half a Brain You'd be Dangerous
17. I Like My Job...It's the Work I Hate!
18. I Love to Suffer...Kick Me!
19. I'm a Psychiatrist...Lie Down
20. I'm a Tiger...on the Prowl.
21. I May Look Busy...But I'm Only Confused!
22. I'm Not Hard of Hearing...I'm Ignoring You
23. It's Not The Ups and Downs That Bother Me...It's the Jerks
24. I Welcome Criticism...Write Yours Here
25. Kwitcherbelliaken
26. Let's Trip the Light - Fantastic
27. My Parents Are in the Iron & Steel Business..My Mother Irons & My Father Steals
28. No Trespassing - Survivors Will Be Prosecuted
29. Official U.S. Taxpayer
30. Of All the No Good Low Down Unscrupulous Coniving Cheap Propositions...I Like Yours the Best
31. Plan Ahead
32. Please Stop Talking While I Interrupt
33. Smile
34. Some People...Can't Ever Do Anything Right
35. Stand Up...Speak Up...Shut Up
36. Take Me To Your Leader
37. Tell Me All You Know...I've Got a Minute to Spare
38. The Creep
39. Think...It May Be a New Experience
40. Use Your Head...It's the Little Things that Count
41. Watch Your Language...Lancoa... Lingua...&*†ssH&x!!
42. We Aim For Accuracy (y is inverted)
43. We Are Sorry There is a Mistake on Your Order...The Man Responsible Will Be Executed Tonight!
44. Well, We Can't All Be Normal!
45. We're Friends Till the End...This Is the End
46. When I Want Your Opinion I'll Give It to You!
47. Wolf Patrol
48. Work Fascinates Me...I Can Sit and Watch It for Hours!
49. You Don't Have To Be Crazy To Work Here...But It Helps!
50. You Here Again?...Another Hour Wasted
51. You Should Be on the Stage...There's One Leaving at Sundown!
52. Your Conversation Has Only One Defect...A Poor Choice of Subject Matter
53. You're Different
54. Your Story Has Touched My Heart... Never Before Have I Met Anyone With More Troubles than You Have
55. Your Visit Has Climaxed an Already Dull Day

GOOFY GOGGLES (12)

"Have Fun and Block The Sun!!" That's the come-on Topps printed on the paper envelope containing a pair of Goofy Goggles. Each package sold for 10 cents and twelve

IRREGULAR

imaginative designs were available. The glasses are made of cardboard and the wearer sees through slits cut into the design. The goggles were made in Japan and all twelve pictured on the back of each wrapper.

ITEM	MINT	EX
Set	265.00	200.00
Goggles	20.00	15.00
Wrapper	--	75.00

Come Fly With Me
Get Lost
Guess Who?
Here's My Heart - Here's My Heart
I'm Cool
I've Got My Eyes On You

Kiss Me
Let's Have A Ball
Please Ignore Me
Stop - Stop
Stop Wasting My Time
What's Cooking

274

GOONIES (86 & 15)

A typical card of this series contains a color photograph from the movie, or an "off-camera" shot, surrounded by "parchment" frame lines and black borders. The backs have a short text and the card number, and there are 84 story cards in all. The first card in the series is a title card which introduces "Goonies" as an "outrageous, thrill-packed adventure movie"; the last card in the set is a checklist. Of the 15 diecut stickers, only one picture (No. 3) is identical to that appearing on a story card. The backs of the sticker-cards are puzzle pieces and there are different pieces possible for Nos. 1-2-4-7-9-10-15. The wrapper depicting "Sloth" is red and the one showing "The Goonies" gang is blue. Note: set price includes stickers.

ITEM	MINT	EX
Set	12.00	9.00
Card	.10	.07
Sticker	.35	.25
Wrappers (2) ea.	--	.35
Box	--	4.00

Special effects artists have been especially prolific in the past two decades with film after film in the science fiction and horror genres requiring their special talents. There was even a movie based on the adventures of a special effects professional ("FX") and some of the scenes from it were both spectacular and hilarious. "Grande Illusions" is a card set, issued in 1988 by Imagine Inc., that spotlights the work of fx specialist Tom Savini. Some of the cards show monsters in complete or semi-complete form, while others picture Savini working on ghouls, goblins, and - occasionally - a live human being (make-up). All of the card fronts are color photographs with "film clip" borders on two sides. The backs are dull compared to the fronts: they have a "Gotcha!" drawing, the set title, the card number, and a few words of text. There are 60 numbered cards in the series, plus four unnumbered cards with advertising for a variety of books, fanzines, etc. None of the cards has a caption or specific title printed on it, yet there is a checklist card (#59) which lists titles and this is the basis for the checklist printed below. For an extra $15, collectors can obtain the regular set plus a special #61 card autographed by Tom Savini. Note: some of the photographs in this series may not be fit for young children or for impressionable individuals of any age.

ITEM	MINT	EX
Sets		
regular	10.00	--
signed	25.00	--

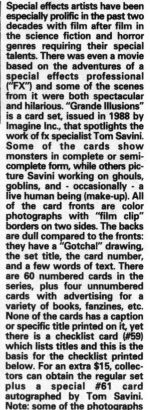

1 Demon I
2 Jason & Me
3 Understructure
4 Grandpa I
5 Baseball Zombie
6 Half-head
7 Japan I
8 Dr. Tongue
9 Babysitter
10 Ax Effect
11 Biker Zombie
12 Brain
13 Zombie I
14 Clowning
15 Shovel Effect
16 3 Heads #1
17 3 Heads #2
18 Zombie 2
19 Martin & Me
20 Operation
21 Raoul
22 Hacksaw
23 Baby Nemo
24 Jason I
25 Bullet Holes
26 Sculpting Lizzy
27 Phantom
28 Creep 1
29 Creep 2
30 Creep 3
31 More Lizzy
32 Lizzy
33 Making Raoul

34 The Spectre
35 Jason 2
36 Severed Head
37 Ben Franklin
38 Marshall Bust
39 Robochimp
40 Happy Snap
41 Zombie 3
42 Japan 2
43 Plate in Head
44 Autopsy
45 Tongue
46 Grandpa 2
47 Zombie 4
48 Lizzy 2
49 Leatherface
50 Morgan
51 George & Fluffy
52 Fangs!
53 Ted
54 Throat
55 Demon 2
56 Creepshow
57 George & Me
58 Two Toms
59 Checklist
60 Spider

61 Autograph
62 listed as Demon 3 but not seen

GREASE (132 & 22)   2 1/2" X 3 1/2"

The Grease set produced by Topps in 1978 consists of 132 cards and 22 stickers issued in two series. The first series cards (1-66) have pink borders and are numbered under the "Grease" logo on the left. The stickers (1-11) are blue-bordered in filmclip style. Second series cards (67-132) have green borders, with the card number once again located underneath the "Grease" logo. Stickers of this series (12-22) have borders of a mustard color. There are 44 poster backs and 22 "Movie Facts" backs in the first series; the second series has 44 poster backs, 17 "Story Summary" backs, and five promotional backs. Note: set and series prices include stickers.

ITEM	MINT	EX
Sets		
Series I	9.00	6.50
Series II	11.00	7.50
Cards (all)	.15	.10
Stickers (all)	.35	.25
Wrappers (2) (ea.)	--	.35
Boxes (2) ea.	--	7.00

1 Danny and Sandy
2 One of the more popular events!
3 The "Grease" Gang
4 Vince Fontaine
5 It's Teen Angel!
6 New arrival at school!
7 Danny Zuko—a track star?
8 Frenchy's fantasy
9 John Travolta as Danny
10 The Thunderbirds!
11 Johnny Casino and the Gamblers (Sha-Na-Na)
12 Stockard Channing
13 Sandy meets the Pink Ladies!
14 The Day of the Greaser
15 Dody Goodman as Blanche
16 Casino and the Gamblers do their thing
17 Rizzo and the Pink Ladies
18 Danny in demand!
19 Looking over the "new" Sandy!
20 A celebration in the sun!
21 Gettin' ready to cream the teacher!
22 A dazzled Danny!
23 Greased Lightning in action!
24 The big rama-lama-ding-dong!
25 Sandy makes the "grade"!
26 Danny and Sandy—made for each other!
27 Trouble at the dance!
28 Putzie and Jan
29 Some encouragement from Sandy!
30 Rizzo imitates Sandy at the sleep-over
31 The Rydell Cheerleaders
32 Sandy's new look!
33 Sandy (Olivia Newton-John)
34 Rizzo flips out!
35 Giving the dancing shoes a workout!
36 Trouble among the cheerleaders!
37 Eve Arden as Principal McGee
38 Joan Blondell as Vi
39 The T-Birds celebrate Summer Nights
40 The sleep-over at Frenchy's
41 The T-Birds!
42 Coach Calhoun and Principal McGee
43 Sandy's big change!
44 Presenting...Greased Lightning!
45 A song of young love
46 Rizzo (Stockard Channing)
47 The T-Birds and their dream car!
48 Dazzled by Vince Fontaine!
49 A real challenge for Coach Calhoun!
50 Rydell High's hottest romance!
51 Black leather Sandy!
52 Together Forever!
53 It's Danny at the bat!
54 Greased Lightning—man, what a car!
55 Sandy and Danny: happy endings!

56 Sandy, Danny and Kenickie
57 The night of the big dance
58 Portrait of a Greaser
59 The fine art of baseball
60 Danny—an unlikely athlete!
61 Thunderbirds are go!!
62 The ever-lovin' Teen Angel!
63 Romance at the dance!
64 A tale of two greasers
65 The auto shop rocks!
66 Danny asks Sandy to wear his school ring

67 Puzzle Piece
68 Puzzle Piece
69 Puzzle Piece
70 Puzzle Piece
71 Creation of a Dream Car!
72 Last Day's Big Bash!
73 In Search of Some Privacy!
74 Danny Gongs It!
75 A Swingin' Celebration!
76 King of the Dance Floor

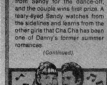

77 Kenickie Asks Danny to Be His "Second"
78 Master of Greased Lightning!
79 Keep "Cool". Danny!
80 Recounting Summer Conquests
81 Fontaine Steals the Scene!
82 All's Well with the Gang!
83 Has Danny Turned Square?
84 Kenickie in Trouble!
85 Lunch with the Pink Ladies

86 Having a Ball at the Frosty Palace
87 Is Sandy too Pure to Be Pink?
88 "Tell Me More, Tell Me More!"
89 Principal McGee Moonlights as a Referee!
90 Craterface and Cha Cha
91 The Rydell High "Jock"
92 It's Danny to the Rescue!

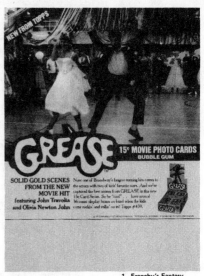

104 World's Greatest Greasers
105 The Soul of Teen Angel
106 "...be a school supporter!"
107 Rizzo—Caught in the Act!
108 Some Advice from Vi
109 Uh-Oh...Trouble!
110 Frenchy's Dream Man
111 Golden Words from Teen Angel
112 Rizzo's Up to Mischief!
113 The Fabulous Fontaine!
114 Pink Thoughts
115 Don't Mess with the Pink Ladies!
116 Cha Cha's Good Luck Kiss!
117 A Man and His Machine
118 Presenting Teen Angel!
119 Jock...or Jerk?
120 Dynamite Sandy!
121 Portrait of Teen Angel
122 Portrait of Stockard Channing
123 Coolest of the Cool!
124 Sandy Superchick!
125 Trying Out for Basketball
126 Danny—a Real Tough Dude!
127 Zuko the Gymnast!
128 Shades of Rizzo!
129 Meet the New, Improved Sandy!
130 Danny at the Wheel
131 Doin' It on the Dance Floor!
132 Rizzo's Fab Four

93 Kids of Rydel!
94 Knocking the Jocks Out of Their Sweatsocks
95 Danny's Summer Romance
96 Three Cheers for Summer Nights!
97 Revealing the Secrets of His Success!
98 Hot Duo: Danny and Cha Cha!
99 The Pinks Make the Scene
100 Casino's Big Night
101 Fun at Frenchy's Sleep-Over
102 Some Unkind Words for Blanche!
103 How Long 'till Summer Vacation

1 Frenchy's Fantasy
2 Johnny Casino and the Gamblers (Sha-Na-Na)
3 Danny Zuko—A Track Star?
4 Vince Fontaine
5 The "Grease" Gang
6 New Arrival at School!
7 John Travolta as Danny
8 The Thunderbirds!
9 It's Teen Angel
10 Danny and Sandy
11 Portrait of Stockard Channing
12 Coach Calhoun and Principal McGee
13 Rizzo's Fab Four
14 The T-Birds and Their Dream Car!
15 Meet the New Improved Sandy!
16 A Real Challenge for Coach Calhoun
17 Danny at the Wheel!
18 Doin' It on the Dance Floor!
19 Sandy's Big Change!
20 Coolest of the Cool!
21 Portrait of a Greaser
22 Shades of Rizzo!

GREAT AMERICANS (30)   2 1/2" X 4"

Another card set inspired by the Bicentennial, "Great Americans" was produced for Big Boy restaurants by CH Trading Card and Poster Society (Summerland, CA). The patriotic theme series has 30 color-artwork portraits surrounded by white borders and thin red and blue framelines. The obverse surface is glossy and the corners are rounded. The subject is named on front and a long biographical sketch is printed in blue ink on the back. The backs are matte finish and also contain the "Big Boy" logo, copyright date and manufacturer identification line, and the card number, and the card number in the set. There are 30 cards in the set.

ITEM	MINT	EX
Set	18.00	12.50
Card	.50	.35

1 Benjamin Franklin
2 Patrick Henry
3 John Hancock
4 George Washington
5 John Paul Jones
6 William Penn
7 Thomas Paine
8 Martha Washington
9 Roger Sherman
10 Thomas Jefferson
11 Nathan Hale
12 James Madison
13 Daniel Boone
14 Andrew Jackson
15 James Monroe
16 Betsy Ross
17 Daniel Webster
18 John Quincy Adams
19 Robert R. Livingston
20 Francis Scott Key
21 Lewis and Clark
22 Booker T. Washington
23 Abraham Lincoln
24 Theodore Roosevelt
25 Clara Barton
26 Alexander Graham Bell
27 John Marshall
28 Thomas Edison
29 George Washington Carver
30 Richard Byrd

GREAT MOMENTS IN AMERICAN HISTORY (24)

The cards of this series were distributed at Esso gas stations in 1969. Each card came attached to another 2-1/2" X 3-1/2" card which contained two prize stamps, part of a contest in play at the time. The trading cards have excellent, multi-color artwork scenes with card numbers and captions printed below. The backs, however, are simply an American history panorama with the set title printed in a black oval at center. The text for each card was printed beneath its numbered space in the paper card album available from Esso dealers (see illustration). There are 24 cards in the set, and for each of these cards Esso also created a very large "fine art" print. Most of the available supply of these cards and prints has surfaced in Houston, the home base of Humble Oil.

ITEM	MINT	EX
Set	40.00	27.50
Card	1.50	1.00
Album	10.00	7.50

(10) ALASKA BECOMES TERRITORY OF THE UNITED STATES (1867)

Collect "GREAT MOMENTS" ALBUM PRINTS
Ask your participating HUMBLE DEALER
for free Collector's Album

Save these Prize Stamps on Prize Stamp Chart,
available free from participating HUMBLE DEALERS.
Rules on Prize Stamp Chart.

PRIZE STAMP   PRIZE STAMP

Punch
Out
Win
Prizes

(23) An American Orbits the Earth

Space capsule Friendship 7, with Astronaut John Glenn still aboard, was hauled from the Atlantic near Grand Turk Island by the Destroyer Noa on February 20, 1962. Glenn had blazed a new trail by successfully completing an 81,000-mile, three-orbit trip around the earth after blasting off from Cape Kennedy, Fla. Three others assigned to Project Mercury also successfully made the orbital journey — Scott Carpenter (3 orbits), Walter Schirra (6), and Gordon Cooper (22).

Gemini followed Mercury. This series of two-man missions was launched to perfect rendezvous and docking maneuvers necessary in the Apollo Project, America's moon mission.

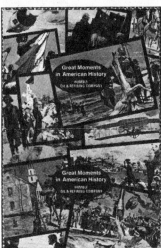

Great Moments
in
American
History

HUMBLE OIL & REFINING COMPANY

© 1969. Marden-Kane, Inc.

GREEN BERETS (66)

2 1/2" X 3 1/2"

The Philadelphia Chewing Gum Company ("Philly Gum," for short) issued this Green Berets series of 66 cards circa 1966. Each card has a black and white photo of Special Forces members and/ or political personalities. A distinctive green panel below the picture contains a caption and the card number. The card backs are color puzzle pieces.

ITEM	MINT	EX
Set	95.00	75.00
Card	1.25	1.00
Checklist	7.50	5.00
Wrapper	--	8.00
Box	--	50.00

1	The Green Berets	23	Double Specialist	45	Jungle Tuxedo
2	Freedom Fighter	24	Jungle Highway	46	Saving a Pal
3	Are You Man Enough?	25	Helicopter Bomber	47	Fast as Lightning
4	Ambush!	26	Airlift to Action	48	Delayed Service
5	Secrets of Survival	27	Silent Destroyers	49	Operation Swift Strike
6	Double Volunteer	28	Deadly Sport	50	Enemy Below
7	Emergency Exit	29	Back from Patrol	51	Scuba Trooper
8	You're Next	30	Equipment Check	52	Uninvited Guest
9	Mapping the Assault	31	Beating the Bugs	53	Deadly Art
10	All Aboard for Action	32	Ready for Anything	54	Jungle Hazard
11	Ready to Go In	33	Water Lift	55	Assault Leader
12	Taking Care of Their Own	34	Look Out Below	56	Express Elevator
13	Disguised Death	35	A New Leader	57	Always Alert
14	Tools of the Trade	36	Mountain Goat	58	Master of Any Weapon
15	Going Where the Trouble Is	37	Without a Shot	59	Teamwork Means Victory
16	Keep It Dry	38	What Hit Me?	60	Guts and Muscle Alone
17	Powerful Punch	39	Tough Training	61	Battle Taxi
18	Weapons Museum	40	Danger Lookout	62	Hit 'Em Hard
19	New Kind of War	41	Guerrillas	63	Modern Swamp Fox
20	Deadly Dozen	42	Signal Shot	64	Wilderness March
21	Fastest Way In	43	Radio Life Line	65	Chow Time
22	Borrowed Weapon	44	Clearing a Swamp	66	Checklist

GREEN HORNET (44)

2 1/2" X 3 1/2"

To gain an edge over competing companies, Donruss issued its Green Hornet cards in wrappers marked "Official Green Hornet Bubble Gum." The cards are color photographs with white borders, and a small logo appears in one corner. The backs are poster pieces and have a green area which contains the number and caption of the card. A line on the reverse reads "Watch the Green Hornet on your local ABC network station."

The Green Hornet and Kato arriving out of the night, surprise the jewel thieves as they are dividing up their loot.

ITEM	MINT	EX
Set	190.00	165.00
Card	3.50	3.00
Wrapper	--	35.00
Box	--	125.00

1 The fantastic crime fighter, The Green Hornet, is played by the television star, Van Williams.

2 Mike Axford, the crime reporter for the Daily Sentinel, does not know of his employer's double life.

3 Miss Case is Britt Reid's secretary at the Daily Sentinel and is one of the three people aware of the identity of The Green Hornet.

4 Kato has proved again the power of Gung-Fu by subduing four vicious criminals.

5 The Green Hornet says to himself, "we must recover the diamonds before the criminals do."

6 The Green Hornet and Kato arriving out of the night, surprise the jewel thieves as they are dividing up their loot.

7 Quickly The Green Hornet and Kato disarm the two notorious jewel thieves.

8 The third jewel thief darting out of the room is apprehended by The Green Hornet who renders him helpless.

9 "All right, fellows, the party's over!" says The Green Hornet arriving out of the stillness of the night.

10 Pointing his pistol at Miss Case, the criminal tells her, "Call The Green Hornet and get him over here!"

11 The Black Beauty entering the hideout is fired upon by the retreating criminals.

12 The Black Beauty has two of the criminals pinned to the wall as The Green Hornet starts after the other criminal.

13 "There he goes!" screams Kato as The Green Hornet leaps over the hood of The Black Beauty in pursuit.

14 "I see him, Kato. We'll soon show him the sting of The Green Hornet."

15 The criminals' leader attacks Kato with a knife and Kato seizing him by the arm throws him to the ground.

16 The leader again rises only to be rendered helpless by another of Kato's Gung-Fu moves.

17 As the Green Hornet closes in, the criminal knows his end has come.

18 "I've got you! Stand up and fight like a man!" yells The Green Hornet

19 With a left to the face, The Green Hornet has again shown his powerful sting.

20 "Well, thanks to you, Miss Case and Kato, we've put away three more criminals.

21 "I saw them running into the house!" says Kato as he hurriedly stops the Black Beauty.

22 Quickly leaving The Black Beauty, The Green Hornet and Kato streak towards the criminal's home.

23 The Green Hornet says to Kato, "Go around back, while I guard the front."

24 The Green Hornet, always ready for action, covers Kato's entrance into the criminal's home.

25 Kato quietly inches his way towards the open door.

26 "Watch it, Kato, I hear someone coming!"

27 Kato, springing into action, disables the attacking criminal with one blow.

28 The Green Hornet quickly tackles the second criminal in a short but deadly battle.

29 The criminals knowing the game is over, start coming out as Kato and The Green Hornet stand ready.

30 "Let's go, Kato, I don't think we'll have anymore interference."

31 The Green Hornet checks the bookshelves looking for the hidden compartment.

32 "Watch it, Kato!" The Green Hornet screams as Kato bolts upright to his defensive position.

33 Kato quickly unleashes a flurry of deadly and decisive blows at the criminal.

34 The final Gung-Fu move lifts the criminal from the floor and the battle is over.

35 Kato, turning quickly, realizes the Green Hornet is trapped and rushes to his aid.

36 As the Green Hornet rescues Miss Case, Kato yells, "Four more of the criminals are getting away!"

37 Kato quickly crosses the street and captures one of the criminals as he is about to steal the police squad car.

38 Another criminal appears from the bushes, but he too is quickly subdued by Kato.

39 "Get the police over here!" yells Kato as two more of the criminals are pinned against the side of the squad car.

40 Seeing the stolen car driving away, Kato unleashes his deadly dart.

41 The dart punctures the tire of the criminal's car—making his get away impossible.

42 "Let's go, Kato, our work is finished here."

43 As quickly as it entered, The Black Beauty fades from sight.

44 The people can sleep well tonight—Kato stands ready to help.

GREEN HORNET PLAYING CARDS (54)

2 1/4" X 3 1/2"

"The Official Green Hornet Playing Cards" were distributed by Ed-U-Cards in 1966 while the television series was stumbling through its first and last season on ABC. The 52 card deck contains "40 official action photos" printed on the ace-through ten cards of each suite, plus Green Hornet character faces superimposed on the standard body designs of the jack-queen-king. The joker card is the most interesting item in the set: it has a nifty color-artwork design which makes the photo-cards look dull in comparison. The small cardboard box is basically green, red, and white and it has a sample card (blank-back) printed on the reverse. The deck is generally found complete and in the box (the latter often has a piece of tape to hold the top closed) and for this reason, only a complete deck price is listed below.

ITEM	MINT	EX
Set in box	27.50	20.00
Box only	7.50	5.00

GREEN HORNET STICKERS (44)   2 1/2" X 3 1/2"

Greenway Productions and 20th Century Fox combined to produce the "Green Hornet" television series from which these stickers were adapted. There are 44 in the set and all the detail appears on the obverse. The designs are both horizontally and vertically aligned and each is numbered. The set was issued by Topps.

ITEM	MINT	EX
Set	275.00	220.00
Sticker	5.00	4.00
Wrapper	--	12.00
29-cent box	50.00	40.00
Display box	--	175.00

GREMLINS (82 & 11)

2 1/2" X 3 1/2"

There are good Mogwai and there are bad Mogwai, and of such "stuff" as this are movies (and bubble gum cards) made. Topps issued this 82-card, 11-sticker set based on the Spielberg film in 1984. The first and last cards are a title card and a checklist; the eighty cards in between have color photographs on the front and a short text on the back. The stickers are numbered and all contain diecut pictures of Gizmo or Stripe and his evil companions. In our display, we have illustrated an uncut sheet of stickers with the 10-piece puzzle on the reverse side. Some blank-backed stickers have been found and there is also a wrapper variety which does not mention stickers (valued at 50 cents). Note: set price includes stickers.

ITEM	MINT	EX
Set	10.00	7.00
Card	.10	.05
Sticker	.35	.25
Wrapper	—	.35
Box	—	5.00

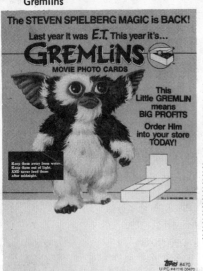

#	Title	#	Title	#	Title
1	Title Card	30	The Science Teacher	59	"The Gremlins Are Inside!
2	A Special Gift?	31	A New Discovery	60	Trapped!!
3	The Old Oriental Man	32	The Caged Mogwai	61	The Unruly Gremlins
4	Rand Peltzer, Inventor	33	(Un)Controlled Experiment	62	Blowing Up The Theater
5	The Mogwai	34	Evil of the Gremlins	63	One Gremlin To Go ...!
6	The Final Warning	35	"They've Hatched!"	64	Toy Department Peril
7	Billy Peltzer	36	Their Home Besieged	65	The Friends Separate
8	Co-worker Kate Beringer	37	Lynn's Big Risk	66	Stripe's Last Stand
9	Nasty Mrs. Deagle!	38	Mashed Gremlin!	67	Brave Billy Peltzer!
10	At Dorry's Pub	39	"Stay Away or I'll Spray!"	68	Hidden Horror!
11	A Present from Dad	40	Attacked!!	69	Gizmo Saves The Day!
12	Introducing Gizmo	41	The Inventor's Convention	70	Stripe's Final Moments
13	Billy's New Friend	42	The Invasion Begins	71	The Good Guys Triumph!
14	Gizmo's Boo-Boo	43	Jamming Traffic!	72	Our Victorious Heroes!
15	Poor Little Gizmo!	44	Deadly Creatures!	73	Return Of The Master
16	3D Comics? Yeech!!	45	Mrs. Deagle's Fate	74	The Peltzers And Kate
17	Best of Friends	46	Scared Silly!	75	Metamorphosis
18	Dad's Latest Invention	47	Crashing Through!	76	Goodbye, Gizmo!
19	Billy and Gizmo	48	Terrified Victim!	77	Artwork: Little Gizmo
20	A Splash of Water	49	Tracking the Gremlins	78	The Frightened Mogwai
21	More Mogwai!!	50	Sling-Shot Defense!	79	Artwork: Evil Stripe
22	Unexpected Guests!	51	Racing Against Time	80	Fiend On The Screen
23	Devious Stripe!	52	"They're Multiplying!"	81	The Young Performers
24	The Nasty Prank	53	Fury Of Stripe	82	Checklist Card
25	Gismo's Fears	54	The Captive Kate		
26	Friend...orFoe?	55	Saved By A Flash!		
27	Thoughts of a Mogwai	56	Kate's Revelation		
28	The Cocoons	57	Along For The Ride!		
29	Enter Roy Hanson	58	A New Plan		

GREMLINS 2 (88/11)

2 1/2" X 3 1/2"

WELCOME TO NEW YORK!

HERE IS WHAT YOUR COMPLETED GREEN BORDER PICTURE WILL LOOK LIKE:

COLLECT ALL 10 CARDS OF PICTURE A.

As if New York wasn't dangerous enough already, here comes Billy Peltzer and Kate Beringer to the Big Apple just in time to interfere in some peculiar laboratory experiments being conducted by the ominous Dr. Catheter. Could those experiments possibly involve Gremlins? You betcha, and soon Manhattan is reeling and squealing from a host of Mogwai misdeeds. Gremlins 2, released in 1990, proves that no movie is too old or too foolish to be "sequelized" and that no one at Topps can refuse a license deal. The two wrappers for the set are yellow, blue, and red and picture Gizmo and Mohawk. The stickers are numbered and captioned and have yellow borders surrounding the picture area. All sticker backs are puzzle pieces except for #11, which has a puzzle preview picture on the reverse. Note: set price includes stickers.

ITEM	MINT	EX
Set	15.00	10.00
Card	.10	.07
Sticker	.35	.25
Wrappers (2) ea.	––	.25
Box	––	2.00

#	Title	#	Title	#	Title	#	Title
1	Title Card	27	Mysterious New Arrival	52	A Definite "Thumbs Down!"	75	Web Worries
2	Gizmo the Mogwai	28	A "Hello" From Gizmo	53	Gremlin's Revenge	76	Spider Gremlin Rampage!
3	Daffy the Mogwai	29	A Boy and His Mogwai	54	Sparking Some Trouble!	77	Gizmo...Marla's Hero!
4	George the Mogwai	30	Clamp Discovers Billy	55	Attacked From On High!	78	We're Not Beaten Yet!
5	Lenny the Mogwai	31	Dinner with Marla	56	Futterman's Triumph	79	Divine, Simply Divine!
6	Mohawk the Mogwai		(& Friend)	57	Buried Alive!	80	On Top of the Trouble!
7	Metamorphosis	32	Birth of New Mogwais	58	Laboratory Lunacy!	81	The Original Party Animals!
8	Lenny and George (Gremlins)	33	Mistaking a Mogwai	59	Dr. Catheter's Demise	82	Having a Gremlin Ball!
9	Daffy the Gremlin	34	Unexpected House Guest	60	Forester's New Girlfriend	83	Zapped by Billy!
10	Mohawk the Gremlin	35	Mogwais on the Loose!	61	Mohawk, The Spider	84	Front-Line Futterman!
11	Billy Peltzer	36	Post-Midnight Snack!!		Gremlin!	85	Don't Rain on our Parade!
12	Kate Beringer	37	The Gremlins are Back!	62	Whooping It Up!	86	Clamp in Command!
13	Mr. Futterman	38	Gremlin Stew!	63	Tourist Attractions	87	A Soggy, Slushly, End
14	Mrs. Futterman	39	Confronting the Little Squirt	64	The Gremlin Shuffle	88	Gizmo's Farewell
15	Daniel Clamp	40	George is Riled!	65	He's Coming For You!		
16	Seductive Marla	41	Marge - Signing Off!	66	Building Under Siege!		
17	Executive Snoop Forster	42	Now You See It...!	67	Marla - Caught in a Web!		
18	Dr. Catheter	43	Clamp's New Secretary	68	She's No Dummy!		
19	Microwave Marge	44	Elevator Assault!	69	The Interview		
20	Grandpa Fred	45	In the Genetics Lab	70	The "Brain" Gremlin		
21	Mr. Wing's Final Stand	46	Animal-Vegetable-Gremlin!	71	Brainy Reflections		
22	A Mogwai in Mourning	47	Lady Gremlin?!	72	Dental Dilemma		
23	Welcome to New York	48	The Bat Gremlin	73	Daffy's Deadly Drill		
24	The Clamp Centre	49	Hit the Road, Bat!	74	Futterman to the Rescue!		
25	Chatting with Grandpa Fred	50	A Batty Escape!				
26	Catheter's Creations	51	"Familiar, Trite, Uninspired!"				

STICKER CHECKLIST;

1 Daffy the Mogwai	6 The Gremlins Have Arrived!
2 Mogwai Invasion	7 Daffy the Gremlin
3 Evil Mogwai Mohawk	8 Lenny & George (Gremlins)
4 George the Mogwai	9 It's After Midnight!
5 Lenny the Mogwai	10 On the Town
	11 The Bat Gremlin

GREMLINS 2 COLLECTORS' EDITION (88/11/22)

2 1/2" X 3 1/2"

According to Topps, this special edition of Gremlins 2 cards "is a must collectible for all Gremlins fans." It contains super glossy versions of the 88 cards of the regular set, the 11 original stickers (now with flat-finish backs), plus 22 "bonus" cards of The New Batch in exclusive "behind-the-scenes" views. The latter, which are lettered A through V, rather than numbered, show director Joe Dante and film technicians framing shots, coaching actors, etc. The box which houses the set has a glossy finish, bears a "Limited Edition" sticker over the top flap, and carries a 19.95 price. The "Gremlins 2 Collectors' Edition" was originally advertised as a mail-in offer on the wrappers of the original set ($19.95 postpaid) but is now readily available through hobby dealers. Note: this item is sold only as a complete boxed set and is assumed to be in "mint" condition (check the seal). The statement on the box that the set contains 22 stickers is incorrect.

ITEM	MINT	EX
Set	20.00	--

THE MOVIES STRIKE BACK!

BONUS CARDS:

A Director Joe Dante
B The Bat Gremlin Attacks!
C High-Flying Gremlin
D Flight Over Hollywood
E Dick Miller and Friend
F Spreading His Wings
G On Top of the World
H Above It All
I The "Secretary" Sequence
J Creature in the Cabinet
K Directing "Grandpa Fred"
L Chris Lee's "Death" Scene
M Lovely Ladies in a Jam!
N "Marla" and the Web
O Directing "Gizmo"
P Finishing Touches
Q The Movies Strike Back!
R Made for Each Other
S Painstaking Creation
T Storyboard: Bat Attack
U Storyboard: Girl Gremlin
V Storyboard: Mohawk/Spider

STORYBOARD: GIRL GREMLIN

FLIGHT OVER HOLLYWOOD

GREMLINS ALBUM STICKERS (180)　　2 1/8" X 3"

The Gremlins album sticker set was manufactured by Panini for Topps, which released it in June 1984. There are 180 stickers in the series, most of which show scenes from the Warner Bros. movie. A 24-page album with text and spaces to affix the stickers was sold for 25 cents. Note: set price includes album.

ITEM	MINT	EX
Set	25.00	18.00
Sticker	.15	.10
Wrapper	---	.50
Album	2.50	2.00

GREMLINS MOVIE STICKERS (5K)　　2 1/2" X 6"

Ziploc Sandwich Bags teamed with Warner Brothers to produce this sticker set for distribution in 1984. One panel of two stickers was inserted inside each box of plastic bags. As you can see by our illustrations, the same sticker could be found in different combinations on various panels. The pictures are color photographs taken from the movie or publicity stills; none are captioned or numbered. The five different scenes pictured here are the only ones on file to date. Note: the prices listed below are for full panels with stickers intact. Detached stickers cannot be graded mint or excellent. The dimensions in the heading refer to a complete panel; individual stickers measure 2-1/16" X 2-1/8" and have rounded corners once they are removed from the backing.

ITEM	MINT	EX
Sticker panel	2.00	1.50

Look for Additional
GREMLINS
Stickers in Special Packages of
Ziploc® Sandwich Bags From Dow
TM & © Warner Bros., Inc. 1984   Form No. 217-206-84

Look for Additional
GREMLINS
Stickers in Special Packages of
Ziploc® Sandwich Bags From Dow
TM & © Warner Bros., Inc. 1984   Form No. 217-206-84

Look for Additional
GREMLINS
Stickers in Special Packages of
Ziploc® Sandwich Bags From Dow
TM & © Warner Bros., Inc. 1984   Form No. 217-206-84

GREMLINS STICKERS (?)

2 5/8″ X 5 5/8″

EeeeK! The Gremlins are in my bathroom! Well, sure they are but they're only stickers which came packaged with Waldorf bathroom tissue in 1984. The stickers were printed in panels of two and they are not numbered or captioned. The format is color artwork and the picture runs right to the edge. Only the panel has the year and copyright holder (Warner Bros.) printed at the bottom. Each sticker measures 2-1/4″ in diameter and detached stickers cannot be graded excellent or mint. The length of the set has yet to be determined.

ITEM	MINT	EX
Sticker panel	2.00	1.50

GREMLINS

TM & © WARNER BROS. INC. 1984

GROOVY STICK-ONS (?)

This interesting series was produced by Topps in 1969. Each "card" is actually composed of smaller cardboard designs (7-13 per card) which have moisten-&-stick backs and scored lines for detaching. The checklist below is arranged according to the first name in a vertical row of names which appears on every card. (When a name is repeated, the one following it in sequence is shown in parentheses.) Some card fronts say "Wet back of labels and paste anywhere" and have a T.C.G. credit; others do not. None of the cards is numbered and the length of the set is unknown.

ITEM	MINT	EX
Card	4.00	3.00
Wrapper	––	40.00

Alec
Alice
Andy
Art
Barbie
Bart
Bob
Chuck
Dottie
Ed
Edna
Elaine
Frank
George
Gertrude
Gregor (Marty)
Gregor (Perry)
Helen
Isabelle
Jacqueline
Jean
Jim
Joan
Joe
Ken
Lil
Lillian
Nancy
Nick
Norman
Paula
Reggie
Tony
Vic
Wally

GROSS BEARS (29)

2" DIA.

In its everlasting struggle against the Forces of Cuteness, Topps launched a new weapon in 1985: Gross Bears. Each "Big Bad Button" is 2" in diameter and consists of a paper disc with artwork enclosed in a plastic holder. There are 29 designs in the set and they were manufactured for Topps in Japan. The buttons were sold, without gum, in small cardboard boxes. The checklist below is taken directly from one of these boxes; the buttons themselves are not numbered.

ITEM	MINT	EX
Set	25.00	17.00
Button	.75	.20
Button box	––	.50
Display box	––	5.00

1 Flare Bear	6 Pig-Out Bear	11 Everywhere Bear	16 B.O. Bear
2 Killer Bear	7 Heady Bear	12 Bonkers Bear	17 Go Bear
3 Flat Bear	8 Ram Bear	13 Spiky Bear	18 Lousy Bear
4 Barf Bear	9 Big Shot Bear	14 Tear Bear	19 Cyclops Bear
5 Goodbye Bear	10 Rug Bear	15 Frankenbear	20 Scar Bear

21 Punk Bear	26 Bat Bear
22 Zit Bear	27 Bicep Bear
23 Melted Bear	28 Butt Bear
24 Bony Bear	29 Bare Bear
25 Trash Bear	

GROSSVILLE HIGH (66)

2 1/2" X 3 1/2"

The Fleer Company—itself no stranger to "grotesque" art—tried to capitalize on the vul-gar fad started by Topps' GPK with this "Grossville High" set distributed in 1987.

The students of this mythical institution are drawn in a blend of "Weird-Oh" and "Weird Ball" art and are shown exhibiting a wide range of reprehensible behavior. Each of the 66 corner-peel stickers is named and numbered. The backs, printed in an unsettling combination of lime green and purple, are filled with miscellaneous features pertaining to Grossville High.

ITEM	MINT	EX
Set	10.00	7.00
Sticker-card	.15	.10
Wrappers (3) ea.	--	.35
Box	--	4.00

GROWING PAINS (66/11)

2 1/2" X 3 1/2"

The "Growing Pains" series of 66 cards and 11 stickers was produced by Topps in 1988, and judging by the results, the company had little enthusiasm for the project. The Seavers, one of television's most photogenic families, suffer through a painful "artistic" interpretation on the wrapper and a series of "mug shots" on the cards. Adding insult to injury, the "captions" are merely a series of mindless cliches that have no bearing to the television show or to the specific scene on each card. Children will no doubt get a few "yuks" out of them, but adults will find them painful. On the plus side, some of the card photos are interesting and the stickers, at least, do some justice to the major players. Ten of the stickers have puzzle piece backs; the reverse of sticker #2 shows a picture of the completed puzzle picture. Note: set price includes stickers.

ITEM	MINT	EX
Set	10.00	7.00
Card	.10	.07
Sticker	.35	.25
Wrapper	--	.35
Box	--	2.50

Growing Pains

1 Growing Pains
2 Alan Thicke As Jason Seaver
3 Joanna Kerns as Maggie Seaver
4 Kirk Cameron as Mike Seaver
5 Tracey Gold as Carol Seaver
6 Jeremy Miller as Ben Seaver
7 It's my new look - "Miami Nice!"
8 Are you sure you followed the recipe? Most cakes don't have brussel sprouts as an ingredient!
9 I'm not angry ... but could you please get off my toe!
10 Grounded again!
11 Yes, dear. You're the fairest of them all. Now can I use the mirror?
12 I know we're all tired. But shouldn't someone turn the TV on?
13 I love you, honey. But please don't glue the silverware to the table.
14 I'm a man of the 80s. I have a real hand in raising my kids.
15 I never met a mirror I didn't like!
16 Have I got a date tonight!
17 Sometimes a guy just has to make sacrifices. I'll only go on two dates this Saturday!
18 A cup of polycarbonate? ... Wait a sec, this is Mike's chemistry book!
19 I hope everyone wanted those burgers well done!
20 I think these high-heels are too high. I'm getting dizzy.
21 Yes, son, that's the best trout imitation I've ever seen!
22 It was either a ghost or I ate too much mocha pistachio ice cream last night!
23 It's not that your grades were bad, Mike. It's just that you failed "Chair Usage 101"!
24 Look for sea shells? Nah, I'm looking for bikinis!
25 It's not a treasure map ... it's directions to New Jersey.
26 That's lovely sweetheart ... but are you trying out for the cheerleading squad or the debate team?
27 Dad, isn't the pancake supposed to come down after you flip it in the air?
28 Three out of four cheerleaders agree! It's me!
29 It sure is quiet. Are the kids out or are we in the wrong house?
30 I'm not mad, Mike. I just think you should ask before renting the house out for a party!
31 I shall return ... my library books
32 C'mon, help me! I put super glue on my fingertips!
33 Don't be afraid, honey! You won't have to eat Daddy's cooking again for a week!
34 Snap the picture already! We can't hold this pose forever!
35 Either this is the wrong shopping bag, or we're eating a TV dinner ... I mean a real TV for dinner!
36 Someday son, we'll own a full-sized dining room table. I promise!

37 It's a cool dance ... now could somebody please help me get up?
38 A toast! ... with extra butter and jam!
39 I can't remember... is that my locker combination or my grade point average?
40 Am I in trouble, Dad? Or do you have lockjaw?
41 Okay, I believe you. You don't wear a toupee!
42 Aloha from the Seavers!
43 I tell ya, it keeps me from getting wrinkles!
44 Don't worry Dad. I saw this move on a wrestling show!
45 How's a guy supposed to look tough with flowers around his neck?
46 Are the kids asleep? Or did you mail them back to the mainland?
47 He's making dinner. Who knows the number for pizza delivery?
48 Okay - who starched my jacket?
49 I cooked dinner, and I get to do the dishes, too!
50 Is this a new look, or are you becoming a mime?
51 We're innocent. We just look guilty.
52 Okay, who left the sprinkler on?
53 What's the meaning of life? More important, do you know a really good place to get dessert?
54 Ready to throw in the towel, honey?
55 2 cool 2 B 4-gotten!
56 No, you cannot swallow goldfish with the other kids!
57 Lights! Action! Cameron!!!
58 Can I ask you a question? Am I cool or what?
59 Love me ... love my snake!
60 A cake only a daughter could love!
61 Trust me, dear, never put asparagus in a dessert!

62 Just what I wanted! A book about the principle exports of Ecuador!
63 When I grow up, will I still have homework?
64 Can we have dessert without dinner tonight?
65 Nah, I don't think it's impossible to be too popular!
66 You kids want to be psychiatrists? Where did I go wrong?

HERE IS WHAT YOUR COMPLETED BLUE BORDER PICTURE WILL LOOK LIKE:

COLLECT ALL 10 CARDS OF PICTURE

GROWING PAINS Stickers

1 Jason Seaver
2 Maggie Seaver
3 Mike Seaver
4 Carol Seaver
5 Ben Seaver
6 Alan Thicke
7 Joanna Kerns
8 Kirk Cameron
9 Jeremy Miller & Tracey Gold
10 Whatta hunk!
11 The Sensational Seavers!

THAT'S LOVELY, SWEETHEART ... BUT ARE YOU TRYING OUT FOR THE CHEERLEADING SQUAD OR THE DEBATE TEAM?

A TOPPS PICTURE CARD SERIES

66 CARDS   11 STICKERS

GRUESOME GREETING CARDS (44)   2 1/2" X 4 11/16"

Very few collectors have ever seen one of these "Gruesome Greeting Cards" distributed by Topps. It is thought they were a Halloween production, or possibly, a non-seasonal "test" issue. No wrapper or box for the set has been reported. The artwork on the fronts of the cards is done in brilliant flourescent colors and every design is captioned. The backs are printed in postcard format and the card number is located below the mailman sketch. There are 44 cards in the set.

ITEM	MINT	EX
Set	800.00	600.00
Card	15.00	10.00

1 You Are a Real Swinger
2 You're My Type
3 Give Me Your Hand
4 I'm Falling for You!
5 I Dig You
6 I Dream of You
7 Hold Me Tight
8 I ve Lost My Head Over You
9 You Bug Me
10 You're My Bag
11 There'll Never Be Another You

12 You Remind Me of My Mummy
13 You Made a Hit With Me
14 You've Got Me in Stitches
15 You Turn Me On
16 I've Got a Crush on You!
17 You've Stolen My Heart!
18 Give Me a Ring
19 You're Hot Stuff
20 You're Cool
21 I Can't Get You Out of My Mind
22 You Warm My Heart

23 Fly Away With Me
24 Beauty Is Only Skin Deep
25 I Missed You
26 I'm Under Your Spell!
27 You're a Real Cut-Up
28 You Go to My Head
29 Charge!
30 I've Got You Under My Skin
31 I'll Keep An Eye Out for You!
32 I've Got You in the Palm of My Hand
33 You Haunt Me

34 You Really Know How to Hurt a Guy
35 Let's Neck
36 You're Yummy!
37 I'm Hung Up Over You!
38 I Get a Kick Out of You
39 I Flipped My Lid Over You
40 You're Out Of This World!
41 You're a Wolf!!
42 You're My Honey!!
43 You Send Me!
44 You're Groovy

GUINNESS WORLD RECORDS (7K)   2 7/16" X 3 7/16"

The card illustrated here is #7 in a series entitled "Guiness World Records" which was packed into loaves of Wonder Bread in 1980. The card front contains a color artwork scene representing the record category and a short text alongside explains the details of the feat and identifies the person[s] who set the standard. The back of each card has spaces to fill in the owner's "personal highs" in the event and advises that "Guiness records are set by people who are much older and [who] have practiced for many years." I guess so ... the basketball free throw record, for example, is 2036 in a row (eat your heart out, Larry Birdl). The length of the set is not known and most cards are found with oil stains from the bread. The prices listed below apply ONLY to cards that are not stained.

ITEM	MINT	EX
Card	2.00	1.50

GUM BERRIES LIDS (55)   1 7/8" DIA.

The lids illustrated below actually capped tubs of two different types of Topps gum: "Gum Berries" and "Rocks O' Gum." There are 55 designs in the set, which was issued in 1971. A recently discovered uncut sheet of 110 Gum Berries cards (two sets) reveals that the 1 7/8" diameter lids were center-cut from 2 1/2" X 3 1/2" cards. This cropping resulted in the loss of a portion of artwork for most of the designs. We have illustrated an original card full size: the "Mr. Gelman" tied up in the chair was then head of the art department at Topps! Note: the checklist is arranged by the initial dialogue on each lid. The tub price is for an intact tub minus the lid.

ITEM	MINT	EX
Set	140.00	100.00
Lid	2.00	1.50
Tub	6.00	5.00

And Just What Prompted Your Decision to Study Mythology, Mr. Green?
Bill's Okay...He's Just a Little Bit Square!
Billy, Is That an Airplane Tattooed on Your Forehead?
Billy's Teacher Says He Ought to Have an Encyclopedia!
Bob, If You Don't Stop Playing Those Drums I'll Go Out of My Mind!
But I Did Shave This Morning Boss!
Can I Make the Five Thirty Train If I Cut Through Your Cow Pasture?
Crunchies — Atomic Submarine
Cultivation Methods in This Area are Hopelessly Outdated. I'd Be Surprised If You Got Three Pounds of Apples off that Tree.
Doctor, I Have the Feeling that People are Taking Advantage of Me!
Doctor, It Hurts Me to Breathe. In Fact, My Only Trouble Now is with My Breathing.
"Going Down"
Good Grief!.....I Need Glasses!!!!
Hair Spray [no dialogue]
"Harold, I Will Not Marry You ... So Quit Hanging Around"
Herman! I Hope I Didn't See you Looking at Joe's Paper!
Hey — How Did Mom Find Out that You Didn't Really Take a Bath?
Honestly, Howard....Sometimes I Think You're Afraid of Your Own Shadow!
How Come Your Hippie Boyfriend Shaved Off His Walrus Mustache?
How Do You Divide Fifteen Apples Evenly Between Four Students?
I Don't Expect to See You in Court Again!
"I Love You, Eileen...You're a Living Doll!"
I'm Going to Open a Pet Shop...Next Time You See Me I'll Be Among All the Dumb Little Animals!
I'm Sorry...I Thought You Were Somebody Else!!!
I'm Sorry...Mr. Gelman Can't Talk to You. He's All Tied Up at the Moment.
I'm Sorry You Can't See the Doctor Now. He's Practicing!
Is She a Tough Teacher?
I Think Your Brother Must Be Shy. He Hasn't Been Out of That Chair All Afternoon!

I Thought I Heard a Mouse Squeak!
"It's The New Improved Model!"
I've Come to Ask for Your Daughter's Hand
If Your Father Earned Four Hundred Dollars a Week, and Gave Your Mother Half, What Would She Have?
Lady I Haven't Eaten in Four Days!
Listen to This, "You're Admired by Girls for Your Good Looks and Personality!"
Miss Jones! I've Never Seen You Without Your Glasses Before! Why—You're Beautiful!
My Cousin Bertha Is So Fat It Takes Two Pennies to Weigh Her!
Name Five Things That Contain Milk.
Now, If I Had Two Hot Dogs and You Had Two Hot Dogs, What Would We Have?
"Okay, Sundog, Reach! This Town Isn't Big Enough for the Two of Us!"
"Pardon Me...Do You Have Any Spare Parts?"
Say, You Don't Seem to be Bothered by the Mosquitoes Around Here at All. Don't You Ever Shoo Them?
So There's a Monster on the Television...So What? Haven't You Ever Seen a Monster on the Television Before?
..."So Use New 'Boo'!...And Wash Your Sheets a Whiter White!"
Teddy — I Heard You Played Baseball Today Instead of Going to School!
That's Funny...I Don't Feel a Draft!
"Waiter! There's a Man in My Soup!"
What a Beautiful Child! He Has His Mother's Eyes and His Father's Nose!
What Did You Learn in School Today, Roy?
What Do Elephants Have That No Other Animals Have?
What's a Nice Girl Like You Doing In a Plate Like This?
What's That In My Soup?
"When I Told You to Wipe that Grin Off Your Face, That's Not What I Meant!"
Why Do You Refer to Your Girl as "My Little Bargain?"
Why Do You Think You Have To Go On a Diet?
Will You Boys in the Back of the Room Stop Passing Notes?

GUMBY AND POKEY TATTOOS (?)　　　1 9/16" X 2 1/2"

This interesting Fleer product was unknown to collectors before its recent discovery in California by Steve Powers. The outer wrappers measure 1 7/16" X 2 1/2" and are white with green and orange accents. They bear a 1968 copyright (Lakesides Industries, Inc.). The tattoos are printed on a slightly larger piece of paper (1 9/16" X 2 1/2") which was wrapped around the gum. The transfer designs illustrated are the only two reported to date, but it is anticipated that others will be found now that they have been identified and listed.

ITEM	MINT	EX
Wrappers (2) ea.	--	25.00
Tattoo	--	3.50

GUMMI BEARS STICKERS (?)　　　1 1/2" X 2"

It's a good thing that more collectors are not interested or aware of this product issued in Jiffy Pop popcorn, because supplies of them in unused condition are sure to be limited. Each 1-1/2" X 2" sticker depicts a Gummi Bear character and has rounded corners. The artwork is by the Disney Studios and their name and the copyright date of this product (1986) are printed below each figure. The backs advertise an instant win game which required peeling the sticker to reveal a prize; naturally, most of the stickers issued were probably "peeled" and have been attached to refrigerators, bedroom walls, doors, etc. for several years. Note: prices listed are for stickers with backing attached; peeled stickers cannot be graded excellent or mint. The set total is unknown at this time.

ITEM	MINT	EX
Sticker	1.50	1.00

"Hang-Ups," a previously unknown test issue from Topps, is being reviewed here for the first time in any publication courtesy of Bob and Jeff Marks. The format is similar to "Batty Book Covers" and "Krazy People Posters": large multicolor artwork drawings with humorous captions. The twelve posters recorded below were all drawn by Basil Wolverton and poster #18 is reported to have been created by Wally Wood. The number of each poster and the initials "TCG" appear in opposite corners at the bottom. Of the few examples known, some have folds — as if actually packed in gum packages — while others do not. It is believed that the posters were printed three to a sheet and that some were actually test-marketed by Topps to test public reaction. Unless more Hang-Ups are discovered, the prices for these unusual posters are likely to remain high as collectors compete for available specimens.

ITEM	MINT	EX
Hang-Up	100.00	75.00

1 You have everything a man wants — a mustache, a beard and sideburns
2
3 Kiss me! ... if you dare!
4 You look like a million — but nobody could be THAT old!
5 You're perfect ... a perfect idiot!
6 I need you like a hole in the head
7 I'll never forget you! ... who could?
8 You're the girl of my dreams
9
10
11 I'm sorry you lost your head over me!
12 Thanks for the lovely gift ... er, what is it!!?
13
14
15 I love you because you're different ... echk, so very different
16 You're too much
17 Your eyes are fascinating ... is that why they keep looking at each other?
18

HANNA-BARBERA MAGIC TRICK CARDS (25)

The title of this series, which was issued by Wonder Bread in 1974, appears only on the unnumbered checklist card (which is not often seen). The fronts of the cards have multi-color, cartoon-style artwork of various Hanna-Barbera characters from several children's shows: The Addams Family, The Harlem Globetrotters, Scooby-Doo, Valley of the Dinosaurs, Goober

and the Ghost Chasers, and Wait 'Til Your Father Gets Home. The card backs seem like an entirely different set: they explain 25 different card tricks and illusions with text and diagrams. Most cards of this series are found with stains as a result of being packed with bread, and cards with stains CANNOT be graded excellent or mint. The set is con-

2 1/2" X 3 1/2"

sidered complete with the 25 numbered cards; the unnumbered checklist card is seldom offered for sale.

ITEM	MINT	EX
Set	45.00	30.00
Card	1.50	1.00
Checklist card	15.00	10.00

1 Disappearing Finger ... Chet
2 X-Ray Glasses ... Pugsley & Cousin Itt
3 Moving Book ... Curley Neal & B.J. Mason
4 Mind-Reading ... Curley Neal & "Geese" Ausbie
5 "Newspaper Stand" ... J.C. Gipson
6 Bottoms Up Glasses ... Shaggy & Velma
7 Disappearing Watch ... Harry & Jamie
8 Color Caper ... Goober
9 See-Through Cup ... Lurch
10 Slick Arithmetic ... Katie & Glump
11 Balancing Bottle ... Tana & Lok
12 Come-Hither Dime ... Fred
13 Hatful of Cards ... Gilly & Ted
14 Got Their Number ... Pablo Robertson
15 Super Straw ... Stegosaurus
16 Paper Bridge ... Meadowlark & Granny
17 Whacky Arithmetic ... Debbie & Tinker
18 Magic Square ... Ted
19 Hocus Pocus ... Fester
20 Magic Seesaw ... J.C. Gipson & Granny
21 Brush-Proof Penny ... Granny & Cousin Itt
22 Hard-Boiled "Top" ... Tyrannosaurus
23 Flip-Flop Dime ... Daphne & Scooby
24 Stand-Up Egg ... Chet & Jamie
25 Diving Seed ... Katie & Greg

HERE'S **ONE** WAY TO SEE WHAT'S UNDER THAT CUP!

LURCH
THE ADDAMS FAMILY

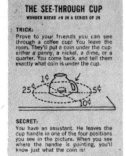

THE SEE-THROUGH CUP
WONDER BREAD #9 IN A SERIES OF 25

TRICK:
Prove to your friends you can see through a coffee cup! You leave the room. They'll put a coin under the cup: either a penny, a nickel, a dime, or a quarter. You come back, and tell them exactly what coin is under the cup.

SECRET:
You have an assistant. He leaves the cup handle in one of the four positions you see in the picture. When you see where the handle is pointing, you'll know just what the coin is!

HANNA-BARBERA 3-D STICKERS (6)

Oral-B
The Brand Dentists' Kids Use
Hanna-Barbera

FREE
3-D Sticker

FRED FLINTSTONE

Oral-B Hanna-Barbera
The Brand Dentists' Kids Use

1 3/4" X 2 3/4"

Wanda Chan, a hologram specialist from New York, brought this series of interesting stickers to our attention. The six stickers, each portraying a Hanna-Barbera cartoon character, were packed with a line of kid's toothbrushes manufactured by Oral-B (the toothbrush bears a color applique of the same character - but not the same pose - as the sticker). Although the expression "3-D" is used on the package to describe the stickers, they are really basic holograms with "depth" added through the use of refraction and design elements. Each sticker is packed in a plastic "bubble" on the cardboard package and this creates a concave edge which disappears once the backing is peeled and the sticker is applied to a surface. Note: stickers which have been peeled and applied cannot be graded excellent or mint.

ITEM	MINT	EX
Set	5.00	2.75
Sticker	.75	.50

Dino
Fred Flintstone
George Jetson
Judy
Scooby Doo
Yogi Bear

HAPPY BIRTHDAY BUGS (240)

2 1/8" X 2 9/16"

"Happy Birthday Bugs," an album sticker set produced by Panini in 1990, is a tribute to Warner Brother's long-playing cartoon character. Of the 240 stickers in the set, 216 have multi-color artwork fronts with peelable backs, and these have corresponding spots in a series of short stories presented in the 32-page album: "Rabbit Fire," "Feed the Kitty," "Birds of a Feather," "Strangled Eggs," "Devil May Hare," "A Pizza Tweety-Pie," "Zoom and Bored," "It's Nice to Have a Mouse Around the House," "Bully for Bugs," "Daffy's Inn Trouble," "For Scent-Imental Reasons," and "Devil's Feud Cake." Another group of 24 front-peel stickers depicts various Warner Bros. characters in poses; these have letters, rather than numbers, and their spots in the album are spread throughout the various pages and stories. The wrapper is yellow and uses the same Bugs Bunny "director's chair" design employed on the more detailed album cover. Note: set price includes album. Peeled stickers cannot be graded excellent or mint.

ITEM	MINT	EX
Set	17.50	13.00
Sticker	.07	.05
Wrapper	--	.20
Album	1.50	1.00

HAPPY DAYS (44 & 11)   2 1/2" X 3 1/2"

The Happy Days series of 44 cards and 11 stickers was issued by Topps in 1976. The cards have blue borders and a white frame line surrounding the color pictures taken from the TV series. The card caption appears on the front in yellow print, and the card number appears on the back. All the card reverses are poster pieces. The sticker set is characterized by a yellow band around the picture and it is numbered. Note: set price includes stickers.

ITEM	MINT	EX
Set	13.00	9.50
Card	.15	.10
Sticker	.50	.35
Wrapper	—	1.00
Box	—	10.00

1 A Chick is Like a Phone...Easy to Pick Up!
2 Richie—You're Such a Turkey!
3 Potzy, What Do You Want to Be if You Grow Up?
4 The President Can't Speak to the Fonz?
5 Cool is a Dying Art!
6 Some Date—We Actually Watched the Movie!
7 Easy Girls, One at a Time!
8 These Kids Today—They Dress Like Clowns!
9 These Are the Kookiest Basketball Uniforms!
10 Sorry Mom—No Kissing! What Would Fonzie Think?
11 Fonzie—The Coolest Thing on Wheels!
12 Aaaay!
13 Aaaay—You're Achin' for a Breakin'!
14 Fixing up Hot Rods is a Real Gas!
15 Take It from the Fonz—Cool is the Rule!
16 If I Were a Disc Jockey I'd Get Some Respect!
17 Sorry Richie—Buy Your Own Hoola Hoop!
18 Girls Are Like Vanilla Shakes—Delicious!
19 I've Got a Date with a Cheerleader—Six Months from Saturday!
20 Here Comes Da Fonz!
21 You're Cruisin' for a Bruisin'!
22 You're Not the Dragons—You Guys Are Just Drags!
23 Now for the $64,000 Question—What's a Nerd?
24 Have No Fear—The Fonz is Here!
25 Ice Cream at Arnold's is Not a Hot Date!
26 This Whole Family is "Cruisin' for a Bruisin"!
27 Eat Your Heart Out, Elvis!
28 Richie is Like an Apple—Rotten to the Core!
29 Whoa!!
30 No Date for Saturday Night—It's Enough to Drive Me to Drink!
31 Chalk up Another One for The Fonz!
32 These Kids Are Cool—But They Can't Charleston!
33 But a Boy Wants to Go Out with a Young Lady—Not a Center Fielder!
34 I've Got Class—And Not the Kind You Get in School!
35 I Just Met the Girl of My Dreams—She's the New Cook at Arnold's!
36 To Be Cool or Not to Be Cool..!
37 I'll Have 6 Burgers and 3 Shakes—Hold the Fries...I'm on a Diet!
38 Love is a Sweet Experience—Just Like Ice Cream!
39 You Can't Beat The Fonz!
40 This Motor Just Isn't Cool!
41 I Can't Fix Your Car, Guys! You'd Be Better Off with an Edsel!
42 If You Had My Looks, Fonzie, Chicks Would Be No Problem!
43 Watch Out Chicks! The Fonz is Dressed to Kill!
44 Big Wheels for the Big Wheel!

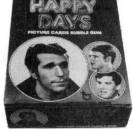

1 The Dynamic Duo
2 Sit on It!
3 The King of Kool!
4 Happy Daze
5 Lock the Fridge, Here Come Potzie!
6 We're Gonna Rock Around the Clock Tonight!
7 Don't Be a Fool...Stay Cool!
8 The Fonz Wants You!
9 Fonzie Forever
10 It's Not the Jacket—It's Who's in It!
11 Calling Mr. C!

HAPPY DAYS "A" SERIES (44 & 11) 2 1/2" X 3 1/2"

The second or "A" series of Happy Days, also distributed by Topps in 1976, has red borders and a white frame line enclosing the color photo on the front. The caption appears below the picture in yellow print. The backs are gray with a blue "Happy Days" title and frame line encircling the text. The cards are numbered 1A to 44A, with the number located on the reverse. The stickers of the A series have a red line enclosing the picture, and white borders. Both series of Happy Days came in the same wrapper. Note: set price includes stickers.

THINGS GO BETTER WITH RICHIE C.!

34A HAPPY DAYS

What is Henry (Fonzie) Winkler's secret love? Girls — of course. But aside from his many dates, Henry really gets a kick out of making all kinds of bowls and plates. One of his neighbors happened to be a pottery teacher, and after the first visit to her class, he was hooked on the hobby! "When you are at the wheel creating, the concentration is total. It takes your mind off everyday problems and pressures."

ITEM	MINT	EX
Set	30.00	22.50
Card	.50	.35
Sticker	.50	.35
Box	—	10.00

1A Here Comes Da Judge
2A I'll Lie Down and Wait for This Younger Generation to Grow Up!
3A Fonz, Why Do You Want 4 Photos of Your Motorcycle?
4A Cool It!
5A Heyyy Man!
6A Hey, Is Everybody Takin' a Holiday from Being Cool?
7A Fonzie's Diary Is Not a Good Subject for a Book Report!
8A Sit on It!
9A I Deserve a Break Today!

10A What's the Perfect Girl? 36—22—36, with Her Own Harley!
11A It's So Nice to Feel Wanted!
12A Mirror, Mirror on the Wall, Who's Coolest of Them All?
13A A Vote for Fonzie Is a Vote for Cool!
14A Hey Day, You're a Real Swinger!
15A I'm the New "Playmate of the Year"!
16A Into the Cooler with Mr. Cool!
17A Live Fast, Die Young, and You'll Leave a Good-Looking Corpse!
18A Only the Fonz Takes Aspirin with No Water!
19A Can I Have a $5 Advance on My 25th Birthday?
20A All Nerds on This Side of the Room!
21A Dad, I Think You Just Ate Your Napkin!
22A Would Somebody Mind Smashing That Alarm Clock?
23A Girls Always Go for a Guy in Uniform
24A "Fonzie Has Birthday Party— Traffic Jam Blocks City"
25A I Got a "C" on this Paper... It Must Stand for Cool!
26A A Harley for Father's Day? Forget It!
27A General Patton...General Eisenhower...General Cunningham?

28A Stealing Hubcaps? That's a Hanging Offense!
29A Hang on to Your Hat, Nobody Else Will!
30A I'm a Man of Few Words— All of Them Cool!
31A Driving Lesson Number One — You Gotta Sit Behind the Wheel
32A Sure I'll Play Ball with You, Where's the Bat?
33A Fonz, I Was Cool...But She Gave Me the Cold Shoulder!
34A Things Go Better with Richie C.!
35A A Chick Is Like a Motorcycle, You've Gotta Rev Her Up!
36A Sorry, This Isn't the County Mental Hospital!
37A Kissing Girls Is a Labor of Love!
38A Bring Me 4 Burgers, 3 Cokes and 2 Waitresses!
39A When I Go to College, I'm Going to Major in Lunch!
40A But I Can't Go On a Blind Date, I've Got 20/20 Vision!
41A Fonzie Sent a List of What He Wants for Breakfast!
42A I Had a Big Date Last Night, She Was 6'2"!
43A Hey Fonz, Let's Double — You Bring the Chicks!
44A Beauty Isn't Everything — But It's Sure Nice to Look at!

HERE COME DA FONZ!

1A To Know Me Is to Love Me!
2A Anyone Care for a Knuckle Sandwich?
3A Cool Is Forever!
4A Here Come Da Fonz!
5A Keep It Cool!
6A Fabulous Fonzie!
7A The Greatest Greaser of Them All!
8A King Kool
9A Fonz — The Man Who Made Milwaukee Famous!
10A Fonzie's Pal Richie C!
11A Whoa!

HAPPY HOROSCOPES (72) 2 1/2" X 3 1/2"

According to the copyright line printed on the back of each card, the Philadelphia Chewing Gum Co. issued Happy Horoscopes in 1972. The fronts of the cards have multi-color sketches and simple fortunes covering a two-month period. There are six cards for every astrological sign, for a total of 72 in the set. The backs contain a variety of features pertaining to the specific sign ("Hang-Ups,"

"Your Favorite Color," etc.) plus a blank line for writing in a name. The card number is located at bottom-right. Note: Sagittarius is misspelled (with two "g's") on all the cards of that sign.

ITEM	MINT	EX
Set	45.00	30.00
Card	.50	.35
Wrapper	—	5.00
Box	—	15.00

Happy Horoscopes

1 Aquarius — Watch Television	25 Gemini — Read 10 Books	50 Saggittarius — Find A New Hobby
2 Aquarius — Find A New Romance	26 Gemini — Show Your Special Talent	51 Saggittarius — Take A Motor Trip
3 Aquarius — Go For A Long Walk	27 Gemini — You Will Win A Contest	52 Saggittarius — Take A Plane Trip
4 Aquarius — Find A Job	28 Gemini — Take Her On A Picnic	53 Saggittarius — Buy A Motorcycle
5 Aquarius — Help Out Mom	29 Gemini — Cut Your Hair	54 Saggittarius — A Friend Will Help You
6 Aquarius — Make New Friends	30 Gemini — Start Your Diet	55 Scorpio — Watch The Stars
7 Aries — Learn To Ski	31 Leo — See An Opera	56 Scorpio — Plant Some Flowers
8 Aries — Visit A Friend	32 Leo — Learn Country Music	57 Scorpio — Get A Sun Tan
9 Aries — Watch For Love	33 Leo — Buy New Records	58 Scorpio — Learn About Horses
10 Aries — Go Fishing	34 Leo — You'll Meet A New Friend	59 Scorpio — Buy Some New Clothes
11 Aries — Join The Circus	35 Leo — Climb A Mountain	60 Scorpio — Eat Big Meals
12 Aries — Have A Party	36 Leo — Watch Out For The Holidays	61 Taurus — Think About Spring
13 Cancer — Go Sledding	37 Libra — Study Hard	62 Taurus — Meet Some New Girls
14 Cancer — Go To The Movies	38 Libra — Write A Book	63 Taurus — Graduate
15 Cancer — Meet A Singing Star	39 Libra — Visit The Zoo	64 Taurus — Enlist In The Marines
16 Cancer — Ask A New Girl For A Date	40 Libra — Take An Ocean Trip	65 Taurus — See A Doctor
17 Cancer — Buy A New Pet	41 Libra — Try Out For A Team	66 Taurus — Help Out Dad
18 Cancer — Learn To Drive	42 Libra — Save Money	67 Virgo — Shovel Snow
19 Capricorn — Take Up Ice Skating	43 Pisces — Plan A Summer Vacation	68 Virgo — Find A New Swim Suit
20 Capricorn — Learn To Dance	44 Pisces — Spend Money	69 Virgo — You'll Have A Surprise
21 Capricorn — Visit A Nudist Camp	45 Pisces — Watch The Moon At Night	70 Virgo — Buy A Hot Rod
22 Capricorn — Buy A Boat	46 Pisces — Stay Healthy	71 Virgo — You'll Grow Taller
23 Capricorn — Take Flowers To The Teacher	47 Pisces — Worry	72 Virgo — See Your Dentist
24 Capricorn — Plan A Big Holiday	48 Pisces — Watch A Basketball Game	
	49 Saggittarius — Make A Friend Happy	

HAPPYSTICKERS (?)

There are three parts to the Happystickers set issued by

Fleer. First, there is a group of 2 1/2" X 3 5/16" "real cloth" stickers (diecut), each containing one large face and one caption. Next, there are cards with a pair of peel-off sticker faces and captions on front (also diecut). Finally,

LARGE STICKERS
Be Happy!
Hello There!
I Love You!
I Should Have Danced All Night!
Joy To The World!
Kiss Me!
Let's Get Together!
Smile!
Smile, It's More Fun!
Smile, Ugly!

TWO-ON-ONE STICKERS
Do You Like me?/Just Ask Me!
How About It?/Let's Get Together!
Kiss Me Baby!/Your Feet Stink!
Let's Get Together!/What If We're Caught?
Let's Go Steady!/Stop!
Like Me?/Nope!
Smile!/I Can't!
Try It!/It's Fun!
You Look Lonely!/Help Me Fix It!

TWO SIZES

there is a series of 2 1/2" X 3 1/2" cards with advice about where to put the stickers (these are printed and do not have peel-off stickers). Our checklist shows all the titles known to date for the three groups of items.

ITEM	MINT	EX
Stickers (all)	1.25	1.00
Card	1.25	1.00
Wrapper	--	3.00

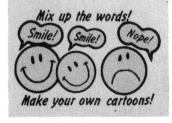

CARDS
Decorate Books and Book Covers!
Decorate Cars and Bikes!
Decorate Dresses and Mirrors!
Decorate Lockers! Use Your Imagination!
Decorate Lunch Boxes and Schoolbags!
Give a Happysticker to a Friend!
Mix Up the Words! Make Your Own Cartoons!
Put a Happysticker on Your Clothes!
Put a Happysticker on Your Hat!!

HARLEM GLOBETROTTERS (84)

The "Harlem Globetrotters" set of 84 cards, created by Fleer, is included in this volume since the basketball magicians are more properly show business entertainers than competitive athletes. The color obverse photos are mostly "mug shots" of individual players and almost every player featured has a run of two cards or more which run in sequence. There are also cards showing two or three players together as they perform one of their amazing tricks or formations. The card backs contain vital statistics and biographical text for players and explanations for tricks and formations. The consensus among collectors is that the cards were poorly designed and the photographs were badly composed. In addition, many of the cards were miscut and are off-center. Fleer also produced a short set of 28 cards for Cocoa Puffs (General Mills) cereal; these are almost identical to the cards of the regular set but have facsimile autographs on front and bear the "Cocoa Puffs" name on back (the numbering sequence is also different). There was a single sticker issued with the Fleer set; many collectors are probably unaware that it exists. Note: cards must be well-centered to be graded mint.

1 Bob "Showboat" Hall	29 Freddie "Curly" Neal	57 Doug Himes
2 Bob "Showboat" Hall	30 Mel Davis and "Curly" Neal	58 Doug Himes
3 Bob "Showboat" Hall	31 Freddie "Curly" Neal	59 Bill Meggett
4 Pablo "Pabs" Robertson	32 Freddie "Curly" Neal	60 Bill Meggett
5 Pablo "Pabs" Robertson	33 Mel Davis	61 Vincent White
6 Pablo "Pabs" Robertson	34 Mel Davis	62 Vincent White
7 Pablo "Pabs" Robertson	35 Mel Davis	63 Pablo and "Showboat"
8 Pablo "Pabs" Robertson	36 Mel Davis	64 Meadowlark, Neal and Ausbie
9 Meadowlark Lemon	37 Mel Davis and Bill Meggett	65 Curley Neal, Quarterback
10 Meadowlark Lemon	38 Mel Davis	66 Ausbie, Meadowlark, and Neal
11 Meadowlark Lemon	39 Bobby Joe Mason	67 Neal and Meadowlark
12 Meadowlark Lemon	40 Bobby Joe Mason	68 Football Routine
13 Meadowlark Lemon	41 Bobby Joe Mason	69 Meadowlark to Neal to Ausbie
14 Meadowlark Lemon	42 Mason and Stephens	70 Meadowlark is Safe at the Plate!
15 Meadowlark Lemon	43 Bobby Joe Mason	71 1970-71 Highlights
16 Meadowlark Lemon	44 Bobby Joe Mason	72 1970-71 Highlights
17 Meadowlark Lemon	45 Clarence Smith	73 Bobby Hunter
18 Curley, Meadowlark and Mel	46 Clarence Smith	74 Bobby Hunter
19 Football Play	47 Clarence Smith	75 Bobby Hunter
20 Meadowlark Lemon	48 Clarence Smith	76 Bobby Hunter
21 Hubert "Geese" Ausbie	49 Jerry Venable	77 Bobby Hunter
22 Hubert "Geese" Ausbie	50 Frank Stephens	78 Jackie Jackson
23 Hubert "Geese" Ausbie	51 Frank Stephens	79 Jackie Jackson
24 Hubert "Geese" Ausbie	52 Frank Stephens	80 Jackie Jackson
25 Hubert "Geese" Ausbie	53 Frank Stephens	81 Jackie Jackson
26 Ausbie and Neal	54 Theodis Ray Lee	82 The Globetrotters
27 Freddie "Curly" Neal	55 Theodis Ray Lee	83 The Globetrotters
28 Freddie "Curly" Neal	56 Jerry Venable	84 Dallas Thornton

ITEM	MINT	EX
Set	200.00	100.00
Card	2.00	1.00
Sticker	5.00	3.50
Wrapper	--	5.00
Box	--	25.00

The "Trotters" are also featured in a Hanna-Barbera set which is reviewed on page 295 of this guide.

CURLEY NEAL   "GEESE" AUSBIE
THE HARLEM GLOBETROTTERS

FLEER

COCOA PUFFS

HARRY & THE HENDERSONS (77 & 22) 2 1/2" X 3 1/2"

Halley's Comet stayed around longer than the movie "Harry and The Hendersons," but that didn't prevent Topps from making a card set based on the film. The front of each story card (75 different) has a color photograph, "vine" frame lines, yellow borders, and a white-print caption in a red panel. The backs are numbered and have a short text. Card No. 1 introduces the set (title card) and No. 77 is a checklist. There are 22 stickers with diecut designs surrounded by yellow frames and green, leafy borders. They are not captioned, and only nine have photos which do not already appear on the cards. The backs of the stickers are puzzle pieces. Note: set price includes stickers.

ITEM	MINT	EX
Set	12.00	9.00
Card	.10	.05
Sticker	.35	.25
Wrapper	--	.35
Box	--	4.00

1 Title Card
2 "Harry"
3 George Henderson
4 Nancy Henderson
5 Teenager Sarah Henderson
6 Young Ernie Henderson
7 Dr. Wrightwood
8 The Hunter, LaFleur
9 Nosey Neighbor Irene
10 George's Dad
11 Ernie's "First Kill"!
12 Oh My Gosh...What Is It?
13 He's Alive!
14 LaFleur On The Trail!
15 Spooky Sounds
16 Hairy Friend...Or Foe?
17 Yum, Yum...Tastes Good!
18 Sarah Gets Riled!
19 Teaching Harry How To Sit!
20 Whoops!
21 Whose House Is It, Anyway?
22 Tanks Alot!
23 Something's Fishy!
24 No Way To Treat An Old Friend!
25 George Strikes Back
26 I Can't Shoot Him!
27 "George, Company's Here!"
28 "Don't Think I'm Crazy, But It's Bigfoot!"
29 Hide In The Cellar!
30 Sniff! Sniff! Yuck!!!
31 Just Getting A Little Exercise!
32 There's Something About You I Like!
33 Hi, Little Guy!
34 What To Do About Harry
35 Care For A Bite?
36 Harry, The Couch Potato!
37 More Munchies, Please!
38 "We Can't Keep Him, Son!"
39 LaFleur At The Henderson Store
40 In Search of Dr. Wrightwood
41 The Bigfoot Museum
42 Bigfoot Biggie
43 Harry Meets Society!
44 That's Not My Drawing!
45 Panic In The Streets
46 Harry Looks For George
47 Garbage Pail Bigfoot!
48 Look Who's Back!
49 We're Just Wild About Harry...
50 ...And Harry's Wild About Us!
51 A Visit From...Whom?
52 Dig Those Wild Sounds!
53 "He Lives Here, With You?"
54 Harry Among Friends
55 A Boy And His Bigfoot!
56 "Don't Look Behind You, LaFleur."
57 Harry Takes A Ride!
58 The Getaway
59 Harry Fakes 'Em Out!
60 Call Of The Wild
61 Hiding From LaFleur
62 Bigfoot Showdown!
63 Harry Gets Even!
64 Harry Takes Charge
65 Harry Hath Tamed The Savage Beast!
66 Dog-Gone It!
67 A Goodbye Kiss From Nancy!
68 Goodbye, Old Friend!
69 Farewell To Harry And His Clan
70 'Till We Meet Again!
71 Director William Dear
72 Setting Up A Shot
73 Behind The Scenes
74 Rick Baker's Creation
75 The Legend Of Bigfoot
76 Portrait Of Harry
77 Checklist

HEE HAW (55)

2 1/2" X 3 1/2"

Most trading card collectors have never seen a specimen of the Hee Haw test set created by Topps. The obverses have color photos from the show, with comic-strip style dialogue

inserted into the picture area. The 3—D backs are bright orange in color; the answer to a "straight line" can be discerned by placing a piece of red cellophane (issued in the pack) over the design. There are 55 cards in the set, with the numbers located on the back. No wrapper or box have been seen for this series.

ITEM	MINT	EX
Set	1375.00	1000.00
Card	20.00	15.00

1 I Keep Hearing These Voices but I Don't See Anyone!
When Does This Happen?
When I'm on the Telephone!

2 Was The Dance Last Night Crowded?
Yep! A Lady Fainted and She Had to Dance for 20 Minutes to Find a Place to Lay Down!

3 They Say a Good Card Player Can Hold Any Kind of Executive Job!
What Would a Good Card Player Want with a Job?

4 What Are We Watching?
I Think It's a Football Game!
Go Team...Go Team!
I Want a Hot Dog!

5 These New Dresses are So Short that I've Seen More Cotton in an Aspirin Bottle!

6 I Heard You Have a New Garbage Disposal!
Yep!..My Brother-In-Law..He'll Eat Anything!

7 If I Was the Red Cross, I'd Declare This a Disaster Area!

8 Say Roy, I Heard the Doctor Sewed You Up and Left a Sponge Inside!
Yep!, It Doesn't Hurt but I Sure Do Get Thirsty!

9 Doc, I Just Got Hit by a Truck and Thrown Fifty Feet!
Gee, You Can Be Sued!...For Leaving the Scene of an Accident!

10 It's Very Difficult to Play Ping Pong with Mashed Potatoes!

11 Here's an Earth-Shattering News Bulletin...But First, a Word from Our Sponsor!

12 What Do You Do When You're in Doubt about Kissing a Girl?
I Usually Give Her the Benefit of the Doubt!

13 When My Aunt Died She Left $1000 Hidden in Her Bustle!
Wow! That's a Lot of Money to Leave Behind!

14 If You Want to Make Anti-Freeze Hide Her Woolen Underwear!

15 My Mama Told Me Too Much Kissing Could Make You Go Blind!
Well, Can't We Just Keep Doing It Till We Need Glasses?

16 You Must Be Crazy About Your Wife... You Always Take Her Everywhere!
Oh, No, I Just Can't Stand Kissing Her Goodbye!

17 I Crossed a Pig with a Porcupine... What Did You Get?
Bacon with Splinters!

18 Do You Miss Your Wife's Cooking?
Oh, Yeah, Every Chance I Get!

19 Grandpa, I Don't Think You Should Marry that 18 Year Old! It Could be Fatal!
Well, If She Dies, She Dies!

20 Are You Sure It Doesn't Hurt When You Give Me a Shot?
Absolutely...Unless I Get Careless and Jab My Finger!

21 What Is It About Me That You Love?
You're a Bachelor!

22 The Man Who Marries My Daughter Will Get a Prize!
Well, I Might Be Interested...May I See It, Please?

23 Four Men Fell in a Creek and Only One Got His Hair Wet!
How Come?
Three of Them were Bald!

24 Is My Face Dirty or Is It My Imagination?
Your Face is Clean! I Don't Know about Your Imagination!

25 Why Does a Stork Stand on One Foot?
If He Lifted the Other One He'd Fall Down!

26 I Crossed an Eagle with a Skunk!
What'd You Get?
I Don't Know, But It Smelled to High Heaven!

27 How Long Has Your Brother Been Out of Work?
We Don't Know...Can't Find His Birth Certificate!

28 That Chicken You Sold Me Yesterday Didn't Have a Wishbone!
Sure, My Chickens Are So Contented They Don't Wish for Anything!

29 My Wife Ought to Be on Records!
Yeah, She's Got a Long-Playing Mouth!

30 I Was Arrested for Kissing a Woman and When the Judge Saw Her He Fined Me $10 for Being Drunk!

31 I Invented a Foolproof Burglar Alarm, But Somebody Stole It!

32 I Saw You Last Night with a Blonde on One Arm and a Brunette on the Other!
Yep...Best Job of Tattooing I Ever Had Done!

33 Sally Refused to Marry Luke and He's Been Drunk for a Month!
Now, I Think that's Carrying a Celebration a Little Too Far!

34 This Morning I Got Up at Dawn to See the Sunrise!
Well, You Sure Picked the Best Time for It!

35 This Is the First Newscast Ever to be Brought to You in Smell-O-Vision!

36 I Fell to Sleep on the Beach and the Sun Burned my Stomach!
I Wish I Could Have Seen Your Pot Roast!

37 My Husband Still Keeps His Old Address Book! Is That Fair?
Sure! When You Buy a New Car You Always Carry a Spare, Don't You?

38 Are Raw Oysters Healthy?
I Think So! I've Never Heard One Complain!

39 What's for Supper?
Chicken Gizards, Rabbit Pot Pies, Corn Pone and Pumpkin Pie!
Yum, Yum!

40 What Do You Think Will Go Good with My Purple and Green Knee Socks?
High Hip Boots!

41 Do You Think Kissing Is Unhealthy?
Well, It Does Leave Me Short of Breath!

42 I'll Be 96 Years Old Tomorrow and I Don't Have an Enemy in the World... I've Outlived 'Em All!

43 Maggie Sure was a Beautiful Bride!
Yep, Her Sweater Matched Her Tennis Shoes!

44 I'm Breakin' My Engagement with Luke! I'm Giving Him Back His Frog!

45 If You Want to Drive Your Wife Don't Talk in Your Sleep...Just Smile!

46 I Still Don't Know What Happened!!!

47 Do You File Your Fingernails?
No, I Throw Them Away after I Cut Them!

48 I Hear You Want to Get Your Brother-In-Law a Gift He'll Love!
Yep! But I Don't Know How to Wrap Up a Saloon!

49 When You're in Love You Feel Jumpy and Miserable and You Ache All Over...
It's a Wonderful Feeling, Honey!

50 I Saw You Plowing and You Handle that Tractor Like a Veteran!
How'd You Know? Did You Ever See Me Handle a Veteran!

51 When I Was a Baby I Cried a Lot, But My Mother Wouldn't Change Me for a Million!
Maybe If She'd Change You, You'd Have Stopped Crying!

52 How Come the Sheriff Called Off Your Wedding to that City Fellow?
Sheriff Found Out My Paw Didn't Have a License for the Shotgun!

53 I Wish I Had a Nickel for Every Girl I've Kissed!
What Would You Do, Buy a Pack of Gum?

54 What Did Your Teenage Daughter Do Last Summer?
Her Hair and Nails!

55 How Do You Like Our New Maple Chair?
Not So Good! The Syrup Stuck to My Dress!

HERE'S BO (72 & 12)

One big happy family.

CARD NO. 69 OF 72

As part of the campaign to make Bo Derek into an international celebrity, the appropriately-named Svengali Pro-

2 1/2" X 3 1/2"

ductions joined with Fleer to produce this 1981 set of 72 cards and 12 paper posters. The color photographs—all taken by husband John—are scenes from the "Tarzan" movie and publicity shots of Bo relaxing, surfing, etc. The cards are numbered on the front. The backs are printed as puzzle pieces, puzzle preview cards, or with a feature entitled "The Life Story of Bo Derek." Collector Kenneth Lunn reports that the puzzle is very difficult to complete because some cards have from two to five different puzzle pieces on the back. For that reason, do not expect to complete a puzzle from a standard 72-card set. The paper posters (7 13/16" X 9 1/2") are not captioned. Note: set price includes posters.

ITEM	MINT	EX
Set	10.00	7.50
Card	.10	.05
Poster	.35	.25
Wrapper	--	.35
Box	--	4.00

1 Good Advice from Daddy!
2 Bo Wipes Out!
3 "Home Movies Anyone?"
4 12-Hour Hairdo for Movie "10"
5 Ain't Puppy Love Great!
6 Bo Pearl Dives in Japan.
7 First Encounter at Camp.
8 Movie "10" Brings International Fame.
9 Bo Is an Excellent Windsurfer.
10 Resting After Jog on Beach.
11 "May the Tooth Fairy Answer My Dreams."
12 "Stand Where I Showed You!"
13 Happiest Girl in the Jungle.
14 "Take Me to Your Leader."
15 Bo Relaxes with Her Mate.
16 "Please Let Me Go."
17 Bo Runs for Her Life.
18 Prepare for the Sacrifice!
19 Bo's Sister Kerry Helps John Shoot.
20 Rafting Down the River.
21 "Don't Touch Me or I'll Shoot!"
22 So This Is the New Crew John Hired?
23 Tender Scene in the Jungle!
24 The Boa Makes a Sneak Attack.
25 Lost and Nowhere to Go.
26 Dressed for Dinner in the Jungle.
27 Lunch Break in Jungle.
28 "Please! Please! Help Me!"
29 "Am I Really Your First Girlfriend?"
30 To the Rescue!
31 Bo's Husband, John Derek.
32 Swinging Through the Trees
33 "Oh, I Hope He's Not Dead."
34 John & Bo Working on Latest Movie.

35 Our Family Portrait.
36 Beauty in the Jungle.
37 Alone on the Beach.
38 Oh, Those Big Blue Eyes.
39 Sweet 16 & Falling in Love!
40 Bo Relaxes with Her Ponies.
41 Adventure in Australia.
42 A Ride in the Surf.
43 Bo Braids Crafts for Relaxation.
44 Jogging Through Central Park, New York.
45 The Jungle Taxi.
46 "O.K. Snap the Shutter."
47 June, 1979.
48 July, 1978.
49 Bo Relaxes in Mexico.
50 Bo Flies Her Hobie Cat.
51 Bo Bo Black Sheep.
52 "Hey, Can You Keep a Secret?"
53 Sailing on America Cup Yacht "Freedom".
54 Bo Exercises and Swims Every Day.
55 Expert Rider on the Beach.
56 "Gimme a Great Big Kiss!"
57 California Girl at 17.
58 Making Friend in Singapore Zoo.
59 Bo Loves Her V.W. Convertible.
60 Captain and Crew on Riverboat.

ASK FOR Heroes JUNGLE ACTION! PHOTO CARDS & POSTERS BY JOHN DEREK!

61 Cornrows... Made Famous by Bo.
62 "Daddy, Is He Really a Savage?"
63 The All American Girl!
64 Saved from the Surf.
65 John's Favorite Photo.
66 One Big Happy Family.
67 C.J. Takes a Stroll.
68 "Burr! The Water Is Cold."
69 Exercising on California Beach.
70 Vacationing in Switzerland.
71 "Hey John, Let Us Help."
72 In Search of the Wild Beast.

HEROES OF THE BLUES (36)

2 3/4" X 3 3/4"

— No. 6 —
JAYBIRD COLEMAN

Burl "Jaybird" Coleman was born in Gainesville, Ala. in 1896 and began playing harmonica around 1908, settling in Bessemer in the early 1920s. Between 1927-1930 he made 11 sides, appearing in the unusual role of a harmonica player accompanying his own vocals. He was largely inactive after 1930 and died in 1950. Of all recorded blues harmonica players Coleman probably developed the richest tone.

This is one of a series of 36 "Heroes of the Blues" trading cards drawn by R. Crumb.
© 1980 by Yazoo Records, Inc.

YAZOO RECORDS INC.
245 Waverly Place,
New York, NY 10014

Complete set: $5.96
A complete set of 36 cards is available by writing to Yazoo Records, Inc.

From the smoky nightclubs of Chicago to the delapidated porches of a field hand's shack in the Mississippi Delta, you'll find all the great blues singers in this 36-card set originally marketed by Yazoo Records in 1980. Renowned artist Robert Crumb created the cards and stylish box for the set. The backs contain the card number, a short biography of the singer, and advertising for Yazoo Records. The set has been reprinted a number of times since 1980 and is currently being sold by Eclipse and Kitchen Sink for $9.95. Note: sold as boxed set only.

1 William Moore
2 Peg Leg Howell
3 Clifford Gibson
4 Blind Blake
5 Frank Stokes
6 Jaybird Coleman
7 Blind Willie Johnson
8 Leroy Carr & Scrapper Blackwell
9 Blind Lemon Jefferson
10 Curley Weaver & Fred McMullen
11 Whistler & His Jug Band
12 Mississippi Sheiks
13 Rube Lacy
14 Skip James
15 Bo-Weavil Jackson
16 Furry Lewis
17 Sam Collins
18 Ramblin' Thomas
19 Sleepy John Estes
20 Cannon's Jug Stompers
21 Memphis Jug Band
22 Big Bill
23 Roosevelt Sykes
24 Blind Gary Davis
25 Papa Charlie Jackson
26 Charley Patton
27 Buddy Boy Hawkins
28 Barbecue Bob
29 Ed Bell
30 Blind Willie McTell
31 Son House
32 Memphis Minnie
33 Mississippi John Hurt
34 Tommy Johnson
35 Peetie Wheatstraw
36 Bo Carter

HEROES OF THE BLUES A SET OF 36 CARDS

HIPPIE TATTOOS (?)

2 3/8" X 3 3/8"

$$$YES ?? $NO

Both wrappers of this Leaf Gum issue depict the same two longhaired youngsters with tattoos on their faces. The premise of the set, according to the red-print instruction card included in every pack, was to "Decorate Yourself." The "tattoos" are printed on clear acetate with adhesive backs and supposedly could be removed "as easy as they go on." The instruction cards have simple sketches indicating places to apply the tattoos. Until recently, only a 5¢ wax pack was known to exist for this set, but collector Mark Angert has come up with a horizontal paper wrapper also bearing a 5¢ price. The price listed below for this new wrapper is a "suggested" retail until it is determined how many more have entered the marketplace.

ITEM	MINT	EX
Sticker	1.25	1.00
Card	1.00	.75
Wax wrapper	--	15.00
Paper wrapper	--	35.00

Hippie Tattoos

HOGAN'S HEROES (66)

2 1/2'' X 3 1/2''

If we get a date for you, we'll make it a double escape

Place backs together to make it a giant photo—55 cards.

The antics of the wise-cracking Colonel Hogan and his zany bunch of POW's are the subject of this Fleer-issued set of 66 cards. Each has a black and white photo from the television series, which is captioned below the picture. The set title is printed in red on the front of the card, and the number is located in a helmet design in one corner. The entire set of 66 backs forms a giant black and white picture-poster.

ITEM	MINT	EX
Set	660.00	500.00
Card	8.00	6.00
Wrapper	--	150.00
Box	--	300.00

1 Lose a Tank Col. Klink?
2 Sir, I Regret to Inform You — None of Our Prisoners Have Escaped.
3 I Wish I Could See If My Shoes Were Shined!
4 What Happened to the Girl I Was Dancing with?
5 I Packed Your Car, General! The Ticking??? Pay No Attention to It!
6 Anybody Would Think There's a War on!
7 It's not a Tunnel, Klink, We're Starting a Victory Garden.
8 Schultz, Make Sure the Eggs Are Fresh This Time!
9 If We Escape... You Want to Come with Us?
10 Col. Klink, in Our Army You'd Be Lucky to Make Corporal!
11 Watch That First Step General, It's a Lulu!
12 And I Say, We Don't Need a Barbecue Pit.
13 Schultz, Watch Where You're Going — You Caved in Another One of Our Tunnels.

14 Folies Bergere? I'd Like to Make a Reservation for Hogans Heroes.
15 Open the Wine Cellar — I Got an Order for Three More Cases.
16 Col. Hogan, I've Got to Keep These Glasses on... Klink Passed Me in the Street Three Times.
17 Klink, I Think Your Sirens Sound Better.
18 You Cook Better Than My Wife! You're Better Looking too!
19 How Do I Know... I Don't Speak German.
20 Carter, How About a Game of Gin Rummy?
21 My Son, the P.O.W.!
22 Schultz, Next Time You Need Money, Come to Me... Don't Sell My Boots.
23 Col. Hogan, You and Your Men Have 24 Hours to Return My Boots.
24 Col. Hogan, This Was a Quiet Camp Until You Got Here.
25 No! No! Don't Take the Freeway.
26 What Do You Mean You Cancelled the Dance?
27 Klink, You're Starting the Christmas Party Early This Year.
28 What Gives You the Idea I Need a Furlough?
29 Put Up a Road Block, My Monocle Is Missing.

30 Don't Worry; I'm Not a Spy. I'm Going to a Halloween Party.
31 How Did I Know It Was a German Uniform??? I Got Dressed in the Dark!
32 Are You the U.S.O. Hostess?
33 I Swear, You're the First Enemy I Ever Kissed.
34 And Boy Can I Do Bird Imitations!
35 And This One Is the Yellow-Bellied Sapsucker!
36 Explain to Klink... It's Not a Tunnel; We're Digging for Clams.
37 I Got It as a Prize in a Cereal Box.
38 I Caught This in a Door.
39 Of Course It's a Funny Hat, But It's Great for Carrying Pizza.
40 Tell the Truth Mate, You've Got a Liverwurst Sandwich in There.
41 If I Can't Have My Afternoon Tea, I'll Shoot My Way Out of Here.
42 I Don't Think Klink'll Miss Either One of Us at Roll Call.
43 Schultz, There's Not a Strand of Barbed Wire Left in This Camp and I'd Like to Know Why?
44 They're Not Wire Cutters Col. Klink. Helga Was Giving Me a Manicure.
45 I Don't Think the Prisoners Would Like It If I Brought You with Me, Col. Klink.

46 I See Nothing... Nothing!
47 Drink That and You'll Be a Bushy Haired Kid Again.
48 The Door Knob Has More Hair Than Klink.
49 It's Growing!!! I Won't Freeze on the Russian Front with Hair.
50 Definite Signs of Dandruff.
51 Col. Hogan, I've Got the Overseas Operator on Your Call to East Peoria.
52 Duck Behind Lebeau — Klink Will Never Notice You.
53 Don't Ask Me, Klink. I Don't Know Whose Side Schultz Is on.
54 If We Get a Date for You, We'll Make It a Double Escape.
55 Don't Worry — Schultz Has Cotton in His Ears.
56 A Boat in a Prison Camp! Please Col. Hogan Hide it.
57 Hail, Hail, the Gang's All Here! But Not for Long!
58 Ah, What Wonderful Sauerkraut Juice.
59 What Do You Mean Lillies for Col. Klink! Let's Get Poison Ivy.
60 Temper! Temper! You'll Fog Up Your Monocle.
61 Why Don't You Get Yourself a Windshield Wiper?
62 And You Didn't Think We Could Make a Do-It-Yourself Airplane.
63 Look at It This Way Klink, It Beats Hiking with a Full Field Pack.
64 Get Away You Big Clown; You're Supposed to Be a Vicious Watch Dog.
65 I've Gained Twenty Pounds Since I Started Eating Your Desserts.
66 He Told Me He Bought It with the Money from His Paper Route.

HOLLYWOOD SLAP STICKERS (66)   2 1/2" X 3 7/16"

What do you get when you take black and white pictures from old movies, tint them in various day-glo colors, and enclose them in "flim clip" style borders? When Fleer did it in 1975, the result was this set of Hollywood Slap Stickers. There are 66 stickers in the series, each showing a scene from a Little Rascals, Marx Brothers, or Laurel and Hardy film. "Humorous" dialogue has been added in cartoon-style dialogue balloons. The stickers are not numbered.

ITEM	MINT	EX
Set	25.00	18.50
Sticker	.35	.25
Wrappers (6)		
1st row, each	--	.50
2nd row, each	--	3.00
Box	--	10.00

Marx Brothers

And It Makes a Great Bread Slicer!
Another Pimple!
Are You Sure He's House Broken?
Bite This Paleface!
But I Used a Leading Mouthwash!
Does He Know Any Beethoven?
Drop Another Water-Bomb and I'll Put Out Your Fire!
Go Play Your Harp Fuzzhead!
Hands Off Fishface!
Harpo (Rifle on Shoulder)
Honk! Honk! Honk! (Lion)
Honk! (Etc.—Typewriter)
I Think I Love You!
I Want to Tickle Your Fancy...
Stop That!
Stop That You Yo-Yo
This May Look Like My Finger But Actually It's My Finger!
Up Your Nose Featherhead!
What's Backwards?
You're Sitting on My Toe!
You're Stepping on My Toe!
You Show Me Yours and I'll Show You Mine!
You Want'em Pretty Beads/You Turkey!

Our Gang

And Someday I'll Be President!
But I Did Take a Bath!
Don't Step in It!
Fat Power!
Go Eat a Bug Fatso!
Hang in There!
Help! Splinters
I Always Knew You Were Henpecked!
I Didn't Do It/It's Not Me
I Hate Spinich Pie!
I Think I'll Have to Blast!
Kiss Me Baby!/a Lover You're Not/Yuck!
Let's Play Hooky Today!
No! She's the Dummy!
Take a Bath Dirtball!
The Great White Whale!/Tidal Wave!
The One on the End!/Yea! He Did It!

This Is Just Like Mom's Oatmeal.
Who Did It? (Blue)
Who Did It? (Green)
Who Did It? (Orange)
Who Didn't Use Deodorant!
Who Said He Was House Broken!
Would You Like a Little?
You Drink Milk?
You Have Bad Breath!
You Told the Teacher What?

Laurel & Hardy

Burp!
But Fat Is Beautiful!
Did You Give My Name to Weight Watcher?
I Think I'm Going to Be 6!
I Think We Won the War!
Keep You Chins Up! Hee! Hee! Hee!
No! No! That's Dishwater!
Now Hit the Nail, Dummy, Not My Finger!
Ouch! She Bit Me!
Quiet!
That's an Elephant Not My Sister!
This Man's a Ding-Bat!
3 Years For Telling Dirty Jokes!
Well This Is Another Fine Mess You've Gotten Me Into!
What Do You Mean? More Salt!
Why It's Just Some Dirty Laundry, Officer!

Disoriented Dad

Hook

Disoriented Dad

It's been a difficult time for Peter Banning; forced to walk the plank by pirates, deposited in a clam by mermaids, and now, most troubling of all, he looks into the youthful faces of the Lost Boys and wonders – is he Peter Pan? In order to rescue his kidnapped kids, he must come to grip with that notion, and somehow win the love and respect of 22 suspicious orphans. . . his pint-sized army in the war against Hook!

8 GLOSSY MOVIE CARDS 1 STICKER

WARNING: any similarity between the characters and scenes in the movie "Hook" and those of the original "Peter Pan" is purely coincidental. That about sums up the content of Steven Spielberg's latest movie fantasy in which a socially-dysfunctional businessman gets in touch with his own feelings after being transported into the tumultous environs of Neverland. Topps decided to produce a card set based upon the movie and this 110-item series was issued in 1991.

The 99 cards feature color photographs from the film surrounded by parchment borders. Each picture is enclosed by a jagged blue frame line and a Peter Pan design is printed in the lower left corner. Collectors will note slight punctuation differences between the front and back captions on some cards. The text on back is printed over a series of varying map designs; the latter can be pieced together to form a larger picture. Nine of the eleven stickers have captionless color pictures, while sticker #1 depicts the "Hook" logo and #6 is an artwork rendition of Julia Roberts. All the sticker backs are puzzle pieces except for #6, which has the completed picture on back. The set was issued in an orange cello pack without gum. Note: set price includes stickers.

ITEM	MINT	EX
Set	15.00	---
Card	.10	---
Sticker	.35	---
Wrapper	---	.10
Box	---	2.00

1 Return to Neverland
2 "Peter Pan": The Play
3 High-Flying Youngsters!
4 Pan vs. Hoo, Kid Style!
5 Peter - Afraid to Fly?
6 Granny Wendy
7 Business or Family Man?
8 The Banquet
9 Tootle's Secret
10 The Past Beckons
11 The Abduction
12 Hooky's Back!
13 The Truth Revealed
14 The Once and Future Pan
15 Tinkerbell's Mission
16 Good Morning, Neverland!
17 Peter the Pirate
18 Hook's Floating Fortress
19 Jack and Maggie - Prisoners!
20 The Captain in Command

21 Pan in a Jam in a Clam
22 The Home of Miss Tink
23 The Nevertree
24 Meet the Lost Boys
25 Disoriented Dad
26 Boy in a Barrel
27 Thud Butt Rebuts
28 Leader of the Pack
29 Enter ... Rufio!
30 The Rivals Meet
31 Is He REALLY Peter Pan?
32 Kill the Lawyer!
33 No Escape From Destiny
34 Arrow Attack!
35 The Scorekeepers
36 Peter's Not Panning Out!
37 Seeing the Child Within
38 The Nefarious Captain and Smee
39 A Hook for All Occasions
40 Getting Down to Business

41 The Captain - Signing Off?
42 A Scheme Most Foul
43 Ponderful Rufio
44 The Ultimate Substitute Teacher
45 In a Class by Themselves
46 Jack - A Pupil With Promise?
47 Getting Into Shape!
48 Happy Landings, Peter!
49 Slingshot Hotshot!
50 Up, Up and Away!!
51 Enslaved Aboard the Jolly Roger
52 The "King of Fun" Strikes
53 A Chip Off the Old ... Hook?
54 Eats and Treats
55 Double Your Appetite!
56 Dishing It Out
57 Food Fighter
58 A Slice of (Former) Life
59 The Revealing Reflex
60 Bedtime in Neverland
61 Small Hope for the Hopeless
62 Maggie's Lullaby
63 Even Hook is Touched
64 To Crow or Not to Crow
65 Field of Far-Out Dreams
66 The Unstoppable Pirates
67 Naturals of Neverland
68 Young Jack's Up at Bat!
69 Hook! Hook! Hook!
70 How Pan Began ...
71 Little Boy Lost
72 Peter Soars Once More
73 Rufios's Pledge
74 Let's Turn Things Around!
75 Lost Boys on the Warpath
76 Tragic Transformation
77 The Return of Peter Pan
78 Swooping Down to Danger
79 This Pan's No Pansy!
80 Slashing and Bashing
81 Carry On, Peter Pan!
82 Never Say Surrender
83 Fighting Back-to-Back
84 Convenient Contraption
85 Assault of the Flying Tomatoes
86 Four Ways to Dye
87 His Final Stand
88 Father and Son Reunited

89 The Lost Boys Triumphant
90 Aftermath
91
92 Thrust and Parry!
93 Clashing Steel!
94 At Each Other's Throats!
95 Croc's Revenge
96 Homecoming
97 Back and Better Than Ever
98 The Family That Flies Together
99 A Farewell to Tootles

Let's Turn Things Around!

SUPER GLOSSY MOVIE CARDS•STICKERS

HORRIBLE HOROSCOPES (72)　　2 1/2" X 3 1/2"

"Your Future Can Be Worse Than You Think!" That's the message Philly Gum delivered with "Horrible Horoscopes," a 72-card set depicting the dark side of the future. The format and artwork are virtually identical to that of "Happy Horoscopes" (including the misspelling of "Sagittarius"): except for the pessimistic tone and the missing "happy face" logo, the sets might be confused with one another. The wrapper for "Horrible" seems to be scarcer than "Happy," although the cards seem to be more common.

ITEM	MINT	EX
Set	40.00	30.00
Card	.50	.35
Wrapper	--	20.00

1　Aquarius — Take Flowers to Teacher
2　Aquarius — Join the School Choir
3　Aquarius — Fall for a New Neighbor
4　Aquarius — You'll Take A Plane Trip
5　Aquarius — A Stranger Loves You
6　Aquarius — Show Your Special Talent
7　Aries — Spend A Day Helping Dad
8　Aries — Take Her On a Picnic
9　Aries — Take Up a New Hobby
10　Aries — Take a Walk in the Woods
11　Aries — Try Out for the Team
12　Aries — Give Mom a Hand
13　Cancer — You'll Win a Award
14　Cancer — You're in the Spotlight
15　Cancer — Become a Teacher
16　Cancer — Babysit with Kid Brother
17　Cancer — You're Ready for the Champ
18　Cancer — Take an Ocean Trip
19　Capricorn — Spend a Day on the Farm
20　Capricorn — Go On a Blind Date
21　Capricorn — Learn a New Dance
22　Capricorn — You'll Join the Rodeo
23　Capricorn — Take Up Painting

24　Capricorn — Learn a New Sport
25　Gemini — Become a Doctor
26　Gemini — You'll Enter a Boat Race
27　Gemini — Visit the Beach
28　Gemini — Loan Your Bike to a Pal
29　Gemini — Bring Home a New Pet
30　Gemini — Visit a Sick Friend
31　Leo — See An Opera
32　Leo — Learn to Sky Dive
33　Leo — Become a Skin Diver
34　Leo — Go Surfing
35　Leo — Get a Healthy Sun Tan
36　Leo — Start a Diet
37　Libra — Become An Astronaut
38　Libra — Learn to Drive
39　Libra — Be A Mountain Climber
40　Libra — Learn to Swim
41　Libra — Compete in the Olympics
42　Libra — Go Horseback Riding
43　Pisces — Take Up Skiing
44　Pisces — You Will Get Needed Help
45　Pisces — You'll Get a Strange Call
46　Pisces — You Will Win a Contest
47　Pisces — You Will Learn to Fly
48　Pisces — Trim the Xmas Tree

49　Saggittarius — Enter the Grand Prix
50　Saggittarius — Go Big Game Hunting
51　Saggittarius — Bake a Birthday Cake
52　Saggittarius — Become a Bird Watcher
53　Saggittarius — Raise Tropical Fish
54　Saggittarius — You'll Become a Big Shot
55　Scorpio — A Visitor Will Call
56　Scorpio — Become An "A" Student
57　Scorpio — Try Out for Rock Group
58　Scorpio — You Will Learn a Secret
59　Scorpio — Be Kind to Animals
60　Scorpio — Relax in the Tub
61　Taurus — Travel Down a Big River
62　Taurus — Become a Magician
63　Taurus — Learn a New Skill
64　Taurus — Your Future is Medicine
65　Taurus — You'll Write a Great Book
66　Taurus — Train Your Dog to Obey
67　Virgo — You'll Decide to Move
68　Virgo — You'll Finally Graduate
69　Virgo — You Will Become Famous
70　Virgo — Do Your Own Thing
71　Virgo — You Will Win a Trip
72　Virgo — Become a Lumberjack

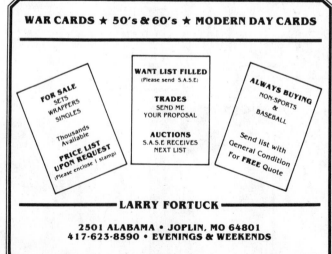

HORROR HEADS (40)

The forty different tattoos in Horror Heads are arranged in pairs: a dotted line is printed to indicate where to cut them

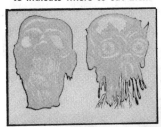

apart. Each design is numbered on the paper backing, but none are captioned. Our illustration shows a pair of tattoos intact and unused as they appear "in reverse" before being applied. A standard size instruction card giving four-step directions for application was included in every pack. Note: a set consists of 20 pairs of tattoos and one instruction card. The "mint" and "excellent" prices for tattoos are for intact sheets with unused designs.

ITEM	MINT	EX
Set	25.00	18.50
Tattoo sheet	1.00	.75
Card	.35	.25
Wrapper	--	5.00
Box	--	20.00

HORROR MONSTER SERIES (146)

Nu-Cards marketed the "Horror Monster Series" in 1961. Cards 1-66 have greenish fronts and red-orange backs and were packaged, without gum, in "Horror Monster" wrappers. The "Horror Monsters" box is orange and bears a 5-cent price on the lid. Cards 67-146 have orange-bordered fronts and green print backs; they apparently were distributed in "Movie Monsters" wrappers (also without gum) and "Shock Monsters" boxes. This box is green and also carries a 5-cent price circle.

A third variety of card is known: it has a blue front and a red print back, and is slightly smaller than the other two types (2 7/16" X 3 3/8"). In our illustration, you will note that the captions of this variety are located in a white panel below the picture and appear to have been written on a typewriter (not typeset). The back design of the blue front cards is the same as that of the green front series, but is printed in red, not orange. The Nu-Card credit line, which appears on both the green and orange series cards, is missing

from those of the blue type. We believe that the blue-front cards are the original issue, which was refined and later reissued in the green and orange colors. The length of the blue series has not been determined. Note: card No. 102 appears with a special bonus back worth 100 wrappers toward premiums offered via the mail. It is not known if any other card numbers appear with bonus backs.

ITEM	MINT	EX
Sets		
Green		
(1-66)	250.00	185.00
Orange		
(67-146)	250.00	185.00
Cards		
Blue	4.00	3.00
Green	3.00	2.25
Orange	2.50	2.00
Bonus card	15.00	12.00
Wrappers (2)		
"Horror"	--	100.00
"Movie"	--	75.00
Boxes		
"Horror"	--	150.00
"Shock"	--	125.00

Green
(1-66)

THE ELECTRONIC MONSTER

Horror Monster Series

Orange (67-146)

Blue

Orange

Green

1 Beast with a Million Eyes
2 Gigantis, The Fire Monster
3 King Kong
4 Gigantis, The Fire Monster
5 The Mummy
6 Teen Age Werewolf
7 The Terror from Beyond Space
8 King Kong
9 Bowery Boy Meets the Monster
10 Return of the Fly
11 Half Human
12 Two-Headed Roe, "Sinbad the Sailor"
13 Horrors of the Black Museum
14 The Giant Behemoth
15 Werewolf of London
16 The Headless Ghost
17 The Mole People
18 Colossus of New York
19 Return of the Fly
20 Werewolf of London
21 Abbott & Costello Meet Frankenstein
22 Man from Planet X
23 Curse of the Faceless Man
24 Dracula
25 Half Human
26 Creature from The Black Lagoon
27 The She Creature
28 Hideous Sun Demon
29 Monster in "Time Machine"
30 How to Make a Monster
31 The Alligator People
32 The Mole People
33 Gigantis the Fire Monster
34 The Dragon from "Sinbad the Sailor"
35 The Mole People
36 Rodan
37 Sinbad Battles the Giant Two-Headed Roc
38 Horror of Dracula
39 The Alligator People
40 Creature from the Black Lagoon
41 The Vampire
42 The Incredible Shrinking Man
43 The Forbidden Planet
44 Dr. Jekyll & Mr. Hyde
45 Frankenstein
46 Creature from the Black Lagoon
47 The Giant Behemoth
48 Strange World
49 Cyclops from "Sinbad the Sailor"
50 The Wolfman

51 Dracula and Frankenstein
52 The Mummy's Curse
53 Blood of the Vampire
54 Monster from Outer Space
55 Monster from "World Without End"
56 Amazing Colossal Man
57 The She Creature
58 Animal Man in "Island of Lost Souls"
59 Vegetable Man, "It Conquered the World"
60 Hunchback of Notre Dame
61 Skeleton Man
62
63 The Man without a Head
64 The Man Who Lost His Skin
65 The Man That Couldn't Die
66 The Unearthly
67 Frankenstein
68 Dragon in Sinbad the Sailor
69 Beginning of the End
70 Look Pa—No Cavities
71 13 Ghosts
72 Amazing Colossal Man
73 The Angry Red Planet
74 The Mysterians
75 The Giant Behemoth
76 Mad Soul
77 Invisible Invaders
78 The Monster That Changed the World
79 Guaranteed to Taste Like the 70 Cents Spread
80 Jack the Ripper
81 The Four Skulls of Jonathan Drake
82 Terror from the Year 5000
83 The Alligator People
84 House of Haunted Hill
85 Monster from Green Hell
86 How to Make Friends and Influence People
87 When You Care Enough to Send the Very Best
88 Find It Fast In the Yellow Pages
89 The Unearthly
90 Invasion of the Saucer Men
91 The Monster of Piedras Blancas
92 Robbie the Robot
93 Aren't You Glad You Used Dile Soap?
94 Nothing Shaves Like a Blade
95 I Ain't Talking While the Flavor Lasts
96 The Bowery Boys Meet the Monsters
97 The Brain from Planet Arous
98 Monster on the Campus

99 The Four Skulls of Jonathan Drake
100 Strange World
101 The Blob
102 The Electronic Monster
103 Hideous Sun Demon
104 The Deadly Mantis
105 The Return of the Vampire
106 Fiend Without a Face
107 The Bride and the Beast
108 Attack of the Green Leeches
109 Look Ma—No Hands
110 The H-Man
111 The Bat Man
112 House of Wax
113 Phantom of the Opera
114 Blood of Dracula
115 You're My Boy
116 This Is No Place For Second Best
117 Put Dancing into Your Life
118 That's One Way to Get Ahead
119 Not a Whisper of Bad Breath
120 From Tarantula
121 From Hell It Came
122 La Casa Del Terror (The House of Terror)
123 The Haunted Stranger
124 Fly Now—Pay Later
125 La Daldicion De La Momia (The Curse of the Mummy)
126 Curse of the Faceless Man
127 If You Care How You Look While You Play
128 You Can Always Tell a Hay Low Girl
129 Like Sleeping on a Cloud
130 Let Hurts Put You in the Drivers Seat
131 Some Things Can't Be Hurried
132 Monster from Outer Space
133 The Creature Walks Among Us
134 The Undead
135 Rodan
136 The Tingler
137 Quick Henry the Flit
138 The Golem
139 The Mummy
140 Queen of Outer Space
141 Wake Up to Tangg
142 Invasion of the Saucermen
143 Not a Whisper of Bad Breath
144 The Mutant
145 The Savage Eye
146 Satan Satellites

HOT HUNKS (7)

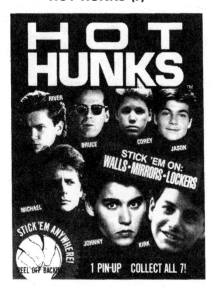

Bruce [Willis]
Corey
Jason [Bateman]
Johnny [Depp]
Kirk [Cameron]
Michael [J. Fox]
River [Phoenix]

4" X 6"

"Hot Hunks" is a classic example of the strange manner in which Topps does business. The company goes to all the trouble and expense of producing a series of large pin-up stickers featuring major-league heart throbs and then deep-sixes the product without seriously testing it in the open market. Each of the seven pin-ups in the series measures about 4" X 6" and has an adhesive surface under a peel off backing ("Stick 'Em Anywhere!"). The large paper wrapper pictures all of the "hunks" and identifies them by their first names, but there are no names on the pin-ups themselves. The illustrations here were provided by John Neuner, who has the only *reported* wrapper and pin-up we know of at this time. Given the current scarcity of this item, we suggest a retail price of $25 per pack, but this would be reduced drastically if any quantity of Hot Hunks turned up.

HOT RODS (66)

Collectors have had a difficult time finding a name for this series since there is no set title printed on the cards and there are five different types of vehicles included in it: hot rods (26), custom cars (14), dragsters (13), dream cars (7) and racers (6). The wrapper, however, bears the title "Hot Rods," and that is how it is listed in this book. Another confusing aspect of this set is that the backs are printed in a variety of colors and shades of colors (pink, yellow, brown, etc.). Regardless of color, every back has a T.C.G. credit line at bottom left, a car drawing at bottom right, and the card number printed in a checkered flag design in the upper left corner.

2 1/2" X 3 1/2"

SURF WOODY

Surf Woody built by Barris Kustom City is made into an AMT model that is also duplicated with a surf hearse. Interior features Muntz Stereo-Pak tape and Sony TV. Completely electronically controlled push button steering, fluorescent headlights, sequential Ford Thunderbird taillights, complete all chrome undercarriage with A. J. knock-off hubs. Gas is consumed from a 10 gallon root beer keg with a Dupree Chrome Dome fuel pump into the dual Paxton blowers on this Ford Cobra engine.

COURTESY—BARRIS KUSTOM CITY

ITEM	MINT	EX
Set	150.00	115.00
Card	2.00	1.50
Wrapper	--	60.00
Box	--	75.00

1 Super Marauder (Custom Car)
2 New Breed T.V. Car (Custom Car)
3 Dragnet 29 (Hot Rod)
4 Li'l Deuce (Hot Rod)
5 T Plus 11 (Hot Rod)
6 Cabriolet (Hot Rod)
7 Rodster (Hot Rod)
8 The Tangerine (Custom Car)
9 Les Po Po (Hot Rod)
10 Li'l Beauty (Hot Rod)
11 Twister "T" (Hot Rod)
12 XPAK 400 (Racer)
13 XMSC 210 (Racer)
14 El Capitola (Custom Car)
15 Life Of Riley T.V. Car (Hot Rod)
16 The Pumpkin (Racer)
17 Mustang (Custom Car)
18 X-Tura (Custom Car)
19 R&C Dream Truck (Custom Car)
20 '57 Thunderbird (Custom Car)
21 Curled Flame (Hot Rod)
22 Surf Woody (Hot Rod)
23 Surf Woody (Hot Rod)
24 Turbo-Sonic (Racer)
25 Drag "T" (Racer)
26 Flaky "T" (Racer)
27 Black Beauty (Custom Car)
28 Ruby "T" (Hot Rod)
29 Bimimi Wagon (Custom Car)
30 Cyclops (Hot Rod)
31 Emperor (Hot Rod)
32 Cosma Ray (Dream Car)
33 Lemans Cadillac (Custom Car)
34 Beatnik Bandit (Dream Car)
35 Rotar (Dream Car)
36 Silhouette (Dream Car)
37 Roanoke Valley Special (Hot Rod)
38 Beach Baron (Hot Rod)
39 Show Boat (Hot Rod)
40 The Mysterion (Dream Car)
41 The Fugitive (Dragster)
42 The Snapper (Hot Rod)
43 Flaming Special (Hot Rod)
44 The Lightning Rod (Dragster)
45 Kamakazi-"1" (Dragster)
46 Little Old Bucket (Hot Rod)
47 Golden Rod (Hot Rod)
48 Bo Weevil (Dragster)
49 Devil Cart (Dragster)
50 Funnel Master (Hot Rod)
51 Modified Dart (Dragster)
52 Newhouse Special (Dragster)
53 The Riviera (Custom Car)
54 The Undertaker (Hot Rod)
55 The Rushin' Roulette (Dragster)
56 T-Bird (Dream Car)
57 Texas Terror (Dragster)
58 Li'l Coffin (Custom Car)
59 The Honey (Custom Car)
60 The Drag Master (Dragster)
61 The Blazer (Dragster)
62 The Streamline (Dragster)
63 The Strip Star (Racer)
64 Li'l Billy (Dragster)
65 The Wild Dream (Hot Rod)
66 The Road Blazer (Dream Car)

HOT SEAT STICKERS

"Give your friend a HOT SEAT" ... "Slip a HOT SEAT on the chair ... watch the rear view action." Such is the inspiration behind this series of day-glo stickers released by Fleer sometime in the early-1970's. Each 5¢ pack contained two strips of three stickers plus a blue and white put-down card bearing a deprecatory joke. The target audience was obviously the preteen crowd and little time or effort was apparently spent in producing either stickers or cards. Neither of the latter items are numbered and we have not seen enough of them in hobby circles to assemble any kind of checklist. The best thing about the entire set is the wrapper, which is not surprising given Fleer's demonstrated excellence in wrapper design. Note: prices are for strips of three stickers with backing intact. Single stickers cut away from the strip or peeled are worth 5¢ each.

ITEM	MINT	EX
Sticker strip	.50	.35
Card	.35	.25
Wrapper	—	3.00

HOT WHEELS (12)   2 7/16" X 3 7/16"

The dimensions stated in the heading refer to the sheet of "Hot Wheels Tattoo Transfers" as it came folded from the package. The sheet opens, accordian style, to 3 7/16" X 14 5/8", and contains six large and eight small designs. These were applied by wetting the skin and pressing the tattoo onto it for a short period of time. There are 12 sheets of tattoos in the set, which was produced by Philly Gum in 1971.

ITEM	MINT	EX
Set	35.00	27.50
Sheet	2.50	2.00
Wrapper	—	12.00

HOWARD THE DUCK (77 & 22)

2 1/2" X 3 1/2"

The trouble with buying license rights for a product based on a film is that you

A COMIC CLASSIC!

sink or swim together. Topps had high hopes for "Howard the Duck" (issued in 1986), but neither the movie or the card set attracted much of a following. There are 75 storycards in the series; these have

photos from the movie on front and text on back. The first and last cards are a title card and a checklist. The 22 stickers have diecut center designs with yellow borders. They are numbered but are not captioned. Eleven stickers have "film clip" side frames; the remaining eleven are photos set on green, blue, or purple backgrounds. Note: set price includes stickers.

ITEM	MINT	EX
Set	15.00	11.00
Card	.10	.07
Sticker	.35	.25
Wrapper	--	.35
Box	--	4.00

1 Howard the Duck
2 Introducing Howard!
3 Beverly Switzler
4 Phil Blumburtt
5 Dr. Jenning
6 Howard on Duck World
7 Duck-O-Vision: The Game Show
8 Duck-O-Vision: Crazy Webby
9 Duck-O-Vision: Teen Bandstand
10 Duck-O-Vision: Medical Program
11 Duck-O-Vision: Public Affairs
12 Duck-O-Vision: Count Duckula
14 Landing on Earth (Plop!)
15 Motorcycle Maniacs!
16 Cherry Bomb's Best Lady!
17 Bev in a Jam!
18 No More Mr. Nice Duck!
19 Little Duck Lost
20 Weird...But Cute!
21 Special Delivery!
22 A Feathered Phenomenon!
23 At The Dynatechnics Lab
24 'Ascent of Duck'
25 Waddling Off in a Huff
26 Bug Off, Blumburtt!
27 Humans...Phooey!
28 So Long, Ducky!
29 How a Duck Can Make a Buck
30 Howard in Hot Water
31 Howie & Bev...Together Again!

32 A Scientist Possessed!
33 Jenning's Mad Lab
34 A Fowl Shakedown!
35 Beverly's Packin'!
36 Master of Quack Fu
37 The Thing within Jenning
38 Diner Dilemma
39 Bottoms Up!
40 Eggs? You're Kidding!
41 Duck Vs. Truckers
42 Stop That Duck!
43 Doctor of Doom!
44 Ketchup Catastrophe!
45 Howard the Swinger!
46 Destroying a Duck
47 He's Not on the Menu!
48 Dr. Destructo!
49 Earth Vs. The Flying Cleavers
50 Howard Gets a Lift!
51 The Dark Overlord
52 Everything's Ducky!
53 "Help Us, Howard!"

54 Hell On the Highway
55 Hit Me with Your Best Shots
56 The Immunity Syndrome
57 Facing the Fiend
58 Howard to the Rescue!
59 How About Plan"B"?
60 The Switzler Sacrifice
61 The Girl Has Problems...
62 Diabolical Dynamo!
63 "He's Unstoppable!"
64 Zapped!!
65 Howard's Last Chance
66 Howard, The Hero!
67 Overloaded Overlord
68 Duck, You Sucker!
69 Spectroscopic Disaster
70 One Last Chance!
71 Ka-Blooey!
72 Quack to Me, Howard!
73 Lord Love a Duck!
74 Cleveland Triumphant!
75 I Want My H-TV!
76 A Comic Classic!
77 Checklist

Produced by Topps in 1976, this is an unusual set, not only because it was issued in both card and sticker formats, but also because the pictures, considered by themselves without the humorous dialogue, stand on their own merits as quality reproductions of famous paintings depicting events in American history. The card version was issued first in a "market test" (note the telltale white wrapper and box with the "Hysterical History" stamp affixed) and card backs are wine colored with gray text areas. The sticker set is the "regular" issue and has lighter pink backs and white text spaces. There are 66 identical titles in each format. Note: stickers missing the detachable corner pieces cannot be graded excellent or mint.

ITEM	MINT	EX
Sets		
Card	50.00	37.50
Stickers	20.00	15.00
Card	.65	.50
Sticker	.25	.20
Wrappers (2)		
Test (card)	--	30.00
Sticker	--	.50
Boxes (2)		
Test (card)	--	50.00
Sticker	--	8.00

1 Signing of the Declaration
2 Penn's Indian Treaty
3 Gov. Shirley's Expedition
4 The Mayflower Compact
5 The Battle of Springfield
6 Captured Flag of Yorktown
7 Paul Revere's Midnight Ride
8 Oklahoma Land Rush (1889)
9 Fort Drummer Indian Attack
10 Henry Hudson, Explorer
11 Abe Lincoln Bids Farewell
12 Washington Meets Lafayette
13 Death of Col. Ephraim Williams
14 Pilgrims Going to Church
15 Landing of William Penn
16 Rescue of Israel Putnam
17 Betsy Ross Shows Stars & Stripes
18 Drafting the Declaration
19 Lincoln and the Contraband
20 Fall of New Amsterdam
21 First Sewing Maching
22 Betsy Ross Displays the Flag
23 Washington Arrives in Manhattan
24 Paul Revere Gives the Alarm
25 Driving the Golden Spike
26 "Let Us Have Peace"
27 The Peacemakers (March 1865)
28 Dealing with the Indians
29 "Remember the Alamo!"
30 Struggle for the New World
31 Lincoln at Independence Hall

32 Battle of Roger's Rock
33 Man on the Moon
34 Battle of Bunker Hill
35 Prairie Buffalo Hunt
36 Capture of Ft. Ticonderoga
37 Lewis and Clark Expedition
38 Home Attacked by Indians
39 John Paul Jones
40 Verrazano Discovers N.Y. Harbor
41 Surrender of General Lee
42 Mt. Vernon Yule Log
43 Capture of Blackbeard the Pirate
44 Disaster at Sea
45 Gilbert Stuart Paints Washington
46 Collecting Money for Revolutionary War
47 Surrender of General Burgoyne
48 Naval Warfare
49 The Spirit of '76
50 Washinton's Inauguration
51 Washington at Valley Forge
52 Paul Revere's Ride
53 Washington Fortifying Dorchester Heights
54 Eli Whitney Invents Cotton Gin
55 Battle of the Big Horn
56 Attack on an Emigrant Train
57 Famous Sea Battle
58 Early American Life
59 Union Army Bonfires
60 Nathan Hale
61 Union in Stone River
62 Washington Crossing the Delaware
63 John Paul Jones Unfurling Flag
64 American Pony Express
65 Norsemen Visit America
66 Columbus Discovers the New Land

IDIOT CARDS (66)

2 1/2" X 3 1/2"

Idiot Cards appears to have been the first Donruss set ever issued. This 66-card set was reported in 1961 by Buck Barker in his 3rd Catalog Additions list. The front of each card has a color, cartoon-like drawing and poses a straight line; the punch line appears on the back (which is red and black on white). The card number, set title, and the advisement "Collect all 66" appear on the back next to the "idiot" logo.

ITEM	MINT	EX
Set	80.00	60.00
Card	1.00	.75
Wrapper	---	35.00

1 I Used to be a Chainsmoker...
2 My Hair Needed Cutting Badly.
3 I Can Stand on My Head
4 These Birds Are For You
5 I Hit Myself with a Hammer
6 Darling
7 Does Your Face Hurt
8 Wanta Know My Secret to Scholastic Success?
9 You Made Me What I Am Today
10 You're a Reg'lar Einstein!
11 To Avoid that Rundown Feeling
12 See Ya Round
13 I Love You Like a Father
14 There's Plenty of Good Fishing Here...
15 I'm Built Upside-Down...
16 I'd Like to Be a Baker
17 She Sure Gave You a Dirty Look
18 Hey Dad! It Followed Me Home

19 You Have the Kind of Face I'd Like
20 You're Far from Dumb...
21 Touche' Nothin
22 Your New Suit Fits Like a Glove
23 When They Passed Out Noses You Tho't They Said Roses...
24 The Squirrels Love You...
25 You're Very Even Tempered
26 I Was Voted Most Likely...
27 Love Me...
28 You've Got a One Track Mind...
29 But Gladys!...
30 You'll Get a Big Bang Out'a This
31 You're No Tarzan
32 No One Cooks Like You Mom
33 You Tell 'em Pieface...
34 I Call My Girl Faucet...
35 Two Heads Are Better than One!
36 Don't Think It Hasn't Been Nice...

37 You Have Only One Equal!
38 I Can't Think Too Well Today
39 You've Got a Point There
40 Hey Frankie—Come Meet Your Biggest Fan
41 You've Got a One-Track Mind
42 If Lincoln Were Alive Today He'd Be a Remarkable Man
43 When They Passed Out Brains You Tho't They Said Trains...
44 Your Name Should Be Glue...
45 You Oughta Be on T.V.!
46 You've Gotta Voice Like a Bird
47 We'll Be Friends Till the End...
48 You've Made Quite an Impression on Me!
49 I'm Not Hard of Hearing
50 You've Got a Head Like a Door Knob...
51 I Ran for President...
52 Are You a Man or a Mouse??
53 We Want You on Our Tug O' War Team...
54 Have an Accident

55 You Musta Got Up Onna Wrong Side of Bed
56 I Just Wanted to Be a Little Boy and Have Fun...
57 I Was Just Admiring Your Picture...
58 Are You Brown from the Sun?
59 Hey Buddy, Wanna Drag?
60 What's That Book About?
61 You're a Perfect Idiot!
62 I Hear You Have the Biggest Collection of Idiot Cards in Town!
63 If Brains Were Dynamite
64 Money Won't Buy Happiness...
65 We're Striking for Shorter Hours!
66 I've Been Catching Up on My Reading!

I LOVE LUCY (110)

2 1/2" X 3 1/2"

Pacific Trading Cards scored a major coup by securing the license to produce this 110-card series based on the classic television series "I Love Lucy." Most of the card fronts (107 in all) contain black & white photographs from various "Lucy" episodes. Only three cards vary from this format: card #1 (illustrated) has a slight tint and card #'s 2 and 3 are in full color. The backs of the cards are white, with pink borders and blue frame lines surrounding the heart-shaped text area. Many of the cards have additional features following the text: quizzes, "Backstage," "Behind The Laughs," "Great Moments," etc. Collectors will find that the card caption is printed only on the front and the card number only on the back.

"Lucy" cards could be obtained by purchasing gumless "wax packs" containing 10 cards or by buying the entire set in a special "Collector Set" box. Both the display box for packs and the smaller set box are pink with white and blue accents. The wrapper is red with blue and white accents, except for the pink heart in the center. Note: since the set was issued in 1991 and could be obtained in mint, boxed sets, we have only listed mint prices for the "set" and "card" categories.

ITEM	MINT	EX
Set	10.00	---
Card	.10	---
Wrapper	---	.15
Set box	---	1.00
Display box	---	2.00

1 Lucy and Ricky
2 The Ricardos and Mertzes
3 Merry Christmas
4 The Mertzes
5 Junior and Senior
6 Bosom Buddies
7 Daydreamin'
8 They Love Lucy
9 Lucy [>[#@!*@!
10 Kissin' Cousins
11 They Call Her Sally Sweet
12 Sour Notes
13 Hillbilly Heaven
14 Lucy Plays Cupid
15 Hoedown!
16 Filling the Bill
17 Mrs. Mayor
18 Mama's Little Man
19 "I'm Your Vitameatavegamin Girl"
20 Hair Today, Gone Tomorrow
21 Queen of the Gypsies
22 Foiled Again
23 "Speed It Up!"
24 Fred's Masterpiece
25 Stirring Up Some Trouble
26 Vacation from Marriage
27 The Boys
28 Lucy the Paperhanger
29 Handy Dandy Lucy
30 Mrs. Mannequin
31 We're Having a Baby
32 Baby Makes Three
33 The Happy Couple
34 Made to Order
35 Squaw-King

36 Dancing Fool
37 Dance, Girl, Dance
38 "Madame, Do You Drink?"
39 The Dress Shop
40 Seeing Double
41 Truth or Consequences
42 Fiddlin' Around
43 Interior Undercoating
44 Friends and Neighbors
45 Lucy Calling!
47 23 Skidoo
48 Charm School Dropouts
49 Say Cheese
50 Lip-Smackin' Lucy
51 Mink's Paradise
52 The Feuding Foursome
54 "It's a Moo-Moo!"
55 Lucy Tees Off
56 Pistol Packin' Mertz
57 All Tied Up
58 Busting Lucy's Budget
59 Partners in Crime
60 Blonde Ambition
61 California, Here We Come!
62 Which Way to Hollywood?
63 Little Ole Pea-Picker, Lucy
64 Starstruck
65 Cyrano de Lucy

66 Making Headway in Hollywood
67 Bronze Goddess
68 Silent Partners
69 "Hi Ethel, It's Lucy."
70 Rock and the Redhead
71 A Routine Souvenir Hunt
72 I Brake for Redheads
73 Heads Up!
74 In the Dog House
75 Fairway Foursome
76 Ricky is a Big Stinker
77 Honeybunch
78 Fred Mertz
79 Lucy the Landlubber
80 "Is Your Cocker Off His Rocker?"
81 Tally Ho!
82 Dressed to Kill
83 Two Heads are Better than One
84 Funny in France
85 Charles Not in Charge
86 Grape Juice, Anyone?
87 "You're Not Even Trying."
88 My Son, the Drumming Doctor
89 Pizza to Go?

90 "Is It Supposed To Do That?"
91 Gone Fishin'
92 Like Father, Like Son
93 Guilty as Charged
94 Puppy Love
95 SUPERLUCY
96 Gabby Gangsters
97 A Rose by Any Other Name
98 Never Can Say Goodbye
99 Mother Hen
100 The Calypso Ricardos
101 Off-Key Ricardo
102 "Surprise!"
103 Ironing It Out
104 Uncementing a Friendship
105 Smile, Lucy.
106 Teaching Lucy a New Trick
107 Yankee Doodle Lucy
108 Fred and Ethel
109 Out on a Ledge
110 Ricky Says Yes

316

I LOVE SNOOPY ALBUM (288) STICKERS

1 15/16" X 2 9/16"

The "I Love Snoopy" introduction inside the front cover of the album designed for this set is well-intentioned but amusing evidence of the need for foreign manufacturers to employ native English speakers to proofread their handi- work. Of the 288 album stickers, 242 have regular glossy surface artwork and 46 are color designs printed on foil. The 32-page album is filled with "I Love Snoopy" captions which are mercifully covered over when the stickers are affixed. Note: set price includes album.

ITEM	MINT	EX
Set	30.00	22.50
Sticker	.10	.07
Wrapper	--	.35
Album	2.00	1.50

INCREDIBLE HULK (88 & 22)   2 1/2" X 3 1/2"

There is no mistaking the Incredible Hulk set marketed by Topps in 1979. The cards have jagged green borders enclosing the color pictures, and they are visible from quite a distance. The captions are printed in yellow and are found alongside the number, right under the picture. A "TV Facts" presentation appears on the back of 10 cards; the remaining 78 backs are poster pieces (four different) and poster preview cards. The numbered stickers have pictures encircled by yellow or pink bands and are uncaptioned. Note: set price includes stickers.

ITEM	MINT	EX
Set	20.00	15.00
Card	.15	.10
Sticker	.35	.25
Wrapper	––	.35
Box	––	8.00

1 No Power to Save Her!	39 Nightmare at the Ranch
2 Experiment: Perilous!	40 Has the Hulk Met His Match?
3 Unearthly Seizure	41 Battle of the Behemoths
4 Birth of the Beast Man	42 Monster in the Mansion
5 This Man...This Monster!	43 No Escape from the Brute
6 Friend...or Fiend?	44 A Titan in Times Square
7 The Hand of Fear	45 Manhattan Mayhem
8 The Creature's Plan	46 The Beast Bursts Through
9 Power of the Brute	47 The 747 Affair
10 To Rescue a Child	48 Stranger at the Door
11 The Make-Shift Bridge	49 Face of Fear
12 The Creature...Shot!	50 The Dark Journey Back
13 Fury of the Hulk	51 Bringing in a 747
14 The Charging Terror	52 "No! It Can't Happen Now!"
15 The Monster Strikes!	53 Caught in Mid-Transformation!
16 In the Clutches of Horror!	54 Banner's Titanic Struggle!
17 The Incredible Man Monster	55 Suppressing the Demon within Him
18 Prehistoric Mutant	56 Creature in the Pilot's Seat!
19 Portrait of a Monster	57 Monster at the Controls
20 Horror in the Woods	58 Panic in the Cockpit
21 Stirrings with the Beast	59 The Life-Saving Thrust
22 The Pawn of Destiny	60 Greetings from Our Captain!
23 Monstrous Reflection	61 Racing Through the Airliner
24 Metamorphosis	62 Stan Lee's Creation...the Hulk
25 Inside the Hyperbaric Chamber	63 Creature on the Runway!
26 Engine of Destruction	64 Nobody Fences in the Hulk!
27 No Walls Can Hold Him!	65 David Banner Confronts... Himself!
28 The Creature Is Loose!	66 Hope Through Hypnotherapy
29 Living Nightmare	67 A Man Possessed
30 The Abomination	68 The Raging Spirit
31 Modified Hulk Make-Up	69 The Humanoid Appears
32 Back from Beyond	70 Tower of Strength
33 Ferrigno in Character	71 No Longer Human
34 Filming the Episode "Married"	72 The Captive Creature
35 The Flame and the Fury	73 The Tranquilizing Gas
36 The Inferno	74 The Two Faces of Dr. Banner
37 Death of Dr. Marks	
38 The Hulk Strikes Back!	

75 Nothing Can Stop the Hulk!
76 Netting the Hulk
77 Sensing Danger
78 The Capture
79 David Banner's Wedding Day
80 The Recurring Dream
81 The Force Inside Banner
82 Demon with a Soul
83 The Mindless Primitive
84 Mightiest Creature on Earth
85 The Monster within Us All!
86 Being of Fantastic Proportions
87 Victim of Gamma Radiation
88 The Eyes of David Banner

1 Modified Hulk Make-Up
2 Metamorphosis
3 Hope Through Hypnotherapy
4 The Hulk Strikes Back!
5 The Monster within Us All
6 Manhattan Mayhem
7 Portrait of a Monster
8 Mightiest Creature on Earth
9 Suppressing the Demon within Him
10 The Monster Strikes!
11 This Man...This Monster!
12 The Creature...Shot!
13 Racing Through the Airliner
14 The Incredible Man Monster
15 Friend...or Fiend?
16 Ferrigno in Character
17 In the Clutches of Horror!
18 A Titan in Times Square
19 Has the Hulk Met His Match?
20 The Pawn of Destiny
21 Experiment: Perilous!
22 The Mindless Primitive

INDIANA JONES & THE (88 & 11) TEMPLE OF DOOM

2 1/2" X 3 1/2"

The story of Professor Jones' visit to the Temple of Doom was hardly the "adventure classic" that the title card of this series claims. The entire run of 86 story cards has monotonous red borders and yellow caption panels which overwhelm the color photos they surround. In fact, the back of the card, with an excellent drawing of "Indy" and crisp layout, is the better side by far. The numbered and captioned stickers are also well-designed: they have diecut color photographs set on a white background and puzzle piece backs (see the uncut sheet of ten stickers illustrated below). Note: set price includes stickers.

ITEM	MINT	EX
Set	12.50	9.00
Card	.10	.07
Sticker	.35	.25
Wrapper	--	.35
Box	--	4.00

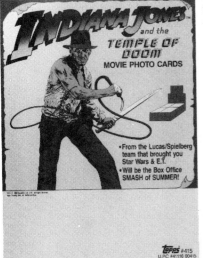

Indiana Jones & The Temple of Doom

1	Title Card	22	The Arrival	43	The Blood of Kali	64	Voodoo Peril!
2	Singer Willie Scott	23	The Palace Banquet	44	Tortured!	65	The Kids Slug it Out!
3	Diamond of Death	24	The Little MAHARAJAH	45	Cage of Death	66	INDY on the Scene!
4	Poisoned!	25	DR. JONES, Banquet Guest	46	Mindless Slave	67	The Mine Adventure
5	The Diamond Seeker	26	A Royal Feast?	47	The Burning	68	Battling Mine Cars!
6	Escape from CLUB OBI WAN	27	Losing Her Appetite	48	SHORT ROUND to the Rescue!	69	Breaking Free!
7	The Car Chase	28	Time Out for Romance	49	Attacking the Guards	70	INDY'S Gamble
8	Flight to Doom	29	Look Out, Behind You!	50	Grabbed by INDY!	71	Deadly Torrents
9	Airborne!	30	Peril in the Palace!	51	INDY is Revived!	72	Hang on, SHORT ROUND!
10	High-Flying Peril!	31	INDY'S Warning	52	Rescuing WILLIE SCOTT!	73	Saved by WILLIE SCOTT!
11	River of Death	32	The Discovery	53	Everything's Okay...	74	The Evil of MOLA RAM
12	Shaman of MAYAPORE	33	Trapped!	54	INDY'S Revenge	75	Don't Mess with INDY!
13	A Village Besieged	34	INDY Gets the Point!	55	The Battle Rages	76	Two Against One...& No Gun!
14	Tales of the MAYAPORE	35	The Spike Chamber	56	Fighting Against Evil!	77	Fantastic Struggle!
15	The Quest Begins	36	WILLIE in the Bug Tunnel	57	Freeing the Children	78	Caught in Between — !
16	To the PALACE of PANKOT!	37	The TEMPLE OF DOOM	58	The Escape Continues!	79	INDY in Action
17	Whoops!	38	The Human Sacrifice	59	The Giant THUGGEE	80	Courage of INDIANA JONES
18	Making Camp	39	The Evil High Priest	60	Incredible Fight!	81	Surrounded!
19	The Dreams of DR. JONES	40	The Flaming Heart	61	INDY'S Fight for Life!	82	The Bridge — Cut!
20	Elephant Ride!	41	INDY'S Discovery	62	Belt to Oblivion!	83	Plunge to Doom!
21	Trek to the Palace	42	INDIANA JONES...Captured!	63	SHORT ROUND'S Chance!	84	INDIANA JONES vs. MOLA RAM
						85	A Day of Rejoicing!
						86	Return of the Stones
						87	The Adventure Concludes
						88	Checklist

INSULT POST CARDS (32)   3 1/8" X 5 1/4"

One of the little-known sets of 1966 is this series of Insult Post Cards produced by Topps. The fronts contain large color drawings with seemingly harmless statements—until the reader puts the two together, thereby forming the intended insult.

The backs are actual post cards, with printed spaces for postage and address, and are numbered in the upper left corner.

ITEM	MINT	EX
Set	150.00	115.00
Card	4.00	3.00
Wrapper	--	20.00
Box	--	50.00

Insult Post Cards

1 I'm Ape Over You!
2 Hi Baby!
3 You Turn Me On!
4 You're One In A Million!
5 I'd Like To Have You For Dinner Sometime!

6 Fangs For The Memory!
7 I Admire Your Open Mind!
8 You're A Dream!
9 I'd Like To Hear From You!
10 You're Out Of This World!
11 Your Teeth Are Like Stars...Pointed!

12 Give Me Your Heart
13 You Were Made For Me!
14 I'm Blue Without You!
15 Let Me Go Lover!
16 You're Sweet!

17 Come Alive! You're In The Monster Generation!
18 Thanks - Your Picture Cured My Hiccups!
19 You're Just What The Doctor Ordered!
20 Look Into My Baby Blue Eye
21 Hey, Lover...We're 2 Of A Kind!
22 Fly Away With Me!
23 I Love Your Curly Locks
24 You're Pretty As A Picture!
25 Take Me In Your Arms
26 You've Got Me Wrapped Around Your Finger!
27 I've Got A Crush On You
28 ...Wish You Were Here!
29 I Wanna Hold Your Hand!
30 Tall, Dark and Hang Some
31 You Swing!
32 You're A Fright For Sore Eyes!

IRAN CONTRA SCANDAL (36)

2 3/4″ X 3 3/4″

OLIVER NORTH

The acid-tipped brush and pen of Salim Yaqub and Paul Brancato found plenty of targets in this politicized treatment of the "arms for hostages" affair. According to a statement printed on the end of the box, "Much of the information on these cards was developed by The Christic Institute, a non-profit public-interest law firm" located on Capitol Hill. Collectors may have a difficult time sorting through the "facts" presented on the backs of the cards, but they are worth reading. The artwork, on the other hand, is not as attractive as that in some other Eclipse sets, since using both caricature and overt symbolism to ridicule often defeats the intended purpose. Originally issued in 1988, the boxed set is still in production and it currently sells for $10.

1 The Iran-Contra Hearings
2 Anastasio Somoza
3 Enrique Bermudez
4 Adolfo Calero
5 William Casey
6 Caspar Weinberger
7 John Singlaub
8 Thomas Posey
9 The La Penca Bomber
10 Rene Corvo & Felipe Vidal
11 The Medellin Cartel
12 John Hull
13 Oliver North
14 Robert Owen
15 Carl "Spitz" Channell
16 Joseph Coors
17 King Fahd
18 Elliot Abrams

19 Richard Secord
20 Albert Hakim
21 Richard Gadd & Robert Dutton
22 Thomas Clines
23 Rafael "Chi Chi" Quintero
24 Theodore Shackley
25 William Buckley
26 Manucher Ghorbanifar
27 David Kimche
28 Robert McFarlane
29 Eugene Hasenfus
30 Felix Rodriguez
31 Donald Gregg
32 George Bush
33 Edwin Meese III
34 Fawn Hall
35 John Poindexter
36 Ronald Reagan

JAKE'S JOKES (121)

2 1/2" X 3 1/2"

What is brown, has a hump, and lives at the North Pole?

1

A Lost camel.

CONTAINS 18 JOKE CARDS

SERIES 1 COLLECT ALL 121

What kind of suit does a duck wear?

3

121

SERIES 1
Checklist

Question: "What do you call a 2,000 pound gorilla?" Answer: "Sir." If cornball humor of this variety tickles your fancy, then "Jake's Jokes" is the series for you! There are 120 joke cards in the set, each with a color drawing and question on the front. The answer is printed on the backs, which have nothing else but a sallow "Jake's Official Jokes" logo, a copyright line for Joseph Rosenbloom, and the card number. Despite the advertising line on the wrapper — "Series 1, Collect All 121," no series 2 has been seen to date. In fact, leftovers of series 1 continue to be sold in variety stores around the country. Each cellophane pack holds 18 cards and advertising for various humor books is printed on the reverse. The checklist card, #121, is nothing more than a list of numbers with boxes alongside.

ITEM	MINT	EX
Set	13.50	10.00
Card	.10	.07
Wrapper	--	.20

What time do ducks get up?

6

1 A lost camel.
2 "Sir."
3 A duck-sedo (Tuxedo).
4 Railroad ties.
5 Cinderelephant.
6 At the quack of dawn.
7 A lawn moo-er.
8 The dentist.
9 A caterpillar.
10 "Jungle Bells."
11 On toadstools.
12 A spelling bee.
13 A purr-a-keet.
14 Water.
15 Road hogs.
16 A horse.
17 A movie star.
18 A clock.
19 Goldfish.
20 A sourpuss.
21 A milk truck.
22 Bluebirds.
23 A garbage truck.
24 A rocket.
25 The Daily Moos.
26 The roller ghost-er.
27 It sounded too fishy.
28 A taxicab driver.
29 In pup tents.
30 A wolfswagen.
31 In snowbanks.
32 A grasshopper.
33 An eye doctor.
34 Sheik-to-sheik (cheek).
35 A horse with a rider.
36 A colonel (kernal).
37 A safe robbery.

38 A centipede with a wooden leg.
39 A mouse going on a vacation.
40 A stamp.
41 On Mummy's Day.
42 Super Pickle.
43 A Santa klutz.
44 Eskimoos.
45 A frog sandwich.
46 A grasshopper with hiccups.
47 A zebra at the North Pole.
48 A zebra on roller skates.
49 An elephant in a Baggie.
50 "Tim..."
51 "Who greased the vine?"
52 The Banana Splits
53 Folling with a bee.
54 A fumble bee.
55 He just fell into it.
56 The big cheese.
57 A purr-snatcher.
58 A toad-em pole.
59 A frog horn.
60 "Hop-in!"
61 It sets a while.
62 Hop rods.
63 20-20-20-20.
64 At the ghost office.
65 A comb.
66 A comb.
67 TP.
68 A box of quackers.
69 An illigator.
70 Porcupine.
71 Your teeth.
72 In the blood bank.
73 He was always horsing around.

74 His fingernail.
75 A lost poiar bear.
76 Time to get a new chair.
77 By school buzz.
78 By rocket sheep.
79 Launch.
80 "Hello, Hello."
81 A big stink.
82 Fangfurters.
83 A bronco-saurus.
84 Bacon and legs.
85 Plunk rock.
86 A school bus full of elephants.
87 New Yolk City.
88 "Toadly awesome."
89 A fresh vegetable.
90 Bat-teries.
91 Moo-sic.
92 A dino-saur.
93 He fell for it.
94 Whooping Cranes.
95 C-A-T.
96 He burned up the road.
97 Boo-ble gum.
98 Jellyfish.
99 Hollow-wienies.
100 Peek-a-Boo.
101 Because two's a crowd.
102 "Ho-Ho-Ho."
103 The Ape-B-C's.
104 Because it was baaa-d.
105 A pancake.
106 Thirst-day.
107 Mouse-tard.

108 A shrunk skunk.
109 The ground.
110 A hot dog.
111 A cold.
112 "Twick or tweet."
113 Frostbite.
114 A quick quack.
115 BOO-ts.
116 An elephant six-pack.
117 No one.
118 Because vacuum cleaners don't have long enough cords.
119 Time to get it fixed.
120 A chair.
121 Checklist card.

JAMES BOND (66)　　　　2 1/2" X 3 1/2"

This Philadelphia Chewing Gum Company set was issued in 1965, and contains black and white photos from three James Bond films: "Dr. No" (1-18), "From Russia With Love" (19-41), and "Goldfinger" (42-66). All other detail save the white-bordered picture is found on the back of the card. The set title is printed in white on a black chevron design, and the number is located in a red target device. The caption lies just over the narrative, which is printed in black ink. Both the credit lines, at the bottom, and the "Secret Agent 007" line at the top, are printed in red.

ITEM	MINT	EX
Set	225.00	190.00
Card	3.00	2.50
Wrapper	—	25.00
Box	—	75.00

1 Debonair But Deadly	19 James Bond, Secret Service Agent 007	33 The Fight with Grant	50 Captured at Last
2 Vacation Over, Back to Work!		34 Hunted by Helicopter	51 The Incredible Laser Ray
3 Trouble in Jamaica	20 The Big Three	35 James Bond Vs. Spectre	52 Spying on a Spy
4 Passions Rise!	21 Dress Rehearsal for Assassination	36 Armed with "Q's" Special Equipment	53 Felix Leiter of the CIA
5 Quarrel			54 The Hood's Convention
6 The Allies Meet	22 Spectre, International Crime Organization	37 Chase by Sea	55 One Good Turn Deserves Another
7 Licensed to Kill		38 Always Burn Your Boats Behind You	
8 Dr. No's Pet	23 Agents of Spectre		56 Goldfinger Vs. the United States
9 Bond Reduces the Enemy by One	24 Graduate of a College for Killers	39 Rosa	
		40 The Dagger Shoes	57 The U.S. Army Strikes Back!
10 The Dragon Tank	25 Kronsteen, the Planner	41 Spectre's Final Effort	58 A Treacherous Escape
11 007's Luck Runs Out, Almost!	26 Looking in on the Russians	42 007 Puts the Heat On	59 Oddjob the Invincible
12 A Prisoner of Dr. No	27 The Lovely Tatiana	43 Gin Rummy by Radio	60 More than a Demonstration
13 Dr. Julius No	28 Double Bait	44 "Not a Personal Affair, 007, a Job!"	61 The Fight with Oddjob
14 Dr. No's Underground Laboratory	29 Head of Secret Service Station "T"		62 Oddjob's Deadly Derby
		45 The Incredible Aston—Martin	63 Death of a Killer
15 Dr. No's Tunnel of Torture	30 Attacked by the Russians	46 A Study in Cheating	64 Racing the Clock at Fort Knox
16 An Anxious Moment for Dr. No	31 "She Should Have Kept Her Mouth Shut!"	47 A Powerful Demonstration	65 Aurie Goldfinger
17 Dr. No's Finish		48 Tilly Masterson	66 The Final Encounter
18 "Where Is She? Quick!"	32 A Taped Message from the Middle East	49 The 24 Carat Rolls Royce	

CARDBOARD HEADER FOR 29¢ CELLOPHANE PACK CONTAINING 36 CARDS.

Like the preceding set, the obverses in this 1966 Philly Gum set have photographs but no other accompanying de-

tail. The pictures in this 66-card series, however, are sepia in tone and depict scenes from the James Bond movie "Thunderball." The reverses are printed entirely in black ink on a white surface. The card number appears in a small square along with a frogman figure. In sequence from top to bottom are found: a wavy black chevron containing the words "James Bond;" the phrase "Secret Agent 007;" the caption; and the narrative. Below this is a "Code Quiz" which required a "Secret Decoder" (inserted into packs) for deciphering.

1	James Bond, Secret Agent 007
2	The Incredible Aston—Martin
3	Never Hit a Lady
4	A Brutal Affair
5	Flying Fists and Figures
6	Defeat of an Assassin
7	A Jet Get Away
8	Flying Solo
9	Let's Get Out of Here!
10	Water, Gentlemen?
11	Hatching an Evil Plot
12	A New Enemy—Emilio Largo
13	A Relaxing Rub-Down
14	A Marked Man
15	Terror on the Traction Machine
16	Heat Treatment Deluxe!
17	Evil Work Ahead
18	Death Dealing Damsel
19	Rockets on the Road
20	Grand Scheme Underway
21	On the Ocean Bottom
22	A New Assignment
23	Felix Leiter, CIA
24	Hardly a Proper Pet!
25	Domino
26	Enemies at the Gambling Table
27	Spectre Fails Again
28	The Disco Volante
29	Underwater Peril
30	Grenades in the Water
31	Fiona Kelley
32	Trapped by Black Suited Killers
33	A Frantic Search
34	Prisoner of Spectre
35	Bold escape Foiled
36	Visions of a Watery Grave
37	Killer of the Deep
38	Q Branch to the Rescue
39	Target for Tonight
40	Going Down for a Close Look
41	Where are the Bombs?
42	An Important Find
43	A New Ally
44	Silencing an Eavesdropper
45	Checking Weapons
46	A Big Job to Do
47	Secret Agent in Disguise
48	An Intruder Discovered
49	'Copter to the Rescue
50	Escape from the Tide
51	Parachuting to Battle
52	No Mercy Expected
53	On the Way to Battle
54	Water Borne Murderers
55	See-Saw Battle
56	Undersea Villainy
57	Defeat for Spectre!
58	There Goes Largo!
59	Ace in the Hole
60	Like Riding a Rocket
61	Final Bid for Freedom
62	Justice Must Prevail
63	Facing Death Weaponless
64	Welcome Assistance
65	Diaster Ahead!
66	Success for James Bond

ITEM	MINT	EX
Set	265.00	225.00
Card	3.50	3.00
Decoder	10.00	7.50
Wrapper	--	25.00
Box	--	100.00

JAWS 2 (59 & 11)

The selling point of the movie Jaws 2 was violent action, and that theme was successfully carried over into the card set issued by Topps in 1978. The color photos have a yellow frame line and black borders. The card number is located in a shark fin design on the front, and the caption (yellow print)

2 1/2" X 3 1/2"

is directly below the picture. The backs are either puzzle pieces (44) or a "Movie Facts" feature (15) done in red, black and yellow colors. The blue-bordered stickers are numbered but are not captioned; the titles for them in the check-list were assigned by comparing them to identical pictures in the card set.

ITEM	MINT	EX
Set	12.00	9.00
Card	.15	.10
Sticker	.35	.25
Wrappers (2)		
"Extra!"	--	3.00
No "Extra!"	--	.35
Box	--	5.00

1 Stalked by the Killer Shark
2 Brody's Leap for Life!
3 Chief Martin Brody
4 Chewing out Mayor Vaughn
5 Remains of a Sea Monster
6 Demolishing a Boat
7 A Close Brush with Death!
8 Beware the Oncoming Horror!
9 Trapped!!
10 Cornered by the Monster!
11 Spotting the Monster Shark
12 Youth of Amity
13 The Calm Before the Storm!
14 Brody's Close Call!
15 The Charging Fury!
16 Dodging the Monster!
17 Shark Alert!
18 Observing the Sea Battle!
19 Too Close for Comfort!
20 The Investigators
21 The Hunted!
22 Shark Fighters of Amity
23 The Devil from the Deep
24 A Cruel and Violent Fate!
25 Rescued from Certain Death!
26 The Shark Closes In...!
27 "Look Out!!!"
28 Capsized!
29 Serene Voyage
30 Night of the Hunter!
31 Scrambling for Their Lives!
32 Horrendous Sights!
33 Trapped in the Inferno!
34 Brody States His Case!
35 The Image of Terror
36 Circling...!
37 Horror of the Seas!
38 The Craft is Sinking!
39 Watching in Horror!
40 Brody at the Beach!
41 Plunge into Death!
42 An Alarmed Chief Brody!
43 Preparing for the Kill!
44 Sitting Ducks!
45 Smashed Like a Matchstick!
46 The Shark's Meal
47 The Monster Attacks!
48 Attacking a Helicopter!
49 The Final Charge!
50 Mauled by the Monster Shark!
51 Shark Prey!
52 Alone Against the Shark!
53 Aiming Against the Monster!
54 Sea Explorer
55 Brody...Clinging to Life!
56 The Supreme Moment of Fear!
57 Roy Scheider
58 Monarch of the Ocean!
59 The Jaws of Death

1 Roy Scheider
2 Monarch of the Ocean!
3 The Jaws of Death
4 Sea Explorer
5 The Monster Attacks!
6 Aiming Against the Monster!
7 Brody...Clinging to Life!
8 Shark Prey!
9 Alone Against the Shark!
10 Mauled by the Monster Shark!
11 The Supreme Moment of Fear!

CHEWING OUT MAYOR VAUGHN

JAWS 3-D (44)

"Sea World...part aquarium, part amusement park...opens with an astounding new exhibit, a captive killer shark." Unfortunately, this is a BABY killer shark, and when it dies, MAMA arrives with a vengeance and starts trashing central Florida. Not a bad idea, really, and Topps decided it had enough merit to produce a 44-card set based on the movie. On the front side of every card there is a color photo with one descriptive sentence. The card number is printed under the jaw of a yellow shark-head design. The more terrifying aspects of the film appear in a series of 3-D sketches on the backs of the cards. These scenes are viewed through 3-D glasses provided in every pack. It is the titles of these 3-D views which make up the checklist printed below. Note: set price includes a 3-D viewer.

ITEM	MINT	EX
Set	6.00	4.50
Card	.15	.10
Glasses	.25	.15
Wrapper	—	.35
Box	—	4.00

1 Header Card	12 Speargun Assault!	23 Bloody Remains!	34 Invading Sea World!
2 Midnight Snack!	13 The Captive Creature	24 The New Peril!	35 The Tunnel In Turmoil!
3 The First Attack!	14 Moving The Behemoth	25 Brody's Warning	36 "Evacuate The Area!"
4 Capsized!	15 The Shark Walkers	26 The Monster Appears!!	37 Madness And Mayhem!
5 Sea Lovers	16 Opening Day!	27 Seeking Human Prey!	38 Fitzroyce Strikes Back!
6 In Search Of Overman	17 Wonders of Sea World!	28 "Everybody Out Of The Water!"	39 Swallowed By The Beast!
7 "Kathryn...Look Out!"	18 Here's Water In Your Eye!	29 Unaware Of Their Peril!	40 Diverting The Monster
8 Rescued By Dolphin Friends!	19 The Major Attraction	30 Zeroing In!	41 The Shark Smashes Through!
9 The Stun-Stick!	20 Startling Exhibit!	31 A Monstrous Demise!	42 The Control Room In Chaos!
10 Facing Savage Death!	21 Terror Of The Tentacles!	32 The Pursued	43 Blasted By A Grenade!
11 Kathryn In Trouble	22 "Oh My God...It's REAL!"	33 At Death's Door!	44 Synopsis/Checklist

JEM ALBUM STICKERS (225)

Jem, the female superstar rocker with "holographic powers," is the lead singer of a "truly outrageous band" called The Holograms. They have signed to make a movie but are threatened by a rival band, The Misfits. That is the story which unfolds, sticker by sticker, in this set issued by Diamond in 1987. The 32-page album is printed in the "coded" style pioneered by Diamond ("Magic Decoder" insert provided). Note: set price includes album.

ITEM	MINT	EX
Set	25.00	18.00
Sticker	.10	.07
Wrapper	—	.35
Album	2.00	1.50
Box	—	2.50

Jem Album Stickers

JET SET STICKERS (40 & 14)   2 1/2" X 3 7/16"

Thirty-nine of the forty sticker sheets in this Fleer set have two separate stickers on the sheet; the large size is a national shield, while the smaller strip sticker at top may or may not have anything to do with the country with which it is paired. Both types of stickers are printed on foil and are set onto a plain brown paper backing. In addition, there is a series of 14 "Fleer Funny Post Cards" printed in gray, black, and shades of red. These cards have titles (but are not numbered) and are blank-backed. Note: set price includes all stickers and cards.

ITEM	MINT	EX
Set	35.00	25.00
Sticker	.75	.50
Post card	.50	.35
Wrapper	--	2.00
Box	--	7.50

Afro - Right On
Argentina - Travel Ambassador
Australia - Down Under
Austria - Goodwill Ambassador
Belgium - Official Pilot
Brazil - Carnival
Canada - Bien Venue
China - Motorcycle For Your Health
Confederate - Dixie Lives
Denmark - Fly Me
England - The Goin's Great
France - Bon Voyage
Germany - Wilkommen
Gibraltar - V.I.P.
Greece - Co-Pilot
Guam - Gone Fishin'
Ireland - Erin Go Bragh
Israel - Shalom
Italy - Arrivederci
Jamaica - Hang 10
Japan - Sayonara
Mexico - Hasta Luego
Morocco - On The Road To Marakesh
Norway - Travel Expert
Philippines - Go! Go! Go!
Poland - Navigator
Puerto Rico - Fun in the Sun
Spain - Ole'
Sweden - Think Snow
Switzerland - Bank On It
Surinam - Welkom!
Trinidad - Surf's Up

Turkey - Ride the Orient Express
U.A.R. - Honorary Stewardess
United Nations - Tourist
Uruguay - I'm Lost
U.S.A. - Keep On Truckin'
U.S.A. - See America 1st
Venezuela - One for the Road
Virgin Islands - Tour Guide

Fleer Funny Post Cards

[Australia — Kangaroo]
Darkest Africa!
Dracula's Castle!
Egypt
Eiffel Tower
Hawaii
New York
Seven Wonders Of The World
Spain
Swat Airlines...
Taj Mahal
The Dirty Post Card!
The Leaning People of Pisa!
Visit The Red Sea

JIGGLY BUTTONS (24)   VARIOUS SIZES

Jiggly Buttons stand out as one of Topps' finest productions ever to be issued without gum. All but one of the 24 buttons is round; the remaining button is rectangular in shape. Each is made of cardboard and each has a base from which a shaped design projects outward on a spring. The buttons are not numbered and were manufactured for Topps in Hong Kong. The "wrapper" is actually a paper envelope and it bears a 10-cent price.

ITEM	MINT	EX
Set	360.00	270.00
Button	12.00	9.00
Wrapper	--	25.00
Box	--	150.00

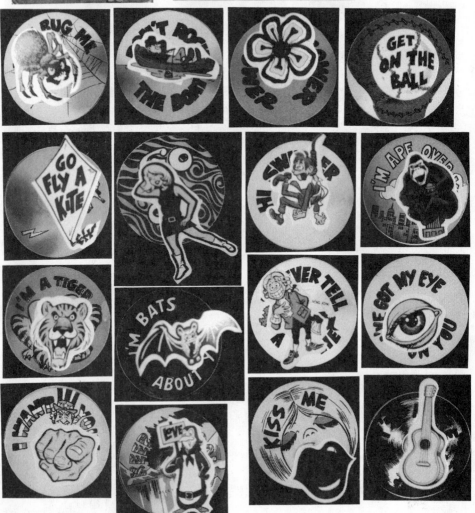

Don't Bug Me	I Want You
Don't Rock the Boat	Keep Cool
Flower Power	Kiss Me
Get On the Ball	Let's Make Music
Go Fly a Kite	Lover
Go Go	Sock It To Me
Hi Swinger	Stop
I'm Ape Over You	What's Shaking Baby?
I'm A Tiger	You Make Me Nervous
I'm Bats About You	You're Off Your Rocker
I Never Tell a Lie	You Shake Me Up
I've Got My Eye On You	You Turn Me On

JOHNNY CLEM (10)   2 1/2" X 3 1/2"

"We're sure you've never seen a set like this before," reads the advertising for the "Johnny Clem Diamond Edition." It continues: "This unique card set is the first SILHOUETTE card set ever produced (as far as we know)" and "High quality and unique graphics make this special 10-card edition a rare collectible item." The producer, Tuff Stuff Magazine, certainly punched all the buttons here in an effort to make Johnny Clem sound attractive. Unfortunately, they're wrong on ALL accounts.

We HAVE seen silhouette cards before. They were produced in the 1890-1910 period as a novelty idea, but the once-popular art form was already on its way out, a victim of the photographic image. Modern collectors seem to be turning up their noses at this attempted revival of "silhouetture" even if the story of Johnny Clem is one to stir the patriotic soul. At the current retail range of $8-$12, the set certainly seems overpriced, and using the "R" word ("rare"), especially in the present tense, is manipulative. The gorgeous full-color, foil-bordered advertising poster is a magnificent contrast to the set itself.

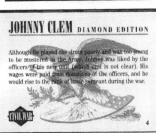

ADVERTISING POSTER

The 66-card Johnson vs. Goldwater set was issued by Topps in 1964 to capitalize on the events and excitement of the presidential compaign. The cards have black and white photographs of the candidates and are white-bordered. The backs, which are printed in blue on a white surface, contain an elephant and a donkey design at the top. The card number and text are found below this design.

ITEM	MINT	EX
Set	150.00	115.00
Card	2.00	1.50
Wrapper	---	6.00
Box	---	60.00

1. President Johnson Often Enjoys a Walk on the White House Lawn as He Takes a Brief Break from His Many Duties.
2. In This Photograph from 1952, Lyndon Johnson Is Being Congratulated By His Mother Rebecca Baines Johnson.
3. United States Attorney General Robert Kennedy Shakes the Hand of President Lyndon Johnson as The Chief Executive Steps Up to a Microphone.
4. Mrs. Goldwater Looks on as Her Husband Campaigns in California Just Before the State Primaries.
5. President Lyndon Johnson Is Pictured with Lynda Bird His Older Daughter and the First Lady.
6. President Lyndon Johnson Arrives at Lambert-St. Louis Field in St. Louis and Is Greeted by a Large Cheering Crowd.
7. A Snapshot from the Johnson Family Album.
8. When World War II Broke Out, Lyndon Johnson Was the First Member of Congress to Become Active in the Armed Forces.
9. Prime Minister of England, Sir Alec Douglas-Home and President Lyndon Johnson Are Shown at the British Embassy in Washington, D.C.
10. Mrs. Lyndon B. Johnson Looks up at Her Husband, the President, as the Famous Couple Arrives at the LBJ Ranch in Johnson City, Texas.
11. Senator Barry Goldwater of Arizona Was Born in Phoenix on January 1, 1909.
12. During Lyndon Johnson's Campaign for the Vice-Presidency in 1960, He Was Opposed by Republican Henry Cabot Lodge.
13. President Johnson Holds an Autographed Baseball, Previously Signed by Presidents Kennedy, Eisenhower and Truman.
14. Major General Barry Goldwater, of the Air Force Reserves, Discussing Training Plans With a Fellow Officer.
15. President Lyndon Johnson in a Family Photograph.
16. President Johnson Strides Briskly Across the White House Lawn to His Waiting Helicopter.
17. Among the President's Daily Duties Is Meeting with Visiting Diplomats from Different Countries.
18. Barry Goldwater, the Senator from Arizona, Is Applauded as He Finishes a Speech in New Hampshire.
19. Lyndon Johnson as a Senator Is Pictured with Fellow Senators Mike Mansfield of Montana and Everett Dirkson of Illinois.
20. Senator Barry Goldwater Is Pictured with His Wife, Peggy Just Before Speaking in New Hampshire.

21. Senator Lyndon Johnson Is Shown Convalescing at His Ranch in Texas Several Weeks after Having Suffered a Heart Attack.
22. Senator Barry Goldwater Puts on a Pair of "Go Goldwater" Campaign Glasses Which Were Distributed during a Campaign Rally.
23. Senator Lyndon Johnson in 1958, Chats with Major General John B. Medaris, Chief of an Army Missile Center.
24. Barry Goldwater Addresses an Outdoor Audience in Southern California as He Begins His Campaign for the State Primaries.
25. Governor Scranton of Pennsylvania Who Was in the Running for the Republican Presidential Candidacy, Meets with Pres. Johnson at the White House.
26. Senator Barry Goldwater of Arizona Arrives in Chicago to Speak at a Fund-Raising Dinner.
27. President Lyndon Johnson Relaxes on His Ranch in Texas, Dressed in the Casual Clothes of a Farmer.
28. President Lyndon Johnson Is Pictured At Work in his "Office in the Sky"-- the Presidential Plane, Air Force 1.
29. President Lyndon Johnson Is Shown Giving a Speech Before the Organization of American States.
30. In 1959 Lyndon Johnson was the Senate Majority Leader.
31. The Goldwater Family of Arizona Arrive in Chicago to Begin Campaigning in the Mid-West.
32. Lyndon Baines Johnson Was Born on a Farm in Texas on August 27, 1908.
33. Arizona Senator, Barry Goldwater, now the Republican Candidate for the U.S. Presidency Speaks at a Dinner in Washington, D.C. Held in His Honor.

34. Senator Barry Goldwater in an Informal Pose with His Family in Washington.
35. Senator Barry Goldwater Is a Native of Phoenix, Arizona.
36. Arizona Senator Barry Goldwater Addresses a Roomful of Newsmen During a Press Conference After Being Nominated as the Republican Presidential Candidate.
37. At a Republican Dinner, Held in Senator Barry Goldwater's Behalf, the Arizonian Speaks with Governor George Romney of Michigan.
38. In 1959, then a U.S. Senator, Lyndon Johnson Is on Hand to Greet Mexico's President Lopez Mateos at Washington National Airport.
39. Republican Presidential Candidate Senator Barry Goldwater Arrives at Kennedy International Airport in New York.
40. Lyndon Johnson at the Age of Six Years on His Father's Farm Near Stonewall, Texas.
41. Senate Majority Leader Lyndon Johnson Jokes with Fellow Congressmen on the Opening Day of Congress in June of 1960.
42. Senator Barry Goldwater Entered Into Politics in 1952 When He Decided to Run for Congress.
43. Lady Bird Johnson Has Always Worked Unceasingly in Behalf of Her Husband During His Political Campaigns.
44. Play Ball!
45. President Lyndon Johnson Poses for Newsmen and Photographers in Washington.
46. In 1942, Lyndon Johnson Was a Lieutenant Commander in the U.S. Navy.
47. Senator Barry Goldwater of Arizona Is in Germany and is Standing in Front of The Berlin Wall Which Divides the City of Berlin.

48 Senator Barry Goldwater Pauses Momentarily in Front of the Capitol Building.
49 President Lyndon Johnson Relaxes on the Johnson Ranch at Johnson City, Texas.
50 In 1956 Senator Barry Goldwater Was Pictured Talking to Senator John F. Kennedy.
51 Senator Barry Goldwater Is a Major General in the United States Air Force Reserves.
52 President Johnson Receives a Pleasant Surprise in His White House Office.
53 President Lyndon Johnson with Labor Secretary Willard Wirtz in April of 1964.
54 President Lyndon Johnson Amuses Several Guests as he Excuses Himself and Stops to Feed the First Family's Pets.

55 "No Words Are Strong Enough to Express Our Determination to Continue the Forward Thrust of America that John Kennedy Began...
56 President Lyndon Johnson Holds Up a Picture of The First Lady in His Private Office on the Johnson Ranch Near Johnson City, Texas.
57 Senator Barry Goldwater Speaks to a Large Audience in California.
58 Senator Barry Goldwater Outlining His Views on Domestic and International Issues for His Presidential Campaign.
59 Senator Barry Goldwater Pauses as His Audience Applauds a Point Made in His Speech at a Rally in Portland.
60 President Lyndon Johnson Speaks in New York at the 180th Anniversary Dinner for the Society of the Friendly Sons of St. Patrick at the Waldorf-Astoria.

61 President Lyndon Johnson Is Caught in a Moment of Concentration on His "LBJ" Ranch.
62 Senator Barry Goldwater Is About to Begin His Speech at the Hilton Hotel in New York City.
63 Senator Barry Goldwater of Arizona Speaks with his Supporters at a Recent Fund-Raising Dinner in New York City.
64 President Lyndon Johnson Rewards The First Lady with a Kiss on Her Forehead.
65 Senator Barry Goldwater Waves to His Friends as He Leaves His Plane in Indiana, the State in Which His Wife Was Born.
66 During President Kennedy's Term, Vice-President Johnson Worked Closely with The Chief Executive.

JULIA (33)

No. 29 in a series of 33 photos

2 1/2" X 3 1/2"

This set was tested by Topps and apparently found lacking since it was never distributed on a regular basis. The fronts of the cards have glossy black & white photos of actors and actresses from the TV show: Diahann Carroll, Michael Link, Marc Copage, and Betty Beaird. A facsimile autograph, printed in blue ink, appears in the field of every picture. The backs contain only a simple box within which is printed the card number and set length and a "Printed in U.S.A." line. No wrapper or box has been reported for this set.

11	Michael Link
12	
13	Diahann Carroll
14	
15	Marc Copage
16	Marc Copage
17	Diahann Carroll
18	
19	
20	Diahann Carroll
21	Diahann Carroll
22	Marc Copage
23	Marc Copage
24	
25	Diahann Carroll
26	
27	Michael Link
28	
29	Diahann Carroll
30	
31	Marc Copagae
32	
33	Marc Copage

1	Diahann Carroll	6	Diahann Carroll
2		7	
3		8	Diahann Carroll
4	Diahann Carroll	9	Diahann Carroll
5		10	Betty Beaird

ITEM	MINT	EX
Set	750.00	550.00
Card	20.00	15.00

JUSTICE LEAGUE OF AMERICA (14) TWO SIZES

The Justice League of America is composed of fantasy heroes from the pages of National Periodical comic books. Fleer Gum obtained a license to create a tattoo series of JLA characters and marketed the set in 1970. With the addition of three more designs sent in by Bob Conway, there are now a total of 17 different tattoos reported for the set. Of these, Batman and Superman have four apiece, with the remainder depicting seven other Justice League members. Each tattoo was folded around the gum inside a yellow or white exterior wrapper. There are six different characters shown on the wrappers and a minimum of three wrappers is needed to have them all pictured at least once. The large item located directly to the right of our wrapper illustrations is a cardboard insert designed to stand up in the back of the display box. Note: no mint prices are given for tattoos since they were folded around the gum.

ITEM	MINT	EX
Tattoo	--	2.00
Wrappers (2)		
yellow	--	5.00
white	--	10.00

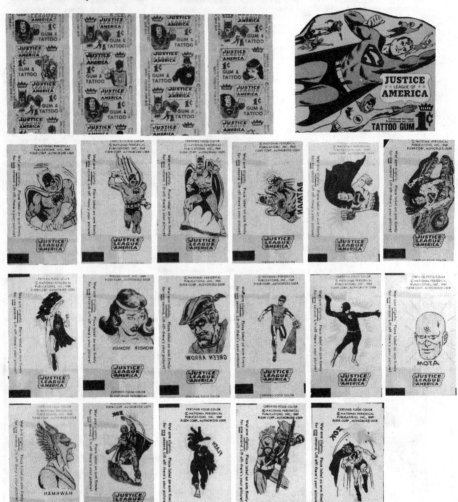

JOHN F. KENNEDY (64)

No type of packaging except the J-hook "Memorial Issue" illustrated has ever been discovered for the "President John F. Kennedy" set produced by Rosan. From the

2 1/2" X 3 1/2"

quantity of cards available today, it is assumed that they were also distributed in cellopacks and via the mail. The obverse pictures are black & white and have white borders. Each back contains a caption, a short text, and the card number. Below this is a line of stars and three drawings (PT-109, a Navy insignia, and the U.S. Capitol).

ITEM	MINT	EX
Set	45.00	35.00
Card	.65	.50
J-hook set	65.00	50.00

MEMORIAL ISSUE OF PRICE PER SET OF 64

PRESIDENT JOHN F. KENNEDY

64 PICTURES - FROM BOYHOOD TO PRESIDENCY
HISTORICAL COLLECTOR'S ITEMS

ROSAN PRINTING CORP., 90 THIRD AVE., BROOKLYN, N.Y. — PRINTED IN U.S.A.

1 Hard At Play
2 Future First Lady
3 Thirty Day Leave Smile
4 PT 109
5 War Hero
6 Venture Into Politics
7 Up With The Sail
8 September Song of Love
9 Tennis Anyone?
10 Mr. & Mrs. John F. Kennedy
11 Cutting The Cake
12 Study Time
13 Work At Capitol
14 The Kennedy Smile
15 Mother and Daughter
16 Family At Home
17 Campaign Wife
18 Giddy Yap
19 Ragga Muffin
20 Autograph Please
21 Riding High
22 Acceptance Speech
23 New Addition
24 Can I Hold Him?
25 The Greatest Day
26 The New President and First Lady
27 Inaugural Parade
28 Presidential Oath
29 Inaugural Cake
30 Stepping Out with My Baby
31 Ouch!
32 Social Engagements
33 No Greater Love
34 In Mother's Shoes
35 Decorating Spaceman
36 Who's Going to Win the Race in 1964?
37 Birthday Party
38 Commander in Chief
39 Kennedy on Crutches
40 Report to the Nation
41 The Eyes Have It
42 A Porthole Look
43 Pony Macaroni
44 India
45 Pakistan
46 The First Family
47 Fire One!
48 Boy's Best Friend
49 Peek-A-Boo
50 Big Chiefs
51 Favored Chair
52 Training Ship
53 Festival Time
54 Jackie in New York
55 Touring
56 Christmas Time
57 Missle Inspections [sic]
58 The Pacesetter
59 Lady of Fashions
60 Play Ball
61 Starting Early
62 Vacation Time
63 Gifts for the President
64 Point of View

JOHN F. KENNEDY (77)

The John F. Kennedy series issued by Topps is easily distinguished from the set of the same name published by

2 1/2" X 3 1/2"

Rosan. The style of the obverses is similar — a black and white photo with white borders — but the Topps photograph is much darker and has more contrast than the Rosan product. The Topps back has a line of stars encircling a sketch of the Capitol building (with clouds overhead), the text, and a line giving the card number and the series total.

ITEM	MINT	EX
Set	115.00	90.00
Card	1.35	1.00
Wrapper	--	30.00
Box	--	100.00

John F. Kennedy [Topps]

1 President John F. Kennedy Meets Lyndon Johnson at the White House. Mr. Johnson had just returned from a mission in Asia.

2 President Kennedy and the first lady lead their two children, Caroline and John Jr., after attending Sunday church services.

3 Senator Kennedy takes a morning stroll with his daughter Caroline. The pair are walking down a street in Georgetown.

4 President John F. Kennedy walks past a line of cadets on a visit to West Point Military Academy in New York.

5 President John F. Kennedy speaks to an attentive audience. In the background is a painting of Abraham Lincoln.

6 The president-elect John Kennedy walks his three year old daughter Caroline near his home in Georgetown.

7 President John Kennedy presents U.S. Astronaut Gordon Cooper with a distinguished service medal in a ceremony at the White House.

8 Congressman John Kennedy and his wife Jacqueline greet vice-president Richard Nixon. The trio are at Midway Airport in Chicago.

9 The Kennedy clan posed for this photo in 1934. John is the first young boy in the rear row.

10 Navy Lt. John Kennedy is congratulated by his captain after receiving the Navy Marine Corps medal for bravery.

11 Senator John Kennedy & his wife Jacqueline arrive at the "April In Paris Ball" at the Waldorf-Astoria Hotel in New York City.

12 Lt. John Kennedy relaxes as he begins his 30 day leave after 11 months of active duty in the South Pacific.

13 President Kennedy reports to the nation by radio and television from his office in the White House.

14 President Kennedy watches John Jr. as the young boy jumps happily along. The chief executive has just attended ceremonies at Arlington Cemetery.

15 President Kennedy enjoys a relaxing game of golf at the Hyannis Port Golf Club in Massachusetts.

16 President John F. Kennedy speaks to a joint session of Congress as he gives his State of the Union Address.

17 President-elect John Kennedy speaks to the pastor after attending a mass prior to the inauguration ceremonies.

18 The First Lady greets King Hassan II of Morocco as her husband, President John F. Kennedy looks on.

19 John Jr. enters the family limousine ahead of his father. President Kennedy is on his way to attend Veteran's Day ceremonies at Arlington Cemetery.

20 President John Kennedy reviews the honor guard just after his arrival at Mexico City, Mexico.

21 President and Mrs. Kennedy leave base hospital on their way to their summer home at Squaw Island in Hyannis Port.

22 President Kennedy and the First Lady are enthusiastically greeted just after their arrival at Bogota, Colombia.

23 President and Mrs. John F. Kennedy walk around the Glenwood Park Course in Middleburg, Virginia.

24 President John F. Kennedy escorts the Grand Duchess of Luxembourg to the state dining room in the White House.

25 President Kennedy and the First Lady wait to greet their guests at an evening function at the White House.

26 President Kennedy speaks before the nation on radio and television asking for public support on his proposed tax cut.

27 President John F. Kennedy is photographed prior to his speech at the Labor Convention held at the Americana Hotel in New York City.

28 President John F. Kennedy addresses the American people on television on his Civil Rights stand.

29 President John F. Kennedy stresses one of his points as he speaks during a Washington News Conference.

30 President John F. Kennedy holds a press conference to speak about his school aid program.

31 President Kennedy speaks before newsmen about the situation in Birmingham during the time of the racial riots in Alabama.

32 Presidential candidates Richard Nixon and John Kennedy debate before a vast television audience in 1960.

33 President John F. Kennedy is photographed during an important news conference concerning recent events in Laos.

34 President Kennedy takes a break from his duties as he lights a cigar during a Washington banquet.

35 At a news conference, President Kennedy tells reports that Soviet forces have been steadily leaving Cuba.

36 President Kennedy answers the many questions that are thrown at him during a Washington press conference.

37 President Kennedy Talks to reporters at a news conference about U.S. plans to halt atmospheric nuclear tests.

38 President Kennedy pauses for a few minutes in front of the White House before returning to work in his office.

39 President John Kennedy greets Yugoslavia's Marshall Tito after his arrival in New York City.

40 President Kennedy and Chancellor Adenauer listen to the U.S. national anthem at Wahn Airport in Bonn, West Germany.

41 John Kennedy was born May 29, 1917 in Brookline, Massachusetts. He was the 2nd of 9 children of Joseph P. Kennedy, former ambassador to England.

42 U.S. Attorney General Robert Kennedy and President John Kennedy discuss a program to help improve the health and fitness of American youth.

43 President John Kennedy and the First Lady get set for an evening out. Admiring reporters look on.

44 President Eisenhower and John Kennedy leave for the Capitol where the new president will take his oath of office.

45 Senator John F. Kennedy, shown as a Democratic Presidential nominee, speaks to his brothers, Robert and Edward.

46 Mrs. Jacqueline Kennedy poses with her two children, John Jr. and Caroline, in a photo taken in November 1961.

47 Senator John F. Kennedy takes a stroll on the beach near his home in Hyannisport, Massachusetts. The two youngsters are Mr. Kennedy's nephews.

48 The Kennedy's two children have returned from a trip to Florida and President Kennedy and his wife are on hand to meet them.

49 John F. Kennedy takes his oath of office and becomes the 35th President of the United States.

50 President John F. Kennedy enjoys a laugh at a news conference held in the nation's capitol.

51 Senator John Kennedy hobbles on crutches, on his way to undergo an operation for an old war injury. Mr. Kennedy has been on crutches for three months.

52 Senator John Kennedy returns to his office at the capitol after an operation on an old World War II spinal injury.

53 Senator and Mrs. John F. Kennedy pose with their two year old daughter, Caroline, in Washington.

54 A brief holiday at Hyannis Port, Mass. shows President Kennedy at the wheel of his golf cart. Caroline, and her friends go along for the ride.

55 President Kennedy points out an interesting site to his wife as the family tours a Civil War battlefield in Gettysburg, Pa.

56 President Kennedy and his wife enjoy a performance by the Black Watch regiment on the South Lawn of the White House.

57 Senator John Kennedy spends a Sunday afternoon in the backyard of his summer home. Caroline is enjoying a brand new picture book.

58 Senator John F. Kennedy, his wife Jacqueline and daughter Caroline leave a plane at Washington Airport.

59 Senator John Kennedy and his wife spend a Sunday afternoon sailing at Hyannis Port, Massachusetts.

60 John F. Kennedy and Jacqueline Bouvier were married at Newport on September 12, 1953.

61 President John Kennedy and his wife Jacqueline acknowledge photographers as they depart in the presidential limousine.

62 It's opening day of the baseball season and President Kennedy tosses out the first ball before a Washington Senators ballgame gets under way.

63 Mrs. Jacqueline Kennedy poses with her son, John Jr., in the first press photo of the youngster.

64 Jacqueline Kennedy gives John Jr. a ride as daughter Caroline sits happily on her pony, Macaroni,

65 President Kennedy has two visitors in his office in the White House. John Jr. performs a dance for his father.

66 John Kennedy (2nd from right, front row) poses with his varsity football team. John is described as "a tiger on defense."

67 President John Kennedy and Vice-President Johnson watch the Inaugural Parade under the Seal of the United States.

68 President Kennedy and the First Lady leave a formal dinner in Paris, hosted by French President DeGaulle.

69 President Kennedy takes time off to make an appearance and a speech at Boston College in Massachusetts.

70 John F. Kennedy enjoys an anecdote from one of his admirers during an afternoon at the ballpark.

71 The First Lady and John Jr. peep out from behind the shrubbery, watching a military ceremony on the grounds of the White House.

72 Sailing is the order of the day as President Kennedy and the First Lady relax on a trip to Hyannis Port.

73 Senator and Mrs. Kennedy exchange fond glances after their marriage ceremony in Newport, Rhode Island.

74 Senator and Mrs. Kennedy ride in a motorcade in New York City during the campaign months of 1960.

75 Senator John Kennedy and Miss Jacqueline Bouvier pose at Hyannis Port shortly after announcing the wedding plans.

76 President Kennedy enjoys a chuckle as he speaks to his daughter, Caroline, during long-distance telephone call.

77 President-elect Kennedy and his wife greet well-wishers after attending a Sunday morning mass.

ROBERT F. KENNEDY (55)

2 1/2" X 3 1/2"

The Robert F. Kennedy set of 55 cards is considered to be scarcer than either of the sets depicting his brother John. The obverse photo is black and white and is surrounded by white borders. The backs bear the title "The Story of Robert F. Kennedy," with the card number in a star just to the right. A sketch of the Capitol dome is located on the left next to a short piece of narrative or a R.F.K. quotation. The cards were issued in 1968 by Philly Gum.

ITEM	MINT	EX
Set	125.00	95.00
Card	2.00	1.50
Wrapper	--	20.00
Box	--	100.00

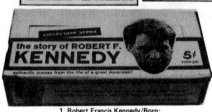

1 Robert Francis Kennedy/Born: November 20, 1925/Died: June 6, 1968

2 Attorney General Robert F. Kennedy congratulates President Johnson following an address to Congress by the Chief Executive. U.N. Ambassador Adlai Stevenson is in the background.

3 Attorney General Robert F. Kennedy discusses civil rights legislation with President John F. Kennedy.

4 Senator Robert F. Kennedy finishes a 15 mile kayak trip through the rapids of the Hudson River.

5 "In the end, in the simplest words, the greatest truth, must be the recognition that in every child, is the potential for greatest—that all are the creatures of God and equal in his sight."—Robert F. Kennedy

6 Senator Robert F. Kennedy walks toward the Capitol—and the Senate Chamber—after announcing he would run for President.

7 Senator Robert F. Kennedy jumps ashore from a rubber raft.

8 Photographer anxious for a close-up climbs on hood of Senator Robert F. Kennedy's car during campaign visit to Denver.

9 "Moral courage is a rarer commodity than bravery in battle or great intelligence."—Robert F. Kennedy

10 Senator Robert F. Kennedy stretches his legs after a kayak ride down the "white water" of Utah's Green River.

11 Senator Robert F. Kennedy and his pet, Freckles, pause to rest during a compaign tour of Portland, Oregon.

12 "Some men see things as they are and say 'Why?' I dream things that never were and say 'Why not?' "—Robert F. Kennedy

13 Attorney General Robert F. Kennedy wears a tank commander's helmet as he sits in a tank during a visit to U.S. Armored units in Germany.

14 Senator Robert F. Kennedy addresses a convention of the Oil, Chemical and Atomic Workers Union in New York City.

15 Senator Robert F. Kennedy concludes an audience with His Holiness The Pope.

16 Robert F. Kennedy brings his campaign for the Senate into New York City.

17 Attorney General Robert F. Kennedy visits United Nations headquarters for a conference.

18 Attorney General Robert F. Kennedy is named 1960 "Father of the Year."

19 Attorney General Robert F. Kennedy joins his brother, President John F. Kennedy, at a White House ceremony.

20 Robert F. Kennedy addresses students at the University of Rochester during his campaign for the Senate.

21 "No one is too young—or too old—to support good and fight against evil."—Robert F. Kennedy

22 Attorney General Robert F. Kennedy grills hamburgers in a fireplace in his office during a picnic for teenagers.

23 Senator Robert F. Kennedy reads while he waits for his turn in the voting booth.

24 Senator Robert F. Kennedy campaigns in the Watts section of Los Angeles.

25 Senate Committee Counsel Robert F. Kennedy takes time out for refreshment.

26 "Like it or not, we live in times of danger and uncertainty. But they are also more open to the creative energies of men than any other time in history."—Robert F. Kennedy

27 Senator Robert F. Kennedy places a flower near the eternal flame on the grave of his brother, the late President John F. Kennedy.

28 Senator Robert F. Kennedy engages in a quiet, thoughtful conversation with his brother, Senator Edward Kennedy.

29 Senator Robert F. Kennedy gets ready to fly to the base camp at Mt. Kennedy in Canada.

30 Attorney General Robert F. Kennedy talks to a meeting of fund raisers for the John F. Kennedy Memorial Library.

31 Attorney General Robert F. Kennedy views the busy harbor on a tour of Hong Kong.

32 Robert F. Kennedy on his wedding day, June 17, 1950.

33 Senator Robert F. Kennedy becomes the first man to reach the top of Mt. Kennedy, the 13,900-foot Canadian peak named in memory of his brother.

34 Senator Robert F. Kennedy reaches out to shake the hands of a crowd of listeners.

35 Senator Robert F. Kennedy attends a dinner for Congressional representatives from New York State.

36 Attorney General Robert F. Kennedy arrives to meet with newsmen gathered outside his office.

37 Senator Robert F. Kennedy exchanges comments with his brother, Senator Edward Kennedy, after they were sworn in as the first pair of brothers to serve in the U.S. Senate since 1803.

38 Robert F. Kennedy addresses a crowd in New York City during his 1964 Senate campaign.

39 Attorney General Robert F. Kennedy receives an Honorary Doctor of Law degree at Marquette University.

40 "I think the motive that should guide all of us, that should guide all mankind, is to tame the savageness of man and make gentle the life of the world."—Robert F. Kennedy

41 Senator Robert F. Kennedy prepares for a ski run at Sun Valley, Idaho.

42 Attorney General Robert F. Kennedy discusses civil rights legislation with Senate leaders.

43 With his pet spaniel Freckles following him, Senator Robert F. Kennedy takes time out for a quiet walk along the Pacific shore.

44 Attorney General Robert F. Kennedy and the Reverend Martin Luther King, Jr. attend a special White House conference on civil rights legislation.

45 Attorney General Robert F. Kennedy arrives in New York City to discuss his race for the Senate.

46 "The future does not belong to those who are content with today...Rather it will belong to those who can blend vision, reason and courage in a personal commitment to the ideals and great enterprises of American society."—Robert F. Kennedy

47 Senator Robert F. Kennedy relaxes during a ski weekend at Mt. Tecumseh, New Hampshire.

48 Senator Robert F. Kennedy applauds during President Johnson's State of the Union message.

49 Senator Robert F. Kennedy walks toward his office in the Senate office building.

50 Senator Robert F. Kennedy waves from a chair lift to the crowd watching him at Tupper Lake, New York ski resort.

51 Attorney General Robert F. Kennedy holds a press conference to give a report on the John F. Kennedy Memorial Library.

52 "The gap between generations will never be completely closed. But it must be spanned."—Robert F. Kennedy

53 Attorney General Robert F. Kennedy smiles to friends outside his office.

54 Attorney General Robert F. Kennedy watches as former President Harry S. Truman signs an autograph for him.

55 Senator Robert F. Kennedy attends a fund raising dinner in New York City.

KIDS AROUND THE WORLD (3K)

2 5/8" X 3 1/2"

"Kids Around the World" is a series of collector cards issued during 1991 in packages of "Kudos" snacks. Each card front has a color picture of a child from around the world and the question "Can you guess my country?" is printed beneath, with a list of four choices. On back at the top, there is a group of clues and right below is a selection entitled "Cool phrases from my country." The basic color scheme front and back is white with lemon-yellow borders containing flecks of green. Both surfaces are glossy. The cards are not numbered and the set total is unknown at this time. Each child's country is printed upside-down in the lower-right corner of the reverse.

	Ivan	Brazil
	Jaime	Spain
	John	Kenya

ITEM	MINT	EX
Card	.35	.25

SERIES 1

1 Piranha	17 Black Widow
2 Radioactivity*	18 Lye
3 Acid Rain	19 Plague*
4 Fear	20 Vacuum of
5 Hypothermia	Space
6 Scorpions	21 Rabies*
7 Cobra	22 Army Ants
8 Here's Our	23 Electricity
Mother Earth*	24 Concussion
9 Jellyfish*	25 Automobiles
10 Vampire	26 Gas
11 Guillotine*	27 Nuclear War
12 Pit Bull	28 Skateboards*
13 Stranger	29 Wood Chipper
14 Guns	30 Teenage Crush
15 Quicksand	31 Killer Whales
16 Fireworks	32 Grizzly Bears
	33 Boomerang

34 Drugs
35 Steel Trap
36 Adrift at Sea
37 Chains
38 Self Discovery*
39 Highway Obstacle Corpse
40 Shark Attack
41 Projectile Vomiting
42 Maggots
43 The Wanderer*
44 Sunburn*
45 Animal Experimentation
-- No number (Note from The Wanderer to Colette)

SERIES 2

1 Skin-Man	24 Mosquitoes
2 Legacy of War	25 Rain Forests
3 Thuggees	26 Dumbcane Plant
4 Ciguatera	27 Texas Horned Toad
5 Tetanus	28 Poison Mushrooms
6 Lightning	29 Hole in the Ozone
7 Avalanche	30 The Geek
8 Leeches	31 Wolf Encounter
9 Tapeworms	32 Spontaneous Human
10 Exploding River Rocks	Combustion
11 Hailstones	33 Polluted Beach
12 Driftnet Fishing	34 Cold Love
13 ATV's	35 Caravan
14 Lyme Disease	36 Rapture of the Deep
15 In the Coils of The	37 Candiru - Arnie, Get
Constrictor	Your Gun
16 Eagles	38 Colette
17 Scalp and a	39 Flatulence
Headcut, Two Bits	40 Drawn and Quartered
18 Swordfish	41 Elephant Poaching
19 Vampires II	42 Talk Radio
20 Rabbit Starvation	43 Van Gogh's Ear
21 Shaman	44 Water Signs
22 Conquistador	45 The Defiler
23 Garbage	

A funny thing happened on the way to the trash can. The artwork of the first series of "Killer Cards" didn't appeal to me at all, but I decided to read some of the backs before dumping the cards into the bottom drawer of my file cabinet. Surprise! There was a serious message being sent, albeit in irreverent fashion, and the blantantly-graphic artwork became less objectionable as I glanced through the remaining cards. Sure, there are a zillion ways to die or be mutilated, or even to be made sick to one's stomach, and none of them is pleasant, but anyone who thinks these cards are operating on superficial sensationalism can't find his cheek with his tongue.

Killer Cards, produced by Warner & Irene, were issued in two sets: Series I, in 1988, and Series II, in 1989. Each consists of 45 numbered cards plus an additional unnumbered card. The text is essentially the chronicle of a world traveler known as "The Wanderer," who just happens to observe and report the multi-faceted forms of human depravity and suffering. Some of these are on the high end of the scale - guillotining, guns, and pit bulls, for example, while others, such as flatulence, skateboards, boomerangs, and exploding river rocks, somehow seem less life-threatening. There is also a love interest: The Wanderer rescues lovely Colette from harm in Costa Rica and we are told that in Series III (when and if it ever appears), he will come face to face with the abomination who killed Colette's father and many other innocents ... The Defiler!

NOTE: the artwork and text of "Killer Cards" may exceed the comprehension levels or standards of taste of some individuals irregardless of age or IQ. This is NOT an "underground" set but you may wish to review before buying. Killer Cards are sold only in complete sets.

ITEM	MINT	EX
Sets		
Series 1	15.00	---
Series 2	12.00	---

KING KONG (55)

In 1965, R.K.O. General sold licenses to both Topps and Donruss to produce card sets based on the original black & white "Kong" movies. The Donruss concept was to put humorous dialogue with each photo, in effect, to create a parody. In contrast, Topps stuck to the original story and employed a narrative style. The cards of this set have captioned black & white photos and a title box on the front.

2 1/2" X 3 1/2"

The backs are printed in chocolate brown on off-white stock and contain the card title, text, card number, and a drawing of Kong atop the Empire State Building. "Bubbles Inc." is listed as the manufacturer and the R.K.O. credit line is dated 1965. The set was "tested" and withdrawn from the market. No wrapper or box have been reported to date and the length of the set has not been confirmed.

ITEM	MINT	EX
Card	35.00	30.00

1	Mysterious Expedition	12	Into the Gorge	23	Attacked	34	Blast Kong	45	Disaster
2	Taken Captive	13	In Hiding	24	Battle	35	Gas Grenades	46	The Mighty Kong
3	Sacrifice to Kong	14	Enemy Approaching	25	Danger from the Sky	36	Kong On Stage	47	Attacking Kong
4	Kong Is Coming	15	Moment of Fear	26	Carried Aloft	37	Stalking City Streets	48	Kong Fights Back
5	Beauty and the Beast	16	Prehistoric Terror	27	Kong to the Rescue	38	In Search of Ann	49	Kong Defiant
6	King Kong	17	Battle to the Death	28	Destroying An Enemy	39		50	
7	Into the Jungle	18	Perilous Perch	29	Escape	40	Face in the Window	51	Out of Action
8	Tree of Terror	19	Trapped	30	Plunge to Safety	41	Captured Again	52	Fight Above The City
9	Island Bridge	20	Kong Triumphs	31	Rescued	42	Rooftop Peril	53	Kong Is Hurt
10	Warning Cry	21	Cry of Victory	32	Kong Returns	43	On The Rampage	54	Dying Kong
11	Danger Ahead	22	In the Hands of Kong	33	Kong Is Loose	44	Tracks of Doom	55	Kong Is Dead

KING KONG (55)

2 1/2" X 3 1/2"

Hey! Here's a great idea. You take an old movie, say King Kong, or Son of Kong, and you get stills of Kong and all those monsters and put funny captions on them! Donruss thought the idea was pretty good and produced this set of 55 cards in 1965. The pictures are black and white with white borders, and the humorous dialogue appears in an oval inserted into the field of the photograph. The card number (0-15, 17-55 — no number 16 issued) and a credit line for RKO General are located on the bottom of the card front. The backs are color puzzle pieces which form a large picture of Kong and a girl (Fay Wray?).

ITEM	MINT	EX
Set	190.00	155.00
Card	3.00	2.50
Wrapper	--	30.00
Box	--	125.00

0 Write Your Own
1 "Okay, So You Won the Tooth Paste Test!"
2 "Just as I Thought—Lights on After Taps Again."
3 "They Told Me This Mattress Was Like Sleeping on a Cloud"
4 "This Is the Best Tooth Brush We Have, Sir."
5 Write Your Own
6 Write Your Own
7 "Don't You Know This Is a Private Beach?"
8 "This Must Be a Dream"
9 "Look, No Cavities!"
10 "Nothing Like a Vacation in the Mountains."
11 "Who Stole My Bubble Gum?"
12 "That Mouth of Yours Could Get You into Trouble Someday."
13 "Just a Quick Trim, Barber."
14 I Said, "Beat It, Mac!"
15 "You Said You Wanted a Really Big Show."
16 Not Issued
17 "I Think You Have Been Eating Onions Again."
18 Write Your Own
19 "Is This Supposed to Be a Puppet Show?"
20 "What Do You Think of My Act?"
21 "But I Just Want to Be Your Buddy."
22 "Where Do I Enlist?"
23 "Get Back in Your Cage"
24 Write Your Own
25 Write Your Own
26 "But I Didn't Expect You to Go Overboard for This Idea!"
27 "Leaping Lizards!!!"
28 "She's Expecting Me on the 5:10"
29 "Just Don't Tickle My Toes!"
30 "What Type of Skin Cream Do You Use?"
31 "I Was a Ninety Pound Weakling Until..."
32 "But I Don't Want to Go Swimming."
33 "I Don't Like the Look on Your Face."
34 "What Else Was It I Was Going to Do Today?"
35 Write Your Own
36 "The Traffic Seems to Be a Little Heavy Up Here."
37 Write Your Own
38 "I Needed Something Stronger So I Tried Your Product."
39 "Oops, That Second Diet Drink!"
40 "So...I Don't Wear Tenny Pumps!"
41 "But It Looks Just Like Tomato Juice"
42 "I Told You to Quit Using My Mouth Wash."
43 "Is This Where They Make the Announcements for Lost Kids?"
44 "Look I Use a Deodorant"
45 "I Only Want a Short Ride."
46 "OK, So It's Not the Best Hotel in Town!"
47 "Look Who's Calling Me Ugly!"
48 "I Told You Three Times You Couldn't Keep any Pets!"
49 "The Toll is 25 cents a Head."
50 Write Your Own
51 "I Don't Like What You Said, Fella!"
52 "I Should Have Taken the Elevator."
53 "Let Hurts Put You in the Driver's Seat"
54 Write Your Own
55 "All Right, Knock It Off, You Cats!"

KING KONG (55 & 11)

2 1/2" X 3 1/2"

In 1976, Dino De Laurentiis released his color version of King Kong to the movie-going public, and Topps issued its card set to the bubble gum chewers of America. The cards (55) have red borders surrounding a color photograph; the caption is located outside the frame line next to the card number. The backs as a group are composed of 44 puzzle pieces and 11 "Movie Facts" features. The stickers (11) are designed in "film-frame" style and are numbered on a diagonal red band. They are not captioned but have been assigned captions taken from identical pictures in the set for purposes of the checklist below. Note: set price includes stickers.

ITEM	MINT	EX
Set	22.00	16.50
Cards		
1-45	.20	.15
46-55	.50	.35
Sticker	.50	.35
Wrapper	--	1.00
Box	--	10.00

1 Kong fights a mighty battle to the death!
2 Kong attacks New York harbor!
3 Kong battles a gigantic serpent!
4 The great wall is smashed by Kong!
5 Kong scales the buildings of New York!
6 Subway trains are demolished by Kong!
7 Speeding toward the fog-shrouded island!
8 The expedition braves dangerous waters!
9 The natives chant, "Kong.. Kong...Kong!"
10 Observing the strange native ritual!
11 Natives wear strange costumes for Kong!
12 Witch doctor dons a terrifying costume!
13 Dwan is kidnapped by the natives!
14 Dwan is dressed in native attire!
15 Dwan, helpless, cannot escape her fate!
16 Beyond the great wall lies... what?

17 Huge doors open and Dwan is carried inside!
18 The lovely Dwan awaits Kong's arrival!
19 The jungle trembles when Kong appears!
20 Dwan watches in horror as Kong approaches!
21 A huge hairy paw lifts Dwan into the air!
22 The mud-covered Dwan is washed clean!
23 Dwan is dazed after being washed by a waterfall!
24 Dwan faints in the great ape's paw!
25 Kong treats his new friend Dwan kindly!
26 Dwan tells Kong she's afraid of heights!
27 A big hand for the little lady!
28 Kong puts the terrified Dwan down!
29 Wilson's men crash to their deaths!
30 Kong is captured when he falls into a pit!
31 Dwan is rescued!

32 Kong is transported to civilization
33 Dwan is present for Kong's debut!
34 King Kong is displayed to the world!
35 The great ape is angered by man's greed!
36 Panic strikes the city as Kong breaks loose!
37 Thousands scream as Kong escapes captivity!
38 Kong rampages through the city!
39 Kong falls from the World Trade Center towers!
40 Actress Jessica Lange
41 Mightiest Monster That Ever Lived!
42 Natives tie Dwan to the sacrificial altar!
43 Dwan helplessly awaits the monster Kong!

44 Kong, Eighth Wonder of the World!
45 Kong prowls New York in search of Dwan!
46 Witch Doctor prepares Dwan for her ordeal!
47 New York trembles as the great ape attacks!
48 A heartbroken Dwan stands by Kong's body.
49 No bars are strong enough to hold Kong!
50 Beauty and the Beast
51 Dwan and Kong make the New York scene!
52 The Lady and the Monster
53 Kong is held captive in Shea Stadium!
54 Reporters try to take Kong's picture!
55 Dwan seems unalarmed as Kong breaks free!

1A Kong fights a mighty battle to the death!
2A Kong attacks New York harbor!
3A The great wall is smashed by Kong!
4A Kong battles a gigantic serpent!
5A Kong scales the buldings of New York!
6A Subway trains are demolished by Kong!
7A Kong is captured when he falls into a pit!
8A Kong is transported to civilization!
9A Kong rampages through the city!
10A Dwan is dazed after being washed by a waterfall!
11A Kong puts the terrified Dwan down!

KISS (132)

2 1/2" X 3 1/2"

The 132-card series featuring the rock band Kiss, marketed by Donruss in 1978, has presented some problems for collectors and researchers over the years. Series 1 cards (1-66) have "sharp" edges on the angles of the framelines surrounding the color photos, while the frameline corners of Series 2 cards (67-132) are rounded. In both series, the card number is printed in the lower right corner of the picture and is not repeated on the back of the card. The 1st series wrapper is blue and the 2nd series wrapper is red. The 2nd series box differs from its 1st series counterpart in print details, but the picture is merely reversed.

In the 1988 volume of this price guide, it was reported that the death of drummer Peter Criss had forced Donruss to alter 21 cards of the first series in a later print run. In fact, Peter Criss merely retired from the band and was replaced by another drummer, Eric Carr. The altered cards, however, were never released to the public until later, when they surfaced, along with leftover stock from other sets, in Donruss "Fun Packs." The Criss replacement cards, 21 in number, are now known to collectors as the "corrected version" set when combined with the 45 cards of the original set that remained unchanged.

The following numbers were "corrected": 2-3-7-9-15-17-22-24-25-33-36-39-42-44-47-51-53-56-57-59-61. The corrected versions of #'s 3, 36, and 39 have new pictures on front and Eric Carr biography on back. The rest of the "corrected" numbers have new pictures on the obverse and new puzzle pieces on the back (so there is an entirely different 18-piece puzzle picture than appeared on the same numbers in the original printing). Although "corrected" cards are in far less supply than their "original" counterparts, there are still enough of them around to sow confusion among collectors and dealers who do not know what happened. Naturally, corrected cards and corrected version sets command a premium in the marketplace.

ITEM	MINT	EX
Original sets		
Series 1	30.00	22.50
Series 2	40.00	30.00
Original cards		
Series 1	.40	.30
Series 2	.50	.35
Corrected set	65.00	47.50
Corrected card	2.00	1.50
Wrappers (2)		
Series 1	--	.35
Series 2	--	.35
Boxes		
Series 1	--	7.00
Series 2	--	7.00

Kiss

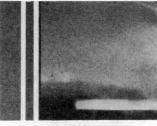

KITCHEN SINK CARDS (36)

2 3/4" X 4 1/8"

This series of 36 cards — "two-color beauties," in the words of the producer — were created for one purpose: as an incentive to purchase items from the Kitchen Sink catalog of magazines, comic books, and related merchandise. One card of your choice was given free for each $5 worth of items ordered. That is not to say that the set is worth $180; it is not. The series features artwork by Will Eisner, R. Crumb, and Jay Lynch, to name a few, plus characters like Steve Canyon, Flash Gordon, and Nancy. Due to individual tastes, collec-tors will find some cards more appealing then others. The card obverses are glossy and have white borders, while the backs are flat-finished and contain information about the artist and his work. Due to the restricted nature of the supply, we recommend a retail value of $1.00 for single cards.

FLASH GORDON

Ming the Merciless pours sweet evilness into lovely Dale Arden's ear in a scene from Alex Raymond's FLASH GORDON, one of the greatest comic strips of all time. Long regarded as the essential cartoon artist, Raymond began FLASH GORDON in 1934, along with JUNGLE JIM and SECRET AGENT X-9. FLASH and JUNGLE JIM ran together as a full page on Sundays, with X-9 running the other six days of the week. After a year, the schedule became too demanding, and Raymond dropped X-9. He continued with FLASH until 1944, when he entered the Marines. FLASH GORDON is world famous for its fantastic art and futuristic stories, many times set on Ming's planet Mongo. Over the years, FLASH GORDON has been rendered by a host of great artists, including Al Williamson, Dan Barry, Frank Frazetta, Harvey Kurtzman, Harry Harrison, Austin Briggs and Mac Raboy. The series is being reprinted by Kitchen Sink Press, most of the material for the very first time.

KITCHEN SINK CARDS: 15 of 36

1 The Spirit
2 Li'l Abner
3 Megaton Man
4 Xenozoic Tales
5 Death Rattle
6 Blab!
7 Twist
8 Steve Rude Sketchbook
9 Kings in Disguise
10 Howard Cruse
11 Male Call
12 Melody
13 Mr. Natural
14 Harvey Kurtzman
15 Flash Gordon
16 Outer Space Spirit
17 Goodman Beaver
18 Omaha
19 City People Notebook
20 Snarf
21 Steve Canyon
22 Caddies & Dinos
23 Denizens of Deep City
24 Moonbeam McSwine
25 A Life Force
26 Jay Lynch
27 Nancy
28 Homegrown
29 Sleazy Scandals
30 Flash Gordon
31 Jungle Book
32 Art of Denis Kitchen
33 Secret of San Saba
34 Omaha 2
35 Curse of the Molemen
36 KSP 20th Anniversary

KNIGHT RIDER (55)

One of the least-inspiring sets in recent memory, "Knight Rider" contains a string of dull, overly-dark photographs taken from the TV show. Every card is numbered on the front (55 in set) and all are horizontally aligned. There are no captions or text and the backs are puzzle pieces. The set was produced by Donruss in 1983.

ITEM	MINT	EX
Set	12.00	9.00
Card	.20	.15
Wrapper	--	.35
Box	--	4.00

KNOW THE PRESIDENTS (42)

2 1/2" X 3 1/2"

A handsome series of presidential portraits issued in Campbell Taggart bakery products during 1984. The fronts of the cards

feature full color artwork of each First Executive, with an interesting scene from his term in the foreground. Each picture is surrounded by thin red and blue framelines and white borders. The backs are well designed and contain an accurate description of "The Man" and "The Administration." The card number is printed in the lower right corner. Oil stains from bread are often found on these cards and stained cards cannot be graded excellent or mint.

ITEM	MINT	EX
Set	15.00	10.50
Card	.35	.25

KNOW YOUR U.S. PRESIDENTS (40)

2 1/2" X 3 1/2"

The fronts of the cards in this presidential set are identical to those in the Campbell Taggart series listed above. However,

"Know Your U.S. Presidents" was issued in 1976, meaning that there are only 40 cards in the set, and it was distributed by both Colonial Baking and "Rainbo" bread. The format of the backs is unimaginative, compared to the CT set previously discussed, but the information provided is accurate and well-written. The words "Colonial" or "Rainbo" are found in a small blue oval on the back. Cards with oil stains from bread cannot be graded excellent or mint.

ITEM	MINT	EX
Set	15.00	10.50
Card	.35	.25

KNOW YOUR 50 STATES (50)

This Colonial Bakery issue of 50 cards dates from 1975. The set title is printed at the top on the obverse of every card. Beneath this, the state flag, bird, flower, and outline are pictured in multicolor artwork and the bird and flower are identified in a divided box at the bottom. The cards are numbered on the back and give the date of entrance into the Union plus the state nickname and a list of demographic information. The "Georgia" card illustrated here is interesting because it has "none" listed for the "Presidents" category. Who would have dreamed that less than a year later, Georgian Jimmy Carter, a virtual unknown, would be sitting in the Oval Office! Although these cards are numbered, we have placed them in alphabetical order in the checklist for your convenience. Cards with oil stains from bread cannot be graded excellent or mint.

1 Delaware	11 New York	21 Illinois	31 California	41 Montana
2 Pennsylvania	12 North Carolina	22 Alabama	32 Minnesota	42 Washington
3 New Jersey	13 Rhode Island	23 Maine	33 Oregon	43 Idaho
4 Georgia	14 Vermont	24 Missouri	34 Kansas	44 Wyoming
5 Connecticut	15 Kentucky	25 Arkansas	35 West Virginia	45 Utah
6 Massachusetts	16 Tennessee	26 Michigan	36 Nevada	46 Oklahoma
7 Maryland	17 Ohio	27 Florida	37 Nebraska	47 New Mexico
8 South Carolina	18 Louisiana	28 Texas	38 Colorado	48 Arizona
9 New Hampshire	19 Indiana	29 Iowa	39 North Dakota	49 Alaska
10 Virginia	20 Mississippi	30 Wisconsin	40 South Dakota	50 Hawaii

ITEM	MINT	EX
Set	12.50	7.50
Card	.25	.15

KOOKIE PLAKS (88)

It required very little effort for Topps to produce "Kookie Plaks" in 1965 since the set was virtually identical to the "Wacky Plaks" series of 1959. In fact, the only details which were changed appear on the back of the cards: the set title, the numbering sequence, and the absence of wavy edges. Even the basic wrapper design is the same except for the title and some minor details. The number in parentheses following each title in our checklist is the card number that design had in Wacky Plaks.

ITEM	MINT	EX
Set	200.00	150.00
Card	2.00	1.50
Wrapper	––	60.00

1 Tell Me All You Know (I've Got a Minute to Spare.) [47]
2 You're Certainly Trying (Very trying) [50]
3 How To Get Good Marks (Cheat) [3]
4 Mistakes Will Happen [52]
5 Looks Aren't Everything (It's a Good Thing You're Rich!) [41]
6 If You Have Nothing to Do. . . (Don't Do It Here!) [1]
7 Thanks (For Seeing Me Through!) [66]
8 I'd Give $1,000 Dollars to Be A Millionaire! [69]
9 Keep Calm! [5]
10 Somebody Goofed [32]
11 Money Isn't Everything (But It's Way Ahead of Whatever's in Second Place!) [43]
12 We're Friends Till The End (This Is The End) [54]
13 Use Your Head! (It's the Little Things that Count.) [81]
14 Time Wounds All Heels [18]

Kookie Plaks

15 If At First You Don't Succeed (To Heck With It!) [39]
16 Be Reasonable (Do It My Way!) [45]
17 Never Do Today What You Can Put Off Till Tomorrow [29]
18 Smile (Even If It Hurts) [78]
19 Think (Before You Louse Things Up!) [7]
20 Join Me For Dinner (At Your House.) [37]
21 Early To Bed Early To Rise (Dull Isn't It!) [16]
22 Plan Ahead [9]
23 In Case Of Fire (Please Yell "Fire") [4]
24 Be Neat [14]
25 Concentrate [68]
26 Whether You're Rich Or Poor It's Good To Have Money [26]
27 Silence [75]
28 Who's Excited? [19]
29 Looking For Someone With A Little Authority? (I Have as Little as Anyone.) [24]
30 Have You Forgotten Anything? [73]
31 I Spend 8 Hours A Day Here (Do You Expect Me to Work Too?) [12]
32 I'm Not Hard of Hearing (I'm Just Ignoring You.) [38]
33 Think You Got Troubles? [11]
34 Think (It May Be a New Experience.) [35]
35 Quiet (Genius At Work) [80]
36 Cleanliness Is Next To Godliness (And Next to Impossible, Too) [76]
37 To Err Is Human (But Why Must You Be So Human?) [83]
38 All People Are Created Equal (Only Some Are More Equal than Others...) [31]
39 If You're So Smart Why Ain't You Rich? [23]
40 Keep Your Eye On The Ball/Keep Your Shoulder To The Wheel/Keep Your Ear To The Ground (Now Try to Work in that Position.) [17]
41 With My Brains and Your Looks (We're in Real Trouble.) [20]

42 Not Everyone Has Your Brains (Some People are Smart.) [79]
43 Absence Makes The Heart Grow Fonder (So Get Lost!) [13]
44 I'd Like To Help You Out (Which Way Did You Come In?) [70}
45 Remember The Old Chinese Saying: [72]
46 Your Visit Has Climaxed An Already Dull Day. [8]
47 Come In (Everything Else Has Gone Wrong Today.) [15]
48 I Never Forget A Face But In Your Case I'll Make An Exception. [21]
49 Do It Tomorrow (You Made Enough Mistakes Today.) [87]
50 Barking Dogs Never Bite (Except When They Stop Barking.) [58]
51 To Be Seen — Stand Up/To Be Heard—Speak Up/To Be Appreciated—Shut Up [77]
52 Work Fascinates Me (I Can Sit and Watch It for Hours.) [10]
53 I'm The Brains Of This Outfit [49]
54 I Am A Self-Made Man. [61]
55 Smile (Later Today You Won't Feel Like It.) [22]
56 If You Ever Need A Friend (Buy a Dog.) [55]
57 Cheer Up! You're Not Completely Worthless. (You Can Always Serve as a Bad Example.) [34]
58 Be An Optimist (So Far Not Bad At All!) [84]
59 Money Can't Buy Poverty [2]
60 You're Tops In My Book [74]
61 Nobody Tells Me What To Do! [82]
62 Don't Let School Work Get You Down (Flunk Now and Get It Over With.) [25]
63 I'm A Genius (Do I Have to Prove It?) [88]
64 I'd Like To See You Get Ahead (You Need One!) [67]
65 The Marines Build Men (But Even They Couldn't Help You!) [36]

66 You Ought To Go To Hollywood (The Walk Would Do You Good.) [65]
67 Stop Worrying (You'll Never Get Out of this World Alive.) [86]
68 Keep Your Temper (Nobody Else Wants It.) [53]
69 No Experience/No Talent (But I'm Willing to Start at the Top.) [71]
70 I Was Born This Way (What's Your Excuse?) [62]
71 Why Be Difficult? (With a Little Effort You Could Be a Real Stinker.) [60]
72 Your Service Was Excellent (Sorry I Don't Believe in Tipping.) [56]
73 I'd Rather Be Handsome Than Rich [33]
74 I May Look Busy (But I'm Only Confused!) [54]
75 Some People Can't Do Anything Right! [42]
76 Are You Looking For An Ambitious Man? (Keep Looking!) [64]
77 Think or Thwin [28]
78 You Must've Been A Beautiful Baby (But What Happened?) [57]
79 The Early Bird Catches The Worm! (But Who Wants Worms?) [27]
80 How To Get Rid Of Ten Pounds of Ugly Fat. (Cut Off Your Head.) [44]
81 Don't Just Do Something (Stand There!) [48]
82 We Aim For Accuracy [6]
83 What's On Your Mind? (If You Will Forgive the Overstatement.) [51]
84 Think (Maybe You Can Dodge This Work.) [59]
85 You're Head and Shoulders Above Everyone. [40]
86 This Is A Non-Profit Organization (We Didn't Plan It That Way.) [85]
87 I'd Like To Compliment You On Your Work (When Will You Start?) [30]
88 Stop Talking When I'm Interrupting [46]

KOOKY AWARDS (44 & 15)

There are two types of cards in the "Kooky Awards" set produced by Topps in 1968. First of all, there is a series of 44 diecut Awards designed to be punched out and applied as stick-ons ("moisten back and press on any surface"). These are numbered (outside the score line) and have a blank space to fill in the name of the person being "honored." Secondly, there is a group of

15 "Shields" printed on thick cardboard; these are numbered (1-15) and also have a fill-in-name line. "Kooky Awards" were tested by Topps before going into full production, so there are two wrappers for the set. Some "Awards" cards (not "Shields") have been found missing the card number, T.C.G. copyright, and application directions; these are believed to be "test" cards.

TWO SIZES

ITEM	MINT	EX
Sets		
Awards	200.00	150.00
Shields	70.00	50.00
Awards		
Test issue	6.00	4.50
Regular	4.00	3.00
Shields	4.00	3.00
Wrappers		
Test	--	175.00
Regular	--	60.00

1 Ugly Award
2 Hippie Award
3 Thrift Award
4 Teacher's Pet Award
5 Physical Fitness Award
6 Sloppy Pig Award
7 Real Dog Award
8 Swell Head Award
9 Booby Prize
10 Disgusting Eater Award
11 Liar's Award
12 Bull Thrower Award
13 Perfect Idiot Award
14 Hollywood Award
15 Champion Kisser Award
16 Most Ambitious Award
17 Pain In The Neck Award
18 Stupidity Award
19 Perfection Award
20 Most Unlikely To Succeed Award
21 Great Lover Award
22 Know It All Award

23 Lousy Driver Award
24 Personality Award
25 Brush & Comb Award
26 Laziness Award
27 Good Neighbor Award
28 Utter Failure Award
29 Cheapskate Award
30 Goof-Off Award
31 Good Guy Award
32 Pigskin Award
33 Nastiness Award
34 Juvenile Delinquency Award
35 Coward Award
36 Champion Cheater Award
37 Most Unpopular Award
38 Rat Fink Award
39 Tattletale Award
40 Patriotism Award
41 Stool Pigeon Award
42 Best Dressed Award
43 Leadership Award
44 Moron Award

Shields

1 Cheerfulness Award
2 Sanitation Award
3 Tough Guy Award
4 Slob Award
5 Confidence Award
6 Fat Slob Award
7 Scholastic Award
8 Water Conservation Award
9 Determination Award
10 Ugliest Girl Award
11 Air Pollution Award
12 Miser Award
13 All-American Award
14 Financial Award
15 Absent-Minded Award

KRAZY KARDS (66)

2 1/2" X 3 1/2"

Who was the copycat? That's the question which springs to mind when reading the card captions in this set, many of which are identical to those in Topps' series of "Giant Plaks." It is a question which may go unanswered given the secretive behavior of the card producers and the lack of information about the Paul A. Price Company, makers of "Krazy Kards." There are two other interesting points about these otherwise dull cards: they could be purchased in sheets and detached into singles (each card has edge "nubs"), and every joke is printed in a variety of ink colors (black, blue, brown, green, purple, and red). Note: this set was issued without gum or wrappers.

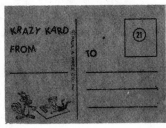

ITEM	MINT	EX
Set	37.50	25.00
Card	.50	.35

KRAZY LITTLE COMICS (16)

2 1/2" X 3 1/2"

Each comic in this series of 16 is eight pages long (counting covers) and spoofs a comic book super hero. Every back cover carries advertising for spurious products and services, such as "Murray Arthur" dance studio and a "Frontier Cabin" complete with "real hostile Indians." Krazy Little Comics was a test issue which was never distributed on a wider basis by Topps. The test wrapper bears a 5-cent price and the set is believed to have been produced in 1967.

Amusing Spider-Guy
Badman
Blunder Woman
Captive America
Fantastic Fear
Incredible Hunk
Jester's League of America
Lone Rancher
Mandrain The Magician
Meekly Thaw
Prince Violet
Stuporman
Sub-Marine Man
Tarsam
The Bantam
The Flush

ITEM	MINT	EX
Set	190.00	140.00
Comic	10.00	7.50
Wrapper	--	150.00
Box	--	200.00

KRAZY PENNANTS (31) 2 1/2" X 3 1/2"

Although this set does not exactly fall within the "non-sports" category, we present it here because it has been repeatedly ignored by "serious" sports card collectors and researchers. Each peel-off pennant is a diecut design approximately 3 1/8" long and has a notched end. Once removed from the paper backing, the pennants "lose" their number, which is printed in the top-right corner of the sheet. There are 31 pennants in the set; they were issued as a "bonus" in packs of 1967 Topps football cards.

ITEM	MINT	EX
Set	70.00	50.00
Pennant	2.00	1.50

1 Navel Academy
2 City College of Useless Knowledge
3 My Teacher Looks Like The Hunchback of Notre Dame
4 Psychedelic State
5 Minneapolis Mini-Skirts Are On The Rise
6 School of Art - Go, Van Gogh
7 Washington is Dead
8 School of Hard Knocks
9 If I See Her Alaska
10 Confused State
11 Yale Locks Are Tough To Pick
12 University of Transylvania
13 Down With Teachers
14 They Caught Me Cheating at Cornell
15 You're a Find If You Don't Root for the Houston Oilers
16 I Flunked Out of Harvard
17 Diskotech
18 Dropout U.
19 Polluted Air Will Force Us to Wear Gas Masks
20 Nutstu U.
21 Michigan State Pen
22 The Girls in Denver Look Like Broncos
23 I Left Buffalo Without Paying My Bills
24 Join the Army of Dropouts
25 In Miami I Was Bitten by Two Dolphins
26 Kansas City Has Too Few Workers and Too Many Chiefs
27 Everything is Banned in Boston Except Patriots
28 Fat People in Oakland are Usually Icebox Raiders
29 I'd Go West If You'd Just Point in the Right Direction
30 New York Skies are Crowded with Jets
31 San Diego Police Will Press Charges

KRAZY PEOPLE POSTERS (24) 9 3/4" X 18 1/2"

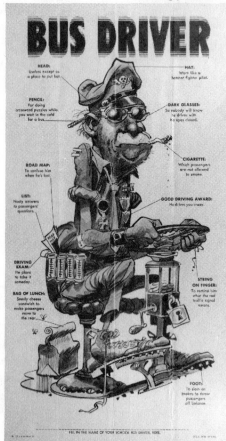

You have to give Topps credit for being persistent. The giant poster format sports a pretty "iffy" track record for success but they refuse to can the idea. If the number of surviving posters is any indication, "Krazy People Posters" must have been terminated shortly after release. Each poster is numbered and depicts specific types of people ("Hippie," "Slob," "Bus Driver," etc.) in caricature. Elements of the person's physical appearance, clothing and habits are pinpointed and ridiculed. If this happens to remind you of someone you know in real life, there is a convenient space provided to fill in their name. Note: posters were pre-folded to fit in small packages, so no mint price is given.

ITEM	MINT	EX
Set	--	285.00
Poster	--	10.00
Wrapper	--	40.00

KRAZY PEOPLE POSTERS
1 Loser
2 Bully
3 School Genius
4 Dunce
5 Rock Group
6 School Safety Patrol Officer
7 Pet Dog
8 Teacher
9 Gym Teacher
10 Father
11 Bus Driver
12 Coward
13 Teenybopper
14 Mailman
15 Scoutmaster
16 Slob
17 Aunt
18 TV Addict
19 Hippie
20 Mother
21 Lazybones
22 Show-off
23 Phoney
24 Doctor

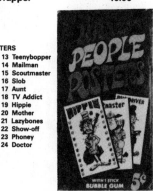

K2 FACTORY WORKERS (56)   2 1/2' 'X 3 1/2''

Corporate America does not often enshrine its employees on bubblegum trading cards. The set of "K2 Factory Workers" is proof positive that it should be done more often. Granted, the sepia-tone photographs are a turn off for many collectors who are accustomed to seeing everything in color, but the text is snappy and well-written ("Gripping tales of romance and adventure from the real lives of K2 employees"). The cards were issued in wrappers, with gum, in stores selling K2 products. Note: card Nos. 54A and 54B have been reported, bringing the set total to 56.

ITEM	MINT	EX
Set	200.00	165.00
Card	3.00	2.50
Wrapper	––	25.00

1 Michael C. Reuter, Parts Department Foreman
2 Karen Olsen Reveals A K-2 Secret
3 Daniel W. Zadra And His Secret Work
4 Robert Beaumont Theriault Admits Error
5
6 Jack Hanson And The K-2 Balloon Race
7 The Other Patti Cotton
8 George Brenno And The Secret Negotiations
9 George P. Yurisich, Jr.
10 Linda Eugenis, Quality Control Inspector
11 Don Andresen And The Hot Dog Racer
12
13
14 Rene Allard, K-2 Racing Director (The King Of Kootchie-Coo)
15
16 Jan Kroger: K-2 And The Single Girl
17 Robert F. Ryan, Quality Control Inspector
18 Carolyn Miller, Shipping Department Silkscreener
19 Craig "Lunk" Jennings And The Prizewinning Essay
20
21
22 Jeffrey P. Bardsley, Finger Hero
23 Bill Kirschner, President
24 Clifford L. Olson, Quality Control Inspector
25 Kenneth Andrew Hill
26 Robert Lee Mello, Fork Lift Driver
27 Edward J. "Gentleman Ed" Norton, National Sales Administrator (The Drummer)
28 Linda Parker, Glue Queen
29 Elmer J. Reed And The Machine Rebellion
30 Steve Millard And The Secret Of Vashon Island
31
32
33 Tom Cecil And The Pyles Mixer
34 Sharon Urban And The Vashon Gnomes
35
36 Dick Anderson, Research And Development Director
37
38 Wallace Bardsley, The K-2 Philosopher
39 Allan Van Buskirk, Foam Hero
40 Wende Browne, Sidepainter
41
42 Richard Eugenis And The Heritage Of K-2
43 The K-2 Volleyball Team
44 Diana Galloway, Career Girl
45 Charles T. Ferries, Executive Vice President
46 How Bob Burns Crossed The Delaware In His Mangusta
47 Vicki Browne And Her Alarming Knees
48 Dick Zue, Violinist
49
50 Jack W. Love And His Pizza
51
52 Delia Corazon Goetz, Grit Heroine
53 Doris Stoltz
54 The Mystery Of The Sheila Butterfields
54A Russ Butterfield And The Butterfield Civilization
54B Michael T. Meyer

KUNG FU – TEST ISSUE (60)   2 1/2" X 3 1/2"

The only difference reported between the cards illustrated here and those of the set immediately following are (1) the blue borders on the reverse, and (2) two asterisks preceding the T.C.G. initials, also on the back. The "regular" issue cards have (1) colorless borders and (2) one asterisk preceding the Topps initials. The picturing and numbering sequence are the same for both varieties. It has been assumed that the blue-bordered cards were a test issue, but no wrapper or box has ever been reported. For the time being, the only fact we know for certain is that they are far scarcer than the regular issue cards.

ITEM	MINT	EX
Card	10.00	8.00

KUNG FU (60)

The television series "Kung Fu" provided the color photo-

2 1/2" X 3 1/2"

graphs used in this Topps set produced in 1973. The obverses have red borders, and the set title is printed in large yellow letters below the picture. Cards one to 44 have poster pieces on the back, while cards 45 to 60 contain either a "Wisdom of Kung Fu" or "Kung Fu" (combat) presentations. Card no. 48 may be found with or without the feature heading on the back. There are 60 cards in the set.

ITEM	MINT	EX
Set	37.50	30.00
Card	.50	.40
Wrapper	--	2.00
Box	--	40.00

1 Caine
2 Caine Using Feet to Stop Firing Gun
3 Caine Dressed in White Gown
4 Caine Surrenders
5 Caine and Horse
6 Caine Traveling through Desert
7 Caine and Woman—Inside House
8 Caine with Kung Fu Class
9 Caine and Woman—Outside House
10 Caine Wearing Hat
11 Caine with Cup
12 Kung Fu Class
13 Caine Holding Hat
14 Caine Pointing Finger
15 Caine and Boy
16 Caine in Woods with Boy
17 Caine in Kung Fu Uniform
18 Foot Stopping Hand Firing Gun
19 Caine and Horse
20 Caine Demonstrating Kung Fu
21 Caine and Horse
22 Caine without Hair
23 Caine Speaking to Man
24 Caine Wearing Green Shirt
25 Woman, Boy and Caine
26 Caine with Mouth Open
27 Caine Wearing Hat
28 Caine Consentrating on Kung Fu Art
29 Caine Looking Forward
30 Woman Hugging Caine and Boy
31 Kung Fu Students
32 Caine Wearing Coat
33 Caine with Hat, Looking Stern
34 Caine in Kung Fu Position
35 Man with Rifle and Caine
36 Caine Lying Down, in Pain
37 Closeup of Caine's Face
38 Caine Meditating
39 Two Hands
40 Wanted Poster of Caine
41 Caine with Brush in Hand
42 Caine Arms Oustretched Baton
43 Caine Using Fighting
44 Caine Standing in Town
45 Caine and Master
46 Two Men Fighting
47 Caine Fighting Man with Rifle
48 Caine Smiling
49 Caine—Side View
50 Caine Holding Arms in Kung Fu Position
51 Caine with Bleeding Face and Arm
52 Caine Wearing Brown Shirt
53 Caine Jumping at Man with Rifle
54 Two Men During Kung Fu Style Fight
55 Caine Holding Pink Cloth
56 Caine in Squatting Position
57 Caine Holding Baton
58 Caine Taking Gun from Man
59 Caine and Man
60 Caine Dressed in Beige Silk and Barefooted

KUSTOM CARS I (30 & 9)

2 1/2" X 3 1/2"

The original series of Fleer's "Kustom Cars" is composed of 30 stickers and nine checklist/puzzle-piece cards. The stickers are found with two varieties of printed backs: one has a simple block containing peel-off directions; the other lists the card title and has text and other details. Stickers with the "simple" back peel from the corners; those with

"text" backs have a score line to allow "bend and peel" removal. All the obverse photos come with both back styles. The puzzle illustrated is made up of nine pieces, all of which have checklist backs (These may be pink or gray in color). Note: set price is for 30 stickers and a complete puzzle (nine cards).

ITEM	MINT	EX
Set	27.50	20.00
Sticker	.65	.50
Puzzle	.50	.35
Wrappers (3)		
Each	--	3.00
Box	--	20.00

FOLD AT CORNER
TO SEPARATE.
PEEL STICKER FROM
BACKING.

ZZR — Spy Rod

ZZR SPY ROD

George Barris designed and built a fantastic James Bond spy spoof hot rod for the UI film "Out of Sight". Extended front fenders have two guns on the ends, and rear fenders have flame throwers. There are also oil squirters, nail spreaders, and other crime fighting accessories.

BEND AT SPLIT TO PEEL
BACKING FROM STICKER
© GEORGE BARRIS
NO. HOLLYWOOD, CALIF. 91605
MFG. by FLEER CORP., PHILA., PA. 19141

Ala Milk Truck
Alvins Acorn
Barber Car
Boothill Express
bugaloo TV Tub
Bunk Bed Buggy
Daktari Jeep
Drag Buggy
Gould Delta Coupe
Hard Hat Hauler
Invader Roadster
Martian Spider
Monster Cycle
Movieland "Hall of Fame"
   Batmobile
Movieland "Hall of Fame"
   Monkeemobile
Pink Panther
Pizza Wagon
Redd Foxx "Li'l Redd Wrecker"
Ronald McDonald "Buggy"
Raiders Coach
Raspberries VW Rolls
Rickshaw Buggy
Romp TV Police Car
Sand Draggin'
Sex Machine
Tastee Big "T"
Twin Bathtub
TV Bearcats
Voxmobile Music Machine
ZZR — Spy Rod

KUSTOM CARS II (39 & 10)   2 1/2" X 3 1/2"

The backs of the stickers in this second series of "Kustom Cars" are identical in format to the "detailed" or "text" variety of Series I. This has created some confusion among collectors, which is easily dispelled by referring to the checklist below. None of the customized vehicles in this second series appeared in the original issue. The 10 stickers marked by an asterisk in the checklist are mounted on cardboard backing rather than paper. The area on the backs of these 10 cards is allocated in a 70/30 ratio to puzzle design and text. Assuming that the stickers had been removed from the front side of the card, the owner had to cut away the "text" area to use the puzzle piece. Since the puzzle has 12 parts, different puzzle pieces are found for the same obverse photo; it is assumed that each picture may also be found with a checklist back. None of the car stickers are numbered, and we have placed the "assigned" number appearing on the checklist card in parentheses. Note: set price is for 49 different sticker fronts and one checklist, plus any extra puzzle backs required to complete the puzzle.

ITEM	MINT	EX
Set	45.00	32.50
Stickers	.65	.50
Cards	1.50	1.00
Wrappers (2)		
Each	--	3.00
Box	--	20.00

Musical Firebird

MUSICAL FIREBIRD

Right out of the "Romp" TV series comes this unique Pontiac convertible painted with the complete musical score used by the famous rock group, Celebration. The wheels are mags with wild, wild tires.

BEND AT SPLIT TO PEEL
BACKING FROM STICKER

© GEORGE BARRIS
NO. HOLLYWOOD, CALIF. 91602
Mfd. by FLEER CORP., PHILA., PA 19141

SUPER MARAUDER—A racing styled Mercury roadster, this Barris special is a two seater with dual extender compartment, open wheels with air braking air vents. The engine has a choke-styled scoop and chrome scoffs-ed into the hood panel. The unique wheel design enhances the beauty of this custom special.

FOLD CORNER FORWARD
FRONT TO SEPARATE
STICKER FROM BACK

© GEORGE BARRIS
N. HOLLYWOOD, CALIF. 91602
MADE BY FLEER CORP.

Super Marauder

Ada's Lincoln (35)
Ala Kart (32)
Anolik Bird (5)
Beach Boys Buggy (38)
Bed Buggy (7)
Bedroom Van (10)
Beverly Hillbillies Car (19)
Bing Crosby's Ala Kart (26)
Bobby Darin's Di-Dia 150 (34)
Bob Hope's Klassic Kart (27)

Chitty Chitty Bang Bang (2)
Covered Wagon (48)*
Daisy Buggy (21)
Dirt Tracker (25)
Dobie Gillis' Car (30)
Everycar (12)
French Bath Tub Buggy (11)
Fun Buggy (18)
Golden Sahara (37)
Good Guys TV Car (28)
Grecian (41)*
Green Hornet (20)
Illusion (45)*

Jackson Five Pantera (43)*
Kopper Kart (46)*
Koratron Toyota (29)
Lloyd Thaxton Hot Rod (23)
Matador (39)
Mattel Bath House Buggy (17)
Mongrel "T" (9)
Moonscope (6)
Movieland Motorcade Van (22)
Murphy's Dune Buggy (15)
Musical Firebird (36)
My Favorite Mustang (42)*
Outhouse Car (8)

Purple Flake (3)
Roarin' Forties (31)
Scallop Truck (44)*
Seymour's Pop-Up Van (1)
Stars and Stripes Van (13)
Super Fly Cadillac (49)*
   Super Marauder (47)*
Thunder Charger (14)
Tommy Steele's Excaliber (24)
Twister "T" (16)
Venturs XX Double Cross (40)*
X.P.A.K. Air Car (33)
Zip Code Mail Truck (4)

Scallop Truck

My Favorite Mustang

Illusion

Jackson Five Pantera

Movieland "Hall of Fame" Batmobile

LABYRINTH (5)

Labyrinth Bubble Gum was produced by Topps in 1986. There are five different characters depicted on the backs of the 2 7/16" X 3 3/8" plastic bags which held the gum. As you can see by the illustrations, each character is named but the artwork suffers from encroachment of the UPC code.

2 7/16" X 3 3/8"

ITEM	MINT	EX
Set	--	6.00
Wrappers (5)		
Each	--	1.00
Box	--	4.00

LAFFS (80)

Released to the public late in 1991, "Laffs" is a series of 80 cards featuring characters and scenes from three of Lorimar Production's most successful television shows. The cards follow this sequence: 1-26 ... Full House; 27-52 ... Family Matters; 53-78 ... Perfect Strangers; 79-80 ... checklists. Both front and back surfaces are super glossy and the color photographs are sharp and well-composed. The text on the reverses is a little "gushy" and superficial but Impel, the manufacturer, made a wise decision in using simple phrases or episode titles ("The Good, The Bad, and The Urkel") for captions. The poly bag "wrapper" is basically yellow, with orange, red, blue and green accents. The display box is also yellow and has three cards, one from each show, on the top (lid) and front panel. A "Laffs Collector's Album" was advertised on the back of the wrapper as a mail premium.

2 1/2" X 3 1/2"

ITEM	MINT	EX
Set	8.00	4.00
Card	.10	.05
Wrapper	--	.15
Box	--	2.00

A "Full House"

Life With Urkel

Larry Appleton

FULL HOUSE
1 Bob Saget
2 Dave Coulier
3 John Stamos
4 Jesse Katsopolis
5 Lori Loughlin
6 Candace Cameron
7 Donna Jo (D.J.) Tanner
8 Jodie Sweetin
9 Stephanie Tanner
10 Mary Kate & Ashley Olsen
11 Michelle Tanner
12 The Tanner Sisters
13 My Three Daughters
14 "Crimes & Michelle's Demeanor"
15 "Working Girl"
16 "Shape Up"
17 "One Last Kiss"
18 "The Wedding"
19 "Ol' Brown Eyes"
20 "Slumber Party"
21 Michelle & Comet
22 "Tanner's Island"
23 "Joey Goes to Hollywood"
24 "Honey, I Broke the House"
25 "Stephanie Plays the Field"
26 A "Full House"

FAMILY MATTERS
27 Jaleel White
28 Steve Urkel
29 Darius McCrary
30 Eddie Winslow
31 Kellie Williams
32 Judy Winslow
33 Jaimee Foxworth
34 arl Winslow
35 Harriette Winslow
36 Mother Winslow
37 Rachel Crawford
38 Bryton McClure
39 Carl & Harriette
40 Life With Urkel
41 "Cousin Urkel"
42 "The Good, The Bad & The Urkel"
43 "Busted"
44 "A Very Winslow Christmas"
45 "Torn Between Two Lovers"
46 "Dog Day Halloween"
47 "The Crash Course"
48 "Rachel's Place"
49 "In A Jam"
50 Laura Winslow
51 "Son"
52 The Winslow Household

PERFECT STRANGERS
53 Bronson Pinchot
54 Mark Linn-Baker
55 Balki Bartokomous
56 Larry Appleton
57 Melanie Wilson
58 Rebecca Arthur
59 Jennifer & Mary Anne
60 Lydia Markham
61 Sam Gropley
62 "Climb Every Billboard"
63 "Hocus Pocus"
64 "A Horse is a Horse"
65 "Great Balls of Fire"
66 "Out of Sync"
67 "This Old House"
68 "Dog Day Afternoon"
69 "Black Widow"
70 "Good Skates"
71 "The Men Who Knew Too Much"
72 "Call Me Indestructible"
73 "Safe At Home"
74 "I Saw This On TV"
75 "See How They Run"
76 "The Sunshine Boys"
77 "New Kid on the Block"
78 Perfect Couples
79 Checklist
80 Checklist

LAND OF THE GIANTS (55)

2 1/2" X 3 1/2"

The Land of the Giants series issued by Topps as a test issue is one of the scarcest of the modern sets. The fronts have color photographs and are captioned in a fancy design at one side of the picture. Backs 45-54 are poster pieces; backs 1-44 have narratives and also contain the card numbers near the credit line at the bottom; card no. 55 has a checklist back. The wrapper is actually a large sticker attached to a piece of waxed paper.

ITEM	MINT	EX
Set	1150.00	750.00
Card	18.00	12.00
Wrapper	--	125.00
Box	--	500.00

1	Dan Erickson	20	Scream of Fear!	38	Courageous Lady!
2	Hide and Seek!	21	A Strange World!	39	Captured!
3	Brave Girl!	22	Magnet of Doom!	40	Alexander Fitzhugh
4	Brave Boy!	23	Alarmed!	41	A Daring Plan!
5	Fire!	24	Bombs Away!	42	Imprisioned!
6	Giant Mouse!	25	Perilous Journey!	43	Back to Safety!
7	Fitzhugh in Flight!	26	Time Running Out!	44	Rough Landing!
8	Prepare for Lift-off!	27	No Joke!	45	The Fire Ball!
9	Move Out Fast!	28	Barry Lockridge	46	Race against Time!
10	Spaceship Pilot!	29	The Giant Watch!	47	Valerie Scott
11	In the Path of Fire!	30	Tiny Plaything!	48	Tunnel to Safety!
12	Steve Burton	31	Tense Moment!	49	The Scavengers!
13	Frightened!	32	Betty Hamilton	50	Furry Menace!
14	Get Inside, Get Inside!	33	Giant Approaching!	51	No Escape!
15	Dangerous Moment!	34	Mark Wilson	52	Race against Time!
16	The Giant Dog!	35	Deadly Experiment!	53	Steve's Plan!
17	Nightmare Alley!	36	Rescued!	54	In the Giant's Clutches!
18	Up, Up and Awaa-a-a-y!	37	Lost!	55	Face of Terror!
19	Return of the Giant!				

LAUGH—IN (77 & 24)

2 1/2" X 3 1/2"

The antics of Rowan & Martin are preserved for card collectors in this 101-item Laugh-In set produced by Topps in 1968. The standard-size cards come in six different formats: regular photo cards (1-33), knock-knocks (34-45), necklaces (46-56), finger puppets (57-62), door cards (63-71), and foldees (72-77). The backs of all the photo cards are puzzle pieces. In addition to the cards, there is a series of stickers, called "Goldie's Laugh-ons." The stickers themselves are peel-off diecut designs centered on 1 15/16" X 2 15/16" yellow cards. They are all captioned but the sticker number is located outside the score line at bottom left. Note: separate set prices are listed for cards and stickers.

ITEM	MINT	EX
Sets		
Cards	250.00	180.00
Stickers	150.00	120.00
Cards		
1-45	2.00	1.50
46-77	4.00	3.00
Sticker	5.00	4.00
Wrapper	--	25.00
Box	--	125.00

Goldie's Laugh-Ons

1 I'm Hot!
2 The Only Way to Fly!
3 Rub Me and Make a Wish
4 Be Nice to Mice
5 Cut Along Dotted Lion

6 Right Now
7 Relax
8 Don't Bug Me
9 Peace
10 Watch It
11 The Court's in Session
12 Flake Off
13 Sock It to Me
14 Verrry Interesting
15 Panic Button
16 Put Your Money Where Your Mouth Is
17 One Way
18 Danger Curves Ahead
19 I'm Hip!
20 Knock Knock
21 Slippery When Wet
22 Heavenly Body
23 I'm A Cut Up!
24 Soft Shoulder

SPECIAL FEATURE: LAUGH-IN RINGS (?) 3/4" DIA.

The L.M. Becker Company (Wisconsin) obtained a license to produce a set of "Laugh-In" rings in 1968. The rings were made of plastic and had famous Laugh-In phrases like "Here Come The Judge," "Verry Innnteresting," and "Sock It To Me" in raised letters on the ring face. One ring was packed, without gum or candy, in each 5¢ paper wrapper. Given the fact that Becker operated in a regional market, it is not surprising that these rings are in short supply today. Suggested values: ring ... $10; wrapper ... $10; display box ... $125.

LAUGH-IN PUZZLES

Laugh-In Topps new checklist
Regular Cards

1 Ooh! That Hurts When We Hug!
2 I Ate Some Seeds and Look What Happened!
3 Are You Worried About Going Up in This Spaceship? No, I'm Worried About Coming Down.
4 When I'm in the Dumps I Get a New Hat...That's Where I Got This One!
5 When We Hold You in Contempt of Court We really Hold You!
6 That's the Last Time I Take on the Whole Team!
7 Bulletin - Russia Has Just Invaded the United States..But First a Word from Our Sponsor!
8 It's Bernie's Engagement Gift...a Tattoo of a Ring!
9 I Like the Shot, But the Chicken Didn't!
10 How Long Were You in Rumania? About as Long as I Am Now!
11 O.K.! Who's the Wise Guy Who Said This Was the Men's Room!
12 Psst, Your Zipper broke!

13 I've Heard of Long Protests But This is Ridiculous!
14 Give Me a Hint...Is the Heart on the Left or Right Side?
15 You Sure This Dance Will Bring Rain?
16 Our Next Act Needs No Introduction! Because They Already Know Each Other!
17 What a Ridiculous Story! It's About a Wolf That Talks!
18 Me? A Woman Athlete? ...I'm the Winner of a Russian Beauty Contest!
19 Take the Picture Already!! The Ink is Drying!
20 Is It Something I Said? No It's Something I Ate!
21 I Predict You'll Soon Meet a Tall Dark Stranger...Who'll Mug You!
22 I Think We'd Make a Lovely Couple! A Couple of What?
23 Verry Interesting!
24 Father...Say Something to Me! Boy, Are You in Trouble!
25 That Rembrandt Was Great! He Covered All the Numbers!
26 Since We've Been Married Dear, You've Grown Another Foot!
27 Gee! That's My Mother-In-Law Standing There! Do You Think You Can Hit Her From Here?
28 If That's a Halo Our Date's Off for Tonight!
29 You Really Have an Open Mind...and a Mouth to Match!
30 Here Come the Judge!
31 You May Hate Me for This, Ma, But You've Got Bad Breath!
32 Why Are You Dressed Like That! I'm a Chain-smoker!
33 Stop! I'm Not Dead Yet! Why Wait Till the Last Minute?
Knock Knocks
34 Isabel Busted? I Came to Fix It.
35 Oliver Troubles Will Soon Be Over
36 Lyndon Bridges Falling Down!
37 Stan Aside, Bud - We're Comin' Through!
38 Jess Li'l Ol' Me!
39 Vera Interesting!
40 Barry Me Not on the Lone Prairie!
41 Clod! Don't You Know Who Abe Lincoln Is?
42 Ivan To Hold Your Hand!
43 Mandy Lifeboats
44 Anita Minute To Think It Over!

45 Saki To Me Baby!

Necklaces
46 Sock It To Me
47 Here Comes The Judge
48 The Court's In Session
49 Flake Off
50 Scoobie Doobie Doo
51 Knock Knock
52 Blast Off
53 Laugh In
54 Verrry Interesting
55 Dumb
56 You Bet Your Sweet Bippy

Finger Puppets
57 I Work For Peanuts
58 Goldie
59 Joanne
60 Uncle Sam Wants You!
61 Ouch!
62 Yellow Pages

Door Cards
63 Sherlock Bones - Private Eye Sickmund Freud - Child Psychiatrist
64 We're About to Discover the Message That Has Been Hidden for 10,000 Years!
65 Do Not Enter This Door Under Any Circumstances
66 Why Does a Stork Stand On One Leg?
67 Why Do Elephants Carry Keys?
68 What's Worse Than a Giraffe with a Sore Throat?
69 How Do You Stop a Charging Lion?
70 What's Black and White and Red All Over?
71 Yacht Club Ku Klux Klan

Foldees
72 Mona Lisa...Joanne Worley...Artie Johnson
73 Artie Johnson...Ruth Buzzi...George Washington
74 Artie Johnson...Monkey Face...Judy Carne
75 Artie Johnson...Ruth Buzzi...Joanne Worley
76 Dick Rowan...Dan Martin...Abe Lincoln
77 Spaceman...Ape Hanging on Branch... Goldie Hahn

LAUGH N' TELL (?)

3/4" X 4 1/4"

Isn't our hobby amazing! The "Laugh N' Tell" series of jokes printed on Sugar Babies (National Biscuit Co.) packages ran through at least six series of 24 jokes each, yet very few collectors know about them today. An offer on the wrapper solicited jokes from the general public; $5 was paid for each joke used and the sender's name and home town were printed along with the gag. The series was first recorded in Barker's "Catalog Additions" of June, 1971 (which indicates a print run of 1970-72). Note: the prices listed below are for nearly complete wrappers (one side cut off to remove contents). Backs only are valued at 50% of list; joke strips cut entirely from the package are priced at 20% of list.

ITEM	MINT	EX
Wrapper	--	5.00

LAUREL & HARDY (25 & 25)

3/4" X 4 1/4"

1 5/8" X 3 3/8"

The confectionary division of Nabisco marketed a variety of cards on the backs of "Junior Mints" and "Pom Poms" boxes during the 1960s and 1970s. One of their best efforts was this Laurel & Hardy production issued in two sets of 25 (one for each brand). The photo and print of each card are sepia-tone and a humorous caption is located beneath the picture. The cards are numbered and there is advertising copy inviting candy eaters to "send in your own funny line for this photo!" Note: cards cut away from boxes cannot be considered mint.

ITEM	MINT	EX
Card	--	3.00
Box	15.00	10.00

LAUREL & HARDY CHECKLIST — JUNIOR MINT SERIES

1 "Positively no collect calls from Calcutta!"
2 "Why can't she elope out the front door?"
3 "Man, that's cross-ventilation!"
4 "What do you mean, you lost the tune?"
5 "Look, you want to play golf or fence?"
6 "I told you short shirts would be in this year."
7 "The train leaves at noon, be under it!"
8 "He says he's willing to settle out of court."
9 "Look, if it cures your warts, it's worth it!"
10 "This is not what is meant by pocket billiards!"
11 "We ate the whole thing!"
12 "Now we have to get another sax player!"
13 "He says they don't deliver pizza on Sundays."
14 "Does she have a friend?"
15 "I told you not to order a hot dog in an Italian restaurant."
16 "... And I don't allow my secretaries to wear pant-suits!"
17 "I'm answering an ad for an apartment with a high ceiling."
18 "I've just been robbed by a man with his finger in his ears."
19 "Are you sure this is the way your mother made rice pudding?"
20 "Are you sure this is how you get filet of sole?"
21 "Excuse me, I think I hear the phone."
22 "You've got to do something about that cough."
23
24
25 "It still hurts, but now I'm getting Channel 2 in Saskatoon."

LAUREL & HARDY CHECKLIST ... POM POMS SERIES

1 "You expect me to believe anybody with a beard that long is under 12?"
2
3 "Make room, buster, this cab is being hijacked!"
4 "I don't want to play anymore!"
5 "And no tip-toeing through the tulips."
6 "Bet my toe cracks louder than yours."
7 "A bird in the hand can be quite a mess."
8 "And this is why it's called hi fi?"
9 "I was just planning a short trip."
10 "OK, OK, I won't spill my milk again."
11 "Now Stanley will explain nuclear fission!"
12 "Tried rubber cement?"
13 "Does this mean we're engaged?"
14 "Did you find it?"
15 "What do you think this is, a 747 stagecoach?"
16 "Another fine mess you've gotten me into ..."
17 "I think I'm frozen to the seat."
18 "These men are guilty officer! Don't try to whitewash them!"
19 "I know where you can get your shoes re-heeled real cheap!"
20 "Say, I think your horn needs a good mouthwash."
21 "He loves stewed rutabagas; he's just a little shy."
22 "You say — he owns the place?"
23
24 "The next time you wash my clothes, be sure I'm not in them!"
25 "Strange, I thought we only get gift wrapped garbage at Christmas."

LEAGUE OF NATIONS - 1ST SERIES (18)

2 1/2" X 3 1/2"

CaliCo Graphics chose an archaic name for the set which marked its debut in trading card production in 1989. The series of 18 cards depicts then-current world leaders in black and white photographs. The country and name of each subject is clearly identified on the fronts of the cards. The reverses are very well composed and present a variety of essential information about the statesman and his nation in very readable form. The cards of this first series are not numbered, so the checklist below appears in alphabetical order. Note: sold in sets only (in clear wrap with label attached).

ITEM	MINT	EX
Set	3.00	--

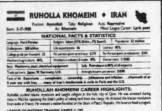

Fahd Bin 'Abdulaziz
Corazon Aquino
Pieter Botha
George Bush
Rajiv Gandhi
Mikhail Gorbachev
Wojciech Jaruzelski
Muammar Khadafi
Ruholla Khomeini
Helmut Kohl
Francois Mitterand
Robert Mugabe
Brian Mulroney
Li Peng
Jose Sarney
Yitzhak Shamir
Noboru Takeshita
Margaret Thatcher

LEAGUE OF NATIONS - 2ND SERIES (54)   2 1/2" X 3 1/2"

Collectors will find plenty to enjoy in this second series of "League of Nations" cards (CaliCo Graphics) once they get past the nonsensical application of baseball terminology ("rookie" and "all-stars") and the inclusion of a Pete Rose card! Ten of the subjects pictured in Series 1 reappear in Series 2 and these are marked with an * in the checklist. All of the cards have color artwork fronts surrounded by red, green, or purple borders. Besides statesmen and women, there are maps, a chess player, theme cards, a preacher-politician, and cards for Dan Quayle and Salman Rushdie. There are even three checklist cards (one is for Series 1). Once again, the card backs are well written and easy to read. CaliCo notes on card 54 that Series 1 subjects Khomeini, Takeshita, Samey, Ghandi, Jaruzelski, Kohl, and Botha either died or retired (voluntarily or otherwise) in a short space of time, and then recites the CaliCo jingle: "Governments may rise and fall, hurry and collect them all." Considering all the changes that have occurred since Series 2 was issued in 1990 (example: no more U.S.S.R. or Gorbachev), maybe it's time for CaliCo to punch out Series 3! The 54 cards of Series 2 were issued only as a set (wrapped in clear plastic with one half the set inside the paper wrapper illustrated below). Note: "Rookie" cards are marked by ** in the checklist.

ITEM	MINT	EX
Set	7.00	---

1	Corazon Aquino*	28	Petroleum All Stars
2	U.S.S.R.	29	Fang Lizhi
3	U.S.A.	30	Japan
4	Fidel Castro	31	Repression
5	Hashemi Rafsanjani**	32	Jessie Jackson
6	Philippines	33	Pakistan
7	Mikhail Gorbachev*	34	Manuel Noriega
8	Poland	35	Mother Theresa
9	George Bush*	36	Libya
10	China	37	Dalai Lama
11	Yitzhak Shamir*	38	Boris Yeltsin
12	South Africa	39	Ronald Reagan
13	Lech Walesa	40	Rich / Poor
14	Wojciech Jarulzelski*	41	Saudi Arabia
15	Nicaragua	42	Li Peng*
16	Fahd Bin Abdulaziz*	43	Desmond Tutu
17	Daniel Ortega	44	Pete Rose
18	Margaret Thatcher*	45	Dan Quayle
19	Yasser Arafat	46	Moammar Khadafi*
20	Gary Kasparov	47	Iran
21	Israel	48	Frederik deKlerk
22	Toshiki Kaifu**	49	Salman Rushdie
23	Raoul Wallenberg	50	Panama
24	U.K.	51	Manufacturing All Stars
25	Cuba	52	Check List 2-A
26	Benazir Bhutto	53	Check List 2-B
27	Ruhollah Khomeini*	54	Check List 1

LEAVE IT TO BEAVER (60)   2 1/2" X 3 1/2"

Amid the jumble of synthetic nostalgia and reprint sets that has deluged our hobby, the "Leave It To Beaver" set produced by Mike Cramer is a refreshing change of pace.

The fronts contain crisp B&W photographs adorned with captions expressed in the ingenuous style that characterized the dialogue of this famous TV show. The backs are numbered and contain a short text or feature. Although the cards were not issued with gum, they were packaged in a red wax wrapper (10 cards per pack, 36 packs per box).

ITEM	MINT	EX
Set	35.00	24.00
Card	.50	.35
Wrapper	---	1.00

Leave it to Beaver

33 School Time
34 Wally's Track Meet
35 Throwing a Pass
36 Beaver at Bat
37 Captain of the Varsity Football Team
38 Beaver's New Bike
39 A Kid Like Eddie Haskell Only Comes Along About Once In a Couple Hundred Years.—Wally
40 Fourth of July
41 June Cleaver
42 Helping Mom
43 A Hug from Mom
44 Catching a Pass
45 Catching Frogs on Miller's Pond
46 Eddie Haskell
47 Smiley and Hoppy
48 Off to School
49 You Know Something, Wally, I'd Rather Do Nothin' with You than Somethin' with Anybody Else.—Beaver
50 I'm Glad We Don't Have a Girl. Our Staircase Isn't Wide Enough for Her to Throw Her Bridal Bouquet From.—June
51 Going Swimming
52 The Haunted House
53 Ward Cleaver
54 He's Got That Little Kid Expression on His Face All the Time, but He's Not Really as Goofy as He Looks.—Wally
55 Beaver's Football Team
56 Theodore Cleaver
57 Gee, I Wouldn't Mind Facin' the Truth If So Much Hollerin' Didn't Go With It—Beaver
58 Please Don't Cry, Mom. I'll Do Anything You Want. I'll Even Kill Myself If You Don't Cry.—Beaver
59 This Is Vacation. You Parents Aren't Allowed to Make You Work All the Time. It's a State Law.—Eddie
60 The Cleaver Family

15 Working Out
16 Where's The Beaver?—June
17 Nobody Can Hurt You When You're Sleepin' in Bed.—Beaver
18 I Guess There's Two Things That'll Always Be in the World...Dirt and Homework.—Wally Cleaver
19 June's Birthday
20 Ward's Baseball
21 Beav, You Sure Get a Lot of Fun Out of Doin' Nothin'.—Wally
22 Ward, I'm Very Worried About The Beaver.—June
23 Hobby Time
24 June and Wally
25 Beaver's Tree
26 Family Time
27 If I Had My Choice Between a Three-Pound Bass and a Girl, I'd Take the Three-Pound Bass.—Beaver
28 Wally's New Suit
29 Thanks an Awful Lot, Dad...It Sure Is Good When Your Father's a Friend—Beaver
30 Wally's Haircomb
31 Beaver's Tree Comes Home
32 Wally and Beaver Ready for Summer

1 The Beaver
2 Mr. and Mrs. Cleaver
3 Fishing at Friends Lake
4 Archery Practice for the Boys
5 Fishing at Shadow Lake
6 Wally Cleaver
7 Wally, I Don't Think This Is Going to Work—Beaver
8 A Valentine for Mom
9 The Hypnotist
10 Beaver, Breakfast Is Not a Race—June
11 St. Patrick's Day
12 Hide and Seek
13 Go See a Girl? I'd Rather Smell a Skunk—Beaver
14 Fun at the Beach

LITTLE MERMAID (90/15/15/7)   2 1/2" X 3 1/2"

The Disney Studios have produced the finest animated films ever seen during their 50 years in the business, and "The Little Mermaid," released in 1991, is destined to become another classic. The card set, issued by Impel, does justice to the original. The 127 "charming and collectible" cards are divided into the following categories: 90 "story" cards, 15 "color-in activity cards," 15 "stand-up activity cards," and 7 "static stick 'ems." The story cards contain lush, borderless artwork from the film on front and have text and a smaller picture set on a multicolor background on the reverse. The stickers are unnumbered and uncaptioned (names provided in our checklist) and the color-ins are simple black & white line drawings awaiting the application of juvenile crayons. The stand-ups are not captioned but have numbers and instructions printed on the back. The poly bag wrapper is mostly blue and a mail-in offer for a Little Mermaid Collector's Album is printed on the reverse. The display box received a 1991 "Gummie Award" for Best Box of 1991. Note: set price includes all stickers, color-ins, and stand-ups.

ITEM	MINT	EX
Set	25.00	18.00
Card	.10	.07
Stand-up	.30	.20
Color-in	.20	.15
Sticker	1.50	1.00
Wrapper	––	.15
Box	––	3.00

Little Mermaid

1 The Little Mermaid
2 King Triton
3 We are the daughters of Triton
4 Sebastian
5 Miles away from the concert hall
6 We really shouldn't be doing this
7 Have you ever seen anything this wonderful
8 Ariel and Flounder swim for their lives
9 Swimming to the surface
10 Furious because Ariel has disobeyed him
11 Sebastian follows Ariel
12 I just don't see how
13 I've got gadgets and gizmos aplenty
14 Ariel gazes longingly at a painting
15 Sebastian is too shocked
16 Just then, the hull of a ship
17 Fireworks blossom in the night sky
18 Sebastian follows Ariel unwillingly
19 On board is the most handsome human
20 It is Prince Eric
21 He's very handsome isn't he
22 Eric's advisor, Grimsby
23 As if responding to Eric's words
24 Fire races through the ship
25 The statue plummets past Ariel
26 Safe ashore
27 Ariel's sisters are amazed
28 King Triton is puzzled
29 Meanwhile, in a sea garden
30 Sebastian is beside himself
31 Sebastian tries talking sense into Ariel
32 Ariel gets into the rhythm
33 Even the seaweed is singing!
34 Everyone on the ocean floor joins the act
35 The ocean floor is really jumping now!
36 Even Ariel can't resist
37 When Sebastian sings,
38 Sebastian winds up for a grand finale,
39 Inside her treasure grotto,
40 Meanwhile, a seahorse messenger has come
41 Sebastian quakes in his shell
42 In a volcanic rage,
43 As father and daughter argue,
44 Ariel collapses as Triton leaves,
45 Unknown to Triton and Ariel,
46 As Ariel sobs,
47 As Ariel approaches Ursula's lair
48 Ariel hesitates before she follows
49 Ursula pretends to offer
50 Take a gulp and take a breath
51 Ursula bends over her teeming cauldron
52 The mists form glowing hands
53 Ursula's spell takes effect
54 Soaked and covered in seaweed,

55 As Ariel happily regards her new legs,
56 Max leads Eric to Ariel,
57 At the palace,
58 Meanwhile, Sebastian, who has hidden
59 As Ariel enters the dining room,
60 Meanwhile, Sebastian isn't having such a good time!
61 Leaping from the pot,
62 Ariel spends a blissful day
63 Time is passing,
64 At least, Sebastian takes matters into his own claws
65 The setting is perfect,
66 Ariel smiles shyly
67 Suddenly the boat tips over,
68 "That was a close one..."
69 With Ariel's beautiful voice
70 As evening falls
71 Scuttle races to warn Ariel
72 Back on shore,
73 Ariel reaches the ship
74 But it is too late!
75 Ursula grabs Ariel
76 Ursula begins to turn Ariel
77 Showing Triton the contract
78 Solemnly, Triton bargains
79 Laughing hideously,
80 Eric dives into the water
81 Eric surfaces and swims
82 Frantically, Eric clambers aboard
83 Beneath the sea,
84 While Eric lies unconscious
85 Ariel is unaware
86 Knowing it means he is giving Ariel away
87 Once again, wedding bells ring out,
88 Even the happiest moments
89 Ariel turns to her father,
90 As the merfolk wave farewell,

COLORING CARDS
1 Ariel & Flounder / Flounder
2 Ariel / Under the Sea
3 Flotsam & Jetsam / Ursula
4 Grimsby / Max
5 Chef Louie & Sebastian / Sebastian
6 Ariel & Flounder / "Under The Sea"
7 Eric & Ariel / Eric & Ariel
8 Ariel & Eric / Eric
9 Ariel & Flounder / Scuttle
10 Ariel / "Under The Sea"
11 Ariel / "Under The Sea"
12 Ariel & Flounder / Flounder
13 Ariel & Flounder / Scuttle
14 Ariel & Flounder / "Under The Sea"
15 Ariel / King Triton

STICKERS
Ariel [full]
Ariel [portrait]
Eric
Flounder
Scuttle
Sebastian
Scuttle

LITTLE MERMAID ALBUM STICKERS (232)   1 15/16" X 3"

Panini purchased a license from Disney Studios to create the Little Mermaid album sticker series, which was released in 1991. The set consists of 232 stickers, of which 202 are the standard color artwork variety, and 30 are die-cut, lift off designs. Each type is numbered and fits on a space with the corresponding number in the 32-page album. The paper wrapper is mostly blue, with mermaid artwork in the center, and has crimped edges which require cutting or tearing to get to the stickers inside. As we went to press, this series was still available in stores for 39¢ per pack (six stickers) and 89¢ per album. This set will undoubtedly follow past market performances for Panini material and settle in at 10¢ per sticker and $15-20 per set as soon as the marketing cycle is finished (Panini normally makes product available for a specific amount of time only).

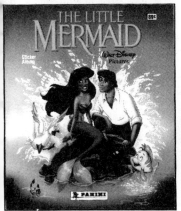

LITTLE SHOP OF HORRORS (44)   2 1/2" X 3 1/2"

When will they learn? The moguls in Tinsel Town have made us laugh for generations with an astonishing variety of humorous films. Every once in a while, however, there is a

real klunker in the can, a tribute to a bad idea made worse by the three lousies: casting, acting, and directing. So, Topps was wrong when it declared (on the wax wrapper) that Little Shop of Horrors was a "New Hit Movie." There are 44 combination sticker/ cards in the set. On the card

side, Nos. 1-32 relate the story in photos and text; Nos. 33-42 are pieces of a 10-part puzzle. On the sticker side, Nos. 1-42 contain peel-off diecut stickers (artwork and photos). The diecut designs are evenly divided between rectangles with rounded corners and irregular shapes. Two unnumbered cards complete the set: they have different diecut stickers on one side, but the same puzzle preview photo on the other (except for the number of stars appearing in the lower-right corner).

ITEM	MINT	EX
Set	8.00	5.50
Sticker/card	.20	.15
Wrapper	--	.35
Box	--	5.00

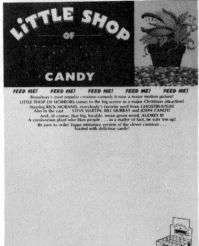

LONE RANGER TATTOOS (?)   1 1/2" X 3 3/8"

The exterior wrappers of this "tattoo transfer" set manufactured by Philly Gum are not dated. There are four basic designs (illustrated), two of which are repeated in another color ("riding" pos and "Indian fight"). Th tattoos on the interior side a printed in five colors an are not numbered or ca tioned (except for occasion "sounds"). Twenty-five diffe ent transfers have been confi med to date, but this set valued more for the exteri wrappers.

ITEM	MINT	E
Wrappers (6)		
each	--	15.0

LOONEY LABELS (50 & 22) 2 5/8" X 3 5/16"

Fleer's "Looney Labels" set is composed of 50 sheets of labels and 22 "eye-teasers" cards. Each label sheet measures 2 5/8" X 3 5/16" and contains two, three, or four "real cloth" designs (front peel). The label sheet has a blank, tan-colored back and some of the individual designs are repreated on other sheets. The "eye-teasers" are a series of optical illusions printed on standard-size cardboard (blank back). Note: the set price listed is for all 72 items:

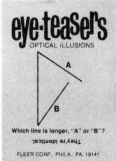

ITEM	MINT	EX
Set	35.00	25.00
Labels	.50	.35
Eye-teasers	.35	.25
Wrapper	--	1.50
Box	--	7.00

LABELS
Ant Farm
Sing Around the Collar
Open at Own Risk

Belly Button Lint
This End Up
Emergency Zipper

B.O. Zone
Condemned by the Board of Health
Wear It With Pride

Button Up for Saftey
Bullet Proof

Censored
Maden From Old Rubber Tires

Danger Warts
Up Your Sleeve

Dingbat Dacron
On the Cuff

Do Not Starch, Dry Clean, Wash or Wear
Inspected By No One
Peel Me

English Tweed
Ataway (He Went Ataway!)

Genuine Artificial Rabbit Fur
Property of Girls Gym
Slightly Irregular

Genuine Irish Linen
Supported by Junkey Shorts

Ground in Dirt
See-Thru
Button Your Lip

Hand Made
Pull to Undress

Hidden Pocket
Sparrow

Horse Blanket
Out Patient

Im Beautiful
My Underwear Is On Backwards
Life Size

Im Beautiful
Designed by Goodwill

I'm Clean
Loggs Sheer Hosejob

Infected By No. 7
Fruit on the Loose

Jive Threads
Protected by Fleas

Keep Away From Open Flame —
  Flammable
Lady Bags
Size [check-off boxes]

Khaki
Pumpers
Drip Dry...You Drip

King Size
Washed by Prison Laundry

King Size
Rainfairy

Levities
Caution Foam Rubber
Perspiration Problem

Made From Bat Wings
Kick Me
Danger Gas

Made in Hong Kong
Worn Out? Wear Haggard Stain-Pressed
Slax

Manhattan (Big Shirts for Big People)
Socks Fifth Avenue

More Bounce to the Ounce
Lady Manhunter

Mudslingwear
Recycled Lint
Danger Warts

My Zipper is Stuck
Straight Jacket
Something Smells

No Sense Pantyhose
Skotch Plaid
Loin Cloth

100% Monkey Hair
Kick Me
Button Your Lip

100% Rubber
Made from Silk Worms
Something Smells

"Peel Me"
Under All This I'm A Stinker

Playflex
This Belongs To [blank]
Slippery When Wet

Push for Action
Bumlon
Property of Reform School

Push to Start
If You Wear This You're Irregular

Recycled Bandages
Don't Use Zippers...Use Belly Buttons
My Girdle is Killing Me

Recycled Penguins
Made Especially for [blank] by Omar the
  Tent Maker
Your Socks Don't Match

Scratch Here
Step Into Puppies Mush

Size [check-off boxes]
Emergency Zipper
I Have Kooties

Space for Rent
Just Wear a Smile...Who Needs Jantsun

Start Unbuttoning Here
My Girdle Is Killing Me
Ouch

Stinko
Bird-Dog Goofman

Super Fly
My Zipper is Stuck
Blue Jeans Forever

Supported by Safety Pins
Hot
Made Especially for [blank] by Omar the
  Tentmaker

Looney Labels

This Suit for Sale
Halfknit for the Halfwit
Use No Hooks

Wash 'N Wear
Wear Dated (Guaranteed One Week)
Wipe Hands Here
Gooster (Tie One On)

Wrinkle Free
See-Thru
High Water Pants

EYE TEASERS

Are The Black Areas the Tops of the Cubes?
Are the Red Lines Curved? [wide pattern]
Are the Red Lines Curved? [narrow pattern]
Do the White Dots Really Move?
Is Line "A" Shorter than Line "B"?
Is the Black Shape Larger?
Is the Center White Rectangle Recessed?
Is the Red Shape an Accurate Circle?
Is the Red Shape an Accurate Square?
Is the Second Telegraph Pole Larger?
Is the Stairway Right-Side-Up?
Is the Top Line Longer than the Others?

The Intersection of the White Strips Appear to Darken.
Tilt the Card and the Lines Will Seem to Move.
Tilt the Card and the Spiral Appears to Spin.
Which Center Circle is Larger?
Which Dot is Larger, the Red or the Black?
Which End of the Box is Closer to You?
Which Hat is Equal in Height and Width?
Which Line is Longer, "A" or "B"?
Which Lines are the Same Length, the Red or the Black?
Which Red Line is Longer?

LOONEY LABELS & STAMPS (99 & 14K)

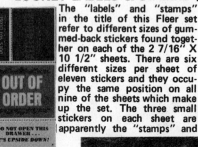

The "labels" and "stamps" in the title of this Fleer set refer to different sizes of gummed-back stickers found together on each of the 2 7/16" X 10 1/2" sheets. There are six different sizes per sheet of eleven stickers and they occupy the same position on all nine of the sheets which make up the set. The three small stickers on each sheet are apparently the "stamps" and

TWO ITEMS

the remaining eight must be "labels." In any case, each sticker is numbered. The stickers were accompanied in the 5-cent packs by a series of calling cards (14 reported to date). These all start with the phrase "This Will Introduce," beneath which is a blank line to fill in a name. The same cards were packed with "Back-Slapper" stickers, but here the print color is red, not black. Note: prices for stickers are for intact sheets of eleven only.

ITEM	MINT	EX
Sticker sheet	1.50	1.00
Card	1.50	1.00
Wrapper	—	10.00
Box	—	15.00

SHEET No. 1
1. This Door Does Not Close (Unless You Slam It Hard!)
2. Attention! (This School Will Be Closed All Next Week)
3. Out Of Order
4. Do Not Open This Drawer...It's Upside Down!
5. This Car Is Owned By a Russian Spy
6. This Phone Is Being Tested (Let It Ring 17 Times Before Answering.)
7. Splat!
8. Stop (This School is a Disaster Area)
9. I Hate Math
10. Mailman: Please Ring The Doorbell Long And Loud!
11. Keep This Refrigerator Closed (Especially you Fatty!)

SHEET No. 2
12. Don't Hog This Drinking Fountain (Save Some Water For Someone Else!)
13. School Closed Tomorrow
14. Knock Ten Times (Then Walk In.)
15. This Phone Will Not Work Unless You Dial Left Handed.
16. No Tipping Permitted
17. Men's Room
18. Wanted (School Teachers Dead or Alive)
19. Caution! (There's A Hidden Tack On This Seat!)
20. George Washington Slept Here! (And They Still Haven't Changed the Sheets!)

21. Whoever Put This Sticker Here (Ought To Be Arrested!)
22. Don't Bother Ringing The Doorbell... Nobody's Home

SHEET No. 3
23. I Have T.B. (Tired Blood)
24. Down With Homework
25. Ladies' Room
26. This School Is Being Torn Down To Build A Hot Dog Stand.
27. Quiet, Moron at Work.
28. This Magazine Was Stolen From Dentist's Office
29. This Bench Reserved For Lovers
30. This Locker is Dirty
31. Dogs In This Neighborhood Would Rather Bite Than Switch
32. Please Walk On The Grass...(If You Want To Get Your Head Handed To You !!!)
33. Smile (You're On Candid Camera)

SHEET No. 4
34. Please Stick Your Gum Under This Table!
35. I Have 98% Fewer Cavities and No Teeth
36. Think Big (Act Small)
37. You Are Hard To Misunderstand
38. Beware Of The Pussy Cat!
39. Make Love Not War!
40. Wet Paint
41. In Case Of Fire...Throw This In
42. I'd Rather Switch Than Fight!
43. Compliments Of A Fiend
44. Gum Chewing Is Permitted

Sheet No. 5
45. The Light Inside This Refrigerator Is On!! (If You Don't Believe It, Open The Door...)
46. Time To Get Your Eyes Examined!
47. Your Move!
48. Attention Post Man: Handle With Care...This Is A Love Letter
49. Do Not Paste Stickers On This Wall
50. Do Not Disturb (Genius At Work)
51. Don't Bug Me
52. Notice (Bank Closed...Out Of Money!)
53. Don't Whisper! (Shout)
54. Don't Ring This Doorbell You'll Get Electrocuted
55. Help Keep This Washroom Clean! (Stay Out)

SHEET No. 6
56. This Chair Is Broken! Sit Somewhere Else!
57. Please Do Not Use This Phone (For Gossiping!)
58. Handle With Care (This Letter Contains A Live Elephant!)
59. This Room Is Off Limits To Parents!
60. Instant Homework: Cheat!
61. Stamp Out Beetles
62. Sorry About That
63. No Girls Allowed In This Room!
64. Caution Motorists! (This Is An Unmarked Police Car!)
65. This Elevator Is Out Of Order...Please Use Stairs
66. This School Book Is Open (Monday Thru Friday; Closed On Weekends!)

Looney Labels and Stamps

SHEET No. 7

67 Be Reasonable (Do It My Way)
68 It's Not The Ups and Downs That Bother Me...It's The Jerks
69 Help Stamp Out Teachers
70 I'm Yours! (If Nobody Claims Me In 30 Days)
71 Meow!
72 Take One! Free Sample!
73 Call Me Stinky!
74 Salt (Is In The Sugar Bowl, Stupid!!)
75 Help Stamp Out School!
76 Think (You Might Like The Change!)
77 Stand Up Speak Up Shut Up

SHEET No 8

78 This Bench Is For The Birds (So Watch Out Where You Sit)
79 Pigs Wouldn't Eat Here
80 I'm A Grouch
81 Kiss Me...You Fool!
82 This Phone Is Out Of Order Please Yell!
83 Help Stamp Out Teachers

84 Ughh!
85 Help Stamp Out Parents!
86 This Movie Is Rotten
87 Out To Lunch (Permanently)
88 Danger (—Falling Dandruff!)

SHEET No. 9

89 This Phone Booth Is Bugged
90 This Is A Safe Car! (As Long As You Don't Drive It!)
91 This Book Was Stolen From The Public Library!
92 Made In U.S.A. (Printed in Japan)
93 Boy, Are You Ugly
94 Pow!
95 Hi Nosey!
96 Quarantine Measles! (In This House
97 Note! (This Parking Meter Is Out Of Order)
98 Use Your Head (It's The Little Things That Count
99 If You Had Brains You'd Be Dangerous

CALLING CARDS

A Born Loser
A Real Moron
Astronaut
Brain Surgeon
Chicken Plucker
Draft Dodger
First-Class Jerk
IQ: Zero
Kindergarten Drop-Out
Professional Bum
Public Nuisance No. 1
Rat Fink
Spoiled Brat
Who Is Really Stupid

LOONEY TUNES MAGIC FUN BOOKS (8)   3" X 4 7/8"

Copyrighted in 1990, this series of Magic Fun Books featuring "Looney Tunes" characters was marketed in Tyson "Looney Tunes Meals" well into 1991. There are eight books in the set.

The "magic" aspect is achieved by rubbing the edge of a coin over the various pictures on the pages, thereby revealing hidden designs plus answers to questions which are printed beneath each one. Each book has a title but is not numbered. The series was brought to our attention by collector Bob Hutchinson.

ITEM	MINT	EX
Set	4.50	3.00
Fun book	.50	.35

Around the World with Bugs Bunny
Fun in the Parks with Yosemite Sam
Jammin' with Tweety
Roadrunner Takes to the Road
Sylvester Takes a Holiday
Speedy Gonzales Takes Up Sports
The Hysterical Historical Daffy Duck
Wile E. Coyote Goes Out of this World

LOONEY TUNES STICKERS & SCENES (6)   3" X 4 3/4"

Basketball
Beach
Picnic
Rock N' Roll
Snow Skiing
Tennis

According to Bob Hutchinson, there are six different scenes and sticker sets in this Looney Tunes theme series packaged inside Tyson frozen kid's meals in 1990 and 1991. One side of each card has four color stickers and advises you to "Create your own comic using these candid captions and cartoon stickers. Simply affix to painted scene on back!" Above each sticker is a dialogue balloon to fill in as you wish, although there isn't enough room to be wordy. The other side of each card has a full color scene onto which the stickers can be fixed, in whatever position or space the owner desires. The prices listed below in both condition grades are for intact sheets with stickers and scenes that have not been used.

ITEM	MINT	EX
Set	3.50	2.25
Card	.50	.35

LOONEY TUNES TRADING CARDS (8)　　2 3/8" X 3 3/8"

"Looney Tunes Trading Cards," a series of eight cards starring famous Warner Brothers cartoon characters, were distributed in Tyson frozen children's meals beginning in late 1990. The cards are slightly smaller than standard size and are printed on thin cardboard stock. Two cards, folded back-to-back in a panel, came in each clear plastic envelope, and -as our illustrations show- different panel combinations exist. The cards are not numbered and the series title appears only on the packaging. The eight different meal boxes -one for each character- are beautifully designed in dark blue with oversize artwork, and these eventually may become more desirable than the cards.

ITEM	MINT	EX
Set	4.50	3.00
Card	.50	.35

LOONEY TUNES TRIVIA GAMES (3K)　　2 9/16" X 4"

This series of "Trivia Games" about Looney Tunes characters was being distributed in Tyson frozen meals as late as January, 1992. Collector Bob Hutchinson believes there are eight games in the series, although only Tweety, Yosemite Sam, and Wile E. Coyote have been confirmed to date. Each game consists of an outer shell or frame with a sliding card inside. A "question" window is located on front and an "answer" window on back. A sequence of five questions and answers can be revealed by pulling the insert card up (or out from the top edge). None of the games is numbered and the set length is not mentioned on the packaging or on the cards.

ITEM	MINT	EX
Trivia game	.50	.35

LOONY SERIES CARDS (66)

2 1/2" X 3 1/2"

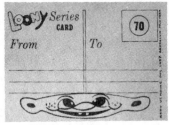

Whoever created the artwork and wrote the captions for the 66-card "Loony Series" appar-ently could not draw or spell very well. However, these deficiencies lend charm to the set, as if it had been con-cocted by a precocious but terribly young child. The cards have a postcard format on back, are numbered (67-132), and were distributed, without gum, by the Abby Vending Company.

ITEM	MINT	EX
Set	75.00	55.00
Card	1.00	.75

67 I'm Twist'in
68 This Is One Way to Shut You Up!
69 I Dig You!
70 You've Got It, and You Can Keep It...
71 What Do Doctors Recommend for You?
72 Behind The 8 Ball?
73 It's Raining Cats & Dogs...
74 Let's Tie the Knot...Around Your Neck
75 How's Fishing?
76 So Get Lost for Awhile!
77 You, Are Your Biggest Fan!
78 You Ought to Be in Horror Pictures
79 You'll Wonder Where the Yellow Went!
80 There's More to You than Meets the Eye
81 I've Got My Eye on You!
82 You've Got a Face Only a Mother Could Have!
83 There's One at Every Party...Wolf
84 So, Who Needs a Permanent?
85 You Should See the One That Got Away!
86 You Belong on the Stage...the First One Out!
87 Don't Take Life Too Seriously, You'll Never Come Out of It Alive Anyway!

88 You're a Natural...Pest
89 Your Out of This World!
90 Go Stand on Your Head!
91 Life Father Like Son!
92 You Have an Ear for Music...
93 Diamonds Are a Girls Best Friend
94 The Charming Miss Universe Year 2003
95 There's Nothing Wrong with You that a New Head Wouldn't Cure.
96 You're Bound to Rise to Great Heights - You're So Full of Hot Air!
97 I'm Pooped
98 How Are You Fixed for Blades?
99 Look Into My Eyes!
100 When Your in Neighborhood Stay There!
101 Whatever You Do, Don't Lose Your Head!
102 You're Quite a Dish, Dirty!
103 I Like You Cause Your Different!
104 I'd Like to Help You Out!
105 Planning a Vacation?
106 What are You Staring At?
107 I've Grown Accustumed to Your Face?
108 Give To The Needy
109 Going My Way?
110 So Who's Nervous!

111 Start the Day with a Smile!
112 See What I Got for Not Keeping My Mouth Shut!
113 I May Not Be Much to Look At But Neither Are You!
114 It's What's Up Front that Counts!
115 In The Doghouse
116 Your a Two-Faced Guy!
117 Your a Real Square!
118 You Don't Stand a Ghost of a Chance
119 Look Pa, No Cavities.
120 Ther's Something Strange About You!
121 Your Real Gone!
122 Do You Love Me, or My Money?
123 Heard You've Been Ill?
124 You're a Real Treasure and Should Have Been Buried Long Ago!
125 Can't You Even Spell
126 You'll Find It in the Yellow Pages
127 Your My Whole World, Big, Fat & Round!
128 I'd Climb the Highest Mountain to Get Away from You!
129 I'll See You in My Dreams - All Nightmares
130 I Hope the Dog Straightens You Out
131 You've Got Everything but Brains, Looks, and Money!
132 Get On The Ball!

LOST IN SPACE (55)

2 1/2" X 3 1/2"

The adventures of the "Space Family Robinson" appear on this Topps set released in 1966. The cards are black and white photos with white borders; they are captioned in a black panel on the front. The backs contain the card number and a story. A small credit line on the bottom carries a "1966 Space Productions" copyright. There are 55 cards in the set.

ITEM	MINT	EX
Set	330.00	265.00
Card	5.00	4.00
Wrapper	--	40.00
Box	--	150.00

1 The World Waits
2 Aliens Are Listening
3 Ready For Take-Off
4 The Pilot Dreams
5 Good-Bye, Earth!
6 Destination—the Stars!
7 Ship Off Course
8 Silence from Earth
9 The Mystery Below
10 Who Goes There?
11 The Stowaway
12 Readying the Robot
13 Fear on Board
14 Terror Strikes
15 Trapped!
16 Two in Danger
17 Danger Ahead
18 A New Peril
19 No Escape
20 Last Chance
21 The Metal Menace
22 Shock Landing
23 Victim of the Crash
24 Opening the Way
25 Robot Research
26 The Strange Planet
27 The Chariot
28 Robot Reporting
29 Alarming News
30 Urgent Warning
31 The Ground Trembles
32 The Deadly Sun
33 Safe from the Sun
34 The Robinsons Report
35 Penny's Pets
36 Where is Penny?
37 The Plants of Peril
38 The Terrible Sight
39 The Plant's Prey
40 Lost in Darkness
41 The Mystery Ship
42 Running for Help
43 The Search
44 In the Lost City
45 The Stranger Helps
46 The Terrible Cold
47 What Was That?
48 One-Eyed Terror
49 The Giant Threatens
50 The Awesome Menace
51 Readying an Attack
52 The Flying Warrior
53 The Battle Begins
54 In Death's Grip
55 Facing the Future

LOVE INITIALS (84?)

2 1/2" X 3 1/2"

"Love Initials" was the original set to use this hippie-related flower motif (Topps used it again for Mod Initials). The "initials" are black-bordered stickers diecut in the shape of letters, numbers, and punctuation marks. Each has a flowery design characteristic of the "mod" or "hippie" style. Neither the stickers or the thin card they sit on are numbered. Collector Clayton Grimm, Jr. reports that 84 different designs have been confirmed in a similar Topps-li- censed set issued in England and it is logical to assume that the U.S. set has the same amount. Note: no set price given since set total is not confirmed.

ITEM	MINT	EX
Sticker	1.25	1.00
Wrapper	--	25.00

LOVE NOTES (6)

3" X 5"

"Love Notes" is a cute set of color cat cards issued by "Tender Vittles" cat food (Ralston) in 1985. Each card is captioned on front and has a heart motif, with "To" and "From" blanks, on back. The set of six came packaged in specially-marked boxes of dry cat food.

ITEM	MINT	EX
Set	3.50	2.25
Card	.50	.35

Cat Got Your Tongue?
Go Cat Go!
You're A Real Pussycat.
You're One Cool Cat.
You're The Cat's Pajamas.
[heart]!

MAD AD FOLDEES (33)

3 1/8" X 5 1/4"

This 1976 Topps set combines the "Foldee" format, used in several previous sets, with the successful "Wacky Packages" theme of satirizing consumer products. The cards were first tested on a limited basis in a white wrapper with the "Bleech Shampoo" design in the center (wrapper code = T-67-5). Since there have been no variations reported among Mad Ad

Foldees cards, it is assumed that the same cards were issued in both the "test" and regular wrappers (the latter has "Buzz-Off" design in center). The cards measure 3-1/8" X 5-1/4" before being folded on the machined score lines. There are 33 basic titles in the set but nine different "Crazy Ad Combinations" are possible for every card. Each card is numbered and bears a

1975 copyright date on the "Collect the entire series of 33 Foldee Ads" panel. Note: mint price applies only to unfolded cards.

ITEM	MINT	EX
Set	27.50	18.00
Card	.75	.50
Wrappers		
Regular	--	3.00
Test	--	35.00
Box	--	20.00

TEST WRAPPER

REGULAR WRAPPER

1 Funny Whip/Buzz-Off/Dry-It
2 Kreemy Butter/Blotto Ink/Zitz Skin Cream
3 Disposo Baby Diapers/Dinosaur Model Kit/Old Fashioned Cookies
4 Bandito Chili/Cherry Flavor Cough Syrup/Greasy Hair Cream
5 Sparko Fireworks/Dento Power/Old Bird Cigars
6 Old Overcoat Whiskey/Sun 'N Surf Swimsuits/Kitty Catnip
7 Silky Soap/Smith's Cement/Perk-It Coffee
8 Hot Dog/Speed-O Gasoline/Golden Gal Suntan Lotion
9 Sleeko Girdles/Circus Peanuts/Handi Shovels
10 Day-Long Deodorant/Sparkle Liquid Detergent/Busy Bee Honey
11 Bubbly Soap/Sticko Glue/Juicy Chewing Tobacco
12 Tastee Corn Flakes/Flakes Laundry Detergent/Puff It Cigatettes
13 Dento Toothpaste/Sunnyfarms Butter/Artistic Oil Paints
14 Parll Perfume/Whiz Car Wax/Poppo Health Tonic
15 Bleech Shampoo/Brown's Rat Poison/Jones' Bacon
16 Slammo Nails/Softee Diapers/Fruitland
17 Go-Go/Bango/Dolphin
18 El Puffo Cigars/Mr. Fresh's Canned Carrots/Mars Pencils
19 Aloha Hawaiian Punch/Champ Tennis Balls/Mr. Krunch Peanut Butter
20 Gooey Jelly Beans/Sherlock Pipe Tobacco/Sudsy Soap
21 Goo-Goo Baby Food/Burpo/Tubby Cat Food
22 Newsweak/Scary Monsters/Playbuy
23 Glugs Fish Food/Majestic Margarine/Health-E Aspirin
24 Cheepo Bird Seed/Neat-Set Hair Spray/Breath-O Mouthwash
25 Old Time Raisins/Creamy Homogenized Milk/Criss-Cross Bandages
26 Gasso Motor Oil/Stewed Pears/Gourmet Brand Frog's Legs
27 Scrubbo Soap Pads/Continental Pure Garlic Powder/Speedy Turtle Food
28 Schmell's Sauerkraut/Glosso Wall Paint/Rosy Dawn Cologne
29 Stogey Cigars/Real Brite Light Blubs/Cheeta Bananas
30 Grandma's Chicken Soup/Stinko Spray Deodorant/Sloppy House Paint
31 Aunt Mary's Fudge/Dr. Jones Diet Pills/The World-Wide Encyclopedia
32 Woof Woof Dog Food/Power House Vitamins/Mama Mia Spaghetti Sauce
33 Greasy Oil Treatment/Stacko Pancake Mix/Vineyard Wine

Mad Ad Foldees

REGULAR ISSUE BOX
(Test box has not been seen)

MAD CARDS (8)

2 1/2" X 3 1/2"

A hilarious set of paper cards which appeared on the back cover of the October 1988 issue of "Mad" magazine (No. 282). The title of the series comes from the sentence "A Mad Card" found printed on each card, not from the "Mad's All-Star Flops" centerpiece on the original cover. The multicolor artwork is well-detailed and is surrounded by attractive graphics and accents. The cards are supposed to be standard size, but dimensions vary slightly due to cover cut and necessary print margins. There are no card numbers and no reverse side (a "Mad Fold-In" is printed on the back of the cover). Interested collectors will find this issue of "Mad" readily available for $2-3 at comic book stores which offer "previously-owned" publications.

MAD MEDALS (14 & ?)

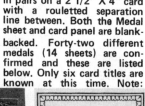

The "Mad Medals" set issued by Fleer was first mentioned in the Barker Updates published in June 1971. Each 5-cent pack contained "3 medals & loser cards." The former are diecut, color designs printed on foil and came three per sheet. The latter were printed in pairs on a 2 1/2" X 4" card with a rouletted separation line between. Both the Medal sheet and card panel are blank-backed. Forty-two different medals (14 sheets) are confirmed and these are listed below. Only six card titles are known at this time. Note:

2 1/4" X 3 3/4"

single cards cannot be graded mint.

ITEM	MINT	EX
Medal Sheet	2.50	2.00
Cards		
single	--	.75
panel	2.50	2.00
Wrapper	--	10.00

Annual Award — Coward
Annual Award — Expert Cheat
Awarded "A" In Recess
Brother Hater
Champion Eraser Snitcher
Champion Fingernail Biter
Champion Interrupter
Class Slob
Dandruff Sweeper
Dirtiest Fingernails
Expert Report Card Forger
1st Prize — Sleeping In Class
1st Prize — Soda Slurper
1st Prize — Spy (Stole Test Papers)
1st Prize — World's Dirtiest Pockets
Greatest Boy Hater
Greatest Girl Hater
Greatest Lover
Hero — Bathes Every Month
Hottest Lips
Indian Giver

Loudest Burper
Loudest Whisperer In Class
Most Cavities
Most Math Mistakes (4—1=2)
Most Often Late For Class
Most Rotten Reader
Most Trips To Lavatory In One Day
Noisiest Eater
President — School Bus Pest Society
Prize Winning Dumbest Student
Prize Winning Stupid Question Asker

Sister Hater
Smelliest Socks
Student Most Likely To Flunk
Teacher's Pest
Winner — Chewed Pencil Collection
Winner — Greasiest Hair
World's Most Clumsy Student
World's Worst Dressed Student
Worst Handwriting
Yellow Teeth Award

MAD MOD BUTTONS (22)

The "Mad-Mod Buttons" of this Philadelphia Gum Company issue are round, peel-off stickers set onto paper sheets. Each numbered sheet contains two buttons plus two 5/8" X 1 5/8" sticker panels bearing humorous expressions. Twenty different sheets have been seen and our checklist contains the two button titles appearing on each sheet.

2 1/2" X 3 1/2"

Note: no set price given since set total is not confirmed.

ITEM	MINT	EX
Sheet	1.50	1.00
Wrapper	--	12.00
Box	--	40.00

1 Don't Blow Your Cool!
   Fat Power
2 U R Gorjuss
   Join Me I'm An Idiot
3 Take Me To Your Leader
   My Button Loves Your Button
4 Be Happy
   Kiss Me Baby
5 Wind Me Up I'm A Living Doll
   The World Is Square
6 Press This Button I'll Scream
   Die—Support Your Florist!
7 Do Nothing Then Rest
   Maybe
8 Tune—Turn On—Drop Out
   Mother Goose Is a Man
9 Reading Rots the Mind
   Ban Buttons

10 I Like Miniskirts!
    Don't Trust Anyone Over 30
11 Boss
    Support Your Local Barber
12 Wink—I'll Do the Rest!
    Brain Control
13 You're Different
    See Next Button
14 I'm a Slob!
    Little Boy Blue Is a Lazy Kid
15 Push Button—Turn Me On
    What's Your Bag?

16 Wake Me Up After School
    Stop the World
17 Kiss Me! (You Fool!)
    You're The Greatest (Slob!)
18 Go Baby Go—
    Advance Progress Drop Dead!
19 You Have One Bad Habit—You
    Breathe!
    Support Your Druggist
20 Flunk Now Avoid The June Rush
    Flower Power

The "Mad Stickers" set produced by Fleer in 1983 is one of the largest single-series issues of recent times. There are 128 numbered "Collector's Stickers" in the set and these are divided into various themes: "Horrifying Cliches", "Family Tree", "Spy vs. Spy", etc. These stickers are of the front-peel, diecut variety and each is assigned a space in the "Mad Sticker Album." Most backs of numbered stickers are black & white puzzle pieces; other backs contain advertising. Another series of 64 unnumbered "Trouble Stickers" was apparently designed for general misuse around the house, school, etc. These have either one or two peel-off stickers per card. The backs are either advertising copy (8) or puzzle pieces (56). Note: set price includes album.

ITEM	MINT	EX
Set	35.00	25.00
Sticker	.20	.15
Album	2.00	1.50
Wrapper	--	.35
Box	--	5.00

MAGIC CARD TRICKS (2K)   2 1/4" X 3 1/2"

It is likely that most collectors never even saw this limited-time promotion run by "Act" dental rinse in 1988. Each cardboard packet had a flap with a special ring to fit over the neck of the bottle; inside the packet was a "Hoyle Magic Card Trick" ex-planation card (two-sided) plus the cards necessary to perform the trick. The numbered instruction card carries the advice: "Remember ... a real magician never tells how he performs his tricks." Magic Card Tricks were available for a short time only and the length of the set is not known (#2 seen). Given the short supply AND limited demand, each complete packet is valued at $2.00 each in "excellent" grade.

MAGIC FUNNY FORTUNES (?)   1 9/16" X 3 1/2"

The exterior, or wrapper, side of this item is yellow with red, blue and white accents. Approximately 40% of the wrapper is devoted to a 3-step set of visual & written instructions for reading the "Funny Fortune" printed on the interior side. Each "Fortune" is designed in the 3-D style of "X-Ray Round Up" and "Isola-tion Booth": the hidden design and punch line are made readable by a red cellophane overlay which came wrapped around the gum. The "Fortunes" are not numbered and the length of the set is unknown.

ITEM	MINT	EX
Wrapper	--	10.00

MAGIC TATOOS (?)   1 9/16" X 3 1/2"

The word "tatoo" is spelled with one "t" in this Topps set. The wrapper is red with yellow, black, and white accents and it has 3-part instructions for applying the transfers. The later are multi-colored designs printed on the interior sides of the wrappers. Above each "tatoo" is a question phrased as an imperative ("Name This Indian Chief"); the answer is located in a panel below the artwork and it appears when the transfer is applied to the skin.

ITEM	MINT	EX
Wrapper	--	10.00

MAGNUM p.i. (66)   2 1/2" X 3 1/2"

One of the "hottest" card sets of 1983 was the 66-card Magnum p.i. series issued by Donruss. The set is divided into (1) a 22-card "episode" related in the first person by Magnum himself and 24- and 20-card groups with puzzle backs. The 24-card group forms a poster of Magnum in a green polo shirt, while the 20-card group pictures him in an adventure scene inside an airplane. The fronts of both puzzle back groups contain color photos from the TV series; these have no "sequence," as do the photos in the 22-card "episode." All the color photographs in the set are enclosed by a red frame line. A Magnum logo and the card number appear in the opposite corners at the bottom of every picture.

ITEM	MINT	EX
Set	10.00	6.50
Card	.15	.10
Wrapper	--	.35
Box	--	5.00

MAGOO TATTOOS (?)   1 9/16" X 3 3/8"

It is assumed that Fleer marketed these "tatoo transfers" sometime close to the copyright date stated on each wrapper (1967). There are six different front designs, each showing the myopic Magoo in imminent danger. The basic wrapper color is white, with blue and pink accents. The multi-color tattoo designs on the interior side have captions preceded by the words "Magoo Sez" and it is confirmed that the same caption can appear on different pictures.

The prices listed reflect a recent "find" which has made this item readily available to collectors.

ITEM	MINT	EX
Wrappers (6)		
each	--	3.00
Box	--	25.00

MAKE YOUR OWN NAME STICKERS (33) 2 1/2" X 3 1/2

According to Topps' records, "Make Your Own Name Stickers" was released to the public in July 1966. The set consists of 33 different hideous faces with a blank name panel underneath. Each 5-cent package included a small sheet of six red or blue-print name stickers ("over 200 names available") to place in the name panel. Each sticker in our visual checklist is numbered, but an identical series without numbers has also been reported. The wrapper is red with a yellow title and green, black, and white accents. Some designs from this set were also used in Topps' 1974 version of "Ugly Stickers." Note: set price is for 33 faces only; the number of names and different name stickers has yet to be determined.

ITEM	MINT	EX
Set	75.00	55.00
Stickers		
Faces	2.00	1.50
Names	1.00	.75
Wrapper	--	15.00
Box	--	65.00

ERIC
MELANIE
DAVID
DONNA
CHRIS
DIANA

NAME STICKERS 5¢

MAN FROM U.N.C.L.E. (55)

2 1/2" X 3 1/2"

Topps produced the 55-card Man From Uncle set in 1966. Each card has a black and white photograph taken from the television show, and a facsimile signature of the star pictured is printed on the photo. The cards have white borders. The backs are pieces of a large black and white poster and the card number is printed near the T.C.G. credit line.

ITEM	MINT	EX
Set	130.00	100.00
Card	2.00	1.50
Wrapper	--	40.00
Box	--	90.00

1 Robert Vaughn	13 Robert Vaughn	23 Robert Vaughn	34 Robert Vaughn	44 Robert Vaughn
2 Robert Vaughn	14 David McCallum	24 David McCallum	35 Robert Vaughn	45 Robert Vaughn
3 Robert Vaughn	15 Robert Vaughn	25 Robert Vaughn	36 Robert Vaughn	46 Robert Vaughn
4 Leo Carroll	16 Robert Vaughn	26 Robert Vaughn	37 No signature	47 Robert Vaughn
5 Robert Vaughn	17 Robert Vaughn	27 Robert Vaughn	38 David McCallum	48 Robert Vaughn
6 Robert Vaughn	18 Robert Vaughn	28 Robert Vaughn	39 David McCallum	49 David McCallum
7 David McCallum	19 David McCallum	29 Robert Vaughn	40 Robert Vaughn	50 Robert Vaughn
8 No signature	20 Robert Vaughn	30 Robert Vaughn	41 David McCallum	51 Robert Vaughn
9 Robert Vaughn	21 Robert Vaughn	31 Robert Vaughn	42 Robert Vaughn	52 Robert Vaughn
10 Robert Vaughn	22 David McCallum	32 Robert Vaughn	43 Robert Vaughn	53 David McCallum
11 Robert Vaughn		33 David McCallum		54 Robert Vaughn
12 David McCallum				55 David McCallum

"Man from U.N.C.L.E." cards were printed in Australia, Great Britain, and New Zealand. These three cards, patterned on the Topps set, were issued under license by Allens & Regina in New Zealand (with "Playtime Gum"). The A&R set contained 72 cards, including 14 standups made by folding the tops of the cards down along pre-scored lines.

MAN ON THE MOON (55) (99)   2 1/2" X 3 1/2"

The Man on the Moon series can be confusing since it was issued twice by Topps. The early set is numbered 1A to 35A and 36B to 55B. The fronts have color photographs of astronauts and the space program; the backs are pieces of 35- and 20-card puzzles ("A" & "B"). The set was extended by the addition of 44 more cards, numbered 56C to 99C, later in 1969 and early 1970. The backs of these cards are pieces of a 44-part puzzle ("C"). However, this third puzzle is extremely difficult to complete because of irregularities: transposed numbers, same fronts with different backs, etc. Numbers 1A to 55B were also reissued but are easily identified by the "99" line, which does not appear on cards of the original set. The boxes for both the original and "extended" issues are the same except that the latter has a red sticker attached to the front. Note: a complete set of original 1A-55B contains two complete puzzles. A set of re-issue 1A-99C does not require a complete "C" puzzle.

ITEM	MINT	EX
1st Issue (55)		
Set	65.00	50.00
Card	1.00	.75
Re-Issue ("99" line)		
Set	120.00	90.00
Card	1.00	.75
Wrapper	--	7.50
Boxes		
No sticker	--	20.00
Sticker	--	15.00

1A	Apollo 10 Emblem	34A	Dark of the Moon!	67C	Aldrin on the Moon
2A	Apollo/NASA Insignia	35A	Launch Control Center!	68C	Pre-launch Activity
3A	Happy Landing	36B	"Welcome Home"	69C	Apollo 11 Insignia
4A	Space Photography	37B	"Spider"	70C	Suited for the Job
5A	Astronaut Lovell	38B	First Manned Mission!	71C	Aboard the USS Hornet
6A	Lunar Test Run	39B	The Saturn V!	72C	1st Lunar Voyage
7A	"Apollo 8 Success"	40B	Official Ceremony!	73C	News Conference
8A	Re-entry	41B	There She Goes!	74C	Aboard the Life Raft
9A	Homeward Bound	42B	The Apollo Orbit!	75C	Left on the Moon
10A	"All Hands on Deck"	43B	Helicopter Recovery!	76C	Taking a Break
11A	Armstrong's Moon Shoes	44B	Briefing Session!	77C	Mother Earth
12A	Command Pilot!	45B	Lift Off!	78C	Honorary Discharge
13A	Rehearsal!	46B	Monitor Countdown!	79C	Lunar Module
14A	Preparation for Flight!	47B	Lunar Base!	80C	Alone in Space
15A	Apollo 8 Insignia	48B	Space Food!	81C	Second Moon Walk
16A	Dress Rehearsal	49B	Splashdown!	82C	Footprints on the Moon
17A	Spacebound	50B	Change Course!	83C	Old Glory
18A	Tiros 1	51B	Hi There!	84C	Apollo 11 Commander
19A	Launching Pad!	52B	Astronaut Aldrin!	85C	North America Under Clouds
20A	Earthbound!	53B	Moon Pilot!	86C	Moon Photo
21A	The Apollo Camera!	54B	Moon Commander!	87C	Recovery
22A	Lunar Study	55B	First Men on the Moon!	88C	Moon Walk
23A	Earthlight!	56C	A Salute	89C	In Quarantine
24A	Training Program	57C	Lunar Seismograph	90C	Ignition
25A	Blast-off	58C	Planting the Flag	91C	Accomplishment
26A	Zero Gravity!	59C	Back to the Module	92C	Tranquility Base
27A	Preparation for Flight	60C	Destination Moon	93C	Moon Print
28A	Bound for Glory!	61C	Presidential Greeting	94C	Moon Work
29A	Capsule Exit	62C	Below the Horizon	95C	First Steps on Earth
30A	Moon Surface	63C	Technical Advice	96C	Historic Steps
31A	Testing a Lunar Module	64C	Launched	97C	Welcome Home
32A	Walk in Space	65C	Back on Earth	98C	Lunar Orbit
33A	Apollo 10!	66C	Training Program	99C	Moon Plaque

THE JOY OF COLLECTING MARS ATTACKS ...

by Russell Roberts

"Wow! Look at all that blood!"

That, in a nutshell, explains why kids in 1962 found Topps' "Mars Attacks" cards so appealing. It was because of the blood - lots and lots of it - that was splashed all over the glorious color cards. Combining buckets of blood with giant insects was a sure-fire way to get kids interested in a card set, and Topps reaped a bonanza at the register before parental pressure finally resulted in a curtailment of the series.

To better understand why cards with ugly, big-headed aliens, disgusting bugs, and yes - all that blood - were so attractive to pre-teens, you have to go back to what America was like in 1962. It was, as the beatniks used to say, "like Dullsville, man." Television was a black and white sea of insipid domestic comedies about perfect families, with fathers who always knew the right thing to say and mothers who always had time to bake cookies. Everyone dressed the same - men wore suits, white shirts, and skinny ties, while women were never seen without a dress and high heels. Their problems were universal. Would Junior's project win the Science Fair? Would the star quarterback ask Sis out to the big dance? And, gosh darn it, what was the family dog burying in the back yard? Except for Elvis, and some obscure blacks singing in smoky night clubs, music was dominated by "squeaky-cleans" like Frankie Avalon, Bobby Darin, and Connie Francis. The closest thing to pornography was a National Geographic magazine article about Africa (Wow! Look at those pictures!).

Mars Attacks slammed into this perfect and extraordinarily bland world like a runaway locomotive.

We had, after all, just been through the sci-fi craze in the movies: film after film introducing some evil alien race from another universe plotting to conquer the earth with death rays and flying saucers. And we were still living in the era of an arms race run amok, with a very real danger that hiding under our desks in school would not, in fact, save us from being horribly mutilated and/or mutated by the effects of an atomic blast. So to the kids in 1962, Mars Attacks cards employed a perfect, if somewhat perverse, logic: aliens invade earth using death rays and giant insects. No problem. Wasn't that pretty much the way things were going in the real world anyway?

Even the conclusion of the Mars Attacks saga, in which earthmen take to their own spaceships and visit the Red

Planet to kick some alien backsides, had a basis in fact. JFK had committed us to the space race and we all thrilled to the exploits of Alan Shepard, John Glenn, and the other astronauts in their tiny Mercury capsules. If man could orbit the earth, our pre-physics minds argued, he could certainly make it to Mars.

It was all too much to resist.

Picture it: you're walking home from school, with a few nickels or dimes in your pocket, when you pass by the little store where you buy all your candy and comic books. There, in the window, is a box of Mars Attacks 5¢ packs with their yellow wrappers, ugly green Martians, and bright red wording that looks like dripping blood. What would you do?

If you were like thousands of other kids back then, you plunked down that loose change in your pocket for as many Mars Attacks packs as you could afford. Then you rushed home, ripped open the packs, immediately threw away the gum and the wrappers, and then feasted your eyes on the bloody mayhem that you held in your hands.

Certain cards were instant favorites, such as #38, "Victims of the Bug," with the giant insect sucking the blood right out of that soldier, and #11, "Destroy the City," with the great pile of charred bones smoldering in the foreground. Others would prompt and renew fierce debates about accuracy and/or believability. Do giant flies really have those huge pincers on either side of their mouth (card #27)? Do spiders (card #30) have all those eyes? And, possibly the most hotly debated question of all: If a person's entire body was burnt up by a heat ray, like the guy in card #19 ("Burning Flesh"), would his eyes still be open so that he could see what was happening to him?

Such were the pursuits of our youth, and we reveled in them. The object of Mars Attacks cards wasn't to have a complete set - everybody had one of those - it was just to have them, period. What could possibly be better than six "Death in the Shelter" cards (#29)? Seven of 'em! Dealer networks, "rare cards," plastic sheets, and all the other trappings of modern card collecting had yet to be invented. This was card collecting on its most basic and satisfying level.

We even dared to use them as toys and diversions, playing "Topsies" and "Leansies" for hours: hundreds of dollars (by today's standards) would change hands in a single afternoon according to the way the wind had whimsically pushed a certain card here or there as it was fluttering to earth. We pasted the cards on the walls of our rooms so they'd be the last thing we saw at night and the first thing we saw in the morning. We featured them in monster museums that we built in dark basements, shining a flashlight on them at just the right moment to scare our "customers." We carried the bloodiest and goriest ones around to show to unsuspecting schoolmates, especially girls.

Of course they were bloody; that was the whole point. You can't bash or fry someone without showing a little blood. We were quick to point out that those "Civil War News" cards our parents had praised as "educational" were equally bloody. Gee, if you don't want us to have these Martian cards, maybe you should take away those great Civil War history lessons as well... Parents have always been suckers for the old "it's educational" excuse.

Eventually, though, parents did get wise and their complaints made Topps pull the cards off the market. But by then it had ceased to matter to us. Other interests - girls, Little League, and looking "cool" - once again superseded bugs and evil aliens. In the end, the Martian menace was defeated not by armies, or parents, but by a much stronger force: adolescent indifference. At some point, without ceremony or regret, most of those Mars Attacks cards were consigned to the closet, or worse, to the trash.

In the years that followed, the cards would occasionally reappear in our lives, like when a friend would write in a high school yearbook upon graduation: "I need Mars Attacks #37. Trade you #9 for it." It may well have been the gradual build-up of moments and memories like these that led many of us, years later, to get back into card collecting. Of course, one of the first orders of business was to reacquire a set of childhood favorites - such as Mars Attacks.

Putting together a set of Mars Attacks cards in the frenetic world of modern card collecting, I was not surprised to find that the series was still a hot topic of conversation. For years a rumor was circulated that the set did not end with card #55, "A Synopsis of Our Story." No, whispered collectors in crowded hallways and back rooms at card shows, there is another card in the set - a #56 that shows Martians gleefully destroying Topps' headquarters. To this the reply would usually be: Horse Hockey! But as the years rolled on, and the unbelievable became commonplace in card collecting, the denials grew fainter and less certain. Finally, the best response seemed to be a paraphrase of Hamlet: "there are more things in cards sets than are dreamt of in your philosophy."

Over time, there have been imitations, spoofs, and spin-offs of the Mars Attacks set. "Uranus Strikes," issued in 1986, also featured aliens bent on conquering the earth. In 1988, Topps tried to catch lightning in a bottle twice with "Dinosaurs Attack," a faux Mars Attacks set in which dinosaurs from the past invade present-day earth, wreaking havoc and munching up plenty of people in the process.

But there's something about Mars Attacks cards that defies duplication. They were the right card at the right time, a counterpoint to the mundane early 1960's and, perhaps, a preview of the violence and bloodshed in the years to come. Along with their savagery, they had a spark of wit and imagination about them that few cards ever have. To kids looking for a little excitement in 1962, this wit and imagination, along with all that blood - made Mars Attacks a set that will live forever.

Art by Wanda Chan

Could this be the missing card?

MARS ATTACKS (55)

2 1/2" X 3 1/2"

The Mars Attacks series of 55 cards ranks as one of the most popular and well-known card sets of the modern era. New evidence, in the form of two "test" boxes bearing the title "Attack from Space," indicates that the cards were distributed on a trial basis before going into full production. Several cards in the original print run that contained artwork with graphic details were withdrawn and replaced by milder versions. Even then, the set did not enjoy a long period of distribution due to complaints from the public. The cards feature sensa-tionalistic color artwork surrounded by white borders. The card number is printed in a red or yellow flying saucer design located next to the red-print caption. On the back, the card number is repeated and the story appears below it. The cards were issued by Topps in 1962, but "Bubbles Inc." (Topps' alter ego) is the company name printed on them. Notes: Collector Ted Knight reports that Mars Attacks was also printed under license in England in smaller card form and that four cards were withdrawn from the series due to objectionable artwork.

Card #1 of the U.S. set carries a premium value of 100%. Checklist cards must be unmarked to qualify for mint and excellent grades.

ITEM	MINT	EX
Set	1450.00	1050.00
Card	20.00	15.00
Checklist	100.00	75.00
Wrapper	--	250.00
Box	--	750.00

Rare 1¢ and 5¢ test boxes of Mars Attacks bear the title "Attack from Space" (illustrations courtesy of Bob Marks). No wrappers with the test title have been found. In addition, no "Mars Attacks" 1¢ wrapper is known to exist, indicating that Topps dropped this price category prior to regular production.

1 The Invasion Begins	16 Panic In Parliament	31 Monster Reaches In
2 Martians Approaching	17 Beast And The Beauty	32 Robot Terror
3 Attacking Army Base	18 Soldier Fights back	33 Removing The Victims
4 Saucers Blast Jets	19 Burning Flesh	34 Terror In Railroad
5 Washington In Flames	20 Crushed To Death	35 The Flame Throwers
6 Burning Navy Ships	21 Prize Captive	36 Destroying A Dog
7 Destroying Bridge	22 Burning Cattle	37 Creeping Menace
8 Times Square Terror	23 The Frost Ray	38 Victims Of The Bug
9 The Human Torch	24 The Shrinking Ray	39 Army Of Insects
10 Skyscraper Tumbles	25 Capturing a Martian	40 High Voltage
11 "Destroy The City"	26 The Tidal Wave	41 Horror In Paris
12 Death In The Cockpit	27 The Giant Flies	42 Hairy Fiend
13 Watching From Mars	28 Helpless Victim	43 Blasting The Bug
14 Charred By Martians	29 Death in The Shelter	44 Battle In The Air
15 Saucers Invade China	30 Trapped!!	45 Fighting Insects
		46 Blast Off For Mars
		47 Earth Bombs Mars
		48 Earthmen Land On Mars
		49 The Earthmen Charge
		50 Smashing The Enemy
		51 Crushing The Martians
		52 Giant Robot
		53 Martian City In Ruins
		54 Mars Explodes
		55 Checklist

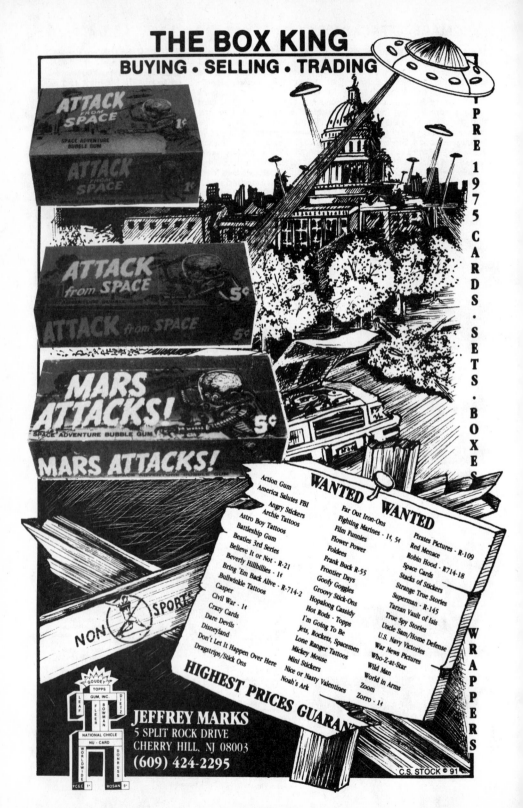

MARS ATTACKS MINI COMIC BOOKS (4)   3" X 4 1/2"

In the trading card business, short-term failures often turn into long-term successes. Perhaps this ambitious Mars Attacks spin-off, marketed by Pocket Comics (Adcor Inc.) in 1988, will at some point achieve the recognition it deserves. Billed as "a collectable within a collectable," the manufacturers had hoped to issue a 54-edition series of Mars Attacks mini comics to tap the "cult following and audience demand that's been swelling for 25 years." They obviously overestimated the attraction and were virtually ignored by both trading card and comic book collectors. Only four issues were produced. Each 32-page comic book contained an original story, comic book style, plus a two-page centerfold of the original Mars Attack card depicted on the cover. Comic #'s 1 & 2 were issued together (25 of each) in two different display boxes; each box had a cut-off card (called a "PREVIEWindow") which itself was designed to be collectable. The boxes holding issue #'s 3 & 4 were similarly designed. Quantities of box #1 (containing comic #'s 1 & 2) were supposedly limited to the amount of pre-orders received, but there is no way to determine if this advertising promise was honored. The print run total for box #2 (holding comic #'s 3 & 4) is also unknown. Pocket Comics obtained a license and actual color film from Topps to produce the series, so the link to the original Mars Attacks is authentic, if somewhat stretched. Collectors will find comic #1 offered at $3.00; comic #2 at $2.00; and comic #'s 3 & 4 at $1.50 each. The display box for #'s 1 & 2 is valued at $10; for #'s 3 & 4, $6.00.

CENTERFOLD PAGE OF COMIC

MARS ATTACKS — THE UNPUBLISHED VERSION (13)   2 1/2" X 3 1/2"

A 1984 set of 13 cards published by Steve Kiviat of Rosem Enterprises. According to Mr. Kiviat, he viewed a collection of original "Mars Attacks" artwork in which thirteen of the paintings were never used in the set released to the public. By arrangement with the owner, Kiviat created a numbered, limited edition set of cards featuring the unpublished artwork on front. The backs bear nothing more than the set title, set total, registration number, and copyright date (no text accompanied the original paintings). Critics of this set point out that the existence of the original artwork on which it is based has not been sufficiently documented, although the official story is that it came from the collection of Woody Gelman (former art director at Topps). At any rate, collectors will likely find this nostalgia set selling in the $25-$30 range and must decide for themselves whether to add it to their card treasury.

MARVEL COMICS (34)   3 5/16" X 3 1/4"

In 1978, Topps issued this set of 34 Marvel Comics with sticks of sugar-free bubble gum. There are four different exterior wrapper designs; the "color comics" are printed on the interior side and each involves a specific Marvel Character. The comic number and a feature entitled "Doctor Strange's Fortunes" are printed below. Our checklist details the character and fortune appearing on each comic. Note: sets of 34 in uncut strips sell for $60. Most comics have a small tear after opening.

ITEM	MINT	EX
Set	--	40.00
Comic	--	1.00
Boxes		
Vertical	--	10.00
Horizontal	--	15.00

1 Sub-Mariner (Your Luck is About to Change.)
2 Doctor Strange (An Artist's Life is in Your Future.)
3 The Incredible Hulk (You Will Have Good Luck in Love.)
4 Silver Surfer (You Will Learn Something Important About Yourself.)
5 The Incredible Hulk (You Will Become a Great Athlete.)
6 The Incredible Hulk (A Major Change is About to Occur.)
7 Iron Man (You Will Have a Career in Hollywood.)
8 Sub-Mariner (A Surprise Gift is in Your Future.)
9 The Fantastic Four (You'll Be Introduced to a New Friend.)
10 The Amazing Spiderman (You Will Hear from Someone You Almost Forgot.)
11 The Amazing Spiderman (A Letter Will Arrive with Important News.)
12 The Incredible Hulk (A Friend Will Give You Some Good Advice.)
13 The Fantastic Four (Be Careful During Your Next Vacation.)
14 Iron Man (A Surprise Awaits You at Home.)
15 The Mighty Thor (Your Lucky Day is Tuesday.)

16 The Incredible Hulk (Your Lucky Number is 4.)
17 The Incredible Hulk (Your Lucky Color is Blue.)
18 Iron Man (Don't Let Your Temper Control You.)
19 Iron Man (This Weekend Will Change the Course of Your Life.)
20 The Fantastic Four (The Most Important Person in Your Life will be the Mailman.)
21 The Incredible Hulk (Someone Older Will Be a Great Help to You.)
22 Captain America (The Thing You Lost Will be Found Again.)
23 Iron Man (Your Father Has a Big Surprise for You.)
24 The Incredible Hulk (Money-Lots of It-Will One Day be Yours.)
25 Iron Man (Your Next Report Card Will Astound Your Parents.)
26 Sub-Mariner (You Have a Talent for Making Friends.)
27 The Incredible Hulk (You Will Get a Phone Call from an Old Friend.)
28 Sub-Mariner (Someone Will Say Something That Gets You Angry.)
29 The Incredible Hulk (You Are at the Beginning of a New Adventure.)

30 The Incredible Hulk (Something Borrowed Will Be Returned.)
31 The Incredible Hulk (Someone is Going to Tell You a Lie. Be Careful.)
32 The Amazing Spider-Man (You Will Have a Future in Space Travel.)
33 The Fantastic Four (You Will Receive a Message from Someone Far Away.)
34 The Thing (Don't Take Chances with Your Money.)

MARVEL COMICS (33)   3" X 3 1/4"

Although it has a different format, this 33-card comic set from 1979 is practically a re-issue of the sugar-free gum set marketed the previous year. One obvious difference is that the exterior wrappers are separate from the comic themselves. However, the 3-panel episodes are identical in both sets, except for numbers 8, 19, & 33. There is no number 30 or 34 in the 1979 set; the former was misprinted as an additional No. 20, and the latter was deleted.

ITEM	MINT	EX
Set	--	40.00
Wrappers (4)		
each	--	1.00
Comics	--	1.00
Box	--	10.00

Marvel Comics

1 Sub-Mariner (Your Luck is About to Change.)
2 Doctor Strange (An Artist's Life is in Your Future.)
3 The Incredible Hulk (You Will Have Good Luck in Love.)
4 Silver Surfer (You Will Learn Something Important About Yourself.)
5 The Incredible Hulk (You Will Become a Great Athlete.)
6 The Incredible Hulk (A Major Change is About to Occur.)
7 Iron Man (You Will Have a Career in Hollywood.)
8 The Thing (Don't Take Chances With Your Money)
9 The Fantastic Four (You'll Be Introduced to a New Friend.)
10 The Amazing Spiderman (You Will Hear from Someone You Almost Forgot.)
11 The Amazing Spiderman (A Letter Will Arrive with Important News.)
12 The Incredible Hulk (A Friend Will Give You Some Good Advice.)

13 The Fantastic Four (Be Careful During Your Next Vacation.)
14 Iron Man (A Surprise Awaits You at Home.)
15 The Mighty Thor (Your Lucky Day is Tuesday.)
16 The Incredible Hulk (Your Lucky Number is 4.)
17 The Incredible Hulk (Your Lucky Color is Blue.)
18 Iron Man (Don't Let Your Temper Control You.)
19 Sub-Mariner (A Surprise Gift Is In Your Future)
20 The Fantastic Four (The Most Important Person in Your Life will be the Mailman.)
20 The Incredible Hulk (Something Borrowed Will Be Returned.)
21 The Incredible Hulk (Someone Older Will Be a Great Help to You.)
22 Captain America (The Thing You Lost Will be Found Again.)

23 Iron Man (Your Father Has a Big Surprise for You.)
24 The Incredible Hulk (Money-Lots of It-Will One Day be Yours.)
25 Iron Man (Your Next Report Card Will Astound Your Parents.)
26 Sub-Mariner (You Have a Talent for Making Friends.)
27 The Incredible Hulk (You Will Get a Phone Call from an Old Friend.)
28 Sub-Mariner (Someone Will Say Something That Gets You Angry.)
29 The Incredible Hulk (You Are at the Beginning of a New Adventure.)
30 The Incredible Hulk (Something Borrowed Will Be Returned.)
31 The Incredible Hulk (Someone is Going to Tell You a Lie. Be Careful.)
32 The Amazing Spider-Man (You Will Have a Future in Space Travel.)
33 The Thing (You Will Receive A Message From Someone Far Away)

MARVEL COMICS (44?) SUPER HEROES TATTOOS

2 1/2" X 3 1/2"

This series of Super Heores skin tattoos was issued by Donruss in 1980. Each pack contained one sheet of tattoos, an instruction card, and a stick of gum. The tattoo sheets are not numbered and it is believed that there are 44 different sheets in the set.

ITEM	MINT	EX
Tattoo	.50	.35
Card	.25	.20
Wrapper	--	1.00
Box	--	5.00

MARVEL FLYERS (12)   IRREGULAR SIZES

Topps took the format of its previously- issued "Flying Things" series to develop this set of "Marvel Flyers." Each "flyer" is a brightly-colored Super Hero character printed on thin styrofoam. By insert- ing a "wing" and "tail" sec- tion, the character becomes a three-dimensional flight mod- el. The models themselves are not captioned or numbered. The underside of the wing and tail sections bear a 1966 copyright and the word "Japan".

ITEM	MINT	EX
Set	200.00	140.00
Flyer	15.00	10.00
Wrapper	--	25.00
Box	--	100.00

Captain America
Dare Devil
Dr. Doom
Human Torch
Iron Man
Spiderman
Sub Mariner
The Angel
The Hulk
The Thing
The Wasp
Thor

MARVEL SUPER HEROES (66)   2 1/2″ X 3 1/2″

Donruss issued the Marvel Super Heroes set in 1966. The 66-card series has eleven cards apiece for the following Super Heroes: Captain American Daredevil, Hulk, Ironman, Spiderman, and Thor. Each card has a color comic-strip style drawing with humorous dialogue, except for 14 cards (3-7-15-18-20-25-30-33-44-45-65-66) which have an empty dialogue balloon designed to allow the collector to fill in his own funny caption. The backs are puzzle pieces which fit together to form a large poster of the Super Heroes. The card number, the subseries identification, and the copyright date are all located on the front in a panel below the picture area.

ITEM	MINT	EX
Set	180.00	145.00
Card	2.50	2.00
Wrapper	--	30.00
Box	--	50.00

CAPTAIN AMERICA
1 I Love These Class Parties!
2 But Lady The Subscription Only Costs $3.98!
3 Write Your Own Caption
4 You're Going to Love our Steam Room!
5 I Told You to Keep Those Pidgeons Out of my Yard.
6 These Class Parties Give Me a Headache!
7 Write Your Own Caption
8 You and Your Fire Sales!
9 Don't Go to Pieces Over the Crab Grass!
10 Write Your Own Caption
11 I Got It for 362 Books of Stamps!

IRON MAN
12 "Get the Lead Out!"
13 I Hate These Toy Kits!
14 Do You Have Iron Deficiency Anemia?
15 Write Your Own Caption
16 To Get Your Atom Smasher Send in 5 Box Tops and $1,000,000.

17 And You Said Add a Little More Lighter Fluid
18 Write Your Own Caption
19 Please, I'd Rather Do It Myself.
20 Write Your Own Caption
21 That Chick Really Puts Me in Orbit!
22 When Did You First Notice Those Stomach Pains?

DAREDEVIL
23 But Halloween Is Next Week!
24 Let Hurts Put in the Drivers' Seat!
25 Write Your Own Caption
26 I'm Sorry I'm Tied-Up This Evening!
27 With These Trading Stamps... You Can Get Anything!
28 He Still Thinks He's in the Circus!
29 Wait 'till I Turn the Antenna!
30 Write Your Own Caption
31 I Didn't Know You Had a Game Room!
32 How's This for a Finish?
33 Write Your Own Caption

SPIDERMAN
34 Next Time I'll Fly the Kite!
35 Next Time You Change the Tire!
36 Write Your Own Caption
37 Just What I Needed, a Bug Bomb!
38 What'ya Mean 50 cents Extra for Gift Wrapping!
39 I Made a Before and After Commercial.
40 This Fly Paper Is Rough on the Hair!
41 Just Fixing a Little!
42 I Meant...Hang Up the Phone!
43 Those Kids & Those Build-It-Yourself A-Bomb Kits!
44 Write Your Own Caption

HULK
45 Write Your Own Caption
46 These P.T.A. Meetings Drive Me Crazy!
47 OK, So You're the Green Giant!
48 When I Was a 82 lb. Weakling.
49 Come on Out and Play
50 But, I wanted an A-Bomb for Christmas!

51 Let's Go Swimming Buddy!
52 From Now on Take Your Coffee Breaks with the Rest of the Guests.
53 This Will Really Curl Your Hair!
54 Watch That First Step!
55 I Don't Believe I've Met You Guys.

THOR
56 She's Always Hiding the Soap!
57 I'd Rather Fight...But I Don't Smoke.
58 The Peasants Are Always Throwing Rocks
59 I Don't Care If You Do Have "We Tried Harder Buttons!"
60 Just, Who Does Your Hair?
61 I Get 8 Shaves from Each Blade Koo-coo!
62 I Think the Trouble Is in the Fuel Pump!
63 So, I Don't Want Any Scout Cookies!
64 We Try Harder...We're Only No. Two
65 Write Your Own Caption
66 Write Your Own Caption

MARVEL SUPERHEROES (60) FIRST ISSUE COVERS

2 1/2" X 3 1/2"

This commemorative issue of 60 cards was produced by the Fantasy Trade Card Co. of Rochester, N.Y. in 1984. The primary retail outlets were comic book stores and card dealers. Two colorful poly bag wrappers were designed for over-the-counter sales. The cards are numbered on back and contain descriptions of the characters portrayed on the fronts. Each of the 59 numbered cards shows a first edition from the Marvel Comics Group. The 60th card is an unnumbered checklist.

ITEM	MINT	EX
Set	9.00	6.00
Card	.15	.10
Wrappers (2)		
each	--	.35
Box	--	4.00

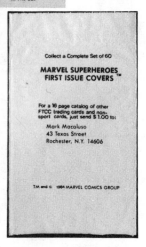

1 The Fantastic Four
2 The Amazing Spiderman
3 Sgt. Fury And His Howling Commandos
4 The Avengers
5 The X-Men
6 Daredevil
7 Ghost Rider
8 Not Brand Echh
9 The Incredible Hulk
10 Captain Marvel
11 Nick Fury, Agent of S.H.I.E.L.D.
12 Doctor Strange
13 Silver Surfer
14 Tales of Asgard
15 Ka-Zar
16 Fear
17 Marvel Spotlight (Captain Marvel)
18 Marvel Feature (Defenders)
19 Marvel Team-Up
20 Marvel Premiere (Warlock)
21 Tomb of Dracula
22 Red Wolf
23 Combat Kelly And The Deadly Dozen
24 Luke Cage, Hero For Hire
25 The Defenders
26 The Cat
27 Shanna The She-Devil
28 Crypt Of Shadows
29 The Monster Frankenstein
30 Man-Thing

31 Marvel Two-In-One
32 Night Rider
33 Giant Size X-Men
34 The Champions
35 The Inhumans
36 Marvel Chillers
37 Iron Fist
38 Howard The Duck
39 The Power Of ...Warlock
40 Black Goliath
41 Nova
42 Peter Parker, The Spectacular Spider-Man
43 Ms. Marvel
44 Spider-Woman
45 Machine Man
46 Devil Dinosaur
47 The Savage She-Hulk
48 Moon Knight
49 Dazzler
50 Marvel Spotlight On...Red Wolf
51 Marvel Fanfare
52 The New Mutants
53 The Thing
54 Alpha Flight
55 Iron Man And Sub-Mariner
56 Chamber Of Darkness
57 Astonishing Tales
58 Amazing Adventures
59 Werewolf By Night
60 Checklist

MARVEL SUPER HEROES (40) STICKERS

2 1/2" X 3 1/2"

Encouraged by the success of "Comic Book Heroes" in 1975, Topps returned in 1976 with the "Marvel Super Heroes" sticker set. As before, there are 40 stickers and nine checklist/puzzle cards. However, this time the stickers have either a plain white card-board back or instructions for peeling the stickers. The puzzle pieces on the checklist cards form the cover of the No. 1 issue of "Conan The Barbarian." Note: set price includes 40 stickers and nine checklist/puzzle cards.

ITEM	MINT	EX
Set	30.00	22.50
Sticker	.65	.50
Card	.50	.35
Wrappers (3) each	--	1.00
Box	--	25.00

387

Marvel Super Heroes Stickers

Blade (I'm a Real Cut-Up!)
Black Goliath (Bowling Sure is Fun!)
Bucky (How'd You Like a Knuckle Sandwich?)
Captain America (I've Got to Stand This Way or My Pants Fall Down!)
Conan (Hold the Pickle...or Else!)
Cyclops (I'm a Sight for Sore Eyes!)
Daredevil (See No Evil!)
Deathlok (I'm the Seven Million Dollar Man!)
Dracula (So This is How You Do the Hustle!)
Dr. Doom (Anyone Out There Have a Can Opener?)
Dr. Strange (Did Anyone See a Flying Sorcerer?)
Galactus (No, I'm Not the Mad Hatter!)
Goliath (Wanna Hear a Tall Story?)
Hercules (Look, I Have a Hang-Nail!)

Howard the Duck (I'm Going Quakers!)
Ice Man (I'll Never Eat Another Frozen Dinner!)
Invisible Girl (I Use Vanishing Cream!)
Iron Man (Quick—Anyone Have an Oilcan?)
Kid Colt (I Am Not Kidding Around!)
Killraven (I'll Teach You to Make Fun of My Hair-do!)
Loki (Who Says I'm Bull-Headed?)
Luke Cage (Like My Denture Work?)
Peter Parker (Peter Parker Picked a Peck of Pickled Peppers!)
Red Skull (What Makes You Think I'm Angry?)
Red Sonja (My Sword Gives Six Extra Shaves!)
Sgt. Fury (War Makes Me Fighting Mad!)
Silver Surfer (You'll Take a Shine to Me!)
Son of Satan (Waiter, Bring Me a Clean Fork!)

Spider-Man (Insects Scare Me Silly!)
Thor (Don't Make Me Thor!)
Tigra (Cat Food For Dinner Again?)
The Angel (I'm Heading South for the Winter!)
The Hulk (Help Cure Athlete's Feet!)
The Human Torch (Who Called Me a Hot-Head?)
The Punisher (Oh Boy! I Win the Kewpie Doll!)
The Thing (Who Said I'm a Falling Rock Zone?)
The Vision (Who Stole My Yo-Yo?)
The Watcher (Hiya Kids! Hiya! Hiya! Hiya!)
Volstagg (Fat is Beautiful!)
Warlock (Stop Me If You Heard This Before...)

MARVEL UNIVERSE I (162)   2 1/2" X 3 1/2"

There is no better example of the "new breed" of cards being produced in the suddenly-competitive non-sports market than this 1990 set of "Marvel Universe" issued by Impel. Each card seems to be a perfect combination of striking color artwork, crisp layout, and pertinent information. The series of 162 is divided into categories: Super Heroes, Super-Villains, Rookies, Famous Battles, M.V.C. (Most Valuable Comics), Team Pictures, and Spider-Man Presents, plus single cards for Stan Lee and the checklist. There is also a subset of five hologram cards which were randomly inserted into packs to promote sales. These have their own numbering system and many collectors consider them to be bonus cards which should not be counted as part of the regular set. For this reason, and because prices for them vary greatly according to individual perspectives, they have been listed separately in the values section below.

The prices listed below reflect the market conditions in December, 1990. Of all the recent sets, it appears that Marvel Universe I and II have captured collector interest and are, at least in the short term, appreciating at a moderate rate. Much of this has to do with the supply, which is perceived to be somewhat limited in respect to current demand. Another factor to consider is that certain cards have been singled out by card-and-comic-book fans as more valuable than others because of the character pictured and a subculture of individual prices for specific heroes and villains has developed. Since every card in the series was produced in the same numbers, this individual card pricing is simply demand-driven by a small group

Marvel Universe I

1 Captain America
2 Spider-Man
3 The Hulk
4 Daredevil
5 Nick Fury
6 The Thing
7 Professor X
8 Cyclops
9 Marvel Girl
10 Wolverine
11 Phoenix
12 Power Man
13 Dazzler
14 Dagger
15 Quasar
16 Sub-Mariner
17 Hulk (Gray)
18 Thor
19 Mister Fantastic
20 Black Panther
21 Archangel
22 Iceman
23 Wolverine
24 Storm
25 Shadowcat
26 Moon Knight
27 Lockheed
28 Aunt May
29 Spider-Man
30 Cosmic Spider-Man
31 Captain America's Motorcycle
32 Silver Surfer
33 Human Torch
34 Doctor Strange
35 Havok

36 Colossus
37 Wolverine (Patch)
38 Nightcrawler
39 She-Hulk
40 Captain Britain
41 Rogue
42 Iron Man
43 Invisible Woman
44 Punisher's Battle Van
45 Longshot
46 The Beast
47 Punisher
48 Storm
49 Elektra
50 Cloak
51 The Wasp
52 Kingpin
53 Baron Zemo
54 Loki
55 Juggernaut
56 Nightmare
57 Sabretooth
58 Electro
59 Doctor Octopus
60 Doctor Doom
61 Ultron
62 Enchantress
63 Magneto
64 Bullseye
65 Mr. Sinister
66 Sandman
67 Lizard
68 Mole Man
69 Dormammu
70 The Leader

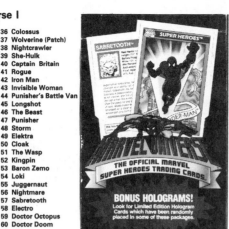

BONUS HOLOGRAMS!
Look for Limited Edition Hologram Cards which have been randomly placed in some of these packages.

of collectors, but card dealers are sure to notice it and some will try to convert it into a generalized trend. In the past, this type of "specialization inflation" has typically run its course and died out as collectors focus on the newer sets coming their way. Until the market sorts it all out, prices for Marvel Universe I and the holograms will probably be "all over the lot," so to speak. NOTE: values are listed for mint cards only; excellent grade cards are rated at 50% of the mint price.

ITEM	MINT	EX
Card set	25.00	---
Card	.15	---
Hologram set	40.00	---
Hologram	7.00	---
Wrapper	---	.15
Box	---	2.00

71 The Blob
72 Black Cat
73 Venom
74 Green Goblin
75 Galactus
76 Mandarin
77 High Evolutionary
78 Mephisto
79 Thanos
80 Apocalypse
81 Red Skull
82 Ghost Rider
83 Deathlok
84 Guardians of the Galaxy
85 New Warriors
86 Nomad
87 Foolkiller
88 The Thing vs. The Hulk
89 Fantastic Four vs. Galactus
90 Fantastic Four vs. Doctor Doom
91 Thor vs. Surtur
92 Spider-Man vs. Kraven
93 Spider-Man vs. Dr. Octopus
94 Daredevil vs. Bullseye
95 Daredevil vs. Kingpin
96 Silver Surfer vs. Mephisto
97 Captain America vs. The Red Skull
98 The Dark Phoenix Saga
99 X-Men vs. The Avengers
100 X-Men vs. Magneto
101 Fantastic Four vs. X-Men
102 Fall of the Mutants
103 The Evolutionary War
104 Atlantis Attacks
105 Acts of Vengeance
106 Spider-Man vs. Venom
107 Nick Fury vs. Hydra
108 The Armor Wars

TEAM PICTURES

X-FACTOR

109 Daredevil vs. Wolverine
110 Daredevil vs. The Punisher
111 Spider-Man vs. Green Goblin
112 Spider-Man vs. Hobgoblin
113 The Hulk vs. Wolverine
114 The Hulk vs. Spider-Man
115 Captain America vs. Wolverine
116 Silver Surfer vs. Thanos
117 X-Factor vs. Apocalypse
118 X-Men vs. Freedom Force
119 Wolverine vs. Sabretooth
120 X-Men in the Savage Land
121 Iron Man vs. Titanium Man
122 Thor vs. Loki
123 The Kree-Skrull War
124 Fantastic Four #1
125 X-Men #1
126 Amazing Fantasy #15
127 The Punisher Vol.2 #1
128 Journey Into Mystery #83
129 Amazing Spider-Man #129
130 Avengers #1
131 Amazing Spider-Man #1
132 Giant-Size X-Men #1
133 Wolverine Limited Series #1
134 Incredible Hulk #181
135 Tales of Suspense #39
136 Avengers #4
137 Fantastic Four
138 Avengers
139 X-Men
140 X-Men
141 Cloak and Dagger

142 New Mutants
143 X-Factor
144 Excalibur
145 Brotherhood of Evil Mutants
146 Sinister Six
147 Hellfire Club
148 Alpha Flight
149 Spider-Man Presents Spider-Man
150 Spider-Man Presents Doctor Doom
151 Spider-Man Presents Doctor Octopus
152 Spider-Man Presents The Hulk
153 Spider-Man Presents Silver Surfer
154 Spider-Man Presents Thor
155 Spider-Man Presents Punisher
156 Spider-Man Presents Magneto
157 Spider-Man Presents Captain America
158 Spider-Man Presents Doctor Strange
159 Spider-Man Presents Iron Man
160 Spider-Man Presents Wolverine

161 Stan Lee
162 Checklist

HOLOGRAMS:
MH1 Cosmic Spider-Man
MH2 Magneto
MH3 Silver Surfer
MH4 Wolverine
MH5 Spider-Man vs. Green Goblin

CHECKLIST

389

MARVEL UNIVERSE II (162)

2 1/2" X 3 1/2"

Impel's second series of Marvel Universe, distributed in 1991, follows the same basic plan of Series I: 162 cards and five holograms. The color scheme is different and there are some interesting improvements in design elements such as heading and picture frames, captioning, and layout. Once again, the cards are grouped into specific categories: Super Heroes, Super-Villains, Arch-Enemies, Weapons, Legends, Rookies, Teams, and Power Ratings, plus a single checklist. The numbering for the holograms is slightly different, H-1 to H-5, than the system used in Series I (MH-1 to MH-5). The three different poly bag wrappers and the display box are all prominently marked with a "SERIES II" panel.

Series II Marvel Universe seems to have been produced in greater quantity than Series I and the May, 1992 price for the regular card set reflects this. The five bonus holograms may be slightly harder to find than their Series I counterparts and they have settled in at the same price level. Once again, many collectors view these and other holograms, "legacy cards," "prototypes," etc., as marketing devices which should be segregated from the regular set. Some people are ignoring them completely, while others collect them exclusively and are not bothering with the normal cards. All this makes for diversity of opinion about their value and collectors must exercise patience and common sense in hunting for them. NOTE: values are listed for mint cards; excellent grade cards are rated at 50% of the mint price.

ITEM	MINT	EX
Card set	20.00	---
Card	.15	---
Hologram set	32.00	---
Hologram	6.00	---
Wrappers		
(3) each	---	.10
Box	---	1.50

Marvel Universe II

1 Spider-Man
2 Daredevil
3 Thing
4 Marvel Girl
5 Phoenix
6 Sub-Mariner
7 Mister Fantastic
8 Iceman
9 Shadowcat
10 Human Torch
11 Nightcrawler
12 Captain Britain
13 Iron Man
14 Punisher
15 Cable
16 Deathlok
17 Gambit
18 Psylocke
19 Vision
20 Hawkeye
21 Silver Sable
22 Night Thrasher
23 Puck
24 Union Jack
25 Quicksilver
26 Scarlet Witch
27 Havok
28 Iron Fist
29 Adam Warlock
30 Wonder Man
31 Sasquatch
32 Firestar
33 Death's Head
34 Speedball
35 USAgent
36 Banshee
37 Meggan
38 Jubilee
39 Ghost Rider
40 Beast
41 Invisible Woman
42 Rogue
43 She-Hulk
44 Dr. Strange
45 Silver Surfer
46 Storm
47 Archangel
48 Thor
49 Quasar
50 Wolverine
51 Cyclops
52 Nick Fury
53 Hulk
54 Captain America
55 Kingpin
56 Sabretooth
57 Magneto
58 Venom

59 Galactus
60 Mandarin
61 Chameleon
62 Super Skrull
63 Grim Reaper
64 Mojo
65 Fin Fang Foom
66 Jigsaw
67 Tombstone
68 Ulik
69 Baron Strucker
70 Mysterio
71 Sauron
72 Annihilus
73 Rhino
74 Absorbing Man
75 Doctor Octopus
76 Baron Mordo
77 Saracen
78 Nebula
79 Puma
80 Deathwatch
81 Kang .
82 Blackout
83 Calypso
84 Ultron
85 Thanos
86 Hobgoblin
87 Lizard
88 Doctor Doom
89 Loki
90 Red Skull
91 Spider-Man vs Venom
92 Fantastic Four vs Skrulls
93 Wolverine vs Sabretooth
94 Silver Surfer vs Galactus
95 Daredevil vs Elektra
96 Avengers vs Kang
97 Human Torch vs Sub-Mariner

98 Spider-Man vs Hobgoblin
99 Captain America vs Baron Zemo
100 Punisher vs Jigsaw
101 X-Factor vs Apocalypse
102 Punisher vs Kingpin
103 Thing vs Hulk
104 Daredevil vs Bullseye
105 Spider-Man vs Doctor Octopus
106 X-Men vs Sentinels
107 Fantastic Four vs Galactus
108 Wolverine vs Hulk
109 Ghost Rider vs Deathwatch
110 Dr. Strange vs Baron Mordo
111 Nick Fury vs Baron Strucker
112 Spider-Man vs Lizard
113 Silver Surfer vs Thanos

114 Avengers vs Ultron
115 Captain America vs Red Skull
116 Daredevil vs Punisher
117 X-Men vs Marauders
118 Iron Man vs Mandarin
119 Hulk vs Leader
120 Thor vs Loki
121 Spider-Man vs J. Jonah Jameson
122 Thor vs Ulik
123 Silver Surfer vs Mephisto
124 Fantastic Four vs Doctor Doom
125 X-Men vs Magneto
136 Daredevil vs Kingpin
127 Captain America's Shield
128 Thor's Hammer
129 Daredevil's Billy Club

130 Ultimate Nullifier
131 Spider-Man's Armor
132 Punisher's Arsenal
133 Iron Man's Armor
134 Infinity Gauntlet
135 Quasar's Quantum Bands
136 Dr. Octopus's Arms
137 Mandarin's Rings
138 Wolverine's Claws
139 Captain Marvel
140 Bucky
141 Green Goblin
142 Original Ghost Rider
143 Kraven
144 Dark Phoenix
145 Darkhawk
146 Sleepwalker
147 Rage
148 X-Force
149 New Fantastic Four
150 Fantastic Four
151 Avengers
152 Avengers West Coast
153 X-Men
154 X-Factor
155 Excalibur
156 New Warriors
157 Masters of Evil
158 Marauders
159 Power Ratings
160 Power Ratings
161 Power Ratings
162 Checklist

HOLOGRAMS

H-1 Spider-Man
H-2 Hulk
H-3 Punisher
H-4 Doctor Doom
H-5 Fantastic Four vs Mole Man

For the past decade, collectors have encountered these fabric iron-on patches of Marvel Super Heroes at shows, flea markets, cards sales, etc., and have wondered about their origin. It has been rumored that they were issued in both cereal and bread, but this has not been confirmed to date. One method of distribution which has been verified is a variety store j-hook package of four iron-ons which we have in The Card Collectors Archive. The plastic bag had a cardboard header and contained two iron-ons each for the Incredible Hulk and Spider-Man. Each fabric patch measures 2" X 2-3/4" and has application instructions printed on the back. The 1979 date on the patches refers to the license arrangement; these j-hook packages were marketed in 1980 for 19¢ each. Current market value = 50¢ per patch.

MASH (66)

With so many card sets over the years featuring short-lived television shows, it is a puzzle to many collectors why it took so long to issue a card set for M.A.S.H. It is ironic that the set was finally produced in 1982, the same year the decision was made to end the show. There are 66 cards in the set; all have color photos taken from the show plus some posed portrait studies. The cards are numbered on the front, and the backs form a large poster of the M.A.S.H. family (same picture as the box).

ITEM	MINT	EX
Set	18.00	13.50
Card	.25	.20
Wrapper	—	.35
Box	—	5.00

MASK ALBUM STICKERS (240)

"Mask," a popular fantasy hero among the younger set, is the focal point of this sticker set produced by Diamond in 1987. There are 240 stickers in the set; of these, 208 have color artwork fronts and 32 are pieces of two "Super 3—D Sticker Puzzles" (see ppg. 16-17 of album). A 3-D format is utilized throughout the 32-page album, which comes with a set of 3-D glasses stapled into the binding. Note: set price includes album.

ITEM	MINT	EX
Set	25.00	17.50
Sticker	.10	.07
Wrapper	—	.35
Album	1.50	1.00

There are six different characters depicted on the backs of these blue poly bags used to market "Eternia Rocks Bubble Gum." The characters are named but the bags are not numbered. Instead of a written checklist, we have provided illustrations of all six drawings. Note: no mint price is given since the bags must be pulled open at the top to remove the gum.

ITEM	MINT	EX
Set	--	7.00
Bags (6) each	--	1.00
Box	--	5.00

MASTERS OF THE (88 & 21) UNIVERSE

2 1/2" X 3 1/2"

The Masters of the Universe set produced by Topps in 1984 chronicles the adventures of Teela and Prince Adam as they battle the evil Skeletor. Cards 1-87 develop the story line while card No. 88 is a simple, number-only checklist. The 21 stickers are all of the front-peel, diecut variety. Stickers 1-10 are untitled "Action Stickers"; Nos. 11-21 depict and name various characters. The backs of stickers 1 & 2 are puzzle previews of two ten-part puzzles; the remaining sticker backs are puzzle pieces. Note: set price includes stickers.

ITEM	MINT	EX
Set	15.00	11.00
Card	.10	.07
Sticker	.35	.25
Wrappers (4)		
each	---	.35
Box	---	4.00

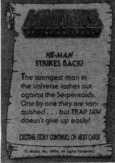

Masters of the Universe

1 Welcome to Eternia!
2 Like Father, Like Daughter!
3 Within These Walls of Evil...
4 Monstrous Alliance!
5 Plan of Skeletor
6 Duo for Destruction!
7 Home of the Brave
8 A New Invention!
9 Gripe of Teela
10 The Adventure Begins!
11 Commanding The Mystic Forces!
12 Metamorphosis!
13 Trusted Ally!
14 Enter...Battle Cat!
15 The Road to Castle Grayskull!
16 Summoned to the Castle!
17 Keeper of the Castle!
18 The Plan of Skeletor Revealed!
19 Three Against Eternia!
20 Final Words of Warning!
21 Fixing the Laser Lasso
22 No Adventure for Teela?
23 He-Man Is Coming!
24 The Monster-Maker!
25 Monarch of Menace!
26 A Friend in Need!
27 The Lasso Test
28 Experiment: Successful!
29 Poor Orko!
30 Dangerous Decision!
31 Orko...Free At Last!
32 Approaching the Fortress
33 Two Determined Heroes!
34 Attack from the Sky!
35 Reeling from the Attack...
36 Device of Doom!
37 The Assault Continues!
38 The Plan to Capture Man-At-Arms!
39 Power of the Bolts!
40 Master of Evil Creatures!
41 Man-At-Arms...Helpless
42 Beast Man Triumphant!
43 Disarmed!
44 And Now...Defeat He-Man!
45 Machine Madness!
46 Nearer to Danger...!
47 Metallic Monster!
48 The Man and the Challenge!
49 A Crushing Defeat?
50 Man Against Monster!
51 He-Man Wins the First Round!
52 Smashed Serpentoid!
53 No Turning Back!
54 The Evil Ones
55 Monsters on the March!
56 He-Man Strikes Back!
57 The Titans Clash!
58 Sneak Attack!
59 Strength of He-Man
60 Surrounded!
61 Teela to the Rescue!
62 Moment of Triumph!
63 Power of the Lasso
64 Snagged!
65 In The Right Hands!
66 Defeat of the Serpentoids
67 Storming the Fortress
68 Mighty Weapon of Teela
69 Bested by our Heroes!
70 Moment of Truth
71 We're Not Through Yet!
72 Outfoxed by Teela!
73 A Cool Reception!
74 Destroying the Machine of Trap Jaw
75 To Rescue a Warrior!
76 Last Minute Rescue!
77 Deadly Device
78 Bravery Wins the Day!
79 Our Friends Re-United!
80 Until Next Time? -- ?!
81 Warning of Skeletor
82 Courage: A Family Tradition!
83 Plight of Orko
84 Look Who's Here!
85 A Royal Put-Down!
86 If Only Teela Knew...!
87 Teela Continues...
88 Checklist

Masters Of The Universe Stickers

1 Action Sticker
2 Action Sticker
3 Action Sticker
4 Action Sticker
5 Action Sticker
6 Action Sticker
7 Action Sticker
8 Action Sticker
9 Action Sticker
10 Action Sticker
11 Guardians Of Eternia
12 Skeletor
13 Teela
14 Man-At-Arms
15 Man-E-Faces
16 Skeletor & Panthor
17 Sorceress
18 Ram-Man
19 He-Man & Battle Cat
20 Teela
21 Evil-Lyn

MASTERS OF THE UNIVERSE (216) ALBUM STICKERS

2 1/8" X 3"

This 216-sticker set, which is based on the animated Masters of the Universe series, was distributed by Panini U.S.A. in 1985. The 36-page album supplements the sticker placements on every page with illustrations and dialogue. Moreover, there is a special four-page section in the center designed to hold 36 diecut character stickers (Nos. 88-123). The stickers themselves are numbered and have the standard multi-language back employed by Panini. Note: set price includes album.

ITEM	MINT	EX
Set	25.00	17.50
Sticker	.10	.07
Wrapper	---	.35
Album	2.00	1.50

395

MASTERS OF THE UNIVERSE (240) 2 1/16" X 2 9/16"
MOVIE ALBUM STICKERS

In the summer of 1987, Cannon Films released a motion picture based on the television series "Masters of the Universe," and right on it's heels came a sticker set issued by Panini U.S.A. The stickers have multi-language backs and are designed to be placed in sequence in a 32-page album. The most impressive element of this set is a 18"

X 19 3/4" wall poster (album insert) designed to hold 15 foil stickers depicting the principal characters (lettered A-O). Note: set price includes album.

ITEM	MINT	EX
Set	25.00	17.50
Sticker	.10	.07
Wrapper	---	.35
Album	2.00	1.50

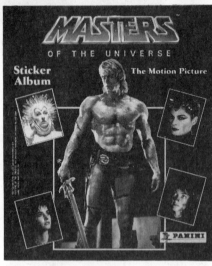  

MASTERS OF THE UNIVERSE
TRADING CARDS (15)

2 1/2" X 3 1/2"

A joint promotion of Mattel Toys and Wonder Bread, this series of 15 cards was issued in 1986.

Fourteen of the cards have color artwork on the front; only "Castle Grayskull" is drawn in black & white. The characters, buildings, and vehicle illustrated in the pictures all correspond to toys manufactured by Mattel. The backs explain about each toy and are printed in gray ink on white stock. Cards that were actually packed in bread may be

found with oil stains and these cannot be graded excellent or mint. Complete sets of cards in new condition were obviously obtained via other channels and some of these will actually have a slight bow, or arc, to them, due to the glossy coating on the surfaces. The cards are not numbered and the captions used in the checklist correspond to those printed on the fronts of the cards.

Castle Grayskull
Dragstor
Eternia Playset
Evil-Lyn
Extendar
He-Man
Hordak
Laser Bolt with He Man

Orko
Rio Blast
Skeletor
Slime Pit
Snout Spout
Stonedar
The Evil Horde

ITEM	MINT	EX
Set	10.00	7.50
Card	.65	.50

MATCHBOX CAR & DRIVER
COLLECTOR CARDS (60)

2 1/2" X 3 1/2"

Very little information has been reported about this series of trading cards found inserted in packages of Matchbox toy cars. The fronts bear color photographs of various automobiles and each car is identified in a stylish white caption panel decorated with green and red stripes. A large yellow and red

"Matchbox" logo is printed to one side on every picture. The backs are blue print on white and contain the caption, card number, set title and pertinent information about each car. Each model car package contained five cards and an album for the set was advertised as "coming

soon." The cards appear to have originated in 1989 and, given the extended shelf life of toys, may still be found today. Checklist furnished by Ted Knight.

ITEM	MINT	EX
Set	18.00	13.50
Card	.25	.20

Car and Driver Collector Cards

101 Ferrari F40
102 Buick LeSabre
103 Nissan 300ZX Turbo
104 Honda Prelude Si
105 Cadillac Allante
201 Lamborghini Countach
202 Porsche 911 Turbo
203 Mazda RX-7 Convertible
204 Toyota Supra Turbo
205 Oldsmobile Toronado
301 Corvette Convertible
302 Mercedes-Benz 300E
303 Porsche 928S4
304 Ford Probe GT
305 Pontiac Turbo Grand Prix
401 Porsche 959
402 Mercedes-Benz 560SEC
403 Ferrari 328GTS
404 BMW 525i
405 Corvette ZR-1
501 Corvette "T" Top
502 Sterling 827SLi
503 Acura Integra GS
504 Audi Coupe Quattro
505 Dodge Viper

601 Ford Bronco II
602 Pontiac Fiero
603 Acura NS-X
604 Merkur XR4Ti
605 Oldsmobile Aerotech
701 Porsche 944 Turbo
702 Lincoln Town Car
703 Dodge Caravan
704 Ford Escort GT

705 Cadillac Seville
801 Camaro Iroc Z
802 Volkswagen GTI 16V
803 Lamborghini LM002
804 BMW 750iL
805 AMG Mercedes Hammer
901 Pontiac Firebird
902 Saab 9000 Turbo
903 Chevrolet Beretta

904 20th Anniversary Trans Am
905 Ford Taurus SHO
1001 Jaguar XJ6
1002 Dodge Daytona Turbo ES
1003 BMW 635CSi
1004 '68 Chevrolet Impala
1005 Toyota MR2 Supercharged
1101 Ferrari Testarossa
1102 Ford Mustang GT

1103 Mazda MX-5 Miata
1104 Peugeot Oxia
1105 Nissan 240SX
1201 Ford T-Bird Turbo Coupe
1202 Chevrolet Blazer
1203 Ford LTD Crown Victoria
1204 Land Rover
1205 Volvo 780

MAX HEADROOM (44)

2 1/2" X 3 1/2"

Many collectors anticipated the arrival of a Max Headroom card set, but it did not appear until November 1987 ... after the TV show had been cancelled. There are 44 numbered sticker-cards in the set, which was produced by Topps. Of these, numbers 1-33 have black-bordered, corner-peel stickers on front and puzzle-piece backs (two 15-part puzzles, and three puzzle preview cards). The obverse designs of numbers 33-44 are printed on foil and also peel from the corner; these cards have a feature entitled "The Origin of Max" on the back. The backs are numbered independently of the front stickers ("1 of 11," etc.) so they can be collated if the stickers are removed. Initially, it was believed that Max Headroom was produced and distributed on an extremely limited basis but new supplies, probably from overstocks, seem to be filtering into the hobby right now. Therefore, it is an opportune time for interested collectors to add the set to their collections while the price is down from previous levels.

ITEM	MINT	EX
Set	25.00	18.50
Sticker / card	.50	.35
Foil	.75	.50
Wrapper	--	.75
Box	--	10.00

MAYA (55 & 16)

2 1/2" X 3 1/2"

The Maya series never achieved the level of popularity which Topps might have envisioned for it, leaving large quantities of mint cards which even now are are so common as to have little value. However, most collectors may not be aware that the set also included 16 "puzzle-piece" cards in which the center designs could be detached to make a jig saw puzzle. The 55 regular cards have color pictures with black frame lines and white borders. The pictures are captioned in a tan panel on the front. The green and white backs have a story narrative and a feature entitled "Mysteries of India." Puzzle cards have a color center and white borders and they are numbered but not captioned. Note: set price does not include puzzle pieces.

ITEM	MINT	EX
Set	16.50	11.00
Card	.30	.20
Puzzle		
piece	5.00	4.00
set	90.00	70.00
Wrapper	--	15.00
Box	--	40.00

1	Headed for India	17	Night Time in India
2	Boy in Bombay	18	Terry and Primo
3	A New Home	19	Primo the Prankster
4	Where Is Dad?	20	Elephant Driver
5	A Tragic Report	21	Mounting Maya
6	Terry in Despair	22	Off to Adventure
7	Desected	23	The Sacred Temple
8	The Search Begins	24	Dense Jungle
9	Jungle Sights	25	The Sacred Elephant
10	Water at Last	26	Sharing Rations
11	Danger Nearby	27	A Worried Boy
12	Boy vs. Beast	28	Bad News
13	Raging Waters	29	Muddy Masquerade
14	Here Comes Raji	30	Terry's Disguise
15	Maya and Raji	31	Maya's Performance
16	Rescued!	32	Riot!
		33	Rush to Safety
		34	Danger Ahead
		35	Rough Ride
		36	Jungle Peril

37	The Missing American
38	Full of Fear
39	Sighted
40	Another Threat
41	Desperate Act
42	To the Rescue
43	The Chase
44	The Evil One
45	Caught in the Act
46	The Battle!
47	Raji in Danger
48	Gleaming Blade
49	Terry's Warning
50	Mission Accomplished
51	New Clothes
52	Goodbye to Primo
53	The Search Continues
54	"Find this Boy"
55	What Lies Ahead?

McHALE'S NAVY (66)

2 1/2" X 3 1/2"

McHale's Navy was another set which the maker — Fleer, in this case — marketed more heavily in vending packs and case lots than in bubble gum packs. The result was a glut of cards which continues to this day. The cards have black and white pictures from the TV series and are white-bordered. The space beneath each picture contains dialogue. The backs are printed in red and blue on white, and the card number is located above a sketch of the three TV series stars.

ITEM	MINT	EX
Set	60.00	47.50
Card	.75	.60
Wrapper	--	10.00
Box	--	60.00

1 The Heroic Commander McHale.
2 The Fearless Leader, Captain Binghamton.
3 Poor Chuck, Did Binghamton Make You Swim Back Again?
4 Skip, I Think My Head Shrank.
5 On You, It Looks Better This Way, Sir.
6 Control Yourself, Tiger... Er I Mean Sir
7 Sir, You Shouldn't say Those Nasty Things. The Shock Will Stunt Parker's Mental Growth.
8 Don't Cry Chuck, Binghamton Won't Keep Your Yo-yo Long. Just Don't Hit Him In The Eye Again.
9 No, It's Not A Rat Knucklehead. I Said I Smell A Rat...McHale.
10 McHale, I'm Afraid Your New Laundry Won't Last.
11 Don't Confuse Me With The Facts...This Is McHale's Fault.
12 Boy, I Can't Get A Drop Out Of This Crazy Straw.
13 Down For The Third Time... McHale Hopes!
14 How Am I Doin' Skip? I Can't See...My Eyes Are Closed.
15 Skip, Is It True The Navy Issues Bathing Suits To The Guys At The North Pole?
16 Anyone Want A Taxi?
17 This'll Put Out That Fire In Your Eyes, Sir!
18 McHale! What Happened... Everything's Gone Blank!
19 Chuck, I Know It's Hard, But You've Just Got To Start Thinking.
20 Here's Your Jeep Sir.
21 Parker, You Knucklehead, I Want To Talk To You!!
22 It's Nice You Learned To Salute, But I Said "At Ease" Ten Minutes Ago!
23 This Combat Zone Duty Is Really Rough!!
24 All Right Captain, Stop Gasping...I'll Throw You Back.
25 Well, I Can Always Try Filet of Sole.
26 Chuck, Are You Sure This Little Red Riding Hood Movie Is For Us?
27 I Taught Him To Salute Myself Sir.
28 Yeh Skip, But Before We Go, Tell Me Again Which Is Port And Which Is Starboard?
29 If He Wasn't Getting Chewed Out, Chuck Would Know Something Was Wrong.
30 Don't Worry Skip...I've Got My Secret Weapon Here.
31 Some After Shave Lotion, Skip?
32 Now Watch You Don't Scratch Up Your Carbine, Skip.
33 After You Give This To Binghamton...Run!
34 Stop Saying You'll Desert To The Enemy...Ensign Parker Is Still In Charge Of This Mission.
35 Gruber, Try Crying Like Ensign Parker Does.
36 Hey, Guys, Look At These Pictures!
37 How About Some Suki Yaki a la Porker?
38 It's No Use McHale, I've Tried...The Infantry Won't Have You Either.
39 McHale's Sidekick...And Somebody's Always Kicking Him In The Side.
40 Skip, Are You Sure He's The Family Doctor?
41 I've Never Seen You Look Better, Captain.
42 I Want To Win The Best Dressed Award.
43 Help, I Want My Mommy!
44 Hey Skip, Can I Have a Bullet for My Gun Now?
45 At Least I'm Not Wet Behind The Ears.
46 This Navy Life Is The Greatest!
47 If We Don't Get All Four, We're Really Going To Declare War...On Binghamton!!
48 Don't Worry Chuck, Flying Is Fun...And Your Arms DON'T Get Tired.
49 Don't Cry Chuck. It Opens Up Just Like A Big Umbrella.
50 You Don't Really Mean Up Thataway!!
51 Remember, If I Think I'm Going To Crash...One If By Land; Two If By Sea.
52 Anything That Covers Up Part Of That Face Is An Improvement!!
53 Parlez-Vous Francais?
54 Boy, You're The Cutest Girl I've Seen On This Island, Man!
55 Aw Skip, Why Is It Always Me? If The Captain Sees Through This Disguise, I'll Get French Fried.
56 Just Call Me Handsome Harry!
57 Do I Have To Say 'I Do' Sir?
58 Get Me To The Church On Time.
59 Oh H-O-W I Wish I Was In The Land Of Cotton...
60 On Guard, Yankee-San!
61 Me Parker-Suki, Japanese Houseboy.
62 You're Standing On My Skirt!
63 Have Kimono, Will Travel!
64 Cheerio, Old Chap!
65 I'm Not A Beatnik...Tell Him McHale!
66 I Don't Care If You Are A Smith Brother...Stop Coughing!!

MEN OF APOLLO XI (?)

2 3/4" SQUARE

This colorful set of small cards printed on thin cardboard stock was issued in Dietzen's Bread and it was first reported to The Card Collectors Bulletin by Bob Stoker of Marion, Indiana in 1973. The number of subjects in the series has not been established, but if it matches other Dietzen sets, there are probably ten. The card illustrated is a color drawing of astronaut Neil Armstrong. The series title is printed vertically on the extra wide left border (5/16" wide); once this is cut away, as the dotted lines indicate, the card would be 2-7/16" X 2-3/4" AND title-less. The back contains the subject's name and rank, biography, and a copyright line for Advico, Inc. Note: cards with the title margin cut away cannot be graded excellent or mint.

ITEM	MINT	EX
Card	2.50	2.00

MEN OF THE OLD WEST (?)

2 3/4" SQUARE

Another Dietzen Bread set reported to The Card Collectors Bulletin in 1973 by Bob Stoker. The card front illustrated is more interesting than that of the preceding set because it has more details in the artwork. The company name is also printed in large script above the picture, which makes it easy to identify. It does not appear that the wide border seen on the Men of Apollo cards was used with this set, although there are some marks and indentations on the left edge which indicate that it was the attachment point (method of attachment unknown). The back has a rustic log design enclosing the biography of the individual named above. The cards are not numbered and there are no other identifying marks, names or dates.

ITEM	MINT	EX
Card	2.50	2.00

MENUDO (66 & 22)   2 1/2" X 3 1/2"

"Menudo has won the hearts of Latin Americans like no other musical group had ever

done before" (card No. 10). After a brief foray into the harsher reality of the U.S. musical marketplace, the boys retreated back to Puerto Rico, leaving no trace except this card set. Produced by Topps

in 1983, with the usual mixture of text and puzzle backs, it contains 66 cards and 22 stickers. The English/Spanish text backs contain some of the most blatantly absurd and unbelievable statements ever printed on trading cards, which gives the set a sort of "campy" appeal.

ITEM	MINT	EX
Set	15.00	11.50
Card	.10	.07
Sticker	.35	.25
Wrapper	--	.35
Box	--	5.00

MICHAEL JACKSON (33 & 33) 1ST SERIES

2 1/2'' X 3 1/2''

The initial print run of Topps' 1984 Michael Jackson 1st series contained picture and print details which were eliminated, by the singer's personal request, on subsequent print runs. On the gum package itself, the "red lips" overlay which attracted so much early attention was removed. Changes in wording —some of them minute— were made on 18 cards, and completely new photos were placed on cards No. 10 and No. 18. Moreover,

the glossy surface on the puzzle piece backs of initial run stickers was later replaced by a dull, flat finish.

The set itself is composed of 33 cards and 33 stickers; the cards have text backs and the sticker backs are puzzle pieces (two 15-part puzzles) or puzzle preview cards (3). The "stick" gum came in a small "chewing gum" style wrapper (pink, red, or orchid). We have illustrated two uncut

sheets of stickers front and back. Note: 1st printing sets (with recalled details) sell for **$40.**
Wording changes: 1-2-3-4-5-7-8-10-12-14-17-18-21-22-25-27-31-32.
Picture changes: 10 & 18.

ITEM	MINT	EX
Set	12.00	9.00
Card	.10	.05
Sticker	.35	.25
Wrappers		
Red lips	––	3.00
regular	––	.35
Box	––	5.00

HERE IS WHAT YOUR COMPLETED BLUE BORDER PICTURE WILL LOOK LIKE:

COLLECT ALL 15 STICKER BACKS OF PICTURE A.

MICHAEL JACKSON (33 & 33)
2ND SERIES

2 1/2" X 3 1/2"

In contrast to the 1st series, there are no variations reported in the 2nd Michael Jackson series, which was also issued by Topps in 1984. The wrapper photo is the same but it has been cropped and the color scheme and print details are altered. The cards are numbered 34-66 and have color photos framed in orange on a green & blue-stripe background. The backs bear questions and answers about the singer's career. The red-border- ed, diecut stickers are also numbered 34-66 and have color photos set in letter shapes (A to Z, plus extras for A-E-I-J-M-O-U). The backs of the stickers are puzzle pieces (two 15-part puzzles and puzzle preview cards.

ITEM	MINT	EX
Set	12.00	9.00
Card	.10	.05
Sticker	.35	.25
Wrapper	--	.35
Box	--	5.00

402

MICHAEL JACKSON (13)
SUPER STICKERS

4 7/8" X 6 7/8"

Topps also took the opportunity to produce these "Super Stickers" in 1984. They were packaged singly in large cellophane "bag" wrappers with crimped ends; no gum was included. There are 13 stickers in the set and all are pictured on the reverse of each card. Some of the photos are identical to those appearing in the card sets previously described, some come from the same photo sequence, and some are entirely new. The photo area is diecut and is set against a black background. The sticker number is located outside the score line at the bottom.

ITEM	MINT	EX
Set	13.00	10.00
Sticker	1.00	.75
Wrapper	--	.50
Box	--	5.00

"Mickey Memorability," a series of 24 very large cards with gorgeous multi-color artwork fronts, is a gem of a set which has managed to elude the attention of most collectors. That's not hard to understand because it was issued simultaneously in two unlikely product areas: as an insert card in boxes of "Disney Cones" (ice cream cones) and as a bonus card attached to certain brands of clothes in large department stores! These are not exactly your usual card sources, and that explains why Memorability cards are so difficult to find. They were distributed in 1988 and come dated (1987) or undated. Those with a center hole at the very top are the type issued with clothes. None of the types is numbered and each has a trivia question (and answer) about Mickey Mouse on the back. The artwork appears to be reproductions of various movie theater cartoon posters.

ITEM	MINT	EX
Set	55.00	42.50
Card	2.00	1.50

MICKEY MOUSE AND HIS (360) FRIENDS

1 3/4" X 2 7/16"

This set of 360 album stickers was marketed in the U.S. on a limited basis by Americana Picture Service of Elizabeth, New Jersey. Each diecut, front-peel sticker contains a photo or artwork from a Disney movie or theme: Olympic Goofy, Mickey and the Ghosts, Donald Duck and the Witch, Snow White, Cinderella, Bambi, The Sword in the Stone, Peter Pan, and Bedknobs and Broomsticks. Four stickers and one piece of "taffy candy" came in each paper wrapper. A colorful "complimentary album" was available to hold the set. Note: set price includes album.

ITEM	MINT	EX
Set	60.00	45.00
Sticker	.15	.10
Album	5.00	4.00
Wrapper	--	3.00
Box	--	15.00

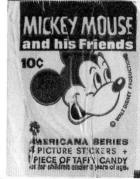

MICKEY MOUSE AND (25) HIS PALS

1 1/8" X 2 3/4"

A set of 25 small cards issued by Nabisco in packages of Sugar Daddy caramel pops. The fronts have drawings of Walt Disney characters set on pastel-colored backgrounds. The card number is located on the back and the set total is stated to be 25.

ITEM	MINT	EX
Set	60.00	45.00
Card	2.00	1.50

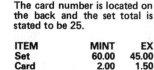

MICKEY STORY (360)

2 1/8" X 2 11/16"

The "Mickey Story" series, distributed in the U.S. by Panini in 1985, appears to be a re-issue of a set marketed several years ago in Europe. The new "American" version is identical to its European counterpart except that the stock is thinner and is white, rather than tan. Both versions bear a Walt Disney copyright from 1978. A beautifully-colored 32-page album designed to hold the set retailed for only 25 cents. Note: set price includes album.

ITEM	MINT	EX
Set	40.00	30.00
Sticker	.10	.07
Album	3.00	2.50
Wrapper	--	2.00

MICKEY'S MAGIC MOMENTS MOBILE (1)   IRREGULAR

Another in the Disney barrage of items released in celebration of Mickey Mouse's 60th anniversary, this mobile - or rather, parts of it - were printed on the fronts and backs of Twix cookie bar boxes in 1988. The back of each box contained four different "Magic Moments" designs complete with dotted lines to aid in cutting them out. Each design has a hole at top for attaching them by thread to the straws which are recommended for use as the cross bars of the mobile. One "Mickey -Sixty Years with You" medallion was printed on each side of the box. These were to be cut out and glued together to serve as the center weight of the apparatus. Sound complicated? Well, each box also carried a full set of instructions to guide you in the construction project. According to a statement on the box, there are "6 Magic Moments" needed to complete the mobile. The four pictured on this box are the only ones reported to date. The retail price for the intact box shown here is $5.00.

MICRO MACHINES (100/100)

Do you like miniature models? OK, do you like trading cards with *pictures* of miniature models?. If you answered yes, then Micro Machines is the set for you. There are racing cars, classic cars, helicopters, fire trucks, street dragsters, vans, semis, motorcycles, bulldozers, tractors, jet fighters, rancheros, propeller aircraft from both world wars, personnel carriers, patrol boats, speedboats, cranes, off-roaders, tugboats, Apollo modules, jeeps, ambulances, a presidential limousine, AND both the B-1 and Stealth bombers, (there is even a tow truck to haul off any of this stuff that breaks down!). In all, there

are 200 cards in the set, divided into Series 1 and Series 2.

Series 1 cards have blue borders surrounding the color pictures of each scale miniature. All the photographs are enclosed by wide framelines of varying colors which are filled with geometric designs. The words "Series 1" are printed in white letters in a red diagonal band in the lower right corner. The set title as it appears on the 100-page companion booklet - "Micro Machines" - is printed next to the card number on the reverse. The backs, printed with black ink on white stock, carry the card title, a short description, plus a "Quick Facts" list of

specifications. Series 1 cards are numbered 1-100 and both surfaces are super glossy.

Series 2 cards fall in the 101-200 sequence, have red borders around the geometric frames and color photos, and are marked "Series 2" in a blue diagonal panel in the lower right corner. They were also packaged in a plastic j-hook bubble pack along with a Series 2 booklet of 100 pages (each interior page shows one model and the real machine it is patterned after). In all other details, they are identical to the cards of Series 1.

Although "Micro Machines" cards are smaller than standard size (1-3/4" X 2-1/2"), they represent an interesting crossover between toy/miniature collectors and trading card enthusiasts. The two companion booklets, both 100 pages long, are filled with interesting color photographs and text. The Series 1 and Series 2 packages (each composed of 100 cards plus the booklet) have appeared quite recently in stores as marked-down overstocks. Collectors are not likely to find them so inexpensive at card shows, where they occasionally turn up in the $6 to $10 range for complete packages. Sets of Series 1 and Series 2 cards without the companion booklets can be found in the $4 to $6 range.

MICRO MACHINES...Series 1

1 1975-85 Ferrari 308 GTB
2 1936 Ford DeLuxe V-8 Cabriolet
3 McDonnell Douglas MD-500 Police Helicopter
4 Firefighters Ladder Truck
5 Pro Circuit Racers 1987 Buick Regal Stock Car
6 1968-69 Pontiac GTO
7 1975-89 Ford E-150 Econoline Van
8 1959 Chevrolet Impala Convertible
9 Heavy Workers Fertilizer Semi-Tanker
10 1955 Chevrolet Corvette
11 Army Reconnaissance Motorcycle
12 Highway Warriors Loader/Dozer
13 Classic Ford Farm Tractor
14 1962-68 Shelby-Cobra
15 Off-Road Heavy-Duty Sleeper Truck
16 Boeing 747
17 Classic Chop-Top V-8 Hot Rod
18 1954 Chevrolet Sedan Delivery
19 1958-60 Thunderbird Convertible

Firefighters "Cherry Picker" Truck #100
This vehicle carries a long, folding "boom" pole. "Cherry picker" basket eases rescue.
QUICK FACTS
Make—LaFrance
Cab—cab-over
Load—boom
Max. wt.—5.5 tons
Engine—gas
Cylinders—V-6
Max. hp—200
Axles—2
Wheels—6
Speeds—4
Service—tilt cab
Max. mph—95
Copyright © 1989 Publications International, Ltd.

20 City Service Police Car
21 Boat Collection Speedboat
22 U.S. Army CH-47D Chinook Helicopter
23 1965-66 Ford Mustang
24 Food Service Milk Semi-Tanker
25 1974-79 Chevrolet Corvette
26 U.S. Air Force B-1 Bomber
27 Pro Circuit Racers Formula 1 Special
28 Case Farm Tractor
29 1957 Chevrolet Bel Air
30 Highway Warriors Loader/Dozer
31 1961-65 Lincoln Presidential Limo
32 Off-Road Heavy Duty Sleeper Truck
33 1974-78 Pontiac Trans Am
34 Super 4x4 Jeep CJ-7
35 U.S. Air Force F-86D Sabre Fighter
36 1978-79 Porsche 928
37 X-29 Forward Swept Wing Fighter
38 1957 Ford Ranchero
39 1955 Chevrolet Corvette
40 1979-85 Mazda RX-7
41 German Messerschmitt 109--Bf109 F-2
42 1976-89 Jaguar XJ-S
43 Sun Color Changers Roller
44 Military "Marauder" Personnel Carrier
45 The Concorde Supersonic Transport
46 1970-71 Plymouth Hemi-Cuda
47 Race Team Flatabed Semi/Formula 1 Race Car
48 Sun Color Changers Chevrolet Corvette
49 1928-31 Ford Model A Roadster Pickup
50 Sun Color Changers Mercedes-Benz 450SLC
51 Helicopter Transport Truck
52 U.S. F-15 Eagle Fighter/Attack Aircraft
53 U.S. Army Bulldozer
54 Sun Color Changers 1979-85 Mazda RX-7
55 1961-74 Jaguar XKE Convertible
56 Construction Collection Crawler Dozer
57 1974-79 Chevrolet Corvette
58 1955-56 Ford Fairlane Crown Victoria 4x4
59 Apollo Lunar Rover Vehicle
60 1973-89 Army Chevrolet Blazer
61 1974-89 Lamborghini Countach
62 1987 Ford Thunderbird
63 Highway Warriors Savage Semi
64 1973-89 Chevrolet Blazer
65 1978-81 Chevrolet Camaro Z-28
66 Construction Collection Tractor/Loader
67 U.S. Air Force Stealth Bomber
68 Hot Bikes Ducati Pantah 750F1 Desmo

69 1984-90 Chevrolet Corvette
70 U.S. Coast Guard Patrol Boat
71 1957 Chevrolet Bel Air Nomad 4x4
72 1982-88 Audi Coupe GT
73 U.S. Army Air Corp #47B
74 Sun Color Changers 1955 Chevrolet Corvette
75 Highway Warriors Savage Semi
76 U.S. Army Medical Evacuation Vehicle
77 U.S. Army Air Corp P-51 Mustang Fighter
78 Classic Hot Rod
79 1971-89 De Tomaso Pantera
80 U.S. Air Force SR-71 Blackbird
81 Highway Warriors Savage Tank
82 1963 Ford Thunderbird Sports Roadster
83 City Service Tow Truck
84 1950 Lincoln Presidential Limo
85 U.S. Army Corp P-38 Lightning Fighter
86 Sun Color Changers Excavator
87 Apollo Lunar Command/Service Module
88 1972-81 Mercedes-Benz 450SLC
89 U.S. Navy F/4U Corsair Fighter
90 1974-78 Pontiac Trans Am
91 1980-90 Ford F-150 4x4 Pickup
92 1932 Packard Twin Six Convertible Sedan
93 Sun Color Changers 1957 Chevrolet Bel Air
94 U.S. Army UH-1 Iroquois Helicopter
95 Highway Warriors Savage Tank
96 1984-90 Chevrolet Corvette
97 1980-90 F-150 4x4 Pickup
98 Sun Color Changers Chevrolet Corvette
99 Curtiss Jenny Jn-4 or 6 World War I Trainer
100 Firefighters "Cherry Picker" Truck

Micro Machines

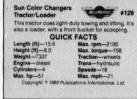

Sun Color Changers Tractor/Loader #129

This tractor does light-duty towing and lifting. It's also a loader, with a front bucket for scooping.

QUICK FACTS

Length (ft)—15.6	Max. rpm—2100
Height (ft)—8.0	Max. torque—158
Weight—7337	Traction—wheels
Engine—diesel	Trans—hydraulic
Cylinders—4	Speeds—18
Max. hp—51	Max. mph—21

Copyright © 1989 Publications International, Ltd.

The first really good, affordable small sports car since the Datsun 240Z. A two-seat hatchback coupe with unique German-designed Wankel rotary engine, improved by this Japanese company. Nimble, speedy, and tons of fun on twisty roads. Well built and very reliable, too.

QUICK FACTS

Length—108.7	Engine type—rotary	0-60 mph (sec)—8.2
Width—65.9	Size—70 cubic inches	0-1/4 mi (sec)—17.0
Height—48.6	Max. horsepower—100	Max. torque—103
Wheelbase—95.3	Max. torque—100	Max. mph—120

40

German Messerschmitt 109—Bf-109 F-2

One of the most famous aircraft of World War II, the German Messerschmitt 109 was one of the deadliest air-to-air combat planes in the Luftwaffe's inventory. The plane was heavily armored to take hits from British or American planes and was armed with a deadly accurate cannon that often cut enemy planes to pieces.

QUICK FACTS

Make—Messerschmitt	Engine—Daimler Benz	Weight—6173 pounds
Model—Bf-109	Size—V-12 liquid	Armament—2
Length—29.0	Max. horsepower—1200	machine guns
Wing span—32.6	Max. mph—373	1 15-mm cannon

41

MICRO MACHINES...Series 2

101 1974-89 Lamborghini Countach
102 F-4 Phantom Attack Aircraft
103 Hot Bikes BMW K100RS
104 Construction Collection Excavator
105 Firefighters Ladder Truck
106 1956 Ford F-100 Pickup
107 U.S. Navy Riverine Patrol Boat
108 Sun Color Changers 1955 Chevrolet Corvette
109 Highway Warriors Laser Raider
110 Lumberjacks Flatbed Logging Semi
111 1965-67 Chevrolet Corvette
112 German Fokker DR-1 Tri-Wing
113 1975-89 Ford E-150 4x4 Van
114 Turbo Wheels 1978-89 Porsche 928
115 1912-16 Ford Model T Runabout
116 Hot Bikes Yamaha Genesis
117 Sun Color Changers 1982-88 Audi Coupe GT
118 F-4 Phantom Attack Aircraft
119 1941 Willys 4x4 Pickup
120 1968-69 Pontiac GTO
121 1958-60 Ford Thunderbird Convertible
122 Case Self-Propelled Windrower
123 Sun Color Changers 1953-55 MG TF
124 Tugboat
125 Turbo Wheels 1971-89 DeTomaso Pantera
126 Long Range Missile Transport
127 1955-56 Ford Fairlane Crown Victoria
128 Sun Color Changers Concorde S.S.T.
129 Sun Colors Changers Tractor / Loader
130 1968-69 Pontiac GTO
131 Highway Warriors Oil Blaster
132 1956-57 Chevrolet Corvette
133 1979-85 Mazda RX-7
134 Race Team Semi
135 Sun Color Changers Plymouth Hemi-Cuda
136 1973-89 Chevrolet 4x4 Blazer
137 Apollo Lunar Landing Module
138 1983-89 Porsche 911 Turbo Cabriolet

139 U.S. Navy F/4U Corsair Fighter
140 1957 Chevrolet Bel Air Nomad
141 City Service Dump Truck
142 Sun Color Changers AH-1W "Super Cobra"
143 Sun Color Changers 1980-85 Renault 5 Turbo
144 U.S. Army M809 (6x6) Cargo Truck
145 1931 Bugatti Type 41
146 Sun Color Changers X-29 Forward Swept Wing
147 1984-90 Chevrolet Corvette
148 NASA 747 With Space Shuttle Orbiter
149 1975-85 Ferrari 308 GTB
150 1957 Ford Ranchero 4x4
151 Construction Collection Cement Mixer Truck
152 1955 Chevrolet Corvette
153 Turbo Wheels 1980-90 Ford F-150 Baja Pickup
154 U.S. Air Force F-15 Fighter / Attack Aircraft
155 1976-80 Plymouth Arrow "Funny Car"
156 U.S. Army Medical Evacuation Vehicle
157 1957 Chevrolet Bel Air
158 Japanese Zero Fighter
159 Turbo Wheels 1973-89 Chevrolet Blazer
160 1965-66 Ford Mustang
161 1976-89 Jaguar XJ-S
162 U.S. Navy SH-3 Sea King
163 1984-90 Chevrolet Corvette
164 1976-80 Jeep CJ-7
165 Pro Circuit Racers Formula 1 special
166 1956 Ford Thunderbird
167 Highway Warriors Oil Blaster
168 1984-86 Ford Mustang SVO
169 Food Service Produce Semi
170 1967-69 Chevrolet Camaro Z-28
171 Military Fast-Attack Jeep
172 Turbo Wheels 1982-88 Audi Coupe GT
173 1965 Lincoln Continental Convertible
174 1980-90 Ford F-150 4x4 Pickup
175 Air Corp B-17G Flying Fortress Bomber
176 Pro Circuit Racers 1987 Buick Regal Stock Car
177 U.S. Army Jeep (4x4) Light Vehicle
178 1957 Chevrolet Bel Air
179 Lumberjack Flatbed Logging Semi
180 Mercedes-Benz 450SLC
181 Classic Chop-Top V-8 Hot Rod
182 City Service Tow Truck
183 U.S. Air Force Stealth Bomber
184 Turbo Wheels 1979 Mazda RX-7
185 U.S. Army Medical Evacuation Vehicle
186 Sun Color Changers 1987 Ford Thunderbird
187 U.S. Navy F / A-18 Hornet
188 1975-89 Ford E-150 4x4 Van
189 1959 Chevrolet Impala Convertible
190 Boeing 747
191 1980-85 Renault 5 Turbo
192 Hot Bikes Kawasaki
193 1959 Cadillac Series 62 Convertible
194 U.S. Army Air Corp P-51 Mustang Fighter
195 1974-79 Chevrolet Corvette
196 U.S. Army M809 (6x6) Cargo Truck
197 1977-79 Lincoln Presidential Limousine
198 1976-80 Jeep CJ-7
199 1956 Ford 4x4 F-100 Pickup
200 U.S. Air Force B-1 Bomber

KIT INCLUDES:
100 Collectible MicroCards™
96 pages of hot Micro Machines

408

RETAILERS!

Are you cutting your profits in half . . .

because you're not selling trading cards by Rosem?

For over seven years, Rosem has been producing some of the most thrilling non-sports cards in the hobby. All of our trading cards are directed toward an older audience and are designed to keep card collectors on the edge of their seats. "Midnight Madness," a recent series of horror trading cards, featured full color artwork by the famous fantasy illustrator Alfredo Osorio. Non-Sport Update Magazine said of the card series, "[Midnight Madness] may certainly be the most popular horror set of the '90s ... Do not miss this set."

We don't hype our cards. We don't offer stickers. And we don't have autographed cards.

We just have cards with exciting, well-written stories and great illustrations; in other words, what non-sports cards should be.

Offer your customers trading cards by Rosem.

For a change.

Rosem Enterprises
P.O. Box 24701
Los Angeles, CA 90024
(310) 478-4699

© Rosem Enterprises

MIDNIGHT MADNESS (72)   2 1/2" X 3 1/2"

Hey there, Bunky. You're looking a mite jaded and bleary-eyed! So you just spent ten hours in a card convention staring at row after row of them new-fangled, high-tech trading cards. You say they all feel like plastic, that you're not interested in photos of dolls and kiddie show cartoon characters and comic books? You say they're turning you into a hobby zombie?? Well, Lugnut, stand up tall, get out the bass drum and strike up the band! It's time for a dose of good old-fashioned trading card artwork, something completely original, not mass-produced. It's time for a visit to The Old Undertaker and his

macabre tales of "Midnight Madness."

Six episodes comprise the set and each 12-card episode is packed in its own ghastly wrapper. The artwork fronts follow classic bubble gum card lines: great color, crisp white borders, and clear captions. The composition and layout of the card backs is simple but stylish. Rosem, the manufacturer, obviously took great pains to appeal to our memories of what it used to be like to collect cards.

The series was originally issued in 1990 and most buyers received their packs in a bag or envelope. For 1991, Rosem has added a sensational new

item: The Old Undertaker display box. In hobby circles, this has already become known as "THE BOX" through word of mouth. It measures an incredible 9" X 13" and features a startling pop-up display and six die-cut windows for viewing the packs inside. According to the manufacturer, each box takes nearly a half hour to assemble before it is shipped. Production of Midnight Madness sets in this special box was limited to 1000 units. Note: prices are listed for mint grade only. Rosem is planning a second series of Midnight Madness which will be sold in wax packs only (no collated sets will be available).

DESERT RATS
1 Drunken Joyride
2 Sacred Grounds
3 "Damn Rat!"
4 Valuable Discovery
5 "Smoke It, Chief!"
6 Splattered
7 The Crash
8 Trapped
9 Crawling Death
10 Rat Attack
11 Aftermath
12 Epilogue

JUNGLE PARASITE
1 The Search
2 "Shut Your Mouth!"
3 Strange Creature
4 Vicious Attack
5 Souvenir Photo
6 "Damn Bugs"
7 "An Allergic Reaction"
8 Infested Wound
9 The Blood Trail
10 Blasting the Creature
11 Jungle Insect
12 Epilogue

ROBOT KILLER
1 Mechanical Soldier
2 Renegade Robot
3 Deadly Weapon
4 Blasted!
5 Fighting Machines
6 Flame of Death
7 Damaged Robot
8 High Impact
9 Fatal Blow
10 Crushed to Death
11 "I Win Again"
12 Epilogue

SHROUD OF THE UNDEAD
1 Gruesome Experiment
2 Sudden Attack
3 The Plan
4 Cemetary Ghouls
5 City Under Siege
6 Bazooka Blast
7 Death in the Air
8 The Bounty Hunter
9 The Flamethrower
10 Defensive Action
11 Awake
12 Epilogue

THE PHARAOH'S REVENGE
1 Museum Visit
2 Digging for Treasure
3 The Lost Tomb
4 The Warning
5 The Death Mask
6 Impending Doom
7 Deadly Greed
8 Running to Safety
9 Blasting the Mummy
10 Machete Attack
11 No Escape
12 Epilogue

THE SURGEON
1 The Seminar
2 Violent Temper
3 The Research Continues
4 Unsuspecting Subjects
5 Midnight Delivery
6 Experimental Surgery
7 Escape
8 Unexpected Visitors
9 Silent Rage
10 Departure
11 The Creatures' Revenge
12 Epilogue

ITEM	MINT
Set in packs	25.00
Set in box	30.00

MIGHTY HERCULES TATTOOS (?)   1 9/16" X 3 3/8"

It is assumed that these tattoos were issued by Fleer in the mid-1960's although the wrapper bears a 1961 copyright date. The wrapper illustrated is blue with pink and black accents and white and black print. The Fleer crown logo is located beneath a set of instructions for applying the tattoos. The latter are tri-colored and are printed on the interior side of the wrapper. They are not numbered or systematically captioned and the length of the set is unknown.

ITEM	MINT	EX
Wrapper	--	10.00

MIGHTY HEROES TATTOOS (?)   1 9/16" X 3 3/8"

There are four different exterior wrapper designs reported for Fleer's "Mighty Heroes" tattoo series. The characters depicted front and back belong to the animated series developed for television by Terrytoons. Each wrapper carries a 1965 copyright date, instructions for applying the "transfers," and the Fleer crown logo. The tattoos on the interior sides of the wrappers are not captioned or numbered and the number in the set is not known.

ITEM	MINT	EX
Wrappers (4)		
each	--	7.50

MIGHTY MOUSE & HIS PALS (?) TATTOOS   1 5/8" X 3 1/2"

Topps produced this set based on the characters developed by Terrytoons, an antimated production division of CBS films. For some time, the Heckle and Jeckle wrapper illustrated in the 1988 volume of this guide was the only one known. It is red with yellow, black and gray accents. The second wrapper pictured here was recently discovered by John Neuner. It is mostly yellow with red, black, green and gray details. The multi-color tattoos on the interior sides are not numbered or captioned and the set total has yet to be determined. The wrappers carry no production codes, which indicates that the series was distributed prior to the summer of 1966.

ITEM	MINT	EX
Wrappers (2),		
each	--	15.00

MIGHTY MOUSE — THE NEW ADVENTURES (6)

2 1/2" X 3 1/2"

As you can see by the illustration, the cartoon artwork of this Mighty Mouse set, produced for distribution in Wendy's kid meals in 1989, is very lush and well-designed. The character is named at the top of every card; a Wendy's logo and the set title are printed opposite one another in the bottom corners. The backs have a basic format with sections giving details about the character and there is a small black and white drawing at the bottom. A line also advises that there are six trading cards in the set (and six "clinger characters" toys to match). The cards are actually printed on glossy paper, rather than cardboard stock, and they are not numbered. The values below reflect the limited supplies indicated by the manner and length of the promotion.

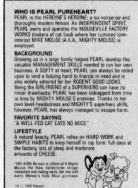

ITEM	MINT	EX
Set	7.00	3.50
Card	1.00	.50

MILITARY EMBLEMS (24)

SIZE UNKNOWN

Here is one of those sets that just zipped on by and nobody noticed. It is a series of Military Emblems made of fabric and designed to "iron on sweaters and shirts." Two emblems were packed in every 25-count, specially-marked box of Bazooka Gum for as long as the promotion ran in 1964. Luckily for us, Topps decided to print pictures of all 24 emblems in color on the back panel of the box, thereby providing us with a checklist which might have otherwise been very difficult to obtain. To show just how much things have changed since 1964, the price of this box and gum was 19 cents!

ITEM	MINT	EX
Set	60.00	45.00
Emblem	2.00	1.50
Box	--	15.00

MILTON THE MONSTER (?) AND FEARLESS FLY

1 9/16" X 3 3/8"

Another tattoo set distributed by Fleer. The one wrapper design reported is white with blue and orange accents and bears a 1967 copyright line for Hal Seeger Productions. The multi-colored tattoos on the interior sides are not numbered or captioned.

ITEM	MINT	EX
Wrapper	––	10.00

MINIATURE COMIC BOOK (6) COLLECTION

2 3/8" X 3 5/8"

Amurol Products marketed the "Miniature Comic Book Collection" in 1981. The comic books were packaged in clear cellophane wraps with a piece of gum inside. There are six different titles in the set and each comic is numbered on the cover. The stories occupy ten numbered pages and the books are center-stapled.

ITEM	MINT	EX
Set	7.00	5.00
Comic	1.00	.75
Box	––	5.00

1 The Amazing Spiderman
2 The Incredible Hulk
3 Captain America
4 Spider-Woman
5 Archie
6 Sabrina The Teen-Age Witch

MINI STICKERS & NUTTY TICKETS (? &24)　TWO SIZES

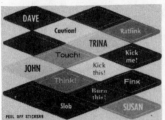

A two-part set issued by Topps in 1968. Each 5-cent pack contained two 16-sticker sheets and one attached pair of "Nutty Tickets." The 16 front-peel stickers on each 2 1/2" X 3 1/2" sheet have various names, words, and phrases printed on several geometric shapes. A pair of cardboard Nutty Tickets meas-

ures 2 1/2" X 4 3/4"; singles are 1 1/4" X 4 3/4". Each ticket is numbered and there are 24 in the set (some tickets are paired in different combinations). Note: no set price given for stickers since length of set is unknown. Detached tickets cannot be graded mint.

ITEM	MINT	EX
Sticker	2.00	1.50
Tickets		
single	--	1.50
pair	5.00	4.00
Wrapper	--	15.00

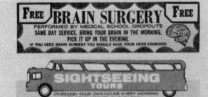

1 Dog Show
2 Inventor's Show
3 Beauty Contest
4 Three Ring Circus
5 Horror Show
6 Antique Show
7
8 Heavyweight Championship
9 Spelling Contest
10 Bus Pass
11 Computer Dating Card
12 Insurance Discount
13 Wrestling Match
14 Free Brain Surgery
15 Fire Sale!
16 Sightseeing Tours
17 Weight Lifting
18
19 Symphony Orchestra
20 Rock n' Roll Concert
21 Alligator Wrestling
22 Art Exhibit
23 Masquerade Party
24 TV Service

MINI—TOONS (12)　　　　3 1/8" X 5 1/4"

Although both the box and The wrapper for this set carry the title "Magic Rub-offs," only the words "Mini-Toons"

appear on the folders themselves. The latter open to 5 1/4" X 6 1/4" and are accompanied by a 2 7/16" X 4 7/8" sheet of "dry transfers" designed to be affixed to the folder scene by following simple directions. There are twelves different folders in the set, which was produced in England by Letraset for Topps. The year of issue was 1970. Note: folders with transfers applied cannot be graded mint.

ITEM	MINT	EX
Set	80.00	65.00
Mini-toon	6.00	5.00
Wrapper	--	15.00
Box	--	40.00

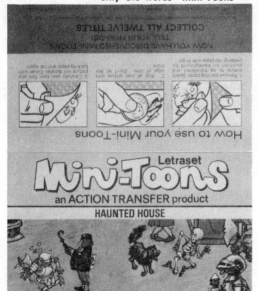

MINNIE 'n ME (160)

Catching Snowflakes

Havin' Fun....

Lacy snowflakes pass my window,
Gently falling to the ground.
I run out and try to catch them,
Watch them land without a sound.

Snowflakes decorate my mittens,
Much too soon they'll disappear.
I'll be sad when they've all melted,
But right now. I'm glad they're here!

©The Walt Disney Company

Catching Snowflakes

2 1/2" X 3 1/2"

Traditional card collectors may question the appeal of a trading card set geared exclusively to little girls, but that's exactly what Impel intended with this 1991 series of "Minnie 'n Me." The cards show strong production values: great color, glossy surfaces, beautiful artwork, and well-composed text which follows specific themes. The first nine cards in the set have characters on one side and puzzle pieces with borders on the other (the borders are NOT meant to be cut away to form the puzzle). Thereafter, the cards run in sequence through five different categories: Heartfelt Moments (10-27), Havin' Fun (28-90), School Days (91-108), Fun Trips (109-144), and Busy Days (145-158). The last two cards in the set are checklists and there is an additional card which is nothing more than an order form for a "Minnie 'n Me Collector Cards Special Poster." The whole set, in effect, is a deck of activity cards designed to keep young hands and minds engaged. This may not attract many adult collectors, but it will delight the kids.

ITEM	MINT	EX
Set	15.00	10.00
Card	.10	.07
Wrapper	––	.15
Box	––	2.00

1 Minnie	11 Open Presents	21 Visiting Grandma	30 Playing With Friends
2 Daisy	12 Make a Wish	22 Pets	31 Hopscotch
3 Minnie's Pet	13 Tea Party	23 Pet Show	32 Paper Dolls
4 Daisy's Pet	14 Slumber Party	24 My Favorite Pet	33 Dancing
5 Clarabelle	15 Vacations	25 New Sister	34 Jumping Rope
6 Heather	16 Mother's Day	26 Helping Hand	35 Jump Rope Song
7 Patti	17 Father's Day	27 Welcome to the	36 Jumping Rope with
8 T.J.	18 Trick or Treat	Neighborhood	Minnie's Pet
9 Lilly	19 Easter Egg Hunt	28 Cooking	37 On the Phone
10 Birthday Party	20 Valentine's Day	29 Dressing Up	38 Dominoes

Minnie 'n Me

39 Hide and Seek
40 Play House
41 Watching T.V.
42 Drawing
43 Dolls
44 Painting
45 Jigsaw Puzzle
46 Collecting Stamps
47 Music
48 Tennis
49 Softball
50 Swimming
51 Sleds
52 Snowmen
53 Playing in the Leaves
54 Sandcastles
55 Collecting Seashells
56 Camp
57 Climbing Trees
58 Pillow Fight
59 Butterflies
60 Bikes
61 Swings
62 Seesaw
63 Jungle Gym
64 Rain Puddles
65 Picking Flowers
66 Cartwheels
67 Somersaults
68 Kickball
69 Playing Store
70 Jacks
71 Marbles
72 Checkers
73 Hand Games
74 Picking Apples
75 Hula Hoop
76 Newspaper Hats
77 Clubhouse
78 Treehouse
79 Skipping
80 Playing Leap Frog
81 Leap Frog Fun
82 Feeding Pigeons
83 Sailing Boats
84 Handshadows
85 Dollhouse
86 Kites
87 Tag
88 Picnic
89 Ice Skating
90 Catching Snowflakes
91 Arts and Crafts
92 Gym

93 School Bus
94 Apple for the Teacher
95 Writing
96 Arithmetic
97 School Plays
98 Music Class
99 Storytime
100 Telling Time
101 Lunch
102 Recess
103 Reading
104 Making New Friends
105 Show and Tell
106 First Day at School
107 Ballet
108 My Locker
109 Off to the Zoo
110 Zoo Animals
111 At the Zoo
112 Circus
113 Feeding the Elephants
114 Under the Big Top
115 Farm
116 In the Barn
117 Barnyard Animals
118 Hayride
119 Movies
120 Shopping for Clothes
121 Amusement Park
122 Water Slide
123 Bumper Cars
124 Country Fair
125 Toy Store
126 Camp
127 Ice Cream Parlor
128 Puppet Show
129 Magic Show
130 Beach
131 Fun in the Surf
132 Swimming Hole
133 Pet Store
134 Restaurant
135 Candy Store
136 Aquarium
137 Boardwalk
138 Country
139 Planetarium
140 Fireworks Display
141 Bar-B-Que
142 Park
143 Summer in the Park
144 Lunch in the Park
145 Stretching
146 Jumping Jacks

147 Exercise Class
148 Receive a Letter
149 Write a Letter
150 Mailing a Litter
151 Bathing Pets
152 Waking Up
153 Pick a Dress

154 Getting Dressed
155 Bubble Bath
156 Setting the Table
157 Help Clean
158 Gardening
159 Checklist
160 Checklist

MOD GENERATION STICKERS (55)   2 1/2'' X 4 11/16''

The "Hippie" generation was the subject of this Topps test set thought to have been issued in 1965 or '66. The fronts contain diecut stickers of various "mod" individuals dressed in outlandish clothes. Each person is named and the sticker number and a Topps copyright line are printed out-side the score line. The backs are devoid of printing and the 5-cent wrapper is actually a large sticker affixed to white wax paper.

ITEM	MINT	EX
Set	650.00	500.00
Sticker	10.00	7.50
Wrapper	--	75.00

1 Alice
2
3 Susan
4 Ray
5 Phil
6 Ann
7 Diane

8 Dave
9
10 Fay
11 Barbara
12 Teddy
13 John
14

15 Paul
16 Helen
17 Pete
18 Fred
19 Jimmy
20 Irv
21 George

22 Millie
23 Jerry
24 Rose
25
26 Louis
27 Natalie
28 Ellen

29
30 Jackie
31 Herb
32 Dotty
33 Shelly
34 Michael
35 Donna

36 Mary
37
38
39 Minda
40
41 Marie
42 Nancy

43 Connie
44 Tony
45 Richard
46 Judy
47 Joe
48
49 Frances

50 Larry
51
52
53
54 Esther
55 Chris

MOD INITIALS (?)

2 1/2" X 3 1/2"

Although conclusive proof has not yet been obtained, it appears that "Mod Initial Stickers" are identical to the "Love Initials" set described earlier in this book (Love Initials issued in 1969; Mod Initials in 1972). The front-peel stickers are diecut letters, numbers, or punctuation marks "filled" with flower artwork. They are not numbered and the length of this Topps set is unknown.

ITEM	MINT	EX
Sticker	1.50	1.00
Wrapper	––	15.00

MOD SQUAD (55)

The Mod Squad card is easily identified by its pink and purple borders. The color photos, selected from the TV show and from publicity stills, are surrounded by white frame lines. Each card is captioned in a red panel below the picture.

2 1/2" X 3 1/2"

The numbered backs are puzzle pieces. Topps issued the set (55 cards) in 1969.

ITEM	MINT	EX
Set	125.00	95.00
Card	2.00	1.50
Wrapper	––	35.00
Box	––	75.00

1 Campsite Meeting!
2 Taking Cover!
3 A New Assignment!
4 Pete's Plan!
5 The Decision!
6 Julie in Disguise!
7 A Familiar Face!
8 Mod Photographer!
9 Pete and Linc Undercover!
10 Julie's Report
11 Planning a Trap!
12 Bewildered Girl!
13 Attacked!
14 The Beating
15 Floored!
16 The Final Blow
17 Comforting Words!
18 Pete's Scheme!
19 On the Beach!
20 Sunbathing Detective!
21 Illegal Entry!
22 Important Discovery!
23 Escape!
24 "Stop or I'll Shoot!"
25 Under Arrest!
26 Disturbed Detectives!
27 Reunion!
28 Final Instructons!
29 Countdown Hour!
30 Trouble Brewing!
31 Riot!
32 The Protesters!
33 Happy Trio!
34 Show Time!
35 Theater Night!
36 At the Museum!
37 A New Caper!
38 Police Doctor!
39 At the Zoo!
40 Taking a Break!
41 Pete's Bag!
42 Julie Unwinds
43 Capt. Adam Greer
44 Linc Hayes
45 Miss Lipton's Day Off
46 Rich Rebel
47 The "In" Crowd
48 Mod Squad's Mentor
49 Hippie Cop
50 Mr. Clarence Williams III
51 Miss Peggy Lipton
52 Mr. Michael Cole
53 Lady Cop
54 The Mod Squad
55 Young Detectives

MONKEES (44)

2 1/2" X 3 1/2"

This series of 44 cards with sepia-tone photographs was the first Monkees set issued by Donruss in 1966. The cards have white borders on the front with a small red "Monkees" logo and facsimile autograph in the picture area. The backs are puzzle pieces. The card number is located in the bottom left corner on the obverse.

ITEM	MINT	EX
Set	125.00	100.00
Card	2.50	2.00
Wrapper	––	15.00
Box	––	75.00

MONKEES—SERIES A (44) B (44) C (44) 2 1/2" X 3 1/2"

The success of the sepia Monkees set prompted Donruss to upgrade to color photos in the next three Monkees issues. The "A" series of 44 cards, with white borders and a black panel, was issued in 1966 in the same box as the sepia series, but with a "2nd Series featuring color photos" sticker affixed to the lid. The "B" series -yellow borders and red panel- used the same box with a "3rd Series" sticker attached (also issued in '66). The "C" series cards have deep pink frame lines front and back and were issued in 1967 in the completely new "More of the Monkees" packaging.

ITEM	MINT	EX
Series (3) each	125.00	100.00
Cards - all	2.50	2.00
Wrappers (3)		
"A"	--	15.00
"B"	--	25.00
"C"	--	8.00
Boxes (3)		
"A" ["2nd"]	--	65.00
"B" ["3rd"]	--	65.00
"C" ["More"]	--	35.00

MONKEES BADGES (44)

2 1/2" X 3 1/2"

To complement its four regular card issues featuring the Monkees, Donruss produced this "novelty" set in 1967. The "badges" are diecut front-peel stickers in the shape of "award ribbons." They are not numbered but every picture has a caption in the "ribbon tails" (which come in different colors). The stickers are mounted on thin white cardboard stock; the backs are blank.

A Gaser	I'm a Monkee Fan	Mike for Me	Real Cool
A Gaser	I Dig Davy	Mike for Me	Real Class
Cool Man	I Flip for Micky	Mike Is Mine Forever	The In Groupe
Davy Baby	I Like Mike	Mike Is Mine Forever	They're Tough
Davy for President	I Love 'Em	Monkees Forever	The Merry Men
Davy Is a Darling	Micky Is a Swinger	Monkees Forever	The Swingers
Davy Is Devine	Micky Is Mine	My Monkee	Think Monkees
Dreamsville	Micky Is Mine	Peter for Principal	Tough
Dynamic Duo	Micky Tickles Me Pink	Peter Is Great	Tough
Dynamic Duo	Mighty Micky	Peter Is Precious	Yea Monkees
Fabulous Four	Mighty Micky	Real Cool	Yea, Yea, Yea

ITEM	MINT	EX
Set	200.00	150.00
Badge	4.00	3.00
Wrapper	--	10.00
Box	--	75.00

MONKEES FLIP MOVIES (16)

2 7/16" X 3 1/2"

Topps got into the Monkee business by issuing this series of 16 "flipbooks" in 1967. Each booklet is numbered and captioned on the front in a television set, the screen of which shows a picture from the sequence of photos inside. The book can be "flipped" from the front (an action sequence) or from the back (a square in which "The Monkees" becomes surrounded by the individual band member's names).

ITEM	MINT	EX
Set	120.00	100.00
Movie	6.00	5.00
Wrapper	--	10.00
Box	--	50.00

1 Pie-Eyed Monkee
2 Four Big Wheels
3 Singing Cyclists
4 Monkeying On A Motor-Bike
5 Geared For Action
6 The Swinger
7 Skateboard To Clarkesville
8 Monkee Matador
9 On Stage
10 Beauties and The Beast
11 Feather-Weight Champ
12 The Monkee Salute
13 The Big Build-Up
14 Davy's Workout
15 The Big Headache
16 Monkey-Shines

MONKEY SHINES (?)

1 5/8" X 3 3/8"

This series of jokes revolving around the lesser primates was first reported to The Card Collectors Bulletin in June, 1971 (it was assigned catalog number R757-9). The measurements in the heading refer to the entire back panel of the "Junior Mints" box since that is the most natural way for this design to be converted into a "card." Each joke is numbered, but there is no mention anywhere of the length of set. Furthermore, it is not known if "Monkey Shines" were also printed on "Pom Poms" boxes of the same period. The answer to each joke was printed on the left closing flap; once that was removed, or the card cut away, the punch line had to be memorized or left to the imagination. As you can see by the illustration, the series was not advertised on the front of the box, making it likely that fewer of these cards and boxes have survived than those from Nabisco sets that had advertising to attract the customer. Note: individual cards cannot be graded mint.

ITEM	MINT	EX
Card	--	2.00
Box	10.00	7.50

MONOGRAM MODELS CARDS (23K)   2 1/2" X 3 1/2"

Aurora, Revell, Testor, and Monogram are four manufacturers of plastic model kits which, in the words of Tom Reed, "took a shot" at producing trading cards in the 1960's and 1970's. These Monogram Models cards of cars were apparently inserted into the kit boxes along with the plastic parts; some may have been

Badman [6747]
Baja Bandito [6759]
Beer Wagon [6736]
Boss "A" Bone [6755]
Boss Mustang [6786]
Cherry Bomb [6761]
Dragon Wagon [6746]
Dune Rat [6784]
Ice "T" [6757]
Li'l Coffin [6749]
Patty Wagon [6741]
Pie Wagon [6738]
Red Baron [6740]
Rommel's Rod [6745]
Sand Crab [6748]
Screamin' Vette [6785]
S'Cool'Bus [6781]
Son of Ford [6754]
Street Fighter [6752]
Swee"T"ee [6756]
Tarantula [6737]
Thunder Bug [6783]
Tijuana Taxi [6743]

stapled to the instruction sheet since they are occasionally found with staple holes in the cardboard. All have multi-color artwork pictures, without captions or any other printing, on the front. The backs contain the name of the car plus a long paragraph describing it. The card in our illustration also has a black & white photo of Tom Daniel on the reverse, and from all reports, this photo appears on every card. In a sense, the cards are numbered by the kit model number listed on the reverse, but we have assembled them alphabetically in our checklist (the kit number is printed in brackets). There are 51 different kit numbers in the span between the first and last cards reported (6736-6786), but only 23 titles have actually been confirmed. Note: cards with staple holes or with scotch tape on them cannot be graded excellent or mint.

ITEM	MINT	EX
Card	3.50	2.50

MONSTER CARDS (84)   2 1/2" X 3 1/2"

If you were looking for a set to use as an example of how trading cards SHOULD NOT be done, "Monster Cards" would be a likely choice. The pictures look like they were photo-copied from magazines and newspapers, the captions were obviously printed on a typewriter with a bad ribbon, and the jokes on back are cornier than Green Giant niblets. Add a blue color which covers the front of the cards like a bad dye job, and what do you get? A darn interesting set of monster cards which has intrigued collectors for years! Some point to the similarities between this set and the Horror Monsters series issued by Nu-Cards as evidence that this blue-tint set may be the

very first Nu-Card set ever issued. That may never be proved since these cards have absolutely no identifying marks and no packaging for them has ever been confirmed. Some cards, #10 and #36 for example, also appear in the "Horror Monster" series. Monster Cards are often found in excellent or "new" condition and collectors are advised that some of the apparent imperfections, like miscut cards, may actually result from the cards not being straight on the original sheet (in other words, they were cut properly but were out of alignment in the first place).

ITEM	MINT	EX
Set	210.00	155.00
Card	2.00	1.50

1 Now Where Was I?
2 Curse of the Faceless Man
3 Gets Me Right Here
4 Bride and the Beast
5 Gramma Will Get You a Cookie
6 Somebody Done This
7 Angry Red Planet
8 Invasion of Saucermen
9 The Golem
10 Haunted Stranger
11 Look Ma — No Feet
12 I Smoke Filter Tips
13 Who's a Cabbagehead?
14 The Mysterians
15 You're Cute Too
16 You're Not My Mummy!
17 Curse of the Mummy
18 Like Man I'm Tired
19 Fiend Without a Face
20 Speak Up, Boy!
21 Mad Soul
22 Hunchback of Notre Dame

23 Here Kitty Kitty!!
24 Phantom of the Opera
25 Hideous Sun Demon
26 It's Only the Avon Lady!
27 Jack the Ripper
28 Look, Pa — No Cavities
29 The Savage Eye
30 Really, Old Chap —
31 I Hate Milk
32 The Deadly Mantis
33 Brain from Planet Arous
34 Don't You Dare Touch Me!!
35 13 Ghosts
36 The Mutant
37 Rodan
38 From Tarantula
39 House of Wax
40 The Tingler
41 Find It Fast in the Yellow Pages
42 I'm Starved
43 Queen of Outer Space

44 Wanna Rassle?
45 Guess Who's Winning?
46 The Blob
47 Hold Still, Now ...
48 You Ain't So Cute Either!
49 Cool It, Man —
50 You've Got Bad Breath
51 Monster From Outer Space
52 Squares Dancing
53 Attack of the Green Leeches
54 I Like Kids (well done)
55 House of Haunted Hill
56 Sinbad the Sailor
57 I Need Vitamins
58 Too Much Pizza, Mom!
59 Fly Now — Play Later
60 I'm Going Batty!!
61 Meanwhile, Back at the Swamp
62 Monster From Green Hell
63 I'm Getting Sick!
64 "Cheese"
65 Strange Earthling

66 You're My Boy
67 The Electronic Monster
68 I'll Carve the Turkey
69 Terror from the Year 5000
70 Dig That Crazy Grasshopper!!
71 Where's That DDT?!
72 Do I Know You?
73 That's One Way to Get Ahead
74 Return of the Vampire
75 Monster on the Campus
76 Shall We Dance?
77 I Smoke Marijuana
78 Satan Satellites
79 The Undead
80 From Hell It Came
81 Blood of Dracula
82 Will It Hurt, Doc? Naw, I'm Just Shrinking Your Head!
83 Aw, Let's Be Friends
84 Sure Beats Stamp Collecting

MONSTER FLIP MOVIES (36)

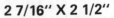

Universal Pictures provided the photos for the "Monster Flip Movies" series produced by Topps in 1963. The flip-books came attached in pairs -a "Monster Double Feature"- in each 5-cent pack. They have 32 pages and are numbered and titled on the red-print cover. The wrapper is black and yellow with a red title. Note: single (separated) books cannot be graded mint.

ITEM	MINT	EX
Sets		
singles	--	260.00
pairs	350.00	300.00
Flipbooks		
singles	--	6.00
pair	16.00	14.00
Wrapper	--	75.00
Box	--	200.00

1 Death Struggle	13 Hurled into the Pool	25 The Club of Frankenstein
2 Futile Battle	14 Electric Shock	26 Frankenstein on the Alert
3 The Mummy Awakens	15 Captured by the Creature	27 Night Attack
4 The Creature Emerges	16 Struggle under the Water	28 Frankenstein Goes Wild
5 The Mummy's Wrath	17 Frankenstein Takes a Bride	29 Anger of the Wolfman
6 No Escape	18 Fiend of the Forest	30 Frankenstein in Hiding
7 Charging the Brute	19 Underwater Combat	31 The Mummy's Master
8 Attack by Fire	20 The Wolfman Goes Berserk	32 Frankenstein Cries Out
9 Frankenstein Attacks	21 Frankenstein's Fight	33 Rage of the Creature
10 The Wolfman Strikes	22 Death of the Wolfman	34 Stalking New Prey
11 Fight to the Finish	23 Here Comes Frankenstein	35 Undersea Menace
12 Kidnapped by Frankenstein	24 The Wolfman Fights Frankenstein	36 The Creature's Capture

MONSTER GREETING CARDS (50) 2 1/2" X 3 1/2"

Topps came up with a monstrous idea in 1965: make a card with a comic art front and a monster punch-line back. The result was this 50-card set of Monster Greeting Cards. The set title does not appear on the cards but is taken instead from the wrapper. The cards are numbered on the back.

ITEM	MINT	EX
Set	90.00	60.00
Card	1.50	1.00
Wrapper	--	45.00
Box	--	150.00

1 I Need You/Like a Hole in the Head!
2 Stay Just Like You Are/Spooky
3 You Have Beautiful Hair!/Whose is it?
4 I Love Your Beautiful Eyes/All Four Of Them!!
5 You Have A Peach Of A Complexion/Hairy!
6 There'll Never Be Another You/Thank Goodness!
7 You're The Caveman Type/Hairy and Ugly
8 Take Me in Your Arms/All Four Of Them
9 If We Combined Your Brains And My Looks.../We'd Make A Stupid Monster!
10 When I Grow Up I'll Be Like You!/Old And Ugly!

11 I Love When You Smile!/I Love Fangs!
12 I Keep Your Picture in My Room./To Scare Off Ghosts
13 I Think Of You As An Old Friend/Very Old!
14 I Dig You/But I Dug Too Far!
15 You've Always Said "Two Heads Are Better Than One."/And You Ought To Know!
16 You Have The Skin I Love to Touch/And Clutch!
17 ...if I Were You.../I'd Do Something About It!
18 I Like Tall Slim Fellows/But You're Too Much!
19 I Love You Because You're Different/Ugh! So Different!
20 I'd Like to Go Out With You/When They Clean You Cage!
21 I Was At A Monster Bazaar/And I Won You!
22 You May Not Be Handsome or Brilliant.../But Nobody's Perfect!
23 You Deserve A Big Hand/Right Across Your Face!
24 You'd Be A Lot Of Fun/If You Were Alive!
25 I Like You/But I Have Strange Tastes!
26 I'd Like To Gaze Into Your Eyes!/if I Could Find The Other One
27 I'd Like To Give You A Big Squeeze/(Woman's Head in Vise)
28 I've Got You Where I Want You/in The Palm Of My Hand!
29 You're A Great Kid/Strange, But Great!
30 When I'm Next To You../Even I Look Good!

31 You Do A Great Twist/At Least Your Nose Does!
32 Come Over To My House/I'd Love To Have You For Dinner!
33 You Look Like A Million Dollars/All Green And Wrinkled!
34 When I Look At You I Can Only Do One Thing!/Run!
35 Isn't it Great To Be Alive?/But How Would You Know?
36 I Admire Your Brains/Whose Are They?
37 You Really Use Your Head/Who Else Would Want To?
38 There's Only One Thing I'd Rather Do Than Go Out With You/Kill Myself
39 Let's Go Out Saturday Night.../We'll Use Your Broom!
40 I'm Ape Over You/Real Ape!
41 You're Out Of This World/Stay There!
42 I'd Love To Visit You!/What's Your Crypt Number?
43 You Have A Great Heart/Too Bad There's A Stake in it!
44 You Do Something To Me/You Make Me Sick!
45 When I'm With You.../I Lose My Head!
46 When I'm With You I Don't Know If I'm Coming Or Going.../No Wonder!
47 Congratulations! You Have Only One Cavity!/In Your Head!
48 Let's Go Out Saturday Night/I'll Bring The Leash
49 If You Work Your Fingers To The Bone, What Do You Get?/Bony Fingers
50 You're Just What The Doctor Ordered/A Shock Treatment!

MONSTER INITIAL STICKERS (132 & 9) 2 1/2" X 3 1/2"

Although the wrapper carries a 1973 production code, Topps did not release "Monster Initial Stickers" to the public until 1974. Two diecut front-peel stickers, in the shape of letters or punctuation marks, are mounted on every card. Each sticker shape contains an artwork monster, many of which are repeated in combination with other letters. There are 132 different letter combinations reported in the set. In addition, there are nine cards with color puzzle piece fronts and a black ink puzzle sketch on back. Note: set price includes all stickers and a complete puzzle. Letter pairs that are repeated in the checklist have different picture combinations.

ITEM	MINT	EX
Set	160.00	55.00
Sticker	1.25	1.00
Card	.75	.50
Wrapper	--	3.00
Box	--	30.00

C-X	G-L	I-A	M-N	R-I	T-!	W-U
C-Y	G-O	I-E	M-T	R-J	U-A	W-X
E-A	G-S	I-K	M-!	R-S	U-E	Z-E
E-A	G-!	I-N	Q-A	R-T	U-I	Z-K
E-D	H-E	I-Y	Q-E	R-U	U-O	Z-N
E-I	H-I	I-!	Q-L	T-A	U-P	Z-P
E-I	H-N	M-A	Q-O	T-O	U-V	Z-T
E-I	H-O	M-E	Q-S	T-P	W-E	Z-Y
E-L	H-V	M-I	Q-V	T-T	W-I	?-A
E-N	H-!	M-K	R-A	T-V	W-O	?-D
E-O					W-S	?-E
E-O						?-I
E-P						?-J
E-P						?-S
E-S						
E-S						
E-T						
E-U						
E-X						
E-Y						
F-I						
F-K						
F-V						
F-Y						
F-!						
G-A						
G-J						

A-A	A-P	A-Y	B-O	C-E
A-D	A-P	A-!	B-S	C-J
A-E	A-S	B-A	B-T	C-J
A-I	A-S	B-A	B-U	C-K
A-K	A-T	B-E	B-X	C-L
A-N	A-V	B-I	B-Y	C-L
A-O	A-V	B-K	C-D	C-O
A-O	A-X	B-N	C-D	C-U

MONSTER IN MY POCKET (48 & 22) 2 1/2" X 3 1/2"

"In February 1991, Matchbook Toys introduced a new collectible line of miniature monster figures to their retail trade. These toys have been released as a limited edition series featuring 48 of the greatest monsters of all time - each with their own legend and lore. The monster toys have each been assigned a point value which is based on their respective strengths and weaknesses. The more powerful "25 point" monsters are rarer than the more common "5 and 10 point" monsters. This feature enhances gaming, trading, and collecting among the target audience." [from Monster In My Pocket Facts and Information, The Source Group, Inc., April 1991.]

The Source Group, a Dallas-based marketing firm, obtained an exclusive license from the Morrison Entertainment Group to create a card set based on the MIMP theme. The series consists of 48 cards and 24 stickers. The cards have multi-color artwork depictions of monsters on the front, with each subject named in large red print. The heading and text on the reverse is framed by a beautiful and intriguing design. The stickers, once assembled correctly, form a 24-piece puzzle picture called "Monster Island," which is rendered in a different style of artwork than that which appears on the cards. Sticker backs contain either a card checklist (according to point values) or a "sticker placement grid." The set was issued in poly bag wrappers holding six cards and two stickers each, with a suggested retail price of 59 cents.

There are two points you should understand about the cards. The monster figures which they are intended to complement were marketed with built-in scarcities: monsters with lower point values (5 & 10) are more common than those with higher point values (15-20-25). The cards are also marked with point values BUT they all appear to have been produced in the same quantities. Secondly, the cards that come in the poly bag wrappers are not numbered; MIMP cards WITH numbers were issued in a promotion with K-Mart and were also

Monster in my Pocket

sent out as preview cards before regular card production began. Given the nature of the non-sport market, it is not likely that the number/no number variations will have much effect on value. Note: we have provided a checklist of the numbered version for those collectors who are trying to assemble a set of this type. There is no sticker checklist since they do not have captions.

ITEM	MINT	EX
Set	12.00	9.00
Card	.15	.10
Sticker	.25	.20
Wrapper	---	.15

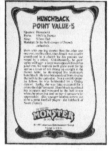

NUMBER ON BACK	COMMON OBVERSE	NO NUMBER ON BACK

1 Great Beast	25 Redcap
2 Hydra	26 Medusa
3 Werewolf	27 Goblin
4 Behemoth	28 Ceberus
5 Griffin	29 Zombie
6 Tyrannosaurus Rex	30 Chimera
7 Cockatrice	31 Ghost
8 Cyclops	32 Hobgoblin
9 Tengu	33 Vampire
10 Triton	34 Roc
11 Kraken	35 Gremlin
12 Jotun Troll	36 Vampiress
13 The Monster	37 Ghoul
14 Manticore	38 The Phantom
15 Karnak	39 Mad Scientist
16 Coatlicue	40 Winged Panther
17 Bigfoot	41 Mummy
18 Baba Yaga	42 Charon
19 Kali	43 The Beast
20 Catoblepas	44 Witch
21 Harpy	45 Spring-Heeled Jack
22 Haniver	46 Invisible Man
23 Ogre	47 Skeleton
24 Windigo	48 Hunchback

MONSTER LAFFS (MIDGEE) (153)   1 9/16" X 2 1/2"

American International Pictures provided the black & white photos for this gallery of monsters issued by Topps in 1963. The cards came packaged in strips of three in a large 5-cent wrapper. Each card has a humorous caption beneath the picture and is numbered in a tombstone design on the back. There are 153 cards in the set. Note: single (separated) cards cannot be graded mint. Panels are valued at the sum of the individual cards plus 25%.

ITEM	MINT	EX
Set	---	250.00
Cards		
1-108	---	1.00
109-153	---	2.50
Wrapper	---	75.00
Box	---	250.00

Monster Laffs (Midgee)

1 Please Show Me to My Room.
2 Want the Name of the Hairdresser?
3 My Ice Cream Melted.
4 Got a 25 Room Apartment for Me?
5 Yoo Hoo, Guess Who's Here!
6 Oh, My Gosh, Dandruff.
7 Nice Puppy!
8 This Beach Used to Be So Crowded.
9 I Stayed in My Bath Too Long.
10 I Lose My Head at Parties.
11 Anyone for a Dip?
12 When We Get a Head Ache, It's a Beauty!!
13 My Tummy Feels Empty.
14 Want to Buy Girl Scout Cookies?
15 Best False Teeth I Ever Had.
16 Mother Please, I'd Rather Do It Myself.
17 Anybody Home?
18 I'll Monkey Around Here a While.
19 Gosh, It's Past My Bedtime!!
20 It Tickles!!
21 Horsepower? I Don't See Horses.
22 When a Dragon Hiccups It Really Burns.
23 I'm the New Truck Inspector.
24 That's Funny My Watch Says (11:30).
25 I'll Crash This Party.
26 He Looks Comfortable.
27 I Got Something in My Eye.
28 Can I Get a Manicure.
29 Let's Stop Playing Leapfrog.
30 I'm Just Falling Apart.
31 Shake Hands Like a Man.
32 Call Me if There's a Full Moon.
33 I Got Some Dentist!!
34 Mommy, I Had a Nightmare.
35 You Should See Me When I'm Angry.
36 Whose the Brains of This Outfit?
37 How Did You Know It Was Poison Ivy?
38 What a Case of Dishpan Hands.
39 I'm a Restless Sleeper.
40 Don't Move, There's a Bug on Your Coat.

41 Now You're as Good as New.
42 Peek a Boo!
43 Hey Watch Those Firecrackers!
44 What Are You Staring At?
45 Got a Fly Swatter?
46 No More Piggyback Rides.
47 The New Rock 'n Roll Quartet.
48 About That Lighter You Sold Me...
49 Life of the Party, Every Halloween.
50 It's Great for Watching Parades.
51 Just Ignore Him and He'll Leave.
52 What a Silly Way to Dry Spaghetti.
53 This'll Cure Your Headache.
54 What Crazy Crabgrass.
55 Give Me a Hand, Will Ya!
56 That New Dog Food Is Fantastic.
57 Boy Have You a Sore Throat!!
58 The Strangest Egg I Ever Laid.
59 Hey, Wait for Me!
60 The Garbage Men Must Be on Strike.
61 Say Uncle!
62 Why Can't I Enter the Beauty Contest?
63 Who Says She Weighs Only 110 Lbs.
64 Break My Dishes, Will You?
65 I Lost My Razor.
66 Why Don't We Ever Have Dates?
67 He's Too Skinny for Our Outfit.
68 Doc, You Goofed!
69 Oops, I Forgot the Marshmallows.
70 Boy These Buses Really Fly.
71 Don't Pinch My Cheek.
72 This Cozy Room Is Ridiculous.
73 I'm Keeping My Eye on You.
74 You Called for a Babysitter?
75 He Was My Friend.
76 Yichh. You're Ugly!!
77 The Soap Was Too Strong.
78 So, That's How You Do the Twist!
79 Meet My Son, the Lobster.
80 I Told You We Were Low on Gas.

81 What a Spooky Town.
82 Yichh, This Man Never Bathes.
83 Where's My Tom Tom?
84 Gee It Looks Bloodshot.
85 Touch My Canary & I'll Scream.
86 Boo!
87 That Lousy Haircut Ruined My Looks.
88 Flying Is the Modern Way to Travel.
89 What Did You Do to My Wrench?
90 Let's Play Charades.
91 No, Stupid I'm Not Santa Claus.
92 Where's My Mickey Mouse T Shirt?
93 Which One Would You Prefer?
94 Who Says I'm Too Young to Shave?
95 "The Attendant Takes Your Car".
96 Ma, Can I Have a Drink of Water?
97 They're Great for an Itch.
98 Smile, You're on Candid Camera.
99 My Hayfever's Killing Me!
100 Let's Be Friends.
101 Smokey the Bear Sent Me.
102 It Only Hurts When I Laugh.
103 A Nice Refreshing Acid Bath.
104 Meet the New Traffic Commissioner.
105 It's a Swell Car, Let's Eat It.
106 I Love to Laugh.
107 I Got My Hands Clasped, Teacher.
108 Dig This Crazy Vegetable Garden.
109 Okay, Okay, You Can Drive!
110 I Have Lousy Luck with Blind Dates.
111 You Got a Cavity in That Molar.
112 Well Shut My Mouth!
113 Wake Up, You're Dreaming.
114 If You Play Rough, I'll Tell My Mother.
115 What a Nutty Home Permanent.
116 You're a Pretty Sloppy Shaver.

117 Wash Your Antenna and Go Right to Bed.
118 Hey, Do Something About Your Breath.
119 The Pet Shop Made a Mistake.
120 Wake Up, Time for School.
121 Shut the Door, There's a Draft.
122 I Got Stabbing Pains in the Head.
123 Guess Who!
124 Okay, You Can Borrow the Car.
125 What a Funny Way to Scratch a Back.
126 Which One Is the 70 ¢ Spread?
127 Glad to See He Can Still Smile.
128 This Won't Hurt a Bit!
129 Oops, Wrong Room.
130 You've Got a Dry Skin Problem.
131 Hey, You're My Girl Friend!
132 You Should See the Other Guy.
133 I See It, but I Still Don't Believe It.
134 You're Just Not My Type!
135 No, I Do Not Want to Dance!!
136 Now You Two Kiss and Make-up.
137 Are We Looking for 2 People?
138 It Goes, One, Two, Cha, Cha, Cha.
139 I Hate These Peeping Toms.
140 Dear, You Look a Sight in the Morning.
141 Hey, No Smoking in Here.
142 Stop Worrying about Getting Dirty.
143 I Fished Her Out of My Glass of Water.
144 Smile, You're on Candid Camera.
145 Shake, Pal.
146 I Had a Great Day Fishing.
147 What Do You Mean, Happy New Year?
148 I Brought a Girl to the Party.
149 He Winked at Me.
150 I Always Wanted a Fur Collar.
151 Still Using Greasy Kid Stuff?
152 Which Car Hit You?
153 Sh! Someone's at the Door.

MONSTER LAFFS (66)

2 1/2" X 3 1/2"

The standard-size cards of this "Monster Laffs" set all contain photos taken from the

WHY DONT WE EVER HAVE DATES?

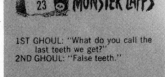

1ST GHOUL: "What do you call the last teeth we get?"
2ND GHOUL: "False teeth."

"midgee" series previously issued by Topps. Since no wrapper or box has been seen, it is assumed that the set was issued in Fun Packs or cellophane during Halloween of 1966 or '67. They were apparently issued in some quantity since sets are readily available today in top condition.

ITEM	MINT	EX
Set	80.00	50.00
Card	1.00	.75

1 I Have Lousy Luck with Blind Dates.
2 He's too Skinny for Our Outfit.
3 You Should See Me When I'm Angry.
4 Where's My Mickey Mouse T Shirt?
5 Boy These Buses Really Fly.
6 What a Spooky Town.
7 Whose the Brains of This Outfit?
8 Mommy, I Had a Nightmare.
9 How Did I Know It Was Poison Ivy?
10 Why Can't I Enter the Beauty Contest?
11 I Got Something in My Eye.
12 You're a Pretty Sloppy Shaver.
13 You Got a Cavity in That Molar.
14 I'll Crash This Party.
15 That New Dog Food Is Fantastic.

16 He Winked At Me.
17 Dig This Crazy Vegetable Garden.
18 Gosh, It's Past My Bedtime!!
19 He Was My Friend.
20 My Ice Cream Melted.
21 Please Show Me to My Room.
22 My Tummy Feels Empty.
23 Why Dont We Ever Have Dates?
24 Smile, You're on Candid Camera.
25 I'm a Restless Sleeper.
26 Now You're as Good as New.
27 I'm Just Falling Apart.
28 It's Great for Watching Parades.
29 Shake Hands Like a Man
30 Flying Is the Modern Way to Travel.
31 Break My Dishes, Will You?
32 It's a Swell Car, Let's Eat It.
33 Hey, You're My Girl Friend!!
34 Smile, You're on Candid Camera.

35 Let's Play Charades.
36 Okay, You Can Borrow the Car.
37 Nice Puppy!
38 Want the Name of My Hairdresser?
39 Sh! Someone's at the Door.
40 Let's Be Friends.
41 Can I Get a Manicure.
42 I Lose My Head at Parties.
43 Call Me if There's A Full Moon.
44 The Pet Shop Made a Mistake.
45 When a Dragon Hiccups It Really Burns.
46 Mother Please, I'd Rather Do It Myself.
47 Oops, I Forgot the Marshmallows.
48 Where's My Tom Tom?
49 I'm Keeping My Eye on You.
50 I Lost My Razor.
51 Yoo Hoo, Guess Who's Here!
52 I Told You We Were Low on Gas.

53 I Fished Her Out of My Glass of Water.
54 The Garbage Men Must Be on Strike.
55 What Are You Staring At?
56 Hey Watch Those Firecrackers!
57 Life of the Party, Every Halloween.
58 Just Ignore Him and He'll Leave.
59 What A Silly Way to Dry Spaghetti.
60 He Looks Comfortable.
61 Got a 25 Room Apartment for Me?
62 Ma, Can I Have a Drink of Water.
63 Wake Up, You're Dreaming.
64 When We Get a Head Ache, It's a Beauty!!
65 This Beach Used to Be So Crowded.
66 No More Piggyback Rides.

MONSTER LEGENDS (?) 3 1/2" X 6 1/2"

Like the "Dino-Mite Facts" wrapper listed elsewhere in this book, "Monster Legends" appears to have failed the marketing test for packaging. "The Story of Jekyll & Hyde" is the only episode reported to date. The front of the colorful wrapper advertises "Drac-Snax Monster Candy" and according to the wrapper code, it was sold in 1977. The candy "tested" here was later marketed by Topps in a smaller wrapper.

ITEM	MINT	EX
Wrapper	--	50.00

MONSTER MARKS (?) 2 1/4" X 3 1/2"

"Monster Marks" were a series of "magic-rub skin tattoos" issued by Fleer in 1968. The tattoos had an adhesive side which allowed them to be applied directly to the skin. The sticky side of the tattoo sheet was protected by cover paper (which makes our illustration dim). A 2 1/2" X 4" instruction card was inserted into the 5-cent package to protect the "Monster Marks" from damage. The tattoo sheet illustrated contains six different designs.

ITEM	MINT	EX
Marks	1.50	1.00
Card	.50	.35
Wrapper	--	15.00
Box	--	40.00

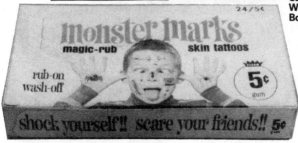

MONSTER TATOO (?) 1 9/16" X 3 1/2"

The spelling of the word "tatoo" with a single "t" marks this as an early Topps issue (possibly 1962). Only the "skull" design has been reported for the exterior wrapper, which is red with black and white accents. The "tattoos" on the interior side are not numbered or captioned and the set total has not been established.

ITEM	MINT	EX
Wrapper	--	15.00
Box	--	150.00

MONSTER TATTOOS (?)

Topps revised the "Monster Tattoo" theme (with a double "tt") in 1975. The exterior side of the wrapper carries a grinning monster design and can be found in four colors: orange, red, yellow, and blue. The tattoos on the "interior" side are not captioned but they are numbered in "A" and "B" series. It is believed that there are 30 tattoos in each series.

1 9/16" X 3 1/2"

ITEM	MINT	EX
Wrapper	——	5.00

MONSTICKERS (68)

2" X 4 3/4"

"Monstickers" is a series of 68 puffy plastic stickers manufactured for Topps in Japan. A three-sticker strip came in every cellophane wrapper. Each monster is named inside the score line but the individual sticker number is printed on the excess plastic between the designs. It appears that some monsters are printed as many as three times in different strips, but relative scarcities are still being researched. A complete set can be made with a minimum of 26 panels and a maximum of 36 panels. Topps issued this product in 1979.

ITEM	MINT	EX
Set	37.50	25.00
Strip	.50	.35
Wrapper	——	1.00
Box	——	7.00

1 Jane	18 Betty	35 Sandy	52 Ken
2 Jennifer	19 Shaun	36 David	53 Joe
3 Lynn	20 Derek	37 Joanne	54 Kay
4 Tom	21 Michael	38 Stuart	55 Paul
5 Carol	22 Sally	39 Nancy	56 Donna
6 Cathy	23 Chris	40 Steven	57 Ray
7 Charlie	24 Eric	41 Jack	58 Jill
8 Bill	25 Kevin	42 Len	59 Liz
9 Vicki	26 Peter	43 Diane	60 Kim
10 Jessica	27 Ronnie	44 Kathy	61 Linda
11 Don	28 Debbie	45 Frank	62 Jim
12 Justin	29 Richard	46 Lois	63 Anne
13 Amanda	30 Beth	47 Greg	64 Ed
14 Jerry	31 Sarah	48 Ted	65 Lisa
15 Susan	32	49 Barbara	66 Tina
16 John	33 Bob	50 Judy	67 Mary
17 Scott	34 Karen	51 Andy	68 Pat

A RECEIPT IS GOOD INSURANCE FOR BOTH BUYER AND SELLER

MOON-MARS (36)

2 1/2" X 3 1/2"

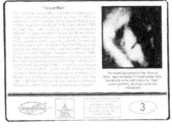

"Moon-Mars," created by Houston-based Space Ventures, is the most lavish space theme series ever produced. Each of the 36 cards in the set is a laser-printed miniature work of art featuring 3-D sculpturing enhanced and protected by UV coating. Subjects include astronaut portraits, the mysterious "Face on Mars," pictures from our triumphant lunar missions, and space art depicting man's future travels to other worlds. The backs carry smaller color pictures and some of the most fascinating text ever printed on trading cards. To date, this is the only trading card set to picture all 11 retired astronauts that walked on the moon. Note: sold as boxed edition only. No single card prices or excellent grade listed below.

ITEM	MINT
Set	30.00

1 The Astronauts Memorial
2 Alan Shawn Feinstein
3 "Face of Mars"
4 Neil A. Armstrong - Apollo 11
5 Neil A. Armstrong - Inside LM on Moon
6 Buzz Aldrin - Apollo 11
7 Buzz Aldrin - Moonwalk
8 Charles "Pete" Conrad, Jr. - Apollo 12
9 Pete Conrad - Holding Camera
10 Alan L. Bean - Apollo 12
11 Alan Bean - Carrying ALSEP

12 Alan B. Shepard, Jr. - Apollo 14
13 Alan Shepard - Holding Flag
14 Edgar D. Mitchell - Apollo 14
15 Ed Mitchell - Consulting Map
16 David R. Scott - Apollo 15
17 Dave Scott - Saluting the Flag
18 James B. Irwin - Apollo 15
19 Jim Irwin - Next to Rover
20 John Young - Jump and Salute
21 Charles M. Duke - Apollo 16
22 Charlie Duke - At Plum Crater

23 Eugene A. Cernan - Apollo 17
24 Gene Cernan - Saluting
25 Harrison "Jack" Schmitt - Apollo 17
26 Jack Schmitt - With Flag and Earthrise
27 Mars - The Red Planet
28 Space Exploration Initiative
29 Viking - On Martian Surface
30 Mars Observer Mission
31 Mission to Mars - Phobos Base
32 U.S.-Soviet Joint Mission to Mars
33 Direct Mission to Mars
34 "The Case for Mars" Mission
35 Mars Mission - Transit System
36 "The Journey"

MOONRAKER (99 & 22)

The James Bond adventure movie "Moonraker" was translated into the trading card medium by Topps in 1979. There are 99 cards in the set; they have blue borders and yellow frame lines encircling color photos. The card number is located in a red design inside the frame line, and each picture is captioned underneath. The backs contain poster pieces (55) and narratives (44). The numbered stickers are color photos edged in red on white backgrounds. They are not captioned but have been assigned titles (from similar pictures in the card series) in the checklist. Note: set price includes stickers.

2 1/2" X 3 1/2"

ITEM	MINT	EX
Set	15.00	10.50
Card	.10	.07
Sticker	.35	.25
Wrapper	—	.35
Box	—	5.00

1 Agent 007
2 Relaxation, Bond-Style!
3 Trapped by Deadly Spies!
4 A Tight Spot for Bond!
5 Thrown from the Plane!
6 Plummeting to Earth!
7 Rescued by Parachute!
8 Jaws Vows Revenge!
9 Reporting to "M"
10 Miss Moneypenny
11 "Q" 's Newest Weapons
12 Enter Drax
13 Fantastic Estate of Drax
14 A Collection of Perfection
15 The Adversaries Meet
16 Holly...Friend or Foe?
17 Deadly Device
18 The Secret Plans
19 Murder in the Canal!
20 Killed by a Living Corpse!
21 Fantastic Chase!
22 Evil Assassin Chang
23 "Kill Bond!"
24 Hired to Kill!
25 The Clock Tower Struggle!
26 The Savage One
27 In Death's Grip!
28 Chang Falls to His Doom!
29 Scientist' Lair
30 The Deadly Fumes!

31 Walls of Destruction!
32 The Lab...Deserted!
33 The Spies Compare Notes!
34 The Man Called "Jaws"
35 Teeth of Steel!
36 Snapping the Cable!
37 Cable Car Peril!
38 Duo for Danger!
39 Holly—Captured by Drax!
40 Bond Undercover!
41 Conferring with "M"
42 Testing New Weapons!
43 Director of "Q" Branch
44 The Menacing Monk!
45 Jaws in Hot Pursuit!
46 A Daring Escape!
47 Bond Glides to Safety!
48 Mysterious Hideout!
49 Beckoned by Beauty!
50 Beautiful but Deadly!
51 The Doom Bridge
52 Icy Waters Below!
53 Bone Crushing Anaconda!
54 Fished Out by Jaws!
55 Less-than-tender Clutches!
56 Escorted by Jaws
57 "Don't Be Foolish, Mr. Bond"
58 Inside the Great Pyramid
59 Drax's "New People"
60 "Launch All Moonrakers!"

61 Bond and Holly on the Run!
62 Commanding Moonraker 6!
63 The Ships Blast Off!
64 Speeding Toward Space!
65 Drax Aboard Moonraker 5
66 Journey Across the Heavens
67 The Incredible Space Station!
68 Docking of the Moonrakers
69 The Drax Empire
70 Peering through the Telescope
71 Mind-boggling Complex!
72 A World in Space!
73 Bond and Holly Arrive
74 Inside the Space Station
75 The People of Tomorrow
76 The Command Chair
77 Spotted by Jaws!
78 Apprehended!
79 The Master Speaks
80 Crazed Genius!
81 Flowers of Death!
82 Hello, Dolly!
83 The Oddest Couple!
84 End of the World!
85 The Craft's Rotation—Stopped!
86 Flying Helplessly through Space!
87 Bond Swings into Action!
88 Arrival of the Earth Forces!
89 Drax's Dream...Up in Smoke!
90 Powerful Karate Chop!
91 Holly Blasts the Enemy!
92 Victorious Astro-fighters!
93 Jaws Saves the Day!
94 Desperate Mission!
95 The Weightless Peril!
96 Destroying the Deadly Globes!
97 Lasers Find Their Mark!
98 The Moonraker in Flight
99 Death of a Mad Dream!

1 Bust of James Bond Holding Gun
2 James Bond in Black Shirt
3 Holly
4 James Bond in Opened Front Shirt
5 James Bond in Leather Coat
6 Murder in the Canal
7 Jaws
8 James Bond Standing with Gun
9 Chang
10 The Man Called "Jaws"
11 Hugo Drax
12 Fished Out by Jaws!
13 Holly and Bond
14 Rescued by Parachute
15 Flying Helplessly through Space!
16 "Don't Be Foolish...Mr. Bond"
17 Inside the Space Station
18 The Incredible Space Station!
19 James Bond in Black Turtleneck
20 Death of a Mad Dream!
21 Crazed Genius!
22 Jaws Saves the Day!

With or without Orkan guidance, Topps produced this 99-card, 22-sticker set based on the television show "Mork and Mindy" in 1978. The cards have color photos and starry, purple borders. Each is numbered on the front in a small circle at the left. On the backs there are 55 poster pieces and 44 "Orkan Reader" features. Stickers one to seven have large photos with plain black borders; eight to 22 have smaller pictures edged in red with starry, black borders. All the stickers are captioned. Note: set price includes stickers.

ITEM	MINT	EX
Set	15.00	12.00
Card	.10	.07
Sticker	.35	.25
Wrapper	—	.35
Box	—	6.00

1. Never Trust a Man with Four Lips! All You'll Get Is Double Talk!
2. Mork, That's the Last Time I Use Your Tailor!
3. My Favorite Dessert...Porcelain!
4. You're in Good Hands with Ork State!
5. Sorry About Last Night—I Made a Real Crimluck Out of Myself!
6. No, Mork—a Double Date Doesn't Mean Going Out with a Two-headed Venusian!
7. Mindy, I'd Like to Take You to a Restaurant with Lots of Atmosphere, Nitrogen!
8. Be It Ever So Humble, There's No Place Like Ork!
9. Mindy, Have You Heard from Trash Gordon Lately?
10. Somebody Just Sold Me Mt. Rushmore..If I Can Buy the Grand Canyon I'll Have Somewhere to Put It!
11. Nice Outfit...But Does It Come with Two Pairs of Pants?
12. Whenever I See a Car Engine I'm Reminded of Home Cooking!
13. Mindy, I Had Thousands of Things to Eat for Lunch! What Did You Have? A Bowl of Rice!
14. I Always Thought Aliens Were Green and Scaly! I've Already Been Through Adolescence!
15. I Come from a Distant Planet! Cleveland?
16. Mork—You're a Man of Few Words—All of Them Weird!
17. Shazbot! I'm at the End of My Rope!
18. Okay, Lefty the Breakout's Set for Tonight!
19. Get Out of Your Shells...Meet People...Tell a Few Yokes!
20. I Just Played the Juke Box—and It Won!
21. No More Furniture Moving Today! I've Got a Cramp in My Finger!
22. My Arms Fell Asleep! Quick—Dip Them in Coffee!
23. I Tell You, Sylvia—We Can't Go on Meeting Like This!
24. You Light Up My Splurg.
25. Mork Acts More and More Human Every Day! Yes—It's Catching!
26. Mork's in the Bathroom! He's Taking a Meteor Shower!
27. I Know You're Watching the T.V.—But I Wish You'd Turn It On!
28. I Feel Like Having Dessert! How About a Bologna Sundae?
29. Some of My Best Friends Are Sandwiches!
30. Mork's a Responsible Guy—Responsible for Lots of Trouble!
31. Mork Is the Cutest Space Creature I've Ever Met!
32. Daddy, How Can You Possibly Wear Such a Silly Outfit?!
33. I Never Met a Spaceman I Didn't Like!
34. I Asked Mork to Take Out the Garbage—He Took It to the Movie!
35. Mork, You're Really Smart! I Should Be—My Great Aunt Was a Computer!
36. You're a U.F.O. Mork—Unbelievable Far Out!
37. I Tried to Report to Orson—But He Kept Me on Hold!
38. Mork—A Blind Date Does Not Mean Going Out in Dark Glasses!
39. Bring Me a Tennis Racket—I Must Toss the Salad!
40. I Wish My Daughter Would Find a Boyfriend Who's More Down to Earth!
41. Greetings, My Main Munchkin!
42. Mindy You're the Nicest Lower Life Form I've Ever Met!
43. Greetings Earthling, Take Me to Your Leader!
44. Cora, Would You Call Me Old-Fashioned?? I Wouldn't Call You at All!
45. I Think I've Just Had a Close Encounter of the Nerd Kind!
46. Hey, This Is Mork's Diary! Is It Written in Crayon?
47. Na No, Na No—Err...I Mean "Hello!"
48. Mork, Did You Take a Shower Last Night? Why, Is There One Missing?
49. Do You Like Your Air Fried or Hard Boiled?
50. Poor Fellow—I'm Afraid He's Lost His Head!
51. Hi There, Plasma! Where It's at! Onk! Onk!
52. I Wish They'd Develop a Vaccine for "Disco Fever!"
53. It's the Only Way to Travel!
54. You Can't Live in the Attic—It's Dirty and Full of Bugs! Will They Split the Rent with Me?
55. Zabah—Next Time I Travel First Class!
56. That's Some Pair of Antennae—Do You Get Good Reception?
57. Smile, Daddy, You're on Candid Hologram!
58. Boy, Was I Ever Bezurd Last Night!
59. I've Caught a Cold! Quick...Get a Jar to Put It in!
60. This Can Has Decided to Have Me Recycled!
61. Shazbot! Those Nimnuls Forgot My Luggage!
62. No, I WII Not Accept a Call from the Planet Ork!
63. Mork—That's Not an Elevator—It's a Washing Machine!
64. Hold the Mayo, Quick!
65. They Must Have Sent You to Finishing School—I Can Still Smell the Varnish!
66. I Can't Stand This Violence on TV! I'll Never Watch Saturday Morning Cartoons Again!
67. Boy, They Sure Have Ugly Girls on this Planet!
68. It's Enough to Drive a Man Ork-Faced!
69. I've Developed a New Slant on Life!
70. I'm Looking Forward to a Certain Letter! How About "K"?
71. Hmm...Reminds Me of a Girl I Once Dated on Venus!
72. If This Is Soap Opera, Mindy, Where Are the Singing Detergents?
73. Take Two Eggs—Add a Scoop of Ice Cream and a Light Bulb...
74. Mindy, I Just Broke a Promise—Where's the Nearest Repair Shop?
75. I've Got a New Boyfriend, Dad! An Earthling? Terrific!
76. I've Discovered a Cure for Hiccups—Unfortunately It's Fatal!
77. Is Mork in Trouble? He's in Over His Head—Literally!
78. Eugene, Here's That Slice of Pizza You Were Looking For!
79. Long Distance? Give Me the Planet Neptune!
80. Ahhh, Peppermint Nail Polish... My Favorite!
81. The Moon Is Full Tonight—It Just Burped!
82. It's All Right, Mork—To Err Is Human! Even If He's Not!
83. Isn't That a Strange Way to Sleep? You're Darn Right It's Strange! Usually He Hangs Upside Down!
84. My First Day on the Job Was Difficult! Like Being Caught In a Meteor Shower without an Umbrella!
85. Mork Are You a Registered Alien? Onk, Onk...Humor!
86. Mork You Can Count on Me! I'd Rather Use My Fingers!
87. I Think I'm Going To Be Sick—I've Just Seen an Egg Beaten to Death!
88. What's a Nice Sausage Like You Doing in a Sandwich Like This?
89. Nice Girl...But She's Suffering from Termites!
90. Mork Does Your Spacesuit Need Ironing? No, I Don't See Any Rust!
91. Have a Seat, Mork! Just Did! It Gave Me Indigestion!
92. It's What the Well Dressed Orkan Is Wearing!
93. These Cups Are a Little Dirty! Then They'll Never Get a G-rating!
94. Are You Okay? Well...It Only Hurts When I Furrp!
95. Mork, I'm Losing My Mind! Perhaps It's in Here!
96. Look, an 8-Armed Namzal—But They Only Live on Ork! No, Mork—That's a Coat Rack!
97. Ah, a Fleet of Fellow Space Travelers! Welcome, Little Nimnuls!
98. Freddie Just Became "Wiener Of the Year!"
99. Mork, You're Really Far Out! Yes, Several Light Years!

1. It Loses Something without Ketchup!
2. Relaxation, Orkan-Style!
3. Mork from Ork Wants You!
4. But Does It Travel Faster Than Light?
5. Skateboard Fever!
6. Have a Chair, Mork!
7. Mork...the (Not So) Easy Rider!
8. Orkan Meets Earthling!
9. Hot Dog Encounter!
10. Greetings, Little Nimnuls!
11. Spaced-Out Mork!
12. Pam Dawber Stars as Mindy
13. TV's Dynamic Duo!
14. Robin Williams & Pam Dawber
15. Friends...or Lovelings?
16. Far-Out Young Star!
17. Na-No, Na-No, Earth Person!
18. Galactic Goof & Girlfriend
19. Disguised as an Earthman!
20. For Me? How...Err...Sweet!
21. Mork Flips His Cork!
22. Beautiful Mindy!

12" X 20"

One of Topps releases of 1981 was this set of 12 full-color Movie Posters. A full 12" X 20" when open, each poster is folded four times to make it fit into the large yellow wrapper-package. Because of this, even posters in the "mint" category will have two long fold lines running vertically and horizontally. Buyers should judge condition accordingly.

ITEM	MINT	EX
Set	12.00	9.00
Poster	1.00	.75
Wrapper	--	.35
Boxes		
30 cents	--	5.00
50 cents	--	35.00

1 Jaws
2 Superman
3 Grease
4 Airplane!
5 Star Wars
6 Rocky
7 Animal House
8 The Empire Strikes Back
9 Young Frankenstein
10 The Blue Lagoon
11 Revenge of the Pink Panther
12 Smokey and the Bandit

MR. FREEZE FUN QUIZ (2K)

2 1/2" X 3 1/2"

Why are the "Mr. Freeze Fun Quiz" cards made out of plastic? They have to be made out of plastic because they're inserted in cartons of Mr. Freeze ice pops. Since the pops are not shipped frozen, there's a certain amount of leakage in the carton when you pull it from the shelf. A cardboard card would self-destruct under such circumstances, so plastic was used. The front of each card has a picture of "Mr. Freeze" himself, is numbered, and asks a question. The flip side also has artwork and answers the question posed on front. Although we have only two titles on record at The Hobby Card Index, it is assumed that all the questions in the series have something to do with temperature (hot temperatures that make you want to reach for a Mr. Freeze frozen confection!). Note: a low supply, low demand item: price per card in excellent grade = 50 cents.

MRS. GROSSMAN'S STICKER ART TRADING CARDS (99K)

2 1/2" X 3 1/2"

Give credit where credit is due. There are zillions of trading cards out there and hundreds of companies vying for hobby dollars, and here comes Mrs. Grossman pulling off a major marketing miracle and getting her "sticker art" card set into variety and greeting card stores all over the country. The executives at some of the major card producers should be so smart! The length of the set is unknown, but card #99 has been seen. The series contains two types of cards: single artwork cards with captions on the back, and puzzle pieces with the name of the puzzle on the back. Some single artwork cards have borders, others do not; all the puzzle piece cards are borderless. The cards were sold in packs of eight wrapped in clear cellophane and a round label on the package advised that it "Contains 8 cards and a FREE surprise." The latter turns out to be a single small sticker cut from another Mrs. Grossman's product, "Stickers by the Yard." A copyright date of 1984 appears on all the cards.

ITEM	MINT	EX
Card	.25	.20
Sticker	.10	.10

MS. PAC MAN (54 & 4)

TWO SIZES

Even if you were not a video game enthusiast, you'd probably admit that the 54 stickers issued by Fleer in the Ms. Pacman set are cute! There are 30 blue stickers, 7 pink stickers, and 17 stickers which have various color combinations. The back of each sticker contains a number, the Fleer logo, and instructions for the rub-off game. The latter is situated on four different game cards which are played by rubbing off the gold coating covering the dots.

ITEM	MINT	EX
Set	9.50	7.00
Sticker	.15	.10
Game	.35	.25
Wrapper	--	.35
Box	--	4.00

Ms. Pac Man

1 Ms. Pac-Man Loves Fruit Salad
2 Ms. Pac-Man Racing Team
3 Call Me Sometime!
4 I Need It Bad
5 I'm a Liberated Woman
6 The Chase Is On! Waka! Waka!
7 Ain't Love Grand
8 Ms. Pac-Man Loves You!
9 Yield... It's More Fun
10 I Completed Ms. Pac-Man Act II
11 Ms. Pac-Man Take the Challenge!
12 I Completed Ms. Pac-Man Act I
13 I'm Not Just Another Pretty Face— For Sure!
14 Ms. Pac-Man Plays Hard to Get
15 Ms. Pac-Man Does It Faster The Nerve!
16 Let's Get Physical

17 Kiss Me Quick— Yuck!
18 Hi Short, Round & Yellow
19 A Marriage Born in Video-Land
20 Ms. Pac-Man
21 Ms. Pac-Man for Ms. America
22 Waka, Waka, Wow!
23 Pucker Up Lover... Out the Side Door!
24 I Want to Hold Your Hand— Do It!
25 Let's Go Steady! No Way!
26 We Make Beautiful Music Together— Hummm!
27 Ms. Pac-Man Fever Is Driving Me Crazy— Tell Me About It
28 I'm a Good Girl
29 Love at First Bite
30 Ms. Pac-Man Has More Fun
31 I'm So Lonely

32 Let's Get Together— What If We're Caught
33 Ready? Are You Kidding
34 It Was Love at First Bite
35 Are You Afraid? No!
36 How Much Do You Love Me— Oh... About 25 Cents Worth
37 How About a Date? See You in Act IV
38 Ms. Pac-Man Operators License
39 Official Ms. Pac-Man Pro
40 Oh! Pac-Man
41 How's My Main Squeeze— Kinky!
42 Doing Anything Tonight? Not with You!
43 Alone at Last— That's What He Thinks!

44 I'm Gonna Get That Ms. Pac-Man
45 Stop... I've Got to Fix My Face— Just Like a Woman
46 I Completed Ms. Pac-Man Act IV
47 Ms. Pac-Man Headquarters
48 I Completed Ms. Pac-Man Act III
49 Faster than a Speeding Electron— My Hero!
50 I Think I'm in Love
51 Stay Away from My Girl! Gulp
52 How About It? Fresh!
53 Here I Come— Go for It!
54 Stop! I Love It

MUNSTERS (72 & 16)   TWO SIZES

The 72 cards of the Munsters set produced by Leaf have black and white photos with white borders and a glossy surface. A line of dialogue sits below the picture. The backs contain a feature entitled "Munsters Mumbles," and the card number is located below this heading. There are 16 unnumbered stickers associated with the set; they have color monster designs. Note: separate set prices listed for cards and stickers.

ITEM	MINT	EX
Sets		
Cards	360.00	315.00
Stickers	100.00	80.00
Card	4.00	3.50
Sticker	5.00	4.00
Wrapper	--	20.00
Box	--	75.00

Car enthusiasts have enjoyed a visual feast in the early part of 1992 with the issuing of two separate sets of trading cards dealing with beefed-up automobiles. The first of these is a series of 104 cards entitled "Muscle Cards," produced by Performance Years Quality Card Company of North Wales, Pa. Of the set total, 102 cards are numbered and the two header/introduction cards are not. The color photographs on the card fronts are enclosed by a neon pink frame line and black borders. Each automobile or engine is dated and identified beneath the picture and the set title in the lower left corner is superimposed onto a distinctive "checkered flag" border.

The card backs have the descriptive text printed on opposing sections with pink and green backgrounds. The upper right section of every card back contains a detail picture of the subject and the power rating of the motor can be found in a tac meter at lower left. The card number appears on the back only and is located in a "burning rubber" design at upper left. Product was distributed in 8-card foil packs (no gum) and our illustration of the wrapper is not clear due to the mostly black color used. The display box has two cards pictured on the lid and has the distinctive checkered flag pattern on all four sides and part of the top. Three types of promotional cards were issued

by PYQCC: (1) marked "prototype" in white letters on the obverse model year line (see Corvette illustration); (2) marked "STATE EXPO" in silver foil letters in the picture area; (3) marked "KING OF THE HILL" in gold foil letters in the picture area. The first two varieties were given away to collectors and to visitors to the Expo; the last type was randomly inserted into foil packs. Note: none of the promotional cards are considered to be part of the regular series and they are not priced below.

ITEM	MINT	EX
Set	15.00	10.00
Card	.15	.10
Wrapper	--	.10
Box	--	1.50

1 1969 ZL1 Camaro	33 1966 Ford Fairlane GTA 390
2 1967 L89 Corvette	34 1967 427 Ford Fairlane XL
3 1967 L78 Chevelle 396	35 1969 Ford Torino Talladega 428
4 1967 Corvette 427 Tri-Power	36 1970 Boss 302 Cougar Eliminator
5 1963 Z/06 Corvette	37 1961 Ford Starliner with 427 SOHC
6 1962 Impala SS 409	38 1969 American Motors SC/Rambler
7 1956 Chevrolet Bel Air	39 1969 AMC AMX 390
8 1970 Hemicuda	40 1968 Shelby Cobra G.T. 350 Fastback
9 1969 Pontiac GTO Judge	41 1968 Mustang GT 428 Cobra Jet
10 1968 Hurst-Olds	
11 1969 Hurst-Olds	
12 1973 Pontiac 455 Trans Am	
13 1966 Shelby G.T. 350H	
14 1968 Shelby Cobra G.T. 500 K.R.	
15 1967 L89 Corvette	
16 1971 Corvette LS6 454 Coupe	
17 1968 Dana 427 Camaro	
18 1966 L79 Nova SS	
19 1969 L89 SS 396 Chevelle	
20 1968 L78 SS 396 Camaro	
21 1969 Camaro Z/28	
22 1972 LS5 Chevelle SS 454	
23 1970 Buick GS 455 Stage 1	
24 1967 Shelby G.T. 500 Fastback	
25 1968 Shelby Cobra G.T. 50	
26 1969 Shelby G.T. 350 Fastback	
27 G.T. 500 Convertible	
28 1966 K-GT Mustang Convertible	
29 1964 289 FIA Cobra	
30 1965 289 Cobra Roadster	
31 1964 Hi-Pro Fairlane	
32 1965 A/FX Falcon	

42 1968 J-Code Mustang GT
43 1970 Hemi Superbird
44 1964 Ford Galaxie R-Code 427
45 1971 Plymouth 'Cuda 44 Six Pack
46 1964 GTO
47 1963 Ford Galaxie Lightweight
48 1970 Buick GSX Stage 1
49 1965 Pontiac Catalina 2+2 Convertible
50 1962 Pontiac Catalina 421
51 1969 Pontiac Trans Am Convertible
52 1967 Dodge Coronet R/T
53 1964 Dodge Race Hemi
54 1971 Pontiac Trans Am 455 HO
55 1972 Buick GS-455 Stage 1
56 1967 Dodge Coronet 440 R/T
57 1967 Hemi GTX
58 1969 Dodge Hemi Daytona
59 1970 Dodge Dart Swinger 340
60 1970 Dodge Super Bee Six Pack
61 1966 427 Cobra Roadster
62 1970 Cougar XR-7 Convertible, 428 CJ
63 1966 Corvette Convertible, 425/427
64 1970 Dodge Super Bee 440 Six Pack
65 1969 Ford Fairlane Cobra
66 1966 Pontiac GTO
67 Hemi Challenger R/T
68 1970 Dodge T/A 340 Six Pack
69 1970 Dodge Challenger Six Pack
70 1966 GT Fastback
71 1970 W30 Oldsmobile 4-4-2
72 1970 Boss 302 Mustang

Muscle Cards

73 1969 Boss 429
74 1970 Mach 1 Twister Special
75 1971 Boss 351
76 1973 Cobra Jet Mach 1 Mustang
77 1970 Nova Yenko Deuce
78 1971 Hemicuda Coupe
79 1970 LS6 454 El Camino
80 1967 Camaro SS / RS 396, L78
81 1969 Boss 302 Mustang
82 1966 Mustang Hi-Po Coupe
83 1970 Plymouth AAR 'Cuda 340 Six Pack
84 1968 Shelby Cobra G.T. 500 KR

85 1969 Dodge Charger RT / SE
86 1966 Dodge Hemi Coronet 500
87 1956 Chrysler 300 Hemi
88 1970 W30 Oldsmobile 4-4-2 Coupe
89 1969 Corvette L89 Convertible
90 1969 427 Camaro SYC
91 1969 Copo 427
92 1967 Ford R-Code 427-8V
93 1970 Buick 455 Stage 1
94 1969 L78 / L89 375 Horse 396
95 1962 Pontiac 421 Super Duty
96 1969 Boss 429
97 1963 426 Stage II Max Wedge
98 1970 Chevrolet LS6 454
99 1969 Chrysler 440 Six Pack
100 1970 Chrysler 426 Hemi
101 1969 Ford 428 Cobra Jet
102 Checklist

MUSCLECARS (100)

The premier edition of "Musclecars" collector's cards focuses on power cars from an eleven-year period, 1964-1974. The card fronts contain full col- or photos of 100 automobiles and each is identified directly below the center of the picture. The frame lines are white, with a black-to-gray bar fade between them and the pure white borders. The set title is printed in blue, stylized letters above each car.

2 1/2" X 3 1/2"

Each card back has a color "detail" photo at top center which is surrounded on both sides and the bottom by specifications. The car is described in technical terms in a text area covering the bottom 40% of the card. The card number is printed on the back only, just above the top right corner of the text. Like the set previously covered, "Musclecars" was distributed in 1992 in a mostly black wrapper, but with nine cards instead of eight. The 36-count display box is also black and the manufacturer is listed as Collect-A-Card Corp. of Greenville, South Carolina. Note: the two checklist cards are included in the set total. They are listed as having numbers, but no numbers are printed on them.

ITEM	MINT	EX
Set	15.00	10.00
Card	.15	.10
Wrapper	—	.10
Box	—	1.50

1 '64 Pontiac GTO
2 '70 Oldsmobile Rallye 350
3 '67 Buick Gran Sport
4 '70 Plymouth Hemi Cuda
5 '69 Buick Gran Sport
6 '71 Buick Gran Sport Stage 1
7 '68 AMC AMX
8 '63 Dodge 426 Ramcharger
9 '69 Chevrolet Camaro Z28
10 '67 Ford Fairlane 500/XL 427
11 '69 Dodge Charger R/T
12 '70 AMC Mark Donahue Javelin
13 '63 Ford Galaxie 427
14 '70 AMC AMX
15 '70 Chevrolet Chevelle SS396
16 '70 AMC Javelin Trans-Am
17 '70 AMC Rebel Machine
18 '69 Chevrolet Corvette L88
19 '69 Ford Mustang Boss 302
20 '67 Chevrolet Camaro Z28
21 '69 Ford Mustang Boss 429
22 '62 Chevrolet Biscayne 409
23 '70 Dodge Challenger R/T
24 '67 Chevrolet Impala SS427
25 '66 Chevrolet Nova SS
26 '65 Ford Mustang 289HP

27 '67 Chevrolet Chevelle SS396
28 '65 Chevrolet Chevelle Z16
29 '69 Ply. Hemi Road Runner
30 '64 Oldsmobile Cutlass 4-4-2
31 '65 Ford Shelby 427 Cobra
32 '70 Mer. Cougar Elim Boss 302
33 '70 Chevrolet Chevelle SS454
34 '70 Ford Torino GT
35 '67 Ford Mustang GT
36 '66 Dodge Charger
37 '69 AMC Rambler/SC
38 '65 Ford Shelby Mustang
39 '64 Ford Shelby Daytona
40 '67 Chevrolet Corvette
41 '69 Chevrolet Camaro SS396
42 '69 Chevrolet Yenko Camaro
43 '69 Dodge Charger 500
44 '69 Ford Talladega
45 '70 Dodge Coronet R/T
46 '70 Chevrolet Camaro Z28
47 '69 Chevrolet Nova SS396
48 '71 Dodge Hemi Challen. R/T
49 '68 Mercury Cougar GT-E
50 Checklist Card #1

51 '71 Dodge Charger
52 '67 Mercury 427 Cyclone
53 '71 Oldsmobile 4-4-2 W30
54 '67 Dodge Coronet R/T
55 '70 Buick GSX
56 '67 Shelby Mustang GT500
57 '68 Dodge Super Bee
58 '64 Ford Galaxie A/Stock
59 '69 Dodge Super Bee 6 Pack
60 '69 Mercury Cougar 428 CJ
61 '69 Dodge Daytona
62 '72 Ford Mustang Mach 1
63 '70 Dodge Challenger 340 T/A
64 '69 Oldsmobile Hurst 4-4-2
65 '72 Dodge Challenge Rallye
66 '69 Torino Cobra 428 SCJ
67 '71 Dodge Demon 340
68 '66 Oldsmobile Cutlass 4-4-2
69 '71 Plymouth Hemi Cuda
70 '69 Mercury Cyclone II
71 '69 Barracuda Formula S
72 '68 Oldsmobile 4-4-2
73 '71 Plymouth Sport Fury GT
74 '72 Oldsmobile Hurst
75 '70 Plymouth AAR Cuda
76 '66 Pontiac GTO

77 '69 Plymouth Road Runner
78 '69 Pontiac Firebird Trans Am
79 '69 Oldsmobile Cutlass S W31
80 '69 Dodge Dart 440 GTS
81 '71 AMC Hornet SC/360
82 '71 Pontiac GTO 455 HO Judge
83 '71 Plymouth Duster
84 '68 Pontiac GTO
85 '70 Plymouth Superbird
86 '70 Pontiac GTO Judge
87 '67 Plymouth Hemi Satellite
88 '71 Plymouth 340 Cuda
89 '67 Pontiac Firebird 400
90 '71 Road Runner 440 6-Barrel
91 '72 Pontiac Trans Am 455 H.O.
92 '67 Plymouth Hemi GTX
93 '74 Pontiac Trans Am 455 SD
94 '70 Plymouth GTX
95 '69 Barracuda Formula 340S
96 '65 Dodge Hemi "Landy's"
97 '64 Ford Falcon A/FX 427
98 '66 Ford Mustang Funny Car
99 '64 Mercury Comet A/FX
100 Checklist Card #2

MY KOOKIE KLASSMATES (9 & 20)　　TWO SIZES

According to Buck Barker, Fleer issued "My Kookie Klassmates" in 1968. The set consists of nine sheets of "autograph stamps with name add-ons" and 20 "insult cards." An intact stamp sheet measures 2 1/2" X 10 1/2" and contains eight 1 1/4" X 2" stamps with spaces to write in names; there are also two columns of 3/8" X 1" name stamps (12) that can be affixed to the name blanks. In all, there are 72 different "autograph stamps" and a total of 108 names (99 different: names appearing twice are marked with an asterisk in the checklist). The "insult cards" are printed in blue ink on white blank-back cardboard and measure 1 3/4" X 2". They were issued in panels of two and are not numbered. Note: set prices include all stickers and cards; separated stickers and cards cannot be graded mint.

ITEM	MINT	EX
Set	25.00	20.00
Cards		
Single	--	.35
Panel	1.00	.75
Sticker		
Sheet	1.50	1.00
Wrapper	--	3.00
Box	--	30.00

CARDS

How Can You Be Both? Ugly and Stupid!
I Could Go for You if You Weren't So Ugly.
If You Had Brains You'd Be Dangerous
Kiss My Foot!
You Are a Saint...St. Bernard.
You Belong in a Nut House!
You Big Jerk!
You Eat Like a Bird...a Vulture!
You Have a Kind Face...the Kind that Makes Me Sick.
You Have Beautiful Eyes...Blood Shot.
You Have B.O.
You Look Like Someone Famous... Frankenstein!
You Make Something Inside Flip: My Stomach!

You're Not Dumb You're Stupid!
Your Feet Stink
Your Face Makes My Heart Jump...From Fright!
Your Mouth's in Gear, and Your Brain's in Neutral.
Your Socks Smell!
You Smell Like a Flower, Stinkweed!
You Stink!

My Kookie Klassmates

STAMPS

Class Actress	Class Highpockets
Class Baby	Class Idiot
Class Back Stabber	Class Jerk
Class Baseball Star	Class Joker
Class Big Mouth	Class Kisser
Class Big Spender	Class Leader
Class Bird Brain	Class Liar
Class Blabbermouth	Class Longhair
Class Boy Chaser	Class Loser
Class Boy Dancer	Class Lover
Class Boy Shrimp	Class Mama's Boy
Class Boy Teaser	Class Mini-skirter
Class Bragger	Class Muscle Man
Class Brain	Class Musician
Class Bubble Head	Class Nice Girl
Class Bully	Class Nice Guy
Class Burper	Class Pencil Chewer
Class Cheater	Class Pest
Class Chowhound	Class President
Class Clock Watcher	Class Romantics
Class Daredevil	Class Showoff
Class Dirty Mouth	Class Singer
Class Dude	Class Sissy
Class Dumbbell	Class Slob
Class Dumbelle	Class Slowpoke
Class Dunce	Class Sneak
Class Flunker	Class Speedster
Class Follower	Class Stinker
Class Girl Chaser	Class Stuck-up
Class Girl Dancer	Class Sweater Girl
Class Girl Shrimp	Class Sweetheart
Class Girl Teaser	Class Teacher Lover
Class Glamor Girl	Class Teacher Hater
Class Gossip	Class Teeny Bopper
Class Gum Chewer	Class Tomboy
Class Hero	Class Whistler

NAME LABELS

Andy	Gene	Mary*
Al	George	Mike
Alice	Greg	Nancy
Ann*	Harry	Nick
Art	Helen	Paul
Barbara	Irene	Pat
Betty*	Jack	Peggy
Bill	Jackie	Pete
Billy	Jane	Phil
Bob*	Jean*	Phyllis
Bonnie	Jeff	Ralph
Bruce	Jerry	Ray
Carl	Jill	Ricky
Cathy	Jim*	Roger
Cheryl	Jimmy	Ronnie
Charlie	Joan	Roy
Cindy	Joe*	Sally
Dan	John*	Sam
Dave	Johnny	Sandy
Debbie	Joyce	Shirley
Diane	Judy	Stan
Dick*	Julie	Steve
Don	Karen	Susan
Donna	Kathy	Ted
Dottie	Ken	Terry
Doug	Kevin	Tim
Ed	Larry	Tom
Frances	Linda	Tony
Frank	Lisa	Vera
Fred	Lois	Wally
Flo	Lou	Walt
Gail	Marie	Wanda
Gary	Marilyn	Will

MY LITTLE PONY (225)

1 3/4" X 2 1/2"

A 1986 Production of Diamond Toy, "My Little Pony" was aimed at the pre-teen sticker-collecting set. There are 225 color artwork stickers in the set, the backs of which carry offers for either a backpack or a "collapsible travel bag." The 32-page album is designed in the "coded" format that has come to characterize Diamond issues. Note: set price includes album.

ITEM	MINT	EX
Set	25.00	18.00
Sticker	.10	.07
Wrapper	--	.35
Album	2.00	1.50

NABISCO'S WILDLIFE (50) CARD COLLECTION

1 1/8" X 2 3/4"

The artwork and text for this 50-card nature series were prepared for Nabisco by H. Wayne Trimm. One card was inserted into each pack of Sugar Daddy or Sugar Mama caramel pops during the distribution period. The "Nabis-co Wildlife Card Collection" was distributed in 1968 as series No. 6 in a continuing nature program. An album could be ordered through the mail to house the set.

ITEM	MINT	EX
Set	35.00	25.00
Card	.60	.45

NASTY NOTES (32)

2 1/2" X 3 1/2"

The size listed in the heading refers to the folded "Nasty Notes" as they came out of the pack. When completely unfolded, the "punch line" and artwork sheet measures 6 7/8" X 9 3/4". Every note is numbered on the nearly-blank panel opposite the original set-up line. Nasty Notes are clearly labelled "a series of 32" and were issued by Topps in 1967. Note: no mint prices given since notes were pre-folded to fit smaller packaging.

ITEM	MINT	EX
Set	--	185.00
Note	--	5.00
Wrapper	--	15.00
Boxes		
No Sticker	--	75.00
Sticker	--	100.00

1 Some Are Called Jim
2 Roses Smell Pretty
3 Horns Make A Blast
4 You Come On Strong
5 I Love Your Style
6 I Love Brown Eyes
7 You're Too Much The Living End
8 You Have The Sweetest Smile
9 You Dress Real Cool
10 You've Got Real Nerve
11 You Have Such Daring
12 You Always Smile
13 The Grass Is Green
14 I Think About You All The Time
15 My Heart Aches For You
16 I'd Like To Build You Some-thing
17 When You Are Speaking...
18 Your Golden Ringlets
19 You're Special
20 You Have A Lot Of Class
21 You're On a Different Wave Length
22
23 There's Something I Must Tell You...
24 As Each Day Dawns
25 You Always Do The Right Thing
26 I Just Can't Go Out With You
27 You Ought To Be In Pictures
28 You're A Special Kind Of Person
29 I Always Said You Had The Build
30 The Beauty Creams They Sell Today
31 Roses Are Blue
32 When I'm With You

NASTY VALENTINE NOTES (30)   2 1/2" X 3 1/2"

Topps revised the "folded note" format for this 30-item set issued in 1971. "Nasty Valentine Notes" have two features which clearly distinguish them from "Nasty Notes": the cupid & hearts design on the panel opposite the set-up line and a stated set total of 30. The wrapper is orange with a deep pink and yellow title. Note: no mint prices given since items were pre-folded to fit smaller packaging.

ITEM	MINT	EX
Set	--	100.00
Note	--	3.00
Wrapper	--	20.00
Box	--	75.00

1 I Think You're Really Groovy
2 You're A Liberated Woman...
3 You're 5-foot-2/Eyes of Blue...
4 You're Concerned About Pollution...
5 You're Really Into Yoga
6 You've Got A Spiffy Motor Bike...
7 You're Always On/You Always Clown
8 Your Groovy Clothes and Freaky Hair...
9 Under Ultra Violet Light We Dance

10 I Love Your Granny Glasses
11 You Made Me Flip When First We Met...
12 If You Were the Only Guy in the World
13 I Love the Odor in Your Room
14 There's Something I Must Ask You...
15 You Remind Me of Great Poetry...
16 You Love to Wander through the Trees...
17 You're Really Quite A Hippie
18 Your Long Hair is a Turn-On
19 You Say City Life's a Drag
20 I've Heard Nobody's Perfect
21 You've Got Quite a Sense of Humor...
22 You Fix the Motor in Your Car...
23 You Dress Just Like An Indian...
24 Your Pocketbook Looks Really Great
25 You're Committed to Causes...
26 To All the World You Are a Saint...
27 You Like Wearing Hot Pants...
28 You 're Always Wearing Bells and Beads
29 You're a Great Freedom Fighter
30 When I Look at You - Time Stands Still...

NATIONAL FUNGUS FOOTBALL LEAGUE (24 & 1)   2 1/2" X 3 1/2"

Out on Fungus Isle they play a pretty mean brand of football and there's quite a rivalry going between the Northern Cave, Eastern Tree, and Southern Swamp teams. This 1991 set of 24 cards from Pyramid Marketing introduces us to various National Fungus Football League personalities: players, a head coach, an official, and the commissoner and founder of the NFFL, Abe Fromage. Not that football is the only thing that concerns the denizens of Fungus Isle. The players also use their amazing skills to thwart the evil schemes of those who would disrupt life and football on the island. An 8-page folding comic book, included with the set, tells us of just such an episode. The neon artwork on the card fronts is surrounded by heavy black borders and the backs provide biographical details for individuals and descriptions of The Power Citadel and of Fungus Isle. Note: values are for mint grade only since NFFL is sold only in set form.

ITEM	MINT	EX
Set	4.00	--

1 Welcome to Fro-Set
2 Zoom - QB
3 Monsoon Kelly - Defense
4 Cyclone - Runningback
5 Mozark - Cornerback / Punter
6 Quadrus - Wide Receiver
7 Flex - QB
8 Grim Brothers - Linebackers
9 Algicus - Multi-Positional
10 Hammer - Runningback
11 Hood - Runningback
12 Abe Formage - Founder / Commissioner
13 Dr. Peter Neuro - Head Coach
14 Corneus - Official
15 Fungus Island
16 Power Citadel
17 Zoom In Action
18 The Infamous Grim Brothers
19 Mozark In Action
20 Hammer vs. Algicus
21 Monsoon In Action
22 Flex In Action
23 Cyclone In Action
24 Super Fungus Bowl Highlights

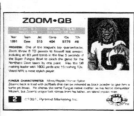

NATIONAL GEOGRAPHIC WORLD (?)

2 1/2" X 3 1/4"

COOLIE

The coolie is one of the most common butterflies in its range. When light strikes this butterfly's wings at a certain angle, shiny patches of purple appear. The coolie lives in the tropics in open spaces along rivers and near houses.

• RANGE – northern South America and Panama

NATIONAL GEOGRAPHIC WORLD Butterfly Series. No. 12

NATIONAL GEOGRAPHIC

world

SEPTEMBER 1979

Casting Tracks
Special Houses
Soccer
Birds That Can't Fly

A series of "collector's cards" issued in 9-card panels in "National Geographic World," a children's magazine, beginning in September, 1979. The cards are slightly smaller than standard size and are printed on thin cardboard stock. All pictures seen to date are color photographs which fall into the following categories: Spacecraft, Cats, House Cats, Butterflies, Horses, Dogs, Birds, and Gemstones. The promotional copy in the magazine states that there are nine subjects per series, but numbers as high as 27 have been confirmed for some. According to the editors, not every copy of the magazine contained the same cards, thereby creating a diversity of titles and establishing an incentive for kids to trade with one another for the cards they needed. At this time, the length of the set is unknown and the cards sell for 25 cents in excellent grade. Intact panels of nine cards are valued at $3.00 (with or without magazine).

NATIONAL PERIODICAL/ WARNER BROS. CARDS (30)

DC HEROES
Aquaman
Batman
Cat Woman
Clark Kent
Lois Lane
Robin
Superman
The Joker
The Penguin
The Riddler
Wonder Woman

WARNER BROTHERS CHARACTERS
Beaky Buzzard
Bugs Bunny
Cool Cat
Daffy Duck
Elmer Fudd
Foghorn Leghorn
Henery Hawk
Honey Bunny
Merlin The Magic Mouse
Pepe Le Pew
Petunia Pig
Porky Pig
Road Runner
Speedy Gonzales
Sylvester
Tasmanian Devil
Tweety
Wile E. Coyote
Yosemite Sam

The manufacturer and method of distribution of this colorful art-work series have yet to been confirmed, but it appears - from stains seen on some of the cards - that it may have come in bread or cereal. The cards fall into two categories: DC Comics charac-ters, which bear a "1974 National Periodical Publications Inc." line on back, and cartoon characters, which have a "1974 Warner Bros. Inc." credit on back. The back of each DC Comic character card has a B&W comic-strip adven-ture involving the hero or villain pictured on front. In similar fashion, there is a B&W comic strip story on the back of each Warner Brothers cartoon character card. Neither variety is numbered and the checklist below contains all the titles reported to The Hobby Card In-dex as of this date. Note: cards with stains cannot be graded ex-cellent or mint.

ITEM	MINT	EX
Card	2.00	1.50

NEW KIDS ON THE BLOCK — SERIES 1 (88 & 11)

Never underestimate the buying power of pre- and barely-teenage girls. The Beatles, The Monkees, and now, New Kids On The Block, are all groups which were propelled to star-dom by screaming mobs wear-ing pony tails and braces. The Beatles, of course, went on to capture the musical minds of adults with their incredible variety and talents. The Monkees turned out to be a purely juvenile fancy which did, indeed, pass and who knows what will become of NKOTB? For the time being, however, they have carved out their own very popular and lucrative niche just outside the realm of mainstream adult music.

Topps Gum decided to ride the NKOTB wave by printing two series of cards about the group. The first series, issued in 1990, consists of 88 cards and eleven stickers. The card fronts bear photographs of two varieties: posed publicity stills and "action" shots from con-certs. Eleven of the photos are black and white; whether this was an attempt to link NKOTB with old time rock 'n roll, or just some composer's attempt to be "arty" is hard to say. Series 1 cards were issued in both wax and cello (99¢) packs and both types appear in two color varieties. As usual, the sticker backs are puzzle pieces, but Topps pulled a fast one by print-ing two different puzzles (red border & yellow border). This means that each sticker front has two separate puzzle piece packs. Many dealers and collec-tors may still be unaware of this deviation from normal Topps procedure, so we have priced card and sticker sets individually below.

ITEM	MINT	EX
Sets		
Cards	8.50	6.50
Stickers		
Yellow puzzle	3.50	2.25
Red puzzle	3.50	2.25
Card	.10	.07
Sticker	.30	.20
Wrappers		
Wax (2) each	--	.35
Cello (2) each	--	.35
Boxes		
Wax	--	2.00
Cello	--	3.00

1 New Kids Mania!!!	44 Jonathan Knight
2 Reluctant Idols	45 Jordan Knight
3 Setting Records	46 Joe Mcintyre
4 Bookin'	47 Hot Moves!
5 Girlfriends	48 Did You Know...
6 Joe Mcintyre	49 On The Road
7 Donnie Walberg	50 Did You Know...
8 Jonathan Knight	51 Romancin' New Kids
9 Danny Wood	52 Good Friends
10 Looks Aren't Everything	53 Smart Guys
11 NKOTB Quiz!	54 Workin' Hard
12 NKOTB Quiz!	55 Funny Guy
13 NKOTB Quiz!	56 Balancing Act
14 NKOTB Quiz!	57 Home Boys
15 NKOTB Quiz!	58 Young Kid
16 NKOTB Quiz!	59 Social Issues
17 NKOTB Quiz!	60 Joe on TV?
18 NKOTB Quiz!	61 They're So Popular
19 NKOTB Quiz!	62 NKOTB Movie?
20 NKOTB Quiz!	63 Dress for Success
21 Message To Fans!	64 Great Shape
22 Bookin' On Tour	65 Stylish
23 Did You Know...	66 Love and Snacks
24 New Kids Have This In Common...	67 The Future
	68 Did You Know...
25 Sports Fans!	69 Going Platinum!
26 Baseball Fan	70 NKOTB Quiz!
27 Jonathan Knight	71 NKOTB Quiz!
28 Jordan Knight	72 NKOTB Quiz!
29 Danny Wood	73 NKOTB Quiz!
30 The Birth of the New Kids on the Block	74 NKOTB Quiz!
	75 NKOTB Quiz!
31 Donnie is Discovered!	76 NKOTB Quiz!
32 Finding the Fab Five	77 NKOTB Quiz!
33 Three More New Kids!	78 NKOTB Quiz!
34 The Sixth New Kid?	79 NKOTB Quiz!
35 Joe Gets His Break!	80 Home Cooking!
36 Newest New Kid	81 Big Time
37 Ambitious!	82 School Days
38 Popular Boys	83 Cover Girl
39 Vital Statistics	84 Dancin'
40 Vital Statistics	85 The Right Fans!
41 Vital Statistics	86 New Kids Have Heart
42 Vital Statistics	87 Peace
43 Donnie Walberg	88 Homeboys

STICKERS
1 Jonathan
2 Danny
3 Donnie
4 Hangin' Tough
5 Joe
6 Jonathan
7 Jordan
8 Joe
9 Donnie
10 Hangin' Tough
11 Jordan

NEW KIDS ON THE BLOCK — SERIES 2
(88 & 11)

2 1/2" X 3 1/2"

Topps followed up with a second series of NKOTB cards (89-176) and stickers (12-22) later in 1990. In comparison to the first series, the front colors of the sequel are more attractive due to the pretty lavender and white borders, although the photographs (82 color, 6 B&W) are more of the same "action" and publicity shots. The backs, which are overlaid with lavender color, continue the style of headings used in Series 1, telling us about the Kids' hopes, habits, work schedule, etc. Once again, the cards were distributed in both wax and cello packs; these have a large "New Pix! 2nd

New Kids on The Block - Series 2

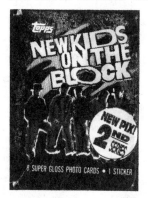

Series" spot on the front. There is only one puzzle picture for the sticker backs since Topps decided to make two different sticker fronts this time around by altering the background details behind each picture. Note: the price differential between Series 1 and Series 2 is due to factors involving product cost, supply, and sort.

ITEM	MINT	EX
Sets		
Cards	10.00	7.50
Stickers (2)		
each	5.00	3.50
Card	.10	.07
Sticker	.35	.25
Wrappers		
Wax (2) each	--	.35
Cello (2) each	--	.50
Boxes		
Wax	--	2.00
Cello	--	3.00

141 Lonely Guys
142 Peacemaker
143 So Little Time
144 Heard Saying...
145 Spicy Smiles
146 Jonathan Knight
147 Peace Lover
148 New Album
149 Maurice Starr
150 Danny Wood
151 Joe's Family
152 Message To Fans
153 Cookie Lover
154 Aware and Concerned
155 Not Perfect
156 Sacrifice
157 Winners!
158 Respect
159 He Tries!
160 NKOTB Quiz
161 NKOTB Quiz
162 NKOTB Quiz
163 NKOTB Quiz
164 NKOTB Quiz
165 NKOTB Quiz
166 NKOTB Quiz
167 NKOTB Quiz
168 NKOTB Quiz
169 NKOTB Quiz
170 Donnie's Wish
171 Giving Guys
172 Phone Calls
173 Together
174 Turning Point
175 Old Times
176 Do Good

89 The Long Road
90 Fun Bunch
91 Smart Danny
92 Chopper Hoppers
93 Danny Wood
94 Thanks Mom!
95 Young Joe
96 Just Say No
97 Jordan Knight
98 Picture Perfect
99 Bros
100 Joe Pro
101 Jordan Knight
102 No Joke
103 Pinball Wizard
104 Down With Racism!
105 Keep Your Head
106 Love Those Fans
107 Street Wise
108 Where'd You Get That Style
109 Hard Workers
110 Homesick
111 Model Son
112 Showtime!
113 Be Donnie's Friend
114 Danny Wood

115 Jonathan Knight
116 Carried Away
117 Character Building
118 Hope For The Future
119 Jordan's Dream
120 NKOTB Quiz
121 NKOTB Quiz
122 NKOTB Quiz
123 NKOTB Quiz
124 NKOTB Quiz
125 NKOTB Quiz
126 NKOTB Quiz
127 NKOTB Quiz
128 NKOTB Quiz
129 NKOTB Quiz
130 New Album
131 Body Building
132 Don't Hurt Him
133 Mean Streets
134 Jonathan Knight
135 Job Well Done
136 Heard Saying...
137 C'Mon Down!
138 Male Mail
139 Come Together
140 Fame Game

STICKERS
12 Danny
13 Donnie
14 Jonathan
15 Jordan
16 Joe
17 Jordan
18 New Kids On The Block
19 Danny
20 New Kids On The Block
21 Donnie
22 New Kids On The Block

HERE IS WHAT YOUR COMPLETED BLUE BORDER PICTURE WILL LOOK LIKE:

COLLECT ALL 21 CARDS OF PICTURE C.

NEW KIDS ON THE BLOCK
ALBUM STICKERS (160)

2 SIZES

Diamond Toy jumped on the NKOTB bandwagon by releasing a 160-piece sticker set about the group in 1990. According to promotional copy on the inside cover of the album, NKOTB "is the most successful band in pop music today. Additionally, these guys are good-looking, streetwise, and smart." Diamond chose to use large color photographs of the group and of individuals on the interior pages; the spots where the stickers are designed to be placed are indicated by numbers and corner guides. There are two sticker sizes: 128 measure 1-15/16" X 2-3/8" and 32 are 2-3/8" X 3-1/2". The album cover has the very same color combinations and geometric designs employed by Topps in their card sets, so we can assume that this style was chosen by NKOTB's agents, not the manufacturers. Each 40¢ packet contained four small stickers and one large one and it had to be cut or torn to remove the contents. The album originally sold for 79¢. Note: peeled stickers and albums with stickers attached cannot be graded excellent or mint. Set price includes album.

ITEM	MINT	EX
Set	35.00	25.00
Stickers		
Small	.15	.10
Large	.35	.25
Wrapper	--	.35
Album	2.50	2.00

NEW KIDS ON THE BLOCK
BUBBLE GUM CASSETTES (24)

Topps ventured beyond their normal trading card format in creating this series of 24 NKOTB "bubble gum cassettes" in 1990. Each cardboard box has a color photograph on the front and a numbered "Kid Quiz" on the back. A miniature plastic cassette case (cello-wrapped) protects the individual boxes and the gum inside. Collectors will find the box reminiscent of the excellent one Topps used to market its baseball pin series in 1956. These novelties were

1 3/4" X 2 3/4"

manufactured for Topps in Taiwan and came packed in 24-count display boxes. It has not been confirmed that each display box held a complete set. Note: prices are for boxes in the original plastic cases. Cases may be scratched and still qualify for both grades as long as the box inside meets the required standards.

ITEM	MINT	EX
Set	20.00	15.00
Box	.75	.60
Display box	--	3.00

NEW YORK WORLD'S FAIR (24)

2 1/2" X 3 1/2"

The Card Collectors Bulletin lists the manufacturer of this set of 24 New York World's Fair cards as Ed-U Cards, although that name is not printed on the cards. The line which does appear on the card backs is totally confusing: "Copyright [symbol] 1961-1963 New York World's Fair 1964-65 Corporation." Most collectors think the series was issued in 1965. The fronts of the cards have uncaptioned color photographs of various pavilions (which is World's Fair terminology for "buildings"). The backs have a large heading followed by several paragraphs of text and the print is black on white stock. There are no card numbers and no packaging has been reported for the set to date.

ITEM	MINT	EX
Set	30.00	22.50
Card	1.00	.75

Bell System Exhibit
Christian Science Pavilion
Coca-Cola Exhibit
Eastman Kodak Pavilion
Festival of Gas Pavilion
Ford Pavilion
General Motors Futurama Building
New York State Exhibit
Plaza of the Astronauts
Port of New York Authority Heliport
7-Up International Sandwich Gardens
Schaefer Center
Sudan Pavilion
Thailand Pavilion
The Hall of Education
The Mormon Pavilion
The National Cash Register Pavilion
The Pavilion of American Interiors
The RCA Pavilion
The Tower of Light
Travelers Exhibit
United States Pavilion
Vatican Pavilion
World's Fair Monorail

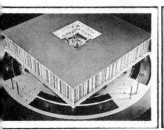

United States Pavilion

The Federal Exhibition is a declaration of faith in the spiritual greatness of the American people. It includes five separate units, each using a different exhibit technique but integrated to express and depict a total story.

An escalator takes the visitor to the upper level where he finds that our journey becomes literal in that he gets into a moving grandstand carrying 60 people that will move as a continuous ride through a series of motion picture experiences throughout the entire upper level.

At the conclusion of the ride the visitor returns to the lower level where children and adults will receive supplementary reference guidance on every subject in the entire exhibition.

The U. S. Pavilion will also sponsor an extensive musical program of performers and groups from throughout the U. S. and possessions.

© 1961-1963 NEW YORK WORLD'S FAIR 1964-1965 CORPORATION

NICE OR NASTY VALENTINES (33)

2 1/2" X 4 3/4"

Since it is impossible to provide a written checklist of the 33 different sticker sheets in this set, we have illustrated them instead. The large sticker in the center of each sheet is designed to be affixed to the Valentine card; the blanks are filled in by selecting words from the 12 choices provided. The Valentine card has a post-card format back for mailing after the front message has been assembled. The set was marketed by Topps in 1971. Note: set prices listed are for 33 intact sticker sheets and one Valentine card.

ITEM	MINT	EX
Set	150.00	115.00
Sticker	4.00	3.00
Card	2.00	1.50
Wrapper	--	10.00

MAKE YOUR OWN VALENTINE CARD

REMOVE MESSAGE FROM STICKER AND STICK IT TO THIS CARD.

REMOVE WORDS FROM STICKER AND STICK THEM TO BLANK SPACES ON MESSAGE.

NICKELODEON (22)

2 1/2" X 3 1/2"

Nickelodeon, one of the hottest kid shows currently on the tube, is the theme of this 22-card set produced as a sales promotion by Capri Sun fruit drinks. The series uses both artwork and color photographs of the various characters appearing on the show and these are accented by orange, blue, and yellow details and green borders. A clear cellophane package containing two cards was inserted into every ten-pack carton of drinks, but as collector Wanda Chan points out, these cards are often found damaged (they are probably twisted as the fruit drinks shift in transit). This may not matter to the targeted juvenile audience but it will frustrate serious hobbyists interested in this set. Luckily, the entire series could be sent for via a mail offer requiring three proofs-of-purchase and $1.59. Our prices are based on 50% of the cost of obtaining a set in this manner: three cartons of drinks at $2.50 each, plus $1.59. Note: even if they come right out of the box, damaged cards cannot be graded excellent or mint.

ITEM	MINT	EX
Set	4.50	3.25
Card	.20	.15

Batly
Brain
Doowopasaurs I
Doowopasaurs II
Doug Funnie
Eureeka
Inspector Gadget
Magellan
Nick is Kids
Patti Mayonnaise
Penny
Phil & Lil DeVille
Porkchop
Rep Style
Ren & Stimpy
Roger & Stinky
Stimpy & Ren
Stu & Didi
Tommy & Chuckie
Tommy & Spike
"Wheels" Lucille
Zardy

NIGHTMARE ON ELM STREET (120 & 10)   2 1/2" X 3 1/2"

HE'S BAAACK! Yes, Freddy Krueger is back and he's brought a set of Impel's trading cards with him. The first thing you should know about this set is that it carries a warning label: "Due to mature subject, material may not be suitable for children." That's appropriate, but it may not go far enough, because some material in this set may not be suitable for adults either. Impel anticipated such concerns and made the series available via catalog only. For $39.95, you received the following: 120 "regular" cards, ten "specialty" cards, two holograms, and "Freddy's own boiler room box" (cardboard coffin). An order form packed inside the box offered the same set, with ten new specialty cards, two new holograms, a "Freddy Cards-Shirt," and a "Freddy Certificate" for an additional $39.95. That means that a Freddy Krueger card collector would have to shell out eighty bucks to complete this line of Impel Elm Street collectibles. Now that's marketing with a capital M! So if you like buckets of blood and bodies bouncing off the walls and ceilings, go take out a loan and buy this set. Note: neither regular or specialty cards are captioned. The numbers on specialty cards are prefixed with the letter "S." One of the holograms in my box was damaged; send damaged cards to Impel for replacement. Sold in boxed sets only.

ITEM	MINT	EX
Set I	40.00	---
Set II	40.00	---

NIGHT OF THE LIVING DEAD (50)   2 1/2" X 3 1/2"

It is fitting that a campy movie be enshrined in a campy card set. "Night of the Living Dead," the low-budget horror tale of ghouls brought back to life by excess radiation in the atmosphere, is the subject of this Rosem set issued in 1987. Looking through the 50 black and white photos in the set, only a handful are as well composed as the card illustrated here. Most are dark, grainy, out-of-focus, off-angle views which, come to think of it, are a perfect mirror of what this amateurish movie was all about. The backs of the cards carry the card number, caption (which is also on front), and a running description of how a bunch of inept, but live human beings fall prey to the ghouls (Some of the recently dead turn ghoulish themselves, just in time to be roasted by the local constabulary). Rosem's Night of the Living Dead was issued in set form only and came packaged in a black wrapper.

ITEM	MINT	EX
Set	8.00	---

Night of The Living Dead

1 Barbara and Johnny
2 Cemetery Visit
3 Attacked!
4 Death Struggle
5 Death in the Cemetery
6 Pursued!
7 Running For Help
8 Refuge
9 Out of Order
10 Grim Discovery
11 Ben Arrives
12 Intruder
13 Barricade
14 Harry and Tom
15 Hiding in the Cellar
16 News Broadcast
17 Police Action
18 Search and Destroy
19 The Plan
20 Wall of Flames
21 Belligerent Foe
22 "Don't Go Out There!"
23 To The Pump
24 Fatal Accident
25 Flames of Death
26 Locked Out!
27 Betrayed
28 Ghouls Approaching
29 Flesh Feast
30 "Oh My God"
31 "Who's Next?"
32 Insatiable Hunger
34 Final Siege
35 Harry's Shot
36 Johnny!
37 Ghoulish Hunger
38 Daughter of Death
39 Karen Attacks
40 Blade of Death
41 The Dead Awake
42 Alive!
43 Ghoul Hunt
44 Gaining Victory
45 Help is Near
46 Careful Aim
47 Friendly Fire
48 Aftermath
49 Pyre
50 Checklist

NIGHT OF THE LIVING DEAD
TRADING CARDS
° ROSEM ENT.

NINTENDO (60 & 33)   2 1/2" X 3 1/2"

Cartophilic computer games are the essence of this Nintendo series issued by Topps in 1989. The 60 cards in the series are divided into six different ten-card categories: Double Dragon, Punch-Out, Super Mario Bros., Super Mario Bros. 2, The Adventures of Link, and The Adventures of Zelda. Each card has a pattern of foil dots laid over an artwork scene (called a "screen") and players must scratch off the covering and reveal the correct sequence of symbols to win the game. There are 60 different scenes and the only ones which are captioned individually belong to the boxers in Punch-Out. The stickers are actually a combination of stickers and cards. The former are die-cut peel-off designs surrounded by yellow margins; the latter are a series of numbered "Tip Cards" printed on the opposite side. Once the sticker is "peeled," only the remaining margin and the Tip Card on the other side are left. Three different 25¢ wax wrappers were issued for the series and each of these packs held 3 game cards and two sticker-cards. In addition, the same designs were used for three 59¢ cellophane packs. These contained six game cards and four stickers and were printed with a "This product is for fun — prizes awarded" line which did not appear on the wax varieties. At the present time, complete 48-count wax boxes of Nintendo are available in the hobby for $5.00 or less (these are mostly overstocks with x'd-out lids) but the collation and the nature of the cards themselves makes sets of unplayed and unpeeled cards and stickers more valuable than the apparent oversupply might indicate. Note: peeled stickers and scratched-off game cards cannot be graded excellent or mint. Boxes with defaced lids (indicating overstocks) cannot be graded excellent.

ITEM	MINT	EX
Set	20.00	13.00
Card	.25	.15
Sticker	.15	.10
Wrappers		
Wax (3) each	--	.10
Cellophane		
(3) each	--	.25
Boxes		
Wax	--	2.00
Cello	--	3.00

NINTENDO ALBUM STICKERS (150)   1 3/4" X 2 1/2"

Diamond Toy's entry into the Nintendo arena was this 1989 set of 150 stickers and album. The stickers may contain an entire small scene or may be a partial design which has to be placed together with other partials to form a picture. Regardless of format, each sticker is numbered and has a corresponding spot marked for it in the album. Diamond used their trademarked 3-D "Magic Decoder" process to create "action" on both the stickers and the album pages. The 24-page album not only has designated sticker spots, but also has a series of games, mazes, and scorecards. The Nintendo packet contained six stickers and sold for 35¢; it required cutting or tearing to remove the stickers. The stickers are printed in both English and French since the product was also distributed in Canada. Note: set price includes album.

ITEM	MINT	EX
Set	35.00	27.50
Sticker	.20	.15
Wrapper	--	.25
Album	2.00	1.50

NUTTY AWARDS (32)   3 1/8" X 5 1/4"

"Nutty Awards," which was distributed by Topps in 1964, adopted the basic "license" format first used on arcade cards by Exhibit Supply and similar companies. Each card has an artwork front with humorous award or license text; the card number is located in a ribbon design. The backs have the set title printed above a standard postcard layout. The wrapper is red with a black title and blue, yellow, and pink accents.

ITEM	MINT	EX
Set	37.50	27.50
Card	1.00	.75
Wrapper	--	25.00
Box	--	75.00

1	Idiot Award	9	Most Unpopular Student Award	17	Conceit Award	25	Know-It-All License
2	Most Unlikely To Succeed Award	10	Back Seat Driver's License	18	Loony Driver Permit	26	Permit Not To Do Homework
3	Right To Be Nasty License	11	License To Take Over TV Set	19	Liars License	27	Great Lover License
4	Permit To Use The Phone	12	Dishonorable Discharge	20	Lateness Award	28	Free Testing License
5	Juvenile Delinquency Award	13	Dog License	21	Disgusting Eater License	29	Truancy License
6	Coward's License	14	Rat Fink Award	22	Teacher's Pet Award	30	Stupid Student Award
7	Cheaters License	15	Cheapskate License	23	Slob Award	31	Pain In The Neck License
8	Permit To Be A Pig	16	Squealer's License	24	Permit To Stay Up Late	32	Bull Thrower's Award

NUTTY INITIAL STICKERS (?)

Topps employed the "initial sticker" format once again in this 1967 issue. The stickers are front-peel designs in the shape of letters and numbers, with each shape containing "weird" (rather than "horror") monster artwork. Photocopies from Topps' archives indicate that each letter of the alphabet is represented at least once by a large design, but that numbers only appear on smaller 4-on-1 sticker sheets. The number of sticker sheets in the set is not yet known. The 5-cent wrapper is black with the title spelled out in letters of different colors.

ITEM	MINT	EX
Sticker	4.00	3.00
Wrappers		
Regular	--	25.00
Test	--	100.00
Box	--	75.00

Regular issue wrapper is one solid color, has "instruction" side panels, & bears the wrapper code 0-417-85-01-7.

Test wrapper is white wax paper with a large sticker affixed to center. The manufacturer and ingredients are printed on a white sticker (used to hold the pack shut) and the wrapper code is T-91-6a.

ODD RODS (5 SETS)

The Odd Rods family of sticker sets is one of the Donruss Company's most popular productions. However, it is also very confusing to collectors because two of the original three sets were reprinted, with the same artwork, under different names. Another set issued later was composed of favorite cards taken from the first three issues, adding to the confusion. Donruss threw in a giant monkey wrench by issuing a "first series" of cards numbered 67-132 and following it with a "second series" numbered 1-66! The layout below was constructed with information provided by Neil Lewis, of Donruss, and collectors Jody Slates and Roxanne Toser.

Odd Rods

A set of 44 numbered stickers believed to have been issued in 1969. The "Fords Breakfast of Chevys" drawing on the back of each card has a "25" printed in the lower right corner. No box has been reported for this set to date.

ITEM	MINT	EX
Set	65.00	50.00
Sticker	1.25	1.00
Wrapper	--	15.00

Odd Rods

1 Bid Daddy	12 Big Fink	23 So What	34 Bug Repellent
2 Mistua Mustang	13 Gas Eater	24 Volks Rule	35 Happiness Is a Low E.T.
3 Gee-Tee-O	14 Chrome Coffin	25 Fords Breakfast of Chevys	36 Mister Lifter
4 Powered By Junk	15 Ram Charger	26 Mini-Quick	37 O.L.T. (Out To Lunch)
5 Bad Start	16 Let's Drag Hog	27 Beach Bunny	38 Weekend Warrior
6 Blower Bracket	17 Rocker Racer	28 Plumbers Delight	39 The Shaker
7 Mad Dragger	18 Draggin Machine	29 Mini Quick	40 Road Runner
8 Hemi Sprint	19 Share Cropper	30 Chevy Killer	41 Bonzai Bomb
9 Hill Climber	20 Mad Shifter	31 Dragon Lady	42 Panic Mouse
10 Super Stuff	21 H2O Go	32 Wild Angle	43 Man Hatcher
11 Imported Animal	22 Super Shift	33 Ford Killer	44 King Cougar

Odder Odd Rods / Fabulous Odd Rods

Odder Odd Rods are a set of 66 stickers thought to have been marketed in 1970. The backs have the statement "Collect All 66 Odder Odd Rods Cards" printed under the hand holding the "Fords" card. Fabulous Odd Rods are a 1973 re-issue of Odder Odd Rods. They have the same obverse designs and numbering sequence of the original set. The backs are different: there is no set title stated and the caption in the card drawing is missing.

ITEM	MINT	EX
Odder Odd Rods		
Set	95.00	75.00
Sticker	1.25	1.00
Wrapper	--	20.00
Box	--	75.00
Fabulous Odd Rods		
Set	75.00	55.00
Sticker	1.00	.75
Wrapper	--	3.00
Box	--	60.00

 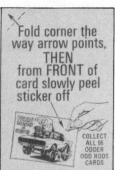  

1 Triumph	14 Head Ache	27 Witch Power	39 4 Forward
2 All Haul	15 Super Fuzz	28 No title (six-eyed monster)	40 Fruit Salad
3 Bonny and Clod	16 No title (five-eyed monster)	29 Slickey	41 No title (U.S. mail)
4 Hippies Delight	17 Straight A's	30 Dragit	42 No title (Roller derby)
5 Javelin	18 Clean Sweep	31 Speed Sicle	43 Clod
6 Swinger	19 Strip Roller	32 Camaro Power	44 No title (golf cart)
7 Cycle Family	20 No title (Roman helmet)	33 Vette	45 Dunce
8 Rubber Laid	21 No title (green toad)	34 Mustang	46 Blow Your Mind
9 Dodge'm	22 Bad Trip	35 Gasser	47 Maverick 429
10 Week-end Warrior	23 No title	36 No Title (Civil War monster)	48 Olds Rule The Street
11 No title (garbage can head)	24 Buried Alive	37 Fly Catcher	49 Double "OO"
12 On the Carpet	25 25 cents Per Quarter Mile	38 Brinks Buggy	50 High Karate
13 Dodge Charger	26 Plain Power		51 You Meet the Nicest People on Honda
			52 Z/28
			53 Tuned For Speed
			54 Legion-Air
			55 California Or Bust
			56 ManXForever
			57 Grrrrrr
			58 Dual Headers
			59 VW
			60 Mole Digger
			61 Speed Demon
			62 Watered Down
			63 No title (red devil)
			64 Cold Power
			65 Medic
			66 Whirly

The estimated date of issue for Oddest Odd Rods is 1970. It is a set of 66 stickers numbered 67-132 and is generally considered by collectors to be the "second series," or continuation, of Odder Odd Rods. The backs have either the standard "peel" instructions (the car drawing is different from previous sets) or a large-scale sketch sent in by Odd Rods fans (with no "peel" directions). Fantastic Odd Rods is a 1973 re-issue of Oddest Odd Rods. The pink coloration added to the background surrounding the artwork makes this set immediately identifiable. The car sketch on the reverse is the original "Fords Breakfast of Chevy's" but without caption or number. The braintrust at Donruss had a short-circuit when they marketed "Fantastic," a remake of a second series set ("Oddest"), as a first series, yet were too lazy to renumber it.

ITEM	MINT	EX
Oddest Odd Rods		
Set	95.00	75.00
Sticker	1.25	1.00
Wrapper	--	20.00
Box	--	75.00
Fantastic Odd Rods		
Set	75.00	55.00
Sticker	1.00	.75
Wrapper	--	5.00
Box	--	35.00

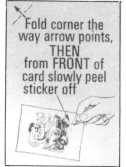

Oddest Odd Rods/Fantastic Odd Rods [Series 1]

67 Stokey Bearly	84 Sissy Slicks	101 no title (jeep & grenade)	117 Power
68 Grimlin Gobbler	85 Street Peace	102 Ratty Randy	118 Monte Carlo Meeny
69 Roiler Derby	86 Dragin Wagon	103 Opel Oger	119 no title (roadrunner)
70 Blower	87 Firebird	104 Cougar Power	120 Hornet Hater
71 no title (pirate kat)	88 Octane Octopus	105 Dealer	121 Mustang Mite
72 Peace	89 no title (pail & shovel)	106 no title (green car)	122 Strip Pest
73 Eats	90 Stinker	107 Cuda Baby	123 Cherry Bomb
74 Purple People Eater	91 No title (VW van)	108 Get Away Man	124 no title (green & yellow trunk)
75 Boss 429	92 Rail Delite	109 Grimlin Grouch	125 Super Souix
76 Fanatic	93 no title (bed)	110 OK Dart	126 no title (ice cream cone)
77 Trans-Am	94 Reel 1	111 Challenger	127 G-Toe
78 Goin Gator	95 AMX Forever	112 Vigorous Vega	128 Cautious Capri
79 Fuzz Bucket	96 Pushin Pinto	113 Super Blower	129 Cougar Crunch
80 Hungry For Fords	97 no title (safari hat)	114 Bad Baron	130 Super Dooper
81 no title (sandman)	98 Dart Doin's	115 No Hands	131 Nit Pix
82 Slugger	99 Reckless Rebel	116 Hornet Honey	132 Orbit Vette
83 Dessert	100 VW Varmit		

Fantastic Odd Rods [Series 2]

The second series of Fantastic Odd Rods, issued in 1973, is probably unique in the annals of card history for being a second series with first series numbers issued after a first series with second series numbers that was a reprint of yet another series. Fortunately, the fronts have completely new artwork (although the backs are identical to "first series" Fantastic Odd Rods) and cards of this set are easily identified by consulting our checklist.

ITEM	MINT	EX
Set	75.00	55.00
Sticker	1.00	.75
Wrapper	—	6.00

1 Sebring	18 Maniac	35 Maverick	51 Cut-Up
2 Nova Nut	19 Trashy Trike	36 Bunyan Bandit	52 Cuda
3 Dodgem	20 Dabon	37 Gremlin	53 El Camino
4 No title (yellow monster, red car)	21 Pinto	38 Chrysler	54 Impala
5 VW	22 Limo	39 Challenger	55 Dodge
6 Dart	23 Oldie Goldie	40 Buick Bandit	56 Finger Likin'
7 Porsche	24 Dig Off	41 HP	57 Charger
8 TR-6	25 Runner	42 We'll Make It	58 No title (cowboy)
9 No title (blue monster with band-aid)	26 Blast Off	43 No title (yellow monster, red car)	59 Oil Burner
10 VW Bus	27 Apollo	44 Cougar	60 Opel
11 Stitches	28 Javelin	45 Omega	61 No title (spotted monster)
12 Gold Duster	29 AMC	46 Eats	62 Camper Scamper
13 Fire Bird	30 T-Bird	47 Jag	63 No title (aviator hat)
14 Montego	31 Lemans	48 To You	64 Pickup Power
15 Treasure Minded	32 Goin Glob	49 Toyota	65 Vette
16 Drag On	33 Squire Fire	50 Fury	66 Eats Cars
17 Vega	34 Super Blown		

Odd Rod All Stars

In 1970, Donruss invited Odd Rods fans to vote for their favorite designs. The results of this promotion were incorporated into a series of 66 stickers issued in 1971. All of the artwork appearing in this set was taken from cards in the "Odd," "Odder," and "Oddest" sets which preceded it, but with new numbers assigned.

ITEM	MINT	EX
Set	95.00	75.00
Sticker	1.25	1.00
Wrapper	—	10.00

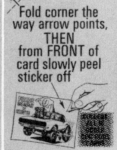

Odd Rods All Stars

1	No title [monster in green shorts]	18	Reckless Rebel	35	Weekend Warrior	51	ManXforever
2	O.T.L. [Out To Lunch!]	19	VW	36	Mister Lifter	52	No title [garbage can head]
3	Mad Shifter	20	Roller Derby	37	H2O Go	53	Blow Your Mind
4	Fruit Salad	21	Grimlin Grouch	38	Purple People Eater	54	Mad Hatcher
5	Mini-Quick	22	Bug Repellent	39	Draggin Machine	55	Big Daddy
6	No title [6-eyed monster]	23	Mustang Mite	40	Super Blower	56	No title [VW hippie van]
7	Mini Quick	24	Triumph	41	Cuda Baby	57	Gas Eater
8	All Haul	25	Vigorous Vega	42	4 Forward	58	Eats
9	Hill Climber	26	Let's Drag Hog	43	Fuzz Bucket	59	Blower
10	Bad Start	27	Peace	44	No title [golfer]	60	Firebird
11	Fly Catcher	28	Dessert	45	Pushin Pinto	61	Week-End Warrior
12	Vette	29	Beach Bunny	46	Cherry Bomb	62	The Shaker
13	Mad Dragger	30	No title [pumpkin car]	47	Wild Angle	63	Bonzai Bomb
14	Big Fink!	31	Maverick 429	48	Super Fuzz	64	California or Bust
15	Chrome Coffin	32	Cycle Family	49	Z/28	65	Challenger
16	Powered By Junk!	33	Super Stuff!	50	Cougar Power	66	Chevy Killer
17	Fords—Breakfast of Chevys	34	Sharecropper				

Ah ha, non-sports aficionados. For years you made fun of "silly" racing cards like Fleer's "Official Drag Champs." Now Bubba B. Collector has come out of the pit stop and is snapping up racing cards right and left, causing prices to escalate. Whoda' ever thunk it?

Although they resemble Fleer's "Drag Nationals" series, the cards of this set have the title clearly printed on the back. The fronts contain uncaptioned color photos of dragstrip action and the pictures are surrounded by white borders. The card caption is located at the very top on the back and beneath it are the set titles, sponsor (AHRA), and sponsor logo. The set was issued in three different wrappers and the cards are not numbered. Note: "Official Drag Champs" were also released in Canada; these cards are numbered and have a "Fleer Ltd., Don Mills, Ontario" line on the back.

ITEM	MINT	EX
Set	145.00	115.00
Card	2.00	1.50
Wrappers		
(3) each	——	15.00
Box	––	35.00

"Akron" Arlen Vanke's 1971 Plymouth Duster
Beyer & Young Top Stock Mercury Cougar
Big John Mazmanian's 1970 Barracuda Funny Car
Bill Hielscher's "Mr. Bardahl" 1970 Camaro Super Stock
Bill Jenkins' "Grumpy's Toy" 1969 Camaro Super Stock
Bruce Dodd's "Spirit" Top Fuel Dragster
Bruce Larson's "U.S.A.–1" 1970 Camaro Funny Car
Candies & Hughes 1970 Barracuda Funny Car
Chris Karamesines' "Chizler" Top Fuel Dragster
C-K-C Chevy II Funny Car
Crietz & Donovan Top Fuel Dragster
Dick Harrell/"Super John" McFadden's Camaro Super Stock
Dick Harrell's "Mr. Chevrolet" 1970 Camaro Funny Car
Dick Landy's 1970 Challenger Super Stock
Dick Loehr's "Stampede" Maverick Super Stock
Don & Roy Gay's "Infinity V" 1970 Firebird Funny Car
Don "Big Daddy" Garlits' "Wynnscharger" Top Fuel Dragster
Don Grotheer's 1970 Barracuda Super Stock
Don Schumacher's "Stardust" 1970 Barracuda Funny Car
Duane Ong's "Torque Pawnbroker" Top Fuel Dragster
"Dyno Don" Nicholson's 1970 Maverick Super Stock
Ed Miller's "Hemi-Duster" 1970 Plymouth Super Stock
Ed Terry's 1970 Mustang Super Stock
Farkonas, Coil, & Minick's "Chi-Town Hustler" Funny Car

"Fast Eddie" Schartman's 1970 Cougar Super Stock
Gary Kimball's Camaro Super Stock
Gary Watson's "Paddy Wagon" Wheelie Van
Gene Snow's "Rambunctious" 1970 Dodge Challenger Funny Car
Harry Schmidt's "Blue Max" 1970 Mustang Funny Car
Hinter & Miller Camaro GT 3
Hubert Platt's "Georgia Shaker" 1970 Mustang Super Stock
Jim Nicoll's Top Fuel Dragster
John Wiebe Top Fuel Dragster
"Jungle Jim" Liberman's 1970 Camaro Funny Car
King & Marshall, "El Diablo" Top Fuel Dragster
K. S. Pittman's " 1970 Super Tiger" Opel G.T.
Larry Christopherson's "Chevy II". Funny Car
Ma & Pa Hoover's Top Fuel Dragster
Mallicoat Bros. 1960 Barracuda Gasser
Mickey Thompson's "Boss Maverick" Funny Car
Mike Burkhart/Mart Higginbotham Camaro Funny Car
Mr. Norm's "Super Charger" 1970 Dodge Charger Funny Car
Norm Tanner's "Tin Indian" GT 2 Firebird
Paul Murphy's "Miss STP" 1970 Duster Funny Car
Prock & Howell's "WarHorse" 1970 Mustang Funny Car

Ray Alley's 1969 "Engine Masters" Barracuda Funny Car
Ray Godman's "Tennessee Boll-Weevil" Top Fuel Dragster
Robert Anderson Top Fuel Dragster
Roland Leong's "Hawaiian" 1970 Dodge Charger Funny Car
Sam Auxier Jr.'s 1970 Maverick Super Stock
Sandy Elliot 1969 Mustang Top Stock
Shirley Shahan's "Drag-On-Lady" 1970 A.M.X. Top Stock
"Sneaky Pete" Robinson's "Tinkertoy" Top Fuel Dragster
Sox & Martin's 1971 Plymouth Barracuda
Steve Carbone's Top Fuel Dragster
Terry Hedrick's "Super Shaker" Chevy II Funny Car
The 1970 A.H.R.A. Grand American Professionals Funny Car Category
The 1970 A.H.R.A. Grand American Professionals Super Stock Category
The 1970 A.H.R.A. Grand American Professionals Top Fuel Category
The Ramchargers' 1970 Dodge Challenger Funny Car
Tommy Ivo's "T.V. Tommy" Top Fuel Dragster
Tony Nancy's "Sizzler" Top Fuel Dragster
Warren Gunter's "Durachrome Bug" 1970 Volkswagen Funny Car

101 DALMATIONS (225) 2" X 2 9/16"

What has 404 legs and 202 eyes and was the subject of a full-length animated movie in 1961? Yes, "101 Dalmations" is the correct answer and it is also the title of this sticker set marketed by Panini U.S.A. in December 1985. There are 225 color artwork stickers in the series, each depicting a scene (or part of one) from the Disney film. The sticker album is 32 pages long and has a blue wrap-around cover. Note: set price includes album.

ITEM	MINT	EX
Set	35.00	25.00
Sticker	.15	.10
Wrapper	––	.35
Album	2.00	1.50

ORDERS AND DECORATIONS (24) OF THE WORLD VARIOUS SHAPES

This wonderful set of 24 replica medals in miniature was distributed in the U.S. by Leaf. Each decoration has a fancy cloth ribbon and a gold-tone plastic disc. The name of the medal is printed in raised letters on the back of the disc. The series was distributed, without gum, in paper envelopes bearing a 10-cent price. A checklist is printed on the back of the envelope. A paper slip identifying the specific medal and explaining its history was inserted in every package.

ITEM	MINT	EX
Set	85.00	70.00
Medal	3.00	2.50
Wrapper	––	4.00
Box	––	25.00

Iron Cross - Germany
Order of Merit - France
Order of St. Olaf - Norway
Order of the Chrysanthemum - Japan
Order of Crown - Belgium
Order of the Elephant - Denmark
Order of the Holy Sepulchre - Vatican
Royal Victorian Order - Great Britain
The Distinguished Service Order (D.S.O.) - United Kingdom
The German Cross - West Germany
The Legion of Honor - France
The Military Order of Italy - Jtaly
The Military Order of William - Netherlands
The Most Noble Order of the Seraphin - Sweden
The Noble Order of the Garter (K.G.) - United Kingdom
The Order of "Arts Et Lettres" - France
The Order of Leopold - Belgium
The Order of Leopold II - Belgium
The Order of Merit - West Germany
The Order of Pius - Vatican
The Order of the Lion - Belgium
The Order of the Palmes Academiques - France
The Order of Victory - Soviet Union
The Victoria Cross - United Kingdom

OSMONDS (66)

2 1/2" X 3 1/2"

Donruss marketed this 66-card set featuring the Osmonds in 1973. The fronts have color photographs surrounded by a deep pink frame line, "mosaic" designs, and white borders. The backs contain the card number plus biographical sketches of, and interviews with, members of the group.

ITEM	MINT	EX
Set	60.00	45.00
Card	.75	.55
Wrapper	--	10.00
Box	--	50.00

1 Donny Osmond Portrait Puzzle	35 Alan
2 Donny Osmond Portrait Puzzle	36 Fan Club Card
3 Donny Osmond Portrait Puzzle	37 Donny
4 Donny Osmond Portrait Puzzle	38 Jay
5 Donny Osmond Portrait Puzzle	39 Jay, Donny & Merrill
6 Donny Osmond Portrait Puzzle	40 Merrill
7 Donny Osmond Portrait Puzzle	41 Donny
8 Donny Osmond Portrait Puzzle	42 Marie
9 Fan Club Card	43 Jay
10 Wayne	44 Donny
11 Fan Club Card	45 Merrill's Vital Statistics
12 Donny	46 Fan Club Card
13 Osmonds Discography	47 Donny's Discography
14 Wayne	48 Osmonds
15 Wayne & Merrill	49 Donny
16 Fan Club Card	50 Donny
17 Jay's Vital Statistics	51 Wayne
18 Donny	52 Donny
19 Alan	53 Donny
20 Donny	54 Wayne's Vital Statistics
21 Marie's Vital Statistics	55 Donny
22 Alan's Vital Statistics	56 Osmonds
23 Osmonds	57 Fan Club Card
24 Wayne	58 Fan Club Card
25 Donny	59 Jimmy
26 Jay	60 Merrill
27 Merrill	61 Fan Club Card
28 Osmonds	62 Donny
29 Alan	63 Jimmy's Vital Statistics
30 Donny	64 Merrill
31 Jay	65 Fan Club Card
32 Osmonds	66 Fan Club Card
33 Wayne	
34 Alan	

OUTER LIMITS (50)

2 1/2" X 3 1/2"

Judging from the cards in this set, there must have been a lot of monsters in the Outer Limits television series! They are pictured here in 50 color drawings, with captions underneath. The cards have black borders and prospective buy-ers should be careful to look for damage to the edges. The card number is located in a meteor design on the reverse. Next to this, the caption is repeated and a story related below. The reverses are dated "1964" and marked "Bubbles Inc."

ITEM	MINT	EX
Set	400.00	310.00
Card	6.50	5.00
Wrapper	--	150.00
Box	--	500.00

1 The Television Terror	6 The Jelly Creature	11 Man from Tomorrow
2 The Radio-active Man	7 The Unstoppable One	12 Monster from Venus
3 Transparent Creature	8 Jelly Man Attacks	13 Horror in the Woods
4 Terror from Space	9 Fangs of Death	14 Hunting New Victims
5 Man from Galaxy "X"	10 Visit from the Future	15 The Brainless Glob

16 Man with Super Sight
17 Not of This World
18 Invasion of the Sea Beast
19 The Sea Beast Strikes
20 Fury of the Sea Beast
21 Prize Catch
22 The Captive Beast
23 Human Insects
24 "Invade Earth"
25 Thing from Mercury
26 The Death Ray
27 The Doom Machine
28 Twin Space Terrors
29 Night of Terror
30 The Invader
31 The Mind Stealer
32 "You Are in My Power"

33 Incredible Ice Man
34 Frozen Terror
35 Plotting Destruction
36 Bring in the Earthmen
37 "You Can't Stop Me"
38 The Brain Destroyer
39 Martian Torture
40 The Touch of Death
41 Fearful Foe
42 Captive Scientist
43 Living Nightmare
44 The Subterraneans
45 The Clay Man
46 Clay Man's Revenge
47 The Clay Man's Next Victim
48 Uninvited Guest
49 The Escape
50 Destruction of the Clay Man

PAC—MAN (54 & 28)   2 1/2" X 3 1/16"

Of the 54 different stickers in the Pac-Man set, 36 have black backgrounds and 18 have backgrounds of various color combinations. Each sticker is numbered on the back, and the fronts contain humorous captions and advertising. The wrapper advises there are 28 different rub-off game cards (2 1/2" X 3 1/2") but these are not included in the set price since they are identical until the designs are revealed by scraping off the dots. The wrapper was printed in two different colors: one is white, the other is yellow. Note: back variations have been reported in print color, location of copyright, and "Pac-Man" design (the so-called "eyes" variety).

ITEM	MINT	EX
Sticker set	10.00	7.50
Sticker	.20	.15
Game card*	.35	.25
*Cannot be scratched off		
Wrappers		
(2) each	--	.35
Box	--	4.00

PARTRIDGE FAMILY (55) (55) (88)   2 1/2" X 3 1/2"

In 1971, Topps issued three series of cards featuring The Partridge Family. Series 1 (1-55) has yellow borders, Series 2 (1A-55A) has blue borders, and Series 3 (1B-88B) has green borders. Three different boxes are now confirmed for this set: two with 5-cent price tabs and one marked 10 cents. In addition, the single known wrapper design has been dis- covered with two different production codes, leading to speculation that a third wrap- per may exist.

GOING ON TOUR

ITEM	MINT	EX
Sets		
Series 1	40.00	30.00
Series 2	40.00	30.00
Series 3	80.00	60.00
Cards		
Series 1 & 2	.65	.50
Series 3	.80	.65
Wrappers		
(2) each	---	7.00
Boxes		
5 cent, Type 1	---	75.00
5 cent, Type 2	---	75.00
10 cent	---	30.00

ELECTRIFYING PERFORMANCE!

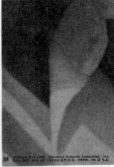

David Cassidy

Portrait Card

JOIN THE PARTRIDGE FAMILY FAN CLUB!

You get: A Free Record autographed photos, complete fact book, membership card, wallet-size photos, mini-poster, stickers, secret decoder plus pouch, much more. Send your name, address and $2.00 to:

PARTRIDGE FAMILY FAN CLUB
Dept. 3B, 5313 Yucca Street, Hollywood, Calif. 90028
ADD 25¢ FOR RUSH HANDLING!

1 David Cassidy as "Keith"
2 Susan Dey as "Laurie"
3 Warming Up
4 Lauri Partridge
5 "Only a Moment Ago"
6 Solo Performance
7 Taking A Break
8 Keith Partridge
9 Musical Discussion
10 "I Think I Love You"
11 "Danny Partridge Speaking!
12 America's Favorite Group
13 The Partridge Family
14 Going On Tour
15 Getting It All Together
16 "Singing My Song"
17 Travelin' Band
18 Rueben & the Kids
19 Danny Disagrees!
20 Home At Last!

21 Berries For Breakfast
22 "To Be Lovers"
23 Relaxing Outdoors
24 Doing His Thing
25 Laurie at the Keyboard
26 "On The Road"
27 The Music Makers
28 Backing the Group
29 "Point Me in the Direction of Albuquerque"
30 Shirley Partridge
31 Getting Involved!
32 Mother of the Group
33 Baseball or Music?
34 Danny Bonaduce as Danny Partridge
35 Proud Mother
36 Laurie's Breakfast
37 "I Can Feel Your Heartbeat"
38 Between Performances
39 Feeling Groovy!
40 Working Out a Song
41 David Makes a Point
42 Popular Teenager

Partridge Family

43 David Stays In Shape
44 Introducing the Act
45 "Bandala"
46 Awaiting His Cue
47 Family Portrait
48 "I Really Want To Know You"
49 "Testing 1-2-3!"
50 Ready to Roll
51 "Somebody Wants To Love You"
52 "Brand New Me"
53 Everybody Pitches In
54 On With The Show
55 Cooking for the Family

1A TV's Favorite Family
2A Partridge Pow-Wow!
3A Beating the Skins!
4A Belting Out a Song!
5A Introducing His Latest Hit!
6A Shirley At The Wheel!
7A Making Sweet Music!
8A David Does a Solo!
9A Electrifying Performance!
10A Arriving in Vegas!
11A 5 Minutes to Showtime!
12A David Spruces Up!
13A Peace Loving Danny!
14A Standing In The Wings
15A Everybody Smile!
16A Happy Times!
17A Keith and Laurie Partridge
18A David Comes Clean!
19A Red Hot Performers!
20A Little Sister
21A Trying Out A Brand New Tune
22A Just David!
23A Pretty Clever Kid!
24A Learning Their Lines!
25A All-American Boy!
26A The Family Pet
27A All Aboard!
28A Showing Up on Schedule
29A Just Before Showtime
30A David On Stage!
31A Performing For Their Fans
32A Keith Makes a Point
33A Spotlight on Danny
34A The Younger Partridges
35A Turned On Performance
36A Singing Up A Storm!
37A Time To Rehearse!
38A Close Friends!

39A A Swinging Singer!
40A Heading Out on Tour
41A Picking Up The Beat!
42A The Lead Singer!
43A Family Discussion!
44A Unwanted Visitor
45A All American Girl
46A Crowded Quarters!
47A What a Groovy Guy!
48A Arriving For Show!
49A Laurie's Got a Date Tonight
50A Leaving Town Today
51A Freckled Face Favorite
52A Reaching Their Destination
53A Keith, Laurie & Danny
54A Laurie and the Younger Set
55A Meet Shirley Jones

1B "Cheer Up, Keith"
2B Mrs. Partridge
3B Outdoor Performance!
4B Discussing Their Next Tour!
5B Danny Trys To Enlist!
6B The Littlest Dodger!
7B Danny Interviews Keith!
8B Showtime!
9B Sharing A Secret!
10B "Back in Five Minutes"
11B "No Pictures, Please!"
12B Danny at the Draftboard!
13B Your Favorite TV Star!
14B "Where To Now, Danny?"
15B "How About This Pose?"
16B Big Sister!
17B "Giddy-Yap, Rueben!"
18B Groovy Guitarist!
19B Time to Laugh!
20B Danny, Laurie and Keith!
21B Mom's Advice
22B Laurie Hides a Smile!
23B Thinking It Over!
24B Before the Cameras!
25B Singing Sensation!
26B "A Close Shave!"
27B Thoughful Moment!
28B Hearing Their New Record!
29B The Partridges at Home!
30B Danny Accepts An Award!
31B Shirley is Pleased!
32B Hitting a High Note!
33B Listening to a Playback!
34B David and Suzanne!

35B The Kids Hold A Meeting
36B The Boys Hit the Sack!
37B "Be Careful, Danny!"
38B Tired of Waiting!
39B Portrait of David!
41B Surrounded By Fans
42B Friendly Enemies!
43B Moment of Decision!
44B TV Superstar!
45B "Holy Cow!"
46B Playing Happy Music!
47B The Great Profile!
48B Belting Out a Song!
49B Daydreamer!
50B Laurie's Favorite Scent!
51B Cool Combination
52B Another Great Performance!
53B All Dolled Up!
54B Laughing It Up
55B Practice Makes Perfect
56B Portrait Card 15 - David Dey
57B Portrait Card 8 - David Cassidy
58B Portrait Card 28 - David Cassidy
59B Portrait Card 11 - David Cassidy
60B Portrait Card 13 - David Cassidy
61B Portrait Card 7 - Shirley Jones
62B Portrait Card 33 - David Cassidy
63B Portrait Card 4 - Danny Bonaduce
64B Portrait Card 19 - Shirley Jones
65B Portrait Card 26 - Suzanne Krough
66B Portrait Card 12 - David Cassidy
67B Portrait Card 17 - Shirley Jones
68B Portrait Card 31 - Dave Madden
69B Portrait Card 24 - David Cassidy
70B Portrait Card 1 - David Cassidy
71B Portrait Card 21 - David Cassidy
72B Portrait Card 29 - Danny Bonaduce
73B Portrait Card 5 - Susan Dey
74B Portrait Card 23 - Jeremy Chelbusks
75B Portrait Card 9 - David Cassidy
76B Portrait Card 3 - Danny Bonaduce
77B Portrait Card 18 - Jeremy Chelbusks
78B Portrait Card 25 - Shirley Jones
79B Portrait Card 32 - David Cassidy
80B Portrait Card 27 - David Cassidy
81B Portrait Card 10 - Danny Bonaduce
82B Portrait Card 14 - David Cassidy
83B Portrait Card 6 - David Cassidy
84B Portrait Card 30 - Susan Dey
85B Portrait Card 22 - David Cassidy
86B Portrait Card 2 - Danny Bonaduce
87B Portrait Card 16 - Suzanne Krough
88B Portrait Card 20 - Shirley Jones

PARTRIDGE FAMILY POSTERS (24) 9 7/16" X 18"

These large paper posters with color photographs of the Partridge Family were distributed by Topps in 1971. Since the posters were folded into gum packs, buyers should take fold lines into consideration when grading these items. There are 24 posters in the set. Note: no mint price given for posters since they were pre-folded to fit into smaller packages.

ITEM	MINT	EX
Set	--	140.00
Poster	--	5.00
Wrapper	--	15.00
Box	--	35.00
Box Sleave	--	25.00

Partridge Family Posters

1	Susan & David	13	David & Shirley—The Partridge
2	To All Our Fans—The Partridge		Family
	Family	14	
3	David	15	David Cassidy
4	David & Danny—The Partridge Family	16	No. 1 Male Vocalist—David Cassidy
5	Laurie—The Partridge Family	17	All My Love—David Cassidy
6	Chris	18	Shirley
7	On Stage—The Partridge Family	19	Susan
8	Laurie & Keith	20	David
9		21	David
10	David Cassidy—The Partridge Family	22	David
11	The Partridge Family	23	
12	Tonight Only!—David Cassidy	24	David

PEANUTS (33)

2 1/2" X 3 1/2"

Promoted as a "Preview Edition" by the manufacturer, Tuff Stuff, this 33-card series of Peanuts trading cards is obviously a forerunner of many more Peanuts cards to come. Except for card #1, which shows a smiling Charles Schulz, the entire set is composed of artwork pictures depicting various Peanuts characters, Snoopy sports, cartoon scenes, slogans, and television specials. The backs contain the card number, caption, some text, and two logos (TSP and Snoopy Doghouse). The copyright dates at the bottom on the reverse vary according to the subject portrayed on the front of the card. A special "Preview Prototype" card (illustrated below) was issued as a promotional item and is not considered part of the regular set. In addition, Schulz signed some cards which were randomly inserted into the boxed sets. Note: available as a boxed set only. At the time this book went to press, the Peanuts set was being offered in the marketplace in the $8-12 range.

PREVIEW PROTOTYPE

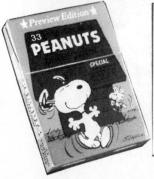

1	Charles Monroe Schulz	17	Spike
2	Snoopy	18	Pigpen
3	Lucy Van Pelt	19	The Psychiatric Booth
4	Charlie Brown	20	Vulture
5	Linus Van Pelt	21	The Literary Ace
6	Peppermint Patty	22	Easter Beagle
7	Schroeder	23	Camping
8	Sally Brown	24	Joe Cool
9	Woodstock	25	Snoopy Kissing Lucy
10	Tennis	26	"You're A Good Man, Charlie Brown"
11	Golf	27	"Happiness Is A Warm Puppy"
12	Basketball	28	Peanuts In Space
13	Ice Hockey	29	The Flying Ace
14	Olympics	30	The Great Pumpkin
15	Marcie	31	"A Boy Named Charlie Brown"
16	Franklin	32	Thanksgiving Special
		33	Christmas Special

PEANUTS CHARACTERS (?)

2 1/4" X 3 1/2"

SNOOPY

Not much is known about this series of color artwork cards showing characters from the cartoon comic series "Peanuts," created by Charles Schulz. They are slightly smaller than standard size and carry a "Dolly Madison" bakery logo in the bottom right corner. The caption is printed below the picture on the left side; the copyright line which is printed below it refers to the original registration, NOT the date of this set. The cards are blank-backed and are printed on thin cardboard stock. They are occasionally seen in flea markets and card shows and are generally priced at 35 cents to 50 cents apiece. Note: cards with oil stains from the bread or cake are worth 10 cents each. The length of the set is unknown.

PEANUTS COMIC CARDS GAME (9K)

2" X 3"

It would be very easy to pass over this clever little set of Peanuts cards because they are hidden inside a drab-looking cardboard packet. This packet has a "Laugh-In" window, i.e., a flap which is lifted up to reveal the card below. Certain cards in the set could be redeemed for prizes (tape players, cameras, inflatable Snoopy dolls) or cash ($1, $5, $10, $25 & $1000). This is a sure indication that many of the cards came in very short supply and chances of finding one of the prize cards (see illustration below) are remote. Collectors are more likely to encounter the cards bearing the "Sorry, This Is Not A Winning Card" line, but even these are seldom seen. Each color artwork card was originally framed by the "window" but the top layer of cardboard may be found removed. The reverse of the card has the contest rules printed in very small wine-colored print. The length of the set is not known. The contest ran in 1978 and appears to have been sponsored by Millbrook Bread. Prices are listed for excellent grade only to allow for the breaking of the flap seal necessary to reveal the card.

ITEM	MINT	EX
Packet	--	2.00
Card only	--	1.00

PEANUTS KLAKKERS (3K)

2 3/4" X 5"

Right about now you may be wondering ... "What on earth is a klakker?" It is a cardboard shape, in this case decorated with characters from the "Peanuts" comic strip, which can be folded and manipulated in a manner which produces a "klakking" sound. Now isn't that special! Millbrook Bread thought so, and brought in Joe Gornall Paper Sculptures, Inc. to engineer the series. Each klakker has a Peanuts character head on one flap and the words "Millbrook Bread" on the other. The noise is created by bending the flaps in toward one another and holding and pressing the edges of the partition area between them. The faster you press, the more noise you make. It doesn't seem like it would work, but ask Mom. She knows. She's probably the reason that there aren't too many klakkers around today! To date, only Snoopy, Charlie Brown, and Lucy klakkers have been confirmed. The Lucy and Charlie Brown each have a word printed on the black color inside portion of the lower flap ("Blockhead!" and "Sigh," respectively). This provided a "visual" effect to go along with the annoying klakking sound. If nothing else, klakkers would be handy items for schools offering "Introduction to the Castanet." Note: mint grade klakkers cannot be bent along the fold lines.

ITEM	MINT	EX
Klakker	2.00	1.00

Peanuts Klakkers

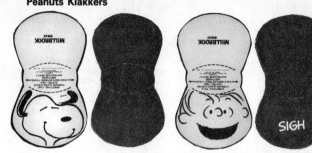
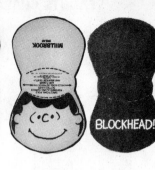

PEANUTS PRESIDENTIAL STICKERS (12)   2 3/8" X 3"

This patriotic set of twelve "vote" stickers appears to have been issued by both Millbrook Bread and Dolly Madison in conjunction with the 1980 presidential elections. Each color artwork sticker has an empty name slot in a sign or at the end of an introductory sentence or dialogue line. Owners could choose from a selection of names printed on the kraft paper backing and the selection had to be carefully positioned onto the adhesive (reverse) side of each sticker so it showed through properly (a task that was probably too difficult for most children AND adults). Collector Warren Hahn provided the stickers which appear in our illustrated checklist. Note: for stickers to be graded excellent or mint, they must have the kraft paper backing intact and be unused.

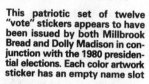

2. Stick name(s) in clear blank space on back of sticker so name shows through front.	JANE	JACK
	MOTHER	BROTHER
	GOVERNOR	CHARLIE
3. Stick anywhere. (removable)	SISTER	SISTER
	JOHN	SAUL
DIRECTIONS (Peel off)	JEFF	SAUL
1. Cut or tear names apart.	ANN	FRANCES
	JIM	CARLOS
2. Stick name(s) in clear blank space on back	BETTY	JANE

ITEM	MINT	EX
Set	6.50	4.50
Sticker	.50	.35

PEE WEE'S PLAYHOUSE (123 ITEMS)

"Pee Wee's Playhouse," issued by Topps in 1988, has to be the most multi-faceted card set ever issued! It contains a variety of different formats and elements, most of which have appeared in previous Topps sets over the years. The diversity of the set may cause confusion for collec-tors so we have decided to describe each category singly. The series was issued in fin packs (which have ridged ends, rather than flaps) and each gumless "Fun Pack" contained "1 Sheet of Tattoos, 3 Picture Cards, 1 Sticker, 1 Wiggle Toy, 1 Activity Card."

VARIOUS SIZES

ITEM	MINT	EX
Set (123 items)*	60.00	45.00
Card	.25	.15
Wiggle toy	.25	.20
Tattoo sheet	.25	.20
Sticker	.35	.25
Activity card	2.00	1.50
Wrapper	--	.50
Box	--	4.00

*This figure is lower than the sum of the com-ponents. The individual prices reflect the dif-ficult collation, the cost of sorting diverse items, and specific card scarcities.

TATTOO SHEETS [3-3/16" X 5-1/4"] Each sheet contains nine tattoos (8 small, 1 large) in the garish colors typical of tattoo issues. There are perforated lines between each tattoo so they can be detached without using scissors. The sheets are numbered in the "Playhouse Tat-toos" panel at top ("1 of 12 sheets," etc.). Individual tattoos are not numbered and they ap-pear to be water-activated, although no instructions are provided.

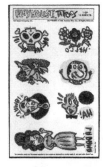 

PICTURE CARDS [2-1/2" X 3-1/2"] A series of 33 color photographs of Pee Wee and his cluttered environment. The borders are blue and the "Pee Wee's Playhouse" panel at bot-tom left is yellow with black print. The cards are numbered on the front only. Eighteen of the backs are puzzle pieces and for once Topps did not provide a card back showing the com-pleted puzzle picture. The re-maining fifteen backs are single features such as "Potato Fun," "Puppetland Poetry," etc.

STICKERS [2-1/2" X 3-1/2"] A series of double-sided items. On one side, there is a card set en-titled "Playhouse Cinema" which is designed to be used as a flip book. The top and bottom halves of each card are a separate "action" scene and you merely reverse position to flip and view the other "movie." Playhouse Cinema cards are numbered 1-40; the remaining four card sides are unnumbered checklists for all the items in the set. The sticker sides of the cards are divided into three categories: nutty initials, characters, and sheets of miniature slogans and pictures. Every one of these sticker sides is repeated twice, without any variation in details, color, or numbering; in other words, there are only 22 different sticker sides backed up to 44 different card sides. This may have saved Topps a bundle in production costs but it has done nothing but confuse and anger potential collectors.

467

WIGGLE TOYS [1-3/4" X 2"] These are a series of what used to be called "vari-vues" - you make a side-to-side motion with them and the picture changes before your very eyes! Each of the twelve numbered "wiggle toys" has alternating images of a Pee Wee character in either photographic or artwork form. The cards feel unusually thick because of the plastic overlay screen necessary to produce the effect. None of the cards is captioned.

ACTIVITY CARDS [3-1/8" X 5-1/4"] Pee Wee's "Activity Cards" present a special problem for collectors. Not only were some of them apparently short-printed (or single-printed), making collation difficult, but the cards themselves were designed to be used as toys, which threatened their survival in the first place. There are five different sub-sets of activity cards, each with their own numbering system: finger puppets (1-5), doors (1-5), flying things (1-4), masks (1-3), and foldees (1-5). If used according to the engineering intent, each of these cards would be folded or have a piece or pieces of the original card removed. Naturally, no card that has been so used can be graded mint or excellent. Sharp-eyed collectors have also noted that each of the three "masks" can be found with slightly different color and intensity, although it would seem that this is merely a natural result of the plate wear in the printing process.

469

PERLORIAN CATS STICKERS (55 & 1)   2 1/2" X 3 1/2"

The concept of dressing cats in "people clothes" and staging them in "people" activities was developed by Satoru Toda of Japan. Topps considered the idea clever enough to merit a sticker series, which the company marketed in 1983. The set is composed of 55 numbered, front-peel stickers and one unnumbered title card. The stickers are either rectangular color pictures with rounded edges (42) or smaller color photos set on solid color, irregular-shaped backgrounds (13). The backs of the cards on which the stickers are mounted are puzzle pieces (50) or puzzle preview cards (5 total, but only 4 different pictures). The cards were marketed in clear cellophane packages devoid of detail.

ITEM	MINT	EX
Set	9.00	6.00
Sticker	.15	.10
Box	--	5.00

PEZ STICKERS (48)   1 1/2" X 1 3/4"

Pez, the company which has become famous for a unique line of candy dispensers, issued a series of "stickers" in refill packs in 1989. The "stickers" are actually more stamp-like in size and appearance and they were printed in strips of two. The only topics advertised to our knowledge were the "Pez Animal Series" and the "Pez Space Series." None of the color or artwork pictures is numbered but all are captioned and all bear the series title and code (1-79 or 4-79). A slip of paper packaged with the stamps reads "Collect All 48" and has a mail-in offer for an album on the back ($2.00 postpaid). It is assumed that there are 24 stamps for each of the two themes.

ITEM	MINT	EX
Sets		
Single stamps	14.00	10.00
Panels	18.00	13.50
Stamp	.25	.20
Panel	.65	.50

PHONEY RECORDS (40 & 15)   TWO SIZES

"Phoney Records," a test issue marketed by Topps in 1967, is rarely seen by collectors. The sticker sheets measure 2 1/2" X 2 5/8" and the "records" on them cannot be "played." The 15 "Stupid Hit Songs" cards are standard size and they spoof popular songs of the period. The "Phoney Records" test wrapper is a color artwork sticker affixed to a piece of wax paper. Note: no set prices given since the card total of 15 has not been confirmed.

ITEM	MINT	EX
Sticker	10.00	7.50
Card	10.00	7.50
Wrapper	--	90.00
Box	--	175.00

PHONEY RECORD STICKERS (40 & 15)   3 3/8" SQ.

The final, or "regular," market version of "Phoney Records" was slightly altered from the "test" variety. Both the "Phoney Record" stickers and the "Stupid Hit Songs" cards were enlarged in size to 3 3/8" square. The wrapper design was completely changed although the price remained at five cents per pack. It is believed that the titles for both cards and stickers are the same in the "test" and "regular" versions.

ITEM	MINT	EX
Sticker	7.50	6.00
Card	7.50	6.00
Wrapper	--	20.00
Box	--	100.00

1 Sunburn in the City ... The Loaded Shovelfull (Kama Kazi)
2 California Screamin' ... The Grandmamas and Grandpapas (Dumbhill)
3 Soil and Perspiration ... Rawchest Brothers (Nerve)
4 I Know a Plague ... Peculiar Clerk (Warring Brothers)
5 Fink of the Road ... Roger Mildew and the Nashville Cats (Mash)
6 Yawn (Go Away) ... Four Seesaws (Phyllis)
7 Irving XI ... Sherman's Sherberts (M-O-M)
8 Winchester Rifle ... Old Audible Band (Funtuna)
9 Did You Ever See Your Father, Baby, Standing in the Shower? ... Falling Stones (Longdumb)
10 I Got the Flu ... Sunny and Fair (Atchoo)
11
12 Reach Out, I'll Be Bare ... Four Topless (Mootown)

Phoney Record Stickers

13 Stop! In the Name of the Law ... Soup Greens (Hicktown)
14 Wooly Blanket ... Stan the Ham and the Sparrows (M-U-M)
15 Split Pea ... Tommy Rot (ABE)
16 I Can't Stop Slugging You ... Ray Charged (APE)
17 Ban! Ban! ... Share (Impossible)
18 Fooey, Fooey ... King Pins (Wind)
19 House of the Rising Slum ... Animules (M-G-D)
20 Last Plane to Clucksville ... Donkees (Coldgerms)
21 Eve of Distraction ... Bury McGuire (Downhill)
22 I Am a Roach ... Slimy and Garfink (Colombia)
23 Good 'n' Yellow ... Down-a-gain (Ape-ic)
24 Your Aunt's Nothin' But a Hound Dog ... Elvis Pretzel (RCG Victory)
25 Glumb All Over ... Dumb Cluck Five (Eechic)
26 I Want to Hold Your Claw ... Beastlies (Capistol)

27 Like a Bouncing Ball ... Bob Dilly (Columbus)
28 Daddy's Got a Brand New Hag ... James Clown (Kink)
29 Everybody Loves Some Boozin' ... Dean Martini (Repiazza)
30 Hello, Doily ... Louis Headstrong (Sapp)
31 Everybody Loves a Clod ... Gary Lousy (Library)
32 A Taste of Money ... Herb Aspirin and the Tijuana Brats (M&A)
33
34 You Don't Have to Say You Loathe Me ... Dusty Springboard (Phil Up)
35 Ballad of the Green Berries ... Sgt. Barry Saddlesore (RGA Victim)
36 Burp Me, Rhonda ... Bleach Boys (Capital)
37 96 Fears ...I and the Miserables (Camera)
38 These Booths are Made for Talking ... Nancy Sinister (Revise)
39 Blowing in the Hanky ... Peter, Paul, and Murray (Worried Brothers)
40 Peephole ... Barbara Strychinne (Carumba)

PIONEERS OF COUNTRY MUSIC (40) 2 3/4" X 3 3/4"

JIMMIE RODGERS

1 Andy Palmer of Jimmie Johnson's String Band
2 Eck Robertson and Family
3 Da Costa Woltz's Southern Broadcasters
4 Gid Tanner and his Skillet Lickers
5 Fiddlin' John Carson & his Virginia Reelers
6 Earl Johnson and his Dixie Entertainers
7 Carter Family
8 Fiddlin' Doc Roberts Trio
9 Ted Gossett of Ted Gossett's String Band
10 Jimmie Rodgers
11 Harry "Mac" McClintock
12 Dr. Humphrey Bate and his Possum Hunters
13 Uncle Dave Macon and his Fruit-Jar Drinkers
14 Burnett & Rutherford
15 Mumford Bean and his Itawambians
16 Shelor Family
17 W.T. Narmour & S.W. Smith
18 Ray Brothers
19 The Tennessee Ramblers
20 Ernest Stoneman and the Blue Ridge Corn Shuckers
21 Shepherd Brothers
22 Taylor-Griggs Louisiana Melody Makers
23 Jimmie & George Carter of Carter Brothers & Son
24 Hoyt Ming and his Pep Steppers
25 Paul Miles and his Red Fox Chasers
26 Roane County Ramblers
27 Frank Blevins and his Tar Heel Rattlers
28 Charlie Poole with the North Carolina Ramblers
29 Al Hopkins and his Buckle Busters
30 Fiddlin' Bob Larkin and his Music Makers
31 East Texas Serenaders
32 "Dock" Boggs
33 Fiddlin' Powers & Family
34 Red Patterson's Piedmont Log Rollers
35 Weems String Band
36 Leake County Revelers
37 Wilmer Watts of Wilmer Watts and The Lonely Eagles
38 South Georgia Highballers
39 Happy Hayseeds
40 Crockett Kentucky Mountaineers

The third and last of the Yazoo Records sets drawn by R. Crumb, "Pioneers of Country Music" was released to the public in 1985. The 40 cards cover the early days of country music in the 1920's and 1930's and modern collectors are not likely to recognize most of the performers featured in the set. Luckily, the bios on the back, written by Rich Nevins, provide a wealth of information about the musicians pictured. The cards are larger than standard size and they are numbered on the back. Sold as a set only, the series is housed in a small box designed by Crumb and retails for $10. Eclipse Books of California has recently obtained the rights to market the set and there are indications that some details of the cards may be changed in future editions.

PIRATES BOLD (66 & 21) 2 1/2" X 3 1/2"

The Pirates Bold set of 66 cards was a serious attempt to impart historical information to the collector. The color pictures of various swashbucklers were imaginative and well drawn. A rope frame and white background surrounded the picture. The backs were a triumph of design, appearing as treasure maps which carried the biography of the subject and a small insert map of his area of operations. The card number was situated in a skull-and-crossbones design and a series of 21 gummed-back paper flags (2 1/4" X 3") was added as a package insert bonus.

WILHELM STOELPER
1671 - 1714

WILHELM STOELPER
1671-1714

FLAGS OF THE SPANISH MAIN

JOLLY ROGER
18TH CENTURY

PLUS PIRATE STICKER

ITEM	MINT	EX
Sets		
Cards	190.00	150.00
Flags	125.00	100.00
Card	2.50	2.00
Flag	5.00	4.00
Wrapper	---	150.00
Box	---	250.00

Argentine Republic	French Western Colonies	Santa Marta
Bolivia	Guatemala	St. Domingo
Brazil	Hayti	Spanish Man of War
British Merchant	Jolly Roger	United States
British Union Jack	Merchant of Spain	United States Excise
Buenos Ayres	Mexico	Uruguay
Cumana	Paraguay	Venezuela

Pirates Bold

1	Rod Mason—1747-1788
2	Frenchy Dulis—1815-1849
3	Pedro Montasques—1547-1581
4	Dannie O'Fain—1754-1777
5	Hendrik Van Broek—1637-1670
6	Rufus Trench—1747-1779
7	Edward Meriwether—1803-1842
8	Raoul Leval—1604-1643
9	Francois Chartre—1711-1755
10	Maurice Lebeq—1551-1586
11	David Henderson—1800-1830
12	Herbert Matteson—1822-1854
13	Juan Delacorte—1575-1598
14	Chief Tom—1840(?)...?
15	Fred Hickey—1804-1832
16	Louis Featherstone—1714-1746
17	Li Fong—(?)-1864
18	Wilhelm Stoelper—1671-1714
19	John Morrisey—1807-1854
20	Jean Lafitte—1780-1826
21	Sir Henry Morgan—1635-1688
22	Francois Lolonois—(?)-1668
23	Captain William Kidd—1645-1701
24	Edward Teach-"Blackbeard"—(?)-1718
25	Anne Bonney — (?) -- 1720
26	Mary Read—(?)-1720
27	Pierre Le Grand—(?)-1685
28	Bartholomew Portuguese—(?)-1669
29	Rock Braziliano—(?)-1670
30	Major Stede Bonnet—(?)-1718
31	Bartholomew Roberts—1682-1722
32	Charles Vane—(?)-1725
33	William Brand—(?)-1723
34	Rod Mason—1747-1788
35	Frenchy Dulis—1815-1849
36	Pedro Montasques—1547-1581
37	Dannie O'Fain—1754-1777
38	Hendrik Van Broek—1637-1670
39	Rufus Trench—1747-1779
40	Edward Meriwether—1803-1842
41	Raoul Leval—1604-1643
42	Francois Chartre—1711-1755
43	Maurice Lebeq—1551-1586
44	David Henderson—1800-1830
45	Herbert Matteson—1822-1854
46	Juan Delacorte—1575-1598
47	Chief Tom—1840-(?)-(?)
48	Fred Hickey—1840-1832
49	Louis Featherstone—1714-1746
50	Li Fong—(?)-1864
51	Wilhelm Stoepler—1671-1741
52	John Morrisey—1807-1854
53	Jean Lafitte—1780-1826
54	Sir Henry Morgan—1635-1688
55	Francois Lolonois—(?)-1668
56	Capt. William Kidd—1645-1701
57	Edward Teach "Blackbeard"—(?)-1718
58	Anne Bonney—(?)-1720
59	Mary Read—(?)-1720
60	Pierre Le Grand—(?)-1685
61	Bartholomew Portuguese—(?)-1669
62	Rock Braziliano—(?)-1670
63	Major Stede Bonnet—(?)-1718
64	Capt. Bartholomew Roberts—1682-1722
65	Charles Vane—(?)-1725
66	William Brand—(?)-1723

PIRATE TATTOO (?) 1 5/8" X 2 1/2"

Although the design of this Fleer wrapper makes it look like a product of the early 1950's, the listing of BHT as a preservative in the ingredients list clearly dates it as a post-1960 issue. The wrapper is yellow with black and red lettering; the treasure chest is drawn in black & white. The words "Fleer Corp., Phila., PA 19141" are printed on the left edge and the numbers "6370" are located to the right of the "cut bar" at top. Judging by the size of the wrapper, the piece of gum inside could hardly have been worth more than a penny. Despite its relatively recent origin, very few specimens are reported in collections as of this time, hence the elevated price.

ITEM	MINT	EX
Wrapper	--	35.00

PIXIES (144) SIZE VARIES

"Pixies" was the title given by designer Jack Wohl to these hold-to-light paper noveties distributed by Fleer in 1968. Thirteen "Pixies" plus a title panel came attached to one another in an accordian format (3" X 20 7/8" long), with score lines between the designs for easy separation. Individual Pixies used letters, numbers, and shapes to pose a riddle: the answer was revealed by holding the paper up to light. There are 144 different riddles in the set and a contest challenged gum chewers to think up their own Pixies ($5 reward). There are four wrappers for this set, differing from one another only by the Pixie design in the center. Note: prices listed are for complete folders; single Pixies are valued at 10 cents each.

ITEM	MINT	EX
Folder	2.50	2.00
Wrappers		
"10" - "H" - "ANT," each	--	10.00
"Y"	--	20.00
Box	--	40.00

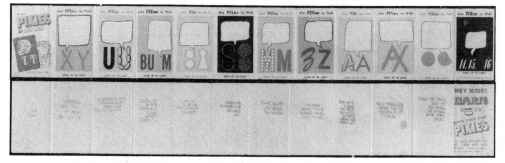

PLANET OF THE APES (44)

2 1/2" X 3 1/2"

This series of 44 cards was marketed by Topps in 1969 and features color photographs taken from the movie

starring Charlton Heston (who does not appear on many cards). The obverse caption is printed in yellow in a wavy red panel. The backs are solid green with the card number and text printed in black.

ITEM	MINT	EX
Set	100.00	75.00
Card	2.00	1.50
Wrapper	--	15.00
Box	--	60.00

1	Crash Landing!	12	No Escape!	23 Words of Anger!
2	Bail Out!	13	Ape Brutality!	24 Human on a Leash!
3	Stranded!	14	Captured!	25 Return to Prison!
4	Spaceman George Taylor!	15	The Victors!	26 Ape Scientist!
5	First Sign of Life!	16	Proud Conquerors	27 Taylor's Escape Fails!
6	Discovery!	17	"Say Cheese!"	28 Zoo Attendant!
7	Man Vs. Beast!	18	Ape Surgeon!	29 Water Torture
8	Captives of the Apes!	19	Taylor's Life Is Saved!	30 Ape Madhouse!
9	Stalking Human Prey!	20	Pleading for Mercy!	31 Manacled!
10	Another Prisoner!	21	Caged!	32 Ape Jury!
11	Nova Is Captured!	22	Taylor's Ally!	33 Speaking Against Taylor!
				34 The Trial Continues!
				35 Ape City!
				36 Deciding Taylor's Fate!
				37 Escape!
				38 The Search!
				39 The Forbidden Zone
				40 "Under Arrest!"
				41 Friends of the Human!
				42 Farewell!
				43 Man's Destiny!
				44 Lights! Camera! Action!

PLANET OF THE APES (66)

2 1/2" X 3 1/2"

The fronts of the 66 cards in this set are identical in format to those of the 1969 set: color pictures, white borders,

and wavy red panels containing printed captions—except that the color photos were taken from the television series. The cards from either set are best distinguished from one another by comparing reverses. The 1969 set has narrative backs only; in this set, the backs are poster pieces with a small narrative area included. The card number appears next to the copyright date (1967—refers to the original material). The set was issued by Topps in 1975.

ITEM	MINT	EX
Set	15.00	12.00
Card	.25	.20
Wrapper	--	1.00
Box	--	30.00

1	Renegade Chimp Galen	23	The Key
2	Comdr. Alan Virdon	24	Shades of the Past
3	Astronaut Peter Burke	25	Storehouse of Facts
4	Dr. Zaius	26	Aiming for Survival!
5	Urko, Gorilla General	27	The Battery Boost
6	The Road to Nowhere	28	"Someone's Coming!"
7	Town of Terror	29	Search the Premises
8	Remnants of Humanity	30	"They're Escaping!"
9	A Mysterious Lead	31	Human Bait
10	The Quest	32	Searching for Virdon
11	In Search of Destiny	33	A Fateful Noise
12	We Must Take Action!	34	Captured!
13	Undeniable Proof	35	The Inquisition
14	Extermination Plans	36	Third Degree!
15	"Find the Humans!"	37	Galen's Plan!
16	Thrill of the Hunt	38	Gorillas Catch On!
17	Visit to a Graveyard	39	Gorillas Coming!
18	Dangerous Climb	40	Horseback Monster
19	Destiny's Door	41	General's Orders!
20	Anticipation	42	Determined Scout
21	A Unique Discovery	43	Potter's Palace
22	Valuable Answers	44	Descent to Danger

45	The Discovery
46	Rescued by Galen
47	Charging the Brute
48	Karate, 3085 A.D.!
49	A Friend in Need!
50	An Uneven Match
51	Team Effort!
52	A Mighty Kick
53	Floored!
54	Urko Takes Off!
55	One for Our Side!
56	Next Stop: Humanity!
57	Roddy McDowall
58	Booth Colman as Zaius
59	Mark Lenard as Urko
60	Ron Harper as Virdon
61	James Naughton
62	Hairy Horseman
63	Relaxing on the Set
64	Marvelous Make-ups
65	Frightful Visage
66	Super-Chimp!

PLAYBOY (72)

2 1/2" X 3 1/2"

While most card sets aimed at the "mature collector" seem to be trying to outdo one another

in terms of graphic content, the Playboy Commemorative series from Star Pics is a splendid example of craftmanship and quality content. To be sure, there are 24 "Playmate Profiles" included in the set, but there is no nudity and the series contains plenty of other interesting cards. The card of Johnny Carson, for example, is one of a handful - almost none of American manufacture - which have been printed for this elusive star. In addition to Carson, there are also cards for Lech Walesa, Fidel Castro, Ferdinand and Imelda Marcos (to name a few), plus 20 magazine covers, including the First Edition featuring Marilyn Monroe. "Favorite Cartoons," Trivia Cards, and a checklist round out the set. The latter lists cards by number but there are no numbers actually printed on the cards. The series is being issued (starting in March, 1992) as a boxed set only. Playboy Magazine has achieved the status of a bona fide American institution and this stylish set certainly does it justice.

ITEM	MINT	EX
Boxed set	20.00	--

1	Checklist	16	Candy Loving
2	Hugh Hefner	17	Candace Collins
3	Rabbit Head Design	18	Shannon Tweed
4	Femlin	19	Cathy St. George
5	Playboy Clubs	20	Marianne Gravatte
6	Playboy Bunny	21	Penny Baker
7	Playboy Mansion West	22	Karen Velez
8	Janet Pilgrim	23	Kathy Shower
9	Donna Michelle	24	Devin DeVasquez
10	Jo Collins	25	Julie McCullough
11	Liv Lindeland	26	Brandi Brandt
12	Lieko English	27	India Allen
13	Cyndi Wood	28	Kimberley Conrad Hefner
14	Marilyn Lange	29	Erika Eleniak
15	Monique St. Pierre	30	Mirjam and Karin van Breeschooten

Playboy

31 Renee Tenison
32 Johnny Carson
33 Tom Hayden
34 Mel Brooks
35 Alex Haley
36 Lech Walesa
37 Fidel Castro
38 Ferdinand and Imelda Marcos
39 Daniel Ortega
40 Lee Iacocca
41 Dec. '53 Cover
42 June '54 Cover
43 May '55 Cover
44 Dec. '55 Cover
45 April '56 Cover
46 Aug. '56 Cover
47 June '57 Cover
48 July '58 Cover
49 Dec. '58 Cover
50 April '60 Cover
51 Aug. '60 Cover
52 Nov. '60 Cover
53 June '61 Cover
54 Dec. '62 Cover
55 May '64 Cover
56 Oct. '71 Cover
57 Dec. '71 Cover
58 May '73 Cover
59 Nov. '76 Cover
60 Jan. '79 Cover
61 Phil Interlandi
62 Gahan Wilson
63 Buck Brown
64 Hap Kliban
65 Eldon Dedini
66 Alden Erikson
67 John Dempsey
68 Don Madden - 1
69 Francis Smith
70 Don Madden - 2
71 Trivia
72 Trivia

POKER HANDS (?)

2 1/2" X 3 1/2"

The Paul A. Price Company of New York appears to have been catering to the gamblers among us with this set of "Poker Hands" issued in the early 1960s. The fronts show different card combinations and are accompanied by "value" circles. The backs bear the set title, a list of hands and their values, and a copyright line. The nubs on the card edges indicate that the set was distributed in sheets. The set total is unknown and no packaging has been reported to date.

ITEM	MINT	EX
Card	.50	.35

POM POM RIDDLES (29K)

1 5/8" X 3 5/8"

This riddle series, first reported in the June, 1971 edition of The Card Collectors Bulletin, was printed on the back of Welch's "Pom Poms" boxes. The design incorporates a rectangular frame, in which the riddle is asked, with a sketch of a child holding a Pom Poms box in his hand to one side. The riddle number is part of the bold print heading which appears inside the frame. The dimensions listed above apply to the panel which comprises the back of the box AFTER it has been cut away. The answer to each riddle is printed on one end flap; after this is torn off, or the box panel removed, there is no way to guess what the answer was (verbatim). Number 29 is the highest riddle confirmed to date and it is assumed that there were at least 30 in the set. Note: "cut" panels cannot be graded mint.

ITEM	MINT	EX
Riddle panel	--	1.50
Complete box	6.00	4.00

POP GUNS (12)

IRREGULAR SIZES

According to the production codes appearing on the wrapper and box, "Pop Guns" were marketed in 1971. Each "gun" is a shaped cardboard design with a trigger hole for gripping. When the gun is snapped down abruptly a paper wedge flies out of the front, accompanied by a "pop." There are 12 designs in the set and all are pictured on the back of the "wrapper" (a large paper envelope). This Topps novelty was manufactured in Japan and was issued without gum.

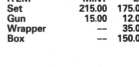

ITEM	MINT	EX
Set	215.00	175.00
Gun	15.00	12.00
Wrapper	--	35.00
Box	--	150.00

POPPLES (225)   2 1/16" X 2 9/16"

"Popples" are the 20th century's version of elves; they are also the subject of an album sticker set issued by Panini in 1987. The great majority of the 225 stickers contain "cute" artwork, although an occasional sticker has an actual posed photograph of a stuffed "Popples" bear. The backs of the stickers have the usual multi-language Panini format and there is a 32-page album offered to house the set. Note: set price includes album.

ITEM	MINT	EX
Set	25.00	18.50
Sticker	.10	.07
Wrapper	--	.25
Album	1.50	1.00

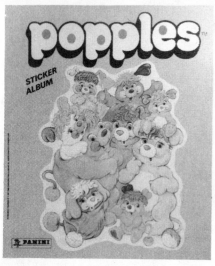 

POP—UPS (12)   2 13/16" X 3 1/2"

"Pull the tab and they Pop their Tops"...how could a kid resist such a novelty for only 10 cents? Each design has a pop-up panel attached inside to a rubber band; when the tab is pulled, up goes the panel to reveal the punch line and artwork. The novelties are numbered on back and and have a safety pin for attaching to clothing. The wrapper is a red and black paper envelope with the title in yellow letters. The packages were gumless and were packed 12 to a box. Eleven of the 12 designs are illustrated below.

ITEM	MINT	EX
Set	110.00	85.00
Pop-up	7.50	6.00
Wrapper	--	20.00
Box	--	75.00

PREHISTORIC SCENES (18)

1 5/8" X 4 3/4"

The color artwork of "Prehistoric Scenes" is a striking departure from the drab sepia tones of most "Pom Pom" candy box card sets. There are 17 different "scenes" plus one checklist card in the series. Aurora Models co-produced the set and the artwork of the cards was probably developed for the boxes of the model kits which are advertised on them. Beneath each scene there is a short text, the card number, and Aurora advertising. Note: cards cut away from the box cannot be graded mint.

ITEM	MINT	EX
Set	--	75.00
Card	--	3.00
Checklist	--	6.00
Complete Box	10.00	7.50

1 Neanderthal Man
2 Cro-Magnon Man
3 Cro-Magnon Woman
4 Cave
5 Saber Tooth Tiger
6 Flying Reptile
7 The Tar Pit
8 Allosaurus
9 Cave Bear
10 Giant Bird
11 Jungle Swamp
12 Three Horned Dinosaur
13 Spiked Dinosaur
14 Giant Woolly Mammoth
15 Armored Dinosaur
16 Sail-Back Reptile
17 Tyrannosaurus Rex

PREMIERE MAGAZINE COLLECTORS' CARDS (72K)

3 3/4" X 5 1/2"

The movies and movie stars have been favorite topics for trading cards ever since moving pictures found commercial success in the 1920's. The majority of such sets issued over the years have featured individual celebrities or action scenes from particular films. To our knowledge, this series of "Collectors' Cards," inserted in four-card sheets in early issues of "Premiere Magazine," is the first set ever to showcase posters from various films. These are not your standard bubblegum package size cards: they are larger than most postcards and are printed on thin cardboard stock. The artwork posters as a group are more interesting than the photographic ones, but movie buffs should be delighted by the entire set. The card backs contain an astonishing amount of information about each movie and its cast. Whatever your taste in films, be it "Action Jackson," "Au Revoir Les Enfants," or somewhere in between, this set has a card for you. Very few "Collector's Cards" have turned up at card shows; we suggest you look for them in back issues of Premiere Magazine. Our checklist contains the 72 titles confirmed as of this date. Note: single cards have been detached and cannot be graded mint.

ITEM	MINT	EX
Single card	--	.25
Sheet (4 cards)	2.00	1.50

Action Jackson
Au Revoir Les Enfants
Babette's Feast
Baby Boom
Batteries Not Included
Beetlejuice
Benji The Hunted
Best Seller
Biloxi Blues
Bright Lights, Big City
Broadcast News
Colors
Consuming Passions
Dark Eyes
Dirty Dancing
D.O.A.
Dominick & Eugene
Empire of the Sun
Frantic
Full Metal Jacket
Gentlemen Prefer Blondes
Good Morning Vietnam
Hairspray
Hellraiser

Hope and Glory
Housekeeping
Ironweed
Julia and Julia
King Lear
Lady and the Tramp
Less Than Zero
Made in Heaven
Matewan
Maurice
Moonstruck
My Life as a Dog
Niagara
Nuts
Off Limits
Overboard
River's Edge
Sammy and Rosie Get Laid
School Daze
September
Shoot to Kill
Stakeout
Star Trek IV
Suspect
Switching Channels

Tampopo
The Big Easy
The Couch Trip
The Dead
The Fox and the Hound
The Glass Menagerie
The Hidden
The House on Carroll Street
The Last Emperor
The Lonely Passion of Judith Hearne
The Milagro Beanfield War
The Moderns
The Princess Bride
The Serpent and the Rainbow
The Unbearable Lightness of Being
The Untouchables
The Witches of Eastwick
Three Men and a Baby
Throw Mama from the Train
Tin Men
Vice Versa
Wall Street
Willow

PRESIDENTIAL SERIES (39)

2" X 2 7/8"

Ziploc Sandwich Bags introduced this series of distinguished looking presidential sticker-cards in the latter part of 1984. The special two-in-one format, which collectors will recognize from similar Kellogg's cereal trading card sets, is a trademarked design of Bates Printing Specialities (Chicago). The sticker portion is an artwork portrait of the president, his term of office, and his place in the sequence of First Executives printed in a ribbon design at bottom. Black borders surround the picture. Pulling the sticker away from the card reveals another design composed of a smaller portrait set onto a background of vignettes relating events which occurred during that subject's term of office. The back of the card has a substantial biography printed in black ink on white stock. A single card, protected by a white paper wrapper, was packed into Ziploc boxes during the promotion. According to an offer printed on the wrapper, an entire set of 39 plus a "colorful collector poster (24" X 36")" was available via the mail for $2.50 and three purchase proofs. Note: prices listed are for complete sticker/card combinations.

ITEM	MINT	EX
Set	20.00	15.00
Card	.50	.35
Wrapper	--	.25

George Washington
John Adams
Thomas Jefferson
James Madison
James Monroe
John Quincy Adams
Andrew Jackson
Martin Van Buren

William Henry Harrison
John Tyler
James K. Polk
Zachary Taylor
Millard Fillmore
Franklin Pierce
James Buchanan
Abraham Lincoln

Andrew Johnson
Ulysses S. Grant
Rutherford B. Hayes
James Garfield
Chester A. Arthur
Grover Cleveland
Benjamin Harrison
William McKinley

Theodore Roosevelt
William Howard Taft
Woodrow Wilson
Warren G. Harding
Calvin Coolidge
Herbert C. Hoover
Franklin D. Roosevelt
Harry S. Truman

Dwight D. Eisenhower
John F. Kennedy
Lyndon Johnson
Richard Nixon
Gerald Ford
James E. Carter
Ronald Reagan

Presidential Series

PRESIDENTS (33)   2 1/2" X 3 1/2"

9   **William Henry Harrison**
1773–1841

"Old Tippecanoe," as Harrison was called, got his nickname from the battle in which he led the army that defeated Tecumseh, an Indian chief. Because of his military success, he was a national hero and easily won the election in 1840. The campaign that year was the first one in which slogans, songs, and parades were used to make the voters interested in the candidates. The most famous slogan was "Tippecanoe and Tyler, too!" Tyler was Harrison's running mate. Unfortunately, Harrison died suddenly after holding office for only one month.

WILLIAM HENRY HARRISON
president 1841

Of the three old style Golden Press sets in this book, only the "Presidents" series is standard card size ("Animals" and "Dinosaurs" are smaller). There are 33 cards to the set and each is a handsome artwork portrait of one of America's First Executives. The term of office for each individual is printed directly below his name in the white panel under the picture area. The backs bear the card number - located in a black shield at upper left - plus the life span of and a short text about each subject. The name "Golden Press" is not printed on the card on either side. Only the rouletted edges (three or four per card) give away the fact that these cards originally came in sheets which essentially were the pages in a 39¢ book targeted at the juvenile market. The set was first reported by Buck Barker in The Card Collectors Bulletin of November, 1960, where it was assigned the catalog number W547. Note: only cards in the original sheets can be graded mint and sheets increase in value by 25%.

ITEM	MINT	EX
Set	47.50	37.50
Card	1.50	1.00
Book	60.00	47.50

1 George Washington	7 Andrew Jackson	13 Millard Fillmore	19 Rutherford B. Hayes	25 Theodore Roosevelt	31 Franklin D. Roosevelt
2 John Adams	8 Martin Van Buren	14 Franklin Pierce	20 James Garfield	26 William Howard Taft	32 Harry S. Truman
3 Thomas Jefferson	9 William Henry Harrison	15 James Buchanan	21 Chester A. Arthur	27 Woodrow Wilson	33 Dwight D. Eisenhower
4 James Madison	10 John Tyler	16 Abraham Lincoln	22 Grover Cleveland	28 Warren G. Harding	
5 James Monroe	11 James K. Polk	17 Andrew Johnson	23 Benjamin Harrison	29 Calvin Coolidge	
6 John Quincy Adams	12 Zachary Taylor	18 Ulysses S. Grant	24 William McKinley	30 Herbert Hoover	

PRESIDENTS AND FAMOUS (44) AMERICANS   2 1/2" X 4 11/16"

Ulysses S. Grant
18th President (1869 1877)

The Barker Updates reported that this Topps set was issued in 1965 (a set of 72 baseball players was also issued in this format the same year). The cards are essentially gold foil "Plaques" with a raised portrait design centered at top. The individual's name and biography, plus the card number, are printed below the foil oval on a solid color area (the color of this "frame" area is noted for each card in the checklist). There are 35 Presidents and nine "Famous Americans" in the set. Note: the surface of these cards are easily damaged; make sure the condition is equal to the price.

ITEM	MINT	EX
Set	200.00	125.00
Card	4.00	2.50
Wrapper	—	20.00

1 George Washington 1st President
(1789-1797) [Blue]

2 John Adams 2nd President
(1797-1801) [Blue]

3 Thomas Jefferson 3rd President
(1801-1809) [Red]

4 James Madison 4th President
(1809-1817) [Blue]

5 James Monroe 5th President
(1817-1825) [Red]

6 John Quincy Adams 6th President
(1825-1829) [Blue]

7 Andrew Jackson 7th President
(1829-1837) [Red]

8 Martin Van Buren 8th President
(1837-1841) [Blue]

9 William H. Harrison 9th President
(1841-1841) [Red]

10 John Tyler 10th President
(1841-1845) [Blue]

11 James K. Polk 11th President
(1845-1849) [Red]

12 Zachary Taylor 12th President
(1849-1850) [Blue]

13 Millard Fillmore 13th President
(1850-1853) [Red]

14 Franklin Pierce 14th President
(1853-1857) [Red]

15 James Buchanan 15th President
(1857-1861) [Red]

16 Abraham Lincoln 16th President
(1861-1865) [Black]

17 Andrew Johnson 17th President
(1865-1869) [Blue]

18 Ulysses S. Grant 18th President
(1869-1877) [Red]

19 Rutherford B. Hayes 19th President
(1877-1881) [Blue]

20 James A. Garfield 20th President
(1881-1881) [Black]

21 Chester A. Arthur 21st President
(1881-1885) [Red]

22 Grover Cleveland 22nd-24th President
(1885-1889) (1893-1897) [Blue]

23 Benjamin Harrison 23rd President
(1889-1893) [Blue]

24 William McKinley 25th President
(1897-1901) [Black]

25 Theodore Roosevelt 26th President
(1901-1909) [Red]

26 William H. Taft 27th President
(1909-1913) [Blue]

27 Woodrow Wilson 28th President
(1913-1921) [Blue]

28 Warren G. Harding 29th President
(1921-1923) [Red]

29 Calvin Coolidge 30th President
(1923-1929) [Blue]

30 Herbert C. Hoover 31st President
(1929-1933) [White]

31 Franklin D. Roosevelt 32nd President
(1933-1945) [Red]

32 Harry S. Truman 33rd President
(1945-1953) [White]

33 Dwight D. Eisenhower 34th President
(1953-1961) [White]

34 John F. Kennedy 35th President
(1961-1963) [Blue]

35 Lyndon B. Johnson 36th President
(1963- [White]

36 Benjamin Franklin Statesman
(1706-1790) [Green]
37 Charles Lindbergh Aviator
(1902- [Green]
38 Alexander Graham Bell Inventor
(1847-1922) [Green]
39 Alexander Hamilton Statesman
(1757-1804) [Green]
40 Albert Einstein Physicist
(1879-1955) [Green]

41 Henry Ford Industrialist
(1863-1947) [Green]
42 Orville Wright Inventor
(1871-1948) [Green]
43 Douglas McArthur General
(1880-1964) [Green]
44 Frank Lloyd Wright Architect
(1869-1959) [Green]

PRESIDENT STICKERS (40)

Do you like unsolved mysteries? There's one in this set of President Stickers issued by Coronet Paper Towels (Georgia Pacific) in 1984. According to advertising copy, there are 40 stickers in the series, yet at the time it was

1 George Washington
2 John Adams
3 Thomas Jefferson
4 James Madison
5 James Monroe
6 John Quincy Adams
7 Andrew Jackson
8 Martin Van Buren
9 William H. Harrison
10 John Tyler
11 James K. Polk
12 Zachary Taylor
13 Millard Fillmore
14 Franklin Pierce
15 James Buchanan
16 Abraham Lincoln
17 Andrew Johnson
18 Ulysses S. Grant

19 Rutherford B. Hayes
20 James A. Garfield
21 Chester A. Arthur
22 Grover Cleveland
23 Benjamin Harrison
24 William McKinley
25 Theodore Roosevelt
26 William H. Taft
27 Woodrow Wilson
28 Warren G. Harding
29 Calvin Coolidge
30 Herbert C. Hoover
31 Franklin D. Roosevelt
32 Harry S. Truman
33 Dwight D. Eisenhower
34 John F. Kennedy
35 Lyndon B. Johnson
36 Richard M. Nixon
37 Gerald Ford
38 Jimmy Carter
39 Ronald Reagan

2″ X 3″

issued, only 39 individuals had been elected to the White House. Since the stickers were issued in panels of two, there is either a repeated sticker or one with an unknown picture. Collectors will find the stickers devoid of any print whatsoever: no numbers, captions, text... nothing to tell you who the president is or who manufactured the set. Even the label on the cellophane packaging is wrong: it calls the paper two-sticker strip a card! Note: prices are for intact panels with two stickers; peeled stickers cannot be graded excellent or mint. No set price will be listed until the twentieth and last panel is identified.

ITEM	MINT	EX
Panel		
(2 stickers)	.50	.35

PRO CHEERLEADERS (44)

One of the hottest sets of 1991 was Lime Rock's "Preview Issue" of "Pro Cheerleaders Trading Cards." The company has arranged for a full-scale series of cheerleader cards to be released in the fall of 1992, and this 44-card edition was issued to test the market and give collectors a taste of things to come. Cheerleading squads representing the Washington Bullets, the Philadelphia 76ers, and the Minnesota Timberwolves are featured in the set (team names

and logos are not used since that would have involved another type of licensing arrangement). There are 41 numbered cards, each picturing an individual cheerleader, plus 3 unnumbered checklist cards. All the color photographs of the Bullettes and the Sixers Dream Team are publicity stills, while the girls of the Reebok Performance Team (Minnesota) are seen in action at a game. "Pro Cheerleaders" was distributed only in foil "fin" packs containing twelve cards and production

2 1/2″ X 3 1/2″

was limited to 2500 cases.

Collectors should be aware of some bonus items and anomalies associated with the Preview Issue. Bonus cards inserted randomly into packs included "instant winners" (two different, for a "team autographed game ball" or an uncut sheet of cards), cards signed by individual cheerleaders, "promo" cards bearing an SCAI St. Louis 1991 show logo on the front, and a "proto type" Larry Bird hologram. In addition, there was a series of promo cards distributed by the company which did not bear the SCA logo on front and one of these, that of Lisa Marie Byram, incorrectly identifies her as Terri Derryberry. Finally, the Minnesota checklist has been found with and without a copyright line on the back. While the Bird hologram is likely to attract some collector interest, the variation and promotional cards listed will probably have very little premium value in the long run.

WASHINGTON BULLETTES
1 Courtney Corry
2 Lynne-Marie Griffin
3 Shelley Cumberland
4 Jodi Stark
5 Stephani Christy
6 Lisa Michelle Randolph
7 Leslie D. Murphy
8 Linda Wells
9 Cewyon Chandler
10 Vihky Smith
11 Kimberly David
12 Monica Gilliam
13 Lisa Marie Byram
14 Marjorie "Twiggy" Black
15 Carrie Smith
16 Felicia "Crickett" Harris
17 Terri Derryberry
18 Donna Clark

ITEM	MINT	EX
Set	7.00	4.50
Card	.15	.10
Wrapper	--	.15
Box	--	2.00

Pro Cheerleaders

SIXERS DREAM TEAM

19 Sheryl M. Washington
20 Jennifer Thomas
21 Robin Amundsen
22 Maryann Wenger
23 Dianemarie Fabiano
24 Michele Ray
25 Darlene Quinn
26 Julie Carmichael
27 Sharon Boschi
28 Kiva Dawson
29 Jyl Kristi Baker
30 Colleen McCullough
31 Sharon Saputelli
32 Michelle R. Daniels
33 Susan Thompson

REEBOK PERFORMANCE TEAM (MINNESOTA)

34 Stephanie
35 Tesha
36 Cari
37 Christine
38 Julie
39 Amy
40 Yvette
41 Janice

MINNESOTA CHECK LIST

483

A novel series in terms of design, "Push-Pull" is an example of how the value of a non-sport set can be radically affected by a few sports cards that appear in it. The cards of Mantle/Berra (#6), Gehrig/Ruth (#17), and Stengel (#19) are no scarcer than any others in the set but are highly prized by sports card collectors. We cannot even give a range of value for these three cards because they are offered almost exclusively in baseball card shows and auctions and opinions about their value differ greatly. Since no established prices for these cards are available, it is impossible to list a set price for Push-Pull. The best we can offer is individual prices for the remaining cards.

Each card in the series has two pictures of people, objects, or places under a black "shutter"; one picture or the other is revealed by pushing or pulling the shutter. While the design is certainly unique among modern card issues, Push-Pull repells as many collectors as it attracts. Note: cards with damaged shutters cannot be graded excellent or mint.

ITEM	MINT	EX
Wrapper	--	200.00
Box	--	250.00

PUSH·PULL

ITEM	MINT	EX
1 Kitty Hawk—Jet Plane	20.00	15.00
2 General Custer—Sitting Bull	20.00	15.00
3 Winston Churchill—Franklin D. Roosevelt	20.00	15.00
4 Uncle Sam—George Washington	20.00	15.00
5 Pres. Johnson (18 mos.)—Pres. Johnson (Today)	20.00	15.00
6 Mickey Mantle—Yogi Berra	SPECULATIVE	
7 Charles Lindbergh—Alexander Graham Bell	25.00	20.00
8 Connie Francis—Bobby Darin	20.00	15.00
9 United States Flag—The Capitol Building	12.00	9.00
10 Mohandas Gandhi—Jawaharlal Nehru	15.00	12.00
11 Mount Rushmore—the White House	12.00	9.00
12 The French Flag—Arch of Triumph	10.00	7.50
13 Empire State Building—the Statue of Liberty	15.00	12.00
14 Paul Anka—Rock Hudson	20.00	15.00
15 Dutch Windmill—Dutch Girl	10.00	7.50
16 Taj Mahal—the Wall of China	10.00	7.50
17 Lou Gehrig—Babe Ruth	SPECULATIVE	
18 Old-Time Automobile—Modern Sports Car	10.00	7.50
19 Casey Stengel Wins—Casey Stengel Loses	SPECULATIVE	
20 Steam Locomotives—Modern Diesel	10.00	7.50
21 John F. Kennedy—Abraham Lincoln	30.00	25.00
22 Eskimos—African Natives	10.00	7.50
23 Nikita Khrushshev—African Gorilla	25.00	20.00
24 Queen Elizabeth—Prince Philip	15.00	12.00
25 Tower of Pisa—Eiffel Tower	10.00	7.50
26 Gen. Douglas MacArthur—Charles DeGaulle	15.00	12.00
27 Mrs. Jacqueline Kennedy—Mrs. Eleanor Roosevelt	20.00	15.00
28 Pres. Lyndon Johnson—Lady Bird Johnson	20.00	15.00
29 Albert Einstein—Thomas Edison	20.00	15.00
30 Whistler's Mother—Mona Lisa	12.00	9.00
31 General Lee—General Grant	35.00	30.00
32 Dwight Eisenhower—Harry Truman	25.00	20.00
33 Clipper Ships—U.S. Destroyers	10.00	7.50
34 Princess Grace—Prince Rainier	25.00	20.00
35 Lincoln Memorial—Washington Monument	12.00	9.00
36 Theodore Roosevelt—Mark Twain	20.00	15.00

Pictures Change Before Your Eyes!

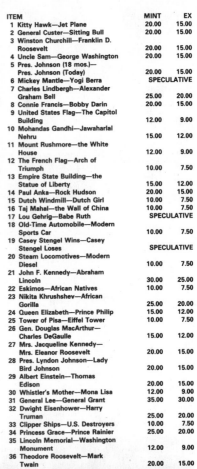

PUT—ON STICKERS (33)

2 1/2" X 3 1/2"

The standard size cards of this set have four to six different front-peel stickers mounted on the obverse (the backs are blank). The great majority of individual stickers have a printed expression or logo, but some only have artwork. Every design has a small "instruction" line about where to place the sticker. Each card is numbered and there are 33 in the set. Collectors will note that some sticker designs appear in other Topps sets: "Stop the Draft" on card No. 28, for example, is from "Angry Stickers."

ITEM	MINT	EX
Set	80.00	60.00
Card	2.00	1.50
Wrapper	--	15.00

1 Guaranteed To Make You Burp
Moth
Pure Catmeat
Bus Leaves in 20 Minutes (Be Under It)
Put a Turtle in Your Tank
2 Give No Quarter!
[worm]
Wooden Nickel
Mad Genius
Watch Your Step
Eeek! Don't Punch Me!
3 No Swimming Allbwed
Clip Joint
Guided Missile
For Adults Only!
4 Worlds Handsomest Person
King Kong Was Here
100%
This Side Up
[mustache]
5 Dry Paint
10 cents
[motorcycle cop]
You Talk Too Much
I Wish I Had a Pot O' Gold
Snake Crossing
6 For Inter-Planetary Mail Only
In Emergency Break Glass
Stomach Pump
Mole
I've Been Robbed!
7 Revolution Now!
Park Chewing Gum Here
[skunk]
Well, What Are You Staring At?
Depressed Area

8 [robot]
Strawberry Fields Forever!
Eek! A Peeping Tom
What's Shakin?
Beware!
9 No Tickee No Washee
Space Bar
Prevent Forest Fires Stay Home!
Lonely? Call the Operator
10 [tack]
[fly]
Out of Order
Idea!
One Way
11 Condemned
'Don't Answer'
.03 cents
Poison
[television]
12 Even The Walls Have Ears
Superguy Was Here!
Danger Explosive
Teechur
13 Go Go
[eye]
[lips]
Remove Your Cap
[earring]
14 [victrola]
I Am The Eggman
Do Your Own Thing
I'm Hung Up!
15 [Chinese symbol]
gLove
Factory Reject
If Found Return to Garbage Can
Tight Squeeze
16 Gadzooka
Hey Fatty! Yer Breaking the Scales
I'm Boiling Mad
You're Too Much!
Nothing Is Real
17 [Lincoln]
Made on Mars
You're Being Watched!
I Work for Peanuts
18 This Record Is Warped!
Slow
Boy Are You Ugly!
Lassie Was Here!
Hard Boiled
19 Don't Sweat It!
I'm a 98 Lb. Wealking
Kiss Me!
Ouch!
Give Me a Ring!
20 Make Reservation
Call Me Stupid!
Bee-In
[money with wings]

21 This Garment Guaranteed to Shrink
Louisville Slugger
You're My Type
Come Clean!
Idea File
22 Want A Date With A Hot Number?
This Book Was Stolen From The
Sing Sing Library
[Spill On Floor]
This Typewriter Only Writes Dirty
Words
23 Don't Pick On Me
[German Cross]
Our Food Untouched by Human Hands
[mosquito]
24 [elephant]
Machines Are Human Too
This Place Fine for Littering
[donkey head]
25 [band aid]
[target]
Patch
Up Up and Away!
[lips]
26 [Car Wreck]
Run, Baby, Run
Contains 96% Grease 4% Fat
Ear Drums (2)
27 You're Driving Me Buggy!
Cute Dish
Get the Point!
Exit
Caution Health May Be Dangerous to
Cigarette Smoking
28 [horns]
This Phone Is Bugged
Stop the Draft!
I'm Cool!
Kick Me!
29 Beware of the Dinosaur
Try Our Meatball Flavored Ice Cream
Boo!
Tilt!
30 Vacancy
This Guitar Case Contains
One Machine Gun
Paid
Don't Look
Aw Dry Up!
31 Father of Our Country
Stop Lifters Beware
Rip This Up!
Shoe Brother
32 Banned in Boston!
I'm Going to Seed
These Boots Were Made for Walking
[keyhole eye]
Get a Haircut!
33 Stolen Car Call Police
Seal of Approval
Quiet!
[two monkeys]

IN DOUBT ABOUT MAKING A PURCHASE? GET A SECOND OPINION.

Back in 1969, if you had a friend that was feeling "down" you could always send him a glossy color 5 X 7 of Quentin to cheer him up. These novelty pictures came in cellophane packs produced by Philly Gum. The card number is located in the bottom left-hand corner on the ob- verse. The reverses are done in post card style with a "Best Wishes To You" message pre- printed and signed by "David (Quentin) Selby." There are 12 cards in the series.

ITEM	MINT	EX
Set	50.00	42.50
Card	3.50	2.50
Wrapper	––	10.00
Box	––	65.00

Gosh dam, every time we collectors get serious about a new type of trading card, somebody starts making fun of it. First they mocked baseball with sets like "Awesome! All-Stars," "Baseball's Greatest Grossouts," "Baseball Weird-Ohs," and "The Baseball Enquirer." Then they went after football, our second "nasnul pastime," with parodies named "Football Stickers" and "Football Super Freaks!" Even basketball was not spared the lash of spoofiness!

But now they have gone too far! They are attacking the most manly sport of all, the epitome of Southern Culture: MOTOR RACING!!! The set is called "Race Toons" and everything and everyone associated with the sport are fair game. From races like the "Instant Grits 500" to racing scenarios like "Major Pile-Up," this set of 77 cards with checkered flag borders has got it all. And talk about all those racing personalities you see on the tube ... now you can buy your very own trading cards of "Motor Home Mama," "Racing Randy," "Billy Bob," "Big Daddy," "Rusty Wrench," "Dixie Trixie," and, of course, the "Pit Bunnies."

This irreverent glimpse into the world of motor racing is brought to us by Carolina Custom Cards. The caricature artwork and sophmoric text may be too lowbrow for collecting purists, but the cards are a good-natured effort by people - obviously racing fans - who are not too uptight to laugh at themselves. My favorite card: "High-Priced Charlie," a racing souvenir dealer who sets up at race tracks with wallet-gouging prices. Finding a Race Toon set may be a problem: they sell for $8-$10, but so far they have only been seen in the south. Note: the information in this presentation was provided by Bill Mullins.

1. Racing Randy
2. Fast Frank
3. Home James
4. Junker Joey
5. Delightful Debbie
6. Lovely Linda
7. Terrible Tammy
8. King Country
9. Billy Bob
10. Badluck Bobby
11. Red Light
12. Fast Eddie
13. Reckless Rex
14. Bumping Benny
15. Gentleman Jim
16. CB Sally
17. Crazy Carl
18. John Money
19. Mr. Green
20. Big Daddy

21. Slick Sally
22. Playboy John
23. Sir Thomas
24. Racing Mama
25. Dream Racer
26. Major Wreck
27. Radical Red
28. Mr. Junkfood
29. Redneck Ron
30. Chewing Charlie
31. Drinking Billy
32. One Shot
33. Beer Belly Billy
34. Motor Home Mama
35. Jamming Jackie
36. Dixie Trixie
37. Tall Todd

38. Betting Bobby
39. Lula
40. South Carolina National
41. North Carolina 500
42. Georgia Cracker Run
43. Rebel Yell 500
44. Instant Grits 400
45. Rachet Face
46. Rusty Wrench
47. Oiley
48. Joe Quick
49. Billy Gas
50. Chief Loud Horn
51. Hauldog Hank
52. Sweeping Sammy
53. Miss Fast Track
54. Miss Bigwheels
55. Miss Racetoons
56. Pit Bunnies
57. Skeeter
58. High-Priced Charlie
59. Upchuck Chuck
60. Fast Cash

61. Restrooms
62. Future Champ
63. Mr. Timmy
64. Miss Muffen
65. Miss Tiffany
66. Miss Taylor
67. Miss Allison
68. Casanova David
69. Mr. Flags
70. Major Pile-up
71. Parking Lot
72. Start of a Race
73. Fast Frank Winning
74. Home James Winning
75. Delightful Debbie, Lovely Linda, and Tammy Wrecked

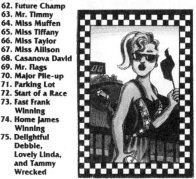

RACE USA (74)

According to details listed on the cards, Fleer's "Race USA" was issued in 1972. The cards are similar to those in "Drag Nationals" and "Official Drag

2 1/2" X 3 1/2"

Champs"—uncaptioned color photos on front and blueprint backs—but the set title is clearly stated on the reverse. The backs contain the card title, specifications list, text, and card number. The two wrappers show different scenes and there are 74 cards in the set.

ITEM	MINT	EX
Set	170.00	125.00
Card	2.00	1.50
Wrappers (2)		
each	---	15.00

1 Tom "The Mongoose" McEwen/1972 Plymouth Funny Car
2 Tom "The Mongoose" McEwen/1972 Plymouth Funny Car
3 Tom "The Mongoose" McEwen/1972 Plymouth Funny Car
4 Don "The Snake" Prudhomme/1972 Plymouth Funny Car
5 Don "The Snake" Prudhomme/1972 Plymouth Funny Car
6 Don "The Snake" Prudhomme/1972 Plymouth Funny Car
7 Mike Randall's "Gremlin 401-XR"/ 1972 Top Stock Gremlin
8 Bill Leavitt's "Quicky Too"/1972 Mustang Funny Car
9 Richard Tharp's "Blue Max"/1972 Mustang Funny Car
10 Bob Lambeck's Pro-Stock Duster/1972 Plymouth Duster
11 Butch Leal's "California Flash Duster"/ 1972 Pro-Stock Duster
12 Dick Landy's Dodge Challenger/1972 Pro-Stock Dodge
13. Dick Landy's Dodge Challenger/1972 Pro-Stock Dodge
14 "Kimball Bros. Camaro"/1972 GT-1 & GT-2 Camaros
15 "Tom Hoover Dragster"/Top Fuel Dragster
16 "White Bear Dodge"/1972 Dodge Funny Car
17 "Dyno-Don's Maverick"/1972 Pro-Stock Maverick
18 Ken Holthe's Camaro/1972 Camaro GT-1
19 Don Grotheer's "Cable Car Barracuda"/ 1972 Top Stock Barracuda
20 "Fast Eddie Schartman's" Comet/ 1972 Top Stock Comet

21 Wayne Gapp's "Shotgun Maverick"/ 1972 Top Stock Maverick
22 Kelly Brown's "Mr. Ed"/1972 Dodge Charger Funny Car
23 Cogo Eads "Boss Hoss" Barracuda/ 1972 Barracuda Funny Car
24 "Gene Dunlap's" Camaro/1972 Camaro GT-2
25 Mart Higginbotham's "RFI Drag-On Vega"/1972 Vega Funny Car
26 "Steve Carbone's" Dragster/Top Fuel Dragster
27 Don Cook's "Southwind Too"/Top Fuel Dragster
28 "Gary Cochran's" Dragster/Top Fuel Dragster
29 "Big Mike Burkhart's" Vega/1972 Vega Funny Car
30 Tom Akin "Lead Sled" Chevrolet/ 1972 Top Stock Chevrolet
31 "Driver of the Year"/Don Garlits
32 "Larry Christopherson's Vega"/1972 Chevy Vega Funny Car
33 "Larry Christopherson's Vega"/1972 Chevy Vega Funny Car
34 Sox & Martin/1972 Pro-Stock Barracuda
35 Sox & Martin/1972 Pro-Stock Barracuda
36 Don Schumacher's Barracuda/1972 Plymouth Funny Car
37 "We Haul Vega"/1972 Pro-Stock Vega
38 "We Haul Vega"/1972 Pro-Stock Vega
39 Scott Shafiroff's Camaro/1972 GT-2 Camaro
40 Berry Setzer's Vega/1972 Vega Funny Car
41 "Chris Karamesines"/Top Fuel Dragster
42 "Dave Russell"/Top Fuel Dragster
43 Twig Zigler's Duster/1972 Plymouth Funny Car

44 Robert Anderson/Top Fuel Dragster
45 Mickey Thompson's Fords/Mustang and Pinto Funny Cars
46 "Mickey Thompson Pinto"/1972 Pinto Funny Car
47 "Mickey Thompson's Mustang"/1972 Mustang Funny Car
48 "Revellution I"/1972 Plymouth Funny Car
49 "Revellution I"/1972 Plymouth Funny Car
50 "Kansas John Wiebe"/Top Fuel Dragster
51 "Paddy Wagon"/Exhibition Wheelstander Vega
52 "Akron Arlen"/1972 Pro-Stock Barracuda
53 "The Whatley Bros."/1972 Hot Rod Camaro
54 "Rapid Ronnie"/Chevy Vega Funny Car
55 "Polaris Racing Team"/Top Stock Mustang
56 "Sandy Elliot"/1972 Pro-Stock Maverick
57 Bobby Yowell's Hemi-Duster/1972 Pro-Stock Plymouth
58 Don Garlits' "Wynn's Charger"/Top Fuel Dragster
59 Don Garlits' "Wynn's Charger"/Top Fuel Dragster
60 Don Garlits' "Wynn's Charger"/Top Fuel Dragster
61 Jeg's Racing Team/1972 Super Stock Dodge
62 Mike Sullivan's "Hemi-Fiat"/Fuel Altered Fiat
63 Jon Petrie's "Cuda"/1972 Pro-Stock Barracuda
64 Bob Riffle's "Rod Shop Dodge"/1972 Dodge Demon Hot Rod
65 Dave Hough's "Nanook"/Fuel Altered Dragster
66 "The Mob"/Fuel Altered Dragster
67 "The Mob"/Fuel Altered Dragster
68 "Praying Mantis"/Top Fuel Dragster
69 "Jim Nicoll"/Top Fuel Dragster
70 Ed Sigmon's Open GT/Altered 1972 Opel
71 Gene Snow's "Revell Snowman"/ 1972 Dodge Charger
72 Gene Snow's "Revell Snowman"/ 1972 Dodge Charger
73 Gene Snow's "Revell Snowman"/ 1972 Dodge Charger
74 Gene Snow's "Revell Snowman/ Top Fuel Dragster

RACING TRACK CARDS (21)
SODA FOUNTAIN CARDS (12)

Both sets of these "jigsaw" format cards were bonus inserts in packs of Topps "Mini Model Cars." The 21 "Racing Track Cards" are numbered and fit together to form a "starting grid" (race course).

The 12 "Soda Fountain Cards," when assembled, depict a scene sure to appeal to youthful collectors: an unsupervised child in an ice cream parlor. Each 10-cent envelope contained a "genuine" miniature model of a "world beating racing car" plus one jigsaw card.

No. 8 in a series of 21 "RACING TRACK" cards

ITEM	MINT	EX
Sets		
Race	120.00	95.00
Soda	50.00	35.00
Cards		
Race	5.00	4.00
Soda	3.50	2.50
Wrapper	--	15.00
Box	--	50.00

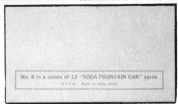

No. 8 in a series of 12 "SODA FOUNTAIN CAR" cards

RAD DUDES (111)

Hey, Dudes, on paper it didn't look like such a bad idea. You take a slice of the old California lifestyle (you know, boards, babes, and ball), put Garbage Pail Kid-like names on the characters, and tell the artist to do them all in neon colors. Pretty rad trip. In fact, it's like, totally tubular, you know? End result: a gnarly jamin' series of 110 cards depicting some of the coolest boys and babes on the Coast. But will it play in Peoria?

Peoria, a.k.a. the card collecting hobby, seems reluctant to embrace Rad Dudes at this point in time. Not that the cards aren't well produced. From a technical standpoint, the series matches or exceeds the quality of other Pacific sets. The theme seems to be the problem, plus the redundancy built into the set. You see, there are only 55 different card fronts; each front has both a text back and a puzzle piece back. That means you have to look at these characters twice and that's too much. The series was issued in 1990 both in wax packs (10 cards, no gum) and as a boxed "Collector Set." Note: a number of words misspelled on the cards were never corrected. An unnumbered checklist card exists, meaning that the set actually contains 111 cards.

1	Cannonball Cory
2	Nerdy Nathan
3	Busted Ben
4	Awesome Volleyball Val
5	Chemical Chris
6	Bored Brandon
7	Mad Mowin' Mike
8	Slamin' Jamin' James
9	Totally Tubular Tiffany
10	Boogie Boardin' Bob
11	Pichin' Pete
12	Boom Box Bryan
13	Running Back Ryan
14	Stunt Bike Steve
15	Skate Board Scott
16	Remote Control Craig
17	Video Mad Vince
18	Mini Video Vinny
19	Awesome B'Ball Blake
20	Downhill David
21	Snow Board Shawn
22	Wave Rippin' Ray
23	Rah Rah Rachael
24	Big Buff Brian
25	Kickin' Kevin
26	Radical Ron
27	Dissecting Dan & Don
28	Hang Ten Tony
29	Back Up Bart
30	Rail Riddin' Ronnie
31	Hand Plant Hank
32	Messy Marty
33	Spikin' Spencer

ITEM	MINT	EX
Set	11.00	5.50
Card	.10	.05

Rad Dudes

34 Funky Fred	45 Knee Board Nick
35 Half Pipe Pat	46 Wipe Out Wayne
36 Crammin' Clint	47 Jason Jock
37 Dodge Ball Doug	48 Surfin' Stacy
38 Checkin' Out the	49 Gnarly Bryan & Trent
Babes Brett	50 Wild Waylon & Willie
39 Poser Pete	51 Clara Cleavage
40 Peekin' Tom & Jimmy	52 Alien Exchange Student Al
41 Teasin' Toby	53 Hurtin' Harry
42 Piggin' Out Owen	54 Totally Buff Tina
43 Cherry Bomb Dudes	55 The Four Rad Dudes
44 Bicep Brothers	

RAIDERS OF THE LOST ARK (88)   2 1/2" X 3 1/2"

THE ARK IS OPENED!

BEAUTIFUL, SPIRITED
Marion Ravenwood

The Topps card set of Raiders of the Lost Ark is as crisp and refreshing as the movie itself: no puzzle backs, stickers, or other unnecessary baggage. Of the 88 cards in the set, 82 are totally devoted to the story line, four introduce the characters, and the remaining two are a checklist and title card. The color photos are from the movie and are surrounded by "snake" frames. The narrative on the back is encased in a red and yellow "Ark," and the card number is located beneath this in the bottom-left corner.

ITEM	MINT	EX
Set	17.50	13.00
Card	.20	.15
Wrapper	––	.35
Box	––	5.00

1 Title Card	29 Deadly Flames!	59 Terror of the Mummies
2 Indiana Jones, Freelance Adventurer	30 The Human Torch	60 "I Hate Snakes!"
	31 The Prize of Agony	61 Indy's Gamble
3 Beautiful, Spirited Marion Ravenwood	32 Escape!	62 Loading the Ark
	33 Fleeing the Blazing Inferno!	63 A Mountain of Muscle
4 Rene Belloq, Indy's Rival	34 Secret of the Medallion	64 Marion Holds Off the Enemy!
5 Indy's Loyal Friend Sallah	35 Attacked by Arab Henchmen!	65 Spectacular Brawl!
6 Valley Mystery	36 The Challenge	66 Exploding Fuel Tank!
7 Temple of the Warriors	37 Master of the Bullwhip	67 Where There's Smoke, There's Indy!
8 Victim of the Gods	38 Where's Marion?	
9 The Priceless Gold Idol	39 Marion Ravenwood... Dead?	68 Destruction of the Flying Wing
10 Removing the Idol	40 The Rivals Meet	69 Race for the Ark!
11 The Collapsing Walls	41 A Valuable Clue for Indy	70 The Chase
12 Chased... by a Boulder!	42 The Tanis Digs	71 Aboard the Bantu Wind
13 Fearsome Hovitos Indians	43 Overseers of Evil	72 Held at Gunpoint by the Nazis
14 Snagged by Belloq	44 Indy and Sallah... in Disguise!	73 Indy Hitches a Ride!
15 Belloq's Prize	45 Inside the Map Room	74 The Arrival of the Ark
16 Escape to the Skies!	46 The Key to Eternity	75 Removing the Precious Cargo
17 Indy's Lecture	47 Indy Zeroes In	76 Yet Another Disguise for Jones
18 Outlining the Quest	48 Well of the Souls	77 The March to Destiny
19 Mystery of History	49 A Very-Much-Alive Marion!	78 Threatened by Indiana Jones
20 The Raven Bar	50 Treacherous Descent	79 Indy's Bluff Is Called
21 The Drinking Contest	51 Chamber of Death!	80 Captives of the Evil One
22 Indy and Marion Reunited	52 Within the Stone Chest	81 The Way to the Altar
23 An Affair to Remember	53 Ark of the Covenant	82 The Ritual Begins
24 The Mysterious Medallion	54 Trapped by Belloq	83 The Awesome Moment
25 The Creature Called Toht	55 Sea Serpents	84 The Ark Is Opened!
26 Marion in a Jam!	56 Our Heroes... Doomed?	85 The Power of God!
27 Jones to the Rescue!	57 Hissing Death!	86 The Adventure Ends... or Does It?
28 Struggle to the Death!	58 Trapped in the Well!	
		87 Destiny of the Ark
		88 Checklist(1-88)

RAMBO (66 & 22)

The adventures of America's fantasy alter-ego, Rambo, are recorded in this card set marketed by Topps in 1985. The fronts of 64 cards have color photographs from the movie "First Blood Part II;" these are captioned and are surrounded by "barb wire" frame lines and red borders. Card No. 1 is a title card and No. 66 is a checklist. The first 65 cards all have story backs. The series of 22 yellow-bordered stickers have different photos than the cards, except for Nos. 7 and 21. The backs of the sticker cards are pieces of a 20-part puzzle, plus two puzzle preview cards. Note: set prices include stickers.

ITEM	MINT	EX
Set	15.00	10.00
Card	.10	.07
Sticker	.35	.25
Wrapper	--	.35
Box	--	5.00

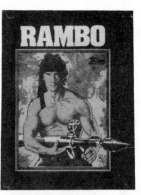

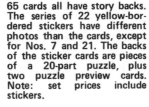

1 Rambo First Blood Part II
2 Caged!
3 Trautman's Offer
4 Is Rambo Reliable?
5 The Strategists
6 For Luck!
7 Friend...Or Foe?
8 Duo For Danger!
9 Rambo's Plan
10 Deathblade!
11 The Prison Camp
12 Rescued!
13 Blow 'em Away!
14 Pirates in Flames!
15 Grip of Death!
16 To The Extraction Site!
17 Surrounded!
18 "Where's Trautman?"
19 Help From Above!
20 Shameful Betrayal!
21 The Bog
22 Killer Leeches!
23 The Prisoner
24 Man with a Mission
25 Pain Is My Ally!
26 The Unkindest Cut!

27 Rambo Gets The Point!
28 Rambo...Tool Of The Enemy?
29 Words of Betrayal
30 Down To The Wire!
31 Escape Through Barbed Wire!
32 The Death of Co Boa
33 Retribution!
34 By Co's Grave
35 Rambo's Revenge!
36 Killing Machine!
37 Hidden Death!
38 Aiming to Win!
39 Up From The Depths!
40 "I'm Coming For You!"
41 Unstoppable!
42 Blasted to Bits!
43 No Escape From Rambo!
44 Bridge - Obliterated!
45 Target: Rambo!
46 Super Bowman!

47 The Enemy Fries!
48 One-Man Army!
49 Blowing The Prison Camp!
50 Escape!
51 Destination: Freedom
52 Warship Battle!
53 Fighting Back!
54 To The Death!
55 Safe At Home!
56 Don't Cross Rambo!
57 Getting Even!
58 "Next Time...You'll Die!"
59 What Rambo Wants
60 "I Want Respect!"
61 Fit For The Part!
62 Julie Nickson Is Co Boa
63 "Action!!"
64 The "Ram-Bow"
65 Awaiting His Next Mission!
66 Checklist

RAMBO ALBUM STICKERS (240) 21/16" X 2 9/16"

Yo, collectors! Can you imagine a world totally dependent upon Rambo to maintain law and order? Can you see him fighting villains in castles with a broadsword one day and sinking enemy battleships with laser missiles the next? How about Rambo as Secretary-General of the U.N.?

Well, they don't go THAT far in this 240-sticker tribute to America's latest matter-over-mind hero, but they do make Rambo into a "man for all seasons." Anyway, the artwork is colorful and there is a 32-page album containing a special bonus wall poster (for mounting a mini-series of 15 foil stickers). Note: set price includes album.

ITEM	MINT	EX
Set	25.00	18.50
Sticker	.10	.07
Wrapper	--	.35
Album	2.00	1.50

RAT FINK GREETING CARDS (40) 2 1/2" X 4 11/16"

According to Topps' records, "Rat Fink" was released for general distribution in September 1965. The "cards" were designed to be actual greeting cards with a "set-up" phrase on the front cover and a "punch line" inside. The back panels were printed with a postcard format and the set title appears in a postage stamp design. The card number and set total are also stated on the back panel.

ITEM	MINT	EX
Set	240.00	190.00
Card	5.00	4.00
Wrapper	--	20.00
Box	--	125.00

Rat Fink Greeting Cards

1 You Sure Know How to Pick a Friend (To Pieces)
2 I'd Like to Keep in Touch with You (But I Lost My Ten Foot Pole)
3 If I Only Had Your Looks, Ability and Personality (I'd Be Worried)
4 You're So Kind and Sweet (You Wouldn't Hurt a Dragon)
5 I Never Thought I'd Miss You (and I Was Right)
6 Let Me Be By Your Side Always (Standing Next to You I Look Good)
7 You Look Much Better (From a Distance)
8 You've Got a Face Only a Mother Could Love (A Mother Gorilla)
9 I Feel Guilty About Not Getting You a Present on Your Birthday (But as Confucious Says, Feeling Guilty is Cheaper than Buying a Present)
10 I'd Like to Get You an Expensive Gift for Your Birthday (...but I'm Too Nervous to Steal)
11 You Can Have Everything I Own (For Cash)
12 You're My Cup of Tea (You Old Bag)
13 There's Only One Thing I Miss More than You (The Money I $pent on this Card)
14 To My Teacher: I Know Why You Look So Busy (You're Just Confused)
15 What Luck to Have a Friend Like You (Bad Luck)
16 Thanks for Making Me a Birthday Cake—Unfortunately My Dog Ate It (Rest His Soul)
17 I Hear When You Grow Up You're Joining the Army (Which Side?)
18 Have Some Good Clean Fun on Your Birthday (Take a Bath for a Change)
19 You Came Along When I Really Needed a Friend (And Scared Him Away)
20 Please Stay the Way You Are...Don't Change a Thing (Except Maybe Your Sox Once in a While)
21 I Wish I Could Give You a Big Kiss— But There Is Only One Thing Holding Me Back (Your Face)
22 Only Once Before Did I Have a Wonderful Friend Like You (But He Gnawed a Hole in His Box and Got Away)

23 I Rushed Out the Last Minute to Buy You a Present and I Was Lucky (All the Stores Were Closed)
24 I Have Come to the Conclusion that Everyone in the World is Crazy Except Us (and I'm Not Sure about You)
25 You Know All the Answers, You Keep Your Desk Neat, You're Never Late, You're Never Absent (You're the Class Fink)
26 Here's a Riddle for You...What's the Difference between a Birthday Card and a Birthday Present ($9.75)
27 I Searched All My Life for Just the Right Person...then I Found You (Instead)
28 You Ain't Seen Nothing Until You See What I Got You for Your Birthday (Then You've Seen Nothing)
29 If You Lost All Your Money and All Your Friends, You'd Still Have Me (and I Don't Like You)
30 Keep Smiling (Your Teacher Loves Grinning Idiots)
31 Do Something Every Day to Make Other People Happy (Leave Them Alone)

32 Some People Are Good and Some People Are Miserable (You're Both Good and Miserable)
33 Dear Friend — Sorry You Had an Accident. It Could Have Been Worse (It Could Have Been Me)
34 You Are Good Looking, Sincere, Clever, Witty (...and Very Conceited If You Believe All This)
35 This Card Isn't Much (But Neither Are You)
36 I Wanted to Take You Out on Your Birthday (But Your Cage Was Locked)
37 Happy Birthday — Great Oaks From Little Acorns Grow (Which Proves Any Nut Can Make It)
38 I Spoke to Your Doctor and I've Got Terrible News for You (You'll Be Back in School in No Time)
39 I Think You Are the Handsomest and the Most Wonderful Boy in the World (It Would Embarrass Me if This Card Fell into the Wrong Hands.— Memorize This Message and Destroy Yourself)
40 You're So Smart — Tell Me: Why Do Bees Hum? (Because They Don't Know the Words)

RAT PATROL (66 & 22)

2 1/2" X 3 1/2"

The Rat Patrol set produced by Topps in 1966 has 66 cards and 22 Army Insignia rings. Each card front contains a color photograph from the television series and has white borders. All other detail—narrative, card number, credit lines, etc.—are located on the back. The backs of the cards are picture puzzle pieces which can be arranged to form a large poster. The set of 22 punch-out Army Insignia rings was distributed as a one-per-pack bonus insert. Note: separate prices are listed for sets of cards and rings. Detached rings cannot be graded excellent or mint.

ITEM	MINT	EX
Set		
Cards	95.00	75.00
Rings	205.00	160.00
Card	1.25	1.00
Ring	7.50	6.00
Wrapper	--	20.00
Box	--	85.00

Hitchcock was a member of The Rat Patrol by his own request. Born in New York City, he was the scholar of the group. All his life Mark had been called a sissy, but as a soldier he'd prove them all wrong.

©1966 by MIRISCH-RICH Television Productions Collect all 66 RAT PATROL Picture Cards.

PUZZLE SEVEN

1 7th Army
2 Army Air Forces
3 H.Q. European Theater
4 2nd Division
5 17th Airborne Division
6 59th Division
7 63rd Division
8 10th Mountain Division
9 11th Airborne Division
10 77th Division
11 187th Airborne Regiment
12 4th Air Force
13 Alaska Air Command
14 Aviation Cadet
15 3rd Observation
16 99th Infantry Battalion
17 442d Regiment Combat Team
18 101st Division
19 Armored Force
20 U.S. Wing Marking
21 VF-2
22 31st Bombardment

REAL CLOTH PATCHES (55 & 12)

2 1/2" X 3 5/16"

A 1973 Fleer set composed of 55 sheets of patches and 12 "credit cards." The "Real cloth" fabric of these patches appears to be made of plastic fibers, but only a chemist could say for sure. Most sheets contain two patches: we have listed both titles where the subject or designs are dissimilar. A (2) indicates two patches with a similar subject or design. The phoney credit cards measure 2 1/2" X 3 1/2" and are blank-backed. There are three yellow wrappers for the set—they are identical except for the patches depicted. Note: set prices listed are for 55 patches and 12 credit cards.

ITEM	MINT	EX
Set	37.50	25.00
Patch	.50	.35
Card	.50	.35
Wrappers (3)		
each	--	3.00
Box	--	15.00

CLOTH PATCHES
Airborne [eagle]
Airborne (AA)
   Airborne/Civil Air Patrol
Air Force (Systems Command)
Air Force (United States Air Force)
American Hot Rod Association
Avis/United
Army (United States Army)
Barnum's Animals
Be My Chum/Harlem Globetrotters
Blue Angels
Boy Scout/United States Auto Club
Brat Boy/Palm Beach Bus Drivers
Brat Girl/[Supergirl emblem]

CAP/[Air Force stripes]
Civil Air Patrol
Civil Air Patrol Emergency Services
Coast Guard
Command/Strategic Air Command
Expert (2)
F.A.A./7up
Fire Dept. (2)
Follow Me (2)
   Frog Man/United States Coast Guard
Good Humor Ice Cream
Guard/PRA
Harley-Davidson/Bic
Liberty (2)
Lipton Tea
Nascar/Pepsi
Navy/United States Navy
Paratroops (2)
Police/New York City Transit Police
Ranger (2)
Rescue/Fleer Rescue Squad

Schlitz
Sea Scout/Tonkin Gulf Yacht Club
Security/USS Intrepid CVS-11
Seventh (2)
Sharpshooter (2)
Sheriff/[Confederate flag]
Ski Patrol/U.S. Mail
Skydiver/Skydiver
Special Forces/U.S. Army Armoured Force
Teacher's Pest/Truant Officer
The Fresh Guys/Nabisco
U.S. Female /Wonder Racing Team
USAF Auxiliary Civil Air Patrol
U.S. Marines (2)
USS Wasp
Weeeeeo!/Fleer Dubble Bubble Gum
[Air Force chevron[
[Army chevron]
[Marine chevron]
[Infantry patch — Indian chief]
CARDS
Air Unravel Card
American Undress
Bell Smellophone
Blue Moss Glue Shield
Cramco
Cart Blank
Faster Charge
Golf
Hexxon
Mobile Gasoline
Social Insecurity
Winners Club

REAL ROAD SIGNS STICKERS (41)

Although it seems to be an unlikely total, there appear to be 41 different combinations on "Real Road Sign" sticker sheets. Each sheet contains one large and two small signs. Two of the large signs—"Garbage Dump" and "Wash Hands Before Eating"—appear twice in combination with two different pairs of small signs. Some of the small signs are repeated in different combinations and some are petite versions of larger signs. Fleer reportedly issued the series in

2 1/2" X 3 1/2"

1978.

ITEM	MINT	EX
Set	20.00	14.00
Sticker	.50	.35
Wrapper	---	2.00
Box	---	12.00

Bear Area (No Looking)
Blasting Area (Wear Gas Mask)
Brothers Keep Out
City Jail (You Are Forbidden to Talk to Inmates)
Criminals Must Register
Danger (Do Not Enter During LOADING OPERATION)
Dangerous Curves (Keep Your Cotton-Picking Hands Off!)
Do Not Touch It (You Don't Know Where It's Been)
Drive-In Movie (Removal of Clothing Prohibited at All Times
Federal Prison (Do Not Talk to the Inmates)
Garbage Dump ["This Locker Condemned"]
Garbage Dump ["Slow It's More Fun"]
Keep Hands Off
Lunch Room (This Food Unfit for Human Consumption
No Parking Anytime (If You're Over 21)

No Stopping Or Standing (Between 9 AM and 11 PM incl. Sat., Sun., and Holidays)
Notice Private Property (All Trespassing Forbidden Under Penalty of the Law)
Official Notice Closed (By Board of Health, Division of Rat, Termite and Garbage Control
Out Of Order
Polluted Water
Rest Area (Close Eyes, and Relax)
School Zone (Busing Prohibited)
Sisters Keep Out
Slippery When Wet
Slow (I'm Enjoying It)
Slow (It's More Fun!)
Slow (Make It Last)
Sound Horn
Stink Factory (Hold Your Nose)
Stop (If You Can)
Stop (In 10 Minutes)
This Locker Condemned
This Room Is a DISASTER AREA
US Capitol Massage Parlor (For Senior Officials Only)
US Congress (Secretary Wanted No Typing Required)
US Senate (Disrobing Prohibited)
Wash Hands Before Eating ["No Parking Anytime"]
Wash Hands Before Eating ["Press Here"]
White House (Quiet! Recording in Session)
Yield (It's More Fun!)
Zoo (Do Not Feed the Teachers)

REAL WOOD PLAKS (66?)
VALENTINE WOOD PLAKS

1 3/8" X 3 1/2"

We have decided to combine the listing for these two sets because they are essentially the same. The plaks are actually made of compressed wood and are approximately 3/32" thick. Both of the wrappers are the same size, have the same price, and both contained two plaks and one piece of gum. The center designs differ significantly but the information on the top panel is identical. We assume, from examples seen, that the plak captions for both sets are identical, but this has yet to be confirmed. The plaks are not numbered and our partial checklist contains 62 captions.

ITEM	MINT	EX
Plak	4.00	3.00
Wrappers		
"Real"	––	25.00
"Valentine"	––	10.00

Always love they neighbor, defend her near and far, It's easy if you live, next to a movie star.

As Eli Whitney once said—Get your cottin pickin hands off.

Be kind to your elders—They can't help it if they're stupid.

Be trustworthy, loyal, helpful, friendly, kind, brave and cheerful—And people will take advantage of you.

Books are good friends—Like checkbooks, bankbooks, etc.

Bored of Education (ho hum)

Do not disturb

Do not feed the animals. The teachers have their own lunchrooms.

"Don't cry over spilt milk" is a saying I like best.

Don't go away angry...just go away.

Do something for your country to make it strong and grand.

Do unto others as they would do unto you—only do it first!

Drive carefully, children at play.

Education is wonderful, it's just school that's miserable.

Food in this school is untouched by human hands, Monkeys make it.

Gather your belongings and move to another land (Outer Mongolia).

Graduate of Alcatraz

I did well on my test. I was the first to leave. It's easy when you have the answers on your sleeve.

I'd like to take a walk with you—Where's your leash?

If ever trouble comes along and pulses begin to quicken, the smartest thing for you to do is immediately turn chicken.

I'll never leave you—Unless you get off my foot

In our classroom you're quite the rage. You're the only girl who sits in a cage.

It is said that one good turn, always deserves another, at lunch you turned my stomach, and did the same to mother.

It's fun to see you happy. I've told all my chums it's fun to see you smile cause all I see is gums.

I wish I had ten friends like you, cause I've got 20 friends like you.

Keep smiling and you'll be known as the grinning idiot

Kiss Me Darling

Kiss me, you fool—Only a fool would kiss me

Look before you leap, then leap, then leap.

Money can't buy happiness—But it makes misery much more fun.

Mother please, I'd rather do it myself

My group had 32% fewer cavities—But we had our gums removed.

My teacher loves me, she thinks I'm a dear, She's kept me with her, for the fourth straight year.

My teacher takes ugly pills

Never hit a man when he's down...Kick him

Never put off till tomorrow what you can do today—Play hookey now.

No dogs allowed—So how'd you get in?

Please shut the door from the outside.

People who live in glass houses shouldn't take baths.

Remember the immortal words of General Custer: Ouch.

Sit on my lap, show me you care. I'm sitting right now in the electric chair.

Support mental health or I'll kill you.

The pen is mightier than the sword. If you know where to stick it.

"There is no place like home," a poet said with grace, I wonder what he'd say, if he lived at my place.

They said it couln't be done. And they were right.

This house condemned by the Board of Health.

This pass plus the price of admission allows bearer to go to the movies.

Three is a crowd, so you two get lost.

To the memory of Irving Glots, Public School 6, who died waiting for the bell.

Two heads are better than one—I was told by my dad but it won't help me much cause both of yours are bad.

We have not yet begun to fight. We're too busy running.

When things look bad don't holler or curse. Think of the future when things will get worse.

"Where there's smoke there's fire" is a saying quite complete—Cause when I'm caught smoking there's fire in my seat.

With your looks you'll go far—But not far enough

You are real solid. All the fellows said I know the reason—You got rocks in your head.

You never get punished for something you don't do. So don't do your homework.

You're pretty blonde braids, are your mom's pride and joy, But people have mentioned, you're a strange looking boy.

You're so different so very different

You're the prettiest girl in the country—But in the city Yich

Your face is your fortune, of this you are sure, just look in the mirror—oh boy, are you poor.

You should get ahead—You need one

RED BARN SPACE CARDS (8)

2 1/4" X 3 3/16"

It is believed that Red Barn Restaurants, a once-popular fast food chain, released this eight-card set of space cards in 1968 in anticipation of the Apollo missions which landed on the surface of the moon in mid-1969. The card fronts are color artwork scenes from various phases of a moon flight and each is captioned inside the field of the picture. Narrow white borders enhance the effect of the drawings. The backs are printed in red ink on white stock and the card number is located in a red barn design at top. The card caption is repeated in large type and there is a short text beneath it. The rest of the card advertises the Red Barn Space Contest and the Red Barn Passport to the Moon promotions.

ITEM	MINT	EX
Set	37.50	27.50
Card	4.00	3.00

REMEMBER PEARL HARBOR (50)

REMEMBER THE SACRIFICE   1

This U.S. poster remembers the dead of Pearl Harbor and reminds Americans of the sacrifice made by many gallant men and women on December 7, 1941. The tattered, but still waving flag, set against the smoking inferno, personifies both the horror of the attack and the courage of the American people.

A Tuff Stuff set of 50 cards, "Remember Pearl Harbor" was issued to coincide with the 50th anniversary of the Japanese attack on the hub of our naval operations in the Pacific. "Relive America's Day of Infamy. Meet the heroes of the attack. See the devastation. Face the fear. Honor those who died so bravely." You can do all these things, according to Tuff Stuff advertising, by owning a set of these cards. The 50 cards are of two types: eleven are artwork or photographs in color and 39 are black and white pictures of various scenes and individuals. The captions, which are printed front and back, are terse. Text is short and to the point. The series was issued only in J-hook "blister packs" containing complete sets and has been selling in the $10 range since it was released. Approximately 5000 large 8-1/2" X 11" advertising cards were also issued as an adjunct to the regular series. It remains to be seen whether or not these larger cards will be popular with collectors.

1 Remember the Sacrifice
2 Takeoff for Attack
3 Ready to Die
4 Final Performance
5 The Mastermind
6 "Day of Infamy"
7 Ships Under Fire
8 Shattered P-40
9 Hangar Destruction
10 Easy Targets
11 One Family's Loss
12 In Her Prime
13 Death for 1,777
14 Fire Pours From Ships
15 The Enemy Attacks
16 Ammunition Explodes
17 War Hero
18 Flag Flies Proudly
19 Failed Effort
20 Smoke Rises From Ships
21 Ford Island Bombarded
22 Hull of USS Oglala
23 Seaplane Wreckage
24 Crashed Japanese Zero
25 Words to Remember
26 Kamikaze Pilot Salutes
27 Crash Landing
28 Spoils of War
29 The Horror Grows
30 Fighting the Fires
31 All That's Left
32 Only One Survived
33 USS Shaw Explodes
34 Saving Burning Plane
35 Air Station Burns
36 Enemy Shot Down
37 Wreckage of P-40
38 Devastation Continues
39 Medal of Honor
40 Trying to Salvage
41 Japanese Loss
42 Bizarre Plan
43 Heroic Rescue
44 Badly Burned B-17C
45 Call to Arms
46 Announcing War
47 Fallen Comrades
48 In Lasting Memory
49 Avenging the Attack
50 Japanese Surrender

RETURN OF THE JEDI I (132 & 33)

The movie sensation of the summer of '83 was Return of the Jedi and Topps was quick to capitalize on its appearance by releasing a 132-card, 33-sticker set at the same time. The cards have red borders, are captioned beneath the color picture, and are numbered on the back. Collectors should note that there are no less than 25 Jedi characters and pieces of hardware drawn in the accent area to the right of the narrative. Of the 132 cards, 130 have narrative backs and two are checklists. The uncaptioned stickers come in six colors (1-11: purple or yellow; 12-22: turquoise or red; 23-33: green or orange) and can be composed into two different 15 piece posters. The remaining three sticker backs are puzzle preview cards. Note: set price includes stickers.

ITEM	MINT	EX
Set	22.00	15.00
Card	.10	.07
Sticker	.35	.25
Wrappers (4)		
each	--	.35
Box	--	5.00

1 Title Card
2 Luke Skywalker
3 Darth Vader
4 Han Solo
5 Princess Leia Organa
6 Lando Calrissian
7 Chewbacca
8 C-3PO and R2-D2
9 The New Death Star
10 The Inspection
11 Toward the Desert Palace
12 Bib Fortuna
13 Court of Evil
14 Jabba the Hutt
15 Intergalactic Gangster
16 Salacious Crumb
17 A Message for Jabba the Hutt
18 Dungeons of Jabba the Hutt
19 Beedo and a Jawa
20 Sy Snootles and the Rebo Band
21 Droopy McCool
22 Sy Snootles
23 Watched by Boba Fett
24 Boushh's Captive
25 The Bounty Hunter Boushh
26 The Villains Confer
27 Han Solo's Plight
28 The Resuer
29 Decarbonized!
30 Princess Leia to the Rescue!
31 Heroes in Disguise
32 The Princess Enslaved
33 Luke Skywalker Arrives
34 The Young Jedi
35 The Court in Chaos!
36 The Rancor Pit
37 Facing Jabba the Hutt
38 The Sail Barge and the Desert Skiff
39 Jabba the Hutt's New Dancing Girl
40 On the Sail Barge
41 A Monstrous Fate!
42 The Battle Begins
43 Lando Calrissian's Flight for Life
44 Fury of the Jedi
45 Princess Leia Strikes Back!
46 The Demise of Jabba the Hutt
47 Boba Fett's Last Stand
48 The Rescue
49 Gamorrean Guard
50 The Deadly Cannon
51 The Raging Battle
52 Princess Leia Swings into Action!
53 Swing to Safety
54 On the Death Star
55 Guards of the Emperor
56 The Deciders
57 The Emperor
58 Yoda the Jedi Master
59 A Word with Ben (OBI-WAN) Kenobi
60 The Allies Meet
61 A New Challenge
62 Pondering the Raid
63 Mission: Destroy the Death Star!
64 Mon Mothma
65 The Friends Depart
66 Benevolent Creature
67 The Plan Begins
68 Forest of Endor
69 Droids on the Move
70 Blasting a Speeder Bike
71 Approaching the Princess
72 A New Found Friend
73 Princess Leia's Smile
74 Under Attack!
75 Imperial Scout Peril!
76 Entering the Throne Room
77 The Skywalker Factor
78 Captured by the Ewoks
79 The Netted Droid
80 All Hail See-Threepio!
81 Royal Treatment
82 Sitting with Royalty
83 Levitated by Luke
84 The Ewok Leaders
85 Logray and Chief Chirpa
86 Help from Princess Leia
87 Will Han Solo Be Dinner?
88 The Baby Ewok
89 The Forest Creatures
90 The Droid and the Ewok
91 R2-D2 Meets Wicket
92 Unexpected Allies
93 Serious Situation
94 Luke Skywalker's Destiny
95 Quiet, See-Threepio!
96 Imperial Biker Scout
97 Biker Scout and the Battlefield
98 Han Solo's Approach
99 The Ultimate Mission
100 Ready for Action!
101 Ambushed by the Empire
102 Observed by the Ewoks
103 The Courageous Ewoks
104 Prisoners
105 Revising Their Plan
106 At-St (All Terrain Scout Transport)
107 The Forest Fighters!
108 Break for Freedom!
109 Artoo-Detoo—Hit!
110 Chewbacca Triumphant!
111 Ewoks to the Rescue!
112 Battle in the Forest
113 Stormtrooper Attack!
114 The Victorious Rebels
115 Time Out for Love
116 Facing the Emperor
117 Master of Terror
118 The Emperor's Offer
119 Battle of the Jedi
120 Lightsaber Battle!
121 Darth Vader Is Down!
122 The Confrontation
123 The Death Star Raid
124 Military Leader Admiral Ackbar
125 Within the Death Star
126 Victory Celebration!
127 Congratulating Wedge
128 The Triumphant Trio
129 The Heroic Droids
130 Toward Brighter Tomorrows
131 Checklist I
132 Checklist II

RETURN OF THE JEDI II (88 & 22)

2 1/2" X 3 1/2"

This 88-card, 22-sticker follow-up to the first "Jedi" series was also issued by Topps in 1983. The blue-bordered cards are numbered 133-220 and all except the Series 2 title card (No. 133) have a "Star Quiz" feature on the back. Stickers 34-44 are close-ups of Jedi characters and equipment set on solid red centers; stickers 45-55 are round-cornered rectangles with blue frames and "film clip" edges. Note: set prices include stickers.

ITEM	MINT	EX
Set	15.00	10.00
Card	.10	.07
Sticker	.35	.25
Wrappers (4)		
each	--	.35
Box	--	5.00

499

133 Title Card	155 Thoughts of a Jedi	177 Confronting Their Destiny	199 Rescuing Han Solo
134 Path to Destiny	156 The Jaws of Death	178 "Where's Princess Leia?"	200 Father Versus Son
135 Captured!	157 Princess Leia Has the Force!	179 Horror From the Pit	201 Luke Skywalker, Jedi Warrior
136 The Courageous Jedi	158 Arrival of the Emperor	180 "Give In to Your Hate!"	202 The Young Jedi Knight
137 The Victors	159 Reunion on Endor	181 Awaiting His Majesty	203 Han Solo Is Alive!
138 Wicket and Princess Leia	160 Toward the Sarlacc Pit	182 A Mother Ewok and Child	204 Lando Calrissian Undercover
139 The Emperor's Arrival	161 Sail Barge Creatures	183 A Concerned Princess Leia	205 Horrendous Creature
140 Sail Barge Battle!	162 Friends of the Alliance!	184 Lead Singer Sy Snootles	206 Corridors of the Imperial Destroyer
141 Luke Skywalker, The Jedi	163 The Dreaded Rancor	185 The Arrival of Boushh	207 Surrounded by Ewoks
142 The Approach of Wicket	164 Face of Terror	186 Master of His Court	208 Gamorrean Guard Profile
143 A Close Call!	165 Inside Jabba the Hutt's Palace	187 Star Lovers	209 Hulking Gamorrean Guard
144 Above the Sarlacc Pit	166 The Ewok Village	188 Luke Skywalker...Now a Jedi!	210 Guests of Jabba the Hutt
145 Admiral Ackbar's Defenders	167 A Collection of Creatures	189 Battle of the Bunker!	211 A Full-Fledge Jedi!
146 R2-D2 on Endor	168 Alert to Danger!	190 Portrait of Wicket	212 Bizarre Alien Creatures
147 Boba Fett Attacks!	169 Walking the Plank!	191 Trapped by the Empire	213 Headquarters Frigate
148 Deadly Plunge!	170 A Gamorrean Guard Emerges	192 Their Secret Revealed	214 TIE Interceptor
149 Lando Calrissian's Disguise	171 The Imperial Fleet	193 Rethinking the Plan	215 The Nearly Completed Death Star
150 Soldiers of the Empire	172 Jabba the Hutt on the Sail Barge	194 Snagged by the Ewoks	216 Rebel Cruiser
151 A Curious Ewok	173 Escorted to the Ewok Village	195 Han Solo's in Trouble!	217 The Interceptor
152 A Pensive Luke Skywalker	174 A Monstrous Guest!	196 Is Han Solo Giving Up?	218 The Emperor's Shuttle
153 The Captive Princess	175 Village of the Ewoks	197 The Royal Droid	219 Portrait of Chewbacca
154 Luke Skywalker Surrenders	176 Aboard the Sail Barge	198 Princess Leia Intercedes	220 Checklist

RETURN OF THE JEDI
ALBUM STICKERS (180)

2 1/8" X 3 1/2"

Topps apparently thought the demand for Return of the Jedi cards would outstrip its 275-item regular series, so the company commissioned Panini to manufacture an album sticker set based on the Jedi theme. The series is composed of 180 stickers containing color scenes from the movie. The backs are numbered and are written entirely in English. A 24-page album to house the set was sold for 25 cents. Note: set prices include album.

ITEM	MINT	EX
Set	30.00	20.00
Sticker	.15	.10
Album	2.00	1.50
Wrapper	--	.35
Box	--	2.00

RETURN TO OZ (44)

2 1/2" X 3 1/2"

A true sticker-card set produced by Topps in 1985. On one side, there is a series of 44 un-numbered, front-peel stickers set on solid red backgrounds. On the other side, there are cards: a title card (No. 1), story cards (2-33), puzzle pieces (34-43) and a puzzle preview card (not numbered). The 42 cards in the 2-43 sequence are divided into "flat" and "glossy" surface finishes. There are four different wrapper designs for the set.

ITEM	MINT	EX
Set	12.00	9.00
Sticker-card	.25	.20
Wrappers (4)		
each	--	.35
Box	--	4.00

RIDDLE FUN (5K)

IRREGULAR SIZE

Glenn Candies, a Buffalo, N.Y. based confectionary firm, produces, among other things, a group of syrup-filled wax figures for the retail trade. In both 1990 and 1991, their Halloween line included an item called "Syrup Filled Ghosts," and the packaging for this product had a feature entitled "Riddle Fun" printed on the back. There are two riddles on every tombstone and five sets of riddles have been reported to date. Riddle Fun would probably not attract most mainstream collectors, but it is an interesting seasonal issue produced by a company with a long tradition in producing cards. Intact Riddle Fun packages currently sell for 50 cents apiece provided they are not stained by syrup.

RIDDLE TIME! (?)

Another riddle series from Glenn Candies: this one is printed on the back of a small carton containing six miniature syrup-filled wax bottles (remember those from when you were a kid?). The carton is red with white letters and the "Riddle Time!" panel is white with red letters. As with "Syrup Filled Ghosts," there are

two riddles on each panel and the latter are not numbered. The number of panels in the set is unknown mainly because boxes of "Nik-L-Nip" always seem to contain the very same carton. An item of limited interest to mainstream collectors: cartons not damagaed by syrup sell for 50 cents each.

RINGER DINGERS (?)

"Ringer Dingers"—produced by Fleer—were first reported in the Barker Updates of June 1971. Each five-cent package contained a paper sheet holding five rings and assorted "add-ons" (used to change the message) and one

2 1/2" X 4 5/16" instruction card. The number of different ring sheets confirmed to exist stands at eight; however, the existence of more is indicated by a series of birthstone rings, for which only seven months are accounted so far.

ITEM	MINT	EX
Ring sheet	2.50	2.00
Card	.75	.50
Wrapper	--	10.00
Box	--	20.00

RIP INTO ROCK (15)

This series of 15 small stickers was distributed in bags of potato chips in the United States (Wise) and Canada (Hostess) beginning in 1988. In contrast to the common sticker format so familiar to collectors - where the sticker is printed on

paper and is pulled from a paper or cardboard backing - "Rip Into Rock" stickers are printed on cardboard, with adhesive backs which are exposed when the paper backing is pulled off. They are not numbered and the groups and individuals pictured include country, pop, heavy metal, blues, soul, and rock performers. Some stickers bear group names only; others picture the entertainer(s). All stickers have rounded corners and glossy surfaces. Note: peeled stickers cannot be graded excellent or mint.

ITEM	MINT	EX
Set	8.00	5.50
Sticker	.50	.35

ROBIN HOOD
PRINCE OF THIEVES (2 SETS)

2 1/2" X 3 1/2"

The year 1991 will go down in history as the year in which Topps Gum achieved the impossible: the company issued two separate card sets for the same motion picture! Somehow the wires between Hollywood and New York got crossed, and Topps produced an 88-card set which the licensor considered to be too lengthy. However, by the

time this conviction was communicated to Topps, a quantity of "88" product had already found its way into the public domain. Collectors were astounded when the 88-card set of Robin Hood vanished into thin air and was replaced by a 55-card version. At the time, very few hobbyists noticed the switch or understood its implications for the future.

Both versions have the same set of nine stickers, although the sequence is not identical. "88" cards bear a "Collect All 88" line; "55" cards read "Collect All 55." All of the "55" cards appear in the "88" set, but most do not share the same number (by comparing the respective checklists, you can see which titles were deleted). In addition,

"55" series cards are marked with one or two asterisks in the lower left corner on the reverse. A single wrapper was used for both versions and it appears that the display box for both sets was also the same. Estimates of how much "88" product actually reached collectors is a matter of speculation; that it will increase in value much faster than the "55" Robin Hood is a matter of fact.

ITEM	MINT	EX
Sets		
"55"	10.00	7.00
"88"	13.50	10.00
Cards		
"55"	.10	.07
"88"	.10	.07
Stickers, all	.35	.25
Wrapper	--	.25
Box	--	2.50

1 Header card	9 England, At Long Last!	16 Enter Mysterious Sherwood Forest!
2 Robin Hood	10 Journey to Locksley Castle	17 Battling Little John
3 Azeem	11 The Evil Guy of Gisborne	18 Robin Gets the Worst of It!
4 Will Scarlet	12 Get the Point, Gisborne?	19 A Great Friendship is Born
5 Maid Marian	13 Danger in the Distance	20 Tempers Flare!
6 Arrows of Justice	14 Ride like the Wind!	21 A Sworn Enemy is Made!
7 The Journey Begins	15 Love at First Sight?	22 Azeem Prays by Night
8 Mysterious Stranger		

23 A Midnight Council of War!	31 Robin Joins the Fray!
24 Leader of the Woodsmen	32 Stealing the Sheriff's Horse
25 A Plan is Hatched	33 Robin Defends His Love!
26 Awaiting Battle	34 The Spoils of War!
27 Weapons of Glory!	35 A Secret Revealed!
28 Surprise Attack!	36 The Sheriff's Plot!
29 Showdown in Sherwood!	37 Gisborne's Revenge!
30 Attack from Above!	38 The Face of Terror!
	39 Sherwood Ablaze
	40 Robin, Trapped?
	41 Escape from Death's Grasp!
	42 Safe At Last!
	43 Bad News!
	44 Friend or Traitor?
	45 The Sheriff and his Bride
	46 Preparations for a Royal Wedding
	47 Captured!
	48 Condemned to Hang!
	49 Robin in Disguise!
	50 Robin Hood, Hero of the Ages!
	51 Make Way for the Beggar!
	52 Battle for Nottingham!
	53 Striking Back!
	54 A Hero's Death!
	55 Happily Ever After!

1 Header card	17 Danger 'Round the Bend!	32 Woodsmen Share a Laugh	46 Robin Joins the Fray!
2 Robin Hood	18 Maiden with a Secret	33 Azeem Prays by Night	47 Expecting the Enemy!
3 Azeem	19 Love at First Sight?	34 A Midnight Council of War!	48 Stealing the Sheriff's Horse!
4 Will Scarlet	20 Enter Mysterious Sherwood Forest!	35 Sure Shot with the Crossbow!	49 Robin Defends His Love!
5 Maid Marian	21 Battling Little John!	36 Leader of the Woodsmen	50 Rob the Rich, Feed the Poor!
6 Arrows of Justice!	22 Robin Gets the Worst of It!	37 Romance in Sherwood	51 The Spoils of War!
7 The Journey Begins	23 A Great Friendship is Born	38 A Plan is Hatched	52 A Secret Revealed!
8 Mysterious Stranger	24 Comrades in Combat	39 Treetop Hideout	53 The Sheriff's Plot!
9 England, At Long Last!	25 Tempers Flare!	40 Awaiting Battle	54 Gisborne's Revenge!
10 Journey to Locksley Castle	26 A Fierce Argument!	41 Weapons of Glory!	55 The Face of Terror!
11 The Evil Guy of Gisborne	27 A Matter of Trust!	42 The Ambush Begins!	56 Battling in Vain!
12 "Taxes" from the Poor	28 Brothers in Arms	43 Surprise Attack!	57 Out of Control!
13 Get the Point, Gisborne?	29 A Challenge is Issued!	44 Showdown in Sherwood!	58 Sherwood Ablaze!
14 Danger in the Distance!	30 Robin's Aim is True!	45 Attack from Above!	59 Run for Your Lives!
15 Ride Like the Wind!	31 A Sworn Enemy is Made!		
16 Betrayed!			

60 Robin Trapped?	
61 Escape from Death's Grasp!	
62 Safe at Last!	
63 Bad News!	
64 Friend or Traitor?	
65 The Sheriff and His Bride?	
66 Preparations for a Royal Wedding	
67 Poised for Killing!	
68 Barrels of Doom!	
69 Killers for Hire!	
70 Captured!	
71 Condemned to Hang!	
72 Sentenced to Death!	
73 Robin in Disguise!	
74 Robin Hood, Hero of the Ages!	
75 Make Way for the Beggar!	
76 Explosions of Freedom!	
77 The Enemy Strikes!	
78 The Death of Duncan	
79 Fists of Fury!	
80 Battle for Nottingham!	
81 Demon of Death!	
82 Striking Back!	
83 A Hero's Death	
84 Victorious!	
85 A Trio of Woodsmen	
86 Mercenary Monsters!	
87 Robin and Marian Unite!	
88 Happily Ever After!	

ROBOCOP 2 (88 & 11)

2 1/2" X 3 1/2"

"Part Man, Part Machine, All Cop." This caption, which appears on the first card of Topps' 1990 series of "RoboCop 2," is the perfect nutshell description of Orion Pictures' heroic law enforcer. RoboCop is a futuristic rendition of the vigilante role perfected by Charles Bronson and the success of the RoboCop movies at the box office proves that the public craves situational drama in which good triumphs decisively over evil.

There are 88 cards and eleven stickers in the "regular issue" set. The fronts of cards 1-80 have color photographs taken directly from the movie and these are captioned underneath the picture area. Jagged red framelines surround the pictures and the borders are yellow. The obverse surface is glossy and there is a RoboCop "shield" logo at bottom-left. The backs of the story cards (1-80) bear a large set title, the card caption, and a short text. The color scheme is dull tones of red, blue and yellow. Cards 81-88 are "storyboards," which are "pre-production renderings that capture the composition and flavor of the finished film." In other words, they are pieces of artwork which are used by the filmmakers as guides to creating the ambiance of the movie. The numbered sticker series (1-11) has color insets on red backgrounds and they have the set title printed on them rather than individual captions. The series was issued in wax packs (with gum) and there are two different wrapper designs. Note: set price includes stickers.

ITEM	MINT	EX
Set	13.00	9.00
Card	.10	.07
Sticker	.30	.20
Wrappers (2), each	---	.35
Box	---	2.50

ROBOCOP, HEAL THYSELF!

RoboCop 2

1 Part Man, Part Machine, All Cop
2 Fatal Malfunction
3 The Price of Progress
4 A Man Named Murphy
5 Boddicker's Butchers
6 Man Without a Hand
7 Murphy - Blown Away
8 The Cop of Tomorrow
9 Partners in Crimefighting
10 "Freeze!"
11 Supermarket Assault!
12 A Lady in Distress
13 Robocop Blasted!
14 Reining in the Madness
15 A Blow Against Evil
16 Memories of Me
17 Man ... or Machine?
18 Taking the Heat
19 His Murders Apprehended
20 The Hidden Directive
21 Correcting His Mistakes
22 ED-209 Missile Assault
23 Dented But Undaunted
24 Slammed by ED-209
25 Robocop, Heal Thyself!
26 Toxic Nightmare
27 Showdown
28 Pummeled from Above
29 Robocop's Revenge
30 Say Goodnight, ED
31 "Or the Old Geezer Gets It!"
32 Murphy's Comeback
33 Duo For Danger
34 "Peace Officer"
35 A Madman Named Cain
36 The Robotics Museum
37 "Get Lost, Robocop!"
38 Lewis vs. Hob
39 A Bad Cop...
40 Duffy's Just Deserts
41 The New Mission
42 Devastating Blasts
43 In the Clutches of Cain
44 Captured!
45 Destruction of Robocop
46 In Need of Repair
47 Living Death
48 Robocop Screw-Up!
49 "You Can't Be Serious!"
50 Only One Way Out...
51 Electrical Purge
52 Cop Comradery
53 Beautiful But Savage
54 The Rebirth of Cain
55 What Was Once, Can Never Be Again
56 Detroit's Action Hero
57 Crusader Against Crime
58 Practice Makes Perfect!
59 Robocop Patrol!
60 Helmeted Hero
61 Officer Anne Lewis
62 No Escape from Robocop!
63 Spectacular Explosion!
64 Hob Bites It
65 Robocop Means Business!
66 Closing In
67 Shielded From Harm
68 Robocop Stunned!
69 Metallic Monster
70 Preparing to Pounce

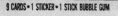

9 CARDS • 1 STICKER • 1 STICK BUBBLE GUM   9 CARDS • 1 STICKER • 1 STICK BUBBLE GUM

0-445-21-01-0

STORYBOARD: STANDING TALL

STORYBOARD: STANDING TALL

71 The Robot Warriors
72 Facing the Enemy
73 Incredible Struggle!
74 Clashing Titans
75 Has Robocop Met His Match?
76 Only One Will Survive...
77 Cain's Brain
78 Robocop ... Triumphant!
79 Bad Day for the Old Man
80 Metal Justice
81 Storyboard: The Shoot-Out
82 Storyboard: Taking the Plunge
83 Storyboard: Suspended in Mid-Air
84 Storyboard: Jolted by Electricity
85 Storyboard: Standing Tall
86 Storyboard: Blocking the Blast
87 Storyboard: Sizing Each Other Up
88 Storyboard: About To Pounce

ROBOCOP 2
COLLECTORS' EDITION (110 & 11)

If you find yourself at the "RoboCop Crossroads," trying to decide which version to buy - the "regular" or "collectors' edition" - here's some advice. The collectors' edition contains all of the cards and stickers issued in the regular series, but in an "enhanced" format which includes glossier surfaces, sharper images, and clear, readable backs. Moreover, the special edi-

2 1/2" X 3 1/2"

tion contains a handsome 22-card subset showing behind-the-scenes photographs of the producer and director composing "shots," supervising FX action, and counseling actors. The "deluxe" Robocop 2 set is much superior to the regular issue and is well worth the extra money. It comes in a factory-sealed box and is currently selling in the $20 range.

A How to Handle Your Gun
B The Predatory Stance
C Death of a Dummy
D Lending as Needed Hand
E Metal Appendage
F Conferring with Kurtwood

G Paul Verhoeven Directs
H Touching Up the Toxic Terror
I Directing ED-209
J Display of Blood
K Shooting a Night Scene
L Readying Robocop for the Cameras
M Director Irvin Kershner
N Fine Tuning
O All Wired Up!
P Making the Unreal Real
Q Nancy Allen as Lewis
R Some Advice for Robocop
S The Human Dimension
T "All Quiet on the Set!"
U Shooting a Shoot-Out!
V A Gathering of Evil

COMPLETE COLLECTORS' EDITION

ROBOT WARS (33 & 4)

Fleer's "Robot Wars" is a visual treat for the hi-tech card collector. The sticker-cards measure 2 1/2" X 3 11/32" and are separated into two types. One variety contains large robot stickers of various shapes (11), while the other type (22) has smaller stickers designed to be placed onto those robots. All 33 sticker backs carry identical advertising for a "Name That Robot" contest. Four different "rub-off" cards complete the set. Note: game cards with silver coatings removed cannot be graded mint. The high set prices indicate a poor distribution

TWO SIZES

of cards within boxes.

ITEM	MINT	EX
Set	15.00	10.00
Sticker	.35	.25
Card	.25	.20
Wrapper	---	.35
Box	---	4.00

ROCKCARDS (288 & 18)

Heavy Metal music, dismissed as a species of sonic adolescent whining in the 1970's and '80's, has become one of the cultural successes of the 1990's. True, the trappings of the old order - outlandish garb and make-up, eardrum-busting volume, anti-culture band names, and un-couth lyrics - are very much alive, but the major bands have proved that a little refinement and image merchandising can score big points with both the public and with music-industry executives. It is no wonder, therefore, that card collectors are seeing more metal-music card sets pop up in the hobby.

By any standards, Brockum's "RockCards" is a major-league card set, with a total of 288 cards and 18 stickers in the series. Released in 1991, the cards feature color photographs of heavy metal band members and bands on front, with color head shots of each subject and biography on back. The card number is located on the back only, next to the "MLE" (Major League Entertainment) holo-gram logo which is printed on every card. The sticker set is blank-backed; the fronts have color artwork which appears to have been used for album covers. The borders are black and there are no numbers. Thir-

teen cards plus one "peel & stick art card" came packed in each holographic package (voted the best wrapper of 1991 by Non-Sport Update subscribers). In ad-dition to these regular issue cards and stickers, a set of nine hologram band logos and a "Legacy Series" subset of ten cards honoring The Grateful Dead were inserted randomly in-to packs. A contest entry card/order form inserted into every pack offered a large color poster showing the 288 regular cards, the "Art Card" stickers, and the "Legacy Series" cards for $3.50 postpaid. Note: Legacy Series cards and band holograms are not considered part of the regular set and are priced separately. Promotional cards handed out at the National Sports Convention have a foil sticker reading "Anaheim 1991" in the lower left corner. Hologram packages had to be cut to remove contents.

ITEM	MINT	EX
Set	30.00	21.00
Card	.10	.07
Sticker	.25	.20
Wrapper	---	.15
Box	---	2.00
Legacy card	3.00	2.50
Legacy set	35.00	27.50
Band hologram	2.00	1.50
Hologram set	20.00	15.00
Poster	4.00	3.00

HOLOGRAM
LOGO STICKERS

AC/DC	Poison
Anthrax	Slayer
Cinderella	Testament
Megadeth	Warrant
Motley Crue	

ART CARDS
Ball and Chain
Berlin Wall
Birth of Vic
Clown's Best Friend
Eddie & The Kid
Freaks from the Fink Dimension
General Vic Launch
Hangar 18
Holy Smoke
In the Heart of the Young
Oxidation of the Nations
Rust in Peace
Sanda Kuwait
Seasons in the Abyss
Souls of Black
Tailgunner
The Album
The Wave

RockCards

1 KIP WINGER	28 VINCE NEIL	55 SCOTT IAN	82 MEGADETH	109 BRIAN BAKER	136 SEBASTIAN BACH
2 VINCE NEIL	29 DAN PRED	56 MALCOLM YOUNG	83 CHARLIE BENANTE	110 ALICE COOPER	137 CHUCK BILLY
3 MICK MARS	30 ACE FREHLEY	57 FRANK BELLO	84 ROD MORGENSTEIN	111 BRET MICHAELS	138 STEVE SOUZA
4 FRED COURY	31 PAUL TAYLOR	58 LOUIE CLEMENTE	85 STEVE SOUZA	112 BRIAN JOHNSON	139 JOEY BELLADONNA
5 WINGER	32 GREG CHRISTIAN	59 CHARLIE BENANTE	86 MARTY FRIEDMAN	113 DAVID ROACH	140 ALICE COOPER
6 CLIFF WILLIAMS	33 CAINE CARRUTHERS	60 AC/DC	87 RACHEL BOLAN	114 PETE McCLANAHAN	141 GARY HOLT
7 TOM KEIFER	34 DAVE MUSTAINE	61 PAUL TAYLOR	88 DAVID ROACH	115 CHUCK BILLY	142 MARK EVANS
8 DAN SPITZ	35 CHRIS SLADE	62 FRED COURY	89 BOBBY DALL	116 POISON	143 KATMANDU
9 JEFF LABAR	36 CLIFF WILLIAMS	63 FRANK BELLO	90 BRIAN JOHNSON	117 DAVID LEE ROTH	144 ERIC PETERSON
10 MEGADETH	37 CHRIS SLADE	64 KIP WINGER	91 MICK MARS	118 LOUIE CLEMENTE	145 STEVIE RAY VAUGHAN
11 CHRIS SLADE	38 MARTY FRIEDMAN	65 REB BEACH	92 PATRICK MUZINGO	119 JUNKYARD	146 RITCHIE BLACKMORE
12 CINDERELLA	39 MIKE ALONSO	66 TOM KEIFER	93 DAVE MUSTAINE	120 JOHN TEMPESTA	147 JON LORD
13 ANGUS YOUNG	40 SCOTT IAN	67 ERIC BRITTINGHAM	94 GREG CHRISTIAN	121 DAVID COVERDALE	148 IAN PAICE
14 NICK MENZA	41 ERIC PETERSON	68 REB BEACH	95 DAN REED NETWORK	122 TOMMY ALDRIDGE	149 JOE LYNN TURNER
15 ALEX SKOLNICK	42 ANGUS YOUNG	69 JEFF LABAR	96 ROB AFFUSO	123 ADRIAN VANDENBERG	150 TICO TORRES
16 DAVE KING	43 DAVID ELLEFSON	70 ALEX SKOLNICK	97 IGGY POP	124 ROB McKILLOP	151 ANDREW ELDRITCH
17 DAN REED	44 NICK MENZA	71 CINDERELLA	98 BRIAN BAKER	125 TESTAMENT	152 KIP WINGER
18 NIKKI SIXX	45 MANDY MEYER	72 ROD MORGENSTEIN	99 MICK MARS	126 CLAY ANTHONY	153 RICK WAKEMAN
19 TOMMY LEE	46 BLAKE SAKAMOTO	73 FRED COURY	100 NIKKI SIXX	127 GARY HOLT	154 RICHIE SAMBORA
20 CHRIS GATES	47 LOUIE CLEMENTE	74 GREG CHRISTIAN	101 CLAY ANTHONY	128 DAVE SABO	155 CHECKLIST/POISON
21 CLIFF WILLIAMS	48 TESTAMENT	75 MALCOLM YOUNG	102 IGGY POP	129 VINCE NEIL	156 STEVE HOWE
22 CHARLIE BENANTE	49 JOEY BELLADONNA	76 TOM KEIFER	103 JOHN RICCO	130 JUNKYARD	157 ROGER GLOVER
23 MALCOLM YOUNG	50 DAN SPITZ	77 ERIC BRITTINGHAM	104 KORY CLARKE	131 WARRIOR SOUL	158 RICK WRIGHT
24 ANGUS YOUNG	51 AC/DC	78 JOEY BELLADONNA	105 DAVE SABO	132 RIKKI ROCKETT	159 RACHEL BOLAN
25 MELVIN BRANNON	52 REB BEACH	79 BRIAN JOHNSON	106 SCOTTI HILL	133 STEVE SOUZA	160 JIMMI BLEACHER
26 CHUCK BILLY	53 FRANK BELLO	80 JEFF LABAR	107 SKID ROW	134 ANTHRAX	161 DANA STRUM
27 ALEX SKOLNICK	54 ACE FREHLEY	81 ERIC BRITTINGHAM	108 ERIC PETERSON	135 PATRICK MUZINGO	162 SCOTTI HILL

163 TIM KELLY	190 BON JOVI	217 JANI LANE	244 SCOTTI HILL	271 DANA STRUM	280 ROD MORGENSTEIN
164 KHURT MAIER	191 CHECKLIST/SALTY DOG	218 RIKKI ROCKETT	245 JOEY ALLEN	272 MICHAEL HANNON	281 BOBBY DALL
165 CHECKLIST/ALICE COOPER	192 BLAS ELIAS	219 BRET MICHAELS	246 ERIK TURNER	273 ALEC JOHN SUCH	282 RICK HUNOLT
166 EXODUS	193 THE SISTERS OF MERCY	220 DAVID LEE ROTH	247 STEVEN SWEET	274 WINGER	283 DAVID BRYAN
167 SEBASTIAN BACH	194 SLAUGHTER	221 BRION JAMES	248 CHECKLIST/DAVID LEE ROTH	275 POISON	284 THE SISTERS OF MERCY
168 MARK SLAUGHTER	195 RICK HUNOLT	222 DAN SPITZ	249 SLAUGHTER	276 PINK FLOYD	285 SEBASTIAN BACH
169 JERRY DIXON	196 ALEC JOHN SUCH	223 DAVID ELLEFSON	250 BLACK SABBATH	277 RACHEL BOLAN	286 C.C. DEVILLE
170 DOUG GORDON	197 CHECKLIST/KORY CLARKE	224 C.C. DEVILLE	251 COZY POWELL	278 MARK SLAUGHTER	287 EXODUS
171 GARRY NUTT	198 ROB McKILLOP	225 GARY HOLT	252 TIM KELLY	279 PAUL TAYLOR	288 TICO TORRES
172 BOB BENDER	199 TOMMY LEE	226 TOMMY LEE	253 WARRANT		
173 JANI LANE	200 BRET MICHAELS	227 ROB AFFUSO	254 JOHN TEMPESTA		LEGACY SERIES
174 MICHAEL LECOMPTE	201 SCOTT IAN	228 TANGIER	255 RICK HUNOLT		
175 JON BON JOVI	202 JOHN TEMPESTA	229 NIKKI SIXX	256 RIKKI ROCKETT	1 JERRY GARCIA	6 VINCE WELNICK
176 RICHIE SAMBORA	203 DAVID BRYAN	230 DAVE SABO	257 DAVE MUSTAINE	2 BOB WEIR	7 MADISON SQ. GARDEN 1990
177 BLAS ELIAS	204 RICHIE SAMBORA	231 ANTHRAX	258 DAVID ELLEFSON	3 PHIL LESH	8 SEVEN-TEN ASHBURY 1967
178 MOTLEY CRUE	205 JON ANDERSON	232 STEVEN SWEET	259 MARTY FRIEDMAN	4 BILL KREUTZMANN	9 EUROPE 1990
179 SKID ROW	206 TONY IOMMI	233 JOEY ALLEN	260 NICK MENZA	5 MICKEY HART	10 SKULL W/TOP HAT
180 IRON MAIDEN	207 DAVID LEE ROTH	234 JERRY DIXON	261 ALEC JOHN SUCH		
181 DEEP PURPLE	208 COZY POWELL	235 WARRANT	262 ROB McKILLOP		
182 MARK SLAUGHTER	209 C.C. DEVILLE	236 ERIK TURNER	263 ROB AFFUSO		
183 JUSTIN HAYWARD	210 JON BON JOVI	237 JANI LANE	264 SALTY DOG		
184 JOHN LODGE	211 TONY IOMMI	238 IRON MAIDEN	265 DAVID GILMOUR		
185 TIM KELLY	212 BLAS ELIAS	239 MOTLEY CRUE	266 ERIK TURNER		
186 GRAEME EDGE	213 BOBBY DALL	240 TICO TORRES	267 STEVEN SWEET		
187 RAY THOMAS	214 BON JOVI	241 JON BON JOVI	268 JOEY ALLEN		
188 DANA STRUM	215 NICK MASON	242 CLARKE-ROTONDO	269 JERRY DIXON		
189 BILL BRUFORD	216 CHECKLIST/MOTLEY CRUE	243 PETE REVEEN	270 DAVID BRYAN		

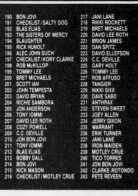

BOB WEIR

JERRY GARCIA

VINCE WELNICK

GRATEFUL DEAD EUROPE 1990

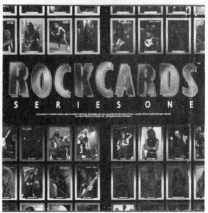

ROCK BOTTOM AWARDS (36)   2 3/4" X 3 3/4"

"BEST HOST"

Richard Nixon, Leona Helmsley, David Letterman, George Bush, Clayton Williams, Nancy Reagan, Imelda Marcos, Milli Vanilli, Arnold Schwarzenegger, George Steinbrenner, Pete Rose, Don King, Jimmy and Tammy Baker, Al Sharpton, Joseph Hazelwood, Zsa Zsa Gabor, Manuel Noriega, Joan Rivers, Madonna, Marilyn and Dan Quayle, Neil Bush, Donald Trump, Bess Myerson, Ted Koppel, John Sunnunu, Ronald Reagan, and Jessie Helms. What

do these people have in common? They are all parodied in "Rock Bottom Awards," a 36-card set produced and distributed by Eclipse Books. The text by Peggy Gordon may be a tad too whimsical for the mainstream card collector but, after all, this is not a mainstream card set. Bill Sienkiewicz did the artwork in his trademark off-center style. Sold only as a boxed set, "Rock Bottom Awards" retails in the $9-$10 range.

1 Opening Party!
2 This is Your Nightmare
3 "Best Breach of Confidentiality"
4 "Best Potential Scam"
5 "Best Host"
6 "Most Imaginative Rip-Off of a Classic"
7 "Best Revenge"
8 Crossover Acts
9 "Most Contemptuous Girl Group of the 80's"
10 "Right Country - Right Time!"
11 "Dangerous Career Move"
12 "If the Shoe Fits..."
13 America's Funniest Prison Videos
14 "Weeping in Tongues"
15 "Bad Shot"
16 "Best Plea for Temporary Insanity"
17 "Worst Actress / Best Publicity"
18 "Best Tap Dance"
19 A Catered Affair
20 "Gimme a Break Today!"
21 "It Sells"
22 "Lifetime Lack of Achievement"
23 "Best Burn"
24 Life Imitating Art Imitating Life
25 Living Sitcoms
26 "The Blunder Years"
27 "Three's (Never Enough) Company"
28 "Fatal Distraction"
29 "The Honkeymooners"
30 Unbelievably Bad Taste
31 "Whoops"
32 "So, What!"
33 "Stick-R-Up"
34 "Who, Us?"
35 "Gosh"
36 "Best Demagogue"

ROCKETEER (99 & 11)   2 1/2" X 3 1/2"

Continued on Card 57.
A Make-Shift Plan

"The Rocketeer," a major motion picture released by Walt Disney in 1991, is the subject of this 99-card/11-sticker series issued under license by Topps Gum. The movie, based on a character drawn

by Dave Stevens (Pacific Comics), was not the dramatic adventure some had hoped it would be, and the pictures of the card set are bland when compared to the brilliant Stevens artwork used to advertise the film and associated items. In fact, some collectors rate the artwork on the Topps stickers as some of the best the company has ever printed. Topps also issued an "Official Movie Souvenir Magazine" in conjunction with the movie / card set ($2.95) and the lead advertisement (inside front cover) offers a "Collectors' Edition" of Rocketeer which has received little attention from collectors. The special edition differs from the regular set in that the cards have super glossy fronts, more readable backs, and there are 22 extra behind-the-scenes cards added as a bonus. This limited edition of 121 cards and eleven stickers, housed in its own sealed box, was available only in comic book stores or through the mail ($20). Note: set price includes stickers. The Rocketeer was issued in cello packages containing eight cards and one sticker (no gum) and there are two different wrapper designs.

ITEM	MINT	EX
Regular set	15.00	11.00
Card	.10	.07
Sticker	.30	.20
Wrappers (2), each	--	.25
Box	--	2.50
Collectors' set	20.00	--

1 Rocketing to the Screen
2 Cliff Secord
3 The Rocketeer
4 Jenny Blake
5 Ambrose "Peevy" Peabody
6 Neville Sinclair
7 Lothar
8 Eddie Valentine
9 At Chaplin Airfield
10 Cliff's Gee Bee
11 A Hail of Bullets
12 The Great Car Chase
13 Switcheroo
14 Occupational Hazard
15 Fitch and the Feds
16 Mayhem on the Runway
17 The Big Bang
18 Rescuing Cliff
19 Retrieving the Prize
20 Instant Enemies
21 "Keep This Guy Alive"
22 Hughes' Invention
23 Mysterious Rocketpack
24 A Turbulent Take-Off!
25 Bigelow's Big Deal
26 Heartthrob. . .or Heel?
27 Lindy's Test Flight
28 Under Police Protection
29 Creeping Assassin
30 His Back. . .Broken!
31 The Man She Loves. . .
32 Nazis in the News!
33 At the Bulldog Cafe
34 Spoofing Sinclair
35 Designing a Helmet
36 Day of the Air Show
37 Malcolm in a Jam!
38 His First Flight
39 Blast Off to Adventure!
40 High-Flying Hero
41 Spectacular Rescue!
42 Dunked in the Duck Pond
43 "I Did It, Peevy!"
44 Bigelow's Bonanza
45 News Travels Fast
46 Another Broken Back
47 Pondering the Future
48 Attacked by Lothar!
49 In the Creature's Clutches

50. Feds to the Rescue!
51 Romanced by Sinclair
52 "Where's Cliff Secord?"
53 Pummeling Peevy
54 Bulldog Brawl!
55 Ready for Action!
56 At the Chinese Theatre
57 A Make-Shift Plan
58 Up the Laundry Chute
59 The Club - Invaded!
60 No Way Out!
61 Netted by Neville
62 Emergency Escape!
63 Blasting Off!
64 The Seduction
65 Jenny's Ploy
66 Nightmare Scenario
67 "I've Got to Save Jenny!"
68 The Rocketeer's Plan
69 At Griffith Observatory
70 The Devils and the Damsel
71 "Sinclair is a Nazi!
72 Hitler's Commandos
73 The Feds Open Fire!
74 Observatory Shootout!
75 "It's the Rocketeer!"
76 A Hero Once Again
77 Danger on All Sides
78 America's Daredevil
79 The Flying Fortress
80 Slip-Sliding Away!
81 Taking on the Enemy
82 Atop the Zeppelin
83 "Oh No, It's Lothar!"
84 Facing the Monster-Man
85 Mid-Air Death Struggle!
86 Down, But Far From Out!
87 Fists of the Flying Man
88 Lother. . .Triumphant?!
89 His Fury Unleashed
90 Helmeted Hero
91 Neville's Last Stand
92. "He's Got the Rocket Pack!"
93. Him Again?!!
94. Escape From Flaming Death
95. A Gift from Howard
96 All's Well That Ends Well!
97 The Future Look Bright!
98 Rocketing Role Model!
99 The Knight of Flight

510

ROCKETEER (2 ITEMS)

The "Rocketeer" promotion at Pizza Hut was so successful that quantities of the kid's meal box and accompanying "Rocketeer" flying model were exhausted in record time. The Dave Stevens artwork on both items is outstanding, especially so on the glossy surface of the box. The promotion ran for a short period in 1991 and at this time there is no

TWO SIZES

way to estimate how many of these items have survived. Note: assembled flyers and flyers detached from the sheet cannot be graded excellent or mint.

ITEM	MINT	EX
Box	3.00	2.00
Rocketeer model	5.00	4.00

ROCKETSHIP X—M (50)
2 1/2" X 3 1/2"

The Fantasy Trading Card Company created this 50-card set based on the science fiction film "Rocketship X-M." The 11 color cards in the set are taken from advertising posters, "effects" sets, and off-camera private shots.

The remaining card fronts have black and white photos (28) or photos with a "filter purple" cast. The cards are numbered on the back, where several lines of text introduce cast members or explain the story. The set was

a production aimed at card and comic collectors rather than the general public, and although a wrapper and box were produced, no gum accompanied the cards. Note: generally found in complete sets.

ITEM	MINT	EX
Set	15.00	10.00
Card	.35	.25
Wrapper	--	1.00
Box	--	7.00

ROCK STARS (66)
2 1/2" X 3 1/2"

Back in 1979 when Donruss marketed its "Rock Stars" set, the company claimed to have cornered "Four of the most Popular Rock Music

Groups in the World!" Donruss left no type of rock unturned with its line-up of Kiss ("theatrical-rock"), Queen ("jazz-rock"), The Babys ("hard-rock"), and the Village People ("disco-rock"). The card fronts show color photos of group members performing or in publicity

poses; the backs are puzzle pieces. The distribution of cards per group is: Kiss—14, Queen—20, The Babys—12, and Village People—20.

ITEM	MINT	EX
Set	20.00	13.50
Card	.30	.20
Wrapper	--	.50
Box	--	8.00

1 Queen	20 Village People		
2 Queen	21 Kiss		
3 Kiss	22 The Babys		
4 The Babys	23 Village People		
5 Village People	24 Village People		
6 The Babys	25 Queen	39 Kiss	53 Village People
7 Village People	26 Queen	40 Queen	54 Queen
8 Village People	27 The Babys	41 Queen	55 The Babys
9 The Babys	28 Village People	42 Kiss	56 Village People
10 Village People	29 Kiss	43 Village People	57 The Babys
11 Kiss	30 Kiss	44 Village People	58 Queen
12 The Babys	31 Queen	45 Queen	59 Kiss
13 Village People	32 Kiss	46 Village People	60 Village People
14 Village People	33 Village People	47 Queen	61 The Babys
15 Village People	34 Kiss	48 The Babys	62 Queen
16 Queen	35 Queen	49 Queen	63 The Babys
17 Queen	36 Village People	50 Kiss	64 Kiss
18 Queen	37 Village People	51 Queen	65 Kiss
19 Queen	38 The Babys	52 Queen	66 Kiss

Rock Stars

ROCK STARS (15)   2 1/2″ X 3 1/2″

  FREE ROCK STAR CARD
IN SPECIALLY MARKED WONDER BREAD PACKAGES

Wonder Bread produced this series of 15 "Rock Star" cards in 1985. The fronts have color pictues of various groups and individual performers and they are named in a diagonal band running through the photograph and the right side border. The cards are printed on thin cardboard and are not numbered. On the backs, we find the performers named again, along with details of their careers and the ad-dresses of their fan clubs. Uncut sheets, such as the one illustrated here, have turned up in the hobby and are selling for about $15. Collectors should beware of oil stains on single cards that were distributed in bread. These cannot be graded excellent or mint.

ITEM	MINT	EX
Set	8.50	5.50
Card	.50	.35

Bon Jovi
Bryan Adams
Culture Club
Deep Purple
Duran Duran
Hall & Oates
Howard Jones
Joan Jet and
   the Blackhearts
Kool & the Gang
New Edition
Night Ranger
Rex
Sheena Easton
'til Tuesday
Triumph

ROCK EXPRESS (3/3/3)

THREE SIZES

Amurol devised an ingenious method to market "Rock Express" gum in 1991. The series was limited to three artists only, M.C. Hammer, Paula Abdul, and Nelson, and each appeared in three distinct formats. In order from smallest to largest, the first format was a 2-5/8" X 3-1/2" metal "band-aid" box with the performer's picture front and back. Inside the box were 24 chewing gum size sticks of bubble gum in individual wrappers. The second largest packaging was a 3-1/2" X 4-7/8" folder which held tear-apart sheets of pre-scored gum. The largest item was a 5" X 7-1/2" double pouch filled with gum nuggets. At the time this book went to press, all three varieties of Rock Express were still being sold in variety and convenience stores for prices ranging from 99¢ to $1.19. Note: a complete set consists of all three artists in all three formats.

ROCKY HORROR PICTURE SHOW (60)

2 1/2" X 3 1/2"

This 60-card set based on the camp movie was not produced by a major gum company and therefore was not released through normal market channels. It was, however, mass produced and sold in bulk, so it is readily available across the country. The fronts have color pictures and white borders. The backs contain the caption, the card number, and a picture of four characters from the film. The copyright date found on the reverse — 1975 — does not refer to the year of distribution, which was 1980.

ITEM	MINT	EX
Set	15.00	12.00
Card	.25	.20
Wrapper	—	.50
Box	—	5.00

1	Tim Curry as Frank N Furter	21	Hi, I'm Brad Majors
2	Richard O'Brian as Riff Raff	22	It's Astounding
3	Susan Sarandon as Janet Weiss	23	Let's Do the Time Warp
4	Barry Bostwick as Brad Majors	24	It's Just a Jump to the Left
5	Peter Hinwood as Rocky	25	Put Your Hands on Your Hips
6	Little Nell as Columbia	26	Dance Time's Over
7	Patricia Quinn as Magenta	27	Say Something Stupid Brad
8	Jonathan Adams as Dr. Everett Scott	28	They're probably Just Rich Weirdos
9	Meatloaf as Eddie	29	How Do You Do
10	Transylvania Groupies	30	I'm One Hell of a Lover
11	Church Caretakers	31	Columbia Does Her Number
12	Tim as Minister	32	Chug It Riff!
13	Ralph and Betty Get Married	33	What Charming Underclothes
14	Nice Going Janet	34	Unconventional Conventionists
15	I Love You Too	35	Oh Brad, You're So Forceful
16	Wedding Car	36	Unveiling the Creation
17	Storytime	37	Making a Man
18	Walking to the Castle	38	Rocky Revealed
19	The Frankenstein Place	39	Happy Birthday Rocky
20	You're Wet	40	One from the Vaults

41	Hot Patootie Bless My Soul
42	Rockin' Their Socks Off
43	Music Critic
44	A Real Mismatch
45	Rocky Escapes
46	Unexpected Visitor
47	Falling in Love
48	Discovery
49	Eddie Didn't Like His Teddy
50	Eddie's Mug Shot
51	Meatloaf Again?
52	The Floor Show
53	Don't Dream It. Be It
54	The Party's Over
55	Take That
56	Your Mission Is a Failure
57	We're Going Home!
58	Blast-Off
59	Lost In Time and Space
60	Checklist

ROCKY II (99 & 22)

2 1/2" X 3 1/2"

There are 99 cards and 22 stickers in the Rocky II set distributed by Topps in 1979. The front of each card contains a color photo from the movie and is characterized by bright yellow borders, a red "Rocky II" panel, and a boxing glove caption design. As a group, the backs are divided between poster pieces (55 cards, two different posters) and story line (44 cards). On cards with poster-piece backs, the card number is located in the red panel on the obverse only; on the storyline-backed cards, the number appears both front and back. The numbered stickers have pictures enclosed by a red boxing glove design and black borders. They have been assigned captions in the checklist from similar card designs. Note: set price includes stickers.

ITEM	MINT	EX
Set	15.00	10.00
Card	.10	.07
Sticker	.35	.25
Wrapper	—	.35
Box	—	5.00

23 Fists of Fury
24 Man Behind the Muscles
25 The Rope Exercise
26 Shapin' Up!
27 Punch that Bag!
28 Rocky's Trainer, Mickey
29 Rocky's Hope
30 Splatter the Stallion!
31 Actor Burgess Meredith
32 "Weighty" Task!
33 The Living Legend
34 Tuning Up!
35 Feelin' Strong Now!
36 Fury of Apollo
37 Demolishing His Opponent!
38 Nothing Can Stop Me Now!
39 Gonna Fly Now!
40 Philly's Favorite!
41 The Big Battle
42 The Square Jungle
43 The Contender
44 Man-Mountain Creed
45 World in His Corner
46 The Gladiators
47 Chin-Up, Rock!
48 It's Now or Never
49 The World's Champ
50 Formidable Foe
51 Stupendous Struggle
52 The Slugfest Continues!
53 Power of Apollo
54 Against the Ropes
55 Stay in Control!
56 Man of Destiny
57 Apollo's Dynamic Fists
58 Bloody Confrontation
59 A Left to Rocky's Chin!
60 Creed...Smashed!
61 The Undefeated Champ

62 Rocky Rocked by Apollo
63 The Raging Giants
64 Fire in Every Muscle
65 In Over His Head!
66 Flesh and Fury
67 Rocky Gets Riled!
68 Rocky on the Offensive
69 Round Nine Coming Up!
70 Bruised but Not Beaten!
71 The Warriors Clash!
72 In the Rock's Corner
73 "I Won't Give Up!"
74 Balboa's Dream
75 The Final Round
76 Creed Creamed!
77 Devastating Sock!
78 Both Men Are Down!
79 The Champ's Been Floored!
80 The Moment of Truth
81 One Last Chance...
82 Summoning Hidden Strengths
83 Hang in There, Rocky!
84 Down for the Count!
85 Four...Five...Six!
86 Do It Rocky!
87 Stumbling to His Feet!
88 The Reeling Champ
89 The Winner!
90 The Victorious One!
91 A Hard-Fought Battle!
92 Moment of Glory
93 Now...Number One!
94 Balboa's Triumph
95 Interviewing the Champ
96 Man of the Hour
97 Face of a Champion
98 High Spirits
99 "We Did It, Adrian."

1 Meet "Rocky"
2 Rocky's Girl, Adrian
3 Stickball Champ!
4 Sultan of Stickball!
5 Yo, Butkus!
6 The Champ and His Dog
7 Rocky Pops the Question
8 Hitched
9 It's Cold Outside!
10 Rocky's Speech
11 Inside the Meat Factory
12 The Rock at Work
13 Rappin' with Paulie
14 Don't Mess with the Rock!
15 Actress Talia Shire
16 Rocky's Training Technique
17 Mrs. Balboa...Expecting!
18 Encouraging Words
19 Visions of Victory
20 The Verbal Bout
21 Training at the Gym
22 "You Can Do It!"

1 "Weighty" Task!
2 The Warriors Clash!
3 Chin-Up, Rock!
4 Meet "Rocky"
5 Man of Destiny
6 Stickball Champ!
7 Face of a Champion
8 Fury of Apollo
9 Formidable Foe
10 Rocky's Trainer, Mickey
11 Bruised but Not Beaten!
12 One Last Chance...
13 Rocky's Hope
14 Feelin' Strong Now!
15 Don't Mess with the Rock!
16 The Living Legend
17 Punch that Bag!
18 Yo, Butkus!
19 Rocky Pops the Question
20 It's Cold Outside!
21 Actress Talia Shire
22 World in His Corner

ROCKY IV (66 & 11)   2 1/2" X 3 1/2"

The politicians and generals of the super powers can put aside their armies and missiles because Rocky Balboa and Drago have already staged "World War III" in the boxing arena. That's the gist of the movie on which

Topps based its "Rocky IV" set released to the public in 1985. The card fronts have color photos from the movie and are captioned in a yellow panel below the picture. A red boxing glove design is located in the bottom-right corner. The card backs contain the series title, card number and text. The series of 11 diecut stickers has uncaptioned color photos with

yellow frame lines and red backgrounds. Two wrappers—both blue in color—portray each of the combatants. Note: set prices include stickers.

ITEM	MINT	EX
Set	10.00	7.00
Card	.10	.07
Sticker	.35	.25
Wrappers (2)		
each	--	.35
Box	--	4.00

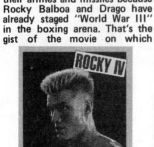

1	Title Card	13	Apollo Wants You!	25	"I Want Balboa!"	37	Jeers, Not Cheers!
2	Rocky Balboa	14	Man-Mountain Creed	26	A Man Determined	38	Balboa vs. Drago
3	Apollo Creed	15	Creed vs. Drago!	27	Welcome to Russia!	39	Man with a Mission!
4	Adrian Balboa	16	Apollo's Gamble	28	In Training!	40	A Dream Realized!
5	Paulie	17	Sizing Up Drago!	29	Power of the Rock!	41	The Battle Begins!
6	The Man Called Drago	18	The Power of Creed!	30	Feelin' Strong Now!	42	Clash of the Super-Powers!
7	Igor Rimsky	19	Dynamic Punch!	31	Russia's Mightiest Man!	43	Man Against Superman!
8	Corner Man Duke	20	A Champion's Fists!	32	Pumping Up!	44	Time Out!
9	A New Challenge!	21	Belted by Drago!	33	A Man of Steel!	45	Drago's Winded!
10	Apollo's Comeback	22	Anyone's Fight!	34	Aided by Science!	46	Two Raging Giants!
11	Happy Birthday!	23	Drago Comes On Strong!	35	For America!	47	Socked!
12	The Fight is Set	24	The Fatal Blow!	36	Night of the Strongmen!	48	Rocky Stymied!

49 Rage of the Rock!
50 Pounded Into Next Week!
51 A Fantastic Fighter!
52 Up, Up and Away!!
53 Drago's Sunday Punch!
54 "I Won't Give Up!"
55 What a Match!
56 Slugging it Out!
57 "Shut Up, Igor!"
58 A Face Made for Punching!
59 Demi-Gods of the Ring!
60 From Russia with Hate!
61 Pandemonium!
62 Rocky's Up, Drago's Down!
63 The Winner!
64 In Praise of Balboa!
65 A Man for All Countries!
66 Checklist

RODDA CARDS (?)

NO. 114

CALIFORNIA SISTER BUTTERFLY

2 1/8" X 2 5/8"

If you like your card sets to be predictable, then Rodda cards are for you. Every year, like clockwork, the Pennsylvania-based candy company produces marshmallow confectionaries keyed to the holidays: white and yellow marshmallow chicks for Easter, orange "Happy Pumpkins" for Thanksgiving, and green and rose snowmen for Christmas. On the back of every one of these boxes are printed small, rounded-corner cards depicting flowers, butterflies, roosters, rabbits, and cats. And year after year, they are the SAME pictures, with absolutely no change in artwork or print details. So what's the fascination, you ask? Well, for one thing, some of the cards are numbered and there are titles missing from the checklist. Were they ever printed? If so, when? That's the element of mystery. Then there's the fatal attraction of waiting for Rodda Candy to break down and actually print different cards. So every year, at Easter, Thanksgiving, and Christmas, a small band of veteran collectors troops down to the grocery store to see what Rodda has printed on the backs of the packages. Will it change this year? I wouldn't bet on it! Meanwhile, on the infrequent occasions when Rodda cards are actually sold, they fetch 10¢ each.

ROGER RABBIT (132 & 22)

"OH NO...IT'S THE TOON SQUAD!"

2 1/2" X 3 1/2"

The answer is: Ishtar, Willow, and Roger Rabbit. You don't have to be Karnak, the soothsayer and seer, to know the question, but I'll tell you anyway. What three movies had the heaviest advance campaigns in the history of filmdom? Of the three, Roger Rabbit enjoyed the most commercial success, although some movie buffs insist that Ishtar and Willow were, in a word, less offensive. I guess it all depends on whether or not you like animation films aimed at adults.

Topps bet that Roger Rabbit would be a hot property and obtained a license to produce a card set based on the movie in

Roger Rabbit

1988. If you liked the movie, you will enjoy these cards. There are 132 in all and each shows a scene from the film. There is a film clip border on the left side and the caption is printed below the picture. On the back, where the cards are numbered, a short text is printed over part of a color artwork sketch of one of the film's cartoon characters. The obverse finish is slightly glossy, while the reverse finish is dull. The 22 stickers in the set are divided into two types. Stickers 1-8 bear artwork depictions of cartoon cast members, while numbers 9-22 are color scenes from the movie. Twenty of the stickers have puzzle piece backs belonging to one or the other of two ten-piece puzzle pictures. The backs of stickers 9 and 11 show what the completed puzzle pictures look like. The Roger Rabbit series was sold in wax packs containing eight cards, one sticker, and one piece of gum. Note: set price includes stickers.

ITEM	MINT	EX
Set	20.00	14.00
Card	.15	.10
Sticker	.35	.25
Wrapper	--	.35
Box	--	2.00

HERE IS WHAT YOUR COMPLETED RED BORDER PICTURE WILL LOOK LIKE

COLLECT ALL 10 CARDS OF PICTURE A.

HERE IS WHAT YOUR COMPLETED BLUE BORDER PICTURE WILL LOOK LIKE:

COLLECT ALL 10 CARDS OF PICTURE B.

SPECIAL STICKER INSIDE!

9 MOVIE PHOTO CARDS • 1 STICK BUBBLE GUM

1 132 Cards - 22 Stickers
2 Toon Superstars
3 Their Latest Cartoon!
4 "Now Be a Good Little Baby!"
5 "He's in Your Hands, Roger!"
6 Never Fear, Roger's Here!
7 Baby Herman Is Loose!
8 Yyyooooooowwwwwwww!!!
9 Baby on the Burners!
10 The Rolling Pin Tumbles!
11 Was This Trip Necessary?
12 Roger Goes to Pot!
13 A Step in the Wrong Direction!
14 One Roasted Rabbit!
15 When You're Hot, You're Hot!
16 "Socket" to Roger!
17 Electrifying!
18 The Cookie Quest Continues!
19 Look Out Below!
20 Utensils Attack!
21 Yikes!!!
22 Sharp Shooters!
23 Whew!!!
24 Whoops!!!
25 Saved by Roger!
26 Roger Gets Clunked!
27 Roger's Tweeting Birds!
28 "Cut!!!"
29 "I Said Stars, Not Birds!"
30 "Gimme One Last Chance!"
31 Eddie Valiant, Private Eye!
32 "Welt Sent Me."
33 Inside the Club
34 "This Way, Mr. Valiant!"
35 The Main Attraction
36 Va-va-va-voom!!
37 Jessica Rabbit Swings Out!
38 Can Jessica Be Trusted?
39 "Don't Monkey With Me!!"
40 Pattycake Betrayal!
41 "I Don't Believe It...!"
42 "I Won't Believe It...!"
43 "I Can't Believe It...!"
44 "I Shan't Believe It...!"
45 A Hasty Retreat!
46 Judge Doom's Latest Victim
47 "Care for a Dip?!"
48 Death of a Toon!
49 Tooned-Out!
50 An Important Clue!
51 Strange Bedfellows!
52 "Get Out, Ya Screwy Toon!"
53 Roger's Love Letter
54 "Funny Meeting You Here!"
55 Handcuffed to a Toon!
56 "We're In This Together, Eddie!"
57 "Hide Me...Quick!"

58 A Panicked Rabbit!
59 "Oh No... It's the Toon Squad!"
60 Those Wily Weasels!
61 "All Right, Where's the Rabbit At?"
62 Damp but Undaunted!
63 Eddie and Roger, Uncuffed!
64 Jessica Meets Valiant in his Office
65 "I'm Not That Kind of Toon!"
66 Jessica Blows a Kiss
67 Those Luscious, Luminous Lips!
68 Nabbed by the Toon Squad!
69 The Judge Gets His Toon!
70 "Into the Dip, Rabbit!"
71 This Drink's for Roger!
72 Toons and Booze Don't Mix!
73 Gangway!!
74 Talk About a Getaway Car!
75 Benny to the Rescue!
76 "They're Gaining on Us!"
77 Bang! Bang! Bang!!
78 Look Oooooouuuuuuttttttt!!!
79 A Narrow Escape!
80 "Oh No...No...No!!!"
81 "We Got 'Em This Time!"
82 Benny's Up for It!
83 The Road to Unreality!
84 Another World...
85 One Heck of a Place to Visit!
86 Toontown Pile-Up
87 In Pursuit of Jessica
88 What Goes Up...
89 Eddie's Hard-Pressed!
90 "Jessica, Is That You?"
91 Look Out Below!
92 Just Hanging Around!
93 Above It All!
94 The Fall of Eddie Valiant
95 Perilous Plunge!
96 Mysterious Back Streets!
97 "Someone's Tailin' Me..."
98 Jessica...Friend or Foe?
99 Aided by a Car-Toon!
100 A Dip-Slicked Road!
101 Poor Benny Crashes!
102 Snagged by the Toon Patrol!
103 "I've Got to Save Them!!"
104 Roger to the Rescue!
105 Trapped by Judge Doom!
106 What a Way to Go!
107 "Don't Try Anything Fancy!"
108 "A Valiant Effort!"
109 What a Crack-up!
110 Alas, Poor Weasel!
111 The Deadly Dip!
112 Say It, Don't Spray It!
113 What a Weird Weapon!
114 Doom on a Roll!

115 Stand Up and Sneer!
116 The Judge Re-Inflated!
117 He's Back & Badder Than Ever!
118 Booing!!
119 The Mad Toon's Fury
120 Eddie Sees The Saw!
121 The Fatal Splash!
122 Crack of Doom!
123 Swing to Safety!
124 Good Morning, Toontown!
125 The Day is Saved!
126 Judge Doom's Demise!
127 Special Tanks From Jessica!
128 A Grateful Roger Rabbit
129 What a Pal!
130 The Mystery is Solved!
131 Love With the Proper Rabbit
132 Made for Each Other!

ROGER RABBIT ALBUM STICKERS (216)   2 1/8" X 2 9/16"

There are 216 stickers in the "Who Framed Roger Rabbit?" series issued by Panini in 1988. Most of these have four white borders surrounding the color artwork, although a few stickers have only two or three white borders so they could be placed together to make larger pictures in the album. Regardless of how many borders a sticker has, it always has a number on the back and this number corresponds to a space in the 32-page album. Stickers were sold in "packets" that were lime-green with Roger Rabbit artwork in the center. The packets had to be cut or torn to remove the contents. Albums retailed for 59¢ and the inside back cover carried an offer to trade stickers with collectors. Note: set price includes album.

ITEM	MINT	EX
Set	30.00	20.00
Sticker	.15	.10
Wrapper	--	.25
Album	2.00	1.50

ROOKIES (44)   2 1/2" X 3 1/2"

Surely one of the most sensational discoveries of 1983 was a small cache of a theretofore unknown Topps test set based on the television show "The Rookies." Each card contains a color photo from the show; "The Rookies" is printed in a red panel inside the picture area, and the card caption is printed in white letters in the blue border at bottom. The card backs are divided on approximately a 60/40 basis between puzzle picture area and narrative. The card number is located on the back and there are 44 cards in the set.

ITEM	MINT	EX
Set	1350.00	1000.00
Card	25.00	20.00
Wrapper	--	150.00

ROOM 222 (44)

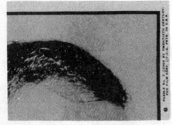

Room 222, a popular TV series which played on ABC from 1969 to 1973, was the subject of a Topps test series believed to have been issued in 1969 or 1970. Both black and white and color versions have been found. The former are either promotional stills or scenes from the show and a facsimile autograph appears on all cards except #'s 11, 37, and 41. Room 222 cards printed in color may be proofs; too few are known to say anything else about them. The test wrapper is a large sticker set on white waxed paper and it does not bear a product code number.

ITEM	MINT	EX
Set (B&W)	750.00	525.00
Cards		
B&W	15.00	12.00
Color	50.00	40.00
Wrapper	--	100.00

1	Pete Dixon	21	Alice Johnson
2	Liz McIntyre	22	Seymour Kaufman
3	Regards, Richie	23	Regards, Richie
4	Seymour Kaufman	24	Seymour Kaufman
5	Alice Johnson	25	Alice Johnson
6	Alice Johnson	26	Seymour Kaufman
7	Seymour Kaufman	27	Seymour Kaufman
8	Pete Dixon	28	Pete Dixon
9	Seymour Kaufman	29	Pete Dixon
10	Regards, Richie	30	Alice Johnson
11	[Walt Whitman High School]	31	Alice Johnson
12	Pete Dixon	32	Pete Dixon
13	Pete Dixon	33	Liz McIntyre
14	Pete Dixon	34	Liz McIntyre
15	Alice Johnson	35	Pete Dixon
16	Alice Johnson	36	Alice Johnson
17	Pete Dixon	37	[Black dude on bench]
18	Pete Dixon	38	Pete Dixon
19	Regards, Richie	39	Seymour Kaufman
20	Regards, Richie	40	Liz McIntyre

41 [Black dude]
42 Pete Dixon
43 Pete Dixon
44 Pete Dixon

ROTTEN EGGS (?)

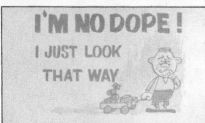

What a great name for a set! Unfortunately for Fleer, the product didn't live up to the name. The "eggs" were "peel off" oval stickers mounted 20 to a sheet. A total of 180 stickers constituted a set but since some stickers are repeated in different combinations, there are more than nine sticker sheets. Each sheet was protected from being bent in the package by a single card bearing a blue-ink joke and sketch. Collectors will recognize that these jokes and illustrations also appeared in another Fleer set, "Back-Slapper Stickers." The number of cards in the set is unknown so no set prices are listed below.

ITEM	MINT	EX
Sticker	2.50	2.00
Card	2.50	2.00
Wrapper	--	12.00
Box	--	35.00

CARDS — PARTIAL CHECKLIST
Find Me in the Yellow Pages. (Under Coward)
Help Stamp Out Children
Help Stamp Out Schools!
I am Not a Girl! I Just Look That Way
I'm No Dope! I Just Look That Way
I've Got B.O.
My Father Can Beat Up Your Mother!
Please Pick My Pockets
You're Looking at the World's Biggest Coward.

SATURDAY NIGHT FEVER (66)

2 1/2" X 3 1/2"

Donruss made a hit with its Saturday Night Fever set in 1978. Each of the 66 cards has a color photograph from the movie, with 21 of the cards showing dance scenes. The obverses have violet borders, and the set title is printed in blue ink just to the left of the card number. The backs are puzzle pieces which, when assembled correctly, form a poster-sized picture of the movie's most famous dance scene. Note: card No. 63 was not issued; instead two cards bear the number 62.

ITEM	MINT	EX
Set	10.00	6.50
Card	.15	.10
Wrapper	--	.35
Box	--	4.00

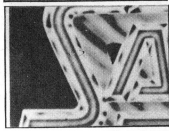

SATURDAY NIGHT LIVE (150)   2 1/2" X 3 1/2"

It occurred to me, as I was looking over the card proofs illustrated here (graciously provided by Star Pics), that Saturday Night Live is a rare old bird among a covey of rather common television fowl. It's difficult to believe, but true, that SNL made its debut *seventeen* years ago in 1975. Only the Tonight Show and 60 Minutes have enjoyed longer careers on the tube. That's an incredible achievement, especially for a live-broadcast, performance-television show.

Has any show in radio or television made such an indelible impression on society? I doubt it. Countless catch words and phrases from it have become ingrained in our speech ("Isn't that special?!") We often mimic characters from it when we want to make a point ("But nooool" or "Nev-er mindl"). And it has served as a stepping stone to fame for a generation of comedians who redefined the very word "comedy" for millions of Americans. If there ever was a show that came upon the scene at the right time, Saturday Night Live was it. As Bill Murray said in the movie "Stripes," 1975 was the year in which America's war record went from "nine-and-oh" to "nine-and-one." SNL helped us weather the psychological shock of the Vietnam disaster and showed us that we could still laugh. That is one reason that the show has such a legendary reputation and such a loyal following among middle-aged Americans.

Card collectors and SNL fans will have the time of their lives with Star Pic's CardArt set of 150 titles. The series is due to be released in June and will be distributed only in packs. The cards themselves will contain color and black & white photographs taken directly from the show. Of course, there will not be any material from the Eddie Murphy/Billy Crystal era (1980-84) - this isn't even available for television reruns - but all the rest of your favorite characters will show up on the Star Pics cards. Modern favorites will include Church Lady, Hans & Franz, Toonces the Cat, and Wayne's World; for older fans there will be cards for the Coneheads, Samurai, The Blues Brothers, Landshark, Baba Wawa, Chico Escuella, Emily Litella, Bass-O-Matic, and Mel's Char Palace, to name a few.

So hear me now and remember me later: this is *THE* fun set of 1992, and possibly, of the decade. Thank you, Star Pics, for making a dream come true!

1 Checklist	39 Nerds	76 Candy Slice	114 Ronald Reagan
2 Checklist	40 Nerds	77 Widettes	115 George Bush
3 Super Fans	41 Nerds	78 Wolverines	116 George Bush
4 Super Fans	42 Samurai	79 Roseanne & Tom	117 Belushi Rant
5 Church Lady	43 Samurai	80 Tammy Faye Bakker	118 Chevy Chase
6 Church Lady	44 Alien Spacewoman	81 Barbara Bush	119 Jane Curtin
7 Church Lady	45 All Things Scottish	82 Carsenio	120 Chico Escuela
8 Stuart Smalley	46 All Drug Olympics	83 Johnny & Ed	121 Al Franken Decade
9 Stuart Smalley	47 Chippendales	84 Cyrano de Bergerac	122 Emily Litella
10 Hans & Franz	48 Chris Farley Show	85 Bette Davis	123 Bill Murray
11 Hans & Franz	49 Coffee Tawk	86 Dylan & Petty	124 Point/Counterpoint
12 Hans & Franz	50 The Devil	87 Harvey Fierstein	125 Point/Counterpoint
	51 Gulf War Briefing	88 Frank & Nancy	126 Roseanne Roseannadanna
	52 Hanukkah Harry	89 Frank & Sammy	127 Annoying Man
	53 Iraqi Pete	90 Saddam Hussein	128 Grumpy Old Man
	54 Lothar	91 Jagger & Richards	129 Dennis Miller
	55 Middle-Aged Man	92 Leona & Zsa Zsa	130 Kevin Nealon
	56 Receptionist	93 McLaughlin Group	131 Queen Shenequa
	57 Simon		132 Victoria Jackson
	58 G.E. Smith		133 Buzz Pen
	59 Sweeney Sisters		134 Chia Head
	60 Lank Thompson		135 Compulsion
	61 Victoria's Secrets		136 Colon Blow
	62 The Blues Brothers		137 Dysfunctional Xmas LP
	63 Chevy Falls		
	64 Chevy's Girls		
	65 Festrunk Brothers		
	66 Franken & Davis		
	67 Killer Bees		
	68 Landshark		
	69 Lifer Follies		
13 I'm Chillin'	70 Irwin Mainway		
14 I'm Chillin'	71 Mr. Mike		
15 Pat	72 Judy Miller		
16 Pat	73 Nick the Lounge Singer		
17 Pat	74 Not Ready ... Players		
18 Pat	75 Olympia Diner		
19 Richmeister			
20 Richmeister		94 Sinead O'Connor	
21 Sprockets		95 Sally Jessy Raphael	
22 Sprockets		96 Regis & Kathie Lee	
23 Sprockets		97 Axl Rose	
24 Toonces		98 Gen. Schwarzkopf	
25 Toonces		99 Gene Shalit	
26 Toonces		100 Clarence Thomas	138 Handi-Off
27 Wayne's World		101 Tonto, Tarzan &	139 Happy Fun Ball
28 Wayne's World		Frankenstein	140 Hedley & Wyche
29 Wayne's World		102 Julia Child	141 Love Toilet
30 Wayne's World		103 Joe Cocker	142 Lung Brush
31 Nat X		104 Kissinger & Nixon	143 Nikey Turkey
32 Nat X		105 Tom Snyder	144 Schmitt's Gay Beer
33 Nat X		106 Star Trek	145 Bass-O-Matic
34 Coneheads		107 Liz Taylor	146 Donuts
35 Coneheads		108 Tina Turner	147 Jewess Jeans
36 Coneheads		109 Baba Wawa	148 Mel's Char Palace
37 E. Buzz Miller		110 Lina Wertmuller	149 Shimmer
38 E. Buzz Miller		111 Richard Nixon	150 Swill
		112 Gerald Ford	
		113 Jimmy Carter	

SATURDAY SERIALS — SERIES 1 (40)

2 1/2" X 3 1/2"

Epic Cards (Minneapolis) invites you to revisit an art form from the glorious days of yesteryear: the Saturday movie matinee serial. Those exciting one chapter adventures which preceded the full-length feature were addictive to kids and adults alike. And they always ended the same way: with the hero and heroine in grave peril of their lives. Would they, could they be saved? Come back next Saturday and find out! In retrospect, this card set also reminds us that the heroes of our youth were not the perfect omnipotent physical and mental specimens we construct today. No Robocops here, ladies and gentlemen. The old Batman's mask had pointy ears; Superman had a gut and baggy drawers; The Spider resembles a slightly deranged interior designer; and Captain Marvel (Tom Tyler) looks like he's doing a Bela Lugosi imitation. The perceptive observer might point out that the Rocket Man's awesome weapon was constructed from golf clubs and vacuum cleaner parts or that Zorro has no business leaping onto 18-wheelers from his horse, but we weren't so picky. These were our heroes, and Epic has reproduced them for us in glorious black and white photos. Each character has a three-card set which relates the titles, chapters, and story of a particular serial. When "Saturday Serials" was first issued in 1988, Epic issued a promotional wrapper containing a sample card and a Lone Ranger sticker. The set you purchase today for $10 has no wrapper or sticker included.

PROMOTIONAL STICKER

1 Batman Titles
2 Batman Chapters
3 Batman Story
4 Atom Man vs. Superman Titles
5 Atom Man vs. Superman Chapters
6 Atom Man vs. Superman Story
7 Radar Men from the Moon Titles
8 Radar Men from the Moon Chapters
9 Radar Men from the Moon Story
10 Flash Gordon Titles
11 Flash Gordon Chapters
12 Flash Gordon Story
13 Zorro Rides Again Titles
14 Zorro Rides Again Chapters
15 Zorro Rides Again Story
16 The Spider Returns Titles
17 The Spider Returns Chapters
18 The Spider Returns Story
19 Captain America Titles
20 Captain America Chapters
21 Captain America Story
22 Mandrake the Magician Titles
23 Mandrake the Magician Chapters
24 Mandrake the Magician Story
25 Adventures of Captain Marvel Titles
26 Adventures of Captain Marvel Chapters
27 Adventures of Captain Marvel Story
28 The Lone Ranger Rides Again Titles
29 The Lone Ranger Rides Again Chapters
30 The Lone Ranger Rides Again Story
31 Green Hornet Titles
32 Green Hornet Chapters
33 Green Hornet Story
34 The Phantom Titles
35 The Phantom Chapters
36 The Phantom Story
37 Blackhawk Titles
38 Blackhawk Chapters
39 Blackhawk Story
40 Checklist

SATURDAY SERIALS — SERIES 2 (40)

2 1/2" X 3 1/2"

Hey, did somebody steal Superman's hand grenade or is he just practicing for Monday Night Football? This histrionic pose is typical of the pictures you'll see in Epic's second series of "Saturday Serials," issued in 1991. Of the 40 cards in the set (numbered 41-80), 36 are black and white photographs from various matinee adventures, while three are multicolor movie posters and one is a multicolor header/checklist card. There are more cards for some of the heros depicted in Series 1, plus some new characters: Buck Rogers, Spy Smasher, The Shadow, Captain Midnight, and Captain Video. So if you adore frumpy heroes in outlandish garb and spine-tingling adventure, Saturday Serials is just the set for you. Note: sold as a set only (in shrinkwrapped plastic); retail price: $10.

41 The Lone Ranger Titles
42 The Lone Ranger Chapters
43 The Lone Ranger Story
44 Drums of Fu Manchu Titles
45 Drums of Fu Manchu Chapters
46 Puzzle Piece
47 Flash Gordon's Trip to Mars Titles
48 Flash Gordon's Trip to Mars Chapters
49 Puzzle Piece
50 Captain Video Titles
51 Captain Video Chapters
52 Puzzle Piece
53 Dick Tracy vs. Crime Inc. Titles
54 Dick Tracy vs. Crime Inc. Chapters
55 Puzzle Piece
56 Zombies of the Stratosphere Titles
57 Zombies of the Stratosphere Chapters
58 Puzzle Piece
59 Superman Titles
60 Superman Chapters
61 Puzzle Piece
62 Captain Midnight Titles
63 Captain Midnight Chapters
64 Puzzle Piece
65 Batman and Robin Titles
66 Batman and Robin Chapters
67 Puzzle Piece
68 The Shadow Titles
69 The Shadow Chapters
70 Puzzle Piece
71 The Green Hornet Strikes Again Titles
72 The Green Hornet Strikes Again Chapters
73 Puzzle Piece
74 Spy Smasher Titles
75 Spy Smasher Chapters
76 Puzzle Piece
77 Buck Rogers Titles
78 Buck Rogers Chapters
79 Completed Puzzle
80 Checklist

SAVINGS & LOAN
SCANDAL TRADING CARDS (40)

2 3/4" X 3 3/4"

THE BANKING BANDITS

Eclipse Enterprises is riding a high wave of publicity right now. Their cards have been advertised in "Playboy," reviewed in "Time" magazine, and psycho-analyzed on network television. In "Savings & Loan Scandal Trading Cards," writers Dennis Bernstein and Laura Sydell and artist Stewart Stanyard turn their acid-tipped pens and brushes to the corporate culprits who sank America's banks. Ronald Reagan, George and Neil Bush, Charles Keating, Adnan Khashoggi, Michael Milken, John Connally and a host of lesser-known figures all appear in the 36-card set. The text examines the roles of the major and minor players in this financial fiasco brought about by deregulation of the banking industry. The series is packaged in a small artwork box and sells for $10 (retail). Reportedly, some of the people named on the cards have ordered sets for themselves and their friends.

CREDIT UNLIMITED

1 The Banking Bandits
2 Credit Unlimited
3 A New Deal
4 The Junk Bond King
5 Tapdancer from Hell
6 A Man of Influence
7 Southern Hospitality
8 A Present for the Pope
9 Party Animal
10 Dustbowl Financier
11 California Scheming
12 Eternal Dental Care
13 The Grove of Academe
14 Pocket Money
15 The Bushkins
16 Read My Lips
17 It's a Wonderful Life
18 A Modern Day Cassandra
19 Finger Puppets
20 Lincoln Logroller
21 Merrill Lynched
22 Cleaning the World
23 Two-Face
24 Watchdog
25 No Money Down
26 Bailout Broker
27 Covert Banking
28 High Stakes Game
29 Company Card
30 The Middleman
31 Cover-Up
32 The Money Machine
33 Junk Food
34 Business Partners
35 The Fed
36 New World Banking Order

COMPANY CARD

SCHOOL DAZE STICKERS (60)

2 1/2" X 3 1/2"

As you can see by the wrappers, this set of 60 stickers is actually a continuation of Fleer's "Back-Slappers." Apart from the style of the artwork, the stickers from either series can be easily identified by consulting the appropriate checklist. The sticker number is printed on the design, so it remains even if the sticker has been removed from the backing.

ITEM	MINT	EX
Set	150.00	110.00
Sticker	2.00	1.50
Wrappers (2)		
each	--	7.50
Box	--	35.00

1 Help Me Think of Something That's Fun For Free
2 My Grades Are Improving...
3 Speling Is My Best Subject
4 This Sticker Covers A Hole In My Clothes
5 I'm Deaf
6 Sure I'm A Loafer
7 Notice My Beautiful Figure
8 Quarantine
9 Official School Blackboard
10 I'm the Class Lover
11 Hold Me, Hug Me, Kiss Me
12 Panic Button
13 Shoot Here!
14 Help!
15 I Bathe Daily...
16 If you think I'm Stuck Up Hold your nose!
17 Call Me Stinky!
18 I'm a V.I.P.
19 Mail Me
20 I'm a Go-Go
21 My Favorite exercise
22 I'm a Catastrophe about to Happen
23 I'll Teach You All I Know
24 Our Principal has an open mind
25 I'm Staying after School
26 Quiet!
27 My Favorite Subjects
28 I Can't Always Be Wrong
29 I'm The Class Idiot
30 Medicare Patient
31 I Hate Girls
32 No. 694832
33 Fragile
34 Flunk Now
35 Your Glasses Are On Backwards
36 Don't just do Something
37 Pardon my Back
38 I Dare You To Mess My Hair
39 Do Not Disturb
40 I Hate Boys
41 I Have All The Answers
42 I Have Personality...
43 Teacher's Pest
44 No Smoking
45 Champion
46 It's Hard To Be Humble!
47 I Made Only 1 Mistake Today...
48 I Got 100 Today
49 Think
50 Go Cart Champ
51 Please put your Bubble Gum Wrapper in my desk
52 I'm beautiful
53 Wake Me!
54 I Gave the Teacher a Worm for her Apple
55 I'M wearing my Mother's Girdle
56 Turn me Around
57 Follow Me
58 Homework Is Fun!
59 I've the biggest
60 I Think Big

SCHOOL STICKERS (72 & 12)　　3 1/2" X 7 7/8"

The measurements in the heading refer to the two large cards as they are found in the pack: one has stickers mounted on it; the other is a panel of "Crazy Cards." Each of the eight different sticker-cards contains nine designs (set total=72); these are checklisted below in alphabetical order according to title of the upper-left sticker. The Crazy Cards are listed singly by title since they may be found cut apart from the original panel. Note: items are not individually priced since complete sets, in gumless cellophane packs, are readily available.

ITEM	MINT	EX
Set	15.00	--
Box	--	5.00

School Stickers

Bear Area No Peeking
Beautiful Body
Careful...the Bus Fairy is Looking
Free Kisses
[blank] Has Frog Breath
[blank] Is an Idiot
This Place is Haunted
This Seat Reserved For Nose Picker

Crazy Cards

Absentee Note
All Purpose Excuse Slip
Cafeteria Credits
Dishonor Student
Failure Notice
Hall Pass
Locker Pass
Playaround Pass
Permission Slip [not signed]
Permission ["Rock N. Roll"]
Special Parking Permit
Student ID

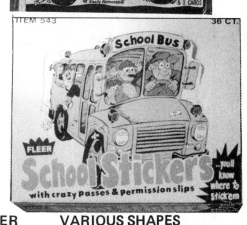

SCREAMIN GLEAMIN GLITTER IRON-ONS (?)

Another tee shirt wrecker from Donruss! The iron-ons were designed to be applied

VARIOUS SHAPES

with a hot iron. The artwork on some is beautifully done and the glitter may dominate some designs or be limited to "accents" and titles on others. The number of iron-ons in the set has not been confirmed. Each pack contained a stick of gum, one iron-on, and an instruction card.

ITEM	MINT	EX
Iron-On	1.00	.75
Card	.35	.25
Wrapper	--	3.00

Screamin' Gleamin Glitter Iron-Ons

SEA WORLD CHARACTER CARDS (12)   3" X 4"

Little Debbie snack cakes and the Sea World parks in San Antonio, Cleveland, Orlando, and San Diego got together in 1990 to produce this series of twelve artwork cards depicting Sea World characters. Actually, only ten of the cards show Sea World characters; the other two card show Little Debbie herself in two different color dresses and these both have a "Cypress Gardens" caption. As you can see by our illustration of the complete box, each card had to be cut away from the package with scissors (dotted lines provided as a guide). Once removed, the cards measure 3" X 4" and they are blank-backed. Collectors were stymied for quite a while because they could only find ten of the twelve cards stated to be in the set. Eventually, Brian Biglow's sharp eyes noticed that Little Debbie had two different dress colors and that Shamu could be found swimming in different directions. Good work, Brian! Note: no mint listing for single cards since they had to be cut away from the boxes.

ITEM	MINT	EX
Set	––	7.00
Card	––	.50
Box	––	1.50

Cap'n Kid   Dolly Dolphin   Little Debbie (2)   O.P. Otter   Penny Penguin   Pete Penguin

Seamore Sea Lion   Shamu (going up)   Shamu (going down)   Sir Winston Walrus   Virgil Pelican

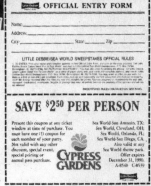

SECRET ORIGIN STORIES (8)

2 3/4" X 4 1/4"

This series of eight miniature comic books was distributed by Leaf in 1981. Each comic has fourteen numbered pages and explains how a specific Super Hero appeared on Earth. The comics are not numbered sequentially; all have a No. 1 label at top right. A plastic bag containing one comic book and a cellophane packet of "tart 'n tangy Comic Book Candy" retailed for 35 cents. The back cover of each comic carries advertising for a "Super Heroes Collector Album" available via the mail.

ITEM	MINT	EX
Set	11.00	8.50
Comic	1.25	1.00
Box	--	10.00

Aquaman	Superman
Bat Man	The Flash
Green Lantern	Wonder Woman
Hawkman	
Justice League of America	

SECRET WARS (180)

1 3/4" X 2 1/2"

Leaf's sole reported entry in the "album sticker" market seems to have been quite a secret itself. Apparently, it was not distributed throughout the United States for it is not widely known by collectors. The 180 stickers have artwork fronts depicting "Marvel Super Heroes" and "Marvel Super Villians" in "their constant battle for the supremacy of the human spirit". Each sticker is numbered on the back and fits into an assigned space in a 24-page album. Note: set price includes album.

ITEM	MINT	EX
Set	80.00	55.00
Sticker	.35	.25
Album	5.00	4.00
Wrapper	--	2.00
Box	--	8.00

SGT. PEPPER'S LONELY HEARTS CLUB BAND (66)

2 1/2" X 3 1/2"

The Sgt. Pepper's Lonely Hearts Club Band set of 66 cards was produced by Donruss in 1978. It features color photographs from the movie enclosed by ornate red frames and white borders. Each card is numbered and captioned on the front. The backs of all 66 cards are pieces of a large color poster.

ITEM	MINT	EX
Set	10.00	6.50
Card	.15	.10
Wrapper	--	.35
Box	--	5.00

Sgt. Pepper's

7 FULL COLOR PHOTOS — BUBBLE GUM CARDS

1. Sandy Farina as Strawberry Fields
2. Barry Gibb as Mark Henderson
3. At the Benefit for Heartland
4. The LHCB Receives a Wire from B.C.
5. George Burns & the LHCB at the Benefit
6. Mr. Kite Dancing in Heartland
7. The Bee Gees as They Appear in the LHCB
8. In Costume Ready to Board the Balloon
9. Paul Nicholas as Dougie Shears
10. Robin Gibb Performing in Heartland
11. Posing in Front of the Heartland Museum
12. Heartland's Hot Air Balloon
13. Peter Frampton as Billy Shears
14. George Burns as Heartland's Mayor, Mr. Kite
15. Dr. Maxwell Edison

16. Un-titled (the Band)
17. Heartland Has Become Sin City
18. Battle Between LHCB & Future Villians
19. B.D. & Lucy Ready to Meet the LHCB
20. Strawberry Looks on as Billy Performs
21. LHCB Cutting Their First Record
22. Clowns at the Benefit
23. The Original Sgt. Pepper's LHCB
24. The Grand Finale
25. The Henderson Brothers
26. Dougie Presents the Instruments to the Museum
27. The Grand Life Style at B.D.'s Mansion
28. LHCB Record Their Demo Record
29. Maurice Gibb as Bob Henderson
30. Billy Preston as the Sgt. Pepper Weathervane
31. LHCB in B.D.'s Oversized Limousine
32. Un-titled (Strawberry & Mark)
33. Billy Shears & Strawberry Fields
34. B. D. Brockhurst with Some of the LHCB
35. Starting the Balloon Chase
36. Steve Martin as the Mad Dr. Maxwell Edison
37. The Sgt. Pepper Weathervane Comes to Life
38. At the Benefit Concert
39. Lucy as Chauffeur for the LHCB in B.D.'s Limo

40. Mean Mr. Mustard in his Van
41. LHCB at the Benefit
42. Leaving Heartland
43. Maurice Gibb Performing in Heartland
44. Father Sun's Temple of Electronic Cosmology
45. The LHCB & the Future Villians
46. Maurice Gibb as Bob Henderson
47. "Lucy in the Sky" Production Number
48. Recording for B.D. Records
49. The Benefit Parade
50. The Parade for the Benefit
51. Mr. Mustard Stealing the Instruments
52. Sgt. Pepper Dies at Cermonies in His Honor
53. Un-titled (Maurice & Barry Gibb)

54. Funeral Procession for Strawberry Fields
55. Future Villians
56. The LHCB in Concert
57. Billy Shears
58. Preston, the Weathervane, Sings "Get Back"
59. B.D. Brockhurst with Some of the LHCB
60. Aerosmith as the Future Villians
61. Donald Pleasence as B.D. the Record Mogul
62. Dianne Steinberg as Lucy
63. Heartland after Mr. Mustard Takes Over
64. Peter Frampton as Billy Shears
65. A LHCB Concert
66. B.D. Brockhurst Played by Donald Pleasence

SHADOWORLD (102)

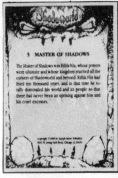

LIMITED EDITION TRADING CARD SET by Joe Sarno & Paul Sonjou

$15.95 SET

Shadoworld

1. The Sage
2. The Finger Writes
3. Design of the Master Dreamer
4. Into a World of Shadows
5. Master of Shadows
6. Messengers in the Shadow
7. Vingil, A Man of Vision
8. Suhalon Village
9. Govan
10. Teacher and Pupil
11. Beginning the Quest
12. Creatures That Burn
13. Creatures That Fly
14. Creatures of the Shadows
15. To Dream New Dreams
16. The Silverwind Sword
17. Dark Crystals
18. Watching Shadows
19. Castle in the Darkness
20. Dwelling of the Mapmaker
21. Mapmakers Hearth
22. Lure of the Spiderqueen
23. Spider's Trap
24. Freedom from Death
25. A Dwarf with Small Powers
26. The Abduction
27. Beast of Burden
28. Creature of the Sea
29. Rilliss of the Sea
30. Strange Wasteland
31. Swallowed by the Earth
32. Chamber of the Green Dragon
33. Must Heroes Turn To Stone
34. Vault of the Blue Dragon
35. Crypt of the Red Dragon
36. The Stone Dragon
37. Master of Dragons
38. Tales of the Dragon Hearth
39. The Dragon Fire of Orex
40. Worlds of Knowledge
41. Puppets of Rillik-Nin
42. Ultimate Danger
43. Black Dragon of the Sea
44. Night Plans and Dark Dreams
45. Cliffs of Doom

46. Castle of Darkness
47. Servant to Linderick
48. Master of Darkness
49. Dining with Demons
50. Maetace
51. Dream Magic
52. Arkvid
53. A Jibberish Thing
54. Spiral Doom
55. Drog Monster
56. Clutching Death
57. Caves of Knowledge
58. Visions of Knowledge
59. Silver Music
60. Stone of Silent Laughter
61. Wall Swallows Sword
62. Winged Menace
63. Evil Waits
64. The Stealth of Trongel
65. An Old Friend
66. Sly Subterfuge
67. The High Tower
68. Clash of Steel
69. Fire and Steel
70. Escaping the Shadowlord
71. New Master
72. Room of One Hundred Mirrors
73. Images of the Soul
74. A Hundred Mirror Images
75. The Maze to Secret Portals
76. Into the Darkness
77. Madness
78. Into Another Madness
79. Light of the Indriss

80. Shadow of the Sindrinn
81. Shadow's Music
82. Moving in Shadow
83. Dragon Reed
84. Doorway into the Dark Abyss
85. Dragon Attack
86. Lair of the Shadow Lord
87. Laughter of Death
88. Light Against Darkness
89. Conquest of Darkness
90. Death of the Shadow Lord
91. Return to Dragon's Lair
92. Lure of the Sindrinn
93. Evil Conquers Light
94. Death Conquers Evil
95. Death of the Indriss
96. Returned to Light
97. Destruction of the Messengers
98. The Rift is Closed
99. Alternate Worlds
100. And Having Writ Moves On

2 1/2" X 3 1/2"

A "Limited Edition" trading card set issued in 1990, "Shadoworld" is the handiwork of Joe Sarno and Paul Sonjou. The series of 100 original artwork cards takes us on a fantasy journey to a parellel world of shadows and the inhabitants who dwell within. We follow Govan on his quest for knowledge and watch him overcome many obstacles and dangers along the way. Fans of fantasy artwork and adventures will find this set a very attractive combination of colorful artwork and well-written text. The obverses have small white borders to maximize the effect of the paintings. The backs are numbered and have an interesting "Shadowland" design around the perimeter. The set, which comes with two identical header cards (unnumbered) and a wide paper band, currently sells for $16.

SHE-RA ALBUM STICKERS (216)

2 1/8"X 3"

Princess Adora, a.k.a. "She-Ra," is the subject of this 216-sticker set released by Panini U.S.A. in 1986. Thirty-six stickers are diecut foils, including 12 circular portraits from the first two album pages, 18 characters designed for the "She-Ra" Action Mobile (in album), and two unnumbered "extra" (bonus) stickers. Both of the latter show the same character, but one is gold and the other is silver. The remaining 180 stickers have color fantasy artwork fronts and Panini multi-language backs. Note: set price includes album.

ITEM	MINT	EX
Set	25.00	18.00
Sticker	.10	.07
Wrapper	--	.35
Album	2.00	1.50

SHOCK THEATER (50)

2 1/2" X 3 1/2"

"Shock Theater" is an unusual set because it was "tested" by Topps in the U.S. market one year, and sold on a regular basis in England the next. The cards of the "test" series bear a 1975 Topps copyright on the back. The wrapper is white wax paper with a large sticker in the center and carries a "T-64-5" production code. The word "Theater" in the title is spelled "American style." There are two cards for No. 17 and no card for No. 47; the designers compounded the mistake by adding an extra card (No. 51). No box has been seen for this set.

ITEM	MINT	EX
Test Issue		
Set	85.00	55.00
Card	1.50	1.00
Wrapper	--	12.50

Shock Theater

1 But I Ordered a Vanilla Shake!
2 I Can't Understand Why Girls Don't Like Me!
3 My Goodness, You've Brainwashed Him!
4 I Get the Feeling the Villagers Don't Like Me!
5 I Think You've Got a Screw Loose!
6 I Cannot Tell a Lie. I Chopped Down the Cherry Tree!
7 Doctor, Will You Please Lend Me a Hand!
8 Nuts! Blew Another Fuse!
9 At Last! I've Invented Lemonade!
10 But All I Asked for Was a Trim!
11 I've Had It with These Cheap Hotel Rooms!
12 Counting Bats Really Puts Me to Sleep!
13 Who Took My Baby Powder!
14 Not Tonight Deary...I Have a Headache!
15 Who Starched My Cape?
16 Hmmm...Dishpan Hands!

17 Pardon Me Miss-I Lost My Contact Lenses!*
17 It's The Heartbreak of Psoriasis!*
18 Care for a Bite?
19 I've Got a Lot at Stake!
20 You Forgot to Wash Behind Your Ears Again!
21 I'm Batty Over You!
22 Only My Dentist Knows for Sure!
23 Sure Doesn't Taste Like Tomato Juice!
24 Like My New Charm Necklace?
25 Don't Be Silly. I'm Jewish!
26 I Sure Got the Point!
27 Quick--Get the Eyedrops!
28 Presenting...The Transylvania Glee Club!
29 Anybody Lose a Knitting Needle?
30 Who Stole My Hair Spray!
31 Does This Mean We're Pinned?
32 Look Ma--No cavities!
33 Let Me Take a Stab at It!
34 I Always Fall Asleep in Church!
35 Who Forgot the Marshmallows?

36 Support Your Local Blood Bank!
37 Clean Up Your Room Before Father Gets Home!
38 I'm the Big Wheel in This Town!
39 Wake Up Dear--Breakfast's Ready!
40 Hap-py Birth-day to You!
41 You've Been Biting Your Nails!
42 Waiter! The Steak Is Too Rare!
43 Yipes! What a Scary Dream!
44 Darling! You've Got to Stop Cooking with Garlic!
45 I Have a Thing for Bloody Marys!
46 But Honey...I Used Mouthwash This Morning!
48 Don't Cook Tonight...Call Monster Delight!
49 This Should Cure Your Hiccups!
50 I'd Say You Had About a 15½" Neck!
51 Those T.V. Doctors Never Had a Case Like This!

The "regular" issue was distributed in England in 1976 and all the cards bear a 1976 copyright date. The designers were able to correct one of their previous goofs -the 51st card- but blundered again by printing two cards for No. 47 but none for No. 17! The only wrapper seen for the 1976 series is a standard full color type with the word "Theatre" in the title spelled "English style." The box for this set is marked "4p" (four pence). It is possible that Topps may have distributed some leftover English version in this country on a limited basis.

ITEM	MINT	EX
Regular Series		
Set	185.00	155.00
Card	3.00	2.50
Wrapper	--	30.00
Box	--	150.00

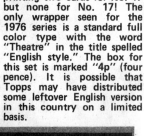

I'M JUST FANG-TASTIC!

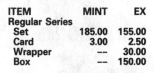

SURE DOESN'T TASTE LIKE TOMATO JUICE!

WITH 1 STICK BUBBLE GUM

1 I Can't Understand Why Girls Don't Like Me!
2 Support Vampire Lib!
3 My Goodness! You've Brainwashed Him!
4 I Get the Feeling the Villagers Don't Like Me!

5 I Think You've Got a Screw Loose!
6 Drac's Snacks!
7 I've Got to Cut Down on My Drinking!
8 Beware of Vampires!
9 Dracula Lives!
10 But All I Asked for Was a Trim!
11 I'm Fed Up with these Cheap Motel Rooms!
12 Counting Bats Really Puts Me to Sleep!
13 Welcome to the Monster Mash!
14 Dear Your Fingernails Are a Disgrace!
15 Who Starched My Cape?
16 Can It Be My Breath?
17 Not Issued (see No. 47)
18 Care for a Bite?
19 The Count Dracula Society Wants You!
20 You Forgot to Wash Behind Your Ears Again
21 Who Said I Have Bad Breath?
22 Only My Dentist Knows for Sure!
23 Sure Doesn't Taste Like Tomato Juice!
24 Down for the Count!
25 Dracula for Parliament!
26 All This Place Needs is a Good Paint Job!
27 Quick Get the Eye Drops!
28 Presenting...The Transylvania Glee Club!

29 Anybody Lose a Knitting Needle!
30 Who Stole My Hairspray?
31 I Travel by Blood Vessel!
32 Look Ma - No Fillings!
33 What am I Bid?
34 That was Some Wild Party!
35 Support Your Local Vampire!
36 Harold, You're Weird!
37 Clean Up Your Room Before Father Gets Home
38 I'm the Big Wheel in this Town
39 Wake Up Dear Breakfasts Ready
40 I'm Just Fang-Tastic
41 I'm Just a Big Cry Baby!
42 Waiter! The Steak is Too Rare!
43 He Sure Got the Point!
44 Darling You've Got to Stop Cooking with Garlic
45 I Ordered "Steak" Not Stake!
46 But Honey I Used a Mouthwash this Morning
47 I Have a Real Drinking Problem!*
47 Pardon Me Miss - I Lost My Contact Lenses!*
48 I'm Batty Over You!
49 This Should Cure Your Hiccups!
50 Equal Rights for Vampires!

SILLY CYCLES (66)

A spin-off from the Odd Rods concept, Silly cycles depicts an assortment of wacky monsters and crazy characters driving strange and unusual motorcycles. The stickers are numbered on the front near the artwork (stickers without numbers may be variations or overseas issue). The backs contain "peel" instructions and a sketch of a helmeted biker driving towards the left. Some stickers have been seen with this biker driving right, but the significance of this reversal has not yet been determined.

ITEM	MINT	EX
Set	95.00	75.00
Sticker	1.25	1.00
Wrapper	--	20.00
Box	--	60.00

#		#		#		#	
1	No title (ape, bone in hand)	10	Charlie CC's	15	Harry Horsepower	19	No title (football players)
2	Super-Cop	11	No title (bug chaser)	16	Hereafter Honda	20	No title (knife in mouth)
3	Wheelie	12	No title (riding backward)	17	Greasy Rider	21	Custom Chopper
4	Teeny Weeny Meeny	13	No title (orange monster)	18	Chrome Bayonet	22	Motor Mouth
5	Uncle	14	No title (green demon)			23	Satan's Dream
6	Honda Hickle					24	Mini Mama
7	Super Chopper					25	Super Torque
8	Trail Boss					26	Groovin
9	Easy Rider					27	Hill Chopper

#		#	
28	Hill Hopper	43	Mini Wheels
29	No title (green-striped monster)	44	Bat Angel
30	Mummy Machine	45	Shifty
31	Road Hog	46	No title (genie monster)
32	Digger	47	Moto Guzzi
33	Sure Footed	48	Just Weird
34	Ronny Rear-Up	49	Midnite Bandit
35	No title (Roman)	50	Billy Blastoff
36	Nose Job	51	No title (gun in right hand)
37	Chopper	52	B.C. Bike
38	BSA	53	Pain Pusher
39	Triumph	54	Ride 'Em or Leave 'Em
40	Mini Mess	55	Cop Watcher
41	Nit Picker	56	Honda Hopper
42	Kawasaki	57	Garbage Delite
		58	No title (polo stick)
		59	2 Wheeler
		60	No title (fork)
		61	Super Hawk
		62	Susie Sazukis
		63	Mounted Monty
		64	Very Interesting
		65	Ugly Duck
		66	Raker

SILLY STICKERS (55)

Some collectors try to label this set "Silly Travel Stickers," but 30 of the 55 stickers in the set have nothing to do with travel. The series predates the era of wrapper production codes and is thought to have been issued in 1965. The stickers are not numbered and the paper backing is prescored for easy removal.

ITEM	MINT	EX
Set	160.00	125.00
Sticker	2.50	2.00
Wrapper	--	25.00

First Place Award in Dog Show
Fly Frightfully Wobbly Airlines
Fly Jet for a Faster Trip to the Graveyard
Graduate of Pig Penn
Havana Is Fun If You Like Firing Squads
I Don't Care If I Never See the Taj Mahal
(...) If You Can Read This, You're Too
Darn Close
If You Fly To Europe Use a Plane
I Go To Harvard Kosher Delicatessen
I Had My Head Shrunk On a Visit to the
Congo

Alaska Is Delightful For Polar Bears
April Is a Lousy Month To Be In Rainy,
Cold, Unfriendly Paris
Arithmetic Is a Waste of Time
Boy, Do I Hate History
Do Not Open Your Big Fat Mouth Till Xmas
Eliot Ness Had Me Deported To Sunny Italy
Enjoy the View of Auto Crashes On the
York State Thruway

I Love My Teacher Like Poison
I Love School! And Measles and Mumps
Cause I'm Nuts
In Case of Fire Yell Fire
I Never Send Flowers By Telephone
They Get Beat Up Going Thru the Wires
I Played Hookey From School and a Police
Patrolman Caught Me

Silly Stickers

I Stayed in Los Angeles City Dump
It's So Darn Sunny in Florida You Get
  Roasted Alive
I Visited Grand Canyon Drop in Sometime
I Visited New York City Sewers
Member Olympic Liars Team
Most Popular Student with Truant Officer
My Compositions Are Lousy
My Pant's Caught Fire in Macy's
  Department Store
My Plane Almost Made It Over the Rocky
  Mountains
Official Monkey Business

Ohio State Prison
One Visit to Russia Is More Than Enough
Only Creeps Like Science
On My Honor As a Student I Hate School
Spelling Puts Me to Sleep
Teachers Pet! So Do Others
They Pushed Me Overboard on the U.S.S.
  America
They Said I Had No Sportsmanship When I
  Punched the Kid Who Won the Award
To Get Me Up in the Air They'd Have To
  Force Me
Visit Hoover Darn Can't Say d..., You
  Know

Visit the Kremlin During Execution Season
Visit Washington Oops, He's Dead
Voted All American Idiot
Voted Most unLikely to Succeed
Voted the Best Nit Wit
Wanted By the Police Department
Who Needs Geography
Why Don't You Jump In Lake Erie
World's Greatest Authority on Nothing
You'll Love Leaving Cuba
You're Lucky If You Get Out of Cape
  Canaveral Alive

SILVER HAWKS ALBUM STICKERS (240)   1 3/4″ X 2 1/2″

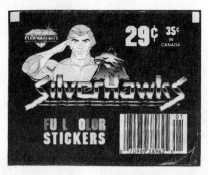

Diamond released the "Silver Hawks" series of 240 album stickers in 1987. Packets containing six stickers sold for 29¢ at variety, convenience, and grocery stores, along with an album which retailed at 49¢. Each sticker is numbered and has a corresponding numbered space in the album. Since some of the album illustrations require that stickers be grouped together, collectors will find some stickers with two or three white borders (instead of four). There are 32 pages in the album and nearly all the page space and the sticker slots have 3-D designs which can be viewed by Diamond's trademarked "Magic Decoder" (attached to each album). Collectors were encouraged to trade their duplicate stickers to the company in exchange for numbers they needed (two dupes for every number requested). Note: set price includes album.

ITEM	MINT	EX
Set	25.00	18.00
Sticker	.10	.07
Wrapper	--	.20
Album	2.00	1.50

SIX MILLION DOLLAR MAN (66)   2 1/2″ X 3 1/2″

The Six Million Dollar Man series of 66 stickers was issued by Donruss in 1975. The stickers, attached to a white card (underneath), have color photos from the television show surrounded by either black or red frame lines and blue borders. They are num-bered and captioned. The card backs form a giant color poster.

ITEM	MINT	EX
Set	25.00	17.50
Sticker	.35	.25
Wrapper	--	1.00
Box	--	10.00

Six Million Dollar Man

1 Steve lifts a timber as though it were a match stick.
2 The Bionic Leg.
3 Steve running at over 50 m.p.h.
4 The Bionic Arm.
5 Austin charging a jungle enemy.
6 The Bionic Eye.
7 Colonel Austin pulling heavy safe out of the floor.
8 Steve hurling a pipe at crooks.
9 Steve using his Bionic Arm to escape.
10 Austin ripping open a gas line to save his life.
11 Steve plunging a huge stake into the ground.
12 Steve throws a table as though it were a match box.
13 Austin in hot pursuit of criminals.
14 Steve can lift a tree as though it were a twig.
15 Steve discovers vital link to save oil refinery.
16 Steve and Oscar discuss plans for capturing aggressors.
17 Austin breaks free from chair.
18 Steve lifts car so Oscar can change the tire.
19 Steve searching for criminals' hideout.
20 Steve at the controls of re-entry vehicle that almost killed him.
21 Steve and Oscar exchange ideas for capturing criminals.
22 Steve being monitored by the scanner.
23 Steve leaping from helicopter.
24 Austin trying to save runaway train.
25 With the Bionic Leg Steve can leap up cliffs.
26 Steve throwing a bale of hay as though it were nothing.
27 Austin extinguishing dangerous electrical fire.
28 Steve spraying deadly gas at crooks.
29 A steel door is no match for Steve's super strength.
30 Steve hurdles fence to head off crooks.
31 The more the merrier for Steve.
32 Steve driving armored truck.
33 Austin kicking the door off a car to escape.
34 A jungle trap is no match for Steve.
35 Austin opens locked door with ease.
36 Mother ship carrying Steve's re-entry vehicle.
37 The Bionic Leg enables Steve to hop over fences.
38 Steve rips off cover of reactor to avert danger.
39 Oscar and Steve discuss plans.
40 Steve fights a secret agent on board an airplane.
41 Colonel Austin awaiting blast-off in re-entry vehicle.
42 Steve de-activates a mechanical man.
43 With the Bionic Arm Steve can throw a steel beam.
44 Steve fighting with secret agent
45 Steve kicking open door to suprise secret agents.
46 Steve photographs secret documents.
47 Austin knocks aggressor off cliff.
48 Steve in early stages of bionic development.
49 B-52 about to launch Steve in the experimental craft.
50 Steve hops over stone wall.
51 Steve keeping in shape with sparring partner.
52 Steve attacking a secret agent.
53 A sword pierced Austin's Bionic Leg.
54 Steve making a believer out of a criminal.
55 Austin easily lifts a car.
56 Oscar ponders the outcome of Steve's mission.
57 Assassin attacks Steve—unaware of Austin's super powers.
58 Steve easily pulls steel post from ground.
59 Austin escapes from handcuffs as though they were string.
60 Steve attacks enemy outpost to rescue an American prisoner.
61 The Bionic strength of Steve can easily break chains.
62 Steve disarms a nuclear reactor.
63 Austin rips open enemy tank.
64 Steve turns over an oncoming car.
65 Steve rips lock off enemy hideout.
66 Steve and Oscar examine research material.

SIX MILLION DOLLAR MAN (55) 2 1/2" X 3 1/2"

Most collectors will never see - much less own - a card from this "Six Million Dollar Man" series test-marketed by Topps in 1974. The Topps cards, with their brilliant blue borders and clear photographs, are a striking con- **trast to the dull tones of the more common Donruss set. The card backs are arranged to be part text and part puzzle piece. Collector Bob Marks reports that the test packs came in a plain white box with a label on one** **end bearing the set name in pencil.**

ITEM	MINT	EX
Set	1350.00	1000.00
Card	20.00	15.00
Wrapper	--	40.00

1 Col. Steve Austin
2 A Fateful Operation
3 New Sights
4 Incredible Transplant!
5 Human Cannonball!
6 A Man of Steel!
7 Steve's Boss
8 Baffling Mystery!
9 Special Production!
10 Death Town!
11 A Sign of Life!
12 Trapped!
13 Fantastic Rescue!
14 The Deadly Sound
15 A Fearful Ultimatum!
16 Austin's Gamble
17 Tricked!
18 A Cool Reception!
19 Deep Freeze!
20 A Trace of Warmth!
21 One Last Hope!
22 Inventive Austin!
23 Once Upon A Chilling!
24 Home-Made Blow Torch!
25 Slicing Through!
26 Breakout!
27 Sound of Death!
28 Racing Against Time!
29 The Final Blow!
30 Flight of Chance!
31 Saved!
32 Steve, The Human Jack!
33 Delayed!
34 His Life at Stake!
35 Struck by Lightning!
36 Engine on Fire!
37 A Serious Situation!
38 Leaping for Life!
39 Campfire Thoughts!
40 Morning Caller!
41 Uphill Racer
42 Majestic Leap!
43 Rescue!
44 Calling for Help!
45 Ominous Mood!
46 Destroying a Snake!
47 Electronic Miracle!
48 Lifesaver!
49 A Happy Ending!
50 Lee Majors
51 Richard Anderson
52 Mechanical Magician!
53 Dangerous Work!
54 Six Million Dollar Outfit!
55 Prime Mover!

SKATEBOARD STICKERS (44)

2 1/2" X 3 1/2"

It is assumed that "Skateboard Stickers" was the first of Donruss' two skateboard theme sets because it is a bare-bones issue compared to "All-Pro Skateboard." The stickers of this set are diecut, front-peel designs that are unnumbered. The cardboard backing is blank on the reverse side and there are 44 stickers in the set. Skateboard Stickers gum packages sold for 10 cents ("All-Pro" retailed for 15 cents).

ITEM	MINT	EX
Set	12.00	9.00
Sticker	.25	.20
Wrapper	––	1.00
Box	––	5.00

Board Spin
Coffin
Cosmic Rider
Curb Crusher
Daffy
Endover
Flash
Get Down!
Gorilla Grip
Handstand
Hang Five
Hang Ten
Headstand Wheelie
Heavy Action
High Energy

High Jumper
Hill Hunter
L-Sit
Mashed Potatoes
Number 1
One Board Daffy
One-Foot Nose Wheels
One-Foot Tail Wheelie
Rim Shot
Rolling Duce
Shooting The Tube
Shoot The Duck (or Christie)
Sidewalk Eagle
Sidewalk Surfer
Sidewalk Warrior
Skateboard Championship
Skateboarders Aren't Crazy But It Helps!
Skateboard Power
Skateboard Purple Heart
Skateboards Forever
Slalom Run
Stoked
Street Demon
Street Fox
This Board Is The Property Of...
Two-Foot Tail Wheelie
V-Sit
Walking The Boards

SLIMER & THE REAL GHOSTBUSTERS ALBUM STICKERS (180)

1 3/4" X 2 1/2"

In 1988, Diamond Toy issued a sticker set based upon the popular "Slimer and The Real Ghostbusters" children's show. The key design feature of the series was Diamond's patented "Slide-O-Scope," which allowed the viewer to see "action" (movement) when looking at pictures in the album or at special "animated" stickers. Collectors will find three kinds of stickers in the set: the small group of "animation" just mentioned; "partials" intended for grouping into larger pictures; and singles with complete pictures and white borders all around. Every sticker is numbered and fits in a corresponding spot on an album page. The album has 24 pages and there is a sticker trading offer printed on the back cover. The packet is lime green and burgundy in color and had to be torn or cut open to release the contents. Note: set price includes album.

ITEM	MINT	EX
Set	24.00	16.00
Sticker	.15	.10
Wrapper	––	.20
Album	2.00	1.50

SLOB STICKERS (44) (44) (44)

2 1/2" X 3 1/2"

In the court battle between Cabbage Patch Dolls and Garbage Pail Kids, Topps introduced "Slob Stickers" - with its "same artwork, different names" format - as a forerunner of GPK. Indeed, the 44 "slobs" depicted in this issue are identical for each number in all three series, except for the name (and the letters "A" and "B" added to the numbers). The "B" series is much scarcer than the other two and we only have a partial checklist for it at this time. Note: series are priced individually since the "degree of difficulty" varies with each one.

ITEM	MINT	EX
Sets		
1st	185.00	155.00
"A"	210.00	185.00
"B"	330.00	275.00
Sticker		
1st	3.50	3.00
"A"	4.00	3.50
"B"	6.00	5.00
Wrapper	--	20.00
Box	--	150.00

1	Jerky Jim	23	Jackass John	1A	Jerky Ed	23A	Jackass Tony	1B		23B	Jackass Jim
2	Smelly Steve	24	Jabbering Jackie	2A	Smelly Sal	24A	Jabbering Joel	2B		24B	
3	Disgusting Donald	25	Jungle Joe	3A	Disgusting Dom	25A	Jungle Lew	3B	Disgusting Donnie	25B	Jungle Jeff
4	Fragrant Fran	26	Lousy Linda	4A	Fragrant Fanny	26A	Lousy Lois	4B	Fragrant Fay	26B	
5	Decaying Debbie	27	Gabby Gail	5A	Decaying Dottie	27A	Gabby Gwen	5B		27B	Gabby Gert
6	Dandruff Dick	28	Maggot Mary	6A		28A	Maggot Mame	6B	Dandruff Dave	28B	Maggot Mame
7	Stinky Sandy	29	Painful Paul	7A	Stinky Ben	29A	Painful Perry	7B		29B	
8	Slippery Sidney	30	Sissy Scott	8A	Slippery Victor	30A	Sissy Sheldon	8B		30B	Sissy Sam
9	Clammy Carl	31	Puffy Pat	9A	Clammy Cliff	31A	Puffy Pauline	9B		31B	
10	Loudmouth Larry	32	Tearful Ted	10A	Loudmouth Leo	32A	Tearful Terry	10B		32B	Tearful Terry
11	Contagious Carol	33	Angry Alan	11A	Contagious Claire	33A	Angry Albert	11B		33B	
12	Chicken Charlie	34	Clumsy Cathy	12A	Chicken Irv	34A	Clumsy Lil	12B		34B	Clumsy Cora
13	Muscles Melvin	35	Dirty Danny	13A	Muscles Marc	35A	Dirty George	13B		35B	Dirty Denny
14	Ecchy Eileen	36	Misfit Michael	14A	Ecchy Edna	36A	Misfit Mac	14B		36B	Misfit Marv
15	Bashful Barbie	37	Sweaty Stan	15A	Bashful Bea	37A	Sweaty Art	15B	Bashful Betty	37B	
16	Phinky Phyllis	38	Beggar Bernie	16A	Phinky Frieda	38A	Beggar Andy	16B		38B	Beggar Barry
17	Hypnotic Helen	39	Brainless Bill	17A	Hypnotic Carol	39A	Brainless Bert	17B	Hypnotic Hilda	39B	
18	Prying Paula	40	Moustache Millie	18A	Prying Ann	40A	Moustache Min	18B		40B	
19	Hot-Head Howie	41	Ghoulish Gerry	19A	Hot-Head Frank	41A	Ghoulish Greta	19B	Hot-Head Henry	41B	
20	Dumb Denny	42	Garlic Gary	20A	Dumb Dwight	42A	Garlic Glenn	20B	Dumb Daniel	42B	Garlic Greg
21	Nasty Nancy	43	Eerie Ellie	21A	Nasty Nellie	43A	Eerie Elaine	21B	Nasty Nora	43B	Eerie Edith
22	Warty Willie	44	Hairy Herbie	22A	Warty Wally	44A	Hairy Ray	22B		44B	Hairy Harvey

SMELLIES (80 & ?)

"Amazing stickers that really smell! —Scratch 'Em!...then smell 'em...PU!" There are 80 different stickers in this 1969 Fleer set. Each is 1" square and came in strips of four. A two-card panel (2 9/16" X 4 1/2") also came in every 10-cent pack and each card had a specific area to attach a "Smellie." These cards are not numbered and only four

TWO SIZES

have been reported to date. Note: single cards cannot be graded mint; separated stickers cannot be graded excellent or mint.

ITEM	MINT	EX
Sticker strip	2.50	2.00
Cards		
Single	--	.75
Panel	2.50	20.00
Wrapper	--	25.00

SMURF ALBUM STICKERS (180)

The characters known as "Smurfs"—created by the Belgian cartoonist Peyo—are the subject of this Topps set first issued in April 1984. The color artwork stickers (180 in all), yellow wrapper, and 32-page album were all manufactured for Topps by Panini. A package containing six

2 1/8" X 3"

album stickers, but no gum, retailed for 25 cents (the album also sold for a quarter). Note: set price includes album.

ITEM	MINT	EX
Set	27.50	18.00
Sticker	.15	.10
Wrapper	--	.35
Album	2.00	1.50

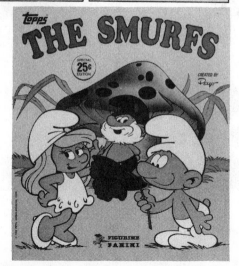

SMURF SUPERCARDS (56)   2 1/2" X 4 7/8"

Topps employs the term "super" to describe almost any type of card that is larger than standard size. The design of this 56-card Smurf set issued in 1982 is similar to other Topps "plaks" sets (Wacky Plaks, Wood Plaks, etc.) in that the color drawings are set against a knotty pine or woodgrain background. Each card carries a humorous caption on front; the card number and the set title are given on the back.

ITEM	MINT	EX
Set	8.00	5.50
Card	.15	.10
Wrappers (2)		
wax	--	.50
cellophane	--	.50
Box	--	3.00

NUMBER 21

1 Keep Talking... I'm Listening!	30 You're So Sweet
2 Let's Be Friends	31 Happy Smurfday
3 T.G.I.F.	32 What's Cookin' Good Lookin'?
4 Stop Look and Listen!	33 Whistle While You Smurf
5 Stay Cool!	34 I Never Met a Smurf I Didn't Like!
6 Recess Is My Favorite Subject!	35 S—M—U—R—F—S Yea Team!
7 Life's a Ball	36 Wanna Smurf Around?
8 Can't You Tell a Superstar when You See One?	37 Want a Present?
9 2 Smurfs Are Better than 1	38 Keep Smurfin'
10 Take a Smurf to Lunch	39 Mind If I Smurf My Own Horn?
11 Have a Smurfy Day!	40 Goin' Smurfin'
12 I Love Smurfing	41 Don't Bother Me I'm Smurfin'
13 Calling All Smurfs	42 Smurfettes Should Be Treated Royally
14 Smurf Fever	43 Come Smurf with Us!
15 Hello Handsome	44 Ever Feel You've Lost Your Last Smurf?
16 Neatness Counts!	45 A Smurf's Work Is Never Done
17 Smurf's Up!	46 I Smurf You
18 Keep on Smurfin'...	47 Come Smurf with Me
19 Welcome to Smurf Country	48 Weekends Are for Smurfin'
20 He Smurfs Me... He Smurfs Me Not	49 Wait Till Tomorrow If You Think Today Is Bad
21 You're Out of This World	50 Let a Smile Be Your Umbrella
22 Nothing's Easy!	51 Lets Have a Smurfy Good Time
23 You Make Me Fell Like a Winner	52 You're In a Class by Yourself
24 Don't Be Shy	53 Have Smurfy Dreams?
25 Home, Smurf Home!	54 She Smurfed Me
26 Who Invented Homework?	55 I Love My Smurfs
27 We Make Great Music Together!	56 Don't Just Stand There Smurf Me
28 Smurf Appeal	
29 Tomorrow's Monday	

SMURF TATTOOS (288)   TWO SIZES

Gee Mom, how would you like the kids to be running around with Smurf tattoos all over their faces and arms and legs? Topps thought it was a good idea—they've produced a lot of tattoo sets over the years—so they made up 12 sheets of Smurf tattoos, 24 tattoos to the sheet, and distributed them in 1982. There are 288 color designs on the 24 sheets (although it appears that some designs are repeated) and these are colored with "food approved colors."

ITEM	MINT	EX
Set	7.00	4.50
Sheet	.50	.35
Wrapper	--	.50
Box	--	2.50

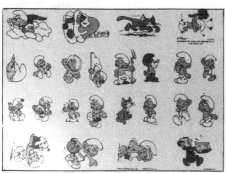

COLLECT ALL 12 DIFFERENT SHEETS

1 SHEET OF 24 TATTOOS
FOOD APPROVED COLORS

SNEEKIES PLASTIC (12 SHEETS) STICKERS

VARIOUS SIZES

The idea behind Fleer's "Sneekies" was simple: replace the traditional, time-consuming methods of mutilating footwear (messy ink pens, etc.) with "instant" plastic grafitti. Each 2 1/2" X 4 1/4" sheet (12 in the set) contained 12 thin plastic stickers of varying sizes. As if the method of application wasn't immediately apparent, an instruction card was inserted in every pack. This card was printed with some impossible preconditions: "sneakers must be dry & free of dust & dirt" —who ever heard of a pair of kid's sneakers that were clean and dry? "Sneekies" was first reported by Barker in his June 1971 "Updates."

ITEM	MINT	EX
Set	27.50	20.00
Sticker sheet	2.00	1.50
Card	1.00	.75
Wrapper	--	5.00

SNOOTS (71K)

2 1/2" X 3 1/2"

Imagine millions of children across the U.S. with "Snoot" cards on their noses, trying to ride bicycles, climb trees, or play soccer. Now imagine thousands of hospital emergency rooms filled with children who had collided with one another or with scores of inanimate objects. Sounds implausible? Maybe so, but this scenario could have come to pass if "Snoots," the "Crazy Collector Cards You Wear On Your Nose" had, for example, become as popular as Garbage Pail Kids were (once upon a time). I can tell you for a fact that very small children would have been the victims because the nose holes in these cards are very small. The series was the brainstorm of the Continental Candy Co. of Denmark and it was also marketed in Canada, Great Britain, Ireland, France, and Australia. Since we have not heard any reports of mass juvenile collisions in those countries, we can assume that "Snoots," had the same commercial success "over there" as they did here. Each color artwork card has a nose hole in the middle and the character and a joke about him are printed on the back. Number 71 is the highest card seen to date. The wrapper is orange, black, purple and white and each pack contained five cards and a stick of gum.

ITEM	MINT	EX
Card	.15	.10
Wrapper	--	.25

SNOTTY SIGNS (24)

4 15/16" SQ.

Topps carried its obsession with "gross" design too far in "Snotty Signs." Three signs were pulled from the original series that was "tested" and they were blacked out by hand on the "test" wrapper (see test Nos. 11, 14, & 19 in checklist). When the "regular" series was released, the wrapper indicated that three more signs (see regular Nos. 1, 4, & 23 in checklist) had been replaced. However, "replacement" sign No. 1, "School Really Stinks" has not been found and collectors have reported finding test titles Nos. 4 & 23 in both test and regular packs. The regular wrapper listing for Nos. 21 & 22 is also incorrect: sign No. 21 is always "Falling Dandruff Zone" and sign No. 22 is always "Roach Resort."

Summary of changes & values: No. 1 in test was theoretically changed but is the only sign found for this number; No. 4 test is confirmed ($4) and may be found in both test & regular packs; No. 11 test has not been confirmed; No. 14 test has not been confirmed; No. 19 test has been found ($8); No. 23 is found in test & regular packs ($4). Note: set prices listed are for "regular" issue signs only.

ITEM	MINT	EX
Set	18.00	14.50
Sign	.75	.60
Wrappers		
Regular	—	1.00
Test	—	12.50
Box	—	15.00

NO. 6 OF 24

PEEL OFF STICKER BACKING.
STICK SIGN ANYWHERE!

DISTRIBUTED BY:
©1986 TOPPS CHEWING GUM, INC.
DURYEA, PA. 18642.
MADE IN TAIWAN.

1   T: School Sucks
    R: School Really Stinks*

2   T: Danger: Zit Zone
    R: Danger: Zit Zone

3   T: Mutants Keep Out
    R: Mutants Keep Out

4   T: Caution: Smart A-- Inside**
    R: Caution: Smart Kid Inside

5   T: No Homework Beyond This Point
    R: No Homework Beyond This Point

6   T: Boogers Are Beautiful
    R: Boogers Are Beautiful

7   T: This Toilet Stinks
    R: This Toilet Stinks

8   T: Smell My Socks
    R: Smell My Socks

9   T: Danger: Human Gas Leak
    R: Danger: Human Gas Leak

10   T: Toxic Waste Area
    R: Toxic Waste Area

11   T: Date In Bed***
    R: Pass Gas on Left

12   T: Condemned By Board of Health
    R: Condemned By Board of Health

13   T: Psycho On Premises
    R: Psycho On Premises

14   T: Horny Child Inside***
    R: Homework Copied Here

15   T: Bed Dangerous When Wet
    R: Bed Dangerous When Wet

16   T: Teacher in Closet
    R: Teacher in Closet

17   T: Nerds Keep Out
    R: Nerds Keep Out

18   T: I Barf For Nerds
    R: I Barf For Nerds

19   T: Dad's Drunk Again***
    R: Hold Nose When Passing

20   T: I [Love] Privacy
    R: I [Love] Privacy

21   T: Falling Dandruff Zone
    R: Falling Dandruff Zone

22   T: Roach Resort
    R: Roach Resort

23   T: Gone To School (Damn It)**
    R: Gone To School (Darn It)

24   T: No Pukes
    R: No Pukes

SNOTTY SIGNS STICKERS (44)   2 1/2" X 3 1/2"

Topps' fascination with some of the grosser liabilities attendant to human existence continued in 1986 with this 44-sticker set. The fronts of the cards have three front-peel stickers —one large and two small. The stickers closely resemble those automobile signs currently in vogue except, of course, for the "shock value" messages they contain. The cardboard backing of the stickers is printed on back with puzzle pieces (36) and puzzle preview cards (eight).

ITEM	MINT	EX
Set	6.50	4.50
Sticker	.15	.10
Wrapper	––	.35
Box	––	5.00

Baby Barf On Bed
Bazooka On Seat
Bed Dangerous When Wet
Boogers Are Beautiful
Born to Cut Class
Caution: School Kills
Caution: Smart Kid Inside
Condemned by Board of Health
Danger: Human Gas Leak
Danger: Zit Zone
Dirty Laundry Under Bed
Don't Slip On Barf
Expensive Radio in Car
Falling Dandruff Zone
Geek Crossing
Gone to School (Darn It)
Hold Nose When Passing
Homework Copied Here
I Barf for Nerds
I Love Privacy
Mutants Keep Out
Nerd Crossing Drive Fast

Nerds Keep Out
No Homework Allowed
No Pukes
One Hour Puking
Pass Gas on Left
Psycho on Premises
Roach Resort
Roaches in Hot Lunch
Say It With Spit
School Lunches Cause Hunger
School Really Stinks
Sis Is Gross
Smelly Socks On Student
Smell My Socks
Snot Under Seat
Teacher in Closet
This Toilet Stinks
Toxic Waste Area
Warning: Cook Spits in Food
Warning: Dog on Doody
Warning: Killer Breath
Zits Popped Here

SNOW WHITE ALBUM STICKERS (225) 2 1/16" X 2 9/16"

Almost 50 years after Walt Disney's classic movie "Snow White and the Seven Dwarfs" made its debut, Panini U.S.A. produced an album sticker set to commemorate the occasion. All of the 225 stickers in the series contain color scenes taken directly from the movie. The sticker backs have the series title printed in six languages, and the sticker number is enclosed in a box. A 32-page album with supplemental text and illustrations retailed for 35 cents. Note: set price includes album.

ITEM	MINT	EX
Set	32.50	22.50
Sticker	.15	.10
Wrapper	--	.35
Album	2.00	1.50

SONGBIRDS OF THE UNITED STATES (50)

1 1/8" X 2 3/4"

This was Series No. 4 in Nabisco's excellent trading card program dedicated to natural history. There are fifty cards in the set, which was marketed in 1965. The artwork and text were once again prepared by H. Wayne Trimm. The birds are identified by their English language names and Latin binomials and are described in a brief text. A wall chart on which to mount the set was available via the mail from Nabisco.

ITEM	MINT	EX
Set	35.00	25.00
Card	.60	.45
Wrapper	—	7.50

1 Red-Headed Woodpecker
2 Scissor-Tailed Flycatcher
3 Catbird
4 Rose-Breasted Grosbeak
5 Eastern Bluebird
6 Redstart
7 Barn Swallow
8 Song Sparrow
9 Red-Bellied Woodpecker
10 Robin
11 Pileated Woodpecker
12 Purple Grackle
13 Cedar Waxwing
14 Red-Winged Blackbird
15 Downy Woodpecker
16 Verdin
17 Varied Thrush
18 Horned Lark
19 Cardinal
20 Prothonetary Warbler
21 Clark's Nutcracker
22 Yellow-Headed Blackbird
23 Mockingbird
24 Dipper
25 Evening Grosbeak
26 Steller's Jay
27 Yellow Warbler
28 Vesper Sparrow
29 Ruby-Throated Hummingbird
30 Mountain Bluebird
31 Dickcissel
32 Goldfinch
33 Lark Bunting
34 House Finch
35 American Magpie
36 Pyrrhuloxia
37 Brown Thrasher
38 Wood Thrush
39 Tufted Titmouse
40 Vermilion Flycatcher
41 Chestnut-Collared Longspur
42 Western Meadowlark
43 Calliope Humming Bird
44 Sage Thrasher
45 Snow Bunting
46 Black-Capped Chickadee
47 Gray-Crowned Rosy Finch
48 Loggerhead Shrike
49 Blue Grosbeak
50 White-Crowned Sparrow

SOUPY SALES (66)

2 1/2" X 3 1/2"

All the black and white photos in this 66-card Topps set seem to have been taken from one episode of the Soupy Sales television show. The obverses have white borders and a facsimile autograph in blue ink. The backs contain a feature called "Soupy Sez;" the card number is located under this. It appears that some 66-card printing sheets were reversed, so that all the cards in the set may be found with two different numbers. Cards made of thin paper were wallet inserts and are not part of this set.

ITEM	MINT	EX
Set	225.00	190.00
Card	3.00	2.50
Wrapper	—	35.00
Box	—	100.00

1 Girdles Don't Lie — They Just Redistribute the Truth!
2 Keep Your Nails Clean — and You Won't Have a Dirty Hammer!
3 Things Always Look Greener — in the Other Guy's Wallet!
4 Let a Smile Be Your Umbrella — If You Like to Gargle Snow!
5 A Good Day's Work Never Hurt Anyone — and Neither Did a Good Day's Rest!
6 When Things Look Black — Send Them to the Laundry!
7 Don't Take a Bath in the Front Room — You Might Leave a Ring Around the Walls!
8 Don't Kiss a Girl Under the Mistletoe — It's More Fun Kissing Her Under the Nose!
9 People Who Live in Glass Houses — Should Dress in the Basement!
10 It's Always Easier to Control Your Temper — When the Other Guy Is Bigger!
11 It's Better to Give Than Receive — Especially If It's a Punch in the Mouth!
12 Don't Tell Anybody That You Have False Teeth — Unless It Comes Out in a Conversation!
13 Don't Bite Your Nails — They're for Hanging Up Things!
14 Look for the Silver Lining — and You'll Have the Most Expensive Jacket in Town!
15 The Way to a Man's Heart Is Through His Stomach — But Don't Let a Doctor Know This!
16 If Your Girl Swears She's Never Been Kissed — She Has a Right to Swear!
17 Don't Bite Your Nails — Especially If You're a Carpenter!
18 If You Can't Brush After Every Meal — Comb!
19 Love Your Enemies — Boy! Will It Confuse Them!
20 Don't Feed Lemons to Your Cat — or You'll Have a Sour Puss!
21 Do a Good Turn Every Day — Even If It Makes You Dizzy!
22 The World Is Your Oyster — But the Pearl Belongs to the Guy Next Door!
23 Never Kick a Man When He's Down — Unless You're a Professional Wrestler!
24 Don't Cry Over Spilled Milk — There's Enough Water in It Already!
25 Don't Let Grass Grow Under Your Feet — It Tickles!
26 Be True to Your Teeth — And They Won't Be False to You!
27 Don't Play with Daddy's Pipe — He Doesn't Smoke Your Toys!
28 If Your Rug Wears Out, Don't Get a New One — Have the Soles of Your Feet Carpeted!
29 Blood Is Thicker Than Water — So Is Toothpaste!
30 Before You Hang Your Clothes — Make Sure They Get a Fair Trial!
31 Show Me a Baby with Fever — and I'll Show You a Hotsy Totsy!
32 If Your Date Won't Kiss You in a Canoe — Paddle Her Back!
33 Show Me a Pineapple That Plays the Trumpet — and I'll Show You a Tutti Fruitti!

Soupy Sales

34 The Best Things in Life Are Free — If You've Got the Necessary Box Top!

35 If Your Wife Wants to Learn How to Drive — Don't Stand in Her Way!

36 Keep Your Chin Up — It'll Keep the Milk from Dripping on Your Clothes!

37 Don't Bite Your Nails — or Your Stomach Will Need a Manicure!

38 Show Me a Beatnik Bird That Sings — and I'll Show You a Hairy Canary!

39 There's Only One Disadvantage in Arriving on Time...There's Nobody There to Appreciate It!

40 If You Want to Be the Center of Attention — Ask for Catsup in a Chinese Restaurant!

41 If You Brush Your Teeth Twice a Year — See Your Dentist Every Day!

42 Never Talk About a Butter Knife — You Know How Those Things Spread!

43 If Your Biscuits Look Pink — Maybe You're Cruller Blind!

44 If You Get the Key to the City — Make Sure You Check All the Locks — and the Bagels, too!

45 Don't Spill Food on the Floor — It Might Give the Termites Indigestion!

46 Don't Drop Out of School — Especially If You're on the Third Floor!

47 Don't Play in the Street — You Might Get That Run Down Feeling!

48 Watch Your Weight — or You'll Have More Chins Than a Chinese Phone Book!

49 If You Want to Create a Big Stir — Build Yourself a Prison!

50 Don't Spread Rumors at the Laundromat — Unless You're Willing to Come Clean!

51 Where There's a Will — There Are Relatives!

52 Don't Kiss Your Girl While She's Brushing Her Teeth — You'll Get a Paste in the Mouth!

53 Cross the Street with the Light — If You Can Rip It Out of the Pavement!

54 Exercise Keeps Germs Away — If You Can Get Them to Do Pushups, You're in!

55 If You Get Tied Up on the Phone — Get Someone to Cut You Loose!

56 People Who Live in Glass Houses — Should Invite Sophia Loren over the the Week-End!

57 He Who Laughs Last — Usually Sits in the Last Row in the Balcony!

58 Here's a Sure Way to Keep Your Bills Down! — Use a Heavier Paperweight!

59 He Who Hesitates — Gets Bumped from the Rear!

60 Girls Who Eat Sweets — Take Up Two Seats!

61 Many a True Word Has Been Spoken — Through False Teeth!

62 If You Try to Pull the Wool Over Someone's Eyes — Don't Use the Wrong Yarn!

63 Music Soothes the Savage Beast — If a Lion Breaks into Your House, Turn Up Your Record Player!

64 Don't Talk About Carousels — You Know How Those Things Get Around!

65 Early to Bed and Early to Rise — And You Won't Have Red in the Whites of your Eyes!

66 It's Easy to Get Kids to Look Up to You — Just Walk in and Turn Off the TV Set!

SPACE CANDY (19K)

A series of smaller-than-standard-size cards manufactured by the Taylor-Reed Corp. of Connecticut, "Space Candy" is somewhat of a mystery set to collectors. The set title is taken from the back of the card but no packaging has been reported to

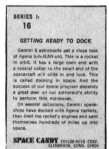

2 1/8" X 3"

date. Each card has two tiny nubs on two sides, indicating that cards were attached to one another in some fashion originally. The color pictures on front seem to be standard NASA pool photos and the date of issue, judging from the Apollo 11 material, would appear to be 1968 or 1969. The card number, caption, text, and the words "Series 1" are printed on the back. Despite the latter, no subsequent series has been reported to the Hobby Card Index as of this time.

ITEM	MINT	EX
Card	1.00	.75

SPACE DEFENDERS (19)

Aris	Matador	Thor
Atlas	Minuteman	Titan II
Blue Scout	Pershing	Titan III
Bomarc	Polaris A-3	TLM-18
Cape Kennedy	Redstone	Transit 4B
Jupiter	Snark	Vanguard
Mace		

2 1/4" X 3 1/4"

One of the first recorded trading cards sets issued within the U.S. Government, "Space Defenders" is the futuristic name of a 19-card series depicting "Military Missiles and Satellites Launched From Cape Kennedy Air Force Station, Florida." The fronts of the cards have black and white photos surrounded by white borders. The backs describe each missile and give pertinent unclassified details as provided by the Office of Information, Patrick Air Force Base, Florida (the installation in charge of the Air Force Eastern Test Range). The cards were printed on thin cardboard stock and came attached in five rows of four cards each. The twentieth card was a header card bearing the set title and description. Note: detached cards cannot be graded mint.

ITEM	MINT	EX
Set	--	22.50
Card	--	1.00

SPACE-PAK (10)

One of the very first non-fiction space sets to hit the hobby was this ten-card series issued by the Space-Pak Company (New York) in 1962. There are nine numbered cards plus one un-

2 1/2″ X 3 1/2″

numbered header/introduction card and the latter is marked "Set #1." (No subsequent sets have been reported.) The advertising copy on the header card reads as follows: "Keep up with America's Space Program - Start your SPACE LIBRARY - Learn to identify AMERICA'S ROCKETS, SATELLITES, SPACE PROBE VEHICLES." Since manned space flight by American astronauts had not yet occurred, all the cards show models or artwork depictions of space activities. The original price in 1962 for a set of ten cards was 10¢; collectors can expect to pay $10-$15 for a set today.

Header card	5 Project Apollo
1 Project Ranger	6 Moon Base
2 Orbiting Geophysical Observatory	7 Exploring Space
3 Building a Lunar Satellite	8 Project Mercury
4 Goose Missile	9 Agena Rocket Engine

SPACE: 1999 (66)

2 1/2″ X 3 1/2″

The Space 1999 series of 66 cards was issued by Donruss in 1976 and was based upon the television series starring Martin Landau and Barbara Bain. The color picture has a black frame line and white borders. The caption and number appear within the field of the picture to the bottom-left. All the reverses are puzzle backs.

ITEM	MINT	EX
Set	15.00	10.00
Card	.20	.15
Wrapper	––	.50
Box	––	10.00

1 Dr. Russell and Paul Morrow Are Frightened by the Unknown.
2 Comdr. Koenig and His Landing Party Are Trapped on a Frozen Alien Planet.
3 Comdr. Koenig and Dr. Russell Investigate a New Planet.
4 Aerial View of Moon Base Alpha.
5 Moon Base Alpha's Communication Devices.
6 Comdr. Koenig Is Kidnapped by an Alien Race.
7 Dr. Helena Russell Aids the Wounded Prof. Bergman.
8 Sandra Is Hurt as Her Eagle Crash-lands on the Moon.
9 Alpha Astronaut Comes to the Aid of a Crashed Eagle.
10 A Gruesome Alien Creature Attacks Eagle 1.
11 Alpha Astronauts Find a Mysterious Container.
12 Alpha Astronauts Check for Radiation Leaks.
13 Comdr. Koenig and Dr. Russell Come Face to Face with Terror.
14 Alpha Astronaut Checking Security System.
15 Eagle's Eye View of Moon Base Alpha.
16 Alpha Astronauts Search for Their Lost Comrades.
17 Dr. Russell Discovers Human Skeleton on an Alien Planet.

18 Comdr. Koenig and Dr. Russell Plead for Safety of Moon Base Alpha with an Alien.
19 Comdr. Koenig Aims His Laser Rifle Against an Enemy Alien.
20 Lt. Carter Holds a Robot Ruler Hostage on an Alien Planet.
21 Comdr. Koenig Saves Dr. Russell from Hostile Enemies.
22 A Fleet of Hawks.
23 Main Mission Control Is Attacked by Deadly Alien Foam.
24 Eagle 1 Preparing to Land.
25 The Beautiful but Deadly Planet Zenno.
26 Comdr. Koenig Prepares Eagle 1 for Lift Off.
27 Alpha Security Men Capture Alien.
28 Prof. Bergman Invents an Anti-Gravitational Device.
29 A Laser Equipped Eagle Attacks an Alien Vessel.
30 Comdr. Koenig's Brain Is Probed as His Companions Look on Helplessly.
31 Lt. Carter Relays a Message to Eagle 1.
32 Main Mission Personnel Combating a Deadly Alien Foam.
33 An Enemy Consuming Monster Threatens Moon Base Alpha.

34 Lt. Carter and Landing Party Are Attacked by a Giant Robot.
35 Alien Space Ship Is Captured.
36 An Eagle Crash Lands on the Moon's Surface.
37 Alpha Astronauts Investigate Nuclear Waste Deposit Area.
38 Dr. Russell and Prof. Bergman Discover a New Form of Life in Outer Space.
39 Comdr. Koenig Searches the Planet Peri.
40 Alpha Astronauts Face Danger As They are Exposed to Radiation.
41 Alpha Crew Lost on the Planet Ultima Thule.
42 Main Mission Crew Fights Deadly Alien Foam.
43 Prof. Bergman Analyzing X-Rays.
44 Prof. Bergman and Comdr. Koenig Discover a Malfunction in the Life Support System.
45 An Alien Killer Escapes from Security Guards.
46 Alpha Astronauts Signaling Danger.
47 Alpha Members Trying to Communicate with a Celestial Being.
48 Alpha Crew Members Bringing Supplies to a Wounded Alien.
49 Main Mission Command Gazes Upon a Possible New Home.

50 Prof. Bergman Welcomes Comdr. Koenig to Moon Base Alpha.
51 Two Alpha Astronauts Discover Magnetic Radiation.
52 Alpha Astronaut Trying to Remove Deadly Canister of Nuclear Waste.
53 Dr. Russell and Comdr. Koenig Aid Paul Morrow.
54 Dr. Russell is Captured by a Race of Cannibals.
55 Alpha Astronauts Calculate Speed of Runaway Moon.
56 Comdr. Koenig Discusses Their Chance for Survival.
57 Dr. Russell and Comdr. Koenig Checking for Water Contamination.
58 Dr. Russell and Comdr. Koenig Face a New Danger.
59 Eagle Lifts Off Launch Pad.
60 Comdr. Koenig Receives a Distress Call from Lt. Carter.
61 Alpha Astronauts Search for Mineral Deposits.
62 Comdr. Koenig and Dr. Russell; Leaders of the Moon Base Alpha Colony.
63 Nuclear Waste Disposal Area No. 2.
64 Alien Invaders Scheme to Take Over Moon Base Alpha.
65 Dr. Russell Analyzes a Medical Computer Readout.
66 On an Alien Planet, Arkadia, Comdr. Koenig Discovers the Origins of the Planet Earth.

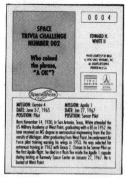

"Space Shots," the first trading card effort of Houston-based Space Ventures, has been acclaimed by collectors as the finest non-fiction space series ever produced. The first edition of 110 cards contains some of the most spectacular color photographs imaginable and these are complemented by authoritative text which is fascinating to read. Every detail on the cards, both front and back, was carefully designed to create a visual feast for the collector. It is a splendid chronicle of our space program, from the appalling moments of tragedy to the splendid triumphs of America's astronauts on the surface of the moon. Twenty-five percent of the profits from the card set have been donated to the Astronauts Memorial Foundation and collectors have been invited to participate in a $150,000 "Space Trivia Challenge" set up by Space Ventures. Series 1 was distributed in 1990 in 12-card gumless foil packages or could be purchased in complete sets from the manufacturer. When pulled up, the lid of the display box is cleverly engineered to present a launch scene in which the top section of the rocket and shuttle extend past the end of the box.

ITEM	MINT	EX
Set	20.00	15.00
Card	.20	.15
Wrapper	--	.25
Box	--	2.50

0001 The Astronauts Memorial
0002 Frank Borman
0003 STS-41B 1st Untethered EVA
0004 Edward H. White II
0005 STS 41-B 1st Landing at KSC
0006 Thomas P. Stafford
0007 STS 41-D "Frisbee" Deployment
0008 James A. Lovell
0009 SKYLAB 1 - After Repair in Orbit
0010 Charles D. Walker
0011 Space Station Freedom
0012 GEMINI 9 - The Approach to Agena
0013 APOLLO 15 - Irwin Salutes The Flag
0014 GEMINI 10 - Launch
0015 GEMINI 11 - Gordon EVA
0016 GEMINI 11 - Agena
0017 APOLLO 7 - Launch
0018 APOLLO 7 - Third Stage Over Cape
0019 APOLLO 8 - Launch
0020 APOLLO 8 - Far Side Of The Moon
0021 FRIENDSHIP 7 - 1st U.S. Orbital Flight*
0022 APOLLO 8 - First Whole Earth
0023 APOLLO 9 - Scott EVA
0024 APOLLO 10 - CSM Over Lunar Surface
0025 APOLLO 10 - Pacific Dawn Landing
0026 APOLLO LUNAR MODULE
0027 FREEDOM 7 1st U.S. Manned Flight
0028 APOLLO 11 - LM Pulls Away From CM
0029 APOLLO 16 - CSM And Earthrise
0030 FAITH 7 - Launch
0031 APOLLO 11 - First Moonprint
0032 APOLLO 11 - Tranquility Base
0033 APOLLO 11 - Lift-off From The Moon
0034 APOLLO 11 - LM Ascent To CM
0035 APOLLO 12 - LM Over Crater Ptolemaeus
0036 APOLLO 13 - Damaged CSM
0037 APOLLO 14 - LM Lift-Off

0038 APOLLO 15 - 1st Lunar Rover
0039 APOLLO 14 - Tracks On Moon
0040 Walter M. Schirra, Jr.
0041 GEMINI SPACECRAFT
0042 APOLLO 15 - Young At Lunar Rover
0043 APOLLO 17 - Schmitt With Flag
0044 APOLLO 17 - Schmitt In Lunar Rover
0045 APOLLO 17 - CM From LM
0046 APOLLO 17 - "Split Rock"
0047 APOLLO 17 - Evans EVA
0048 STS 61-B EVA Assembly Of EASE
0049 SKYLAB 1 - EVA Repair
0050 JUPITER - The Giant Planet
0051 SKYLAB 3 - Solar Flare
0052 LUNAR ROVING VEHICLE
0053 THE SHUTTLE - On Pad At KSC
0054 STS 1 1st Shuttle Launch
0055 STS 1 1st Shuttle Landing
0056 APOLLO 1 - Crew
0057 NEPTUNE - The Blue Planet
0058 APOLLO 8 - A Mission Of Firsts
0059 SATURN - From Hubble
0060 GEMINI 4 - Crew
0061 Checklist
0062 Alan L. Bean
0063 VENUS - The Sister Planet
0064 Donald "Deke" Slayton
0065 URANUS - From Voyager 2
0066 Eugene A. Cernan
0067 STS 41-G 1st Female EVA
0068 STS 51 - A Rescue of Westar
0069 STS 51-A "For Sale"
0070 STS 51-1 Rescue of Leasat-3
0071 STS 51-1 Fisher On RMS Arm
0072 MARS - The Red Planet
0073 STS 26 "Return To Flight"
0074 APOLLO 17 - Cernan On Lunar Surface

0075 NEW YORK - From Space
0076 SKYLAB 2 - Moonrise
0077 GEMINI 3 - Launch
0078 GEMINI 4 - 1st Self-Propelled EVA
0079 GEMINI 4 - Inside Capsule
0080 SAN FRANCISCO - From Space
0081 STS 30 Magellan Deployment
0082 GEMINI 7 - First Rendezvous
0083 SKYLAB 3 - Approach To Skylab
0084 Walter Cunningham
0085 APOLLO/SOUYUZ TEST MISSION
0086 MERCURY SPACECRAFT
0087 APOLLO 16 - Jump And Salute
0088 GEMINI 9 - "Angry Alligator"
0089 STS 2 Launch
0090 STS 5 1st Satellite Deployment
0091 APOLLO 14 - Shepard On The Moon
0092 STS 6 1st Shuttle EVA
0093 STS 7 Challenger From SPAS
0094 STS 8 Night Launch
0095 SKYLAB - The Craft
0096 STS 41-B MMU
0097 APOLLO 17 - Last Earthrise
0098 STS 41-C Capture Of Solar Max
0099 APOLLO 11 - Launch
0100 Alan B. Shepard, Jr.
0101 FREEDOM 7 - Shepard's Recovery
0102 Michael Collins
0103 GEMINI 6 - 1st Rendezvous
0104 Charles "Pete" Conrad, Jr.
0105 APOLLO 8 - 1st Earthrise
0106 Richard F. Gordon, Jr.
0107 APOLLO 11 - Aldrin Moonwalk
0108 James A. McDivitt
0109 GEMINI 4 - 1st U.S. Spacewalk
0110 Buzz Aldrin

SPACE SHOTS — SERIES 2 (110)   2 1/2" X 3 1/2"

The second series of "Space Shots," advertised as a "Commemorative Edition" by the manufacturer, made its debut in 1991. Among the 110 cards in the set are 20 marking the anniversary of specific NASA missions (0136-0155), plus more astronaut portraits and breathtaking views from space. As with Series 1, Space Ventures offered Series 2 in two ways: in 12-card packs and as complete sets. The wrapper is the same color as previously used but the shuttle design in center is now an actual photograph rather than artwork. The words "Series Two" are clearly printed at the bottom. The display box is a deeper shade of blue, and while it does not have the striking launch graphic used on the first series box, it is decorated with entirely new card images from Series 2. Space Ventures also made some worthwhile changes in its factory set, replacing the clear plastic case with a handsome small box and inserting a "Moon-Mars" cards as a bonus. For this reason, the factory set is listed at a slightly higher price than sets assembled from individual packs. Note: Series 1 factory sets were "sealed" with a plain foil sticker; Series 2 factory set boxes are made of cardboard and are not sealed.

APOLLO 11 - Aldrin Near LM Leg

ITEM	MINT	EX
Factory set	20.00	—
Set (from packs)	18.00	11.50
Card	.15	.10
Wrapper	—	.15
Box	—	2.00

0111 Neil A. Armstrong
0112 Apollo 11 Crew
0113 Virgil I. Grissom
0114 Gordon L. Cooper, Jr.
0115 Scott M. Carpenter
0116 Bill Dana, A.K.A. Jose Jimenez
0117 James R. Irwin
0118 Harrison "Jack" Schmitt
0119 Charles M. Duke, Jr.
0120 Edgar D. Mitchell
0121 Alfred M. Worden
0122 Stuart A. Roosa
0123 Fred W. Haise, Jr.
0124 Owen K. Garriot
0125 Edward G. Gibson
0126 Pogue and Carr - "Magic Trick"
0127 Jack R. Lousma
0128 Mike Mullane - Onboard Atlantis
0129 John M. Fabian
0130 Bruce McCandless II
0131 George "Pinky" Nelson
0132 Joe Allen - On Columbia's Flight Deck
0133 Bill Nelson
0134 Bobko and Williams - Juggling Fruit
0135 Leonov and Slayton - Apollo-Soyuz
0136 30th Anniversary - Mercury 2
0137 30th Anniversary - Freedom 7
0138 30th Anniversary - Liberty Bell 7
0139 25th Anniversary - Gemini 8
0140 25th Anniversary - Surveyor 1
0141 25th Anniversary - Gemini 9
0142 25th Anniversary - Gemini 10
0143 25th Anniversary - Gemini 11
0144 25th Anniversary - Gemini 12
0145 20th Anniversary - Apollo 14
0146 20th Anniversary - Apollo 15
0147 20th Anniversary - Mariner 9

0148 15th Anniversary - Viking 1
0149 15th Anniversary - Viking 2
0150 10th Anniversary - STS 1
0151 10th Anniversary - STS 2
0152 10th Anniversary - Voyager 2 At Saturn
0153 5th Anniversary - STS 61C
0154 5th Anniversary - Voyager 2 At Uranus
0155 5th Anniversary - STS 51L - Challenger
0156 Gemini 4 - White EVA
0157 Gemini 9 - Cernan Spacewalk
0158 Apollo 7 - After Liftoff
0159 Apollo 8 - Full Moon
0160 Apollo 9 - LM From CM
0161 Apollo 10 - Whole Earth
0162 Apollo 11 - Liftoff
0163 Apollo 11 - Aldrin Near LM Leg
0164 Apollo 11 - Setting Up Flag
0165 Apollo 11 - LM With Earthrise
0166 Apollo 11 - LM Inside Third Stage
0167 Apollo 12 - Bean Deploying ALSEP
0168 Apollo 12 - Conrad At Suveyor 3
0169 Apollo 13 - Launch
0170 Apollo 16 - Duke At Rover
0171 Apollo 17 - Whole Earth
0172 Apollo 17 - Cernan Salutes Flag
0173 Apollo 17 - Schmitt Drives Rover
0174 Skylab 2 - Garriot EVA
0175 Apollo-Soyuz - Soyuz Launch
0176 STS-1 - On Pad With Superimposed Moon
0177 STS 41B - Stewart with MMU
0178 STS 41C - Tumbling EVA
0179 STS 41C - Nelson At Solar Max
0180 STS 41C - LDEF Deployment
0181 STS 51A - Allen Maneuvers Satellite
0182 STS 51D - Working On RMS Arm
0183 STS 51J - Atlantis' Maiden Voyage
0184 STS 51J - Atlantis Climbs Into Orbit

0185 STS 61B - Checking Joints On ACCESS
0186 STS 30 - Deployment Of Magellan
0187 STS 34 - Galileo Deployment
0188 STS 32 - LDEF Recovery
0189 STS 31 - Hubble Deployment
0190 STS 31 - Hubble In Orbit
0191 STS 41 - Ulysses Deployment
0192 STS 35 - Astro Deployed
0193 STS 37 - Gamma Ray Observatory
0194 Moon From Galileo
0195 Galileo - Color Visualization Of Moon
0196 Neptune From Voyager 2
0197 Jupiter From Voyager 1
0198 Solar Flare From SKYLAB 3
0199 Mars From Hubble
0200 Mars - Olympus Mons
0201 Saturn "Burps"
0202 Mercury Mosaic
0203 Jupiter's Moon Io
0204 Venus From Magellan
0205 Jupiter Moon Montage
0206 Saturn Moon Montage
0207 Voyager 2 - Uranus Flyby
0208 Solar Sail
0209 Biosphere 2
0210 Spacecraft at Neptune
0211 Galileo Passing Io
0212 Omega Centauri From Astro
0213 Galaxy M-81 From Astro
0214 Supernova 1987A From Hubble
0215 Redesigned Space Station Freedom
0216 Industrial Space Facility
0217 Mars Observer Mission
0218 Astronauts Exploring Mars
0219 The Astronauts Memorial
0220 Checklist - Series 2

SPEC SHEET (66)

Although the wrappers and box for this Donruss product say "Hot Rod," the series is called "Spec Sheet" by collectors because that is the heading which appears on the back of the cards. The set was first reported in the Barker Updates of January 1966, so it was issued in 1965. There are 88 cards in the set. The fronts have uncaptioned color photos of hot rods; the backs contain the card number, a descriptive text, and advertising for "Hot Rod Magazine."

ITEM	MINT	EX
Set	150.00	110.00
Card	2.00	1.50
Wrappers (2)		
each	--	20.00
Box	--	50.00

1	Bonneville Streamliner	23	Well Dressed Mill
2	Ready to Go	24	Custom Pick-Up
3	Blown Ford Engine	25	Bob-Tailed "T"
4	"Triple Threat 'vette"	26	Fiery Chevy
5	1925 "T" Roadster	27	Offy Engine
6	Show Winner	28	334 Cubic Inches
7	Ageless Street Rod	29	Points Champion
8	315 Horsepower	30	Abandoned
9	700 Horsepower	31	Salt Flats
10	Hot Rod Fever	32	Experimental Roadster
11	East African Safari	33	Modified Sport Car
12	Beauty and Comfort	34	Instant Roadster
13	Record Runs	35	1923 Dodge
14	Pair Duces	36	L.A. Roadsters
15	Six Pots	37	137 Quarter
16	'64 Buick Mill	38	A Real Winner
17	What a Machine	39	Cruising Model A
18	Dodge Super Stock	40	Mark 27
19	Kurtis Roadster	41	Owners Pride
20	World's Fastest Class A Coupe	42	Roman Red
21	Super Super Stock	43	Flamed Roadster
22	Hot Rod Dictionary	44	Hot Rod Dictionary
45	Detailed Custom	
46	306 Streamliner	
47	The Wedge	
48	The Oakland National	
49	Hill Climb Champ	
50	Off the Line	
51	Hot Rod Dictionary	
52	Record Holder	
53	Pikes Peak Champ	
54	National Championship	
55	Hot Rod Dictionary	
56	"Boss"	
57	"Indianapolis 500"	
58	Hot Rod Dictionary	
59	Nitro Loaded	
60	Off the Line	
61	Starlighter	
62	National Drags	
63	'35 Custom	
64	Going Cart	
65	Hot Rod Dictionary	
66	Hot Rod Dictionary	

SPEED WHEELS (24)

In 1974, Topps contracted with the English firm "Letraset" to manufacture "Speed Wheels." The package design is very clever: after the pre-scored top, bottom, and right borders are detached, the "package" becomes a "folder" and the enclosed sheet of decals is freed. The two interior pages of the folder make up a color-artwork piece of a 24-part racing course (illustrated on the back of each folder). The enclosed sheet of decals (3 5/32" X 3 11/16") is numbered (24 in set) and contains a selection of color "rub-offs" to be positioned on the track. No gum was packaged with this product. Note: mint prices apply only to packages with borders intact. Decal sheets can be removed from the pack without detaching the borders.

ITEM	MINT	EX
Sets		
Track	85.00	55.00
Decals	70.00	55.00
Track	3.00	2.00
Decal sheet	2.50	2.00
Box	--	30.00

SPOOKING SIZE CANDY CIGARETTE BOXES (?)

2 1/8" X 3 1/4"

This clever group of candy cigarette boxes was distributed by the Four Star Candy Co. The large front and back panels on each box measure 2 1/8" X 3 1/4" and contain the title and artwork for a specific "scare-filtered" brand. Seven different brands have been reported and each has its own "endorsement" by a spooky character (or characters) located on an 11/16" X 3 1/4" side panel. Note: price applies to full box or box carefully flattened with all parts intact.

ITEM	MINT	EX
Box	--	20.00

Spooking Size Candy Cigarettes

Ann Emie (Booport)
Ben Hearse (Ghoul)
Jerkel And Hide (Old Mold)
Licey Roy (Liceroys)
Mort Teeshan (Scent)
Spraynd Bac (Pottersfield)
Stan Van Pyre (Scar 'em)

SPOOK STORIES (144 & ?)

Universal Pictures supplied the "genuine authentic photographs" used by Leaf in this 144-card set issued over a three-year period (1963-65). Each card has a black & white picture that is captioned underneath. The backs are entitled "Spook Stories" and contain a monster-related joke. A black box design in the lower right corner holds the card number and another title, "Spook Talk" (seldom used by collectors). A series of 2 1/4" X 3" gummed-back stickers was also inserted in the packs. These are uncaptioned, so we have illustrated all the known designs.

Cards 1-72 were issued in

"Spook Theatre" wrappers and boxes; Nos. 73-144 were issued in "Son of Spook Theatre" wrappers and boxes. There are a number of color, material, and print variation among the wrappers, so we have assigned a code to each to help with identification and pricing ("1" wrappers are Series 1 and "2" wrappers are Series 2).

1A — Glossy paper & reddish-orange color; no "Bubble Gum" under title; "Authentic Photographs" near shoulder; sign on chest reads "Three Spook Cards In This Package."
1B — Wax wrapper & orange color; words "Bubble Gum" under title; "Genuine Authentic Photographs" near shoulder; sign on chest reads "Extra! Spook Sticker In This Package."

2 1/2" X 3 1/2"

1C — Identical to 1B except no "Bubble Gum" under title.
1D — Identical to 1C except color is lavender.

2A — Wax wrapper is lavender in color.
2B — Wax wrapper is orange in color.

Note: two different pictures reported for No. 12.

ITEM	MINT	EX
Sets		
Series 1	210.00	165.00
Series 2	295.00	260.00
Cards		
Series 1	2.50	2.00
Series 2	3.50	3.00
Sticker	6.00	5.00
Wrappers		
1A	--	200.00
1B	--	85.00
1C	--	60.00
1D	--	60.00
2A	--	80.00
2B	--	110.00
Boxes		
1-"Spook"		
"Bubble Gum"	--	350.00
2-No gum	--	200.00
3-"Son of Spook"		
Regular	--	150.00
4-"All New"	--	250.00

I TOLD THIS WISE GUY NOT
TO TAKE MY PARKING PLACE

SPOOK STORIES

1ST GHOST: That witch is chicken.

2ND GHOST: How do you know?

1ST GHOST: She uses foul language.

Spook Stories

1A

1B

1C

1D

2A

2B

Notice: Beware of counterfeit stickers which have been reproduced on color copiers.

Spook Stories

1. 1961—I Must Have Overslept a Couple of Years!
2. I Brush After Every Meal
3. I Brush Twice a Day!
4. What Are You? Chicken or Something?
5. Mother Said Spinach Puts Hair on Your Chest—But This Is Ridiculous
6. Throw Me the Beach Ball, Dad
7. Whaddaya Mean—Pruneface?
8. Hurry Up Buster My Broomstick Is Double Parked
9. All Right—Where's the Wise Guy with the Soap?
10. Boy—With You on Our Side We'll Have the Best Football Team in the 6th Grade
11. I Hate This Feeling of Something Hanging Over My Head
12. Please Hand Me the Bubble Bath
13. You Knew What I Was When You Married Me—Why Are You Backing Out?
14. You Wont Believe This—But I Have a Cold
15. Relax, Mr. Jones—One More Squeeze and Your Sore Throat Will Be Gone!
16. Watch the Birdie!
17. Did You Say Fish for Dinner—Anyone I Know?
18. I'm Really a Nice Boy—But I Got in Bad Company
19. That Boy Never Could Keep His Feet on the Ground
20. Take It Easy—I Told You I'd Give You the Shirt Off My Back
21. Now Will You Take Your Castor Oil?
22. Last One in Is a Sissy!
23. Don't Get Excited It's Only Your Mummy!
24. I'm Not Very Pretty—But I'm Mighty Cute!
25. Oh! Oh! Now I Really Put My Foot in It!
26. There's a Full Moon Tonite—and I Turn into a People!
27. My, What Big Tonsils You Have!
28. I Paid for Dance Lessons—So Let's Dance
29. Tell Your Friend to Quit Hanging Around
30. What Are You Fishing Around for?
31. That's What I Call a Real "Rock Head"
32. May I Have the Next Dance?
33. Please Mommy, Buy Me a Catcher's Mitt
34. Shut Off That Air Conditioner
35. Honey—Please Change Laundries
36. Anybody Lose a Second Grade Teacher?
37. No, Sonny—I Don't Want the Ladies Home Journal!
38. That's What I Mean by a Chain Smoker
39. Don't Laugh—Yul Brynner Started Out This Way!
40. Worst Case of Athlete's Feet I've Ever Seen
41. If I Say It Is a Cha-cha—It's a Cha-cha!
42. When Did You First Notice Your Dry Skin Problem?
43. I Said "Spoon" Not "Swoon"
44. No—I'm Not Like All Teachers!
45. I Can't Marry You Baby! I've Got a Career!
46. Yea, But You Should See the Other Guy!
47. Sometimes These Tricks Don't Work!
48. I'm So Mad I Could Slap Your Wrists
49. Dessert, Anyone?
50. Darling, Where Is My Tie?
51. But This Is the New Look
52. But I'll Be Late for School!
53. Doctor—Why Do I Get This Ringing in my Ears?
54. Darling Did You Use My Razor to Shave Your Legs Again?
55. I Said Cut a Rug—Not Cut a Mug
56. Lost a Little Weight, Haven't You Sam?
57. I Think We Dug Too Deep
58. Tricks or Treat?
59. I'm in First Grade, Too
60. Plant You Now Dig You Later!
61. Altogether Now—Three Cheers for the Principal
62. Every Time I Flip that Coin—It Comes Up Heads!
63. I Told This Wise Guy Not to Take My Parking Place
64. I'm Starring in a New TV Show—Father Knows Bats
65. But Mudpacks Are Good for You
66. Look Ma, No Cavities
67. She Tried to Make a Monkey Out of Me
68. Gee, Pop—I Don't Want to Get a Haircut
69. For the Last Time—Stop Talking and Go to Sleep
70. Mother Doesn't Want to Cut Off My Curls!
71. How's This for Size?
72. Look Sharp—Feel Sharp—Be Sharp!
73. This Acts So Much Faster than Aspirin
74. Aren't You Too Old for Blind Man's Bluff?
75.
76. You Didn't Have to Starch the Pajamas!
77. C'mon, Cut It Out!
78. Who Threw That Spitball?
79. Now, Sing Along with Mitch
80. I'll Huff and I'll Puff and I'll Blow Your House Down
81. Don't Fight It—It's Bigger than Both of Us!
82. After 3,000 Years in a Tomb, What Did You Expect?
83. But It's Only 20 Calories!
84. All Right, Martha, I'll Wear a Wedding Ring
85. Make Up Your Mind—I'm Tired of Moving Furniture!
86. Heavens! I Need a Manicure!
87. Coffee, Tea or Milk?
88. These High Notes Sure Are a Strain
89. Eeek! That Ice Cube Was Cold!
90. They Call It the Cleopatra Cut
91.
92. Who Said I'm Bad Luck
93. Party Pooper!
94.
95. They Told Me Stripes Are the Fashion This Year
96. Try Brushing These 3 Times a Day
97. Wow! I Thought You Said This Pool Was Heated!
98. Come Out and Play, Red Riding Hood
99.
100. They Said a Little Dab Will Do It—So What Happened?
101. Oh George—You're So Virile—So Dominating!
102.
103. Who Pulled the Plug?
104. Welcome to the Haunted Hilton
105. Who Let That Cat Out of the Bag?
106. Look, Ma! I'm Flying!
107.
108.
109. Boy—These Texas Dust Storms Are Really Something
110. Teacher—May I Be Excused?
111. It's Not Your Looks, Harold—It's Your Personality
112. Of Course, I'll Volunteer
113. Don't Interrupt Me—I'm Making a Fiery Speech!
114. Flying a Little Low, Weren't You?
115. I'm Here for My Dental Appointment, Miss Jones
116. Hold Still While I Get That Fly
117. I Can't Afford a Candelabra
118. Smile, Darn You—Smile!
119. How Do You Change the Bulb in This Thing?
120. Scratch a Little Lower, Please
121. Quit It, Fellows, I'm Ticklish!
122. Don't Just Stand There—Call the Vet
123. This Is Worse than a Cold on the Chest
124. Don't Just Stand There Grinning—Throw Me a Rope!
125. How Did I Get Roped into This Deal?
126. They Sure Don't Build Them Like They Used to
127. You Said If I Had Talent—Looks Don't Count
128. Tell Me—Is Mommy Still Mad at Me?
129. I Said Fish Fry—Not Fish Fly!
130. Hurry Up Sis—You'll Be Late for Work
131. Mother, Please I'd Rather Do It Myself!
132. You Missed the Apple!
133. Can't You Wait 'til Recess?
134. This Is My Last Blind Date!
135. It Was a Rotten Fight, Ma—I Lost!
136. And I Make 56 Varieties!
137.
138. You Plant Tomatoes, I'll Plant People. O.K.?
139. Did You Ever Have the Feeling Someone Was Staring at You?
140. All Right, Harvey, It's My Turn to Get into the Tub
141. I Told You Goldfish Would Make Better Pets
142.
143. Sir, I'd Like You to Meet Our New Brain Surgeon
144. Look Sharp! Feel Sharp! Be Sharp!

1. • Bubble Gum

2. • No Gum Variety

3. • Regular Issue

4. • "Spook Box" covered with "Son of Spook" sticker

SPORT GOOFY TRADING CARDS (3K)

Collecting "Sport Goofy Trading Cards" can be hazardous to your pocketbook. A single card of this series was printed on 9-pack cartons of Minute Maid fruit drinks and each carton cost between $3.60 and $5.00 (depending on the flavor and the store you bought it in). The company did not offer complete sets, or even tell you how many cards were in the set. Moreover, they printed the cards on the bottom of the packages where they were easily damaged (the sides would have offered more protection). Each Disney artwork scene shows Goofy participating in a specific sport and the cards measure a mere 1/16" more than standard size. Since Sport Goofy cards had to be cut away from the boxes they were printed on, you can also expect to find them with less-than-perfect edges. Very few have reached the hobby at this time and single cards in excellent grade are selling for $1.50 to $2.00 apiece, depending on the sport involved. Note: set issued in late 1990 and early 1991; some may still be on store shelves as of this date.

HISTORY OF GYMNASTICS:

The modern development of gymnastics started in the 19th century. Gymnastics came to be recognized as a form of physical exercise, having not only recreational but therapeutic value and offering a means of developing a high degree of discipline of both mind and body.

The countries that have been strongest in competitive gymnastics in recent years are Japan, the Soviet Union, the United States, East and West Germany and Romania.

SPORTS CARS (66 & 20)

Topps issued the 66-card "Sports Car" series in 1961. Each card measures 2 1/2" X 4 3/4" and has a large color artwork illustration of a snappy "sports" automobile. The titles in our checklist correspond to the large-print portion of the caption which appears under each picture. The license plate stickers advertised on the wrapper measure 1 13/16" X 4 1/4" with the end tab intact and have gummed backs. In the June 1961 Barker Updates, it was reported that there were 24 stickers in the set. However, the 20 which appear in our checklist are the only ones confirmed to date and it is assumed that this is a complete set. Note: card and sticker sets are priced individually.

ITEM	MINT	EX
Sets		
Cards	150.00	110.00
Stickers	100.00	75.00
Card	2.00	1.50
Sticker	4.00	3.00
Wrapper	--	40.00
Box	--	200.00

LOTUS SEVEN SPORTS ROADSTER GREAT BRITAIN

Sports Cars

1 Lotus Seven	13 MGA Twin Cam	25 Porsche 718 RSK	37 Sunbeam Alpine	47 Guilietta Sprint	57 Aurelia 2500GT
2 Abarth-Fiat	14 Mark III	26 Borgward	38 Denzel	48 Ferrari 4.9	58 Gregoire
3 Maserati 3500 GT	15 Moretti	27 Renault	39 Talbot	49 Giulietta Spider	59 Lancia Appia
4 A.C. Aceca	16 Aston-Martin DBR1	28 Borgward RS	40 DKW-1000	50 Ferrari Sports	60 Jaguar XK
5 Maserati 200 SI	17 Morgan	29 Scarab	41 Triumph TR-3	51 Alvis	61 Lister-Chevy
6 Firebird III	18 Austin-Healey	30 Bocar	42 Dual Ghia	52 Testa Rosea	62 Jaguar XK-SS
7 Maserati 5000 GT	19 OSCA 750	31 Simca	43 Volkswagen	53 Elva Courier	63 M-B 300 SL
8 A.C. Ace	20 Sprite	32 Corvette SS	44 Facel Vega	54 Frazer-Nash	64 Jensen 541
9 M-B 190 SL	21 Peerless GT	33 Skoda	45 Volvo P-1800	55 Ferrari 250GT	65 M-B 300 SLR
10 Alfa-Romeo 2000	22 Bentley	34 Stingray	46 Ferrari 250	56 Goggomobil	66 Lotus Elite
11 Austin-Nash	23 Porsche 356 B	35 Stanguellini			
12 Asardo	24 BMW 507	36 Daimler			

Alabama	Minnesota
California	New Jersey
Florida	New York
Georgia	North Carolina
Illinois	Ohio
Indiana	Pennsylvania
Iowa	Tennessee
Kentucky	Texas
Louisiana	Virginia
Massachusetts	Wisconsin

STACKS OF STICKERS (44)

When Topps says "Stacks of Stickers" they mean it! Each sticker card (44 in all) holds 16 5/8" X 7/8" stickers, and if every sticker on every card is different (not confirmed), that makes a total of 704!

According to the production code on the wrapper, the set was issued in 1970. Neither the sheets holding the stickers or the stickers themselves are numbered. Our checklist is arranged alphabetically by the title of the top left sticker on every sheet.

2 1/2" X 3 1/2"

ITEM	MINT	EX
Set	100.00	75.00
Sticker sheet	2.00	1.50
Wrapper	--	25.00

Aaargh	Good Morning!
Blown Mind	Good Noose!
Booby Hatch!	I Can't Stomach You!
Call Me Up	I'm a Little Teapot
Check Your Teeth!	I'm a Swinger
Class Nit Wit	Lend an Ear
Cool It!	Let's Shake!
Compulsive Eater	Nature Abhors a Vacuum
Don't Bolt Your Food!	On Your Toes!
Drive Carefully	Overcharged $5.98
Drop Dead!	Road Hog!
Drop Me a Line!	Shakespeare Wrote Hamlet
Dynamite	The Fuzz
Edison Was a Blub Snatcher	This End (Up)
Eggs-Actly!	Topless Waitress
Far Out	Why Not?
Fish Can't Swim!	You Get My Goat
Fork in the Road	You Turn Me On!
Frankie	Your Days Are Numbered
Get a Haircut!	You're a Nightmare!
Gift Wrap Your Garbage!	You're an Eyesore
Go Fly a Kite	You're Chicken Hearted

STARCOM STICKERS (?)

"DASH"—Col. James Derringer"
© 1987 Coleco Industries, Inc.

Look for additional
STARCOM Stickers in specially marked packages of ZIPLOC® Sandwich Bags

"StarCom Stickers," issued by Ziploc Sandwich Bags in 1987, is a neat little series based on the toy line developed by Coleco. Each Ziploc box contained a 2 1/2" X 6" strip carrying two different types of peel-off stickers. The top sticker measures 2" X 2 13/16" and depicts a StarCom character. It has rounded corners and the character's name is printed beneath the artwork picture. The lower sticker also has rounded corners but is smaller (about 1 7/8" X 2") and is either a named or unnamed StarCom insignia. The color artwork of both types is most attractive. Unfortunately, Ziploc made no mention of the set total on either the sticker strip or the package. Note: prices are for strips with both stickers intact. Peeled stickers cannot be graded excellent or mint.

ITEM	MINT	EX
Strip	1.25	1.00

TWO SIZES

"CANNON"—PFC. Al Evans"
© 1987 Coleco Industries, Inc.

Look for additional
STARCOM Stickers in specially marked packages of ZIPLOC® Sandwich Bags

Look who's reading *Non-Sport Update!*

STAR TREK (72)   2 3/8" X 3 7/16"

This 72-card Star Trek set issued by Leaf in 1967 was withdrawn from the market because of contractual problems and is consequently of short supply. The cards are printed on thin stock and feature black and white photographs taken from the television series. Each photo is captioned in a black panel beneath the picture. The horizontally-aligned backs contain the card number (inside the arrowhead) and a story.

ITEM	MINT	EX
Set	1500.00	1250.00
Card	18.00	15.00
Wrapper	--	250.00
Box	--	600.00

1 No Time for Escape	25 You're Kidding	49 Into a New World
2 Attempted Mutiny	26 Beam Out	50 Tranquilized
3 A Grup Appears	27 Burn Out	51 Time for Shore Leave
4 Come In, Captain Kirk	28 Interference Out	52 Ice Age
5 Murasaki Mischief	29 Not So Funny	53 Ambushed
6 Beam Down to Dawn	30 Prisoner of the Mind	54 Pain of Victory
7 Beside Himself	31 Stalking a Killer	55 Cornered
8 Back Through Time	32 The Earth Killer	56 Jungle Hunt
9 Horta Emerging	33 Fight for Lithium	57 Collision Course
10 Spock's Box	34 Destruction Decision	58 Corbomite Maneuver
11 Spock in Command	35 "Return my Ship"	59 You Give Me a Headache
12 Spock in Command	36 Frozen at the Controls	60 Shore Leave Surprise
13 Befuddled Bones	37 Christmas Present	61 Killer Aboard
14 Prepare to Fire Phasers	38 Amnesia Victim	62 Mindless Man
15 Command Decision	39 Decoy	63 Pirates at Bay
16 Kirk Battles a Gorn	40 Beyond Tomorrow	64 Off Course
17 Phaser Daser	41 Trapped	65 Attack by Nothing
18 Space Race	42 Kirk Outside Spock Inside	66 Funny Little Enemies
19 Fight Fire with Fire	43 Spock Takes a Job	67 Poison Attack!
20 Captain's Bluff	44 Kirk Held Hostage	68 Warp Out for Rescue
21 Underground Pursuit	45 Big Joker	69 Out of Control
22 The Bird	46 A Scream of Pain	70 Return to the Living
23 Teeny Bopper	47 Captain's Statue	71 Space Prisoner
24 Time Warp	48 Call Me Senator	72 Raspberries

STAR TREK (88 & 22)

2 1/2" X 3 1/2"

This Star Trek card set composed of 88 cards and 22 stickers was issued by Topps in 1976. It features color photos from the television

show; captions appear on the picture, which is enclosed by white borders. The backs are entitled "Captain's Log" and consist of narrative and character profiles. The stickers are numbered and captioned, with the color photos encircled by green, orange, and yellow lines. They have "universe" backgrounds and black borders. Note: set price includes stickers.

ITEM	MINT	EX
Set	125.00	95.00
Card	.75	.60
Sticker	2.00	1.50
Wrapper	--	1.00
Box	--	10.00

7 Ensign Chekov	
8 The Phaser—Tomorrow's Weapon	
9 The Shuttle Craft	
10 Opponents	
11 Energize!	
12 The Alien Mr. Spock	
13 Men of the Enterprise	
14 Story of Voyage One	
15 "Live Long and Prosper"	52 Ordeal on Rigel Seven
16 View from the Bridge	53 Capturing the Keeper
17 Toward the Unknown	54 Blasted by the Enemy
18 Enterprise Orbiting Earth	55 Trapped by the Lizard Creature
19 The Purple Barrier	56 The Gorn Strikes!
20 Outwitting a God	57 Earthman's Triumph
21 Planet Delta Vega	58 Specimen: Unknown
22 Charlie's Law	59 Mirror, Mirror
23 Mysterious Cube	60 Spock's Wedding
24 Dwarfed by the Enemy	61 Strangled by Mr. Spock
25 Balok's Alter-Ego	62 Grasp of the Gods
26 Last of Its Kind	63 The Monster Called Nomad
27 Frozen World	64 The Companion
28 Spock Loses Control	65 Journey to Babel
29 The Naked Time	66 Death Ship
30 The Demon Within	67 The Tholian Web
31 "My Enemy...My Self!"	68 The Architects of Pain
32 Monster Android	69 The Mugato
33 Korby's Folly	70 The Deadly Years
34 The Duplicate Man	71 Ancient Rome Revisited
35 Balance of Terror	72 The Melkotian
36 Attacked by Spores	73 The Vulcan Mind Meld
37 Spock Unwinds!	74 Possessed by Zargon
38 Duel at Gothos	75 Creation of a Humanoid
39 Timeship of Lazarus	76 Captured by Romulans
40 Dagger of the Mind	77 A War of Worlds
41 The Lawgivers	78 Space of Brains
42 Hunting the Tunnel Monster	79 I, Yarneg!
43 Battling the Horta	80 Death in a Single Cell
44 Strange Communication	81 The Uninvited
45 A Startling Discovery	82 The Lights of Zetar
46 McCoy...Insane!	83 Invaded by Alien Energy
47 The Guardian of Forever	84 Kirk's Deadliest Foe
48 Visit to a Hostile City	85 The Trouble with Tribbles
49 Mystery at Star Base 6	86 The Nazi Planet
50 Fate of Captain Pike	87 The Starship Eater
51 The Talosians	88 Star Trek Lives!

LIEUTENANT UHURA

1 The U.S.S. Enterprise	1 James Kirk	12 The Keeper
2 Captain James T. Kirk	2 Mr. Spock—Unearthly!	13 Commander Balok
3 Dr. "Bones" McCoy	3 Spock of Vulcan	14 The Mugato
4 Science Officer Spock	4 Dr. "Bones" McCoy	15 Lal, the Interrogator
5 Engineer Scott	5 Engineer Scott	16 The Parallel Spock
6 Lieutenant Uhura	6 Lieutenant Uhura	17 Ambassador Gav
	7 Ensign Chekov	18 Alien Possission!
	8 The Starship Enterprise	19 Spock Lives!
	9 Kirk Beaming Up!	20 Evil Klingon Kang
	10 Star Trek Lives!	21 Spock Forever!
	11 "Highly Illogical!"	22 The Romulan Vessel

STAR TREK (88 & 22)　　　　2 1/2" X 3 1/2"

In 1979, Topps issued another Star Trek set. In it are 88 cards with color scenes from the film, each surrounded by a blue, red, or yellow frame line and white borders. The captions can be found resting on these frame lines, and the card numbers are located just to the right. A synopsis of the card backs reveals the following categories: puzzle pieces — 68; "Story Summary" — 5; actor profiles — 12; "Star Quotes" — 2; and one checklist. The purple-bordered stickers are numbered and also have puzzle backs. (They have been assigned captions.) Note: set price includes stickers.

ITEM	MINT	EX
Set	20.00	14.00
Card	.15	.10
Sticker	.35	.25
Wrapper	--	.35
Box	--	5.00

1　Star Trek The Motion Picture
2　Toward the Unknown
3　Space Intruder
4　Fate of the Klingons
5　Warning from Space
6　"Our Starcrafts---Annihilated!"
7　Enterprise in Drydock
8　Rebuilding the Enterprise
9　Filming 'Drydock' Sequence
10　James T. Kirk
11　Captain Kirk's Mission
12　Dr. 'Bones' McCoy
13　Executive Officer Decker
14　Navigator Ilia
15　Uhura
16　Helmsman Sulu
17　Engineer Scott
18　Security Chief Chekov
19　Dr. Christine Chapel
20　Janice Rand
21　The Vulcan Mr. Spock
22　Spock on Planet Vulcan

23　The UFP Assembled
24　Being from Beyond
25　The Face of Terror
26　Lizard-like Diplomat
27　Not of This Earth
28　Alien Insectoid
29　The Unearthly
30　The Andorians
31　Advanced Life Form
32　Betel's Attendant
33　Andorian—Close-Up
34　The U.S.S. Enterprise
35　Back in Operation!
36　Refurbished Starship
37　Enterprise—Rear View
38　Return to the Bridge
39　The Senior Officers
40　View from the Bridge
41　Scotty's Domain
42　Fantastic New Devices
43　The Engineering Deck
44　Investigating a Malfunction

45　Heart of the Starship
46　Incredible Explosion!
47　Starship Under Attack!
48　Assault on Chekov!
49　Half Human
50　Spock's Fight for Life
51　Into the Nameless Void
52　Terror in the Transporter Room
53　The Surak Craft
54　Transporter Malfunction
55　Zero Gravity Adventure
56　Symbol of Her People
57　Exotically Beautiful Ilia
58　Spock's Discovery
59　The Phaser Battle!
60　Ilia in Sick Bay
61　Stamina of the Alien
62　Filming the Shuttlecraft
63　Star Explorer
64　Alien Menace
65　Star Challengers
66　"Beam Me Down, Scotty"

67　The Landing Party
68　Portrait of a Vulcan
69　Beyond Infinity
70　The Encounter
71　Its Secret Revealed
72　On Spock's Native World
73　Spectacular Starship
74　Welcoming Dr. McCoy Aboard
75　Kirk's Last Stand
76　Landscape of Vulcan
77　Klingon Warship—Rear View
78　The Final Frontiersmen
79　Klingon Warship
80　Vulcan Starship—Overhead View
81　Pride of the Starfleet
82　Duo for Danger
83　The Unearthly Mr. Spock
84　Woman from Planet Delta
85　New Starfleet Uniforms
86　Men with a Mission
87　The Deltan Beauty
88　Klingon Commander

1　Engineer Scott
2　Janice Rand
3　On Spock's Native World
4　Security Chief Chekov
5　Navigator Ilia
6　Helmsman Sulu
7　Star Explorer
8　Dr. Christine Chapel
9　Portrait of a Vulcan
10　Dr. 'Bones' McCoy
11　Uhura
12　The Deltan Beauty
13　The Face of Terror
14　Being from Beyond
15　Advanced Life Form
16　Executive Officer Decker
17　Betel's Attendant
18　Lizard-like Diplomat
19　Pride of the Starfleet
20　Klingon Warship
21　The Surak Craft
22　Spectacular Starship

STAR TREK (33)

2 1/2" X 3 1/2"

One of the most interesting of all the modern bread issues is this set of 33 Star Trek cards distributed jointly by "Rainbo," "Kilpatrick," and "Colonial" in 1976. Collectors will find that the set is really more of a promotion to attend the movie than a complete story in itself. Consider the "Story Summary" cards, for example. There are two identical sets of five (meaning that each specific summary is printed on two different card numbers) and we are left dangling at the conclusion of summary no. 5 with Kirk and the Enterprise warp-driving toward "an alien entity with the most incredible, most destructive power ever encountered!"If you wanted to find out what happened, you had to go see the film, or talk to one of your friends who already went. This clever bit of manipulation was probably very effective within the target market.

The rest of the cards are divided into three types: character photos with actor identifications and credits on the back; scenes from the film which all have an identical photo on the reverse (same picture as on the obverse of card #18); and two cards with scenes on front and profiles of Director Robert Wise and Producer Gene Roddenberry on back. Collectors will note the obvious similarity in style and format between these cards and those of the Topps regular issue Star Trek series (see side-by-side illustrations of header cards from the two sets). The major difference between the two sets is that Topps obviously had many more cards and scenes, although 68 of these had puzzle backs, and that two cards with "Star Quotes" are missing from the bread sets. Other than that, the number of "Story Summary" and actor-producer-director cards is the same. Each one of the bakery brands, of course, placed its own logo on the cards (see illustration).

The cards marked by an asterisk in our checklist all have the identical group picture on the back. Although individual cards were packed into bread loaves by the various companies, large quantities of complete sets in excellent or better grade have found their way into the hobby. These are generally priced in the $6-$10 range and specialists may want to collect a set with the logos of all three brands of bread. Cards with oil stains resulting from being packed in the bread cannot be graded excellent or mint.

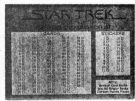

Cropped version of photo on front of card #18 appears on backs of ten different cards.

1 Header / Checklist
2 Toward the Unknown
3 "Our Starcrafts — Annihilated!"
4 Filming 'Drydock' Sequence
5 James T. Kirk
6 Captain Kirk's Mission*
7 Dr. 'Bones' McCoy
8 Executive Officer Decker
9 Navigator Ilia
10 Helmsman Sulu
11 Security Chief Chekov
12 Dr. Christine Chapel
13 Janice Rand
14 The Vulcan Mr. Spock*
15 Lizard-Like Diplomat*
16 Andorian — Close-up*
17 Return to the Bridge*
18 The Senior Officers
19 Scotty's Domain
20 Investigating a Malfunction
21 Starship Under Attack!
22 Assault on Chekov!
23 The Surak Craft
24 Transporter Malfunction*
25 Zero Gravity Adventure*
26 Ilia in Sick Bay*
27 The Landing Party*
28 Spectacular Starship
29 Welcoming Dr. McCoy Aboard*
30 Klingon Warship - Rear View
31 The Unearthly Mr. Spock
32 Woman from Planet Delta
33 New Starfleet Uniforms

STAR TREK II
WRATH OF KAHN (30)

Star Trek II, produced by FTCC, is a set of 30 large (5" X 7") color photographs taken from the movie of the same name. These photos are not captioned but they are numbered on the front at bottom-left. The backs contain a black and gray "space" design with the set title in the center and the copyright line in the border below.

ITEM	MINT	EX
Set	22.50	18.00
Card	.75	.60
Wrappers (4)		
each	--	.50
Box	--	3.00

**ALWAYS OBTAIN A RECEIPT FOR UNUSUAL ITEMS
SUCH AS UNCUT SHEET OF CARDS AND UNCREASED WRAPPERS**

STAR TREK III
SEARCH FOR SPOCK (60 & 20)

2 1/2" X 3 1/2"

A set of 80 cards issued without gum by FTCC (Fantasy Trading Card Co.). The sixty numbered story cards have color photographs enclosed by white borders on front. The backs contain the series title, the card caption, number, and copyright credits. An additional series of cards, numbered 1-20, picture various spacecraft from the movie.

ITEM	MINT	EX
Set	16.00	12.00
Card	.20	.15
Wrapper	--	.50
Box	--	3.00

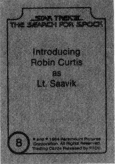

STORY CARDS

1. William Shatner Stars as Admiral James T. Kirk
2. Leonard Nimoy as Captain Spock
3. DeForest Kelley Stars as Dr. Leonard "Bones" McCoy
4. Chief Engineer Montgomery Scott Played by James Doohan
5. Captain Hikaru Sulu Played by George Takei
6. Acting Science Officer Commander Pavel Chekov Played by Walter Koenig
7. Nichelle Nichols as the Beautiful Uhura
8. Introducing Robin Curtis as Lt. Saavik
9. Ambassador Sarek, Spock's Father Portrayed by Mark Lenard
10. Vulcan High Priestess T'Lar Played by Dame Judith Anderson
11. Starfleet Commander Morrow Played by Robert Hooks
12. Klingon Battle Commander Kruge Played by Christopher Lloyd
13. Kruge's Pet, Warrigul
14. The Enterprise Returning Home for Repairs
15. The Enterprise Berthed Next to the Excelsior Inside Spacedock
16. Sarek Mind-Melds with Kirk
17. Kirk Replaying the Enterprise's Engine Room Flight Records
18. Kirk Reviewing the Tape of Spock Transferring His Katra to Bones
19. Morrow Tells Kirk the Bad News—Genesis is Off Limits
20. Conspirators in Conference
21. Visiting Bones in Prison
22. Liberating Bones from Prison
23. Sabotaging the Prison's Communications Console
24. Kirk and Crew Find Saavik and Spock Held Prisoner by Klingons
25. Commander Chekov at the Helm
26. Lt. Saavik and Dr. David Marcus, Kirk's Son, View the Genesis Planet from the Grissom
27. Dr. David Marcus Arrives on His Creation, the Genesis Planet, with Lt. Saavik
28. Locating Spock's Torpedo Tube Coffin
29. Spock's Burial Robe, but No Body
30. What Could Have Happened to Spock's Body?
31. Tracking ... Spock?
32. The Spock Child Lost in the Snow
33. Rescuing the Spock Child from Hostile Elements
34. Uncloaking Itself, Kruge's Klingon Ship Fires on the Grissom
35. The Spock Child Resting in Saavik and David's Makeshift Camp
36. Klingon Landing Party
37. Kruge Subduing a Genesis Mutation
38. Kruge Planning His Next Strategy Against the Enterprise
39. Deadly Enemies Crippled in Space
40. Scotty and Chekov Worrying Over Instrument Readings
41. Young Spock in the Agony of Pon Farr
42. Saavik Soothing Young Spock from the Effects of Pon Farr
43. Spock, Now a Young Adult, and Still Aging Along with the Genesis Planet
44. Which One Shall I Execute?
45. David Attracts the Klingon's Fatal Hand to Save Saavik and Spock
46. Turning Certain Death into a Fighting Chance at Life
47. Watching the Starship Enterprise Blaze into History
48. Kruge in Rage After Kirk Outwits Him
49. Kirk and Kruge Duel as Gensis Convulses
50. Fighting on the Brink of Destruction
51. The Death Throes of Genesis
52. Kirk Bargaining for the Lives of His Crew
53. Escaping the Exploding Genesis Planet
54. The Enterprise Crew and Their Stolen Bird of Prey Land Safely on Vulcan
55. The Enterprise Crew Returning Spock to His Vulcan Home
56. Sarek, at the Foot of Mount Seleya, Asking T'Lar to Initiate the Rite of Fal Tor Pan
57. McCoy's Friendship for Spock is Put to the Ultimate Test
58. T'Lar Performs the Ritual of Fal Tor Pan—the Refusion
59. Spock and Kirk Face to Face After Fal Tor Pan
60. Spock's Memories Finally Restored; the Search is Over

SPACESHIP CARDS

1. U.S.S. Enterprise NCC–1701
2. U.S.S. Enterprise Rear View
3. U.S.S. Enterprise Leaving Spacedock Pursued by the Excelsior
4. U.S.S. Enterprise Front View
5. Spacedock Earth's Orbiting Space Station Top View
6. Spacedock Side View
7. NX–2000 U.S.S. Excelsior The New Generation of Starfleet Spaceships Equipped with Trans-warp Drive.
8. U.S.S. Excelsior Right Rear View
9. U.S.S. Excelsior Top View
10. U.S.S. Excelsior Bottom View
11. The Merchantman—Merchant Ship Destroyed by Kruge
12. The Merchantman Bottom View
13. The Merchantman Top View
14. The Merchantman Rear View
15. Kruge's Ship Klingon Bird of Prey
16. Klingon Bird of Prey Captured by Kirk and the Enterprise Crew
17. U.S.S. Grissom NCC–638 Destroyed by Kruge as it Orbited the Genesis Planet
18. U.S.S. Grissom Rear View
19. U.S.S. Grissom Top View
20. U.S.S. Grissom Bottom View

STAR TREK IV
THE VOYAGE HOME (60)

The fronts of the cards in this latest FTCC issue share the same format as those of Star Trek III: color photos surrounded by white borders.

The backs have a nifty design in which the card caption is superimposed over a sketch of Planet Earth. The card number is located in a small "rocket" design at bottom left. The first card in the series is an unnumbered checklist. A poly bag wrapper was printed for pack sales although the cards are more often found in sets.

ITEM	MINT	EX
Set	12.00	9.00
Card	.20	.15
Wrapper	--	.50
Box	--	3.00

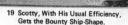

Checklist

2 Admiral James T. Kirk Played by William Shatner.
3 Captain Spock in Vulcan Robes Played by Leonard Nimoy.
4 Dr. Leonard "Bones" McCoy Played by DeForest Kelley.
5 Chief Engineer Montgomery Scott Played by James Doohan.
6 Commander Chekov Played by Walter Koenig.
7 Klingon Ambassador Played by John Schuck.
8 Amanda, Wife of Sarek and Mother of Spock, Played by Jane Wyatt.
9 Federation Headquarters
10 Alien Visitor to Star Fleet.
11 The Klingon Ambassador Presents Information on the Genesis Torpedo to a Gallery of Representatives in Federal Council Chambers.
12 Extraterrestrials Witness the Impressive Spectacle of Genesis.
13 The Klingon Ambassador Demands the Extradition of Admiral Kirk.
14 Sarek, Spock's Father, and Commander Chapel Walk Toward Council Chambers.
15 Alien Representatives Listen to Sarek Defending Kirk.
16 Spock Tests His Memory Using Vulcan Computers.
17 Admiral Kirk Verifies His Ship's Status Shortly Before His Departure from Vulcan.
18 Bridge Equipment on the Bird of Prey, "H.M.S. Bounty."

19 Scotty, With His Usual Efficiency, Gets the Bounty Ship-Shape.
20 Leaving Vulcan; Heading for Earth.
21 Captain Spock, With His Katra Restored, Prepares to Leave for Earth.
22 A Mysterious Alien Probe Orbits Earth. Its Powerful Signal Disrupts Communications for Parsecs.
23 The President of Earth Broadcasts a Warning for All Starships to Stay Clear of Earth.
24 Matching Whale Songs With the Emenations From the Probe.
25 Kirk Discusses the Possibility of Bringing Home Humpback Whales From the Past to Save Earth.
26 Bones Tries to Talk Kirk Out of His Mad Scheme to Bring Whales From the Past.
27 Warping Towards a Time Jump.
28 During Time Travel, Kirk Experiences a Series of Hypnotic Dream Sequences.
29 Disembarking at Night in Golden Gate Park.
30 Scotty Explains That the Dilithium Crystals Are De-Crystalizing.
31 Experiencing 20th Century San Francisco First Hand.
32 Kirk Tells the Crew That He'll Have to Find Money to Use While in the 20th Century.
33 An Antique Store Provides a Place for Kirk to Hock His 18th Century Spectacles for $200.
34 Gillian and Kirk Drop Spock Off at the Park Before They Go Out For Pizza.
35 Now What Do I Do?
36 Gillian Discovers Kirk's Invisible Spaceship.
37 A Call for Help Gets Gillian "Beamed Up"
38 Uhura and Chekov Waiting for Their Proton Collector To Do Its Job.
39 Bones and Kirk Ask Gillian to Help Them Rescue Chekov.

40 Chekov's Rescue From 20th Century Medicine Allows the Bounty to Resume Its Mission.
41 Watching Spellbound as the Bounty's Crew Efficiently Does Its Job.
42 Free in the Sun, Oblivious to the Imminent Danger.
43 Scaring the Pants Off the Whales' Would-Be Executioners.
44 Seeing the Whales in Their Space-Bound Aquarium, Gillian Tells Mr. Scott He's Performed a Miracle.
45 Scotty, Amazed at the Sight of the Whales, Tells Kirk That They're Safely Aboard.
46 Kirk Tells Gillian That Mankind Was Destroying Its Own Future by Killing the Whales.
47 After Re-entry in Time, the Bounty Is Rocked By Probe-Generated Turbulence.
48 Abandoning Ship.
49 The Whales Are Set Free in the 23rd Century.
50 Making Sure Everyone Is Safely Out.
51 The Whales Sing Their Song. The Rain Stops, and the Probe Departs As Mysteriously as It Came.
52 The Enterprise Crew on Trial in Federation Council Chambers.
53 Kirk Is Demoted From Admiral Back to Captain and Is Given Command of a New Starship.
54 Gillian and Kirk Say Their Farewells — Each Heading for Their Respective Starship.
55 The Enterprise Crew Shuttling to Its New Commission, Speculating That It Will Probably Be a Freighter.
56 Coming Home to the New "U.S.S. Enterprise, NCC 1701-A".
57 Bridge Control Panel on the New Enterprise.
58 Sulu Comtemplating Going Boldly Where No Man Has Gone Before.
59 Uhura Ready at Her New Communications Console.
60 Kirk and Crew Ready for the Unknown.

STAR TREK 1991 — SERIES 1 (160)   2 1/2″ X 3 1/2″

Captain's Log, Stardate 4373.2: the rescue party returning from the abandoned Terran freighter reports finding a curious artifact. It seems to be a box containing small pieces of cardboard with pictures and writing on the surfaces. I asked Dr. McCoy to scan them in the quarantine chamber for possible contamination. Mr. Spock is suspicious. He says that the numbering sequence on the objects implies order, and

therefore, intelligence, but he cannot discern any practical application for them. The writing appears to be Old Earth but is faded. Uhura says the computer bank has identified a single word which appears on all the objects: "Impel." I've notified Starfleet Command of our findings and asked for data assistance. Meanwhile, we can only wait and wonder ...

Had Captain Kirk been around in 1991, he would have recognized the "ar-

tifact" as a shoe box full of Impel's 1991 Star Trek trading cards. This series of 160 cards is divided into two distinct categories: all odd number cards depict characters and scenes from the original TV series, and all even number cards feature the adventures and characters of "The Next Generation." "Original" cards have dark blue borders and "Next Generation" cards have burgundy borders, and each subset has its own checklist card and personalized wrapper (same design, but different color and logo-title). The display box has a card from each subset on the lid but is otherwise undistinguished. To promote sales of the product, Impel randomly inserted two Star Trek holograms inside the poly bag packs. These are not considered part of the regular set and at the time this book went to press (Spring, 1992), the "asking" price for a single hologram fell in the $20-$25 range.

ITEM	MINT	EX
Set	15.00	8.00
Card	.10	.05
Wrappers (2)		
each	--	.15
Box	--	2.00

1 Where No Man Has Gone Before
2 The Last Outpost
3 Space Seed
4 Where No One Has Gone Before
5 The Corbomite Maneuver
6 Haven
7 Mudd's Women
8 Code of Honor
9 The Enemy Within
10 The Naked Now
11 The Man Trap
12 Encounter at Farpoint
13 The Naked Time
14 Lonely Among Us
15 Charlie X
16 Justice
17 Balance of Terror
18 The Battle
19 What Are Little Girls Made Of?
20 Hide and Q
21 Dagger of the Mind
22 Too Short a Season
23 Miri
24 The Big Goodbye
25 The Conscience of the King
26 Datalore
27 The Galileo Seven
28 Symbiosis
29 Court-Martial
30 We'll Always Have Paris
31 The Menagerie
32 The Neutral Zone
33 Shore Leave
34 Where Silence Has Lease
35 The Squire of Gothos
36 Conspiracy
37 Arena
38 Elementary, Dear Data
39 The Alternative Factor
40 The Outrageous Okona
41 Tomorrow is Yesterday
42 The Schizoid Man
43 The Return of the Archons
44 The Measure of a Man
45 A Taste of Armageddon
46 The Dauphin
47 This Side of Paradise
48 Contagion
49 The Devil in the Dark
50 The Arsenal of Freedom
51 Errand of Mercy
52 Skin of Evil
53 The City on the Edge of Forever
54 Heart of Glory
55 Operation — Annihilate!
56 Coming of Age
57 Catspaw
58 When the Bough Breaks
59 Metamorphosis
60 Home Soil
61 Friday's Child
62 11001001
63 Who Mourns for Adonais?
64 Angel One
65 Amok Time
66 Loud as a Whisper
67 The Doomsday Machine
68 Unnatural Selection
69 Wolf in the Fold
70 A Matter of Honor
71 The Changeling
72 The Royale
73 Mirror, Mirror
74 The Child
75 The Deadly Years
76 Pen Pals
77 The Trouble with Tribbles
78 Time Squared
79 Bread and Circuses
80 The Icarus Factor
81 The Apple
82 Warp Drive
83 Transporter
84 The Continuing Voyages
85 Tribbles
86 A Place for Families
87 Communications
88 The Prime Directive
89 Communications
90 U.S.S. Enterprise
91 Tricorder
92 U.S.S. Enterprise
93 Phasers
94 Dilithium Crystals
95 Spock
96 Ten-Forward
97 James T. Kirk
98 Transporter
99 Pavel Chekov, Navigator
100 Shuttlecraft
101 Sulu, Chief Helmsman
102 Diagnostic Bed
103 Montgomery Scott, Chief Engineer
104 Defensive Shields
105 Uhura, Communications
106 Holodeck
107 Leonard McCoy, Physician
108 Medical Tricorder
109 Vulcan
110 Lieutenant Worf
111 Klingons
112 Geordi LaForge, Lt. Commander
113 Gorn
114 Deanna Troi, Counselor
115 Talosians
116 Dr. Beverly Crusher, Physician
117 Captain James T. Kirk
118 The Ferengi
119 Commander Spock
120 Wesley "Wes" Crusher, Ensign
121 Montgomery "Scotty" Scott
122 Guinan
123 Dr. Leonard "Bones" McCoy
124 Captain Jean-Luc Picard
125 Andorians
126 Commander William T. Riker
127 Uhura
128 Romulans
129 Pavel Andreievich Chekov
130 Patrick Stewart
131 Worldsinger
132 Jonathan Frakes
133 Enemy Unseen
134 Michael Dorn
135 The Argon Affair!
136 Marina Sirtis
137 Fast Friends
138 Levar Burton
139 ...Gone!
140 Brent Spiner
141 A Piece of the Action
142 Wil Wheaton
143 The Pandora Principle
144 Gates McFadden
145 Amok Time
146 Doomsday World
147 Journey to Babel
148 The Derelict
149 Phasers
150 The Gift
151 The Devil in the Dark
152 The Weapon
153 Beaming Down
154 Contamination
155 Ghost-Walker
156 The Eyes of the Beholders
157 Home is the Hunter
158 Exiles
159 Star Trek Checklist
160 Star Trek, The Next Generation Checklist

This group of the world's finest people all subscribe to NON-SPORT UPDATE!

If you want quality and up-to-date information, NON-SPORT UPDATE is the magazine for you.

$16 - 1 year subscription (4 issues) - U.S.

(PA residents MUST add $1.00 magazine tax)

$25 - 1 year subscription (4 issues) - Foreign (bulk rates upon request)

Subscribe by fax with VISA or MasterCard
1-717-238-3220

Member
(order with confidence)

Make checks payable to:

NON-SPORT UPDATE
4019 Green St. - Dept. G
PO Box 5858
Harrisburg, PA 17110

Subscribe by phone or call for additional information
1-717-238-1936

Series 2 of Impel's 25th anniversary salute to Star Trek was also issued in 1991 and has ten less cards in it than Series 1. Once again, the cards dealing with the original series have blue borders and odd numbers (161-309), while "The Next Generation" sequence is even-numbered (160-310) and has burgundy borders. Each sequence includes its own color-coded checklist card. While the 75 cards dealing with "The Next Generation" all contain color or pictures from various episodes, there are several sub-groups of "original" cards which deal with Star Trek insignia, engineering blueprints, and "TV Credit Cards." Series II wrappers have black fronts, in contrast to the silver foil of Series I, and they bear the statement "Completes 25th Anniversary Collector Set."

Two holograms (H-3 and H-4) were randomly inserted into packs as bonuses for collectors. These, like the H-1 and H-2 holograms found in Series I packages, are not considered to be part of the regular set and will not be priced below. Impel has categorically denied printing a Gene Roddenberry hologram, so collectors encountering this item, cleverly marked H-5, are looking at a bogus card. A small packet containing three cards from a "Star Trek - The Next Generation" set were distributed as a promotion in subscriber copies of the April issue of Non-Sport Update magazine. This set, from Skybox International (Impel's new company name), was scheduled for a June, 1992 release and is not connected in any way to the "Star Trek 1991" series in any way.

ITEM	MINT	EX
Set	15.00	8.00
Card	.10	.05
Wrappers (2) each	--	.10
Box	--	2.00

161 I. Mudd
162 Q Who
163 Journey to Babel
164 The Samaritan Snare
165 A Private Little War
166 Up the Long Ladder
167 The Gamesters of Triskelion
168 Manhunt
169 Obsession
170 The Emissary
171 The Immunity Syndrome
172 Peak Performance
173 A Piece of the Action
174 Shades of Gray
175 By Any Other Name
176 The Ensigns of Command
177 Return to Tomorrow
178 Evolution
179 Patterns of Force
180 The Survivors
181 The Ultimate Computer
182 Who Watches the Watchers
183 The Omega Glory
184 The Bonding
185 Assignment Earth
186 Booby Trap
187 Elaan of Troyius
188 The Enemy
189 Spectre of the Gun
190 The Price
191 The Paradise Syndrome
192 The Vengeance Factor
193 The Enterprise Incident
194 The Defector
195 And The Children Shall Lead
196 The Hunted
197 Spock's Brain
198 The High Ground
199 Is There in Truth No Beauty?
200 Deja Q
201 The Empath

202 A Matter of Perspective
203 The Tholian Web
204 Yesterday's Enterprise
205 For the World is Hollow and I Have Touched the Sky
206 The Offspring
207 The Day of the Dove
208 Sins of the Father
209 Plato's Stepchildren
210 Allegiance
211 Wink of an Eye
212 Captain's Holiday
213 That Which Survives
214 Tin Man
215 Let That Be Your Last Battlefield
216 Hollow Pursuits
217 Whom Gods Destroy
218 The Most Toys
219 The Mark of Gideon
220 Sarek
221 The Lights of Zetar
222 Menage a Troi
223 The Cloudminders
224 Transfigurations
225 The Way to Eden
226 The Best of Both Worlds, Part I
227 Requiem for Methuselah
228 The Best of Both Worlds, Part II
229 The Savage Curtain
230 Suddenly Human
231 All Our Yesterdays
232 Brothers
233 Turnabout Intruder
234 Family
235 U.S.S. Enterprise: One of the Vanguard

236 Remember Me
237 Deck 1: The Riddle
238 Legacy
239 Bridge: Main Viewscreen
240 Reunion
241 Transporter Room
242 Future Imperfect
243 Transporter Controls
244 Final Mission
245 Corridor
246 The Loss
247 Shuttlecraft
248 Data's Day
249 Shuttlecraft Hangar Deck
250 The Mission Continues
251 Engineering Plans of the U.S.S. Enterprise
252 Turbolift
253 NCC-171
254 Battle Section
255 Hypospray
256 Ship's Computer
257 Command Insignia
258 Technology Unchained
259 Sciences Insignia
260 The Main Bridge: Command Area
261 Engineering Insignia
262 The Main Bridge: Forward Stations
263 William Shatner
264 The Main Bridge: Aft Stations
265 Leonard Nimoy
266 The Dress Uniform
267 Deforest Kelly
268 Picard & Riker
269 James Doohan
270 Picard & Q
271 Nichelle Nichols
272 Riker & Troi

273 George Takei
274 Picard & Troi
275 Walter Koenig
276 Riker & Geordi
277 The Origins of Star Trek
278 Picard & Wesley
279 TV Credit Card - #1
280 Riker & Data
281 TV Credit Card - #2
282 Picard & Data
283 TV Credit Card - #3
284 Troi & Dr. Crusher
285 TV Credit Card - #4
286 Picard & Sarek
287 TV Credit Card - #5
288 Picard & Worf
289 TV Credit Card - #6
290 Picard & Dr. Crusher
291 Nacelles
292 Picard & Guinan
293 United Federation of Planets
294 Data
295 Neutral Zone
296 The Borg
297 Environmental Suit
298 Dr. Kate Pulaski
299 Vulcan Lyrette
300 Dr. Leah Brahms
301 The Melkot
302 K'ehleyr
303 Harcour Fenton "Harry" Mudd
304 Vash
305 Horta
306 Armus
307 Captain Christopher Pike
308 Gene Roddenberry & Crew
309 Star Trek Checklist
310 Star Trek: The Next Generation Checklist

STAR TREK — THE NEXT GENERATION ALBUM STICKERS (240)

1 15/16" X 2 9/16"

Of all the album sticker sets issued by Panini in the United States over the years, this 1988 series of "Star Trek - The Next Generation" is probably the most sought after and the hardest to find. This is a result not only of tremendous collector interest in all items pertaining to Star Trek, but also to Panini's sales strategy of rotating sets in and out of their market countries on a schedule. That means that regardless of how well a product is selling in any country, when the timetable says "end of promotion" it is no longer offered. So, by the time the general collecting public becomes aware of a certain Panini set, it is usually gone out of market already and is only available through dealers.

The series contains 240 stickers which are divided into two groups: single complete pictures with four white borders and partial pictures with two or three white borders. The former have small spaces allotted in the album, while the latter are designed to be placed together to form larger two- or four-part pictures (see illustration below). The wrapper is basically blue with pink lettering and the standard yellow Panini logo. The album covers follow the same color scheme and the 32 pages within are compartmentalized into seven specific adventures, after a one-page introduction to "Next Generation" characters. Note: set price includes album.

ITEM	MINT	EX
Set	50.00	36.00
Sticker	.20	.15
Wrapper	––	.25
Album	2.50	2.00

STAR WARS (330 & 55)

The success of the Topps Star Wars series in the trading card and bubble gum market might have approached the movie's success in the film world. There are five series totaling 330 cards and 55 stickers. The border colors for the five series are as follows: 1st (1-66) — blue; 2nd (67-132) — red; 3rd (133-198) — yellow; 4th (199-264) — green; 5th (265-330) — brown. Stickers one to 22 (1st and 2nd series) have black borders; numbers 23 to 55 are done in "film-frame" style. Note: series prices include stickers.

ITEM	MINT	EX
Sets		
Series 1	27.50	20.00
Series 2	24.00	18.00
Series 3	22.00	16.50
Series 4	22.00	16.50
Series 5	22.00	16.50
Cards (all)	.25	.20
Stickers		
Series 1	1.00	.75
Series 2	.75	.55
Series 3-4-5	.50	.35
Wrappers		
Series 1	--	1.50
Series 2-3	--	1.00
Series 4-5	--	.75
Boxes		
Series 1	--	10.00
Series 2	--	7.50
Series 3-4-5	--	5.00

STAR WARS
Luke Skywalker

1 Luke Skywalker
2 See—Threepio and Artoo—Detoo
3 The little droid, Artoo-Detoo
4 Space pirate Han Solo
5 Princess Leia Organa
6 Ben (Obi-Wan) Kenobi
7 The villainous Darth Vader
8 Grand Moff Tarkin
9 Rebels defend their starship!
10 Princess Leia-captured!
11 Artoo is imprisoned by the Jawas
12 The droids are reunited!
13 A sale on droids!
14 Luke checks out his new droid
15 Artoo-Detoo is left behind!
16 Jawas of Tatooine
17 Lord Vader threatens Princess Leia!
18 Artoo-Detoo is missing!
19 Searching for the little droid
20 Hunted by the Sandpeople!
21 The Tusken Raiders
22 Rescued by Ben Kenobi
23 See-Threepio is injured!
24 Stormtroopers seek the droids!
25 Luke rushes to save his loved ones
26 A horrified Luke sees his family killed
27 Some repairs for See-Threepio
28 Luke agrees to join Ben Kenobi
29 Stopped by stormtroopers
30 Han in the Millennium Falcon
31 Sighting the Death Star
32 Lord Vader's Guards
33 The droids in the Control Room
34 See-Threepio diverts the guards
35 Luke and Han as stormtroopers
36 Blast of the laser rifle!
37 Cornered in the labyrinth
38 Luke and Han in the refuse room
39 Steel walls close in on our heroes!
40 Droids rescue their masters!
41 Facing the deadly chasm
42 Stormtroopers attack!
43 Luke prepares to swing across the chasm
44 Han and Chewie shoot it out!
45 The light sabre
46 A desperate moment for Ben
47 Luke prepares for the battle
48 Artoo-Detoo is loaded aboard
49 The rebels monitor the raid
50 Rebel leaders wonder about their fate!

51 See-Threepio and Princess Leia
52 Who will win the final Star War!
53 Battle in outer space!
54 The victors receive their reward
55 Han, Chewie and Luke
56 A day of rejoicing!
57 Mark Hamill as Luke Skywalker
58 Harrison Ford as Han Solo
59 Alec Guinness as Ben Kenobi
60 Peter Cushing as Grand Moff Tarkin
61 Mark Hamill in Control Room
62 Lord Vader's stormtroopers
63 May the Force be with you!
64 Governor of Imperial Outlands
65 Carrie Fisher and Mark Hamill
66 Amazing robot See-Threepio

STAR WARS
"May The Force be with you!"™

67 See-Threepio and Luke
68 The Millennium Falcon
69 Threepio's desert trek!
70 Special mission for Artoo-Detoo!
71 The incredible See-Threepio!
72 Ben Kenobi rescues Luke!
73 The droids wait for Luke
74 Luke Skywalker on Tatooine
75 Darth Vader strangles a rebel!
76 Artoo-Detoo on the rebel starship!
77 Waiting in the control room
78 Droids to the rescue!
79 Preparing to board Solo's spaceship!
80 "Where has R2-D2 gone?"
81 Weapons of the Death Star!
82 A daring rescue!
83 Aboard the Millennium Falcon
84 Rebel pilot prepares for the raid!
85 Luke on the sand planet
86 A mighty explosion!
87 The droids try to rescue Luke!
88 Stormtroopers guard Solo's ship
89 The imprisoned Princess Leia
90 Honoring the victors!
91 Solo and Chewie prepare to leave Luke
92 Advance of the Tusken Raider
93 Stormtroopers blast the rebels!
94 Interrogated by stormtroopers!
95 Sighting Artoo-Detoo!
96 The droids on Tatooine
97 Meeting at the cantina
98 See-Threepio
99 Ben with the light sabre!

100 Our heroes at the spaceport
101 The Wookiee Chewbacca
102 Rebels prepare for the big fight!
103 Stormtroopers attack our heroes!
104 Luke's uncle and aunt
105 Imperial soldiers burn through the starship!
106 A message from Princess Leia!
107 The Tusken Raider
108 Princess Leia observes the battle!
109 Ben turns off the Tractor beam
110 Threepio fools the guards!
111 Chewie and Han Solo!
112 Threatened by Sandpeople!
113 Ben hides from Imperial stormtroopers
114 Planning to escape!
115 Hiding in the Millennium Falcon!
116 Honored for their heroism!
117 Chewbacca poses as a prisoner!
118 R2-D2 and C-3PO
119 Threepio, Ben and Luke!
120 Luke destroys an Imperial ship!
121 Han Solo and Chewbacca
122 The Millennium Falcon speeds through space!
123 Solo blasts a stormtrooper!
124 Threepio searches for R2-D2
125 Luke in disguise!
126 A quizzical Threepio!
127 The Rebel Fleet
128 Roar of the Wookiee!
129 "May The Force be with you!"
130 Pursued by the Jawas!
131 Spectacular battle!
132 Lord Vader and a soldier

STAR WARS
The evil Grand Moff Tarkin

133 Ben and Luke help C-3PO to his feet
134 Luke dreams of being a star pilot
135 Cantina troubles!
136 Danger from all sides!
137 Luke attacked by a strange creature!
138 On the track of the droids
139 Han Solo...
hero or mercenary?
140 "R2-D2,
where are you?"
141 Some quick-thinking by Luke!
142 Darth Vader inspects the throttled ship

143 Droids on the sand planet
144 Harrison Ford as Han Solo
145 Escape from the death Star!
146 Luke Skywalker's aunt preparing dinner
147 Bargaining with the Jawas!
148 The fearsome stormtroopers!
149 The evil Grand Moff Tarkin
150 Shoot-out at the chasm!
151 Planning an escape!
152 Spirited Princess Leia!
153 The fantastic droid Threepio!
154 Princess Leia comforts Luke!
155 The Escape Pod is jettisoned!
156 R2-D2 is lifted aboard!
157 "Learn about the Force, Luke!"
158 Rebel victory
159 Luke Skywalker's home
160 Destroying a world!
161 Preparing for the raid!
162 Han Solo cornered by Greedo!
163 Caught in the tractor beam!
164 Tusken Raiders capture Luke!
165 Escaping from stormtroopers!
166 A close call for Luke and Princess Leia!
167 Surrounded by Lord Vader's soldiers!
168 Hunting the fugitives
169 Meeting at the Death Star!
170 Luke and the princess... trapped!
171 "The walls are moving!"
172 Droids in the Escape Pod
173 The stormtroopers
174 Solo aims for trouble!
175 A closer look at a "Jawa"
176 Luke Skywalker's dream
177 Solo swings into action!
178 The Star Warriors!
179 Stormtroopers search the spaceport!
180 Princess Leia honors the victors
181 Peter Cushing as Grand Moff Tarkin
182 Deadly blasters!
183 Dave Prowse as Darth Vader
184 Luke and his uncle
185 Luke on Tatooine
186 The Jawas
187 Threepio and friend
188 Starship under fire!
189 Mark Hamill as Luke
190 Carrie Fisher as Princess Leia
191 Life on the desert world
192 Liberated Princess!
193 Luke's uncle buys Threepio!
194 Stormtroopers attack!
195 Alec Guinness as Ben Kenobi
196 Lord Darth Vader
197 Leia blasts a stormtrooper!
198 Luke decides to leave Tatooine!

Star Wars

199 The star warriors aim for action!
200 C-3PO searches for his counterpart
201 Raid at Mos Eisley!
202 Inquiring about Obi-Wan Kenobi
203 A band of Jawas
204 Stalking the corridors of Death Star
205 Desperate moments for our heroes!
206 Searching for the missing droid
207 C-3PO (Anthony Daniels)
208 Luke Skywalker on the desert planet
209 The Rebel Troops
210 Princess Leia blasts the enemy
211 A proud moment for Han and Luke
212 A stormtrooper is blasted!
213 Monitoring the battle
214 Luke and Leia shortly before the raid
215 Han bows out of the battle
216 Han and Leia quarrel about the escape plan
217 The Dark Lord of the Sith
218 Luke Skywalker's home.. destroyed!
219 The swing to freedom!
220 "I'm going to regret this!"
221 Princess Leia (Carrie Fisher)
222 "Evacuate? In our moment of triumph?"
223 Han Solo covers his friends
224 Luke's secret yen for action!
225 Aunt Beru Lars (Shelagh Fraser)
226 Portrait of a princess
227 Instructing the Rebel pilots
228 R2-D2 is inspected by the Jawas
229 Grand Moff Tarkin (Peter Cushing)
230 Guarding the Millennium Falcon
231 Discussing the Death Star's future
232 The Empire strikes back!
233 Raiding the Rebel starship
234 Envisioning the Rebel's destruction
235 Luke Skywalker (Mark Hamill)
236 Readying the Rebel fleet
237 The deadly grip of Darth Vader
238 Uncle Owen Lars (Phil Brown)
239 The young star warrior
240 Artoo's desperate mission!
241 The Rebel fighter ships
242 Death Star shootout!
243 Rebels in the trench!
244 Waiting at Mos Eisley
245 Member of the evil Empire
246 Stormtrooper—tool of the Empire
247 Soldier of evil!
248 Luke suspects the worst about his family
249 Ben Kenobi (Alec Guinness)
250 Luke and Ben on Tatooine
251 An overjoyed Han Solo!
252 The honored heroes!
253 R2-D2 (Kenny Baker)
254 Darth Vader (David Prowse)
255 Luke poses with his weapon
256 The marvelous droid See-Threepio!
257 A pair of Jawas
258 Fighting impossible odds!
259 Challenging the evil Empire!
260 Han Solo (Harrison Ford)
261 Fury of the Tusken Raider
262 Creature of Tatooine
263 The courage of Luke Skywalker
264 Star pilot Luke Skywalker!

265 Anxious moments for the Rebels
266 Threepio and Leia monitor the battle
267 No-nonsense privateer Han Solo!
268 Ben prepares to turn off the tractor beam
269 Droids on the run!
270 Luke Skywalker: farmboy-turned-warrior!
271 "Do you think they'll melt us down, Artoo?"
272 Corridors of the Death Star
273 "This is all your fault, Artoo!"
274 Droids trick the stormtroopers!
275 Guarding the Millennium Falcon
276 It's not wise to upset a Wookiee!
277 Bizarre Inhabitants of the cantina!
278 A narrow escape!
279 Awaiting the Imperial attack
280 "Remember Luke, The Force will be with you"
281 A monstrous thirst!
282 "Hurry up, Luke—we're gonna have company!"
283 The Cantina musicians
284 Distracted by Solo's assault
285 Spiffed-up for the Awards Ceremony
286 Cantina denizens!
287 Han and Chewie ready for action!
288 Blasting the enemy!
289 The Rebel Fighters take off!
290 Chewie aims for danger!
291 Lord Vader senses The Force
292 The stormtroopers assemble
293 A friendly chat among alien friends!
294 Droids make their way to the Escape Pod
295 Han and the Rebel Pilots
296 Artoo-Detoo is abducted by Jawas!
297 Inside the Sandcrawler
298 Chewie gets riled!
299 Leia wishes Luke good luck!
300 A crucial moment for Luke Skywalker
301 Luke, the Star Warrior!
302 Threepio and Artoo
303 Various droids collected by the Jawas
304 The Jawas ready their new merchandise
305 Director George Lucas and "Greedo"
306 Technicians ready C-3PO for the cameras
307 A touch-up for Chewbacca!
308 Directing the Cantina creatures
309 The birthday celebration for Sir Alec Guinness
310 Filming the Awards Ceremony
311 The model builders proudly display their work
312 Using the "blue screen" process for X-wings
313 The birth of a droid
314 Shooting in Tunisia
315 Inside the Millennium Falcon
316 Photographing the miniature explosions
317 Filming explosions on the Death Star
318 "Make-up" for the Bantha
319 Dave Prowse and Alec Guinness rehearse
320 Flight of the Falcon
321 George Lucas directs his counterpart "Luke"
322 Constructing the Star Destroyer
323 Aboard the Millennium Falcon

324 Chewie takes a breather between scenes
325 The princess gets the brush!
326 Animating the "chessboard" creatures
327 Filming the Sandcrawler
328 X-wings positioned for the cameras
329 Sir Alec Guinness and George Lucas
330 Filming Luke and Threepio in Tunisia

STICKER CHECKLIST

1 Luke Skywalker
2 Princess Leia Organa
3 Han Solo
4 Chewbacca the Wookiee
5 See—Threepio
6 Artoo—Detoo
7 Lord Darth Vader
8 Grand Moff Tarkin
9 Ben (Obi-Wan) Kenobi
10 Tusken Raider
11 Battle in Outer Space
12 Han and Chewbacca
13 Alec Guinnes as Ben
14 The Tusken Raider
15 See—Threepio
16 Chewbacca
17 Threatened by Sandpeople
18 The Rebel Fleet
19 The Wookiee Chewbacca
20 R2-D2 and C-3PO
21 The Millennium Falcon Speeds Through Space!
22 Spectacular Battle!
23 Dave Prowse as Darth Vader
24 Droids on the Sand Planet
25 The Escape Pop is Jettisoned
26 The Fantastic Droid Threepio
27 A Closer Look at a "Jawa"
28 Peter Cushing as Grand Moff Tarkin
29 Han Solo Hero or Mercenary?
30 The Fearsome Stormtroopers

31 Princess Leia Comforts Luke
32 Preparing for the Raid!
33 Solo Aims for Trouble!
34 The Star Warriors Aim for Action!
35 Han Solo (Harrison Ford)
36 Star Pilot Luke Skywalker!
37 The Marvelous Droid See—Threepio!
38 R2-D2 (Kenny Baker)
39 Creature of Tatooine
40 Darth Vader (David Prowse)
41 A Pair of Jawas
42 Luke Poses with his Weapon
43 Stormtrooper - Tool of the Empire
44 Monitoring the Battle
45 A Cruicial Moment for Luke Skywalker
46 Chewie Aims for Danger!
47 Droids on the Run!
48 Inside the Sandcrawler
49 Luke, the Star Warrior!
50 Director George Lucas and "Greedo"
51 Technicians Ready C-3PO for the Cameras
52 The Jawas Ready Their New Merchandise
53 Directing the Cantina Creatures
54 Leia Wishes Luke Good Luck!
55 A Touch-Up for Chewbacca!

STAR WARS (16)　　　　2 1/2" X 3 1/2"

This interesting little 16-card "Star Wars" series was issued by Wonder Bread in 1977. The fronts are a stylish combination of color photographs, black borders, and bright yellow caption panels, and the series name running vertically up the right margin adds a dramatic air. The backs are as dull as the fronts are interesting, with simple black-print text laid down unceremoniously on white stock. The card numbers, which appear only on the reverse of each card, are spelled out. Some blank-backed cards are known to exist but these have not attracted any extra interest or value. Complete sets are quite easily found in the hobby and retail for $10 or less in excellent or mint condition. Individual cards sell for 50¢ each. No packaging has been reported to date.

HAN SOLO
HARRISON FORD

Han Solo, the daring captain of the Millennium Falcon, a Corellian pirate starship, outwits and outraces the space fleet of the Empire.

Four

© 1977 Twentieth Century-Fox Film Corp., Inc.

SEE-THREEPIO
C-3PO

1 Luke Skywalker
2 Ben (OBI-WAN) Kenobi
3 Princess Leia Organa
4 Han Solo
5 Darth Vader
6 Grand Moff Tarkin
7 See-Threepio
8 Artoo-Detoo
9 Chewbacca
10 Jawas
11 Tusken Raiders
12 Stormtroopers
13 Millenium Falcon
14 Star Destroyer
15 X-Wing
16 TIE - Vader's Ship

STAR WARS MOVIE PHOTO PIN-UPS (56)　　　2 7/8" X 3 5/16"

There are two sides to this "Star Wars" set marketed by Topps in 1978. Wrapper collectors are interested in the four different exterior designs and the large foil wrapper in which some boxes were packed. Science fiction and "Star Wars" enthusiasts like the color photos printed on the interior side of every wrapper. These photographs are numbered but are not captioned. A large quantity of unfolded wrappers has appeared in the hobby but most cannot be graded mint because they have small tears in the right margin.

ITEM	MINT	EX
Set	--	125.00
Pin-up	--	2.00
Foil wrapper	--	10.00
Boxes (2) each	--	20.00

Star Wars Movie Photo Pin-Ups

⊑⊑⊑⊑⊑ THE WRAPPER ⊑⊑⊑⊑⊑⊑⊑

⊑⊑⊑⊑⊑⊑⊑⊑ THE WRAPPER 1978–1991 ⊑⊑⊑⊑⊑

STATE LICENSE PLATES (70) 2 7/16" X 3 11/16"

Although the "State License Plate" series has been on the market for several years, it is not well known by collectors. One license plate comes with every package of "Super Sips," which are wax containers filled with sugary syrup. There are 70 different U.S. and Canadian license plate stickers in the set and each is numbered. The dimensions in the heading refer to the plate itself without the extra 1 5/16" X 2 7/16" ingredient tab. Note: prices listed are for unpeeled stickers complete with tabs.

ITEM	MINT	EX
Set	30.00	21.00
Sticker	.35	.25
Box	---	10.00

1	Alabama	18	KY [Kentucky]	35	N. Dakota	
2	Alaska	19	Louisiana	36	Ohio	
3	Arizona	20	Maine	37	Oklahoma	
4	Arkansas	21	Maryland	38	Oregon	
5	California	22	Massachusetts	39	Pennsylvania	
6	Colorado	23	Michigan	40	Rhode Island	
7	Connecticut	24	Minnesota	41	South Carolina	
8	Delaware	25	Mississippi	42	South Dakota	
9	Washington D.C.	26	Missouri	43	Tennessee	
10	Florida	27	Montana	44	Texas	
11	Georgia	28	Nebraska	45	Utah	
12	Hawaii	29	Nevada	46	Vermont	
13	Idaho	30	New Hampshire	47	Virginia	
14	Illinois	31	N.J. [New Jersey]	48	Washington	
15	Indiana	32	New Mexico	49	West Virginia	
16	Iowa	33	New York	50	Wisconsin	
17	Kansas	34	North Carolina	51	Wyoming	

52	American Samoa	61	Manitoba
53		62	New Brunswick
54	Guam USA	63	Newfoundland And Labrador
55	Puerto Rico	64	Nova Scotia
56	Virgin Islands	65	Ontario
57	Chippwea Indians MN	66	Prince Edward Island
58	US Forces Korea	67	Quebec
59	Alberta	68	Saskatchewan
60	British Columbia	69	Northwest Territories Canada
		70	Yukon

STICK — ITS (120 & 13?) 2 1/2" X 3 1/2"

If the statement on the wrapper is accurate —"Collect All 120 Crazy Stickers"— there must be 60 different sticker sheets in this set. Each sheet holds two stickers: one measures 2 3/16" X 2 1/2"; the other is 15/16" X 2 1/2". The space in between is occupied by a strip (1/4" X 2 1/2") bearing a Fleer crown logo, a suggestion on where to place the stickers, and the words "Peel Here." Almost 50 percent of these strips also carry a number to the left of the crown logo (the significance of which has yet to be discovered). The partial checklist below lists the known "Stick-Its" sheets alphabetically by the title of the large sticker. (The "peel-strip" directions and number are also listed along with the title of the smaller sticker). A series of "Notice of Violation" cards was also packaged with the stickers. The 13 known titles for these sticker sheets appear below. Three sticker sheets and one card came in each pack.

ITEM	MINT	EX
Sticker	2.00	1.50
Card	1.00	.75
Wrapper	---	3.00
Box	---	15.00

STICK-ITS

1 STICK GUM

Atomic Powered
Stick-its for Decorations [2]
Disaster Area

Bathroom Award
Stick It to Your Book [3]
I'm Turned On

Big Ham
Stick It Pal!
The End

Blind Date
Stick It to a Friend [1]
I Need a Diet

Broken Zipper
Stick It to Your Jacket [1]
Call Me Jumbo

Class Burper
Stick It to a Bumper
Weirdo

Class Loudmouth
Stick It to a Bumper [2]
Turn Me On

Class Slob
Stick It to Your Pants
Push

Detention King
Stick It to a Bumper [3]
B.O.

Don't Litter — Pick Me Up
Stick 'Em Everywhere
Slap Here

Egghead
Stick It to Your Pants
Unfair to Students

Flunkie
Stick It to Your Book [1]
I Hate [blank]

I Hate Boys!
Stick It to Your Pants [2]
So Do I

I Hate Girls!
Stick It? [2]
Please Steal This Book

I'm a Worm
Stick-its are Fun [3]
I'm Cute - Kiss Me

It Must Be My Breath
Stick It Pal! [2]
Eat Here

No Brain No Pain
Stick It to a Friend [3]
Kiss Me

I'm Boy Crazy
Stick 'Em Everywhere
Bite Here

Jock
Stick-its are Fun [2]
Peep Hole

No Smoking
Stick It to your Book
King Size

I'm Boy Crazy
Stick It to Your Book
Please Steal This Book

Kick Me
Stick It Where It Hurts [3]
This is a Dirty Book

School Bus Bully
Stick It to Your Book
[blank] Has Kooties!

CARDS

I'm Dy-No Mite
Stick It to a Bumper [1]
Dropout

Low Life
Stick It Where It Hurts
Stick-it

Teacher's Spy
Stick It?
Fink

I'm Fragile
Stick-its are Fun [3]
2000 Volts

Lunch is My Favorite Subject
Stick It to a Bumper
Just Call Me Fats!

There's More Bounce to the Ounce
Stick It Where It Hurts
Foam Rubber

A Jock Your Not! (NOT378516)
As a Lover Your a Bummer! (LOV231476)
As a Lover Your a Bummer! (BUM2467)
Future All-Time Dunce! (DUN8967)
Get Off Your End and Do Some Work!
(END167360)
On School Bus (BUS867516)
Personal Appearance [Boys] (PA167516)
Personal Appearance [Girls] (PA1675167)
Playground Violations (PLA451278)
Rest Room Violations (RR3215670)
Slow Down You Idiot! (ID782316)
That Was Some Boo-Boo Baby!
(BOO196701)
To a Future Fatty! (FAT8816732)

I'm the Class Bully
Stick It to a Bumper
Fool [purple]

Mystery Meat Served Here
Stick 'Em Everywhere
Boys Locker Room

Weight Watcher
Stick-its are Fun
10th Wonder of the World

I'm the Class Bully
Stick-its are Fun [1]
Fool [blue]

STICK-IT-TO-EM (66)
INSULT STICKERS

2 1/2" X 3 3/8"

You have to give Fleer credit for using the old noggin on this one. Once you peel off the sticker in most sets, you're left with no record of what it looked like. However, peeling a sticker in this set still leaves you with a card on the other side. These cards have the same designs as the stickers, but identical designs do not appear back-to-back. Fleer did exaggerate on the wrappers, which claim there are "6 stickers ... plus 6 cards" in every pack. Both wrappers are yellow with identical layouts except for the two stickers below the title.

ITEM	MINT	EX
Set	18.00	15.00
Sticker-card	.25	.20
Wrappers (2)		
each	--	.35

1 Dentist Office Closed
2 Janitors Room
3 I'm the Class Slob
4 Gas Station
5 Smoking Allowed
6 I'm the Class Dirty-Mouth
7 I'm the Class Cheat
8 I'm the Class Stool-Pigeon
9 Warning — Student Driver
10 Sisters and Other Nerds Keep Out
11 Brothers Keep Out
12 No Tipping Permitted
13 This Shoe Store Sells Torture Devices!
14 Study Hall
15 Warning — Our Cook Has Poison Ivy
16 I'm the Class Jock
17 This Fire Hydrant Squirts Back
18 I'm the Class Pick-Pocket
19 Reject!
20 I'm the Class Brat
21 Smile
22 Health Notice
23 This Machine Takes Pennies
24 Chocolate Covered Roaches

25 Phone Calls
26 This Pay Phone is Bugged
27 The Lunch Box
28 I'm the Class Blabbermouth
29 Taxi
30 Don't Eat Here
31 World's Greasiest Food Sold Here!
32 Speak Loud (Shout!)
33 This M.D. Flunked Out with Frankenstein
34 I'm the Class Show-Off
35 Do Not Eat
36 I'm the Class Sneak
37 Lunch Room Food
38 I'm the Class Idiot
39 I'm the Class Stuck-Up
40 We Serve 100% Recycled Food
41 Girls Wanted
42 Boys Wanted
43 This Dry Cleaner Employs Hungry Moths
44 I Need a Bath
45 Don't Laugh...Guess Who's Inside?
46 Disco Died Here

47 This Bread Is For the Birds
48 Danger Zone Wear Gas Mask
49 Dirty Truck
50 This Motel Is Bed Bug Approved
51 Teachers Room
52 This Car Is Not a Wreck
53 Bathroom Permanently Out of Order
54 This Room Is Not a Disaster Area
55 Doctors Office Closed
56 This Parking Meter Out of Order
57 Free Samples!
58 Beware This Barber
59 Who Did It?
60 This Butcher Sells Pure Horsemeat
61 Principals Office
62 School Bus Driver Is Insane
63 This Lunch Room Managed by the Sanitation Department
64 I've Got B.O.
65 Our Hamburgers Are Rotten!
66 This Mirror Tells No Lies — You're Ugly!

STICKY FEET (?)

"Feet are Funny," intoned one of the Head Honchos at Fleer, so the art department worked day & night to devel-

2 1/4" X 3 1/2"

op a set based on that idea. What they came up with was very simple: foot stickers and foot cartoons. The "stickers" are black, foot-shape designs mounted 10 to a 2 1/4" X 3 1/2" paper sheet. The standard size cards have uncomplicated black ink sketches and dialogue. Neither the sticker sheets or cartoon cards are numbered and the set totals for each are unknown. Also inserted into the packs were cards advising where to put the stickers.

ITEM	MINT	EX
Sticker sheet	2.00	1.50
Foot cartoon	1.25	1.00
Advice card	.50	.35
Wrapper	––	12.00

STOP STAMPS (?)

"More Fun From Fleer" proclaimed the "Stop Stamps" wrapper, and sure enough, inside each package they provided merriment aplenty with three sheets of stamps (six stamps per sheet) and a "Summons" card. The former were actual stamps, mind you, with gummed backs and rouletted edges. On each was printed a stop sign containing a humorous expression—just the thing to decorate the house, your books, school, any-

thing! The 2 1/2" X 3 1/2" "Summons' card had blank spaces to fill in the names of the tormented and the tormentor, plus a space to affix a "Stop Stamp." The set totals for stamps and cards are not known at this time.

2 5/16" X 3 1/32"

ITEM	MINT	EX
Stamp sheet	1.25	1.00
Card	.60	.45
Wrapper	––	4.00

STUPID BUTTONS (?)

If you have the notion that you've seen this set before, you're half right: Philly Gum did issue a very similar series called "Mad-Mod Buttons." The sticker sheets of both sets have the same format: large round "buttons" and small rectangles in oblique corners. However, the "Mad-Mod Buttons" have a flowery design above and below

2 1/2" X 3 1/2"

the number, while the sheet number in "Stupid Buttons" is enclosed by a circle. The length of the set is not known but No. 33 has been confirmed. The series was first reported in the Barker Updates of June 1971.

ITEM	MINT	EX
Sticker	2.00	1.50
Wrapper	––	20.00
Box	––	35.00

Stupid Buttons

STUPID SCRATCH—OFFS (44) 2 1/2" X 3 1/2"

It's a plain and simple fact: "Stupid Scratch-offs" are a mystery. No wrapper or box has ever been associated with the cards and most collectors assume that Topps issued them in fun packs or tested them as a surprise insert in a regular card series. Each card is numbered and the set total is stated as 44. One side of the card poses a question, a la Jeopardy; the "answer" is revealed by scratching off several black bands coating the surface on the other side of the card. Note: mint cards have black bands intact.

ITEM	MINT	EX
Card	10.00	7.50

STUPID SMILES STICKERS (44) 2 1/2" X 3 1/2"

The "dirty tricks" department at Topps must be proud of the set entitled "Stupid Smiles" because of all the confusion it has caused for collectors. The basic premise of the set was simple: make up "241 vile smiles" stickers in different sizes and with different captions and arrange them on 44 cards. Voila, you have a parody of the "Mr. Happy Face," the symbol which has achieved an almost transcendental status among the "have a nice day" crowd.

It seems like the project to deride Mr. Happy Face was not embraced by the public since Stupid Smiles was withdrawn from the marketplace after a brief period of test marketing in 1989. This explains why supplies of it are short and why most people in the hobby have never heard of the set. To make things worse, the backs of most of the sticker cards are puzzle pieces which can be combined to make four distinct puzzle pictures (see illustrations). Since the same puzzle back has been found with two different sets of stickers on front, collectors are also unsure of exactly how many stickers constitutes a set. Answer: 44 different fronts, plus enough puzzle piece backs to assemble all four puzzles, plus at least one puzzle preview back for all four puzzles. Confusing? You bet, probably too much so for a set that has attracted little attention or demand. Stupid Smiles sets have been advertised in the $35-$50 range, with the four different wrappers at $1-$2 each and the box at $7-$10. At those prices, only specialized collectors will consider adding this set to their collections.

Stupid Smiles Stickers

STUPID SOAPS (27)

How many different types of soap are there? Probably many more than are parodied in this clever Philadelphia Gum series of 27 gum wrappers, but hey, there's no need for overkill. After all, the braintrust at Philly Gum probably put away some soapy ideas for a future revival. By the way, did you catch the double-entendre involved here? Remember the standard cure for kids using foul language? Wash out their mouths with soap! Well, here's bubble gum wrapped like soap and don't believe for one second that the kids who chewed it weren't aware of the joke. At any rate, the series consists of 27 different wrappers with names that poke fun at established brands of hand, cosmetic, medicinal, dish, and laundry soaps. They are numbered, for example, as "No. 24 of 27," etc., and the set title is not printed on any of the wrappers. The large display box was designed to be "popped up" into a tub scene and the gum packages (36 per box) were displayed inside the tub!

Bait	Feels-Nasty	Loafboy
Bone	Feeto	Palm-Off
Camelhay	Gagaton	Peeled
Carcass	Gross	Rusty Spring
Clucks	Hives	Shakehard
Cootiescrub	Itchy Flea Soap	Sweat Hard
Cup 'O' Swill	Jerky's	Trash Can Banquet
Deal	Liver	U.S. Army Issue
Duck	Livery	Zits

1 1/2" X 2 1/2"

ITEM	MINT	EX
Set	30.00	22.00
Wrapper	1.00	.75
Box	––	10.00

STUPID STAMPS (108 & 18?) — 1 7/16″ X 10 1/2″

The contents of one five-cent pack of Fleer's "Stupid Stamps" was one sheet of 12 stamps and one panel of two cards. The stamp sheets, like those of "Looney Labels & Stamps," contain several different sizes of gummed-back stamps bearing humorous expressions. Each stamp is numbered. The two-card panel is 2 1/2″ X 3 1/2″ overall and a score line between the cards permits easy separation. The titles are printed in blue and the backs are blank. In the checklist, the cards marked by one asterisk are those reported with frames only; two asterisks indicate a card title which has been seen both framed and unframed. Note: separated cards cannot be graded mint; individual stamps are valueless.

ITEM	MINT	EX
Stamp sheet	1.25	1.00
Cards		
Single	--	.35
Panel	1.25	1.00
Wrapper	--	7.50
Box	--	15.00

STAMPS

1 Lick Other Side
2 Salt
3 Pepper
4 No Smoking
5 Cereal Grows Hair
6 This Desk Contains Love Letters
7 Watch Out For Cockroaches
8 Check Your Zipper
9 Throw Cigarette Butts Here
10 You Have Dirty Ankles
11 Lavatory Closed (For Inspection)
12 Quiet Teacher Asleep
13 Use Revolving Door
14 Official Blockhead
15 Wash Me!
16 Free Root Beer
17 Exit Only
18 Can the Teacher Pass the Test??
19 No Teachers' Pets Allowed
20 Push
21 Pull
22 Very Ignorant Pupils
23 You're A Bird - Pigeon Toed with a Big Beak!
24 Sale! ½ Price Today!
25 Please Wash Your Socks
26 Open Here — Use Brick Only
27 You Need A Bath
28 Down Only
29 Up Only
30 Clean Socks Cause Rickets
31 Boys Are Lousy
32 No School Today
33 Watch Out For Birds
34 Pure Dishwater
35 Rush — Pony Express
36 Squeeze Me Tight
37 Danger 5,000 Volts
38 Pull Then Run!
39 Leave Water On
40 Dry Paint
41 Stop Air Pollution — Don't Breathe
42 Tests Are Unfair!
43 Girls Have Fleas
44 Out Of Order
45 Deposit Dime — Kick Bottom
46 This Kid Cheats
47 Principal's Office Closed!
48 Push Plunger — Blow Up Town!
49 No Lunch Today
50 Hot
51 Cold
52 Be Sure Refrigerator Light Is Out
53 This Locker Is Bugged
54 Sour Milk
55 No Teachers Allowed
56 Girls' Dressing Room
57 Boys' Dressing Room
58 I'm Locked In!
59 For Adults Only, Stupid!
60 This Book Banned!
61 My Nose Is Bald!
62 No Girls Allowed
63 No Boys Allowed
64 This Brain Is For Hire
65 Brushing Teeth Rattles Brains
66 Please Wear Pajamas
67 All Comic Books 3 cents
68 Walk Softly — Yell a Lot!
69 Pinch Girls This Week
70 Your Girdle Is On Backwards
71 Teachers Cheat (They Know the Answers)
72 Tie Your Shoe Laces — I'm Tripping Over Your Tongue
73 My Mother Loves Idiots
74 I Hate Cats
75 My Sister Is A Boob!!!
76 My Sister Is A Bum
77 Soap Rots Skin
78 This Clock 1 Hour Slow
79 It's An Emergency — Scream!
80 Mothers Like Fat Kids
81 Doink!
82 My Legs Just Look Crooked 'Cause My Head's Small
83 I'm Not Fat — I'm Healthy
84 Who's Complaining?
85 Count Your Change — This Store Is A Big Gyp!
86 I Can't Hear Me
87 Morons Are My Best Friends
88 If Your Feet Smell and Your Nose Runs You're Built Upside Down
89 Lunch Bag
90 Garbage Bag
91 Brothers Are Stupid
92 You Must Be 21 To Read This Book
93 Girls Talk Funny
94 Teachers Drink Warm Milk
95 Keep Off The Water
96 To Open Without Key Use Crow Bar
97 Free Sample Take One.
98 Down With [blank]
99 I Hate School
100 Poison
101 Slow — Air Mail
102 Polluted — Not Fit for Drinking
103 Man Eating Plant
104 Write Your Complaints Here
105 Down With Report Cards
106 Student Power!
107 This Locker Contaminated
108 Hang On

CARDS

All Work and No Play Stinks!
A Stitch in Time Makes Your Clothes Itch
Be Kind To Animals...or They Might Bite You!
Don't Bend Over — Your Pants Are Too Tight
Don't Cry Over Spilt Milk — It Was Probably Sour, Anyway
Eat Carrots and Go Blind
Eat Green Vegetables and You'll Turn Into a Rabbit
Evil Is The Root of All Money
Fresh Air Is Full of Germs
Get Plenty of Exercise and You'll Be Pooped!
Give an Athlete an Inch and He'll Take a Foot...That's Alright — Who Wants Athlete's Foot Anyway?*
I Could Go For You — If You'd Wear a Sock Over Your Head
If At First You Don't Succeed — You're Stupid!
If You Had Brains You'd Be Dangerous
National Gorilla Week...Give One To a Friend!**
Respect Your Elders or They'll Beat You
Smile and the World Thinks You're Nuts**
You Have Everything — Brains, Good Looks, Personality, Dandruff & B.O.*

SUPER CYCLES (66)

2 1/2" X 3 1/2"

The similarity between "Super Cycles" and "Choppers and Hot Bikes" is confusing to collectors, but it's easy to tell them apart. "Choppers" are cards and have a line which says "Collect all 66 cards;" "Super Cycles" are stickers on cardboard backing and their line reads "Collect all 66 stickers." [Of course, it doesn't help that the "Cycles" wrapper says "Bubble Gum Stickers" in the title and "gum...and picture cards" in the ingredients section.] The sticker number is printed only on the reverse of the cardboard backing. The fronts show motorcycles, logos and action racing scenes; the backs list statistics or have text related to the picture on front (some backs merely have advertising). It appears that the set was issued by Donruss in 1972.

ITEM	MINT	EX
Set	95.00	75.00
Sticker	1.25	1.00
Wrapper	--	10.00

FOLD CORNER TO SEPARATE SLOWLY PEEL STICKER FROM BACKING

RD 350
The first in the Yamaha line of two-strokes with a six-speed transmission and front disc brake.

COLLECT ALL 66 STICKERS

35

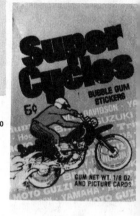

1	Benelli Panther 125	26	Don Emde...
2	Honda XL-250 First—Baja 500	27	AMA Youth Division
3	Kenny Roberts and Ron Pierce...	28	The Hot One Triumph
4	Moto Guzzi	29	Kawasaki
5	Hodaka	30	Canadian National Champion...
6	Frank Gillespie...	31	Yamaha CT3 150cc Enduro
7	AMA Youth Division	32	Ron Pierce...
8	Moto Guzzi Vee-eight	33	Hodaka Super Rat
9	Kawasaki	34	Honda SL-70
10	Honda Motosport 100	35	Yamaha RD 350
11	American Motorcycle Association	36	Suzuki MT-50J Trailhopper
12	Kenny Roberts...	37	Rex Beauchamp...
13	Suzuki RV-90J Rover	38	Benelli
14	Tom Rockwood...	39	Honda Mini Trail 50
15	T.T. specialist Mark Williams...	40	Kawasaki
16	Kel Carruthers...	41	Gene Romero...
17	What The Critics Say About BMW	42	Hodaka Super Rat
18	Moto Guzzi	43	Benelli Super Sport 250
19	Yamaha	44	Let's Boogie With Wombat
20	American Motorcycle Association	45	Chuck Palmgren...
21	Suzuki Trail Hopper	46	Yamaha
22	Yamaha TX 650	47	Harley-Davidson Shorster
23	Benelli	48	Kawasaki
24	Harley-Davidson XR-750	49	Motto Guzzi
25	Honda	50	Moto Guzzi

51	Chuck Palmgren...
52	Honda 350/Honda Motosport 250
53	Hodaka Wombat 125
54	BMW
55	Harley-Davidson Leggero
56	Benelli Enduro 175
57	Suzuki
58	World's Fastest Motorcycle!! Harley-Davidson 265.492 MPH!
59	Kawasaki
60	BMW
61	BMW
62	Honda Motosport 125
63	Suzuki TM-250J Champion
64	The Tough, Durable BMW Engines
65	Harley-Davidson
66	Don Castro...

SUPER DEFENDERS (?)

2 1/2" X 3 1/2"

So there! The Japanese may make better automobiles but we make better trading cards. That is not to say that this series of "Super Defenders" doesn't have its good points. The artwork is striking and well-detailed and the use of different color cubes behind each character is very stylish. However the backs of the cards are, in a word, dull. Dull print, dull pictures, dull information (those of you who have other Japanese trading cards in your collections know how really boring the backs can be). Of course, it doesn't help that the specs are expressed in metric terms, but that's a minor point. To get these cards, you had to buy packages of Super Defender toys and they were not inexpensive (I suspect that most card collectors didn't know they existed). The length of the set is unknown and the odd cards which do pop up in the hobby generally sell for 50¢ each.

SUPERGIRL (44)

2 1/2" X 3 1/2"

Leave it to Hollywood to reduce decades of wondrous exploits by a classic Super Heroine down to 120 minutes of catfight between a Caped Bimbo and her adversary

Selena, "a vicious, frustrated small-time witch..." Nevertheless, the sharp new format and colors of this 44 card set are impressive, even if the plot and dialogue aren't. Cards 1-33 have story fronts, cards 34-43 have puzzle piece fronts, and the front of card No. 44 is a puzzle preview picture. The backs of all these cards contain diecut stickers.

ITEM	MINT	EX
Set	6.50	4.50
Sticker	.15	.10
Wrapper	--	.35
Box	--	4.00

SUPER HEROES (30)

2 1/4" X 3"

"Super Heroes" is a series of colorful stickers marketed in 1978 by several bread companies. The individuals featured are all trademarked heroes and villains of DC Comics. There are 30 stickers in the set; more than half of these picture characters from the story of Superman. About a dozen lines of text on each back gives details about the character pictured on the front. The stickers are numbered on the back only in the "No. ___ in a Series of 30" format. These are true stickers with thin kraft paper backing, not a card with a sticker on the front. The sticker is removed by bending it at the pre-scored crack and pulling the backing away. Super Heroes have been reported with both "Taystee" and "Sunbeam" brand names printed on the front, and with no brand as well (the latter may be proofs). A ten-page folder entitled "Super Heroes Fun Book & Checklist" contains a visual checklist plus games and features. Note: peeled stickers and stickers with oil stains cannot be graded excellent or mint.

ITEM	MINT	EX
Set	17.50	12.00
Sticker	.50	.35
Folder	3.00	2.50

Aquaman
Batgirl
Batman
Batman & Robin
Clark Kent
Good vs. Evil
Green Lantern
Hawkman
Jimmy Olsen
Jonathan & Martha Kent
Jor-El & Lara
Krypto
Leaving Krypton

Lex Luthor
Lois Lane
More Powerful Than a Locomotive
Perry White
Plastic Man
Superman
Superman & Lois Lane
Superman & Supergirl
The Flash
The Green Arrow
The Joker
The Man of Steel
The Penguin
The Riddler
The Super Heroes
The Villains
Wonder Woman

SUPER HERO STICKERS (55)   2 1/2" X 3 1/2"

The "Super Heroes Stickers" set distributed by the Philadelphia Chewing Gum Company in 1967 has 55 titles. The sticker fronts are numbered, have a 1967 copyright line, and depict various Super Heroes—all identified—saying or asking humorous things. The tan paper backing on the stickers has a heavy separation line which is usually visible from the front. In addition, many stickers are found miscut, causing them to appear crooked. Note: miscut stickers cannot be graded excellent or mint.

ITEM	MINT	EX
Set	150.00	120.00
Sticker	2.50	2.00
Wrapper	--	15.00
Box	--	60.00

1 The Human Torch — I Must Get That Roof Fixed!
2 The Human Torch — How Do You Like Your Hamburgers?
3 Daredevil — It Might Have Been Easier to Take the Elevator
4 Thor — That's Right, This Big! But It Got Away!
5 The Hulk — My Father Can Lick Your Father!
6 But — I Thought You Took the Garbage Out!
7 The Thing — It's Clobberin' Time!
8 The Thing — No Fair Using Water-Guns!
9 The Human Torch — I Wish I'd Used That Sun Tan Lotion!
10 Iron Man — What If I Am a High School Drop-Out?
11 Daredevil — Taxi!
12 Spider-Man — Some Web Shooter! I Can't Shut It Off!
13 Thor — You Sent for a Carpenter?
14 Submariner — I'm the Only Wash-and-Wear Hero in Town!

15 Submariner — Yipe! That Water's Cold!
16 The Human Torch — Butter-Fingers!
17 The Thing — Stop Talking! While I'm Interupting
18 Daredevil — Now--Where Did I Leave My Clothes!
19 Thor — Why, Yes, I Do Set My Hair Myself!
20 The Thing — I'm Not Fat! I'm Just Short for My Width!
21 Spider-Man — Aren't We a Little Too Old to Play Leapfrog, Herman?
22 The Hulk — Which Hand Has the Chocolate Candy?
23 Daredevil — Who Moved the Trapeze?
24 Dr. Strange — All I Get is Nag, Nag, Nag!
25 The Thing — That Dry Skin Cream is Just No Good!
26 Submariner — Who Stole My Pants?

Super Hero Stickers

27 Daredevil — Darn! Missed the Bus Again
28 Iron Man — Well, There Goes My Last Roll of Caps!
29 Spider-Man — But Mother, I'm Too Old for Dancing Lessons!
30 The Hulk — What Do You Mean You Don't Have My Shoe Size?
31 The Hulk — Who Used Up the Hot Water?
32 The Thing — Clyde! How You've Changed!
33 The Hulk — Ouch! Bwang!
34 Dr. Strange — If You Can't Beat 'Em-- Call Them Names
35 Captain America — No, Lady, This Isn't Your Trash Can Lid!
36 The Thing — I May Not be Brave, But I'm Handsome!

37 Iron Man — Let's See Now -- What's Good for Rust?
38 The Hulk — This is the Last Time I'll Babysit!
39 Spider-Man — I Must Have Made a Wrong Turn
40 Iron Man — My Work is So Secret, Even I Don't Know What I'm Doing!
41 Thor — Turn That Air Conditioner Off!
42 Your Friendly Neighborhood Spider-Man — Smile! Later Today You Won't Feel Like It
43 Spider-Man — May I Leave the Room?
44 Iron Man — They Just Don't Make Chains the Way They Used To!
45 The Hulk — Rah! Rah! Team!
46 Submariner — Which Way is the Men's Locker Room?

47 The Hulk — The Dance is Tonight! Why Isn't My Suit Ready?
48 The Hulk — One, Two Cha Cha Cha!
49 Spider-Man — Hey, Lady - You Dropped Your Package!
50 Captain America — Regular Aspirin Just Isn't Enough!
51 We're That New Singing Group -- "Him, Her and It"
52 Thor — One More Word Out of You, Charlie, and You Get It!
53 Captain America — Jay Walker! Wok!
54 Captain America — May I Take Two Giant Steps?
55 The Human Torch — Don't You Call Me a Slob!

SUPER POWERS STICKERS (?)

Don't believe for a moment that H.J. Heinz has "57 Varieties" of products! It's probably more like 1057 varieties because in today's competitive marketplace, innovation is as important to the consumer as tradition. So in 1984, the product development and marketing team at Heinz came up with a clever idea: contact DC Comics for a license to use Superman on a new item called "Superman Hot Cocoa Mix." Not that the cocoa itself would be any better or worse than other brands in the hot chocolate section, but it MIGHT sell better if it had The Man of Steel on the label instead of, for example, a silly rabbit. And to add to the appeal, why not put a series of "Super Powers" stickers inside the box? Alas, not

2" SQUARE

even this inducement helped with sales. In fact, the Superman brand of cocoa disappeared so fast that very few collectors (or grocery shoppers) ever knew it existed. So fast, indeed, that even a sharp-eyed collector like myself only managed to buy two boxes before it departed to never-never land. In each box, I found the very same sticker of Superman. Were there any more characters of different poses? None have been reported to date. Occasionally, you'll see one of these blank-backed, 2" square stickers for sale at a card convention or yard sale for anywhere from 5¢ to 50¢. That's not much to pay for a "Cinderella" collectible.

SUPERMAN (4)

It is believed that this 1979 "Krypton Bubble Gum" set of four Superman pictures was the first "poly-bag" set ever

2 1/2" X 3 5/8"

issued by Topps. The bags are blue and have the distinctive "S" logo printed on the front in bright orange and yellow colors. The Superman figures on back are surrounded by white outlines which make them stand out brightly from the blue background of the bag. Each bag bears a 1979 copyright and production code, and these four designs are the only ones reported to date.

ITEM	MINT	EX
Set	--	11.00
Bag	--	2.50
Box	--	7.50

SUPERMAN (66)   2 1/2" X 3 1/2"

Judging from the range of back variations recently reported by collector Bob Marks, it appears that Topps may have distributed this 66-card series over a period of several years beginning in 1966. Each card sports a black and white photo from the TV show. There are three types of backs: (1) completely white; (2) dull orange with copyright beneath text; (3) dull orange with "Watch Superman On T.V." under text and copyright on right border. The first variety is scarce; the others are common. The series may have once been issued with gum, but only gumless packs have been found in recent years.

ITEM	MINT	EX
Set	225.00	190.00
Cards		
White back		Speculative
All others	3.00	2.50
Wrapper	--	20.00
Box	--	100.00

1 "Krypton is Doomed"	23 Crushing Blow	45 Super Safecracker
2 Destination: Earth	24 Seeing with X-ray Eyes	46 Interviewing the Chief
3 Superman's Parents	25 Saved by Superman	47 Superman's Pet
4 Ace Reporter	26 Safe at Last	48 At the Police Station
5 Superman	27 Superman's Peril	49 Capturing the Crooks
6 A Job for Superman	28 Jimmy, Superman & Perry	50 The Alien Arrives
7 The Man of Steel	29 Great Caesar's Ghost	51 Superman Gets His Man
8 Superman's Strength	30 Bullets Bounce Off Him	52 Jor-El on Krypton
9 Metropolis' Hero	31 In the Nick of Time	53 Jimmy Behind Bars
10 The Threat	32 Superman & the Savages	54 "Help Me, Superman"
11 Plotting Lois' Death	33 Superman Leaps In	55 Lois Threatened!
12 Lois in Trouble	34 Superman to the Rescue	56 Superman's Search
13 Lois is Kidnapped	35 Superman's Problem	57 Pa Kent Finds Superboy
14 Jimmy and Clark	36 The Challenge	58 Held as a Hostage
15 "He's Been Shot"	37 The Pirates' Decision	59 Rocket from Krypton
16 Clark Gets a Lead	38 It's Superman!	60 Flight over Metropolis
17 "No False Moves, Kent"	39 Helping Hand	61 The Kryptonite Ray
18 "You're Finished, Kent"	40 Superman & the Cavemen	62 Superman as a Baby
19 Superman in Action	41 Facing the Death Ray	63 Ruler of Krypton
20 Futile Fight	42 Superman's "Wedding"	64 Superman's Father
21 Superman's Warning	43 Happy Ending	65 Visitor from Space
22 The Backfire	44 Reporter Clark Kent	66 Harmless Blow

SUPERMAN IN THE JUNGLE (66) 2 1/2" X 3 1/2"

This 66-card set appears to be yet another Topps production that was tested on the market and then disappeared. Each card has a color drawing surrounded by white borders on the front; the caption is located in a panel within the picture area. The backs are green and contain the card number and text. We have no information about the "full-color jigsaw puzzle" advertised on the wrapper.

ITEM	MINT	EX
Set	4000.00	3000.00
Card	50.00	40.00
Wrapper	--	400.00
Box	--	600.00

Superman in the Jungle

1 Assignment - Africa
2 Luthor Escapes
3 A Job for Superman
4 A Jungle Inferno
5 Superman to the Rescue
6 Snuffing Out the Flames
7 Steel on Steel
8 A Grateful People
9 A Leopard Lurks
10 The Leopard Leaps
11 Luthor's Laboratory
12 The Ghastly Gorilla
13 Jimmy in Jeopardy
14 Rocking the Rhino

15 The Perilous Panther
16 Fangs of Death
17 Escape by X-Ray
18 Crisis on the Congo
19 In the Nick of Time
20 Jungle Ambush
21 Blasting the Python
22 The Evil Luthor Lurks
23 The Lost City
24 Kidnapping Congo Style
25 Into the Lost City
26 Jimmy on the Spot
27 Before Mighty Kryptonia
28 A Blade in the Back

29 Head-on Collision
30 The Sinister Plotters
31 Surprise! Surprise!
32 Useless Attack
33 Demolishing the Sun
34 Zoruk the Terrible
35 Round One to Superman
36 Kryptonite Kayo
37 The Unconscious Superman
38 Luthor Triumphant
39 Powerless Before Kryptonia
40 Superman Nears Death
41 Miraculous Madness
42 Superman Unchained

43 Lois Poses a Puzzle
44 One Down - One to Go
45 Luthor's Last Trick
46 The Awesome Android
47 Stunned Superman
48 Prehistoric Peril
49 Out of Harm's Way
50 A Trap is Sprung
51 An Awesome Apparition
52 The Dragon Disappears
53 Duel of Titans
54 Superman Strikes
55 The Arms of Death
56 Clouted by Kryptonius
   ("Kryptoninus" on back)
57 The Chilling Climax
58 And New - Attack
59 Snatched from the Sky
60 The Secret is Spilled
61 Victory at Last
62 Verdict for a Villain
63 A Final Vow
64 Taking Precautions
65 A Puzzling Mystery
66 The Astonishing Answer

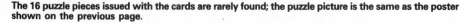

The 16 puzzle pieces issued with the cards are rarely found; the puzzle picture is the same as the poster shown on the previous page.

SUPERMAN TATTOOS (?)

A set first reported by Buck Barker in his 4th Updates (July 1962). The yellow exterior wrapper depicts "The Man of Steel" snapping chains in two; the letters of the title are red and gray. The multi-colored tattoos on the interior side of the wrapper are neither captioned or numbered and the set total is unknown.

ITEM	MINT	EX
Wrapper	--	10.00
Box	--	100.00

SUPERMAN, THE MOVIE (165 & 28)

The series Superman The Movie — a Topps product issued in 1978-79 — contains 165 cards, 12 color stickers, and 16 foil stickers. The first series of white-bordered cards (1—77) has color photos enclosed by red frame lines. Both the blue-bordered stickers (6) and the foil stickers (6) are unnumbered. Second series cards (78—165) have blue frame lines and red borders. There are ten foil stickers and six regular red-bordered stickers, all unnumbered. First series reverses fall into three types: "Story Summary" (3), "Movie Facts" (30), and puzzle backs (44). The backs on the second series cards are either "Movie Facts" (44) or puzzle pieces (44). Note: set prices include stickers.

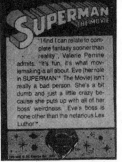

ITEM	MINT	EX
Sets		
Series 1	18.00	14.00
Series 2	20.00	15.00
Cards (all)	.15	.10
Stickers	.35	.25
Foil stickers	.50	.35
Wrappers		
(each)	--	.35
Boxes (2) each	--	5.00

Protector of the Peace

TM and ® DC Comics Inc. 1978   20¢

1 Christopher Reeve as The Man of Steel
2 Christopher Reeve as Clark Kent
3 Margot Kidder as Lois Lane
4 Zooming Across the Sky
5 Valerie Perrine as Eve
6 Ned Beatty as Otis
7 Jackie Cooper as Perry White
8 Editor and Staff of the Daily Planet
9 Susannah York as Lara
10 Marc McClure as Jimmy Olsen
11 Glenn Ford as Jonathan Kent
12 The Majestic Planet Krypton
13 Incredible Laboratory of Jor-El
14 Lois Lane In a Jam!
15 A Study in Villainy
16 Arch Criminals on Trial
17 Briefing Military Police of Krypton
18 A World Torn Asunder...!
19 The Spaceship Blasts Off!
20 Protector of the Peace
21 The Might of Superman
22 A Final Farewell from Lara!
23 The Death Throes of Planet Krypton!
24 Clark Kent, Ace Reporter!
25 Destruction of a World in Space!
26 Aerial Adventure!
27 Escape from Destruction
28 Journey Across the Gulf of Space!
29 Superbaby arrives on Earth!
30 Observing Landing of a Spaceship
31 Adopting a Space Child
32 Young Clark Kent (Jeff East) and his Foster Dad
33 The Passing of Jonathan Kent
34 The Youthful Lois Lane and her Parents
35 Superman Makes the Headlines!
36 Paying a Call on Lois Lane
37 Night Flight
38 Flight Over Metropolis
39 Perils of The Big City!
40 The Man of Steel In Flight
41 Panic In the Jam!
42 Amazing Strength of the Star Child
43 Sole Survivor of Krypton

44 Preparing to Leap Skyward
45 Facing Incredible Odds!
46 Trial By Fire!
47 On the Trail of Lex Luthor
48 The Icy Peril
49 Ready for Action!
50 Heroic Stranger from the Stars
51 The Amazing Man of Steel
52 Interview with Superman
53 The incredible Scoop of Lois Lane
54 Superman Leaps Into Action!
55 Superman To The Rescue!
56 A Daring Rescue!
57 Lois Lane thanks Superman
58 Rescued by the Man of Steel!
59 Superman (Christopher Reeve)
60 Confronting the Arch-Criminal Lex Luthor
61 Portrait of a Hero
62 Protector of Truth and Justice
63 All-American Hero!
64 First Appearance In the Comics (1938)
65 Soaring Above The City
66 Landing of the Spaceship
67 Nefarious Plan of Lex Luthor
68 The Scheme to Destroy Superman
69 Marlon Brando as Jor-El
70 Jor-El and Lara... Their Final Moments!
71 The Projection of Jor-El
72 Doomsday On Krypton!
73 Life-Saving Spaceship of Jor-El
74 The Infant Son of Jor-El
75 Lex Luthor and Eve... Companions in Villainy!
76 Gene Hackman as Lex Luthor
77 Conversing With The Elders

78 Rushing to the Rescue!
79 Phyllis Thaxter Plays Martha Kent
80 Sunset in Smallville
81 Fabulous Lair of Lex Luthor
82 The Villains Discuss Their Plan
83 Christopher Reeve Plays Superman
84 A Razzled Lois Lane!
85 Inside the Fortress of Solitude

86 A Low Moment for Clark Kent!
87 Ace Bumbler Otis!
88 The Dynamic Duo of Villainy
89 Lovely Lois Lane (Margot Kidder)
90 Clinging to Life!
91 Clark Kent as a Young Man (Jeff East)
92 The Family of Jor-El on Krypton
93 Superman in a Pensive Mood
94 Sarah Douglas Plays Ursa
95 Eve's Part in the Lex Luthor Plan
96 Clark Kent of the Daily Planet
97 Director Richard Donner
98 Christopher Reeve Plays Clark Kent
99 Accident on the Road
100 Ned Beatty Plays Otis
101 Saved by the Man of Steel!
102 Marc McClure Plays Jimmy Olsen
103 Face of Anger
104 Farewell to Smallville
105 Glenn Ford Plays Jonathan Kent
106 "And Who, Disguised as Clark Kent..."
107 Superman Visits the Fortress of Solitude
108 Maria Schell Plays Vond-Ah
109 Incredible Display of Strength!
110 Jack O'Halloran Plays Non
111 Spotting the Man of Steel
112 Destruction of the Dam!
113 The Chamber of the Council of Elders
114 Fleeing the Destruction of Krypton!
115 Superman in Metropolis
116 The One-And-Only Lois Lane!
117 Johathan Kent in Smallville
118 Repairing the Twisted Train Rails!
119 Terence Stamp Plays General Zod
120 Mysterious Hunt for Lex Luthor
121 The World's Most Diabolical Villain
122 Lex Luthor Wants You
123 Time for a Quick Change!
124 200 Feet Below Grand Central Station!
125 Cub Reporter Jimmy Olsen
126 Flight Around Metropolis
127 Condemned to the Phantom Zone
128 Eve Teschmacher: Dizzy, Devious and Delightful!
129 Our Hero in Civilian Clothes
130 Clark Kent Transforms into Superman!
131 Jor-El in the Trial Chamber
132 Jackie Cooper Plays Perry White
133 The Incredible Scheme Begins
134 Eve and Her Mentor, Lex Luthor
135 John Barry, Mastor of Illusion
136 Amazing Hearing Powers of Superman
137 Ursa—Villainess Supreme
138 Might of the Man of Steel
139 Valerie Perrine Plays Eve
140 Lovers from Different Worlds
141 Suzannah York Plays Lara
142 Gene Hackman Plays Lex Luthor
143 Vond-Ah and Jor-El
144 Valerie Perrine, Featured as Eve
145 The Farm of Jonathan Kent in Smallville
146 The Stupendous Man of Steel
147 Young Clark Kent and the Mysterious Crystal
148 Superman Spots a Crime
149 Can This Be the End of Lois Lane?
150 Night Heist
151 Flying Over the Dam
152 The Movie Set for Krypton

153 A Cowardly Blow from Behind!
154 Mission for a Bumbler
155 Visitor from Another Planet
156 Lex Luthor: Madman or Brilliant Scientist?
157 Deceiving His Military Foes
158 Soaring to New Heights!
159 'Copter Atop the Daily Planet
160 Death of an Exotic World
161 "How Did You Know the Exact Contents of My Purse?"
162 Threatened by a Mugger!
163 On His Way to the Lair of Lex Luthor
164 The Objective of Lex Luthor
165 Saving a Power Plant!

PORTRAIT OF JIMMY OLSEN ™
TM and ® DC Comics Inc. 1978

Superman Insignia
The Amazing Man of Steel
The Might of Superman
Night Flight
Protector of Truth and Justice
Zooming Across the Sky

The Man of Steel
Portrait of Clark Kent
Portrait of Jimmy Olsen
Portrait of Lois Lane
Portrait of Lara
Portrait of Superman
Christopher Reeve Plays Superman
Superman in a Pensive Mood
Christopher Reeve Plays Clark Kent
Superman Visits the Fortress of Solitude
Incredible Display of Strength!
Mysterious Hunt for Lex Luthor
Might of the Man of Steel
Soaring to New Heights!
On His Way to the Lair of Lex Luthor
Superman Insignia

Villainess Ursa
Evil Criminal Non
Young Clark Kent
Lovely Lois Lane
General Zod
The Man of Steel

SUPERMAN — THE MOVIE (24)

Drake's Cakes produced its own "Superman, The Movie" card set in 1978 as a promotion to spur sales of its bakery goods. Single cards were inserted in packages of ten different Drake's items: Coffee Cake Jr., Creme Fingers, Cup Cakes, Devil Dogs, Funny Bones, Pound Cake, Ring Ding Jrs., Swiss Rolls, Yankee Doodles, and Yodels. The card fronts have Drake's orange & blue logo colors in the center between the black (top half) and silver (bottom half) borders. Each picture is numbered ("Scene 1," etc.) on the front but is not captioned. A sentence on the back describes the scene on front.

ITEM	MINT	EX
Set	36.00	24.00
Card	1.50	1.00

SUPERMAN II (88 & 22)

The Superman II set was issued in the summer of 1981 by Topps and is based on the movie of the same name. The cards have color photographs from the film, which are enclosed with yellow frame lines and red borders. The stickers have color photos and designs inside blue accent lines; they have yellow borders and are numbered but not captioned. Captions have been assigned in the checklist below. The puzzle-backs of the cards and stickers, when arranged correctly, form six different poster pictures. There are no foil cards associated with this set. Note: set price includes stickers.

ITEM	MINT	EX
Set	15.00	10.00
Card	.10	.07
Sticker	.35	.25
Wrapper	--	.35
Box	--	4.00

Superman II

1 Superman II — Title Card
2 The Man of Steel
3 Clark Kent, Reporter
4 Newswoman Lois Lane
5 General Zod
6 The Monstrous Non
7 Beautiful but Deadly Ursa
8 Lara, Mother of Superman
9 Bumbling Crook Otis
10 Editor Perry White
11 Young Jimmy Olsen
12 Superman to the Rescue!
13 Zooming into the Sky!
14 Trapped by Terrorists!
15 Phantom Zone Villains Released
16 Clark Kent Smells a Scoop!
17 They Don't Make Taxi Cabs Like They Used to!
18 Terror on the Moon
19 Hulking Villain from Krypton
20 The Fortress of Solitude
21 The Niagara Falls Affair
22 Undercover Assignment!
23 A Child in Danger!
24 Saved from Certain Death!
25 Reporters on the Job!
26 Rescued by... Clark Kent?
27 His Secret Revealed
28 Flying to Superman's Pad
29 Sky Trek
30 Inside the Fortress of Solitude
31 A Very Special Mission
32 The Fastest Boyfriend on Earth!
33 Dinner for Two!
34 Villains Arrive on Earth
35 Snake Trouble!
36 Ursa's Deadly Heat Rays
37 Non Tests His Powers
38 Welcome to Our Country!
39 Bullets Have No Effect!
40 Superman's Great Sacrifice
41 A Message from Beyond
42 Inside the Mysterious Chamber
43 The Strength-Removing Process Begins
44 Superman... Now a Mere Mortal!

45 A New Beginning... or End?
46 Villains Wreak Havoc!
47 The Unstoppable Non!
48 Changing the Face of the World
49 Belted by a Bully!
50 A Desperate Appeal!
51 The Crystal Survives!
52 Back in Action
53 Master of the World?
54 Raiding the Daily Planet!
55 The Destructors
56 Perry White Hits the Ceiling!!!
57 The Bringers of Hate
58 Holding Lois Lane Hostage
59 The Man of Steel Returns!
60 The Destructive Heat Rays!
61 The Coolest Man in Town!
62 Panic in Metropolis
63 Battle of the Kryptonians
64 Superman Cages Non!
65 A City in Shambles!
66 One Way to Catch a Bus!
67 Ursa Hurls a Deadly Lid
68 Has Superman Been Defeated?
69 Destructive Winds
70 Destroying Metropolis
71 Reflecting the Villain's Powers
72 A Fight to the Finish!
73 Spectacular Battle!
74 Ring-Side Seats!
75 Speeding Across the World
76 Invading Superman's Home
77 Showdown at the Fortress of Solitude
78 The Villains' Trump Card
79 The Final Stand
80 Lois Lane... Hostage!
81 A Clever Trick!
82 Getting a Boot Out of Ursa!
83 The Tables Are Turned!
84 Kiss of Forgetfulness
85 Getting Even, Superman Style!
86 Defender of Liberty
87 Until Next Time...!
88 Checklist Card

1 Superman
2 Clark Kent
3 Lois Lane
4 Non
5 General Zod
6 Jimmy Olsen
7 Ursa
8 Perry White
9 Otis
10 Man of Steel
11 Phantom Zone Villains
12 Battle of the Kryptonians
13 Inside the Fortess of Solitude
14 Superman's Great Sacrifice
15 Superman Vs. the Villains
16 The Tables Are Turned!
17 Defender of Liberty
18 Superman in Flight
19 Superman Emblem
20 Superman II Logo
21 Double Emblem
22 The Staff of the Daily Planet

SUPERMAN III STICKERS (12)   2 5/8" X 6"

Although each of the "Superman III" stickers in this Ziploc Sandwich Bag series is marked "1982," the set was issued in 1983 in conjunction with the movie (1982 was the year in which the license was obtained from DC Comics). There are twelve unnumbered stickers in the set. Of these, ten are color photographs of The Man of Steel

and other characters from the film, and two are logos. There are no captions, so we have illustrated all twelve designs as they appeared in the original strips for collectors to use as a visual checklist. The dimensions listed in the heading refer to a three-sticker strip. The stickers themselves are 1 3/4" X 1 7/8" and have rounded corners. To

peel off a sticker, you simply bend the strip slightly and one of the rounded edges would pop up. Note: peeled stickers cannot be graded excellent or mint and only intact strips are priced below.

ITEM	MINT	EX
Set	10.00	7.00
Strip	2.00	1.50

Superman III Stickers

SUPERMAN III (99 & 22)　　　　　　2 1/2" X 3 1/2"

Topps immortalized the 1983 movie "Superman III" for card collectors with this 99-card, 22-sticker set issued during the summer of that year. The card fronts have color photos from the movie; the frameline is yellow and the borders are black. The "S" logo appears on all card fronts with the exception of the checklist. No. 1 is a title card and no. 99 is a checklist; the remaining 97 cards carry narrative on the back. The backs have red borders and a picture of Pryor and Reeve. The card caption is printed both front and back, but the number is located on the back only. There are 22 stickers in the set; they have color photos encased in wide blue frames and have red and white striped borders. All stickers are numbered, but only the first ten are captioned, so the remaining twelve have been assigned captions for checklisting purposes. The sticker backs can be arranged to form two different 10 piece puzzles. Note: set price includes stickers.

ITEM	MINT	EX
Set	15.00	10.00
Card	.10	.07
Sticker	.35	.25
Wrapper	--	.35
Box	--	4.00

GUS GORMAN

1 Title Card
2 A Comic Catastrophe!
3 Has Superman Been Snagged?
4 Soaring Through The City!
5 The Crime-Fighter From Krypton
6 A New Kind Of 'Car Pool'!
7 Clark To The Rescue!
8 A Nimble Feat—Almost
9 A Gloomy Gus Gorman
10 Computer Whiz!
11 In Perry White's Office
12 Lois Lane And Jimmy Olsen
13 Smallville's Finest
14 Off On Vacation
15 On The Road To Smallville
16 The Chemical Plant Disaster
17 A Job For Superman
18 Courageous Photographer
19 The Resourceful Superman
20 Slide To Safety
21 Jimmy Olsen—Injured!
22 Into The Fray
23 Rescuing Jimmy Olsen
24 In The Nick Of Time!
25 Astounding Ice-Breath
26 The Enormous Ice Platter!
27 A Dapper Clark Kent!
28 The Smallville High Reunion
29 Greeting Lana Lang
30 Gus Has A Plan
31 Millionaire Ross Webster
32 Gus And Lorelei Ambrosia
33 Clark Kent 'Bumps' Into Gus
34 The Picnic
35 Ricky In The Wheat Fields
36 Terror Of The Thresher
37 Saving Ricky's Life

38 A New Found Friend
39 At The Bowling Alley
40 Creepy Brad Wilson
41 Gus Gorman's Ploy
42 The Way To Brad's Heart
43 The Ski Resort Penthouse
44 Gus Describes The Hurricane Affair
45 Lorelei Ambrosia
46 Skiing In Metropolis?
47 Smallville Honors Superman
48 The Esteemed Speaker
49 General Gus Gorman!
50 The Deadly Gift
51 Friends...Or Foes?
52 De-Leaning The Pisa Tower
53 The Villains Exercise Their Options
54 Goodness At The Crossroads
55 The 'Ultimate Computer' Scheme
56 Awaiting Superman's Arrival
57 A Disgraceful Superman
58 Spotting Superman
59 An Evil Superman?
60 Challenged By Clark Kent
61 The Man Of Steel Vs. Himself
62 Dastardly Nemesis
63 Clark Kent—Defeated?
64 Car Crusher Terror
65 Clark Kent's Fight For Life!
66 Goodness Triumphant!
67 A Hero Once Again
68 Back In Action!
69 Righting Wrongs With Heat-Vision
70 In Search Of Ross Webster
71 Balloon Escape
72 The Only Way To Travel!
73 The Fantastic Computer
74 Confronting His Foes

75 The Computer Attacks!
76 Controlling The Computer
77 Trapped!!
78 Strength Of The Man Of Steel
79 The Kryptonite Ray
80 Enveloped By The Ray!
81 Gus Gorman Turns On His Creation!
82 Is Superman Doomed?
83 Vera's Monstrous Fate!
84 Robotized!
85 Attacking Lorelei Ambrosia!
86 Robot On The Rampage
87 Gus Gorman Is Zapped!
88 Allies At Last!
89 The Plan Of Superman
90 Acid Indigestion Death!
91 Destruction Of The Ultimate Computer
92 Giving Gus Gorman A Lift!
93 Stopping Off At The Coal Mine
94 Transforming Coal Into A Diamond
95 The Friends Depart
96 A Gift From Superman
97 Lana Lang At The Daily Planet
98 Superman Flies Again!
99 Checklist

STICKERS

1 The Man of Steel
2 Lana Lang
3 Ross Webster
4 Gus Gorman
5 Lorelei Ambrosia
6 Vera Webster
7 Jimmy Olsen
8 Lois Lane
9 Clark Kent
10 "General" Gus Gorman
11 (Superman Flying Right)
12 (Superman Flying Left)
13 Smallville's Finest!
14 The Resourceful Superman
15 Astounding Ice-Breath!
16 The Picnic
17 Friends...or Foes?
18 Righting Wrongs with Heat-Vision
19 The Computer Attacks!
20 Strength of the Man of Steel
21 Enveloped by the Ray!
22 Robotized!

SUPER PAC-MAN (53 & ?)

The progression of this video game series is almost biblical: first "Pac-Man," then "Ms Pac-Man," and finally, "Super Pac-Man." Marketed by Fleer in 1983, the final series has a total of 53 unnumbered stickers. The backs of the sticker cards carry promotional photos and copy for a "Design Your Own Pac-Man Posters Contest." Each pack contained three sticker-cards and three 2 1/2" X 3 1/2" game cards. The latter have rub-off dots which reveal different game conditions; they are, however, indistinguishable from one another before the coating is removed, so dealers generally include several "unrubbed" cards with each set of stickers.

ITEM	MINT	EX
Sticker set	12.00	9.00
Sticker	.25	.20
Game	.15	.10
Wrapper	--	.35
Box	--	3.00

SUPER SNEEKIES (16)

How, you might ask, could Fleer ever hope to improve on the original "Sneekies?" Well, improve they did by printing new "Super Sneekies" in psychedelic colors designed to glow in the dark. Every five-cent pack contained one sheet of Super Sneekies stickers (12 stickers per sheet) and one slip of paper with instructions about applying the stickers and making them glow. There are 16 different sticker sheets in the set, which was first reported in the Barker Updates of June 1971.

ITEM	MINT	EX
Set	37.50	27.50
Sticker sheet	2.00	1.50
Paper sheet	.50	.35
Wrapper	--	5.00
Box	--	15.00

SUPERSTAR MUSICARDS (260)   2 1/2" X 3 1/2"

Pro Set's "Super Stars MusiCards," issued in 1991, contains 260 cards. When the set was first announced, collectors entertained visions that it might emerge as a truly classic anthology of the best musical performers from whatever period of time that Pro Set cared to review. The finished product, however, more resembles a catch-all collection of various pop, rock, and rap artists than a thoughtful review of music history. The people pictured in the set are those who were "available" and the missing performers clearly were not. That's understandable in light of the egos and licensing arrangements involved but it also diminishes the end product. What sense does it make, for ex-

ample, to have a "Legend" card of John Lennon in a set in which the Beatles are sadly absent? [Or a set of heavy metal cards, like Brockum's "RockCards," that's missing Guns N' Roses?] Oh well, I guess that's just the "music biz."

Collectors will find plenty to like in the Pro Set series. Many top groups and singers in pop, rock, soul, rap, and reggae are represented, from M.C. Hammer to Bonnie Raitt. Catering to the superstar mentality, Pro Set produced multiple cards of the more famous celebrities like Paula Abdul, Hammer, Cher, George Michael, Madonna, etc. Not all of the photographs in the set are well composed, but these are more than compensated for by some striking poses which exist throughout the series. The "Historic Concerts" subset is a puzzler: all of the concerts listed occurred at the Winterland Arena, the Fillmore

West, or the Fillmore East. That's a very biased perspective, as anyone who attended a Beatles concert or Woodstock would agree.

At least two groups of promotional cards (numbered & unnumbered) were produced in advance of the regular set. Most of these were handed out to table holders at sports card conventions and prices for them vary greatly according to rumors and personal whims. Since they are not part of the regular set, we will not attempt to price them here. The regular series was distributed in poly bag packages containing ten cards each; please note that these bags had to be cut or torn to remove the contents. Super Stars MusiCards were also released in England (in a ten-card foil package) and these not only have text revised to suit English tastes but also have some photos of performers not in the American set. Note: the first print run of Super Stars MusiCards contained two cards with the number 86, and no card number 90; the second print run corrected this mistake.

ITEM	MINT	EX
Sets		
1st run	30.00	22.50
2nd run	25.00	18.00
Card	.10	.07
Wrapper	—	.10
Box	—	2.00

AMERICAN - PROMO CARD

AMERICAN - REGULAR ISSUE

ENGLISH - REGULAR ISSUE

Super Stars MusiCards

SERIES I

1 Allman Brothers Band
2 Eric Clapton
3 Eric Clapton
4 Crosby, Stills & Nash
5 Doobie Brothers
6 The Doors
7 The Doors
8 The Doors
9 The Doors
10 Jimi Hendrix
11 Jimi Hendrix
12 Jefferson Airplane
13 Jefferson Airplane
14 B.B. King
15 John Lennon
16 Bob Marley
17 Jimmy Page
18 Jimmy Page
19 The Who
20 The Who
21 Led Zeppelin
22 Led Zeppelin
23 Led Zeppelin
24 Led Zeppelin
25 Led Zeppelin
26 Paula Abdul
27 Paula Abdul
28 Paula Abdul
29 Adamski
30 Adamski
31 The Alarm
32 Bad English
33 Basia
34 Michael Bolton
35 Bobby Brown
36 Belinda Carlisle
37 Belinda Carlisle
38 Cher
39 Cher
40 Taylor Dayne
41 Dino
42 Debbie Gibson
43 Debbie Gibson
44 Debbie Gibson
45 Debbie Gibson
46 Gipsy Kings
47 The Go-Go's
48 Hall & Oates
49 Hall & Oates
50 HooDoo Gurus
51 Bruce Hornsby & The Range

52 Hothouse Flowers
53 Indecent Obsession
54 Information Society
55 INXS
56 Janet Jackson
57 Janet Jackson
58 Janet Jackson
59 Janet Jackson
60 Janet Jackson
61 Lenny Kravitz
62 Patti LaBelle
63 Huey Lewis
64 Linear
65 Madonna
66 Madonna
67 Madonna
68 Madonna
69 Madonna
70 Ziggy Marley
71 Martika
72 Richard Marx
73 Ian McCulloch
74 George Michael
75 George Michael
76 George Michael
77 George Michael
78 George Michael
79 Morrissey
80 Alannah Myles
81 Alannah Myles
82 Nelson
83 Nelson
84 Nelson
85 New Edition
86 Maxi Priest
87 The Party
88 The Party
89 Poco
90 The Party
91 Lionel Richie
92 Lionel Richie
93 Roxette
94 Simple Minds
95 Sting
96 Tiffany
97 Tina Turner
98 Tina Turner
99 Tina Turner
100 Tina Turner
101 U2
102 UB40
103 Jody Watley
104 Karyn White
105 Paul Young
106 U2
107 Al B. Sure!
108 Al B. Sure!

109 Bell Biv DeVoe
110 Bell Biv DeVoe
111 Big Daddy Kane
112 Biz Markie
113 Boogie Down Productions
114 BulletBoys
115 De La Soul
116 Digital Underground
117 En Vogue
118 EPMD
119 Eric B. & Rakim
120 Force M.D.'s
121 Johnny Gill
122 M.C. Hammer
123 M.C. Hammer
124 M.C. Hammer
125 M.C. Hammer
126 M.C. Hammer
127 Heavy D. & The Boyz
128 Kool Moe Dee
129 L.L. Cool J
130 L.L. Cool J
131 Teddy Pendergrass
132 Perfect Gentlemen
133 Perfect Gentlemen
134 RUN-DMC
135 Soul II Soul
136 3rd Bass
137 Tone Loc
138 Tone Loc
139 Troop
140 Luther Vandross
141 Vanilla Ice
142 Vanilla Ice
143 Vanilla Ice
144 Vanilla Ice
145 Vanilla Ice
146 Young MC
147 24-7 Spyz
148 Alias
149 Annihilator
150 Annihilator
151 Blue Tears
152 Blues Traveler
153 Bonham
154 Cheap Trick
155 Circus of Power
156 The Clash
157 Crimson Glory
158 Cromags
159 The Cult
160 D.A.D.
161 Damn Yankees
162 Dangerous Toys
163 Death Angel
164 Doro

165 Dread Zeppelin
166 Dread Zeppelin
167 Steve Earle
168 Dave Edmunds
169 Electric Boys
170 Energy Orchard
171 Enuff Z' Nuff
172 Europe
173 Excel
174 Extreme
175 Fates Warning
176 Fleetwood Mac
177 Forbidden
178 Lita Ford
179 Giant
180 Goo Goo Dolls
181 GWAR
182 Hanoi Rocks
183 Heart
184 Hericane Alice
185 House of Lords
186 Hunters & Collectors
187 Billy Idol
188 Billy Idol
189 Bill Idol
190 Colin James
191 Colin James
192 Jeff Healy Band
193 Jetboy
194 King's X
195 Kings of the Sun
196 Kiss
197 Kiss
198 Kix
199 Law and Order
200 Little Feat
201 Living Colour
202 Living Colour
203 The London Quireboys
204 Lord Tracy
205 Lynch Mob
206 Yngwie Malmsteen
207 Steve Miller
208 Jefferson Airplane - '66
209 Eddie Money
210 Motorhead
211 Mr. Big

212 Ted Nugent
213 Ted Nugent
214 Ozzy Osbourne
215 Ozzy Osbourne
216 Michael Penn
217 Tom Petty
218 Tom Petty
219 The Pretenders
220 The Pretenders
221 Pretty Boy Floyd
222 Bonnie Raitt
223 Bonnie Raitt
224 Ratt
225 REO Speedwagon
226 Randy Rhoads
227 Sacred Reich
228 Saigon Kick
229 Sanctuary
230 Santana
231 Joe Satriani
232 Savatage
233 Scorpions
234 Shy
235 Paul Butterfield - '67
236 The Sisters of Mercy
237 The Smithereens
238 Soundgarden
239 Starship
240 Steelheart
241 Suicidal Tendencies
242 Trouble
243 Vio-lence
244 Voivod
245 Zakk Wylde
246 Zakk Wylde
247 Winterland Arena
248 Santana - '69
249 Jimi Hendrix - '68
250 Muddy Waters -'66
251 Cream - '67
252 The Who- '67
253 B.B. King/Albert King - '70
254 Big Brother & The Holding Co. - '68
255 The Doors - '70
256 The Byrds - '70
257 The Who - '69
258 Led Zeppelin - '69
259 Jefferson Airplane - '68
260 Jimi Hendrix - 68

FIRST EVER SERIES

ProSet

MusiCards

10 POP, ROCK & RAP MUSICARDS

ENGLISH WRAPPER

HISTORIC CONCERTS
NEW YEAR'S EVE 1967-1968

ProSet

MusiCards™

AMERICAN WRAPPER

SERIES II

261 Bo Diddley
262 Bo Diddley
263 Lynyrd Skynyrd 1991
264 The Ventures
265 Adam Ant
266 C + C Music Factory
267 C + C Music Factory
268 Deee-Lite
269 Donny Osmond
270 Grayson Hugh
271 The Hooters
272 Keith Sweat
273 Keith Sweat
274 Linda Ronstadt
275 Madonna
276 Madonna

277 MC Skat Kat
278 MC Skat Kat
279 Men At Work
280 Milli Vanilli
281 Paula Abdul
282 Paula Abdul
283 Roxette
284 Sheena Easton
285 Steve Winwood
286 Steve Winwood
287 Stevie Nicks
288 Stevie Nicks
289 Vinx
290 Alyson Williams
291 Alexander O'Neal
292 The Beastie Boys
293 Biscuit

294 Bootsy Collins
295 The Commodores
296 Guy
297 Ralph Tresvant
298 Ralph Tresvant
299 Pat Benatar
300 Big Country
301 Britny Fox
302 BulletBoys
303 Diving For Pearls
304 Divinyls
305 Divinyls
306 Extreme
307 Firehouse
308 Flesh For Lulu
309 Foreigner

310 Foreigner
311 Hanoi Rocks
312 Havana Black
313 Henry Lee Summer
314 INXS
315 Ivan Neville
316 Journey
317 Journey
318 Kingofthehill
319 Metal Church
320 Metal Church
321 The Neville Brothers
322 The Neville Brothers
323 Pantera
324 The Police
325 The Police
326 Primus

327 Psychedelic Furs
328 Rigor Mortis
329 The Romantics
330 Screaming Trees
331 Sonic Youth
332 Sonic Youth
333 Starship
334 Steve Earle
335 Stevie Salas
336 Styx
337 Twisted Sister
338 Twisted Sister
339 Tyketto
340 The Toll

SUPERSTAR TATTOO TRANSFERS (12)

3 7/16" X 14 5/8"

Each of the 12 long (3 7/16" X 14 5/8") sheets of tattoos in Philly Gum's "Superstar" set contains 14 different transfers (two different sizes). The sheets are numbered in the "header" area but the individual designs are not. One sheet, folded accordian style, was issued in each pack. The wrapper is red with blue and yellow accents; it has a "Swell" logo above the title and a 1972 copyright.

ITEM	MINT	EX
Set	27.50	20.00
Sheet	2.00	1.50
Wrapper	—	12.50

TAC-IT-TO-ME-SPOOKY TATTOOS (40) 2 5/16" X 3 3/16"

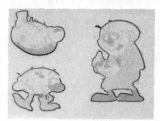

This series employs a standard format used by Donruss in several sets: a sheet of three tattoos (two small, one large) with gummed fronts protected by a paper overlay, plus a cardboard "instructions" card. The tattoo designs in this case are "spooky" monsters, monster parts, etc., and they were manufactured in Spain by Ortega. Neither the individual tattoos or the sheets carrying them are numbered, but the total number of sheets (40) is stated on the back. The 2 1/2" X 3 1/2" instruction card bears the title "Tac-It-To-Me Tattoos" (no "Spooky") but differs from the instruction card of that set by virtue of the patent line at bottom.

ITEM	MINT	EX
Set	22.50	16.00
Tattoo	.50	.35
Card	.35	.25
Wrapper	—	3.00
Box	—	20.00

TAC-IT-TO-ME TATTOOS (63)

2 5/16" X 3 1/4"

The tattoos and cards of this set are easily distinguished from their "Spooky" cousins. The paper backing is clearly marked "Collect all 63 sets" and "Made in U.S.A.," and the tattoos themselves are normal objects like the bell, train, and eggplant illustrated here. Furthermore, the overlay protecting the tattoos is made of clear wax paper, not the brown paper of the "Spooky" set. Finally, the instruction card is missing the patented, "Tattoo Made in Spain" line which appears on its "Spooky" counterpart.

ITEM	MINT	EX
Set	42.50	32.50
Tattoo	.60	.45
Card	.50	.35
Wrapper	—	8.00

Tac-It-To-Me Tattoos

TACKY TATTOOS (63)
TICKY TACKY TATTOOS (80)

2 5/16" X 3 1/4"

The title of this Donruss set— "Tacky Tattoos"—is printed on the back of every tattoo sheet. The set total is stated to be 63 sets and the tattoos, manufactured in Spain by Ortega, are protected by a brown paper overlay. The instruction card is entitled "How To Apply Tattoos" and warns "Do Not Apply To Face!" We recently opened a pack of "Ticky Tack Tatos" and found the sheet inside marked "Tacky Tattoos." However, it also carries the statement "Collect All 80 Sets," as opposed to the "63 Sets" line appearing on authentic "Tacky" sheets. This leads us to believe that most of the transfer designs referred to are shared by both sets.

ITEM	MINT	EX
Tattoos (all)	.50	.35
Instruction card	.35	.25
Wrappers (each)	--	2.00
Boxes (each)	--	20.00

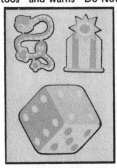

TALE SPIN ALBUM STICKERS (180)

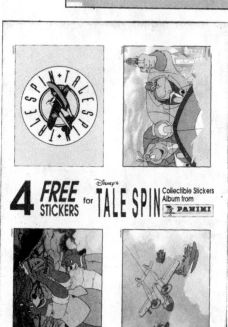

The "Talespin" saga revolves around the exploits of Baloo the Bear and Kit Cloudkicker as they encounter incredible adventures while working for Rebecca Cunningham's air freight company. This animated television series is produced by Disney and Panini obtained a license to create an album sticker set based upon it in 1991. There are 180 stickers in the set. Most of these are rectangular and have either two, three, or four white borders, depending upon how they are postioned in the album. The final eight stickers in the series (173-180) are round. Each sticker is numbered on the back and has a corresponding numbered spot on an album page. As usual, the text for each sticker, or group of stickers, is printed directly on the appropriate page. The album is 32 pages long and is divided into four separate stories. The centerfold pages have four cut-out-and-assemble Talespin air-craft models plus an "air skier." The four-sticker panel illustrated below was a special promotional insert distributed in the April 1991 issue of "Disney Adventures" magazine. Note: set price includes album.

ITEM	MINT	EX
Set	20.00	14.00
Sticker	.10	.07
Wrapper	––	.10
Album	1.50	1.00

TARZAN (66)   2 1/2" X 3 1/2"

This 66-card Tarzan set was marketed by Philadelphia Gum in 1966. Each card has a color drawing depicting the adventures of the Ape Man in the jungle. The card number and caption appear together in a white and red circle on the front of the card. White borders and a red frame line enclose the picture area. The reverse has a detailed jungle sketch running from side to side. The text, caption and card number are located above this sketch.

ITEM	MINT	EX
Set	190.00	150.00
Card	2.50	2.00
Wrappers		
Wax (5¢)	--	35.00
Cello (10¢)	--	100.00
Box	--	125.00

1 Call of the Jungle
2 Human Sacrifice
3 Idol Returned
4 Tarzan Vs. Tarzan
5 Nearly Entombed
6 Inches from Death
7 Death Charge
8 No Time to Lose!
9 Unexpected Detour
10 The Mad Elephant
11 Fire from Space
12 Everybody Out!
13 Death Ride
14 Grim Ending
15 Terror in the Trees
16 Tug of Death
17 Fiery Finish?
18 Watery Grave
19 Good Vs. Evil
20 Desperate Gamble
21 Danger Lurks Above
22 Prisoner of the Lost Tribe
23 Stowaway!
24 Strike First or Die
25 The Ape Arena
26 Daring Rescue
27 Lightning Attack
28 Frozen Stiff
29 Gamble with Death
30 The Giant Spider
31 At the Brink
32 Nick of Time
33 Over the Falls
34 Black Fury
35 Man Against Beast
36 Peril in the Pit
37 Acid Bath
38 One Chance!
39 From Another Age
40 Jaws of Death
41 Jet-Powered Thieves
42 Dive to Danger
43 Vines of Death
44 Kill or be Killed
45 Madman's Machine
46 Sentenced to Death
47 Battle in the Clouds
48 Squeeze Play
49 Battle in the Bucket
50 Toppled Tyrant
51 Cage of Death
52 King Against King
53 Landslide Terror
54 Terror of the Skull
55 Tarzan, the Ape-Man
56 Dungeon Duel
57 Turtle Taxi
58 Program Interrupted
59 The Q-Ray
60 Justice from the Trees
61 Death Trap!
62 Ambushed
63 Interrupted Cat Nap
64 Escaping the Man-Eaters
65 Speak Now or Die!
66 Lord of the Jungle

TEDDY BEAR COLLECTOR CARDS (3)   2 1/8" X 2 3/4"

The second, in alphabetical order, of three different "minisets" issued by Kraft in 1991 on the backs of "Macaroni & Cheese Dinner" boxes. The cards are smaller than standard size and have blank backs. The card fronts depict three different bear characters in multicolor artwork, with caption and a short text underneath each picture. As you can see from our illustration, the principal card on each box is "layered" over the other two cards in the set. Collectors should be on the lookout for complete boxes since there are other "bear" features printed on them. Please note that these are cut-out cards. For this reason, single cards in "mint" grade should have super-straight edges.

ITEM	MINT	EX
Set of complete boxes	2.00	1.50
Set of cards	1.00	.75
Complete box	.65	.50
Card	.35	.25

TEENAGE MUTANT NINJA TURTLES
SERIES 1 (88 & 11)   2 1/2" X 3 1/2"

AMERICAN VERSION

ENGLISH VERSION

"Teenage Mutant Ninja Turtles," one of the hottest concepts to hit the children's market in the last decade, is the subject of this Topps' set issued in 1989. There are 88 cards and eleven stickers in the series, which is based on the animated cartoon airing on network television. Each card has an artwork picture which is surrounded by lime-green, turtle-shell borders. The card caption is printed on both sides of the card (all captions except #1 are identical front and back). The backs have a short text printed in a yellow rectangle and the cardboard stock is a dull gray color. The card number, located in a turtle shell design, is printed front and back. The eleven stickers are basically yellow, with artwork centers, and all save one are captioned in some manner. Ten of the sticker backs are puzzle pieces; the remaining sticker back shows the completed puzzle picture.

ITEM	MINT	EX
Set	15.00	10.50
Card	.10	.07
Sticker	.35	.25
Wrapper	--	.25
Box	--	2.00

Teenage Mutant Ninja Turtles — Series 1

1 The Epic Begins
2 Crime City!
3 The Art of Crime
4 "Get April O'Neil!"
5 Mysterious Rescuer!
6 Monitoring the Turtles
7 A Special Wake-Up Call!
8 The Perfect Host
9 Pizza for Breakfast
10 The Slice that Satisfies!
11 Splinter's Crew
12 It Began in Japan...
13 Ninjas in Training
14 Framed by a Foe!
15 The Fateful Stumble
16 A Man and His Turtles
17 Metamorphosis
18 Humanoid Turtles!
19 Man-Into-Ratman!
20 Splinter's Skill
21 Donatello!
22 Raphael!
23 Leonardo!
24 Michaelangelo!
25 The Shredder
26 The Master's Plan
27 Ready for Action!
28 Underground Heroes!
29 The Ninjas Emerge
30 "Turtles! No Way!!"
31 "Here's Looking at You, Kid!"
32 Our Kinda Town!
33 Ninja Pizza Coming Up!
34 April ... Kidnapped!
35 The Shredder's Evil Gang
36 Let's Rock 'N' Roll!
37 High Flyin' Hero!
38 Time to Fight, Dudes!
39 Clobbered!
40 Turtle Threat
41 Power of the Enemy
42 Zapped!
43 A Narrow Escape!
44 Tumble That Wall!
45 The Rescue of April
46 Trapped by Their Foe
47 Making a Splash!
48 "Water? No Prob!"
49 Unsinkable April
50 Sword of Justice

51 Death-Defying Escape!
52 Turtles Triumphant
53 The Fearless Foursome
54 Rockabye Turtle!
55 Another Day, Another Battle!
56 Action-Packed Workout!
57 Hero in a Half-Shell
58 A Tasty Treat!
59 "Err...Ahh...No Thanks!"
60 Technodrome Terror
61 In Cahoots with Krang
62 Diabolical Duo!
63 "What About My Story?!"
64 Jive Turtles!
65 "Sorry About That, April!"
66 Madness at the Zoo
67 New Mutant Henchmen

68 Up From The Depths
69 Rocksteady's Revenge
70 When Mutants Collide!
71 The Long Journey
72 Courage of the Master
73 Snagged by the Shredder
74 Turtles to the Rescue!
75 "Looks Like Another Trap!"
76 Surrounded!
77 Danger on All Sides!
78 Mechanical Monsters
79 Turtle Power!
80 Roused and Riled!
81 His Best Foot Forward
82 Smashed to Smithereens!
83 The Assault Continues
84 A Mean Green Machine!

85 The Rage of Krang
86 "Next Time, Turtles...!"
87 "Cowabunga! It's Meal Time!"
88 Savoring Their Reward

Stickers
1 Raphael
2 Michaelangelo
3 Donatello
4 Leonardo
5 The Shredder
6 Splinter
7 Cowabunga!
8 Turtle Power
9 [no title]
10 Teenage Mutant Ninja Turtles
11 "We're Out to Battle the Forces of Evil..."

TEENAGE MUTANT NINJA TURTLES SERIES 1 COLLECTOR'S EDITION (110 & 11)

2 1/2" X 3 1/2"

Bonus Cards
A "Yarghi!"
B "Battle for the Sewers"
C "Ambushed by the Shredder"
D "Trashing the Transmat"
E "Ninja Sunset"
F "Battle Above The Streets"
G "Mouser Attack"
H "Alien Encounter"
I "Possessed"
J "The Unmentionables"
K "Stone Sleep"
L "Leap Into Battle"
M "Leatherhead"
N "Day of the Dragon"
O "Dream Flight"
P "Battle in the Arena"
Q "Barroom Brawl"
R "Walk on the Wild Side"
S "Galactic Conflict"
T "Warrior Woman from Beyond the Stars"
U "Brothers Under the Spell"
V "Night of the White Ninja"

Good deal! Those two words describe what TMNT fans will get if they buy this "Collectors' Edition" rather than the regular set issued to the general public. Not only are the cards more attractive, with their super-glossy fronts and crystal-clear text on pure white cardboard backs, but the set also includes a bonus series of 22 cards. The latter are "spectacular comic book cover paintings from Mirage Studios," and they are dramatically framed by red accent lines and black borders. The bonus cards are not numbered, but have letter designations instead (A-V). These cards have not been reprinted anywhere else, so they are well worth the differential between the price of the Collectors' Edition and that of the regular-issue set. Note: the Collectors' Edition was sold as a boxed set only in 1989 by Topps.

ITEM	MINT	EX
Boxed set	20.00	--

TEENAGE MUTANT NINJA TURTLES
SERIES 2 (88 & 11)

Those "Heroes in a Half-Shell" just don't get any time off! Topps issued Series 2 based on the animated television series in 1990 and the cards are numbered from 89 to 176. There are two separate stories involved: the first describes the Turtles' attempts to socialize a Ninja Rabbit who they mistakenly pull in from another dimension. The second plot revolves around an archeologist turned into a human fly by the evil Krang. All of these cartoon cards have red framelines and black borders with green accent swirls. The backs are the same dull gray stock used for regular-issue Series 1. Paradoxically, Topps did not number the blue-border stickers of this series 12-22, but used the 1-11 sequence all over again. Ten of the sticker backs are puzzle pieces; the back of sticker #10 shows what the completed puzzle picture looks like. Note: set price includes stickers.

ITEM	MINT	EX
Set	15.00	10.50
Card	.10	.07
Sticker	.35	.25
Wrapper	--	.25
Box	--	2.00

89 Our Story Opens
90 Pulling the Switch
91 Usagi Yojimbo
92 Unbelievable!
93 The Tortoise and the Hare
94 Defeated by Donatello
95 A New Caper
96 Turtles Undercover
97 Hare Today, Gone Today
98 Rabbit About Town
99 Rabbit Transit
100 Welcome to the Hutch
101 Rabbit Rampage
102 Turtles to the Rescue
103 Studying the Screen
104 The Plot Heats Up!
105 Quakes and Shakes
106 Enter The Dragon
107 Flaming Fangs
108 The Dragon Master
109 A Possible Solution
110
111 An Old Flame
112 Defeating the Dragon
113 Usagi Triumphs
114 Praise from Shredder
115 A Monster Egg
116 Obento's Thanks
117 A Hare Out of Place
118 A New Problem
119 Turtle-Robics
120 No Pain, No Fame
121 TV Time
122 Dig This
123 Worried Turtles
124 Return of the Fly

125 Buzzing Baxter
126 Fly Trap
127 Angry Krang
128 A Gift from a Fly
129 Follow The Fly
130 Heading for their Hide-Out?
131 Back to the Sewer!
132 Gearing Up
133 Sewer Surfing
134 Without a Paddle
135 Sinister Surfers
136 Goons and Harpoons
137 Down Goes Donatello!
138 Taking the Plunge
139 The Last of the Turtles?
140 Donatello's Discovery
141 Paddling Pals
142 A Shortcut!
143 A Piece of the Rock
144 A Familiar Place
145 Home of the Fly
146 Man Into Fly
147 Fly VS. Turtles
148 Blam!
149 Ninja Gerbil!
150 A Reluctant Rodent
151 A Buzzing Boss
152 Saving Michaelangelo
153 Dancin' Bebop
154 Will the Fly Flee?
155 Turtle and Gerbil
156 Getting Bugged
157 No Time To Lose!
158 Conquering the Computer
159 Not So Fast, Fly!

160 Who's in the Suits?
161 Insect Aside
162 Down the Tube!
163 Chefs of the Future
164 Too Many Cooks
165 The Kithen of Doom!
166 Chop Chop!
167 A Turtle Once More!
168 Speeding Turtles
169 A Shaky Situation
170 A Finale for the Fly?
171 The Missing Piece
172 Not Quite Shipshape
173 Bye Bye Fly!
174 Pretty Please
175 Back Home Again
176 Saved by Science!

TEENAGE MUTANT NINJA TURTLES
THE MOVIE — SERIES 1 (132 & 11)

After the success of the television cartoon series, it was really no surprise that Mirage Studios and New Line Cinema teamed up in 1990 to produce a full-length motion picture starring the Heroes on a Halfshell. Topps, naturally, followed suit with a card set composed of 132 cards and eleven stickers. The plot revolves around the perils of Channel 3 News reporter April O'Neil as she attempts to expose the seedy side of crime-crazed New York City. The turtles are kept busy rescuing her from various sticky situations and fighting off their own set of arch criminals ("The Shredder," Tatsu, etc.). Each card has a color photograph taken from the movie, with number and title printed below. The backs contain a TMNT design at left and white print text on a purple background at right. The stickers have red borders with oval color pictures in the center and all have the very same back (no puzzle). Note: set price includes stickers.

ITEM	MINT	EX
Set	20.00	14.00
Card	.10	.07
Sticker	.30	.20
Wrapper	--	.25
Box	--	2.00

Teenage Mutant Ninja Turtles, The Movie — Series 1

1 The Turtles Have Arrived!
2 Leonardo
3 Michaelangelo
4 Donatello
5 Raphael
6 Master Splinter
7 Reporter April O'Neil
8 Crimefighter Casey Jones
9 Danny Pennington
10 The Shredder
11 Tatsu
12 Chief Sterns
13 Crime-Crazed City
14 Phantom Rescuers
15 "Underground" Heroes!
16 A Respectful Bow
17 Master of the Sewer Den
18 "And Remember ... No Anchovies!"
19 Turtle-About-Town!
20 Hungry Mike
21 Just Hangin'!
22 Turtle Soul Food!
23 Raphael Under Cover!
24 The Masked Vigilante
25 Casey in Action!
26 "Who's the Champ, Pal?"
27 "Tough Rocks, Raphael!"
28 April's Boss in a Snit
29 Watching from Below
30 Fencing with O'Neil
31 April in a Jam!
32 Courage of April
33 Subway Assault!
34 Decked by the "Foot"!
35 Raphael to the Rescue!
36 One Dangerous Dude!
37 Airborne Hero!
38 Stepping on the "Foot"!
39 April Gets Carried Away
40 Pursued by the Enemy
41 Back from Oblivion
42 Furry Friend or Foe?
43 Startled by Splinter
44 Pow-Wow in the Sewer!
45 Splinter's Story
46 Mutant Turtle Baby!
47 Through a Sewer Darkly
48 Up, Up and Away!
49 Coming Up in the World
50 April's Pad

51 Unusual Houseguest
52 Distant Cousins?
53 A Frozen Pizza Party!
54 Their First Human Friend
55 The Sewer Den ... Trashed!
56 "Where's Master Splinter?!"
57 The Rat Man Manacled!
58 Tatsu and his Evil "Foot"
59 Approach of the Evil One
60 Master of Plunder!
61 Danny is Nabbed!
62 Dejected Heroes
63 April on the Air
64 Watch Out Behind You ...!
65 Spotted by Casey!
66 Against the "Foot" Army!
67 Utterly Outnumbered!
68 Check Out the Tube!
69 Raphael Holds His Own!
70 Fine Place For a Nap!
71 April's Guided Tour
72 The O'Neil Junk Store
73 Topsy-Turvy Turtle!
74 Special Delivery!
75 Creeps from on High!
76 Crashing April's Party
77 Protecting Raphael
78 Fighting for Their Lives!
79 The Battle Rages On!
80 The Apartment - Invaded!
81 "Let's Split!"
82 Escape from New York
83 Tatsu's Failure
84 An Evil Reprimand
85 Reaching Out to Danny
86 "I Will Listen, My Son!"
87 Bathtub Vigil
88 Casey — Mr. Fix-It!
89 "It'll Never Work!"
90 Whoops!
91 Raphael Revives!
92 Raph's Gonna Be Okay!
93 Brotherly Love, Turtle-Style!
94 What To Do Next...?
95 In Tune with the Infinite
96 Message from Beyond
97 The New Fighting Method!
98 Tuning Up!
99 Ready for a Rematch!
100 "It's Time to Go Back!"
101 Danny ... Ally or Spy?

102 "Kill Splinter!"
103 Surprise for the "Foot"!
104 The Soprano Maker Strikes!
105 "Shelling" It Out!
106 The Battle with Tatsu
107 "Fore!"
108 Armed and Anxious!
109 A Foot for the "Foot"!
110 Turtle Power!
111 Rooftop Assault!
112 The Shredder Pours It On!
113 "We've Got a Problem Here!"
114 The Face of Oroku
115 Saki on the Rampage
116 Outwitted by Splinter!
117 The Final Confrontation
118 The Shredder's Great Fall
119 Dying ... without Honor!
120 The Victor
121 "Thank You, My Children!"
122 Father and Son Reunited
123 The Birth of Cowabunga
124 April O'Neil ... Signing Off!
125 He Loves Being a Turtle!
126 Until Next Crime ...!
127 Clowning with Leonardo
128 The Comics Come to Life!
129 Preparing for "Battle"
130 Shooting Splinter
131 Last Minute Costume Check
132 The Gang's All Here!

1 Splinter
2 Shredder
3 April
4 Raphael
5 Leonardo
6 April
7 Raphael
8 Tatsu
9 Michaelangelo
10 Donatello
11 Casey Jones

TEENAGE MUTANT NINJA TURTLES THE MOVIE — SERIES 1 COLLECTOR'S EDITION (132)

LEONARDO
He wears a blue mask and wields "katana" (Ninja swords). Leonardo is the unofficial leader of the Teenage Mutant Ninja Turtles. He is disciplined, calculating and cool under fire...

CONTINUED ON CARD #3:
MICHAELANGELO

LEONARDO

2 1/2" X 3 1/2"

No doubt about it, the boys in the merchandising department down at Topps were grasping for straws when they decided to issue a "Deluxe Edition" of Series 1 TMNT, The Movie. What's so "deluxe" about this copycat reprint of the regular series? It has the super-glossy obverse surfaces and more readable backs that we've come to appreciate with Topps' special printings, but there are no bonus cards AND no stickers included with the set. That means that for once the regular series of cards is a better deal for collectors than the so-called Deluxe Edition, especially since both varieties sell for the same price: $20. We have not included a checklist with this presentation since the titles of cards in the Deluxe Edition are identical to those which appear in the regular series.

ITEM	MINT	EX
Boxed set	20.00	---

Yo dudes, here is a movie about four really cool turtles named Raph, Don, Mikey and Leo. They live in a sewer, but that's cool because they're mutants, and besides, the city above is a cesspool of crime and violence anyway. These turtle dudes are always trying to help out their friend and mentor, April O'Neil, a courageous and beautiful television news reporter who is not afraid to confront the criminal element led by arch-villain, The Shredder. TMNT II was a full-length motion picture relating the adventures of the "Heroes in a Halfshell" as they fought against Shredder and his newest mutant henchcreature, "Tokka the Terrible."

Having produced four - count 'em - four card sets about the TMNT previously, Topps did not hesitate to create yet another for this movie when it appeared in 1991. There are 99 cards in the set, each with a color photo from the film on the front. The card caption is printed in a "canister" design on front and the obverse number is located at the bottom of a stream of green ooze (lower left corner). The backs are vertically-aligned and carry the movie title, card caption, text, and a "continuation" line. The eleven stickers bear color photos on lime green backgrounds; they are numbered, but are not captioned. Ten of the sticker backs are puzzle pieces and one back shows the complete puzzle picture. Only one wrapper has been reported for series. Note: set price includes stickers.

ITEM	MINT	EX
Set	20.00	14.00
Card	.10	.07
Sticker	.35	.25
Wrapper	---	.10
Box	---	2.00

1 Exactly One Year Later ...
2 Raph
3 Don
4 Mikey
5 Leo
6 Splinter
7 April O'Neil
8 The Shredder
9 Rahzar
10 Tokka
11 Special Pizza Delivery!
12 Clobered by Keno!
13 Turtles to the Rescue!
14 "Take Cover, Kid!"
15 Brawl in the Mall!
16 "Let's Improvise, Guys!"
17 Deli Dilemma!
18 At April's Apartment
19 A Turtle's Life
20 The Evil One Returns
21 Interviewing the Professor
22 Junk Food Fanatic!
23 The Clean-up Brigade!
24 Kitchen Catastrophe!
25 Rooftop Meeting
26 "Seek Your Answers!"
27 The Original Canister
28 Mysterious Green Ooze
29 Their Latest Mission
30 In the T.G.R.I. Lab
31 Startling Discovery!
32 The Pizza Boy is Back!
33 A Lesson from Splinter
34 April Showers!
35 A Bogie-man Farewell
36 On the Track of a New Home
37 Prof. Perry - Kidnapped!
38 Questionable Creations
39 Masters of Darkness
40 "They're ... Babies!!"
41 Nabbed by the Baddies
42 Shredder's Captive
43 "We've Gotta Save Ralph!"
44 The Rescue Party
45 "A Trap! I Knew It!!"
46 Netting Our Heroes
47 Triumphant Villain
48 Splinter's Steady Arrow
49 Ready For Action!
50 The Mutants Appear!
51 Weird Henchcreature
52 Tokka the Terrible
53 "They're Not So Tough!"
54 Beastial Bellow
55 No Match for Rahzar
56 No Stopping the Monster!
57 A Hasty Retreat
58 Man in the Manhole!
59 "Four ... Turtles!"
60 Underground Escape!
61 Home Sweet Home?!
62 Secret of their Origin
63 Mutant Attack!

64 Rahzar on the Rampage!
65 April Held Hostage!
66 A Message from Shredder
67 Lab Assistants!
68 The Anti-Mutagen
69 Pizza Break!
70 A Dough-nutty Idea
71 "Let the Games Begin!"
72 Traditional Pre-Fight Doughnut!
73 "This Better Work!"
74 "MMMMMMMM ...!"
75 Invading a Rap Club!
76 Taking on the Terror
77 One Tossed Turtle!
78 The Monster Mash
79 Crashing the Party
80 Makeshift Experiment!
81 Seltzer Bottle Attack!
82 The Mutants — Neutralized!
83 Tackling the Foot Soldiers
84 Tatsu is Flattened!
85 The Birth of "Ninja Rap"!
86 Rockin' and Rappin' Heroes!
87 The Showdown
88 "Cool It, Keno!"

89 Blasting the Shredder
90 All's Well that Ends ... Well?
91 Turtles on the Edge
92 Their Final Obstacle
93 Mutated Supershredder
94 Supershredder Terror!
95 Outmatched?!
96 Tackling the Monster
97 Turtles Triumphant!
98 The Morning After
99 "Can You Believe It?!"

TEENAGE MUTANT NINJA TURTLES
ALBUM STICKERS (180)

1 3/4" X 2 1/2"

Diamond Toy obtained a license from Mirage Studios to produce this 180-sticker series, based on the animated television series, in 1989. There are two types of stickers in the set: conventional artwork with two, three, or four white borders (depending on whether they stand alone or are grouped) and "3-D" designs. Each sticker is numbered and matches up with a corresponding number on an album page.

The 3-D "action" is achieved by using the "Slide-O-Scope" inserted in the 24-page album and there are 3-D illustrations printed on the album pages. Collectors could order groups of ten or twenty stickers of their choice by sending $1.00 or $2.00 and a list of numbers to the Diamond Sticker Trading Club. The packet used to distribute the stickers is mostly yellow with a TMNT

design in the center. The series was also distributed in Europe as you can see by the illustration of the German/Swedish wrapper. Note: set price includes album.

ITEM	MINT	EX
Set	36.00	25.00
Sticker	.20	.15
Wrapper	---	.20
Album	2.00	1.50

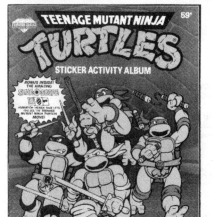

AMERICAN WRAPPER

GERMAN WRAPPER

TEENAGE MUTANT NINJA TURTLES
THE MOVIE — ALBUM STICKERS (180)

1 11/16" X 2 1/2"

They said it couldn't be done! They were wrong. You can dress up four guys in turtle outfits and have them springboard their way through a series of totally unbelievable movie scenes and make a zillion dollars. TMNT, The Movie is proof of that. Following up on their cartoon-based TMNT set of 1989, Diamond produced this 180-sticker series based on the movie in 1990. Each sticker has a color photograph on front and a number on the back. The 24-page album contained numbered spots for each sticker (some were combined to form

larger pictures) plus a centerfold poster in full color (stickers 97-102 fit here). The usual offer to purchase specific stickers, in groups of ten or twenty, is printed on the back cover of the album. The packet used for the series is black; the center design shows the Ninja Turtles emerging from a sewer grate. Note: set price includes album.

ITEM	MINT	EX
Set	30.00	20.00
Sticker	.15	.10
Wrapper	---	.15
Album	1.50	1.25

TEENAGE MUTANT NINJA TURTLES II ALBUM STICKERS (150)

1 3/4" X 2 1/2"

The halfshell heroes returned to the silver screen in 1991 to discover "The Secret of the Ooze," and Diamond was right there to follow up its previous two TMNT sets with a series based upon this movie epic. Collectors will have no difficulty identifying TMNT II stickers from those of the previous movie issue: they have bright yellow borders on front and slime-green print on the back. The set total this time around was 150, a drop of 30 stickers from the two previous sets. Each sticker is numbered and has a corresponding spot in the 24-page album.

The color poster in the center of the album has spaces for four stickers (75-78) and the back cover has the usual Diamond Sticker Trading Club mail offer to sell specific stickers in groups of ten or twenty. The packet is black and pictures the Ninja Turtles hovering over a glowing container which closely resembles a giant automobile fuse (old style). Note: set price includes album.

ITEM	MINT	EX
Set	22.50	15.00
Sticker	.15	.10
Wrapper	––	.10
Album	1.25	1.00

TEENAGE MUTANT NINJA TURTLES
ACTION FIGURES (4)

4 3/8" X 6 1/2"

The best TMNT collectible of the 1989-1991 period was created for McCain-Ellio's Pizza: a series of giant cut-out figures of the four halfshell heroes. The Raphael figure illustrated here is 4 3/8" wide at the base and measures 6 1/2" tall at the highest point. The wavy lines around the figure are the "suggested" cut lines; the dotted lines at bottom define the folding base which allows the figure to stand by itself. The action figure series adorned pizza boxes in 1990 and it is assumed, but not confirmed, that all four Ninja Turtles were produced and distributed. Figures that are cut away from the box are valued at $1.00 each; intact boxes are worth $2.00.

TEENAGE MUTANT NINJA TURTLES COLLECTOR CARDS (17)

4 3/8" X 5 1/4"

McCain-Ellio's Pizza also issued a series of 17 "movie scene" cards in 1990 in conjunction with the first TMNT film. The cards could be obtained in two ways. The first, or hard way, was to assemble a set by cutting individual cards off the pizza cartons purchased in the frozen foods section of the grocery. This was certainly a hit-or-miss method, especially since the same card was likely to appear on all the boxes in a particular shipment. It was far easier to obtain a complete set by sending in three purchase proofs and $3.00 (you also received a 22" X 32" poster and $1.00 worth of coupons in the deal). The cards printed on the boxes had dotted lines to aid in their removal; please note that the caption panel had separate lines for cutting it away from the picture. Each scene is numbered in an orange colored block inside the picture area and the backs of the cards are blank. Note: no mint prices are given for package back cards and no single prices are given for cards in the mail-order set.

ITEM	MINT	EX
Mail-order set	12.00	9.00
Box card set	––	8.50
Box card	––	.50

FRONT OF CARD (BACK IS BLANK)

PANEL WITH MAIL-IN OFFER FOR SET

604

TEENAGE MUTANT NINJA TURTLES STICKERS (18)

1 5/8" X 3 1/2"

This series of 18 small stickers, marketed by Conusa in packages of "Bonkers" fruit candies, has

April O'Neil	Michaelangelo (left hand down)
Bebop	Raphael
Donatello	Rocksteady
Foot Soldier	Shredder
Fresh From The Sewer	Splinter
Krang	Teenage Mutant Ninja Turtles
Leonardo (sword to right)	(group)
Leonardo ("Cowabunga")	Turtle Blimp
Leonardo (resting on sword)	Turtle Party Wagon ("Let's
Michaelangelo (left hand up)	Party Dude!")

probably eluded the attention of most collectors. On the fronts are artwork pictures of various TMNT characters and vehicles, plus one slogan (other TMNT catchphrases are printed on several stickers that also show a character or vehicle). Each sticker has a paper backing which is imprinted on the opposite side with two mail offers and an address blank. A small notice about the stickers is located on the front of two different Bonkers wrappers: the "assorted" wrapper is yellow and the "grape" wrapper is purple. The series was issued in 1989 as a tie-in with the successful television cartoon featuring the TMNT's. Note: the stickers have rounded corners and peeled stickers cannot be graded excellent or mint.

ITEM	MINT	EX
Set	12.00	9.00
Sticker	.50	.35
Wrappers (2)		
each	––	.50

TEENAGE MUTANT NINJA TURTLES STICKERS (5)

2 1/2" X 3 1/2"

The Continental Baking Company created a specialty item called "Teenage Mutant Ninja Turtle Pies" to sell under the "Hostess" brand name in 1991. The pies were sold in four different yellow packages, each picturing one of the TMNT turtles. Packed inside with each pie was a large glossy-surface sticker

with a clear acetate backing. There are five stickers in the set and none are numbered or captioned. Each of the four turtles is featured on a single sticker; the fifth and last sticker is a group picture. Turtle Pies made their debut as early as February but the duration of the promotion has not yet been establish-

ed. Since the stickers are not captioned, we have illustrated them as a visual checklist. Note: peeled stickers cannot be graded excellent or mint.

ITEM	MINT	EX
Set	3.00	2.00
Sticker	.50	.35
Wrappers (4)		
each	––	1.00

TEENAGE MUTANT NINJA TURTLES MOVIE STICKERS (5)

2 1/2" X 3 1/2"

At the very same time that Continental Baking was distributing the cartoon artwork TMNT series previously described, the company also issued a series of five TMNT "cards" based on the "Secret of the Ooze" film about to be released in March, 1991. The yellow "Hostess" wrappers used for the artwork set were refitted with a larger red advertising seal on the front to attract more attention to the insert cards and the upcoming movie. The five "cards" in the set are printed on very thinstock; the material actually seems to be some form of acetate and the cards can be folded in different directions without being harmed. They are not numbered or captioned, but they do have printed backs which advertise the TMNT II movie. Each card shows a color scene from the movie, with a "slime" border inside the black frameline and white borders on the outside. Only one wrapper design has been confirmed to date but it is assumed that there are four different ones.

ITEM	MINT	EX
Set	3.00	2.00
Card	.50	.35
Wrappers (4)		
each	---	1.00

TEENAGE MUTANT NINJA TURTLES VENDING MACHINE STICKERS (15)

2" X 2 3/4"

Bebop
Casey Jones
Donatello
Krang
Leatherhead
Leonardo
Michaelangelo
Mondo Gecko
Raphael
Rocksteady
Shredder
Splinter
Teenage Mutant Ninja Turtles (vertical)
Teenage Mutant Ninja Turtles (horizontal)
Teenage Mutant Ninja Turtles (Heroes in a Half Shell)

The fifteenth and final TMNT listing in this book is a series of foil stickers sold in vending machines in 1990. We have 15 different titles in our checklist and this appears to constitute a set, although there is some question about a color and size variation for "Donatello." The stickers are not numbered and the only print on them is a credit line for Mirage Studios. They have a plain white paper backing with a pre-scored line down the middle for easy removal. These stickers came folded inside plastic containers and sold for 25¢ each in vending machines placed in variety and grocery stores. From a supply point of view, it is probably very difficult to assemble a set and each sticker ALWAYS has creases as a result of the way it was packed. Single stickers retail for 25¢ each; a set of 15 is valued at $7.50.

TERMINATOR 2 (44)

2 1/2" X 3"

It's not often that two competing companies decide to offer sets about the same subject, like Topps and Impel did for the movie "Terminator 2." Impel probably paid the most money to get its license from Carolco Pictures, since trading cards, not stickers, are the format of choice. But give Topps credit: limited to the sticker format, they came up with an interesting and well-designed series.

All 44 stickers have vibrant blue borders and hi-tech red and black framelines enclosing color pictures from the film. There are two types of backs.

1	"I'll Be Back"
2	Terminator
3	Sarah Connor
4	Young John Connor
5	The T-1000
6	L.A. 2029
7	Men vs. Machines
8	Endoskeleton Patrol
9	In Search of John
10	Sarah's Nightmare
11	A Date with Destiny
12	Big-Rig Pursuit
13	Fiery Escape

Stickers 1-38 have "Sequence" backs featuring another, smaller color picture and several lines of text (yes, the LED light is in the "armed" box on ALL of the backs). The reverses of stickers 39-44, however, are puzzle piece sections which make up a six-part picture. Impel's 140-card T2 set seems to be the major reason that this Topps' issue hasn't received much attention from collectors, but from a historical perspective, that's a mistake. Stickers are more fragile than cards and they always are priced higher on a per-unit basis, so T2 by Topps seems undervalued at this time. Note: peeled stickers cannot be graded excellent or mint.

ITEM	MINT	EX
Set	7.00	4.50
Sticker	.15	.10
Wrapper	---	.10
Box	---	2.00

14 "We Gotta Rescue Mom"	19 Not-So-Friendly Persuasion	24 Battering Van	29 Battered but Unbowed
15 Protector ... or Assassin?	20 Armed and Dangerous	25 The T-1000's Aerial Exit	30 Warrior Out of Time
16 Programmed to Kill	21 Guardian of Tomorrow	26 Road Warriors	31 A Clash of Titans
17 The Refuge	22 The Combatants	27 Blasting a Big-Rig	32 Against the Mercury Man
18 Saving Sarah from Herself	23 "No Problemo"	28 Besting the Behemoth	33 Sarah Faces Death
			34 The Deception
			35 "Hasta La Vista, Baby"
			36 A Final Farewell
			37 Programmed to Protect
			38 More than a Machine
			39 Adult John Connor
			40 Cycling Cyborg
			41 Mankind's Enemy
			42 "I Need a Vacation"
			43 Saviors of the Earth
			44 The Killing Machine

TERMINATOR 2 (140)

2 1/2" X 3 1/2"

In one of the neatest switches in movie history, Carolco Pictures brought back the awesome villain of "The Terminator" and turned him into the hero of "Terminator 2." Arnold Schwarzenegger plays a T-800 model cyborg "recruited" by the resistance to prevent the assassination of John Connor by another cyborg sent into the past by Skynet. Impel successfully captured the action and special effects of the movie in its 140-card T2 series issued in 1991. The stylish card fronts display an excellent blend of color and design in the framing of each color photograph from the film. The card backs are equally impressive: a small color picture (part of the front image) is inset into the text area. The combination of white print on gray backgrounds makes for easy reading. Of the 140 numbered cards in the series, 132 are story cards, six depict the actors, producer-director, and the T2 movie sign, and two are checklists. In addition to the regular cards, Impel also packed ten different merchandise cards into T2 packs. These offer buttons, a hat, a poster (showing all the cards), a pen & pencil set, a mug, an emblem, a set of action photos, a jacket, laser t-shirts, and a sweatshirt. Merchandise cards are not considered part of the regular card set although they are a reminder of Impel's marketing background.

ITEM	MINT	EX
Set	22.50	15.00
Card	.15	.10
Wrapper	--	.10
Box	--	2.00

1 The Cyborg Returns	37 "You Can't Just Go Around Killing People."
2 Terminator 2: Judgment Day	38 "Talk To Us. Don't You Care?"
3 Terminator's Creator	39 The Pescadero State Hospital For The Criminally Insane
4 On The Battlefield	40 The T-1000 Dispatches Lewis The Guard
5 Score One For The Resistance	41 The Face Of Sarah's Worst Nightmares
6 Armed And Ready	42 "Come With Me If You Want To Live."
7 "I Can't Let You Take The Man's Bike, Son."	43 The Escape Is Almost Complete, When...
8 What Terminator Wants, Terminator Gets	44 "Go! Run!"
9 Terminator Begins His Mission	45 Firing At Point Blank Range
10 The Unstoppable T-1000	46 A Close Call
11 John Connor, Not So Average American Kid	47 John Stares At The Unstoppable T-1000
12 Sarah Connor, Former Waitress	48 Terminator Sews Up Sarah's Wound
13 Observing A Mental Patient	49 "Does It Hurt?"
14 Dreams Meet Reality For Kyle And Sarah	50 Terminator's Switch Is Reset To "Learn"
15 "I Feel Much Better Now..."	51 Resetting Terminator's Computer Chip
16 "You Have To Let Me See My Son."	52 Keeping Watch
17 Officer X Stalks Its Prey	53 "Miles Dyson," Computer Genius
18 Hunting For John	54 Sunday Morning At The Home Of Miles Dyson
19 Terminator Carries Roses For His "Date"	55 James Cameron Directs At The "Compound"
20 If John Thinks This Game Is Intense, Just Wait...	56 Going For Guns
21 The T-1000 Closes-in On John	57 "Oye, Big John. Who's Your Large Friend?"
22 Terminator Explodes Through The Shop Window	58 Enrique Salceda's Compound: An "Oasis" In The Desert
23 A Rough Landing	59 "Drop By Any Time..."
24 Terminator Gets Back Up	60 High-Five
25 Exiting The Parking Garage	61 Ready For War
26 Director James Cameron Stages The "Tow-Truck From Hell" Scene	62 Ready To Cruise
27 How Fast Can This Bike Go?	63 "No Fate"
28 Terminator Searches For John	
29 700 Pounds of Airborne Harley	
30 Too Hot To Handle?	
31 Terminator And John Escape Again	
32 When Cops Are Everywhere, It's Easy To Blend In	
33 Who Is This Guy I'm Riding With?	
34 Terminator	
35 Terminator And John Infiltrate Pescadero	
36 "You Have To Do What I Say?!"	

Terminator 2

64 Sarah Takes Aim At Dyson
65 "Mom? You Okay?"
66 James Cameron Directs Schwarzenegger
67 Terminator Is Prepared To Go To Extremes
68 The Truth Is Revealed
69 Maybe This Will Convince Dyson To Help
70 "We Have To Destroy Everything!"
71 "Evening, Paul. These Are Friends Of Mine..."
72 Are These Authorized Personnel?
73 "Let Me Try Mine."
74 Armed And Dangerous
75 Can They Change The World's Fate?
76 Will The Destruction Of Cyberdyne Save The World?
77 "Give Me That Thing A Second."
78 John's Auto-Teller Experience Pays Off
79 Filming The Siege Of Cyberdyne
80 Cyberdyne Is Under Siege
81 Human Casualties: 0
82 The Vault Is Opened
83 Handing Over The Evidence
84 Sarah Confronts The Swat Team
85 "Go," Dyson Tells Sarah
86 For Miles Dyson, The End Is Near

87 Termination Override
88 The Swats Can't Save Him
89 "I'll Be Back," Terminator Says Again
90 A Total Rout
91 The Swat Van Crashes Into The Lobby
92 Airborne Kawasaki
93 Inside A Rolling Armory
94 The T-1000 Prepares To Fire Again
95 Sarah Fires On The T-1000's Chopper
96 "Come On, Mom, We Gotta Keep Moving..."
97 T-1000 Commandeers A Tanker
98 "Faster, He's Right On Us."
99 "Drive For A Minute."
100 The T-1000 Borrows A Tanker Truck
101 Terminator Rides The Tanker
102 "Hasta La Vista, Baby."
103 The T-1000 Reforms Once More
104 "Come On, Mom, You Can Do It!"
105 The T-1000 Sticks To Its Mission
106 The Gun Points Right At The Audience
107 Steel Fingers Aim The M-79
108 The Battle Is Joined
109 John Finds His Mother Among The Machines
110 Terminator Frees Himself From The Machine's Jaws
111 Terminator Goes After The T-1000
112 Sarah Shoots The T-1000

113 The Stiletto Goes In
114 The T-1000 Skewers Sarah
115 Will This Stop The T-1000?
116 The T-1000 Strikes Back
117 The T-1000 Hammers Terminator
118 The Eye Servo Glares Red
119 Terminator Drags Himself After The T-1000
120 The Real Sarah Connor Seals Her Fate
121 The Grenade Explodes Inside The T-1000
122 The End Of The T-1000
123 It's Over
124 The T-1000 Meets A Fiery Fate
125 Director And Actor Confer
126 "Please Don't Go"
127 "I Know Now Why You Cry."
128 The Final Good-Bye
129 "Are You Afraid?"
130 The Endoskeleton Shows Through
131 Into The Fire
132 Mission Completed
133 Producer-Director James Cameron
134 Arnold Schwarzenegger, "Terminator"
135 Linda Hamilton, "Sarah Connor"
136 Edward Furlong, "John Connor"
137 Robert Patrick, "T-1000"
138 Movie Credits
139 Checklist
140 Checklist

TERRORIST ATTACK (35)   2 1/2" X 3 1/2"

My how times have changed! In 1987, "Terrorist Attack" was not only one of the first, but also one of the most controversial "collector's sets" to hit the non-sport hobby. The creators, a midwestern collector and Den's Collectors Den, even hid their identities behind the apocryphal "Piedmont Candy Company" listed on the wrapper and box. The set was advertised as "Educational Trading Cards" to downplay the violence portrayed on the artwork fronts. Compared to some of today's themes - mafia hit men, mass murderers, freaks, etc. - Terrorist Attack, with its jingoistic Kadaffi-bashing and unfulfilled prophecies, seems almost passe. In 1992, sensationalism is equated with innovation, and a horde of private card producers has overwhelmed the hobby with lurid topics which once were unprin-table. Compared to them, Terrorist Attack, a set virtually unknown to most collectors, is a good deal more interesting and, even better, is still moderately priced. Note: sold as set only.

ITEM	MINT	EX
Set	8.00	---
Wrapper	---	1.00
Box	---	4.00

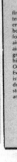

In April of 1986, the United States finally got fed up with Libya and Kaddafi's terrorist policies. Using F-III fighter bombers based in Britain, the United States bombed Libya, attacking a training camp for terrorists, the section of the Tripoli airport which stored terrorists' transport aircraft, and Kaddafi's personal campground. While Kaddafi survived the raid, his young adopted daughter was killed. Only one U.S. plane was lost in the attack. Ever since Kaddafi was bombed, the terrorist attacks sponsored by Libya have dropped off markedly. Would similar strategies work on Syria, South Yemen and Iran!

Kadafi Gets His!

© 1987 PIEDMONT CANDY COMPANY

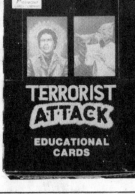

TERRORIST ATTACK
EDUCATIONAL CARDS

TERRORIST ATTACK

1 Header Card
2 Checklist
3 Mad Dog Kaddafi
4 The Ayatollah Speaks
5 On The Front Line
6 Mastermind of Terror
7 A Sadistic Ritual
8 Madman in Munich
9 The Brutal Dictator
10 American Terrorist
11 The Training Camp
12 Suicide Driver!
13 A Sad Day for America
14 Guards Kill Gandhi
15 Innocent Tortured!
16 The President Slain!
17 The Pope Shot!
18 Caught!
19 Making a Bomb!
20 A Bomb For Thatcher
21 Demands Are Ignored
22 Looking for Publicity
23 (untitled)
24 Kaddafi Gets His!
25 Target U.S.A.
26 Attack on Liberty!
27 Sneak Attack!
28 Goodbye!
29 The End of New York!
30 Will It Ever End?
31 Missiles in Space
32 Poison Gas Attack
33 "Run, Children, Run!"
34 America Under Guard
35 No More Muammar!

The Pope Shot!

On May 13th, 1981, the unthinkable almost happened. Pope John Paul II, a religious leader of peace, loved by millions, was shot and nearly killed by a fanatic Arab gunman named Mehmet Ali Agca. The incident occurred at St. Peter's Basilica during a regularly scheduled Wednesday afternoon papal general audience.

While slowly driving around the square greeting children and well-wishers from around the world, shots rang out and the Pope collapsed. After being rushed to a hospital where his life was saved, he generously forgave the gunman who meant to take his life.

The incident is still considered one of the most outrageous terrorist acts ever committed, and seemed to shatter a taboo that even assassins should observe.

© 1987 PIEDMONT CANDY COMPANY

TERROR MONSTERS (130)

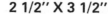 **2 1/2" X 3 1/2"**

From a technical point of view, it is difficult to say anything polite about the "Terror Monsters" series distributed by Rosan in 1963. Take the pictures, for example: some appeared previously in Nu-Card's "Horror Monster Series" (1961); others, as our illustration shows, were repeated. Several of the captions are misspelled. Series 1 cards are numbered 1-64 and have green borders on front and black-print backs. Series 2 cards are numbered 67-132 and have purple borders on front and purple-print backs. Despite their obvious flaws, Terror Monsters are popular among collectors. They were not issued with gum and no wrapper or box for them has been seen to date. Note: the so-called "not printed" cards (Nos. 65 and 66) may have been converted into the two unnumbered "bonus" cards which accompany this set.

ITEM	MINT	EX
Sets		
1-64	185.00	145.00
67-132	185.00	145.00
Cards		
Numbered	2.50	2.00
"Bonus" (2) each	20.00	15.00

1 Konga	34 How To Make A Monster	67 One Eyed Monster Strikes	100 Goliath And The Dragon
2 The Red Planet	35 The Claw	68 The Cruel Terror	101 The House of Usher
3 I Was A Teenage Frankenstein	36 The Werewolf And Frankenstein	69 Konga	102 The Tingler
4 Amazing Colossal Man	37 Teenage Werewolf	70 The Terror Beyond Space	103 Return of the Fly
5 Invasion Of Saucerman	38 Werewolf Meets Teenage Frankenstein	71 Invasion Of The Saucer Men	104 The Blood Of Dracula
6 Konga	39 Invasion Of Saucerman	72 Invasion Of The Saucer Men	105 Invasion of the Saucer Men
7 Night Of The Blood Beast	40 Phantom Of The Opera	73 Teenage Werewolf	106 The Mad Scientist
8 The Undead	41 The She Creature	74 Rodan	107 Curse Of The Mummy
9 Goliath And The Dragon	42 The Hook	75 Creation Of Frankenstein	108 The Aligator People
10 The Blood Of Dracula	43 Unknown Terror	76 I Was a Teenage Frankenstein	109 Invasion Of The Saucer Men
11 War Of The Colossal Beast	44 Horrors Of The Black Museum	77 Goliath And The Barbarians	110 The Amazing Colosal Man
12 The Blood Of Dracula	45 She Werewolf	78 I Was A Teenage Frankenstein	111 The Witch Strikes
13 Konga	46 The Zombie	79 I Was A Teenage Frankenstein	112 Konga
14 Terror From Year 5,000	47 The Phantom	80 Konga	113 The Hook
15 Return Of Saucerman	48 The Living Dead	81 Teenage Werewolf Meets Frankenstein	114 Konga
16 Headless Ghost	49 Frankenstein	82 Goliath And The Dragon	115 The Educated Skeleton
17 Goliath And The Barbarians	50 The Ghoul	83 Satan's Curse	116 Mumy's Curse
18 Konga	51 She Cyclopse	84 The Cruel Monster	117 The Devil's Curse
19 Goliath And The Dragon	52 Vampire	85 The Cruel Monster	118 Goliath And The Barbarians
20 The Apeman	53 The Sea Monster	86 The She Creature	119 The Blood Of Dracula
21 Educated Skeleton	54 She Face Of Death	87 The Colossal Man	120 Half Human
22 The She Creature	55 The Martian Monster	88 The Head Shrinker	121 The Blood Of Dracula
23 The Head Shrinker	56 "Kauna" The Ape	89 Konga	122 The Fire Monster
24 The Giant Lizzard	57 The Shrunken Head	90 The 13th Ghost	123 Skeleton Man
25 Teenage Frankenstein	58 The Fiend	91 The Apeman	124 The Voo Doo Man
26 Cruel Terror	59 The Mummy	92 The Chocker	125 The Giant Lizzard
27 How To Make Monster	60 The Melting Man	93 The Aligator People	126 The Phantom of the Opera
28 Creation Of Frankenstein	61 The Giant Bat	94 The Claw	127 Rodan
29 Skeleton Woman	62 The 6 Eyed Creature	95 Frankenstein	128 Time Machine
30 The Blood Of Dracula	63 Death	96 Frankenstein	129 The Spider
31 The Voo Doo Man	64 The Cobra Woman	97 Return Of The Fly	130 The 13th Ghost
32 The Devil's Curse	65 Not Printed	98 The Angry Red Planet	131 The She Creature
33 Invasion Of Saucerman	66 Not Printed	99 Skeleton Man	132 The She Creature

TERROR TALES (88)

Topps got together with American International Pictures to produce this gruesome set in 1967. The original black and white photos from the

2 1/2" X 3 1/2"

movies appear in a sickly shade of green on the card fronts; a humorous piece of dialogue is located within a conversation balloon in the picture area. The backs are purple and have the set title "Terror Tales" at top. Below this is narrative and the question "Did It Ever Happen?" The card number is situated in a skull in the bottom-right corner. The wrapper is entitled "Movie Monsters."

ITEM	MINT	EX
Set	550.00	440.00
Card	5.00	4.00
Wrapper	--	35.00
Box	--	300.00

1 Don't Move, There's a Bug on Your Coat.
2 This Is a Nice City to Visit—But I Wouldn't Wanna Live Here.
3 Wow—a Fire Sale!
4 Let's Play Charades!
5 Let's Stop Playing Leapfrog.
6 Daddy, Tell Me a Bedtime Story.
7 I Hate Visiting the Dentist.
8 Stop That Snoring.
9 What's a Nice Girl Like You Doing in a Place Like This?
10 Funny—I Smell Burning Ape Fur!
11 What A Beautiful Head—I Can Use It As A Paperweight.
12 Mommy, I Had a Nightmare!
13 Who Says I'm too Young to Shave.
14 Miss, Could You Spare $50 For A Face Lift?
15 Drat It! We Lose More Astronauts by Feeding Them K-Ratons.
16 Remember, Only You Can Prevent Forest Fires
17 I Told You We Were Low on Gas.
18 Yiich! This Man Never Bathes!

19 Ah, These Massages Are So Invigorating
20 Let's Tell Scary Stories.
21 You Go to My Head.
22 I Can't Get a Date, Do You Think It's My Breath?
23 My Ice Cream Melted.
24 My Father Worked in a Peanut Brittle Factory.
25 Quick, Henry...the Flit
26 See, I Told You My Hair Restorer Would Work.
27 I Think I'll Go See a Horror Movie Today.
28 Ok, Who Called My Friend "Ugly"
29 Peek-A-Boo! I'm Watching You!
30 I Better Stop Washing My Room...It Keeps Shrinking.
31 Okay Junior, You Can Have the Car!
32 I Must Do Something about These Peeping Toms.
33 The Soap Was too Strong!
34 Ah Ha, and Your Secretary Told Me You Weren't in!
35 Strangest Egg I Ever Laid.
36 Say Uncle!
37 I'm a Restless Sleeper.

38 Ah—That's a Load Off My Mind.
39 Dear, Your Mother's Here.
40 Ok, Mr. Gulliver, Time for Your Polio Shot.
41 What a Crazy Way to Dry Spaghetti
42 Good Grief, I've Got Dandruff!
43 Hey, You Broke My Wrench!
44 This Is the Last Time I Pick Up a Hitchhiker.
45 I Wonder if These Isometric Exercises Will Help!
46 I Wouldn't Date You If You Were the Last Ape on Earth!
47 Next Time Park Where You're Supposed to.
48 I Warn You—I Know Judo!
49 That Lousy Haircut Ruined My Looks!
50 It's a Swell Car—Let's Eat It.
51 It Only Hurts When I Laugh.
52 What a Case of Dishpan Hands.
53 My Wife Is Always Fainting.
54 I Always Lose My Head at Parties.

55 Touch My Canary and I'll Scream.
56 I Just Got A Loan At The Blood Bank.
57 I Love Taffy Pulls.
58 Well, It Beats Lifting Weights
59 That's the Last Time I Let You Give Me a Haircut.
60 This Is the Last Time I Go on a Blind Date.
61 Peek A Boo
62 Why's Everybody Running Away?
63 Are You Trying to Make a Monkey Out of Me?
64 I've Got to Go Home...It's Past My Bedtime.
65 One Moment Sir, I'll Transfer Your Call.
66 I'll Monkey Around Here Awhile
67 Come on Dear, the Groom Has to Carry the Bride Over the Threshold.
68 I Better Stop Taking Those Reducing Pills.
69 I'm Sorry to Bust in on You Like This...
70 So This Is How You Do the Frug.

71 Who Took My Tom-Tom?
72 Those Picnickers Always Litter the Park.
73 I Used to Be a 98 Pound Weakling.
74 Which One Would You Prefer?
75 ...And Leave the Driving to Us
76 Hey, My Watch Is Slow
77 So, Big Deal! You've Got a Headache
78 Hey, How Come Everybody Left the Beach?
79 About that Lighter You Sold Me...
80 Sorry, We're Looking For Smugglers.
81 G-Gosh, I Hope This Park is Free of Muggers.
82 Hi, I'm Your New Roommate.
83 There, There...You'll Outgrow Your Acne.
84 Phew, I Wish You'd Use a Mouth Wash.
85 Worst Sore Throat I Ever Had.
86 Trick or Treat.
87 Bellhop, Show Me to My Room
88 I Hate Doing Dishes!

THE AIR POWER SERIES (12)

Although the exact date of issue of "The Air Power Series" has not been established, we know for certain that it was reported in the Barker Updates printed in the July 25, 1962 edition of The Card Collectors Bulletin. The card fronts have excellent, finely-detailed artwork pictures of various aircraft in flight. Some of the planes date back to World War II, while others are more

2 1/2" X 3 15/16"

modern (jets). The identifying caption and card number are printed on the back along with a considerable amount of text. The cardboard stock is thin and both front and back surfaces are glossy. The cards came attached in panels of two and were part of a folder inserted into model plane boxes. The folder states that there are 24 different

cards in the series, but the cards themselves have a line which reads "Limited Edition of 12 Historic Collectors Cards." Note: detached cards cannot be graded mint.

ITEM	MINT	EX
Card	--	4.00
Panel	12.00	10.00
Flyer & panel	15.00	12.00

1 Northrop F-89D Scorpion
2 Boeing B-52 Bomber with the North American X-15
3 Convair F-106A, Delta Dart
4 Boeing B-29 Bomber
5 Lockheed Hercules C-130A Combat Transport
6 North American B-25 Mitchell Bomber
7 Lockheed F-104A Starfighter
8 Convair B-58 Hustler
9 Convair B-36 Bomber
10 Republic 105B Thunderchief
11 Boeing B-47 Bomber
12 Boeing KC-135 Stratotanker

THE AMAZING OCEAN (3)   2 5/8" X 4 1/4"

I hope you like fish, or have children, friends or cats who like fish, because fish is what you're going to have to buy to assemble a set of "The Amazing Ocean" collector cards by Gorton. The Massachusetts-based fish company has made it easy for you, however, because the set consists of only three cards and they are printed on the backs of the packages, so you can pick the ones you need right out of the freezer case (they were still available when this book went to press). The card fronts are nicely-colored artwork studies of a manatee, a nautilus, and a sea otter and there are bold dotted lines to help you cut them off the boxes. The cards have blue print backs on white stock and the inside of the package has more information, plus other games and features. A single card is valued at 50¢; a complete box is worth $1.00.

THE CALIFORNIA RAISINS (?) (4)　　2 1/2" X 3 1/2"

Collectors looking for Hardee's "California Raisins" cards are going to have their work cut out for them. In the first place, the cards were distributed in short-run promotions, and secondly, there are two distinct series. The first, or earliest, type of card has excellent color artwork pictures which have a "1988 Calrab" copyright line printed in the lower left corner, inside the frame line. The back has a "Hardee's Presents" heading, a description of the character depicted on front, and a 1988 copyright line for Hardee's Food Systems, Inc. In fact, the 1988 date is repeated once again under "The California Raisins" title at bottom. The second, or latest, variety of card uses a harsher artwork style and coloration; there are no dates printed on either side and the sub-heading on the back invites you to "Meet The Family Of The 90's." A statement on the front of these cards reads "Limited Edition Series/Collect All Four." Given the method and duration of distribution, collectors can expect to pay $2.00 each for cards of either series in excellent grade (beware of food stains and one-surface wrinkles!).

TYPE 1

TYPE 2

THE CALIFORNIA RAISINS ALBUM STICKERS (180)　　1 3/4" X 2 1/2"

There are three different kinds of stickers in "The California Raisins" series issued by Diamond Toy in 1988. Type 1 has the regular cartoon-style artwork on front; type 2 is a 3-D design; and type 3 contains color photographs of Raisin models and characters. All 180 are numbered on the back and fit into the spaces with identical numbers in the 24-page album. Some of the stickers are grouped together to form bigger pictures on the album pages, so collectors will notice that some stickers have four white borders, while others have three, two, or only one. The artwork on the album pages is "3-D" and a "Slide-O-Scope" animator was included with the album to make these drawings and the 3-D stickers "move." An offer on the inside back cover of the album allowed groups of ten or twenty stickers (your choice of numbers) to be ordered for 10¢ each. Note: set price includes album.

ITEM	MINT	EX
Set	30.00	18.00
Sticker	.15	.10
Wrapper	--	.20
Album	1.50	1.25

THE CIVIL WAR (100)

1-10	...	Fort Sumter
11-20	...	Brother Against Brother
21-30	...	Bull Run
31-40	...	Shiloh
41-50	...	Peninsula Campaign
51-60	...	Jackson's Valley Campaign
61-70	...	Fair Oaks (Seven Pines)
71-80	...	Seven Days I
81-90	...	Seven Days II
91-100	...	Second Bull Run

Civil War buffs and card collectors alike will admire this handsome 110-card series issued by Tuff Stuff in 1991. Unlike other sets dealing with the War Between The States, each battle is examined in depth via ten-card subsets. Hence this "First Series" of 10 cards covers only a small portion of the conflict and we can expect to see additional series in the future. The card fronts are a mixture of sepia-tone photos, colorized engravings and portraits, and maps. The back text is short but factual and is printed over an eagle-and-shield design. Complete sets, packed in j-hook bubble packs, are the only reported method of distribution. Although the series title as it appears on the package is "Famous Battles of the Civil War," the title on the cards has been shortened to "The Civil War" (see lower left corner on reverse).

ITEM	MINT	EX
Set	12.00	--

THE DEAN GUNNARSON COLLECTION (41)

Coffin Escape I. Coffin Escape II. Sounds like a couple of cheap horror movies, doesn't it? Well they're not, they're cards explaining an escape performed by the amazing Dean Gunnarson, and they are part of this 1991 series produced by Escape Cards International. Gunnarson is a disciple of Houdini and eventually hopes to surpass the master and become the greatest escape artist of all time. Wrapped in chains and/or hand cuffs, he has eluded confinement, perhaps even death, in a car crusher, a falling parachute, a crate immersed in the Bermuda Triangle, a giant milk can, and yes, in a coffin sunk in a river. There are 41 cards in the series and 40 show a candid photograph of Gunnarson or Houdini memorabilia. According to the manufacturer, the set is a limited edition (65,000) for which the printing plates have been destroyed. Although there is a display box (illustrated below), to date we have only seen complete sets shrink-wrapped in plastic. Each set comes with an unnumbered checklist card which has a "certificate of authenticity" and a serial number printed on the other side. As a bonus, 500 cards autographed by Dean Gunnarson were randomly inserted into product.

ITEM	MINT	EX
Set	12.00	--

Welcome to the
Mystical World of
DEAN GUNNARSON

this is the one card
collectors have been
waiting for!

1 To Be The Greatest
2 Car Crusher
3 Doors of Death
4 The Final Countdown
5 Handcuff Collecting
6 Harry Houdini
7 Tribute to Houdini
8 The Thrill of Victory
9 The Search for Houdini
10 Milk Can Escape
11 Houdini's Milk Can
12 Coffin Escape I
13 Coffin Escape II
14 World Record
15 Dire Straits
16 Family Ties
17 Hocus Pocus
18 Mystical Portrait
19 Bridge Jump
20 The World's Smallest Magic Trick
21 Always Escaping
22 No Escape
23 Shark Cage
24 Breathless
25 Cowboys and Indians
26 Buried Alive
27 The Houdini Collection
28 Portrait in Blood
29 Torture Crib
30 The Great Niagara
31 The World's Handcuff King
32 Bermuda Triangle
33 Houdini's Last Escape?

34 Many Sleepless Nights
35 Daring Adventures
36 The Ride of His Life
37 Free Falling
38 The Great Escape
39 The Final Curtain - October 31, 1926
40 Facing the Future
Checklist card / Certificate

THE NEW ARCHIES (180)

1 3/4" X 2 1/2"

Let's face it, adults who remember the original Archie, Jughead, Veronica, and Betty won't much care for the redesigned version which emerged in 1989, but then adults won't be watching television animation (cartoons) on Saturday mornings. Diamond Toy employed the talents of Jay Lynch, Jim Engel, et al., to produce this series of 180 stickers based on the TV show. Most of the stickers have conventional artwork fronts, but a few were rendered in Diamond's patented 3-D process for viewing with the "Slide-O-Scope" included with the album. The latter has 24 pages with numbered spots for stickers and 3-D illustrations on most of the pages. The sticker backs and album text are written in both French and English since the product was also marketed in Canada. Note: set price includes album.

ITEM	MINT	EX
Set	27.50	18.00
Sticker	.15	.10
Wrapper	---	.15
Album	1.25	1.00

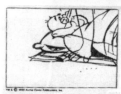

THE REAL GHOSTBUSTERS (180)

1 3/4" X 2 1/2"

A 1986 production by Diamond Toy, "The Real Ghostbusters" album sticker set is based on the animated TV show of the same name. The stickers were manufactured in Italy by Euro Flash and there are 180 in the set. They are numbered on the back and have a corresponding "story frame" in a 24-page album designed to hold the set. The album is filled with "hundreds of hidden surprises" (coded frames) which are read with the aid of an enclosed "Magic Decoder." The wrapper is a paper packet which holds seven stickers, but no gum. Note: set prices include album.

ITEM	MINT	EX
Set	20.00	14.50
Sticker	.10	.07
Album	2.00	1.50
Wrapper	---	.15
Box	---	2.00

THE SIMPSONS (88 & 22)

2 1/2" X 3 1/2"

8 DYNAMIC CARDS
1 CRUMMY STICKER

8 FABULOUS CARDS
1 LOUSY STICKER

"The Simpsons," a kind of animated "All in the Family" in which Bart Simpson takes over the crude role of Archie Bunker, is the subject of this Topps set released in November, 1990. There are 88 cards and 22 stickers in the set. The card fronts have a TV set format with dialogue-laced artwork pictures on the screen (the way the TV is drawn, it looks like it came right out of the Flintstones!). The backs are divided into puzzle pieces (40), puzzle preview pictures (4), or five different trivia features: "Bart's Bafflers" (12), "Homer's Homeroom" (8), "Lisa's Lowdown" (8), "Maggie's Mutterings" (8), and "Marge's Mind-benders" (8). The 22 stickers have artwork designs laid on gray backgrounds and are both numbered and captioned. The series was issued in gum packs with two different wrappers (each pack contained "8 dynamic cards / 1 crummy sticker"). For once, the backs of the stickers were not puzzle pieces; instead, each has a picture of Bart at the class blackboard writing punishment sentences ("Hamsters do not eat onion rings," etc.). Note: set price includes stickers.

ITEM	MINT	EX
Set	15.00	10.00
Card	.10	.07
Sticker	.30	.20
Wrappers (2)		
each	--	.25
Box	--	2.00

The Simpsons

1. "Don't Forget Your Lunches!"
2. "Suck!"
3. "I'm Lisa Simpson - I'm Above Domestic Cleaning!"
4. "I'm Bart Seemp-Seau, Famous Underwater Explorer!"
5. "No More Television - For All Eternity!"
6. "I Have an Announcement to Make: I'm Bored!"
7. "Marge - You're My Wife, But Cupcakes are My Mistress!"
8. "Calm Down, Boy! It was Just a Nightmare!"
9. "Comics are for Kids, Boy!"
10. "Time for Our Favorite Cartoon, 'Itchy & Scratchy.'"
11. "The Family that Mambos Together, Stays Together!"
12. "Bart!!" "Uh, oh..."
13. "Are We at Weenie Barn Yet?"
14. "We're the Grown-Ups and You're the Children - Understand?"
15. "Help, I'm a Fully Developed Female Trapped Inside the Body of a Child!"
16. "Suck! Suck!"
17. "Now Get in There and Clean Up that Mess!"
18. "Come Back Here, You Little Smartass!"
19. "Tolstoy Schmolstoy! Space Mutants II is What I Call a Work of Genius!"
20. "I'm No Supervising Technician ... I'm a Technical Supervisor."
21. "All Right! America's Most Armed and Dangerous is On!"
22. "Ha! Ha! Ha! Ha!"
23. "Suck! Suck! Suck!"
24. "Homework is Society's Way of Torturing Their Young!"
25. "No Reststops for the Next 16 Hours!"
26. "Zee Brave Undair Sea Exploraire Wrestles Ze Yuge Sea Monstair to Zee Better End."
27. "Look Homer, Clean as a Whistle!"
28. "We Can Never Let Him Down. He'll Kill Us."
29. "Don't Bug Me. I'm Studying, Man!"
30. "And Don't Come Out till You Sparkle, Boy!"
31. "Maggie? Lisa? You in There?"
32. "Should I Turn on the TV?"
33. "Don't Have a Cow, Man!"
34. "Bart! Get Back Here!!!"
35. "Anybody Seen Maggie?!"
36. "Marge, Let's Run Away from Home."
37. "She's Such an Adorable Infant!"
38. "It's the Bart Simpson Show, Starring Bart Simpson, and Featuring the Bart Simpson Orchestra and the Bart Simpson Dancers."
39. "Quiet! Genius at Work, Man!"
40. "Shut Up Back There, You Little Smart Alecks!"
41. "Bart! Did You Eat All the Pork Rinds?!"
42. "What'll It Be Tonight, Marge?"
43. "Suck! Suck! Suck!"
44. "March Your Butts Straight Up to Bed, You Little Hellions! Pronto!"
45. "Happy Father's Day, Dad!"
46. "Stand Back, Comrades!"
47. "There's Nothing More Disheartening to Young Fertile Minds than the 5:00 News Hours!"
48. "Right On, Dude!"
49. "Who Do You Think You Are, Thomas Edison?!"
50. "This Looks Like the Work of One Bartholomew J. Simpson!"
51. "You Said 'Left.'" "I Said 'Right.'"
52. "It's Quiet." "Yeah. Too Quiet!"
53. "Kids Out There in T.V. Land ... You're Being Duped!"
54. "There's Only So Much One Hell Raisin' Kid Can Take, Man!"
55. "It's Amazing How Much Beauty and Intelligence Can Fit into Such a Petite Frame!"
56. "AAAUUUGHHH!"
57. "Who Ate My Cookies?"
58. "Back Off Homer."
59. "I Said Knock It Off!!"
60. "Don't Blame Us, Dad!"
61. "Go to Bed! Go to Bed Right Now!!"
62. "There's Only One Cookie Left!"
63. "I Didn't Do It"
64. "Gangway Man!"
65. "Which One of You Ate My Last Donut!"
66. "Bart?" "Uh Oh Gotta Hide."
67. "Last One to the Breakfast Table is a Wimp, Man!"
68. "God Help Me."
69. "Bart, You're Such a Dimwit!"
70. "I'm Bart Simpson, Who the Hell are You?"
71. "Your Father's Chasing After Bart Because He Loves Him."
72. "BBAARRTTTT!!"
73. "I Can't Wait to See the Happy Little Elves!"
74. "Why You Little ...!!!"
75. "For the Last Time, I'm the Parent and You're the Children!"
76. "I Think It's Time to Go Down to the Dairy Den for Some Frosty Chocolate Milkshakes!"
77. "Let's Take Turns Yelling into the Canyon, Lisa, You Start."
78. "Marge! Where's the Personals Section of Today's Paper?!"
79. "We Have No Idea Who Made This Mess."
80. "This is the Life, Man!"
81. "Me, Bartunga!" "Me, Leesumba!"
82. "Unga, Bunga, Yunga, Ho!"
83. "There is Justice in the World, Maggie."
84. "Suck, Suck, Suck, Suck, Suck."
85. "Uh, Oh ..."
86. "Another Day of Parental Oppression."
87. "Aye Carumba!"
88. "Apple Polisher!"

STICKERS

1. Bartman
2. "Underachiever"
3. Peace, Man.
4. Bart Simpson
5. Maggie Simpson
6. Marge Simpson
7. Homer Simpson
8. The Simpsons
9. All-American Dad
10. [family portrait in frame]
11. "I'm Bart Simpson."
12. War is Hell, Man.
13. There Was a Little Accident at the Power Plant Today ...
14. Go For It, Dude!!
15. No Way, Man!
16. Cowabunga, Man!
17. I'm Going to Tell Mom and Dad!
18. The All-American Family
19. Queen of the Blues
20. Suck Suck Suck
21. Fun Has a Name and It's Bartholomew J. Simpson
22. That's My Boy!

THE SIMPSONS ALBUM STICKERS (150)   1 3/4" X 2 9/16"

The rights to produce "The Simpsons" in album sticker format were obtained by Diamond Toy and the series was released in 1990. There are 150 stickers in the set; 126 of these are artwork types with two, three, or four borders (depending on how they are grouped in the album) while the remaining 24 are "3-D" designs which require the "Slide-O-Scope" viewer to give the impression of motion. The album has 24 pages and there are 3-D illustrations on nearly all of them; there are also two game/puzzle pages at the very end. All the stickers are numbered and each has a corresponding numbered space in the album. A special "Sticker Starter Set With Album," containing six packets of stickers plus an album, was packaged for sale in variety stores. Collectors report that it still can be found in some stores at a highly discounted price. Note: set price includes album.

ITEM	MINT	EX
Set	24.00	16.00
Sticker	.15	.10
Wrapper	--	.15
Album	1.25	1.00

THE SIMPSONS & BART BUBBLE GUM (?)   THREE SIZES

Collectors who like fancy packaging will appreciate this group of Amurol items marketed in 1990 and 1991. The first type of package is a small box measuring 2-5/8" X 3-5/8"; there are four known designs, two each for "The Simpsons" and for "Bart." The second style of package is the standard Amurol "chewing tobacco pouch" which the company has used successfully over the years. The dimensions here are 4-1/2" X 5-1/2" and the only designs seen to date are the two illustrated here for "Bart Bubble Gum." The final item is a 3 1/2" X 4-7/8" folder which contained flat sheets of bubble gum inside. The "Bart" design illustrated is the only one reported so far. It is possible that some of these packages may still be in circulation. As collectibles, they are valued (with bubble gum removed) at 50¢ apiece.

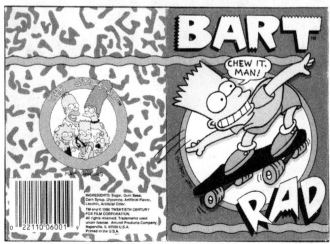

THE TRUE WEST (10)

PARTIAL CHECKLIST

1 Sitting Bull	6 Chief Joseph
2	7
3	8 Billy the Kid
4 Geronimo	9 Buffalo Bill Cody
5 Wild Bill Hickok	10 Annie Oakley

2 1/4" X 3"

The origin of "The True West" series is clouded right now. Some collectors say it came in bread, others say in cereal. Visual Panographics, the company which composed the set for whomever marketed it, has worked for both cereal and bread firms. The only "fact" we can point to with certainty is that there is a 1977 copyright date on all the cards. The color artwork on the front of the cards is surrounded by white borders and the set title and the subject's name are printed in a brass panel within the picture area. The color of the text print on the back is brown and the cardboard stock is off-white. After the last paragraph of text, there is a line that reads "Biography by the Editors of The World Book Encyclopedia." Below this, in the bottom right corner, is the card number. The copyright line referred to earlier is in the bottom left corner.

ITEM	MINT	EX
Set	12.00	9.00
Card	1.00	.75

THREE'S COMPANY (44 & 16)

The Three's Company set produced by Topps contains 44 stickers and 16 puzzle cards. The stickers have color photos taken from the television series as well as promotional poses. Nos. 1-3 and 5-27 are front-peel types with pink or violet accents; Nos. 4 and 28-44 are corner-peel types

2 1/2" X 3 1/2"

with yellow corner accents. Fifteen of the puzzle cards have puzzle pieces on both sides: puzzle "A" is pink and puzzle "B" is blue. The 16th puzzle card is a double-sided preview card. Note: set price includes all stickers and puzzle cards.

ITEM	MINT	EX
Set	14.00	10.00
Card	.50	.35
Sticker	.15	.10
Wrapper	—	.35
Box	—	5.00

1 Talented Stars of "Three's Company"
2 Dreamgirl Chrissy!
3 Suzanne (Chrissy) Sommers
4 Pert Chrissy!
5 The Gang's All Here!
6 Portrait of Janet
7 Trio for Fun!
8 John Ritter as Jack
9 John Ritter Is Jack
10 The "The Three's Company" Gang
11 Three Smart Cookies!
12 Suzanne Sommers Is Chrissy
13 Mr. and Mrs. Roper
14 The Zany Threesome!
15 Portrait of Chrissy
16 The Terrific Trio!
17 The Irresistible Chrissy
18 Wacky Roommates!
19 Adorable Chrissy!
20 Having Her Ups and Downs!
21 Janet, Jack and Chrissy
22 Joyce DeWitt Is Janet
23 Gorgeous Roommate!
24 Chrissy—One in a Million!
25 Three for the Show!
26 Zany Bachelor Jack!
27 Norman Fell Is Mr. Roper
28 Executive Sweet!
29 We've Finally Got Our Relationship Ironed Out!
30 The Giggling Gourmet!
31 I've Got a Big Surprise for You, Mrs. Roper—the Rent!
32 And I Thought All You Could Serve Was an Eviction Notice!
33 Mr. Roper Is a Man of Few Words—All of Them Nasty!
34 I Hate to Say This, Jack, But There Are Easier Ways to Count!
35 I've Heard of Putting Your Best Foot Forward, But This Is Ridiculous!
36 "Dear Abby, I Have This Weird Tenant..."
37 So I'm a Sight for Sore Eyes, Eh?
38 "Now Let's Move the Couch into the Bathroom!
39 Exercising Is Fine Jack—But Can You Stretch Our Budget?
40 Golly, Jack, You Make a Great Certerfold!
41 All Girls Put Me on a Pedestal!
42 Jack, You Should Go Far in Life—the Farther the Better!
43 Sure, I'll Fix Your Leaky Faucet—After You Move!
44 Look Dear—Jack Can Read without Moving His Lips!

THREE STOOGES (66)
2 1/2" X 3 1/2"

This black and white Fleer set of 66 Three Stooges cards — issued in 1966—is not as popular as the 1959 color set, but it still is very much in demand. The fronts have a sallow yellow cast; the dialogue appears beneath each picture and the card number is located inside the frame line. The backs are puzzle pieces. Note: while single cards are moderately priced, complete sets are in high demand and command a very high premium.

ITEM	MINT	EX
Set	525.00	400.00
Card	4.00	3.00
Wrapper	--	10.00
Box	--	100.00

1 Mac: How's This for a "Natural...
2 Joe: Do You Know What They Call...
3 Larry: You Got It Backwards...
4 Simple Way to Get Around...
5 Moe: No Wonder These Two...
6 Joe: I Realize You Interns...
7 Larry: Lay Off, Moe! We...
8 "My Latest Investion—Power...
9 Joe: This Ain't a Space Gun,...
10 Moe: These Martians Will Have to Call Off Their Invasion...
11 Moe: If You Think Those...
12 Joe: The Instrument Panel...
13 Larry: I'll Hafta Jump the...
14 Joe: Underneath It All,...
15 Wearing Bunny Suits Doesn't...
16 Moe: Do It Yourself, We...
17 Moe: Singing's Just Another...
18 Moe: It's Supposed to Be...
19 Moe: But, Landlady, You...
20 Joe: We Would Have Made...
21 Joe: So We Get Life for...
22 Moe: To Heck with...

23 Moe: Just Our Casual Things for...
24 Joe: We Better Blow the...
25 Moe: They Said We'd Make...
26 Initiation Night—Not into the...
27 Joe: It's a Wrist Watch with...
28 Larry: So We're Gonna Be...
29 Moe: Talk About Luck,...
30 Moe: Grand Vizier, Shmizier— I Give the Orders...
31 Moe: If This Doesn't Give...
32 Moe: Thought I Might Raise...
33 Larry: These Chinese May...
34 Larry: They Say Paintin'...
35 Joe: We'd Like a Patent for...
36 Moe: The Way Joe Explains...
37 Moe: A "Pal" Shipped Him...
38 Joe: Pioneerin' Suits Me...
39 Joe: Meebe We Oughta...
40 Moe: Thanks, Ma'am, for...
41 Moe: Calm Down! That...
42 Moe: Since We've Been...
43 Moe: Take That Back or...
44 Joe: We'll Be Safe as Long...
45 Larry: These Horse Pistols Will Do...

46 Moe: It's More Comfortable...
47 Moe: There's Gonna Be Law...
48 Joe: Larry, Here, Was a...
49 You Can Lead a Stooge to...
50 Joe: We Want a Raise or...
51 Joe: You Only Get Out of...
52 Joe: You're Gettin' Closer...
53 Joe: You're Just the Type...
54 Bartender: Drink Up, Boys— We Call It...
55 Joe: I Thought These...
56 Moe, I Wish I Knew...
57 Moe: Begin Operation Meat-Grinder. If Bullets...
58 Joe: The Redskins Are...
59 Joe: Him Called Chief Mangy Bear Because...
60 Moe: We're New Sioux. Wanted to Join...
61 Moe: I Was Lookin' for...
62 Joe: Dinner Wouldn't Have...
63 Moe: Think I'll Spring...
64 Joe: When the Human Bulldozer Leaves...
65 Joe: I Know My Own Truck...
66 Moe: Only One Reason I...

THUNDERCATS (264)
1 15/16" X 2 9/16"

Panini U.S.A. began distributing the Thundercats album sticker series in June 1986. Of the 264 stickers in the set, 24 are printed on foil: Nos. 1-6, which belong on page 1 of the album, and Nos. 122-139, which attached to an 18 3/8" X 20 1/8" wall poster (inserted in the album). All the stickers, regular and foil, have Panini's standard multi-language back. Note: set price includes album.

ITEM	MINT	EX
Set	25.00	17.50
Sticker	.10	.07
Wrapper	--	.25
Album	1.25	1.00

STICKER ALBUM WITH POSTER

Thundercats Album Stickers

TINY TOON ADVENTURES (77 & 11)   2 1/2" X 3 1/2"

From an adult point of view, the folks at Warner Brothers have lost their grip on reality. How on earth can you produce a bunch of cartoons based on parodies of Orson Welles movies??? Well, for one thing, if you have a "hot" new set of cartoon characters based on Tiny Toons, you could probably cast them in "War and Peace" or in "The Day The Earth Stood Still" and kids wouldn't care. Nobody that watches Saturday morning television gives a hoot about Citizen Kane, The Magnificent Ambersons, or The Lady From Shanghai. Now, give 'em "Citizen Max," "The Magnificent Amberducks," and "The Bunny From Shanghai" and that's a different story (literally)! Then the little monsters

will chant dialogue verbatim, scream and holler for "Tiny Toons" cereal at lunch and dinner, and deplete your patience and pocketbook buying a zillion "officially-licensed" items at the local Toysmart.

Topps issued its Tiny Toons Adventures series of 77 cards and eleven stickers in 1991. The number 1 card is a header/introduction and the 17 cards which follow (2-18) introduce the Toons themselves. In case you haven't heard, these characters are pint-sized relations of classic Warner legends like Bugs Bunny, Elmer Fudd, Daffy Duck, etc. The next nine cards (19-27) are a brief look at some of the characters in action, while the rest of the set (28-77) is

devoted to a satire of Citizen Kane. The stickers are all numbered and captioned and have the characters set on a concentric circle design at center. Each sticker front has two different backs and it is possible to have a complete set of eleven without having the back which shows the completed ten-part puzzle picture. Note: set price includes stickers and the stickers must complete the puzzle.

ITEM	MINT	EX
Set	12.00	9.00
Card	.10	.07
Sticker	.35	.25
Wrapper	--	.10
Box	--	2.00

1 Tiny Toon Adventures!
2 Buster Bunny
3 Babs Bunny
4 Plucky Duck
5 Hamton
6 Dizzy Devil
7 Montana Max
8 Fifi
9 Elmyra
10 Sweetie
11 Furrball
12 Gogo Dodo
13 Calamity Coyote
14 Little Beeper
15 Shirley the Loon
16 Sneezer
17 Concord Condor
18 Bookworm
19 School's Out
20 Wackyland or Bust!
21 Surf's Up!
22 A Multi-Flavored Romance
23 Hit the Ice!
24 Duck-A-Muck!
25 Dancin' in the Rain
26 TV or Not TV!
27 Hamton Meets His Match!
28 A "Tiny Toon" Adventures Classic!
29 "Citizen Max"
30 The Last Word: "Acme!"
31 News on the March
32 Montana Max - Expelled!!
33 Empire of Montana Max
34 "We Need an Angle..."
35 Investigating Montana Max
36 "I Remember Montana Max..."
37 A Pair of Poor Pals
38 A Surprise
39 Unstoppable Montana Max
40 Food for Thought
41 "Acme? Never Heard of It!"
42 A Looney Education
43 The Plucky Interview
44 Plucky Duck for Hire!
45 Buster Wows 'Em!
46 Campaign Con Job!
47 Plucky Streak!
48 Moneybags Montana Max!
49 Media Blitz!
50 No Escape from Montana Max
51 The Great Debate
52 Lunch Scheme!
53 A Dizzy Delight!
54 Master Mudslinger!
55 Tracking the Race

56 Ahead in the Polls!
57 Buster Bunny ... Framed!
58 Buster's Fall From Grace
59 "Now It's Personal!"
60 Elmyra's Story
61 Plucky to the Rescue
62 Exposing the Creep!
63 Freezing the Frame-Up!
64 Montana's Big Day
65 Babs in Disguise
66 Something's Fishy!
67 A Blast from Babs
68 Triumph ... or Travesty?
69 The Truth Hurts!
70 The Hero is a Heel!
71 Tomato Salesman Plucky!
72 Monty is Clobbered!
73 The Acme Mystery Solved!

74 What Montana Max *Really* Lost ...
75 "Not Acme ... Acne!!"
76 "Now He Tells Me!"
77 With Apologies to Orson

STICKERS
1 Tiny Toon Adventures
2 Buster Bunny
3 Babs Bunny
4 Plucky Duck
5 Hamton
6 Dizzy Devil
7 Montana Max
8 Fifi
9 Elmyra
10 Sweetie
11 Calamity Coyote / Little Beeper

TINY TOON ADVENTURES ALBUM STICKERS (200)

1 15/16″ X 2 3/4″

"Tiny Toons," a clever Warner Brothers spinoff from its lineup of famous cartoon characters, is the subject of this Panini album sticker series issued in 1991. The Tiny Toons are 17 relations of Bugs Bunny, Elmer Fudd, Daffy Duck, etc., and they attend Acme University, where their elders teach courses such as "Introduction to Wabbits" and "Varmint Blasting." Naturally, riot and mayhem ensue. The 200 color artwork stickers in the set are all numbered on back and match up with numbered spots on the album pages. The album, one of the best that Panini has ever done, is 32 pages long and has specific sections: "School Faculty," "Student Body," "Her Wacky Highness," "Test Stressed," and "Acme University Awards." Not all the stickers are rectangular: #'s 97-112 fit onto irregular spaces on album pages 16 & 17. Note: set price includes album.

ITEM	MINT	EX
Set	20.00	14.00
Sticker	.10	.07
Wrapper	--	.15
Album	1.25	1.00

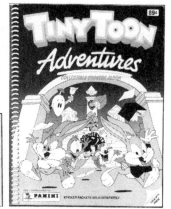

TOM AND JERRY TATTOOS (?)

1 5/8″ X 3 1/2″

The exterior wrapper of this 1965 Topps set is blue with yellow, gray, and white accents and the design illustrated is the only one seen to date. A series of multi-colored tattoos were printed on the interior sides; they are not numbered or captioned, and the set total is not known.

ITEM	MINT	EX
Wrapper	--	15.00

TOP PILOT CARDS (5 SETS)

2 1/2″ X 3 1/2″

Top Pilot, a San Diego based company, has quickly gained a reputation among aviation buffs for producing quality color photographic cards of aircraft of different types and from different eras. The company's greatest coup, perhaps, was their timely release of card sets for both the B-2 Stealth Bomber and the F-117A Stealth Fighter. On the other hand, the backs of the cards have shown some confusing inconsistencies which Top Pilot, with little experience in trading card production, is attempting to overcome. For example, after numbering its first set 1-15, with two unnumbered cards, and using a 1-31 sequence for the second, Top Pilot decided to start its third series at #49 and continue on consecutively thereafter. Does this mean that there is one big set, containing five sub-sets, or are there five individual sets, of which three just happen to have sequential numbering? In addition, what the company calls its "Cover Card" is more commonly known in the hobby as a "header" and it should come at the front of each series, not at the end. Despite these problems, hobbyists who like airplanes will find these sets to be attractive and informative additions to their collections. Note: each set (or subset) is priced individually. All cards sold in sets only (sealed in plastic or in plastic boxes).

Top Pilot Cards

B-2 STEALTH BOMBER
Issue date 1990
Set length . . . . .7 cards
Set price 2.00

CHECKLIST:
49 B-2 Advanced Technology Bomber
50 B-2 Advanced Technology Bomber
51 B-2 Advanced Technology Bomber
52 The Triad
53 B-2 Predecessor / The YB-35 and XB-35
54 B-2 Predecessor / The YB-49
55 Covercard / Checklist

F-117A STEALTH FIGHTER
Issue Date 1990
Set length . . . . .7 cards
Set price 2.00

CHECKLIST:
56 F-117A Stealth Fighter
57 F-117A Stealth Fighter
58 F-117A Stealth Fighter
59 F-117A Stealth Fighter
60 F-117A Stealth Fighter
61 F-117A Stealth Fighter
62 Covercard / Checklist

COMBAT HELICOPTERS
Issue date 1991
Set length . . . . .14 cards
Set price 4.00

CHECKLIST:
63 AH-1S Hueycobra   70 SH-60B Seahawk
64 AH-1W Supercobra   71 UH-1H Huey
65 AH-64A Apache   72 A 129 Mongoose
66 AH-64A Apache   73 Battlefield Lynx
67 530MG Defender   74 MI-24 Hind-D
68 OH-58D Kiowa   75 PAH-1
69 SH-2F Seasprite   76 Cover Card / Checklist

MACH 1 EDITION
Issue date 1989
Set length . .17 cards
Set price 5.00

CHECKLIST:
1 F-15 Eagle
2 F-14 Tomcat
3 F-16 Fighting Falcon
4 F/A-18 Hornet
5 F-4 Phantom II
6 F-5 Freedom Fighter
7 F-104 Starfighter
8 F-111 Raven
9 A-4 Skyhawk
10 B-1
11 SR-71 Blackbird
12 AV-8 Harrier II
13 Hawk
14 F-14 Tomcat
15 B-1
Checklist card
Header Card

WARBIRDS EDITION
Issue date 1990
Set length . . . . .31 cards
Set price 5.00

CHECKLIST:
1 A-2A Havoc   21 TBD-1 Devastator
2 A-26B Invader   22 TBF-1 Avenger
3 B-17G Flying Fortress   23 D.H. 98B.35 Mosquito
4 B-24J Liberator   24 Hurricane Mark I
5 B-25J Mitchell   25 Spitfire Mark XIV
6 B-26G Marauder   26 Bf. 109E Messerschmitt
7 B-29 Superfortress   27 Fw. 190D-9 Focke-Wulf
8 F2A-3 Buffalo 1   28 Me. 262A-1a Swallow
9 F4F-4 Wildcat   29 A6M5 Zero
10 F6F-3 Hellcat   30 D3A2 Val
11 FG-1D Corsair   31 Cover Card / Checklist
12 P-38J Lightning
13 P-39D Airacobra
14 P-40E Warhawk
15 P-47D Thunderbolt
16 P-51D Mustang
17 P-61B Black Widow
18 PBY-5A Catalina
19 SB2C-3 Helldiver
20 SBC-2 Dauntless

TOPPS PAK O' FUN (42)

3 1/8" X 5 1/4"

"EARTH MONSTERS! FULL SPEED BACK TO MARS."

'TSK, TSK! HOW SILLY CAN TV GET?'

This series of 42 cards is one of Topps' most brilliant cartophilic achievements, yet it is so obscure that few collectors know of its existence. In general, the "Fun Pack" issues (including "Pak O'Fun) are limited in time of distribution (and therefore, in quantity) to certain holidays: Valentine's Day, Halloween, and Christmas. Judging from the number of cards we have seen, "Pak O'Fun" must have had a very short "run" in 1969.

The cards of this set are seven different types which all appeared, at one time or another, in other Topps sets. The types are: "Necklaces," "Flying Things," "You'll Die Laughing" (original Funny Monsters version), "Foldees," "Funny Doors," "Finger Puppets," and Hold-To-Light cards. Every card

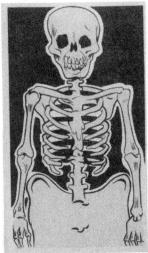

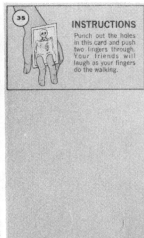

is numbered and each bears a "Set of 42" line. The "You'll Die Laughing" cards come in two-card panels (single cards measure 2 5/8" X 3 1/4") and each card is individually numbered. [The artwork is identical to the corresponding card in the original set (R-78-5).] It is confirmed that some of these cards are paired in more than one panel combination. Two "Pack O' Fun" wrappers have been found: one, thought to be the test issue, is made of plain paper, while the "regular" wrapper is made of standard wax paper.

Notes: Single "You'll Die Laughing" cards cannot be graded mint. The set contains 30 large cards (#'s 1-12 and 25-42) and six two-card panels (#'s 13-24, in various combinations). Set price depends on quantity of intact "You'll Die Laughing" panels included.

ITEM	MINT	EX
Cards 1-12		
& 25-42	18.00	13.50
Two-card panels		
(cards 13-24)	20.00	15.00
Single cards		
from 13-24		
sequence	--	6.00
Wrappers		
Plain paper	--	150.00
Wax paper	--	100.00
Box	--	250.00

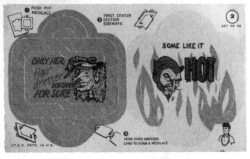

TOPPSCIENCE (24)

3" X 6 1/4"

"See Mom, I toldja', gum cards are educational!" Topps provided children with this instant excuse in 1967 by printing a series of 24 science experiments on the back of Bazooka Gum 25-count boxes. Each card is actually the entire back panel of the box and bears the production code 1-190-38-01-7. The card in our illustration is mostly yellow, with red print headings and black print text. The "Toppscience" panel at top left and the offer panel at bottom right are black with white print and the drawing is black and white. Each experiment is numbered next to the "Toppscience" logo. Note: detached cards cannot be graded mint.

ITEM	MINT	EX
Card	--	1.50
Card set	--	27.50
Box	--	5.00
Set of boxes	--	150.00

TOPPS SCRATCH-OFFS (6?)　　　2 1/2" X 3 1/2"

John Neuner, "The Wrapper King," reports that this series of six scratch-off game cards was distributed in packs of Bazooka Cherry and Fruit flavor bubble gum in 1979. These packs have a "Comics/Fortunes/Prizes" label on the front, and contained Bazooka Joe cards as well as these game cards. There are only six card designs confirmed and we have illustrated them all here. The game cards are not numbered but they do have individual titles. Note: game cards with coatings removed cannot be graded excellent or mint.

ITEM	MINT	EX
Set	14.00	10.00
Card	2.00	1.50
Wrappers (2)		
each	--	2.00

"GHOST HUNTER" GAME INSTRUCTIONS

There's a ghost haunting Grimley Manor. But you're not scared. Can you find it?

FOR 2 PLAYERS
Take turns scratching off windows. Whoever finds the ghost first wins.

FOR 1 PLAYER
How many tries does it take you to find the ghost?

1 try	EXORCIST
2 tries	A MIGHTY HUNTER
3 tries	WIZARD
4 tries	EXTRA SENSORY PERSON
5 tries	SORCERER'S APPRENTICE
6 tries	MEDIUM
7 tries	HAUNTED HUNTER
8 tries	SPOOKED OUT
9 tries	SCARED STIFF
10 tries	VAMPIRE BAIT
11 tries	AIEEEE!

"CASTLE OF DOOM" GAME INSTRUCTIONS

The peasants are revolting. The evil wizard has terrorized the village long enough. Can you help them capture him?

FOR 2 PLAYERS
Take turns scratching away windows. Whoever finds the wizard first wins.

FOR 1 PLAYER
How many tries does it take you to find the wizard?

1 try	KNIGHT OF THE ROUND TABLE
2 tries	DRAGON SLAYER
3 tries	GOOD KNIGHT
4 tries	PLEASANT PEASANT
5 tries	TARNISHED ARMOR
6 tries	COURT JESTER
7 tries	DOOMED TO THE DUNGEON
8 tries	DROWNED IN THE MOAT
9 tries	TURNED INTO A FROG

"STAKE-OUT" GAME INSTRUCTIONS

The cops have finally cornered escaped murderer "Scarface" Smith. He's holed up in a downtown tenement. Catch him before he kills again!

FOR 2 PLAYERS
Take turns scratching away windows. Whoever finds "Scarface" first wins.

FOR 1 PLAYER
How many tries does it take you to find "Scarface"?

1 try	HEADLINE HERO
2 tries	MEDAL FROM THE MAYOR
3 tries	POLICE ACADEMY AWARD
4 tries	TOP COP
5 tries	PLAIN OLD PLAINCLOTHESMAN
6 tries	JUST A ROOKIE
7 tries	FAULTY FLATFOOT
8 tries	DEFECTIVE DETECTIVE
9 tries	BACK ON THE BEAT
10 tries	OUT OF WORK

"KIDNAPPED IN SPACE" GAME INSTRUCTIONS

Captain Starr must find the kidnapped space princess. He's traced her to one of these space ships. Help him find which one.

FOR 2 PLAYERS
Take turns scratching away squares. Whoever finds the princess first wins.

FOR 1 PLAYER
How many tries does it take you to find the princess?

1 try	GALACTIC GALAHAD
2 tries	FOUR STAR HERO
3 tries	THREE STAR HERO
4 tries	FALLING STAR
5 tries	COSMIC CLOWN
6 tries	RUSTY RAY GUN
7 tries	LOST IN SPACE
8 tries	SPACED OUT

"SKY TERROR" GAME INSTRUCTIONS

A crazed hi-jacker carrying a bomb is aboard this trans-continental flight. Can you find him before the bomb explodes?

FOR 2 PLAYERS
Take turns scratching away windows. Whoever finds the hi-jacker first wins.

FOR 1 PLAYER
How many tries does it take you to find the hi-jacker?

1 try	FIRST CLASS
2 tries	SMOOTH FLYING
3 tries	ON SCHEDULE
4 tries	FASTEN YOUR SEATBELTS
5 tries	BUMPY FLIGHT
6 tries	AIR SICK
7 tries	FEAR OF FLYING
8 tries	CLOSE CALL
9 tries	TICK-TICK-TICK
10 tries	BOMBS AWAY!

"NEPTUNE'S TREASURE" GAME INSTRUCTIONS

You're 20,000 leagues below, searching for a lost treasure chest from the pirate ship Neptune. Find it before you run out of air!

FOR 2 PLAYERS
Take turns scratching away squares. Whoever finds the treasure first wins.

FOR 1 PLAYER
How many tries does it take you to find the treasure?

1 try	STRIKE IT RICH
2 tries	JACKPOT
3 tries	FISTFUL OF DOLLARS
4 tries	SMALL CHANGE
5 tries	BELOW "C" LEVEL
6 tries	ALL WET
7 tries	WATER LOGGED
8 tries	OUT OF AIR
9 tries	DEAD FISH

TOPPS WINNERS (?)

An unusual series which will never be described in a "legitimate" sports card guide, "Winners" was obviously a promotional item designed to generate goodwill for Topps. The cards are dated 1971 and the samples examined appear to have been issued in the Pittsburgh area. It is not known at this time whether similar sets were developed for other cities.

ITEM	MINT	EX
Card	2.00	1.50

TOTAL RECALL (110)

2 1/2" X 3 1/2"

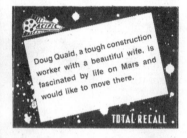

Doug Quaid, a tough construction worker with a beautiful wife, is fascinated by life on Mars and would like to move there.

TOTAL RECALL

1 Header Card
2 Mars Red Rocket Desert
3 The Dream
4 Quaid Wakes Up
5 Doug Quaid - Construction Worker
6 Trouble on Mars
7 "Move to Mars"
8 "The War Effort Depends on Mars"
9 Off to Work
10 A Dream Vacation from Rekall Incorporated
11 Construction Site
12 "RekallRekallRekall"
13 Rekall Building
14 "What About a Trip to Saturn?"
15 First Class Memories
16 Quaid...Secret Agent?
17 Rekall Memory Studio
18 Something's Wrong!
19 The Cover Up at Rekall
20 "We've Never Heard of Douglas Quaid"
21 "How Was Your Trip to Mars?"
22 "You Blabbed About Mars!"
23 Quaid Escapes
24 "I Got a Trip to Mars!"
25 "I'm Not Your Wife!"
26 "If I'm Not Me Who Am I?"
27 Lori's an Agent?
28 The Escalator Shootout
29 Experience Space Travel

There is an ancient Chinese paradox about reality: did I dream that I was a butterfly, or am I a butterfly dreaming that I am a man? Doug Quaid, the leading character in the movie Total Recall, has a similar problem. Is he a construction worker on Earth or a rebel leader on Mars? By the end of the film, Quaid has sorted it all out and dealt with his opponents in traditional Arnold Schwarzenegger form.

Pacific Trading Cards issued its "Total Recall" series of 110 cards in 1990. The card fronts have starry black borders surrounding color photographs taken from the film. The backs also have a starry black background, with the card number at top-right and an angled text panel in the center. Pacific packaged the set in an imaginative way: the small box contains not only cards, but a ticket to Mars, an "Official Mars Rock," a "Rekall" sheet, and a stack of Martian money. The series has settled in, price-wise, at the original retail figure of $20.

Total Recall

30 "In an Hour He Could Have Total Recall"
31 "They've Got You Bugged"
32 Quaid Meets Stevens
33 "We Hope You Enjoyed the Ride"
34 What is in the Suitcase?
35 "You're Not You. You're Me."
36 Who is Hauser?
37 "Get Rid of That Bug in your Head"
38 "Get Yourself to Mars"
39 Richter's Too Late; Quaid is Off to Mars
40 Mars Space Port
41 The Fat Lady
42 "It's Quaid"
43 On The Martian Subway
44 The Mars Pyramid Mine
45 Cohaagen's Headquarters
46 Quaid Arrives at the Hilton Hotel

47 Quaid Meets Benny
48 Venusville Plaza
49 Madame Fatima's Daughter
50 The Last Resort
51 "Hauser?"
52 "Melina, I Don't Remember You!"
53 Melina Turns on Quaid
54 Cohaagen Delivers a Speech
55 (Dr. Edgemar, From Rekall.)
56 "Oh, I Get it; I'm Dreaming!"
57 "You Paid to be a Secret Agent"
58 "It's All a Dream?"
59 "I'm Still at Rekall?"
60 Return to Reality?
61 Quaid is Torn with Doubt
62 Dr. Edgemar Dies
63 Quaid is Captured
64 Melina to the Rescue
65 The Chase
66 The Crash

67 Quaid and Melina Escape at the Last Resort
68 The Shootout
69 The Call from Cohaagen
70 The Air on Mars Stops
71 The Catacombs of Mars
72 Mutant Lieutenant
73 Benny
74 Mars Rebel Headquarters
75 "It's up to Kuato"
76 Quaid meets Kuato
77 The Mutant - Rebel Leader
78 Quaid Hypnotized
79 The Reactor Cavern
80 The Rebel Headquarters is Attacked
81 Benny the Villain
82 Kuato Dies
83 "So This is the Great Man"
84 Hauser Volunteered?
85 "Too Perfect!"
86 The Holovision
87 Cohaagen's Implant Lab
88 Suffocating in Venusville
89 Re-programming

90 Quaid Breaks Loose
91 "Let's Get Out of Here!"
92 The Elevator Fight
93 "Let's Get to the Reactor"
94 The Mole
95 The Alien Reactor
96 Oxygen for Mars
97 Time is Running Out
98 "Quaid's got a Hologram"
99 Richter's Death
100 Reactor core/control room
101 "I am Quaid!"
102 Instant Tornado on Mars
103 Cohaagen Decompresses
104 Pyramid Mountain Blows Up
105 Mars near Death
106 The Reactor Makes Air
107 Mars is Saved
108 Was it all a Dream?
109 Get Ready for the Ride of Your Life
110 Arnold Schwarzenegger as Doug Quaid

TOXIC CRUSADERS (88 & 8)   2 1/2" X 3 1/2"

The storyline of Topps' "Toxic Crusaders" is succinctly stated on the back of card #1: "In order to save Tromaville and the rest of the planet, the Toxic Crusaders must thwart the plans of the evil Dr. Killemoff and his heinous henchmen. The Toxic Crusaders have arrived! It's clean up time!" The hero of this environmental morality play is one Melvin Junko, former janitor at the Tromaville Health Club, who after falling into a barrel of Grossolium 90 while wearing a tutu, emerges as "a hideously deformed creature of superhuman size and strength." The altered Melvin Junko, now known as "Toxie," has one goal in life: to outwit habitual polluters led by Dr. Killemoff.

The 88 cards in the set follow the adventures of Toxie and his mutant canine ally, "Junkyard." The artwork fronts are surrounded by "slime" framelines and neon color borders. The backs contain slogans, text, the card number, and a bio grid or one of "Toxie's Tips." Eight numbered holografic stickers were issued with the cards and these were produced in quantity, not withheld as "special" bonus items like the majority of other holograms produced in recent years. Note: examine hologram surfaces for scratches and marks which must lower condition grade and value.

ITEM	MINT	EX
Set	10.00	7.50
Card	.10	.07
Hologram	.50	.35
Wrapper	--	.15
Box	--	2.00

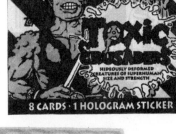

1 The Toxic Crusaders
2 Toxie
3 Nozone
4 Major Disaster
5 Headbanger
6 Junkyard
7 Dr. Killemoff
8 Psycho
9 Bonehead
10 Radiation Ranger
11 Killemoff's Scheme
12 Destination: Tromaville
13 Junko the Nerd
14 A Present for Melvin
15 The Horrible Accident
16 Goodbye, Melvin Junko
17 Hello, Toxie!
18 Advice from Toxie's Mom
19 Toxie's Little Buddy
20 Crusader on the Job
21 An Unscheduled Flight
22 Acid Rain on Bonehead's Parade
23 Toxie Gets Tough!
24 That Strange Sensation
25 Clobbering a Creep
26 Ranger Attack!
27 No Chance Against Toxie
28 Hurray for You Know Who!
29 An American Hero
30 Bonehead's Revenge
31 Cycling Sicko

32 That Run-down Feeling
33 One Good Turn ...
34 Confronting Killemoff
35 Meet the Bug-Man!
36 Toxie's Crusade
37 The New Recruits
38 Disaster's Awesome Power
39 Branching Out!
40 Polluto Strikes!
41 Sneeze Power!
42 K'O'ed by Kitty Litter!
43 Toxie Triumphant
44 Yvonne's Latest Ditty
45 Job-Hunting Heroes
46 Greedy Mayor Grody
47 Demented Genius
48 Dim-witted Messenger
49 Trapped in the Atom Smasher!
50 Fender-Bender
51 Toxie The Ice Cream Man
52 Bender's Foul Brew
53 The Contaminators
54 This Spud's For You!
55 Nozone The Magician
56 Killemoff Takes Over!
57 Captured Crusader
58 Nozone in a Jam
59 Emergency Plan "B"
60 Grand Gobbler
61 "Thanks a Lot, Mop!"
62 Headbanger Goes Straight

63 Aerial Assault!
64 Battlefield: New Jersey
65 The Big Sneeze
66 Nozone Blows 'Em Away!
67 Killemoff's Cruel Plot
68 Psychic Psycho
69 Hot-headed Headbanger
70 Bikin' Bonehead
71 The Crusaders Heed the Call!
72 Psycho Blasts Off!
73 Getting a Lift from Toxie
74 A Strange Reward
75 Ride the Toxic Surf

76 Bonehead at the Controls
77 A Stranger Swims Ashore
78 Short-Circuiting Bonehead
79 Lending a Helping Paw
80 The Hobo and the Hound
81 Birth of a Hero
82 Mutated Mutt
83 Junkyard Joins the Fray!
84 Polutto Strikes Again
85 A Taste of Bad Medicine
86 Turning the Toxic Tide
87 Junkyard's Oath
88 Canine Crusaders

TOXIC HIGH (88)

2 1/2" X 3 1/2"

Topps clearly demonstrated why it is the industry leader with its initial set of 1992: "Toxic High." There are 65 cards and 33 sticker-cards in the set and each and every one is a hilarious satire of the worst side of high school existence. Teachers, coaches, teams, clubs, cheerleaders, science fairs, class trips - all are fair game for the warped imaginations of Topps' editorial staff. True, there is the usual over-kill concerning bodily excretions, and some of the card backs are too obscure to read properly, but the wealth of detail and design is overwhelming. Numbers 1-64 and number 88 are cards; numbers 65-87 are four-in-one stickers that read like a series of yearbook pictures. I guarantee you will recognize some of the "types" depicted on the stickers and some of the characterizations on the cards will also ring true. It's too soon to tell whether Toxic High will go on to glory as the "Garbage Pail Kids" of the 1990's or whether it will sink into undeserved obscurity like "Dinosaurs Attack!" Only time will tell, but meanwhile, grab a set and have some fun.

ITEM	MINT	EX
Set	10.00	7.50
Card	.10	.07
Wrappers (2) ea.	--	.25
Box	--	2.00

1 Toxic High - School Symbol
2 Welcome to Toxic High!
3 Our Principal:
4 Arno Fleck: R.I.P.
5 Cleon Jarvis: R.I.P.
6 Margie Lowin: R.I.P.
7 Faculty Mailboxes:
8 The Forgotten Locker:
9 The Toilet Overflowed Again.
10 Selling Test Answers:
11 The Food Fight:
12 A Hallway Romance:
13 School Nurse:
14 Hygiene Class:
15 Career Counselor:
16 School Bus Driver:
17 School Librarian:
18 School Chef:
19 Kitchen Staff:
20 English Class:
21 Shop Class:
22 Science Class:
23 Substitute Teacher Arrives:
24 Art Class:
25 French Class:
26 Photography Class:
27 Music Class:
28 Drivers Ed:
29 Home Ec:
30 Those Who Ignore History Class Are Doomed to Repeat It.
31 Math Class:
32 School Janitor:
33 Science Fair:
34 Science Fair:
35 Science Fair Losers:

36 Track Team:
37 Basketball Team:
38 Wrestling Team:
39 Our Coach:
40 The Cheerleaders:
41 Football Team:
42 Swim Team:
43 Warren Forgot His Gym Suit ...
44 Class Trip:
45 Class Trip:
46 Class Trip:
47 Class Trip:
48 Sr. Prom:
49 Sr. Prom:
50 Sr. Prom:
51 Sr. Prom:
52 Acne Club:
53 Nose Picking Club:
54 Debate Club:
55 Astronomy Club:
56 Drama Club:
57 Smoking Club:
58 The Party Line Club:
59 Oatmeal Club:
60 Toe Nail Clipping Club:
61 Puberty Club:
62 Left Back Club:

63 Goodbye Toxic High Club:
64 Toxic High Senior Class
65 A-B-C-D
66 A-B-C-D
67 A-B-C-D
68 A-B-C-D
69 A-B-C-D
70 A-B-C-D
71 A-B-C-D
72 A-B-C-D
73 A-B-C-D
74 A-B-C-D
75 A-B-C-D
76 A-B-C-D

77 A-B-C-D
78 A-B-C-D
79 A-B-C-D
80 A-B-C-D
81 A-B-C-D
82 A-B-C-D
83 A-B-C-D
84 A-B-C-D
85 A-B-C-D
86 A-B-C-D
87 A-B-C-D
88 Toxic High Senior Class Poster Offer

TOXIC WASTE ZOMBIES (41)

2 3/4" X 3 3/4"

There isn't one of us who hasn't heard or read about the countless pollutants that are destroying the planet and creating health problems for all living creatures. Mother Productions has done us all a service by personifying some of these forces into characters that appear on trading cards in their series of "Toxic Waste Zombies." Issued in 1991, the set consists of 40 unnumbered cards, plus a checklist. A glance at the alphabetical checklist will reveal a host of clever names and double-entendres. But this is not mere riposte: the card backs

Toxic Waste Zombies

Acid Rain Duane
Amos and Arco The Sludge Twins
Armondo the Slasher
Big Baby Dewkie
Burnie Furnace
Buzz Acres
Capt. Slick and Oily Boyd
Chewy Chokinbreath
Chlorine Bleachmen
Col. Stuffy Carcass
Corrosive Bob and PeeWee
Dead Louie Lungchunk
Delbert Brewsky
Dewey Vapors
Dr. Buster Bloodvessel
Dr. George Fishbone

Dynah Cancer
Eugene Peckerwood
Harley Death-Hard
Heidi Deadskins
Lawn Gauger 2000
Lester Footfester

John Q. Public
Misty Ozone
Noxious Eddie
Oilvis
Pee-Air LaTrien
Percy the Scumsucker

Porkly Brothers
Prof. Wiggley Cortex
Rat Master Floyd
Ray Nukem
Snappy Hipone
Snotty Waters

Sparky Fryman
T-Bone Slaughter
Tex T-Rexaco
Thelonious Stenchmeister
Thruston Thirtyweight
Toxic Snarffy
Checklist card

contain some sobering facts about our wasteful habits and the "Zombie Quiz" feature on each card is, in fact, a reality check for each one of us who reads it. In the right hands, these cards would be much more effective than a legion of braying politicians and scientists. At the retail price of $10-$12, this is a set well worth having!

TRADING CARD TREATS (36)　　　2 1/2" X 3 1/2"

Topps Gum has a long tradition of issuing theme sets and fun packs for Halloween, but along came Impel in 1991 to show them how to REALLY do the job right. Impel's idea was simple: make up six mini-sets of cards covering a range of characters and juvenile tastes and package them up in inexpensive 24-pack bags. Each clear cello pack contained three cards and could be handed out to Halloween participants as "trading card treats," rather than candy or food treats. The six different mini-sets are: Archie, Inspector Gadget, Marvel Superheroes, Super Mario Bros., Universal Monsters, and Widget. The Archie, Gadget, Mario, and Monster cards had regular story backs; the backs of Marvel and Widget carried "Traffic Safety" and "Bicycle Safety" tips, respectively. All the cards have the glossy surfaces and excellent artwork and format details for which Impel has already become famous. They are not captioned, however, so no written checklist is available.

ITEM	MINT	EX
Set of 36	4.00	--
Card	.10	--
Bags (6) each	--	.50

TRANSFORMERS (225)　　1 3/4" X 2 1/2"

Can the Autobots, the Junkions and the Dinobots withstand the relentless attacks of the Decepticons, Quintessons, Sharktacons, and the Unicon? To answer this, you must use your magic decoder and follow the story of the Transformers as it is presented in Diamond's 32-page album. There are 225 stickers in the set; each has an ad for a "Transformers Backpack" on the reverse. The set was released to the public by Diamond in January 1987. Note: set price includes album.

ITEM	MINT	EX
Set	25.00	17.50
Sticker	.10	.07
Wrapper	—	.25
Album	1.25	1.00

TRIVIA BATTLE (132 & 11 & 2)　　2 1/2" X 3 1/2"

Back in 1984, when adults were shelling out big bucks to buy trivia board games, the bubble gum crowd could purchase an impressive trivia game of their own for a fraction of the cost. Each pack of Topps "Trivia Battle" contained eight question cards, one game card, one sticker card, and gum —all the items necessary to play a quiz round according to the rules on the back of the "game" and sticker cards. There are 264 question cards in the set; these originally came in 132 two-card panels with a scored center line for easy separation. The game cards are rub-off dots with colors coded to categories underneath the coating. Each sticker card is numbered on the border and has two front-peel stickers designed for ornamental purposes only. The back of the sticker card contans Game Rules for one player. Two-player game rules are printed on the backs of the rub-off-the-dots game cards. Each game card has questions in six categories: people, books, TV-film, hi IQ, music, and sports; there are a total of 1584 different questions in a complete set. Note: set prices include 132 cards, 11 sticker cards, and a minimum of two game cards. Separated question cards cannot be graded mint.

ITEM	MINT	EX
Set	20.00	15.00
Card	.10	.07
Sticker	.35	.25
Wrapper	—	.35
Box	—	3.00

TRIVIA QUIZ (24 & 24)　　1 1/8" X 2 11/16"

Set "A" of "Trivia Quiz" first appeared in packages of Sugar Daddy caramel pops in 1985. Each card measures 1 1/8" X 2 11/16"; three questions are posed on front and the answers are given on back. Nabisco followed up with the "B" set of 24 cards in 1986. All Trivia Quiz cards are numbered and are clearly marked "Set A" or "Set B." However, the series title only appears on the wrapper. Only the checklist for the "B" series was available at press time.

ITEM	MINT	EX
Sets		
A	5.50	4.00
B	5.50	4.00
Cards (all)	.20	.15
Wrapper	—	1.00

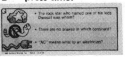

1 If March comes in like a lion, it goes out like a [ ]?
2 Do animals' temperatures go up or down when they hibernate?
3 The Sun has been burning how many years — about 50 million, 500 million or 5 billion?
4 A sparrow's foot has how many toes facing forward?
5 "Black Ghosts" and "dojos" are what?
6 If you find a "spud" in a garden, what should you do — kill it, cook it or mow it?
7 What state is the Great Lakes state?
8 A gallon contains how many pints?
9 Houseflies are deaf. True or false?
10 There are more sheep than people in New Zealand. True or false?
11 What popular food is named for the Italian word for "pie"?

12 The front teeth that a beaver flashes are what color — green, white or orange?
13 Which is the biggest — the Sun, the Moon or Earth?
14 If a French horn was uncurled, how long would it be — 3 feet, 7 feet or 11 feet?
15 Does the male or female canary sing?
16 A North American stop sign has how many edges?
17 What famous song that asks questions was written for Walt Disney's "Three Little Pigs"?

18 Rock & roll's first superstar was whom?
19 Which ocean is deeper — the Pacific or the Atlantic?
20 TV's Mr. Rogers wears what style of sweater?
21 Often called a bear, what large animal is actually related to the racoon?
22 Who lives under the bridge that the Three Billy Goats have to cross?
23 What creature can have as many as 710 legs?
24 The fence behind a baseball home plate is called what?

TRON (66 & 8)

There are 66 cards and eight stickers in the Tron set distributed by Donruss in 1982. The series was based upon the Walt Disney animated film feature of the same name, and for

2 1/2" X 3 1/2"

some collectors, the cards (in "stop-action") are easier to look at than was the movie. Each card is numbered on front and has a puzzle piece back. The eight stickers are front-peel designs depicting video games (directions on back) or characters and equipment (blank backs). Special note: there are two different cards printed with the number 6 and there is no number 9.

ITEM	MINT	EX
Set	8.00	6.50
Card	.10	.07
Sticker	.35	.25
Wrapper	--	.35
Box	--	4.00

TANK MAZE

Tron drives a red tank through the maze, watching for Sark's blue enemy tanks. Tron's tank has the unique ability to fire bouncing energy pellets, can fire around corners and has a rotating turret. The enemy tanks can fire only in the direction of travel, and must be hit three times to be destroyed. The number of enemy tanks increases as a player earns higher racks. Tron has one other advantage: the pink diamond "random relocator" in the center of the maze can relocate him to a random location in the maze when entered.

TRUCKIN' (44)

The "Truckin'" series produced by Donruss shows 44 different customized vans and trucks prepared for show competition by their owners. The color pictures on front are surrounded by fancy frames and white borders. Each vehicle is described on back and all the photos were provided by "Truckin' Magazine." Our checklist is made up of owner's names and home towns as they are listed on the card backs. Every card is numbered except one, which should be the "missing" No. 2.

ITEM	MINT	EX
Set	9.00	6.50
Card	.20	.15
Wrapper	--	1.00
Box	--	7.00

2 1/2" X 3 1/2"

1 Ed Ham (Santa Ana, California)
2 Richard Delgadillo (Hacienda Heights, California)
3 Don Burks (Santa Ana, California)
4 Brian Holmes (Salinas, Kansas)
5 Tom Anderson (Bonner Springs, Kansas)
6 Richard Bettencourt (Gilroy, California)
7 Daryl Eve (Newport Beach, California)
8 Jim Witzig (Anaheim, California)
9 Larry Ask (Billings, Montana)
10 B.J. Kennemore (Florence, Alabama)
11 Bill White (San Carlos, California)
12 Tony Cardenas (Denver, Colorado)
13 Jim Haid (Anaheim, California)
14 Ray Gossett (Anaheim, California)
15 Bill Sadler (San Jose, California)

16 Ron Vargas (Hayward, California)
17 Jim Thor (Los Angeles, California)
18 Bob Dunn (Grand Junction, Colorado)
19 Frank Roberts (Las Vegas, Nevada)
20 Joe Eddy (Rosemead, California)
21 Vini Bergeman (Anaheim, California)
22 Tom McMullen (Fullerton, California)
23 Dave Williams (Placentia, California)
24 Bill Gerry (San Jose, California)
25 Tom McMullen (Fullerton, California)
26 Tom Woodling (Upland, California)
27 Steve Maraggio (Fullerton, California)
28 Hi Enterprises (Garden Grove, California)
29 Jerry Wesseling (Cerritos, California)
30 Bobby Ramey (Spring, Texas)
31 Ralph Humrick (Minneapolis, Minnesota)

32 Jake Cushingham (Cathedral City, California)
33 Sharon Rickel (Lemon Grove, California)
34 Jerry Tetting (Jefferson, Wisconsin)
35 Chuck Payne (Cypress, California)
36 Paul Marquez (Chula Vista, California)
37 Winston Mitchell (Ellenwood, Georgia)
38 George Zarounian (Visalia, California)
39 Dan Stoner (Princeton, Illinois)
40 Herman Johnson (Eau Claire, Wisconsin)
41 Greg Smith (Akron, Ohio)
42 Yosemite Sam's (Detroit, Michigan)
43 Jack Courville (Ontario, Canada)
44 Don Hastings (Albuquerque, New Mexico)

TRUE FACT SERIES (5K)   2 3/8" X 4 7/16"

Another mystery set from Topps, the "True Fact Series" was brought to our attention by Mike Gallela and Roxanne Toser. TFS is a group of miniature comic books covering sports and non-sports subjects. Their physical dimensions are too large to fit into standard packaging and that led researchers to the conclusion, now confirmed, that the comics were a bonus item packed specifically for retailers. Each comic has 16 pages and is filled with excellent artwork and text. The books were prepared for Topps by Custom Comics of New York City.

ITEM	MINT	EX
Comic	12.50	10.00

No. 1 The Story of Baseball and Football
No. 2 The Wright Brothers
No. 3 Prehistoric Beasts
No. 4 Magellan, The Great Explorer
No. 5 They Served The Nation

TSR TRADING CARDS (750)   2 1/2" X 3 1/2"

My vote for Best Set of 1991 doesn't go to a card series based on comic books, movies, television shows, or the war in the Persian Gulf. Instead it belongs - lock, stock and barrel - to a set based on a theme about which I know nothing: Fantasy Games. People who play these games invariably speak of the wonderful characters, complicated intrigues, and a wide range of maneouvers which keep them coming back for more. Now, at last, we card collectors have a glimpse of what makes Fantasy Games so popular.

While examining the cards, I was literally and figuratively overwhelmed by the variety and depth of the elements on which they draw: religion, history, mythology, folklore ... and yes, even science fiction and popular heroes (real and fictional). A list, abandoned after a few moments when I realized how immense it was going to be, cited the following sources for characters seen on the cards: Dark Shadows, Tarzan, Robin Hood, Norse mythology, Shogun, King Arthur & Camelot, Charles "The Hammer" Martel, Dracula, witches, ghouls, vampires, elves, dwarfs, trolls, Vietnam, the Conquistadors, Sinbad the Sailor, and professional wrestling. I swear there is even a picture of Gabriella Sabatini! The TSR characters are new, yet familiar; they have specific propensities for good or evil, and the artists who drew them are truly talented.

There are seven Fantasy Games represented in the TSR "Premier Edition Factory Set": Advanced Dungeons & Dragons (472 cards), Forgotten Realms (129 cards), Dragon Lance (79 cards), Greyhawk (33 cards), Spelljammer (20 cards), Ravenloft (16 cards), and Dark Sun (1 card). Collectors not familiar with Fantasy Game jargon will probably skip the proficiency lists of each character (level, armor class, hit points, etc.) and go right to the "Background" description printed for each subject. The cards were originally designed, says a company spokesman, "to provide quick information that is easily used in a night's adventuring," without having to refer to standard reference manuals. Card collectors will want them for the lush artwork, the great value (see price below), AND for the humor.

Yes, the humor. You see, not all of the cards in the series are stirring examples of manly men or breathtaking women, or dragons, wizards, and trolls. There are many cards which simply display an inanimate object used as a game piece, the possession of which endows the holder with specific (and usually temporary) powers. There is, for example, a Horn of Bubbles, a Hat of Stupidity, and an Amulet of Inescapable Location. Although these items have specific and serious applications in fantasy campaigns, you may find yourself convulsed with laughter when you see them.

The TSR factory set described here is a parallel issue to the regular production TSR series released over a period of time in 1990 and 1991. Most "regular" TSR cards, which have gold symbols in the lower right corner, came in foil packs and were primarily sold in comic book stores and magazine outlets. However, some sequences of regular TSR cards were only available as magazine inserts, and it is these groups of "rare" cards that have caused severe problems for collectors trying to complete the gold-symbol set. As a gesture of goodwill, TSR created the parallel silver-symbol factory set to provide a low-cost alternative to the regular series and also to replace the gold-symbol cards which were being handled and used for fantasy gaming. We will not attempt to evaluate the regular series of TSR cards in this volume because prices are not firmly established for the so-called "rarities." The TSR factory edition, however, came into the marketplace at a suggested retail of $24.95 and has been selling in the $25-$30 range ever since. That comes out to about 4¢ per card, which we think is a very good deal.

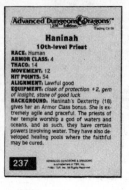

1 Alias
2 Bruenor
3 Dragonbait
4 Midnight
5 Tristan
6 Robyn
7 Shandril
8 Olive
9 Raistlin
10 Caramon
11 Tika
12 Tasslehoff
13 Tanis
14 Goldmoon
15 Laurana
16 Kitiara
17 Aldarr
18 Dalamar
19 Imp
20 Elkoremarr
21 Firbolg
22 Hill Giant
23 Pyrosternia
24 Chlormordia
25 Dagaronzie
26 Ar-Kane
27 Renwood
28 Crystal Ball
29 Gem of Insight
30 Talamar Thraydin
31 Sorvani
32 Boris Nahal
33 Mara Korvin
34 Nastorrian
35 Jalen Lang
36 Dwyam Marz
37 Shonorr
38 Candle of Invocation
39 Ring of Fire Resistance
40 Water Weird
41 Hawk
42 Zollrendar
43 Santis
44 Tarninia
45 Alyssa
46 Snakes, Giant
47 Kagon
48 Randoer
49 Drent
50 Bylquore
51 Wand of Frost
52 Gauntlets of Dexterity
53 Sword +2, Giant Slayer
54 Cloak of Elvenkind
55 Vandrillon
56 Baron Rykoffe
57 Panndallor
58 Smilodon
59 Lizard Man King
60 Lich
61 Death Knight
62 Heucuva
63 Dagger of Venom
64 Quiver of Ehlonna, Bow +1
65 Bledorown

66 Liliornin
67 Morrandar
68 Amberstar
69 Anatoly Crarr
70 Gargoyle
71 Max Rinnen
72 Frost Giant
73 Cloak of Protection +2
74 Sword +3, Frost Band
75 Helm of Opposite Alignment
76 Helm of Underwater Action
77 Seragrimm
78 Drendar
79 Norsinnow
80 Hell Hound
81 Chhe Phou
82 Krazzora
83 Lakkonon
84 Zendhora
85 Gorsomm
86 Short Sword of Quickness
87 Helm of Teleportation
88 Brazier Commanding Fire Elements
89 Neerga
90 Azurem
91 Kapak Draconian
92 Bozak Draconian
93 Glaze
94 Magma
95 Amulet of Inescapable Location
96 Horn of Fog
97 Gunthar Ironbeard
98 Thraygar Blackbeard
99 Persephone
100 Gimballon
101 Garth
102 Uthrac
103 Staff of Curing
104 Bracers of Archery
105 Drakkimor
106 Elianna
107 Owlbear
108 Talamius
109 Salem Ironring
110 Bartolus Menk
111 Donorow
112 Borak
113 Masakito
114 Takako
115 Randron
116 Talthoron
117 Gem of Seeing
118 Libram of Gainful Conjuration
119 Sword +2, Nine Lives Stealer
120 Thunderstorm
121 Ettin
122 Klarenden
123 Nobilius
124 Oni
125 Orsos
126 Staff of Power
127 Pouch of Accessibility
128 Axe of Hurling +4

129 Helm of Comprehending Languages & Reading Magic
130 Cloak of Displacement
131 Mirror of Opposition
132 Heronimus
133 Oriana
134 Mardus
135 Checklist
136 Checklist
137 Checklist
138 Skie, Blue Dragon
139 Fewmaster Toade
140 Lord Verminaard
141 Ember, Red Dragon
142 Vaporighu
143 Maelephant
144 Bebilith
145 Boccob's Blessed Book
146 Boots of Levitation
147 Boots of Speed
148 Cloaker
149 Thri-kreen
150 Meazel
151 Orc
152 Prince Torvil
153 Oceana, Blue Dragon

Kagon

154 Sword of the Planes
155 Wand of Illusion
156 Flask of Curses
157 Gloves of Missile Snaring
158 Crysania
159 Puccalli
160 Beholder
161 Fejyelsae
162 Ogre
163 Gully Dwarf
164 Martin

165 Krazen
166 Allisa of the Mists
167 Bowl Commanding Water Elements
168 Censor of Summoning Hostile Air Elementals
169 Warrior, Skeleton
170 Dergard, Red Dragon
171 Izz'teri
172 Tessen Leder
173 Grazaria, Green Dragon
174 Unicorn
175 Palin Majere
176 Dougan Redhammer
177 Princess Linea
178 Hettman Dorbin Tsurin
179 Mika
180 Sysania
181 Wolf
182 Marshana, Green Dragon
183 Pryessant
184 Chandalar
185 Mind Flayer
186 Orkondon
187 Michaela
188 Geoff of Easlon
189 Torrince
190 Sakornia
191 Alazar
192 Eriadne
193 Sword +1, Cursed
194 Rod of Terror
195 Staff of Withering
196 Bag of Holding
197 Bucknard's Everfull Purse
198 Boots of the North
199 Wand of Fear
200 Scroll, Protection from Magic
201 Wand of Enemy Detection
202 Broom of Flying
203 Decanter of Endless Water
204 Tome of Clear Thought
205 Skikkin Wu, Shen Lung Dragon
206 Go-Zu-Oni
207 Jiki-ketsu-gaki
208 Rod of Smiting
209 Cloak of the Bat
210 Cyan Bloodbane
211 King Lorac Caladon
212 Riverwind
213 Jarak-Sinn
214 Griffon
215 Waldo
216 Blaze
217 Korumundu
218 Blizzard
219 Onyx
220 Elspeth
221 Smolder
222 Valdemari

TSR Trading Cards

223 Zadoc
224 Tyrinon
225 Odin
226 Doral
227 Ragna
228 Bruinthor
229 Arax
230 Helm of Telepathy
231 Dagger +2, Longtooth
232 Larage shield +1, +4 vs. missiles
233 Sword +1, flame tongue
234 Bracers of Defense
235 Bag of Transmuting
236 Pearl of Wisdon
237 Haninah
238 Dirck of Wildspace
239 Inferno
240 Pegasus
241 Azurem
242 Iduna
243 Casimir
244 Fire Giant, Undead
245 Malchus
246 Ayamee
247 Philemon
248 Flame
249 Aurum
250 Ren o' the Blade
251 Dracolich
252 Chou Ling
253 Drizzt Do' Urden
254 Wulfgar
255 Checklist
256 Checklist
257 Checklist
258 Necklace of Adaptation
259 Robe of Stars
260 Gauntlets of Ogre Power
261 Astral Dreadnought
262 Claudanius
263 Nanzar
264 Shabala
265 Korindell
266 Sukari
267 Ki-rin
268 Bayalun
269 Ranach
270 Dhoran
271 Yamun Khahan
272 Samuel
273 Carmen
274 Werebear
275 Dwarinom
276 Finder Wyvernspur
277 Grypht
278 Giogioni Wyvernspur
279 Mind Flayer
280 Neogi
281 Giff
282 Sonya Dell' Anar
283 Cork Renford
284 Orog
285 Boots of Dancing
286 Cloak of Poisonousness
287 Morning Star +3
288 Sword +5, Holy Avenger
289 Bracers of Defenselessness
290 Hat of Disguise
291 The Pereghost
292 Khoman
293 Dazar
294 Chalak
295 Githyanki Knight
296 Githyanki Mage
297 Eldred Treydarr
298 Edomira
299 Mist Wolf
300 Sea Zombie
301 Swordwraith
302 Arina
303 Kendallar
304 Quagmiela
305 Killan
306 Static
307 Crimson
308 Gauntlets of Swimming and Climbing
309 Jewel of Attacks
310 Brooch of Shielding
311 Harp of Charming
312 Mirror of Mental Prowess
313 Arrow of Direction
314 Staff-Spear
315 Robe of Vermin

Panndallor

316 367lott
317 Joliet
318 Malakan
319 Makenzie
320 Pallandra
321 Tysiln San
322 Elephant
323 Xanthom
324 Elad Edals
325 Miltiades
326 Goram
327 Varalla
328 Pseudodragon
329 Sandor
330 Werewolf
331 Hilmar
332 Kraiton
333 Emilia
334 Ian Jytman
335 Julius
336 Finian Garwoode
337 Marquis
338 Mavis
339 Ramsey
340 Avildar
341 Einar
342 Carolyn
343 Volmer
344 Catriona
345 Emerentia
346 Anuirin
347 Wand of Metal and Mineral Detection
348 Cloak of the Manta Ray
349 Sword +2, Dragon Slayer
350 Manual of Stealthy Pilfering
351 Beaker of Plentiful Potions
352 Axe +2, Throwing
353 Sword +4, Defender
354 Amulet of Life Protection
355 Trystan
356 Miles
357 Thorvid
358 Chad
359 Yara
360 Jewel of Flawlessness
361 Universal Solvent
362 Efreeti Bottle
363 Keoghtom's Ointment

364 Ghengal
365 Sandiraksiva
366 Cephus
367 Nolzur's Marvelous Pigments
368 Poresche
369 Calandria
370 Gulian
371 Wendel
372 Zombie
373 Candace
374 Sturm Brightblade
375 Checklist
376 Checklist
377 Checklist
378 Sithel
379 Sithas
380 Kith-Kanan
381 Meredoth
382 Grim Reaper
383 Werebat
384 Bussengeist
385 Minotaur of Taladas
386 Carpet of Flying
387 Manual of Bodily Health
388 Talisman of Pure Gold
389 Pipes of Haunting
390 Gem of Brightness
391 Staff of Striking
392 Robe of Powerlessness
393 Stone of Good Luck
394 Wand of Secret Door and Trap Location
395 Necklace of Strangulation
396 Periapt of Wound Closure
397 Obliviax
398 Mummy
399 Mud-man
400 Mold, Brown
401 Mold, Yellow
402 Mimic
403 Kobold
404 Jermlaine
405 Martel
406 Gruendar
407 Staenorr
408 Tevra
409 Trent
410 Darrick
411 Halvor II
412 Verdantia
413 Gloriana
414 Gabriel
415 Ambrose
416 Barent
417 Duncan
418 Reginald
419 Kereth
420 Maelstrom
421 Stone of Weight
422 Ring of Blinking
423 Oil of Timelessness
424 Eversmoking Bottle
425 Boots of Varied Tracks
426 Oil of Fumbling
427 Scroll of Protection from Cold
428 Talisman of Ultimate Evil
429 Octopus, Giant
430 Badger
431 Troll
432 Shambling Mound

433 Satyr
434 Spider, Giant
435 Aboleth
436 Air Elemental
437 Earth Elemental
438 Scroll of Protection from Acid
439 Potion of Clairaudience
440 Ring of Djinni Summoning
441 Ring of Invisibility
442 Potion of Extra-Healing
443 Scroll of Protection from Petrification
444 Elixir of Health
445 Scroll of Protection from Plants
446 Gorgosaurus
447 Hyena
448 Vattaan
449 Silvara
450 Tinuel
451 Kendal
452 Oran Firehammer
453 Quintin
454 Huma
455 Huma's Silver Dragon
456 Seiroku Ashida
457 Goblin Spider
458 Ring of Shocking Grasp
459 Ring of Sustenance
460 Scroll of Protection from Water
461 Peregrine
462 Allene
463 Rufus Thistlebee

Geoff of Easlon

464 Tobias
465 Barracuda
466 Bulette
467 Carrion Crawler
468 Catoblepas
469 Chimera
470 Axebeak
471 Triceratops
472 Dryad
473 Ettercap
474 Ghost

475 Galeb Duhr
476 Goblin
477 Sea Hag
478 Matron Grazia Drodeen
479 Alodia Drodeen
480 Mind Flayer
481 Gabrielle Aderre
482 Azalin
483 Vlad Drakov
484 Lord Wilfred Godefroy
485 Hazlik
486 Harkon Lukas
487 Frantisek Markov
488 Yagno Petrovna
489 Strahd Von Zarovich
490 Jovena
491 Geritt
492 Wilhelm
493 Theodoric
494 Mordenkainen
495 Checklist
496 Checklist
497 Checklist
498 Rod of Beguiling
499 Wand of Earth and Stone
500 Wand of Magic Detection
501 Wand of Negation
502 Amulet of Proof Against
    Detection and Location
503 Boots of Elvenkind
504 Drums of Deafening
505 Eyes of Charming
506 Umber Hulk
507 Displacer Beast
508 Camel
509 Cat
510 Horse
511 Ape, Carnivorous
512 Margoyle
513 Bat, Giant
514 Lorin
515 Marith
516 Niles
517 Intellect Devourer
518 Hasan Balu
519 Noble Djinni
520 Quiornim
521 Charles
522 Vance
523 Gershom
524 Eyes of the Eagle
525 Girdle of Giant Strength
526 Harp of Discord
527 Hat of Stupidity
528 Horn of Bubbles
529 Incense of Obsession
530 Libram of Silver Magic
531 Potion of Delusion
532 Vampiric Mist
533 Blood Sea Imp
534 Yeth Hound
535 Eyewing
536 Fetch
537 Sabrita
538 Disir
539 Crypt Thing
540 Elixir of Madness
541 Oil of Disenchantment
542 Philter of Stammering and
    Stuttering
543 Potion of Sweet Water
544 Ring of Delusion
545 Ring of Human Influence
546 Ring of Mammal Control
547 Ring of Mind Shielding
548 Wasp
549 Man-O-War
550 Nautiloid
551 Dragonfly
552 Tradesman
553 Neogi Mindspider
554 Neogi Deathspider
555 Hammership
556 Squid Ship
557 Lander
558 Koresh
559 Swendi
560 Joseph

Miltiades

561 Pteranodon
562 Cairn
563 Ireisal
564 Ghoul
565 Sim Paing
566 Ring of X-Ray Vision
567 Scroll of Protection
    from Dragon Breath
568 Scroll of Protection
    from Electricity
569 Scroll of Protection
    from Elementals
570 Scroll of Protection
    from Fire
571 Scroll of Protection
    from Gas

Minotaur of Taladas

572 Kech
573 Kappa
574 Hook Horror
575 Fire Elemental
576 Water Elemental
577 Gelatinous Cube
578 Green Slime
579 Piercer

Strahd Von Zarovich

Jovena

580 Roper
581 Rust Monster
582 Treant
583 Xorn
584 Yuan-ti
585 Yeti
586 Kaz the Minotaur
587 Leofric
588 Volita
589 Garic Stonefoot
590 Romney
591 Stribling
592 Kelton
593 Halden
594 Olivia
595 Nameless Priest of Zard
596 Emerald
597 Averill
598 Guntar Griswold
599 Hubadai
600 Elminster
601 Ruga
602 Autumn
603 Winslow
604 Selim
605 Darbee
606 Carcavulp
607 Worden Ironfist
608 Vasos Flameslayer
609 Udall Granitecrusher
610 Tibold Hillmover
611 Strahd
612 Rat, Common
613 Curcio
614 Uthgar
615 Checklist
616 Checklist
617 Checklist
618 Frog, Giant
619 Pixie
620 Iron Golem

621 Stirge
622 Asperii
623 Brownie
624 Couatl
625 Darkenbeast
626 Brontosaurus
627 Iguanodon
628 Rod of Rulership
629 Wand of Lightning
630 Wand of Magic Missiles
631 Wand of Paralyzation
632 Horn of Goodness / Evil
633 Manual of Quickness of
    Action
634 Maul of the Titans
635 Murlynd's Spoon
636 Pearl of the Sirines
637 Pipes of Sounding
638 Doppleganger
639 Eagle, Giant
640 Shrieker
641 Cloud Giant
642 Korred
643 Trapper
644 Weretiger
645 Priest of Milil
646 Priest of Lathander
647 Priest of Torm
648 Priest of Waukeen
649 Priest of Gond

650 Priest of Silvanus
651 Priest of Mask
652 Priest of Talona
653 Priest of Malar
654 King Azoun IV
655 Princess Alusair
656 Torg mac Cei
657 Dwarf of Earthfast
658 Emperor Kai Tsao Shou Chin
569 Batu Min Ho
660 Lady Batsu Hsuang Wu

Yeti

661 Mandarin Ting Mei Wan
662 Mymph
663 Black Pudding
664 Dun Pudding
665 Giant Shark
666 Slithering Tracker
667 Sprite
668 Living Web
669 Wraith
670 Rope of Climbing
671 Scarab of Enraging Enemies
672 Scarab of Insanity
673 Wind Fan
674 Rug of Smothering
675 Potion of Diminution
676 Elixir of Youth
677 Philter of Glibness
678 Neirgral
679 Maison Thorvold
680 Eleazar Clyde
681 Kienan
682 Oorag
683 Aeriell
684 The Magister
685 Takhisis
686 Firestar
687 Gnoll
688 Merman
689 Myconid
690 Topaz
691 Turqual
692 Fizban
693 Lord Gunthar
694 Giltarald
695 Vampire
696 Okuma
697 Toraga
698 Min Lang

Leofric

TSR Trading Cards

699 Grogan
700 Belkarall
701 Theros Ironfeld
702 Potion of Rainbow Hues
703 Potion of Vitality
704 Ring of Free Action
705 Ring of Jumping
706 Ring of Swimming
707 Ring of Warmth
708 Ring of Water Walking
709 Fistandantilus
710 Lord Soth
711 Scroll of Protection
    from Lycanthropes
712 Scroll of Protection
    from Poison
713 Scroll of Protection
    from Undead
714 Scroll of Protection
    from Possession
715 Scroll, Cursed
716 Trooper Herphan Gomja
717 Captain Hemar
718 Teldin Moore
719 Pheragas
720 Kiiri of the Sirines
721 The Red Minotaur
722 Pegataur
723 T'Laan
724 Halloran
725 Erixitl of Palul
726 Captain Daggrande
727 Amerigo
728 Gultec
729 Qotal
730 Takto and Loktil
731 Darien
732 Bishou Domincus

733 Lactun
734 Zocon
735 Checklist
736 Checklist
737 Checklist
738 Arialana
739 Belgora
740 Sword of Life Stealing
741 Domarlynnas
742 Kyrrolla
743 Cytulliar
744 Poliamus
745 Zerrannon
746 Neeva
747 Fallon
748 Indirion
749 Baloriek
750 Gort

Nymph

Captain Daggrande

Weretiger

The Red Minotaur

Gultec

TV CARTOON TATTOOS (16)   2 7/16" X 3 7/16"

The dimensions in the heading refer to the folded sheet of tattoos as it came in the pack: an unfolded sheet measures 3 7 1/16" X 14 1/4". There are 14 tattoo designs per sheet (six large, eight small) and a total of 224 different tattoos in the set. Only the "header" portion of the sheet is numbered. The shared borders between tattoos are pre-scored to permit easy separation. The set was issued by Topps in 1976. Note: prices listed are for intact sheets only.

ITEM	MINT	EX
Set	55.00	45.00
Sheet	3.00	2.50
Wrapper	--	6.00
Box	--	65.00
Box Sleeve	--	35.00

48-CT. DUAL DISPLAY UNIT

TV'S BEST-LOVED CARTOON CHARACTERS

TESTED FOR REPEAT SALES!
Re-order as soon as your first box is sold!

TV SMELLY AWARDS (64) 2 1/2" X 3 7/16"

When Fleer decided to make a sticker set satirizing television, they not only went after the shows, but the commercials as well. That's why you'll find titles like "Burger Kink" and "Badyear Tires" mixed in with show spoofs like "Sappy Daze" and "Mission Improbable." The fronts of the sticker-cards are television sets with captioned, color artwork "pictures." The sticker number and set total are stated in the upper right corner. The backs are designed as a write-in ballot for the owner to make his own "Smelly Award" choices.

ITEM	MINT	EX
Set	16.00	12.50
Sticker	.25	.20
Wrapper	––	2.00
Box	––	7.00

1 Sappy Daze
2 Six Dollar Man
3 Brawl In The Family
4 Sanford & Bum
5 The Jerkersons
6 Kojerk
7 Birdetta
8 Chicken & The Man
9 Bob Oldheart Show
10 Lone Stranger
11 Wring Around The Collar
12 Badyear Tires
13 To Tell A Lie
14 Squirmin Toilet Tissue
15 Hondo Motorcycles
16 Caressed Bath Soap
17 Binocker Mouthwash
18 Freaks of San Francisco
19 Toidy Bowl
20 Berny Mailer
21 Crunch Toothpaste
22 Anguish Pain Reliever
23 Petrosilly
24 Mary Taylor Less
25 Mucky Mouse
26 Emergence
27 Dynamite Detergent
28 Bananaz
29 Good Crimes
30 Ratman & Bobbin
31 Don Atom's Scream Test
32 M*U*S*H
33 Husky & Starch
34 Lavoine & Shoiley
35 Columbum
36 Shingles Potato Chips
37 Ignited Airlines
38 Burger Kink
39 Kentucky Fried Children
40 Sister Rogers
41 Sappy Days
42 I Dream of Jennie
43 Rude-ah
44 Easy-Oof Oven Cleaner
45 Fraud
46 Vomit Cleanser
47 Boo Knight
48 Dummy & Mary Show
49 Mary Heatburn
50 Little Louse On The Prairie
51 Mission Improbable
52 Sunny & Sure
53 Please Woman
54 Phony Orland & Yawn
55 Grogan's Zeros
56 Star Truck
57 Elementary Queen
58 Welcome Back Klodder
59 Medic Central
60 Goober Pile
61 Sillygan's Island
62 Canned Camera
63 Mary Heartless
64 Chicken &The Man

24 TATTOOS (12) 6 7/8" X 9 5/8"

In 1983, Topps revived the "24 Tattoos" format it had previously used in 1971. The modern version was packaged in a large blue paper wrapper with crimped edges at top and bottom. The tattoo sheet measures 6 7/8" X 9 5/8" when open (it is folded in half to fit the pack). The individual tattoos are not numbered but the sheet number and the line "Collect All 12 Sheets" are printed on each piece.

ITEM	MINT	EX
Set	9.00	6.00
Sheet	.75	.50
Wrapper	––	.50
Box	––	5.00

A Non-Sport Mystery:
THE CASE OF THE MISSING TATTOOS

Here we have a genuine mystery. Two clues from the past - part of a box and a wrapper - are evidence that these two Topps sets did exist, but nobody has reported finding any of the tattoos. The first set, entitled "21 Tattoos," obviously predates the switch from 5¢ to 10¢ gum packs (1964). The wrapper is deceiving because it has a standard production code for 1971 printed at the bottom (0-412-21-01-1), which might indicate an American product, but the ingredients list is written in English, French, German, and Dutch. It probably was an export item that was never sold in the United States. Trading cards hold many mysteries for the collector and solving them, however long it takes, is one of the activities which makes our hobby so much fun.

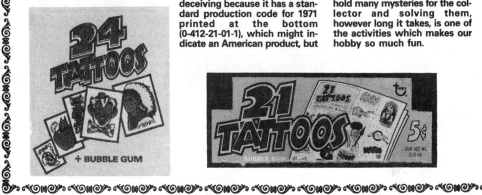

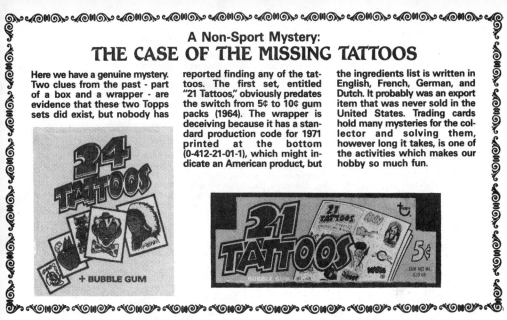

21 JUMP STREET (44)

2 1/2" X 3 1/2"

A modern-day retread of the old "Mod Squad" idea, "21 Jump Street" was the hottest show on the Fox Network (a.k.a. The California Culture Channel) when Topps produced this set in 1988. Alas, fame is fleeting but we will always have these 44 sticker-cards to remind us of the glorious past. The obverses contain corner-peel stickers with color publicity stills set at a slight angle in the center. The frameline is red and the background is a brick wall. The number is printed in the lower left corner to the left of the yellow caption panel. Speaking of captions, Topps pulled out all the creative stops in this area, coming up with dingers like "What a Hunk!," "What a Fox!," and "Lighten Up!" The backs fall into three categories: 18 bio/promo blurbs, 24 puzzle pieces, and two "completed" puzzle pictures. Note: peeled stickers cannot be graded excellent or mint.

1	Five for Danger!
2	Proud and Fearless
3	Cops Who Care!
4	Officer H.T. Ioki
5	Officer Judy Hoffs
6	At the Rifle Range
7	A Man, His Duty
8	High School Cops!
9	Officer Tom Hanson
10	Time for Fun!
11	The City Beat
12	Hanson & Hoffs
13	One Cool Cop!
14	Undercover!
15	Judy's Dream
16	Captain Adam Fuller
17	On the Job!
18	"To Protect & Serve"
19	Duo for Danger!
20	Fuller in Charge!
21	Dynamite Duo!
22	Jump Street's Finest
23	What a Cop!
24	Ioki's Gamble
25	A Fast Lane Life!
26	The New Case
27	Hot Night Out!
28	Huggable Hoffs!
29	Man and the Mission
30	Hot Young Star
31	Hanson Takes a Break!
32	A Laugh Between Jobs
33	Hanson Undercover
34	Officer Doug Penhall
35	Top Secret!
36	What a Fox!
37	Lighten Up!
38	Teen Patrol
39	Schoolyard Blues
40	Officer H.T. Ioki
41	Officer Tom Hanson
42	What a Hunk!
43	Freeze!
44	Officer Doug Penhall

ITEM	MINT	EX
Set	8.00	6.00
Sticker	.20	.15
Wrapper	--	.25
Box	--	2.00

TWIN PEAKS (76)   2 1/2" X 3 1/2"

Let's face it, "Twin Peaks" was never a mainstream American phenomenon. Oh, it had its moments, especially in the early episodes when Agent Dale Cooper arrived in town to investigate the death of Laura Palmer. There were "Twin Peaks" parties with fans gathering around TV sets on Thursday nights, eating cherry pie and drinking coffee. But as the show played on, the plots became more twisted and bizarre, as if Mark Frost and David Lynch couldn't help reverting to the irritating form exhibited in movies like Blue Velvet. The ratings, never healthy, began to slide, the show was switched to another night, and then was cancelled. Given one last episode to tie up loose ends, the creators opted to

alienate even die-hard "Peakies" with a mindless, "Last Year at Marienbad" show which ended with "Killer Bob" taking demonical possession of Agent Cooper himself!

Star Pics produced a 76-card series about Twin Peaks in 1991. The portrait cards in the series are far more attractive than the movie scene cards, many of which are blurry. A clever touch was the inclusion of cards showing cherry pie, the log lady's log, Agent Cooper's tape recorder, the heart locket, and a cup of coffee. Three cards are given over to trivia questions and there is one for "Production Notes" and another with the set checklist. The well-designed card backs have interesting biography, dialogue, episode notes, descrip-

tions, etc., and a majority of them also have eerie-looking picture negatives miniaturized on one edge. The series was marketed in complete-set form in its own special box and for this reason there are no prices given for single or for excellent grade cards. Star Pics issued a two-card panel as a promotion in advance of the set and also arranged for Twin Peaks actors and staff to autograph some of their cards, which were then randomly inserted into sets. Note: autographed cards have premium value and are not considered part of the regular set.

ITEM	MINT	EX
Set	20.00	—

1 Welcome to Twin Peaks	16 James Hurley	31 RR Diner
2 Checklist	17 Dr. Jacoby	32 Norma Jennings
3 Bird	18 Diary	33 Coffee
4 Agent Cooper	19 Dr. Hayward	34 Shelley Johnson
5 Tape Recorder	20 Donna Hayward	35 Leo Johnson
6 "Diane, 2:15 in the afternoon..."	21 Pierre Tremond	36 Bobby Briggs
7 Cherry Pie	22 Madeleine Ferguson	37 Ed Hurley
8 Sheriff's Station	23 Pete Martell	38 Big Ed's Gas Farm
9 Sheriff Truman	24 Fish	39 Nadine Hurley
10 Deputy Brennan	25 Catherine Martell	40 "I'm going to have the world's ..."
11 Lucy Moran	26 "Everything smells like fish..."	41 "One day my Log will have
12 Deputy Hawk	27 Packard Saw Mill	something to say ..."
13 Corpse	28 Josie Packard	42 The Log Lady
14 Laura Palmer	29 "Man ... smell those trees ..."	43 Log
15 Heart Locket	30 Pine Cone	44 The Roadhouse

45 One-Eyed Jack's
46 Benjamin Horne
47 Audrey Horne
48 Jerry Horne
49 Horne's Department Store
50 Richard Tremayne
51 Great Northern Hotel
52 Whitetail Falls
53 "The owls are not ..."
54 Jean Renault
55 "The Giant"
56 "He is Bob ..."
57 "The One-Armed Man"
58 "Killer Bob"
59 Leland Palmer
60 Sarah Palmer
61 Ceiling Fan
62 "Maybe that's all Bob is ..."
63 Agent Rosenfield
64 Major Briggs
65 Owl
66 "Local legend. The White Lodge ..."
67 "Don't let 'em rattle you, Coop ..."
68 Trivia
69 Trivia
70 Trivia
71 Production Notes
72 Mark Frost
73 David Lynch
74 Angelo Badalamenti
75 Jennifer Lynch
76 Julee Cruise

This spring, Star Pics, in cooperation with David Lynch and Mark Frost, will introduce a Twin Peaks Collectible Card Art set.

Are you ready for this?

IT CAME FROM ▲ TWIN PEAKS ▲

Twin Peaks Collectible CardArt™ by Star Pics.
Quirky. Bizarre. Off-the-wall. Images and facts from
America's most talked about TV show.

200 YEARS OF FREEDOM (45)

Early in February 1992, a letter arrived from Bill Hongach of Capital Cards (New York): "Recently I came across some Bicentenniel sets I made in 1976 (I was partners with Mike Aronstein of TCMA in SSPC - Sports Stars Publishing Co.). This 45-card set was made for the 4th of July celebration in N.Y. City when the tall ships came into New York harbor." That, in a nutshell, tells how these cards came into being.

Collectors will have no difficulty in identifying this set because the title is printed three times on the front of every card. The center ilustrations are scenes of revolutionary battles, events, and leaders and all are printed in a blue cast. The caption for every card is printed in red ink below the picture. Turning to the back, we find a U.S. "76" flag flanked by the dates "1776" and "1976" and text which describes the subject depicted on the front. The card number is printed in red in the lower left corner; in the bottom right corner is a copyright line with the SSPC initials and a 1976 date. Sold only in complete sets, "20 Years of Freedom" currently retails in the $10-$12 range.

 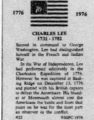

1 The Declaration of Independence	24 John Paul Jones
2 The Declaration of Independence	25 Serapis vs. Bonhomme Richard
3 George Washington	26 Battle of Saratoga
4 Paul Revere	27 Nathan Hale
5 Minutemen	28 Benjamin Lincoln
6 Battle of Lexington	29 John Adams
7 Ben Franklin	30 Casimir Pulaski
8 Sam Adams	31 Battle of Princeton
9 Patrick Henry	32 Death of Mercer at Princeton
10 The Battle of Bunker Hill	33 Anthony Wayne
11 Thomas Paine	34 Betsy Ross
12 Thomas Jefferson	35 John Stark
13 John Hancock	36 Battle of Monmouth
14 Nathaniel Greene	37 Francis Marion
15 Robert Morris	38 Valley Forge
16 Marquis de LaFayette	39 Frederich Von Steuben
17 Henry Knox	40 Comte De Rochambeau
18 Washington Crosses The Delaware	41 "We fight, get beat, rise and fight again"
19 Capture of Hessians at Trenton	42 Cornwallis Surrenders at Yorktown
20 Horatio Gates	43 Resignation of Washington
21 Alexander Hamilton	44 George Washington
22 Charles Lee	45 Spirit of '76
23 Benedict Arnold	

UGLY BUTTONS (24)

The artwork and captions on the buttons and the production code printed on the wrapper suggest that "Ugly Buttons" were issued during the 1966 Halloween season. The "wrapper" is a glossy paper packet with a five-cent price. The buttons are made of tin and are approximately 2" in diameter. They are not numbered but the word "Japan" is printed on the inside rim. The attachment device is a tabbed half-moon straight pin with an angled safety bar.

ITEM	MINT	EX
Button	5.00	4.00
Wrapper	--	15.00
Box	--	150.00

Photo courtesy of Robert Marks

Be Kind To Animals
Brush After Every Meal
Come On Down
Don't Be Nosey
Don't Bug Me
Give Me A Great Big Kiss!
Here's Looking At You
Here's Mud In Your Eye
Hold Me
I'm A Cool Ghoul
I'm Super
I Use Greasy Kid Stuff

Keep Our City Clean
License To Kill
National Blemish Week
98 Pound Weakling
Peek-A-Boo
Respect Your Elders
Visit Your Dentist Twice A Year
Watch The Birdie
What Ever Happened To Baby Sister
You Kill Me
You're Driving Me Bats
You're Just My Type

UGLY STICKERS (3 SETS)

2 1/2" X 3 1/2"

Topps issued Ugly Stickers on three separate occasions: 1965, 1973-74, and 1976. The series is popular among collectors who appreciate the handiwork of famous artists Basil Wolverton and Wally Wood, among others. Our prices reflect a substantial premium value for stickers in new or like-new condition, and prospective buyers should insist that condition match the price being asked.

1965 Series: Consists of 164 different names distributed among 44 numbered pieces of artwork. Each number except 29, 30, 32, and 40 has four different names for the same design (all set on white backgrounds); Nos. 29, 30, 32, and 40 have a single name only and have black or painted backgrounds. All 1965 Ugly Stickers are numbered and have tan paper backs separated into two parts. The wrapper for this series is brownish-maroon and carries a 5-cent price. Note: numbered stickers without names were issued in England and are not variations.

ITEM	MINT	EX
Set	470.00	375.00
Sticker	2.50	2.00
Wrapper	--	25.00
Box	--	200.00

EUGENE

ISABELLE

MELVIN

NICHOLAS

1	Arthur	4	Ann	7	Henry	10	Adam
	Edith		Red		Lester		Brenda
	Jim		Sy		Marv		Dan
	Terry		Will		William		Steve
2	Carl	5	Emily	8	Brian	11	Barry
	Jose		Joan		Irene		Donald
	Leslie		Lou		Kenneth		Florence
	Nancy		Rich		Victor		Wendy
3	Edward	6	Diana	9	Don	12	Arleen
	Harvey		Gail		Ed		Fay
	Jacqueline		Gene		Lil		Inez
	Sandy		Howard		Ruth		Pete

Ugly Stickers

13 Elizabeth / Lewis / Stan / Walt
14 Andrew / Harv / Susan / Sylvia
15 Ben / Bonnie / Eleanor / Shelly
16 Irving / Jess / Patricia / Walter

17 Belle / Julie / Ken / Leonard
18 Bill / Harold / Keith / Malcolm
19 Cynthia / Jeff / Laurie / Pat
20 Barbara / Frank / Marg / Vincent

21 Albert / Charles / Muriel / Ron
22 Catherine / Clifford / Loretta / Richard
23 Drew / Fred / Iris / Joel
24 Bert / Eileen / Jessica / Marty

25 Artie / Beth / Susan / Grace
26 Ana / James / Joe / John
27 Al / Amy / Les / Vi
28 Carl / Caroline / Lillian / Mike

29 Doc
30 Granny
31 Daniel / Dean / Mark / Vince
32 Tommy
33 Art / Cheryl / Fay / Michael
34 Helen / Jane / Lois / Robert

35 Carol / George / Marvin / Minda
36 Cliff / Doris / Margaret / Mitch
37 Eugene / Isabelle / Melvin / Nicholas
38 Alice / Betty / David / Gloria

39 Alan / Anthony / Nan / Rita
40 Charlie
41 Bruce / Henry / Peter / Vic
42 Josephine / Marie / Paul / Rob

43 George / Joseph / Stanley / Ward
44 Bob / Dorothy / Evelyn / Renee

1973-74 Series: Composed of 110 names on 55 unnumbered stickers, two names for each Ugly character. The backs are a single sheet of brown paper and the sticker designs on the front are diecut. Each sticker carries either one or two stars before the Topps copyright line: a one-star name always shares the same artwork with a two-star name. [No stars printed on "Granny" and "Millie."] Efforts to distinguish the 1973 group from that of 1974 are still on-going. One puzzle piece printed on 2 1/2" X 3 1/2" cardboard was inserted into every 1974 pack (not reported for 1973 packs). The wrappers for both years share the same basic design but have different panel details and production codes. The box in our display is from the 1974 set. Note: set price includes puzzle.

ITEM	MINT	EX
Set	175.00	135.00
Sticker	1.25	1.00
Puzzle Parts (12) each	1.00	.75
Wrappers (2) each	--	6.00
Box	--	60.00

AGNES

CATHY

Ugly Stickers

KIDS: COLLECT ALL 12 PIECES TO COMPLETE YOUR UGLY JIGSAW PUZZLE

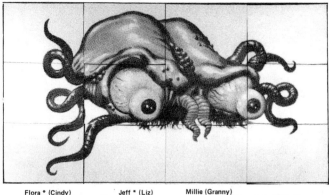

Agnes * (Cathy)
Alvin ** (Harold)
Andy * (Doug)
Artie ** (Felix)
Barbara * (Karen)
Barney ** (Elliott)
Ben * (Roy)
Bill * (Dom)
Bobby * (Elmer)
Brian * (Tony)
Bridget * (Connie)
Bruno ** (Glenn)
Buddy ** (Oliver)
Carl ** (Pete)
Cathy ** (Agnes)
Charlie * (Murray)
Chris [yellow eyes] * (Jean)
Chris [red eyes] ** (Frank)
Cindy ** (Flora)
Cliff * (Ralph)

Connie **(Bridget)
Craig ** (Stan)
Dale ** (Irene)
Dave ** (Leon)
Doc * (Stu)
Dom ** (Bill)
Donna * (Helen)
Doris * (Lenny)
Dorothy ** (Jennifer)
Doug ** (Andy)
Ed * (Pat)
Edith ** (Steve)
Eleanor * (Sandy)
Elliott * (Barney)
Elmer ** (Bobby)
Emily * (Mary)
Emma * (Joan)
Eva * (Jane)
Evelyn ** (Glenda)
Felix * (Artie)

Flora * (Cindy)
Frank * (Chris [red eyes])
George * (Harvey)
Glenda * (Evelyn)
Glenn * (Bruno)
Granny (Millie)
Guy ** (Joe)
Harold * (Alvin)
Harry ** (Ida)
Harvey ** (George)
Hazel * (Melvin)
Helen ** (Donna)
Henry ** (Oscar)
Hugo ** (Keith)
Hymie * (Mitch)
Ida * (Harry)
Irene * (Dale)
Iris * (Lou)
Irv ** (Jill)
Jane ** (Eva)
Jean ** (Chris [yellow eyes])

Jeff * (Liz)
Jennifer * (Dorothy)
Jill * (Irv)
Jim ** (Ron)
Joan ** (Emma)
Joe * (Guy)
Joel ** (Judy)
Judy * (Joel)
Karen ** (Barbara)
Keith * (Hugo)
Leon * (Dave)
Lenny ** (Doris)
Leroy * (Paul)
Liz ** (Jeff)
Lloyd * (Walt)
Lou ** (Iris)
Mark ** (Nick)
Mary ** (Emily)
Mary Ann * (Paula)
Melvin ** (Hazel)
Mike ** (Neal)

Millie (Granny)
Mitch ** (Hymie)
Murray ** (Charlie)
Nancy ** (Susan)
Neal * (Mike)
Nick * (Mark)
Norman * (Tommy)
Oliver * (Buddy)
Oscar * (Henry)
Pat ** (Ed)
Paul ** (Leroy)
Paula ** (Mary Ann)
Pete * (Carl)
Phil ** (Rich)
Ralph ** (Cliff)
Rich * (Phil)
Ron * (Jim)
Roy ** (Ben)
Sandy ** (Eleanor)
Sid * (Sy)
Stan * (Craig)

Steve * (Edith)
Stu ** (Doc)
Susan * (Nancy)
Sy ** (Sid)
Tommy ** (Norman)
Tony ** (Brian)
Walt **(Lloyd)

1976 Series: Identical to the 1973-74 stickers in all details EXCEPT that the card back is thin white cardboard rather than brown paper. The wrapper design and color are also identical but the panel details and production code are different. This wrapper states that the 1976 Ugly Sticker series was "Made & Printed In U.S.A. By Topps For Trebor Sharps Ltd., Maidstone," thereby indicating that this white-back set was distributed primarily in England. It is also probable that some overstock was issued in the U.S. in Fun Packs (Bay City Rollers and Spook Theatre were also released in America in this manner). The fact that no box has been reported to date supports this theory. Note: no puzzle has been found for this issue.

ITEM	MINT	EX
Set	125.00	90.00
Sticker	1.00	.75
Wrapper	--	5.00

FLORA

CINDY

UNDERDOG (?)

The exterior—or wrapper—side of "Underdog" is yellow with orange, red, blue, and green accents. The design illustrated is the only one reported to date for this set. A 1966 copyright line for "Leonardo-T.T.V." sits above the title and a red Fleer "crown" is at bottom left. The tattoos on the interior side of the wrappers are not captioned or numbered (total in set unknown).

ITEM	MINT	EX
Wrapper	——	15.00

UNIVERSAL MONSTERS (6 & 6)   TWO SIZES

One of the neatest sets of 1991 came and went so swiftly that it is doubtful that most collectors know anything about it. "Universal Monsters" was a joint promotion of Doritos and Pepsi Cola, who targeted Halloween for the start-up of their "Play Monster Match For Monster Money" campaign. Specially-marked bags of Doritos contained a plastic packet with contest rules, one-half of a Monster Money banknote, and a color artwork sticker of a famous Universal Studios monster. Although the banknotes might be considered a collectible item, we cannot imagine anyone ignoring the cash prizes that a match of left and right sides would bring (and collecting halves isn't very interesting). The stickers, however, are a different story. Although they measure 2-1/2" square, the artwork centers are designed to be viewed like a baseball diamond. There are six characters in the set: Frankenstein, The Bride of Frankenstein, The Wolfman, The Creature from the Black Lagoon, The Mummy, and Dracula. When they can be found, they are selling in the range of 50¢ to $1.00 each.

Far more difficult to obtain are the "window pictures" of the same six monsters which were printed on 12-pack Pepsi cartons. From all reports, many stores never even received any of these great-looking cartons, while others had some cartons, but not others. Each "window picture" measures 7-1/2" X 10" and owners were advised to "Cut out and hang in your window. You could be visited by a Monster Spotter with Monster Money prizes!" According to our information, specific monsters came only on cartons of specific products: Frankenstein and Bride of Frankenstein on Pepsi; Dracula and The Wolfman on Diet Pepsi; The Mummy on Caffeine Free Diet Pepsi; and Creature from the Black Lagoon on Mountain Dew. Prices for intact cartons are as follows: Frankenstein & Bride of Frankenstein, $3.00 each; Dracula & The Wolfman, $4.00 each; Creature from the Black Lagoon, $5.00; and The Mummy, $6.00. Window pictures cut away from the box are worth 50% of these values. Note: the same six monsters appeared in the "Trading Card Treats" series by Impel.

DIET PEPSI

Cut out and hang in your window. You could be visited by a Monster Spotter with Monster Money prizes!

UNTOUCHABLES (16 & 16)　　　　2 9/16" X 4 5/8"

Leaf issued this series of 16 Untouchables booklets in gum packages and collectors should be wary about stains when buying this item. The booklets have eight pages, counting covers, and each relates an "Official Eliot Ness Adventure Story." One of a series of 16 gummed-back stickers depicting the shields and emblems of U.S. and international law enforcement agencies was also inserted as a bonus in every pack. Note: separate set prices apply for booklets and stickers.

ITEM	MINT	EX
Sets		
Booklets	95.00	75.00
Stickers	95.00	75.00
Booklet	5.00	4.00
Sticker	5.00	4.00
Wrapper	—	15.00
Box	—	75.00

Ain't We Got Fun
Jamaica Ginger
Little Egypt
Masterpiece
Mexican Stakeout
Purple Gang
The Antidote
The Bugs Moran Story
The Larry Fay Story
The Lily Dallas Story
The Nick Moses Story
The Organization
The Otto Frick Story
The Tri-state Gang
3000 Suspects
Vincent "Mad Dog" Coll

Central Intelligence Agency	Italian Police	Texas Rangers
Department of Justice	Japanese Police	Treasury Department Bureau of
Federal Bureau of	Mexican Police	Narcotics
Investigation	Royal Canadian Mounted Police	U.S. Board of Parole
German Police	Scotland Yard British Police	U.S. Coast Guard
Interpol International Police	Surrete French Police	U.S. Customs Police

URANUS STRIKES (36)　　　　2 1/2" X 3 1/2"

One of the best trading card sets of 1986, this science fiction spoof was privately produced by collector Bob Ting. The 36 color artwork cards and accompanying text relate the horrific details of an Earth invaded by hostile Uranians. Each card is numbered and captioned on front; the backs contain a preview sketch of the next card in sequence. Most backs also have an added feature, such as "Yuks from Uranus," puzzle pieces, etc. A glossy paper wrapper was designed to hold the entire set. Note: cards issued to the hobby in complete sets only; set price incudes wrapper.

ITEM	MINT	EX
Set	25.00	—

1 Operation Flaming Coffin!	19 Nature Strikes Back!
2 Lost in Space!	20 Torture!
3 Earth is Alerted!	21 Lynch Mob!
4 Killing Spree!	22 Laughed to Death!
5 Earth Strikes––Out!	23 Pest Control Squadron!
6 Nowhere to Hide!	24 Infiltrating Enemy!
7 Halloween Trick!	25 Fate of Mankind!
8 Fatal Atmosphere!	26 Remember the Alamo!
9 Airwave Takeover!	27 Uranus Victorious
10 Horror in Fantasyland!	28 Surprise Counterattack!
11 War Souvenirs!	29 Earth Hits 'Em Home!
12 Attack at Sea!	30 Hand to Claw Combat!
13 Prize Captive!	31 Uranus Crumbles!
14 Traitors!	32 Dog Fight!
15 Youths Fight Back!	33 Terrifying New World!
16 Fleeing the Fleas!	34 Man's Final Gesture!
17 Humongous Insects!	35 This Fireball Earth!
18 In Their Own Image!	36 Invasion Synopsis!

U.S. CONGRESS CARDS (535) (535)　　2 1/2″ X 3 1/2″

With all the Congress-bashing going on these days, there is sure to be heightened collector interest in the Congressional card sets which the National Educational Association issued in 1989 and 1991. These sets were brought to our attention by Bill Mullins and Gordon Burns, and Mullins has written the following description: "The NEA cards were issued in 1989 and 1991 for the 101st and 102nd sessions of Congress. They feature a black and white photo of a Senator or Representative on front, along with his or her party affiliation and district represented. The backs contain facts such as education, year of birth, mailing addresses, and committee assignments. Created as a lobbying tool for the NEA, there were 535 cards issued in each year. Non-sport collectors may have to compete with sports enthusiasts for some NEA cards: ex-Knick Bill Bradley and ex-Tiger Jim Bunning, for example. Also among the group are Fred Grandy ("Gopher" from the "The Love Boat"), Ben Jones ("Cooter" of "The Dukes of Hazzard") and astronauts John Glenn, Jake Garn, and Bill Lee. The 1989 set even has an error: Rep. Tommy Robinson (R-Ark.) changed parties in the midst of production, and his cards list him as a Democrat." Pictured: former Senator John Heinz of Pennsylvania, who died in a plane crash; Maryland Representative Kweisi Mfume, whose recent articles about greed and incompetence in upper management have pinpointed the single greatest factors in America's economic decline.

ITEM	MINT	EX
1989 Set	85.00	--
1991 Set	75.00	--

U.S. CUSTOMS CANINE ENFORCEMENT (81) 2 1/2″ X 3 1/2″

When collectors first heard about this set of 81 dogs depicting drug-sniffing dogs, it was considered a regional issue limited to the Southwest U.S. only. Packets containing nine cards, plus a "header," were handed out at anti-drug clinics and demonstrations at schools in Texas. The original printing of two million cards appears to have been distributed in this piecemeal fashion. Only recently, we have discovered that another series, or perhaps several series, have been released in different parts of the U.S.; cards have been seen with dogs representing the Pacific coast, New York, and Virginia. To compound matters, Customs finalized that long-rumored deal with "Milk Bone" brand dog snacks to issue a 24-card version entitled "All-Star Drug Detecting Dogs,"

Of the three types described, the Milk Bone issue will be the easiest to collect since it is available as a set for $1.00 and six purchase proofs (approximately $9.00 worth of product). The 81-card Southwest Region set is far more difficult to obtain

and the limited supply that has reached the hobby is selling for $1.00 per card and $100 per set. The cards from other U.S. locations are scarce at this time and are valued at $2.00 each. Only the Milk Bone set has blue borders with white stars; the other two versions have white borders with blue stars. The title used in our heading comes from the header card of the Southwest Region set.

U.S. OF ALF (51)

2 1/2" X 3 1/2"

Diamond Toy's beautifully designed "U.S. of Alf" set was released to the public in January 1988. There are 50 corner-peel stickers in this initial series, one for each state in the Union. The brilliant color artwork and snappy humorous dialogue are a pleasing contrast to some of the uninspired non-sports sets of recent years. Each sticker is assigned a number which is printed on the card back above a list of basic facts about each state. The 51st card in the set is an unnumbered checklist card with Alf pictured on the front in "Uncle Sam" attire.

ITEM	MINT	EX
Set	7.50	5.00
Sticker	.15	.10
Wrapper	--	.25
Box	--	4.00

U.S. PRESIDENTS (43 & 15)

2 1/2" X 3 1/2"

The artwork used by both Bowman and Topps in previous presidential sets was revived by Topps in 1972 for the first 33 cards of this series. New artwork was created for cards 34-36 and a "candidate" series (37-43) was added. Topps also inserted one 4-7/8" X 6-15/16" paper "campaign poster" as a bonus in each pack. SPECIAL NOTE: Topps apparently reprinted the series in 1976 for the Bicentennial Celebration and modified it by adding a "resignation line" to the Nixon card and by deleting Shirley Chisholm (#37) and replacing her with Gerald Ford. A moderate supply of these two cards has surfaced and at the present time they are valued at $5.00 each.

ITEM	MINT	EX
Card set	25.00	18.00
Poster set	--	25.00
Cards		
1-36	.50	.35
37-43	.75	.60
Wrapper	--	4.00
Box	--	30.00

EDMUND MUSKIE

Cards

1. George Washington
2. John Adams
3. Thomas Jefferson
4. James Madison
5. James Monroe
6. John Quincy Adams
7. Andrew Jackson
8. Martin Van Buren
9. Wm. Henry Harrison
10. John Tyler
11. James K. Polk
12. Zachary Taylor
13. Millard Fillmore
14. Franklin Pierce
15. James Buchanan
16. Abraham Lincoln
17. Andrew Johnson
18. Ulysses S. Grant
19. Rutherford B. Hayes
20. James A. Garfield
21. Chester A. Arthur
22. Grover Cleveland
23. Benjamin Harrison
24. William McKinley
25. Theodore Roosevelt
26. William H. Taft
27. Woodrow Wilson
28. Warren G. Harding
29. Calvin Coolidge
30. Herbert C. Hoover
31. Franklin D. Roosevelt
32. Harry S. Truman
33. Dwight D. Eisenhower
34. John F. Kennedy
35. Lyndon B. Johnson
36. Richard M. Nixon
37. Shirley Chisholm
38. Hubert Humphrey
39. John Lindsay
40. George McGovern
41. Edmund Muskie
42. Edward Kennedy
43. George Wallace

Posters

1. Lincoln
2. Taft
3. Kennedy
4. Truman
5. Eisenhower
6. Coolidge
7. Johnson, L.
8. Grant
9. Wilson
10. Washington
11. Roosevelt, T.
12. Jefferson
13. Roosevelt, F.
14. Hoover
15. Adams, J. Q.

V (66 & 22)

Fleer brought the popular television series "V" to card collectors with this series of cards and stickers issued in

UNMASKED

1984. The story cards are numbered 1-66 and have color photos with captions on front. The backs contain the card number and a single sentence of text, except for Nos. 9, 25, 27, 35, 60, and 62, which have more. Card No. 28 was never printed. Instead, there are two cards bearing the number 38;

the sentence on the backs of both cards is the same, but the pictures on front are different. The 22 numbered sticker cards have diecut photo areas on front and puzzle or puzzle preview backs (the puzzle has 15 parts). The sticker cards measure 2 1/2" X 3 3/8" and are not cap-

TWO SIZES

tioned. Special note: the uneven distribution of stickers in packs makes sticker sets much more difficult to assemble and has resulted in separate prices for cards and sticker sets. A complete run of 22 sticker fronts may not have the necessary pieces to complete the puzzle on back.

ITEM	MINT	EX
Sets		
Cards	10.00	6.50
Stickers	25.00	18.00
Card	.15	.10
Sticker	1.00	.75
Wrapper	--	.35
Box	--	4.00

They're Here!

STICKER NO. 21 OF 22

They're Here!
TRADING CARDS AND STICKERS
WITH BUBBLE GUM
10 CARDS, 1 STICKER & 1 STICK GUM
FLEER

1	Ready For A Chase	15	Fire!	30	Evasive Action	49	The Evil Eye
2	Visitor Roadblock	16	Mike Donovan—The Cameraman	31	On The Dark Side Of The Moon	50	Halt!
3	Julie—The Brave Resistance Leader	17	Diana's Favorite Torture Chair	32	Diana Escapes	51	Awaiting A Message
4	Sparks Are Flying	18	Standing Guard	33	Near Miss	52	In For A Landing
5	Fried Lizard	19	Unmasked	34	Visitor Shuttle Craft	53	Julie Parrish
6	Outside Refinery	20	Deadly Pair	35	Snack Time	54	Stand By To Open Fire!
7	Blasting Through	21	Ready For Action	36	Stand Back!	55	Sneaking Past Alien Guards
8	Hot Pursuit	22	Donovan In Disguise	37	A Quiet Moment	56	Kyle And Ham
9	The Conversion	23	Freeze!	38	Good And Evil	57	Oh! Those Eyes
10	Close Up View	24	Willie's Our Friend	38	Mother & Daughter Reunited	58	Diana Looks Under The Hood
11	Bullseye	25	Robin Maxwell	39	Attention!	59	Not Bad Looking For A Lizard
12	View From Inside	26	Diana Looks For New Conquests	40	Into A Snake Pit	60	Kyle And Elizabeth Run For Their Lives
13	The Hanger Deck	27	Elizabeth and Kyle	41	Meeting With The Enemy	61	Don't Let Them Get Away!
14	Diana At The Controls	29	Lydia Taking Aim	42	Ham Tyler	62	Kyle Bates
				43	Diana Runs For Cover	63	Some of "V's" Famous Cast
				44	Time To Chow Down	64	It's Donovan...After Him!
				45	The Planning Never Stops	65	Take Us Home Martin
				46	A Face You Can't Forget!	66	A Fearless Resistance Fighter
				47	Lead And Lasers For The Visitors		
				48	Mike Pulls The Switch		

VALENTINE FOLDEES (55) (55)   2 1/2" X 4 11/16"

"Valentine Foldees" has proved confusing to collectors because the series was issued on two separate occasions by Topps. However, the cards and wrappers of each type are easily distinguished from one another. The set was first marketed in January 1963 in a vertically-aligned five-cent wrapper. The 55 cards from this year are known as the "wheel" variety

because of the ornate circle designs on every card. The set that was re-issued in 1970 came in a horizontal wrapper bearing no price. Cards of this set are identical in artwork and captions to the 1963 issue, except that the "wheel" designs were replaced by the so-called "banana" pattern. Note: the "wheel" variety is more commonly found than the "banana," yet prices for both are the same because of

the age differential. Cards that have been folded (all score lines broken) cannnot be graded mint.

ITEM	MINT	EX
Sets		
"wheel"	190.00	155.00
"banana"	190.00	155.00
Cards (all)	3.00	2.50
Wrappers		
1963	--	60.00
1970	--	15.00
Box		
1970	--	75.00

Valentine Foldees

1 You're Popular Like Richard D. Nixon
   I Admire You Like John F. Kennedy
   You're A Hero Like Dwight D. Eisen-
   hower

2 A 70 Year Old Millionaire Marries
   22 Year Old Hollywood Movie Starlet
   In Maine a 9 Year Old Boy Graduates
   with Honors From High School
   A Small Tan Cocker Spaniel Gives
   Birth to Twenty Healthy Puppies

3 You're Cute as a 6 Year Old Riding
   on Daddy's Back
   You're Jolly as Santa Claus. Driving
   His Reindeer.
   You're Clever as Jesse James. Robbing
   a Bank

4 U.S. Senators Will Meet in the New
   Session of Congress
   Cops Break Up Fight in Bloody High
   High School Football Game
   Citizens Complain About Mess in the
   Smelly, Dirty City Sewers

5 Your Skin is as Smooth as... a 6
   Month Old Baby
   You are Wise Like an Old Hermit
   To Win Your Love I'd Fight a Big
   Gorilla

6 You'd Make a Better Soldier than
   General Grant
   You're More Intelligent than Betsy
   Ross
   You'd Make a Bigger Hit with Me than
   Babe Ruth

7 Former President of the U.S.A. Called
   in for a White House Conference
   12 Year Old Ballet Dancer will Dance
   at Opera House in New York City
   French Horse Named Pierre Takes
   Spill and Breaks Leg in Kentucky
   Derby

8 You Make My Heart Beat Faster.
   You're as Lovely as...Miss America.
   I'll Always Love You Even when I
   Become...a Wrinkled Old Man.
   I'd Fight for You even Against...a
   Horrible Monster.

9 You're a Cute Skinny Kid
   You're Honest as an Old School
   Teacher
   You Have a Figure Like a Bathing
   Beauty

10 Use Joan's Soap and Have a Face of
   Smooth Feminine Skin
   Fitz Skin Cream Gets Rid of Your
   Unsightly Pimples
   Ace Footballs Are Made of Genuine
   Pigskin

11 You're a Leader like Winston
   Churchill
   You Charm Me Like Queen Elizabeth
   You're Powerful like a Ferocious
   Bulldog

12 Use Jones' Ointment to Prevent
   Getting Painful Blisters and Infec-
   tions
   Use Mel's Dog Powder and Your Dog
   Will Have Thick Fur All Over the
   Body
   Use Klotz Hair Remover and You'll
   Have Legs like a Movie Star

13 I Think of You before I go to Sleep!
   When You Tell Jokes I...Go Crazy!
   If You Ever Left Me I'd...Jump off a
   Cliff!

14 Daredevil Dives 150 Feet into 6 Foot
   Deep Flaming Tank of Water
   Kids Enjoy Bathing in a Shallow
   Rubber Wading Pool
   Boy Rushed to Hospital after
   Swallowing a Small Cast Iron
   Thimble

15 I Love to Sink my Teeth into...a Steak
   You Cooked.
   You Look Just Like...Your Mother.
   I Get Scared when I See...a Movie
   Monster.

16 You're Kind Like Abraham Lincoln
   You're Honest Like George Wash-
   ington
   You're Courageous Like Franklin D.
   Roosevelt

17 Stick Pictures on Your Wall with Ace
   Thumb Tacks
   Fill Holes in Your Driveway with
   Mason's Cement
   Kids Love to Have a Mouthful of
   Burpy Mashed Potatoes

18 You Can Sing Better than...Elvis
   Presley.
   You're Cuter than...Prince Charles.
   You're Cleverer than...Thomas
   Edison.

19 Muriel Eye Wash Works like Magic
   when Applied to Tired Eyes
   Whiz Floor Wax is Great when
   Rubbed on Kitchen Floors
   Limburger Cheese is Delicious on
   Crackers

20 You're as Smart as an Absent Minded
   Professor
   You're as Strong as a Viking
   You're as Beautiful as Cleopatra

21 Give Your Smelly Pet a Bath with
   Fay's Dog Soap
   For Mother's Day Give Dear Old Mom
   A Big Kiss and a Pair of Nylon
   Stockings
   Take Strongheart's Muscle Course and
   You can Beat a Bully by Giving Him
   a Punch in the Nose!

22 Famous Baby Doctor Treats 3 Year
   Old Son of a Local Congressman
   Olympic Star Set to Wrestle a 650
   Pound Ferocious Alligator
   Zoo's Anteater Arrives to Eat Bugs
   in the Counties New Park

23 Why Do You Avoid Me Like...Poison
   Ivy
   You're as Refreshing as...a Clean Shower.
   If Anyone Annoyed You I'd Give
   Him...a Hole in the Head.

24 I Love Your Adorable Teeth!
   You're as Faithful as my Bird Dog!
   I Love Your Hairy...Mustache!

25 You're as Cute as a...Toy Poodle.
   Your Strength Reminds Me of a...
   Wrestler.
   You're Smart Like a...College
   Professor.

26 Brigitte Bardot Isn't Prettier than
 You.
 Whistler's Mother wasn't Sweeter than
 You.
 John L. Sullivan wasn't Stronger than
 You.
27 Talent Contest Winner Gets a Prize of
 a $10,000 Beautiful Mink Coat
 Man Ruled Insane After Giving Wife a
 Bone Crushing Punch in the Nose
 United States President asks Congress
 for Another New $50,000,000
 Atomic Sub
28 You're Fast as a Galloping Horse
 You're Brave Like a Fearless General
 You're Charming as a Lovely Lady
29 An Allen Girdle gives You a Figure
 like a Curvy Movie Star
 The Apex Disposal Unit Grinds Up
 Even a 200 Pound Bag of Garbage
 With a Crane Model Kit You Can Make
 Your Own Navy Blimp
30 Smith's Cream Cheese is Delicious in
 Sandwiches
 Nilson's Iodine is Wonderful when
 Applied to Cuts and Bruises
 Gordon's Flea and Tick Killer Kills on
 Contact
31 You're Popular like Eleanor Roose-
 velt.
 You're Lovely like Mamie Eisen-
 hower.
 You're Glamourous as Jackie
 Kennedy.
 32 You're Strong as a 500 lb. Gorilla
 You're Cute as a Hopping Kangaroo.
 You're Clever as Napoleon
33 You're a Real Old Trickster
 You're Strong as a Bald Bone Crusher
 You're a Lovely Shapely Doll
34 You're Distinguished like Teddy
 Roosevelt
 You're Smart like Benjamin Franklin
 You're a Champ like Babe Ruth
35 You're as Brave as Paul Revere on
 Horseback!
 You're More Daring than Tarzan King
 of the Apes.
 You're Funnier than Charlie Chaplin
 the Tramp!
36 Brush Your Teeth Twice a Day with
 Shiny Tooth Paste
 Patch Up Holes in Your Roof with
 Black Tar
 Shine Your Shoes with Nifty Shoe
 Polish

37 A Tornado Blows Down Our Towns
 Year Old School House
 Mayor to Get Rid of Top of Our
 Towns Local Police Department
 Womens' Group Ask Action Against
 Teenagers Skimpy Bikini Bathing
 Suit
38 You're Wise as an Old Philosopher
 You're Cute as a Drolling Baby
 You're as Attractive a Beauty Queen
39 Kill Off Pesty Rodents with Brown's
 Rat Poison
 Police Need the Best! They Always
 Use a "Quick-Firing" Revolver
 Surprise Guests Who Drop in Un-
 expectedly with Woodbury's Liquor
40 Principal Asks Help with Our Towns
 Juvenile Delinquents
 Man Injured Trying to Kiss Wife Who
 Objects to His Being Drunk
 Zoo Keeper Eaten by Ferocious Man-
 Eating Bengal Tiger
41 You're as Cute as a Cuddly...Baby
 You're Strong as a Slugging...Ball
 Player
 You're as Clever as a Mad...Scientist
42 If We Were Married I'd Take Out...Old
 Dirty Garbage.
 Here's a Great Pair: Your Looks and
 My Brains
 Marry Me and You Will Have Every-
 thing Including a German Shepherd.
43 Millionaire to Live Near the Newly
 Elected Mayor and His Wife
 Astronaut Lands Safely on the Far
 Surface of the Moon
 Garbage to be Unloaded on the City's
 New Downtown Garbage Dump
44 You Make Me Laugh Harder then
 W.C. Fields
 You've Made Me Richer than John D...
 Rockefeller
 You've Made More Followers than
 Sitting...Bull
45 Marry Me and We will Live in...Your
 Folks' House.
 If You Ever Left Me, I'd Throw My-
 self into...the City Sewer.
 Let's Take a Walk and See the Ani-
 mals in...the Monkey House.
46 You're as Fearless as...a Lion
 You're as Strong as...Mr. Universe
 You're a Smart Dresser like...a Male
 Model

47 You look Just Like...a Beautiful
 Movie Star!
 You'll Love Me When I Grow Side-
 burns Like...My Father!
 To See You I'd Fight...A Lion!
48 I'd Love to Take You Driving in a...
 New Automobile.
 When You Go to the Store, Please Let
 Me Push Your...Shopping Cart.
 To prepare for Our Date, I Spent
 Hours Bathing in My Bath Tub.
49 George Washington's Valentine
 Martha Washington
 Buffalo Bill's Sweetheart Calamity
 Jane
 Frankenstein's Heart Throb Mrs.
 Frankenstein
50 Your Pens Write Smoother Filled with
 Waterburys Black Ink
 For a Quick Snack, Try a Sandwich
 Made of Creamy Peanut Butter
 Komfy Beach Chairs are Great when
 You are Sitting in Sand
51 You're as Lovely as...Cleopatra
 You're More Famous than...the Statue
 of Liberty.
 You're Cuter than...Caroline Kennedy
52 You Look So Manly When You Wear
 Your Football Uniform
 I'd Love to See You at the Beach in a
 Bikini Bathing Suit.
 You Look So Refined When You
 Walk Down the Street in Your Mink
 Coat.
53 For Valentine's Day I'd Like to Give
 You...a Rare Tropical Fish.
 You Remind Me of My Grandmother!
 If Someone Wanted to Steal You from
 Me I'd Give Him a Punch in the
 Mouth!
54 You Remind Me Of...My Mother.
 To Win Your Love I'd Fight...a 300
 LB. Wrestler.
 Let's Go to the Zoo, We'll Feed Pea-
 nuts to...a Ring Tail Monkey.
55 When I See You I Think Of...The
 Queen of Sheba.
 You Sing Like...An Opera Star
 You're Funnier Than...A TV Comic

VALENTINE POSTCARDS (33) 3 1/8" X 5 1/4"

The wrapper for this Topps series is black with an orange and blue title and it bears a 1970 production code number. There are 33 cards in the set: all have humorous color-artwork fronts and postcard format backs. Each card is numbered in a heart design located on the back.

ITEM	MINT	EX
Set	150.00	112.50
Card	4.00	3.00
Wrapper	--	15.00
Box	--	75.00

1. I'm Blue Without You! (So Be My Valentine)
2. You're Really Something to Crow About! (So Be My Valentine!)
3. You're Dynamite! (So Be My Valentine!)
4. Love Me a Lot...There's a Lot of Me to Love!
5. I'm Down in the Dumps without You! (So Be My Valentine)
6. You're a Charmer! (So Be My Valentine!)
7. I'm Your Baby! (So Be My Valentine!)
8. You Turn Me On! (So Be My Valentine!)
9. If You Won't Be My Valentine, I'll Croak!
10. I'm One of a Kind (...So Be My Valentine!)
11. I'm a Groovy Chick! (Be My Valentine!)
12. You're Really a Peach! (So Be My Valentine!)
13. Let's Horse Around! (You're My Valentine)
14. You're a Knockout! (So Be My Valentine!)
15. I'm a Dreamboat! (So Be My Valentine!)
16. You Drive Me Nuts! (Please Be My Valentine!)
17. When I See You I Melt! (So Be My Valentine!)
18. You're A Real Doll! (So Be My Valentine!)
19. I'm Stuck on You
20. Is There a Ghost of a Chance...That You Might Be My Valentine?!?
21. I'm Crazy About You! (Be My Valentine)
22. I Can't Bear to Be Without You! (Be My Valentine!)
23. I'm Nothing Without You! (So Be My Valentine!)
24. You've Really Got It! (Be My Valentine!)
25. You're a Turtledove! (Please Be My Valentine!)
26. I'm a Farout Cat! (So Be My Valentine)
27. Hi, Honey... ...Bee Mine!
28. I'd Ask You to Be My Valentine But... ...I'm Chicken
29. You're a Cute Dish (So Be My Valentine!)
30. I'm a Cute Little Devil! (Be My Valentine!)
31. I'm a Prisoner of Your Heart! (Be My Valentine)
32. Let's Neck! (You're My Valentine!)
33. You're Really Something Else! (So Be My Valentine!)

VALENTINE STICKERS (43?)

"Valentine Stickers" are similar in format to the "Frankenstein Stickers" series described earlier in this guide. Each front-peel sticker has color artwork and humorous dialogue within a diecut shape (heart, rectangle, etc.) and is mounted on plain brown paper backing. The designs are not numbered; the checklist below contains 43 captions and may possibly be missing one title for a complete set. The series was produced by Topps.

2 1/2" X 3 1/2"

ITEM	MINT	EX
Sticker	3.00	2.50
Wrapper	--	20.00
Box	--	65.00

Darling, Could I Have a Lock of Your Hair? (I'm Stuffing a Mattress.)
Darling, I Love You for What You Are (Rich!)
Darling, I'm Miserable When You're Away! (Fortunately I Found Someone to Keep Me Company.)
Darling, I Would Give You the Shirt Off My Back! (Please Wash and Iron It!)
Darling, There's Only One Thing Wrong with Your Face (It Sticks Out of Your Collar.)
Darling, You've Got Something (I Hope It Isn't Catching.)
Dearest, All the Kids Call Me Names but You Don't (You Don't Even Talk to Me!)
Dearest Valentine Having a Wonderful Time! (Wish You Were Here!)
Dearest Valentine I'm Crazy About Your Looks I'm Crazy About Your Voice (My Sister's Crazy Too!)
Dearest Valentine You're Mine! (Until Something Better Comes Along.)
Dear, The Next Time You're in the Neighborhood...(Don't Stop!!)
Don't Act Kittenish (You Haven't Got the Puss for It!)
Don't Forget To Write (Just Forget to Mail It.)
I Couldn't Ask for a Sweeter Girl (But I'd Like To!)
I Don't Know What I'd Do Without You! (But I'm Going to Find Out!)
I'd Like to Get Something for You (But Nobody Will Make an Offer.)
I Dreamed I Married You and Was Happy! (When I Woke Up.)
I'll Never Forget You (Who Could?)
I Miss You (Every Chance I Get!)
I Need You (Like an Iron Parachute!)
I Never Thought I'd See Anything Like You (Without Digging!)
I Want to Send You a Valentine Gift! (How Do You Wrap a Time Bomb?)
Sweetheart, You're Just My Type! (A Girl!)
There are 2 Things I Like About You (Your Heads!)
Too Bad You Can't Get A Girl to Love You (The Way You Love Yourself!)
Two Can Live as Cheap as One! (But Not as Long!)
When I Met You It was Love at First Sight! (Then I Took a Second Look.)
Where Have You Been All My Life? (And When Are You Going Back?)

Would You Take a Walk With Me? (I'm Supposed to Exercise with Dumbbells!)

You Deserve a Big Hand (Across Your Mouth!)

You Have a Mind Like a Streak of Lightning (Fast and Crooked.)

You Have Quite a Head on Your Shoulders! (Who Does It Belong To?)

You Look Like a Million (But Nobody Could Be That Old!)

You Made Me The Happiest Boy in the World (When You Said Goodbye!)

You Ought to Be in Pictures (With Numbers Across the Bottom.)

You Remind Me of Lincoln (He's Dead Too!)

Your Golden Hair is Like Dandelions (Black at the Roots!)

Your Health Has Me Worried Dear (It's Always Good!)

You'd Look Perfect in Something Long and Flowing (Like the Hudson River.)

You're a Boy with Horsesense! (And a Face to Go With It!)

You've Got Everything! (I'd Like to Get Some of It Back.)

You've Got a Mind of Your Own (Who Else Would Want It?)

You've Got a Winning Smile (And a Losing Face.)

VALENTINE WOOD PLAKS — SEE "REAL WOOD PLAKS"

VETTE SET (100)

This gorgeous 100-card set of trading cards is a pictorial history of America's foremost sports car, the Corvette. From the earliest models (1953) to the present, all the body types and special production models are presented in beautiful color photographs. The backs of the car cards, which are as impressive as the fronts, are divided into two sections: a facts

2 1/2" X 3 1/2"

and figures list on top and one or two color "detail" pictures beneath. In addition to the cars, there are cards showing various Corvette emblems and a special six-card subset devoted to Mario Andretti. The manufacturer, Collect-A-Card, has arranged for 2500 cards to be personally signed by Andretti and these have been inserted randomly into packs. The series was distributed in ten-card foil packages (no gum) with a red Corvette in the center. The display box is also black, but has a different model car (white) on the lid. Note: autographed Andretti cards are not part of the regular set and prices for them have yet to be established.

ITEM	MINT	EX
Set	20.00	15.00
Card	.20	.15
Wrapper	--	.10
Box	--	2.00

1.	1953 Convertible	18.	1966 Sport Coupe	35.	1972 Convertible	52.	1981 Sport Coupe	68.	1988 Convertible
2.	1954 Convertible	19.	Flag Emblem #2	36.	1973 Sport Coupe	53.	1982 Sport Coupe	69.	1989 Sport Coupe
3.	1955 Convertible	20.	1966 Convertible	37.	Flag Emblem #6	54.	1982 Coll. Coupe	70.	1989 Convertible
4.	1956 Convertible	21.	1967 Sport Coupe	38.	1973 Convertible	55.	Flag Emblem #9	71.	1990 Sport Coupe
5.	1957 Convertible	22.	1967 Convertible	39.	1974 Sport Coupe	56.	Flag Emblem #10	72.	1990 ZR-1 Coupe
6.	1958 Convertible	23.	Flag Emblem #3	40.	1974 Convertible	57.	1984 Sport Coupe	73.	Flag Emblem #13
7.	1959 Convertible	24.	1968 Sport Coupe	41.	1975 Sport Coupe	58.	1985 Sport Coupe	74.	1990 Convertible
8.	1960 Convertible	25.	1968 Convertible	42.	1975 Convertible	59.	1986 Sport Coupe	75.	1991 Sport Coupe
9.	1961 Convertible	26.	1969 Sport Coupe	43.	1976 Sport Coupe	60.	1986 Convertible	76.	1991 ZR-1 Coupe
10.	1962 Convertible	27.	1969 Convertible	44.	1977 Sport Coupe	61.	1986 Pace Car	77.	1991 Convertible
11.	1963 Sport Coupe	28.	Flag Emblem #4	45.	Flag Emblem #7	62.	1987 Sport Coupe	78.	Flag Emblem #14
12.	Flag Emblem #1	29.	1970 Sport Coupe	46.	Flag Emblem #8	63.	1987 Convertible	79.	1991 Callaway Turbo
13.	1963 Convertible	30.	1970 Convertible	47.	1978 Sport Coupe	64.	Flag Emblem #11	80.	Aerovette Showcar
14.	1964 Sport Coupe	31.	1971 Sport Coupe	48.	1978 Anniv. Coupe	65.	1988 Sport Coupe	81.	1990 Corv III
15.	1964 Convertible	32.	1971 Convertible	49.	1978 Pace Car	66.	1988 Anniv. Coupe	82.	Flag Emblem #15
16.	1965 Sport Coupe	33.	1972 Sport Coupe	50.	1979 Sport Coupe	67.	Flag Emblem #12	83.	Stingray Race Car
17.	1965 Convertible	34.	Flag Emblem #5	51.	1980 Sport Coupe				

84.	1967 Le Mans
85.	Mario Andretti #1
86.	Mario Andretti #2
87.	1971 XP-895
88.	1986 ASC Geneve
89.	Flag Emblem #16
90.	Corv. Challenge
91.	Greenwood Custom
92.	**Corvette Jet Boat**
93.	Mako Shark Show
94.	Mario Andretti #3
95.	Mario Andretti #4
96.	Mario Andretti #5
97.	Mario Andretti #6
98.	Callaway Speedster
99.	1953 & 1991 Indy
100.	Checklist Card

VIDEO CITY (26 & 4)

This **1983** Topps set is ideal for the video game enthusiast. In truth, the cards and stickers are nothing more than advertising for promoting four specific games: Donkey Kong Junior, Fogger, Turbo, and Zaxxon. There are 26 front-peel stickers in the set but only 21 different fronts, since five obverses appear with two different backs each. The reverses of the stickers contain puzzle pieces, tips on improving game scores, and advertising for "Electronic Games" magazine. There is also one rub-off-the-dots game card for each of the four video games showcased by the set. Note: game cards with dot coatings removed cannot be graded mint. Uneven distribution of stickers within boxes has resulted in high set values relative to individual sticker and card prices.

ITEM	MINT	EX
Set	10.00	7.00
Sticker	.35	.25
Game	.25	.20
Wrapper	—	.25
Box	—	4.00

VIETNAM FACT CARDS — VOLUME I (66)

SURROUNDING THE FRENCH
LES FRANÇAIS ENCERCLÉS

Vietnam will always be a controversial and unpleasant topic for most Americans. Some might even argue that it is not an appropriate subject for a trading card set. When it was announced in 1988 that Dart Flipcards, a Canadian company, was about to release a 66-card set about Vietnam, there was an initial wave of protest, no doubt magnified by the stereotypical coverage of the electronic and print media. Had any other card manufacturer produced the set, the criticism might have been warranted, but once the set was made public, the derision turned to admiration. This was not a set that glorified war in artwork or in word, nor propaganda on behalf of either side. Instead, Dart created a trading card set based on nothing but the facts, and in so doing, established a benchmark for exellence and a reputation for integrity.

The series consists of 66 titles and all the card fronts have color artwork pictures with red-print captions located inside yellow boxes. The backs have gray-stock text areas layered over green "jungle" backgrounds and the card number is printed on the helicopter hovering in the top left corner. Most of the captions and all of the text descriptions are printed in both English and French since the series was sold in Canada as well as the U.S. Cards could be purchased in 6-count cello packs (no gum) or in complete, boxed sets. The quality built into this set has made it a favorite with collectors and the fact that it was produced on a limited basis (the printing plates AND the film were destroyed) suggests that demand for it will continue to rise on a steady basis. Note: Dart also marketed a green "Vietnam" binder which it originally sold for $8.50.

ITEM	MINT	EX
Set	25.00	17.50
Card	.35	.25
Wrapper	—	.50
Box	—	3.00

Vietnam Fact Cards — Series 1

1 Title Card
2 Vietminh Victory!
3 Ho Chi Minh
4 French Return
5 War Begins!

6 General Giap
7 Dien Bien Phu
8 Preparing for Battle
9 Surrounding the French
10 Parachute Drops
11 No Retreat!
12 French Surrender
13 Vietnam Split!
14 Joining Forces
15 Village Defense
16 Gangsters Attack!
17 Shocking Public Suicides
18 President Kennedy
19 Leaders Assassinated
20 President Johnson
21 Bombs Away!
22 "Maddox" Attacked
23 Taking Action
24 North Vietnam Bombed
25 Surprise Attack!
26 Terrorists Bomb Cafe
27 "Flaming Dart"
28 Operation "Rolling Thunder"
29 Christmas in Vietnam
30 General Westmoreland
31 Search and Destroy
32 Medevac
33 Checklist #1
34 Black Market

35 Tunnel System
36 Tunnel Rats
37 Ho Chi Minh Trail
38 Attacking the Trail!
39 Pointman
40 Agent Orange
41 Perils in the Jungle
42 Captured!
43 Huey
44 Danger!
45 The B-52 Stratofortress
46 The SAM Missile
47 Khe Sanh
48 M-16 vs. AK-47
49 Cities Attacked!
50 Riverboats

51 The Death Card
52 "Hamburger Hill"
53 Brutal Captors
54 Protest at Home
55 Emergency!
56 Ambushed!
57 Transfer of Duties
58 Easter Invasion
59 Hanoi Bombarded
60 Briefing the President
61 Frantic Refugees
62 The Battle of Xuan Loc
63 Make Room!
64 Last Huey
65 Saigon Falls
66 Checklist #2

VIETNAM FACT CARDS — VOLUME II (100) 2 1/2" X 3 1/2"

In late 1991, Dart Flipcards released "Volume II" of its "Vietnam Factcards" series. The new format uses photo-journalism pictures taken directly from UPI and Bettman Archive files. The wide framelines are a sort of clear-coat metallic bronze color and they encompass both the caption and set title which are printed on every card. The layered effect is capped by the outer white borders, giving the card fronts a very crisp look. The text area on back is printed on white stock and the words are easier to read than the descriptions of Series 1, which were printed on gray cardboard. Dart also abandoned the French language translation for this series, resulting in more information on every card. The card number now resides in a helicopter hovering in the upper right corner. Each card carries a 1991 copyright date and a "Printed in Canada" line. There are 100 cards in the series and collectors are advised that some show graphic scenes from battlefield situations. Volume II of "Vietnam Factcards" is being sold in complete, boxed sets and production was limited to 15,000.

ITEM	MINT	EX
Set	18.00	--

1 Introduction
2 President Kennedy
3 M48 Patton Tank
4 Missing In Action
5 155mm Howitzer
6 Recon Patrol
7 South Vietnamese Infantryman
8 Robert McNamara
9 Rules of Conduct
10 Troop Escalation
11 A Soldier's Christmas
12 Da Nang Air base
13 USS Enterprise
14 Night Flights
15 Supply Lines at Sea
16 All Systems Go
17 B-52 Bomber
18 Radio Man
19 1st Cavalry Division
20 VC Stronghold Destroyed
21 Women at War
22 Flares Over Da Nang
23 Deadly Reminder
24 Guarding The Mekong
25 Ambush on Hill 861
26 The M16 Controversy

27 People Sniffer
28 Battlefield Medic
29 The Battle Below
30 Pacification Program
31 M60 Machine Gun
32 Attack on Da Nang
33 Nguyen Cao Ky
34 CH-53 Sea Stallion
35 Tragedy at Sea
36 Vietcong Captured
37 Phantom of the Skies
38 Flaming Arrow
39 Hill of Angels
40 A Nation Divided
41 The Dragon's Jaw
42 Deathtrap at Hill 875
43 Air Support
44 President Johnson
45 Firebase Defenses
46 Montagnards
47 Flame Thrower
48 Armored Personnel Carrier
49 House-to-House Fighting
50 Ancient City Besieged
51 Brutal Battle for Hue
52 City Ablaze

53 Civilians Seek Refuge
54 Battle for the Citadel
55 Target of Terror
56 Smart Bomb
57 Doomed Khe Sanh Flight
58 Whispering Death
59 F-4B MiG Killer
60 Bull's-eye
61 A Shau Valley
62 Secret Bombings
63 199th Light Infantry
64 Postmark: Khe Sanh
65 Saigon's Black Market
66 Siege at Khe Sanh
67 The Paths of War
68 Battlefield Landing
69 Change of Command
70 Cholon Devastated
71 Mobile River Force
72 USS New Jersey
73 A-4 Skyhawk
74 Mortar Attack
75 Battlefield Indochina
76 "Frogmen of the Delta"
77 Ho Chi Minh
78 Cambodian Stronghold

79 Chasing Charlie
80 President Nixon
81 Vietnamization
82 My Lai
83 President Nguyen Van Thieu
84 Tiger Cages
85 Raid on Son Tay POW Camp
86 War Reporters
87 Vulnerable Existence
88 Workhorse of War
89 M41A3 Walker Bulldog
90 The Easter Offensive
91 Ammo Dump Blasted
92 Assault on Quang Tri
93 Christmas Bombings
94 Tragedy of War
95 Medals of Honor
96 Paris Peace Talks
97 The Boat People
98 The Final Chapter
99 The Wall
100 Checklist

VOLTRON ALBUM STICKERS (216)   1 15/16″ X 2 3/4″

The "union of science with the primitive" has given "new life to the story of the eternal conflict between good and evil...." That's how the creators of "Voltron, Defender of the Universe," introduce their robohero in the 32-page album made to house this sticker set. Of the 216 stickers, 200 have color artwork and 16 are foils. Panini U.S.A. began distribution of Voltron in March 1986. Note: set price includes album.

ITEM	MINT	EX
Set	24.00	17.00
Sticker	.10	.07
Wrapper	––	.25
Album	1.25	1.00

VOLTRON TATTOOS (?)   6 7/8″ X 9 5/8″

When Topps released the Voltron Tattoos issue in 1985, it hoped to attract fans of "The most popular Robot Toy Series and T.V. Cartoon Adventure Show of Them all!" The format is identical to other Topps issues already described: "Smurf Tattoos" and "24 Tattoos." The large yellow "Voltron" wrapper is a paper packet, or bag, with crimped edges top and bottom. The pack contained one sheet of 24 tattoos (eight large, 16 small) but no gum. Neither the sheets nor the individual tattoos are numbered. The set was produced in 1985 and the number of different sheets and tattoos is not confirmed.

ITEM	MINT	EX
Tattoo sheet	.35	.25
Wrapper	––	.35

VOTE (33)

2 1/2" X 3 1/2"

Donruss produced this patriotic set in 1972. It is composed of 33 different corner-peel stickers drawn in America's colors: red, white and blue. Each sticker is numbered on the back above the "peel" instructions. The packs came in 24-count boxes and retailed for five cents each.

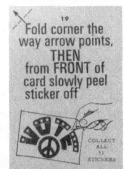

ITEM	MINT	EX
Set	15.00	10.00
Sticker	.50	.35
Wrapper	--	2.00
Box	--	15.00

VOYAGE TO THE BOTTOM OF THE SEA (66)

2 1/2" X 3 1/2"

This 66-card set based on the television series was issued by Donruss in 1964. The cards have black and white photos with white borders. The card number, caption, and text are printed on the back, which is dark blue and white in color. A line on the reverse reads "Watch Voyage to the Bottom of the Sea on Your Local ABC Station." The statement "Series I Numbers 1-66" indicates a second series was contemplated, but it was never issued. Cards with a red "printed in U.S.A." line were issued in Canada.

ITEM	MINT	EX
Set	225.00	190.00
Card	3.00	2.50
Wrapper	--	25.00
Box	--	125.00

1 Admiral Harriman Nelson	23 Bull's Eye	45 Launch Missles
2 Commander Lee Crane	24 Narrow Escape	46 Clear Horizons
3 The Seaway	25 Putting to Sea	47 Well Done
4 Ears of the Seaview	26 Zero Hour	48 On Patrol
5 Eyes of the Seaview	27 Top Secret	49 Working Parties
6 The Main Deck	28 Plotting the Course	50 Fuel Cell Reading
7 Emergency Call	29 Sonar Contact	51 Command Decision
8 Fastest Course	30 Death Sign	52 Orders from Washington
9 Atomic Engine Control Room	31 The Blackwitch	53 Detour to the North Pole
10 'copter on the Way	32 Torpedoes Away!	54 Surface at the North Pole
11 Reporting	33 Blast Damage	55 Hull Damage?
12 War Conference	34 Seaview Strikes Back	56 An Icy Swim
13 Motorcycle Escort	35 Death Shot	57 Arctic Operations
14 A Sniper	36 Scratch One Sub	58 Fuel Cell Away
15 Close Call	37 Clear Sailing Again	59 Setting the Timer
16 Hidden Tape Recorder	38 Torpedo Loading	60 Injured Man
17 Dr. Gamma and Professor X	39 What Happened?	61 Icebound
18 Preparing for the Long Voyage	40 Periscope Depth	62 Leave without Us!
19 Frogmen Away!	41 Condition Red	63 Not a Minute to Spare!
20 Hull Check	42 Up Periscope	64 Going Ashore
21 Attach of the Giant Squid	43 The Enemy Above	65 Debriefing
22 First Shot	44 Enemy Eyes	66 Battle Report

WACKO-SAURS (48)

2 9/16" X 3 3/8"

Diamond Toy's 1987 series entitled "Wacko-Saurs" blends the current public fascination with dinosaurs with the formats of Perlorian Cats and Garbage Pail Kids. The obverses have wavy-edge, front-peel stickers depicting dinosaurs in a variety of improbable situations. Each picture appears in both the 24-card "A" and "B" series with a different name. The cardboard backing is printed with puzzle pieces, "Design-a-Dino" parts, or "Pre-Hysterical Humor." Five stickers came in each gumless packet (25 cents retail). The wrapper is marked "1st Series" but no second series appears to be in the works.

ITEM	MINT	EX
Set	10.00	7.00
Sticker	.20	.15
Wrapper	--	.25
Box	--	4.00

1A	Frizzy Liz	1B	Wailin' Wally
2A	Rick Wrecks	2B	Wreckin' Becky
3A	Fired-Up Fran	3B	Birth Dave
4A	Sandy Claws	4B	Ho Ho Howard
5A	Shoppin' Sean	5B	Maggie Baggy
6A	Hang-Ten Ken	6B	Surf's-Up Suzie
7A	Stone Joan	7B	Monty Rushmore
8A	Mary Mee	8B	Greg Groom
9A	Skate Kate	9B	Scott Board
10A	Astro Nate	10B	Tracey Spacey
11A	Star Spangled Brenda	11B	Yankee Doodle Danny
12A	Jeff Chef	12B	Barbie Q.
13A	Pete Beat	13B	Cybil Cymbals
14A	Tom Bomb	14B	Bombs Away Kay
15A	Harry Housewife	15B	Homemaker Heather
16A	Fine Artie	16B	Moaner Lisa
17A	School Bess	17B	Russ Bus
18A	Wheelin' Willie	18B	Peddlin' Paula
19A	Eileen Eyestrain	19B	Foul-Ball Bill
20A	Ice Cream Joan	20B	Ice Cream Joan
21A	Mummy Mia	21B	Gary Gauze
22A	Live-Bait Bob	22B	Reelin' Celia
23A	Egg Shelly	23B	Cracked-Shell Mel
24A	Alpha Betty	24B	Arthur Teacher

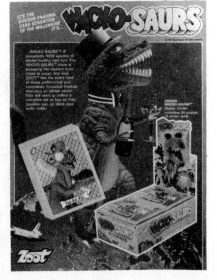

WACKY BASEBALL PLAYERS (9)　　　2 1/2" X 3 1/2"

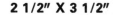

One of the most exciting "grocery store moments" of 1990 came when we discovered that Sunkist was inserting "Wacky Player" baseball cards in their "Fun Fruit" packages. Not only did the cards look interesting, but they were standard size (plenty of food companies give away cards, but the great majority of these do not measure 2-1/2" X 3-1/2"). The fronts have color artwork drawings of different baseball characters and all (except the ump) are dressed in WP (Wacky Player) uniforms. Each character is named below his picture and a "WP" symbol is printed to one side in a star design. The backs carry a statistic grid and a paragraph of "Highlights" for each individual and, naturally these are rendered in facetious terms. The cards are numbered by the last two digits of a production code located at lower right but we think it's easier to list them alphabetically. A complete set of nine cards could be ordered by sending three proofs of purchase in to Sunkist. The prices listed below are based on a simple 50% of retail price of the products required to obtain a complete set.

Brickwall Bob
Dusty Diving Dan
Fireball Phil
Homerun Harold
Lumpy The Ump
Micky Megaphone
Sneaky Pete
Walking Wally

ITEM	MINT	EX
Set	3.50	2.50
Card	.35	.25

WACKY BASKETBALL PLAYERS (9)　　　2 1/2" X 3 1/2"

Although it is listed second in our alphabetical line-up of "Wacky Players" cards, this basketball series is the third and most recent of the Sunkist sets. The card fronts depict one coach and eight players in cartoon art-work style and each picture is surrounded by dark green borders. Each individual is named beneath his likeness and the initials "WP" are printed in a basketball design to one side. The backs contain a statistic grid and a biographical paragraph which are quite amusing. Once again, we have arranged the checklist alphabetically although the cards are numbered at the end of the production code number in the bottom right corner. The cards are dated 1991 and a complete set could be obtained through the mail for three proofs of purchase.

Can-Do Carl
Dribblin' Dave
Lanky Frankie
Nothin' But Net Nick
Slammin' Jammin' Jerome
Small-Fry Bry
Stompin' Rompin' Ralph
The Twin Towers
"The Wall"

ITEM	MINT	EX
Set	3.50	2.50
Card	.35	.25

WACKY FOOTBALL PLAYERS (9)　　　2 1/2" X 3 1/2"

The second Sunkist set to be issued, in chronological terms, "Wacky Football Players" appeared in boxes of "Wacky Players Fun Fruits" in the fall of 1990. You can be sure that this series of nine grotesque gridiron greats will never make it into the standard football card price guides. The cards have orange borders and red frame lines enclosing the artwork characters pictured in the center. The players are wearing "WP" uniforms and their name and position are printed below. The initials "WP" also appear on a football helmet design located in the bottom left corner. The backs have a statistic grid and a paragraph of description and they are a riot to read. Of the three Sunkist sets, this is the best in terms of artwork. The last two digits of the production code in the lower right corner are the card numbers and for this series they run from 10 to 18 (the basketball series issued later started all over again at 01-09). Three proofs of purchase were all that was required to have a complete set mailed from the company.

PARTIAL
CHECKLIST
–Coach
Piled-On Pete
The Crusher

ITEM	MINT	EX
Set	3.50	2.50
Card	.35	.25

Take a good look at the items illustrated in this layout because you will probably never see them outside of this book.

"Wacky Labels" was test-marketed by Topps in 1966 (the wrapper code is 325-001-1-6) and very few specimens have survived. There are two components to the set. The first is the wrapper, which is mostly yellow with the product name in red and the words "Bubble Gum" in black. The second element is the

wacky label itself; it measures 1-1/8" X 2-9/16" and sits on a piece of paper which is 1-11/16" X 2-9/16" in size. The label is actually a small sticker which was designed to be removed from its paper backing and stuck to an appropriate (or inappropriate!) surface. It is not numbered and there is no clue as to how many different ones were produced. The wrapper and label pictured here come from the collection of John Neuner, "The Wrapper King." Since they are essentially "one-of-a-kind" collectibles, the values listed for them will remain high unless more find their way into the hobby.

ITEM	MINT	EX
Wrapper	--	75.00
Label	--	15.00

WACKY PACKAGES
STICKERS AND RELATED SETS

One of the most popular themes ever introduced by Topps, Wacky Packages have been spoofing various food and household products since 1967. Although the original Wacky die-cuts set of 1967 was not a tremendous market success, the company returned to the concept in 1973 and enjoyed sensational sales which resulted in 16 separate series being issued over a two and one-half year period. In 1974, Wacky Packages achieved the remarkable distinction of outselling Topps' baseball series, the only time in company history that a non-sport set proved more popular than the baseball line. Even the fabulously-successful Garbage Pail Kids never accomplished that!

Over the years, Topps has produced more than 30 sets based on the "Wacky Packages" theme, in every medium at its disposal: die-cuts, paper and cloth stickers, posters, patches, tattoos, album stickers, and even cereal box designs. Since we did not cover Wacky Packages in the 1988 Price Guide, we will concentrate on the so-called "mainstream" sets in this volume and cover the lesser-known issues in future editions.

Issuing card sets which satirize established consumer products is not without its pitfalls. Topps has survived several lawsuits challenging specific satires and through actual or threatened litigation has removed, retouched, or replaced certain designs. This accounts for the scarcity and elevated values of a number of stickers and the blank spaces on checklists and uneven set totals for some series. A key element of EVERY Wacky set is the inclusion of a design which satirizes a Topps product. This is a "safety valve" device which seriously diminishes (but does not remove) the chances of proving malice or intentional copying of trademark in a commercial court of law.

As far as our layouts are concerned, we have abandoned our traditional "text plus pictures" format for the "original" Wacky Packages stickers sets in favor of a statistical item list for each series. We feel that a standardized item list for each set makes more sense, especially for newcomers and collectors not familiar with "Wackys." We have also decided not to illustrate most of the wrappers known to us since many are simple repeats of the same design with slight changes in color, minor details, and production codes. Wrappers are probably the most confusing element of the Wacky Packages universe, since some were used for as many as three different series. The confusion which this repetition has engendered is the principal reason that Wacky Packages wrappers are not highly valued.

For their special assistance with the information presented in this section, we wish to thank Roxanne Toser, author of "Wacky Packages ... The Beat Goes On," and Bob Marks and his friends: Phil Carpenter, Robert Hamilton, and Mark Macaluso.

WACKY ADS (36)

3 1/8" X 5 1/4"

This 36-card set, issued by Topps in 1969, is a large card spin-off of the "Wacky Packages" series. There are two different types of cards in the set: 30 cards have a single "Wacky" product spoof, while six others have four different satirized products on each card. Every product design is a diecut piece with pre-scored borders that allow it to be completely removed from the card. The backs are coated with adhesive which is activated by water. Each card is numbered, but the designs themselves are not. Note: Card No. 25 is scarce.

ITEM	MINT	EX
Set	250.00	200.00
Cards		
1-24, 26-36	5.00	4.00
No. 25	30.00	25.00
Wrappers		
5-cent	---	50.00
10-cent	---	20.00
Boxes		
5-cent	---	150.00
10-cent	---	75.00

1 Melty Way (The Candy Bar That's Out of This World)
2 Plastered Peanuts (You'd Have To Be Nuts To Eat Plastered Peanuts!)
3 Minute Mud (You'll Go Hog Wild Over...)
4 Gloom Toothpaste (Gloom Reduces Cavities by Reducing Your Teeth!)
5 Vile Soap (Use Vile Soap for 24 Hour Protection)
6 Ajerx (Gets Rid of Dirt and Grime... and the Competition)
7 Blunder (Build Your Body Eight Crazy Ways with Blunder Bread)
8 Metrekill Diet Drink (I Got Rid of 200 Lbs. of Ugly Fat with Metrekill)
9 Ultra Blight (End Toothaches Once and For All!)
10 Boo-Hoo (Drink One and You'll Cry for More)
11 Hurts Pasty Tomatoes (The Tomato Paste That Really Sticks to Your Ribs!)
12 Guerilla Milk [cartoon]
13 Chicken Fat Laundry Detergent (For a Wash You'll Never Forget...)
14 Garbage Baby Foot (Which of these 3 Babies Ate Garbage Baby Food?)
15 Blecch Shampoo (Beautiful Hair Bleech)
16 Tied Detergeant...Cover Ghoul... Quacker Oats...Band-Ache
17 Duzn't...Horrid...Pure Hex...Canada Wet Fink
18 Schtick Blades (Sal Clodhopper All-Star Shortstop Uses Schtick Blades)
19 Nertz [cartoon]
20 Minute Lice...Dopey Whip...Hostage Cupcakes...Chock Full of Nuts and Bolts
21 Paul Maul...Spray Nit...Mutt's Apple Juice...Lavirus
22 Ditch Masters (Sammy Clod, World Famous Ditchdigger Sez, Don't Get In a Rut! Smoke...)
23 Poopsi-Cola (Come Alive! You're in the Diaper Generation)
24 Cap'n Crud (Have a Pirate for Breakfast)
25 Good and Empty (The Between Meal Treat That's Good for Your Teeth!)
26 Kook (3 Out of 4 Penguins Prefir...)
27 Exceedrin (Exceedrin Will Cure Any Headache)
28 Sludgesickle (Eat the Stick and Throw Away the Sludge!)
29 Weakies...Crust...Gadzooka...Kook-Aid
30 Commie Cleanser (Keep America Clean with Commie Cleanser)
31 Sailem (You Can Take Sailem Out of the Country But—You Can't Take the Country Out of Sailem)
32 Botch Tape (Botch Up the Job with Botch Tape...)
33 Kooloff's All-Brain (You'll Blow Your Brain Eating All-Brain Cereal)
34 Pest Awful Bits (Spell Naughty Words With...)
35 Fish-Bone (Fish-Bone Russian Dressing is Great on Everything)
36 Skimpy...Mrs. Klean...6up...Breadcrust Corned Beaf Hash

WACKY PACKAGES ALBUM STICKERS (120)

2 1/8" X 3"

Of the seven album sticker sets manufactured by Panini for Topps, only "Wacky Packages" was an original Topps design. It was released to the public in July 1982, and consists of 120 diecut stickers and a 24-page album. The inside page of the front cover is interesting because is has a checklist of titles and the following disclaimer: "Hey, the stickers that Topps... created are all in fun. The products we're spoofing—including our own—are all good ones, no kidding." Note: set price includes album.

ITEM	MINT	EX
Set	50.00	35.00
Sticker	.35	.25
Wrapper	—	1.00
Album	4.00	3.00

1 (Puzzle Piece)
2 (Puzzle Piece)
3 (Puzzle Piece)
4 (Puzzle Piece)
5 Crookie Crisp
6 Creature Crackers
7 Cram
8 Chock Full of Nuts and Bolts
9 Oscar Moron
10 Laffelos
11 Brittle
12 Liptorn
13 Shot Tissue
14 Belchs
15 Kook
16 Muleburro
17 Sell'em
18 Camals
19 Windstun
20 Bandage
21 Dampers
22 Scratchy Blades
23 Screech
24 Cult 45
25 Jerky Fruits
26 Clunky
27 Gadzooka
28 Mr. Goodbye
29 Lifeservers
30 Easy Cuss-Words
31 Unpopular Mechanics
32 Mod
33 Shorts Illustrated
34 Seventon

35 Playbug
36 My Sink
37 Soft-Head Bulbs
38 Pollydent
39 Fearstone
40 Mashbox
41 Squabble
42 Beastball
43 Playskull
44 Killy Putty
45 Koduck
46 Chimpanzee
47 Neveready
48 Bloodweiser
49 Bit-O-Money
50 Pounds (candy)
51 Foolball
52 Milk Muds
53 Yicks
54 Cracked
55 Peter Pain
56 Hurtz
57 Pupsi Cola
58 Dinky Gonuts
59 Wormy Packages
60 Armor
61 Plaster Chips
62 Whale O's
63 Alpoo
64 Feetena
65 Windaxe
66 Petley
67 Scary Lee
68 Slaytex
69 Mutt's

70 Heavy
71 Blunder
72 Fright Cocktail
73 Hardly Wrap
74 Ivery Snow
75 Choke King
76 Hopeless
77 Pepto-Dismal
78 Paid
79 L'oggs
80 Ditch Masters
81 Contrac
82 Fright Guard
83 Medi-Quak
84 No Tips
85 Schnozmopolitan
86 Snort
87 Nooseweek
88 Crocked
89 Family Circuit
90 TV Garbage
91 Greaseline
92 Bear
93 Blisterine
94 Hex-Lax
95 Lavirus
96 Stinkertoy
97 Brandy Land
98 Shot Wheels
99 Crakola
100 Fishey-Prize Toys
101 Gloom
102 Rabid Shave
103 Vile
104 Head & Boulders

105 Kleenaxe
106 Arise
107 Ain't
108 Flare
109 Hostage
110 Creep
111 Cheap Stick
112 Pounds (cream)
113 Fearasil
114 Irish Ring
115 Schtick
116 Ram-a-liar
117 Tied
118 Hawaiian Punks
119 Dr. Popper
120 Mr. Mean

Another "Wacky Packages" spinoff, these large paper posters came folded into much smaller packs in 1973 and '74. Each poster has one large artwork design and the poster number is located in the lower right corner. The yellow wrapper is marked with a 1973 production code and the blue wrapper is coded 1974. Note: no mint prices listed since posters were prefolded to fit smaller packaging.

ITEM	MINT	EX
Set	--	140.00
Poster	--	5.00
Wrappers (2)		
each	--	8.00
Box	--	20.00

1 Log Cave In Syrup
2 Koduck
3 Blast Brew Ribbon Beer
4 Neveready Assaulted Battery
5 Kook
6 Hiptorn Tea Bags
7 Camals
8 Gadzooka
9 Crakola Crayons
10 Milk Foam
11 Ivery Snow
12 Plop Sikle
13 Wacky Garbage
14 Burpsi-Cola
15 Mex-Pax
16 Hurtz
17 Jail-O
18 STD
19 Hawaiian Punks
20 Slopicana Orangutan Juice
21 Ditch Boy Paint
22 Fang
23 Lipoff Cup-a-Slop
24 Glutton

WACKY PACKAGE DIE-CUTS

Year 1967
Set total . . . . 44 (numbered)
Wrapper color/code . . yellow/0-414-90-01-7
Box color/code orange-red/1-414-37-01-8
Box size/price . . . . 24 packs/5¢
Anomalies: As many as three different titles can be found for some numbers (see checklist).

DIE-CUT SERIES VALUES (excellent grade)
Set price . . . . $200 (does not include Cracked Animals or Ratz Crackers)
Single die-cut . . . . $4 each
Exceptions:
   Cracked Animals . . $25
   Ratz Crackers $25
   Boredom's Instant Coffee $8
Wrapper $20
Box Price $100

1	Boredom's Instant Coffee
2a	Fearstone
2b	Duzn't Do Nuthin
3a	Vicejoy
3b	Jolly Mean Giant
4	Camals
5a	Campy
5b	Chock Full of Nuts and Bolts
6a	Slum-Maid Raisins
6b	Grave Train
7	Spray Nit
8	Lavirus
9	Paul Maul
10	Dopey Whip
11	Cracked Jerk
12	Crust
13	Kook-Aid
14	Alcohol Seltzer
15a	De-mented Rotten Tomatoes
15a	Skimpy
16	Pure Hex
17	Weakies
18a	Schmutz
18b	Quacker Oats
19	Minute Lice
20	Gadzooka*
21a	Moron Salt
21b	Jolly Mean Giant
21c	Maddie Boy
22	Liptorn
23a	Muller
23b	6 Up
24	Band-Ache
25	Chock Full of Nuts and Bolts
26	Tied
27	Mrs. Klean
28	Breadcrust Corned Beef Hash
29	Cover Ghoul
30	Horrid
31	Jail-O
32a	Ratz
32b	Weakies
32c	Chock Full of Nuts and Bolts
33	Grave Train
34a	Duzn't Do Nuthin
34b	Paul Maul
35	Fink
36	Maddie Boy
37a	Coronation Milk
37b	Breadcrust Corned Beef Hash
38	Cracked Jerk
39	Hostage Cupcakes
40	Mutt's
41a	6 Up
41b	Spray Nit
42	Skimpy
43a	Jolly Mean Giant
43b	Maddie Boy
43c	Breadcrust Corned Beef Hash
44	Quacker Oats

WACKY PACKAGES STICKERS — 1st Series

Year 1973
Set total . . . . 30 stickers
Wrapper color/code . . red/0-422-21-01-03
Box color/code . . . . . . dark purple/1-422-40-01-3
Box size/price . . . . 48 packs/5¢
Checklist color . . . . . . orange
Puzzle . . . . Gadzooka Gum
Anomalies: Each sticker can be found in three back varieties — white, tan, & "Ludlow."

1ST SERIES VALUES (excellent grade)
Sets:
   white back $90
   tan back $180
   "Ludlow" $260
Stickers:
   white back . . . . . . $2 each
   tan back . . . . $4 each
   "Ludlow" . . . . $6 each
Checklists . . . . 50¢ each
Checklist set (9) $5
Wrapper $10
Box $75
Premium value stickers:

Duzn't Detergent . .	W = $4	T = $8	L = $10
Lavirus	W = $6	T = $12	L = $14
Paul Maul	W = $8	T = $16	L = $18
Mutt's Juice	W = $8	T = $16	L = $18
Band-Ache Strips . .	W = $12	T = $24	L = $26

Band-Ache Strips	Lavirus
Bread Crust Hash	Liptorn Soup
Camals	Maddie Boy
Chock Full O'Bolts	Minute Lice
Cover Ghoul (tan bottle)	Mrs. Klean
Crust Toothpaste	Mutt's Juice
Dopey Cream	Paul Maul
Duzn't Detergent	Pure Hex
Fink Beverage	Quacker Oats
Gadzooka Gum (no date)*	6-Up Beverage
Grave Train	Skimpy
Hostage Cupcakes	Spray Nit
Horrid Deodorant	Tied Detergent
Jail-O Dessert	Vicejoy Cigarettes
Kook-Aid	Weakies Cereal

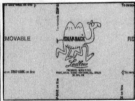

LUDLOW BACK

WACKY PACKAGES STICKERS — 2nd Series

Year 1973
Set total . . . . .33 stickers*
Wrapper color/code . .red/0-422-85-01-3
Box color/code purple/1-422-40-01-3
Box label code 5-438-46-01-1
Box size/price . . . . . .48 packs/5¢
Checklist color . . . . . . .orange
Puzzle . . . . .Sugarmess Bubble Gum
*Anomalies: Each sticker can be found in three
    back varieties: white, tan, & "Ludlow."

2ND SERIES VALUES (excellent grade)
Sets:
    white back $80
    tan back $80
    "Ludlow" $170
Stickers:
    white back . . . .$2 each
    tan back . . . .$2 each
    "Ludlow" . . . .$6 each
Checklists . . . . .50¢ each
Checklist set (9) $5
Wrapper $10
Box $75
Premium value stickers:
    Dull Pineapple . . . .W&T = $6 L = $15
    Gurgle Baby Food .W&T = $4 L = $12
    Run Tony Shells . .W&T = $8 L = $20

Ajerx
All-Brain Cereal
Awful Bits
Bleech Shampoo
Blunder Bread
Boo-Hoo Drink
Botch Tape
Brittle Soap Pads
Cap'n Crud
Chicken Fat
Commie Cleanser
Ditch Masters
Dull Pineapple
8-Lives Tuna Bones
Exceedrin
Fish Bone Dressing

Gloom
Gurgle Baby Food
Gyppy Pop Corn
Hurts Tomatoes
Kook Cigarettes
Log Cave-In Syrup
Minute Mud
Nertz
Plastered Peanuts
Poopsie
Putrid Cat Chow
Run Tony Shells
Sailem
Schtick Blades
Sugarless Bubble Gum*
Ultra Bright
Vile Soap

WACKY PACKAGES STICKERS — 3rd Series

Year 1973
Set total . . . . .30 stickers*
Wrapper color/code . .red/0-422-21-01-3
Box colors/codes . . . .(1) purple/1-422-40-01-3
                 (2) blue/1-436-40-01-3
Box labels codes . . . . .(1)
                 (2) no label
Box sizes/prices . . . . .(1) 48 packs/5¢
                 (2) 48 packs/5¢
Checklist color . . . . . . .orange
Puzzle . . . . .Beanball Bubblegum
*Anomalies: each sticker can be found with
    either a white or a tan back. Spic & Spill
    found with & without "Spic & Span" on lid.

3RD SERIES VALUES (excellent grade)
Sets:
    tan back $80
    white back $150
Stickers:
    tan back . . . .$2 each
    white back . . . . . .$4 each
Checklists . . . . .50¢ each
Checklist set (9) $5
Wrapper $4
Boxes: (1) purple . .$35
       (2) blue $35
Premium value stickers:
    Dr. Ono $3
    Harm & Hammer . .$4
    Rice-A-Phony $3
    Spic & Spill
    (both versions) . .$5 each
    Sweat-Hard $3

Argh
Beanball Bubble Gum*
Busted-Finger Candy
Choke King
Crakola Crayons
Dr. Ono
Drowny Softener
Foolball Bubble Gum*
Fright Guard
Harm & Hammer
Hawaiian Punks Juice
Hired Root Beer
Hungry Jerk
Hurtz Bird-Seed
1-A Sauce

Koduck Photos
Lova Soap
Lucky Stride Cigarettes
Moonshine Crackers
Motorzola
Neveready Battery
No Tips
Rabid Shave
Raw Leaves Cigarettes
Rice-A-Phony
Sledge
Snatch-A-Pack
Spit & Spill Cleanser
Sweat-Hard Soap
Windchester

WACKY PACKAGES STICKERS — 4th Series

Year 1973
Set total ....32 stickers (tan backs)*
Wrapper colors/codes (1) yellow/0-436-85-01-3
   (2) yellow/0-436-21-01-3
Box colors/codes ....(1) blue/1-436-40-01-3
   (2) yellow/1-436-40-01-3
Box labels/codes ....label on both reads
   5-433-46-01-2
Box sizes/prices .....both: 48 packs/5¢
Checklist color ......orange
Puzzle ....Wormy Packages
*Anomalies: Two different checklists exist. One
  has Mess Clairoil and Windhex; the other
  has Choke Wagon and Bum Chex. The latter pair of stickers are more difficult to find
  and including them raises the set total to
  34 and the set price by $10.

4TH SERIES VALUES (excellent grade)
Sets:
  w/Mess Clairoil &
    Windhex $80
  w/Choke Wagon
    & Bum Chex $90
Stickers ....$2 each
Checklists ....50¢ each
Checklist sets (9 each) $5 each
Wrapper $4
Box $25
Premium value stickers:
  Milk Foam $3
  Mess Clairoil $8
  Windhex $8
  Choke Wagon.....$10
  Bum Chex........$10

Armor Hot Dogs	Heave Cigarettes
Bald Detergent	Hipton Tea Bags
Bent Cigarettes	Hyde's Rox Cookies
Blue Beanie Margarine	Land O Quakes Butter
Brute 88	Liquid Bomber
Bum Chex	Mess Clairoil
Cheapios Cereal	Milk Foam
Chef Girl-ar-dee	Mustard Charge
Choke Wagon	Nestree
Dampers	Nutlee's Quit
Escuire Foot Polish	Quake n' Ache
Fang	Raw Goo Sauce
Freetoes	Rinkled Wrap
Gatoraid	Taster's Choke
Grass Wax	Windhex
Grazin' Bran	Wormy Packages*

WACKY PACKAGES STICKERS — 5th Series

Year 1974
Set total ....32 stickers (tan backs)
Wrapper colors/codes (1) blue/0-462-85-01-3
   (2) blue/0-462-85-02-3
Box colors/codes ....(1) blue/1-436-40-01-3
   (2) yellow/1-462-40-01-3
Box labels/codes ....(1) 5th/5-434-46-01-2
   (2) 5th/5-434-46-01-2
Box sizes/prices .....(1) 48 packs/5¢
   (2) 48 packs/5¢
Checklist color ......orange
Puzzle ....Big Baddy
Anomalies: A space between Cram and Pounds
  Candy on the checklist indicates that a
  sticker was pulled from the set.

5TH SERIES VALUES (excellent grade)
Set $55
Sticker $1.50
Checklist...........50¢ each
Checklist set (9) $5
Wrapper $3
Boxes:
  (1) blue $25
  (2) yellow $25
Premium value stickers:
  Betty Crooked
    Sludge $3

Achoo	Moobeline
Betty Crooked Sludge	Muleburro Cigarette
Big Baddy*	Old Spit Cologne
Chumps Candy	Plopsikle
Clank Bar	Pounds Candy
Cover Ghoul (green bottle)	Secrets
Cram	Shots Candy
Fatina Cereal	Shot Wheels
Glutton Mustard	Sicken of the Sea
Graft Cheese	Slaytex Gloves
Ha Ha Crackers	Smith Sisters
Head and Boulders	Stiffords Glue
Hungry Jerk	Swiss Mess Cocoa
Knuckles Candy	Tijuana Smells
Krazy Crackers	Triks Cereal
Light and Dizzy Yoga	White Fowl Cigars

WACKY PACKAGES STICKERS — 6th Series

Year 1974
Set total . . . . .33 stickers (tan backs)
Wrapper colors/codes (1) blue/0-462-85-02-3
                     (2) blue/0-462-21-02-3
Box colors/codes . . . .(1) blue/1-462-40-01-3
                     (2) yellow/1-462-40-01-3
Box labels/codes . . . .(1) 6th/5-435-46-01-2
                     (2) 6th/5-435-46-01-2
Box sizes/prices . . . . .(1) 48 packs/5¢
                     (2) 48 packs/5¢
Checklist color . . . . . . .blue*
Puzzle . . . . .Mold Rush Gum
*Anomalies: One checklist variety reads Goon-
   man's Looney Noodles and Spills Bros;
   these stickers exist. A second checklist
   variety has *Goodman's* and *Spills Bad*, but
   these stickers apparently were never
   printed.

6TH SERIES VALUES (excellent grade)
Set $55
Sticker $1.50
Checklists:
   (1) Goonman's/Spills Bros . . . 50¢ each
   (2) Goodman's/Spills Bad . . . $1 each
Checklist sets (9 each):
   (1) Goonman's/Spills Bros . . . $5
   (2) Goodman's/Spills Bad . . . $10
Wrappers (2) . . . .$3 each
Boxes:
   (1) blue $25
   (2) yellow $25
Premium value stickers:
   Mold Rush $3
   Fruit of the Tomb . .$3
   Truant $3

Airraid Deodorant
Baby Runt
Bar-Kist
Bit-O-Money
Blisterine
Broomo Seltzer
Bum Bums Candy
Clammy Soap
Cut-Rong Hacked Paper
Ditch Boy Paint
Eviltime
Footsie Roll
Fruit of the Tomb
Goonman's Looney Noodles (1)
Jerken's Soap
Mold Rush Gum*
Monotony
My Sink Perfume
Peter Pain Peanut Butter
Piwi Blecch
Play Dumb Clay
Run-A-Way Vitamins
Scare-Deal Notebook
Snarlamint Cigarettes
Sneer
Soft-Head Bulbs
Spills Bros. (1)
Sugar Cigar Crisp
Sugar Daffy
Truant Cigarettes
Valveater Cheese
Virginia Slums
What Man's Simple Candy

WACKY PACKAGES STICKERS — 7th Series

Year 1974
Set total . . . . .33 stickers (tan backs)*
Wrapper colors/codes (1) blue/0-462-85-01-3
                     (2) blue/0-462-21-01-3
Box colors/codes . . . .(1) yellow/1-455-40-01-4*
                     (2) yellow/1-462-40-01-3
                     (3) yellow/1-462-40-01-4
Box labels/codes . . . .(1) no label
                     (2) 7th/5-463-46-01-3
                     (3) 7th/5-463-46-01-3
Box sizes/prices . . . . .(1) 24 packs/5¢
                     (2) 48 packs/5¢
                     (3) 48 packs/5¢
Checklist color . . . . . . .green
Puzzle . . . . .Boozo Gum
*Anomalies: The 24-count yellow box was
   issued with gumless packs as an experi-
   ment. "Grime" sticker comes in two ver-
   sions: "Dusty-Greasy Chunks" (easy) and
   "Heavy Chunks" (difficult).

7TH SERIES VALUES (excellent grade)
Set $55
Sticker $1.50
Checklist . . . . .50¢ each
Checklist set (9) $5
Wrappers (2) . . . .$3 each
Boxes:
   (1) 24 ct/no gum . .$100
   (2) yellow/-3 . . . . .$50
   (3) yellow/-4 . . . . . .$35
Premium value stickers:
   Big Muc $3
   Baked Bears $3
   Grime
   ("Heavy Chunks") . .$10

Alpoo Dog Food
Big Banana Pen
Big Muc Hamburger
Blank Crows
Blast Blew Ribbon Beer
Boozo Gum*
Caged Dog Food
Contrac
Creature Crackers
Dimwit Sugar Dots
Dums (For The Dummy)
El Polluto Cigars
Emptimo Cigars
Feetena Cereal
Fibby's Juice
Grime Dog Food
Gurgle Cereal
Hag & Hag Tobacco
Hurtz Baked Bears
Hurtz Tomato Ketchup
Leek Oil Dripper
L'Oggs Panty Hose
Marshmallow Flopp
Medi-Quak
Mex-Pax Coffee
Mr. Goodbye Candy
Murial Bland Cigars
My-T-Fink Desert
Oh Hairy Candy Bar
Slopicana Juice
Soggy Babies Candy
Sorry Wrap
Top Slob Cleanser

WACKY PACKAGES STICKERS — 8th Series

Year 1974
Set total . . . . 30 stickers (tan backs)
Wrapper colors/codes (1) orange/0-465-85-02-4
                                (2) orange/0-465-21-02-4
Box color/code green/1-465-40-01-4
Box label/code 8th/
Box size/price . . . . 48 packs/5¢
Checklist color . . . . dark red
Puzzle . . . . Kong Fu Bubble Gum
Anomalies: none reported

8TH SERIES VALUES (excellent grade)
Set $55
Sticker $1.50
Checklist . . . . 50¢ each
Checklist set (9) $5
Wrappers (2) . . . . $3 each
Box $30
Premium value stickers:
    Burpsi Cola $3
    Daffy Baking
      Powder $3
    Knots Gelatine $3
    Kentucky Fried
      Fingers $3
    Paid Killers $3

Bam
Biva Towels
Bone Ami
Burpsi-Cola
Canadian Clod
Cheep Detergent
Choke-Up Toothpaste
Daffy Baking Powder
Dr. Popper
Hardly Wrap
Hex-Lax
Hopeless Snow Balls
Hostile Thinkies
Ivery Snow
Kentucky Fried Fingers
Kleenaxe Tissues
Knots Gelatine
Kong Fu Bubble Gum*
Lipoff Cup-A-Slop
Mop & Glop Cleaner
Paid Killers
Rolaches
Scary Lee
Scorch Mouthwash
Shot Tissue
Smoocher's Jam
STD Oil Shortage
Suffertone
Yicks Cough Drops
Yubum Coffee

WACKY PACKAGES STICKERS — 9th Series

Year 1974
Set total . . . . 29 stickers (tan backs)*
Wrapper colors/codes (1) green/0-407-85-01-4
                                  (2) yellow/0-478-85-01-4
Box color/code orange/1-407-40-01-4
Box label/code 9th/5-473-46-01-4
Box size/price . . . . 48 packs/5¢
Checklist color . . . . yellow
Puzzle . . . . Hookey Bubble Gum
*Anomalies: The checklists have a blank space
  at the end of the 3rd column where a
  sticker was apparently deleted from the
  set.

9TH SERIES VALUES (excellent grade)
Set $80
Sticker $2
Checklist . . . . 50¢ each
Checklist set (9) $5
Wrappers (2) . . . . $3 each
Box $25
Premium value stickers:
    Bear Aspirin $4
    Easy Cough Cleaner . . . $4
    Foolite $4
    Killy Putty $4
    Moscow Syrup $4
    6-Urp $4

Bear Aspirin
Belch's Grape Jelly
Cents
Czechlets
Delinquent Spinich
Ducko Cement
Easy Cough Cleaner
Foolite
GI Toe
Goon's Farm Wine
Heartburn Cereal
Hookey Bubble Gum*
Ivy Soap
Jerky Fruits
Kick A Man Sauce
Killy Putty
Messy Marker
Moscow Syrup
Mrs. Small's Fish
Paper Wate Pen
Pig Pen Oil
Raggedy Ant Doll
Shake and Skip Ink
6-Urp
Squabble Word Game
Stickers
Taxim
3 Mosquitoes
Windstun Cigarettes

WACKY PACKAGES STICKERS — 10th Series

Year 1974
Set total . . . . .30 stickers (tan backs)*
Wrapper colors/codes (1) blue/0-477-85-01-4
(2) blue/0-477-21-01-4
Box color/code blue/1-477-40-01-4
Box label/code 10th/5-477-46-01-4
Box size/price . . . . . .48 packs/5¢
Checklist color . . . . . . .orange
Puzzle . . . . .Batzooka Gum
*Anomalies: Pupsi Cola does not appear on
some checklists; it is considered scarce and
most 10th series sets are sold without it.

10TH SERIES VALUES (excellent grade)
Sets:
with Pupsi Cola . . . $90
w/o Pupsi Cola . . . $70
Sticker $2
Checklists:
with Pupsi Cola . . . $1
w/o Pupsi Cola . . . 50¢ each
Checklist sets (9 each)
with Pupsi Cola . . . $10
w/o Pupsi Cola . . . $5
Wrappers (2) . . . . $3 each
Box $25
Premium value stickers:
Mountain Goo $4
Pupsi Cola $20

Batzooka Gum*	Mold Power
Bigtumi Spaghetti Sauce	Mountain Goo
Bum Baked Beans	Nutt's Apple Sauce
Casket Soap	Oscar Moron Bacon
Caraid Bandages	Painters Peanuts
Clunky Candy	Pepto Dismal
Coffin-Mate	Pooped Ridge Farms
Diet Frite Cola	Pupsi Cola**
Fishey-Prize Toys	Ruden's Cough Drops
Greaseline	Scary Jane Candy
Hairy Lee Cake	Stove Glop
Heavy Trash Bags	Sunsweat Prune Juice
Life Servers Candy	Tic-Toc Candy
Lox Soap	Underworld Ham
Milk of Amnesia	Uncle Bum's Rice

WACKY PACKAGES STICKERS — 11th Series

Year 1974
Set total . . . . .30 stickers (tan backs)
Wrapper color/code . .green/0-407-21-01-4
Box color/code black/1-478-40-01-4
Box label/code 11th/5-478-46-01-4
Box size/price . . . . . . .48 packs/5¢
Checklist colors . . . . . .light or dark orange
Puzzle . . . . .Planet of the Grapes
Anomalies: None reported.

11TH SERIES VALUES (excellent grade)
Set $70
Sticker $2
Checklist . . . . 50¢ each
Checklist set $5
Wrapper $3
Box $30
Premium value stickers:
Alpain Cereal $4
Easy-Cuss Words . . $4
Saturday Evening
Ghost $4

Alpain Cereal	Easy Cuss-words
Bash Detergent	Family Circuit
Bird Brain Burned Leftovers	Fib Falsehood Detergent
Chaffed and Sunburn Coffee	Gulp Oil
Chimpanzee Spark Plug	King O'Scare Sardines
Comit Cleanser	Moron Chicken Dinner
Cult 45 Witches Brew	Mr. Bog Wet Bread
Decay Toothpaste	Mud
Dizzie Cups	Muler's Dregg Noodles
	National Geografink
	Planet of the Grapes
	Progreaso Raw Clammy Sauce
	Saparin Coffee
	Seventon
	61 Magazine
	Sleepy
	Stinkertoy
	Swiss Fright Cheese
	The Saturday Evening Ghost
	TV Garbage
	Unpopular Mechanics

WACKY PACKAGES STICKERS — 12th Series

Year 1975
Set total . . . . 27 stickers (tan backs)
Wrapper color/code . . green/0-407-85-1-4
Box color/code white/1-476-40-01-4
Box label/code 12th/5-476-46-01-4
Box size/price . . . . . . 48 packs/5¢
Checklist colors . . . . . . red or white
Puzzle . . . . Sootball Bubble Gum
Anomalies: None reported.

12TH SERIES VALUES (excellent condition)
Set $70
Sticker $2
Checklist . . . . 50¢ each
Checklist set (9) $5
Wrapper $3
Box $30
Premium value stickers:
    Battle Caps $4
    Creep Toothpaste . . $4
    Toad Bubble Bath . $4
    Wash 'n Fly $4

Aquax Cleaner
Battle Caps
Barman Barroom Tissue
Brandy Land Game
Buz Detergent
Creep Toothpaste
Duck and Hide

Dud Laundry Soap
Dud's Boot Beer
Flare Pen
Hav-A-Temper Cigars
Killette Hair Spray
Martian Hats
Milk Muds Candy
Mr. Mean
Paydough Candy
Pieces Candy
Pollydent
Robot Burns Cigars
Shock Dispenser
Siesta Crackers
Sootball Bubble Gum*
Stingline Staple Gun
Toad Bubble Bath
Wash 'n Fly
Weak Germ
Wrecko Candy

WACKY PACKAGES STICKERS — 13th Series

Year 1975
Set total . . . . 30 stickers (tan backs)
Wrapper colors/codes (1) orange/0-483-85-01-5
               (2) orange/0-483-21-01-5
Box color/code orange/1-407-40-01-4
Box label/code 13th/5-483-46-01-4
Box size/price . . . . . . 48 packs/5¢
Checklist color . . . . green
Puzzle . . . . Beastball Bubble Gum

13TH SERIES VALUES (excellent grade)
Set $80
Sticker $2
Checklist . . . . $1 each
Checklist set (9) $10
Wrappers (2) . . . . $3 each
Box $25
Premium value stickers:
    Battle Ball $4
    Doomed Matches . $4
    Sore Deodorant . . . $4

Ale Detergent
Ape Green Beans
Bathless Ribbons
Battle Ball
Beastball Bubble Gum*
Brain Power
Bug Wally
Bum's Life Magazine
Crocked Magazine

Doomed Matches
Don't-Touch-Mee Tea
Doesn't Delight
Drainola Cereal
Dumb and Crazy Salt
Hazel Mishap Lipstuck
Icicle Playing Cards
Jerk in Jail Magazine
Le Rage's
National Spittoon Magazine
Nooseweek
Playskull
Rowdy Gelatine
Scream Sicle
Screech Tape
Shorts Illustrated
Shrunken Donuts
Sneezer Dressing
Sore Deodorant
Umbrella Magazine
Windaxe

WACKY PACKAGES STICKERS — 14th Series

Year 1975
Set total . . . . 30 stickers
  (white & tan backs)*
Wrapper colors/codes (1) tan backs:
  yellow/0-489-21-01-5
  (2) white backs:
  yellow/0-489-85-01-5
Box color/code blue/1-477-40-01-4
Box label/code 14th/5-489-46-01-5
Box size/price . . . . . . 48 packs/5¢
Checklist color . . . . . . yellow
Puzzle . . . . Rotsa Root Candy
*Anomalies: Gadzooka Bubble Gum also
  appeared in 2nd Series Wacky Packages
  Stickers. The 2nd Series sticker is *not*
  dated; the 14th Series sticker is.

14TH SERIES VALUES (excellent grade)
Sets:
white backs $80
  tan backs $105
Stickers:
  white back $2
  tan back $3
Checklist . . . . $1 each
Checklist set (9) $10
Wrappers (2) . . . . $3 each
Box $25
Premium value stickers:
  Balding Football $4
  Gadzooka Bubble Gum . . . $4
  Rebell Jet $4

Ain't Toothpaste
Balding Football
Battletime Beer
Canquit Chicken Pie
Duxie Cups
Fanatical Sickly Fiction
Fearasil
Flunk Mushmallow
Gadzooka Bubble Gum*
Hippy Trash Bags
Irish Ring Soap
IOU Magazine
Messquire Magazine
Moldy Bride Magazine
Mrs. Poles Sticks
Nose-X Tissue
Oscar Mayor Baloney
Playbug Magazine
Polarbearoid Film
Promesso Sauce
Rebell Jet
Rotsa Root Candy
Satan Wrap
Sealva Thins
Sell 'Em Cigarettes
Slayer Aspirin
Snort Magazine
Taffy Cat Food
Totarillo Cigars
Weakinson Blades

WACKY PACKAGES STICKERS — 15th Series

Year 1975
Set total . . . . 30 stickers
  (white & tan backs)
Wrapper colors/codes (1) blue/0-490-85-01-5
  (2) blue/0-490-21-01-5
Box color/code black/1-478-40-01-4
Box label/code 15th/5-490-46-01-5
Box size/price . . . . . . 48/5¢
Checklist color . . . . . . blue
Puzzle . . . . Iron Ons
Anomalies: None reported.

15TH SERIES VALUES (excellent grade)
Sets:
  white backs $90
  tan backs $180
Stickers:
  white backs $2.50
  tan backs $5
Checklist . . . . $1 each
Checklist set (9) $10
Wrappers (2) . . . . $3 each
Box $50
Premium value stickers:
  Hacks Cough
    Drops $4

Bandage Cigarettes
Bawl Park Franks
Bloodweiser
Blurine
Bum and Mabel
Catgobite Detergent
Cheap Stick
Dynamites
Earth Barn Shampoo
Electric Slave
Famous Mobster's
Fang Edward
Gums
Hacks Cough Drops
Hamel Cigarettes
Iron-Ons*
Jean Nutty Bubbles
Jerkitol
Mare Cigarettes
Mashbox Toys
Moron Beef Pot Pie
Petley Flea Bags
Pound's Cream
Shingle's Plaster Chips
Slam Jim Snacks
Slayskool
Smell Motor Oil
Sore Mel Chili
Ultrasheep Shampoo
View Monster

WACKY PACKAGES STICKERS — 16th Series

Year 1977
Set total . . . . 30 stickers (white backs)
Wrapper color/code . . red/0-495-21-01-7
Box colors/codes . . . . (1) red/1-495-70-01-7*
. . . . (2) red/1-495-70-01-7
Box labels/codes . . . . (1) white/no code #
. . . . (2) no label
Box sizes/prices . . . . . (1) 36 packs/5¢
. . . . (2) 36 packs/10¢
Checklist color . . . . wine
Puzzle . . . . Real Garbage Candy
*Anomalies: Both boxes have the same box
code, but the 5¢ variety with the white
label is considered a "test" issue. The box
with no label contained 10¢ packs, the first
time an original series (1973-1977) gum
pack cost more than 5¢.

16TH SERIES VALUES (excellent grade)
Set $90
Sticker $2.50
Checklist . . . . $1 each
Checklist set (9) $10
Wrapper $4
Boxes:
. . (1) white label/5¢ . $100
. . (2) no label/10¢ . . $50
Premium value stickers:
. . Bleed's Candy $4
. . Fool Guard $4
. . Regal Clown $4
. . Similecch Squid . . . $4
. . Smartz Collar $4

Arise Cream	Fool Guard	Regal Clown
Bleed's Candy	Ghoul Humor	Scoot Mouthwash
Clubbed Canadian	Gillo Port	Seven Spies
Copperbone Lotion	Horsey Feed Bags	Similecch Squid
Cracked Lighter	Jungle Potion	Smartz Collar
Dirty Cell Battery	Krummies Diapers	Sucker Twin
Dr. Nest's Toothpaste	Old Grand-Mom Whiskey	Sufferin Coffee
Earth Bum Shampoo	Prowl Shampoo	Suspect Deodorant
Fling 'Ems Candy	Ram-A-Liar Syrup	Tipsy Roll Pop
Floral Cigarettes	Real Garbage Candy*	Yichs Sign-X

ALPHABETICAL DIRECTORY
Series 1-16 "Original" Wacky Packages Stickers
Reprinted from "Wacky Packages ... The Beat Goes On," courtesy of Roxanne Toser

STICKER TITLE	SERIES
Achoo	5
Ain't Toothpaste	14
Airraid Deodorant	6
Ajerx	2
Ale Detergent	13
All-Brain Cereal	2
Alpain Cereal	11
Alpoo Dog Food	7
Ape Green Beans	13
Aquax Cleanser	12
Argh	3
Arise Cream	16
Armor Hot Dogs	4
Awful Bits	2
Baby Runt	6
Bald Detergent	4
Balding Football	14
Bam	8
Band-Ache Strips	1
Bandage Cigarettes	15
Bar-Kist	6
Barman Barroom Tissue	12
Bash Detergent	11
Bathless Ribbons	13
Battle Ball	13
Battle Caps	12
Battletime Beer	14
Batzooka Gum	10
Bawl Park Franks	15
Beanball Bubble Gum	3
Bear Aspirin	9

STICKER TITLE	SERIES
Beastball Bubble Gum	13
Belche's Grape Jelly	9
Bent Cigarettes	4
Big Baddy	5
Big Banana Pen	7
Big Muc Hamburger	7
Bigtumi Spaghetti Sauce	10
Bird Brain Leftovers	11
Bit-O-Money	6
Biva Towels	8
Blank Crows	7
Blast Blew Ribbon Beer	7
Blecch Shampoo	2
Bleed's Candy	16
Blisterine	6
Bloodweiser	15
Blue Beanie Margarine	4
Blunder Bread	2
Blurine	15
Bone Ami	8
Boo-Hoo Drink	2
Boozo Gum	7
Botch Tape	2
Brain Power	13
Brandy Land Game	12
Bread Crust Hash	1
Brittle Soap Pads	2
Broomo Seltzer	6
Brute 88	4
Bug Wally	13
Bum Baked Beans	10

WACKY PACKAGES ALPHABETICAL DIRECTORY

STICKER TITLE	SERIES
Bum Bums Candy	6
Bum Chex	4
Bum and Mabel	15
Bum's Life Magazine	13
Burpsi-Cola	8
Busted-Finger Candy	3
Buz Detergent	12
Caged Dog Food	7
Camals	1
Canadian Clod	8
Canquit Chicken Pie	14
Cap'n Crud	2
Caraid Bandages	10
Casket Soap	10
Catgobite Detergent	15
Cents	9
Chaffed & Sunburn Coffee	11
Cheap Stick	15
Cheapios Cereal	4
Cheep Detergent	8
Chef Girl-ar-dee	4
Chicken Fat	2
Chimpanzee Spark Plug	11
Chock Full O'Bolts	1
Choke King	3
Choke Wagon	4
Choke-Up Toothpaste	8
Chumps Candy	5
Clammy Soap	6
Clank Bar	5
Clubbed Canadian	16
Clunky Candy	10
Coffin-Mate	10
Comit Cleanser	11
Commie Cleanser	2
Contrac	7
Copperbone Lotion	16
Cover Ghoul (Green Bottle)	5
Cover Ghoul (Tan Bottle)	1
Cracked Lighter	16
Crackola Crayons	3
Cram	5
Creature Crackers	7
Creep Toothpaste	12
Crocked Magazine	13
Crust Toothpaste	1
Cult 45	11
Cut-Rong Hacked Paper	6
Czechlets	9
Daffy Baking Powder	8
Dampers	4
Decay Toothpaste	11
Delinquent Spinich	9
Diamond Matches	13
Diet Frite Cola	10
Dimwit Sugar Dots	7
Dirty Cell Battery	16
Ditch Boy Paint	6
Ditch Masters	2
Dizzie Cups	11
Doesn't Delight	13
Don't-Touch-Mee Tea	13
Doomed Matches	13
Dopey Cream	1
Dr. Nest's Toothbrush	16
Dr. Ono	3
Dr. Popper	8
Drainola Cereal	13
Drowny Softener	3
Duck and Hide	12
Ducko Cement	9
Dud Laundry Soap	12

STICKER TITLE	SERIES
Dud's Boot Beer	12
Dull Pineapple	2
Dumb and Crazy Salt	13
Dums (For the Dummy)	7
Duxie Cups	14
Duzn't Detergent	1
Dynamites	15
Earth Barn Shampoo	15
Earth Bum Shampoo	16
Easy Cough Cleaner	9
Easy-Cuss Words	11
Eight (8-Lives Tuna Bones)	2
El Polluto Cigars	7
Electric Slave	15
Emptimo Cigars	7
Escuire Foot Polish	4
Eviltime	6
Exceedrin	2
Family Circuit	11
Famous Mobster's	15
Fanatical Sickly Fiction	14
Fang	4
Fang Edward	15
Fatina Cereal	5
Fearasil	14
Feetena Cereal	7
Fib (FIB Detergent)	11
Fibby's Juice	7
Fink Beverage	1
Fish Bone Dressing	2
Fishey-Price Toys	10
Flare Pen	12
Fling 'Ems Candy	16
Floral Cigarettes	16
Flunk Marshmallow	14
Fool Guard	16
Foolball Bubble Gum	3
Foolite	9
Footsie Roll	6
Freetoes	4
Fright Guard	3
Fruit of the Tomb	6
Gadzooka Bubble Gum (dated)	14
Gadzooka Gum (undated)	1
Gatoraid	4
Ghoul Humor	16
Gi (GI Toe)	9
Gillo Port	16
Gloom	2
Glutton Mustard	5
Goodman's Looney Noodles*	6
Goon's Farm Wine	9
Goonman's Looney Noodles*	6
Graft Cheese	5
Grass Wax	4
Grave Train	1
Grazin' Bran	4
Greaseline	10
Grime Dog Food	7
Gulp Oil	11
Gums	15
Gurgle Baby Food	2
Gurgle Cereal	7
Gyppy Pop Corn	2
Ha Ha Crackers	5
Hacks Cough Drops	15
Hag & Hag Tobacco	7
Hairy Lee Cake	10
Hamel Cigarettes	15
Hardly Wrap	8
Harm & Hammer	3
Hav-A-Temper Cigars	12

675

STICKER TITLE	SERIES	STICKER TITLE	SERIES
Hawaiian Punks Juice	3	Messquire Magazine	14
Hazel Mishap Lipstuck	13	Messy Marker	9
Head and Boulders	5	Mex-Pax Coffee	7
Heartburn Cereal	9	Milk Foam	4
Heave Cigarettes	4	Milk Muds Candy	12
Heavy Trash Bags	10	Milk of Amnesia	10
Hex-Lax	6	Minute Lice	1
Hippy Trash Bags	14	Minute Mud	2
Hipton Tea Bags	4	Mold Power	10
Hired Root Beer	3	Mold Rush Gum	6
Hookey Bubble Gum	9	Moldy Bride Magazine	14
Hopeless Snow Balls	8	Monotony	6
Horrid Deodorant	1	Moobeline	5
Horsey Feed Bags	16	Moonshine Crackers	3
Hostage Cupcakes	1	Mop & Glop Cleaner	8
Hostile Thinkies	8	Moron Beef Pot Pie	15
Hungry Jerk (hockey pucks)	5	Moron Chicken Dinner	11
Hungry Jerk (pancakes)	3	Moscow Syrup	9
Hurts Tomatoes	2	Motorzola	3
Hurtz Baked Bears	7	Mountain Goo	10
Hurtz Bird Seed	3	Mr. Bog Wet Bread	11
Hurtz Tomato Ketchup	7	Mr. Goodbye Candy	7
Hyde's Rox Cookies	4	Mr. Mean	12
Icicle Playing Cards	13	Mrs. Klean	1
Iou (IOU Magazine)	14	Mrs. Poles Sticks	14
Irish Ring Soap	14	Mrs. Small's Fish	9
Iron-ons	15	Mud	11
Ivery Snow	8	Muleburro Cigarettes	5
Ivy Soap	9	Muler's Dregg Noodles	11
Jail-O Desert	1	Murial Bland Cigars	7
Jean Nutty Bubbles	15	Mustard Charge	4
Jerk in Jail Magazine	13	Mutt's Juice	1
Jerken's Soap	6	My Sink Perfume	6
Jerkitol	15	My-T-Fink Desert	7
Jerky Fruits	9	National Geografink	11
Jungle Potion	16	National Spittoon Mag.	13
Kentucky Fried Fingers	8	Nertz	2
Kick A Man Sauce	9	Nestree	4
Killette Hair Spray	12	Neveready Battery	3
Killy Putty	9	No-Tips	3
King O'Scare Sardines	11	Nooseweek Magazine	13
Kleenaxe Tissues	8	Nose-X Tissue	14
Knots Gelatine	8	Nutlee's Quit	4
Knuckles Candy	5	Nutt's Apple Sauce	10
Koduck Photos	3	Oh Hairy Candy Bar	7
Kong Fu Bubble Gum	8	Old Grand-Mom Whiskey	16
Kook Cigarettes	2	Old Spit Cologne	5
Kook-Aid	1	One (1-A Sauce)	3
Krazy Crackers	5	Oscar Mayor Baloney	14
Krummies Diapers	16	Oscar Moron Bacon	10
Kung Fu Bubble Gum	8	Paid Killers	8
L'Oggs Panty Hose	7	Painters Peanuts	10
Land O Quakes Butter	4	Paper Wate Pen	9
Lavirus	1	Paul Maul	1
Le Rage's	13	Paydough Candy	12
Leek Oil Dripper	7	Pepto Dismal	10
Life Servers Candy	10	Peter Pain Peanut Butter	6
Light and Dizzy Yoga	5	Petley Flea Bags	15
Lipoff Cup-A-Slop	8	Pieces Candy	12
Liptorn Soup	1	Pig Pen Oil	9
Liquid Bomber	4	Piwi Blecch	6
Log Cave-In Syrup	2	Planet of the Grapes	11
Lova Soap	3	Plastered Peanuts	2
Lox Soap	10	Play Dumb Clay	6
Lucky Stride Cigarettes	3	Playbug Magazine	14
Maddie Boy	1	Playskull	13
Mare Cigarettes	15	Plopsikle	5
Marshmallow Flopp	7	Polarbearoid Film	14
Martian Hats	12	Pollydent	12
Mashbox Toys	15	Pooped Ridge Farms	10
Medi-Quak	7	Poopsi	2
Mess Clairoil	4	Pound's Cream	15

WACKY PACKAGES ALPHABETICAL DIRECTORY

STICKER TITLE	SERIES	STICKER TITLE	SERIES
Pounds Candy	5	Snatch-A-Pack	3
Progreaso Sauce	11	Sneer	6
Promesso Sauce	14	Sneezer Dressing	13
Prowl Shampoo	16	Snort Magazine	14
Pupsi Cola	10	Soft-Head Bulbs	6
Pure Hex	1	Soggy Babies Candy	7
Putrid Cat Chow	2	Sootball Bubble Gum	12
Quacker Oats	1	Sore Deodorant	13
Quake 'n Ache	4	Sore Mel Chili	15
Rabid Shave	3	Sorry Wrap	7
Raggedy Ant Doll	9	Spills Bad*	6
Ram-a-liar Syrup	16	Spills Bros.*	6
Randy Gelatin	13	Spit and Spill Cleanser	3
Raw Goo Sauce	4	Spray Nit	1
Raw Leaves Cigarettes	3	Squabble Word Game	9
Real Garbage Candy	16	Std Oil Shortage	8
Rebell Jet	14	Stickers	9
Regal Clown	16	Stiffords Glue	5
Rice-A-Phony	3	Stingline Staple Gun	12
Rinkled Wrap	4	Stinkertoy	11
Robot Burns Cigars	12	Stove Glop	10
Rolaches	8	Sucker Twin	16
Rotsa Root Candy	14	Sufferin Coffee	16
Rowdy Gelatin	13	Suffertone	8
Ruden's Cough Drops	10	Sugar Cigar Crisp	6
Run Tony Shells	2	Sugar Daffy	6
Run-A-Way Vitamins	6	Sugarmess Bubble Gum	2
Sailem	2	Sunsweat Prune Juice	10
Saparin Coffee	11	Suspect Deodorant	16
Satan Wrap	14	Sweat-Hard Soap	3
Saturday Evening Ghost	11	Swiss Fright Cheese	11
Scare-Deal Notebook	6	Swiss Mess Cocoa	5
Scary Jane Candy	10	Taffy Cat Food	14
Scary Lee	8	Taster's Choke	4
Schtick Blades	2	Taxim	9
Scoot Mouthwash	16	Three (3 Mosquitoes)	9
Scorch Mouthwash	8	Tic-Toc Candy	10
Scream Sicle	13	Tied Detergent	1
Screech Tape	13	Tijuana Smells	5
Sealva Thins	14	Tipsy Roll Pop	16
Secrets	5	Toad Bubble Bath	12
Sell'em Cigarettes	14	Top Slob Cleaner	7
Seven Spies	16	Totarillo Cigars	14
Seventon	11	Triks Cereal	5
Shake and Skip Ink	8	Truant Cigarettes	6
Shingle's Plaster Chips	15	Tv (TV Garbage)	11
Shock Dispenser	12	Ultra Blight	2
Shorts Illustrated	13	Ultrasheep Shampoo	15
Shot Tissue	8	Umbrella Magazine	13
Shot Wheels	5	Uncle Bum's Rice	10
Shots Candy	5	Underworld Ham	10
Shrunken Donuts	13	Unpopular Mechanics	11
Sicken of the Sea	5	Valveater Cheese	6
Siesta Crackers	12	Vicejoy Cigarettes	1
Similecch Squid	16	View Monster	15
Six (6-Up Beverage)	1	Vile Soap	2
Six (6-urp (dash is a dot)	9	Virginia Slums	6
Sixty-one (61 Magazine)	11	Wash 'n Fly	12
Skimpy	1	Weak Germ	12
Slam Jim Snacks	15	Weakies Cereal	1
Slaver Aspirin	14	Weakinson Blades	14
Slayskool	15	What Man's Simple Candy	6
Slaytex Gloves	5	White Fowl Cigars	5
Sledge	3	Windaxe	13
Sleepy	11	Windchester	3
Slopicana Juice	7	Windhex	4
Sludge (Betty Crooked)	5	Windstun Cigarettes	9
Smartz Collar	16	Wormy Packages	4
Smell Motor Oil	15	Wrecko Candy	12
Smith Sisters	5	Yichs Sing-X	16
Smoocher's Jam	8	Yicks Cough Drops	8
Snarlamint Cigarettes	6	Yubum Coffee	8

WACKY PACKAGES 1979-1980

After a four year interval, Topps issued another group of Wacky Packages Stickers in 1979-1980. Many collectors refer to these as "reissues" because a great majority of the titles were previously used in the "original" 16 series released in 1973-1975. All of the stickers in the '79-'80 series are numbered and all have puzzle picture pieces or checklists printed on the back, so they are easily distinguished from their predecessors. The stickers were issued in four series of 66 titles and each series has its own wrapper. Wrapper codes and colors are as follows: Series 1 ... red / 0-483-21-01-9; Series 2 ... yellow / 0-484-21-01-9; Series 3 ... blue / 0-485-21-01-0; Series 4 ... green / 0-489-21-01-0. Sharp-eyed collectors will see, from the box illustrations shown below, that the price of a package changed from 20 cents in 1979 to 25 cents in 1980. The backs of the stickers in each series form a puzzle, as follows: Series 1 ... Gadzooka Bubble Gum; Series 2 ... Wormy Packages; Series 3 ... Beastball Bubblegum; Series 4 ... Real Garbage Candy.

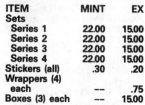

ITEM	MINT	EX
Sets		
Series 1	22.00	15.00
Series 2	22.00	15.00
Series 3	22.00	15.00
Series 4	22.00	15.00
Stickers (all)	.30	.20
Wrappers (4)		
each	--	.75
Boxes (3) each	--	15.00

SERIES 1

1 Camals
2 Mrs. Klean
3 Chock Full O'Bolts
4 Vicejoy
5 Liptorn
6 Hostage Cupcakes
7 Tied
8 Crust
9 Gadzooka
10 Botch Tape
11 Plastered Peanuts
12 Ultra Blight
13 Ditch Masters
14 Gloom
15 Schtick
16 Boo Hoo
17 Fish Bone
18 Vile
19 Blunder Bread
20 Gyppy Popcorn
21 Ajerx
22 Lucky Stride
23 Rabid Shave
24 Koduck
25 Neveready
26 Neveready
27 Hurtz
28 Hawaiian Punks
29 Drowny
30 Rice-A-Phoni
31 Busted Finger
32 Fright Guard
33 Rinkled Wrap
34 Chef Girl-Ar-Dee
35 Dampers
36 Armor
37 Land-O' Quakes
38 Moonshine Hydrox
39 Raw Goo
40 Wormy Packages
41 Blast Blue Ribbon
42 Smith Sisters
43 Head & Boulders
44 Slay-Tex
45 Shots
46 Shot Wheels
47 Ha Ha Crackers
48 Piwi
49 Peter Pain
50 Sugar Daffy
51 Generally Demented
52 Goonmans
53 Baby Runt
54 Footsie Roll
55 Bit O'Money
56 Blisterine
57 Ditch Boy
58 Medi-Quak
59 Sunstroke
60 Top Slob
61 Contrac
62 My-T-Fink
63 Dums
64 Slopicana
65 Feetena
66 Loggs

SERIES 2

67 Scary Lee Cake
68 Lipoff Cup A Soup
69 Daffy Baking Powder
70 Hopeless Snowballs
71 Mop & Glop
72 Suffertone
73 Ivery Snow
74 Paid Killers
75 Canadian Clod
76 Hostile Thinkies
77 Hardly Wrap
78 Yicks Cough Drops
79 Cheep
80 Kleenaxe Tissues
81 Scorch Mouthwash
82 Smoocher's Jam
83 Rolaches
84 Horrid
85 Duzn't
86 Spraynit
87 Lavirus
88 Mutt's Apple Juice
89 Sailem Cigarettes
90 Kook Cigarettes
91 Nertz Mints
92 Blecch Shampoo
93 Chicken Fat
94 Commie Cleanser
95 Brittle
96 Raw Leaves
97 No-Tips
98 Wheez-It Crackers
99 Sledge
100 Sweathard Soap
101 Rice-A-Phoni
102 Motorzola
103 Choke King
104 Windstun
105 Grass Wax
106 Esquire Foot
107 Bald
108 Swiss Mess
109 Jerky Fruits
110 Big Baddy
111 Krazy Crackers
112 Muleburro
113 Clank
114 White Fowl
115 Secrets
116 Glutton
117 Cram
118 Chumps
119 Moobeline
120 Old Spit
121 Achoo
122 Tijuana Smells
123 Eviltime
124 Airraid
125 Snarlamint
126 Broomo Seltzer
127 Virginia Slums
128 Clammy
129 My Sink
130 Oh Hairy!
131 Belch's Jelly
132 Sorry Wrap

WACKY PACKAGES 1979-1980

SERIES 3

133 Czechlets	159 Mr. Mean
134 Cents	160 Beastball
135 Ivy Soap	161 Shorts Illustrataed
136 Killy Putty	162 Screech
137 Raggedy Ant	163 Playskull
138 Clunky	164 Ale
139 Scary Jane	165 Sore
140 Mold Power	166 Nooseweek
141 Heavy Trash Bags	167 Playbug
142 Life Servers	168 Balding
143 Casket	169 Fearasil
144 Tic Toc	170 Slayer Aspirin
145 Mud Magazine	171 Irish Ring
146 Nat. Geografink	172 Mashbox
147 Fib	173 Bandage
148 Seventon	174 Hamel
149 Stinkertoy	175 Shingle's
150 Stingline	176 Copperbone
151 Barman	177 Cracked
152 Pollydent	178 Ram-a-liar
153 Weak Germ	179 Underworld Ham
154 Flare	180 Hairy Lee
155 Buz	181 Pepto Dismal
156 Toad	182 Oscar Moron
157 Brandy Land	183 Robot Burns
158 Creep	184 Duck and Hide

185 Ape Green Beans	192 Sufferin
186 Ain't	193 Ghoul Humor
187 Sell Em	194 Hiccups
188 Duxie	195 Smartz 2 in 1
189 Cheap Stick	196 Shock
190 Electric Slave	197 Progreaso
191 Earth Bum	198 Milk Muds

SERIES 4

199 Alpain Cereal	225 Dynamites	251 Real Garbage Candy
200 Aquax Cleanser	226 Famous Mobster	252 Ruden's Cough Drops
201 Arise Cream	227 Fanatical Sickly	253 Saparin Coffee
202 Bash Detergent	228 Fibby's Juice	254 Scare Deal Notebook
203 Bawl Park Franks	229 Flunk Marshmellow	255 Scoot Mouthwash
204 Beanball	230 Fool Guard	256 Seven Spies
205 Bear Aspirin	231 Gulp Oil	257 Shrunken Donuts
206 Big Banana Pen	232 Gums	258 Siesta Crackers
207 Bleed's Candy	233 Hag & Hag	259 Slam Jim Snacks
208 Blue Beanie	234 Hazel Mishap	260 Stiffords Mucilage
209 Blunder Bread	235 Ice Krunkles	261 Sucker Twin
210 Blurine	236 Jerkins	262 Suspect Deodorant
211 Brain Power	237 Jerkitol	263 Windchester
212 Bug Wally	238 Killette	264 Yichs Sign-X Spray
213 Bum Bums	239 King O'Scare	
214 Bum's Life	240 Krummies Diapers	
215 Chafed & Sunburn	241 Lova Soap	
216 Choke King	242 Lox Soap	
217 Clubbed Canadian	243 Moonshine Wheez-it	
218 Comit Cleaner	244 Moron Beef Pot Pie	
219 Cover Ghoul	245 Muriel Blands Cigars	
220 Creature Crackers	246 National Spittoon Mag.	
221 Crocked Magazine	247 Oscar Mayor Baloney	
222 Ditch Boy Paint	248 Paydough	
223 Don't Touch Mee Tea	249 Promesso Sauce	
224 Dud Laundry Soap	250 Prowl Shampoo	

WACKY PACKAGES 1985

Topps waited until 1985 to unleash another set of Wacky Packages stickers to delight children and torment mothers and teachers everywhere. The series consisted of 44 numbered stickers which the company heralded as "all new" designs.

The backs of the stickers are puzzle pieces which form two different puzzles: Beastball (blue borders) and Batzooka (red borders). The wrapper for the set is red and carries a "25¢ cheap" price (the package contained 5 stickers & one piece of gum). A statement on one side panel reads as follows: "Hey, the stickers that Topps Chewing Gum created are all in fun. The products we're spoofing - including our own - are all good ones, no kidding. So enjoy!" The box is clearly marked 1985 and features a goofy-looking kid carrying a bag of groceries which has just broken through the bottom and are spilling out towards the viewer.

ITEM	MINT	EX
Set	12.00	9.00
Sticker	.25	.20
Wrapper	--	.35
Box	--	5.00

Wacky Packages 1985

1 T.V. Ghoul
2 Stinky
3 Mr. Pig Tissue
4 Burger Thing
5 National Retirer
6 Loafing Cow Cheese
7 Aqua-Flush Toothpaste
8 Puritan Oil
9 Hottest Coal Cakes
10 Reaganets
11 Grave Cat Food
12 G.I. Toe
13 Pimple Magazine
14 Beak Shaver
15 Terrier Water
16 Chock Full O'Guts
17 Soapy Washman
18 Cannon Yogurt
19 Pupto-Dismal
20 Itch'N Chaps Cookies
21 Mr. Clown
22 Frisk
23 Lumps Diapers
24 Bla Yogurt
25 Waffle Ball
26 Greaser's Pieces
27 Muggies Diapers
28 Mr. Stubble
29 Red Hoss Salt
30 Tobacco Juice

31 Dr. Pooper
32 Ghost Soap
33 Velaphants
34 Peter Panic Peanut Butter
35 Bananacin
36 Lazy Goo
37 Hamel Cigarettes

38 Snoot Powder
39 Beastball Gum Cards
40 Chimpwich Ice Cream
41 Badzooka Bubble Gum
42 Kid Kud
43 Go Bums
44 Everdeady Battery

WACKY PACKAGES STICKERS 1991

1 Keggs Draft Brew
2 Badzooka Cement Gum
3 Trucker's Strawberry Traffic Jam
4 Stupid Moron 2
5 Boozco
6 Snakes
7 Char Boy
8 Mentals
9 Vlad
10 Tragedy Ann
11 Yuppie Chow
12 Scrawny
13 Famished Amish Cookies
14 Popps Magazine
15 American Distress
16 Original Stench Dressing
17 Squelch's Ape Juice
18 Prez Broccoli Dispenser
19 Reckboks
20 Space-Out Time
21 Bambo
22 Pego Building Set
23 Zenergizer
24 Barf Wimpson
25 Pigtionary
26a Tattoo Skins
26b Barf's Rot Beer

27 Hobo Cop
28 Newpork Pig Cigs
29 Kitty Zitter
30 Saneball
31 Little Dead Kitten
32 Pit
33 Retch A Sketch
34 Fatman
35 The Real Gross Blisters
36 Oldage Mutant Nasty Turkeys
37 Nude Kids on the Block
38 Cup O'Poodles
39 Flea-Wee's Flop-House
40 Duck Bar
41 Wheel of Torture

42 Old El Gaso
43 Scumby
44 Dr. Sushi
45 Blubber Worth's
46 The Rat in the Cat
47 Coorpse Light
48 Sick Tracy
49 Mummorex
50 Drunken' Donuts
51 Snot 'N Blow
52 Barfield
53 The Baby Splitters Club
54 Microbe Machines
55 Donkey Nose Pizza

The "Great Wacky Packages Debate of 1990-91" centers about the year of issue and the number of stickers in the set. Topps decided to test-market this latest series of "Wackys" in the fall of 1990, setting off a mini-panic among Wacky collectors who did not reside in the geographical areas selected for the experiment. For a while, the series was scarce, but the company decided to mass produce the issue and it appeared in quantity in 1991. The shift from "test" to "regular" marketing produced only two anomalies. One of these is the existence of two separate display boxes: the "test" box held 60 packs and is coded 1-481-44-01-0; the "regular" box contained 48 packs and bears a 1-481-40-01-1 production code. Of more interest to collectors is the switch in sticker #26. In the original "test" series and the initial printing of the "regular" set, it was entitled "Tattoo Skins"; this design was removed from subsequent printings and replaced by "Barf's Rot Beer." It appears that the Barf's sticker is somewhat scarce and would not normally be included in sets. In addition, eleven stickers have two backs: text and puzzle piece. The set price listed is for 55 stickers and DOES NOT include both sets of backs, but does include all the puzzle pieces.

ITEM	MINT	EX
Set	8.00	--
Sticker	.15	--
Wrapper	--	.20
Boxes (2)		
test	--	5.00
regular	--	3.00

WACKY PACKAGE TATTOOS (57)   1 9/16" X 3 1/2"

By comparing records among collectors, it has recently been concluded that numbers 12A, 13B, and 23B of this Topps series were never issued. The exterior wrapper design illustrated is the only one reported to date; it is blue, with the title and packages printed in various colors. The tattoos on the interior sides of the wrappers are numbered 1-30 in "A" and "B" groups. The series was marketed in 1973. Note: all wrappers seen to date have a small tear at the attachment point.

ITEM	MINT	EX
Set	--	210.00
Wrapper	--	3.00
Box	--	50.00

1A Snarlsmint Sicker-Echs!
2A Gadzooka Bubble Gum
3A Cover Ghoul Murk Up
4A Grasin Bran
5A Jail-O Prison Desert
6A Sunshine Krazy Crackers
7A Peter Pain Peanut Butter
8A Dopey Whip
9A Stupid Beanball
10A Dampers
11A Blue Beanie Margarine
12A Not issued
13A Girl-Ar-Dee Spaghetti
14A Spills Bros Coffee
15A Brittle Sop Pads

16A Wierdo Smith Sisters Cough Drops
17A Crust Poo-Paste
18A Glutton Hot Mustard
19A Kook-Aid Mixed-Up Drink
20A Liquid Bomber
21A Ditch Masters Cheap Cigars
22A HaHa Crackers
23A Rabid Shave
24A Wormy Packages Stinky Gum
25A Triks
26A Cram
27A Nevereright Battery
28A Liptorn Soup
29A Gloom Toothpaste
30A No title [cereal package]

1B Bum Bums
2B Moonshine Wheez-It
3B Sweathard Odorous Soap
4B No-Tips For Slobs
5B Kook Mental Cigarettes
6B Super Cigar Crisp
7B Chicken Fat (For Fat Hens)
8B Vile Soap (For Stinkers)
9B Ill Tempered Sneer
10B Mrs. Kleen
11B Pest Awful Bits
12B Crakols Broken Crayons
13B Not issued
14B Ditchboy Paint
15B Bit-O-Honey

16B Camals Jerkish Blend
17B Hipton Teabags
18B Gadzooka Sugarmess Bubble Gum
19B Moldy Clay
20B Ajerx Cleanser
21B Grass Wax Grass Cleaner
22B Tied (You'll Go Knots)
23B Not issued
24B Blecch Shampoo (For Hippies)
25B Sailem (Don't Smoke 'Em, Sail 'Em)
26B Horrid Deodorant
27B Raw Goo Spaghetti Sauce
28B Mold Rush
29B Bald Toupee Cleanser
30B Milk-Foam

WACKY STICKERS (23)

1 1/16" X 2 11/16"

Nabisco distributed "Wacky Stickers" in Sugar Daddy caramel pops during 1983-84. Each sticker has a simple combination of color artwork plus a phrase or expression. A 1983 copyright line, set identification ("A"), and sticker number are located below the design. The backing is tan paper with a scored center line for removal. There are 23 stickers in the set and all we have seen to date belong to "Set A."

ITEM	MINT	EX
Set	6.50	5.00
Sticker	.25	.20
Wrapper	––	1.00

WACKY TV SHOW CARDS (48)

2 1/4" X 3 1/4"

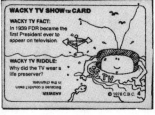

Collecting non-sports cards is fun and sets like "Wacky TV Show Cards," although not as sophisticated as most other issues, can be a real hoot. The cards bear a 1978 copyright date and the initials C.B.C. (Continental Baking Company) on the back and they were issued in 3-card panels on the box backs of "Hostess" brand bakery products. Since they are "package design" cards — meaning that they had to be cut away from the original box — it is likely that collectors will encounter them with uneven edges. For this reason, we will not list values for mint grade cards (if you find intact panels, simply total single card prices and add 50%). According to our records, there are 48 cards in the set, but since we do not have a complete checklist available, we will list the numbers and titles that have been confirmed so far. The cards have printed backs with numbers, interesting "Wacky TV Facts," and "Wacky TV Riddles."

PARTIAL CHECKLIST
(Provided by Brian Bigelow & Gordon Burns)

4	To Smell The Truth
5	The Cod Couple
6	Roper Room
19	Tar Trek
20	The Hatch Game
21	The Flintrocks
22	Thunder Dog
24	Brawl In The Family
28	Candied Camera
29	Bad Times
34	She Haw
45	Hollywood "Scares"
36	Barney Chiller
37	Little Mouse On The Prairie
38	The Arfies
39	The Souper Bowl
40	Flea's Company
41	The Bratty Bunch
42	Blunder Woman
43	The Six Million Dollar Mess
44	Eight Is Too Much
45	Wild World Of Shorts

ITEM	MINT	EX
Set	––	27.50
Card	––	.50

WALT DISNEY CHARACTERS TATTOOS (?)

1 9/16″ X 3 1/2″

We have illustrated all four of the exterior wrappers known for this Disney tattoo set produced by Topps. All of them are yellow with red print titles and black-color characters. The tattoos on the interior sides are not numbered but the characters are named. The total number of tattoos in the set has yet to be determined. Advertising for the Disney movie "Summer Magic" indicates that this set was distributed in 1963.

ITEM	MINT	EX
Wrappers (4)		
each	--	12.00

WALT DISNEY'S CHARACTER (90) COLLECTING CARDS

2 1/2″ X 3 9/16″

A series of 90 trading cards marketed by Treat Hobby Products in 1982. There are five different sets of 18 cards featuring a specific Disney character: Mickey Mouse, Donald Duck, Bambi, Goofy, and Snow White. The card number, series and set identification, and a short line of text appear on the back of every card. Each 18-card set was sold, without gum, in a cardboard J-hook package.

ITEM	MINT	EX
Set of 90	20.00	15.00
Card	.20	.15

WALTONS (50)

One of the more elusive Topps sets of the 1970's is the Waltons set of 50 cards issued in 1973. The card has a color picture from the television show enclosed in a white frame line and purple borders. "The Waltons" is printed in large yellow letters across the front of the card. Approximately 65 percent of the reverse area is given to a puzzle piece, while the remaining 35 percent contains the card number and a short text. Waltons gum packs came stacked in a plain white box without any identification on it. Gum pack wrappers are coded T-8-5-A and say "Bubble Gum" on the front; another variety wrapper reads "America's Favorite TV Show" under the picture and carries a T-8-5-B code.

ITEM	MINT	EX
Set	1600.00	1100.00
Card	25.00	18.00
Wrappers		
T-8-5-A	--	100.00
T-8-5-B	--	125.00

WANTED POSTERS

"Wanted Posters" must be an all-time favorite at Topps because they have issued it on three separate occasions: 1967, 1975, and 1980. As far as we can determine, the same 24 titles with identical artwork appear in each of the sets, although the wording beneath the picture may vary slightly in some cases. Our checklist enumerates the titles alphabetically; the numbers of the 1980 posters are in brackets.

The 1967 wrapper is red with a woodgrain pattern background (production code: 0-420-91-01-7) and has uncaptioned "Kid Brother" artwork in the center. The posters are printed on tan paper stock and measure 10" X 18 1/2"; they are not numbered and have an undated copyright line in the bottom right corner.

Baby-Sitter [24]
Barber [9]
Big Brother [8]
Big Sister [13]
Butcher [5]
Candy Store Owner [20]
Cheapskate [10]
Class Bully [23]
Dentist [4]
Doctor [21]
Father [22]
Garbageman [11]
Kid Brother [2]
Kid Sister [15]
Liar [18]
Librarian [19]
Mother [6]
Next Door Neighbor [12]
Principal [19]
School Flirt [1]
Slob [14]
Teacher [16]
Teacher's Pet [17]
T.V. Repairman [7]

The 1975 wrapper is yellow with a woodgrain pattern background (production code: 0-419-21-01-5) and also has uncaptioned "Kid Brother" artwork in the center. The posters are printed on white paper stock and are simply cropped versions of those of the 1967 series, measuring 9 7/16" X 18 1/16".

The 1980 wrapper is red and yellow and has no woodgrain pattern (production code: 0-450-212-01-0)' The center design is a captioned "Class Bully." The posters measure 12" X 20" and are printed on white paper stock. Each poster is numbered at bottom-left and has a 1980 copyright line at bottom-right. Posters from this set also have a production code number printed inside the lower right frame line.

Note: no mint prices are listed for folders since uncreased specimens have not been seen.

ITEM	EX
1967 Set	165.00
1967 Poster	6.00
1967 Wrapper	60.00
1967 Box	100.00
1975 Set	80.00
1975 Poster	3.00
1975 Wrapper	15.00
1975 Box	35.00
1980 Set	35.00
1980 Poster	1.25
1980 Wrapper	4.00
1980 Box	10.00

WANTED STICKERS (42)

"Wanted Stickers" is a set of 42 paper stickers and nine checklist cards produced by Topps in 1975. The wrapper is "tiger orange" in color with a woodgrain background and un-captioned "Class Bully" artwork in the center. The artwork on the unnumbered stickers resembles that of "Wanted Posters," and a few designs are shared by both sets (None of the "Wanted Stickers" are numbered and all have plain brown paper backing. There is only one American series of "Wanted Stickers": those with white paper backs were issued in England and have a 1976 copyright date.) Each of the nine puzzle piece cards has a checklist printed on back. Note: set prices include a complete puzzle.

2 1/2'' X 3 1/2''

ITEM	MINT	EX
Set	35.00	27.50
Sticker	.65	.50
Card	.50	.35
Wrapper	--	3.00
Box	--	35.00

Baby
Baby Sitter
Barber
Big Brother
Big Sister
Bus Driver
Butcher
Cafeteria Cook
Candy Store Owner
Chainsmoker
Cheapskate
Class Bully
Dentist
Disc Jockey
Doctor
Door-To-Door Salesman
Father
Fatso
Garbageman
Kid Brother
Kid Sister
Lazybones
Liar
Librarian
Maid
Mechanic
Mother
Next Door Neighbor
Pet Cat
Pet Dog
Plumber

Policeman
Postman
Principal
School Nurse
Slob
Taxi Cab Driver
Teacher
Teacher's Pet
Telephone Operator
T.V. Repairman
Wise Guy

WAR BULLETIN (88)

The Philadelphia Chewing Gum Company issued the War Bulletin set in 1965. Each of the 88 cards has a black and white photo of a World War II event, which is captioned in a red panel on the picture. The back of the card has a red border, a red number box, and the set name printed in red. The set is sometimes referred to as "World War II" from the title on the wrapper.

2 1/2'' X 3 1/2''

ITEM	MINT	EX
Set	220.00	165.00
Card	2.00	1.50
Wrapper	--	25.00
Box	--	100.00

War Bulletin

	21 Silent Sentinel	
	22 Bullseye!	
	23 Sole survivor	
	24 Il Duce	
	25 Death in the Ruins	
	26 Inch by Inch	
	27 Bombs Away	
	28 Over the Side	
	29 Unseen Death	
	30 We're Hit!	
	31 Passing the Ammo	
	32 Long Wet Walk	
	33 Help, Medic!	
	34 One Less Jap	
	35 Ocean-Going Garage	55 Battle of the Bulge	75 Run for the Hills
	36 Pinned Down	56 House to House	76 Nazi Give Up
	37 Smoked Out	57 Wading Party	77 Tears of Joy
	38 Killing a Killer	58 Torch of Liberation	78 Kamikaze!
	39 Softening up	59 Big Three	79 Tokyo Express
	40 Leapfrog Landing	60 Dodging Death	80 Manmade Earthquake
	41 D-Day at Last	61 Assault From Above	81 Cat and Mouse
	42 A Word From Ike	62 Beachhead Bottleneck	82 Divine Wind
	43 Ready to Fight	63 The Dragon's Teeth	83 Champion of Liberty
	44 Storm and Steel	64 Ready to Quit	84 Aussies Wade In
Europe Beware	45 Tools of Victory	65 Help From a Buddy	85 Super Bomb
Heil Hitler	46 Crawling Ashore	66 Floating Inferno	86 Living Legend
Terror in the Sky	47 Flaming Meatball	67 Squeeze Play	87 Surrender!
The Invader	48 Secret Weapon	68 Broadside	88 Check List
End Run	49 Flush Them Out!	69 Buffalo Round-Up	
The War-Makers	50 Paris Freed	70 The Navy's Might	
London Blitz	51 Home Again	71 Kamerad!	
Cossack Patrol	52 What Hit Me?	72 Headed for the Bottom	
Day of Infamy	53 I Have Returned	73 Ghost Town 1945	
10 Hit and Run	54 Stubborn Enemy	74 Hot on Their Heels	

	11 Victory at Sea	
	12 Desert Danger	
	13 The Enemy Below	
	14 Wooden Weapon	
	15 Stop the Nazis	
	16 Fox on the Run	
	17 Flying Tigers	
	18 Blizzard of Steel	
	19 Jackal at Bay	
	20 The Noose Tightens	

WASHINGTON DUDES (8K)   2 1/2" X 3 1/2"

What can we tell you about the card series entitled "The Washington Dudes Baseball Club?" Well, for one thing, the cards were printed by Signet Magazine as a promotion for an

Augie A. August, Owner
Aurelio Dominguez "Smith"
Big Bubba Bassoon, Catcher
Chi Chi Blanco, Centerfielder
Gabby Smith, Shortstop
Gather P. Morse, Pitcher
Melinda
Rod Smith, Third Baseman
"Soul Chink," Rightfielder
Tony Santucci "Smith"

upcoming issue. Secondly, the people in the baseball uniforms were probably all Signet staff members. Other than that, we can only physically describe the cards. They are standard size, have black & white photos on front, and are not numbered. The borders are black (title & names are in white) and the backs all contain the same advertising copy for the upcoming issue of "Signet." The year and method of issue remain unknown at this point in time; reports that a wrapper exists have not been confirmed. Value of a single card in excellent condition: $3.00.

WATER WORLD HEROES (50)   1 1/16" X 2 3/4"

"Water World Heroes" is the ninth set in Nabisco's natural history series. Published in 1972, it has a total of 50 cards and the artwork and text were once again prepared by H. Wayne Trimm. The card fronts have a

tiny copyright line located under the picture. The card caption, number, and text appear on the green-print back. A 24" X 36" wall chart could be obtained from Nabisco via an offer in Sugar Daddy and Sugar Mama caramel pops.

ITEM	MINT	EX
Set	35.00	30.00
Card	.60	.45

PARTIAL CHECKLIST	13 Lungfish	26 Krill	39 Horseshoe Crab
1 Red Salmon	14 Shellfish Seashells	27 Sea Snake	40 Narwhal
2 Belted Kingfisher	15 Kelp	28 Gulf Stream - Sargasso Sea	41 Blue Whale
3 Mink Frog	16 Sea Urchin	29 Peruvian Booby	42 Alaska King Crab
4 Killifish	17 Fiddler Crab	30 Marine Iguana	43 California Flying Fish
5 Great Blue Heron	18 Sandworm	31 Puffin	44 Killer Whale
6 Mayfly	19 Hermit Crab	32 Wandering Albatross	45 Portuguese Man-Of-War
7 Freshwater Zooplankton	20 Sea Squirt	33 Leatherback Turtle	46 Coral Reef
8	21 Sea Anemone	34 Manta Ray	47 Crown-Of-Thorns Starfish
9 Electric Eel	22 Common Octopus	35 Abalone	48 Giant Clam
10 Basilisk Lizard	23 Prehistoric Sea Life	36	49 Ocean Depths
11 Piranha	24 Saltwater Phytoplankton	37 Common Skate	50
12 Jacana	25 Saltwater Zooplankton	38 Common Lobster	

WAY OUT WHEELS (36 & 22)

"Way Out Wheels" is an excellent example of the competition between card companies and how individuals with a "hot item" can exploit that rivalry. George Barris specialized in customizing automobiles for the Hollywood crowd and it appears that both Topps and Fleer ("Kustom Cars") produced sets featuring his cars at the same time! Ten of the 36 titles in Way Out Wheels are identical to those in Kustom Cars, and a number of other cards, with name changes, appear in both sets. The 22 "Auto Stickers" that accompanied these cards as bonus inserts have the same format as those issued later with "Evel Knievel," but are easily identified by their white, rather than tan, backs. Note: separate set prices are listed for cards and stickers.

ITEM	MINT	EX
Sets		
Cards	80.00	60.00
Stickers	50.00	37.50
Card	2.00	1.50
Sticker	2.00	1.50
Wrapper	---	12.00

1 Calico Surfer	7 Alvin's Acorn	13 Mongrel T	19 Daroo 1	25 Mini Surfer	31 Ala Kart
2 Bed Buggy	8 Bev. Hills 442	14 Turbo-Sonic	20 Speed Coupe	26 Cyclops Deuce	32 Dragnet 29
3 Moonscope	9 Barris T Buggy	15 ZZR ZZR	21 Sonny's Mustang	27 AMX 400	33 Flaky T
4 Voxmobile	10 Raiders Coach	16 Munster Drag-U-La	22 Barris' Ricksha	28 Daktari Jeep	34 Beau-T
5 Fuzz G.T.O.	11 Panel Buggy	17 Surf Woody	23 Aerodynamic	29 Expo 67X	35 Flushes Yamaha
6 Fiberfab	12 Psychedelic Firebird	18 V-8 Roadster	24 Mod Mail Truck	30 Excalibar	36 X Pak Air Car

WEIRD BALL TRADING CARDS (42)

Mel Appel combined the elements of Garbage Pail Kids, Ugly Stickers, and Wacky Packages to create this 42-card set in 1986. The artwork pictures on front are a series of gross-looking individuals with clever names like Rusty Badwrench, Paco Taco, and Sleaze E. Rider. The card number is printed in the upper right corner of the picture area and a wide black diagonal band angled across the upper left corner contains the set title. The frame lines are white and black and the borders are red.

There are three different types of backs. Fifteen cards have puzzle piece backs which can be assembled into a large picture. Five other backs have a joke and answers to jokes printed on the reverse. On 21 of the backs, you will find product parodies and funny certificates. The final card, #7, has a checklist back. Although the red and black display box has a "Gross Series No. 1" seal printed on it, no additional series have been seen.

ITEM	MINT	EX
Set	12.50	8.00
Card	.30	.20
Box	---	5.00

Weird Ball Trading Cards

1 Doc Shrink Head	4 Bonehead
2 Sludgehead	5 Spitball Louie
3 Sewer Face Sam	6 Spitball Louie, Jr.

7 Warthog Bundy	
8 Warthog Berry	
9 Freddy Fling-it	

10 Kleen N. Jerk	27 Sewer Face Sam
11 Cheapskate Charlie	28 'The' Slob
12 Izzy Gone	29 Blambo
13 Chuck Chopper	30 'Frog' Leggs
14 Cool Hand Duke	31 Wrong Stuff Williams
15 I.B. Emms	32 Sergeant Pork
16 Runnin' Ralph	33 Pullet N. Bailout
17 None Chuck	34 Biff Beamer
18 Karate Sid	35 R.V. Harvey
19 Humungasaki	36 Sleaze E. Rider
20 Doctor Screw Loose	37 BMX Boger
21 Kid Snot Nose	38 'Sting' Ray
22 Clark Cable	39 Roto Scooter
23 Rusty Badwrench	40 Tennesee
24 'Superfly' Dumper	41 U.R. Starr
25 Paco Taco	42 Philo Soote
26 Eddy Spaghetti	

WEIRD-OHS (66)

2 1/2" X 3 1/2"

PLAYERS NEVER HAVE SEEN THE LIKES.. OF OLD POP FLY AND HIS SWITCH BLADE SPIKES !!

The wrapper design tells you at a glance what the "Weird-Ohs" set is all about: a monster wearing an "SCTA" hat (Society for Cruelty To Animals) is apparently flagging down prospective victims. The other bizarre characters in the set have similar professions and proclivities. The cards are clearly marked "Weird-Ohs" on the green-print back and they were distributed in 1965 (a year before "Baseball Weird-Ohs" was marketed). The monsters were based on characters created by the Hawk Model Company.

ITEM	MINT	EX
Set	150.00	115.00
Card	2.00	1.50
Wrapper	--	10.00
Box	--	65.00

1 Wade A. Minut	20 Kooky Klancy
2 Huey Hut Rod	21 Sooty Sam
3 Francis The Foul	22 Leaky Boat Louie
4 Davey	23 Wade A. Minut
5 Sling Rave Curvette	24 Huey Hut Rod
6 Endsville Eddie	25 Francis The Foul
7 Terry Tent	26 The Psycho Cyclist
8 Sarge Barge	27 Sling Rave Curvette
9 Tex Tumbleweed	28 Endsville Eddie
10 Digger	29 Terry Tent
11 Shorty Shotgun	30 Sarge Barge
12 Drag Hag	31 Tex Tumbleweed
13 Pop Fly	32 Digger
14 Daddy	33 Shorty Shotgun
15 Count Von Frankfurter	34 Drag Hag
16 Donald The Duffer	35 Pop Fly
17 Killer McBash	36 Daddy
18 Freddy Flameout	37 Count Von Frankfurter
19 Speed Downhill	38 Donald The Duffer

39 Killer McBash	
40 Freddy Flameout	
41 Speed Downhill	
42 Kooky Klancy	
43 Sooty Sam	
44 Leaky Boat Louie	
45 Wade A. Minut	
46 Huey Hut Rod	
47 Francis The Foul	
48 Davey	
49 Sling Rave Curvette	

50 Endsville Eddie	
51 Terry Tent	
52 Sarge Barge	
53 Tex Tumbleweed	
54 Digger	
55 Shorty Shotgun	
56 Drag Hag	
57 Pop Fly	
58 Daddy	
59 Count Von Frankfurter	
60 Donald The Duffer	
61 Killer McBash	
62 Freddy Flameout	
63 Speed Downhill	
64 Kooky Klancy	
65 Sooty Sam	
66 Leaky Boat Louie	

WEIRD WHEELS STICKERS (55)

2 1/2" X 3 1/2"

"Weird Wheels" is Topps' answer to the "Odd Rods" series produced by Donruss. The 55 artwork designs are pictures of

FOLD CORNER ON DOTTED LINE
•
Slowly peel sticker from FRONT of card.

various monsters causing mayhem from behind the wheel. The stickers are corner-peel types with cardboard backing; the number and a 1980 copyright line are printed on front. The cardboard backs contain checklists, puzzle pieces, or peel-off instructions.

ITEM	MINT	EX
Set	8.50	5.50
Sticker	.15	.10
Wrapper	--	.50
Box	--	5.00

6 STICKERS • 1 STICK OF BUBBLE GUM

1 Hunchback of Notre Drag	22 Witch's Wheels
2 Hot Rabbit	23 Hearse of Horror
3 Loco-motive	24 Creep In A Jeep
4 Putrid Porsche	25 Meat Wagon
5 Slab Cab	26 Old-Old-Olds
6 Samurai Subaru	27 Blackhound
7 Voo Doo Vette	28 Motorat
8 Doom Buggy	29 Big Swarm
9 Bone Dragger	30 Zom B Zee
10 Dynosaur	31 Swamp Buggy
11 Stingray	32 U.F.O.
12 Bad Brat	33 Screamin Demon
13 Drag-On!	34 Flying Dutchman
14 Mob Mobile	35 Hun On A Honda
15 Killer Bee	36 Motor Mummy
16 Pony Car	37 Rolls Roach
17 Vampire Van	38 Teacher's Screecher
18 Fast Frank	39 Big Bad Bug
19 Crash Cobra	40 Killdozer
20 Racin' Robot	41 Psyclops Cycle
21 Octo-Rod	42 The Blobb

43 Punk Junk	
44 Black Hawk	
45 Howlin' Wolf	
46 Grease Mobile	
47 Hot Shoe	
48 Chopped Hog	
49 Model T'NT	
50 Psycho Cycle	
51 Space Stude	
52 Bad Humor Truck	
53 Spyder	
54 Boo-Ick	
55 Konk Kar	

WELCOME BACK KOTTER (53)   2 1/2" X 3 1/2"

There are 53 cards in the Welcome Back Kotter set marketed by Topps in 1976. The format consists of a color photo from the television series with humorous dialogue inserted in a dialogue balloon. The obverse borders are red. The backs are divided among poster pieces (eight cards) and a feature labeled "The Sweat-Hogs Speak" (45 cards). The card number is located on the reverse.

ITEM	MINT	EX
Set	15.00	10.00
Card	.30	.20
Wrapper	--	1.00
Box	--	10.00

1 Up Your Nose with a Rubber Hose!
2 Gabe, When You Take Out the Garbage, Don't Forget Horshack!
3 Three O'clock and All's Well!
4 I've Heard of Homeroom...But This is Ridiculous!
5 This is the Happiest Day of My Life...Saturday!
6 Can Mr. Kotter Come Out and Play?

7 Cheer Up, Mr. Woodman....Us Sweat-Hogs Will Never Leave Ya!
8 Who Said I Looked Like a Penguin?
9 To Be or Not to Be...A Sweat-Hog?
10 I Thought You Said Doing the Hustle Was Easy!
11 Horshack, You Don't Have an Inferiority Complex--You're Genuinely Inferior!
12 Hi There!
13 Woodman Charged Me with Cheating! Yeah? How Much?
14 You'll Look Sexier if You Wipe Your Nose!
15 But Why Can't I Pledge to Brooklyn
16 You Sweat-Hogs Are a Bunch of Lazy, Sloppy Loudmouths... But Nobody's Perfect!
17 I Went to the Playground-- Someone Stole All the Hoops!
18 There's a School Bus Leaving in 20 Minutes--Try and Be under It!
19 I'd Throw You a Kiss--But It's Been a Hard Day!
20 Sorry I'm Late--The School Bus Was Hijacked to Cuba!
21 Schools Have Changed Since Your Day--We Don't Kill Students, We Fail Them!

22 Our Report Cards Sunk-- They're Below "C" Level!
23 Kotter Wants to Know Where Asia Is--Where'd You Put It?
24 I Failed French--It's All Greek to Me!
25 O.K. Girls--Form a Double Line!
26 Too Bad They Haven't Got a Course in Good Looks!
27 I Don't Hate School--It's Just the Principal of the Thing!
28 You Sweat-Hogs Should Go Far--The Farther the Better!
29 Hail the Honorary Sweat-Hog!
30 Me, Me! Him, Him!
31 From the Shores of Montezuma to the Halls of Buchanan High!
32 Today Buchanan High School-- Tomorrow the World!
33 Which Sweat-Hog Wrote His Composition in Invisible Ink?
34 When I Want Your Advice, Kotter, I'll Rattle Your Cage!
35 How Long Can a Man Live Without a Brain? I Don't Know--How Old Are You?
36 Ooh! Oooh! Ooh! Ooh!
37 Darn--We Gotta Let Her Play-- It's Her Ball!
38 This is One Way of Getting a Balanced Education!

39 Your Uncle Hershey Did What?
40 Even in the New Math, 2 + 2 Doesn't Equal Five!
41 Horshack, Your Deodorant Failed--And You Might Too!
42 The Meeting of the Barbarino Fan Club Will Now Come to Order!
43 Who Said I'm All Wet?
44 Other Kids Have Teachers... We Have Mr. Kotter!
45 You're in a Class by Yourself-- And I Wish You'd Stay That Way!
46 Horshack, Nowadays Charm and Intelligence Just Aren't Enough!
47 Do You Feel Like a Glass of Juice? No--Do I Look Like One?
48 The Three Musketeers... ...One For All... ...And All for Lunch!
49 Mr. Kotter Says He Can't Teach Us Anything--We Must Be Geniuses!
50 Ooh! Ooh! Ooh! Ooh!
51 I Was Gonna Cut Class, but Someone Stole My Pocket Knife!
52 But How Can Anybody Fail Lunch?
53 In This School You've Gotta Be Crazy...Or You'll Go Nuts!

WENDY'S OLD WEST TRADING CARDS (10) 2" X 2 5/8"

This interesting series of ten "Old West Trading Cards" was given away at Wendy's fast food restaurants (year unknown). The cards are "vari-vues," meaning that they have two different pictures: a primary one which is normally visible, and an underlying one which is revealed by tilting the card a certain way. The "Kit Carson" portrait illustrated here is paired with a four-in-one view of Carson (same picture, but smaller), Buffalo Bill, and two Indians. The backs have the set title at top and a considerable amount of text, prepared "by the Editors of The World Book Encyclopedia," below. The card number is located in the bottom right corner. Note: if the plastic overlay on front of the card is cracked, it cannot be graded excellent or mint.

ITEM	MINT	EX
Set	22.00	17.00
Card	2.00	1.50

WHAT'S MY JOB? (72 & 16)   2 1/2" X 3 1/2"

Leaf issued this 72-card set in 1965 according to Buck Barker (8th Catalog Additions). The front of each card has a color drawing which depicts a person engaged in some form of activity; the large white border at bottom contains the question which also serves as the set title—"What's My Job?". The gray-colored backs have "Clues" to be used when using the set as flash cards. Sixteen gummed-back stickers (2 1/4" X 2 15/16") were issued with the cards as an insert bonus. They are all marked "A-16" on one border and are not captioned. Our sticker checklist, which is missing one title, is composed of descriptions of the characters depicted. Note: separate set prices are listed for cards and stickers.

ITEM	MINT	EX
Sets		
Cards	105.00	85.00
Stickers	80.00	55.00
Card	1.25	1.00
Sticker	4.00	3.00
Wrapper	—	35.00

1 Fish Canner	19 Teacher	37 Steno	55 Bartender	Arab
2 Cookie Inspector	20 Bullfighter	38 Rustler	56 Taffy-Puller	Convict
3 Head Hunter	21 Poodle Clipper	39 Baseball Umpire	57 Olive Stuffer	Flapper (cigarette in holder)
4 Cracker Stacker	22 Camel Driver	40 Ditch Digger	58 Grave Digger	French Gendarme
5 Man of Distinction	23 Carpenter	41 Witch Doctor	59 Cub Reporter	German General
6 Business Executive	24 Executioner	42 House Hunter	60 Gold Digger	Guardsman
7 Cobbler	25 Belly Dancer	43 Fisherman	61 Bell-Hop	Hobo
8 Chinmey Sweep	26 Limburger Cheese Maker	44 Roofer	62 Fireman	Indian
9 Pig Sticker	27 Diary Maid	45 Rabbit Breeder	63 Beautician	Merry Man (arrow in hat)
10 Banker	28 Snake Charmer	46 Bricklayer	64 Ham Actor	Native (fruit basket hat)
11 Dog Catcher	29 Tea-Taster	47 Dog Trainer	65 Purse Snatcher	Pharoah
12 Seamstress	30 Manicurist	48 Ballet Dancer	66 Bulb Snatcher	Pirate
13 Pretzel Bender	31 Undertaker	49 Turtle Painter	67 Private Eye	Sherlock Holmes
14 Spy	32 Beachcomber	50 Pickle Packer	68 Ghost Writer	Singing Girl
15 Baby Sitter	33 Wine-Taster	51 Chef	69 Moon Shiner	Viking
16 Hog Caller	34 Tree Surgeon	52 Chicken Plucker	70 Head Shrinker (Psychiatrist)	
17 Pea Picker	35 Housewife	53 Bee Keeper	71 Card-Shark	
18 Cat Breeder	36 Beat Poet	54 Sewer Digger	72 Nurse	

WHEELS, WINGS AND THINGS (54)

For a set with 54 titles, cards from "Wheels, Wings and Things" are sure hard to come by. Each card formed the entire back of a Pom Poms candy box and dotted lines on either side showed the owner where to cut the box to remove the card. The pictures are color or artwork scenes and each is numbered and described below. There is no writing on the back of the cards and a small advertising block for the set is printed on the front of the box. It is not known if the series also appeared on boxes of "Junior Mints." Note: cards cut from boxes cannot be graded mint. No set price is given because all 54 titles have not been confirmed to exist.

ITEM	MINT	EX
Card	--	1.00
Box	8.00	6.00

WHERE'S WALDO? (128)

What an appropriate name for this set! Mattel, the manufacturer, has in a short time acquired a dismal reputation among collectors for producing large sets that are very expensive to complete. Take their "Barbie" cards, for example: two series of 300 cards each that sorted miserably and are of questionable future interest to most card collectors. "Where's Waldo?" also sorts badly and telephoning the company about this has only revealed their indifference to the problem. The set consists of 128 cards which can be assembled into 16 different scenes: the gimmick is to spot Waldo in amongst all the other characters and details. Mattel used blue poly bag fin packs (crimped edges up and down) to distribute the cards and the wrapper bears the explanation "Randomly Packed." Too random, in fact, for us to suggest what a set price might be, so we will only price individual cards. "Where's Waldo?" is really a set of cardboard toys for children, rather than real trading cards, and the manner in which they are being marketed has already led many collectors to answer the question "Where's Waldo?" with a hearty "Who Cares!"

ITEM	MINT	EX
Card	.10	.05
Wrapper	--	.15
Box	--	2.00

WHO AM I? (44)

The initial print run of "Who Am I?"—distributed by Topps in 1967—contained cards of famous people with scratch-off disguises hiding their features and clues overhead. It was later re-issued without those devices, so cards with or without the coating may be graded as mint. Unfortunately for non-sports collectors, this set contains pictures of Ruth (No. 12), Mantle (No. 22), Mays (No. 33), and Koufax (No. 41). The speculative prices that baseball card dealers charge for these cards makes set completion very expensive. Note: prices listed are for non-baseball cards.

ITEM	MINT	EX
Card		
Coating	3.00	2.50
No coating	2.00	1.50
Wrapper	--	35.00
Box	--	150.00

Who Am I?

1 Clue........Nobody Ever Called Me a Liar.
Answer...George Washington
2 Clue........I Fought the Indians Before
Becoming U.S. President.
Answer...Andrew Jackson
3 Clue......In 1823, I Halted Colonization
of North and South America.
Answer...James Monroe
4 Clue......A Vision Convinced Me that I
Could Save the Nation.
Answer...Joan of Arc
5 Clue......I Became Famous for My
Fiddle Playing in Ancient
Rome.
Answer...Nero
6 Clue......I Was the Only U.S. President
Elected Four Times.
Answer...Franklin D. Roosevelt
7 Clue......There Was a Famous Rock n'
Roll Song Written About Me.
Answer...Henry VIII
8 Clue......I Was a Famous Playwright in
the 15th Century.

Answer...William Shakespeare
9 Clue......I Organized the American Red
Cross in the 19th Century.
Answer...Clara Barton
10 Clue......Though Just 5'2" I Stood Tall
as the Emperor of France.
Answer...Napoleon Bonaparte
11 Clue......Piano Playing was My Trade-
mark While in the White
House.
Answer...Harry Truman
12 Clue......I Was Baseball's Original Home
Run Champion.
Answer...Babe Ruth
13 Clue......Everyone Flipped Their Wigs
over a Document I Wrote.
Answer...Thomas Jefferson
14 Clue......I Was a Famous Washington
Hostess in the 19th Century.
Answer...Dolly Madison

15 Clue......I Was Assassinated by My
Most Trusted Friend.
Answer...Julius Caesar
16 Clue......Long John Silver was a Char-
acter in One of My Novels.
Answer...Robert Louis Stevenson
17 Clue......I Declared War on Germany in
1917.
Answer...Woodrow Wilson
18 Clue......I Earned My Nickname by
Refusing to Retreat.
Answer...Stonewall Jackson
19 Clue......I Was a General and Later
President of France.
Answer...Charles DeGaulle
20 Clue......My Father and I Both Served
Our Nation in the White
House.
Answer...John Quincy Adams
21 Clue......A Spanish Queen Financed My
Sailing Trip to the West Indies.
Answer...Christopher Columbus
22 Clue......I Have Many Baseball Awards
on my Mantlepiece.
Answer...Mickey Mantle
23 Clue......Science and Math Became My
Formula for Success.
Answer...Albert Einstein
24 Clue......When I was Told "Go Fly a
Kite" I Did.
Answer...Benjamin Franklin
25 Clue......I Was the President During the
Civil War.
Answer...Abraham Lincoln
26 Clue......In 1000 A.D. my Viking Ship
Reached America.
Answer...Leif Ericson
27 Clue......I Spent Forty Days Alone at
the South Pole.
Answer...Adm. Richard Byrd
28 Clue......I Raided Ships off the
American Coast in the 17th
Century.
Answer...Capt. Kidd

29 Clue......My Brightest Idea Lit Up the
Whole World.
Answer...Thomas A. Edison
30 Clue......President Lincoln Appointed
Me Head of his Army.
Answer...Ulysses S. Grant
31 Clue......I Am the Female Ruler of a
Large Empire.
Answer...Queen Elizabeth II
32 Clue......My Invention Started Bells
Ringing All Over the World.
Answer...Alexander Graham Bell
33 Clue......I Stand as a Giant among Men
in my Sport.
Answer...Willie Mays
34 Clue......I Recognized Panama and
Brought About the Canal.
Answer...Teddy Roosevelt
35 Clue......I Conquered Central Asia in
the 13th Century.
Answer...Genghis Khan
36 Clue......After Fighting Indians I
Looked for New Frontiers Out
West.
Answer...Daniel Boone
37 Clue......I Was a Statesman who Led
Britain through World War II.
Answer...Winston Churchill
38 Clue......A Current Pop Music Group
has my Name.
Answer...Paul Revere
39 Clue......My Parents were Shocked
when I Decided to Become a
Nurse.
Answer...Florence Nightingale
40 Clue......Generally Speaking, I Had a
Military and Political Career.
Answer...Dwight Eisenhower
41 Clue......I Never Hit My Enemies, I'd
Fan Them Instead.
Answer...Sandy Koufax
42 Clue......As First Lady I Supervised
the Refurnishing of the White
House.
Answer...Jackie Kennedy
43 Clue......My Husband is a Famous
World Leader
Answer...Lady Bird Johnson
44 No clue
Answer...Lyndon Johnson

WIERD WORLD OF BASEBALL (40)   2 1/2" X 3 1/2"

Here is another set of baseball cards which has been ignored by the baseball card hobby simply because it has comic artwork on the card fronts. That's a shame, because the card fronts and backs contain a series of questions about baseball which would require a solid knowledge of baseball history to answer. The manufacturer is listed as Funky Sales Corp. and the date of issue as 1976. The set may be better known as "Funky Facts," the trademarked identification which appears on the front of every card, but our title is taken from the display box. The cards were apparently distributed in clear cellophane since no printed, color wrapper has been seen.

1 Who holds the Major League record for being hit by pitches?
2 What active pitcher used hypnotism to end a slump?
3 When did snowballs end a Major League game?
4 Who successfully threw pitches 25 feet high?
5 The language of baseball. Holding the runner on base. Dusting the batter off.
6 What team hired a midget as a pinch hitter?
7 Clues for names and nicknames.
8 Hall of Famers find 'em puzzle.
9 What Major League team was known as "dem bums"?
10 When did players first "get away with" wearing gloves?
11 A fan sat on a flagpole 117 days till what team regained first place?
12 Who was most valuable player in both leagues?
13 What Hall of Fame pitcher started his career as a Kansas Bloomer Girl?
14 What playoff team drenched the base paths to slow the speedy opposition?
15 What was Pasqual's raid?
16 What player was fined $5000 for contempt (of fans)?
17 Who was pitching when Norm Cash came to bat with a piano leg?
18 What Met star ran around the bases backwards?
19 Who invented "hot dogs"?
20 What Hall of Famer had 4 brothers in the Major Leagues?
21 How did shoe polish affect the outcome of the World Series? (1968)
22 Which NBA superstar pitched for the White Sox?
23 What ML player hit pitches while hanging upside down on a trapeze?
24 How did 3 Dodger runners end up on 3rd base?
25 What was the smallest paid attendance at a game?
26 What team hired an "evil eye" to put the whammy on opposing pitchers?
27 Who outran Phllie 3rd baseman, Hans Lobert, around the bases?
28 What did Dodger manager Wil Robinson say when the dropped grapefruit splattered on his head?
29 Which Pirate hurler was charged with walking a batter he never faced?
30 Why did Red's star Ernie Lombardi take a snooze in the 1939 World Series?
31 Who caught the most men trying to steal bases in one game?
32 How was Giant's Mel Ott prevented from winning a home run title?
33 Pitching Grips.
34 In the 1933 W.S. 1st baseman Terry robbed 2 runners of hits. How?
35 Which Boston hurler hit 3 batters in one inning?
36 Who had 3 hits in one inning?
37 Name the 2 great Yankee sluggers who played most of their careers with their legs bandaged?
38 What big leaguer pitched lefty and righty?
39 Nicknames
40 Unnumbered card with title "International Baseball."

ITEM	MINT	EX
Set	10.00	8.00
Card	.25	.20
Box	--	10.00

WILD ANIMALS (25)   1 1/2" X 2 3/4"

It's easy to see how some collectors have mistakenly identified this series of "Wild Animals" as a Nabisco "Sugar Daddy" issue. The cards of this set and those of the "Wildlife Baby Animals" series which follows are, for example, very similar in format and details. Even artist Wayne Trimm, who prepared the paintings and text for "Wild Animals," has performed the very same tasks for several series of Sugar Daddy cards. However, "Wild Animals" was distributed in "Dutch Maid Cookies," a brand of the Federal Sweets & Biscuit Co., in 1968. There are 25 numbered cards in the set and an album to house them could be obtained through the mail for 25¢. A line on the back reads "Series No. 1," but no subsequent issues are known to exist. The cards are about the same size as Sugar Daddy cards on the long axis, but are substantially wider on the shorter plane.

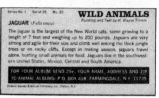

1 Tiger	6 American Elk or Wapiti	11 Cape Buffalo	16 African Elephant	21 Caribou
2 Puma	7 Red Fox	12 Timber Wolf	17 Otter	22 Zebra
3 Indian Mongoose	8 Antelope or Pronghorn	13 Grizzly Bear	18 Wolverine	23 Jaguar
4 Giraffe	9 Rhinoceros	14 Impala	19 Raccoon	24 Moose
5 Blackbuck	10 Cheetah	15 Bison	20 African Lion	25 Black Bear

ITEM	MINT	EX
Set	30.00	22.50
Card	1.00	.75

"WILDLIFE" BABY ANIMALS (50)   1 1/8" X 2 3/4"

The seventh series in the Nabisco nature program, "Wildlife" Baby Animals was distributed in Sugar Daddy and Sugar Mama caramel candy in 1969. The artwork and text for the 50-card set were created by Charles L. Ripper. The card number, series title, card caption, and text are all printed in blue ink on the back. A 24-page album to house the set was available via a mail offer from Nabisco.

ITEM	MINT	EX
Set	35.00	25.00
Card	.60	.45

WILD WHEEL COLLECTOR CARDS (3)   2 1/8" X 2 3/4"

CUT'EM OUT
COLLECT ALL 3!

WILD WHEEL STORIES

The first wheel was used more than 5,000 years ago.
KRAFT began making Wheel shaped Macaroni
and Cheese five years ago!

Some of the first wheels were made of wood. KRAFT
Wild Wheels are made from wheat!

MISSING A WHEEL

Match the wheel
to its vehicle.

Airplane
Dune Buggy
Skateboard

At the time this book went to press (May, 1992), Kraft Macaroni & Cheese Dinner boxes with "Wild Wheels Collector Cards" on the back were still available in grocery stores. Each multi-color artwork card had dotted lines around the perimeter for cutting it away from the package. The three pictures in the set are anthropomorphic versions of different methods of transportation: skateboard, airplane, and dune buggy. As you can see in the illustration, each card is layered over parts of the other two cards in the set. The text beneath each picture is informative and there are other features and games on the package itself (which is another reason to keep the box intact). The cards have no writing on the back and are not numbered. To be graded mint, single cards must be precisely cut along each edge.

ITEM	MINT	EX
Set of complete boxes	2.00	1.50
Set of cards	1.00	.75
Complete box	.65	.50
Card	.35	.25

WILD WONDERS ANIMAL CARDS (9)   2 3/8" X 3 3/4"

Brian Bigelow and Bill Mullins reported this 1991 set of "Wild Wonders Animal Cards" to The Hobby Card Index almost simultaneously. The cards are beautiful multi-color paintings of nine different endangered species and each is accompanied by the appropriate Latin binomial and a short text. Three-card panels, with dotted lines as cutting guides, were printed on the package backs of "Wild Wonders" shortbread cookies boxes. The cards are blank-backed and are not numbered (the numbered checklist on the side panel of the box refers to the animal montage on front, NOT to the cards themselves).

Single cards cannot be graded mint unless they are very carefully and precisely cut and have straight edges.

ITEM	MINT	EX
Sets		
Cards	3.25	2.25
Panels	4.50	3.00
Card	.35	.25

Clip out and collect all 9 WILD WONDERS animal cards!

Hawaiian Monk Seal *(Monachus schauinslandi)*
If you were in Hawaii, you might like to lie on the beach all day — so do Hawaiian monk seals! They soak up sunshine each day, and hunt in the warm waters at night for slow-swimming octopuses and fish.

Black Rhinoceros *(Diceros bicornis)*
Black rhinos love to roll in mud — it keeps them cool on hot days, and keeps flies away. So even though their skin is black, they usually look gray, or brown, or rust-colored, depending on the color of the mud!

African Elephant *(Loxodonta africana)*
Even if he wanted to, a big male elephant from Africa probably couldn't fit in your living room! He stands thirteen feet tall, and weighs up to six tons—the African elephant is the biggest land animal in the world.

African Elephant
Bald Eagle
Bengal Tiger
Black Rhinoceros
Eastern Gray Kangaroo
Giant Panda
Hawaiian Monk Seal
Koala
Mountain Gorilla

WILLOW ALBUM STICKERS (240)

1 15/16" X 2 9/16"

I'm sure that all of you who regularly go to the movies remember the relentless promotional campaign which preceded Willow. According to George Lucas' advertising agency, the film was going to be an epic adventure of Star Wars magnitude. According to box office receipts, however, it achieved nothing more than an equal footing with Ishtar (and at least Ishtar had one very funny scene). None of this stopped Panini from producing a set of 240 album stickers about the film in 1988. To be truthful, the artwork drawn for the album cover, header page, and sticker pages is excellent; the color photography of the movie and its script are no where near as good. Each sticker is numbered and shows a scene, or part of a scene, from the film. The number of white borders on any sticker depends on whether it stands alone in the book or is grouped with other stickers. Collectors could trade stickers (up to 30 at a time) with the company by simply paying a $1.00 handling fee with each exchange. Note: set price includes album.

ITEM	MINT	EX
Set	30.00	21.00
Sticker	.10	.07
Wrapper	--	.25
Album	2.00	1.50

WILLOW MOVIE STICKERS (10)

2" X 3"

Hobbyists who wanted to add these "Willow Movie Stickers" to their collections had to make the ultimate sacrifice: they had to buy a three pound loaf of Velveeta processeed cheese just to get a single sheet bearing two stickers. Considering that each sticker, once pulled from the sheet, only measured 1" X 1-1/2", the ratio of cheese to sticker was wildly disproportionate. Each front-peel sticker bears a color scene from the movie and the two stickers on every sheet share a common caption. The paper on which the stickers rest has a printed back with the set title, text, and a "Collect All 10 Willow Movie Stickers" line. Note: prices are for intact sheets of two stickers. Single (cut) or peeled stickers cannot be graded excellent or mint.

ITEM	MINT	EX
Set of 5 sheets	8.00	5.50
Sticker sheet	1.50	1.00

WILLOW TRADING CARDS (6)

2 1/2" X 5"

Ziploc Sandwich Bags produced a series of six Willow cards as a promotion in 1988. Although the cards are standard width, they are five inches tall and are printed on thin cardboard stock. The fronts bear captioned, color photographs from the film under a very large "Willow" heading. On the back, there are several paragraphs of text describing the subject pictured on the front, plus a line which reads "Collect all 6 Willow Trading Cards." One card was inserted in each box of sandwich bags. The characters seen to date are: Queen Bavmorda, Sorsha, and Willow Ufgood.

ITEM	MINT	EX
Set	7.00	5.00
Card	1.00	.75

WINDOW PAINS (57? & 13?)

2 1/2" X 3 5/16"

The set totals of 57 stickers and 13 cards for "Window Pains" were reported by a collector and have not yet been confirmed. The "see-through" stickers have humorous artwork and wording printed on a clear acetate sheet with an adhesive back. Many of the designs and jokes have appeared in other Fleer sets. The "Sorry You Lost" cards are another format used repeatedly by Fleer; in this set, the large patterned borders are printed in red ink and the message in black.

ITEM	MINT	EX
Sticker	1.25	1.00
Card	.65	.50
Wrapper	--	7.00
Box	--	20.00

WINGS OF FIRE (101)

2 1/2" X 3 1/2"

Panini, the Italian sticker manufacturer, has now branched out into making cards under the "Action" brand name. "Wings of Fire" (Alies de Feu) is a 100-card series now being distributed in Canada which will no doubt make its way across the border into the U.S. The cards are simply designed on front, with no more than a color picture of aircraft in flight, a caption, and the set title on a wing-pin emblem. The backs are headed at top by the very same emblem and basic data about the plane is summarized in both English and French. A 1992 copyright line for Panini and the "Action" logo are located in the bottom corners. Both surfaces are glossy, giving the cards that "plastic" feel which the industry has favored thus far in the 1990's. The actual set total is 101 cards since the checklist card is not numbered. The set is so new that we have listed prices for mint grade only.

ITEM	MINT	EX
Set	12.00	--
Card	.10	--

1 F-14A Tomcat
2 EC-135 Looking Glass
3 A-10 Warthog
4 A-7K Corsair II
5 SR-71 Blackbird
6 C-2 Cod
7 CF-5 Tiger II
8 C-5B Galaxy
9 Snowbirds
10 A-3 Skywarrior
11 F-14 A-Plus Super Tomcat
12 F-21 Kfir
13 E-2C Hawkeye
14 UV-1 Mohawk
15 RC-135V
16 MH-60 Pave Hawk
17 C-130 Hercules Transport
18 C-9 Nightingale
19 A-3 Skywarrior
20 H-3 Sea King
21 F-4C Phantom II
22 F / A-18 Hornet
23 WC-130 Hercules
24 HC-130 Hercules
25 C-141 Starlifter
26 AC-130 Specter
27 P-3C Orion
28 US Customs Service P-3
29 LC-130 Hercules
30 C-130 Hercules
31 TA-4 Skyhawk
32 Canadair CL-215-T
33 F-106 Delta Dart
34 UH-1 Huey
35 KA-3

36 A-7E Corsair II
37 OV-10 Bronco
38 T-38 Talon
39 KC-135R Stratotanker
40 C-22 Transport
41 C-21
42 MH-53E Sea Dragon
43 Ch-53A Sea Stallion
44 AH-1T Cobra
45 UH-1N Huey
46 KA-6D Intruder
47 A-6E Intruder
48 SH-60B Sea Hawk
49 Pioneer
50 EA-6A Prowler
51 EF-111A Raven
52 HU-25A Falcon
53 E-4 "Kneecap"
54 E-6 Tacamo
55 SH-3 Sea King
56 C-12
57 De Havilland Buffalo
58 Blue Angels
59 F-4D Phantom
60 Thunderbirds
61 RF-4B Phantom II
62 F-16B Falcon
63 F-4E Phantom II
64 F-4S Phantom
65 F-16A Falcon
66 F-15 Eagle
67 F / A-18D Hornet

68 TA-4 Skyhawk
69 MC-130E Combat Talon II
70 CH-53E Super Stallion
71 AH-64 Apache
72 UH-60 Black Hawk
73 MH-53J Pave Low
74 OH-6 Cayuse
75 T-33 Thunderbird
76 B-1B Bomber
77 B-52H Stratofortress
78 A-4 Superfox Skyhawk
79 RC-135U
80 F-15E Eagle
81 F-117A Stealth Fighter
82 CF-18 Hornet
83 F-16N Falcon
84 S-3A Viking
85 RF-4C Phantom II
86 F-5E Tiger II
87 F-111F Aardvark
88 FB-111 Aardvark
89 A-4M Skyhawk
90 AV-88 Harrier II
91 HH-65 Dolphin
92 EA-6B Prowler
93 AH-1W Cobra
94 CH-46 Sea Knight
95 F / A-18 Hornet

96 F-4G Wild Weasel
97 KC-130T Hercules
98 KC-10 Extender
99 E-3A Sentry
100 EC-130E Hercules

WINGS OF GOLD (19)

2 1/2" X 3 1/2"

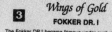

Wings of Gold

FOKKER DR. I

The Fokker DR.I became famous under such pilots as Werner Voss and Manfred Von Richthofen (The Red Baron). Able to outrun and outclimb almost any allied fighter of its time, the tri-wing Fokker could rarely be shaken off except with a high speed dive. The Red Baron scored a total of 80 victories with his final 21 in a Fokker DR.I until he was shot down by Canadian pilot A. R. Brown in the battle which cost the Baron his life.

FOKKER DR.I

| Span | Length | Height | Weight | Max. MPH |
| 23'7¾" | 18'11½" | 9'8¼" | 1,289 | 103 |

Eagle Trading Card Co.© 1991 Series I

A creation of the Eagle Trading Card Company, "Wings of Gold" is a nostalgic look at some of best fighting aircraft of the first and second World Wars. Cards 1-4 show WWI aircraft, while 5-18 depict WWII types. The fronts of the cards have multi-color flight or action scenes surrounded by black borders. All other information and details - set title, card caption, text, and stats - are printed on the card backs. The 19th card is an un-numbered header/checklist. The series was distributed in 1991 and is sold only in complete sets, with a paper "Certificate of Authenticity" included. It is marked "Series I," but as of this date no subsequent sets have been reported. Note: packaged in clear hard-plastic cases.

1 Nieuport XI
2 Spad
3 Fokker DR.1
4 Sopwith Camel
5 Supermarine Spitfire
6 A 6M2 Zero-Sen
7 F6F Hellcat
8 P-40 Warhawk (Tomahawk)
9 Stuka JU 87
10 P-47 Thunderbolt
11 BF-109 Messerschmitt
12 P-38 Lightning
13 F-4U Corsair
14 F4F-4 Wildcat
15 Nakajima KI-43
16 Yakovlev Yak-9
17 B-24 Liberator
18 B-17 Flying Fortress
Series 1 Checklist

ITEM	MINT	EX
Set	7.00	--

WISECRACKERS (72)

2 1/2" X 3 1/2"

DON'T THINK IT HASN'T
BEEN PLEASANT
TO MEET YOU

BECAUSE IT HASN'T

The person who designed "Wise-crackers" must have had a very tight budget! The cards are nothing more than cardboard blanks with a funny expression printed on the front in black ink. Many of the jokes which appear here also show up in a number of Topps sets. Wise-crackers was reportedly issued by Rosan and the anonymous format is evidence that Rosan, not Topps, was the copycat. Whether intentional or not, an identical card—"Mistakes Will Happen"—was printed for Nos. 34 and 70.

ITEM	MINT	EX
Set	27.50	20.00
Card	.35	.25

1 A Calling Card for Narrow Minded Kids
2 Don't Think It Hasn't Been Pleasant to Meet You (Because It Hasn't)
3 Don't Go Away Mad (Just Go Away)
4 Do It Tomorrow (You've Made Enough Mistakes Today)
5 You Should Be Nice to Me (Good Men Are Hard to Find)
6 Knowinguisan Experience
7 God Made Man and Rested (God Made Heaven & Earth and Rested—Then God Made Women—Since Then No One Has Rested)
8 How to Save On Taxes (Don't Work!!)
9 I Am Somewhat of a Liar Myself, But Go On With Your Story (I'm Listening)
10 Pardon Me (But May I Buy My Introduction back?)
11 Quiet! (Ulcers At Work)
12 You Can't Fight City Hall
13 Is It Tax Deductible?
14 Stick With Me (And You'll Wind Up Wearing Stripes)
15 My Wife Doesn't Understand Me
16 Think or Thwim
17 I May Look Busy...But I'm Only Confused
18 I'm Not At All Well
19 You Don't Have to Hunt to Shoot the Bull
20 If You Ever Need a Friend (Buy a Dog)
21 Don't Fwown—Smile
22 How should I Know? (I Only Work Here)
23 I Hate My Boss
24 Don't Write—Send Money
25 What's In It For Me?
26 Don't Just Do Something (Stand There)
27 Price Is No Object (As Long As It's Cheap)

28 Even Your Best Friends Won't Tell You
29 You Should Live So Long
30 My Intentions Are Strictly Dishonor-able
31 I'm Too Light for Heavy Work and Too Heavy for Light Work
32 My Card
33 I Was Born This Way—What's Your Excuse?
34 Mistakes Will Happen (But Must You Give Them So Much Help?)
35 My Best Is Never Too Good—Don't Bring Out the Worst In Me.
36 Time Wound All Heels!
37 Who Died and Left You Boss?
38 I Need a Vacation
39 This Work Is Interfering with Our Coffee Break
40 Hereby I Publicly Acknowledge Every-thing I Owe, I Owe Because of My Wife
41 Stop Smiling (Don't You Have Enough Work to Do?)
42 This Is a Non-profit Organization (We Don't Plan It That Way but It Is!!)
43 Be Reasonable...Do It My Way
45 What? (You Here Again—Another Half Hour Shot to...!)
46 Think! (Maybe We Can Dodge This Work)
47 If You Have a Minute to Spare (Tell Me All You Know)
48 Here Lies My Boss (Here Let Him Be—Now He's at Rest—and So Am I)
49 When I Am Right No One Remembers (When I Am Wrong No One Forgets)
50 Somebody Goofed ["F" Inverted]
51 Use Your Head (It's the Little Things That Count)
52 Let's Get Down to Business...unless You Have Another Good Story

53 Plan Ahead
54 Flattery Will Get You Somewhere (Start Talking)
55 Money Isn't Everything (But It's Away Ahead of Whatever Is in Second Place)
56 Dog Tired at Night? (Maybe You've Been Growling too Much during the Day)
57 Smile! Later Today You Won't Feel Like It
58 I Spend 8 Hours a Day Here (Do You Expect Me to Work too?)
59 What's on Your Mind (If You Will Forgive the Overstatement)
60 Looking for Someone with a Little Authority? I Have as Little as Anyone
61 Anything Worth While Is Worth Doing for Money
62 I'd Like to Compliment You on Your Work. When Will You Start?
63 I'm Fairly Intelligent Myself (but I Have a Lot of Stupid Help)
64 You're Certainly Trying (Very Trying)
65 How to Succeed in Business (Cheat)
66 All the Things I Really Like to Do Are Either Immoral, Illegal, or Fattening—Alexander Woolcott
67 There Was a Cannibal Without Any Hates—He Just Stayed in His Hut—Eating His Dates
68 As an Outsider (What Do You Think of the Human Race)
69 Some Girls Are like a Cold (Easy to Catch—Hard to Get Rid Of)
70 Mistakes Will Happen (But Must You Give Them So Much Help)
71 Why Be Difficult (When with Just a Little More Effort—You Can Be Impossible)
72 Wise Is the Fool Who Knows...Enough to Keep His Mouth Shut

WISE GUY BUTTONS (24)

2" DIAMETER

It is believed that "Wise Guy Buttons" were distributed by Topps in 1965. Each tin button measures 2" in diameter and has the word "Japan" printed on the inside rim. The buttons are not numbered and they were marketed in gumless paper packets with a pull-open flap on back. This packet is blue with a large yellow circle holding the red-print title and price.

ITEM	MINT	EX
Set	140.00	110.00
Button	5.00	4.00
Wrapper	--	25.00
Box	--	125.00

Double Your Pleasure — Kiss Me Twice
Down With Everything
Down With Homework
Fight Physical Fitness
Fink University
Get Off My Back
Handle With Care!
Have No Fear — I Am Here

I Am The Greatest
I Found My Ideal — Me
I Love Me
I Was Born This Way — What's Your Excuse?
Keep Off
Kiss Me, You Fool!
Offishal Speling Champ

Same To You, Buster!
Scram
Shhh!! You'll Wake Me Up
Stamp Out Good Sportsmanship
Stamp Out Report Cards
Support Sloppiness
Think You Got Troubles?
Wanna Fat Lip?
When You Say That — Smile

WISE TIES (12)

One of the strangest Topps issues of all time! This series of 12 ties (manufactured in Hong Kong) was sold in large (gumless) paper envelopes for 10 cents each. The ties are made of thin plastic felt and have a rolled elastic neck strap attached to the knot. The measurements in the heading refer to the distance between the longest and wid-

3 3/4" X 9 1/2"

est points. Each artwork picture is multi-colored and is set on a solid-color background (some designs seen with two different background colors).

ITEM	MINT	EX
Set	215.00	170.00
Tie	15.00	12.00
Wrapper	--	75.00
Box	--	150.00

Don't Bug Me
Genuine Hand Painted Tie
Get Lost
Homework Destroys Brain
I Hate School
I Love You
Kiss Me
Pizza Stained Tie
Shut Up!
What'cha Lookin' At
You Make Me Sick!
You Turn Me On

WIZARD OF OZ (110)

There has been a glut of trading cards based on specific movies in recent times, but very few films of Hollywood's Golden Age

have been captured on cardboard. That is why Pacific Trading Card's "Wizard of Oz" series, issued in 1990, is such a

2 1/2" X 3 1/2"

welcome addition to our hobby. Collectors will find the cards divided into three different front formats: color scenes (94), black and white scenes (12), and artwork portraits (4). Regardless of type, each card has the series title and four miniature head shots of Dorothy and her companions on the front. The backs are mostly dialogue or song lyrics, although there are some exceptions (prologue, cast identification, etc.). There is a tall but narrow scene panel to the left of the text rectangle on every card:

Wizard of Oz

on cards with color fronts, this is a yellow-cast picture of Dorothy and her pals on the yellow brick road approaching Oz; on the twelve black and white cards, this panel is a scary blue and it depicts the Wicked Witch of the West gazing into her crystal ball. Pacific marketed the series in two ways: in gumless wax packs and as a boxed collector's edition.

ITEM	MINT	EX
Set	11.00	7.50
Card	.10	.07
Wrapper	--	.25
Display box	--	2.00
Collector's box	1.00	.75

1 Introduction
2 Dorothy and Toto Escape Miss Gulch
3 The Farm House
4 Your Head Ain't Made of Straw
5 Dorothy Falls Into the Pig Pen
6 Mrs. Gale Feeds the Hired Hands
7 A Place Far, Far Away
8 Somewhere Over The Rainbow
9 Miss Gulch Bicycles to the Farm
10 Destroy That Dog!
11 Toto Escapes from the Basket
12 The Professor's Crystal Ball
13 The Professor Speaks!
14 I've Got to Go Home Right Away
15 It's a Twister
16 Dorothy and Toto Inside the Cyclone
17 We're Not in Kansas Anymore
18 Munchkinland
19 I'm Not a Witch At All
20 Kansas is the Name of the Star
21 The House Began to Pitch
22 Ding Dong, The Witch is Dead
23 The Wicked Old Witch is Dead
24 We Welcome You to Munchkinland
25 The Lollypop Guild
26 The Ruby Slippers
27 The Ruby Slippers Are on Dorothy's Feet
28 The Wizard of Oz?
29 The Yellow Brick Road
30 Follow the Yellow Brick Road
31 Dorothy Meets the Scarecrow
32 I Haven't Got a Brain
33 I Can't Even Scare a Crow
34 Do? Why, If I had a Brain I Could...
35 Where's Kansas
36 Doroth and Scarecrow Off to Oz
37 Off To See The Wizard
38 Dorothy and the Apple Trees
39 The Tin Man
40 I've Held that Ax Up for Ages
41 No Heart?
42 If I Only Had a Heart
43 Come With Us and Ask the Wizard for a Heart
44 The Wicked Witch Appears
45 To Oz!
46 Lions and Tigers and Bears!
47 They Meet the Lion

48 The Cowardly Lion
49 I'm Afraid of 'Em
50 The Wizard Will Give You Some Courage
51 If I Only Had the Nerve
52 Poppies! Poppies! Poppies Will Put Them to Sleep
53 The Emerald City
54 This Is a Spell
55 The Good Witch Breaks the Spell
56 To Emerald City
57 The Gates of the Emerald City
58 Well Bust My Buttons!
59 Horse of a Different Color
60 The Merry Old Land of Oz
61 That Certain Air of Savoir-Faire
62 Surrender Dorothy
63 Nobody Can See the Great Oz!
64 But She's Dorothy
65 King of the Forest
66 Imposterous!
67 Courage!
68 I Had an Aunt Em Myself
69 I'm Still Scared
70 The Great Power of Oz
71 I Mean ... Your Wizardry!
72 Bring Me Her Broomstick!
73 The Haunted Forest
74 The Winged Monkeys
75 They Tore My Legs Off!
76 In the Witch's Castle
77 Run, Toto, Run!
78 I'm Frightened, Auntie Em
79 Dorothy's In That Awful Place
80 Rescue Dorothy!
81 In the Wicked Witch's Castle
82 The Escape From the Witch's Castle
83 Ring Around the Rosy
84 The Wicked Witch is Dead!
85 They Return to Oz
86 The Wizard is Exposed
87 I'm a Humbug!

88 I'm Just a Very Bad Wizard
89 I've Got a Brain
90 A Member of the Legion of Courage
91 Look! It Ticks!
92 Dorothy Next!
93 Balloon Trip
94 Toto Jumps From the Balloon Basket
95 The Good Witch Glinda Helps
96 What Have You Learned?
97 Toto Too!
98 Goodbye. I'll Miss You
99 There's No Place Like Home
100 Oh, Auntie Em, It's You!
101 She's Got Quite a Bump
102 But It Wasn't a Dream!
103 Oh, But Anyway, Toto, We're Home
104 The Wizard of Oz...
105 A little girl ...
106 Dorothy Gale's 'Wiz Quiz
107 Cowardly Lion 'Wiz Quiz
108 The Tin Woodman 'Wiz Quiz
109 The Scarecrow 'Wiz Quiz
110 The Wizard of Oz - The Cast

WNEW SUPERSTARS (5K)

GENE
'End-over-end'
KLAVAN

Ht: 6'4" Wt: 215
Time Slot: 5:20-10 AM
School: Johns Hopkins Univ.
Home: Long Island

GENE IS ALWAYS FIRST
ONE UP FOR THE GAME.

Captain of the WNEW Superstars, Klavan first saw action with his home-town club, the Baltimore "Ozones". A WNEW starter for 20 years, zany Gene shared the turf with veteran QB Dee Finch who retired in '68. Since then, Klavan has run amuck alone as an un-predictable triple threat. Known for his dazzling end-over-end passing style, he also confuses the opposition by assum-ing a variety of identities, such as Trevor Traffic and Close Shave.

1 WNEW SUPERSTARS

2 1/2" X 3 1/2"

Help! Someone from New York, please tell us when this deejay set from WNEW was issued and how many cards there are in the set (the highest we have seen is #5). The cards have col-or photos on front and each deejay is dressed in a sports uniform. His "posi-tion" and radio show times are printed below the set title. The backs give vital statistics and have promotional text about each subject. The cards are numbered and they are printed on thin cardboard stock. The few specimens we have encountered at card shows sell in the $1.50-2.00 range (excellent grade.).

WOODY WOODPECKER TATTOOS (?)

That Woody Woodpecker is a fickle guy! When collectors saw him first, he was on a tattoo series issued by Topps Gum in 1959. Only nine years later, Woody was the basis for another tattoo series, but this time the producer was Fleer. The wrapper for the set is white with yellow blocks and red and black accents. The print running along the edges identifies Fleer as the manufacturer, Walter Lantz as the licensor, and 1968 as the year in which the license was granted (and in which the set, presumably, was issued).

Strange as it may seem, the tattoo is bigger than the wrapper, but that's because it was folded over long-ways and draped around the gum. Although this Fleer issue is more recent than the Topps series, it is far more difficult to find, resulting in a higher price. Note: since both wrapper and tattoos were folded, prices are listed for excellent grade only.

ITEM	MINT	EX
Wrapper	--	25.00
Tattoo	--	10.00

WORLD OF STAMPS

STAMP ALBUM ORDER FORM

Please send me the WORLDWIDE STAMP ALBUM plus 25 Assorted Stamps, for which I enclose 25c with this card.

Name

Address

City   Zone   State
Mail Card and money to:
STAMPS, Donruss Co., Memphis 2, Tenn.

WRAPPER ONLY

Donruss dabbled in the stamp hobby with this interesting approach: stamps sold in gum packs. Each five-cent package contained a small glassine envelope of cancelled stamps from around the world, plus one stick of gum. A stamp album order form printed on a 2 1/2" X 3 1/2" card was the package "stiffener." We list the set here for the benefit of wrapper collectors.

ITEM	MINT	EX
Wrapper	--	5.00
Box	--	7.00

WORLD WAR II (110)

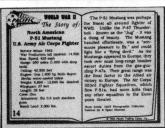

The fiftieth anniversary of the attack on Pearl Harbor and the entry of the United States into World War II prompted Pacific Trading Cards to issue this 110-card series in early 1992. The set is compartmentalized into four basic topics: Allied and enemy aircraft (1-16); statesmen, military leaders, and heroes (17-55); war scenes of Europe, the Pacific, and the Home Front (56-94); and propaganda and patriotic posters (95-110). Although Pacific's "Super Hi-Gloss" cards have some very nice format designs and graphics, the series falls short of being a classic treatment of World War II. For one thing, many of the candid photos on cards 17-94 are much too dark and there aren't enough battle scenes to give the reader any perspective of the scope of the war. Moreover, the numerical sequence of the cards seems out of synch with the chronological events of the war which, along with one major spelling error we spotted, indicates a lack of editorial overview. Finally, the nicest cards in the set - the propaganda and patriotic posters on #'s 95-110 - may appear in another set about to be released by a competitor. Still in all, "World War II," which Pacific made available in wax packs plus a Collector Set, is moderately priced and there is a Hitler card in the set (Mussolini, JFK, and Audie Murphy too!). Note: no values given for excellent grade since most cards encountered at this point in time should be mint.

ITEM	MINT	EX
Set	10.00	--
Card	.10	--
Wrapper	--	.10
Display box	--	2.00
Collector Set box	--	.50

World War II

1 PBY Catalina
2 Messerschmitt ME. 109
3 Supermarine Spitfire
4 C-47 Dakota
5 P-40 Warhawk
6 B-17 Flying Fortress
7 A6M Zero
8 Focke-Wulf FW. 190
9 B-26 Marauder
10 B-25 Mitchell
11 B-24 Liberator
12 P-38 Lightning
13 TBF Avenger
14 P-51 Mustang
15 B-29 Superfortress
16 F6F Hellcat
17 Franklin D. Roosevelt
18 Harry S. Truman
19 Winston S. Churchill
20 Adolf Hitler
21 Benito Mussolini
22 Marshall Joseph Stalin
23 General Hideki Tojo
24 Kichisabura Nomura
25 General George C. Marshall
26 Gen. Dwight D. Eisenhower
27 General Omar Bradley
28 General Courtney Hodges
29 General George S. Patton
30 General Curtis LeMay
31 General Henry Arnold
32 General Mark Clark
33 General Mathew Ridgeway
34 Maj. Gen. James M. Gavin
35 Maj. Gen. Maxwell Taylor
36 Maj. Gen. Claire L. Chennault
37 Lt. Gen. James Doolittle
38 Lt. Gen. Jonathan Wainwright
39 Lt. Gen. Holland Smith
40 Lt. Gen. Alexander Vandegrift
41 General Douglas MacArthur
42 General Joseph Stillwell
43 Vice Admiral Raymond Spruance
44 Admiral Chester W. Nimitz
45 Fleet Admiral Ernest J. King
46 Admiral William Halsey
47 Admiral Frank J. Fletcher
48 Colonel Benjamin O. Davis
49 The Sullivan Brothers
50 Lt. John F. Kennedy
51 2nd Lt. Audie Murphy
52 Colonel Paul Tibbets

53 Col. Oveta C. Hobby
54 Admiral Isoroku Yamamoto
55 Kamikaze Pilot
56 The Artic Convoy Battles
57 The Battle for the Atlantic
58 Bombers Over Germany
59 Operation Torch
60 The Invasion of Sicily
61 The Italian Campaign
62 D-Day: Assault on Nazi Europe
63 The Normandy Breakout
64 The Battle of the Bulge
65 Operation Market Garden
66 Fighting in Germany
67 After the Battle
68 On Fire and Sinking
69 Along the March of Death
70 Doolittle Raid on Tokyo
71 USS Lexington at Coral Sea
72 Crash Landing
73 Japanese Cruiser Mikuma Burns at Midway
74 American Tanks on Guadalcanal
75 USS Wasp Explodes at Guadalcanal
76 Mopping Up on Bougainville
77 Returning from the Attack
78 Marines Head for the Beaches
79 Kamikazes Go After the Carriers
80 Carriers on the Offensive
81 Flag Raising on Iwo Jima
82 "I Have Returned"

83 The Battle for Wana Ridge
84 The Japanese Surrender
85 USS Washington Waiting for Action
86 The "Big E" is Hit
87 Supplying the Allies
88 The Home Front
89 Defending the Hornet
90 The Silent Service
91 The American Fighting Spirit
92 The Real Cost of War
93 War Factory Workers
94 M4 "Sherman" Medium Tank
95 They're Fighting!
96 ... and WE talk about sacrifice
97 Stop Him!
98 Man the Guns
99 Remember Dec. 7th!
100 We Can Do It
101 A Careless Word...
102 I Want You
103 Keep This Horror From Your Home
104 This Is Your Scrap!
105 Do With Less-
106 Buy War Bonds
107 Stop This Grab
108 They're Watching Us ... Plenty!
109 Loose Lips Might Sink Ships
110 For Your Country's Sake Today -

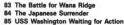

WORLD WAR II PROPAGANDA (1) (15) (120)   2 1/2" X 3 1/2"

The Second World War probably seems like ancient history to most modern-day collectors, especially after the technological blitz we witnessed in the Persian Gulf. Half a century has passed since America entered the conflict and even now we tend to forget that some of the nations of Europe and Asia had been fighting for years before December 8, 1941. The scope and the harsh realities of this global conflict have only occasionally been properly recorded on cards, in sets such as "Horrors of War," "War Gum," and "Battle." We've waited a long time for a World War II set of major significance to arrive and it finally has: "World War II Propaganda" by Tuff Stuff.

To enjoy this set, however, you will first have to endure the manufacturer's own marketing propaganda: "When the Propaganda set becomes available, demand will spread through the hobby like wildfire," for example.

Trying to create speculation and relentlessly reminding us that two elements of the Propaganda set are "limited" - all that is promotional claptrap designed to produce advance sales. The truth is, these cards will sell themselves, not only because of their "unique designs" and "startling messages," but more importantly because they convey the experience of global war in a compelling fashion. This isn't the first war poster set - there have been others - but it is the best we've ever seen.

The "Propaganda Series" contains three elements. The first of these is an 8-1/2" X 11" advertising card - sort of a giant "header card" or lobby card for the set - which has the famous "Skull" poster on one side and Tuff Stuff propaganda on the other. It is a cousin, so to speak, of the Johnny Clem advertising card pictured elsewhere in this book, and the print run was "limited" to "less than 5,500." The

World War II Propaganda

DIAMOND EDITION CHECKLIST

Adolf Hitler ist der Sieg!
[Allied hands breaking apart the Swastika]
American Relief for Holland
Ecco il Nemico
Every Canadian Must Fight
Fuori i Tedeschi
Get a War Job!
Greece Fights On
India Needs YOU
The Downfall of the Dictators is Assured
The Fighting Filipinos
To Have and To Hold!
[Unity]
We Will Destroy the [Nazi] Cross
What Do YOU Say, America?

second component of the series is a 15-card "Diamond Edition" of standard-size cards showing propaganda posters which are "international favorites" (by whose standards, we wonder?). Unlike the regular series cards, these have wide gold borders and production was limited to "less than 55,000 sets." Finally, there is a regular issue of 125 cards which, although advertised for a November, 1991 release, had yet to be distributed by the time this book went to press.

Regular issue cards have white borders surrounding the front pictures (see illustration of uncut sheet) but we have no other details at this time.

VALUES: since the "Propaganda Series" was not yet in distribution when this book went to press, we can only suggest the following values, which are based on the performance of previous Tuff Stuff sets: "Skull" advertising card ... $8-$10; "Diamond Edition" ... $7.00; "Regular Set" ... $10-$12.50.

One of the newest sets from Impel, "X-Men," made its debut in mid-February 1992. To describe the series, we have assembled the following excerpts from Impel's press releases: "A clandestine group of Good Mutants, the X-Men were born with unique abilities that give them superhuman powers. Their mission is to save mankind from the threat of Evil Mutants led by the malevolent Magneto. Jim Lee, the ever-popular X-Men artist, has created all new art for this premiere edition of X-Men trading cards. The 100-card set includes innovative categories, new action holograms, and the introduction of a brand new character. The categories include: Super Heroes (40 cards); Villains (30 cards); Teams (10 cards); Allies (5 cards); Ex-X-Men (5 cards); Action Holograms (5 cards); The Danger Room (a 9-card picture puzzle); and a checklist card. Card backs include a Cerebro Scan which provides vital statistics and power ratings of the comic book characters, as well as background information and a fascinating 'X-tra Fact.' As an industry first, five specially-designed, limited edition gold foil holograms will be randomly inserted in the six-card X-Men Trading Card packs. Artist Jim Lee signed 2000 autographed cards which will also be randomly inserted into X-Men packs."

Values: Since the X-Men series had not been released before we went to press, the following values are suggested until the market is established for these cards. Note: holograms and autographed cards are not part of the regular set. Set ... $12 (mint); Card ... 10¢ (mint); Wrapper ... 10¢; Display box ... $2.

1 Beast	39 Maverick	
2 Wolverine	40 Cerise	
3 Havok	41 Magneto	
4 Iceman	42 Mr. Sinister	
5 Phoenix	43 Deadpool	
6 Nightcrawler	44 Proteus	
7 Cannonball	45 Mojo 2	
8 Wolfsbane	46 Juggernaut	
9 Siryn	47 Sentinels	
10 Lockheed	48 Gideon	
11 Professor X	49 Masque	
12 Psylocke	50 Shiva	77 Mutant Liberation Front
13 Domino	51 Apocalypse	78 Brotherhood of Evil Mutants
14 Storm	52 Sabretooth	79 Upstarts
15 Meggan	53 Mojo	80 Technet
16 Feral	54 Caliban	81 Sunspot
17 Cyclops	55 Gatecrasher	82 Dark Phoenix
18 Gambit	56 Brood	83 Longshot
19 Cable	57 Blob	84 Magik
20 Archangel	58 Stryfe	85 Dazzler
21 Banshee	59 Warwolves	86 Starjammers
22 Shadowcat	60 Omega Red	87 Imperial Guard
23 Kylun	61 Black Tom	88 Lilandra
24 Jean Grey	62 Mystique	89 Weird Happenings Organization
25 Colossus	63 Sauron	90 Roma
26 Warpath	64 Saturnyne	91 Danger Room
27 Polaris	65 Toad	92 Danger Room
28 Boom Boom	66 Shadow King	93 Danger Room
29 Jubilee	67 White Queen	94 Danger Room
30 Shatterstar	68 Mastermind	95 Danger Room
31 Strong Guy	69 Deathbird	96 Danger Room
32 Captain Britain	70 Lady Deathstrike	97 Danger Room
33 Forge	71 X-Men "Gold"	98 Danger Room
34 Madrox	72 X-Men "Blue"	99 Danger Room
35 Quicksilver	73 X-Factor	100 Checklist
36 Rogue	74 X-Force	
37 Widget	75 Excalibur	
38 Bishop	76 Hellfire Club	

M.C. HAMMER

The original idea at Pro Set was to include rap artists in the "SuperStars MusiCards" Series 1, but at the last moment they were spun off into a separate set. Part of the reasoning behind this decision was the realization that rap is a specialized form of musical expression of limited interest to "pop" music fans. A more compelling motivation, however, was the furor over rap lyrics caused by Public Enemy and groups making names for themselves with obscene language. The "Yo! MTV Raps" series turned out to be a series of the good, the bad, and the ugly in rap music, running the gamut from Hammer to Vanilla Ice to Public Enemy. The cards have a "Laverne" (after the character performed by Cher) sense of fashion and color, with color photos on the front and text on the back. Series 1 cards are numbered 1-100 (in white print) on the back next to the small color photos. They were issued in green poly bag packages containing ten cards each during 1991. Pro Set apparently was satisfied with sales, since the company announced Series 2 of Yo! MTV Rap cards (101-150) in its "Pro Set Gazette" of February, 1992. The new series has a few holdovers from Series 1 ranks, but is mainly composed of new faces.

FAB FIVE FREDDY

TED DEMME

SERIES 1

1 Bell Biv DeVoe	66 RUN-DMC
2 Bell Biv DeVoe	67 RUN-DMC
3 Bell Biv DeVoe	68 RUN-DMC
4 Bell Biv DeVoe	69 RUN-DMC
5 Big Daddy Kane	70 Paris
6 Big Daddy Kane	71 Slick Rick
7 Big Daddy Kane	72 Slick Rick
8 Big Daddy Kane	73 Stetsasonic
9 Biz Markie	74 Super Lover Cee &
10 Boogie Down	Casanova Rud
Productions	75 Super Lover Cee &
11 Boogie Down	Casanova Rud
Productions	76 Ted Demme
12 Chuck D.	77 Terminator X
13 De La Soul	78 3rd Bass
14 De La Soul	79 3rd Bass
15 Digital Underground	80 Three Times Dope
16 Digital Underground	81 Three Times Dope
17 Digital Underground	82 Tone Loc
18 Digital Underground	83 Tone Loc
19 Dr. Dre & Ed Lover	84 Tone Loc
20 Dr. Dre & Ed Lover	85 Tone Loc
21 Dr. Dre & Ed Lover	86 Vanilla Ice
22 Dr. Dre & Ed Lover	87 Vanilla Ice
23 EPMD	88 Vanilla Ice
24 EPMD	89 Vanilla Ice
25 EPMD	90 Vanilla Ice
26 EPMD	91 Vanilla Ice
27 Eric B. & Rakim	92 Vanilla Ice
28 Eric B. & Rakim	93 Vanilla Ice
29 Eric B. & Rakim	94 Whodini
30 Eric B. & Rakim	95 Young Black
31 Eric B. & Rakim	Teenagers
32 Fab 5 Freddy	96 Young Black
33 Fab 5 Freddy	Teenagers
34 Fab 5 Freddy	97 Young MC
35 Fab 5 Freddy	98 Young MC
36 Flavor Flav	99 Young MC
37 Heavy D. & The Boyz	100 Young MC
38 Heavy D. & The Boyz	
39 Heavy D. & The Boyz	
40 Heavy D. & The Boyz	
41 Kool Moe Dee	
42 Kool Moe Dee	
43 KRS-1	
44 L.L. Cool J	
45 L.L. Cool J	
46 L.L. Cool J	
47 L.L. Cool J	
48 L.L. Cool J	
49 L.L. Cool J	
50 L.L. Cool J	
51 M.C. Hammer	
52 M.C. Hammer	
53 M.C. Hammer	
54 M.C. Hammer	
55 M.C. Hammer	
56 M.C. Hammer	
57 M.C. Hammer	
58 M.C. Hammer	
59 Public Enemy	
60 Public Enemy	
61 Public Enemy	
62 Public Enemy	
63 Public Enemy	
64 Public Enemy	
65 Public Enemy	

ITEM	MINT	EX
Sets		
Series 1	10.00	--
Series 2	5.00	--
Series 1 wrapper	--	.10
Series 1 box	--	2.00

BELL BIV DEVOE

SERIES 2

101 A Tribe Called Quest	126 Kool Moe Dee	140 Rappin' Is Fundamental
102 The Beastie Boys	127 L.A. Posse	141 Slick Rick
103 The Beastie Boys	128 L.A. Posse	142 Slick Rick
104 Black Sheep	129 Leaders Of The New School	143 T-Money
105 Black Sheep	130 Leaders Of The New School	144 The Afros
106 Brand Nubian	131 Main Source	145 The Afros
107 Brand Nubian	132 Main Source	146 3rd Bass
108 BWP	133 Nikki D	147 3rd Bass
109 BWP	134 Nikki D	148 Tony D
110 Craig G	135 Oaktown's 3.5.7	149 Tony D
111 Daddy-O	136 Oaktown's 3.5.7	150 YO! Posse
112 Daddy-O	137 Queen Latifah	
113 Def Jef	138 Queen Latifah	
114 Def Jef	139 Queen Latifah	
115 Doctor Dre and Ed Lover		
116 Doctor Dre and Ed Lover		
117 Doctor Dre and Ed Lover		
118 Doctor Dre and Ed Lover		
119 Ed O.G. & Da Bulldogs		
120 Ed O.G. & Da Bulldogs		
121 Fab 5 Freddy		
122 Heavy D. & The Boyz		
123 Kid Capri		
124 KMD		
125 KMD		

YOU'LL DIE LAUGHING - 1973 (128)   2 1/2" X 3 1/2"

This is the second set, in terms of sequence, to become known to collectors as "You'll Die Laughing" from the title of the monster-humor feature on the back of the card. The obverse picture is black and white and is captioned in the wide white border underneath. The backs are purple on gray and bear the T.C.G. initials and a credit line for American International Pictures. The card number is located in a circle in the upper-left corner on the back. The set was distributed by Topps in 1973. The wrapper is entitled "Creature Feature" and this name does appear on the card reverse in small print; however, most collectors refer to the set by the large title at top.

COME ON IN ! THE WATER'S FINE !

ITEM	MINT	EX
Set	75.00	55.00
Cards		
1-60	.35	.25
61-128	.65	.50
Wrapper	--	4.00
Box	--	35.00

1 Would Somebody Tell Me a Scary Story?
2 Please... Not on Our First Date!
3 The Laundry Man Is Here for the Sheets, Dear!
4 I Think My Deodorant Failed!
5 That's the Most Ridiculous Face I Ever Saw!
6 This Terrible Haircut Just Ruins My Good Looks.
7 I Warn You, Frankie, Smoking Will Stunt Your Growth.
8 And We'll Put the New Chair in That Corner!
9 Lullaby and Goodnight
10 O.K. O.K. YOU Pitch and I'LL Play Right Field.
11 My Boy, I Don't Think You're Cut Out for Medical School!
12 I Take It You Didn't Like the Meal, Sir!
13 If It Comes with Two Pair of Pants, I'll Take It.
14 All Right... Bring Back the Lighter for a Refund!
15 And Your Secretary Told Me You Weren't In!
16 If You Don't Like This Carpet I'll Show You Something in Red.
17 Watch Out for That Mole on the Back of My Neck!
18 And Papa Bear Said "Somebody Ate My Porridge, too!"
19 No Sleeping in a Public Park, Lady!
20 I See a Tall, Dark Stranger in Your Future!

21 Could You Direct Me to the Olympic Stadium, Sir?
22 But I Used a Mouthwash This Morning!
23 Maybe It Was a Mistake to Keep You After School!
24 Oh Darling, You've Cut Yourself Shaving Again!
25 One—Two—Cha—Cha—Cha!
26 You're Not Going to That Women's Lib Meeting and That's Final!
27 Okay, Okay, You Can Have the Car Tonight!
28 I Wish She'd Stop Falling Asleep in Front of the T.V.!

29 Pssst! Wanna Buy a Good Watch?
30 Gee Kid, You Weigh a Ton!
31 What Do You Mean My Mother Has a Mustache?
32 I Guess It's Time to Give Up Those Reducing Pills!

33 My Girdle Is Killing Me!
34 Who Took My Right Guard?
35 I Wonder If She Noticed My Dandruff?
36 Wait Till They Find Out I'm the New Baby Sitter!

37 Who Says I'm too Young to Shave?
38 One More Acupuncture and You'll Be a New Man!
39 Who Fooled Around with My Butane Lighter?
40 Watch It Lady! I'm the Store Detective!
41 O Solo Mio
42 Look Dad, No Cavities
43 Ho Hum... Must Have Overslept!
44 Can You Spare $50 for a Face-Lift?
45 Ring Around the Collar! Ring Around the Collar!
46 You—Hoo... Ice Cream Man!
47 I'm Sure My Ball Rolled Under This Car!
48 Boy, They've Sure Got Some Ugly Girls in This Neighborhood!
49 Will Someone Turn the Thermostat Down?
50 My Sinuses Have Been Acting Up Again!
51 If You Want Anything, Just Scream!
52 Come on In! The Water's Fine!
53 I Can't Understand Why Girls Don't Like Me!
54 What Do You Mean I'm Not Your Type, Susan?
55 O.K. Buddy, Let's See Your Driver's License!
56 How's the Skin Treatment Going, Darling?
57 The Doctor Says It's Poison Ivy!
58 Last One in the Water Is a Rotten Egg!

59 Chocolates Just Ruin My Complexion!
60 My Nose Is Itchy!
61 Wait Till I Get My Hands on That Travel Agent!
62 Wake Up Miss, We've Rented Your Room!
63 But Dear... There Must Be an Easier Way to Hang a Picture!
64 Taxi!
65 She's Gonna Have to Join Weight-Watchers
66 Good Heavens... Dishpan Hands?
67 "I Love You Tru—ly"
68 Look Albert... A Hamburger Stand!
69 But WE'RE Supposed to Pick YOU up!
70 An' a One An' a Two...
71 Who Threw That Mudball?
72 Burp! Excuse Me!
73 Wait'll I Get My Hands on That Hair Styler!
74 Just Where Does Your Tummy Hurt, Junior?
75 You Oughta See the Other Guy!
76 I've Heard of Hangovers, But This Is Ridiculous!
77 No Thanks... I Quit Smoking a Year Ago!
78 Try It... You'll Like It!
79 But I Don't Want to Dance Anymore!
80 Okay... Who Put Starch in My Pants Again!
81 Maybe We Are Rushing Things, Frankie!
82 Mary, We're Out of Toilet Paper Again!

83 I Told You Not to Go Out Without a Hat!
84 The Contract Says I Get Top Billing!
85 C'mon Irving... Just One More for the Road!
86 You Forgot Your Oil Can Again, Dear!
87 These Vitamins Really Work!
88 Gosh, I'll Never Find That Fuse Box!
89 Hey, Charlie... Time to Get Up!
90 ... and for My Next Shadow Picture...!
91 This Exercise Is Killing Me!
92 Do You Have Dishpan Hands?
93 Gee... I Hope She's House Broken!
94 Try to Give Me the Brush-Off, Eh?
95 "Me... and My Sha—dow"
96 Congratulations, Larry... She's a Great Little Gal!
97 Isn't There an Easier Way to Remove a Mole?
98 Aw, C'mon Frankie, You Always Get to Bat First!
99 But I Gave at the Office!
100 Remember... Only You Can Prevent Forest Fires!
101 Man, That's Coffee!
102 Well, I'll Be a Mummy's Uncle!
103 Horror Comics Sure Have Some Scary Characters!
104 Fools! You're Singing Off-Key Again!
105 Aw C'mon... Tell Me One More Bedtime Story!
106 What's the Matter? Haven't You Seen a Canary Before?

107 I Won't Dance with You and That's Final!
108 Does This Mean We're Engaged!
109 Brand "A" Gives Faster Relief Than the Other Leading Brand!
110 How Do You Like My New Charm Bracelet?
111 But You Knew I Snored Before You Married Me!
112 Smile!... You're on Candid Camera!
113 I've Had It with Those Piano Lessons!
114 You've Been in the Water So Long Your Skin's Wrinkled!
115 Quick, Honey, Get the Raid!
116 These Old Horror Movies Sure Are Ridiculous!
117 How Long Does It Take Till This Nail Polish Dries?
118 I Gotta Lay Off Those Sweets!
119 Who Put All That Pepper on My Eggs?
120 Honey, I Have an Axe to Grind with You!
121 Don't Take too Much Off the Top, Dear!
122 Wait Till I Find the Guy Who Sold Me That Hair Restorer!
123 But Judge... I Was Only Doing Thirty!
124 Agnes, I Warned You About Those Diet Pills!
125 I've Heard of Close Shaves But This Is Ridiculous!
126 ...I'll Be Done Cutting Your Hair in a Moment!
127 Wanna Neck?
128 ...Maybe It's My Breath!

YOU'LL DIE LAUGHING - 1980 (88 & 22) 2 1/2" X 3 1/2"

HI! I'M THE NEW BABY SITTER!

After lying dormant for seven years, the Creature Feature/ You'll Die Laughing idea rose again from the vaults at Topps in 1980. Out came those old black and white photos from Universal Studios decorated with monster-art frames in various colors. An added bonus was a color sticker set composed of various monsters and monster-movie posters and lobby cards, plus a title/checklist card. The card backs contain the very same monster drawing used in 1959 and 1973, but the back coloration this time around is a truly monstrous combination of red, green and yellow. Note: Set Price includes stickers.

ITEM	MINT	EX
Set	18.00	14.00
Card	.15	.10
Sticker	.35	.25
Wrappers (4)		
each	--	.75
Box	--	10.00

You'll Die Laughing - 1980

1. Creature Feature
2. A Little Off the Top, Please!
3. Sheesh! I Better Join Weight Watchers!
4. Well I'll Be a Mummy's Uncle!
5. Hi! I'm the New Baby Sitter!
6. Come On In...The Water's Fine!
7. You Can't Boogie in Size 10 Shoes!
8. But Judge—I Was Only Doing 30!
9. I Zapped the Zits—But They Zapped Me Back!
10. Okay—Who Put the Starch in My Pants Again!
11. Oh No...Dishpan Hands!
12. Nobody Move! I Dropped a Contact Lens!
13. Will You Please Turn Down That Disco Music!
14. You Oughtta See the Other Guy!
15. I Just Got a Face Lift with a Steam Shovel!
16. Who Called Me a Big Drip!
17. Clothes Make the Monster!
18. Buddy, Can You Spare a Dime?
19. You Can't Make a Monkey Out of Me!
20. I Misplaced My Nail Polish Again!

21. But Why Can't I Get into Studio 54?
22. They're Really Biting Today!
23. I Feel Like a Fish Out of Water!
24. Do You Have a Pair of Pants My Size?
25. Allright Officer—I'll Come Quietly!
26. Good Heavens...A Wart!
27. I'll Look Better After My Nose-Job!
28. My Face Feels Like I Slept in It!
29. There's Something about You That I Like!
30. This Is a Hairy Situation!
31. I've Heard of Hangovers, but This Is Absurd!
32. "...And for My Next Shadow-Picture"
33. What Do You Mean You Can See Right through Me?
34. No Job Is Too Big for Your Exterminator!
35. Trick or Treat!
36. "You Light Up My Life"
37. This Terrible Haircut Just Ruins My Good Looks!
38. I Ask You...What Becomes a Legend Most?

39. Who Stole My Rubber Duck?
40. This Acne Is Getting Out of Hand!
41. Be My Ghoul Friend!
42. Who Sold Me That Hair Restorer?
43. Which Way to the Pajama Party?
44. I Told Those Kids to Clean Out the Pool!
45. Max Really Lost His Head This Time!
46. How Do You Like My New Charm Bracelet?
47. Who Fooled Around with My New Butane Lighter?
48. I Tell You, Rover...It's a Dog-Eat-Dog World!
49. Like My New Nail Polish?
50. You Should Have Seen the One That Got Away!
51. Wait'll I Get My Hands on That Travel Agent!
52. I Tell You, That Nuclear Plant Is Safe!
53. Spray Starch? I Thought It Was Underarm Deodorant?
54. "Fly the Friendly Skies..."
55. But I Gave at the Office!
56. Those Darn Weight-Reducing Pills!
57. Gosh, I'll Never Find That Fuse Box!
58. Who Took My Deodorant?
59. What Do You Mean, My Mother Has a Moustache?
60. My Girdle Is Killing Me!
61. I Love to Play in the Sandbox!
62. Yoo Hoo...Ice Cream Man!

63. Only You Can Prevent Forest Fires!
64. Who Threw That Mudball?
65. Hi, It's the Tidy Bowl Man!
66. I Wonder if She Noticed My Dandruff?
67. Will Somebody Tell Me a Scary Story!
68. Hey Baby—Lets Boogie!
69. I'm Available for Blind Dates!
70. He Accused Us of Police Brutality? Get Him!!
71. Will This Cure My Hiccups?
72. Man, That's Coffee!
73. Must Have Been Someone I Ate!
74. Just Where Does Your Tummy Hurt, Junior?
75. I Want My Mummy!
76. I'm the Head of My Family!
77. "Oh Sole Mio..."
78. I'll Get the Drinks—Type A or Type O?
79. I've Got My Eye on You!
80. Is This the Right Way to Pick Up a Girl?
81. Look Ma—No Cavities!
82. I Gotta Lay Off Those Sweets!
83. Well, There Goes the Neighborhood!
84. Can You Spare a Dime for a Bite?
85. I'm a Brain!
86. Who Says I'm Too Young to Shave?
87. They Sure Have Ugly Girls in This Town!
88. Kid, You Weigh a Ton!

1. The Mummy
2. Frankenstein's Monster
3. The Invisible Man
4. The Hunchback
5. Mr. Hyde
6. The Mad Scientist
7. The Werewolf
8. Terrifying Monsters from a Lost Age!
9. Blood of the Vampire
10. Full Figure—Creature from the Black Lagoon
11. The Mummy
12. The Mole Man
13. The Creature
14. The Mutant
15. The Masked Phantom
16. The Phantom
17. The Wolf Man
18. Giant Spider Strikes!
19. The Land Unknown

20. Revenge of the Creature
21. Bust—Creature from the Black Lagoon
22. The Incredible Shrinking Man

YOUR LATEST PICTURE (8?)

2" X 3"

The title for this set of "insult" cards comes from the panel at the bottom of every card. The designs illustrated here are the only ones reported to date. The cards are not numbered: the small number next to the Four Star copyright (1, 2 or 3) is a production code of undetermined significance. Each card has a blank space to fill in "My Pal's Name."

ITEM	MINT	EX
Card	2.00	1.50

YUCKIES (24)

1 Addie Airhead
2 Greta Gossip
3 Paula Punk
4 Clara Clumsy
5 Nancy Nerd
6 Murfy Mess
7 Neil Know-It-All
8 Billy Broke
9 Waldo Wild
10 Louie Loudbox
11 Larry Loser
12 Stacey Stuck-Up
13 Bobby Braces
14 Freddy Foulmouth
15 Peter Party
16 Tommy Timid
17 Henrietta Hairspray
18 Bernie Burnout
19 Dee-Dee Doo-Doo
20 Ollie Upbeat
21 Gwendolyn Gimme
22 Sheri Shaape-Up
23 Spencer Spittle
24 Massively Cool Clyde

2 1/2" X 3 1/2"

"Yuckies," a 1990 series patterned after Garbage Pail Kids, was manufactured by Gumsters Inc. The title, the company informed us, is an acronym standing for "Young, Unruly, Creepy Kids of Yuppies." The cards are standard size and feature simple color artwork caricatures which fall far short of the quality found in GPK. One two-card panel of "Yuckies" (with a 2 1/2" X 5 " contest panel at bottom) was packaged in a large red wrapper containing approximately 25 gum balls and a prize. The set length was advertised as 75 cards, but only 24 were ever printed. In their exuberance, Gumsters Inc. even created a large lapel button as a bonus for wholesale clients. Note: single cards, which are detached from two-card panels, cannot be graded mint.

ITEM	MINT	EX
Sets		
Single cards	--	8.50
In panels	18.00	12.00
Card	--	.35
Panel	1.50	1.00
Wrapper	--	1.00
Box	--	2.50
Button	--	3.00

ZERO HEROES (66)

"Zero Heroes" are just what the name implies: a bunch of Fantastic Foul-Ups tripping over their own "feet" all over the galaxy. The artwork is excellent, but most of it is wasted on sterile white backgrounds. Each design is a diecut, front-peel sticker; the backs carry brief descriptions of the "Zero" pictured, plus the card number. The eight numbers missing from the number sequence correspond to a set of Zero Hero signs. These are not numbered, however, and have a different back format than the numbered stickers. The set was produced by

2 1/2" X 3 1/2"

Donruss and has three different wrappers.

ITEM	MINT	EX
Set	10.00	6.50
Sticker	.15	.10
Wrappers (3)		
each	--	.50
Box	--	4.00

Award -- Zero Hero Crime Fighter
Do Not Enter Protected By Zero Heroes
Secret Society of Zero Heroes
Super Turkey
Warning! This Vehicle Protected By Zero
  Heroes
Zero Hero
Zero Hero Official I.D. Card
Z Team

Zero Heroes

1 The Fantastic Fast Guy
2 No Card
3 Muscle Man
4 Put-Down Man
5 Brand X Man
6 Power Baby
7 Rat Man
8 Milkman
9 No Card
10 Lard Lady
11 Ape Man
12 The Silver Screamer
13 Hen Boy
14 Video Boy
15 No Card
16 Great Gobbler
17 Egbert, The Barbarian
18 No Card
19 Commander Bigfoot

20 Wonder Richguy
21 Colossal Cockroach
22 Commander Clown
23 Captain Cement
24 The Silver Skunk
25 Yellowbelly
26 Captain Ugly
27 Amazing Fantastic Colossal Power Zapper Wonder Man
28 Power Punk
29 Super Sneezer
30 Space Slug
31 No Card
32 Super Surfer
33 The Human Flashlight
34 Super Swine
35 Captain Clod
36 The Caped Cucumber
37 Toad Man

38 Captain Long-Distance
39 Power Pinhead
40 Dazzling Dog
41 Valley Girl
42 The Fantastic Flea
43 No Card
44 The Z-Team

45 Captain Forgetful
46 Thunder Thighs
47 No Card
48 Garlic Gal
49 Mean Man
50 Fall Person
51 Lead Head
52 Bullet Boy
54 Commander Cheese
55 Fancy Man
56 Wonder Weakling
57 Steel Putty Man
58 Beetle Man
59 Creampuff Man
60 The Caped Computer
61 Greased Lightning
62 Jet Boy
63 The Caped Rock Head
64 Bird Boy
65 Electric Man
66 The Incredible Bulk

ZILLY-ZEREAL BOXES & STICKERS (36 & 12) TWO SIZES

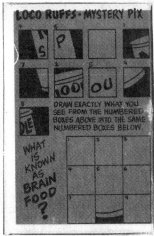

The "Zilly-Zereal" series of 36 cereal brand spoofs was issued by the now-defunct Fun Foods, Inc. in 1985. Each 2" X 3" artwork-decorated box has a silly cereal satire on front and a feature or puzzle on the back. The boxes themselves are not numbered, although there is a mysterious small number printed on the left small flap at top. All of the boxes have the sentence "This Is The Bottom, Stupid!" printed on the bottom outside flap. The "free prize" advertised on the fronts of the cereal boxes turned out to be a series of small (1" X 1-1/2") stickers with funny sayings. These have split backs for easy peeling and the twelve which are recorded on our checklist are the only titles that have been found to date. Note: box and sticker sets are priced separately.

ITEM	MINT	EX
Sets		
Boxes	--	60.00
Stickers	7.00	4.50
Box	--	1.50
Sticker	.50	.35

Big Wormy Apple
Do Not Lick This Sticker! You Have *Bad Breath*
I Love Rock 'N Roll
I Love Skool Lunch!
Kiss Me
Nutice / This Sticker Is So Secret It Should Not Be Read! / Notice!
Save Energy / Close This Skool!
Stop Living and Start *Worrying*
Veterinarians Endorse Burgers
Warning! Reading This ... Will Make You Late!
Witches Are Good In Skool ... They Get "A" In Spell!
You Are Off Your Rocker!

ZOO CARD SERIES (12)

2 7/8" X 4 1/8"

 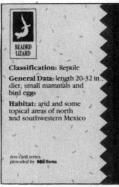

Bearded Lizard
Dolphin
Greater Kudu
Humboldt Penguin
Indian Fruit Bat
Lion Fish
Malayan Tapir
Meerkat
Ostrich
Peafowl
Red Kangaroo
Scorpion

A project of the Milwaukee County Zoo, this "Zoo Card Series" was released in 1988 and was funded by M&I Banks. The card fronts have smallish center pictures of animals set upon modern decorator backgrounds. The only other writing on the obverse is the "Milwaukee County Zoo" line in the bottom right corner. On the back, there is an outline of each animal and three categories of details: classification, general data, and habitat. A small line at bottom credits M&I banks for funding the series. Only the twelve cards listed have been reported for this series to date.

ITEM	MINT	EX
Card	.50	.35

ZOO LIFE ZOO CARDS (72)

2 1/2" X 3 1/2"

One of the nicest animal sets of recent times, this series of 72 cards was issued as bonus inserts in copies of 1990 and 1991 "Zoo Life" magazine. There were nine cards per issue and these came in sheet form near the end of the magazine. Pre-scored lines between the individual cards made removal easy. Each sheet consisted of eight numbered animal cards and one un-numbered "Quiz" card with questions about each of the animals pictured. The center illustrations are captioned color photographs which have marbled green orders. The card backs summarize vital details at top and follow these with a paragraph of descriptive text. The card number is located in an angled block. Since the front photos were obtained from a variety of zoological parks and facilities, each card identifies the source of the illustration. Collectors who encounter single cards may notice that there is some variation in measurement on the long plane, from 3-1/2" to 3-5/8". This is a natural consequence of how the insert sheet was produced. Note: single cards cannot be graded mint.

ITEM	MINT	EX
Set		
Cards	--	20.00
Sheets	35.00	27.50
Card	--	.25
Sheet	4.00	3.00

Zoo Life Zoo Cards

1 Lesser Panda
2 Wholpin
3 Collared Lizard
4 Marabou Stork
5 Great Indian Hornbill
6 Giant Pacific Octopus
7 Geoffroy's Marmoset
8 Javanese Leaf Insect
- Quiz Card
9 Crowned Crane
10 Corn Snake
11 Bison
12 Great Blue Heron
13 Golden Lion Tamarin
14 White Tiger
15 Bongo
16 Blue-Girdled Angelfish
- - Quiz Card
17 Ring-Tailed Lemur
18 Rocky Mountain Goat
19 Blue Tang
20 Blue-Tongued Skink
21 Hooded Merganser
22 Lionfish
23 Surinam Horned Frog
24 Rajah Brooke's Birdwing
- - Quiz Card
25 Grevy's Zebra
26 Hyacinth Macaw
27 Komodo Dragon
28 Patagonian Cavy
29 Sumatran Orang-utan
30 Spotted Scorpionfish
31 Barred Owl
32 Lacewing Butterfly
- - Quiz Card
33 Crested Forest Lizard
34 Stuart's Milksnake
35 Sea Pen
36 wild Turkey
37 Musk Ox
38 Hamadryas Baboon
39 Scarlet Macaw
40 False Killer Whale
- - Quiz Card
41 Spotted Jaguar
42 Saiga
43 Kemp's Ridley Turtle
44 Squarespot
45 Scheepmaker's Crowned Pigeon
46 Emerald Tree Boa
47 Opalescent Nudibranch
48 Toco Toucan
- - Quiz Card
49 Great Horned Owl
50 Slow Loris
51 Black Rhinoceros
52 Blackbuck
53 Chimpanzee
54 Secretary Bird
55 Clown Anemonefish
56 Bearded Dragon
- - Quiz Card
57 Arabian Oryx
58 Purple Striped Jellies
59 Micronesian Kingfisher
60 Walrus
61 Maned Wolf
62 Aldabra Giant Tortoise
63 King Vulture
64 North American River Otter
- - Quiz Card

ZOO-PER CARD SERIES (12)   2 1/4" X 3 1/2"

This series of twelve cards depicting vanishing animals, created as handouts for the Milwaukee County Zoo, was sponsored by the MCZ Educa-

Asian Elephant
Arctic Wolf
Bactrian Camel
Cheetah
Golden Monkey
Gorilla
Polar Bear
Ruppell's Griffon Vulture
Swamp Rattler
Trumpeter Swan
Victoria Crowned Pigeon
White Rhinoceros

tion Department, Zoo Pride, and Marshall & Ilsley Bank. The cards were given away free in sets of four to zoo visitors from June 1st to September 7th of an unidentified year. They are smaller in physical size than the Milwaukee Zoo Card series previously listed in this book, but have the same MCZ logo on front. The backgrounds on which the color photographs rest are very interesting: they are, in fact, close-ups of the skin and fur of the animals pictured. On the back of each card there is a list of details about the subject animal. This is the second series of twelve cards produced by the Milwaukee County Zoo that has been reported to The Hobby Card Index and we assume that others may exist.

ITEM	MINT	EX
Set	7.00	4.50
Card	.50	.35

ZOO'S WHO (40 & 18)   2 1/2" X 3 1/2"

Natural history buffs who applaud Topps for creating this set of 36 "Animal Stick-ons" must also wonder why the company left such glaring errors in it. Cards 14 and 22 refer to Koalas as bears, which they are not; card No. 21 should read "Proboscis Monkey" (not "Probiscis"). The stickers also suffer from the imposition of the two back "break & peel" lines onto the picture. A series of 18 cards with puzzle piece fronts and checklist backs rounds out the set. Note: the puzzles are more difficult to complete than the stickers; the set prices listed are for stickers only.

ITEM	MINT	EX
Sets		
Stickers	22.00	15.00
Cards	21.50	16.00
Sticker	.50	.35
Card	1.00	.75
Wrapper	--	5.00
Box	--	30.00

1 Giraffe	14 Koala Bear No. 1	27 Mountain Lions
2 Toucan	15 Ocelot	28 Monkey and Offspring
3 Lion	16 Owls	29 Leopard
4 Bobcat	17 Chinchilla	30 Grinning Monkey
5 Panda	18 Elk	31 Basset Hound
6 Cattle	19 Hare	32 Squirrel Monkey
7 Frog	20 Pandas	33 Pony
8 Pigs	21 Probiscis Monkey [sic]	34 Zebra
9 Bushbaby	22 Koala Bear No. 2	35 Tabby Cat
10 Monkey	23 Fawn	36 Tabby Cat and Butterfly
11 Tamarin	24 English Bulldog	37 Squirrel
12 Peacock	25 Lynx	38 Dachsund
13 Bear	26 Baboon	39 Rabbits
		40 Hamster

MANUFACTURER'S INDEX

ANONYMOUS
Bicentennial Daze 76
Civil War Picture Cards 103
Horror Heads 309
Monster Cards 421
National Periodical / Warner Bros. Cards 443
Teenage Mutant Ninja Turtles
Vending Machne Stickers 606
The True West 618
Wisecrackers 698
AAA SPORTS
Operation Yellow Ribbon 146
ABBY VENDING
Looney Series Cards 365
ACT DENTAL RINSE
Magic Card Tricks 371
ACTION .... see "Panini"
ADCOR
Mars Attacks Mini Comic Books 381
AMERICANA PICTURE SERVICE
Mickey Mouse and His Friends 405
AMERICA'S MAJOR PLAYERS
Desert Storm Card & Map Set 140
AMUROL
Dungeons & Dragons 178
Miniature Comic Book Collection 413
Rock Express 514
The Simpsons / Bart Bubble Gum 617
ARGUS
Garfield NFL Mini Posters 257
BAZOOKA .... see "Topps"
BECKER (L.M.)
Elephant Jokes 181
Laugh-In Rings 354
BIG BOY RESTAURANTS
Great Americans 278
BON AIR
Birds and Flowers 78
BONKERS .... see "Conusa"
BONOMO'S
Exciting Science Facts 196
BROCKUM
Rockcards 507
BUBBLES INC. .... see "Topps"
BURGER KING
Everybody Wins Trading Cards 196
CALICO GRAPHICS
Endangered Species Trading Cards 189
League of Nations, 1st Series 356
League of Nations, 2nd Series 357
CAMPBELL TAGGART
Know The Presidents 342
CAPITAL CARDS
200 Years of Freedom 642
CAPRI SUN
Nickelodeon 449
CAROLINA CUSTOM CARDS
Race Toons 487
CHEETOS .... see "Frito-Lay"
COLLECT-A-CARD
Muscle Cars 437
Vette Set 655
COLECO
Cabbage Patch Kids Trading Cards 92
COLONIAL BREAD
Busch Gardens Cards 90
Know Your U.S. Presidents 342
Know Your 50 States 343
Star Trek 557
COMIC IMAGES
Boris 83
Feature Story 106
CONFEX
Garbage Pail Kids Chewy Candy 253
CONTINENTAL BAKING
Funny Cars 227
Teenage Mutant Ninja Turtles Stickers 605
Teenage Mutant Ninja Turtles
Movie Stickers 606
Wacky TV Show Cards 682
CONTINENTAL CANDY
Snoots 538
CONUSA
Teenage Mutant Ninja Turtles Stickers 605
CORONET PAPER TOWELS
President Stickers 482
COUNTRY OVEN
Dinosaurs Cutouts 156
CROWN SPORTS CARDS
Landforce 145
Seaforce 147
Skyforce 147
The Desert Storm Card Collection 148
Victory 149
DART FLIPCARDS
Beetlejuice 70
FernGully 205
Gulf War Fact Cards 143
Vietnam, Volume 1 656
Vietnam, Volume 2 657
DELISH-US CHIPS
Civil War Scenes 103
DIAMOND TOY
Alf Album Stickers 18
An American Tail — Fievel Goes West
Album Stickers 25
Dinosaurs Album Stickers 160
Garfield Album Stickers 257
G.I. Joe Album Stickers 263
Jem Album Stickers 326
Mask Album Stickers 392
My Little Pony 439
New Kids On The Block Album Stickers 446
Nintendo Album Stickers 452
Silver Hawks Album Stickers 532
Slimer & The Real Ghostbusters
Album Stickers 534
Teenage Mutant Ninja Turtles
Album Stickers 601
Teenage Mutant Ninja Turtles
Movie Album Stickers 601
Teenage Mutant Ninja Turtles II
Album Stickers 602
The California Raisins Album Stickers 612
The New Archies 614
The Real Ghostbusters 614
The Simpsons Album Stickers 616
Transformers 630
(DIAMOND TOY continued)
U.S. of Alf 649
Wacko-Saurs 660
DIETZEN'S BREAD
Men Of Apollo XI 399
Men Of The Old West 399
DISNEY CONES
Mickey Memorabilty 404
DOLLY MADISON
Peanuts Characters 465
Peanuts Presidential Stickers 466
DONRUSS
Addams Family 14
Alf-Pro Skateboard 22
Andy Gibb Posters 26
Awesome! All-Stars 40
Baseball's Greatest Grossouts 48
Baseball Super Freaks, 1st Series 49
Baseball Super Freaks, 2nd Series 50
Bionic Woman 77
BMX Bikes 81
CB Convoy Code 94
Chips 100
Choppers & Hot Bikes 101
Combat 108
Crazy Hang Ups 119
Dallas 124
Dark Crystal 126
Disneyland 166
Dukes of Hazzard (1980) 174
Dukes of Hazzard Stickers 175
Dukes of Hazzard (1983) 175
Elvis Presley 183
Fiends and Machines 207
Flower Power 216
Flying Nun 216
Football Super Freaks 221
Freddie & The Dreamers 222
Galaxy Wars 232
Green Hornet 280
Idiot Cards 315
King Kong 338
Kiss 340
Knight Rider 342
Magnum p.i. 372
Marvel Comics Super Heroes Tattoos 383
Marvel Super Heroes 385
MASH 392
Monkees 417
Monkees, Series A-B-C 418
Monkees Badges 419
Odd Rods 453
Odder Odd Rods / Fabulous Odd Rods 454
Oddest Odd Rods / Fantastic Odd Rods 455
Fantastic Odd Rods, 2nd Series 456
Odd Rod All Stars 456
Osmonds 460
Rock Stars 512
Saturday Night Fever 521
Screamin Gleamin Glitter Iron-Ons 525
Sgt. Pepper's Lonely Hearts Club Band 527
Silly Cycles 531
Six Million Dollar Man 532
Skateboard Stickers 534
Space: 1999 544
Spec Sheet 547
Super Cycles 576
Tac-It-To-Me Spooky Tattoos 582
Tacky Tattoos / Ticky Tacky Tattoos 583
Tron 632
Truckin' 632
Vote 659
Voyage To The Bottom Of The Sea 659
World of Stamps 701
Zero Heroes 710
DORITOS
Universal Monsters 646
DRAKE'S CAKES
Superman, The Movie 585
D.S.I.
Desert Storm Weapons Set 142
DYNAMITE MAGAZINE
Dynamite Sports Cards / Dynamite
Trading Cards 179
EAGLE TRADING CARD CO.
Wings of Gold 698
ECLIPSE
Bush League 90
Coup D'Etat 115
Friendly Dictators 223
Iran Contra Scandal 321
Rock Bottom Awards 509
Savings & Loan Scandal Trading Cards 524
ED-U CARDS
Green Hornet Playing Cards 281
New York World's Fair 447
ENVIROMINTAL CANDY CO.
Environmints 190
EPIC
Saturday Serials, Series 1 523
Saturday Serials, Series 2 523
ESCAPE CARDS
The Dean Gunnarson Collection 613
ESSKAY
Airplanes 15
ESSO
Great Moments in American History 279
EVEREADY BATTERIES
Family Fun Games 199
FANTASY TRADING CARD CO. .... see "FTCC"
FEDERAL SWEETS & BISCUIT CO.
Wild Animals 694
FFV
Wild Wonders Animal Cards 695
FOUR STAR
Spooking Size Candy Cigarette Boxes 548
Your Latest Picture 708
FRITO-LAY
Chester Cheetah Cards 99
FTCC
Alien Nation 21
Marvel Superheroes First Issue Covers 386
Rocketship X-M 512
Rocky Horror Picture Show 515
Star Trek II - Wrath of Kahn 558
Star Trek III - Search For Spock 559
Star Trek IV - The Voyage Home 560
FLEER
Alvin Tattoos 23
Back-Slapper Stickers 43
Baseball Stickers 49
Baseball Weird-Ohs 50
Basketball Stickers 51
Beautiful People 68
Believe It Or Not 71
Belly Buttons 73
Body Shop 83
Bugs Bunny Tattoo Transfers 89
Bullwinkle Tattoo Transfers 89
Bumper Stickers 89
Button Factory 91
CB Talk 95
Cover Ups 115
Cracked Magazine 116
Crazy Labels Stickers 119
Crazy Magazine Covers 120
Drag Nationals 169
Dragon's Lair 169
Dragstrips / Stick Shift 170
Dumb Dabs / Dumb Dots 176
Dumb Dabs 176
Dune 177
50 Fun Stamps 207
Football Stickers 220
Glitter Glove 268
Glow Worms 269
Gomer Pyle 270
Gong Show 271
Goofy Gags 274
Grossville High 289
Gumby and Pokey Tattoos 293
Happy Stickers 299
Harlem Globetrotters 300
Here's Bo 303
Hogan's Heroes 305
Hollywood Slap Stickers 306
Hot Seat Stickers 312
Jet Set Stickers 327
Justice League of America 332
Kustom Cars I 346
Kustom Cars II 349
Looney Labels 361
Looney Labels & Stamps 362
Mad Medals 369
Mad Stickers 370
Magoo Tattoos 373
McHale's Navy 398
Mighty Hercules Tattoos 411
Mighty Heroes Tattoos 411
Milton the Monster & Fearless Fly 413
Monster Marks 427
Ms. Pac-Man 433
My Kookie Klassmates 438
Official Drag Champs 458
Pac-Man 461
Pirates Bold 472
Pirates Tattoo 473
Pixies 473
Race USA 488
Real Cloth Patches 494
Real Road Signs Stickers 495
Ringer Dingers 502
Robot Wars 506
Rotten Eggs 520
School Daze Stickers 524
School Stickers 525
Smellies 536
Sneekies 538
Stick-Its 570
Stick-It-To-Em Insult Stickers 571
Stick Shift 170
Sticky Feet 572
Stop Stamps 572
Stupid Stamps 575
Super Pac-Man 589
Super Sneekies 589
Three Stooges 619
TV Smelly Awards 638
Underdog 646
V 651
Weird-Ohs 689
Window Pains 697
Woody Woodpecker 701
FUN FOODS
Fun Buttons 225
Fun N' Donuts 227
Zilly-Zereal Candy Boxes 711
FUN FRUITS .... see "Sunkist"
FUNKY SALES CORP.
Wierd World of Baseball 694
GAMECRAFT
Bicentennial Daze 76
GLENN CONFECTIONS
Dinosaurs 157
Fun Gum Monsters 226
Riddle Fun 501
Riddle Time 502
State License Plates 570
GOLDEN PRESS
Animals 32
Dick Tracy Collector Cards 152
Dinosaurs 159
Presidents 481
GORTON'S
The Amazing Ocean 611
GUMSTERS INC.
Yuckies 709
HARDEE'S
The California Raisins 612
HARRIS, ARNOLD
Bicentennial Daze 76
HASBRO
G.I. Joe 265
HEINZ
Super Powers Stickers 579
HERSHEY
Empire Strikes Back 183
E.T. Stickers 194
HIRES
Famous American Indian Chiefs 200
HISTORICAL IMAGES
Defenders of Freedom 132
HOLLOWAY
Believe It Or Not 72

MANUFACTURER'S INDEX

HOSTESS
Rip Into Rock 502
Teenage Mutant Ninja Turtles Stickers 605
Teenage Mutant Ninja Turtles II Stickers 606
Wacky TV Show Cards 682
ILLUMINATIONS
Dinosaur Action Card Collection 155
IMAGINE INC.
Grande Illusions 276
IMPEL / SKYBOX
An American Tail - Fievel Goes West 24
D.C. Cosmic Cards 129
Disney Collector Cards 164
G.I. Joe 265
Laffs 351
Marvel Universe I 388
Marvel Universe II 390
Minnie 'N Me 415
Nightmare On Elm Street 450
Star Trek 1991 - Series 1 561
Star Trek 1991 - Series 2 563
Terminator 2 607
Trading Card Treats 629
X-Men 704
INTERNATIONAL GAMES
Jake's Jokes 322
JASINSKI
Flash Gordon 214
JIFFY POP
Gummi Bears Stickers 293
JOE LOWE
Popsicle Space Cards 37
JUNIOR MINTS ..... see "Nabisco"
KELLOGG'S
Future of Rock 231
KILPATRICK'S BREAD
Star Trek 557
KITCHEN SINK
Kitchen Sink Cards 341
KRAFT
Dinomac Collector Cards 154
Teddy Bear Collector Cards 596
Wild Wheels Collector Cards 695
Willow Movie Stickers 696
KUDOS ..... see "Mars, Inc."
K-2
K-2 Factory Workers 347
LEAF
Fink Buttons 208
Flags of All Nations 210
Garrison's Gorillas 258
Good Guys & Bad Guys 271
Hippie Tattoos 304
Munsters 434
Orders and Decorations of the World 459
Secret Origin Stories 527
Secret Wars 527
Spook Stories 549
Star Trek 554
Untouchables 647
What's My Job? 691
LETRASET
Mini-Toons 414
LIME ROCK
Dream Machines 171
Heroes of the Persian Gulf 143
Pro Cheerleaders 482
LITTLE DEBBIE
Sea World Character Cards 526
LUCKY LEAF
Duck Tales 173
MAD MAGAZINE
Mad Cards 368
MARS, INC.
Kids Around The World 336
MATCHBOX TOY
Matchbox Car & Driver Collector Cards 396
MATTEL
Barbie Trading Cards - Series 1 46
Barbie Trading Cards - Series 2 47
Where's Waldo? 692
McDONALD'S
Dick Tracy Crimestopper Game Cards 153
McCAIN / ELLIO'S
Teenage Mutant Ninja Turtles
Action Figures 603
Teenage Mutant Ninja Turtles Movie
Scene Cards 604
MEL APPEL
Weird Ball Trading Cards 688
MICRO MACHINES
Micro Machines 407
MILLBROOK BREAD
Peanuts Comic Cards Game 465
Peanuts Klakkers 465
Peanuts Presidential Stickers 466
MILWAUKEE COUNTY ZOO
Zoo Card Series 712
Zoo-Per Card Series 714
MILWAUKEE PUBLIC MUSEUM
Dinosaurs 159
MINUTE MAID
Flag Stickers & International Communities 212
Sport Goofy Trading Cards 552
MONOGRAM
Monogram Models Cards 421
MOTHER PRODUCTIONS
Toxic Waste Zombies 628
MOTHER'S COOKIES
Flintstones Cards 214
MR. FREEZE
Mr. Freeze Fun Quiz 433
MRS. GROSSMAN
Mrs. Grossman's Sticker Art Trading Cards 433
MUNDUS AMICUS
Environmental Action Cards 190
NABISCO
African Wild Animals 14
American Zoo Animals 23
Animal Heroes Card Collection 30
Animal and Flags of the World 32
Elephant Laughs 182
Fantastic First In Sports 203
Fantastic Fun With Science 203
Fool 'Ems 220
Laugh N' Tell 356
Laurel & Hardy 356
Mickey Mouse and His Pals 405
(NABISCO continued)
Monkey Shines 420
Nabisco's Wildlife Card Collection 440
Pom Pom Riddles 476
Prehistoric Scenes 479
Songbirds of the United States 542
Trivia Quiz 631
Wacky Stickers 682
Water World Heroes 687
Wheels, Wings and Things 692
"Wildlife" Baby Animals 694
NATIONAL EDUCATION ASSOCIATION
U.S. Congress Cards 648
NATIONAL GEOGRAPHIC
National Geographic World 442
NEW YORK WORLD'S FAIR CORPORATION
New York World's Fair 447
NU-CARDS
Dinosaur Series 162
Horror Monster Series 309
OCEAN SPRAY
Fun Cards 226
ORAL-B
Hanna-Barbera 3-D Stickers 295
PACIFIC TRADING CARDS
Andy Griffith - 1st Series 27
Andy Griffith - 2nd Series 28
Andy Griffith - 3rd Series 29
I Love Lucy 315
Leave It To Beaver 357
Operation Desert Shield 145
Rad Dudes 489
Total Recall 626
Wizard of Oz 699
World War II 701
PANINI
Animals of the World Album Stickers 33
Aristocats 36
Barbie Album Stickers (1987) 45
Barbie Album Stickers (1989) 46
Barbie Trading Cards 47
Beetlejuice Album Stickers 71
Brave Star Album Stickers 85
Care Bears 93
Chip 'N Dale Rescue Rangers 99
Cinderella Album Stickers 101
Darkwing Duck 128
Dick Tracy Giant Stickers & Poster Set 154
Dinosaurs 157
Duck Tales Album Stickers 173
Flashdance Stickers 213
Ghostbusters Album Stickers 260
Happy Birthday Bugs 296
I Love You Snoopy Album Stickers 317
Little Mermaid Album Stickers 359
Masters of the Universe Album Stickers 395
Masters of the Universe
Movie Album Stickers 396
Mickey Story 405
101 Dalmations 459
Popples 478
Rambo Album Stickers 492
Roger Rabbit Album Stickers 519
She-Ra Album Stickers 529
Snow White Album Stickers 541
Star Trek, The Next Generation
Album Stickers 564
Talespin Album Stickers 594
Thundercats 619
Tiny Toon Adventures Album Stickers 621
Voltron Album Stickers 658
Willow Album Stickers 696
Wings of Fire 697
PAPERCRAFT
E.T. Stand-Ups 193
PAUL A. PRICE
Krazy Kards 345
Poker Hands 476
PEPSI COLA
Universal Monsters 646
PERFORMANCE YEARS QUALITY
CARD CO.
Muscle Cards 436
PEZ
Pez Stickers 470
PHILADELPHIA CHEWING GUM
Blackstone's Magic Tricks 79
Crazy Comic Stick-Ons 118
Daktari 124
Dark Shadows - Pink 126
Dark Shadows - Green 127
Dark Shadows Giant Pinups 128
Green Berets 280
Happy Horoscopes 298
Horrible Horoscopes 308
Hot Wheels 312
James Bond 323
James Bond - Thunderball 324
Robert F. Kennedy 335
Lone Ranger Tattoos 360
Mad Mod Buttons 369
Quentin 486
Stupid Buttons 572
Stupid Soaps 574
Super Hero Stickers 578
Superstar Tattoo Transfers 592
Tarzan 595
War Bulletin 686
PIEDMONT CANDY CO.
Terrorist Attack 608
PIZZA HUT
An American Tail - Fievel Goes West 25
Rocketeer 511
POCKET COMICS ..... see "Adcor"
POM POMS ..... see "Nabisco"
POTSHOT PRODUCTIONS
Damn Saddam - The Wacky Iraqi 131
PREMIERE MAGAZINE
Premiere Magazine Collector's Cards 480
PRO SET
Beauty and the Beast 69
Bill & Ted's Excellent Adventure &
Bogus Journey 76
Desert Storm 133
Dinosaurs 160
Little Mermaid 358
SuperStars MusiCards 590
Yo! MTV Raps 705
PYRAMID MARKETING
National Fungus Football League 441
RAINBO BREAD
Busch Gardens Cards 90
Know Your U.S. Presidents 342
Star Trek 557
RALSTON
Love Notes 366
RED BARN
Red Barn Space Cards 496
REESE'S PIECES
E.T. Magic Motion Stickers 192
E.T. Rainbow Reflection Stickers 193
REVELL
Development of Naval Flight 150
The Air Power Series 610
RODDA CARDS
Rodda Cards 517
ROSAN
Famous Monsters Series 202
John F. Kennedy 333
Terror Monsters 609
ROSEM
Mars Attacks - The Unpublished Version 381
Midnight Madness 410
Night Of The Living Dead 450
ROSENBLOOM, JOESEPH
Jake's Jokes 322
SCHAFER BREAD
Flags of America 210
SCHOLASTIC MAGAZINE
American History Trading Cards 23
SARNO & SONJU
Shadoworld 528
SIGNET
Washington Dudes Baseball Club 687
SMALL WORLD ..... see "Tree of Life"
SPACE-PAK
Space-Pak 544
SPACE VENTURES
Moon-Mars 429
Space Shots - Series 1 545
Space Shots - Series 2 546
SPECTRA STAR
Desert Storm Trading Cards 140
S.S.P.C. ..... see "Capital Cards"
STAR PICS
All My Children 21
Playboy 475
Saturday Night Live 522
Twin Peaks 640
SUGAR DADDY &
SUGAR MAMA ..... see "Nabisco"
SUNBEAM BREAD
CB Jeebies Iron Ons 94
Super Heroes 577
SUNKIST
Dinosaurs 158
Funny Fotos 229
Wacky Baseball Players 661
Wacky Basketball Players 661
Wacky Football Players 661
SUPER DEFENDER TOYS
Super Defenders 576
TAYLOR-REED CORP.
Space Candy 543
TASTEE BREAD
Super Heroes 577
TESTOR
Air-Lines Cards 15
THE SOURCE GROUP
Monster in My Pocket 424
TING, BOB
Uranus Strikes 647
TIP TOP BREAD
CB Stickers 95
TNTL STUDIOS
Triumphs & Horrors of the Gulf War 149
TOP PILOT
Top Pilot Cards 621
TOPPS GUM
Addams Family 13
Alf - 1st Series 16
Alf - 2nd Series 17
Alien 20
Angry Stickers 30
Animal Postcers 31
Annie Album Stickers 34
Archie Tattoos 35
Astro Boy Tattoos 36
Astronauts 37
A-Team 38
Autos of 1977 39
Baby 42
Back To The Future II 43
Barbie Album Stickers 44
Batman 52
Batman - A Series 52
Batman - B Series 53
Batman Deluxe Reissue Edition 53
Batman - Riddler 54
Batman - Color Photos 54
Batman Movie - 1st Series 54
Batman Movie - 1st Series Collectors' Edition 56
Batman Movie - 2nd Series 56
Batman Movie - 2nd Series Collectors' Edition 57
Battle 58
Battlestar Galactica 59
Batty Book Covers 61
Batty Buttons 62
Bay City Rollers 62
Beatles - B&W 63
Beatles - Color 64
Beatles Diary 65
Beatles Movie - "A Hard Day's Night" 65
Beatles Plaks 67
Beverly Hillbillies 74
Beverly Hills 90210 75
Big Bad Buttons 76
Black Hole 78
Blockheads 80
Bobby Sherman "Getting Together" 81
Bobby Sherman Plaks 82
Brady Bunch 84
Buck Rogers 86
Bugs Bunny Roadrunner Tattoos 87
Bugs Bunny Tattoos 88
Captain Nice 92

MANUFACTURER'S INDEX

(TOPPS GUM continued)
Casey & Kildare ... 93
Charlie's Angels ... 97
Civil War News ... 102
Close Encounters ... 105
Comic Book Foldees ... 111
Comic Book Foldees ... 112
Comic Book Heroes Stickers ... 113
Comic Book Tattoos ... 114
Comic Cover Stickers ... 114
Crazy Cards ... 117
Crazy Stick-Ons ... 121
Crazy TV ... 122
Cyndi Lauper ... 123
Dallas Cowboy Cheerleaders ... 125
Daniel Boone ... 125
Desert Storm - 1st Series ... 134
Desert Storm - "Victory" ... 138
Desert Storm - "Homecoming" ... 139
Dick Tracy ... 151
Dick Tracy Deluxe Collector's Edition ... 151
Dino-Mite Facts ... 155
Dinosaurs Attack! ... 161
Disgusting Disguises ... 163
Doctor Dolittle Tattoos ... 167
Donkey Kong ... 167
Dopey Books ... 168
Duran Duran ... 179
Empire Strikes Back ... 184
Empire Strikes Back Giant Photo Cards ... 187
E.T. ... 191
E.T. Album Stickers ... 191
Evel Knievel ... 195
Fabulous Rock Records ... 197
Famous Americans ... 201
Fancy Pants ... 202
Far-Out Iron-Ons ... 204
Fighter Planes ... 208
Flag Midgee Cards ... 209
Flags of the World ... 211
Flash Gordon ... 213
Flipper ... 215
Flipper's Magic Fish ... 215
Flip-Ups ... 215
Flying Things ... 217
Fold-A-Roos ... 218
Foldees ... 219
Frankenstein Stickers ... 221
Fright Flicks ... 223
Funny Doors ... 227
Funny Li'l Joke Books ... 229
Funny Rings ... 230
Funny Travel Posters ... 230
Fun Projects ... 231
Garbage Pail Kids ... 235
Garbage Pail Kids Buttons ... 253
Garbage Pail Kids Giant Stickers ... 253
Garbage Pail Kids Giant Stickers ... 254
Garbage Pail Kids Posters ... 255
Garbage Pail Kids 3-D Wall Plaks ... 256
Get Smart ... 259
Ghostbusters II ... 260
Giant Plaks ... 261
Giant Size Funny Valentines ... 263
Gilligan's Island ... 267
Go-Go Buttons ... 269
Good Times ... 272
Goofy Goggles ... 274
Goonies ... 275
Grease ... 277
Green Hornet Stickers ... 282
Gremlins ... 283
Gremlins 2 ... 284
Gremlins 2 Collectors' Edition ... 285
Gremlins Album Stickers ... 286
Groovy Stick-Ons ... 288
Gross Bears ... 288
Growing Pains ... 289
Gruesome Greeting Cards ... 291
Gum Berries Lids ... 292
Hang-Ups ... 294
Happy Days ... 297
Happy Days "A" Series ... 298
Harry & The Hendersons ... 301
Hee Haw ... 302
Hook ... 307
Hot Hunks ... 311
Hot Rods ... 311
Howard The Duck ... 313
Hysterical History ... 314
Incredible Hulk ... 318
Indiana Jones & The Temple of Doom ... 319
Insult Post Cards ... 320
Jaws 2 ... 325
Jaws 3-D ... 326
Jiggly Buttons ... 328
Johnson vs. Goldwater ... 330
Julia ... 331
John F. Kennedy ... 333
King Kong (1965) ... 339
King Kong (1976) ... 339
Kookie Plaks ... 343
Kooky Awards ... 344
Krazy Little Comics ... 345
Krazy Pennants ... 346
Krazy People Posters ... 346
Kung Fu - Test Issue ... 347
Kung Fu ... 348
Labyrinth ... 351
Land of the Giants ... 353
Laugh-In ... 353
Little Shop of Horrors ... 360
Lost In Space ... 366
Love Initials ... 366
Mad Ad Foldees ... 367
Magic Funny Fortunes ... 371
Magic Tattoos ... 371
Make Your Own Name Stickers ... 374
Man From UNCLE ... 375
Man on the Moon ... 376
Mars Attacks ... 379
Marvel Comics (1978) ... 382
Marvel Comics (1979) ... 382
Marvel Flyers ... 384
Marvel Super Heroes Stickers ... 387
Masters of the Universe ... 393
Masters of the Universe ... 394
Max Headroom ... 397

(TOPPS continued)
Maya ... 398
Menudo ... 400
Michael Jackson - 1st Series ... 401
Michael Jackson - 2nd Series ... 402
Michael Jackson Super Stickers ... 403
Mighty Mouse & His Pals Tattoos ... 411
Military Emblems ... 412
Mini Stickers & Nutty Tickets ... 414
Mini-Toons ... 414
Mod Generation Stickers ... 416
Mod Initials ... 417
Mod Squad ... 417
Monkees Flip Movies ... 419
Monster Flip Movies ... 422
Monster Greeting Cards ... 423
Monster Initial Stickers ... 424
Monster Laffs - Midgee ... 425
Monster Laffs ... 426
Monster Legends ... 427
Monster Tatoo ... 427
Monster Tattoos ... 428
Monstickers ... 428
Moonraker ... 430
Mork & Mindy ... 431
Movie Posters ... 432
Nasty Notes ... 440
Nasty Valentine Notes ... 441
New Kids On The Block - Series 1 ... 443
New Kids On The Block - Series 2 ... 444
New Kids On The Block Bubble Gum Cassettes ... 446
Nintendo ... 451
Nice Or Nasty Valentines ... 447
Nutty Awards ... 452
Nutty Initial Stickers ... 453
Outer Limits ... 460
Partridge Family ... 462
Partridge Family Posters ... 463
Pee Wee's Playhouse ... 467
Perlorian Cats Stickers ... 470
Phoney Records ... 471
Phoney Record Stickers ... 471
Planet of the Apes (1969) ... 474
Planet of the Apes (1975) ... 475
Pop Guns ... 477
Pop-Ups ... 478
Presidents and Other Americans ... 481
Push-Pull ... 484
Put-On Stickers ... 485
Racing Track Cards / Soda Fountain Cards ... 489
Raiders of the Lost Ark ... 49
Rambo ... 491
Rat Fink Greeting Cards ... 492
Rat Patrol ... 494
Real Wood Plaks / Valentine Plaks ... 496
Return of the Jedi I ... 497
Return of the Jedi II ... 499
Return of the Jedi Album Stickers ... 500
Return to Oz ... 501
Robin Hood, Prince of Thieves ... 503
Robocop 2 ... 504
Robocop 2 Collectors' Edition ... 506
Rocketeer ... 509
Rocky II ... 515
Rocky IV ... 516
Roger Rabbit ... 517
Rookies ... 519
Room 222 ... 520
Shock Theater ... 529
Silly Stickers ... 531
Six Million Dollar Man ... 533
Slob Stickers ... 535
Smurf Album Stickers ... 536
Smurf Supercards ... 537
Smurf Tattoos ... 537
Snotty Signs ... 539
Snotty Signs Stickers ... 540
Soupy Sales ... 542
Speed Wheels ... 547
Sports Cars ... 552
Stacks of Stickers ... 553
Star Trek (1976) ... 555
Star Trek (1979) ... 556
Star Wars ... 565
Star Wars Movie Photo Pin-Ups ... 568
Stupid Scratch-Offs ... 573
Stupid Smiles Stickers ... 573
Supergirl ... 577
Superman (1979) ... 579
Superman (1966) ... 580
Superman In The Jungle ... 581
Superman Tattoos ... 583
Superman, The Movie ... 583
Superman II ... 585
Superman III ... 588
Teenage Mutant Ninja Turtles - Series 1 ... 596
Teenage Mutant Ninja Turtles - Series 1 Collector's Edition ... 597
Teenage Mutant Ninja Turtles - Series 2 ... 598
Teenage Mutant Ninja Turtles Movie - Series 1 ... 598
Teenage Mutant Ninja Turtles Movie Collector's Edition ... 599
Teenage Mutant Ninja Turtles II ... 600
Terminator 2 ... 606
Terror Tales ... 610
The Simpsons ... 615
Three's Company ... 618
Tiny Toon Adventures ... 620
Tom and Jerry Tattoos ... 621
Topps Pak-O-Fun ... 622
Toppscience ... 624
Topps Scratch-Offs ... 625
Topps Winners ... 626
Toxic Crusaders ... 627
Toxic High ... 628
Trivia Battle ... 630
True Fact Series ... 633
TV Cartoon Tattoos ... 637
24 Tattoos ... 638
21 Jump Street ... 639
Ugly Buttons ... 642
Ugly Stickers (1965) ... 643
Ugly Stickers (1973 / 74) ... 644
Ugly Stickers (1976) ... 645
U.S. Presidents ... 650
Valentine Foldees ... 651

(TOPPS continued)
Valentine Postcards ... 653
Valentine Stickers ... 654
Video City ... 656
Voltron Tattoos ... 658
Wacky Ads ... 663
Wacky Labels ... 662
Wacky Packages Album Stickers ... 664
Wacky Packages Posters ... 665
Wacky Package Die-Cuts ... 666
Wacky Packages Stickers ... 666
Wacky Packages Tattoos ... 681
Walt Disney Characters Tattoos ... 683
Waltons ... 684
Wanted Posters (1967) ... 684
Wanted Posters (1975) ... 685
Wanted Posters (1980) ... 685
Wanted Stickers ... 686
Way-Out Wheels ... 688
Weird Wheels Stickers ... 689
Welcome Back Kotter ... 690
Who Am I? ... 692
Wise Guy Buttons ... 699
Wise Ties ... 699
You'll Die Laughing (1973) ... 706
You'll Die Laughing (1980) ... 707
Zoo's Who ... 714

TREAT HOBBY PRODUCTS
Walt Disney's Character Collecting Cards ... 683

TREE OF LIFE
Endangered Animals ... 188

TSR
TSR Trading Cards ... 634

TUFF STUFF
Johnny Clem ... 329
Peanuts ... 464
Remember Pearl Harbor ... 497
The Civil War ... 613
World War II Propaganda ... 702

TWIX
Mickey's Magic Moments Mobile ... 406

TYSON
Looney Tunes Magic Fun Books ... 363
Looney Tunes Stickers & Scenes ... 363
Looney Tunes Trading Cards ... 364
Looney Tunes Trivia Games ... 364

UNIVERSE GAMES
Classic Aircraft Collector Cards ... 104

UPPER DECK
Comic Ball 1 ... 109
Comic Ball 2 ... 110

U.S. GOVERNMENT
Space Defenders ... 543
U.S. Customs Canine Enforcement ... 648

VIRGINIA HOBBY SUPPLY
Birds and Flowers ... 78

WALDORF
Gremlins Stickers ... 287

WARNER & IRENE
Killer Cards ... 337

WENDY'S
Mighty Mouse - The New Adventures ... 412
Wendy's Old West Trading Cards ... 691

WILLIAMSON
Astronauts ... 38

WILLY WONKA
Dinosaurs ... 158

WISE POTATO CHIPS
Rip Into Rock ... 502

WNEW
WNEW Superstars ... 700

WONDER BREAD
Battlestar Galactica ... 60
Close Encounters ... 105
Crazy College Pennant Stickers ... 118
Guiness World Records ... 291
Hanna-Barbera Magic Trick Cards ... 295
Masters of the Universe Trading Cards ... 396
Rock Stars ... 513
Star Wars ... 568

WORLD CANDIES
Beatles Candy Boxes ... 68
Dinosaur Bones ... 156

WOW MAGAZINE
Cowboy & Cowgirl Trading Cards ... 116

YAZOO RECORDS
Early Jazz Greats ... 181
Heroes of the Blues ... 304
Pioneers of Country Music ... 472

ZIPLOC
Gremlins Movie Stickers ... 286
Presidential Series ... 480
Starcom Stickers ... 553
Superman II Stickers ... 586
Willow Trading Cards ... 696

ZOO LIFE
Zoo Life Zoo Cards ... 712

ZOOT ... see "Diamond Toy"

ADVERTISER'S INDEX

ARLINGTON CARDS ... 438
CHRIS BENJAMIN ... 232, 256, 264, 293, 331
BRIAN BIGELOW ... 96 & 287
CALIFORNIA NON-SPORTS ... 19
DART ... 720
LARRY FORTUCK ... 308
LASTING IMAGES ... 91
MIKE GORDON ... 206 & 457
MARK MACALUSO ... 435
BOB & JEFFREY MARKS ... 380
BILL MULLINS ... 127 & 252
JOHN NEUNER ... 338 & 393
BILL NIELSEN ... 87
NON-SPORT UPDATE ... 562
PHILLY NON-SPORT SHOW ... 400 & 681
CHARLES REUTER ... 413
ROSEM ENTERPRISES ... 409
SPACE VENTURES ... Inside Front Cover
STAR PICS ... Inside Back Cover
THE WRAPPER ... 569
ROXANNE TOSER ... 66
MARYANN WOLF ... 33

CONDITION GUIDE

MINT (M OR MT)
A card with no defects. A card that has sharp corners, even borders, original gloss or shine on the surface, sharp focus of the picture, smooth edges, no signs of wear, and white borders. There is no allowance made for the age of the card.

EXCELLENT (EX OR E)
A card with very minor defects. Any of the following qualities would be sufficient to lower the grade of a card from mint to the excellent category: very slight rounding or layering at some of the corners, a very small amount of the original gloss lost, minor wear on the edges, slight unevenness of the borders, slight wear visible only on close inspection; slight off-whiteness of the borders.

VERY GOOD (VG)
A card that has been handled but not abused. Some rounding at all corners, slight layering or scuffing at one or two corners, slight notching on edges, gloss lost from the surface but not scuffed, borders might be somewhat uneven but some white is visible on all borders, noticeable yellowing or browning of borders, pictures may be slightly off focus.

GOOD (G)
A well handled card, rounding and some layering at the corners, scuffing at the corners and minor scuffing on the face, borders noticeably uneven and browning, loss of gloss on the face, notching on the edges.

FAIR (F)
Round and layering corners, brown and dirty borders, frayed edges, noticeable scuffing on the face, white not visible on one or more borders, cloudy focus.

POOR (P)
An abused card, the lowest grade of card, frequently some major physical alteration has been performed on the card, collectible only as a fill-in until a better condition replacement can be obtained.

Categories between these major condition grades are frequently used; such as, very good to excellent (VG--E), fair to good (F–G), etc. The grades indicate a card with all qualities at least in the lower of the two categories, but with several qualities in the higher of the two categories.

THE CREASE
The most common physical defect in a trading card is the crease or wrinkle. The crease may vary from a slight crease barely noticeable at one corner of the card to a major crease across the entire card; therefor, the degree that a crease lowers the value of the card depends on the type and number of creases. On giving the condition of a card, creases should be noted separately. If the crease is noticeable only upon close inspection under bright light, an otherwise mint card could be called excellent; whereas noticeable but light creases would lower most otherwise mint cards into the VG catagory. A heavily creased card could be classified fair at best.

GLOSSARY

This glossary defines many common terms frequently used in the collecting hobby of trading cards and closely associated material. There are exceptions to some of the definitions presented; however, to list all of the exceptions would only tend to confuse the reader and detract from the usefulness of the glossary.

ALBUM— A paper book of varying size issued by a card manufacturer to house the cards of a specific series. Generally available as a mail-in, premium offer only, but sometimes sold in retail stores.

BACKLIST or BACKLISTED— Refers to the practice of listing the cards of a set on the back of each card in that set, in effect, providing a checklist on each one. Backlisting is generally found in 19th century tobacco issues.

BREAD END LABEL— The paper label found on the end of a loaf of bread. Since the 1930's, many baking companies have issued bread with sets of cowboy, comic, etc. labels as a promotional device.

CABINETS— Very popular and highly valuable large cards on thick card stock produced in the 19th and early 20th century.

CAPTION— The title of a card as it appears under the illustration and/or on the back. It generally describes or identifies the subject(s) pictured but may also be a line of dialogue.

CHECKLIST— a) A list of the cards contained in a particular set. The list is always in numerical order if the cards are numbered or in alphabetical order if the particular set is unnumbered.

b) A book containing a number of set checklists.

COLLECTOR— A person who engaged in the hobby of collecting non-sport card for his own enjoyment, without a profit motive.

COLLECTOR ISSUE— A set produced for the sake of the card itself, with no product or service sponsor. It derives its name from the fact that most of these sets are produced by collector - dealers.

CONVENTION— A large weekend gathering at one location of dealers and collectors for the purpose of buying, selling, and sometimes trading of non-sport cards. Conventions are open to the public and sometimes feature celebrities, door prizes, films, contests, etc.

CORNER CLIP— The design in the corner(s) of a wrapper which is specifically designed to be cut off and sent in as proof of purchase in a premium offer.

COUPON— A printed advertisement or form, found on older gum and candy wrappers and boxes, which could be cut out as proof of purchase and redeemed for prizes, premiums, etc.

CREASE— A wrinkle on the card, usually caused by bending the card.

DEALER— A person who engages in the buying, selling and trading of non-sport cards who anticipates a profit, direct or indirect, from each transaction. A dealer may also be a collector, but as a dealer, he anticipates a profit.

DIE-CUT— A card which by design has its stock partially cut through for removal or folding of one or more parts to the card. After removal of these parts and appropriate folding, the remaining part of the card can be made to stand-up.

EMBOSSED— Refers to a card on which the design has been stamped into the cardboard surface of the card from the rear, thereby giving the obverse surface a raised, or "relief" effect.

EXHIBIT— The generic name given to thick stock, post card sized cards with single color obverse pictures. The name is derived from the Exhibit Supply Co. of Chicago, the principal manufacturer of this type of card.

FRAME LINE— A line of varying thickness and color which is printed around the picture area of a card to accentuate the main design and to separate it from the borders, or margins.

GRAVURE or PHOTOGRAVURE— A card printed by a specific process in which the ink on the card itself is actually raised slightly above the surface on which it is printed, thereby accentuating the design.

HIGH NUMBER— The cards in the last series of numbers in a year in which the higher numbered cards were printed or distributed in significantly fewer amounts than the lower numbered cards. The high number designation refers to a scarcity of the high numbered cards. Not all years have high numbers in terms of this definition.

INSERT— A card of a different type, a poster, or any other collectible contained and sold in the same package along with a card or cards of a major set.

ISSUE— Synonomous with set, but usually used in conjunction with a manufacturer, e.g. a Topps issue.

LATIN BINOMIAL— The two Latin words which comprise the scientific name (genus and species) for a plant or animal.

LAYERING— The separation or peeling of one or more layers of the card stock, usually at the corner of the card.

LEGITIMATE ISSUE— A set produced to promote or boost sales of a product or service, e.g. bubble gum, cereal, cigarettes, etc. Most collector issues are not legitimate issues in this sense.

MATTE or MATT— Refers to the dull or flat finish on the surface of a card, as opposed to a glossy or shiny surface.

MISCUT— A card that has been cut unevenly at the manufacturer's cutting stage.

NOTCHING— The grooving of the edge of a card, usually caused by the fingernail, rubber bands, or bumping the edge against another object.

OBVERSE— The front, face or pictured side of the card.

PANEL— An extended card that is composed of two or more individual cards. Often the panel forms the back part of the container for the product being promoted.

PLASTIC SHEET— A clear vinyl page (normally using 6–8 mil plastic and punched for insertion into a binder with standard 3–ring spacing) containing pockets for insertion of cards. Many different styles of sheets exist with pockets of varying sizes to hold different sizes of cards.

PICTURE— The main design or illustration on a card, whether it be a drawing, a painting, or a photograph.

POSTER PIECE or PUZZLE PIECE— The back of a card containing a partial design which, when joined properly with similarly designed pieces, forms a large picture or poster.

PREMIUMS— Cards, pictures, gifts or any other items offered as a promotional device in conjunction with a card set.

PUZZLE PIECE— See POSTER PIECE.

PUZZLE PREVIEW CARD or PUZZLE PROMOTION CARD— The side of a card — generally the back — which shows the completed puzzle or poster which can be made by properly assembling the various puzzle-backed cards in the set.

RARE— A card or series of cards of very limited availability. Unfortunately "rare" is a subjective and rather nebulous term sometimes used indiscriminately. "Rare" cards are harder to obtain than "scarce" cards.

REVERSE— The back or narrative side of the card.

SCARCE— A card or series of cards of limited availability. A subjective and nebulous term sometimes used indiscriminately to promote value. Scarce cards are not as difficult to obtain as rare cards.

SEPIA— A dark reddish-brown coloration used in some card sets instead of traditional black-and-white.

SERIES— a) The entire set of cards issued by a particular producer in a particular year e.g., the 1933 Indian Gum series.

b) Within a particular set, a group of consecutively numbered cards printed at the same time, e.g., the first series of Charlie's Angels.

SET— One each of the entire run of cards of the same type produced by a particular manufacturer during a single year. A complete set does not include error or variation cards unless specified.

SKIP-NUMBERED— A set that has many card numbers not issued between the lowest number in the set and the highest number in the set. A major set in which a few numbers were not printed is not considered to be skip-numbered.

STICKER— A card with a removable layer that can be adhered to (stuck onto) another surface.

STIPPLE— Refers to the process by which a painting or drawing is created by using dots rather than lines.

STOCK— The cardboard or paper on which the card is printed.

STRIP CARDS— A sheet or strip of cards, particularly popular in the 1920's and 1930's, with the individual cards separated by a broken or dotted line.

TAB— a) A part of a card set off from the rest of the card, usually with perforations, that may be removed without damaging the central character or event depicted by the card.

b) The grasping nib of a lid.

TEST SET— A set, usually containing a small number of cards, issued by a national card producer and distributed in a limited section or sections of the country. Presumably, the purpose of a test set is to "test" market appeal for this particular type of card.

TEXT— The principal written material on a card as distinguished from card titles, set titles, headings, numbers, advertisements, etc. It may be a narrative, a small scientific treatise, or simple dialogue.

TRIMMED— A card cut down from its original size.

UNCUT SHEET— (Also called full sheet) A complete sheet of cards that has not been cut up into individual cards by the manufacturer.

VARIATION— One of two or more cards from the same series with the same number (or player with identical pose if the series is unnumbered) differing from one other by some aspect, the different feature stemming from the printing or stock of the card, not from an alteration.

ABBREVIATIONS

ACC	— The American Card Catalog
ATC	— American Tobacco Company
BGHLI	— Bowman Gum
E(card)	— The ACC reference letter for pre-1930 candy and gum cards
ITC	— Imperial Tobacco Company
LBI	— Leaf Brands Inc.
IWC	— The Illustrated Wrapper Checklist
N(card)	— The reference letter denoting 19th Century tobacco cards
T(card)	— The ACC reference letter for 20th Century tobacco cards
TCG	— Topps Chewing Gum
V(card)	— The ACC reference letter for Canadian candy and gum cards
3-D	— Three-dimensional